Dietary Reference Intakes: RDA, AI*

Life Stage Group	Calcium (mg/d)	Chromium (µg/d)	Copper (µg/d)	Fluoride (mg/d)	Iodine (µg/d)	Iron (mg/d)	Magnesium (mg/d)	Manganese (mg/d)	Molybdenum (µg/d)	Phosphorus (mg/d)	Selenium (µg/d)	Zinc (mg/d)	Potassium (g/d)	Sodium (g/d)	Chloride (g/d)
Infants															
0–6 mo	200*	0.2*	200*	0.01*	110*	0.27*	30*	0.003*	2*	100*	15*	2*	0.4*	0.12*	0.18*
6–12 mo	260*	5.5*	220*	0.5*	130*	**11**	75*	0.6*	3*	275*	20*	**3**	0.7*	0.37*	0.57*
Children															
1–3 y	**700**	11*	**340**	0.7*	**90**	**7**	**80**	1.2*	**17**	**460**	**20**	**3**	3.0*	1.0*	1.5*
4–8 y	**1,000**	15*	**440**	1*	**90**	**10**	**130**	1.5*	**22**	**500**	**30**	**5**	3.8*	1.2*	1.9*
Males															
9–13 y	**1,300**	25*	**700**	2*	**120**	**8**	**240**	1.9*	**34**	**1,250**	**40**	**8**	4.5*	1.5*	2.3*
14–18 y	**1,300**	35*	**890**	3*	**150**	**11**	**410**	2.2*	**43**	**1,250**	**55**	**11**	4.7*	1.5*	2.3*
19–30 y	**1,000**	35*	**900**	4*	**150**	**8**	**400**	2.3*	**45**	**700**	**55**	**11**	4.7*	1.5*	2.3*
31–50 y	**1,000**	35*	**900**	4*	**150**	**8**	**420**	2.3*	**45**	**700**	**55**	**11**	4.7*	1.5*	2.3*
51–70 y	**1,000**	30*	**900**	4*	**150**	**8**	**420**	2.3*	**45**	**700**	**55**	**11**	4.7*	1.3*	2.0*
>70 y	**1,200**	30*	**900**	4*	**150**	**8**	**420**	2.3*	**45**	**700**	**55**	**11**	4.7*	1.2*	1.8*
Females															
9–13 y	**1,300**	21*	**700**	2*	**120**	**8**	**240**	1.6*	**34**	**1,250**	**40**	**8**	4.5*	1.5*	2.3*
14–18 y	**1,300**	24*	**890**	3*	**150**	**15**	**360**	1.6*	**43**	**1,250**	**55**	**9**	4.7*	1.5*	2.3*
19–30 y	**1,000**	25*	**900**	3*	**150**	**18**	**310**	1.8*	**45**	**700**	**55**	**8**	4.7*	1.5*	2.3*
31–50 y	**1,000**	25*	**900**	3*	**150**	**18**	**320**	1.8*	**45**	**700**	**55**	**8**	4.7*	1.5*	2.3*
51–70 y	**1,200**	20*	**900**	3*	**150**	**8**	**320**	1.8*	**45**	**700**	**55**	**8**	4.7*	1.3*	2.0*
>70 y	**1,200**	20*	**900**	3*	**150**	**8**	**320**	1.8*	**45**	**700**	**55**	**8**	4.7*	1.2*	1.8*
Pregnancy															
14–18 y	**1,300**	29*	**1,000**	3*	**220**	**27**	**400**	2.0*	**50**	**1,250**	**60**	**12**	4.7*	1.5*	2.3*
19–30 y	**1,000**	30*	**1,000**	3*	**220**	**27**	**350**	2.0*	**50**	**700**	**60**	**11**	4.7*	1.5*	2.3*
31–50 y	**1,000**	30*	**1,000**	3*	**220**	**27**	**360**	2.0*	**50**	**700**	**60**	**11**	4.7*	1.5*	2.3*
Lactation															
14–18 y	**1,300**	44*	**1,300**	3*	**290**	**10**	**360**	2.6*	**50**	**1,250**	**70**	**13**	5.1*	1.5*	2.3*
19–30 y	**1,000**	45*	**1,300**	3*	**290**	**9**	**310**	2.6*	**50**	**700**	**70**	**12**	5.1*	1.5*	2.3*
31–50 y	**1,000**	45*	**1,300**	3*	**290**	**9**	**320**	2.6*	**50**	**700**	**70**	**12**	5.1*	1.5*	2.3*

Note: This table (taken from the DRI reports, see www.nap.edu) presents Recommended Dietary Allowances (RDAs) in **bold type** and Adequate Intakes (AIs) in ordinary type followed by an asterisk (*). An RDA is the average daily dietary intake level sufficient to meet the nutrient requirements of nearly all (97–98 percent) healthy individuals in a group. It is calculated from an Estimated Average Requirement (EAR). If sufficient scientific evidence is not available to establish an EAR, and thus calculate an RDA, an AI is usually developed. For healthy breast-fed infants, an AI is the mean intake. The AI for other life stage and gender groups is believed to cover the needs of all healthy individuals in the groups, but lack of data or uncertainty in the data prevent being able to specify with confidence the percentage of individuals covered by this intake.

Data from: DIETARY REFERENCE INTAKES series, National Academies Press. Copyright ©1997, 1998, 2000, 2001, 2005, and 2011, by the National Academy of Sciences. These reports may be accessed via www.nap.edu. Courtesy of the National Academies Press, Washington, DC. Reprinted with permission.

Dietary Reference Intakes: RDA, AI*

Vitamins

Life Stage Group	Vitamin A (µg/d)[a]	Vitamin C (mg/d)	Vitamin D (µg/d)[b,c]	Vitamin E (mg/d)[d]	Vitamin K (µg/d)	Thiamin (mg/d)	Riboflavin (mg/d)	Niacin (mg/d)[e]	Vitamin B6 (mg/d)	Folate (µg/d)[f]	Vitamin B12 (µg/d)	Pantothenic Acid (mg/d)	Biotin (µg/d)	Choline (mg/d)[g]
Infants														
0–6 mo	400*	40*	10*	4*	2.0*	0.2*	0.3*	2*	0.1*	65*	0.4*	1.7*	5*	125*
6–12 mo	500*	50*	10*	5*	2.5*	0.3*	0.4*	4*	0.3*	80*	0.5*	1.8*	6*	150*
Children														
1–3 y	**300**	**15**	**15**	**6**	30*	**0.5**	**0.5**	**6**	**0.5**	**150**	**0.9**	2*	8*	200*
4–8 y	**400**	**25**	**15**	**7**	55*	**0.6**	**0.6**	**8**	**0.6**	**200**	**1.2**	3*	12*	250*
Males														
9–13 y	**600**	**45**	**15**	**11**	60*	**0.9**	**0.9**	**12**	**1.0**	**300**	**1.8**	4*	20*	375*
14–18 y	**900**	**75**	**15**	**15**	75*	**1.2**	**1.3**	**16**	**1.3**	**400**	**2.4**	5*	25*	550*
19–30 y	**900**	**90**	**15**	**15**	120*	**1.2**	**1.3**	**16**	**1.3**	**400**	**2.4**	5*	30*	550*
31–50 y	**900**	**90**	**15**	**15**	120*	**1.2**	**1.3**	**16**	**1.3**	**400**	**2.4**	5*	30*	550*
51–70 y	**900**	**90**	**15**	**15**	120*	**1.2**	**1.3**	**16**	**1.7**	**400**	**2.4**[h]	5*	30*	550*
>70 y	**900**	**90**	**20**	**15**	120*	**1.2**	**1.3**	**16**	**1.7**	**400**	**2.4**[h]	5*	30*	550*
Females														
9–13 y	**600**	**45**	**15**	**11**	60*	**0.9**	**0.9**	**12**	**1.0**	**300**	**1.8**	4*	20*	375*
14–18 y	**700**	**65**	**15**	**15**	75*	**1.0**	**1.0**	**14**	**1.2**	**400**[i]	**2.4**	5*	25*	400*
19–30 y	**700**	**75**	**15**	**15**	90*	**1.1**	**1.1**	**14**	**1.3**	**400**[i]	**2.4**	5*	30*	425*
31–50 y	**700**	**75**	**15**	**15**	90*	**1.1**	**1.1**	**14**	**1.3**	**400**[i]	**2.4**	5*	30*	425*
51–70 y	**700**	**75**	**15**	**15**	90*	**1.1**	**1.1**	**14**	**1.5**	**400**	**2.4**[h]	5*	30*	425*
>70 y	**700**	**75**	**20**	**15**	90*	**1.1**	**1.1**	**14**	**1.5**	**400**	**2.4**[h]	5*	30*	425*
Pregnancy														
14–18 y	**750**	**80**	**15**	**15**	75*	**1.4**	**1.4**	**18**	**1.9**	**600**[j]	**2.6**	6*	30*	450*
19–30 y	**770**	**85**	**15**	**15**	90*	**1.4**	**1.4**	**18**	**1.9**	**600**[j]	**2.6**	6*	30*	450*
31–50 y	**770**	**85**	**15**	**15**	90*	**1.4**	**1.4**	**18**	**1.9**	**600**[j]	**2.6**	6*	30*	450*
Lactation														
14–18 y	**1,200**	**115**	**15**	**19**	75*	**1.4**	**1.6**	**17**	**2.0**	**500**	**2.8**	7*	35*	550*
19–30 y	**1,300**	**120**	**15**	**19**	90*	**1.4**	**1.6**	**17**	**2.0**	**500**	**2.8**	7*	35*	550*
31–50 y	**1,300**	**120**	**15**	**19**	90*	**1.4**	**1.6**	**17**	**2.0**	**500**	**2.8**	7*	35*	550*

Note: This table (taken from the DRI reports, see www.nap.edu) presents Recommended Dietary Allowances (RDAs) in **bold type** and Adequate Intakes (AIs) in ordinary type followed by an asterisk (*). An RDA is the average daily dietary intake level sufficient to meet the nutrient requirements of nearly all (97–98 percent) healthy individuals in a group. It is calculated from an Estimated Average Requirement (EAR). If sufficient scientific evidence is not available to establish an EAR, and thus calculate an RDA, an AI is usually developed. For healthy breast-fed infants, an AI is the mean intake. The AI for other life stage and gender groups is believed to cover the needs of all healthy individuals in the groups, but lack of data or uncertainty in the data prevent being able to specify with confidence the percentage of individuals covered by this intake.

[a] As retinol activity equivalents (RAEs). 1 RAE = 1 µg retinol, 12 µg β-carotene, 24 µg α-carotene, or 24 µg β-cryptoxanthin. The RAE for dietary provitamin A carotenoids is two-fold greater than retinol equivalents (RE), whereas the RAE for preformed vitamin A is the same as RE.

[b] As cholecalciferol. 1 µg cholecalciferol = 40 IU vitamin D.

[c] Under the assumption of minimal sunlight.

[d] As α-tocopherol. α-Tocopherol includes *RRR*-α-tocopherol, the only form of α-tocopherol that occurs naturally in foods, and the *2R*-stereoisomeric forms of α-tocopherol (*RRR*-, *RSR*-, *RRS*-, and *RSS*-α-tocopherol) that occur in fortified foods and supplements. It does not include the *2S*-stereoisomeric forms of α-tocopherol (*SRR*-, *SSR*-, *SRS*-, and *SSS*-α-tocopherol), also found in fortified foods and supplements.

[e] As niacin equivalents (NE). 1 mg of niacin = 60 mg of tryptophan; 0–6 months = preformed niacin (not NE).

[f] As dietary folate equivalents (DFE). 1 DFE = 1 µg food folate = 0.6 µg of folic acid from fortified food or as a supplement consumed with food = 0.5 µg of a supplement taken on an empty stomach.

[g] Although AIs have been set for choline, there are few data to assess whether a dietary supply of choline is needed at all stages of the life cycle, and it may be that the choline requirement can be met by endogenous synthesis at some of these stages.

[h] Because 10 to 30 percent of older people may malabsorb food-bound B12, it is advisable for those older than 50 years to meet their RDA mainly by consuming foods fortified with B12 or a supplement containing B12.

[i] In view of evidence linking folate intake with neural tube defects in the fetus, it is recommended that all women capable of becoming pregnant consume 400 µg from supplements or fortified foods in addition to intake of food folate from a varied diet.

[j] It is assumed that women will continue consuming 400 µg from supplements or fortified food until their pregnancy is confirmed and they enter prenatal care, which ordinarily occurs after the end of the periconceptional period—the critical time for formation of the neural tube.

Data from: DIETARY REFERENCE INTAKES series, National Academies Press. Copyright ©1997, 1998, 2000, 2001, 2005, and 2011, by the National Academy of Sciences. These reports may be accessed via www.nap.edu. Courtesy of the National Academies Press, Washington, DC. Reprinted with permission.

Bring your nutrition course
INTO FOCUS

Nutrition & You

THIRD EDITION

FOCUS on Visualizing

The Third Edition of **Nutrition & You** provides students with a personalized approach to nutrition and helps them become informed consumers of nutrition information through interactive lessons, practical applications, and visual study tools.

NEW! Visual Chapter Summaries contain important art and photos from the chapter text to reinforce key concepts and serve as concise study tools. ▼

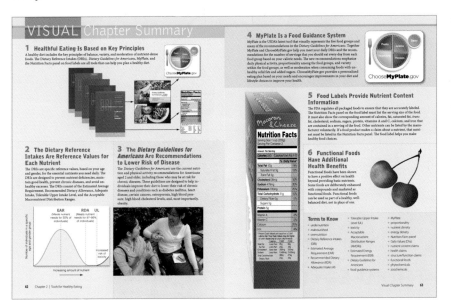

- Including art and photos with content summaries prompts student engagement and provides visual cues to reinforce important concepts.
- Numbered sections correspond to Learning Objectives and chapter headings.
- Alternating background colors aid navigation and keep each summary point separate and distinct.
- Key terms lists provide quick reference for study.

Exploring Micronutrients sections incorporate photos, illustrations, and text to present each vitamin and mineral. Each micronutrient is discussed using the same categories (functions, daily needs, food sources, toxicity and deficiency symptoms) and are accompanied by Table Tips for a consistent and easy-to-study format. ▶

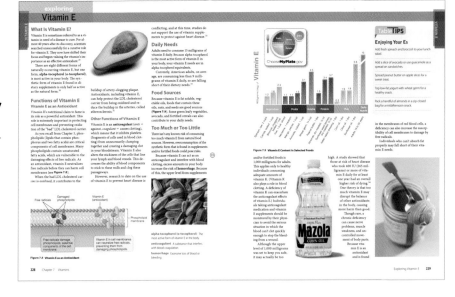

Information

NEW! Focus Figures explore targeted and integrated topic areas through visual information displays that are bold, clear, and detailed. These full-page figures also have corresponding tutorials in MasteringNutrition™.

Introductory text explains how the figure is key to other concepts students will learn in this chapter and future chapters. ▶

The pairing of dynamic art and photographs provides students with the visual reinforcement needed for concepts to come alive. ▶

Large figures depict macro-to-micro levels of explanation for complicated topics. ▶

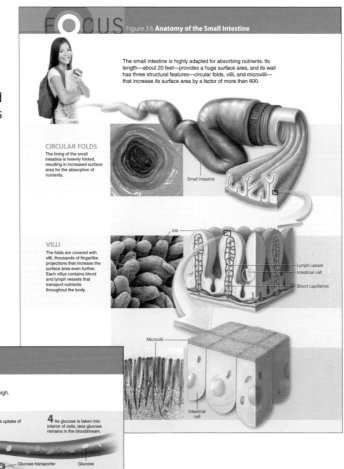

◀ Stepped-out art guides the eye through complex processes, breaking them down to make concepts easier to teach and understand.

◀ Intuitive layouts facilitate comparison and comprehension of related processes.

MasteringNutrition™

Mastering is the most effective and widely used online homework, tutorial, and assessment system for the sciences. It delivers self-paced tutorials that focus on your course objectives, provide individualized coaching, and respond to each student's progress.

FOR STUDENTS

Proven, assignable, and automatically graded nutrition activities reinforce course learning objectives.

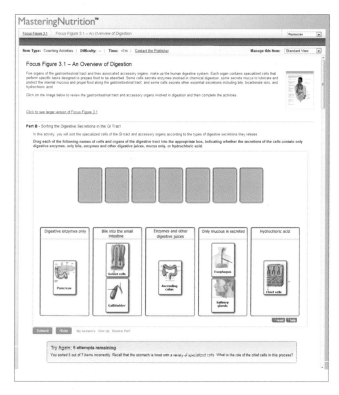

Focus Figure Coaching Activities ▲

Coaching activities guide students through key nutrition concepts with interactive mini-lessons that provide hints and feedback.

NutriTools Build-A-Meal Activities ▲

These unique activities allow students to combine and experiment with different food options and learn firsthand how to build healthier meals.

Other automatically graded nutrition activities include:

- MyDietAnalysis Case Study Activities
- Calculation Corner Activities
- Reading Quizzes
- ABC News Videos
- Chapter Tutor Session MP3s
- Get Ready for Nutrition

Nutrition Animations ▲

Animations built specifically for nutrition help students master tough topics with assessment and feedback.

DO YOUR STUDENTS WANT TO PRACTICE ON THEIR OWN?

The MasteringNutrition Study Area also provides students with the tools to study effectively and practice on their own time at their own pace.

eText ▲

The Pearson eText gives students access to the text whenever and wherever they can access the Internet. The eText can be viewed on PCs, Macs, and tablets, including iPad and Android.

Get Ready for Nutrition helps students get up to speed for their course by covering study skills, basic math, chemistry, and biology basics. ▲

◄ MyDietAnalysis

MyDietAnalysis is now available as a single sign on to MasteringNutrition.

For online users, a new mobile website version of MyDietAnalysis is available. Students can track their diet and activity intake accurately, anytime and anywhere, from their mobile device.

▲ NEW! Dynamic Study Modules enable

students to study effectively on their own in an adaptive format. Students receive an initial set of questions with a unique answer format asking them to indicate their confidence level. Once completed, reviews include explanations using materials taken directly from the text. These modules can be accessed on smartphones, tablets and computers.

The Study Area also includes: Cumulative Test, RSS Feeds, Audio Case Studies, ABC News Videos, Animations and book specific activities.

Easy to Get Started, Use,

MasteringNutrition™

FOR INSTRUCTORS

MasteringNutrition helps instructors maximize class time with easy-to-assign, customizable, and automatically graded assessments that motivate students to learn outside of the class and arrive prepared for lecture.

Calendar Feature for Instructors and Students ▶

The Course Home default page now features a Calendar View displaying upcoming assignments and due dates.

- Instructors can schedule assignments by dragging and dropping the assignment onto a date in the calendar.

- The calendar view lets students see at-a-glance when an assignment is due, and resembles a syllabus.

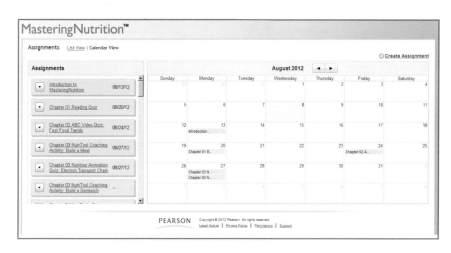

Customize Publisher-provided Problems or Quickly Add Your Own ▲

MasteringNutrition™ makes it easy to edit any questions or answers, import your own questions, and quickly add images or links to further enhance the student experience.

Learning Outcomes ▶

Tagged to book content and tied to Bloom's Taxonomy, Learning Outcomes are designed to let Mastering do the work in tracking student performance against your learning outcomes. Mastering offers a data supported measure to quantify students' learning gains and to share those results quickly and easily:

- Add your own or use the publisher-provided learning outcomes.

- View class performance against the specified learning outcomes.

- Export results to a spreadsheet.

and Make Your Own

Now that students come more prepared to class with MasteringNutrition,
FLIP YOUR CLASSROOM

▲ NEW! LEARNING CATALYTICS™

Learning Catalytics allows students to use their smartphones, tablets, or laptops to respond to questions in class. With Learning Catalytics you can:

- Use a wide variety of question types to engage students: multiple choice, word clouds, sketch a graph, annotate art, highlight a passage, compute a numeric answer, and more.

- Use multiple question types to get into the minds of students to understand what they do or don't know and adjust lectures accordingly.

- Access rich analytics to understand student performance.

- Add your own questions to make Learning Catalytics fit your course exactly.

- Assess and improve students' critical-thinking skills, and so much more.

Learning Catalytics is included with the purchase of MasteringNutrition with MyDietAnalysis.

Everything You Need to Teach in One Place!

▲ Teaching Toolkit DVD for Nutrition & You

The Teaching Toolkit DVD replaces the former printed Teaching Toolbox by providing everything you need to prep for your course and deliver a dynamic lecture in one convenient place. Included on 3 disks are these valuable resources:

Disk 1: Robust media assets for each chapter:

- 36 ABC News Lecture Launcher videos
- Practical Nutrition Tips videos
- Nutrition Animations
- PowerPoint® Lecture Outlines
- Media-only PowerPoint slides for easy importing of videos, animations, and Nutritools
- PowerPoint clicker questions and Jeopardy-style quiz show questions

- Files for all illustrations and tables and selected photos from the text
- Transparency Masters

Disk 2: Comprehensive Test Bank:

- Test Bank in Word and RTF formats
- Computerized Test Bank, which includes all the questions from the test bank in a format that allows you to easily and intuitively build exams and quizzes

Disk 3: Additional innovative supplements for instructors and students:

For Instructors:

- Instructor's Resource Support Manual
- Introduction to MasteringNutrition

- Introductory video for Learning Catalytics
- Great Ideas in Teaching Nutrition

For Students:

- Eat Right! Healthy Eating in College and Beyond
- Food Composition Table

User's Quick Guide for *Nutrition & You*

This easy-to-use printed supplement accompanies the Teaching Toolkit and offers easy instructions for both experienced and new faculty members to get started with the rich Toolkit content, how to access assignments within MasteringNutrition, and how to flip the classroom with Learning Catalytics.

Nutrition & You

THIRD EDITION

Joan Salge Blake, MS, RD, LDN

Boston University

PEARSON

Boston Columbus Indianapolis New York San Francisco Upper Saddle River Amsterdam
Cape Town Dubai London Madrid Milan Munich Paris Montréal Toronto Delhi
Mexico City São Paulo Sydney Hong Kong Seoul Singapore Taipei Tokyo

Executive Editor: *Sandra Lindelof*
Project Editor: *Kari Hopperstead*
Director of Development: *Barbara Yien*
Editorial Assistant: *Tu-Anh Dang-Tran*
Managing Editor: *Mike Early*
Assistant Managing Editor: *Nancy Tabor*
Program Manager: *Susan Malloy*
Project Manager: *Beth Collins*
Director of Digital Product Development: *Lauren Fogel*
Executive Content Producer: *Liz Winer*
Associate Content Producer: *Lauren Hill*
Copyeditor: *Anna Reynolds Trabucco*
Production Manager and Compositor: *S4Carlisle Publishing Services*

Design Manager; Interior and Cover Designer: *Side by Side Studios*
Art Development Editor: *Kelly Murphy*
Illustrator: *Precision Graphics*
Senior Image Project Manager: *Maya Melenchuk*
Photo Researcher: *Carolyn Arcabascio, PreMediaGlobal*
Senior Procurement Specialist: *Stacey Weinberger*
Executive Marketing Manager: *Neena Bali*
Text Printer: *Courier/Kendallville*
Cover Printer: *Lehigh-Phoenix*
Cover Photo Credit: © *FoodCollection/SuperStock*

Library of Congress Cataloging-in-Publication Data
Blake, Joan Salge, author.
  Nutrition & you / Joan Salge Blake, MS, RD, LDN, Boston University. — Third edition.
    pages cm
  Revision of: Nutrition and you. 2nd ed. 2012; originally published under: Nutrition & you.
  Includes bibliographical references and index.
  ISBN-13: 978-0-321-91040-0
  ISBN-10: 0-321-91040-0
  1. Nutrition—Textbooks.   I. Title.   II. Title: Nutrition and you.
  RA784.B552 2015
  613.2—dc23
                                                                        2013035734

ISBN 10: 0-321-91040-0; ISBN 13: 978-0-321-91040-0 (Student edition)
ISBN 10: 0-321-96088-2; ISBN 13: 978-0-321-96088-7 (Instructor Review Copy)
ISBN 10: 0-321-96091-2; ISBN 13: 978-0-321-96091-7 (Books A La Carte edition)

Credits and acknowledgments borrowed from other sources and reproduced, with permission, in this textbook appear on the appropriate page within the text or on p. CR-1.

Many of the designations used by manufacturers and sellers to distinguish their products are claimed as trademarks. Where those designations appear in this book, and the publisher was aware of a trademark claim, the designations have been printed in initial caps or all caps.

MasteringNutrition is a trademark, in the U.S. and/or other countries, of Pearson Education, Inc. or its affiliates.

4 5 6 7 8 9 10—CRK—17 16 15

Brief Contents

Contents

4

Carbohydrates: Sugars, Starches, and Fiber   96

What Are Carbohydrates and Why Do You Need Them?   98

What Happens to the Carbohydrates You Eat?   102

How Does Your Body Use Carbohydrates?   105

How Much Carbohydrate Do You Need and What Are the Best Food Sources?   108

What's the Difference between Natural and Added Sugars?   113

What Are Sugar Substitutes and What Forms Can They Take?   126

5

Fats, Oils, and Other Lipids   140

6

Proteins and Amino Acids   182

7

Vitamins 222

8

Minerals and Water 278

9

Alcohol 336

10

Weight Management and Energy Balance 364

11

Nutrition and Fitness 412

14

Life Cycle Nutrition: Pregnancy through Infancy   522

15

Life Cycle Nutrition: Toddlers through the Later Years   560

16
Hunger at Home and Abroad 594

Appendices

Special Features

self-Assessment

Table TIPS

MADE over MADE better

POINTS OF VIEW

About the Author

Joan Salge Blake is a clinical associate professor and dietetics internship director at Boston University's Sargent College of Health and Rehabilitation Sciences. She teaches both graduate and undergraduate nutrition courses, and has been a guest lecturer at both the Boston University Goldman School of Dental Medicine and the Boston University School of Medicine. She received the Whitney Powers Excellence in Teaching Award from Boston University. Joan completed her MS at Boston University and is currently working toward her doctorate.

Joan is a member of the Academy of Nutrition and Dietetics (AND; formerly the American Dietetic Association) and the Massachusetts Dietetic Association (MDA). She has been a presenter and presiding officer at both the AND Annual Meeting and the MDA Annual Convention, and she was previously named the MDA's "Young Dietitian of the Year," Outstanding Dietitian (2009), and Outstanding Dietetic Educator (2007). Joan has served on the MDA board for more than a decade in many roles, including past MDA Director of Education and Nominating Committee Chairperson.

In addition to teaching and writing, Joan is also an AND National Media Spokesperson, responsible for representing the association in the media and promoting its initiatives. She is often asked to translate complex nutritional issues in popular terms and has conducted more than 1,000 media interviews. Her nutrition segments can be seen regularly on Fox25 television in Boston. Joan is also the nutrition blogger for the *Boston Globe*'s Boston.com website.

Why I Wrote
Nutrition & You

"You'll probably finish this class with a whole new outlook on diet and exercise . . . and you'll probably be a lot healthier!"

"Professor Salge Blake makes the material seem like the most interesting material in the universe."

—Excerpts from student comments about my nutrition class at Boston University, courtesy of ratemyprofessor.com

I wrote *Nutrition & You* for you. It is all about you. For more than a decade, I have taught an Introduction to Nutrition course to a packed classroom of almost 200 students, at the unseemly hour of 8 A.M. The students keep coming year after year because I not only deliver accurate nutrition science and information in an easy-to-understand, entertaining format, but more importantly, I personalize the information for them so that they can immediately apply it to their own lifestyles.

As a college student, you are exposed to a steady stream of nutrition and health information from the media, your family and friends, and the Internet. While you may think Google has the answer to your nutrition questions, I have seen students frequently fall victim to misinformation found via a quick Web search and a few glitzy websites. So I designed *Nutrition & You* to be as user friendly as possible, packed exclusively with sound nutrition information. The text goes beyond basic nutrition science and provides realistic advice and strategies to help you easily incorporate what you learn into your busy life. The text is written to meet *your* nutritional concerns and answer *your* questions.

As you read *Nutrition & You,* I want you to feel as though you are sitting in my class being entertained and informed. For this reason, I wrote the text in a conversational tone, and we designed it to visually communicate complex nutrition science and topics in an easy-to-understand way.

The information in this textbook is arranged in a deliberate **"What," "Why,"** and **"How"** format. Each chapter will tell you:

➤ **"What"** the nutrition concept is;
➤ **"Why"** it is important and the role it plays in your body; and then, most importantly,
➤ **"How"** to easily adjust your lifestyle based on what you just learned.

Remember, nutrition matters to *you!* What you eat today and tomorrow will affect you and your body for years to come. Just as important, what you learn about nutrition today will enable you to make a positive effect on the lives of others from now on.

Joan Salge Blake

New to This Edition

➤ **MasteringNutrition™** is an online homework, tutorial, and assessment product designed to improve results by helping students quickly master concepts. You will benefit from self-paced tutorials that feature immediate wrong-answer feedback and hints that emulate the office-hour experience to help keep students on track. With a wide range of interactive, engaging, and assignable activities, it encourages you to actively learn and retain tough course concepts.

➤ **Focus Figures** teach key concepts in nutrition. These full-page figures explore targeted and integrated topic areas through visual information displays that are bold, clear, and detailed. These figures also have corresponding coaching activities in MasteringNutrition.

➤ **Visual Chapter Summaries** are structured to mirror the organization of the chapter content and numbered to correspond with the chapter objectives. They contain important art and photos from the main chapter text and serve as concise study and review tools.

➤ **Health Connection** features highlight diseases and disorders in which nutrition plays a major role, as well as nutritional practices that offer unique health benefits.

➤ **Examining the Evidence** features look at the latest research on controversial or confusing "hot" topics in nutrition today and include critical-thinking questions. These features guide you to making better, informed choices in your personal nutrition, and becoming a critical media consumer of nutrition information.

➤ **Organizational changes** tie the learning objectives, chapter headings, and summary sections together to provide a strong pedagogical structure that promotes comprehension and facilitates study and review.

➤ **MyDietAnalysis mobile website** is now available, so you can track your diet and activity accurately, anytime and anywhere, from your mobile device.

Other Key Features

➤ **Exploring Micronutrients** within Chapters 7 and 8 are self-contained sections that incorporate photos, illustrations, and text to present each vitamin and mineral. Each micronutrient is discussed using the same categories (forms, functions, daily needs, food sources, toxicity and deficiency symptoms) for a consistent and easy-to-study format. These enable you to identify at a glance the key aspects of each nutrient.

➤ **Two Points of View** at the end of each chapter contains a summary of opposing viewpoints on a timely topic. This feature will encourage you to think critically about pro and con arguments on a given issue and decide for yourself which side you agree with. You will be applying the critical-thinking skills that you learned in the chapter as you think through each point of view presented.

➤ **True or False?** pretests open each chapter with 10 true/false statements that help you realize that the things you think you know about nutrition aren't always accurate. Answers are given at the end of the chapter, and a true/false icon emphasizes locations of answers within the chapter.

➤ **Nutrition in the Real World** features take a closer look at some of the ways nutritional information and issues affect daily life.

➤ **Practical Nutrition videos** show the dynamic and ever-interesting Joan Salge Blake walking you through making better eating choices in familiar environments, based on a choice related to the chapter topic. Examples include a pizza parlor, deli, coffee shop, breakfast choices on the go, fitness smoothies, and much more. QR codes appear throughout the text for direct links to the videos.

- **Table Tips** give practical ideas for incorporating adequate amounts of each nutrient into your diet using widely available foods.
- **Self-Assessments** throughout the book ask you to think about your own diet and behaviors and how well you are meeting your various nutrient needs.
- **Made Over, Made Better** food comparisons at the end of Chapters 4 through 11 can help you visually see how to make more nutritious decisions.
- **eLearn activities** within the chapters direct you to a website to complete an animated activity, assessment, or worksheet.

Key Content Updates

Both nutrition research and personalized applications are continually expanding this dynamic science. To keep pace, we have reorganized the content, visually improved the figures and tables, and added new features to each chapter in the third edition of *Nutrition & You*. Some of the key content updates include:

- The latest statistics on such key topics as the obesity epidemic, consumption trends, incidences of nutrition-related diseases, physical activity, hunger, and food insecurity
- Updates on official data and recommendations, including DRIs, dietary guidelines, physical activity guidelines, *Healthy People 2020* objectives, eating disorder diagnostic criteria, and hydration recommendations
- New coverage of fundamental nutrition concepts including calculating the energy content of foods, nutrient absorption, identifying saturated fats, essential fatty acids, avoiding nutrition scams, and vitamin D and calcium functions
- Fifteen full-page Focus Figures on key nutrition topics, including DRIs, macronutrient digestion overviews, glucose regulation, diabetes, lipoprotein transport, atherosclerosis, energy balance, and fluid and electrolyte balance
- New hot topics added to text and features include the effect of meal timing on health, high-fructose corn syrup and obesity, nutrition labeling at restaurants, bans of super-sized sodas, the paleo diet, calorie restriction, and orthorexia
- Updated coverage of popular topics including sugar substitutes, mercury in fish, the Mediterranean diet, protein supplements, remedies for the common cold, popular weight-loss diets, the fat-burning zone, bottled water, vegetarianism, binge drinking, weight-loss strategies, body image disorders, the health benefits of exercise, genetically modified foods, sustainable agriculture, organic foods, nutritional needs during pregnancy, and geriatric nutritional needs
- Health Connection features contain updated coverage of nutrition-related health topics including celiac disease, lactose intolerance, diabetes, heart disease, hypertension, osteoporosis, food allergies, and cancer prevention.

Digital Learning Products

MasteringNutrition™

www.masteringhealthandnutrition.com

MasteringNutrition is an online homework, tutorial, and assessment product designed to improve results by helping students quickly master concepts. Students benefit from self-paced tutorials that feature immediate wrong-answer feedback and hints that emulate the office-hour experience to help keep students on track. With a wide range of interactive, engaging, and assignable activities, students are encouraged to actively learn and retain tough course concepts.

- ➤ **Focus Figure coaching activities** guide students through key nutrition concepts with interactive mini-lessons that provide hints and feedback.
- ➤ **NutriTools Build-a-Meal coaching activities** allow students to apply nutrition concepts to improve their health through interactive mini-lessons that provide hints and feedback.
- ➤ **Math activities** provide hands-on practice in important calculations with helpful wrong-answer feedback.
- ➤ *ABC News* videos bring nutrition to life and spark discussion with up-to-date hot topics that occur in the nutrition field. These are accompanied by multiple-choice questions with wrong-answer feedback.
- ➤ **Animations** explain big-picture concepts that help students learn the hardest topics in nutrition.
- ➤ Other graded activities include **Chapter Reading Quizzes, Chapter MP3s, Math and Chemistry Review,** and **MyDietAnalysis Case Study activities.**

MyDietAnalysis

www.mydietanalysis.com

MyDietAnalysis was developed by the nutrition database experts at ESHA Research, Inc. and is tailored for use in college nutrition courses. This software system allows students to complete a diet assignment by keeping a diary of food intake and exercise and then creating a variety of reports (for example, the balance between fats, carbohydrates, and proteins in the diet; how many calories eaten vs expended; whether the student is meeting the RDAs for vitamins and minerals; and so on). It has been updated to include a **mobile version** so students can access it from their smartphones to easily track food, drink, and activity on the go, 24/7.

Teaching Toolkit DVD for *Nutrition & You* (for instructors)

The Electronic Teaching Toolkit DVD replaces the former printed Teaching Toolbox by providing everything an instructor needs to prep for the course, and deliver a dynamic lecture, in one convenient place. Resources include:

- ➤ NEW! 51 *ABC News* Lecture Launcher videos, with air dates from 2010 to 2013
- ➤ Practical Nutrition Tips videos
- ➤ Clicker questions
- ➤ Quiz Show questions
- ➤ PowerPoint® Lecture Outlines (including Media-only PowerPoints)
- ➤ PowerPoint step-edit Image Presentations
- ➤ Files for all illustrations and tables and selected photos from the text
- ➤ Transparency Masters
- ➤ Microsoft® Word files for the *Instructor Resource and Support Manual* and the Test Bank
- ➤ Computerized Test Bank, which includes all the questions from the printed test bank in a format that allows instructors to easily and intuitively build exams and quizzes
- ➤ Printed *User's Quick Guide* with easy instructions for both experienced and new faculty members to get started with the rich toolkit content

Additional digital instructor and student resources include PDFs of:

- ➤ *NEW! Step-by-step MasteringNutrition tutorials*
- ➤ *Great Ideas in Teaching Nutrition*
- ➤ *Eat Right! Healthy Eating in College and Beyond*
- ➤ *Food Composition Table*

Acknowledgments

It takes a village, and then some, when it comes to writing a dynamic textbook. *Nutrition & You* is no exception. I personally want to thank all of those who passionately shared their expertise and support to make *Nutrition & You* better than I could have envisioned.

Beginning with the dynamic staff at Pearson, I would like to thank Sandy Lindelof, who helped make my vision for this textbook a reality. Revising a text of this nature takes a lot of coordination, and Project Editor Kari Hopperstead managed to keep us on track which still applying her eagle eye to every aspect of the revision. Program Manager Susan Malloy and Assistant Editor Meghan Zolnay were invaluable in lending an extra set of eyes and an additional pair of hands when needed. Crackerjack Editorial Assistant Tu-Anh Dang-Tran, Content Producer Lauren Hill, and Project Managers Lauren Beebe and Kyle Doctor all worked diligently to create the best supplements for *Nutrition & You*. Thanks also to Editorial Assistant Briana Verdugo for her many contributions.

A very special thanks to Beth Collins and Megan Power, Project Managers extraordinaire, and Mary Tindle, Senior Project Editor at S4Carlisle Publishing Services, for all of their hard work shepherding this book through production. My humble appreciation also goes to Kelly Murphy, Art Development Editor, for developing our stunning new Focus Figures; to Carolyn Arcabascio and Kristin Piljay for obtaining the most vivid and unique photos available; and to Design Manager Mark Ong, whose design made the text, art, and photos all come alive and whom I must thank for the book's gorgeous cover.

Marketing takes energy, and that's exactly what Executive Marketing Manager Neena Bali and her team seem to generate nonstop. The many instructors who reviewed this book and supporting media, and who provided good insights and suggestions are listed on the following pages; I am grateful to all of them for helping to inform the development of the third edition of *Nutrition & You*.

The village also included loyal contributors who lent their expertise to specific chapters. They are: Kathy Munoz at Humboldt State University, who revised the chapter on the basics of digestion; Tara Smith at East Carolina University, who revised the nutrition and fitness chapter as well as the disordered eating section of the weight-management chapter; Elizabeth Ward, who revised the two "life cycle" chapters; Heidi Wengreen at Utah State University, who revised the food consumerism chapter; and Claire Alexander, who updated the hunger chapter as well as the Two Points of View features. Many thanks also to my accuracy reviewers, Joanne DeMarchi of Saddleback College, Milli Owens of College of the Sequoias, and Esther Okeiyi of North Carolina Central University.

A heartfelt thank you goes to my research assistant, Corcoran Downey, who helped me with the research needed to keep the science up to date. Lastly, an endless thanks to my family, **A**dam, **B**rendan, and **C**raig, for their love and support when I was working more than I should have been.

Joan Salge Blake

Reviewers

Liane Summerfield
Marymount University

Jo Taylor
Southeast Community College

Norman Temple
Athabasca University

Gabrielle Turner-McGrievy
University of Alabama

Simin Vaghefi
University of North Florida

Amy Vaughan
Radford University

John Warber
Morehead State University

Dana Wassmer
Cosumnes River College

Diana Watson-Maile
East Central University

Beverly Webber
University of Utah

Annie Wetter
University of Wisconsin, Stevens Point

Fred Wolfe
University of Arizona

Maureen Zimmerman
Mesa Community College

Donna Zoss
Purdue University

Second Edition

Barbara Bernardi
Lincoln Land Community College

Tracey Brigman
University of Georgia

Linda Brothers
Indiana University—Purdue

Lisa Duich-Perry
Chaminade University of Honolulu

Jerald C. Foote
University of Arkansas

Boyd Foster
Gonzaga University

Carol Friesen
Ball State University

Krista Jordheim
Normandale Community College

Lorri Kanauss
Western Illinois University

Kathleen M. Laquale
Bridgewater State College

Linda Johnston Lolkus
Indiana University—Purdue

Raymond McCormick
University of South Florida

Owen Murphy
University of Colorado, Boulder

Cheryl Neudauer
Minneapolis Community and Technical College

Patricia Plavcan
Cooking and Hospitality Institute of Chicago

Ramona Rice
Georgia Military College

Lisa Sasson
New York University

Tiffany Shurtz
University of Central Oklahoma

Priya Venkatesan
Pasadena City College

Third Edition

Lisa Aberle
Heartland Community College

Andrea Altice
Florida State College at Jacksonville

Joanne DeMarchi
Saddleback College

Linda Fleming
Middlesex Community College

Carol Friesen
Ball State University

Alvin Furiya
Indiana University—Purdue University Indianapolis

Vijay Ganji
Georgia State University

Scott Johnson
Wake Technical Community College

Kathleen Laquale
Bridgewater State University

Esther Okeiyi
North Carolina Central University

Ryan Paruch
Tulsa Community College

Teresa Peeples
The College of Coastal Georgia

Janet Yarrow
Housatonic Community College

MasteringNutrition™ Faculty Advisory Board

Brian Barthel
Utah Valley College

Melissa Chabot
University at Buffalo—The State University of New York

Julia Erbacher
Salt Lake Community College

Carol Friesen
Ball State University

Urbi Ghosh
Oakton Community College

Judy Kaufman
Monroe Community College

Michelle Konstantarakis
University of Nevada, Las Vegas

Milli Owens
College of the Sequoias

Janet Sass
Northern Virginia Community College

Dana Sherman
Ozarks Technical Community College

Priya Venkatesan
Pasadena City College

I am nothing without
my ABCs.

Thanks.

1

What Is Nutrition?

True or False?

1. **Habit** is the the number-one determinant of what you eat. T|F p. 5

2. Heart disease is the leading cause of **death** in the United States. T|F p. 8

3. The energy in food is commonly measured in **calories**. T|F p. 9

4. **Vitamins** provide you with energy. T|F p. 10

5. **Water** is an essential nutrient. T|F p. 11

6. Taking a **vitamin supplement** ensures that your diet is healthy. T|F p. 12

7. Meats, poultry, and fish are good sources of **fiber**. T|F p. 12

8. More than **50 percent** of Americans regularly spend money on daily supplements. T|F p. 13

9. The number of **obese** Americans is lower today than it was ten years ago. T|F p. 13

10. You can get good nutrition advice from anyone who calls himself a **nutritionist**. T|F p. 21

See page 27 for the answers.

1. **Discuss the factors that influence your food choices.**

2. **Define the term *nutrition*.**

3. **Differentiate between the six categories of essential nutrients found in food and in the body.**

4. **Understand the importance of a well-balanced diet in meeting your daily nutrient needs.**

5. **Discuss the current nutritional state of the American diet.**

6. **Understand the scientific method that is involved in nutrition research and identify reliable sources of nutrition information.**

From the minute you were born, you began performing three automatic behaviors: You slept, you ate, and you expelled your waste products . . . often while you were sleeping. You didn't need to think about these actions, and you didn't have to decide to do them. You also didn't need to make choices about where to sleep, what to eat, or when to go to the bathroom. Life was so easy back then.

Now that you're older, these actions, particularly the eating part, are anything but automatic. You make numerous decisions every day about what to eat, and you make these decisions for reasons that you may not even be aware of. If your dietary advice comes from media sound bites, you may get constantly conflicting information. Yesterday's news flash announced that eating more protein would help you fight a bulging waist. Last week's headline boldly announced you should minimize *trans* fats in your diet to avoid a heart attack. This morning, the TV news lead was a health report advising you to eat more whole grains to live longer, but to hold the line on sodium, otherwise your blood pressure may go up.

You may find it frustrating that dietary advice seems to change with the daily news (though it actually doesn't), but this bombardment of nutrition news is a positive thing. You are lucky to live in an era when so much is known and being discovered about what you eat and how it affects you. Today's research validates what nutrition professionals have known for decades: Nutrition plays an invaluable role in your health. As with any science, nutrition is not stagnant. Exciting discoveries will continue to be made about the roles that diet and foods play in keeping you healthy.

Let's find out more about nutrition, why it's so important to your health, and how you can identify sound sources of nutrition information. We'll start with the basic concept of why you eat and how this affects your nutrition.

What Drives Our Food Choices?

What did you have for dinner last night? Where did you eat it? Who were you with? How did you feel?

Do you ever think about what drives your food choices? Or are you on autopilot as you stand in line at the sub shop and squint at yet another menu board? Do you adore some foods and eat them often, while avoiding others with a vengeance? Perhaps you have a grandparent who encourages you to eat more (and more!) of her traditional home cooking. You obviously need food to survive, but beyond your basic instinct to eat, there are many other factors that affect what goes into your stomach. Let's discuss some of these now.

We Need to Eat and Drink to Live

All creatures need fuel in order to function, and humans are no exception. We get our fuel from food in the form of chemical compounds that are collectively known as **nutrients**. These nutrients work together to provide energy, growth, and maintenance, and to regulate numerous body processes. Three of the six classes of nutrients—carbohydrates, fats (part of the larger class of lipids), and protein—provide energy in the form of **kilocalories**. Two other classes of nutrients, vitamins and minerals, help regulate many body processes, including **metabolism**. Some also play other supporting roles. The last class of nutrient, water, is found in all foods and beverages, and is so vital to life that you couldn't live more than a few days without it.

Foods also provide nonnutrient compounds that help maintain and repair your body in order to keep it healthy. We will explore each of these nutrients in more depth later in this chapter, and in much more depth throughout the book.

Beyond the basic need to replenish our bodies with daily fuel are other factors that drive our food choices.

We Choose Foods for Many Other Reasons

Your favorite foods taste delicious—that's why they're your favorites. You also choose certain other foods because they're staples of your culture, or they've become an important aspect of your social life. Some of your food selections are determined by trends, influenced by media messages, or reflect the amount of time or money you have available (**Figure 1.1**). Sometimes, you choose a food just because it's there. Let's explore each of these factors more closely.

Figure 1.1 Many Factors Influence Your Food Choices

Taste and Culture

Research confirms that when it comes to making food choices, taste is the most important consideration.[1] This shouldn't be too much of a surprise, considering that there are at least 10,000 taste buds in your mouth, mainly on your tongue. Your taste buds tell you that chocolate cheesecake is sweet, fresh lemon juice is sour, and a pretzel is salty.

What you choose to put on your plate is often influenced by your culture. If you were a student in Mexico, you may be feasting on a dinner with corn tortillas and tamales, as maize (corn) is a staple of Mexican cuisine. In India, meals commonly include lentils and other legumes with rice and vegetables, whereas Native Americans often enjoy stews of mutton (sheep), corn, and other vegetables. In China, rice, a staple, would be front and center on your plate.

A culture's cuisine is greatly influenced by the environment. This includes not only the climate and soil conditions but also the native plants and animals, as well as the distance people live from rivers, lakes, or the sea. People tend to consume foods that are accessible and often have little experience eating foods that are scarce. For example, native Alaskans feast on fish because it is plentiful, but eat less fresh produce, which is difficult to grow locally. For most Americans, this is less of an issue today than in the past, due to global food distribution networks. However, it still rings true for some food items. People living in landlocked states may have less access to fresh fish, for example, while those outside the south may not see collard greens or beignets on local store shelves as often as their Gulf State counterparts do.

One in four Americans is of Hispanic, Native American, Asian, or African descent. Cultural food preferences often influence food choices.

Social Reasons and Trends

Eating is an important way to bond with others. Every year, on the fourth Thursday in November, over 85 percent of Americans gather with family and friends to consume close to 736 million pounds of turkey as they celebrate Thanksgiving.[2] A person is likely to eat more on Thanksgiving than on any other Thursday, and this is

nutrients Compounds in foods that sustain your body processes. There are six classes of nutrients: carbohydrates, fats (lipids), proteins, vitamins, minerals, and water.

kilocalories The measurement of energy in foods. Commonly referred to as *calories*.

metabolism The numerous reactions that occur within the cell. The calories in foods are converted to energy in the cells of the body.

Food, friends, and football . . . a way of life.

While brown rice is a healthy whole-grain addition to any meal, it can take close to an hour to cook. For time-strapped consumers, food manufacturers have developed instant brown rice that cooks in 10 minutes, and a precooked, microwavable variety that reheats in under 2 minutes.

partly because of all the other people eating with them. Eating dinner with others has been shown to increase the size of the meal by over 40 percent, and the more people present, the more you'll eat.[3]

For many people, activities like watching a football game with fellow fans or going to a movie with friends often involve particular foods. According to the National Restaurant Association, one out of six individuals who order takeout or delivery on Super Bowl Sunday order pizza.[4] Movie theater owners bank on your buying popcorn, candy, and beverages at their concession stands before heading in to watch the picture. Revenue from these snack items can account for up to 50 percent of a theater's profits. If you're with a group of friends, you're even more likely to buy these snacks. Research shows that movie concession snacks are more often purchased when people are socializing in a group.[5] For instance, chances are that you'll choose a popcorn and soda at the theater, even if you are not hungry, because everyone else is having a snack.

Your food choices are also affected by popular trends. For instance, home cooks in the 1950s bought bags of newfangled frozen vegetables in order to provide healthy meals in less time. A few decades later, vegetables went upscale and consumers bought them as part of ready-to-heat stir-fry mixes. Today, shoppers pay a premium price for bags of fresh veggies, like carrots, that have been prewashed and peeled, sliced, or diced. Similarly, decades ago, the only way to enjoy iced tea was to brew it and chill it yourself. Now most markets provide dozens of choices in flavored and enhanced bottled teas, a popular beverage for many college students. As food manufacturers pour more money into research and development, who knows what tomorrow's trendy food item will be?

Cost, Time, and Convenience

According to the United States Department of Agriculture, almost 15 percent of American households did not have access to enough healthy foods to satisfy their basic, daily food needs in 2012, often because of limited financial resources.[6] It's not surprising, then, that many people may be forced to base their food choices on cost. The large, store-brand bag of potato chips, on sale, may appear to be an economical way for a struggling family on a tight budget to fill a dinner plate, rather than with more nutritious fresh or frozen vegetables, which are assumed to be more expensive. The good news is that research has shown that many fruits and vegetables can actually be cheaper per serving than unhealthy junk foods that are high in fat, sugar, and sodium. Buying produce in season and using frozen varieties can actually be very economical ways to consume fruits and vegetables.[7]

For those with adequate food budgets, time is often at a premium. Because of this, the types of foods that many people choose have changed. Research shows that Americans, especially working women with families, want to spend less than 15 minutes preparing a meal.[8] Consequently, supermarkets have changed the types of foods they sell as well as how the food is presented.

If chicken is on the menu tonight, you can go to the poultry section in the store and buy it uncooked. Or you can go to the takeout section of the store and buy it hot off the rotisserie, precooked and stuffed with bread crumbs, or grilled with teriyaki sauce. You can also probably get the cooked vegetables and rice side dishes to take home and reheat with the chicken.

Convenience also influences food choices. Foods that are easily accessible to you are more likely to be eaten. Let's say you have a long walk back to your dorm building after your last class of the day. On the way, you pass a food stand selling slices of delicious-looking pizza. The wonderful smell reminds you that you are hungry, so you buy a slice, or two. Or consider coffee. Decades ago, the most convenient way to get a hot cup of coffee was to brew it yourself. Americans today are more likely to get their java from one of the 27,000 coffee shops, carts, and kiosks across the United States.[9] Pizza and coffee are just two examples of a broad trend of Americans spending more of their household food budget on eating out.

Habits and Emotions

Many people start their day with a bowl of cereal and a glass of orange juice. In fact, ready-to-eat cereals are the number-one breakfast food choice among Americans, and citrus juice is the top juice choice for most people in the morning.[10] Why? For many, the only answer is habit.

Your daily routine and habits can dictate not only what you eat but also *when* you eat. When you get home from work or school, do you head straight for the refrigerator, whether or not you're hungry? Do you always snack when you watch television at night? Or when you're studying?

Emotions also influence your food choices. When the going gets tough, the tough often eat. For many, food is used as an emotional crutch during times of stress, sadness, or joy. Happiness can also trigger eating. Many people celebrate their end-of-term good grades or a promotion at work with a celebratory meal with friends or family. On vacation, you likely reward yourself with fun, relaxation, and, of course, good food. No matter your mood, food is often part of how you express your emotions.

The Take-Home Message Food provides the nutrients that your body needs to function, and the foods that you choose are influenced by many factors. Taste is the primary reason why certain foods have become your favorites. The availability of certain foods has made them a part of your culture and a habitual part of your day. Food trends, cost, limits on your time, convenience, and your emotions all can influence your food choices.

What Is Nutrition and Why Is Good Nutrition So Important?

Whereas food is the source of nutrients that your body needs, **nutrition** is about more than just food. Nutrition is the science that studies how the nutrients and compounds in foods nourish you, help you function, and affect your health.

nutrition The science that studies how the nutrients and compounds in foods that you eat nourish and affect your body functions and health.

self-Assessment

What Does the Health of Your Family Tree Look Like?

Is there a history of heart disease, diabetes, or obesity in your family? What about other chronic diseases or conditions? Before you read this textbook and learn about the role that good nutrition plays in preventing chronic diseases and maintaining overall good health, ask your parents and grandparents about your family's health history. If there are certain diseases or conditions that run in your family, you'll want to pay particular attention to these as you read about them in this book.

An easy way to manage information about your family's health history is by visiting My Family Health Portrait at http://familyhistory.hhs.gov. When you input your family medical history, it provides a family tree report. Save a copy of this family health history for future reference.

This isn't exactly what's meant by the phrase "You are what you eat," but it's close.

Your body needs all the nutrients to function properly. An acute deficiency of even one nutrient will negatively affect your body's ability to function in the short term. Chronic deficiencies, excesses, and imbalances of many nutrients can also affect your long-term health.

Good nutrition plays a role in reducing the risk of four of the top ten leading causes of death in the United States—heart disease, cancer, stroke, and diabetes. (Table 1.1).[11] Nutrition also plays an important role in preventing other diseases and conditions that can impede your lifestyle. A healthy diet can help keep your bones strong and reduce your risk of osteoporosis. Eating right will help you better manage your body weight, which in turn will reduce your risk of developing obesity, diabetes mellitus, and high blood pressure.

You are a product of what you eat, what you *don't* eat, or what you may eat *too much* of. You want to eat the best combination of a variety of foods to meet your nutritional needs and to be healthy. To do that, you need to understand the roles of the essential nutrients in your body and which foods to eat to get them.

The Take-Home Message Nutrition is the scientific study of how the nutrients and compounds in foods nourish your body. Good nutrition plays a role in reducing the risk of many chronic diseases and conditions. Long-term imbalances of many nutrients will affect your health.

Table 1.1

Leading Causes of Death in the United States

Disease/Cause of Death	Nutrition Related
Heart Disease	X
Cancer	X
Respiratory Diseases	
Stroke	X
Accidents	
Alzheimer's Disease	
Diabetes	X
Influenza/Pneumonia	
Kidney Disease	
Intentional Self Harm	

Source: Based on "Leading Causes of Death," Centers for Disease Control and Prevention website, 2012.

What Are the Essential Nutrients and Why Do You Need Them?

The classes of nutrients that we introduced earlier are all *essential* because you must have them in order to function. (Alcohol, in contrast, is not an essential nutrient; even though it provides energy in the form of kilocalories, your body does not need it to function.) Your body is, in fact, made up of the same essential nutrients that are found in foods (see **Figure 1.2**).

Carbohydrates, lipids (fats), and proteins are called **macronutrients**, because you need higher amounts of them in your diet. Vitamins and minerals, though equally important to your health, are considered **micronutrients** because you need them in lesser amounts. You need to consume the final nutrient, water, in copious amounts daily so that you are well hydrated.

Kilocalories from the macronutrients are used as energy during the process of metabolism, and many vitamins and minerals are essential to this process. Vitamins and minerals are also needed for growth and reproduction and to help repair and maintain your body (**Figure 1.3**).

Although each nutrient is unique, they are all equally important, as they work together in numerous ways to keep you healthy. An imbalance of just one will affect your health. Let's take a closer look at the macro- and micronutrients, and water.

Carbohydrates, Fats, and Proteins Provide Energy

Carbohydrates, fats (lipids), and proteins are the energy-providing nutrients, because they contain calories. When we talk about energy, we mean that your body breaks down these nutrients and "burns" them to fuel your activities and internal functioning. One kilocalorie equals the amount of energy needed to raise the temperature of 1 kilogram of water 1 degree Celsius. (Note that *kilocalories* are commonly referred to as *calories,* which is the term used in this book.) Carbohydrates and protein provide 4 calories per gram, and fats provide 9 calories per gram. The

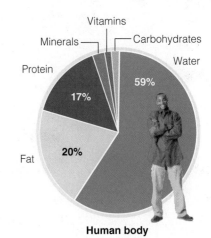

Human body

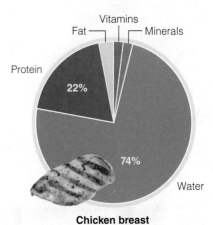

Chicken breast

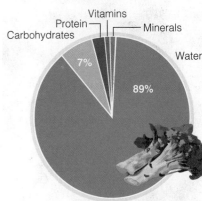

Broccoli (raw)

Figure 1.2 Nutrients in Foods and in the Body
The nutrients found in the foods that you eat are the same ones that provide structure for your body and allow your normal body processes to occur.

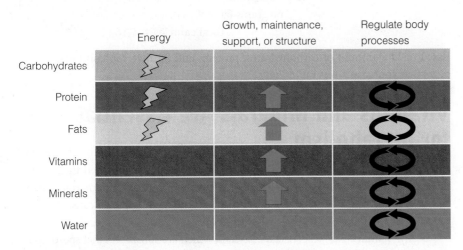

	Energy	Growth, maintenance, support, or structure	Regulate body processes
Carbohydrates	⚡		
Protein	⚡	⬆	🔄
Fats	⚡	⬆	🔄
Vitamins		⬆	🔄
Minerals		⬆	🔄
Water			🔄

Figure 1.3 Nutrients and Their Functions
Nutrients work closely together to provide energy, structure, and support, and to regulate body processes.

macronutrients The energy-containing essential nutrients that you need in higher amounts: carbohydrates, lipids (fats), and proteins.

micronutrients Essential nutrients that you need in smaller amounts: vitamins and minerals.

number of calories in a given food can be determined by measuring the weight, in grams, of each of the three nutrients in one serving of the food.

The amount of calories that you need daily to maintain your weight is estimated based on your age, gender, and activity level. However, you need these nutrients for many reasons beyond providing energy. You must consume a healthy combination of carbohydrates, fats, and protein so that excesses, deficiencies, and imbalances don't occur that may increase your risk of chronic diseases.

Carbohydrates supply the simple sugar, called glucose, that your cells use as the major energy source to fuel your body. Most of your daily calories should come from carbohydrates. Fats are another major fuel source. They also help cushion your organs to prevent damage and act as insulation under your skin to help maintain your body temperature. Proteins can be used as energy, but are better used to build and maintain your tissues, muscles, and organs. You also need protein to make most enzymes and some hormones, to help transport other nutrients, and for a healthy immune system. A healthy diet should provide adequate amounts of carbohydrates and fats for energy, and enough protein to maintain and repair your body.

Carbohydrates, fats, and proteins are all **organic** because they contain the element carbon. They also contain two other elements, hydrogen and oxygen. Proteins also contain nitrogen, while carbohydrates and fats do not.

You Can Calculate the Amount of Energy a Food Provides

The number of calories in one serving of a given food can be determined based on the amount (weight in grams) of carbohydrates, protein, and fat in the food. For example, suppose you ate an entire bag of potato chips and drank a 16-ounce cola for a snack. Together these two items contain 144 grams of carbohydrate (in the cola and chips), 12 grams of protein (from the chips), and 60 grams of fat (also in the chips). How many calories did you consume?

To find this out, you need to multiple the total grams of each energy-yielding nutrient times the number of calories per gram of that nutrient. Remember, a gram of carbohydrates and protein each contain 4 calories and a gram of fat contains 9 calories. Let's do some simple math to find out the total calories in the snack:

$$144 \text{ grams carbohydrates} \times 4 \text{ calories} = 576$$
$$12 \text{ grams protein} \times 4 \text{ calories} = 48$$
$$60 \text{ grams fat} \times 9 \text{ calories} = 540$$
$$\textbf{Total calories} = \textbf{1,164}$$

Based on the amount of carbohydrates, protein, and fat that you consumed, it appears that your snack was rather hefty.

Vitamins and Minerals Are Essential for Metabolism

Even though vitamins and minerals do not provide calories, you need them to use the carbohydrates, fats, and proteins you consume and to sustain numerous chemical reactions in your body. A deficiency of vitamins and minerals can cause ill effects ranging from fatigue to stunted growth, weak bones, and organ damage.

Many vitamins and minerals aid **enzymes**, which are substances that speed up reactions in your body. For example, many of the B vitamins function as coenzymes in the metabolism of carbohydrates and fats. Many minerals, such as calcium and phosphorus,

Do you know how many calories are in your chips and soda "study snack"?

organic Containing carbon.

enzymes Substances that speed up chemical reactions in your body.

work with protein-containing hormones and enzymes to maintain and strengthen your teeth and bones. The fate of carbohydrates, protein, and fats in your body is very much dependent upon your consuming enough vitamins and minerals in your daily diet.

Vitamins are organic compounds that usually have to be obtained from your foods. Your body is able to make some vitamins, such as vitamin D, but sometimes cannot make enough of it to maintain good health. In these situations, your diet has to supplement your body's efforts.

Minerals are **inorganic** substances that play a role in body processes and are key to the structure of some tissues, such as bone. A deficiency of any of the minerals can cause disease symptoms. Anyone who has ever suffered from iron-deficiency anemia can tell you that falling short of your daily iron needs, for example, can cause fatigue and interfere with your ability to function.

Water Is Vital for Many Processes in Your Body

(T/F) Although plain water does not provide energy or calories, it is vital to many key body functions, and staying hydrated is therefore an important part of staying healthy. As part of the fluid medium inside your cells, water helps chemical reactions, such as those involved in the production of energy, take place. Water also bathes the outside of your cells, playing a key role in transporting vital nutrients and oxygen to, and removing waste products from, your cells. Water helps maintain your body temperature and acts as a lubricant for your joints, eyes, mouth, and intestinal tract. It surrounds your organs and cushions them from injury.

The Take-Home Message Your body needs carbohydrates, fats (lipids), protein, vitamins, minerals, and water to survive. These six classes of nutrients have specific roles in your body, and you need them in specific amounts for good health. While carbohydrates, fats, and protein provide energy, vitamins, minerals, and water are needed to use the energy-producing nutrients and to maintain good health. The amount of calories you consume can be calculated based on the grams of carbohydrates, protein, and fat in the foods and beverages that you eat. Water is part of the medium inside and outside your cells that carries nutrients to, and waste products from, your cells. Water also helps maintain your body temperature and acts as a lubricant and protective cushion.

How Should You Get These Important Nutrients?

There is no question that you need all six classes of nutrients to function properly. But is there an advantage to consuming them through food rather than taking them as supplements? Is there more to a healthy diet than just meeting your basic nutrient needs? Let's look at these questions in more detail.

The Best Way to Meet Your Nutrient Needs Is with a Well-Balanced Diet

Many foods provide a variety of nutrients. For example, low-fat milk is high in both carbohydrates and protein and provides a small amount of fat. Milk is also a good source of the vitamins A, D, and riboflavin, as well as the minerals potassium and

Low-fat milk provides a whole host of nutrients.

inorganic Not containing carbon. Inorganic compounds include minerals, water, and salts.

calcium, and is approximately 90 percent water by weight. Whereas milk contains a substantial variety of all six classes of nutrients, a single food item doesn't have to provide all nutrients in order to be good for you. Rather, a well-balanced diet composed of a variety of foods can provide you with all of these important nutrients.

A well-balanced diet will also provide other dietary compounds, such as **phytochemicals** and **fiber**, that have been shown to help fight many diseases. At least 900 different phytochemicals have been identified in foods and more are likely to be discovered. However, don't assume that these compounds can be extracted from foods, put in a pill, and still produce the same positive effect on your health. The disease-fighting properties of phytochemicals likely go beyond the compounds themselves, and work with fiber, nutrients, or unknown substances in foods to provide a synergistic, positive effect on your health. Ⓣ Ⓕ

Fiber is the portion of plant foods that isn't completely digested in the stomach and Ⓣ Ⓕ small intestine. Some foods, such as whole grains, fruits, and vegetables, that are high in fiber are also phytochemical powerhouses. Studies have shown that diets rich in these plant-based foods fight many diseases. Fiber is not found in meat, poultry, or fish.

Also, let's not forget some of the obvious benefits of getting your nutrients from food. The delicious texture and aroma of foods, coupled with the social interaction of meals, are lost when you pop a pill to meet your nutrient needs. That said, some individuals *should* take a supplement if food alone can't meet their needs.

You Can Meet Some Nutrient Needs with a Supplement

Although many people can get all their nutrients through their diet, others have diet restrictions or higher nutrient needs such that they would benefit from taking a supplement in addition to consuming a healthy diet. For example, someone who is lactose intolerant (meaning they have difficulty digesting milk products) may have to meet his or her calcium needs from other sources. A calcium supplement could be an option for these individuals. Pregnant women should take an iron supplement because their increased need for this mineral is unlikely to be met through the diet alone. As you can see, a well-balanced diet and dietary supplements aren't mutually exclusive. In some situations, they should be partnered as the best nutritional strategy for good health.

The Take-Home Message A well-balanced diet will likely meet all of your nutrient needs and also provide a variety of compounds that may help prevent chronic diseases. People who cannot meet their nutrient needs through food alone may benefit from taking a supplement.

A well-balanced, healthy diet can help reduce the risk of heart disease, cancer, stroke, and diabetes, which are leading causes of death among Americans.

phytochemicals Nonnutritive compounds in plant foods that may play a role in fighting chronic diseases.

fiber The portion of plant foods that isn't digested in the small intestine.

How Does the Average American Diet Stack Up?

The food supply in the United States provides an array of nutritious choices to meet the dietary needs of most Americans. Fresh fruits and vegetables, whole grains, and lean meats, fish, and poultry are usually easily accessible and affordable through grocery stores and farmers' markets. Yet, with such an abundance of healthy foods to choose from, are Americans adopting healthy diets?

The Quality of the American Diet

In general, Americans eat too much added sugar, sodium, and saturated fat, and too little fiber and some vitamins and minerals. Our low fiber intake is partly due to our inadequate consumption of fruits and vegetables and our overconsumption of refined rather than whole grains.[12] At the same time, while dietary fiber intakes are below recommended levels, added sugars account for an average of 16 percent of Americans' daily calories.[13] This is largely due to Americans' love of soft drinks and other sugary beverages, as well as sweets and treats. For most of us, our fat intake is at the higher end of the recommended range, at about 33 percent. We eat too much saturated fat, and many of us exceed the recommended dietary cholesterol intake of less than 300 milligrams per day.[14]

With regard to the micronutrients, American men meet their recommendations for most vitamins and minerals but women often fall short of many—including iron, for example. Americans, in general, eat too much sodium, but not enough vitamin D, potassium, and calcium.[15] In an attempt to balance our lack of healthy food choices, more than 50 percent of Americans take at least one dietary supplement per day.[16]

The lack of a healthy diet may also be due to *where* we eat. Americans spend over 40 percent of their food budget consuming food outside the home.[17] As mentioned earlier, many of us buy prepared foods from the supermarket or takeout meals from restaurants. If you don't prepare a meal yourself, it can be more difficult to keep track of how much sugar, sodium, or saturated fat you're consuming. Research shows that prepared foods purchased outside the home tend to be less nutritious than those foods prepared in the home.[18,19] Eating one or more fast-food meals a week can increase the risk of weight gain, overweight, and obesity.[20]

Skipping breakfast may also hinder control of your waistline. Research suggests that children and adolescents who do not eat breakfast are at a higher risk for overweight and obesity.[21]

Rates of Overweight and Obesity in Americans

Americans have been battling the bathroom scale for decades, and the scale is winning. The prevalence of both **overweight** and **obesity** has become epidemic in the United States (see **Figure 1.4**). As people take in more calories than they burn, usually due to more sedentary lifestyles, they create a recipe for poor health. Over 65 percent of American adults are overweight and of those, approximately 36 percent are considered obese.[22] Whereas the latest statistics indicate that the epidemic of obesity may be slowing, the rate is still too high, and reducing it is a top health care priority.

Unfortunately, the rate of excessive weight gain is increasing for younger Americans. Currently, 12 percent of children aged 2 to 5 years and 18 percent of those aged 6 to 19 are considered obese.[23] Along with the weight gain have come higher rates of type 2 diabetes, particularly among children, and increased rates of heart disease, cancer, and stroke.

Ironically, being overweight doesn't necessarily mean being well fed. In fact, many of the poorest Americans are obese and malnourished. The Nutrition in the Real World feature "Poor, Obese, and Malnourished: A Troubling Paradox" looks at this growing problem among Americans.

1990

2000

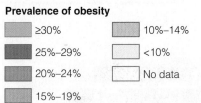

2011

Prevalence of obesity

≥30%	10%–14%
25%–29%	<10%
20%–24%	No data
15%–19%	

Figure 1.4 Obesity Trends among U.S. Adults
Over the last two decades, rates of overweight and obesity have risen significantly in the United States.

Source: Adaptations of "Prevalence of Self-Reported Obesity among U.S. Adults," "Percent of Obese (BMI = 30) in U.S. Adults: 1990," and "Percent of Obese (BMI = 30) in U.S. Adults: 2000," from Centers for Disease Control and Prevention website, 2013.

overweight Carrying extra weight on your body in relation to your height. Clinically defined as having a body mass index (BMI) of 25 to 29.9.

obesity Carrying an excessive amount of body fat above the level of being overweight. Clinically defined as having a body mass index (BMI) of 30 or higher.

Poor, Obese, and Malnourished: A Troubling Paradox

Food costs money, so people who are poor typically have less money to buy food. Therefore, people who are poor are less likely to be overweight or obese—right? Makes sense, but the conclusion is wrong.

In survey after survey, rates of obesity turn out to be highest among people with the lowest incomes. The numbers are greater for women than for men, but for both genders, Americans living near or below the poverty level have much higher rates of obesity than affluent Americans. While households with limited funds for monthly groceries tend to buy *less* of a variety of foods, the *quality* of the foods tends to be low in nutrients and high in calories.[1] When food insecurity, or the inability to satisfy the basic food needs of individuals, exists in the home, the goal is to fill the stomach, not necessarily nourish the body.

Obesity aside, children who are food insecure are more likely to be deficient in iron, have colds and headaches, and even have delayed cognitive development. These children are at risk for behavioral problems such as irritability, performing poorly academically, and being disruptive in class compared with their well-nourished peers.[2]

In addition to the lack of funds to buy adequate food, researchers have uncovered other factors that can lead to obesity for those who are food insecure, including:[3]

> **Inconsistent Meal Patterns.** Homes with food insecurity often experience "feast or famine" episodes in the kitchen. In other words, there may be times during the month when the kitchen shelves are full of food, only to have other days, and even weeks, where the pantry is bare. When food is plentiful, children often feast heartily, knowing that famine is just around the corner. Researchers speculate that these wide swings in the consumption of calories may wreak havoc with a person's metabolism as well as promote the storage of fat in the body.

> **Household Stress.** In addition to food insecurity, financial constraints also threaten a stable home and access to adequate health care, both of which can contribute to a stressful environment. Stress, anxiety, and depression can cause unhealthy eating, which can perpetuate obesity.

Individuals living in low-income neighborhoods also tend to have limited access to supermarkets to purchase healthy foods at a reasonable cost. In addition, poorer neighborhoods tend to be surrounded by convenience stores and fast-food restaurants, so high-fat, high-calorie foods may be plentiful but nutritious foods scarce. When money is scarce, the stage is set for the paradox of being poor, obese, and malnourished.

Practical Nutrition VIDEO

Shop Smart

Is it possible to eat healthfully on a tight budget? Take a trip to the supermarket with Joan to find out! Scan this QR code with your mobile device to access the video. You can also access the video in MasteringNutrition™.

Healthy People 2020 A set of disease prevention and health promotion objectives for Americans to meet during the second decade of the new millennium.

Improving Americans' Diets Is One Goal of *Healthy People 2020*

The U.S. Surgeon General has issued calls for a nationwide health improvement program since 1979. The latest edition of this report, *Healthy People 2020*, contains a set of health goals and objectives for the nation to achieve over the second decade of the twenty-first century.[24]

Healthy People 2020 focuses on several overarching goals:

> Attain high-quality, longer lives free of preventable disease, disability, injury, and premature death.
> Achieve health equity, eliminate disparities, and improve the health of all groups.
> Create social and physical environments that promote good health for all.
> Promote quality of life, healthy development, and healthy behaviors across every stage of life.

There are more than 35 topic areas in *Healthy People 2020*, ranging from ensuring that Americans have adequate access to health services to improvements in their diets and physical activity. Objectives are developed within each topic area.

Table 1.2

Healthy People 2020 Nutrition and Weight Status Objectives

Objectives	Target for Americans (%)	Status of Americans (%)
Increase the proportion of adults who are at a healthy weight	33.9	30.8
Reduce the proportion of adults who are obese	30.5	33.9
Reduce the proportion of children and adolescents who are considered obese	14.5	16.1
Increase the contribution of fruits to diets of the population age 2 years and older	0.9 cups/ 1,000 calories	0.5 cups/ 1,000 calories
Increase the variety and contribution of vegetables to the diets of the population age 2 years and older	1.1 cups/ 1,000 calories	0.8 cups/ 1,000 calories

Source: *Healthy People 2020*, U.S. Department of Health and Human Services, 2012.

For example, current research indicates that Americans' body weights are increasing rather than decreasing. Thus, "Nutrition and Weight Status" is one topic area. Its goal is to promote health and reduce chronic diseases associated with diet and weight. There are numerous objectives developed within this topic area that, if fulfilled, will help Americans improve their diet and reduce their weight. See Table 1.2 for the list of a few objectives in this area of focus.

As you can see from the table, consuming adequate amounts of fruits and vegetables is beneficial to managing one's weight. Americans should increase their intake of both of these food sources to help them improve their nutrition and weight status.

The Take-Home Message Incidences of overweight and obesity among Americans are prevalent, yet many people are falling short of some nutrient needs. *Healthy People 2020* is a set of health objectives for the nation to achieve over the second decade of the twenty-first century.

The incidence of overweight and obesity among adults and children is becoming more prevalent in the United States.

What's the Real Deal When It Comes to Nutrition Research and Advice?

If you "Google" the word *nutrition*, you will get a list of about 391,000,000 entries instantly. Obviously, the world is full of nutrition information.

Just ask anyone who is trying to lose weight and that person will probably tell you how hard it is to keep up with the latest diet advice—because it seems to keep changing. In the 1970s, waist watchers were told that carbohydrates were the bane of their existence and that a protein-rich, low-carbohydrate diet was the name of the game when it came to shrinking their waistlines. A decade later, avoiding fat was the key to winning the battle of the bulge. By 2000, carbohydrates were being ousted yet again, and protein-rich diets were back in vogue. But now protein-heavy diets seem to be fading out of the limelight and higher carbohydrate diets—with plenty of fiber,

Nutrition-related research findings are often lead stories in newspapers, magazines, and on websites.

fruits, and vegetables—are becoming the way to fight weight gain. So . . . are you frustrated yet?

Even though popular wisdom and trends seem to change with the wind, scientific knowledge about nutrition doesn't change this frequently. While the media publicizes results from studies deemed newsworthy, in reality it takes many, many affirming research studies before a **consensus** is reached about nutrition advice. News of the results of one study is just that: news. In contrast, advice from an authoritative health organization or committee, such as the American Heart Association or the Dietary Guidelines Advisory Committee, which is based on a consensus of research information, is sound information that can be trusted for the long term. Headlines in newspapers, lead articles on websites, and the sound bites on television often report the results of a single, recent research study. The Examining the Evidence feature "How Can I Evaluate Nutrition News?" discusses how to scrutinize information about current research findings and not get caught up in the media hype.

Sound Nutrition Research Begins with the Scientific Method

Research studies that generate enough information are based on a process called the **scientific method**. Scientists are like detectives. They observe something in the natural world, ask questions, come up with an idea (or **hypothesis**) based on their observations, test their hypothesis, and then see if their idea is correct. There are many steps in the scientific method and many adjustments made along the way before a scientist has gained enough information to support his or her hypothesis. In fact, the entire process can take years to complete.

Let's walk through a nutrition-related study in which scientists used the scientific method to study rickets. Rickets is a potentially severe and even fatal disease in children, whereby the bones throughout the body weaken. For instance, the spine and rib cage can become so distorted that breathing is impaired. The leg bones can become so weakened that they are unable to hold up the child's body weight, and they curve outward ("bow legs"). In the nineteenth century, parents often relied on folk remedies to treat diseases; in the case of rickets, they used cod-liver oil because it seemed to prevent the disorder as well as cure it, although no one knew how.

The first steps of the scientific method are to make an observation and ask questions (**Figure 1.5**). Originally, scientists were piqued by the cod-liver oil curing phenomenon. They asked themselves why cod-liver oil cured rickets. In the second step of the scientific method, a hypothesis is formulated. Because cod-liver oil is very rich in vitamin A, scientists initially thought that this vitamin must be the curative factor. To confirm this, scientists proceeded to the next step in the scientific method, which was to conduct an experiment.

Observe and ask a question
Why does cod-liver oil cure rickets?

Formulate a hypothesis
The vitamin A in cod-liver oil is the curative factor.

Conduct an experiment
Feed rats with rickets cod-liver oil that contains no vitamin A.

Hypothesis supported
Rats were not cured.

Hypothesis not supported
Rats were cured.

Revise or formulate a new hypothesis

Figure 1.5 Steps of the Scientific Method
The scientific method is used to conduct credible research in nutrition and other scientific fields.

consensus The opinion of a group of experts based on a collection of information.

scientific method A stepwise process used by scientists to generate sound research findings.

hypothesis An idea generated by scientists based on their observations.

How Can I Evaluate Nutrition News?

August 30, 2012

Chocolate May Lower the Risk of Stroke in Men

Loren Grush, *FoxNews.com*

Based on this headline, you may be tempted to run out immediately and get yourself a couple of chocolate bars. However, you would be doing a disservice to your health if you didn't read below this tantalizing headline, to assimilate and analyze the evidence on which the headline is based.

The media are routinely bombarded by press releases sent from medical journals, food companies, organizations, and universities about research being conducted and/or conferences being sponsored by these institutions. These releases are sent for one reason: to gain publicity. Reputable news organizations that report these findings will seek out independent experts in the field to weigh in on the research and, just as importantly, explain how these findings relate to the public. If you don't read beyond the headlines, you are probably missing important details of the story. Even worse, if you begin making dietary and lifestyle changes based on each news flash, you become a scientific guinea pig.

When a headline piques your interest, read the article with a critical eye, and ask yourself the following questions.

1. Was the Research Finding Published in a Peer-Reviewed Journal?

You can be confident that studies published in a peer-reviewed journal have been thoroughly reviewed by experts in this area of research. If the research isn't published in a peer-reviewed journal, you have no way of knowing if the study was conducted in an appropriate manner and whether the findings are accurate. A study about the possible virtues of chocolate in fighting heart disease that is published in the *New England Journal of Medicine* has more credibility than a similar article published in a baking magazine.

2. Was the Study Done Using Animals or Humans?

Animals are animals and humans are humans. Experiments with animals are often used to study how a particular substance affects a health outcome. But if the study is conducted in rats, it doesn't necessarily mean that the substance will have the same effect if consumed by humans. This doesn't mean that animal studies are frivolous. They are important stepping stones to designing and conducting similar experiments involving humans.

3. Do the Study Participants Resemble Me?

When you read or hear about studies involving humans, you should always seek more information about the individuals who took part in the research. For example, were the people in the chocolate studies college-aged subjects or older individuals with heart disease and high blood pressure? If older adults were studied, then would these findings be of any benefit to young adults who don't have high blood pressure or heart disease?

4. Is This the First Time I've Heard about This?

A single study in a specific area of research is a lonely entity in the scientific world. Is this the first study regarding the health benefits of chocolate? If

the media article doesn't confirm that other studies have also supported these findings, this one study may be the *only* study of its kind. Wait until you hear that these research findings have been confirmed by a reputable health organization, such as the American Heart Association, before considering making any changes in your diet. Reputable organizations will only change their advice based on a consensus of research findings.

In your lifetime, you are going to read thousands of newspaper and website headlines, as well as watch and listen to who-knows-how-many similar television and radio reports. Your critical thinking skills in evaluating the sources and information presented will be your best friend when it comes to deciding which blurbs to believe. These skills may also save you considerable money by helping you avoid nutrition gimmicks. When it comes to assessing nutrition information in the media, it's worth your time and effort to find out where it came from and why (or if) you should care.

What Do You Think?

1. Have you ever changed your food purchasing or consuming habits as the result of a story in the media?
2. What criteria did you use to evaluate that nutrition news?
3. What ethical obligations do news organizations have to protect the public from unreliable nutrition information?

Figure 1.6 A Hypothesis Can Lead to a Scientific Consensus
When a hypothesis is supported by research, the results are published in peer-reviewed journals. Once a theory has been developed and supported by subsequent experiments, a consensus is reached in the scientific community.

peer-reviewed journal A research journal in which fellow scientists (peers) review studies to assess if they are accurate and sound before they are published.

laboratory experiment A scientific experiment conducted in a laboratory. Some laboratory experiments involve animals.

observational research Research that involves looking at factors in two or more groups of subjects to see if there is a relationship to certain outcomes.

epidemiological research Research that looks at populations of people; it is often observational.

experimental research Research involving at least two groups of subjects.

experimental group The group given a specific treatment.

control group The group given a placebo.

placebo A sugar pill that has no impact on the individual's health when ingested.

The scientists altered the cod-liver oil to destroy all of its vitamin A. The altered oil was given to rats that had been fed a diet that caused rickets. Surprisingly, the rats were still cured of rickets. This disproved the scientists' original hypothesis that vitamin A was the curative factor. They then needed to modify their hypothesis, as it was obvious that there was something else in the cod-liver oil that cured rickets. They next hypothesized that it was the vitamin D that cured the rats, and conducted another experiment to confirm this hypothesis, which it did.

The next step in the scientific method involves sharing these findings with the scientific community. What good would it be to make this fabulous discovery if other scientists couldn't find out about it? To do this, scientists summarize and submit their research findings to a **peer-reviewed journal** (**Figure 1.6**). Other scientists (peers) then look at the researchers' findings to make sure that they are sound. If so, the research study is published in the journal. (If this relationship between vitamin D and rickets were discovered today, it would probably be the lead story on CNN.)

As more and more studies were done that confirmed that vitamin D can cure and prevent rickets, a theory developed. We now know with great certainty that vitamin D can prevent rickets and that a deficiency of vitamin D will cause this type of deformed bones in children. Because of this, there is a consensus among health professionals as to the importance of vitamin D in the diets of children.

Research Studies and Experiments Confirm Hypotheses

Scientists can use different types of experiments to test hypotheses. The rickets experiment just described is called a **laboratory experiment**, as it was done in the confines of a lab. In the fields of nutrition and health, laboratory experiments are often conducted using animals, such as rats. Research conducted with humans is usually observational or experimental.

Observational Research

Observational research involves looking at factors in two or more groups of subjects to see if there is a relationship to a certain disease or another health outcome. For example, researchers might study rates of breast-feeding in infants with and without rickets, to see if breast-feeding influences the incidence of the disease.

One type of observational research is **epidemiological research**, which looks at populations of people. For example, scientists may look at people who live in Norway and notice that there is a higher incidence of rickets among children there than in Australia. Through their observation, they may find a relationship between the lack of sun exposure in Norway and the high incidence of rickets there compared with sunny Australia. However, the scientists can't rule out the possibility that the difference in the incidence of rickets in these two populations may also be due to other factors in the subjects' diet or lifestyle.

Experimental Research

Experimental research involves at least two groups of subjects. One group, the **experimental group**, is given a specific treatment, and another group, the **control group**, isn't. For instance, after hypothesizing that vitamin D cures rickets, scientists would have randomly assigned children with rickets to two groups. They would have given a vitamin D supplement to the children in the experimental group but would have given the children in the control group a substance, called a **placebo**, that looked just like the vitamin D supplement but contained only sugar or some other nonactive ingredient. If neither of the two groups of subjects knew which substance they received, then they were "blind" to the treatment. If the scientists who were giving the placebo and the vitamin D supplement also couldn't distinguish between the two treatments and didn't know which group received which, this would be called a **double-blind, placebo-controlled study**.

The scientists would also have to make sure that all other significant factors were the same for both groups during the experiment. For example, because the scientists knew that sun exposure has a therapeutic effect on rickets, they couldn't let the children in the control group go outside in the sunshine while keeping the children in the experimental group inside. The exposure to sunshine would change the outcome of the experiment. Similarly, they'd have to ensure that the children were eating exactly the same diet for the duration of the study.

A double-blind, placebo-controlled study is considered the "gold standard" of research, because all of the factors that might influence the study results are kept the same for the groups of subjects, and neither the subjects nor the researchers are biased, as they don't know which group has received which treatment (**Figure 1.7**).

Although the results of many experiments fail to support the initial hypotheses, a great many discoveries are made. With continuing research, one discovery builds upon another. Though it may seem frustrating when the findings of one research study dispute the results of another from just a few months before, even contradictory findings help advance scientific knowledge, in part because of the questions they raise. Why did the first study show one result and a second study something different? In tackling such questions, scientists continue to advance our understanding of the world around us, and within us. For example, scientists are asking intriguing research questions about nutritional genomics. The Health Connection feature "What Is Nutritional Genomics?" discusses this fascinating area of nutritional science.

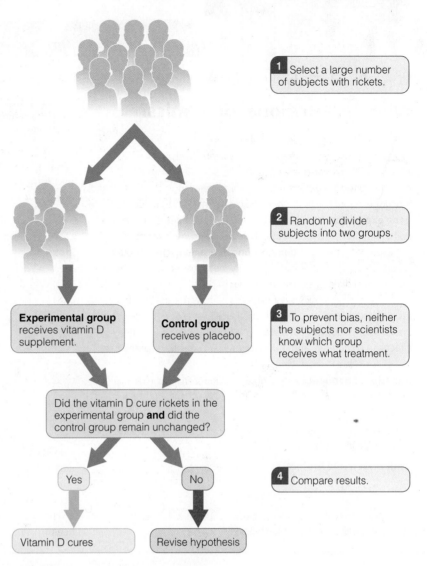

Figure 1.7 Controlled Scientific Experiments
Scientists use experimental research to test hypotheses.

You Can Trust the Advice of Nutrition Experts

If you want legal advice, you seek the expertise of a lawyer. If you need a knee operation, you should visit an orthopedic surgeon. If you want nutrition advice, to whom should you turn? Of course you want to speak with a credible expert who has training in the field of nutrition. So, who are these people and where do you find them?

One option is to seek the expertise of a **registered dietitian nutritionist (RDN)**. The RDN has completed at least a bachelor's degree at an accredited university or college in the United States that has incorporated specific coursework and supervised

double-blind placebo-controlled study When the scientists and subjects in a research experiment can't distinguish between the treatments given to the subjects and don't know which group of subjects received which treatment.

registered dietitian nutritionist (RDN) A health professional who has completed at least a bachelor's degree in nutrition from an accredited university or college in the United States, completed a supervised practice, and passed an exam administered by the Academy of Nutrition and Dietetics (AND).

What Is Nutritional Genomics?

As we learn more about nutrition from ongoing research, we are likely to find even more ways in which what we eat affects our personal health. One exciting area of research now is **nutritional genomics**. Genomics is the study of genes, their functions in your body, and how the environment may influence **gene expression**. Your genes determine your inherited, specific traits. With the completion of the **Human Genome Project**, the complete sequencing of **deoxyribonucleic acid (DNA)** in your cells is now known. Your DNA contains the genetic instructions needed to develop and direct the activities of your body.

Nutritional genomics is concerned with how the specific components in foods that you eat interact on a cellular level with the expression of your genes. Certain dietary components can cause different effects on your genes, and thus, initiate a very specific response in

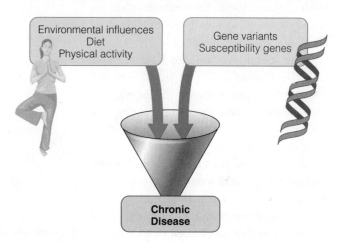

Chronic disease is caused by a mixture of genetic and environmental influences.

nutritional genomics A field of study that researches the relationship between nutrition and genomics (the study of genes and gene expression).

gene expression The processing of genetic information to create a specific protein.

Human Genome Project A project sponsored by the United States government to determine the complete set and sequencing of DNA in human cells and identify all human genes.

deoxyribonucleic acid (DNA) Genetic material within cells that directs the synthesis of proteins in the body.

your body that could be different from the response it initiates in another person. For example, nutritional genomics will help determine the specific dietary combination of types of fats that you should consume to lower your risk of heart disease based on your genetic makeup.[4] Most chronic diseases stem from the interplay between genetic makeup, environment, and diet (see figure). As more becomes known about the application of nutritional genomics, you will have more control over how your diet affects your long-term health.

practice that have been approved by the accrediting body of the Academy of Nutrition and Dietetics (AND). RDNs have also passed a national exam administered by the credentialing body of AND. They have an understanding of **medical nutrition therapy**, which is an integration of nutrition counseling and dietary changes based on an individual's medical history and current health needs to improve that person's health.

RDNs work with their patients to make dietary changes that can help prevent diseases such as heart disease, diabetes, stroke, and obesity. Many physicians, based on the diagnoses of their patients, refer them to RDNs for nutrition advice and guidance. RDNs must participate in continuing professional education in order to remain current in the fast-changing world of nutrition, medicine, and health and maintain their registration. RDNs work in hospitals and other health care facilities, private practice, universities, medical schools, professional athletic teams, food companies, and other nutrition-related businesses.

Individuals with advanced degrees in nutrition can also provide credible nutrition information. Sometimes physicians may have taken a nutrition course in medical school and gone on to get a master of science in public health (MPH), which involves some nutrition courses, or a master's degree in nutrition at an accredited university or college.

medical nutrition therapy The integration of nutrition counseling and dietary changes based on an individual's medical and health needs to treat a patient's medical condition.

nutrition
IN THE Real World

Don't Be Scammed!

Consumers beware. The snake oil salespeople of yesteryear never left the building. They just left the oil behind and moved on to selling nutrition supplements and other products that are not based on science. These skilled salespeople introduce health fears into your mind and then try to sell services and products to allay these newly created fears. They make unrealistic promises and guarantees.

To avoid falling for one of their shady schemes, there are certain "red flags" that should alert and warn you to be leery of infomercials, magazine ads, mail-order catalogs, and websites that try to convince you that:

➢ There is a quick fix for what ails you.
➢ Their product is all natural and miraculously cures.

➢ One product does it all.
➢ You can lose a lot of weight in a short amount of time and without dieting or exercising.
➢ The product contains a secret ingredient.
➢ The product shrinks tumors.
➢ There is no risk, as there is a money-back guarantee. (Good luck getting your money back!)

Don't be a victim of health fraud scams. Be smart, be aware, and be careful. To report a problem, contact the FDA at www.fda.gov/Safety/ReportaProblem or call 1-888-463-6332.

Source: U.S. Department of Health and Human Services, U.S. Food and Drug Administration. 2011. *Health Fraud Scams. . . . Are Everywhere. Get the Facts.* Available at www.fda.gov. Accessed February 2013.

Some **public health nutritionists** may have an undergraduate degree in nutrition but didn't complete a supervised practice, so are not eligible to take the RDN exam. These individuals can work in the government organizing community outreach nutrition programs, such as programs for the elderly.

In order to protect the health of the public receiving nutrition information, more than 30 states in the United States currently license nutrition professionals who must meet specified educational and experience criteria to be considered experts in the field of nutrition. A person who meets these qualifications is a **licensed dietitian nutritionist (LDN)** and so will have the letters "LDN" after his or her name. Because RDNs have completed the rigorous standards set forth by the AND, they automatically meet the criteria for LDN and often will have both "RDN" and "LDN" after their names.

Be careful when taking nutrition advice from a trainer at the gym or the person who works at the local health food store. Whereas some of these people may be credible, many are not, and thus, less likely to give you valid information that's based on solid scientific evidence. Anyone who calls himself or herself a **nutritionist** may have taken few or no accredited courses in nutrition.

You also need to beware of individuals who specialize in health quackery or fraud. Such scammers will try to persuade you with false nutrition claims and anecdotal stories that aren't backed up by sound science and research. Americans spend billions of dollars annually on fraudulent health products, an injustice that the Food and Drug Administration (FDA) has been trying to fight for decades. The FDA's health fraud scams website helps consumers identify quackery and health fraud and make educated decisions about health-related information and products. Common deceptive statements made by health quacks are included in the Nutrition in the Real World feature "Don't Be Scammed!"

Identifying quackery and fraud is important not only when you are seeking out an expert for advice, but also when you read about nutrition on the Internet. The Web is overflowing with nutrition information and *mis*information.

public health nutritionist An individual who may have an undergraduate degree in nutrition but isn't an RDN.

licensed dietitian nutritionist (LDN) An individual who has met specified educational and experience criteria deemed necessary by a state licensing board to be considered an expert in the field of nutrition. An RDN would meet all the qualifications to be an LDN.

nutritionist A generic term with no recognized legal or professional meaning. Some people may call themselves nutritionists without having any credible training in nutrition.

You Can Obtain Accurate Nutrition Information on the Internet

When surfing the Internet for nutrition information, look for a credible, reliable site with up-to-date information.

Mark Twain once said, "Be careful about reading health books. You could die of a misprint." If he were alive today, he probably would have included websites that dole out health advice. Approximately 60 percent of American adult Internet users have surfed millions of websites looking for health information.[25]

Don't assume that a slick website is a sound website. Although many websites, such as Let's Move! (www.letsmove.gov) and *Web*MD (www.webmd.com) provide credible, reliable, up-to-date nutrition information, many, many others do not. Remember, anyone with computer skills can put up a website. The National Institutes of Health (NIH) has developed 10 questions that you should consider when viewing a nutrition- or health-related website:[26]

1. Who Runs the Site?

Credible websites are willing to show their credentials. For example, the National Center for Complementary and Alternative Medicine (www.nccam.nih.gov) provides information about its association with the NIH and its extensive ongoing research and educational programs. If you have to spend more than a minute trying to find out who runs the website, you should click to another site.

2. Who Pays for the Site?

Running a website is expensive, and finding out who's paying for a particular site will tell you something about the reliability of its content. Websites sponsored by the government (with URLs ending in .gov), or an academic institution (.edu) are more reliable than many commercial websites (.com or .net). Some commercial websites, such as *Web*MD, carry articles that can be reliable if they are written by credible health professionals, but other websites may be promoting information to suit a company's own purposes.

For example, if the funding source for the website is a vitamin and mineral supplement company, are all the articles geared toward supporting the use of supplements? Does the website have advertisers, and do their products also influence the content on the website? You need to investigate whether the website content may be biased based on the funding source.

3. What Is the Purpose of the Site?

After you answer the first two questions, look for the "About This Site" link. This will help you understand the website's purpose. For example, at Nutrition.gov, the purpose is to "provide easy access to the best food and nutrition information across the federal government." This website doesn't exist to sell you anything, but to help you find reliable information.

4. Where Does the Information Come From?

You should always know who wrote what you are reading. Is the author a qualified nutrition expert, or did she or he interview qualified individuals? If the site obtained information from another source, was that source cited?

5. What Is the Basis of the Information?

Is the article's information based on medical facts and figures that have references? For example, any medical news items released on the American Heart Association website (www.americanheart.org) will include the medical journal from which the information came. In fact, the website will often include the opinion of experts regarding the news items.

6. How Is the Information Selected?

A physician who is a well-known medical expert for a major television network once commented that he spends most of his time not delivering medical advice, but trying to stop the networks from publicizing health news that isn't credible. Always look to see if the website has an editorial board of medical and health experts and if qualified individuals review or write the content before it is released.

7. How Current Is the Information?

Once a website is on the Internet, it will stay there until someone removes it. Consequently, the health information that you read may not be the most up to date. Always check to see when the content was written, and if it is over a year old, whether it has been updated.

8. How Does the Site Choose Links to Other Sites?

Some medical sites don't like to link to other sites, as they don't have control over other sites' credibility and content. Others do link, if they are confident that these sites meet their criteria. Some sites receive financial reimbursement from the links that they post. Don't always assume that the link is credible.

9. What Information Is Collected about You and Why?

Websites track the pages that you click on in order to analyze their more popular topics. Sometimes, they elicit personal information such as your gender, age, and health concerns. After collecting data on your viewing selections and your personal information, they can sell this information to interested companies. These companies can create promotional materials about their goods and services targeted to your needs. Credible sites should tell you about their privacy policy and if they will or will not give this information to other sources. A website's privacy policy is often found in a link at the bottom of its screens.

10. How Does the Site Manage Interactions with Visitors?

You should always be able to easily find the contact information of the website's owners should you have any concerns or questions that you want answered. If the site has a chat room or ongoing discussion group, you should know how it is moderated. Read the discussion group dialogue before you jump in.

The Take-Home Message Sound nutrition advice is based on years of research using the scientific method. You should only take nutrition advice from a credible source, such as a registered dietitian or other valid nutrition expert. When obtaining nutrition information from the Internet, you need to carefully peruse the site to make sure that it is credible, it contains up-to-date information, and its content isn't influenced by those that fund and support the website.

Should Food Advertising to Children Be Regulated by the Government?

In 2012, the Better Business Bureau, working with several food industry companies, agreed to adhere to the Children's Food and Beverage Advertising Initiative, a voluntary program that was designed to "shift the mix of foods advertised to children under 12 to encourage healthier dietary choices and healthy lifestyles."[1] Still, children's advocacy groups argue that this isn't enough; they say we need laws that govern food advertising to children. Should the government regulate food advertising to children? Read the arguments, then consider the critical-thinking questions and decide for yourself.

yes

- Strong scientific evidence shows that the marketing of unhealthy foods to children is a significant risk factor contributing to childhood obesity.[2]

- Studies have shown that even at 10 years of age, children may not understand the persuasive intent of advertisements.[3]

- Cognitive research shows that young children don't understand that ads are trying to persuade them, nor can they evaluate commercials critically. Given that earlier legal cases set the precedent that it is OK for the government to restrict inherently misleading speech, it should be allowed to restrict advertising to children.[4]

- Dietary patterns that begin in childhood give shape to the health profiles of Americans at all ages. Dietary patterns reflect the influence of our culture, and our social and economic environments. Ensuring that these environments support good health is a fundamental responsibility, requiring leadership and action from all of us—not just parents.[5]

no

- Currently, advertisements to children are protected speech, under the First Amendment.[6]

- Parents can monitor how much TV their child is actually watching so that they are not overexposed to ads, and there are resources to help them sort out how to do this.[7]

- In 2011, McDonald's defended its right to advertise freely, insisting that it is a company's right to advertise so it can stay in business, and the consumer's right to make responsible personal choices.[8]

- Studies have shown that even though Sweden and Quebec have banned TV food advertising to children for over a decade, obesity rates are still comparable to those in the rest of Europe and Canada.[9]

what do you think?

1. Do you support the idea of regulating food advertising to children? **2.** Does food advertising really impact what children eat, given that parents are doing the shopping? **3.** How much impact should advertisers be allowed to have on children, whose minds can't discriminate the way adults' can?

1 Multiple Factors Influence Food Choices

Food choices are influenced by personal taste, culture, social life, accessibility, cost, and time constraints. You eat out of habit, in response to your emotions, and, of course, because food is delicious. However, taste is the most important consideration influencing what you eat.

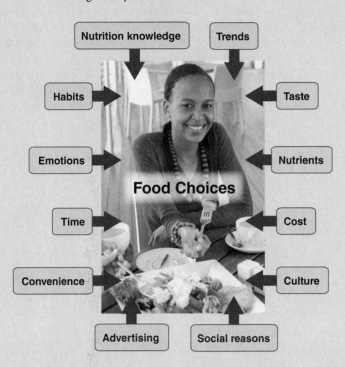

Nutrition knowledge — Trends — Habits — Taste — Emotions — Nutrients — **Food Choices** — Time — Cost — Convenience — Culture — Advertising — Social reasons

2 Nutrition Is the Science of Food

Nutrition is the science that studies how the nutrients and compounds in foods nourish you, help you function, and affect your health. Good nutrition plays an important role in preventing many of the leading causes of death in the United States, including heart disease, cancer, stroke, and diabetes.

3 There Are Six Categories of Nutrients

Nutrients are classified as carbohydrates, lipids (fats), proteins, vitamins, minerals, and water. Carbohydrates, fats, and proteins provide the energy (calories) that your body needs. Carbohydrates are the body's preferred source of energy. Fats insulate the body and cushion internal organs. The primary role of dietary protein is to build and maintain body tissues. Protein also acts as enzymes that catalyze chemical reactions. Vitamins and minerals do not provide energy, but are important for metabolism and to properly utilize carbohydrates, fats, and protein. Many vitamins aid enzymes in your body. Water is an essential nutrient that is vital for many functions. It bathes the inside and outside of your cells, helps maintain your body temperature, and acts as a lubricant and protective cushion.

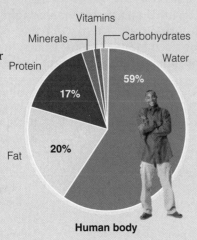

Vitamins — Minerals — Carbohydrates — Protein — Water 59% — 17% — 20% — Fat

Human body

4 A Well-Balanced Diet Will Provide the Nutrients Your Body Needs

Your body needs a mixture of the six categories of nutrients in specific amounts to stay healthy. Eating a well-balanced diet is the best way to meet your nutrient and health needs. Vitamin and mineral supplements can help complete a healthy diet but should not replace foods.

5 The American Diet Doesn't Stack Up

Most Americans are not meeting all their nutrient needs without exceeding their calorie requirements. The average American diet is high in protein, sugar, sodium, saturated fat, and calories, but low in vitamin E, calcium, and fiber. In addition, the rates of overweight and obesity among Americans are too high. Nutrition plays an important role in preventing many of the leading causes of death in the United States, including heart disease, cancer, stroke, and type 2 diabetes.

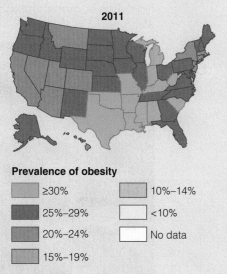

2011

Prevalence of obesity

≥30%		10%–14%	
25%–29%		<10%	
20%–24%		No data	
15%–19%			

6 Nutrition Is a Science and New Discoveries Are Continually Being Made

Sound nutrition information is the result of numerous scientific studies that are based on the scientific method. These research findings should be reviewed by and shared with the medical and scientific community. You should never change your diet or lifestyle based upon the findings of just one or a few studies. The science of nutritional genomics studies how diet may modify the way genes work and how genetic makeup affects nutrient requirements. Nutritional advice should come from credible sources. Individuals who call themselves nutritionists may or may not have a credible nutrition education.

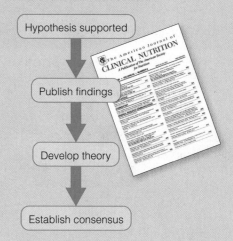

Hypothesis supported

Publish findings

Develop theory

Establish consensus

Terms to Know

- nutrients
- kilocalories
- metabolism
- nutrition
- macronutrients
- micronutrients
- organic
- enzymes
- inorganic
- overweight
- obesity
- *Healthy People 2020*
- scientific method
- hypothesis
- observational research
- epidemiological research
- experimental research
- experimental group
- control group
- placebo
- registered dietitian nutritionist (RDN)
- nutritional genomics
- gene expression

MasteringNutrition™ Want extra practice with key terms in this chapter? Or, would you like additional questions to prep for an exam? Check out the Study Area of MasteringNutrition at www.masteringhealthandnutrition.com (or www.pearsonmastering.com). There you'll find everything from pre-built flashcards that can be downloaded to your smartphone for studying on-the-go to chapter reading quizzes that assess your knowledge of the chapter—and so much more!

Check Your Understanding

1. Megan picks up a sandwich at the campus food truck after class every afternoon before dashing off to her part-time job. Which of the following most likely influences Megan's food choices in this situation?
   a. her ethnic background
   b. her busy schedule
   c. her emotions
   d. her limited budget
2. Nutrition is
   a. the study of genes and their function in the body.
   b. the study of how the body functions.
   c. the scientific study of how compounds in foods affect body functions.
   d. the study of hormones and how they function in the body.
3. The energy in foods is measured in carbohydrates.
   a. true   b. false

4. The majority of your daily calories should come from
   a. fats.
   b. minerals.
   c. vitamins.
   d. carbohydrates.
5. Which nutrients may help enzymes function in your body?
   a. carbohydrates
   b. vitamins
   c. fat
   d. protein
6. Everyone needs to take vitamin and mineral supplements to be healthy.
   a. true   b. false
7. Over _____ percent of American adults are overweight.
   a. 35   b. 45   c. 55   d. 65
8. A cookie with 13 grams of carbohydrates, 4 grams of fat, and 1 gram of protein contains
   a. 54 calories.
   b. 65 calories.
   c. 70 calories.
   d. 92 calories.
9. The first step in the scientific method is to
   a. make observations and ask questions.
   b. form a hypothesis.
   c. do an experiment.
   d. develop a theory.
10. Which of the following individuals would be the best to approach for nutritional counseling?
   a. a health food store employee
   b. your personal trainer at the gym
   c. a licensed dietitian
   d. your roommate, who runs for the campus track team

Answers

1. (b) While ethnic background, emotions, and costs all can influence food choices, in Megan's case her very busy schedule influences her food choices for a quick dinner.
2. (c) Nutrition is about how nutrients affect your body and health. The study of genes is genetics. Physiology is the study of how the body functions. The study of hormones is endocrinology.
3. (b) False. Carbohydrates are a source of energy in your foods. The energy in your foods is measured in units called calories.
4. (d) The majority of your daily calories should come from carbohydrates. Vitamins and minerals don't provide calories. Fats do contain calories, but they shouldn't be the main source of energy in your diet.
5. (b) Vitamins can aid enzymes in your body. Carbohydrates, fat, and protein need enzymes to be properly metabolized.
6. (b) False. Many people can meet their vitamin and mineral needs with a well-balanced diet. Those who can't should take a supplement in addition to eating a healthy diet.
7. (d) Unfortunately, over 65 percent of American adults are overweight.
8. (d) Since both carbohydrates and protein have 4 calories per gram and fat has 9 calories per grams, the cookie contains 92 calories.
9. (a) The scientific method begins with scientists observing and asking questions. They then form a hypothesis and test it using an experiment. After many experiments confirm their hypothesis, a theory will be developed.
10. (c) Unless the salesperson, personal trainer, your aunt, and your roommate are all licensed dietitians, they are not qualified to provide nutrition counseling.

Web Resources

- Academy of Nutrition and Dietetics: www.eatright.org
- Agricultural Research Service: www.ars.usda.gov
- Center for Science in the Public Interest: www.cspinet.org
- Centers for Disease Control: www.cdc.gov
- Food and Drug Administration: www.fda.gov
- Food and Nutrition Information Center: fnic.nal.usda.gov
- National Institutes of Health: www.nih.gov
- Tufts University Health & Nutrition Newsletter: www.tuftshealthletter.com
- U.S. Department of Agriculture, Nutrition Information for You: www.nutrition.gov

1. **False.** There are many outside factors that stimulate and motivate you to eat, but taste, not habits, is the most important consideration. To find out what the other factors are, turn to page 5.
2. **True.** Heart disease is the leading cause of death among Americans. The good news is that your diet can play an important role in preventing it. For more information, turn to page 8.
3. **True.** The energy in foods is measured in calories. To find out more, turn to page 9.
4. **False.** Vitamins do not provide calories so don't provide energy in the diet. Turn to page 10 to learn more.
5. **True.** Although water is often overlooked as an essential nutrient, it shouldn't be. To learn about the important roles water plays in your body, turn to page 11.
6. **False.** A supplement can augment a healthy diet, but it can't replace it. To find out why, turn to page 12.
7. **False.** Although lean meats, poultry, and fish are excellent sources of protein, they don't contain fiber. To find out how to get your fill of fiber, turn to page 12.
8. **True.** Shocked? Americans spend an enormous amount of money shopping for supplements. Turn to page 13.
9. **False.** Currently, obesity is at epidemic proportions in the United States, and it isn't just affecting adults. Turn to page 13 for more information.
10. **False.** Anyone can call himself or herself a nutritionist. To find out whose advice you can trust, turn to page 21.

Tools for Healthy Eating

True or False?

1. There isn't any risk to **overconsuming** the essential nutrients in your diet. T/F p. 34

2. About 40 percent of your daily calories should come from **protein-rich** foods. T/F p. 34

3. The *Dietary Guidelines for Americans* were designed for only healthy Americans to follow. T/F p. 36

4. Solid fats should be **increased** in your diet. T/F p. 40

5. **Healthy oils** are an important food group on MyPlate. T/F p. 41

6. To ensure that your diet is healthy, you should follow **MyPlate** exactly every day. T/F p. 43

7. All packaged foods must contain a **food label**. T/F p. 46

8. A **nutrient claim** on a food label tells you how healthy that nutrient is in the food. T/F p. 53

9. A **health claim** must state the beneficial component that the food contains and the disease or condition that it can improve. T/F p. 54

10. Adding **functional foods** to your diet will ensure that your diet is healthy. T/F p. 58

See page 65 for the answers.

1. **Describe the three key principles of a healthy diet and the tools you can use to help guide you.**

2. **Explain what the DRIs are and the differences between the EAR, AI, RDA, UL, and AMDR.**

3. **Describe the principles in the 2010 *Dietary Guidelines for Americans*.**

4. **Explain the concept of MyPlate and name the five food groups and the typical foods represented in each group.**

5. **Identify the required components of a food label and how to use it.**

6. **Explain the role of functional foods in the diet.**

Many Americans believe that to eat a healthful diet means giving up their favorite foods. Nothing could be farther from the truth! With a little planning, you can still occasionally eat almost any food even if it contains added sugars and fat and is high in calories. All it takes are the right tools to balance those higher calorie foods with more nutritious choices each day.

In this chapter, we'll discuss the various guidelines that exist to help you construct a healthy diet, as well as the tools, including food guidance systems and food labels, you can use to make the best food choices. At first, deciphering the information on the food label might seem confusing. But once you've cracked the code, you'll be able to confidently decide which foods to buy and which to leave on the store shelf.

What Is Healthy Eating and What Tools Can Help?

Healthy eating involves the key principles of balance, variety, and moderation. As a student, you are probably familiar with these principles from other areas of your life. Think about how you balance your time between work, school, and your family and friends. You engage in a variety of activities to avoid being bored, and you enjoy each in moderation, since spending too much time on one activity (such as working) would reduce the amount of time you could spend on others (such as studying, socializing, or sleeping). An unbalanced life soon becomes unhealthy and unhappy.

Likewise, your diet must be balanced, varied, and moderate in order to be healthy.

➤ A balanced diet includes healthy proportions of all nutrients. For instance, a student subsisting largely on bread, bagels, muffins, crackers, chips, and cookies might be eating too much carbohydrate and fat but too little protein, vitamins, and minerals.

➤ A varied diet includes many different foods. A student who habitually chooses the same foods for breakfast, lunch, and dinner is not likely to be consuming the wide range of phytochemicals, fiber, and other benefits that a more varied diet could provide.

➤ A moderate diet provides adequate amounts of nutrients and energy. Both crash diets and overconsumption are immoderate.

In short, you need to consume a variety of foods, some more moderately than others, and balance your food choices to meet your nutrient and health needs.

A diet that lacks variety and is unbalanced can cause **undernutrition**, a state in which you are not meeting your nutrient needs. If you were to consume only grains like white bread and pasta, and avoid other foods such as milk products, fruits, vegetables, and meats, your body wouldn't get enough fiber, calcium, protein, and other important nutrients. You would eventually become **malnourished**.

In contrast, **overnutrition** occurs when a diet provides too much of a nutrient such as iron, which can be toxic in high amounts, or too many calories, which can lead to obesity. A person who is overnourished can also be malnourished. For example, as you read in the previous chapter, a person can be overweight on a diet

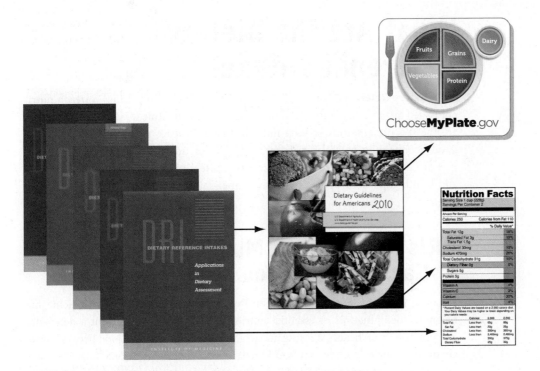

Figure 2.1 Dietary Recommendations and Implementation Tools
The science-based DRIs serve as the basis for information found in the *Dietary Guidelines*, MyPlate, and the Nutrition Facts panel.

Sources: USDA Choose MyPlate website and U.S. Food and Drug Administration.

laden with less nutritious snack foods and sweets—foods that should be eaten in moderation—because he or she is taking in more calories than needed. These foods often displace more nutrient-rich choices, leaving the person malnourished.

Fortunately, the U.S. government provides several tools that can help you avoid both under- and overnutrition, including:

➤ The *Dietary Reference Intakes (DRIs)*, which provide recommendations regarding your nutrient needs

➤ The *Dietary Guidelines for Americans*, which provide broad dietary and lifestyle advice

➤ *MyPlate*, part of the ChooseMyPlate.gov Web-based initiative, which is designed to help you eat healthfully and implement the recommendations in the DRIs and the advice in the *Dietary Guidelines*

➤ The *Nutrition Facts panel* on food labels, which contains the Daily Values, and which can help you decide which foods to buy.

Together, these tools help you plan a balanced, moderate, and varied diet that meets your nutrient and health needs (**Figure 2.1**).

Let's look at each of these tools, beginning with the DRIs.

The Take-Home Message
A healthy diet is balanced, moderate, and varied. The U.S. government provides several tools to assist you in planning a healthy diet. These include the Dietary Reference Intakes, the *Dietary Guidelines for Americans*, the Nutrition Facts panel on food labels, and ChooseMyPlate.gov, the focal point for a multilevel, Web-based initiative that includes the MyPlate food guidance system.

Healthy eating is a way of life.

undernutrition A state of inadequate nutrition whereby a person's nutrient and/or calorie needs aren't met through the diet.

malnourished The long-term outcome of consuming a diet that doesn't meet nutrient needs.

overnutrition A state of excess nutrients and calories in the diet.

What Are the Dietary Reference Intakes?

The **Dietary Reference Intakes (DRIs)** are specific reference values for each nutrient issued by the U.S.' National Academy of Sciences' Institute of Medicine. The DRIs are the specific amounts of each nutrient that one needs to consume to maintain good health, prevent chronic diseases, and avoid unhealthy excesses.[1] The Institute of Medicine periodically organizes committees of U.S. and Canadian scientists and health experts to update these recommendations based on the latest scientific research.

DRIs Tell You How Much of Each Nutrient You Need

Since the 1940s, the Food and Nutrition Board, part of the Institute of Medicine, has recommended amounts of essential nutrients needed daily to prevent a deficiency and promote good health. Because nutrient needs change with age, and because needs are different for men and women, different sets of recommendations were developed for each nutrient based on an individual's age and gender. In other words, a teenager may need more of a specific nutrient than a 55-year-old (and vice versa) and women need more of certain nutrients during pregnancy and lactation, so they all have different DRIs. Since the 1940s the DRIs have been updated more than ten times.

In the 1990s, nutrition researchers identified expanded roles for many nutrients. Though nutrient deficiencies were still an important issue, research suggested that higher amounts of some nutrients could play a role in disease prevention. Also, as consumers began using more dietary supplements and fortified foods, committee members grew concerned that excessive consumption of some nutrients might be as unhealthy as, or even more dangerous than, not consuming enough. Hence, the Food and Nutrition Board convened a variety of committees between 1997 and 2010 to take on the enormous task of reviewing the research on vitamins, minerals, carbohydrates, fats, protein, water, and other substances such as fiber, and developing the current DRI reference values for all the nutrients. As research evolves, changes are made in the DRIs.

DRIs Encompass Several Reference Values

The DRIs comprise five reference values: Estimated Average Requirement (EAR), Recommended Dietary Allowance (RDA), Adequate Intake (AI), the Tolerable Upper Intake Level (UL), and the Acceptable Macronutrient Distribution Range (AMDR) (**Figure 2.2**). Each of these values is unique, and serves a different need in planning a healthy diet. It may seem like a lot to remember, but you will use only the RDA or AI (not both), the AMDR, and the UL to assess whether your diet is meeting your nutrient needs. The EAR is the starting point in the process of determining the other values. Let's look at how the values are determined.

The DRI committee members begin by reviewing a variety of research studies to determine the **Estimated Average Requirement (EAR)** for the nutrient. They may look at studies that investigate the consequences of eating a diet too low in the nutrient and the associated side effects or physical changes that develop, as well as how much of the nutrient should be consumed to correct the deficiency. They may also review studies that measure the amount a healthy individual absorbs, stores, and

Dietary Reference Intakes (DRIs) Reference values for the essential nutrients needed to maintain good health, to prevent chronic diseases, and to avoid unhealthy excesses.

Estimated Average Requirement (EAR) The average amount of a nutrient that is known to meet the needs of 50 percent of the individuals in a similar age and gender group.

Dietary Reference Intakes (DRIs) are specific reference values for each nutrient issued by the United States National Academy of Sciences, Institute of Medicine. They identify the amounts of each nutrient that one needs to consume to maintain good health.

DRIs FOR MOST NUTRIENTS

EAR The Estimated Average Requirement (EAR) is the average daily intake level estimated to meet the needs of half the people in a certain group. Scientists use it to calculate the RDA.

RDA The Recommended Dietary Allowance (RDA) is the average daily intake level estimated to meet the needs of nearly all people in a certain group. Aim for this amount!

AI The Adequate Intake (AI) is the average daily intake level assumed to be adequate. It is used when an EAR cannot be determined. Aim for this amount if there is no RDA!

UL The Tolerable Upper Intake Level (UL) is the highest average daily intake level likely to pose no health risks. Do not exceed this amount on a daily basis!

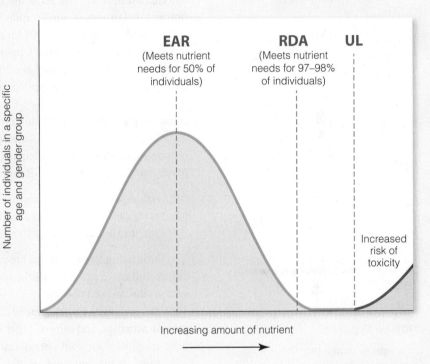

DRIs RELATED TO ENERGY

AMDR The Acceptable Macronutrient Distribution Range (AMDR) is the recommended range of carbohydrate, fat, and protein intake expressed as a percentage of total energy.

EER The Estimated Energy Requirement (EER) is the average daily energy intake predicted to meet the needs of healthy adults.

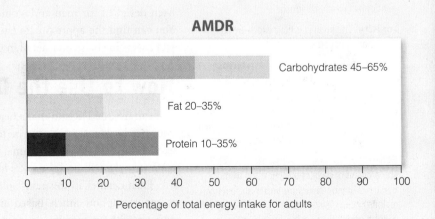

maintains daily. Additionally, they look at research studies that address the role the nutrient plays in reducing the risk of associated chronic diseases, such as heart disease. After a thorough review process, the EAR for the nutrient is determined.

The EAR is the average amount of a nutrient that is known to meet the needs of 50 percent of the individuals in a similar age and gender group. The EAR is a starting point to determine the amount of a nutrient an individual should consume daily for good health. As you can see from Figure 2.2, if a nutrient's requirements were set using the EAR, 50 percent of the individuals would need more than this amount to meet their needs. This is where the **Recommended Dietary Allowance (RDA)** comes in. The RDA is based on the EAR, but it is set higher. It represents the average amount of a nutrient that meets the needs of nearly all (97 to 98 percent) of the individuals in a similar group.

If there is insufficient scientific information to determine the EAR for a nutrient, the RDA can't be developed. When this happens, an **Adequate Intake (AI)** is determined instead. The AI is the next best scientific estimate of the amount of a nutrient that groups of similar individuals should consume to maintain good health.

Because consuming too much of some nutrients can be harmful, the committees developed the **Tolerable Upper Intake Level (UL)**. The UL refers to the highest amount of a nutrient that is unlikely to cause harm if the amount is consumed daily. The higher the consumption above the UL, the higher the risk of **toxicity**. You should not try to consume the UL of a nutrient. There isn't any known benefit from consuming a higher amount, and it may cause health problems.

The DRI committee also developed a range of intakes for the energy-containing nutrients, carbohydrates, proteins, and fats. These ranges are called the **Acceptable Macronutrient Distribution Ranges (AMDR)** and are as follows:

➤ Carbohydrates should comprise 45 to 65 percent of your daily calories.
➤ Fat should comprise 20 to 35 percent of your daily calories.
➤ Proteins should comprise 10 to 35 percent of your daily calories.

Consuming these nutrient types in these ranges will ensure that you meet your calorie and nutrient needs, and reduce your risk of developing chronic diseases such as heart disease and obesity.

Although dietary recommendations have been established for carbohydrate, fat, protein, vitamins, and minerals that meet the optimal intake of nutrients, no DRI has been established for your energy (calorie) intake. The method used to determine the amount of energy you need, or your **Estimated Energy Requirement (EER)**, uses a different approach than the RDAs or AIs. In addition to taking into account your age and gender, the EER is calculated based on your height, weight, and activity level, and indicates the amount of energy *you* need daily to maintain energy balance. Individuals who consume more energy than they need will gain weight. Equations have been designed for men and women to provide a general estimate of energy needs. You can find the approximate amount of energy you require daily in Table 2.1. We will cover this in greater detail in Chapter 10.

How to Use the DRIs

You can use the DRIs to make healthy food choices and plan a quality diet. To meet your needs, your goal should be to meet the RDA or the AI of all nutrients, but not exceed the UL. Table 2.2 summarizes the DRIs for you. On the inside cover of your textbook, you will find the DRIs for all the nutrients that you need daily.

Each chapter in this textbook will further explain what each nutrient is; why it is important; how much, based on the DRIs, you need to consume; and how to get enough, without consuming too much, in your diet.

Recommended Dietary Allowance (RDA) The average amount of a nutrient that meets the needs of 97 to 98 percent of individuals in a similar age and gender group. The RDA is higher than the EAR.

Adequate intake (AI) The *approximate* amount of a nutrient that groups of similar individuals are consuming to maintain good health.

Tolerable Upper Intake Level (UL) The highest amount of a nutrient that can be consumed daily without harm in a similar age and gender group of individuals.

toxicity The level at which exposure to a substance becomes harmful.

Acceptable Macronutrient Distribution Range (AMDR) A healthy range of intakes for the energy-containing nutrients—carbohydrates, proteins, and fats—in your diet, designed to meet your nutrient needs and help reduce the risk of chronic diseases.

Estimated Energy Requirement (EER) The amount of daily energy needed to maintain a healthy body weight and meet energy (calorie) needs based on age, gender, height, weight, and activity level.

Table 2.1

How Many Calories Do You Need Daily?

The amount of calories you need daily is based upon your age, gender, and activity level.*

	Males				Females		
Age	Sedentary	Moderately Active	Active	Age	Sedentary	Moderately Active	Active
16–18	2,400	2,800	3,200	**16–18**	1,800	2,000	2,400
19–20	2,600	2,800	3,000	**19–20**	2,000	2,200	2,400
21–25	2,400	2,800	3,000	**21–25**	2,000	2,200	2,400
26–30	2,400	2,600	3,000	**26–30**	1,800	2,000	2,400
31–35	2,400	2,600	3,000	**31–35**	1,800	2,000	2,200
36–40	2,400	2,600	2,800	**36–40**	1,800	2,000	2,200
41–45	2,200	2,600	2,800	**41–45**	1,800	2,000	2,200
46–50	2,200	2,400	2,800	**46–50**	1,800	2,000	2,200

Source: U.S. Department of Agriculture, *Dietary Guidelines for Americans, 2010.* Available at www.health.gov.
*Note: These calorie levels are based on the Institute of Medicine's Estimated Energy Requirements from the *Dietary Reference Intakes: Macronutrients Report, 2002.*
Sedentary: Partaking in less than 30 minutes a day of moderate physical activity in addition to daily activities.
Moderately Active: Partaking in at least 30 minutes and up to 60 minutes a day of moderate physical activity in addition to daily activities.
Active: Partaking in 60 or more minutes a day of moderate physical activity in addition to daily activities.

Table 2.2

The Do's and Don'ts of the DRIs

The Reference Values and Their Meaning	When Planning Your Diet
Estimated Average Requirement (EAR)	**Don't** use this amount.
Recommended Dietary Allowance (RDA)	**Do** aim for this amount!
Adequate Intake (AI)	**Do** aim for this amount if an RDA isn't available.
Tolerable Upper Intake Level (UL)	**Don't** exceed this amount on a daily basis.
Acceptable Macronutrient Distribution Range (AMDR)	**Do** follow these guidelines regarding the percentage of carbohydrates, protein, and fat in your diet.

Source: "The Do's and Don'ts of the DRIs" from Dietary Reference Intakes: Applications in Dietary Planning by Institute of Medicine of the National Academies. Reprinted with permission from the National Academies Press. Copyright © 2003, National Academy of Sciences.

Whereas the DRIs were released to prevent undernutrition, the *Dietary Guidelines for Americans* were developed out of concern over the incidence of overnutrition among Americans. Let's now look at the second tool that can help you attain a healthy diet and lifestyle, the *Dietary Guidelines for Americans*.

The Take-Home Message The Dietary Reference Intakes (DRIs) are specific reference values that help you determine your daily nutrient needs to maintain good health, prevent chronic diseases, and avoid unhealthy excesses. The reference values include the EAR, RDA, AI, UL, and AMDR. Try to meet your RDA or AI and consume below the UL for each nutrient daily. The EER is calculated according to your height, weight, and activity level, in addition to your age and gender.

TableTIPS

Tip-Top Nutrition Tips

Use traffic light colors to help you vary your lunchtime veggie choices. Add tomato slices (red) to your sandwich and carrots (yellow/orange) to your tossed salad (green).

Pop a snack-pack size of light microwave popcorn for a portion-controlled whole-grain snack.

Say "so long" to the elevator and hoof it up the stairs to work some extra physical activity into your day.

To keep your sweets to a discretionary amount, read the nutrition label and stick to a single serving that is no more than about 100 calories. Note that many big bars and bags contain more than double this amount.

Plan your dinner using at least one food from each of the food groups. Add tomato-pepper salsa (vegetables) and a can of rinsed black beans (meat and beans) to your macaroni (bread) and cheese (dairy), and include an orange (fruit) for dessert to create a complete Mexican-influenced meal.

eLearn

Healthy Eating on a Budget

Healthy eating is not only better for your body, it's better for your wallet. According to the USDA, an individual between the ages of 20 and 50 can eat a healthy diet for as little as about $35 to $40 a week. If you want to learn how to eat healthfully and shop smart on a budget, visit www.pearsonhighered.com/blake.

The *Dietary Guidelines for Americans* at a Glance

Whereas past versions of these dietary guidelines were intended for *healthy* Americans aged 2 and older, this edition was released during a time when a poor diet and the sedentary habits of Americans have become associated with chronic poor health and reduced longevity. The science-based *Dietary Guidelines for Americans, 2010* are intended for those who are 2 years of age and older, *including* those who may also be at risk for chronic diseases. The following is a short overview of the recommendations. The complete guidelines and more information are available at http://health.gov/dietaryguidelines.

There are two overarching concepts in the *Dietary Guidelines for Americans, 2010*:

1. **Maintain calorie balance over time to achieve and sustain a healthy weight.**
   The Health Concern in a Nutshell: Many Americans are in calorie imbalance, consuming more calories than they are expending daily.
   It's Recommended That You: Eat a well-balanced, calorie-appropriate diet, coupled with regular physical activity, to achieve and maintain a healthy body weight.
2. **Consume more nutrient-rich foods and beverages.**
   The Health Concern in a Nutshell: Many Americans are consuming too much sodium and too many calories from solid fats (which are sources of saturated and *trans* fats), as well as added sugars and refined grains, such as those in cakes and cookies. At the same time, they are not consuming enough fiber, vitamin D, calcium, and potassium.
   It's Recommended That You: Routinely follow a healthy, well-balanced, plant-based eating pattern rich in vegetables, fruits, and whole grains. You should consume adequate amounts of lean dairy and protein-rich foods (lean meat, poultry, fish, eggs, nuts, seeds, and dried peas), along with some heart-healthy unsaturated fats. This eating pattern will help you meet nutrient needs without exceeding daily calorie needs.

There are key recommendations provided in the *Dietary Guidelines* to help you do the above:

Balance Calories to Manage Weight

➤ Prevent and/or reduce overweight and obesity through improved eating and physical activity behaviors.
➤ Control total calorie intake to manage body weight. For those overweight or obese, this means consuming fewer calories from foods and beverages.
➤ Increase physical activity and reduce the time spent in sedentary behaviors.

➤ Maintain appropriate calorie balance during each stage of life—childhood, adolescence, adulthood, pregnancy and breast-feeding, and older ages.

Foods Components to Reduce

➤ Daily sodium intake should be less than 2,300 milligrams (mg). Intake should be further reduced to 1,500 mg among people who are 51 and older, and those of any age who are African-American or have hypertension, diabetes, or chronic kidney disease. This 1,500-mg recommendation applies to about half of the U.S. population.
➤ Consume less than 10 percent of your daily calories from saturated fatty acids by replacing them with monounsaturated and polyunsaturated fatty acids.
➤ Consume less than 300 mg of dietary cholesterol daily.
➤ Keep *trans* fatty acid as low as possible by limiting foods that contain synthetic sources of *trans* fats, such as partially hydrogenated oils, and by limiting other solid fats.
➤ Reduce the calories from solid fats* and added sugars.

What Are the *Dietary Guidelines for Americans?*

By the 1970s, research had shown that Americans' overconsumption of foods rich in fat, saturated fat, cholesterol, and sodium was increasing their risk for chronic diseases, such as heart disease and stroke.[2] In 1977, the U.S. government released the *Dietary Goals for Americans*, which were designed to improve the nutritional quality of Americans' diets and to try to reduce the incidence of overnutrition and its associated health problems.[3]

Amid controversy over the scientific validity of the goals, the government asked scientists to lend credence to the goals and provide dietary guidance. Their work culminated in the 1980 *Dietary Guidelines for Americans*, which emphasized eating a variety of foods to obtain a nutritionally well-balanced daily diet. Since 1990, the

- Limit the consumption of foods that contain refined grains, and especially of refined-grain foods that contain solid fats, added sugars, and sodium.
- Consume alcohol in moderation, if at all—up to one drink per day for women and two drinks per day for men—and only if you are an adult of legal drinking age.**

Foods and Nutrients to Increase

In order to consume a well-balanced, healthy eating pattern that meets your daily calorie needs:

- Increase your vegetable and fruit intake.
- Eat a variety of vegetables, especially dark-green and red and orange vegetables and beans and peas.
- Consume at least half of all your grain choices as whole grains.
- Increase the intake of fat-free or low-fat milk and milk products such as milk, yogurt, cheese, or fortified soy beverages (soy milk).
- Choose a variety of protein foods, including seafood, lean meat and poultry, eggs, beans and peas, soy products, and unsalted nuts and seeds.
- Increase the amount and variety of seafood consumed by choosing seafood in place of some meat and poultry.
- Replace protein foods higher in solid fats with choices lower in these solid fats and calories.
- Use oils to replace solid fats where possible.
- Choose foods that provide more potassium, dietary fiber, calcium, and vitamin D. These foods include vegetables, fruits, whole grains, and milk and milk products.

Note: There are recommendations for specific groups such as women capable of being pregnant, pregnant and breast-feeding women, and individuals who are 50 years of age and older. (See Chapters 15 and 16.)

Build Healthy Eating Patterns

- Select an eating pattern that meets nutrient needs over time at an appropriate calorie level.
- Account for all foods and beverages consumed and assess how they fit within a healthy eating pattern.
- Follow food safety recommendations when preparing and eating foods to reduce the risk of foodborne illness.

While the above may seem like a "mouthful," the good news is that the chapters in this textbook have been written to help you meet these dietary guidelines, *one bite at a time.*

*Solid fats are not liquid at room temperature; these contain more saturated and *trans* fatty acids. Solid fats include butter, meat fat, coconut and palm oils, shortening, and margarine. Common food sources of solid fats include full-fat cheese, whole milk, fatty cuts of meat, poultry skin, and many baked goods.

**See Chapter 9 for additional guidance, as there are many circumstances in which individuals should avoid alcohol consumption entirely.

U.S. Department of Agriculture (USDA) and the Department of Health and Human Services (DHHS) have been mandated by law to update the guidelines every five years. The guidelines serve as one governmental voice to shape all federally funded nutrition programs in areas such as research and labeling, and to educate and guide consumers about healthy diet and lifestyle choices.[4]

The **Dietary Guidelines for Americans, 2010** reflect the most current nutrition and physical activity recommendations based on science for good health. They are designed to help individuals aged 2 and older improve the quality of their diet and lifestyle to lower their risk of chronic diseases and conditions, such as high blood pressure, high blood cholesterol levels, diabetes mellitus, heart disease, certain cancers, and osteoporosis. These most recent guidelines are different from previous reports, as they address the obesity epidemic that is occurring among Americans.[5] The Nutrition in the Real World feature "The *Dietary Guidelines for Americans* at a Glance" provides an overview of the current guidelines.

Dietary Guidelines for Americans, 2010
Guidelines published every five years that provide dietary and lifestyle advice to individuals aged 2 and older to maintain good health and prevent chronic diseases.

What Are MyPlate and ChooseMyPlate.gov?

With so many nutrient and dietary recommendations in the DRIs and the *Dietary Guidelines*, you may be wondering how to keep them straight and plan a balanced diet that meets all of your nutritional needs. Luckily, there are several carefully designed **food guidance systems** to help you select the best foods for your diet. These illustrated systems picture healthy food choices from a variety of food groups from which you can select, and show you how to proportion your food choices. Many countries have developed food guidance systems based on their food supply, cultural food preferences, and the nutritional needs of their population (**Figure 2.3**).

Some researchers have also developed food guidance systems to help individuals reduce their risk of certain diseases. For example, the DASH (Dietary Approaches to Stop Hypertension) diet is based on an eating style that has been shown to significantly lower a person's blood pressure. High blood pressure is a risk factor for heart disease and stroke.[6] (The DASH diet is discussed in more detail in Chapter 8.) The Mediterranean-style eating pattern is another food guidance system that emphasizes a plant-based diet rich in vegetables and fruits, nuts, olive oil, grains, and smaller amounts of meats and dairy. A Mediterranean-style eating pattern (discussed in Chapter 5) has been associated with a lower risk of heart disease.

MyPyramid was a food guidance system previously released by the USDA. Using a pyramid-based visual model, it depicted the recommendations in the 2005 *Dietary Guidelines for Americans*. In 2011, the USDA released the website www.ChooseMyPlate.gov and the tool MyPlate to reflect the new recommendations in the 2010 *Dietary Guidelines for Americans*.

MyPlate serves as an icon to remind consumers to eat healthfully. It depicts the five food groups using a familiar mealtime visual, a place setting (see **Figure 2.4**). MyPlate is the focal point for a larger, Web-based communication and education initiative at ChooseMyPlate.gov that provides information, tips, and tools to help you build a healthier diet based on the *Dietary Guidelines for Americans, 2010*. Also available at ChooseMyPlate.gov is an interactive food guidance system that is based on the USDA Food Patterns, which will provide you with a personalized food plan based on the latest nutrition and health recommendations. Consuming a calorie-appropriate, balanced diet that includes a variety of foods in moderation will also allow you to meet the DRIs for your nutrient needs and better manage your health and weight.

MyPlate and ChooseMyPlate.gov Emphasize Changes in Diet, Eating Behaviors, and Physical Activity

In addition to showing a variety of food groups that can make up a healthy diet, the tool MyPlate and the supporting information at ChooseMyPlate.gov promote proportionality, moderation, variety, and personalization.

As you can see from Figure 2.4, MyPlate shows a place setting split into sections, with each colored section representing one of five food groups: fruits, vegetables, grains, protein foods, and dairy. While oils are an important part of a healthy diet,

Figure 2.3 Healthy Eating around the World Many countries have developed their own food guidance systems, and they have a lot in common. For example, in Sweden, the Food Circle shown here is similar to MyPlate as it emphasizes a plant-based diet with plenty of grains, fruits, vegetables, and moderate amounts of milk products, meat, poultry, and fish.

food guidance systems Visual diagrams that provide a variety of food recommendations to help create a well-balanced diet.

MyPlate A tool that depicts five food groups using the familiar mealtime visual of a place setting. It is part of a USDA Web-based initiative to provide consumer information with a food guidance system to help you build a healthy diet based on the current *Dietary Guidelines for Americans*.

self-Assessment

Does Your Diet Have Proportionality?

Answer yes or no to the following questions.

1. Are grains the main food choice at all your meals?
   Yes ☐ **No** ☐

2. Do you often forget to eat vegetables?
   Yes ☐ **No** ☐

3. Do you typically eat fewer than three pieces of fruit daily?
   Yes ☐ **No** ☐

4. Do you often have fewer than three cups of milk daily?
   Yes ☐ **No** ☐

5. Is the portion of meat, chicken, or fish the largest item on your dinner plate?
   Yes ☐ **No** ☐

Answers

If you answered yes to three or more of these questions, it is very likely that your diet lacks proportionality.

---

they are not represented on the plate, as they are not considered a food group.

You can now easily see **proportionality** in how these food groups should dominate your diet. Half of your plate should be devoted to waist- and heart-friendly vegetables and fruits, with a smaller portion for grains (preferably whole grains) and lean protein foods such as fish, skinless poultry, lean meats, and dried beans and peas. The blue circle next to the plate is a visual reminder to make sure that fat-free and low-fat dairy foods such as milk should not be forgotten at mealtimes. With the majority of Americans overweight, this shift of food proportionality on your plate can have a dramatic effect on your calorie intake. Devoting more than half of the surface of the plate to low-calorie fruits and vegetables should crowd out higher calorie grains and protein food choices. Take the Self-Assessment above to see how well-proportioned your diet is.

There are several important nutrition messages at ChooseMyPlate.gov based on the current *Dietary Guidelines*, which emphasize moderation in your diet and eating behaviors. The messages are based on three general areas of recommendation:

1. Balance Calories
   - Enjoy your food, but eat less.
   - Avoid oversized portions.
2. Foods to Increase
   - Make half your plate fruits and vegetables.
   - Make at least half your grains whole grains.
   - Switch to fat-free or low-fat (1%) dairy products.
3. Foods to Reduce
   - Compare sodium in foods like soup, bread, and frozen meals—and choose the foods with lower numbers.
   - Drink water instead of sugary drinks.

These messages not only emphasize that you should balance your calories daily to better manage your weight but also that you should choose mostly nutrient-dense foods from each food group. **Nutrient density** refers to the amount of nutrients a food contains in relationship to the number of calories it contains. More

Figure 2.4 MyPlate
The MyPlate icon reinforces important concepts of meal planning, healthful choices, proportionality, and moderation to be used in planning a healthful diet.

Source: USDA Choose MyPlate website.

proportionality The relationship of one entity to another. Vegetables and fruits should be consumed in a higher proportion than dairy and protein foods in the diet.

nutrient density The amount of nutrients per calorie in a given food. Nutrient-dense foods provide more nutrients per calorie than less nutrient-dense foods.

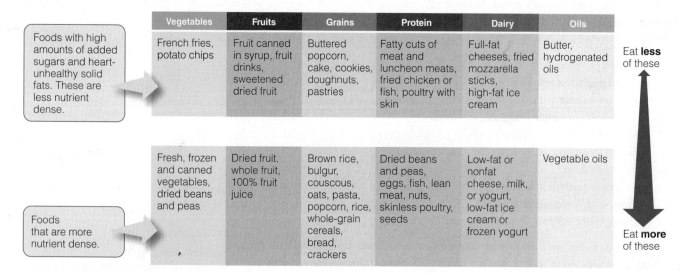

nutrient-dense foods provide more nutrients per calorie (and in each bite) than less nutrient-dense foods, and so are better choices for meeting your DRIs without exceeding your daily calorie needs.

The foundation of your diet should be nutrient-dense foods with little solid fats and added sugars. Solid fats are solid at room temperature and contain a high percentage of heart-unhealthy saturated and/or *trans* fatty acids. Solid fats include butter, beef fat, chicken fat, pork fat (lard), stick margarine, and shortening. The fat in milk is also considered a solid fat, as it is solid at room temperature. Because of the homogenization process involved in processing milk, the solid fat is evenly dispersed and suspended in fluid milk, which masks its solid density. Saturated fat–laden coconut, palm, and palm kernel oils, as well as partially hydrogenated oils, which contain *trans* fatty acids, are also considered solid fats. Added sugars include sources such as brown sugar, corn syrup, molasses, and table sugar (you will learn about other sources in Chapter 4). Foods within each food group that contain solid fats and added sugars should be eaten in moderation because they add calories that are less nutrient dense to your diet.

Let's compare the nutrient density of two versions of the same food: a medium baked potato and an ounce of potato chips (**Figure 2.5**). Both have about the same number of calories, but the baked potato provides much more folate, potassium, and vitamin C, and is therefore much more nutrient dense, than the deep-fried chips. If you routinely choose foods with a lot of added sugar and solid fats, you will have to reduce your food intake elsewhere to compensate for the extra calories. This could cause you to displace healthier foods in your diet. If you don't adjust for these extra calories, but eat them in addition to your normal diet, you will soon experience weight gain.

In contrast to nutrient density, **energy density** refers to foods that are high in energy but low in weight or volume, such as that potato chip. A serving of deep-fried chips weighs much less than a plain baked potato, but is considerably higher in solid fats and calories. Therefore, the chip contains more calories per gram. A big, leafy green salad, on the other hand, is large in volume but low in energy density, due to its high water content. Most higher-fat foods and sweets and treats, such as fried foods and candy, are considered energy dense.

Individuals who choose low-energy-dense and high-nutrient-dense foods will generally have diets that are lower in solid fats and added sugars and higher in nutrient content. **Figure 2.6** helps you compare some nutrient-dense food choices to less healthy food choices in each food group.

Figure 2.5 Which Is the Healthier Way to Enjoy Your Potatoes?
While one ounce of potato chips and one medium baked potato have similar amounts of calories, their nutrient content is worlds apart. A baked potato is more nutrient dense than potato chips.

*Note: Based on the percentage of the DRI for 19–50-year-old males. All these percentages apply to females in the same age range except for vitamin C. Females have lower vitamin C needs than males, so a baked potato provides more than 20 percent of the DRI for this vitamin for women.

	Vegetables	Fruits	Grains	Protein	Dairy	Oils	
Foods with high amounts of added sugars and heart-unhealthy solid fats. These are less nutrient dense.	French fries, potato chips	Fruit canned in syrup, fruit drinks, sweetened dried fruit	Buttered popcorn, cake, cookies, doughnuts, pastries	Fatty cuts of meat and luncheon meats, fried chicken or fish, poultry with skin	Full-fat cheeses, fried mozzarella sticks, high-fat ice cream	Butter, hydrogenated oils	**Eat less** of these
Foods that are more nutrient dense.	Fresh, frozen and canned vegetables, dried beans and peas	Dried fruit, whole fruit, 100% fruit juice	Brown rice, bulgur, couscous, oats, pasta, popcorn, rice, whole-grain cereals, bread, crackers	Dried beans and peas, eggs, fish, lean meat, nuts, skinless poultry, seeds	Low-fat or nonfat cheese, milk, or yogurt, low-fat ice cream or frozen yogurt	Vegetable oils	**Eat more** of these

Figure 2.6 Nutrient-Dense Food Choices
Nutrient-dense foods provide more nutrition per calorie and fewer solid fats and added sugars.

Eating a variety of foods among and within the food groups highlighted in MyPlate will increase your chances of consuming all 40 of the nutrients your body needs. Because no single food or food group provides all the nutrients, a varied diet of nutrient-dense foods is the savviest strategy. **Figure 2.7** provides tips on how to choose a variety of foods from each food group. The interactive website ChooseMyPlate.gov is designed to help you plan a personalized food plan based on your dietary and lifestyle needs. We will discuss this in more detail later in the chapter.

Lastly, physical activity is an important component in the *Dietary Guidelines*. Being physically active helps you stay fit and reduce your risk of chronic diseases such as heart disease and cancer. Advice regarding physical activity can also be found at ChooseMyPlate.gov.

Remember, "Rome wasn't built in a day." Adopting a healthier diet and lifestyle, and changing long-term eating habits, takes time. Taking small steps of improvement every day can be less overwhelming and will ultimately be beneficial to your health.

Let's next look at the foods of each food group, and why each group is uniquely important to you.

How to Use MyPlate and ChooseMyPlate.gov

You now know to eat a variety of nutrient-dense foods to be healthy, and that MyPlate reminds you to eat a diverse group of foods, but you may be wondering how much from each food group *you*, personally, should be eating. The ChooseMyPlate.gov interactive website will give you the exact numbers of servings to eat from each food group based on your daily calorie needs.

Recall that your calorie needs (your EER) are based upon your age and gender (two factors beyond your control) and your activity level (a factor you can control). As you just read, the more active you are, the more calories you burn to fuel your activities, and the more calories you can (and need to) consume in foods.

At the website, you will enter your age, gender, and activity level. Based on this information, your daily calorie needs will be determined and your personalized eating plan, specifying the exact number of servings from each of the five food groups, will be provided. (Oils are not considered a food group but should be added to your diet for good health.) With this information, you can plan your meals and snacks for the day. If you cannot go to the website, you can obtain similar information by using Tables 2.1 and 2.3 in this chapter. Let's use the tables to obtain your recommendations.

The first step in creating your personalized daily food plan is to figure out how many calories you should be eating daily. To do this, you need to find out how active you are. If you participate in activities such as water aerobics, play doubles tennis, enjoy ballroom dancing, garden at home, or walk briskly, you are likely moderately active. You could consider yourself vigorously active if, for example, you race-walk,

Focus on fruits. Eat a variety of fruits—whether fresh, frozen, canned, or dried—rather than fruit juice for most of your fruit choices. For a 2,000-calorie diet, you will need 2 cups of fruit each day (for example, 1 small banana, 1 large orange, and ¼ cup of dried apricots or peaches).

Vary your veggies. Eat more dark green veggies, such as broccoli, kale, and other dark leafy greens; orange veggies, such as carrots, sweet potatoes, pumpkin, and winter squash; and beans and peas, such as pinto beans, kidney beans, black beans, garbanzo beans, split peas, and lentils.

Get your calcium-rich foods. Get 3 cups of low-fat or fat-free milk—or an equivalent amount of low-fat yogurt and/or low-fat cheese (1½ ounces of cheese equals 1 cup of milk)—every day. For kids aged 2 to 8, it's 2 cups of milk. If you don't or can't consume milk, choose lactose-free milk products and/or calcium-fortified foods and beverages.

Make half your grains whole. Eat at least 3 ounces of whole-grain cereals, breads, crackers, rice, or pasta every day. One ounce is about 1 slice of bread, 1 cup of breakfast cereal, or ½ cup of cooked rice or pasta. Look to see that grains such as wheat, rice, oats, or corn are referred to as "whole" in the list of ingredients.

Go lean with protein. Choose lean meats and poultry. Bake it, broil it, or grill it. And vary your protein choices—with more fish, beans, peas, nuts, and seeds.

Know the limits on fats, salt, and sugars. Read the Nutrition Facts label on foods. Look for foods low in saturated fats and *trans* fats. Choose and prepare foods and beverages with little salt (sodium) and/or added sugars (caloric sweeteners).

Figure 2.7 Mix Up Your Choices within Each Food Group

Source: USDA, "Finding Your Way to a Healthier You." Based on the *Dietary Guidelines for Americans* and MyPlate.gov.

energy density A measurement of the calories in a food compared with the weight (grams) or volume of the food.

Portion Sizes

Who says you shouldn't eat with your hands? Let Joan show you how your hands can help you keep portions under control. Scan this QR code with your mobile device to access the video. You can also access the video in MasteringNutrition™.

A woman's palm is the size of approximately 3 ounces of cooked meat, chicken, or fish

a

A woman's fist is the size of about 1 cup of pasta or vegetables (a man's fist is the size of about 2 cups)

b

The "O" made by a woman's thumb and forefinger is the size of about 1 tablespoon of vegetable oil

c

Figure 2.8 What's a Serving? Eat with Your Hands!
Your hands can guide you in estimating portion sizes.

Table 2.3

How Much Should You Eat from Each Food Group?

The following are suggested amounts to consume daily from each of the basic five food groups and healthy oils based on your daily calorie needs. Remember that most of your choices should contain little solid fats and added sugar.

Calorie Level	Vegetables (cups)	Fruits (cups)	Grains (oz eq)	Protein (oz eq)	Dairy (cups)	Oil* (tsp)
1,600	2	1.5	5	5	3	5
1,800	2.5	1.5	6	5	3	5
2,000	2.5	2	6	5.5	3	6
2,200	3	2	7	6	3	6
2,400	3	2	8	6.5	3	7
2,600	3.5	2	9	6.5	3	8
2,800	3.5	2.5	10	7	3	8
3,000	4	2.5	10	7	3	10
3,200	4	2.5	10	7	3	11

Vegetables: Includes all fresh, frozen, canned, and dried vegetables, and vegetable juices. In general, 1 cup of raw or cooked vegetables or vegetable juice, or 2 cups of raw leafy greens, is considered 1 cup from the vegetable group.

Fruits: Includes all fresh, frozen, canned, and dried fruits, and fruit juices. In general, 1 cup of fruit or 100% fruit juice, or ½ cup of dried fruit, is considered 1 cup from the fruit group.

Grains: Includes all foods made with wheat, rice, oats, cornmeal, or barley, such as bread, pasta, oatmeal, breakfast cereals, tortillas, and grits. In general, 1 slice of bread, 1 cup of ready-to-eat cereal, or ½ cup of cooked rice, pasta, or cooked cereal is considered 1 ounce equivalent (oz eq) from the grains group. *At least half of all grains consumed should be whole grains such as whole-wheat bread, oats, or brown rice.*

Protein: In general, 1 ounce of lean meat, poultry, or fish, 1 egg, 1 tablespoon peanut butter, ¼ cup cooked dry beans, or ½ ounce of nuts or seeds is considered 1 ounce equivalent (oz eq) from the protein foods group.

Dairy: Includes all fat-free and low-fat milk, yogurt, and cheese. In general, 1 cup of milk or yogurt, 1½ ounces of natural cheese, or 2 ounces of processed cheese is considered 1 cup from the dairy group.

Oil: Includes vegetable oils such as canola, corn, olive, soybean, and sunflower oil, fatty fish, nuts, avocados, mayonnaise, salad dressings made with oils, and soft margarine.

*Oils are not considered a food group but should be added to your diet for good health.

Source: Adapted from "Daily Plans & Worksheets," from U.S. Department of Agriculture, www.ChooseMyPlate.gov.

jog, run, swim laps, play singles tennis, or bicycle 10 miles per hour or faster. Based on these examples, are you moderately or vigorously active? Refer back to Table 2.1 on page 35 for the number of calories you need based on your activity level, age, and gender. When you know the number of calories you need daily, **Table 2.3** will tell you how many servings from each food group you should consume to healthfully obtain those calories. This is the equivalent of *your* personalized daily food plan.

Let's say that you are a moderately active female who needs 2,000 calories daily. To healthfully meet this level, you should consume each day:

➤ 6 servings from the grains group
➤ 2½ cups of dark green, orange, starchy, and other vegetables, and some legumes
➤ 2 cups of fruits
➤ 3 cups of fat-free or low-fat milk and yogurt
➤ 5½ ounces of lean meat, poultry, and fish or the equivalent in meat alternatives such as beans
➤ You should also add 6 teaspoons (2 tablespoons) of vegetable oils to your diet over the course of the day.

If you are having difficulty figuring out what 1 cup of vegetables, 3 ounces of meat, or 1 tablespoon of salad dressing looks like, use **Figure 2.8**. It provides an easy way to eyeball your serving sizes. Keep in mind that if you consistently eat oversized portions that are larger than those suggested in your daily food plan, you will consume too many calories and may gain weight. The Nutrition in the Real World feature "When a Portion *Isn't* a Portion" on pages 46–47 takes a look at how portion sizes have changed over the years, and how portion distortion can adversely affect our health.

If all of your food selections are low in solid fat and added sugars, the above menu will provide a total of about 1,740 calories. This means that, after meeting your nutrient requirements, you have a maximum of about 260 of your 2,000 calories left (see **Figure 2.9**). You can "spend" these calories on extra servings of foods such as grains, fruits, and/or vegetables, or on occasion, on a food such as a sweet or dessert that has added solid fats or added sugars. The calorie levels and distribution of food groups in daily food plans are calculated using the leanest food choices with no added sugars. So if you pour whole milk (high in solid fats) over your sweetened cereal (added sugars) instead of using skim milk (fat free and low in solid fats) to drench your shredded wheat (no added sugars), you will have added a fair amount of calories from solid fats and added sugars. As you can see from **Table 2.4**, your food choices could quickly provide less healthy calories from solid fats and added sugars and cause your diet to be less nutrient rich per bite.

Let's now use these recommended amounts of servings from each food group and plan a 2,000-calorie menu. **Figure 2.10** on page 44 shows how servings from the various food groups can create well-balanced meals and snacks throughout the day.

Although this particular menu is balanced and the foods are nutrient dense, it is unlikely that every day will be this ideal. The good news is that your nutrient needs are averaged over several days, or a week, of eating. If one day you eat insufficient servings of one food group or a specific nutrient, you can make up for it the next day. For example, let's say that you don't eat enough fruit one day but do eat an extra serving of grains. The next day you can adjust your diet by cutting back on your grain servings and adding an extra serving of fruit. Should you worry about *when* you eat? Read more about the time of day you should eat in Examining the Evidence feature "Does the Time of Day You Eat Impact Your Health?" on pages 49–50.

If the foods at your meals are sometimes mixed dishes that contain a combination of ingredients, such as pizza, then they probably contribute servings to more than one food group. **Table 2.5** on page 45 provides examples of foods that contribute servings from multiple groups.

Now that you know what constitutes a healthy diet, the next step is to go food shopping. As you shop, you'll want to make sure you know the nutrient and calorie contents of the foods you buy. The food label will give you this information, and more.

260 kilocalories (added fats and sugars)

1,740 kilocalories (lean foods without added sugars)

2,000 total daily kilocalories

Figure 2.9 How Solid Fats and Added Sugars Fit into a Healthy Diet
If you select mostly nutrient-dense, lean foods that contain few solid fats and added sugars, you may have leftover calories to "spend" on extra helpings or a small sweet dessert.

Full-fat cheese is the number-one source of solid fats in the diets of Americans.

Table 2.4
Choose Right!

As you can see, your daily food plan could provide a fair amount of solid fats and added sugars, depending on your food selections.

Choosing . . .	Over . . .	Will Cost You
Whole milk (1 cup)	Fat-free milk (1 cup)	65 calories of solid fats
Roasted chicken thigh with skin (3 oz)	Roasted chicken breast, skinless (3 oz)	70 calories of solid fats
Glazed doughnut, yeast type (3¾" diameter)	English muffin (1 muffin)	165 calories of sold fats and added sugars
French fries (1 medium order)	Baked potato (1 medium)	299 calories of solid fats
Regular soda (1 can, 12 fl oz)	Diet soda (1 can, 12 fl oz)	150 calories of added sugars

Source: Adapted from "Empty Calories: How Do I Count the Empty Calories I Eat?" from U.S. Department of Agriculture, MyPlate. Available at www.ChooseMyPlate.gov.

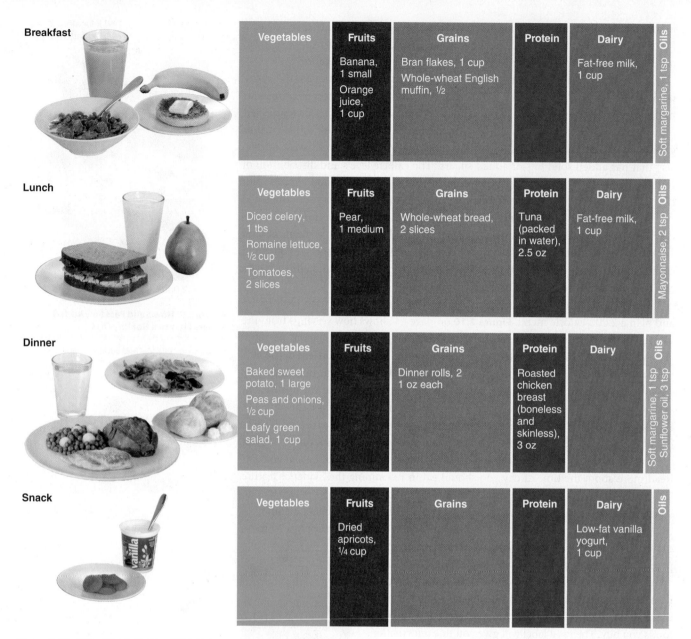

Breakfast

Vegetables	Fruits	Grains	Protein	Dairy	Oils
	Banana, 1 small Orange juice, 1 cup	Bran flakes, 1 cup Whole-wheat English muffin, ½		Fat-free milk, 1 cup	Soft margarine, 1 tsp

Lunch

Vegetables	Fruits	Grains	Protein	Dairy	Oils
Diced celery, 1 tbs Romaine lettuce, ½ cup Tomatoes, 2 slices	Pear, 1 medium	Whole-wheat bread, 2 slices	Tuna (packed in water), 2.5 oz	Fat-free milk, 1 cup	Mayonnaise, 2 tsp

Dinner

Vegetables	Fruits	Grains	Protein	Dairy	Oils
Baked sweet potato, 1 large Peas and onions, ½ cup Leafy green salad, 1 cup		Dinner rolls, 2 1 oz each	Roasted chicken breast (boneless and skinless), 3 oz		Soft margarine, 1 tsp Sunflower oil, 3 tsp

Snack

Vegetables	Fruits	Grains	Protein	Dairy	Oils
	Dried apricots, ¼ cup			Low-fat vanilla yogurt, 1 cup	

Figure 2.10 A Healthy Daily Food Plan
A variety of foods from each group creates a well-balanced diet.

The Take-Home Message MyPlate depicts the five food groups using the familiar mealtime visual of a place setting. It is part of the USDA Web-based initiative at ChooseMyPlate.gov, providing information, a food guidance system, and a personalized daily food plan to help you build a healthy diet based on the 2010 *Dietary Guidelines for Americans*. The concepts of nutrient density and energy density refer to the amount of nutrients per bite of food and the number of calories per gram of food. You want to consume nutrient-dense foods such as fruits, vegetables, whole grains, and lean dairy and protein foods, but limit energy-dense foods, which provide calories from solid fats and added sugars but little nutrition. Daily physical activity is encouraged to better manage your weight and health.

A Few Words about the Exchange Lists

The **Exchange Lists for Meal Planning** were designed in 1950 to give people with diabetes a structured eating plan. The lists are still in use. The Exchange Lists group foods together according to their carbohydrate, protein, and fat composition and provide specific portion sizes for each food. This assures that each food in the group contributes a similar amount of calories per serving.

Some weight-loss programs have adopted a similar meal planning tool to help their members manage their weight by controlling the number of calories that they consume. Because of the similarity of the foods within each group, foods can be exchanged or swapped with each other at meals and snacks. This flexible meal plan is a useful tool to control calorie, carbohydrate, protein, and

fat intakes. Appendix B provides more information on the Exchange Lists.

Exchange Lists for Meal Planning
A grouping of foods, in specific portions, according to their carbohydrate, protein, and fat composition to ensure that each food in the group contributes a similar amount of calories per serving.

Table 2.5

A Combination of Good Food

Many of the foods you eat are probably mixed dishes that contain servings from multiple food groups. The following list should help you estimate the servings from each food group for some popular food items. Because the preparation process can vary greatly among recipes, these are only estimates.

Food and Sample Portion	Vegetable Group (cups)	Fruit Group (cups)	Grains Group (oz eq)	Protein Group (oz eq)	Dairy Group (cups)	Estimated Total Calories
Cheese pizza, thin crust (1 slice from medium pizza)	⅛	0	1	0	½	215
Macaroni and cheese (1 cup, made from packaged mix)	0	0	2	0	½	260
Bean and cheese burrito (1)	⅛	0	2½	2	1	445
Chicken fried rice (1 cup)	¼	0	1½	1	0	270
Large cheeseburger	0	0	2	3	⅓	500
Turkey sub sandwich (6 inch)	½	0	2	2	¼	320
Peanut butter and jelly sandwich (1)	0	0	2	2	0	375
Apple pie (1 slice)	0	¼	2	0	0	280

Source: U.S. Department of Agriculture, Mixed Dishes in MyPyramid. Available at www.ChooseMyPlate.gov.

What Is a Food Label and Why Is It Important?

Imagine walking down the supermarket aisle and finding that all the foods on the shelves are packaged in plain cardboard boxes and unmarked aluminum cans. How would you know if a brown box contained one pound of pasta or of crackers? Do the blank cans hold chicken noodle soup or crushed pineapple?

Food labels don't just make food shopping easier, they also serve important functions that make them helpful tools for anyone who wants to eat a healthy diet. First and foremost, they tell you what's inside the package. Second, they contain a Nutrition Facts panel, which identifies the calories and nutrients in a serving of the food. Third, they list Daily Values (DVs), which help you determine how those calories and nutrients will fit into your overall diet.

When a Portion *Isn't* a Portion

Comparison of Portion Sizes of Common Foods

Food	Typical Portion	Recommended Serving Size	FDA Label
Cooked pasta	2.9 cups	0.5 cup	1.0 cup
French fries	5.3 oz	10 fries	2.5 oz
Bagel	4.4 oz	1.0 oz	2.0 oz
Muffin	6.5 oz	1.5 oz	2.0 oz
Cookie, chocolate chip	4.0 oz	0.5 oz	1.1 oz

Source: Data from L. R. Young and M. Nestle, "Expanding Portion Sizes in the U.S. Marketplace: Implications for Nutrition Counseling," *Journal of the American Dietetic Association* 103 (2003): 231–234.

What is a portion of pasta? The answer depends on who is serving you the pasta. A *portion* is the amount of food eaten at one sitting. At home, a portion of pasta would be the amount that you heap on your plate. In a restaurant, it's the amount brought out on your plate, which can vary enormously among eating establishments.

On the other hand, the FDA defines a *serving size* as a standard amount of food that is customarily consumed. The FDA groups foods together into similar categories and standardizes the serving sizes of the foods within each group. These reference serving sizes are used on the Nutrition Facts panel of the food label. For example, the serving size for pasta is one cup, no matter what brand of pasta you purchase. Standardizing serving sizes among similar foods not only allows for consistency when choosing foods in the supermarket, but also helps the consumer get a ballpark idea of what a typical serving should be.

However, when following the online MyPlate recommendations, the portion size for pasta is only half a cup. Why the difference between the food label and this tool for healthy eating? The MyPlate materials set portion sizes based on many different factors, one of which is the nutrient and calorie content of the foods in each group. All the

foods in the grains group, which contains foods such as pasta, bread, and rice, provide similar amounts of nutrients and calories. The calories in half a cup of pasta are similar to the calories of the other foods in the group, such as a slice of bread.[1]

As you can see from the table, most times, the portions of the foods that you eat

The Food Label Tells You What's in the Package

To help consumers make informed food choices, the Food and Drug Administration (FDA) regulates the labeling of all packaged foods in the United States.[7] Currently, the FDA has mandated that every packaged food be labeled with:[8]

➤ The name of the food
➤ The net weight of the food (the weight of the food in the package, excluding the weight of the package or packing material)
➤ The name and address of the manufacturer or distributor
➤ A list of ingredients in descending order by weight, with the heaviest item listed first
➤ Nutrition information, which lists total calories, calories from fat, total fat, saturated fat, *trans* fats, cholesterol, sodium, total carbohydrate, dietary fiber, sugars, vitamin A, vitamin C, calcium, and iron

don't coincide with the standard serving size on the food label or the portion sizes recommended. A generous helping of cooked pasta that spills over the edge of a plate is probably equal to about 3 cups, which is triple the amount listed on the food label and six times the recommended serving size.

How Have Portion Sizes Changed?

The restaurant industry has appealed to your desire to get the most food for your money by expanding restaurant portion sizes, especially of inexpensive foods, such as fast foods.[2] When McDonalds first introduced french fries in 1954, the standard serving weighed 2.4 ounces.[3] Although a small 2.5-ounce size (230 calories) is available on the menu today, you can also choose the medium french fries weighing 4.1 ounces (380 calories) or the large at 5.4 ounces (500 calories). The difference in costs to the restaurants for the larger sizes is minuscule compared with the perceived "value" of the larger portion to the consumers.[4] Customers will frequent a restaurant more often if they think they are getting a bargain for their buck.

Unfortunately, from a health standpoint, research shows that even slight changes in the portion sizes of foods can lead to increased calorie intake and weight gain.[5] As you have read, being overweight increases the risk of developing heart disease, diabetes, joint problems, and even some types of cancers.[6] Downsizing your portions could downsize your health risks.

Here are some tips to help you control your portion sizes:

Controlling Portion Size

When You Are:	Do This:
At Home	Measure your food until you develop an "eye" for correct portion sizes. Use smaller plates so portions appear larger. Plate your food at the counter before sitting down at the table or in front of the television. Store leftover foods in portion-controlled containers. Don't eat snacks directly from the box or bag; measure a portion first, then eat only that amount. Cook smaller quantities of food so you don't pick at the leftovers.
Eating Out	Ask for half orders when available. Order an appetizer as your main entrée. Don't be compelled to "clean your plate"; stop eating when you're full and take the rest home.
Food Shopping	Divide a package of snacks into individual portion sizes and consume only one portion at any one sitting. Be aware of the number of servings in a package; read the labels. Buy foods in preportioned servings such as a 1-ounce sliced cheese or snack and 100-calorie microwave popcorn.

➤ Serving sizes that are uniform among similar products, which allows for easier comparison shopping by the consumer
➤ An indication of how a serving of the food fits into an overall daily diet
➤ Uniform definitions for descriptive label terms such as "light" and "fat-free"
➤ Health claims that are accurate and science based, if made about the food or one of its nutrients
➤ The presence of any of eight common allergens that might be present in the food, including milk, eggs, fish, shellfish, tree nuts (cashews, walnuts, almonds, etc.), peanuts, wheat, and soybeans

Very few foods are exempt from carrying a Nutrition Facts panel on the label. Such foods include plain coffee and tea; some spices, flavorings, and other foods that don't provide a significant amount of nutrients; deli items, bakery foods, and other ready-to-eat foods that are prepared and sold in retail establishments; restaurant meals; and foods produced by small businesses (companies that have total annual sales of less than $500,000).[9]

Figure 2.11 Out with the Old and In with the New (a) A cereal box from the 1920s carried vague nutrition information. (b) Today, manufacturers must adhere to strict labeling requirements mandated by the FDA. Source: U.S. Food and Drug Administration.

The **Nutrition Facts panel** lists standardized serving sizes, specific nutrients, and shows how a serving of the food fits into a healthy diet by stating its contribution to the percentage of the Daily Value for each nutrient. The old cereal box doesn't contain this information.

The **name** of the product must be displayed on the front label.

The **ingredients** must be listed in descending order by weight. This format is missing in the old box. Whole-grain wheat is the predominant ingredient in the current cereal box.

The **net weight** of the food in the box must now be located at the bottom of the package.

Nutrition Facts panel The area on the food label that provides a uniform listing of specific nutrients obtained in one serving of the food.

Compare the two food labels in **Figure 2.11**. Note that the amount and type of nutrition information on the 1925 box of cereal is vague and less informative than the more recent version, which meets the FDA's current labeling requirements. Whereas raw fruits and vegetables and fresh fish typically don't have a label, these foods fall under the FDA's voluntary, point-of-purchase nutrition information program. Under the guidelines of this program, at least 60 percent of a nationwide sample of grocery stores must post the nutrition information of the most commonly eaten fruits, vegetables, and fish near where the foods are sold.[10] Nutrition labeling is mandatory for meat and poultry, which is regulated by the USDA. Meat and poultry items that are prepared and sold at the supermarket, such as take-out cooked chicken, do not have a nutrition label.[11]

The Food Label Can Help You Make Healthy Food Choices

Suppose you're in the dairy aisle of a supermarket trying to select a carton of milk. You want to watch your fat intake, so you have narrowed your choices to reduced-fat 2% milk or nonfat milk. How do they compare in terms of calories, fat, and other nutrients per serving? How do you decide which is more healthful? The answer is simple: Look at the labels. All the information that you need to make a smart choice is provided on one area of the label, the **Nutrition Facts panel**.

On the Label: The Nutrition Facts Panel

The Nutrition Facts panel provides a nutritional snapshot of the food inside a package. By law, the panel must list the following per serving of the food:

- ➤ Calories and calories from fat
- ➤ Total fat, saturated fat, and *trans* fat
- ➤ Cholesterol
- ➤ Sodium
- ➤ Total carbohydrate, dietary fiber, and sugars
- ➤ Protein
- ➤ Vitamin A, vitamin C, calcium, and iron

Does the Time of Day You Eat Impact Your Health?

We are all creatures of habit. Some of these habits, such as the time of day we eat, can either enhance or detract from overall health. Do you typically eat breakfast? Do you often snack after dinner or late at night? Do you overload on high-fat or fried foods, when you go out on the weekends? The choice to skip breakfast, eat later in the day, or overeat on the weekend can impact your nutrient intake, appetite, and body weight.

Eating Breakfast Means More Energy and Fewer Calories throughout the Day

You probably know that grabbing a latte on the way to your morning class is not a healthy breakfast, but do you understand how such a habit impacts your overall nutrient intake? For one thing, skipping breakfast may affect the total number of calories you consume the rest of the day. Dr. John de Castro evaluated the timing of food intake in 867 people over a seven-day period and found that people who ate a larger proportion of food earlier in the day had a significantly lower intake of total calories.[7] In other words, if you eat breakfast, you are more likely to eat less by the end of the day than if you skip this important meal.

The reduction in total calories when you eat breakfast may be due to the size of the meal and how satisfied you feel. Most of us eat smaller meals at breakfast and more food at lunch and dinner. We also appear to spend less time eating breakfast than other meals. In Dr. de Castro's study, both of these factors affected satiety. Satiety ratios, or the time between meals based on the size of the previous meal, decreased over the day from breakfast through late-evening snacks.[8] Thus, a more substantial breakfast is more satiating than the evening meal.

One reason breakfast may be more satiating involves the types of foods consumed. Holt and colleagues investigated the effects of a high-fat breakfast versus a high-carbohydrate meal on the amount of snacking reported later in the day (see the figure).[9] If the breakfast included higher fiber foods, such as cereal, and a good protein source, the subjects ate less later in the day. Breakfast foods including potatoes, eggs, and high-fiber cereals ranked higher than doughnuts or white bread for satiety.

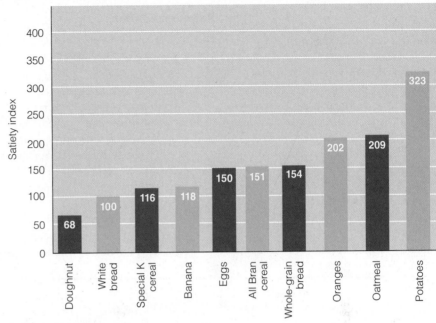

Satiety Index of Different Foods

Subjects were asked to rate their feelings of hunger every 15 minutes for 2 hours after eating 240-calorie portions of specific foods. All foods were compared with white bread, which scored a satiety index of 100.

Data from S. H. Holt, J. C. Miller, P. Petocz, and E. Farmakalidis, "A Satiety Index of Common Foods," *European Journal of Clinical Nutrition* 49 (1995): 675–690.

What if you skip breakfast? Not only will you eat more during the day, chances are you will choose less-nutrient-dense foods. Those who eat breakfast, lunch, and dinner tend to have higher calcium and iron intakes than individuals who skip breakfast.[10,11]

Eating breakfast may also be a good strategy for weight control. Several studies have reported higher BMIs and body weight in subjects who don't consistently eat breakfast compared with their breakfast-eating counterparts.[12] In addition, eating breakfast helps maintain weight loss.[13]

Eating More during Evenings and Weekends Can Lead to Overconsumption of Calories

Do you eat after 7:00 p.m.? Most young adults do, especially during the weekend.[14] For most students, eating schedules are influenced by hunger, pressures from work and school, convenience, and social habits. Regardless of why you eat at various times, the timing of your meals can affect body weight, the level of hormones in the blood, body temperature, and blood pressure.[15] Because eating later is less satisfying, you are likely to

eat more food, and hence consume more calories, particularly from carbohydrates and fats in the evening hours.

Though there is no current evidence that eating later in the day increases BMI or

CONTINUED

the risk of obesity,[16] timing of meals may impact changes in body composition during a weight-loss program. In a controlled metabolic ward study, overweight women who ate the bulk of their calories in the morning hours had a slightly greater weight loss than when the bulk of the calories was consumed later in the day. However, when they ate more of their calories later in the day, they retained more lean muscle mass.[17] More research is needed before any strong conclusions can be drawn from these results.

Weekend eating patterns can also influence overall dietary intake. Haines reports that people in that study ate an average of 82 calories more per day on Friday, Saturday, and Sunday compared with weekdays.[18] These increases in calories were mostly due to an increase in fat (approximately 0.7 percent) and

alcohol (1.4 percent); carbohydrates decreased by 1.6 percent. Over time, this increase in calorie intake may lead to weight gain.

Recommendations

Based on the current research on eating and time of day, it is recommended that you:

➤ Start your day with a nutrient-dense breakfast as part of a healthy eating pattern. Many breakfast foods, such as dry whole-grain cereals, fresh fruit, or whole-grain toast or bagels with low-fat cream cheese, can be eaten on the go. You'll have more energy and will most likely eat fewer total calories by the end of the day.

➤ Choose breakfast foods that are more satisfying to improve your appetite control throughout the day. Enjoy

foods such as whole-grain cereals and whole fruits, which are higher in fiber, protein, and water, and lower in fat and sugar.

➤ Control calorie intake on nights and weekends. Monitor your weekend eating habits to maintain a consistent balance of carbohydrates, fats, and proteins and to reduce alcohol consumption.

What Do You Think?

1. What makes certain foods more satiating than others?
2. Have you ever significantly changed the timing or content of your meals?
3. What effects did you notice in your levels of hunger, satisfaction, and energy as a result of this change?

Virtual Food Label Fun

Take this virtual shopping trip challenge to see how food label–savvy you really are. Visit www.accessdata.fda.gov/videos/CFSAN/HWM/hwmintro.cfm for some comparison-shopping fun!

If an additional nutrient, such as vitamin E or vitamin B_{12}, has been added, or if the product makes a claim about a nutrient, then that nutrient must also be listed. Other nutrients, such as additional vitamins and minerals, can be listed by the manufacturer on a voluntary basis. The majority of the packaged foods you purchase will contain this nutrition information.

Let's learn how to decipher the Nutrition Facts panel (**Figure 2.12**). At the top of the panel is the serving size. By law, the serving size must be listed both by weight in grams (less useful to you) and in common household measures, such as cups and ounces (more useful to you). Because serving sizes are standardized among similar food products, you can compare one brand of macaroni and cheese with a different brand to assess which one better meets your needs.

The rest of the information on the panel is based on the listed serving size (in this case, one cup) of the food. For example, if you ate two servings (two cups) of this macaroni and cheese, which is the number of servings in the entire box, you would double the nutrient information on the label to calculate the calories as well as the fat and other nutrients. The servings-per-container information is particularly useful for portion control.

Below the serving size is listed the calories per serving. The calories from fat give you an idea of what proportion of the food's calories comes from fat. In this box of macaroni and cheese, 110 out of a total of 250 calories—that is, nearly half—are from fat.

Next are the nutrients that you should limit or add to your diet. Americans typically eat too much fat, including saturated fat, *trans* fat, and cholesterol, and too much sodium. In contrast, they tend to fall short in dietary fiber, vitamins A and C, calcium, and iron. These are on the label to remind you to make sure to eat foods rich in these substances. A food manufacturer voluntarily may list other nutrients that it is important to consume in sufficient amounts, such as potassium and vitamin D. The Nutrition Facts panel can be your best shopping guide when identifying and choosing foods that are low in the nutrients you want to limit (like saturated fat) and high in the nutrients that you need to eat in higher amounts (like fiber).

Are you wondering what determines if a food contains a "high" or "low" amount of a specific nutrient? That's where the Daily Values come into play.

On the Label: The Daily Values

Unlike the DRIs, which are precise recommended amounts of each nutrient that you should eat, the **Daily Values (DVs)** listed on the Nutrition Facts panel are general reference levels for the nutrients listed on the food label. The DVs give you a ballpark idea of how the nutrients in the foods you buy fit into your overall diet.

For example, if calcium is listed at 20 percent, a serving of that food provides 20 percent of most adults' daily requirement for calcium. However, if you are under 19 years of age or older than 70, your calcium needs are higher than the reference number used on the DV. Because the DVs on the food label are based on a 2,000-calorie diet, if you need more or fewer than 2,000 calories daily, some of your DV numbers may be higher or lower than those listed on the Nutrition Facts panel.

The DVs are based on older reference levels and are not as current as the DRIs. For example, whereas the DRIs recommend an upper level of dietary sodium of no more than 2,300 milligrams (daily), the DVs use less than 2,400 milligrams as the reference level.

There are no DVs listed on the label for *trans* fat, sugars, and protein. This is because there isn't enough information available to set reference values for *trans* fat and sugars. Although there are reference values for protein, consuming adequate amounts of protein isn't a health concern for most Americans over age 4, so listing the percent of the DV for this nutrient isn't warranted on the label. The DV for protein will only be listed if the product is being marketed for children under the age of 4, such as a jar of baby food, or if a claim is made about the food, such as that it is "high in protein."[12]

If a serving provides 20 percent or more of the DV, it is considered high in that nutrient. For example, a serving of this macaroni and cheese is high in sodium (not a healthy attribute) and is also high in calcium (a healthy attribute). If you eat this entrée for lunch, you'll need to eat less sodium during the rest of the day. However, the good news is that a serving of this pasta meal also provides 20 percent of the DV for calcium.

If a nutrient provides 5 percent or less of the DV, it is considered low in that nutrient. A serving of macaroni and cheese doesn't provide much fiber, vitamin A, vitamin C, or iron. You will need to add other foods to supply these nutrients to your diet on the days that you eat macaroni and cheese.

Lastly, depending on the size of the food package, there may be a footnote at the bottom of the label. This provides a summary of the DVs for a 2,000-calorie diet as well as

Figure 2.12 Understanding the Nutrition Facts Panel

Source: Data from "How to Understand and Use the Nutrition Facts Label" from the FDA's Center for Food Safety and Applied Nutrition website, 2009.

Daily Values (DVs) Established reference levels of nutrients, based on a 2,000-calorie diet, that are used on food labels.

Practical Nutrition VIDEO

Reading a Food Label

The Nutrition Facts panel is easy to read—once you know what to look for. Scan this QR code with your mobile device to access the video. You can also access the video in MasteringNutrition™.

a 2,500-calorie diet. This area of the panel provides you with a little "cheat sheet" to help you when you are shopping so that you don't have to memorize the values. As you can see from the footnote, you should try to keep your sodium intake to less than 2,400 milligrams daily. Because you know that this macaroni and cheese is high in sodium, providing 20 percent of the DV, or 470 milligrams, of sodium, you should try to keep the sodium in your remaining food choices during the day to less than 2,000 milligrams.

Now that you know how to read the Nutrition Facts panel, let's return to the milk question posed at the beginning of this section and use what you've learned to compare the reduced-fat 2% and nonfat milk labels in **Figure 2.13**.

Let's start at the top:

a. Both cartons have the same standardized one-cup serving, which makes the comparison easy.

b. The reduced-fat milk has 50 percent more calories than the nonfat milk; almost 40 percent of the calories in the reduced-fat milk are from fat.

c. Use the percent of the DV to assess whether the milk is considered "high" or "low" in a given nutrient. For instance, a serving of reduced-fat milk provides more than 5 percent of the DV for both total and saturated fat (as well as cholesterol), so it isn't considered "low" in these nutrients. In fact, the saturated fat provides 15 percent of the DV, which is getting close to the definition of "high" (20 percent of the DV). In contrast, the nonfat milk doesn't contain any fat, saturated fat, or cholesterol, so it appears so far to be the healthier choice.

d. However, since being low in fat doesn't necessarily mean being healthier, let's make sure that the nonfat milk is as nutritious as the reduced-fat variety. Comparing the remaining nutrients, especially calcium and vitamin D, confirms that the nonfat milk has all the vitamins and minerals that reduced-fat milk does, but

Figure 2.13 Using the Nutrition Facts Panel to Comparison Shop
The Nutrition Facts panel makes comparison shopping between types and brands of foods easier for the consumer.

Source: U.S. Food and Drug Administration.

with fewer calories and less fat, saturated fat, and cholesterol. In fact, both milks provide a "high" amount of calcium and vitamin D. So, when it comes to choosing milk, the nonfat version is the smarter choice.

While the Nutrition Facts panel on the side or back of the package can help you make healthier food choices, some foods carry claims on their front labels that may also influence your decision to buy. Let's look at these next.

On the Label: Label Claims

In the 1980s, the savvy Kellogg Company ran an ad campaign for its fiber-rich All Bran cereal reminding the public of the National Cancer Institute's recommendation to eat low-fat, high-fiber foods, fresh fruits, and vegetables to maintain a healthy weight. According to the FDA, sales of high-fiber cereals increased over 35 percent within a year.[13] Manufacturers realized that putting nutrition and health claims on labels was effective in influencing consumer purchases. Supermarket shelves were soon crowded with products boasting various claims.

So, can you feel confident that the jar of light mayonnaise is really lighter in calories and fat than regular mayonnaise? Yes, you can. The FDA mandates that all claims on labels follow strict guidelines.

Currently, the FDA allows the use of three types of claims on food products:

1. nutrient content claims
2. health claims
3. structure/function claims

Cereal-box readers will read the information on the box as many as 12 times before they consume the last spoonful!

All foods displaying these claims on the label must meet specified criteria. Let's look at each of these claims closely.

Nutrient Content Claims

A food product can make a **nutrient content claim** about the amount of a nutrient it contains (or doesn't contain) by using descriptive terms such as *free* (fat-free yogurt), *high* (high-fiber crackers), *low* (low saturated fat granola), *reduced* (reduced-sodium soup), and *extra lean* (extra lean ground beef) as long as it meets the strict criteria designated by the FDA. These terms can help you identify at a glance the food items that best meet your needs.

Look at the labels of the canned soups in **Figure 2.14** on page 54. If you want a chicken soup with the least amount of sodium based on the three choices, look for the "low sodium" label on the can, as this nutrient claim means that the soup cannot contain more than 140 milligrams of sodium per serving. A next best choice would be the soup with the term "less sodium" on the label, which means that it must contain at least 25 percent less sodium than the regular variety. The classic can of chicken soup contains almost 900 milligrams for a serving, which is likely the same or even more sodium you may consume at a meal. **Table 2.6** on page 55 provides some of the most common nutrient claims on food labels, the specific criteria that each claim must meet as mandated by the FDA, and examples of food products that carry these nutrient claims.

Health Claims

Suppose you are sitting at your kitchen table eating a bowl of Cheerios in skim milk, and staring at the front of the cereal box. You notice a claim on the front of the box that states: "The soluble fiber in Cheerios, as part of a heart healthy diet, can help you lower your cholesterol." Do you recognize this as a health claim that links Cheerios with better heart health?

nutrient content claims Claims on the label that describe the level or amount of a nutrient in a food product.

a. Because this can of chicken noodle soup displays the "low sodium" nutrient claim, it can't provide more than 140 milligrams of sodium in a serving.

b. This can of soup has more than 25 percent less sodium than the classic version, so the term "less" can be displayed on its label.

c. The classic variety of chicken noodle soup has the most sodium per serving.

Figure 2.14 Soup's On!
Nutrient claims on the food label must meet strict FDA criteria.

Source: U.S. Food and Drug Administration.

health claims Claims on the label that describe a relationship between a food or dietary compound and a disease or health-related condition.

structure/function claims Claims on the label that describe how a nutrient or dietary compound affects the structure or function of the human body.

A **health claim** must contain two important components:

1. a food or a dietary compound, such as fiber, and
2. a corresponding disease or health-related condition that is associated with the claim.[14]

In the Cheerios example, the soluble fiber (the dietary compound) that naturally occurs in oats has been shown to lower blood cholesterol levels (the corresponding health-related condition), which can help reduce the risk of heart disease.

There are three types of health claims: (1) authorized health claims, (2) health claims based on authoritative statements, and (3) qualified health claims. The differences between them lie in the amount of supporting research and agreement among

Table 2.6

What Does That Labeling Term Mean?

Nutrient	Free	Low	Reduced/Less	Light
Calories	< 5 calories (cal) per serving	≤ 40 cal per serving	At least 25 percent fewer calories per serving	If the food contains 50 percent or more of its calories from fat, then the fat must be reduced
Fat	< 0.5 grams (g) per serving	≤ 3 g per serving	At least 25 percent less fat per serving	Same as above
Saturated Fat	< 0.5 g per serving	≤ 1 g per serving	At least 25 percent less saturated fat per serving	N/A
Cholesterol	< 2 milligrams (mg) per serving	≤ 20 mg per serving	At least 25 percent less cholesterol per serving	N/A
Sodium	< 5 mg per serving	<140 mg per serving	At least 25 percent less sodium per serving	If the sodium is reduced by at least 50 percent per serving
Sugars	< 0.5 g	N/A	At least 25 percent less sugar per serving	N/A

Other Labeling Terms

Term	Definition
"High," "Rich in," or "Excellent source of"	The food contains 20 percent or more of the DV of the nutrient in a serving. Can be used to describe protein, vitamins, minerals, fiber, or potassium.
"Good source of"	A serving of the food provides 10–19 percent of the DV. Can be used to describe meals or main dishes.
"More," "Added," "Extra," or "Plus"	A serving of the food provides 10 percent of the DV. Can only be used to describe vitamins, minerals, protein, fiber, and potassium.
"Lean"	Can be used on seafood and meat that contains less than 10 g of fat, 4.5 g or less of saturated fat, and less than 95 mg of cholesterol per serving.
"Extra lean"	Can be used on seafood and meat that contains less than 5 g of fat, less than 2 g of saturated fat, and less than 95 mg of cholesterol per serving.

Note: N/A = not applicable

Source: Data from "Guidance for Industry: A Food Labeling Guide" by U.S. Food and Drug Administration, from the FDA website. Originally published September 1994; Revised April 2008 and October 2009.

scientists about the strength of the relationship between the food or dietary ingredient and the disease or condition. See **Table 2.7** for a definition of these claims and examples of each.

Structure/Function Claims

The last type of label claim is the **structure/function claim**, which describes how a nutrient or dietary compound affects the structure or function of the human body.[15] The claims "calcium (nutrient) builds strong bones (body structure)" and "fiber (dietary compound) maintains bowel regularity (body function)" are examples of structure/function claims. Structure/function claims cannot state that the nutrient or dietary compound

In one consumer survey, more than 40 percent of respondents said that they had purchased foods that claimed to reduce the risk of heart disease and more than 25 percent had chosen items that claimed to reduce the risk of cancer. Health claims do influence food decisions.

Table 2.7

Sorting Out the Label Claims

Type of Claim	Definition	Examples (Claims of links between . . .)
Authorized health claims (well-established)	Claims based on a well-established relationship between the food or compound and the health benefit. Food manufacturers must petition the FDA and provide the scientific research that backs up the claim. If there is significant agreement among the supporting research and a consensus among numerous scientists and experts in the field that there is a relationship between the food or dietary ingredient and the disease or health condition, the FDA will allow an authorized health claim. Specified wording must be used. The FDA has approved 12 authorized health claims.	• Calcium and osteoporosis • Sodium and hypertension • Dietary fat and cancer • Dietary saturated fat and cholesterol and risk of coronary heart disease • Fiber-containing grain products, fruits, and vegetables, and cancer • Fruits, vegetables, and grain products that contain fiber, particularly soluble fiber, and the risk of coronary heart disease • Fruits and vegetables and cancer • Folate and neural tube defects • Dietary noncarcinogenic carbohydrate sweeteners and dental caries • Soluble fiber from certain foods and risk of coronary heart disease • Soy protein and risk of coronary heart disease • Plant sterol/stanol esters and risk of coronary heart disease
Health claims based on authoritative statements (well-established)	Claims based on statements made by a U.S. government agency, such as the Centers for Disease Control and Prevention (CDC) and the National Institutes of Health (NIH). If the FDA approves the claim submitted by the manufacturer, the wording of these claims must include "may," as in "whole grains may help reduce the risk of heart disease," to illustrate that other factors in addition to the food or dietary ingredient may play a role in the disease or condition. This type of health claim can only be used on food and cannot be used on dietary supplements.	• Whole-grain foods and risk of heart disease and certain cancers • Potassium and risk of high blood pressure • Fluoridated water and risk of dental caries • Saturated fat, cholesterol, and *trans* fat and risk of heart disease
Qualified health claims (less well-established)	Claims based on evidence that is still emerging. However, the current evidence to support the claim is greater than the evidence suggesting that the claim isn't valid. These are allowed in order to expedite the communication of potentially beneficial health information to the public. They must be accompanied by the statement "the evidence to support the claim is limited or not conclusive" or "some scientific evidence suggests. . . ." Qualified health claims can be used on dietary supplements if approved by the FDA.	• Selenium and cancer • Antioxidant vitamins and cancer • Nuts and heart disease • Omega-3 fatty acids and coronary heart disease • B vitamins and vascular disease • Monounsaturated fatty acids from olive oil and coronary heart disease • Unsaturated fatty acids from canola oil and risk of coronary heart disease • 0.8 mg folic acid and neural tube birth defects • Green tea and cancer • Chromium picolinate and diabetes • Calcium and colon/rectal cancer and calcium and recurrent colon/rectal polyps • Calcium and hypertension, pregnancy-induced hypertension, and preeclampsia • Tomatoes and/or tomato sauce and prostate, ovarian, gastric, and pancreatic cancers • Corn oil and corn oil–containing products and risk of heart disease

can be used to treat a disease or a condition (see **Figure 2.15**).[16] These claims can be made on both foods and dietary supplements. Unlike the other health claims, structure/function claims don't have to be preapproved by the FDA. They do have to be truthful and not misleading, but the manufacturer is responsible for making sure that the claim is accurate. These claims can be a source of confusion. Shoppers can easily fall into the trap of assuming that one brand of a product with a structure/function claim on its label is superior to another product without the claim. For instance, a yogurt that says "calcium builds strong bones" on its label may be identical to another yogurt without the flashy label claim. The consumer has to recognize the difference between claims that are supported by a significant amount of solid research and approved by the FDA, and structure/function claims that don't require prior approval for use.

If a dietary supplement such as a multivitamin is to contain a structure/function claim, its manufacturer must notify the FDA no later than 30 days after the product has been on the market. Dietary supplements that use structure/function claims must display a disclaimer on the label that the FDA did not evaluate the claim and that the dietary supplement is not intended to "diagnose, treat, cure, or prevent any disease." Manufacturers of foods bearing structure/function claims do not have to display this disclaimer on the label, just on dietary supplements.

All foods that boast a health claim and/or a structure/function claim can also be marketed as **functional foods**. The Health Connection feature "Functional Foods: What Role Do They Play in Your Diet?" discusses this trendy category of foods.

Although keeping the types of health and structure/function claims straight can be challenging, here's one way to remember them:

➤ Authorized health claims and health claims based on authoritative statements are the strongest, as they are based on years of accumulated research or an authoritative statement.

➤ Qualified health claims are less convincing. They are made on potentially healthful foods or dietary ingredients, but, because the evidence is still emerging, the claim has to be "qualified" as such.

➤ Structure/function claims are the weakest claims, as they are just statements or facts about the role the nutrient or dietary ingredient plays in your body. They can't claim that the food or dietary ingredient lowers your risk of developing a chronic disease such as heart disease or cancer. As you read the claims on the labels, you will quickly see that those with less established scientific evidence behind them have the weakest wording.

Table 2.8 on page 60 summarizes the various areas of information you can use to help you achieve a healthful diet.

The Take-Home Message The FDA regulates the labeling on all packaged foods. The Nutrition Facts panel and the Daily Values are found on all food labels. Every food label must include the name of the food, its net weight, the name and address of the manufacturer or distributor, a list of ingredients, and standardized nutrition information. The FDA allows and regulates the use of nutrient content claims, health claims, and structure/function claims on food labels. Any foods or dietary supplements displaying these claims on the label must meet specified criteria and be truthful.

Figure 2.15 A Structure/Function Label Claim
The structure/function claim is that the antioxidants added to this cereal support the immune system. The manufacturer cannot claim that the food lowers a consumer's risk of a chronic disease or health condition.

Practical Nutrition **VIDEO**

Understanding Food Claims

Not all label claims are created equal! Let Joan show you how to recognize the different types. Scan this QR code with your mobile device to access the video. You can also access the video in MasteringNutrition™.

functional foods Foods that have a positive effect on health beyond providing basic nutrients.

Functional Foods: What Role Do They Play in Your Diet?

Have you ever eaten broccoli? Odds are that you have, but you may not have known that you were eating a functional food. In fact, some people have even called broccoli a su-perfood. Although there isn't a legal definition for either of these terms, a commonly used definition for a *functional food* is one that has been shown to have a positive effect on your health beyond its basic nutrients ("superfood" is a more trendy term often used in the media to highlight that a food has functional and healthy proper-ties).[19] Broccoli is a functional food because it is rich in beta-carotene, which, in addition to being a key source of vitamin A, helps protect your cells from damaging substances that can increase your risk of some chronic diseases, such as heart disease. In other words, the beta-carotene's function goes beyond its basic nutritional role as a source of vitamin A, because it may also help fight heart disease. Broccoli is also a cruciferous vegetable, which, along with cauliflower and brussels sprouts, is part of the cabbage family. These vegetables contain compounds such as isothiocyanates, which may also be "super" at fighting cancer. Oats are also a functional food and some-times also referred to as a superfood, because they contain the soluble fiber beta-glucan, which has been shown to lower blood cholesterol levels. This can play a positive role in lowering the risk for heart disease.[20]

If the beneficial compound in the food is derived from plants, such as in the case of beta-carotene, isothiocyanates, and beta-glucan, it is called a **phytochemical** (*phyto* = plant). If it is derived from animals it is called a **zoochemical** (*zoo* = animal). Heart-healthy omega-3 fatty acids, found in fatty fish such as salmon and sardines, are considered zoochemicals. The accompanying table provides a list of currently known compounds in foods that have been shown to provide positive health benefits. Manufacturers are promoting foods containing naturally occurring phyto-chemicals and zoochemicals and have also begun fortifying other food products with these compounds. You can buy margarine with added plant sterols and a cereal with the soluble fiber, psyllium, which both help to lower blood cholesterol levels, as well as pasta and eggs that have had omega-3 fatty acids added.

phytochemicals
Plant chemicals that have been shown to reduce the risk of certain diseases such as cancer and heart disease. Beta-carotene is a phytochemical.

zoochemicals
Compounds in animal food products that are beneficial to human health. Omega-3 fatty acids are an example of zoochemicals.

Are People Buying Functional Foods?

Yes, people are buying them. Consumers in United States annually spend more than $15 billion on these foods.[21] In one survey of 1,000-plus American adults, between 43 and 85 percent of those surveyed were aware that food components such as omega-3 fatty acids and fiber can provide health benefits.[22]

Baby boomers, in particular—the generation of people born be-tween 1946 and 1964—are eager not only to live longer than their parents, but also to live better. They are turning to functional foods to fight heart disease, aid in diminishing joint pain, prevent memory loss, and help them keep their eyesight healthy.[23]

What Are the Benefits of Functional Foods?

Functional foods are being used by health care professionals to thwart patients' chronic diseases and, in some situations, as an eco-nomical way to treat a disease. For example, many doctors send their patients to a registered dietitian nutritionist (RDN) for diet advice to treat specific medical conditions, such as an elevated blood choles-terol level, rather than automatically prescribing cholesterol-lowering medication. Eating a diet that contains a substantial amount of cholesterol-lowering oats or plant sterols is less expensive, and often more appealing, than taking costly prescription medication. Ideally, the RDN, who is trained in the area of nutrition, can recommend the addition of functional foods to the diet based on the person's own medical history and nutritional needs.

However, problems can arise when consumers haphazardly add functional foods to their diets.

What Concerns Are Associated with Functional Foods?

With so many labeling claims now adorning products on supermarket shelves, consumers have an array of enhanced functional foods from which to choose. Having so many options can be confus-ing. Consumers often cannot tell if a pricey box of cereal with added "antioxidants to help support the immune sys-tem" is really better than an inexpensive breakfast of oatmeal and naturally antioxidant-rich orange juice. There is also a concern that after eating a bowl of this antioxidant-enhanced cereal, consum-ers may think they are "off the hook" about eating healthfully the

Your Guide to Functional Foods

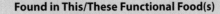

This Compound	Found in This/These Functional Food(s)	May Have This Health Benefit
Beta-carotene	Carrots, pumpkin, cantaloupe, broccoli	Functions as an antioxidant in the body
Lycopene	Tomatoes, tomato sauce	May lower risk of prostate cancer
Soy protein	Tofu, soy milk	Lowers risk of heart disease
Beta-glucan	Oatmeal, oats, oat bran	Lowers blood cholesterol
Plant sterol and stanol esters	Fortified margarines, like Benecol spreads	Lowers blood cholesterol
Omega-3 fatty acids	Salmon, sardines, tuna	May reduce the risk of heart disease
Whole grains	Whole-wheat bread, brown rice, popcorn	May reduce the risk of some cancers and heart disease
Flavanols	Dark chocolate, green apples	May contribute to heart health
Anthocyanins	Berries, red grapes, cherries	Act as antioxidants, may contribute to brain function
Probiotics	Active cultures in fermented dairy products such as yogurt	Support intestinal health

Source: Based on "International Food Information Council (IFIC) Foundation Functional Foods Component Chart" from the IFIC website, accessed March 2013.

rest of the day. Often, more than one serving of a functional food is needed to reap the beneficial effect of the food compound, but the consumer hasn't been educated appropriately about how much of such a food to consume. Finally, while functional foods do convey health benefits, they are not magic elixirs that can negate a poor diet. The best way to use functional foods is as part of a healthy diet that can help *prevent* adverse health conditions from occurring in the first place.

As with most dietary substances, problems may arise if too much is consumed. For example, whereas consuming some omega-3 fatty acids can help reduce the risk of heart disease, consuming too much can be problematic for people on certain medications or for those at risk for a specific type of stroke.[24] A person can unknowingly overconsume a dietary compound if his or her diet contains many different functional foods enhanced with the same compound. Also, functional beverages, such as herbal beverages or vitamin-enhanced water, can have more calories and added sugar than soft drinks.

How to Use Functional Foods

Functional foods can be part of a healthy, well-balanced diet. Keep in mind that whole grains, fruits, vegetables, healthy vegetable oils, lean meat and dairy products, fish, and poultry all contain varying amounts of naturally occurring phytochemicals and zoochemicals and are the quintessential functional foods. If you consume other, packaged functional foods, take care not to overconsume any one compound. Seek out an RDN for sound nutrition advice on whether you would benefit from added functional foods, and, if so, how to balance them in your diet.

Table 2.8

A Summary of Tools for Healthy Eating

	DRIs	Dietary Guidelines for Americans, 2010	MyPlate	Nutrition Facts Panel	Label Claims
What Are They?	Specific reference values, for each nutrient by age and gender	Reflect the most current nutrition and physical activity recommendations for good health	A representational icon that depicts five food groups using the familiar mealtime visual of a place setting	Contains important nutrition information to be used to compare food products	There are three types of claims: 1. Nutrient content claims 2. Health claims 3. Structure/function claims
How Do They Guide You in Healthy Eating?	DRIs provide recommendations to prevent malnutrition and chronic diseases for each nutrient. The upper level is designed to prevent overnutrition or toxicity.	The *Dietary Guidelines* emphasize healthy food choices, maintaining healthy weight, and physical activity. Guidelines for types of foods, moderate alcohol intake, and food safety are also included.	MyPlate is the focal point for the Web-based ChooseMyPlate.gov initiative, which provides information to build a healthy diet based on the *Dietary Guidelines for Americans, 2010.*	You can use the Nutrition Facts panel to compare the nutrient density of foods.	You can use these label terms to help you choose foods that may contain a specific amount of a nutrient or compound to improve your diet.
What Are They Made Up Of?	EARs, RDAs, AIs, ULs, and AMDRs	The recommendations are guided by two overarching concepts: 1. Maintain calorie balance over time to achieve and sustain a healthy weight. 2. Consume more nutrient-rich foods and beverages.	Recommendations are made for physical activity as well as five food groups, plus oils: 1. Vegetables 2. Fruits 3. Grains 4. Protein 5. Dairy 6. Oils	Information is presented about: 1. Serving size 2. Servings per package 3. Total calories and calories from fat 4. Macronutrients 5. Vitamins and minerals 6. % Daily Values	1. Nutrient content claims describe the level or amount of a nutrient in a food product. 2. Health claims describe a relationship between a food or dietary compound and a disease or health-related condition. 3. Structure/function claims describe how a nutrient or dietary compound affects the structure or function of the body.

Will Posting Nutritional Content in Restaurants Have a Positive Impact on the Obesity Epidemic?

The Patient Protection and Affordable Care Act of 2010, also known as "Obamacare," has a provision that forces restaurants with more than 20 locations to disclose calories on the menu board and in written form by the end of 2013.[1] The idea behind this provision is that if people know what is in a food, they will make healthier choices. Is this true? Will posting this information make a dent in the obesity epidemic? Take a close look at the arguments for both sides and see what you think.

yes

- In 2009, a Healthy Eating Research review found that menu labeling reduces intentions to order high-calorie items.[2]

- Several studies reveal that people generally underestimate the calories and fat content in restaurant menu items.[3] If the nutrition information is provided, they will be able to adjust their choices accordingly.

- The Act requires a short statement about daily caloric intake, similar to that on the Nutrition Facts label, that helps consumers understand the calorie information within the context of a total daily diet.[4] Based on that information, they will be able choose a selection with an appropriate amount of calories.

- Having to post nutrition information may encourage restaurant owners to provide and promote healthier fare, as they seek to attract customers.[5]

- Some early studies show that posting caloric content and daily recommended intake does impact the amount of calories purchased.[6] A 2011 study from Stanford found that consumers purchased 6 percent fewer calories per transaction with menu labeling.[7]

no

- Most of the people who read and follow nutrition labels already do so as part of a healthy lifestyle.

- Posting nutritional content has had mixed results with Nutrition Facts labels in supermarkets. One analysis by the USDA's Economic Research Service found that Nutrition Facts label use was associated with higher fiber and iron intake, but not with reduced intake of calories, saturated fat, or cholesterol.[8]

- Surveys conducted about restaurant food choices show mixed results when people are given nutritional information. Some people make the healthier choice, and some don't depending on other factors, such as interest in losing weight.[9]

- A small study from Drexel University points out that while some restaurants add healthy choices to their menus, they also add unhealthy choices, which negates the positive change.[10]

- The groups of people impacted by menu labeling are already lean, already use nutrition labels to make healthy choices, and are, as a result, not part of the obesity epidemic.

what do you think?

1. Do you think that posting nutritional information will solve our obesity epidemic? **2.** Does reading nutritional information override the compulsion to order something unhealthy? **3.** How do you decide what to order in a restaurant?

1 Healthful Eating Is Based on Key Principles

A healthy diet includes the key principles of balance, variety, and moderation of nutrient-dense foods. The Dietary Reference Intakes (DRIs), *Dietary Guidelines for Americans*, MyPlate, and the Nutrition Facts panel on food labels are all tools that can help you plan a healthy diet.

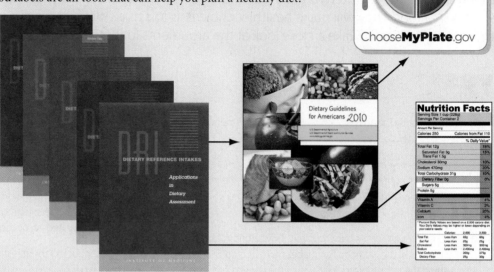

2 The Dietary Reference Intakes Are Reference Values for Each Nutrient

The DRIs are specific reference values, based on your age and gender, for the essential nutrients you need daily. The DRIs are designed to prevent nutrient deficiencies, maintain good health, prevent chronic diseases, and avoid unhealthy excesses. The DRIs consist of the Estimated Average Requirement, Recommended Dietary Allowance, Adequate Intake, Tolerable Upper Intake Level, and the Acceptable Macronutrient Distribution Ranges.

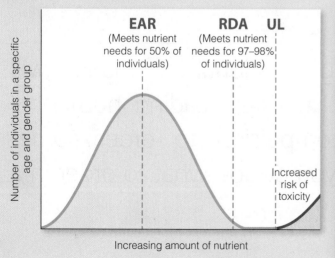

3 The *Dietary Guidelines for Americans* Are Recommendations to Lower Risk of Disease

The *Dietary Guidelines for Americans* are the current nutrition and physical activity recommendations for Americans aged 2 and older, including those who may be at risk for chronic diseases. These guidelines are designed to help individuals improve their diet to lower their risk of chronic diseases and conditions such as diabetes mellitus, heart disease, certain cancers, osteoporosis, high blood pressure, high blood cholesterol levels, and, most importantly, obesity.

4 MyPlate Is a Food Guidance System

MyPlate is the USDA's latest tool that visually represents the five food groups and many of the recommendations in the *Dietary Guidelines for Americans*. Together MyPlate and ChooseMyPlate.gov help you meet your daily DRIs and the recommendations for the number of servings that you should eat every day from each food group based on your calorie needs. The new recommendations emphasize daily physical activity, proportionality among the food groups, and variety within the food groups, as well as moderation when consuming foods with unhealthy solid fats and added sugars. ChooseMyPlate.gov provides a personalized eating plan based on your needs and encourages improvements in your diet and lifestyle choices to improve your health.

ChooseMyPlate.gov

5 Food Labels Provide Nutrient Content Information

The FDA regulates all packaged foods to ensure that they are accurately labeled. The Nutrition Facts panel on the food label must list the serving size of the food. It must also show the corresponding amount of calories, fat, saturated fat, *trans* fat, cholesterol, sodium, sugars, protein, vitamins A and C, calcium, and iron that are contained in a serving of the food. Other nutrients can be listed by the manufacturer voluntarily. If a food product makes a claim about a nutrient, that nutrient must be listed in the Nutrition Facts panel. The food label helps you make healthy food choices.

6 Functional Foods Have Additional Health Benefits

Functional foods have been shown to have a positive effect on health beyond providing basic nutrients. Some foods are deliberately enhanced with compounds and marketed as functional foods. Functional foods can be used as part of a healthy, well-balanced diet, not in place of one.

Macaroni & Cheese

Nutrition Facts

Serving Size 1 cup (228g)
Serving Per Container 2

Amount Per Serving

Calories 250 Calories from Fat 110

	% Daily Value*
Total Fat 12g	18%
Saturated Fat 3g	15%
Trans Fat 3g	
Cholesterol 30mg	10%
Sodium 470mg	20%
Potassium 700mg	20%
Total Carbohydrate 31g	10%
Dietary Fiber 0g	0%
Sugars 5g	
Protein 5g	
Vitamin A	4%
Vitamin C	2%
Calcium	20%
Iron	4%

* Percent Daily Values are based on a 2,000 calorie diet. Your Daily Values may be higher or lower depending on your calorie needs:

	Calories:	2,000	2,500
Total Fat	Less than	65g	80g
Sat Fat	Less than	20g	25g
Cholesterol	Less than	300mg	300mg
Sodium	Less than	2,400mg	2,400mg
Total Carbohydrate		300g	375g
Dietary Fiber		25g	30g

Terms to Know

- undernutrition
- malnourished
- overnutrition
- Dietary Reference Intakes (DRI)
- Estimated Average Requirement (EAR)
- Recommended Dietary Allowance (RDA)
- Adequate Intake (AI)
- Tolerable Upper Intake Level (UL)
- toxicity
- Acceptable Macronutrient Distribution Ranges (AMDRs)
- Estimated Energy Requirement (EER)
- *Dietary Guidelines for Americans*
- food guidance systems
- MyPlate
- proportionality
- nutrient density
- energy density
- Nutrition Facts panel
- Daily Values (DVs)
- nutrient content claims
- health claims
- structure/function claims
- functional foods
- phytochemicals
- zoochemicals

Check Your Understanding

1. The *Dietary Guidelines for Americans* recommend that you
   a. maintain calorie balance over time and sustain a healthy weight.
   b. stop smoking and walk daily.
   c. sleep eight hours a night and jog every other day.
   d. consume adequate nutrients within your calorie needs and stop smoking.

2. The Dietary Reference Intakes (DRIs) are reference values for nutrients and are designed to
   a. only prevent nutritional deficiency.
   b. provide a ballpark range of your nutrient needs.
   c. prevent nutritional deficiencies by meeting your nutrient needs as well as prevent the consumption of excessive and dangerous amounts of nutrients.
   d. outline the health benefits of specific nutrients.

3. The Estimated Average Requirement (EAR) is
   a. the estimated amount of a nutrient that you should consume daily to be healthy.
   b. the amount of a nutrient that meets the average needs of 50 percent of individuals in a specific age and gender group.
   c. the amount of a nutrient that meets the average needs of 100 percent of individuals in a specific age and gender group.
   d. the maximum safe amount of a nutrient that you should consume daily.

4. A three-ounce serving of cooked chicken is approximately the size of
   a. a 5-year-old's palm.
   b. your adult brother's palm.
   c. your adult sister's palm.
   d. your great-uncle's palm.

5. Which of the following are the food groups in MyPlate?
   a. grains, vegetables, dairy, sweets, protein
   b. grains, fruits, alcohol, sweets, protein
   c. grains, vegetables, fruits, dairy, protein
   d. grains, vegetables, oils, dairy, protein

6. Which of the following foods is most nutrient dense?
   a. an orange ice pop
   b. an orange
   c. orange-flavored punch
   d. orange sherbet

7. By law, which of the following MUST be listed on the food label?
   a. calories, fat, and potassium
   b. fat, saturated fat, and vitamin E
   c. calories, fat, and saturated fat
   d. calories, sodium, and vitamin D

8. The bran cereal that you eat in the morning carries a "high-fiber" claim on its label. This is an example of a
   a. nutrient claim.
   b. structure claim.
   c. health claim.
   d. function claim.

9. The yogurt that you enjoy as a morning snack states that a serving provides 30 percent of the Daily Value for calcium. A serving of this yogurt is considered
   a. low in calcium.
   b. high in calcium.
   c. an insignificant source of calcium.
   d. a good source of both calcium and vitamin D.

10. Oatmeal is a functional food. It contains a soluble fiber that can help lower your
    a. blood pressure.
    b. red blood cells.
    c. pulse.
    d. blood cholesterol.

Answers

1. (a) The *Dietary Guidelines for Americans, 2010* recommend that you maintain calorie balance over time and sustain a healthy weight. Though the *Dietary Guidelines* do not specifically address stopping smoking, this is a habit worth kicking. Walking or jogging daily are wonderful ways to be physically active. Sleeping eight hours a night isn't mentioned in the *Dietary Guidelines* but is another terrific lifestyle habit.

2. (c) The DRIs tell you the amount of nutrients you need to prevent deficiencies, maintain good health, and avoid toxicity.

3. (b) The EAR is the amount of a nutrient that would meet the needs of half of the individuals in a specific age and gender group. The EAR is used to obtain the Recommended Dietary Allowance, which is the amount of a nutrient that you should be consuming daily to maintain good health. The Tolerable Upper Intake Level is the maximum amount of a nutrient that you can consume on a regular basis that is unlikely to cause harm.

4. (c) A three-ounce serving of cooked chicken (or meat and fish, for that matter) is approximately the size of an adult woman's palm.

5. (c) Vegetables, fruits, grains, protein, and dairy are the five basic food groups in MyPlate. Sweets and alcohol are not food groups and should be limited in the diet. Oils are essential components of a healthy diet, but are not considered a food group.

6. (b) While an orange ice pop and orange sherbet may be refreshing treats on a hot day, the orange is by far the most nutrient-dense food among the choices because it provides the most nutrients for the fewest calories. The orange-flavored punch is a sugary drink with orange flavoring.

7. (c) The Nutrition Facts panel on the package must contain the calories, fat, and saturated fat per serving. Vitamins E and D and potassium do not have to be listed

unless they have been added to the food and/or the product makes a claim about them on the label.

8. (a) This high-fiber cereal label boasts a nutrient claim and is helping you meet your daily fiber needs.

9. (b) If you consume 20 percent or more of the Daily Value for a nutrient, it is considered "high" in that nutrient. If a nutrient provides 5 percent or less of the Daily Value, it is considered "low" in that nutrient. This doesn't make any reference to the vitamin D content of the serving of yogurt.

10. (d) Functional foods go beyond providing basic nutrients and also provide other health benefits. Oats contain the soluble fiber beta-glucan, which has been shown to help reduce blood cholesterol levels. Because of this, oatmeal is considered a functional food.

Web Resources

- For more tips and resources for MyPlate, visit www.ChooseMyPlate.gov
- For more on dietary guidelines, functional foods, nutrition needs across the lifespan, and other nutrition topics, visit USDA's Food and Nutrition Information Center at http://fnic.nal.usda.gov
- For more on food labels, visit www.fda.gov

1. **False.** Because consuming too much of some essential nutrients can be harmful, the Tolerable Upper Intake Level (UL) of the DRIs was established for many nutrients. To learn more, turn to page 34.

2. **False.** Proteins should comprise only 10 to 25 percent of your daily calories. To find out why, turn to page 34.

3. **True.** The *Dietary Guidelines* are intended for those who are 2 years of age and older, including those who may also be at risk for chronic diseases. To learn more, turn to page 36.

4. **False.** Solid fats are less nutrient dense, so should be reduced in your diet. Turn to page 40 to find out the sources of solid fats that you may be consuming.

5. **False.** Oils are not considered a food group but you should add some daily for good health. Turn to page 41 to find out more.

6. **False.** The good news is that your nutrient needs are averaged over several days or a week of eating, so your plate doesn't have to perfectly match MyPlate daily. Turn to page 43 to learn how to do this.

7. **True.** The FDA requires a food label on all packaged food items, and specific information must be included. To find out exactly what must be disclosed on the food label, turn to page 46.

8. **False.** A nutrient claim uses descriptive terms to make a claim about the amount of a nutrient a serving of food contains (or doesn't contain). To find out what those terms are, turn to page 53.

9. **True.** However, more than one type of health claim is allowed on a label. Turn to page 54 to learn about the types of claims that food manufacturers may use.

10. **False.** Eating functional foods can have numerous health benefits, but they are not a magic potion. Find out which foods are functional foods, and why they are beneficial, on page 58.

3

The Basics of Digestion

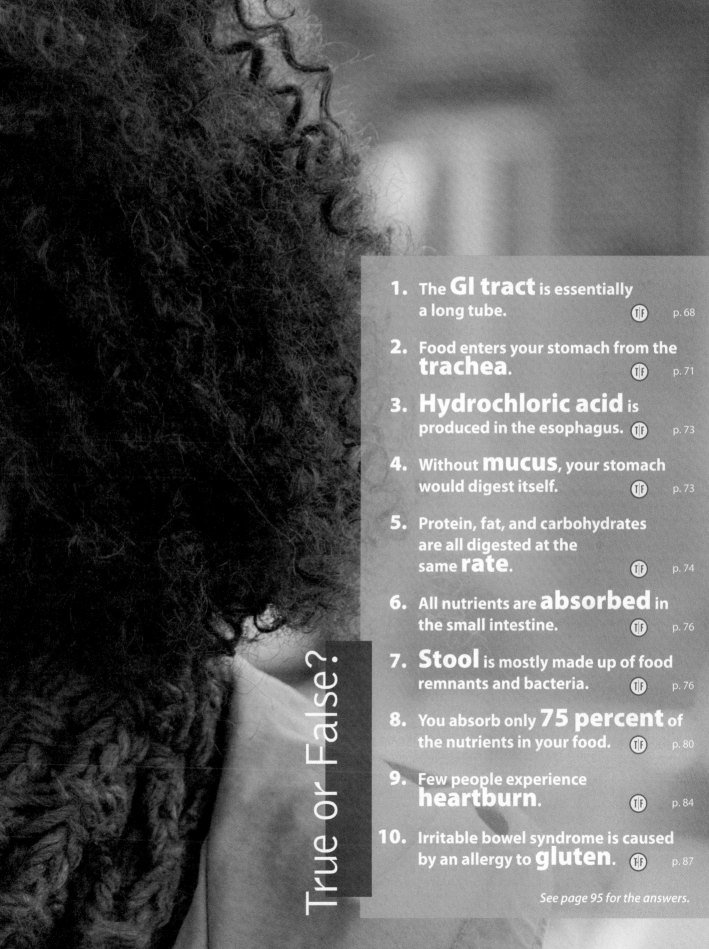

True or False?

1. The **GI tract** is essentially a long tube. T/F *p. 68*

2. Food enters your stomach from the **trachea**. T/F *p. 71*

3. **Hydrochloric acid** is produced in the esophagus. T/F *p. 73*

4. Without **mucus**, your stomach would digest itself. T/F *p. 73*

5. Protein, fat, and carbohydrates are all digested at the same **rate**. T/F *p. 74*

6. All nutrients are **absorbed** in the small intestine. T/F *p. 76*

7. **Stool** is mostly made up of food remnants and bacteria. T/F *p. 76*

8. You absorb only **75 percent** of the nutrients in your food. T/F *p. 80*

9. Few people experience **heartburn**. T/F *p. 84*

10. Irritable bowel syndrome is caused by an allergy to **gluten**. T/F *p. 87*

See page 95 for the answers.

1. Define digestion and the processes involved in preparing food for absorption.

2. Describe the organs involved in digestion and their primary functions.

3. Explain the function of enzymes, hormones, and bile in digestion, including their primary action and their source of origin.

4. Describe the process of absorption.

5. Explain how the circulatory and lymphatic systems transport absorbed nutrients throughout the body.

6. Describe the role of the nervous system and the endocrine system in keeping your body nourished.

7. Describe the symptoms and causes of the most common digestive disorders.

Even before you take your first bite of food, the process of digestion begins. Just the smell of warm bread fresh out of the oven or the sight of homemade apple pie stimulates saliva to be released in the mouth. The secretion of saliva and other digestive juices sets in motion a cascade of events that prepares the body to digest your favorite foods. In this chapter you will explore the processes included in digestion and absorption, the organs involved, and the other biological mechanisms that regulate how you process the foods you enjoy. We'll also discuss the causes and treatments of some common gastrointestinal conditions and disorders.

What Is Digestion and Why Is It Important?

The simple definition of digestion is the breaking down of foods into absorbable components in the **gastrointestinal (GI) tract**. Through a multistep **digestive process**, food is softened with moisture and heat, and then broken down into smaller particles by chewing and exposure to enzymes.

Digestion Occurs in the GI Tract

The GI tract consists of the mouth, esophagus, stomach, small intestine, and large intestine. Outside the GI tract are *accessory organs*—the pancreas, liver, and gallbladder—that aid in digestion by secreting digestive juices through ducts into the small intestine. The main roles of the organs of the GI tract are to (1) break food down into its smallest components; (2) absorb the nutrients; and (3) prevent microorganisms or other harmful compounds consumed with food from entering the tissues of the body.[1]

The GI tract is a muscular tube that coils and twists, beginning with the mouth and ending with the anus. The GI tract is nearly 30 feet long in a cadaver; it is significantly shorter in a living person because of muscle tone.[2] Stretched vertically, the GI tract would be about as high as a two-story building. The many circular folds, grooves, and projections in the stomach and intestines provide an extensive surface area over which absorption can occur. The cells lining your GI tract have a very brief life span. They function for three to five days and then they are shed into the **lumen** (interior of the intestinal tract) and are replaced with new, healthy cells.

Digestion Is Mechanical and Chemical

There are two forms of digestion: mechanical and chemical. **Mechanical digestion** involves chewing, grinding, and breaking food apart in, and then moving it through the GI tract. **Chemical digestion** involves digestive juices and enzymes breaking down food into absorbable nutrients that are small enough to enter the cells of the GI tract, blood, or lymph tissue.

Both mechanical and chemical digestion occur in various organs throughout the GI tract. After food has been chewed and ground up in the mouth, mechanical digestion continues with wavelike actions of the muscles throughout the GI tract, called peristalsis, segmentation, and pendular movement. The muscular activity and rhythmic contractions, or **peristalsis (Figure 3.1)**, occurs throughout the GI tract and helps mix food with digestive secretions and propel the mixture from the esophagus through the large intestine.

Segmentation is a "sloshing" motion that thoroughly mixes food with chemical secretions in the small intestine. Segmentation is different from peristalsis in that food is shifted back and forth along the small intestine to increase the time food comes into contact with the intestinal walls. **Pendular movement** is a constrictive wave that involves both forward and reverse movements and enhances nutrient absorption in the small intestine. Together, these three actions move chyme at a rate of 1 centimeter per minute.[3] Depending on the amount of food and the type of food consumed, the contact time in the small intestine is about 3 to 10 hours.[4]

The process of chemical breakdown can be interrupted. For example, the weight-loss drug orlistat, sold over the counter as Alli, interferes with the chemical digestion of fat (see the Nutrition in the Real World feature "Tinkering with Your Body's Digestive Process" on page 70).

Before we examine the individual roles of the organs, take a look at **Figure 3.2** and refresh your memory of how organs are built from cells and tissues and how they work together in various body systems. Understanding how cells build tissues will help you understand how digestion and absorption happen in the body.

The Take-Home Message Digestion is a multistep process that takes place in the GI tract. Digestion is comprised of mechanical and chemical processes that break food into smaller units until it can be absorbed for use by the body. Food is propelled along the GI tract by peristalsis. Segmentation and pendular movement move chyme back and forth to allow mixing with the secretions of the small intestine.

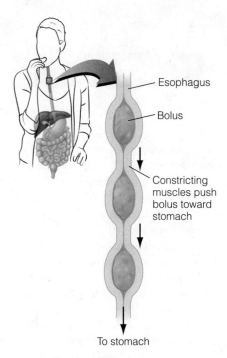

Figure 3.1 Peristalsis
Muscles around the organs of the GI tract constrict in a wavelike manner to help move food along.

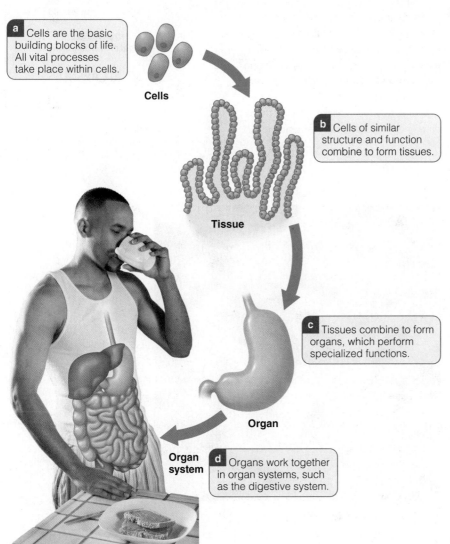

a Cells are the basic building blocks of life. All vital processes take place within cells.

Cells

b Cells of similar structure and function combine to form tissues.

Tissue

c Tissues combine to form organs, which perform specialized functions.

Organ

d Organs work together in organ systems, such as the digestive system.

Organ system

Figure 3.2 From Cells to Organs and Organ Systems

gastrointestinal (GI) tract Body area containing the organs of the digestive tract. It extends from the mouth to the anus.

digestive process The breakdown of foods into absorbable components using mechanical and chemical means.

lumen The interior of the digestive tract, through which food passes.

mechanical digestion Breaking food down through chewing and grinding, or moving it through the GI tract with peristalsis.

chemical digestion Breaking down food with enzymes or digestive juices.

peristalsis The forward, rhythmic motion that moves food through the digestive system. Peristalsis is a form of mechanical digestion because it influences motion, but it does not add chemical secretions.

segmentation A "sloshing" motion that thoroughly mixes chyme with the chemical secretions of the intestine.

pendular movement A constrictive wave that involves both forward and reverse movements of chyme and enhances nutrient absorption.

What Is Digestion and Why Is It Important? **69**

Tinkering with Your Body's Digestive Process

If you're like a lot of people, you may have considered using a weight-loss aid at some point. One of those aids, Alli, has popped up in many drugstores in recent years. How does this drug work, and will it help you lose weight? Is the potential for weight loss worth the side effects and costs?

Let's find out. Alli (pronounced AL-eye) is the first Food and Drug Administration (FDA)–approved, over-the-counter drug containing orlistat. This version has 60 milligrams of orlistat versus 120 milligrams in the prescription form, Xenical. When taken with a meal, orlistat helps prevent some dietary fat from being absorbed into your body. Orlistat works its magic by preventing lipase, the enzyme secreted from the pancreas, from breaking down dietary fat in the small intestines. If the fat isn't broken down, your body can't absorb it, and it will pass through the GI tract and be eliminated in stool. Alli blocks the absorption of about 25 percent of the fat at a meal. If you are taking Alli and eat a slice of pepperoni pizza containing 189 calories from fat for lunch, you will only absorb about 140 of them. Because fat—a hefty source of calories—isn't absorbed by your body, your body can end up with significantly fewer calories to potentially store as body fat.

Unfortunately, because this unabsorbed fat has to be eliminated from your body, there may be some not-so-pleasant side effects, including oily spotting, gas with discharge, the feeling of having to go to the bathroom immediately, fatty/oily stools, and frequent bowel movements. Interestingly, because these side effects are so unpleasant, they may actually help an individual adhere to a well-balanced, low-fat diet (approximately 30 percent of calories from fat) when taking the drug. Orlistat taken with a very high-fat meal will make these side effects more pronounced.

Orlistat also reduces the absorption of some fat-soluble vitamins as well as beta-carotene. Consequently, individuals taking the drug are advised to take a supplement that contains the fat-soluble vitamins A, D, E, and K and the antioxidant beta carotene.

According to the FDA, Alli is indicated for obese individuals or for people who are overweight and have other risk factors such as diabetes, high cholesterol, and elevated blood pressure. However, taking the drug won't let you off the hook when it comes to managing your weight. If you replace the unabsorbed fat calories with excess nonfat calories, such as from sweets, pretzels, and soda, or with hefty snacks between meals, you'll end up getting nowhere fast. There is also a cost factor. A month's supply of Alli costs approximately $50.

There isn't any quick fix when it comes to weight loss. Although Alli has been approved to help those who are obese, in the long term, eating healthfully, changing eating habits and behaviors, and exercising regularly are still, and always will be, the cornerstones and the *least expensive* methods of long-term weight management—for everyone.

REFILL PACK SEE SIDE OF PACKAGE FOR LISTING OF CONTENTS

alli®
Orlistat 60mg Capsules
Weight Loss Aid

FDA approved
non-prescription
weight loss aid

*Helps you lose more
weight than dieting alone*

120 CAPSULES

Alli, the non-prescription version of the drug orlistat, was FDA-approved for sale over-the-counter in 2007.

The drug orlistat prevents some of the fat in foods from being absorbed. This isn't a free ticket to eat a lot of fat-laden foods like pizza, however. Any fat that is consumed but not absorbed will be passed out of the body, potentially causing some unpleasant side effects.

Digestion converts whole foods into individual nutrients that can be used by the body's cells.

The smell, sight, and taste of food, such as freshly baked bread, triggers the release of saliva and other digestive juices.

What Are the Organs of the GI Tract and Why Are They Important?

Figure 3.3 on page 72 illustrates the organs of the GI tract and the unique and crucial role each organ plays in digestion. Let's begin with your first bite and follow the process of digestion through the entire GI tract.

Digestion Begins in the Mouth

Both mechanical and chemical digestion begins in the mouth. Glands in your mouth release **saliva**, a watery fluid that will help soften the food you are about to eat. Once you take a bite and begin to chew, your teeth, powered by your jaw muscles, cut and grind the food into smaller pieces and with your tongue mix it with saliva. Saliva helps dissolve small food particles and allows you to comfortably swallow dry food. In addition to water, saliva contains electrolytes, a few enzymes (including amylase, which begins to break down carbohydrate), and **mucus**. The mucus helps lubricate the food, helps it stick together, and protects the inside of the mouth. Once food has been adequately chewed, it's pushed to the back of the mouth and through the **pharynx** by the tongue.

Swallowing seems simple because we do it hundreds of times a day, but it is actually a complicated process. Pushing chewed food to the pharynx is a voluntary act—that is, you control it. Once the food mass (now called a **bolus**) enters the pharynx, the swallowing reflex kicks in, and you no longer control the action.

You have probably experienced an episode of "swallowing gone wrong" in which you've accidentally propelled food down the wrong pipe. When this happens (and you find yourself in a coughing fit trying to expel the item), it is because the normal

> You produce 1 to 1.5 liters of saliva every day.

saliva Watery fluid secreted by the salivary glands in the mouth. Saliva moistens food and makes it easier to swallow.

mucus Viscous, slippery secretions found in saliva and other digestive juices.

pharynx The throat. Passageway for the respiratory (air) and digestive tracts (food and beverages).

bolus Chewed mass of food.

The human digestive system consists of the organs of the gastrointestinal (GI) tract and associated accessory organs. The processing of food in the GI tract involves ingestion, mechanical digestion, chemical digestion, propulsion, absorption, and elimination.

ORGANS OF THE GI TRACT

MOUTH

Ingestion Food enters the GI tract via the mouth.

Mechanical digestion Chewing tears, shreds, and mixes food with saliva, forming a bolus.

Chemical digestion Carbohydrate enzymes secreted by the salivary glands begin carbohydrate breakdown.

PHARYNX AND ESOPHAGUS

Propulsion Swallowing and peristalsis move the bolus from mouth to stomach.

STOMACH

Mechanical digestion Mixes and churns the bolus with acid, enzymes, and gastric fluid into a liquid called chyme.

Chemical digestion Stomach enzymes begin the digestion of proteins.

Absorption A few fat-soluble substances are absorbed through the stomach wall.

SMALL INTESTINE

Mechanical digestion and **Propulsion** Segmentation mixes chyme with digestive juices; peristaltic waves move it along tract.

Chemical digestion Digestive enzymes from pancreas and small intestine digest most classes of food.

Absorption Nutrients are absorbed into blood and lymph through the intestinal cells.

LARGE INTESTINE

Chemical digestion Some remaining food residues are digested by bacteria.

Absorption Reabsorbs salts, water, and some vitamins.

Propulsion Compacts waste into feces.

RECTUM

Elimination Temporarily stores feces before voluntary release through the anus.

ACCESSORY ORGANS

Salivary glands

LIVER

Produces bile to digest fats.

GALLBLADDER

Stores bile before release into the small intestine through the bile duct.

PANCREAS

Produces digestive enzymes and bicarbonate ions that are released into the small intestine via the pancreatic duct.

mechanism that protects your trachea (or windpipe) didn't engage properly. Usually, a small flap called the **epiglottis** closes off your trachea during swallowing (**Figure 3.4**). The epiglottis ensures that food and drink go down the correct pipe—the **esophagus**—rather than down the trachea. When the epiglottis doesn't work properly, food can get lodged in the trachea, which can potentially result in choking.

Once swallowed, a bolus of food is pushed down your esophagus by *peristalsis* (refer again to Figure 3.1). When the bolus of food reaches the stomach, the lower part of the esophagus relaxes, allowing the bolus to enter the stomach. Solid or partially chewed food passes through the esophagus in about 8 seconds. Soft food and liquids pass through in about 1 to 2 seconds.[5]

The esophagus narrows at the bottom (just above the stomach) and ends at a sphincter, or ring of muscle, called the **lower esophageal sphincter (LES)**. Under normal conditions, when we swallow food, the LES relaxes and allows food to pass into the stomach. The stomach also relaxes to comfortably receive the food.[6] After food enters the stomach, the LES should close. If it doesn't, hydrochloric acid from the stomach may flow back into the esophagus and irritate its lining. This is called *heartburn* because it causes a burning sensation in the middle of the chest.

Chronic heartburn and the reflux of stomach acids are symptoms of gastro-esophageal reflux disease (GERD). The condition, GERD, and the treatment for it will be discussed later in this chapter.

The Stomach Stores, Mixes, and Prepares Food for Digestion

(T/F) The **stomach** is a muscular organ that continues mechanical digestion by churning and contracting to mix food with digestive juices (see **Figure 3.5**). The food is continuously mixed for several hours. The stomach also has a role in chemical digestion in that it produces powerful digestive secretions. These secretions include **hydrochloric acid (HCl)**, various enzymes, mucus, intrinsic factor (needed for vitamin B_{12} absorption), and the stomach hormone, **gastrin**. The swallowed bolus of food soon becomes **chyme**, a semiliquid substance that contains digestive secretions plus the original food. The stomach can expand to hold 2 to 4 liters of chyme.

(T/F) Hydrochloric acid has important digestive functions. You might think that such a strong chemical would "digest" the stomach itself, but mucus produced in the stomach acts as a barrier between the HCl and the stomach lining, protecting the lining from irritation or damage. Hydrochloric acid activates enzymes, including

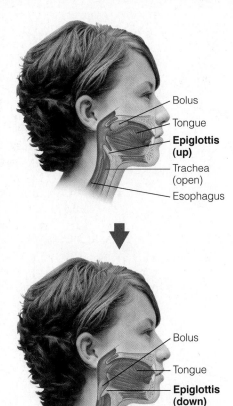

Figure 3.4 The Epiglottis
The epiglottis prevents food from entering the trachea when you swallow.

epiglottis Flap of tissue that protects the trachea while swallowing.

esophagus Tube that extends from the throat to the stomach.

lower esophageal sphincter (LES) A circular band of muscle between the esophagus and the stomach that opens and closes to allow food to enter the stomach.

stomach Digestive organ that holds food after it's moved down the esophagus and before it is propelled into the small intestine.

hydrochloric acid (HCl) A powerful acid made in the stomach that has digestive functions. It also helps to kill microorganisms and lowers the pH in the stomach.

gastrin A digestive hormone produced in the stomach that stimulates digestive activities and increases motility and emptying.

chyme The semiliquid, partially digested food mass that leaves the stomach and enters the small intestine.

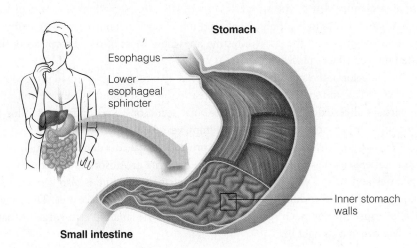

Figure 3.5 Anatomy of the Stomach

the protein-digesting enzyme **pepsin**, enhances the absorption of minerals, breaks down the connective tissue in meat, and destroys some ingested microorganisms.[7]

Have you ever noticed that some foods keep you feeling full longer than others? Foods high in carbohydrate exit the stomach faster, and therefore make you feel less full, than foods high in protein, fat, or fiber. Most liquids, carbohydrates, and low-fiber foods require minimal digestive activity, are easier to absorb, and have less surface area due to low fiber content.

Similarly, low-calorie foods exit the stomach faster than concentrated, high-calorie foods. This is because low-calorie foods frequently require minimal digestion. For example, a lightly sweetened cup of tea, a lower calorie beverage, requires less digestion than a higher-calorie, nutrient-dense milkshake. Digesting the tea involves only the breakdown of the sugar. In contrast, digesting the milkshake involves breaking down fat, protein, and carbohydrates.

As digestion continues, peristaltic contractions push the chyme toward the lower part of the stomach. As the chyme accumulates near the **pyloric sphincter**, the muscular sphincter relaxes and the chyme gradually enters the small intestine. Approximately 1 to 5 milliliters (1 teaspoon) of chyme are released into the small intestine every 30 seconds during digestion.[8] The pyloric sphincter prevents chyme from exiting the stomach too soon, and it prevents intestinal contents from returning to the stomach.

Most Digestion and Absorption Occurs in the Small Intestine

The **small intestine** is a long, narrow, coiled chamber in the abdominal cavity. The "small" in "small intestine" refers to its diameter, not its length, which accounts for about 20 feet of the GI tract. It consists of three segments—duodenum, jejunum, and ileum—and extends from the pyloric sphincter to the beginning of the large intestine. The first segment, the duodenum, is the shortest portion of the small intestine, followed by the jejunum, and finally the longest segment, called the ileum. While digestion continues along the small intestine, the duodenum is the primary site for food digestion within the human body.

The remarkable surface area (enough to cover a tennis court) of the folds and crevices of the small intestine lining allows for a continuous, efficient absorption of virtually all digested nutrients (**Figure 3.6**). The small intestine has tremendous surface area compared with the stomach, and its digestive secretions do most of the work when it comes to breaking down food into absorbable nutrients. The jejunum and ileum segments of the small intestine are where most of the absorption of digested nutrients takes place.

The interior of the small intestine is covered with thousands of small projections called **villi**. The villi increase the surface area of the small intestine's lining and mix the partially digested chyme with the intestinal secretions. Each individual villus is adjacent to a cluster of blood capillaries, lymph vessels, and nerve fibers.

The villi are covered by even smaller projections called **microvilli**, which provide additional surface area through which nutrients are absorbed into the blood capillaries and lymph vessels. The lining of the small intestine is also arranged in unique, circular folds, which further increase the absorptive surface area. The circular folds cause the chyme to spiral forward through the small intestine, rather than merely move in a straight line.

There are more microorganisms than human cells in your body, and many of them are located in your large intestine.

pepsin A digestive enzyme produced in the stomach that breaks down protein.

pyloric sphincter Sphincter in the bottom of the stomach that separates the pylorus from the duodenum of the small intestine.

small intestine Comprised of the duodenum, jejunum, and ileum, the small intestine is the longest part of the GI tract. Most of the digestion and absorption of food occurs in the small intestine.

villi Projections on the walls of the small intestine that increase the surface area over which nutrients can be absorbed.

microvilli Tiny projections on the villi in the small intestine that increase the surface area even more.

The small intestine is highly adapted for absorbing nutrients. Its length—about 20 feet—provides a huge surface area, and its wall has three structural features—circular folds, villi, and microvilli—that increase its surface area by a factor of more than 600.

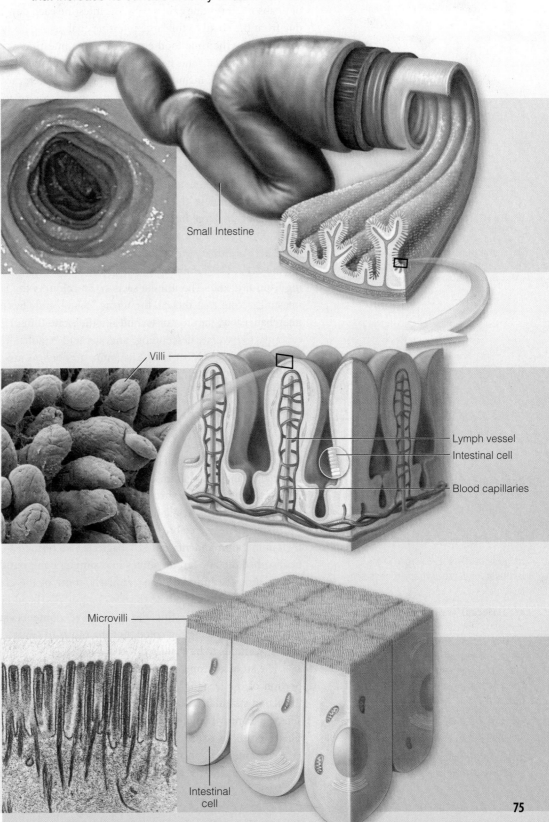

CIRCULAR FOLDS

The lining of the small intestine is heavily folded, resulting in increased surface area for the absorption of nutrients.

Small Intestine

VILLI

The folds are covered with villi, thousands of fingerlike projections that increase the surface area even further. Each villus contains blood and lymph vessels that transport nutrients throughout the body.

Villi

Lymph vessel

Intestinal cell

Blood capillaries

MICROVILLI

The cells on the surface of the villi end in hairlike projections called microvilli that further increase the surface area of the small intestine.

Microvilli

Intestinal cell

The Large Intestine Eliminates Waste and Absorbs Water and Some Nutrients

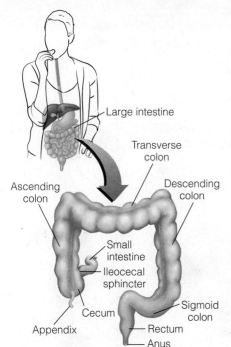

Figure 3.7 Anatomy of the Large Intestine
By the time chyme reaches the large intestine, most of its nutrients have been absorbed. However, water and some electrolytes are absorbed in the colon. The final waste products of digestion pass out of the body as stool through the anus.

ileocecal sphincter Gateway between the end of the small intestine and the beginning of the large intestine. The sphincter prevents backflow of fecal contents from the large intestine into the small intestine.

large intestine Final organ of the GI tract. It consists of the cecum, appendix, colon, and rectum.

stool (feces) Waste products that are stored in the large intestine and then excreted from the body. Consists mostly of bacteria, sloughed-off gastrointestinal cells, inorganic matter, water, unabsorbed nutrients, food residue, undigested fibers, fatty acids, mucus, and remnants of digestive fluids.

rectum The lowest part of the large intestine, continuous with the sigmoid colon and the anus.

anus The opening at the end of the rectum where waste is eliminated from the body.

Once the chyme has passed through the small intestine, it comes to the **ileocecal sphincter**, which serves as the gateway to its next digestive destination, the **large intestine**. The primary purpose of the ileocecal sphincter is to prevent backflow of fecal contents from the large intestine into the ileum. In general, this sphincter is quite strong and resists reverse pressure. About 750 milliliters (approximately 3 cups) of unabsorbed residue enters the large intestine each day. The slow entry of this residue from the small to the large intestine enables the body to maximize nutrient absorption.[9] By the time food enters the large intestine, it has been digested and the majority of the nutrients have been absorbed. But the large intestine serves some important functions, including the absorption of water, production of a few vitamins, absorption of important electrolytes, and the formation and storage of fecal material.

At approximately 5 feet long, the large intestine is one quarter the length of the small intestine, but it has twice the diameter. The structure of the large intestine borders the small intestine on three sides and unlike the small intestine, is not tightly coiled, nor does it secrete or use digestive enzymes. Rather, the chemical digestion that takes place in the large intestine is due to the efforts of bacteria. The large intestine produces mucus that protects the cells and acts as a lubricant for fecal matter. The cells of the large intestine absorb water and electrolytes much more efficiently than do the cells of the small intestine.

There are three segments of the large intestine: the cecum, colon, and rectum (**Figure 3.7**). The cecum is a small, pouchlike area that has the appendix hanging from one end. The middle section, or colon, is the largest portion of the large intestine. (Note that though the terms "colon" and "large intestine" are often used interchangeably, they're not technically the same thing.) The colon includes the ascending, transverse, descending, and sigmoid regions. These regions are relatively long and straight. Most of the vitamin production and absorption of water and electrolytes occur within the first half of the colon. The last half of the colon stores fecal matter.

The colon receives about 1 liter (about 1 quart) of fluid material each day from the cecum, consisting of water, undigested or unabsorbed food particles, indigestible residue, and bacteria. It slowly and gently mixes these intestinal contents and absorbs the majority of the fluid. The colon gradually produces a semisolid material that is reduced to about 200 grams (about 7 ounces) of fecal matter (**stool, or feces**). The intestinal matter passes through the colon within 12 to 70 hours, depending on a person's age, health, diet, and fiber intake.[10]

Bacteria in the colon play a role in producing some vitamins, including the B vitamin biotin and vitamin K.[11] Bacteria also ferment some of the undigested and unabsorbed dietary carbohydrates into simpler compounds, including methane gas, carbon dioxide, and hydrogen. Similarly, some of the colon's bacteria break down undigested fiber and produce various compounds, including hydrogen and sulfide.

As in the small intestine, the colon moves contents via peristalsis. Peristalsis occurs within the ascending colon, but the waves of contraction are quite slow, which allows the fluids to be absorbed.[12]

The stool is propelled forward until it reaches the **rectum**, the final eight-inch portion of the large intestine, where it is stored. When stool distends the rectum, the action stimulates stretch receptors, which in turn stimulate the defecation reflex. This causes nerve impulses of the rectum to communicate with the rectum's muscles. The end result is relaxation of the internal sphincter of the anus.

The **anus** is connected to the rectum and controlled by two sphincters: an internal and an external sphincter. Under normal conditions, the anal sphincters are closed. Periodically, the anal sphincters will relax, stool will enter the anal canal, and defecation will occur. The final stage of defecation is under our voluntary control and influenced by age, diet, prescription medicines, health, and abdominal muscle tone.

The Liver, Gallbladder, and Pancreas Are Accessory Organs

Although food doesn't pass through the liver, gallbladder, or pancreas during digestion, these three accessory organs are still essential to the process (**Figure 3.8**).

Weighing in at about three pounds, the **liver** is the largest gland in the body. It is so important that you couldn't survive without it. The liver produces about 500 to 1,000 milliliters (about 2 pints) of bile each day[13] and helps regulate the metabolism of carbohydrates, fats, and protein. The liver also stores several nutrients, including vitamins A, D, and E; the minerals iron and copper; and glycogen, the storage form of glucose. The liver is essential for processing and detoxifying alcohol. You'll learn about each of these functions in more depth in later chapters of this book.

Once bile is formed in the liver, it is collected, drained, and released into the gallbladder to be stored. The **gallbladder** is attached to the liver and stores approximately 30 to 50 milliliters (1 to 2 ounces) of concentrated bile at a time.

The **pancreas** is an organ about the size of your hand that produces hormones, including the two blood glucose–regulating hormones, insulin and glucagon. It also produces digestive enzymes and bicarbonate that are delivered into the small intestine through the pancreatic duct. Bicarbonate neutralizes the acid found in the chyme (raises the pH), creating a neutral environment. This protects certain enzymes that would otherwise become inactivated in an acidic environment.

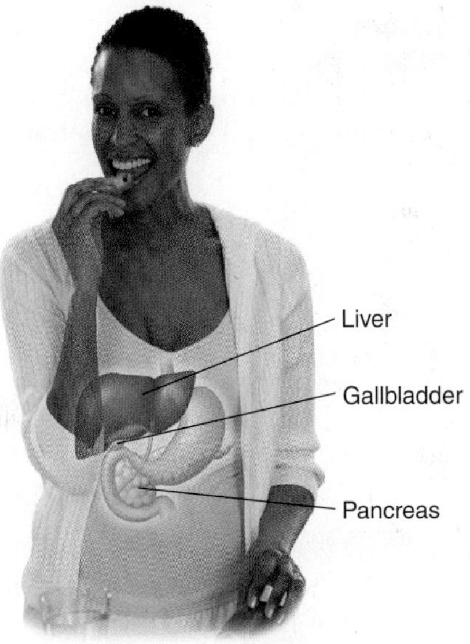

The Take-Home Message In the mouth, saliva mixes with food during chewing, moistening it and making it easier to swallow. Swallowed food that has mixed with digestive juices in the stomach becomes chyme. Maximum digestion and the absorption of digested nutrients occur in the small intestine. Undigested residue next enters the large intestine, where additional absorption of water and electrolytes occurs. Eventually, the remnants of digestion reach the anus and exit the body in stool. The liver, gallbladder, and pancreas are important accessory organs. The liver produces bile and the gallbladder concentrates and stores it. The pancreas produces enzymes and hormones.

Figure 3.8 The Accessory Organs
The liver, gallbladder, and pancreas produce digestive secretions that flow into the small intestine through various ducts.

How Do Hormones, Enzymes, and Bile Aid Digestion?

The complete digestion of chyme requires chemical secretions, including hormones, enzymes, and bile. Supportive digestive organs such as the pancreas, liver, and gallbladder contribute or concentrate many of these fluids. The stomach and small intestine also produce digestive enzymes. **Table 3.1** summarizes the organs, secretions, and functions that take part in digestion as it proceeds from beginning to end.

Hormones Regulate Digestion

Hormones, released from endocrine glands scattered throughout the lining of the stomach and the small intestine, don't digest food, but regulate the activity of other cells. Eating or not eating stimulates the release of hormones from these glands.

liver The largest gland of the body. It aids in digestive activity and is responsible for metabolism of nutrients, detoxification of alcohol, and some nutrient storage.

gallbladder A pear-shaped organ located behind the liver. The gallbladder stores bile produced by the liver and secretes the bile through the bile duct into the small intestine.

pancreas Accessory organ of digestion that produces hormones and enzymes. It's connected to the duodenum via the bile duct.

hormones Chemical substances that regulate, initiate, or direct cellular activity.

Table 3.1

Functions of Digestive Secretions

Secretion	Secreted From	Function
Saliva	Glands in the mouth	Moistens food, eases swallowing, contains the enzyme salivary amylase
Mucus	Stomach, small and large intestines	Lubrication and coating of the internal mucosa to protect it from chemical or mechanical damage
Hydrochloric acid (HCl)	Stomach	Activation of enzymes that begin protein digestion
Bile	Liver (stored in the gallbladder)	Emulsifies fat in the small intestine
Bicarbonate	Pancreas	Raises pH and neutralizes stomach acid
Enzymes (amylases, proteases, and lipases)	Stomach, small intestine, pancreas	Chemicals that break down food into nutrient components that can be absorbed
Hormones (gastrin, secretin, cholecystokinin, and ghrelin)	Stomach, small intestine	Chemicals that regulate digestive activity, increase or decrease peristalsis, and stimulate various digestive secretions

For example, when food reaches your stomach, *gastrin* is released to signal the rest of the GI tract to prepare for digestion. Gastrin stimulates the stomach to release HCl, increases gastric motility and emptying, and increases the tone of the LES.[14] Gastrin also causes the release of gastric secretions that contain the enzyme gastric lipase. When you haven't eaten, the hormone *ghrelin* is released to stimulate hunger.

The small intestine secretes the hormone *secretin* when acidic chyme enters the duodenum. Secretin in turn stimulates the pancreas to release *bicarbonate ions* to neutralize the HCl present in the chyme. When partially digested protein and fat enter the small intestine, the intestinal cells secrete the hormone *cholecystokinin*. This powerful hormone also stimulates the pancreas to secrete digestive enzymes, controls the pace of digestion, and contributes to meal satisfaction.

Enzymes Drive the Process of Digestion

The process of digestion is driven by a group of proteins called **enzymes**. Digestive enzymes speed up the chemical reactions that break apart food particles into smaller, unbound nutrients that can be easily absorbed. All macronutrients—carbohydrates, fats, and proteins—are broken down by their own specific enzymes without changing or consuming the enzymes in the process. For example, the enzyme *amylase,* secreted in saliva, starts digesting starch, whereas in the stomach, a *protease* or protein-digesting enzyme called *pepsin* and a fat-digesting enzyme called *gastric lipase* begin breaking down protein and a few fats. The pancreas produces the majority of digestive enzymes. These enzymes include *amylase*, which digests carbohydrate; *lipase*, which digests fat; and *trypsin, chymotrypsin,* and *carboxypeptidase*, which digest protein. The enzymes from the pancreas are responsible for the digestion of almost all (90 percent) of ingested fat, about half (50 percent) of all ingested protein, and half (50 percent) of all carbohydrates.[15]

Bile Helps Digest Fat

Bile, the yellowish-green substance made in the liver and stored in the gallbladder, helps digest fat. This dilute liquid consists of water, bile acids (and/or salts), various fats including cholesterol, and pigments. Bile is released from the gallbladder into the small intestine through the bile duct.

enzymes Substances that produce chemical changes or catalyze chemical reactions.

bile A yellowish-green fluid made in the liver and concentrated and stored in the gallbladder. It helps emulsify fat and prepare it for digestion.

Table 3.2

Organs of Digestion and Their Functions

Organ or Tissue	Function	How They Work Together to Digest a Peanut Butter Sandwich
Mouth	Begins breaking down food into components through chewing	Saliva moistens the sandwich as your teeth grind the food. Amylase begins to break down the carbohydrate in the bread.
Esophagus	Transfers food from the mouth to the stomach	Bolus of sandwich moves through the esophagus to the stomach.
Stomach	Mixes food with digestive juices; breaks down some nutrients into smaller components	The HCl activates pepsin to begin digesting the protein in the sandwich. Gastric lipase starts breaking down the triglycerides in the peanut butter.
Small intestine	Completes digestion of food and absorbs nutrients through its walls	The carbohydrates, proteins, and fat are broken down further with the help of bile and enzymes so they can be absorbed.
Large intestine	Absorbs water and some nutrients; passes waste products out of the body	The fiber in the bread leaves the body in the stool.
Accessory organs	Release enzymes, bile, and bicarbonate ions	
liver		The liver produces the bile and regulates the metabolism of the absorbed nutrients.
gallbladder		The gallbladder releases stored bile into the small intestine to emulsify the fat in the peanut butter sandwich.
pancreas		The pancreas produces bicarbonate ions to neutralize the chyme, and the enzymes amylase, lipase, and protease to digest the sandwich.

Bile breaks down large fat globules into smaller fat droplets much like dishwashing detergent breaks up the grease in a frying pan. This allows the fat-digesting enzymes to make contact with the fat and break it down to be absorbed.

Unlike other digestive juices, bile can be reused. From the large intestine, bile is recycled back to the liver through *enterohepatic* (*entero* = intestine, *hepatic* = liver) *circulation*. This recycling allows bile to be reused up to 20 times.

Table 3.2 not only summarizes the organs of the GI tract and their functions but also shows you how these organs work together to digest a peanut butter sandwich. The next several chapters will further illustrate how the specific nutrients in foods that you eat, such as pasta and pizza, travel through your GI tract and are digested, absorbed, and or/eliminated from your body.

The Take-Home Message Hormones regulate digestion by stimulating secretions from the stomach, small intestine, pancreas, and gallbladder. They also control the pace of digestion. Specific digestive enzymes speed up the process that breaks apart food particles without being changed or consumed in the process. Bile breaks large fat globules into smaller fat droplets.

⊙Learn

Take a Ride through the GI Tract

Want to learn even more about the organs of the GI tract? Visit MasteringNutrition™ and slide through the organs and their functions.

How Are Digested Nutrients Absorbed?

Digestion is the forerunner to **absorption**. Once the nutrients have been completely broken down, they are ready to be used by the cells of the body. In order to reach the cells, however, they have to leave the GI tract and move to the other parts of the

absorption The process by which digested nutrients move into the tissues where they can be transported and used by the body's cells.

body. To accomplish this, nutrients are absorbed through the walls of the intestines and into the body's two transport systems: the circulatory and lymphatic systems. They are then taken to the liver for processing before moving on to their destination. The body is remarkably efficient when it comes to absorbing nutrients. Under normal conditions, you digest and absorb 92 to 97 percent of the nutrients from your food.[16]

Digested Nutrients Are Absorbed by Three Methods

Once digested nutrients reach the small intestine, they are absorbed by three methods: **passive diffusion**, **facilitated diffusion**, or **active transport** (**Figure 3.9**). Another method of absorption, called *endocytosis*, occurs when whole proteins, such as immunoglobin from breast milk, are absorbed intact.

Passive diffusion is a process in which nutrients are absorbed due to a concentration gradient. When the concentration is greater in the GI tract than inside the intestinal cell, the nutrient is forced across the cell membrane. This simple process doesn't require energy or a special protein carrier to help the nutrient to cross inside the intestinal cell.

Facilitated diffusion is similar to passive diffusion in that nutrients are absorbed from a high to a low concentration and the process does not require energy. But facilitated diffusion does require a specialized protein to carry the nutrients across the cell membrane.

Active transport is different from both passive and facilitated diffusion. In this form of absorption, digested nutrients are absorbed from a low to a high concentration. This process requires both a carrier and energy to shuttle nutrients across the cell membrane.

passive diffusion The process of absorbing nutrients across the intestinal cell membrane from a high concentration to a low concentration.

facilitated diffusion The process of absorbing nutrients across the intestinal cell membrane with the help of a carrier molecule.

active transport The process of absorbing nutrients across the intestinal cell membrane with the help of a carrier molecule and energy.

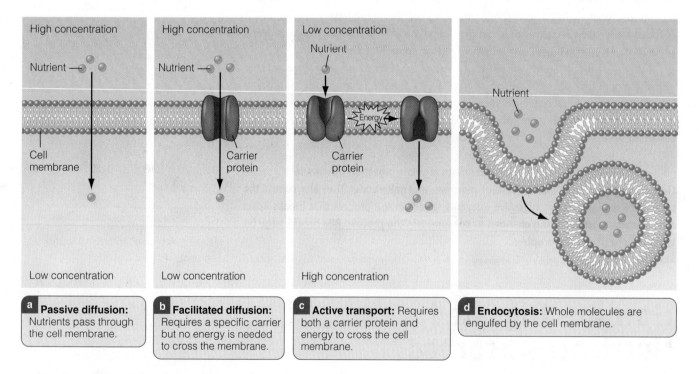

a **Passive diffusion:** Nutrients pass through the cell membrane.	**b** **Facilitated diffusion:** Requires a specific carrier but no energy is needed to cross the membrane.
c **Active transport:** Requires both a carrier protein and energy to cross the cell membrane.	**d** **Endocytosis:** Whole molecules are engulfed by the cell membrane.

Figure 3.9 Absorption Methods in the Small Intestine

What Happens to Nutrients after They Are Absorbed?

Now that you know how the body digests and absorbs the nutrients from foods, you might be wondering what happens to the nutrients once they are absorbed. Once the nutrients are absorbed, they must be transported to the cells before they can be used by the body. Nutrients are transported either through the veins and arteries of the circulatory system or through the lymphatic vessels.

The Circulatory System Distributes Nutrients through Your Blood

Water-soluble nutrients are picked up through the capillary walls in the intestinal villi and are transported to the bloodstream. These nutrients circulate through the bloodstream to the liver. The liver regulates the use of the nutrients depending on your needs. Some of the nutrients may be stored in the liver while others are released into the circulation and delivered to the cells of your body. The blood is the body's primary transport system, shuttling oxygen, nutrients, hormones, and waste products throughout the body (**Figure 3.10**). Without the circulatory system, nutrients

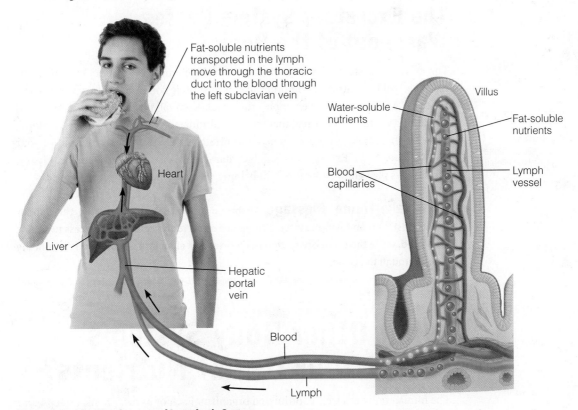

Fat-soluble nutrients transported in the lymph move through the thoracic duct into the blood through the left subclavian vein

Heart

Liver

Hepatic portal vein

Blood

Lymph

Villus

Water-soluble nutrients

Fat-soluble nutrients

Blood capillaries

Lymph vessel

Figure 3.10 The Circulatory and Lymphatic Systems
Blood and lymph are fluids that circulate throughout the body. They both distribute nutrients to cells and blood also picks up waste products for excretion.

that you eat would not reach your cells. Equally important, the blood removes excess water and waste products from the cells and brings these substances to the kidneys for excretion.

The Lymphatic System Distributes Some Nutrients through Your Lymph Vessels

The lymphatic system is a complex network of capillaries, small vessels, valves, nodes, and ducts that helps maintain the internal fluid environment. Some absorbed nutrients, such as the products of fat digestion, must pass through the lymphatic system before they enter the bloodstream because they are too large to enter the bloodstream directly. Lymph also transports absorbed fat-soluble vitamins from the intestinal tract to your blood. The lymph eventually connects with the blood near the heart.

Your Body Can Store Some Surplus Nutrients

Whereas some nutrients are used immediately for energy and other functions, your body can store other, surplus nutrients to be used when you need them. For example, some excess carbohydrate is stored in your liver and muscles in a form called *glycogen*, to be available when you don't eat, such as between meals. Other excess energy (calories) is stored in the form of fat cells. Some vitamins and minerals can also be stored. For example, storing calcium in your bones will help keep them strong. However, storing excessive amounts of fat-soluble vitamins, such as vitamin A, and some minerals, such as iron, can be toxic.

The Excretory System Passes Waste out of the Body

The excretory system eliminates wastes from the circulatory system. After the cells have gleaned the nutrients and other useful metabolic components they need, waste products accumulate. For example, the breakdown of proteins creates nitrogen-containing waste, such as urea, that must be eliminated. The kidneys filter the blood, allowing these waste products to be concentrated in urine and excreted out of your body (**Figure 3.11**). Excess water-soluble vitamins are also excreted in urine. Finally, the kidneys play an important role in helping the body maintain water balance.

The Take-Home Message Absorbed nutrients are transported throughout the bloodstream and lymph systems to be delivered to the cells. Some excess nutrients are stored, while the excretory system helps filter and eliminate waste products from the blood through the urine.

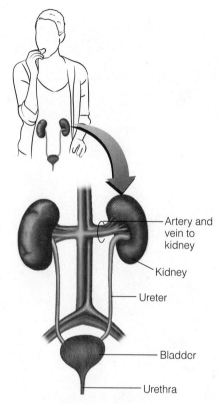

- Artery and vein to kidney
- Kidney
- Ureter
- Bladder
- Urethra

Figure 3.11 The Excretory System
Water and waste products from cells are filtered from your blood in the kidneys and expelled from your body in urine.

What Other Body Systems Affect Your Use of Nutrients?

The human body is a well-coordinated organism. Each of us eats, drinks, sleeps, and lives a normal existence without too much thought about what we are consuming. We don't have to constantly worry about keeping ourselves nourished, or distributing nutrients to our cells, because numerous body systems are doing this work for us.

The Nervous System Stimulates Your Appetite

The main role of the nervous system in keeping you nourished is to let you know when you need to eat and drink and when to stop. Your brain, with the help of hormones, plays a central role in communicating and interpreting the message of hunger and encouraging you to seek food. For example, when your stomach is empty, the hormone ghrelin signals your brain to eat. If you ignore the signals of hunger or thirst sent by your nervous system, you may experience a headache, dizziness, or weakness. The nervous system helps each of us make daily decisions regarding what to eat, when to eat, where to eat, and, perhaps most important, when to stop eating.

The Endocrine System Releases Hormones That Help Regulate the Use of Absorbed Nutrients

The endocrine system consists of a series of glands, including the pancreas, the pituitary, the thyroid, and the adrenal glands, that release hormones into the bloodstream. The hormones regulate growth, reproduction, metabolism, and the cells' use of absorbed nutrients. For example, the hormones insulin and glucagon help regulate blood levels of glucose. When blood glucose levels get too high, the pancreas releases insulin, which directs the glucose out of the blood and into cells. On the flip side, if blood glucose levels dip too low, the body releases glucagon, which directs the release of the body's stored glucose to increase the levels in blood. We will learn more about the important roles of hormones in future chapters.

The Take-Home Message In addition to the digestive system, other body systems help us use the nutrients we take in from foods. The nervous system lets us know when we need to eat or drink, the blood and lymph systems deliver absorbed nutrients to cells, and the endocrine system releases hormones that regulate nutrient use in cells.

What Are Some Common Digestive Disorders?

Generally, the digestive tract works just fine. As a matter of fact, it doesn't usually require tinkering or medications to be healthy. But sometimes the digestive tract gets "off track" and the resulting symptoms can quickly catch your attention. Some of the problems are minor, like occasional heartburn or indigestion. Other problems such as ulcers or colon cancer are very serious.

Disorders of the Mouth and Throat

Oral health involves healthy teeth, gums, and supporting tissue. Maintaining a healthy oral environment is important because these tissues are used to bite, chew, taste, speak, smile, swallow, and communicate through facial expressions. Properly

Table TIPS

Digest It Right!

Eat and drink slowly and thoroughly chew your food. This will cut down on the amount of air you take in, and may reduce the need for belching later on.

Watch your portion size and stop eating when you are full. You are less likely to feel uncomfortable and won't have to unbutton that top button of your jeans!

Set aside time to eat. Don't eat your meals while you are doing something else, like watching television or driving to work or school. You will be more aware of your body's cues to stop if you are paying attention.

Be aware of foods that don't agree with you. If spicy foods irritate your stomach, eat those items less frequently or in smaller amounts to avoid discomfort.

Get plenty of fiber and fluid. This will help help you stay regular and avoid uncomfortable bouts of constipation.

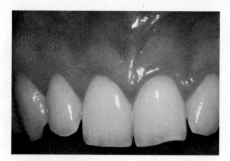

Gingivitis causes redness and swelling of the gums and can lead to more serious gum disease and tooth loss.

nourishing yourself can be difficult if you have chronic oral disease or extensive dental problems. There are many oral diseases, but we will only review some of the most common ones in this section.

Gingivitis and Periodontal Disease

In addition to tooth decay, which we'll discuss in depth in Chapter 4, common oral health problems include gingivitis and periodontal disease. Gingivitis is an early form of periodontal disease that involves gum swelling, bleeding, and oral pain. Periodontal disease is an inflammation of the gums that leads to multiple dental diseases. It is caused by infections or by plaque that adheres to the surface of the teeth, and is a common problem for adults over age 35.[17] Periodontitis results in a gradual loss of teeth as they loosen or partially separate from the gums and jawbone. Even though these conditions are serious, they are treatable with various dental procedures, optimal food choices, and excellent oral hygiene. Other oral health problems include dry mouth, inflamed oral tissue, cold sores, soft tissue ulceration, oral cancers, fungal infections, or various abnormalities of the tongue.

Swallowing Problems

Under some circumstances the ability to swallow is compromised. Difficult swallowing, or **dysphagia**, can have mechanical causes such as tumors, scar tissue, obstruction, cancer, trauma, or other barriers in the throat. Dysphagia can also result from nerve damage or a stroke.

Swallowing problems can lead to malnutrition, respiratory problems, tooth decay, nasal regurgitation, and compromised health. Various health care professionals are trained to help a person overcome swallowing difficulties.

Certain foods and lifestyle factors contribute to heartburn.

Esophageal Problems

Several esophageal problems can lead to annoying symptoms such as belching, hiccups, burning sensations, or uncomfortable feelings of fullness. Some serious esophageal problems include cancer, obstruction from tumors, faulty nerve impulses, severe inflammation, and abnormal sphincter function.

One of the most common problems involving the esophagus is **heartburn**, or *reflux disease.* About 7 percent of the population experiences daily heartburn, about 20 percent of adults report frequent heartburn, and 25 to 35 percent of adults have occasional symptoms.[18] Collectively, this adds up to millions of people experiencing heartburn symptoms.

Heartburn, also known as indigestion or acid reflux, is caused by hydrochloric acid flowing from the stomach back into the esophagus or even the throat. The acid causes a lingering, unpleasant, sour taste in the mouth. Other symptoms include nausea, bloating, belching, a vague burning sensation, or an uncomfortable feeling of fullness. Chronic heartburn can lead to a condition called **gastroesophageal reflux disease**, or **GERD**, when the acidic stomach contents reflux into the esophagus.

A weak lower esophageal sphincter is often the culprit in acid reflux, because it sometimes permits this backflow of stomach fluids into the esophagus. Certain foods, including chocolate, fried or fatty foods, coffee, soda, onions, and garlic, seem to be associated with this condition.[19] Lifestyle factors also play a role. For example, smoking cigarettes, drinking alcohol, wearing tight-fitting clothes, being overweight or obese, eating large evening meals, and reclining after eating tend to cause or worsen the condition. If dietary changes and behavior modification are insufficient to relieve the heartburn, over-the-counter antacids or prescription drugs may help. In rare circumstances, surgical intervention is required to treat severe, unrelenting heartburn.

dysphagia Difficult swallowing.

heartburn A burning sensation originating in the esophagus. Heartburn is usually caused by the reflux of gastric contents from the stomach into the esophagus. Chronic heartburn can lead to gastroesophageal reflux disease (GERD).

gastroesophageal reflux disease (GERD) The backward flow of stomach contents past the lower esophageal sphincter into the esophagus.

Esophageal cancer is another medical condition that has serious consequences. According to the National Cancer Institute, esophageal cancer is one of the most common cancers of the digestive tract, and the seventh leading cause of cancer-related deaths worldwide. In the United States, this type of cancer is typically found among individuals older than 50 years, men, those who live in urban areas, long-term smokers, and heavy drinkers.[20] Treatments include surgery, radiation, and chemotherapy.

Disorders of the Stomach

Does your stomach ever "growl"? A rumbling stomach, or *borborygmus,* isn't really a disorder (though if it's accompanied by pain or vomiting, it can be a sign of a larger problem, such as a mechanical obstruction).[21] Rather, the gurgling is due to the gas and air pockets that form as chyme is pushed through the stomach and small intestine. The best way to quiet the noise is to eat or drink something, or to apply mild pressure to the abdomen. Other stomach problems can range from the trivial, like an occasional stomachache, to life-threatening complications such as bleeding ulcers or stomach cancer.

At some point in time, everyone has had a stomachache. Common causes include overeating, gastric bloating, or eating too fast. Other possible causes include eating foods that are high in fat or fiber, eating spicy foods, lactose intolerance, or swallowing air while eating. More serious causes of a stomachache include the flu or consuming food or water that is contaminated with bacteria. Stomach flu or **gastroenteritis** is an inflammation of the stomach or intestines caused by a virus or bacteria. Flu symptoms include nausea, vomiting, diarrhea, and abdominal cramping. Sometimes the problem requires medical intervention, but usually rest, oral rehydration therapy, and a soft-food diet will help with the symptoms of this type of flu. (*Note:* The stomach flu is not the same as influenza (flu), which is a respiratory illness caused by the influenza virus.)

Peptic ulcers occur in the lower region of the stomach.[22] A peptic ulcer is a sore or erosion in the stomach or intestinal lining caused by drugs, alcohol, or, more often, the *Helicobacter pylori* bacterium. Symptoms of an ulcer include abdominal pain, vomiting, fatigue, bleeding, and general weakness. Medical treatments may consist of prescription drugs and dietary recommendations, such as limiting alcohol and caffeine-containing beverages, and/or restricting spices and acidic foods.

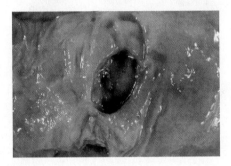

An ulcer is created when the mucosal lining of the GI tract erodes or breaks.

Gallbladder Disease

One common problem of an unhealthy gallbladder is the presence of **gallstones**. Most people with gallstones have abnormally thick bile, and the bile is high in cholesterol and low in bile acids. Over an extended period of time, the high-cholesterol bile forms crystals, then sludge, and finally gallstones. Some individuals with gallstones experience no pain or mild pain. Others have severe pain accompanied by fever, nausea, vomiting, cramps, and obstruction of the bile duct.

Medical treatment for gallstones may involve surgery to remove the gallbladder, prescription medicine to dissolve the stones, shock-wave therapy (a type of ultrasound treatment) to break them up, or a combination of therapies. If surgery is required to remove the gallbladder, patients typically recover quickly. After gallbladder removal surgery, the anatomy of the biliary tract adapts. The liver continues to produce the bile and secrete it directly into the duodenum. Interestingly, the remaining bile duct dilates, forming a "simulated pouch" that works in a manner very similar to the original gallbladder.

Gallstones result from the crystallization of salts and other compounds in bile.

gastroenteritis Formal term for "stomach flu." Caused by a virus or bacteria and results in inflammation of the stomach and/or intestines.

peptic ulcers Sores, erosions, or breaks in the mucosal lining of the stomach.

gallstones Small, hard, crystalline structures formed in the gallbladder or bile duct due to abnormally thick bile.

Disorders of the Intestines

Disorders of the intestines can occur anywhere along the length of the small and large intestines. Common, temporary problems can include gassiness, diarrhea, constipation, and hemorrhoids; more serious disorders include celiac disease and Crohn's disease.

Flatulence

Flatulence is the release of intestinal gas from the rectum. It can be uncomfortable and sometimes embarrassing (but normal). Intestinal gas is produced for a variety of reasons, and most adults release it 10 to 20 times a day! Eating too fast, or drinking beverages with added air, such as beer and carbonated beverages, can result in the intake of air that makes its way through the GI tract. Legumes such as beans and lentils can lead to gas production because they contain indigestible carbohydrates that are fermented by intestinal bacteria. The bacteria produce the gas as a by-product. The gas is a mixture of carbon dioxide, hydrogen, nitrogen, oxygen, and methane. The offending odor comes from the gases that contain sulfur. Using products such as Beano, eating smaller meals, adding fiber gradually in your diet, and increasing your fluid intake can all help reduce the amount of gas produced.

Constipation and Diarrhea

Constipation is caused by excessively slow movements of the undigested residue through the colon, and is often due to insufficient fiber or water intake. Consuming an adequate amount of dietary fiber daily can help prevent constipation. Stress, inactivity, or various illnesses can also lead to constipation. It is usually treated with increasing the fiber and fluids in the diet. Daily exercise, establishing eating and resting routines, and using over-the-counter stool softeners are usually recommended to treat this condition.

Diarrhea is the passage of frequent, watery, loose stools. It is considered more serious than constipation because of the loss of fluids and electrolytes. If the diarrhea continues for an extended period of time, you may malabsorb additional nutrients, which can lead to malnutrition. There are many causes of diarrhea, including contaminated water, various microorganisms, stress, or excessive fiber intake. Diarrhea is generally treated with fluid and electrolyte replacement. Most physicians identify the cause(s) of the diarrhea in addition to treating the symptoms.

Hemorrhoids

Hemorrhoids are a condition in which pressure in the veins in the rectum and anus causes swelling and inflammation. The walls of the veins dilate, become thin, and bleed. As the pressure builds, the vessels protrude. Straining to pass dry stools, pregnancy, chronic constipation or diarrhea, and aging are all factors that can contribute to hemorrhoids. You may never know that you have hemorrhoids unless they begin to bleed (following a bowel movement), itch, or become painful. As with constipation, increasing both your fiber and fluid intake can treat hemorrhoids. Sometimes surgery may be necessary to remove hemorrhoids.

More Serious Intestinal Disorders

The more serious small intestine and large intestine problems, such as irritable bowel syndrome, celiac disease, Crohn's disease, and colon cancer, tend to involve nutrient malabsorption, which can cause severe health consequences. The symptoms of these diseases vary, but they include abdominal pain, nausea, vomiting, bloating, loss of

Products like Beano contain enzymes that help reduce the production of gas in the large intestine.

flatulence Production of excessive gas in the stomach or the intestines.

constipation Difficulty in passing stools.

diarrhea Frequent, loose, watery stools.

hemorrhoids Swelling in the veins of the rectum and anus.

appetite, diarrhea, anxiety, weight loss, and fatigue. The medical problems that have to be addressed include various anemias, gastrointestinal blockages, inflammation, malnutrition, growth failure, vitamin and mineral deficiencies, and other medically complicated challenges.

Irritable Bowel Syndrome (IBS)

Approximately 20 percent of, or one in five, American adults have symptoms of **irritable bowel syndrome (IBS)**. In fact, it is one of the most common disorders diagnosed and treated by doctors.[23] IBS is a functional disorder that involves changes in colon rhythm; it is not an actual disease. People with IBS overrespond to colon stimuli. This results in alternating patterns of diarrhea, constipation, and abdominal pain. The exact cause of IBS is unknown, but low-fiber diets, stress, consumption of irritating foods, and intestinal motility disorders are all suspected factors. Medical management includes dietary modification, stress management, and occasional use of prescription drugs.

Celiac Disease

Celiac disease is an autoimmune, genetic disorder that causes a person's own immune system to damage the small intestine when gluten, a protein in wheat and other grains, is consumed. People with celiac disease must make many dietary adjustments. The Health Connection feature "Celiac Disease: An Issue of Absorption" on page 88 explains this intestinal disorder in greater detail. Note that celiac disease is not the same thing as **gluten intolerance**, which does not involve the immune system or damage the wall of the small intestine. However, individuals with gluten intolerance can experience symptoms such as stomachaches, diarrhea, bloating, and tiredness if gluten is consumed.

Crohn's Disease

Crohn's disease, or inflammatory bowel disease, is the general name for diseases that cause swelling in the intestines. Crohn's disease can affect any area of the GI tract, from the mouth to the anus, but it typically affects the ileum and the colon. The swelling can cause pain and diarrhea. Bleeding from the rectum, weight loss, and anemia are just some of the symptoms that can occur. Though there isn't a cure for Crohn's disease, medication, nutritional and dietary supplements, and/or surgery are currently used to manage the disease.[24]

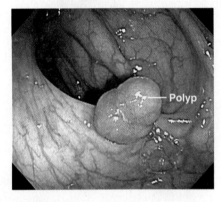

Polyps, or abnormal growths, on the lining of the large intestine may indicate early stages of colon cancer.

Colon Cancer

Colon cancer is one of the leading forms of cancer and the second leading cause of cancer deaths. Fortunately, colon cancer is one of the most curable forms of cancer, if it is detected in the early stages.

Colon cancer often begins with polyps on the lining of the colon. They vary in size from that of a small pea to that of a mushroom or plum. The good news is that polyps can be removed surgically, and they are often small and benign. If the polyps are not removed or change to cancerous tumors, colon cancer can be more difficult to cure.

Individuals diagnosed with colon cancer may require radiation therapy, chemotherapy, and surgery to remove part of the colon or the entire colon. After surgery, patients are given dietary advice regarding the foods that would be the most comfortable to eat. Survival rates vary depending on the individual's age, health, treatment response, and stage of cancer diagnosis.

Table 3.3 on page 90 summarizes common digestive disorders.

irritable bowel syndrome (IBS) A functional disorder that involves changes in colon rhythm.

celiac disease An autoimmune disease of the small intestine that involves the inability to digest the protein gluten.

gluten intolerance A sensitivity to the protein gluten, which is found in wheat and other grains. Symptoms include stomachaches, diarrhea, bloating, and tiredness.

Crohn's disease An inflammatory bowel disease involving inflammation and swelling of the intestines.

Celiac Disease: An Issue of Absorption

One of the more serious malabsorption conditions to occur in the small intestine is celiac disease. A healthy small intestine contains numerous villi and microvilli that efficiently and exhaustively absorb nutrients from food. In people with celiac disease (about 1 in 133 Americans), the lining of the small intestine flattens out due to an autoimmune reaction to gluten, a protein found in wheat, rye, and barley. This reduces the intestine's ability to absorb nutrients.

What Causes Celiac Disease?

The exact cause of celiac disease is unknown, but it is believed to be genetic, and is more common among people of European descent. The risk for the disease may be decreased by breast-feeding rather than bottle-feeding infants. Celiac disease is sometimes detected or caused by surgery, pregnancy, a viral infection, or severe emotional stress.

What Are the Symptoms of Celiac Disease?

The classic celiac symptoms include reoccurring abdominal bloating, cramping, diarrhea, gas, fatty and foul-smelling stools, weight loss, anemia, fatigue, bone or joint pain, and even a painful skin rash. Some people develop the symptoms of celiac disease in infancy or childhood. Others develop the disease later in life, after being misdiagnosed with irritable bowel syndrome or various food intolerances. Diagnosing celiac disease is sometimes difficult because it resembles other very similar malabsorption diseases. Depending on the length of time between symptom development and diagnosis, the complications from celiac disease can be serious. They include increased incidence of osteoporosis from poor calcium absorption, diminished growth because of nutrient malabsorption, and even seizures due to inadequate folate absorption.

How Is Celiac Disease Treated?

The only treatment for celiac disease is a gluten-free diet. This should stop the symptoms from progressing, allow the intestines to heal, and prevent further damage. The symptoms often improve within a few days after beginning the gluten-free diet. Within three to six months, the absorption area of the intestinal tract often returns to normal status, if the diet is faithfully followed. Depending on the age at diagnosis and the severity of the disease, there may be some permanent health problems such as delayed or stunted growth.

Adhering to a gluten-free diet, which means avoiding all gluten-containing foods, can be challenging. All breads, pasta, cereals, and other foods made with wheat, barley, or rye must be eliminated. However, there are many gluten-free foods to choose from, such as meat, milk, eggs, fruit, and vegetables. These foods are permissible in any quantity. Rice, potatoes, corn, and beans, as well as grains such as quinoa, amaranth, and millet, do not contain gluten and are also acceptable. The Academy of Nutrition and Dietetics maintains a comprehensive list of foods allowed on a gluten-free diet on its website, www.eatright.org.

Due to an increased awareness of celiac disease and gluten intolerance, the demand for gluten-free products has exploded. Gluten-free products are now easier to find in your local markets and there is a wider range of choices. There are now smart phone apps to locate

Popcorn is a gluten-free snack that people with celiac disease can safely enjoy.

Rice noodles are a good gluten-free substitute for pasta.

Eat Gluten Free

Be a label reader to avoid products that contain all forms of wheat, barley, rye, triticale, or their hybrids.

Substitute whole-wheat bread with breads made from gluten-free whole grains, such as quinoa, buckwheat, amaranth, sorghum, and millet.

If you like a hot cereal for breakfast try teff, a nutritious cereal grain from Ethiopia with a nutty, chewy texture.

Avoid packaged foods that contain modified food starch, dextrin, malt, or malt syrup, as these ingredients may be sourced from gluten-containing grains.

Enjoy coffee, tea, sodas, fruit juices, and even fermented or distilled beverages, such as wine, sake, and distilled spirits, on a gluten-free diet. But avoid coffee flavorings or creamers.

Look for either the GFCO or CSA Seal of Recognition marks on labels to assure the product is gluten free.

Maintain a high fiber intake by incorporating gluten-free fresh fruits, vegetables, beans, peas, and lentils into your diet.

Consume calcium-rich dairy or calcium-fortified gluten-free products, such as orange juice, soy products, or non-milk beverages made from rice or nuts.

Snack on gluten-free nuts, fruits, popcorn, raisins, rice cakes, and fruit smoothies.

Enjoy homemade meals to control gluten intake and eat a variety of nutrient-dense foods.

a wider range of choices. There are now smart phone apps to locate gluten-friendly restaurants, even while traveling to another country. The most problematic feature of the diet is avoiding the multiple foods that contain "latent," or hidden, sources of gluten. Individuals with celiac disease need to read food labels carefully.

Celiac disease is a manageable condition. Individuals with celiac disease can live normal lives. They can learn about their condition by talking to health care professionals. Researchers are currently working to determine the exact component in gluten that causes celiac disease, and to develop enzymes that would destroy these immuno-toxic peptides.

Table 3.3

Common Digestive Disorders

Site	Disorder	Symptoms	Causes	Treatment
Esophagus and stomach	Gastrointestinal reflux disease (GERD)	Sore throat, burning sensation in the chest (heartburn)	Poor eating habits; overeating; other lifestyle choices	Eat smaller meals; eat more slowly; decrease fat and/or alcohol intake; quit smoking
Stomach or small intestine	Gastric and duodenal ulcers	Bleeding, pain, vomiting, fatigue, weakness	Multiple causes	Prescription drugs and an as-tolerated diet
Gallbladder	Gallstones	Cramps, bloating, intense abdominal pain, diarrhea	The concentration of high-cholesterol-containing bile that crystallizes and forms stones in the duct	Gallbladder removal, medication, or shock-wave therapy
Small intestine	Celiac disease	Malabsorption	Error of gluten metabolism	Gluten-free diet
Small intestine	Crohn's disease	Pain, diarrhea, rectal bleeding, weight loss, anemia	Swelling of the intestines	Medication, nutritional or dietary supplements, surgery
Large intestine	Constipation	Cramping, bloated uncomfortable feeling in abdomen	Too little water or too little fiber; inactivity	More water, fiber, and exercise
Large intestine	Diarrhea	Too-frequent, loose bowel movements	Multiple causes	Water and electrolyte replacement
Large intestine	Irritable bowel syndrome (IBS)	Diarrhea and constipation in alternating sequence; pain	Unknown cause(s); stress worsens the condition	Self-management with fiber therapy, stress relief, and good sleep habits
Large intestine	Colon cancer	Symptoms are often silent; may include weight loss, internal bleeding, iron-deficiency anemia, fatigue	Multiple causes (genetics, various colon diseases, smoking, exposure to dietary carcinogens)	Radiation therapy, chemotherapy, surgery

Practical Nutrition VIDEO

Probiotics: Do You Need Them?

Many products on the shelves today claim to have probiotics that aid digestion. But what are they? Joan takes a look. Scan this QR code with your mobile device to access the video. You can also access the video in MasteringNutrition™.

The Take-Home Message Gastrointestinal diseases and digestive disorders include less serious conditions, like heartburn, GERD, indigestion, stomach flu, flatulence, constipation, diarrhea, and hemorrhoids, and more serious conditions, such as esophageal cancer, gastric ulcers, irritable bowel syndrome, celiac disease, Crohn's disease, and colon cancer. Disorders of the small intestine may result in malnutrition.

POINTS OF VIEW

Probiotics: Do You Need Them? Probiotics are live microorganisms, usually bacteria, mainly found in cultured dairy foods.[1] Some research indicates that probiotics can have health benefits for the immune and digestive systems. However, the research is not conclusive, and some experts feel adding probiotics to the diet is ineffective at best and possibly harmful at worst. Should you seek out fortified yogurt or probiotic supplements, or can you get along fine without them? Read the arguments below, then consider the critical-thinking questions and decide for yourself.

yes

- Research suggests that regular consumption of certain probiotics helps maintain the normal functioning of the digestive system. Studies indicate that probiotics can help in the prevention or treatment of antibiotic-associated disorders, in the treatment (and to a lesser extent prevention) of gastroenteritis (stomach inflammation) and diarrhea, and in the alleviation of lactose intolerance.[2]

- Some specific strains of probiotics have been shown to increase regularity in some people who have occasional constipation. Other strains have been studied for their role in decreasing the frequency of irritable bowel syndrome and some inflammatory bowel conditions.[3]

- Probiotics are generally considered safe. Their safety is somewhat evident by the fact that they have a long history of use in dairy foods like yogurt, cheese, and milk.[4]

- Though the burden lies with the manufacturer to make sure that the correct probiotic is added to the product and in adequate amounts, there is some regulation of probiotic labeling.[5] The FDA requires that the food label of these products contain accurate and relevant information.[6]

no

- We do not have sufficient information to say that probiotics are always beneficial and never harmful. Research is promising in several areas of digestive health but more research is needed to confirm their effectiveness, safety, and optimal dosage and duration.[7]

- Some products have been evaluated in well-controlled human studies, while others have no or not enough research to support their efficacy.

- Some consumers could experience gas or bloating when consuming probiotic products. The microorganisms may also have the potential to cause more serious side effects, especially in people with underlying health conditions.[8]

- People who have short bowel syndrome, a weakened immune system, a damaged intestinal lining, or are recovering from surgery are at a higher risk for side effects. These individuals should take probiotics only under the advice of a health care provider.

- Due to lack of strict FDA regulation, various probiotic products may not consistently contain the correct type of probiotics or enough of the probiotic to have an effect. Further, probiotics are not always delivered in an effective vehicle (foods versus supplements) and may be of variable quality.[9]

what do you think?

1. Do you think you should add probiotics to your diet? Why or why not? **2.** Which is the most compelling argument for taking probiotics? Which is the most compelling reason not to take them? Explain your rationale. **3.** Do you think we know enough about probiotics to recommend them to the public?

1 Digestion Breaks Down Foods for Absorption

Digestion is the process of breaking down whole food into absorbable nutrients. There are both mechanical and chemical aspects of digestion. Mechanical digestion includes chewing, peristalsis, segmentation, and pendular movement. Chemical digestion involves mixing consumed food with enzymes and gastric juices to break it down.

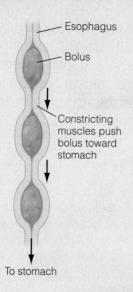

Esophagus

Bolus

Constricting muscles push bolus toward stomach

To stomach

2 The Organs of the GI Tract and Their Accessory Organs Are Involved in Digestion

Digestion takes place in the organs of the GI tract—particularly the stomach and small intestine. Digestion begins in the mouth as chewing breaks down food and mixes it with saliva. Swallowing is a coordinated process that involves the mouth, throat, and esophagus. The stomach mixes food with enzymes and stores it before propelling it into the small intestine, where most of the digestion takes place. The large intestine absorbs water and some nutrients, before pushing waste through the colon and out of the body via the anus. Several sphincters control the entry and exit of food and chyme through the organs of the GI tract.

The accessory organs include the liver, gallbladder, and pancreas. The liver produces bile and stores it in the gallbladder. The pancreas produces both hormones and enzymes that play roles in digestion.

3 Hormones Regulate Digestion, Enzymes Chemically Digest Food, and Bile Aids in Fat Digestion

Hormones, enzymes, and bile are necessary for efficient digestion. Hormones are chemical messengers that direct enzymes that do the actual work of breaking down food into smaller pieces for efficient absorption. Bile breaks large fat globules into smaller fat droplets to allow fat-digesting enzymes to come into contact with the fat.

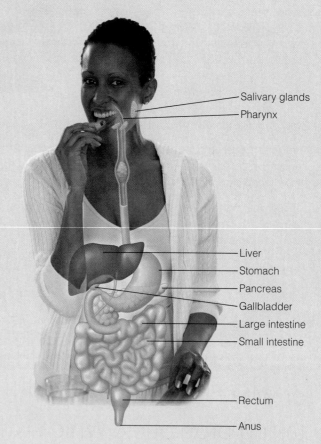

Salivary glands
Pharynx

Liver
Stomach
Pancreas
Gallbladder
Large intestine
Small intestine

Rectum

Anus

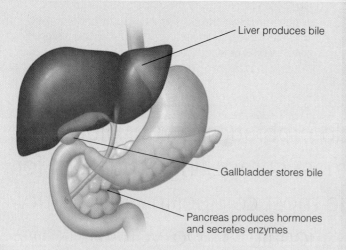

Liver produces bile

Gallbladder stores bile

Pancreas produces hormones and secretes enzymes

4 Nutrients Are Absorbed through the Small Intestine

The walls of the small intestine are covered with villi, which greatly increase its surface area and facilitate absorption. Digested nutrients pass through the small intestinal wall either by passive diffusion, facilitated diffusion, or active transport. Endocytosis is the process in which whole proteins, such as immunoglobulins, are absorbed intact.

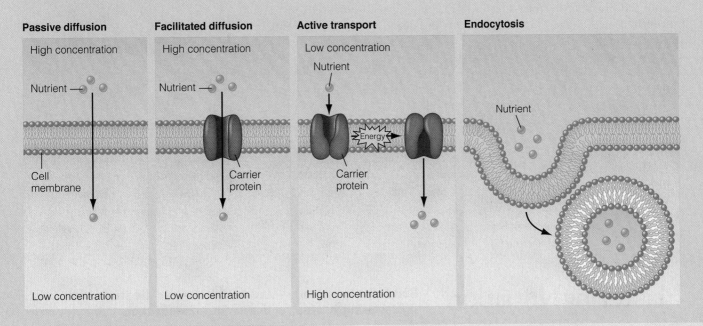

Passive diffusion
High concentration
Nutrient
Cell membrane
Low concentration

Facilitated diffusion
High concentration
Nutrient
Carrier protein
Low concentration

Active transport
Low concentration
Nutrient
Carrier protein
Energy
High concentration

Endocytosis
Nutrient

5 Nutrients Are Transported through the Circulatory and Lymphatic Systems

Water-soluble nutrients absorbed through the villi of the small intestine are transported through the circulatory system to the liver. Fat-soluble nutrients are transported through the lymphatic system before they enter the bloodstream.

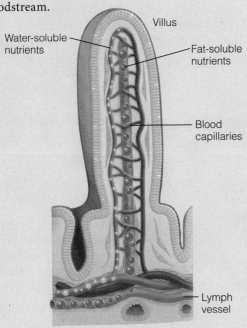

Villus
Water-soluble nutrients
Fat-soluble nutrients
Blood capillaries
Lymph vessel

6 Other Body Systems Help You Use Digested Nutrients

Body systems other than the digestive system help you use the nutrients you eat. Your nervous system lets you know when you are hungry or thirsty. The endocrine system releases hormones that regulate the cells' use of nutrients.

7 There Are Many Digestive Disorders

Heartburn, constipation, diarrhea, and hemorrhoids are common digestive disorders. The more serious disorders such as ulcers, colon cancer, and even diarrhea can be potentially life-threatening. Colon cancer begins with polyps but is treatable if caught early. The causes of IBS and Crohn's disease are unknown but can lead to malabsorption and malnutrition. The autoimmune disorder celiac disease results in damage to the villi of the small intestine due to gluten, and can result in malabsorption.

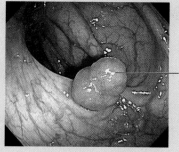
Colon polyp

Terms to Know

- gastrointestinal (GI) tract
- lumen
- mechanical digestion
- chemical digestion
- peristalsis
- segmentation
- pendular movement
- saliva
- mucus
- pharynx
- bolus
- epiglottis
- esophagus
- lower esophageal sphincter (LES)
- stomach
- hydrochloric acid (HCl)
- gastrin
- chyme
- pepsin
- pyloric sphincter
- small intestine
- villi
- ileocecal sphincter
- large intestine
- stool (feces)
- rectum
- anus
- liver
- gallbladder
- pancreas
- hormones
- enzymes
- bile
- absorption
- passive diffusion
- facilitated diffusion
- active transport
- dysphagia
- gastroesophageal reflux disease (GERD)
- gastroenteritis
- peptic ulcers
- gallstones
- flatulence
- constipation
- diarrhea
- hemorrhoids
- irritable bowel syndrome (IBS)
- celiac disease
- gluten intolerance
- Crohn's disease

MasteringNutrition™ Build your knowledge—and confidence—in the Study Area of MasteringNutrition with a variety of study tools.

Check Your Understanding

1. Food is moved through the GI tract by muscular waves called
   a. segmentation.
   b. peristalsis.
   c. bowel movement.
   d. pendular movement.
2. _____ is the process that breaks down food into absorbable units.
   a. Circulation
   b. Digestion
   c. Absorption
   d. Excretion
3. Chemical digestion begins in the
   a. liver.
   b. stomach.
   c. mouth.
   d. colon.
4. The name of the protective tissue that covers the trachea when you swallow is the
   a. esophagus.
   b. tongue.
   c. pharynx.
   d. epiglottis.

5. What causes heartburn?
   a. improper relaxation of the lower esophageal sphincter
   b. improper contraction of the lower esophageal sphincter
   c. improper and rapid swallowing
   d. improper breathing and chest congestion
6. The name of the secretion produced in the stomach that helps break down protein and activates pepsin is
   a. hydrochloric acid (HCl).
   b. amylase.
   c. bile.
   d. gastrin.
7. The sphincter that separates the stomach from the duodenum is the
   a. lower esophageal sphincter.
   b. ileocecal sphincter.
   c. pyloric sphincter.
   d. colon sphincter.
8. The compounds that help break down foods during digestion are
   a. enzymes.
   b. hormones.
   c. proteins.
   d. bicarbonate ions.

9. Which of a following is a function of the pancreas?
   a. to make bile
   b. to neutralize acidic chyme in the duodenum
   c. to absorb proteins
   d. to secrete hormones
10. Which of the following is true regarding the small intestine?
    a. The small intestine has a vast digestive surface area.
    b. The small intestine has minimal digestive surface area.
    c. The small intestine has access to lymph tissue, but not to the bloodstream.
    d. The small intestine is unimportant in the process of digestion.

Answers

1. (b) Peristalsis is the process that moves food through the entire GI tract. Segmentation and pendular movements move food back and forth along the small intestine. A bowel movement involves peristalsis moving the feces through the large intestine.

2. (b) Digestion. Circulation is the process of distributing blood or lymph throughout the body. Absorption is the process of nutrients passing from the GI tract into the body. Excretion is the passing of waste products out of the body.

3. (c) Chemical digestion begins in the mouth, when the enzyme amylase secreted in the saliva begins to chemically break down carbohydrates. The liver is an accessory organ to digestion. The stomach and colon (part of the large intestine) are organs in the GI tract.

4. (d) Epiglottis. The esophagus is a tube that connects your mouth with your stomach. The tongue is a muscle that pushes food to the back of the mouth into the pharynx. The pharynx is a chamber that food passes through just before being swallowed.

5. (a) Heartburn occurs when the lower esophageal sphincter allows acid from the stomach back into the esophagus.

6. (a) Hydrochloric acid (HCl) is part of the gastric juices produced in the stomach; it activates pepsin, breaks down connective tissue in meat, and destroys some ingested microorganisms. Amylase is an enzyme in the mouth that begins breaking down carbohydrates. Bile is made by the liver and emulsifies fat. Gastrin is a hormone in the stomach that stimulates digestive activity.

7. (c) The pyloric sphincter allows chyme to pass from the bottom of the stomach to the beginning of the duodenum, the first part of the small intestine. The lower esophageal sphincter is between the mouth and the stomach. The ileocecal sphincter separates the ileum from the colon. The colon sphincter is also called the anal sphincter and it is the last part of the GI tract.

8. (a) Enzymes such as amylase and lipase break down the individual nutrients during digestion. Hormones are chemical messengers that regulate activities such as metabolism and the cells' use of nutrients. Protein is a macronutrient, and bicarbonate ions are released from the pancreas into the duodenum of the small intestine to neutralize the acids found in chyme.

9. (b) The pancreas produces bicarbonate ions, which are released through the pancreatic duct into the duodenum of the small intestine where they neutralize the acidic chyme. The liver makes the bile in dilute, liquid form. Proteins are absorbed along the small intestine and hormones that control digestion are secreted from the stomach and the small intestine.

10. (a) With numerous villi and microvilli along its interior wall, the small intestine indeed has a vast surface area that enhances digestion. Nutrients are absorbed through these projections and are transported through the blood and lymph throughout the body. The small intestine is critical to the process of digestion.

Web Resources

- To find out more about celiac disease, visit www.celiac.org
- To learn about numerous types of cancer, cancer treatments, and preparation for treatment, visit www.cancer.gov
- To learn more about GI concerns, diseases, conditions, medicines, procedures, and treatments, go to www.medicinenet.com
- The National Library of Medicine is an abundant Internet resource for health care professionals, the public, researchers, and librarians; visit it at www.nlm.nih.gov
- To learn more about various digestive diseases, go to http://digestive.niddk.nih.gov

1. **True.** The gastrointestinal, or GI, tract runs through the body and connects the mouth to the anus. Turn to page 68 to find out more about the organs that make up the GI tract.

2. **False.** The trachea is the windpipe. To find out what happens if food mistakenly enters it, turn to page 71.

3. **False.** Hydrochloric acid is only produced in the stomach. For more about digestive juices, turn to page 73.

4. **True.** The stomach secretes a powerful acid, HCl, which is strong enough to damage the stomach wall. A thick layer of mucus protects it. Turn to page 73 to find out more.

5. **False.** Fats and protein take longer to digest than carbohydrates. Turn to page 74 to find out why.

6. **False.** Though most absorption does take place in the small intestine, some nutrients, particularly water, are absorbed in the large intestine. Turn to page 76 to learn more.

7. **True.** Stool (or feces) contains leftover food residue, nondigestible fibers, bacteria, gases, and sloughed-off intestinal cells. Turn to page 76 to find out more about the waste products of digestion.

8. **False.** Your body is very efficient and absorbs more than 90 percent of the nutrients in food. To find out how this happens, turn to page 80.

9. **False.** Approximately 20 percent of adults experience heartburn every day. Turn to page 84 to learn what causes it.

10. **False.** The exact cause of irritable bowel syndrome is unknown. To find out more, turn to page 87.

4

Carbohydrates:
Sugars, Starches, and Fiber

True or False?

1. People who are **lactose intolerant** need to avoid all dairy products. ⓉⒻ   p. 104

2. You need to eat a **minimum** of carbohydrates daily for good health. ⓉⒻ   p. 108

3. Americans do not consume **enough fiber**. ⓉⒻ   p. 109

4. There is more fiber in dark-colored **bread** than in white bread. ⓉⒻ   p. 110

5. **Carbohydrates** make you fat. ⓉⒻ   p. 115

6. Sugar causes **diabetes**. ⓉⒻ   p. 120

7. Sugar causes **cavities**. ⓉⒻ   p. 121

8. **High-fructose corn syrup** causes weight gain. ⓉⒻ   p. 124

9. **Sugar free** equals calorie free. ⓉⒻ   p. 128

10. Saccharin causes **cancer** in humans. ⓉⒻ   p. 128

See page 139 for the answers.

1. **Describe what carbohydrates are and why you need them.**

2. **Explain the process of digesting dietary carbohydrates.**

3. **Explain how the body uses carbohydrates and regulates blood glucose levels.**

4. **Describe the guidelines for carbohydrate intake, including the AMDR for carbohydrates, the DRI for fiber, and the recommendation for consuming added sugars.**

5. **Describe the difference between natural and added sugars in the diet.**

6. **Define type 1 and type 2 diabetes and describe how the types differ.**

7. **List alternative sweeteners used as sugar substitutes.**

8. **Describe the importance of fiber in the body and diet.**

Carbohydrates are essential nutrients that make up the foundation of diets the world over. They are predominant in plant-based foods such as grains (rice and pasta), fruits, vegetables, nuts, and legumes (dry beans and peas), but are also found in dairy products such as milk and yogurt. These foods are staples in cuisines from Asia to Latin America, the United States to the Mediterranean. In Asia, rice is a dietary staple, and in Latin America, carbohydrate-laden bananas and nuts adorn most dinner plates. In the Mediterranean, grain-based pastas, breads, and couscous are plentiful, and here in the United States, many people consume bread on a regular basis.[1] In this chapter, you will learn about different types of carbohydrates and the functions they perform in the body. We will also discuss how we digest carbohydrates, how the body metabolizes glucose, and what happens when metabolic control fails, as in the disease diabetes mellitus. You will learn the role that certain types of carbohydrates can play in fighting obesity, heart disease, cancer, and diabetes. Finally, we will explore how to incorporate a rich balance of carbohydrates into your daily diet.

What Are Carbohydrates and Why Do You Need Them?

Carbohydrates are the most desirable source of energy for your body. Providing four calories of energy per gram, their main role is to supply fuel, primarily in the form of **glucose**, the predominant sugar in high-carbohydrate foods, to your cells. Your brain in particular relies on glucose to function, as do your red blood cells.

The carbohydrates you eat come mostly from plant foods. Plants make carbohydrates to store energy and to build their root and stem structures. Animals, including humans, also store energy as carbohydrates, but in limited amounts. The storage form of carbohydrates in animals breaks down when the animal dies, so eating meat and poultry will not supply carbohydrates to our diets. Plants form the basic carbohydrate, glucose, in a process called **photosynthesis (Figure 4.1)**. During photosynthesis, plants use the **chlorophyll** in their leaves to absorb the energy in sunlight. The absorbed energy splits water in the plant into its component parts: hydrogen and oxygen. Glucose is formed when the hydrogen joins with carbon dioxide that the plant has taken in from the air. The oxygen is released as a waste product.

Glucose is the most abundant carbohydrate in nature, and plants use it as energy, or combine it with minerals from the soil to make other compounds, such as protein and vitamins. They also link glucose units together and store them in the form of starch. Plants synthesize an estimated 145 billion tons of carbohydrates a year. This equals about 23 tons per person in the world.[2]

Carbohydrates are divided into two categories based on the number of units that are joined together. **Simple carbohydrates** include **monosaccharides** (*mono* = one, *saccharide* = sugar) and **disaccharides** (*di* = two), and **complex carbohydrates** include **polysaccharides** (*poly* = many).

Simple Carbohydrates Contain One or Two Sugar Units

Three monosaccharides are found in foods. In addition to glucose, which we just discussed, there are **fructose** and **galactose** (**Figure 4.2** on page 100). Fructose is the

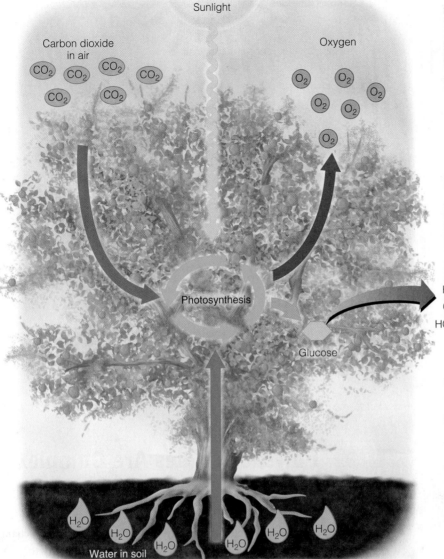

Sunlight

Carbon dioxide in air

CO_2 CO_2 CO_2 CO_2 CO_2 CO_2

Oxygen

O_2 O_2 O_2 O_2 O_2 O_2 O_2

Photosynthesis

Glucose

H_2O H_2O H_2O H_2O H_2O H_2O

Water in soil

CH₂OH — this appears as CH_2OH with structural formula showing H, C, O, OH, HO, C, OH groups

Figure 4.1 Photosynthesis: How Glucose Is Made
During photosynthesis, the leaves of green plants absorb the energy from sunlight. This energy splits six molecules of water (H_2O) into hydrogen and oxygen. The hydrogen joins with carbon dioxide in the plant to create glucose. In this process, six molecules of oxygen are released into the air. Glucose is the most abundant sugar in nature and the optimal fuel for your body.

glucose The most abundant sugar in foods and the primary energy source for your body.

photosynthesis A process by which green plants create carbohydrates using the energy from sunlight.

chlorophyll The green pigment in plants that absorbs energy from sunlight to begin the process of photosynthesis.

simple carbohydrates A category of carbohydrates that contain a single sugar unit or two sugar units combined. Monosaccharides and disaccharides are simple carbohydrates.

monosaccharide One sugar unit. There are three monosaccharides: glucose, fructose, and galactose.

disaccharide Two sugar units combined. There are three disaccharides: sucrose, lactose, and maltose.

complex carbohydrates A category of carbohydrates that contain many sugar units combined. A polysaccharide is a complex carbohydrate.

polysaccharide Many sugar units combined. Starch, glycogen, and fiber are all polysaccharides.

fructose The sweetest of the monosaccharides; also known as fruit sugar.

galactose A monosaccharide that links with glucose to create the sugar found in dairy foods.

sucrose A disaccharide composed of glucose and fructose; also known as table sugar.

maltose A disaccharide composed of two glucose units joined together.

lactose A disaccharide composed of glucose and galactose; also known as milk sugar.

sweetest of the simple sugars and is found abundantly in fruit. For this reason, it is often referred to as fruit sugar. Galactose is found in dairy foods. From these three sugars, the disaccharides can be created:

➤ When glucose and fructose join together, the disaccharide **sucrose**, or table sugar, is formed.
➤ When two glucose units join together, the disaccharide **maltose** is created. Maltose is the sugar found in grains, such as barley. It is used in the process of brewing beer.
➤ When glucose and galactose join together, the disaccharide **lactose** is created. Lactose is often called *milk sugar*, as it is found in dairy foods.

Foods high in carbohydrates are staples in many of the world's cuisines.

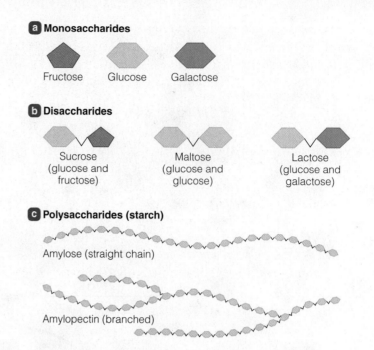

a Monosaccharides

Fructose   Glucose   Galactose

b Disaccharides

Sucrose
(glucose and
fructose)

Maltose
(glucose and
glucose)

Lactose
(glucose and
galactose)

c Polysaccharides (starch)

Amylose (straight chain)

Amylopectin (branched)

Figure 4.2 Creating Monosaccharides, Disaccharides, and Polysaccharides
(a) Fructose, glucose, and galactose are the three monosaccharides that are found in nature. **(b)** The disaccharides sucrose, maltose, and lactose are created from the monosaccharides. **(c)** The polysaccharide, starch, is composed of many glucose units joined together.

Unripe fruit tastes more starchy than sweet. As fruit ripens, its complex carbohydrates are broken down into simple sugars, including fructose. The more it ripens, the more fructose it has.

Polysaccharides Are Complex Carbohydrates

Polysaccharides consist of long chains of monosaccharides linked together. As you can see in Figure 4.2c, these chains contain many combined glucose units, which is why they are called complex carbohydrates. **Starch**, **fiber**, and **glycogen** are the three groups of polysaccharides.

Starch Is the Storage Form in Plants

Plants can store thousands of straight or branched glucose units strung together as starch. The straight chains of glucose units in starch are called amylose, whereas branched chains are called amylopectin. The many branches in amylopectin enable the body to break it down quickly and easily compared with amylose because there are so many sites where the enzymes can attach (Figure 4.2c). Starchy foods with highly branched amylopectin, such as potatoes, rice, bread, pasta, and cereals, are digested more rapidly than foods rich in amylose, such as legumes (dried peas, beans, and lentils).

Fiber Is Nondigestible but Important

Humans lack the digestive enzyme needed to break down fiber, so for the most part, fiber is the part of the plant that we eat but cannot digest. Plant components like cellulose, hemicellulose, lignins, gums, and pectin are all types of fibers.

starch The storage form of glucose in plants.

fiber A nondigestible polysaccharide.

glycogen The storage form of glucose in humans and animals.

Dietary fiber is found naturally in foods and **functional fiber** is added to food for a specific, beneficial effect. For example, psyllium is a functional fiber derived from wheat husks. It can be added to breakfast cereals to help promote regular bowel movements. Together, dietary and functional fibers account for the *total fiber* that you eat.

Many compounds can be classified as both dietary fiber and functional fiber, depending on how they are used. Pectin occurs naturally in foods such as apples and citrus fruits and would be considered a source of dietary fiber. However, pectin can also be isolated and added to foods, such as nonfat yogurt, to add texture. In this situation, pectin is considered a functional fiber.

Fiber is sometimes also classified by its properties when combined with water. **Soluble fiber** dissolves in water, whereas **insoluble fiber** does not. Soluble fiber can be viscous (though not all soluble fibers are viscous); that is, it can have gummy or thickening properties. For example, the viscous soluble fiber in oats and beans thickens cooked oatmeal and bean chili. When you eat such foods, their soluble fiber is fermented (or digested) by bacteria in your large intestine. In contrast, insoluble fiber, found in foods such as bran flakes, is not viscous and is fermented less readily by bacteria.

A fiber's solubility affects how quickly it moves through the digestive tract. This classification system isn't exact, as most plant foods typically contain both types of fiber (**Figure 4.3**), and some fibers can have multiple effects in your body. In general, insoluble fibers include cellulose, hemicellulose, and lignins and are found in the bran portion of whole grains, cereal fiber, seeds, and in many fruits and vegetables. They typically move more quickly through your intestinal tract, so can have a laxative effect. Soluble fiber—like pectin in fruits and vegetables, beta-glucan in oats and barley, gums in legumes, and psyllium—is more viscous and moves slowly through your digestive system. Meat and dairy products do not contain fiber. Even though fiber is mostly nondigestible, it can have powerful health effects. We will discuss some of its effects in depth later in the chapter.

Figure 4.3 Most Plant Foods Contain Both Soluble and Insoluble Fibers
The skin of an apple is high in cellulose, an insoluble fiber, while the pulp is high in pectin, a soluble fiber.

Glycogen Is the Storage Form in Animals

Glycogen is the storage form of glucose in humans and animals and is found in the liver and in muscle cells. Glycogen is branched glucose similar to amylopectin. Humans store only limited amounts of glycogen in their bodies, but it can be an important source of glucose for the blood. People can't access the carbohydrates stored in meats and poultry because the glycogen stored in animals breaks down when the animals die.

The Take-Home Message Carbohydrates are found abundantly in plant-based foods. Your body cells use them for energy. Carbohydrates are divided into two categories: simple and complex. Simple carbohydrates include the monosaccharides and disaccharides; complex carbohydrates include polysaccharides. Glucose, fructose, and galactose are the three monosaccharides. Sucrose, lactose, and maltose are the three disaccharides. Starch, fiber, and glycogen are all polysaccharides. Dietary fiber occurs naturally in plant-based foods. Functional fiber has been added to foods because it has been shown to have a specific, functional effect. The total fiber in your diet is a combination of dietary and functional fiber. Viscous, soluble fiber has thickening properties and can be fermented by intestinal bacteria, and moves slowly through your intestinal tract. Insoluble fiber typically moves more quickly through your digestive system, so it can have a laxative effect.

dietary fiber Nondigestible polysaccharides found naturally in foods.

functional fiber The nondigestible polysaccharides that are added to foods because of a specific desired effect on health.

soluble fiber A type of fiber that dissolves in water and is fermented by intestinal bacteria. Many soluble fibers are viscous and have gummy or thickening properties.

insoluble fiber A type of fiber that doesn't dissolve in water and is not fermented by intestinal bacteria.

What Happens to the Carbohydrates You Eat?

When you eat plant foods, your body breaks down the carbohydrates for energy. Let's look at how your body digests a sandwich.

You Digest Carbohydrates in Your Mouth and Intestines

The digestion of carbohydrates starts in your mouth (**Figure 4.4**). The act of chewing mixes the saliva in your mouth with the food. Your saliva delivers a powerful enzyme called amylase (*ase* = enzyme), which starts breaking down the starch in the fiber-rich whole-wheat bread in the sandwich, specifically the amylose and amylopectin, into smaller starch units. Some of the starch is broken down to the disaccharide, maltose.

This mixture of starch and amylase, along with the maltose and the fiber, travels down to your stomach. The amylase continues to break down the starch until your stomach acids deactivate this enzyme. Once the food leaves your stomach, it moves through your small intestine. The arrival of the food in the small intestine signals the pancreas to release another enzyme, pancreatic amylase. The pancreatic amylase breaks down the remaining starch units into maltose.

All the disaccharides—maltose, lactose, and sucrose—are absorbed in your small intestine. The disaccharides brush up against the lining of your digestive tract. A variety of enzymes such as maltase, lactase, and sucrase, called brush border enzymes, are housed in the microvilli in your small intestine. These enzymes break down the disaccharides into monosaccharides, specifically glucose, fructose, and galactose. (Some people lack sufficient lactase and have difficulty digesting lactose. See the Health Connection feature "What Is Lactose Intolerance?" on page 104 for more about this condition.)

Once the dissacharides are broken down into monosaccharides, they are absorbed into the blood and travel to the liver. There the fructose and galactose are converted to glucose. The glucose is either stored in the liver or shipped back out into the blood for delivery to your cells.

The fiber continues down to the large intestine, where some of it is metabolized by bacteria in your colon. However, the majority of the fiber is eliminated from your body in stool.

The Take-Home Message The digestion of carbohydrates begins in your mouth and continues in your stomach and small intestine. Enzymes help break down the carbohydrates into disaccharides and then monosaccharides so that they can be absorbed. All the monosaccharides are converted to glucose in your liver to be used as energy by your cells or stored as glycogen or fat. Fiber travels to your colon and then most of it is eliminated from your body.

 Figure 4.4 **Carbohydrate Digestion and Absorption**

Carbohydrate digestion begins in the mouth and ends with the absorption of the monosaccharides glucose, fructose, and galactose in the small intestine.

ORGANS OF THE GI TRACT

ACCESSORY ORGANS

MOUTH

Mastication mixes food with saliva. Salivary amylase breaks down amylose and amylopectin into smaller chains of carbohydrates.

Amylose → Smaller chains

Amylopectin → Smaller chains

SALIVARY GLANDS

Produce salivary amylase.

STOMACH

The acidity of the stomach inactivates the salivary amylase; thus, very little digestion of carbohydrates occurs in the stomach.

SMALL INTESTINE

Pancreatic amylase breaks down the amylose, amylopectin, and smaller chains of carbohydrates into maltose, a disaccharide.

Smaller amylose chains → Maltose

Smaller amylopectin chains → Maltose

Brush border enzymes break down all disaccharides to the monosaccharides glucose, fructose, and galactose, which are then absorbed into the bloodstream.

Sucrose → Glucose Fructose

Maltose → Glucose

Lactose → Glucose Galactose

PANCREAS

Produces pancreatic amylase that is released into the small intestine via the pancreatic duct.

LIVER

Glucose is taken up by the liver from the blood. Most glucose is returned to the blood to be picked up and used by body cells, or the body can use glucose for energy, convert it to glycogen, or store it as fat.

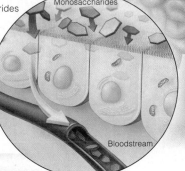

Monosaccharides

Bloodstream

LARGE INTESTINE

All starches and simple sugars are broken down and absorbed in the small intestine; only fiber passes into the large intestine. Bacteria in the colon metabolize some of the fiber. The majority of fiber is eliminated in the stool.

What Is Lactose Intolerance?

Lactose, or milk sugar, is the principal carbohydrate found in dairy products such as milk, yogurt, and cheese. People with a deficiency of the brush border enzyme lactase cannot properly digest lactose.

Lactose maldigestion is a natural part of the aging process and affects diverse populations in the United States, including people of Asian, African, Hispanic, and Native American backgrounds.[1] In fact, as soon as a child stops nursing, his body makes less lactase.

Though the term lactose maldigestion may sound serious, it doesn't mean that dairy foods have to be eliminated from the diet. In fact, the latest consensus is that people with lactose maldigestion can enjoy a serving of milk, yogurt, or cheese, especially with a meal or snack, without any problems or unpleasant side effects.[2] This is good news, as dairy products can be an important source of calcium and vitamin D in the diet.

However, in some individuals the amount of lactase in the digestive tract decreases so much that they start to experience distressing symptoms. The undigested lactose draws water into the digestive tract, causing diarrhea. To make matters worse, once the lactose reaches the colon, the bacteria that normally live in the colon ferment this sugar and produce various gases. For some lactose-sensitive individuals, bloating, flatulence (gassiness), and cramps can sometimes be an unpleasant reminder that they ate lactose-containing foods. When these symptoms occur within two hours after eating or drinking foods that contain lactose, these people may be **lactose intolerant**.

You should never self-diagnose lactose intolerance, or any other medical condition. This could not only cause you to inflict unnecessary dietary restrictions on yourself, it could delay you from receiving an accurate diagnosis of a potentially more serious medical condition. It is best to leave medical diagnosis to your physician.

(T)(F)

People with lactose maldigestion have varying thresholds for tolerating lactose-containing foods and beverages. Research suggests that these individuals can ingest at least 12 grams of lactose, the amount found in a cup of milk, with few or no symptoms (see Table).[3] Consuming smaller amounts of dairy foods throughout the day can be better tolerated than having a large amount at one time.

Eating these foods with a meal or snack, rather than by themselves, can also influence how much can be tolerated. People tend to respond differently to various dairy foods. Whole milk tends to be better tolerated than skim milk. Cheeses (especially hard, aged cheeses, such as Swiss and cheddar) typically have less lactose than milk, and so are better tolerated. Yogurts that contain active cultures are better tolerated than skim or low-fat milk.

For those who want to enjoy dairy foods without worrying about developing the unpleasant side effects, lactose-reduced dairy products such as milk, cottage cheese, ice cream, and other items are available in many supermarkets. Lactase pills are available that can be consumed with meals containing lactose.

lactose maldigestion The inability to digest lactose in foods due to low levels of the enzyme lactase.

lactose intolerant When maldigestion of lactose results in symptoms such as nausea, cramps, bloating, flatulence, and diarrhea.

Many products are available to help those who are lactose intolerant enjoy dairy foods.

How Much Lactose Is in Your Foods?

Food	Amount	Lactose (grams)
Milk	1 cup	12
Yogurt, low fat	1 cup	11
Ice cream	½ cup	4
Cottage cheese	½ cup	3
Lactaid milk	1 cup	0
Soy milk	1 cup	0
Provolone, Cheddar, Parmesan cheese	1 oz	<1

Don't Forget These Hidden Sources of Lactose

Baked goods	Instant potatoes
Baking mixes	Lunch meats
Bread	Margarine
Breakfast drinks	Salad dressings
Candies	Soups
Cereals, processed	

Source: The National Digestive Diseases Information Clearinghouse, *Lactose Intolerance* (National Institutes of Health Publication No. 09-2751). Available at http://digestive.niddk .nih.gov. Accessed March 2013; National Institutes of Health, "NIH Consensus Development Conference: Lactose Intolerance and Health," 2010. Available at http://consensus .nih.gov. Accessed March 2013; Joneja, J., *The Health Professional's Guide to Food Allergies and Intolerances* (Chicago: The Academy of Nutrition and Dietetics, 2013).

How Does Your Body Use Carbohydrates?

Your body uses carbohydrates—specifically glucose—for energy (**Figure 4.5**). Chemical messengers called **hormones** that regulate the amount of glucose in your blood. Hormones are like traffic cops, directing specific actions in your body. Let's take a closer look at how this works.

Insulin Regulates Glucose in Your Blood

After you eat a carbohydrate-heavy meal, your blood is flooded with glucose. To lower your blood glucose level, your pancreas releases the hormone **insulin** into the blood. Insulin helps direct the uptake of glucose by cells and also determines whether it will be used immediately as energy or stored for later use (**Figure 4.6**). When your cells need fuel, insulin stimulates the conversion of glucose to energy. If the amount of glucose in your blood exceeds your body's immediate energy needs, insulin directs it to be stored as glycogen and/or as fat if glycogen stores are maximized.

As mentioned, the surplus of glucose is stored in long, branched chains called glycogen. (Recall that plants store glucose as starch. Animals and humans store glucose as glycogen.) This process of generating glycogen for later use is called **glycogenesis** (*glyco* = sugar/sweet, *genesis* = origin). Glycogenesis occurs only in your liver and muscle cells. Whereas plants have an unlimited capacity to store glucose as starch, you can't squirrel away unlimited extra energy in the form of glycogen.

However, your body can store energy in another form: fat. Insulin can direct the conversion of the excess glucose to fat. In fact, most of the energy stored in your body is in the form of fat. Very little of it is in the form of glycogen. (Fat is covered in detail in Chapter 5.)

Carbohydrates Fuel Your Body between Meals and Help Spare Protein for Other Uses

Both glycogen and fat are important sources of stored fuel that meet your body's energy needs. These storage forms come in handy between meals when you aren't eating but your body continues to need fuel. Remember, your red blood cells and your brain,

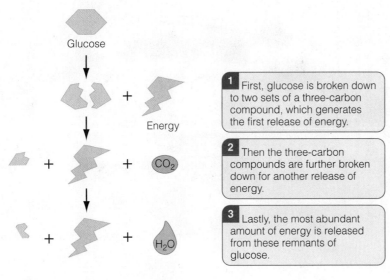

1 First, glucose is broken down to two sets of a three-carbon compound, which generates the first release of energy.

2 Then the three-carbon compounds are further broken down for another release of energy.

3 Lastly, the most abundant amount of energy is released from these remnants of glucose.

Figure 4.5 Generating Energy from Glucose
When your body needs to break down glucose for energy, it begins a three-step process in your cells.

hormones Protein- or lipid-based chemical substances that act as "messengers" in the body to initiate or direct actions or processes. Insulin, glucagon, and estrogen are examples of hormones.

insulin The hormone, produced in and released from the pancreas, that facilitates the movement of glucose from the blood into cells.

glycogenesis The process of converting excess glucose into glycogen in your liver and muscle.

Our bodies regulate blood glucose levels within a fairly narrow range to provide adequate glucose to the brain and other cells. Insulin and glucagon are two hormones that play a key role in regulating blood glucose levels.

HIGH BLOOD GLUCOSE

1 Insulin secretion: When blood glucose levels increase after a meal, the pancreas secretes the hormone insulin into the bloodstream.

2 Cellular uptake: Insulin travels to the tissues where it alters the cell membranes to allow the transport of glucose into the cells by increasing the number of glucose transporters on the cell membrane.

3 Glucose storage: Insulin also stimulates the storage of glucose in body tissues. Glucose is stored as glycogen in the liver and muscles (glycogenesis), and is stored as triglycerides in fat tissue (lipogenesis).

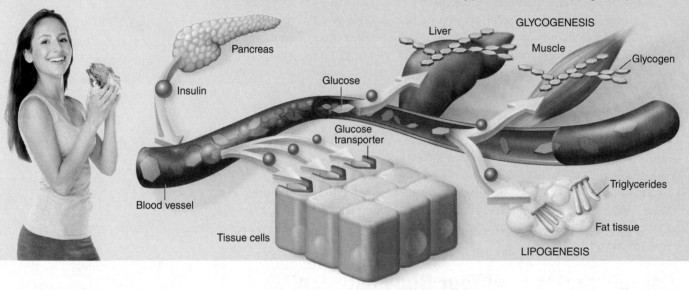

LOW BLOOD GLUCOSE

1 Glucagon secretion: When blood glucose levels are low, the pancreas secretes the hormone glucagon into the bloodstream.

2 Glycogenolysis: Glucagon stimulates glycogenolysis in the liver to break down stored glycogen to glucose, which is released into the blood and transported to the cells for energy.

3 Gluconeogenesis: Glucagon also activates gluconeogenesis in the liver, stimulating the conversion of amino acids to glucose.

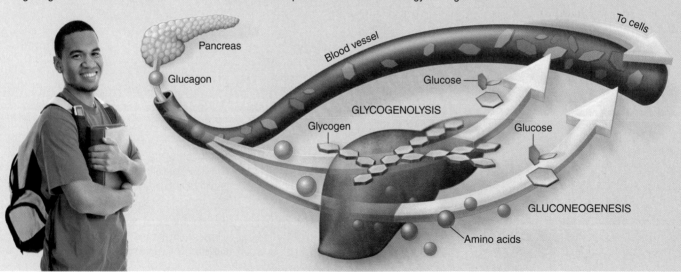

as well as the rest of your nervous system, rely on a steady supply of glucose to function properly. When your blood glucose level dips too low, such as if it has been longer than four hours since your last meal, your body calls upon its glycogen reserves to supply glucose to your blood. The glycogen in your liver is used to maintain your blood glucose level, and your muscle glycogen is used exclusively by the muscles for fuel. During this time, your body will also break down your fat stores to provide the energy for your tissues, such as your muscles. For example, let's say that your nutrition class is at 8 a.m. and that you overslept and didn't eat breakfast. The last time you ate was at dinner last night—more than 12 hours ago. As your blood glucose level begins to drop, your pancreas releases another hormone, **glucagon**, which directs the release of glucose from the stored glycogen in your liver to help raise your blood glucose level. This breakdown of glycogen is called **glycogenolysis** (*lysis* = loosening) (see Figure 4.6).

In addition to directing the breakdown of glycogen, glucagon signals the liver to start **gluconeogenesis** (*gluco* = sugar/sweet, *neo* = new, *genesis* = origin). This is the creation of glucose from noncarbohydrate sources, mostly from protein. Gluconeogenesis can only occur in your liver and kidneys, as these are the only organs that have all the enzymes needed. Most of the time, this glucose-generating process occurs in your liver. Gluconeogenesis kicks in from the kidney only after long periods of fasting. In times of deprivation, your body dismantles protein, using specific remnants (amino acids, which we will discuss in Chapter 6) to generate the glucose that it needs. If you don't feed your blood with glucose, your body will attempt to feed itself. Thus, consuming adequate amounts of carbohydrates is important to *spare* protein from being broken down to make glucose. You will learn in Chapter 6 that protein has so many other important functions in your body that you want to preserve it, rather than use it to make glucose. Once your blood glucose returns to normal, glucagon will no longer be released.

In addition to glucagon, other hormones can increase your blood glucose level. Epinephrine and norepinephrine, also known as adrenaline, act on the liver and muscle cells to stimulate glycogenolysis to quickly flood your blood with glucose. Emotional and physical forms of stress, such as fear, excitement, and bleeding, will increase your body's output of adrenaline. For example, if an aggressive dog was chasing you down the street, your body would be pumping out adrenaline to help provide the fuel you need to run. For this reason, epinephrine and norepinephrine are also referred to as the "fight-or-flight" hormones.

A low blood glucose level can also trigger the release of epinephrine. In fact, some of the symptoms that you may experience when your blood glucose level dips too low, such as anxiety, rapid heart beat, turning pale, and shakiness, are caused by the release of epinephrine.

Carbohydrates Fuel Your Body during Fasting and Prevent Ketosis

Skipping breakfast is one thing; fasting, or not eating for long periods of time, is quite another. After about 18 hours of fasting, your liver's glycogen stores are depleted, so your body must rely solely on fat and protein for fuel.

To burn fat thoroughly, you need adequate amounts of glucose. Without it, excessive amounts of **ketone bodies**, by-products of the incomplete breakdown of fat, are created and spill out into your blood. Because most ketone bodies are acids, excessive amounts can cause your blood to become slightly acidic. After about two days of fasting, the number of ketone bodies in your blood is at least doubled, and you are in a state of **ketosis**. Individuals who fast or follow strict low-carbohydrate diets are often in ketosis because they consume inadequate amounts of carbohydrates.

glucagon The hormone that directs glycogenolysis and gluconeogenesis to increase glucose in the blood. Glucagon is produced in and released from the pancreas.

glycogenolysis The breakdown of glycogen to release glucose.

gluconeogenesis The creation of glucose from noncarbohydrate sources, predominantly protein.

ketone bodies The by-products of the incomplete breakdown of fat.

ketosis The condition of increased ketone bodies in the blood.

Although the term *ketosis* sounds scary, the condition is not necessarily harmful as long as you are otherwise healthy.

During extended fasting, while your body continues to break down fat for fuel, it also breaks down the protein from your muscles and organs to generate glucose. If you continue to fast, your body's protein reserves will reach a dangerously low level and death will occur.

The Take-Home Message After a meal, when your blood glucose level begins to rise, the hormone insulin is released from the pancreas, directing glucose into your cells to be used for energy. Excess glucose is stored as glycogen or as fat. When your blood glucose drops too low, the hormone glucagon directs the release of glucose from glycogen in your liver to increase the glucose in your blood. Glucagon will also signal the start of gluconeogenesis in the liver, which is the creation of glucose from noncarbohydrate sources, such as protein. Epinephrine also plays a role in increasing your blood glucose level. When you fast, stored fat and ketone bodies become the primary source of energy to fuel your body. This spares your protein-rich tissues by reducing the amount of protein that needs to be broken down to generate glucose. If the fasting continues, death is inevitable.

How Much Carbohydrate Do You Need and What Are the Best Food Sources?

Although your body has mechanisms in place to provide the energy it needs on demand, you have to feed it the proper fuel to keep it running efficiently. Consequently, the question of how much carbohydrate you should consume daily has two answers. The first refers to the minimum amount of carbohydrates that you should eat to provide adequate fuel for your body, specifically your brain, to function efficiently. The longer, and more challenging, answer relates to the best type and source of carbohydrates that you should eat daily for long-term health. First, let's look at the amount of carbohydrates that you should eat daily.

You Need a Minimum Amount of Carbohydrates Daily

The latest Dietary Reference Intakes (DRIs) for carbohydrates recommend that adults and children consume a minimum of 130 grams daily. This is based on the estimated minimum amount of glucose your brain needs to function efficiently. This may sound like a lot, but 130 grams is less than the amount you would consume by eating the minimum recommended daily servings for each food group in MyPlate, that is, 6 servings from the grain group, 3 servings each from the vegetable and dairy groups, and 2 servings from the fruit group (**Figure 4.7**).

If your diet is well balanced, feeding your brain should be a no-brainer. In the United States, adult males consume, on average, just under 300 grams of carbohydrates daily, whereas adult females eat slightly over 200 grams daily, well over the minimum DRI.[3]

Recall from Chapter 2 that the AMDR for carbohydrates is 45 to 65 percent of your total daily calories. Adults in the United States consume about half of their calories from carbohydrate-rich foods, so they are easily meeting this optimal range.

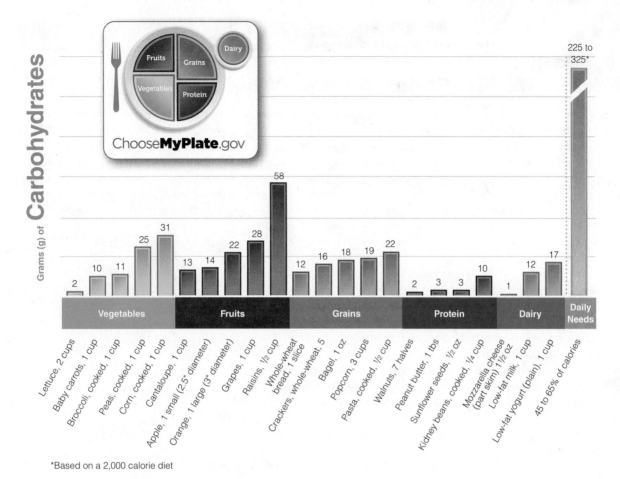

Figure 4.7 Food Sources of Carbohydrates
You need to eat at least 130 grams of carbohydrates daily.* Eating the minimum recommended servings from the grains, vegetables, fruits, and dairy groups will meet this need.

*Based on a 2,000-calorie diet.

For fiber, the current DRIs recommend that you consume 14 grams for every 1,000 calories you eat, to promote heart health. For example, individuals who need 2,000 calories daily to maintain their weight should consume 28 grams of fiber daily. Because few people know the exact number of calories they consume daily, the recommendations for fiber are categorized by both age and gender so that your estimated needs can be determined (**Table 4.1**). Unfortunately, most Americans fall short of this goal and consume approximately 15 to 18 grams of fiber a day, on average.[4]

The Best Carbohydrates Are Found in These Foods

Now let's turn to the second part of our answer and look at the best type and source of carbohydrates to choose for long-term health. As with other nutrients, not all carbohydrate-laden foods are created equal. For example, eating high-sugar foods containing lots of calories and saturated fat, but few other nutrients, can lead to weight gain and promote heart disease. It's best to choose carbohydrates from a variety of nutrient-dense, low-saturated-fat foods whenever possible. In general, the best strategy for long-term health is to eat a diet with fewer (low to moderate amounts of) simple carbohydrates and more complex carbohydrates.

Table 4.1

What Are Your Fiber Needs?

	Grams of Fiber Daily*	
	Males	**Females**
14 through 18 years old	38	26
19 through 50 years old	38	25
51 through 70+ years old	30	21
Pregnancy		28
Lactation		29

*Based on an Adequate Intake (AI) for fiber.

Source: Institute of Medicine, *Dietary Reference Intakes for Energy, Carbohydrate, Fiber, Fat, Fatty Acids, Cholesterol, Protein, and Amino Acids* (Washington, D.C.: The National Academies Press, 2005).

nutrition
IN THE
Real World

Grains, Glorious Whole Grains

Grains are not only an important staple in the diet but also a wonderful source of nutrition. Americans' consumption of wheat, corn, oats, barley, and rice products has increased by over 40 percent since the 1970s. The consumption of grain products is estimated to be approximately 134 pounds per person each year, or the equivalent of 7.5 MyPlate servings daily.[4]

There are three edible parts in a kernel of grain: the bran, the endosperm, and the germ (see the figure). The **bran**, or outer shell of the wheat kernel, is rich in fiber, B vitamins, phytochemicals, and trace minerals such as chromium and zinc. The **germ**, or seed of the kernel, is a nutritional powerhouse providing vitamin E, heart-healthy fats, phytochemicals, and plenty of B vitamins. The **endosperm**, or starchy component of the grain, contains protein, B vitamins, and some fiber, although not as much as the bran.

Depending upon which parts of the kernel are used, grain products can be divided

into two main categories: **refined grains** and **whole grains**. In refined grains, such as wheat or white bread and white rice, the grain kernel goes through a milling process that strips out the bran and germ, leaving only the endosperm of the kernel in the end product. As a result, some, though not all, of the B vitamins, iron, phytochemicals, and dietary fiber are removed. Though refined grains can still be a good source of complex carbohydrates, you can think of *refined* as having left some of the nutrition *behind*. From a health standpoint, what was left behind may end up being the most important part of the kernel.

To restore some of the nutrition lost from refined grains, **enriched grains** have folic acid, thiamin, niacin, riboflavin, and iron added to them. This improves their nutritional quality somewhat, but the fiber and the phytochemicals are lost.

Whole-grain foods, such as whole-wheat bread, white whole-wheat bread, brown rice, and oatmeal, contain all three parts of the kernel. (Note: White whole-wheat bread *is* a whole-grain product. It is made from a lighter variety of wheat, so although the bread is lighter in color, it has the same whole-grain nutrition as darker whole-wheat bread.) Whole grains are potential disease-fighting allies in the diet.[5] Research has shown that consuming whole grains protects against heart disease and may help individuals better manage their weight.[6] Several research studies have also shown that the fiber in whole grains may help reduce the risk of diabetes.[7] Because whole grains are abundant in vitamins, minerals, fiber, and phytochemicals, it is uncertain which of these substances are the disease-fighting

heroes, or if some or all of them work in a complementary fashion to provide the protection.[8]

The consumption of whole grains in the American diet has been steadily increasing. There was a 20 percent increase in whole-grain consumption from 2005 to 2008.[9] The good news is that it's easy to incorporate more grains into your diet. When it comes to whole grain, you have a lot of choices:

- ➤ Brown rice
- ➤ Bulgur (cracked wheat)
- ➤ Graham flour
- ➤ Oatmeal
- ➤ Popcorn
- ➤ Pearl barley
- ➤ Whole-grain cornmeal
- ➤ Whole oats
- ➤ Whole rye
- ➤ Whole wheat

Dark bread is not necessarily whole-grain bread. Bread made with refined wheat flour can have caramel coloring added to give it a darker brown appearance.

bran The indigestible outer shell of the grain kernel.

germ In grains, the seed of the grain kernel.

endosperm The starchy part of the grain kernel.

refined grains Grain foods that are made with only the endosperm of the kernel. The bran and germ are not included.

whole grains Grain foods that are made with the entire edible grain kernel: the bran, the endosperm, and the germ.

enriched grains Refined grain foods that have folic acid, thiamin, niacin, riboflavin, and iron added.

Whole Grains Can Help Meet Starch and Fiber Needs

Starch is the primary complex carbohydrate found in refined grains, while fiber is found in whole grains. Select whole-grain breads and cereals that have at least 2 to 3 grams of total fiber per serving, such as quinoa, whole-wheat bread, bulgur, brown rice, and whole-wheat pasta. See the Nutrition in the Real World feature "Grains, Glorious Whole Grains" for more on what constitutes a whole grain.

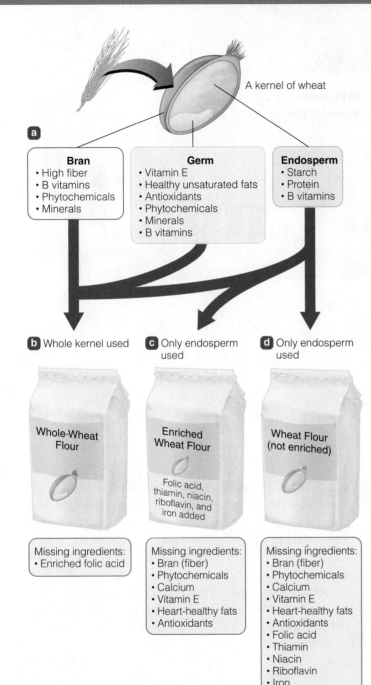

a A kernel of wheat

Bran
- High fiber
- B vitamins
- Phytochemicals
- Minerals

Germ
- Vitamin E
- Healthy unsaturated fats
- Antioxidants
- Phytochemicals
- Minerals
- B vitamins

Endosperm
- Starch
- Protein
- B vitamins

b Whole kernel used

c Only endosperm used

d Only endosperm used

Whole-Wheat Flour

Enriched Wheat Flour
Folic acid, thiamin, niacin, riboflavin, and iron added

Wheat Flour (not enriched)

Missing ingredients:
- Enriched folic acid

Missing ingredients:
- Bran (fiber)
- Phytochemicals
- Calcium
- Vitamin E
- Heart-healthy fats
- Antioxidants

Missing ingredients:
- Bran (fiber)
- Phytochemicals
- Calcium
- Vitamin E
- Heart-healthy fats
- Antioxidants
- Folic acid
- Thiamin
- Niacin
- Riboflavin
- Iron

From Wheat Kernel to Flour
(a) The wheat grain kernel has three parts: the bran, germ, and endosperm. **(b)** Whole-wheat flour is made using the entire grain kernel. It is not enriched. **(c)** Enriched wheat flour doesn't contain the bran and germ, so it is missing nutrients and phytochemicals. Some nutrients, including folic acid, thiamin, niacin, riboflavin, and iron, are added back to the flour during an enrichment process. **(d)** Wheat flour that is not enriched lacks not only the bran and germ, but also many nutrients and phytochemicals.

TableTIPS

Ways to Enjoy Whole Grains

Choose whole-grain cereal such as shredded wheat, bran flakes, raisin bran, and oatmeal in the morning.

Combine a 100% whole-wheat English muffin and low-fat cheddar cheese for a hearty breakfast cheese melt.

Enjoy your lunchtime sandwich made with a whole-wheat pita or 100% whole-grain bread.

Try instant brown rice for a quick whole grain at dinner.

Snack on popcorn or 100% whole-wheat crackers for a high-fiber filler in the afternoon.

Fruits and Vegetables Provide Simple Sugars, Starch, and Fiber

Whole fruits, 100-percent fruit juices, and vegetables are naturally good sources of simple carbohydrates. The flesh of fruit, for example, is rich in simple sugars, including fructose and glucose. Though you can also get simple sugars from processed foods and sweets, the higher calorie and lower nutrient levels in these foods make them a less healthy option (you'll learn more about the pros and cons of natural and

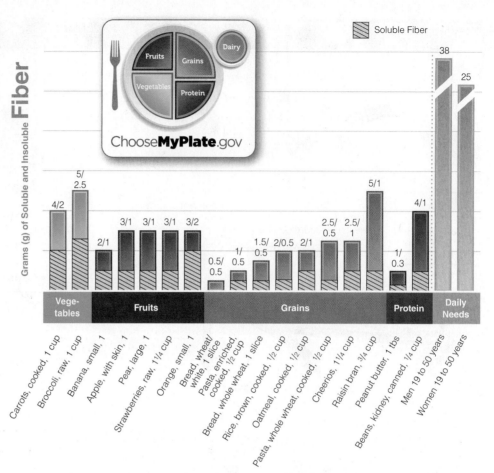

Figure 4.8 Food Sources of Fiber
Adults need to consume about 21 to 38 grams of fiber daily. Foods are a combination of soluble and insoluble fiber.

Source: Harvard University Health Services. "Fiber Content of Foods in Common Portions." 2004. Available at www.huh.harvard.edu; Tufts University School of Medicine. HIV Resources: Fiber. www.tufts.edu.

An orange has four times the fiber of six ounces of orange juice.

added sugars in the next section). The skins of many fruits contain cellulose (a type of insoluble fiber), so eat unpeeled (but cleaned and scrubbed) fruit more often. Another type of fiber, pectin (a type of soluble fiber), is found in the flesh of fruit, and makes up about 15 percent to 30 percent of the fiber in fruit. Fruit overall contains about 2 grams of dietary fiber per serving (**Figure 4.8**). When selecting fruit, choose fresh or frozen versions over canned, but if canned is your only option, choose fruit packed in fruit juice rather than heavy syrup, to cut down on added sugar.

Vegetables contain abundant amounts of complex carbohydrates, including starch and fiber. A serving of vegetables contains approximately 2 grams of fiber. In general, starchy vegetables, such as corn and potatoes, contain more carbohydrate per serving than nonstarchy vegetables like green beans or carrots.

Legumes, Nuts, and Seeds Are Excellent Sources of Carbohydrates and Fiber

Legumes, such as kidney beans and chickpeas, are rich sources of both carbohydrates and fiber. Nuts and seeds are also good sources of fiber, providing over 1 gram in a ½ ounce or small handful. A ½ ounce of nuts is about 15 peanuts, 7 walnut halves, or 24 shelled pistachios. See the High Five! Table Tips for some ways to add legumes and other fiber-rich foods to your diet.

Low-Fat and Fat-Free Dairy Products Provide Some Simple Sugars

Milk and milk products, including cheese and yogurt, contain approximately 1 to 12 grams of lactose per serving. Choose low-fat or fat-free dairy products whenever possible, for the sake of your heart health. The lactose content is the same regardless of the fat content.

Packaged Foods Can Also Provide Carbohydrates

Packaged and processed foods, such as ready-to-eat cereals, crackers, and savory snacks, can be good sources of carbohydrate, but can also contain fair amounts of added sugar, salt, and fat. When selecting these packaged foods, choose products that contain at least 2 grams of dietary fiber per serving and be aware of the amounts of added sugar, salt, fat, and total calories. Choose whole-grain cereals with lower amounts of added sugar, whole-grain crackers, and baked rather than fried snacks. The Nutrition Facts panel and ingredients listings on the product can help you to choose healthier packaged foods.

The Take-Home Message You need to consume a minimum of 130 grams of carbohydrates daily to provide adequate glucose for your brain. It is recommended that 45 to 65 percent of your daily calories come from carbohydrates. You should consume 14 grams of fiber for every 1,000 calories you eat. Whole grains, whole fruits and vegetables, legumes, and lean dairy products are the best food sources of simple carbohydrates and starch. Whole grains, fruits, vegetables, legumes, nuts, and seeds are excellent sources of fiber. Packaged foods can be good sources of carbohydrate, but the added sugars, fat, and total calories in such foods should be monitored.

Table TIPS

High Five! Five Ways to Increase Fiber Daily

Choose only whole-grain cereals for breakfast.

Eat two pieces of whole fruit daily as snacks.

Use only 100% whole-wheat bread for your lunchtime sandwich.

Layer lettuce, tomatoes, or other vegetables on your sandwich.

Eat a large salad topped with chickpeas with dinner nightly.

What's the Difference between Natural and Added Sugars?

Finding the taste of sweet foods pleasurable is an innate response. A child being fed puréed applesauce for the first time will probably show his pleasure with a big smile. You're not likely to see the same smile when Junior is eating plain oatmeal.

You don't have to fight this taste for sweetness. A modest amount of sweet foods can easily be part of a well-balanced diet. However, some sources of sugar provide more nutrition than others.

Your taste buds can't distinguish between **naturally occurring sugars**, which are found in foods such as fruit and dairy products, and **added sugars**, which are added by manufacturers to foods such as soda or candy. From a nutritional standpoint, however, there is a big difference between these sugar sources. Foods that contain naturally occurring sugar tend to be nutrient dense and thus provide more nutrition per bite. In contrast, foods that contain a lot of added sugar tend to give little else. The calories in foods with added sugars are often called **empty calories** because they provide so little nutrition.

naturally occurring sugars Sugars such as fructose and lactose that are found naturally in fruit and dairy foods.

added sugars Sugars that are added to processed foods and sweets.

empty calories Calories that come with little nutrition. Jelly beans are an example of a food that provides lots of calories from sugar but few nutrients.

Foods with Natural Sugars Usually Contain More Nutrients for Fewer Calories

Just one bite into a ripe peach, a crisp apple, or some chilled grapes will confirm that fruit can taste sweet, and not surprisingly, can contain more than 15 percent sugar by weight. There are many nutritional advantages of satisfying your sweet tooth with fruit rather than sweets with added sugar. Let's compare slices from a fresh navel orange with candy orange slices (**Figure 4.9**).

Six slices of a navel orange provides about 65 calories, more than 100 percent of the daily value for vitamin C, and 3.5 grams of fiber, which is more than 10 percent of the amount of fiber that many adults should consume daily. These juicy slices also provide fluid. In fact, more than 85 percent of the weight of the orange is water. The hefty amounts of fiber and water make whole fruits such as oranges a hearty, sweet snack that provides bulk. This bulk can increase eating satisfaction, or satiation. When you eat fruit, you not only satisfy your urge for a sweet, but you will also feel full before you overeat.

In contrast, six candy orange slices provide 300 calories of added sugar and little else. The candy is quite energy dense. It provides more than four times as many calories as the fresh orange. However, as it provides no fiber and only negligible amounts of water, it contains a concentrated amount of calories in relationship to the volume of food in the serving. You wouldn't likely feel satiated after consuming six candy orange slices. To consume close to the 300 calories found in the six pieces of candy, you would have to eat more than four oranges. It would be easier to overeat candy orange slices than fresh oranges.

Fiber-abundant whole fruits (and vegetables, for that matter) are not only very nutritious, but they are also kind to your waist, as their bulk tends to fill you up

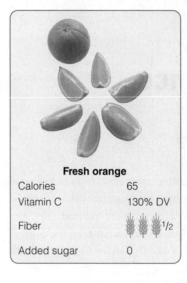
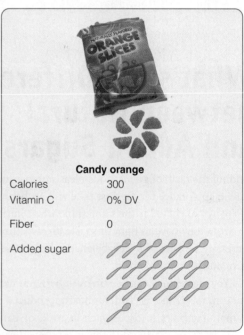

Fresh orange		Candy orange	
Calories	65	Calories	300
Vitamin C	130% DV	Vitamin C	0% DV
Fiber	🌾🌾🌾½	Fiber	0
Added sugar	0	Added sugar	

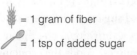

🌾 = 1 gram of fiber

🥄 = 1 tsp of added sugar

Figure 4.9 Slices of an Orange versus Orange Slices
A fresh orange provides more nutrition for fewer calories and without any added sugars compared with candy orange slices.

before they fill you out. In other words, it is more difficult to overconsume calories from fruits and vegetables because you will feel full and stop eating before you take in too many calories. In fact, eating adequate amounts of fruits and vegetables as part of a well-balanced diet is recommended to better manage your weight.[5] Substituting lower-calorie fruit for higher-calorie cake or other sweets on the dessert plate is a sweet way to cut calories.

Processed Foods and Sweets Often Contain Added Sugars

Americans have a sweet tooth. Unfortunately, our yearly consumption of added sugars is higher than it was in 1970.[6] Sugars are added to foods for many reasons. In baked goods, they can hold onto water, which helps keep the product moist and soft. They help provide a golden brown color to the finished product. Sugars function as preservatives and thickeners in foods such as sauces. Fermenting sugars in dough produce the carbon dioxide that makes yeast breads rise. And of course, sugars make foods taste sweet.

Are Added Sugars Bad for You?

Sugar has been blamed for everything from hyperactive children to diabetes, but are these claims myths or facts? Let's look at the most common claims:

- ➤ "Sugar causes hyperactivity in kids." Adults often point to sugary foods as the culprit behind the overly excited behavior of children at parties and holidays. However, research does not support the theory that sugar makes kids hyperactive.[7] The excitable behavior in the kids is more likely due to the festivities of the day rather than the sweets being consumed.
- ➤ "Eating too much sugar causes diabetes." Contrary to popular thought, sugar doesn't necessarily cause diabetes mellitus, as discussed in the Health Connection feature, "Diabetes Mellitis, A Growing Epidemic" on pages 116–120.
- ➤ "Too much sugar can contribute to dental caries." This is certainly true, but so can other sources of carbohydrates. See the Nutrition in the Real World feature, "Avoiding a Trip to the Dentist" on page 121 for information on how to prevent tooth decay.

Though these claims don't hold up, a high-sugar diet has been associated with some real health risks:

- ➤ Too much sugar in the diet can increase your blood level of triglycerides, the primary form of fat in your body. At the same time, it can lower the level of your "good" HDL cholesterol. Together, these changes may increase your risk for heart disease.[8] (This is discussed in Chapter 5.) Luckily, a reduction in dietary sugar coupled with an increase in dietary fiber can typically alleviate this problem.
- ➤ Consuming too much sugar can make weight management challenging. Eating sugar won't cause you to gain weight as long as you do not exceed the number of total calories that you need daily. However, it is easy to overeat high-calorie, sugary foods and quickly add excess calories to your diet. Added sugars are considered "empty calories" as they add calories to food but add few or no nutrients.

Lowering Your Added Sugars

Mix chocolate milk with an equal amount of regular low-fat milk.

Mix equal amounts of sweetened cereal with an unsweetened variety for a breakfast cereal with half the added sugar.

Drink water rather than soda or sweetened beverages throughout the day.

Buy sweets such as candy and cookies in individual serving sizes rather than large packages. The less you buy, the less you'll eat.

Choose canned fruit packed in juice rather than syrup.

Practical Nutrition VIDEO

Satisfy a Sweet Tooth

Hungry for something sweet? Look to nature for some of the sweetest treats around! Scan this QR code with your mobile device to access the video. You can also access the video in MasteringNutrition™.

Diabetes Mellitus, A Growing Epidemic

Diabetes mellitus, or *diabetes*, is becoming so common that it would be rare if you *didn't* know someone who has it. An estimated 25.8 million American adults—more than 8.3 percent of the population—have diabetes.[10]

> *Mellitus* is Latin for "honey-sweet," which is what the blood and urine of a person with diabetes might be, due to the increased amount of glucose.

Recall that the hormone insulin directs glucose into the cells to be used as immediate energy or stored in another form for later use. Individuals develop diabetes because they aren't producing enough insulin and/or they have developed **insulin resistance**, such that their cells do not respond to the insulin when it arrives.[11] In essence, insulin is available in the blood, but the cells' decreased sensitivity interferes with its ability to work properly. Hence, the bloodstream is flooded with glucose that can't get into the cells. In this situation, the body thinks that it must be fasting and shifts into fasting mode. The liver begins the process of breaking down its glycogen stores (glycogenolysis) and making glucose from noncarbohydrate sources (gluconeogenesis) in an attempt to provide the glucose for its cells. This floods the blood with even more glucose. Eventually, the level of glucose builds up in the blood and some of it spills over into the urine and leaves the body.

At the same time, the body has called on its energy reserve, fat, to be used as fuel. The body needs glucose in order to thoroughly burn fat; otherwise, it makes ketone bodies. In poorly managed diabetes, when glucose is unable to get into the cells, acidic ketone bodies build up in the blood to dangerous levels, causing diabetic **ketoacidosis**. Diabetic ketoacidosis can cause nausea and confusion, and in some cases, if left untreated, could result in coma or death. (Note: Although ketosis can develop in individuals who are fasting or consuming a low-carbohydrate diet, ketoacidosis only occurs when insulin is lacking in the body. Ketosis is not the same as diabetic ketoacidosis, nor is it life-threatening.)

diabetes mellitus
A medical condition whereby an individual either doesn't have enough insulin or is resistant to the insulin available, causing the blood glucose level to rise.

insulin resistance
The inability of cells to respond to insulin.

ketoacidosis The buildup of ketone bodies to dangerous levels, which can result in coma or death.

type 1 diabetes
Autoimmune form of diabetes in which the pancreas does not produce insulin.

type 2 diabetes
Form of diabetes characterized by insulin resistance.

Supreme Court Justice Sonia Sotomayor has type 1 diabetes and maintains good control by following a proper diet.

What Are the Forms of Diabetes?

All forms of diabetes involve insulin and unregulated blood glucose levels. Some are due to insulin resistance, as just described, and others are due to a lack of insulin production. Still another form occurs only during pregnancy. The most prevalent types of diabetes are type 1 and type 2 (see **Figure 1**).

Type 1 Diabetes Is an Autoimmune Disease

Type 1 diabetes is considered an *autoimmune* disease and is the rarer of the two forms. It usually begins in childhood and the early adult years and is found in about 5 to 10 percent of the individuals with diabetes in the United States.[12] The immune system of type 1 diabetics actually destroys the insulin-producing cells in the pancreas. Symptoms such as increased thirst, frequent urination, constant blurred vision, hunger, weight loss, and fatigue are common, as the glucose can't get into the cells of the body. If not treated with insulin, the person is susceptible to the dangers of ketoacidosis. Individuals with type 1 diabetes must take insulin every day in order to live a normal life.

Type 2 Diabetes Is More Common

Type 2 diabetes is the more common form of diabetes and is seen in people who have become insulin resistant. It accounts for 90 to 95 percent of diagnoses of the disease. Being overweight increases the risk of type 2 diabetes.[13] People with type 2 diabetes typically produce insulin but have become insulin resistant. After several years of exhausting their insulin-producing cells in the pancreas, their production of insulin decreases to the point where they have to take medication and/or insulin to manage their blood glucose level.

One of the major problems with type 2 diabetes is that this condition can go undiagnosed for some time. Whereas some

Diabetes is a chronic disease in which the body can no longer regulate glucose within normal limits, and blood glucose becomes dangerously high.

NORMAL

1 Liver releases glucose into bloodstream.

2 The cells of the pancreas release insulin into bloodstream.

3 Insulin stimulates uptake of glucose into cells.

4 As glucose is taken into interior of cells, less glucose remains in the bloodstream.

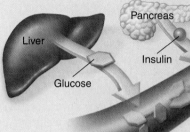
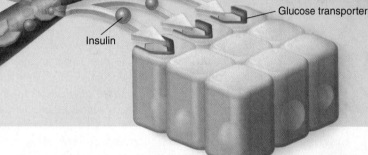

Pancreas

Liver

Insulin

Glucose

Insulin

Glucose transporter

Glucose

TYPE 1 DIABETES

1 Liver releases glucose into bloodstream.

2 The cells of the pancreas are damaged or destroyed. Little or no insulin is released into bloodstream.

3 In the absence of insulin, glucose is not taken up by cells.

4 High levels of glucose remain in the bloodstream.

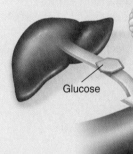

Glucose

TYPE 2 DIABETES

1 Liver releases glucose into bloodstream.

2 The cells of the pancreas release insulin into bloodstream.

3 Insulin is present, but cells fail to respond adequately. Progressively higher amounts of insulin must be produced to stimulate cells to uptake glucose.

4 High levels of glucose remain in the bloodstream.

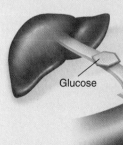

Insulin

Glucose

Insulin

CONTINUED ▶

There are many ways for an individual to monitor his or her blood glucose levels.

people may have symptoms such as increased thirst, others may not. Consequently, diabetes can silently damage a person's vital organs without his or her being aware of it. Because of this, it is recommended that everyone 45 years of age and older undergo testing for diabetes. However, if a person is at a higher risk for developing diabetes, he or she shouldn't wait until age 45 to be tested. Take the Self-Assessment to see if you are at risk.

Because the hormone insulin is derived from the components of protein, it can't be taken orally, as it would be broken down in the same manner that other protein-containing foods are digested. Therefore, most individuals who need to take insulin have to inject themselves with a syringe. Researchers are continually testing alternative ways for those with diabetes to self-administer insulin. New methods include insulin pens, insulin jet injectors, and insulin pumps. Researchers hope that someday those with diabetes will no longer have to use needles to obtain the insulin they critically need.

Prediabetes Can Be a Precursor to Type 2 Diabetes
Individuals with prediabetes have a blood glucose level that is higher than it should be but not yet high enough to be classified as diabetic. About 80 million people age 20 years and older have prediabetes and are at a higher risk of developing not only diabetes, but also other health issues such as heart disease and stroke. Unfortunately, only about seven percent of people with prediabetes know that they have it. If no changes are made in their diet and lifestyle to improve their health, it is estimated that up to 30 percent of people with prediabetes will develop full-fledged type 2 diabetes within 5 years.[14]

hypoglycemia A blood glucose level that drops to lower than 70 mg/dl. Hunger, shakiness, dizziness, perspiration, and light-headedness are some signs of hypoglycemia.

What Effects Does Diabetes Have on Your Body?

Constant exposure to high blood glucose levels can damage vital organs over time. Diabetes, especially if it is poorly managed, increases the likelihood of a multitude of dire effects, such as nerve damage, leg and foot amputations, eye diseases, including

blindness, tooth loss, gum problems, kidney disease, and heart disease.[15]

The longer the person has diabetes, the greater the risk for nerve damage. Numbness in the toes, feet, legs, and hands, as well as changes in bowel, bladder, and sexual function, are all signs of damage to nerves. This nerve damage can affect the ability to feel a change in temperature or pain in the legs and feet. A cut or sore on the foot could go unnoticed until it becomes infected. The poor blood circulation common in those with diabetes can also make it harder for sores or infections to heal. The infection could infiltrate the bone, causing the need for an amputation.

Diabetes can also damage the tiny blood vessels in the retina of the eye, which can cause bleeding and cloudy vision, and eventually destroy the retina and cause blindness. A high blood glucose level can cause tooth and gum problems, including the loss of teeth, and damage to the kidneys. If the kidneys are damaged, protein can leak out into the urine, and at the same time, cause a backup of wastes in the blood. Kidney failure could result.

Diabetes is a risk factor for heart disease. The excess amount of fat often seen in the blood in poorly managed diabetes is most probably an important factor in the increased risk of heart disease in those with diabetes. Fortunately, good nutrition habits play a key role in both the prevention and management of diabetes.

Low Blood Sugar Levels Can Also Be Dangerous
Whereas a high level of glucose in your blood on a regular basis isn't healthy, a blood glucose level that is too low, or **hypoglycemia**, can be unpleasant for many of us and downright dangerous for some with diabetes. Individuals who experience hypoglycemia may feel hungry, nervous, dizzy, light-headed, confused, weak, or shaky, and even begin to sweat. Eating or drinking carbohydrate-rich foods, such as hard candies, juice, or soda, can relieve these symptoms quickly and raise the blood glucose level to a normal range.

Those with diabetes who need to use insulin and/or blood glucose–lowering medications daily are at risk of hypoglycemia if they skip meals and snacks or if they don't eat enough to cover the effects of the medication. If these individuals ignore their symptoms, their blood glucose level can drop so low that they could faint, or slip into a coma.[16] Those with diabetes need to eat regularly to maintain blood glucose levels that coincide with their medication. A change in their activities or exercise level can also lower the blood glucose level. Diabetics need to check their blood glucose level before they exercise to determine if a snack is needed.

Though not common, people without diabetes may also experience bouts of hypoglycemia after meals, better known as reactive hypoglycemia, which may be hormone related. Another type of hypoglycemia, called fasting hypoglycemia, can occur in individuals without diabetes in the morning, after fasting throughout the night. It can also occur during long stretches between meals or after exercise.

How Is Diabetes Treated and Controlled?
For years, people with diabetes have been advised to keep their blood glucose level under control. In the early 1990s, the research

Are You at Risk for Type 2 Diabetes?

Take the following quiz to assess if you are at a higher risk for developing type 2 diabetes. Whereas this list contains the presently known risk factors for type 2 diabetes, there may be others. If you have questions or doubts, check with your doctor.

1. Do you have a body mass index (BMI) of 25 or higher*?
   Yes ☐   No ☐

2. Does your mom, dad, brother, or sister have diabetes?
   Yes ☐   No ☐

3. Do you typically get little exercise?
   Yes ☐   No ☐

4. Are you of African-American, Alaska Native, Native American, Asian-American, Hispanic-American, or Pacific Islander–American descent?
   Yes ☐   No ☐

5. Have you ever delivered a baby that weighed more than 9 pounds at birth?
   Yes ☐   No ☐

6. Have you ever had diabetes during pregnancy?
   Yes ☐   No ☐

7. Do you have a blood pressure of 140/90 millimeters of mercury (mmHg) or higher?
   Yes ☐   No ☐

8. Have you been told by your doctor that you have too much fatty triglycerides (fat) in your blood (more than 250 mg/dl) or too little of the "good" HDL cholesterol (less than 35 mg/dl)?
   Yes ☐   No ☐

9. Have you ever had blood glucose test results that were higher than normal?
   Yes ☐   No ☐

Answers

If you answered "yes" to any of the above questions, you could benefit from speaking with your doctor.

*BMI is a measure of your weight in relationship to your height. See Chapter 10 for a chart to determine your BMI.
Source: American Diabetes Association, "Risk Factors," 2013. Available at www.diabetes.org. Accessed March 2013.

---

community gathered the evidence to back up that advice. The groundbreaking Diabetes Control and Complications Trial (DCCT), conducted from 1983 to 1993, involved more than 1,400 people with type 1 diabetes. It showed that controlling the level of blood glucose with an intense regimen of diet, insulin, and exercise, along with monitoring blood sugar levels and routinely visiting health care professionals, slowed the onset of some of the complications of diabetes. In this study, it was shown that reducing high blood glucose helped lower the risk of eye disease by 76 percent and the risk of kidney and nerve disease by at least 50 percent. However, because some of the individuals in this study experienced bouts of hypoglycemia, this type of intense regimen is not recommended for children under age 13, people with heart disease or advanced complications of heart disease, older people, and those prone to frequent bouts of severe hypoglycemia.[17]

The nutrition and lifestyle goals for individuals with type 1 or type 2 diabetes are the same: to minimize the complications of diabetes by adopting a healthy, well-balanced diet and participating in regular physical activity that maintains a blood glucose level in a normal or close to normal range. The ADA recommends that individuals with diabetes meet with a registered dietitian for individualized instruction regarding weight management, diet, and lifestyle changes.[18]

Whereas monitoring the overall amount of carbohydrate within a healthy diet along with weight management are key factors in managing diabetes, the glycemic index (GI) and glycemic load (GL) may also modestly help those with diabetes, according to the ADA.[19]

The GI and GL can be used to classify the effects of carbohydrate-containing foods on blood glucose. The GI refers to the measured upward rise, peak, and eventual fall of blood glucose following the consumption of a carbohydrate-intense food. Some foods cause a sharp spike and rapid fall in blood glucose levels compared with others that cause less of a spike and a more gradual decline.[20] The index ranks high-carbohydrate foods according to their effect on blood glucose levels compared with that of an equal amount of white bread or pure glucose.

If a carbohydrate-rich food causes your blood glucose level to produce a curve with a larger area than the standard curve of white bread, the food is considered a high-GI food. A carbohydrate-containing food that produces a smaller blood glucose level curve than that of white bread would be considered a low-GI food. For example, 50 grams of white bread have a glycemic index of 100. A 50-gram portion of kidney beans has a GI of 42, whereas the same amount of puffed wheat cereal has a GI of 105. Consequently, the kidney beans are considered a low-GI food compared with the white bread, while puffed wheat is considered a high-GI food (see **Figure 2**). The problem with use of the GI is that 50 grams of puffed wheat would be more than 4 cups of cereal, an amount that is unlikely to be eaten in one sitting. The glycemic load (GL) adjusts the GI to take into account the amount of carbohydrate consumed in

CONTINUED

a typical serving of a food, and in the case of puffed wheat cereal would lower its effect on blood glucose dramatically.

Other factors can also affect the GI of a food. Overripe fruits have more easily digested sugar and a higher GI than underripe ones. Both cooking and food processing change the structure of foods and make them more easily digested, increasing the GI compared with raw, unprocessed equivalents. Larger chunks or bigger particle sizes of food contribute to slower digestion and lower GI than the same foods chopped into smaller pieces. Foods with viscous, soluble fiber tend to be absorbed more slowly, so will have a lower GI than refined carbohydrates. In general, whole grains, vegetables, whole fruit, and legumes tend to have a low GI.[21] Lastly, eating carbohydrate-heavy foods with protein and/or fat can also lower the GI.[22]

Though sugar was once thought of as a "diabetic no-no," it can now be part of a diabetic's diet. Research has found that eating sucrose doesn't cause a rise in a person's blood glucose level to any greater extent than does eating starch, so avoidance of sugar isn't necessary. Nor does eating a lot of sugar cause diabetes. However, being overweight is a risk factor for developing type 2 diabetes. And weight management is often a concern for diabetics, so there isn't room for a lot of sweets and treats in a diabetic diet (or *anyone's* diet, for that matter).

Why Is Diabetes Called an Epidemic?

The incidence of adults being diagnosed with diabetes in the United States has more than tripled since the early 1980s.[23] Our aging population is one of the reasons for this increase, as the occurrence of diabetes is about seven times as high for those 65 years of age or older as it is for younger adults aged 20 to 44 years.[24] Diabetes is the seventh leading cause of death in the United States. Diabetes is not only a deadly disease but also an extremely costly one. Disability insurance payments, time lost from employment, and the medical costs associated with diabetes cost the United States $245 billion annually.[25]

The number of people who have diabetes is not only strikingly high, but it's rising, particularly among children. Type 1 diabetes was formerly the only type of diabetes prevalent in children. Over the years, type 2 diabetes has been steadily increasing among children and adolescents in the United States.[26] Developing diabetes at a younger age means longer exposure to the disease and its medical complications.[27]

Can Type 2 Diabetes Be Prevented?

Recent research has suggested that shedding some excess weight, exercising regularly, and eating a balanced, high-fiber, healthy diet may be the best strategy to lower the risk of developing diabetes. A landmark study by the Diabetes Prevention Program of more than 3,000 individuals with prediabetes showed that those who made

The Glycemic Index of Foods

Foods	GI*
Rice, low amylose	126
Potato, baked	121
Cornflakes	119
Jelly beans	114
Green peas	107
Cheerios	106
Puffed wheat	105
Bagel, plain	103
White bread	100
Angel food cake	95
Ice cream	87
Bran muffin	85
Rice, long grain**	80
Brown rice	79
Oatmeal	79
Popcorn	79
Corn	78
Banana, overripe	74
Chocolate	70
Baked beans	69
Sponge cake	66
Pear, canned in juice	63
Custard	61
Spaghetti	59
Rice, long grain***	58
Apple	52
Pear	47
Banana, underripe	43
Kidney beans	42
Whole milk	39
Peanuts	21

*GI = Glycemic Index
**Boiled for 25 minutes.
***Boiled for 5 minutes.

Figure 2 The Glycemic Index of Commonly Eaten Foods

changes in their lifestyle, such as losing weight, exercising 2.5 hours a week, eating a plant-based, heart-healthy diet, and meeting with a health professional for ongoing support and education, were 58 percent less likely to develop type 2 diabetes than those who did not partake in such intervention.[28] When it comes to winning the battle against diabetes, a healthful diet and lifestyle is the best game plan.

Avoiding a Trip to the Dentist

Carbohydrates play a role in the formation of dental caries. Over the past few decades, the incidence of **dental caries** (tooth decay) in the United States has decreased as the use of fluoride has increased.[29] (The mineral fluoride is covered in more detail in Chapter 8.) Though things are improving in the world of dental health, an estimated 42 percent of children age 2 to 11 still have dental caries, and by the time these children reach age 19, almost 59 percent will have experienced a cavity, the later stage of dental caries. By age 64, over 90 percent of adults will have had dental caries in their permanent teeth.[30] To avoid dental caries, you need to understand the role your diet plays in tooth decay.

Sticky foods like dried fruits can adhere to teeth and promote decay.

Feeding into Dental Caries

(T/F) If you constantly eat carbohydrate-heavy foods, such as cookies, candy, and crackers, you are providing a continual buffet of easily fermentable sugars and starches to the bacteria that bathe your teeth. A study of American diets found that adults who drank sugary sodas three or more times daily had 60 percent more dental caries than those who didn't drink any soda. To make matters worse, soft drinks often contain phosphoric acid and citric acid, which can also erode teeth if consumed over a prolonged time.[31] Soft drinks are not the only beverage that may damage your teeth. Sports drinks, including energy drinks and vitamin waters, if consumed often, have been shown to be even more damaging to your teeth than soft drinks.[32]

Eating three balanced meals daily is best for minimizing tooth decay. Snacks should be kept to a minimum, and you should choose fruit or vegetables over candies or pastries. Whole fruits and raw vegetables tend not to cause tooth decay, so snack on these to your teeth's content.

Sticky foods like dried fruits, such as raisins and figs, can adhere to your teeth, so their fermentable sugars hang onto the tooth for longer periods. The longer the carbohydrate is in contact with your tooth, the more opportunity there is for the acids to do damage. Eating sticky foods in combination with other foods will discourage

their adherence to your teeth. Drinking water after you eat will help by rinsing your teeth.

Fruit juice, even unsweetened juices, may be a problem for teeth, especially in small children. A child who routinely falls asleep with a bottle in his mouth that contains carbohydrate-containing beverages is at risk for developing **early childhood tooth decay** (also called baby bottle tooth decay) because the baby's teeth are continually exposed to fermentable sugars, especially during sleep.[33] Children need adequate amounts of fluids, such as water, but they should not be given a continual supply of sweetened beverages.

Foods That Fight Dental Caries

There are actually some foods that may help reduce the risk of acid attacks on your teeth. The texture of cheese stimulates the release of cleansing saliva. Cheese is also rich in protein, calcium, and phosphorus, all of which can help buffer the acids in your mouth following a meal or snack. The calcium can also assist in **remineralization** of your teeth. Eating as little as half an ounce of cheese after a snack, or eating cheese with a meal, has been shown to protect your teeth.[34] Chewing sugarless gum can also be a healthy ending to a meal or snack if you can't brush your teeth. It encourages the production of saliva and provides a postmeal bath for your teeth. Xylitol, a sugar substitute often found

in sugarless chewing gum, may even help with remineralization.[35]

With regular visits to your dentist, good dental hygiene, and a healthy diet, you can reduce the risk of dental caries. Follow these Do's and Don'ts to keep your teeth healthy:

DO eat three solid meals daily but keep snacks to a minimum.
DON'T graze all day long!
DO snack, if necessary, on whole fruit, raw vegetables, and low-fat cheese, which tend to be friendlier to your teeth.
DON'T munch on sugary foods such as candy, cookies, and other sweets.
DO drink plenty of water.
DON'T drink a lot of sugar-sweetened beverages.
DO chew sugarless gum or eat a piece of low-fat cheese after meals and snacks when you can't brush your teeth.
DON'T think that sugarless gum and cheese can replace a routine of brushing and flossing.
DO brush your teeth at least twice a day and floss daily.
DON'T forget this!

dental caries The decay or erosion of teeth.

early childhood tooth decay The decay of baby teeth in children due to continual exposure to fermentable sugary liquids.

remineralization The repairing of teeth by adding back the minerals lost during tooth decay. Saliva can help remineralize teeth.

Finding the Added Sugars in Your Foods

While sucrose and fructose are the most common added sugars in our foods, sugars can appear on the food label under numerous different names. **Figure 4.10** includes some of the most common added sugars in foods.

Honey should never be given to children younger than one year of age, as it may contain spores of the bacterium *Clostridium botulinum*. These spores can germinate in the immature digestive tracts of babies and cause deadly botulism. Adults do not face this risk.

Over the years, honey has been publicized in the popular press as being more nutritious than table sugar. This is an exaggeration. Honey provides a negligible amount of potassium, and it actually has more calories than sugar. A teaspoon of honey contains 21 calories. The same amount of sugar provides only 16 calories. High-fructose corn syrup (HFCS), a sweetener produced from modified corn and composed of glucose and fructose, has also made media headlines because it has been blamed as a culprit in obesity. HFCS is less expensive than sucrose, and thus has replaced sucrose in some processed foods such as pastries, sweets, and soft drinks. Based on current research, the American Medical Association and other major health organizations suggest that it is unlikely that HFCS contributes more to obesity than any other sweetener in the diet.[9] See the Examining the Evidence feature "Is High-Fructose Corn Syrup Causing the Obesity Epidemic?"

a Sugar can be called a number of different names on ingredient lists and labels.

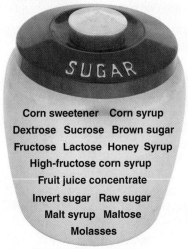

Corn sweetener   Corn syrup
Dextrose   Sucrose   Brown sugar
Fructose   Lactose   Honey   Syrup
High-fructose corn syrup
Fruit juice concentrate
Invert sugar   Raw sugar
Malt syrup   Maltose
Molasses

b You can also look on the Nutrition Facts panel to see the total grams of sugar.

Nutrition Facts

Serving Size 1 Bar (24g)
Servings Per Container 10

Amount Per Serving

Calories 90	Calories from Fat 20

	% **Daily Value***
Total Fat 2g	3%
Saturated Fat 0.5g	3%
Trans Fat 0g	
Sodium 80 mg	3%
Total Carbohydrate 19g	6%
Dietary Fiber 1g	3%
Sugars 7g	
Protein 1g	

Calcium	8%	•	Iron	4%

Not a significant source of Cholesterol, Vitamin A, Vitamin C

* Percent Daily Values are based on a 2,000 calorie diet. Your Daily Values may be higher or lower depending on your calorie needs:

	Calories:	2,000	2,500
Total Fat	Less than	65g	80g
Sat Fat	Less than	20g	25g
Cholesterol	Less than	300mg	300mg
Sodium	Less than	2,400mg	2,400mg
Total Carbohydrate		300g	375g
Dietary Fiber		25g	30g

Ingredients: Granola (whole grain rolled oats, sugar, rice flour, whole grain rolled wheat, partially hydrogenated soybean and cottonseed oils* with TBHQ and citric acid added to preserve freshness and/or sunflower oil with natural tocopherol added to preserve freshness, whole wheat flour, molasses, sodium bicarbonate, soy lecithin, caramel color, barley malt, salt, nonfat dry milk), corn syrup, crisp rice (rice, sugar, salt, barley malt), semisweet chocolate chunks (sugar, chocolate liquor, cocoa butter, soy lecithin, vanillin [an artificial flavor]), sugar, corn syrup solids, glycerin, high-fructose corn syrup, partially hydrogenated soybean and/or cottonseed oil*, sorbitol, fructose, calcium carbonate, natural and artificial flavors, salt, soy lecithin, molasses, water, BHT (a preservative), citric acid.

* Adds a dietarily insignificant amount of *trans* fat.

Figure 4.10 Finding Added Sugars on the Label
A food is likely to contain a large amount of sugar if added sugars appear first or second on the ingredients list and/or if many varieties of added sugars are listed.

Is High-Fructose Corn Syrup Causing the Obesity Epidemic?

When high-fructose corn syrup (HFCS) was first introduced, in 1970, U.S. adults consumed approximately 85 pounds of sweeteners per year, most of which was refined sugar. Since 1970, the consumption of sweeteners has risen to more than 100 pounds per year, mostly due to the increase in HFCS (27.6 pounds per individual per year in 2011).[36] At the same time that our consumption of HFCS has increased, obesity rates among Americans have also skyrocketed.[37] Is this a coincidence or is HFCS to blame?

What Is High-Fructose Corn Syrup?

HFCS is a sweetener produced from modified corn and composed of glucose and fructose. Because glucose and fructose are in a "free" state, the syrup is stable and easy to handle in food processing—a plus for manufacturers. HFCS is less expensive than sucrose, which is probably the reason HFCS has replaced sucrose as the most common sweetener in processed foods, including baked goods, sweets, and soft drinks. In baked products, HFCS gives cookies and snacks their chewy, soft texture, and makes bread brown better. HFCS inhibits the growth of microbes by reducing the availability

of water and thus improves freshness and extends the shelf life of many food products. It's no wonder that HFCS is estimated to represent the highest percentage—more than 40 percent—of added sugar in the food supply.[38] The question is, has our increased consumption of this particular sweetener led to our expanded waistlines?

Does HFCS Consumption Lead to Weight Gain?

Two theories have been proposed to explain the possible connection between weight gain and the increased consumption of HFCS. One theory suggests that HFCS is sweeter than sucrose, resulting in an increased consumption of calories.[39] A second theory posits that the increase in HFCS means an increase in fructose consumption, which may stimulate appetite and alter insulin metabolism.[40] Research exploring both of these theories has yielded some interesting results.

HFCS Is Not Sweeter than Sugar

Monosaccharides and disaccharides vary in their level of sweetness. Fructose is the sweetest monosaccharide, and sucrose,

because of its high fructose content, is the sweetest of the disaccharides.

Sucrose contains 50 percent glucose and 50 percent fructose—one molecule of glucose for every molecule of fructose. HFCS comes in two different forms: HFCS-42 and HFCS-55. HFCS-42 is 42 percent fructose and 58 percent glucose. This version is used in bakery products, jams and jellies, canned fruit, and dairy products. HFCS-55 is 55 percent fructose and 45 percent glucose and is used to sweeten beverages, including soft drinks and sweetened teas. Essentially, HFCS has the same composition as sucrose. Thus, despite its name, HFCS is not dramatically higher in fructose than sucrose and therefore is not any sweeter than sucrose.

HFCS May Impact Satiation

Some researchers have suggested that HFCS may change our appetite control mechanisms, resulting in less satiation and a greater intake of calories. This theory is based on earlier studies conducted with pure crystalline fructose (not HFCS), which reported that fructose ingestion resulted in a decrease in the hormones insulin and leptin. Both of these hormones increase satiety. Fructose does not increase insulin levels because it does not depend on insulin to enter the liver cell. Whereas glucose stimulates satiety, fructose does not.

This is significant in that insulin stimulates the release of leptin, a hormone that decreases appetite.[41] These two hormones also suppress the release of ghrelin, another hormone that stimulates our appetite. If insulin is reduced, then leptin is reduced and ghrelin is not suppressed, which leads to feeling hungry and eating more calories. Thus, if pure fructose reduces the release of appetite-suppressing hormones, then does high-fructose corn syrup increase appetite?

Based on research, the answer is no, because HFCS does not cause the same reaction as pure fructose does in the body. Remember, HFCS is approximately 50 percent fructose and 50 percent glucose. If HFCS did increase appetite, research subjects would report a decrease in satiety and an increase in calorie intake compared with

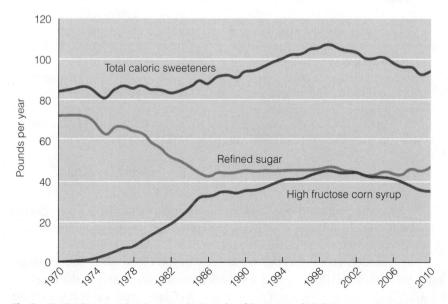

The Per Capita Consumption Patterns, in Pounds, of Sucrose and High-Fructose Corn Syrup

Data from the U.S. Department of Agriculture, Economic Research Service, Table 51—Refined Cane and Beet Sugar: Estimated Number of Per Capita Calories Consumed Daily, by Calendar Year; Table 52—High-Fructose Corn Syrup: Estimated Number of Per Capita Calories Consumed Daily, by Calendar Year; Table 53—Other Sweeteners: Estimated Number of Per Capita Calories Consumed Daily, by Calendar Year. *Sugars and Sweeteners Yearbook*, 2011.

CONTINUED ▶

otherwise sweetened drinks. A recent study showed no significant differences in hunger or satiety ratings, or in the amount of calories eaten at a later meal, when subjects drank a beverage sweetened with HFCS, low-fat milk, or orange juice.[42] Nor did a beverage with HFCS increase the amount of food eaten later in the day when compared with a beverage containing sucrose.[43]

How Does the Body Metabolize HFCS?

Because HFCS contains fructose and glucose, the metabolism of this sweetener is generally the same as the metabolism of each individual monosaccharide.

As soon as it is absorbed, fructose is transported to the liver where it is metabolized. During metabolism, fructose can be converted to intermediate substrates used by the liver for energy production or used as the starter molecules for fat synthesis. Because fructose metabolism in the liver is almost entirely used for glycogen or fat synthesis, when intake of fructose is very high, there is a *potential* that the liver may accumulate higher than normal levels of stored fat and increase the formation of lipoproteins in the blood, leading to increased risk of cardiovascular disease.[44] However, remember that HFCS is not 100% fructose, but rather it contains both fructose and glucose. Thus, when HFCS is consumed, the liver is not overloaded with pure fructose. The glucose in the sweetener appears to have a tempering effect on the metabolism of fructose in the liver. The glucose itself can be utilized by the liver for energy or glycogenesis or contribute to the blood

glucose levels.[45] The current evidence suggests that HFCS and sucrose are metabolized in a similar way once the monosaccharides have been absorbed.[46]

Different Sweeteners and Insulin Production

Whether the sweetener is sucrose or HFCS, they both trigger an insulin response. Pure glucose stimulates the greatest release of insulin; pure fructose stimulates the least. Because HFCS and sucrose contain approximately the same ratio of glucose to fructose, they trigger a similar, intermediate release of insulin. Fructose is generally eaten as part of a food, such as fruit, or as part of a sweetener, such as sucrose or HFCS. The composition of the entire meal, rather than just the type of monosaccharide, also affects the release of insulin in the body.

The Bottom Line: Does HFCS Cause Obesity?

Currently, there is no evidence that HFCS consumption contributes more to obesity than do other sweeteners or energy sources.[47] In fact, obesity has increased sharply in countries where beverage consumption is lower than in the United States and HFCS is not a common sweetener.[48] One expert review of the research literature on the dietary role of HFCS found insufficient support for the theory that HFCS could play a role in obesity. The report states that there are many other "plausible explanations for rising overweight and obesity rates" in the United States, including a reduction in smoking, a decrease in physical activity, including reduced physical education programs in schools, an increase in technology,

which leads to more sedentary activities, and watching television, for the rise in obesity rates.[49]

Although HFCS may not be the main culprit in the dramatic rise in obesity, it likely does play a role in Americans' overall increased caloric intake, including from energy-dense sweets, snacks, and baked goods, which contain more calories than nutrient-dense fruits and vegetables. The DRIs recommend reducing all refined sugars, regardless of whether the sweetener is fructose, sucrose, or HFCS.

What Do You Think?

1. What do you think about the current evidence to blame high-fructose corn syrup for the rise in obesity among Americans?
2. Should food manufacturers should stop using high-fructose corn syrup in their products? Why or why not?
3. What roles does the overall consumption of energy-dense sweets such as baked goods play in the current high level of obesity seen among Americans?

To find the amount and type of added sugars in the foods that you eat, read the ingredients on the food label. If added sugars appear first or second on the list or if the product contains many varieties of added sugars, it is likely to be high in sugar.

The Nutrition Facts panel that is currently used on food labels doesn't distinguish between naturally occurring and added sugars. For example, the nutrition labels on ready-to-eat cereals such as raisin bran and dairy products such as milk list 21 grams of sugars for raisin bran and 12 grams for low-fat milk. This can be misleading, as the grams of sugars listed for the raisin bran cereal include both the amount of naturally occurring sugars from the raisins and the sugars added to sweeten the cereal. For the milk, the sugar listed on the Nutrition Facts panel is just the naturally

Table 4.2

Sugar Smacked!

Food Groups	Teaspoons of Added Sugar
Bread, Cereal, Rice, Pasta	
Bread, 1 slice	0
Cookies, 2 medium	🥄 (1)
Doughnut, 1 medium	🥄 (1)
Cereal, sweetened flakes	🥄🥄🥄 (3)
Cake, frosted, 1/16 average	🥄🥄🥄🥄 (4)
Pie, fruit, 2 crust, 1/6, 8" pie	🥄🥄🥄🥄🥄 (5)
Fruit	
Fruit, canned in juice, ½ cup	0
Fruit, canned in heavy syrup, ½ cup	🥄🥄🥄 (3)
Milk, Yogurt, and Cheese	
Milk, 1% fat, 1 cup	0
Chocolate milk, 2% fat, 1 cup	🥄🥄🥄 (3)
Yogurt, low fat, plain, 8 oz	0
Yogurt, fruit, sweetened, 8 oz	🥄🥄🥄🥄🥄🥄 (6)
Chocolate shake, 10 fl oz	🥄🥄🥄🥄🥄🥄 (6)
Other	
Energy drink, 8 oz	🥄🥄🥄🥄🥄🥄 (6)
Chocolate bar, 2 oz	🥄🥄🥄🥄🥄 (5)
Fruit drink, ade, 12 fl oz	🥄🥄🥄🥄🥄🥄🥄🥄🥄🥄 (10)

🥄 = 1 teaspoon of sugar

Source: USDA, *Dietary Guidelines for Americans,* 5th ed. (Home and Garden Bulletin No. 232, 2000); Manufacturers' labels.

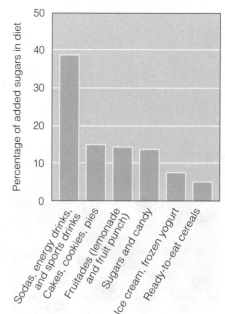

Figure 4.11 Where Are All These Added Sugars Coming From?
Sodas, energy drinks, and sports drinks are the number-one source of added sugars in American diets. Desserts, candy, fruit drinks, and some grains are also sources of added sugars.

Source: *Dietary Guidelines for Americans, 2010.*

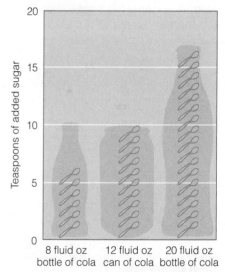

Figure 4.12 The Many Sizes of Soft Drinks
A bottle or can of soda can provide from 6 to 17 teaspoons of added sugars, depending on the size of the container.

occurring sugar, lactose. With the growing concern about the rising levels of added sugars in the diets of Americans, various health professionals and organizations have pressured the FDA to require that all *added* sugars be disclosed on the food label. A final decision by the FDA is pending.

As you know, added sugars come from many sources and are found in many products. In fact, most Americans don't eat the majority of the added sugars in their diets—they drink them. The number-one source of added sugars in the United States is sweetened sodas, energy drinks, and sports drinks (**Figure 4.11**). This fact isn't too surprising when you look at the size of the sweetened beverages that Americans consume. A classic 8-ounce bottle of cola provides approximately 6 teaspoons of added sugars. In today's vending machine, you are more likely to find a 12-ounce can or a 20-ounce bottle. People typically consume the entire can or bottle, regardless of its size, so they consume more sugar (**Figure 4.12**). In addition to beverages, added sugars are hidden in many other foods (**Table 4.2**).

> A super-large soda at the movie theater can be as large as 64 ounces! This giant beverage contains more than 800 calories and 50-plus teaspoons of added sugars.

How Much Added Sugar Is Too Much?

The DRI recommends that added sugars make up no more than 25 percent of your daily calories, but the *Dietary Guidelines for Americans, 2010* suggest that no more than 5 to 15 percent of your daily calories come from a combination of added sugars *and* solid fats. As mentioned, Americans, on average, consume 16 percent of their daily calories from added sugars alone![10] Many Americans, especially women, sedentary individuals, and older adults who have lower daily calorie needs, would benefit from reducing the amount of added sugars in their diet. These individuals need to make sure that they are getting a substantial amount of nutrition from each bite of food. Eating excess amounts of foods with added sugars such as soda can displace more-nutritious food choices, such as skim milk, in the diet.[11]

Concerned with the prevalence of obesity in Americans, the American Heart Association has recommended women consume no more than 100 calories (6 teaspoons) of added sugar daily and that men consume no more than 150 calories (10 teaspoons) of added sugar daily.[12] American adults consume approximately 21 teaspoons of added sugars daily.[13] Eating this much added sugar can have a major impact on daily nutrition and is one of the many reasons Americans are overweight.

The Take-Home Message Your taste buds can't distinguish between naturally occurring and added sugars. Foods with naturally occurring sugars, such as whole fruit, tend to provide more nutrition and satiation than empty-calorie sweets such as candy. Sugar can contribute to dental caries, an elevated level of fat in your blood, and a lowering of the "good" HDL cholesterol. Foods with added sugars may displace more nutritious foods and quickly add excess calories to your diet. The current recommendation is to lower consumption of added sugars in the diet, as they are considered empty calories.

What Are Sugar Substitutes and What Forms Can They Take?

Because eating too much sugar can be unhealthy, what's a person with a sweet tooth to do? Americans have looked to sugar-free beverages and foods over the years to limit their sugar intake while satisfying their yen for sugar (**Figure 4.13**). Such items

Practical Nutrition VIDEO

How Much Hidden Sugar Is in Soda?

Do you like to drink soda? Let Joan show you how much sugar you are consuming with each gulp. Scan this QR code with your mobile device to access the video. You can also access the video in MasteringNutrition™.

Figure 4.13 Growing Interest in Sugar-Free Foods and Beverages
The use of sugar-free products has more than doubled since 1986.

Source: Calorie Control Council, "Trends and Statistics," 2012. www.caloriecontrol.org.

Millions of adult Americans consuming sugar-free products

Year	Value
1986	78
1991	101
1996	151
2004	180
2010	187

Table 4.3

Oh So Sweet!

Sweetener	Calories/Gram	Trade Names	Sweetening Power	The Facts
Sucrose	4	Table Sugar	—	Sweetens food, enhances flavor, tenderizes, and contributes browning properties to baked goods
Reduced-Calorie Sweeteners				
Sorbitol	2.6	Sorbitol	50–70% as sweet as sucrose	Found in foods such as sugarless chewing gum, jams, baked goods, and candy. May cause diarrhea when 50 grams (about 15 sugar-free candies) are consumed.
Mannitol	1.6	Mannitol	50–70% as sweet as sucrose	Found in foods such as chewing gum, jams, and as a bulking agent in powdered foods. Excessive amounts may cause diarrhea.
Xylitol	2.4	Xylitol	Equally sweet as sucrose	Found in foods such as chewing gum, candies; also in pharmaceuticals and hygiene products
Hydrogenated Starch Hydrolysates (HSH)	3.0	HSH	50–70% as sweet as sucrose	Found in confections and can be used as a bulking agent
Tagalose	1.5	Naturlose	92% as sweet as sucrose	Texture and taste similar to sucrose
Calorie-Free Sweeteners				
Saccharin	0	Sweet'N Low	200–700% the sweetness of sucrose	Retains its sweetening power at high temperatures such as baking
Aspartame	4*	Nutrasweet, Equal	Approximately 200% the sweetness of sucrose	Sweetening power is reduced at high temperatures such as baking. Can be added at end stages of recipes such as cooked puddings if removed from heat source. Individuals with PKU need to monitor all dietary sources of phenylalanine, including aspartame.
Neotame	0	Neotame	7,000–13,000% the sweetness of sucrose	Retains its sweetening power at high temperatures
Acesulfame-K	0	Sunette	200% the sweetness of sucrose	Retains its sweetening power at high temperatures
Sucralose	0	Splenda	600% the sweetness of sucrose	Retains its sweetening power at high temperatures
Rebaudioside A	0	Truvia, PureVia	200% the sweetness of sucrose	Retains its sweetening power at high temperatures
Monk fruit	0	Nectresse	150–300% the sweetness of sucrose	May have an aftertaste

*Since so little aspartame is needed to sweeten foods, it provides negligible calories.

contain **sugar substitutes** that are as sweet as—or sweeter than—sugar but contain fewer calories.

All sugar substitutes must be approved by the FDA and deemed safe for consumption before they are allowed in food products sold in the United States.[14] Several sugar substitutes are presently available to consumers, such as polyols, tagalose, saccharin, aspartame, acesulfame-K, sucralose, rebaudioside A, and neotame. Polyols don't promote dental caries and cause a slower rise in blood glucose than sugar does. Saccharin, aspartame, acesulfame-K, sucralose, rebaudioside A, tagalose, and neotame also won't promote dental caries and have the added advantage of not affecting blood glucose levels. All these sugar substitutes are either reduced in calories or are calorie free. See Table 4.3 for a comparison of available sweeteners.

sugar substitutes Alternatives to table sugar that sweeten foods for fewer calories.

Polyols Are Sugar Alcohols

Polyols are often called sugar alcohols because they have the chemical structure of sugar with an alcohol component added. Whereas polyols such as sorbitol, mannitol, and xylitol are found naturally in plants, they are also produced synthetically and are used as sweeteners in foods such as chewing gum and candies. They can be used tablespoon for tablespoon to substitute for sucrose. Sorbitol and mannitol are also less likely to promote dental caries because the bacteria on your teeth metabolize them so slowly. (Humans lack the enzyme needed to ferment xylitol.) Their slower absorption means that they do not produce a spike in blood glucose, which is a benefit for those with diabetes.

Chewing gums and candies that contain sugar alcohols can be labeled "sugar free" and boast that they don't promote tooth decay. Keep in mind, though, that even though these products are sugar free, they are not necessarily calorie free. Even more importantly, because polyols are incompletely absorbed in your digestive tract, they can cause diarrhea. For this reason, they should be used in moderation. Ⓣ Ⓕ

Another type of polyol is hydrogenated starch hydrolysates (HSH), which are made by partially breaking down corn, wheat, or potato starch into smaller pieces and then adding hydrogen to these pieces. The end product is a wide range of polyols, including those that can be strung together and used commercially. HSH adds sweetness, texture, and bulk to many sugarless products such as baked goods and candies.[15]

Tagalose is about 90 percent as sweet as sucrose and contains fewer calories per gram (see Table 4.3). It is derived from lactose that can be found naturally in some dairy products.

Saccharin Is the Oldest Sugar Substitute

Saccharin was first discovered in 1879, and during the two World Wars, when sugar was being rationed, it was used as a sugar substitute in the United States and Europe. Today, you probably know saccharin as those little pink packets often found on coffee shop counters or diner tables. It has been used in foods, beverages, vitamins, and pharmaceuticals. Because saccharin is not metabolized in your body, it doesn't provide any calories.

In 1977, the FDA banned saccharin due to reports from the research community that it could cause bladder cancer in rats. Congress immediately implemented an 18-month moratorium on this ban through the Saccharin Study and Labeling Act. This allowed the continued commercial use of saccharin, but required that any saccharin-containing products bear a warning label stating that saccharin was potentially hazardous to your health, as it caused cancer in laboratory animals.

In 2000, the National Toxicology Program (NTP) removed Ⓣ Ⓕ saccharin from the list of substances that could potentially cause cancer. After extensive review, the NTP determined that the observed bladder tumors in rats were actually from a mechanism that wasn't relevant to humans.[16] The lesson learned from this is that though you can safely consume saccharin in moderation, you shouldn't feed it to your pet rat. Saccharin is used in more than 100 countries in the world today.

A variety of sugar substitutes is available to the consumer.

Aspartame Is Derived from Amino Acids

In 1965, a scientist named James Schlatter was conducting research on amino acids in his quest to find a treatment for ulcers. To pick up a piece of paper in his laboratory, he licked his finger and stumbled upon a sweet-tasting compound.[17] It was the "lick" that was soon to be "tasted" around the world. Schlatter had just discovered aspartame, a substance that would change the world of sugar substitutes.

Aspartame is composed of two amino acids: a modified aspartic acid and phenylalanine. Enzymes in your digestive tract break down aspartame into its components, and the amino acids are absorbed, providing 4 calories per gram. Consequently, aspartame has the potential to provide calories to foods as an added sweetener. However, as aspartame is 200 times sweeter than sucrose, only a small amount is needed to sweeten a food.

In 1981, the FDA approved aspartame for use in tabletop sweeteners such as Equal and Nutrasweet, and for various other uses, such as to sweeten breakfast cereals, chewing gums, and carbonated beverages. The majority of the aspartame that is consumed in the United States is in soft drinks. In 1996, the FDA gave the food industry carte blanche to use aspartame in all types of foods and beverages. It is currently used as a sweetener in more than 100 countries, and can now be found in more than 6,000 foods, as well as pharmaceuticals and personal care products, sold in the United States.

Aspartame has undergone continual, vigorous reviews to ensure that it is safe for human consumption. The FDA considers it one of the most thoroughly studied and tested food additives approved by the agency. It is not associated with any adverse effects in the general population, including children.[18]

Individuals with a rare, inherited disorder known as phenylketonuria (PKU) are unable to metabolize one of the amino acids in aspartame, phenylalanine, and must adhere to a special diet.[19] PKU affects about 1 out of every 10,000 to 15,000 infants in the United States. While PKU can happen to anyone, it is more common in those who are Native American and Northern European.[20] It is the result of a deficiency of phenylalanine hydroxylase, an enzyme needed to properly metabolize phenylalanine.[21]

People with PKU need to control all dietary sources of this amino acid, including aspartame as well as protein-rich foods such as meat, milk, eggs, and nuts. These individuals do not necessarily have to avoid aspartame, but they need to monitor it as an additional source of phenylalanine in their diet. Because of the seriousness of this disorder, the FDA mandates that all food products that contain phenylalanine carry a label declaring its content.

Foods and beverages that contain aspartame must carry a warning label that says phenylalanine is present.

> Substituting sweeteners for sugar isn't shaving off the pounds. Although the consumption of low-calorie sweeteners has tripled since 1980, the prevalence of overweight and obese Americans has increased by 60 percent.

Neotame Is Also Made from Amino Acids

Neotame, which the FDA approved in 2002, comprises the same two amino acids—aspartic acid and phenylalanine—as aspartame, but they are joined together in such a way that the body cannot break them apart. So, individuals with PKU can use neotame without concern. Neotame is completely eliminated in either the urine or stool. It has been approved as a sweetener and for a variety of uses, such as chewing gum, frostings, frozen desserts, puddings, fruit juices, and syrups.[22]

Acesulfame-K Contains Potassium

While less than sweet sounding, acesulfame-K (the K refers to the potassium component) is about twice as sweet as sucrose. It is available as a tabletop sweetener, called

Sunette, and is currently used in chewing gum, candy, desserts, yogurt, and alcoholic beverages. Your body does not metabolize acesulfame-K.

Sucralose Is Made from Sucrose

Sucralose was developed in 1976 by slightly changing the structure of the sucrose molecule. Unlike sucrose, sucralose isn't absorbed by your body—it is excreted in your urine. In 1998, sucralose was approved as a tabletop sweetener, and it's available commercially as Splenda.

Rebaudioside A Is Derived from the Stevia Plant

Rebaudioside A is a combination of a sugar alcohol with an extract from the stevia plant. Extracts from the stevia plant, which is native to Brazil and Paraguay, are currently used in Brazil and Japan as tabletop sweeteners and in some products, such as teas and yogurt. This zero-calorie sweetener is approximately twice as sweet as sugar and is available under trade names such as Truvia, Sun Crystals, and PureVia. It doesn't affect blood glucose levels, so those with diabetes can use it.

Monk Fruit Is the Newest Sugar Substitute

A new addition to the world of sugar substitutes is the extract of the luo han guo fruit, commonly called monk fruit. The name came from the Buddhist monks who discovered the fruit centuries ago. It is up to 150 to 300 percent the sweetness of sucrose but can have a lingering aftertaste when consumed in large amounts. It can be found in both foods and beverages.

The Take-Home Message Millions of Americans consume reduced-calorie or calorie-free sugar substitutes. The FDA has approved polyols, tagalose, saccharin, aspartame, acesulfame-K, sucralose, neotame, rebaudioside A, and monk fruit to be used in a variety of foods. These sugar substitutes do not promote dental caries and can benefit those with diabetes who are trying to manage their blood glucose.

Why Is Fiber So Important?

Even though fiber is a nondigestible substance that is resistant to being broken down in your small intestine, it can have many powerful health effects in your body. Fiber has been shown to help lower your risk of developing constipation, diverticulosis, obesity, heart disease, cancer, and diabetes mellitus (Table 4.4). Let's look closely at how this works.

Fiber Helps Prevent Constipation and Diverticulosis

More than 4 million Americans complain about being constipated, with women, especially pregnant women and adults 65 years of age and older, experiencing it more

Table 4.4

Type-Casting Fiber

Type	Found in	Can Help Reduce the Risk of
Insoluble Fiber		
Cellulose Hemicellulose Lignins	Whole grains, whole-grain cereals, bran, oats, fruit, and vegetables	Constipation Diverticulosis Certain cancers Heart disease Obesity
Soluble, Viscous Fibers		
Pectin Beta-glucan Gums Psyllium	Citrus fruits, prunes, legumes, oats, barley, brussels sprouts, carrots	Constipation Heart disease Diabetes mellitus Obesity

often than others. The uncomfortable, bloated, and sluggish feelings of constipation compel Americans to spend approximately $725 million each year on laxative products.[23] Because a diet lacking sufficient high-fiber whole grains, fruits, and vegetables and abounding in cheese, eggs, and meats is a recipe for constipation, many people would be better off spending time in the produce and whole-grain aisles of the supermarket rather than shopping for laxatives.

As remnants of food move through your colon, water is absorbed, which causes the formation of solid waste products (stool). The contractions of the muscles in your colon push the stool toward your rectum to be eliminated. If these muscle contractions are sluggish, the stool may linger too long in your colon, which can cause too much water to be reabsorbed. This can create hard, dry stools that are more difficult and painful to expel. A diet adequate in insoluble fibers such as bran, whole grains, and many fruits and vegetables will help keep things moving along in your digestive tract and decrease your likelihood of becoming constipated. (Note: Some soluble fibers, such as psyllium, can also be an aid in relieving constipation, as its water-attracting capability allows the stool to increase in bulk and form a gel-like, soft texture, which makes it easier to pass.)

Constipation can become more frequent during different stages of your life. During pregnancy, hormonal changes as well as the pressure of the growing baby on the intestine can make regular bowel movements more difficult. As you age, your metabolism slows, which results in a slower-moving digestive tract as well as loss of intestinal muscle tone. Unfortunately, abusing laxatives can damage the nerve cells in the colon and disrupt the colon's natural movements. This can cause you to depend on laxatives in order to bring on a normal bowel movement.[24]

Long-term constipation can lead to a disorder called **diverticulosis** (*osis* = condition). Constipation is the main cause of increased pressure in the colon and may cause the weak spots along your colon wall to bulge out, forming **diverticula** (**Figure 4.14**).

Infection of the diverticula, a condition known as **diverticulitis** (*itis* = inflammation), can lead to stomach pain, fever, nausea, vomiting, cramping, and chills. Though not proven, it is believed that the stool and its bacteria in the colon may get stuck in the diverticula and cause the infection in approximately 50 percent of Americans over age 60.[25] The disorder is more common in developed countries, such as the United States and England, and is rarely found in areas where high-fiber diets are more commonplace, such as Asia and Africa. Consuming a diet with

diverticulosis The existence of diverticula in the lining of the intestine.

diverticula Small bulges at weak spots in the colon wall.

diverticulitis Infection of the diverticula.

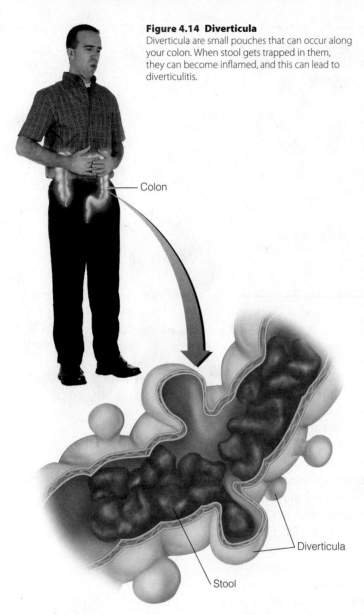

Figure 4.14 Diverticula
Diverticula are small pouches that can occur along your colon. When stool gets trapped in them, they can become inflamed, and this can lead to diverticulitis.

Colon

Diverticula

Stool

adequate fiber may reduce the symptoms associated with diverticulosis. The best way to prevent diverticulosis is to eat a diet that is generous in fiber to avoid constipation and to keep things moving through your system.

Fiber Helps Prevent Obesity

A fiber-rich diet can also be kind to your waistline. As mentioned earlier, high-fiber foods, such as whole grains, fruits, and vegetables, can add to satiation so that you need to eat fewer calories to feel full. Research studies suggest that this can aid in weight management.[26] Whereas some weight-loss diets restrict carbohydrates, these plans would work better if they *increased* high-fiber carbohydrates.

Fiber Helps Prevent Heart Disease, Diabetes, and Cancer

Viscous, soluble fibers have been shown to help lower elevated blood cholesterol levels. A high blood cholesterol level can increase the risk of heart disease. It is believed that viscous fiber interferes with the reabsorption of bile acids in the intestines. Bile acids are high in cholesterol and are released into your intestine by your gallbladder to help with the digestion of fat. The bile acids are likely "grabbed" by the fiber before they can be reabsorbed by the body. They then end up being excreted along with the fiber in your waste products. Your body replaces these lost bile acids by removing cholesterol from the blood to generate new bile acids in the liver. Blood cholesterol levels are lowered as a result.

Slow-moving, viscous, soluble fibers may reduce the rate at which fat and carbohydrates are absorbed from your meals. Delayed absorption can lower the surge of fat in your blood after a meal, and may help improve sensitivity to the hormone insulin. Both high levels of fat in the blood and a decreased sensitivity to insulin are considered risk factors for heart disease.

Viscous, soluble fiber may not be the only type of fiber that can promote heart health. Several research studies have shown that cereal and grains, which contain insoluble fiber, may help to lower the risk of heart disease.[27] Fiber from cereal has been associated with a reduction in blood pressure.[28] High blood pressure is a risk factor for both heart disease and stroke.

Viscous, soluble fibers have also been shown to help individuals with diabetes mellitus. They slow the release of food from your stomach, and thus slow down the digestion and absorption of glucose. This could help avoid a large spike in blood glucose after eating and help those with diabetes improve the long-term control of their blood glucose level.[29] Fiber may also play a role in preventing diabetes. Research suggests that diets that provide 30 to 50 grams of fiber from food sources daily can help lower blood glucose levels, reducing the risk of diabetes.[30]

Fiber is thought to have many positive and protective effects in the fight against certain cancers. Fiber from cereals has been shown to help lower the risk of breast cancer.[31] Research also suggests that as fiber consumption increases, the incidence of colorectal cancer is reduced.

Four mechanisms may account for fiber's role in fighting cancer:

➤ Fiber increases the bulk of stool, which can dilute cancer-promoting substances in the colon.

➤ Fiber helps keep things moving through the digestive tract so that potential cancer-promoting substances spend less time in contact with the intestinal lining.

➤ Fiber encourages the growth of friendly bacteria in the colon and their fermentation by-products, both of which may have cancer-fighting potential.

➤ Fiber binds with acids in bile, a substance produced by the liver and important in fat breakdown. This causes the acids to be expelled from the body in the stool, rather than being reabsorbed. Because an increased amount of bile acids in the colon is thought to be associated with colon and rectal cancer, fiber's ability to reduce the concentration of these acids is viewed as a cancer deterrent.[32]

Whole fruits and vegetables, whole grains, and legumes are the best food sources of fiber.

While over the years, some studies have challenged fiber's protective role against colorectal cancer, current research supports the cancer-fighting potential of fiber.[33] A large research study involving over 500,000 individuals recruited from 10 European countries showed that individuals who consumed the most fiber (35 grams of fiber daily, on average), compared with those eating the least amount of fiber daily (15 grams, on average), reduced their risk of colorectal cancer by about 40 percent.[34] The dietary sources of fiber were varied among the countries and included fiber from cereal, vegetables, fruits, and legumes. Because this large study was done with high-fiber foods and not fiber supplements, it is difficult to tease out if the potential cancer-fighting substance in these foods is only the fiber, or the other nutrients and phytochemicals in these plant-based foods operating in concert with the fiber.

Once again, the best advice is to eat a varied, balanced, plant-based diet rich in whole grains, fruits, vegetables, and legumes. This type of diet is also good for weight management. Obesity increases the risk of colorectal cancer.[35]

Too Much Fiber Can Cause Health Problems

A word of caution: Initially, a high-fiber diet can have negative side effects (flatulence and bloating). Consuming too much fiber can reduce the absorption of some vitamins and minerals and may cause diarrhea in some individuals.[36] Gradually increasing the fiber in your diet, rather than suddenly adding large amounts, will allow your body to adjust to the increased amount of fiber and minimize the side effects. A small, steady increase of fiber will be easier on your colon and on those around you. As you add more fiber to your diet, you should also drink more fluids.

The Take-Home Message Fiber is a nondigestible substance that can help reduce the risk of constipation, diverticulosis, heart disease, obesity, diabetes mellitus, and certain cancers. Increasing fiber intake too quickly can cause diarrhea, constipation, and gassiness, so consumption should be increased gradually and be accompanied by plenty of fluids.

MADE over MADE better

Americans, on average, are consuming only about half of the amount of fiber recommended daily. Making some easy food substitutions can quickly bump up your daily fiber intake. Here are some typical foods made over and made nutritionally better!

If you like this. . .	Try this to boost your fiber intake!

Special K cereal
Serving size: 1 cup
Total Fiber: 1 gram

Wheaties cereal
Serving size: 1 cup
Total Fiber: 4 grams

Cheez-It
Serving size: 27 crackers
Total Fiber: 1 gram

Triscuit
Serving size: 6 crackers
Total Fiber: 3 grams

White bread
Serving size: 2 slices
Total Fiber: 1.2 grams

100% Whole-wheat bread
Serving size: 2 slices
Total Fiber: 8 grams

Pretzels
Serving size: 10 pretzels
Total Fiber: 0.9 grams

Popcorn
Serving size: 100-calorie
microwave popcorn bag
Total Fiber: 4 grams

Source: USDA National Nutrient Database for Standard Reference, www.nal.usda.gov/fnic; manufacturers.

Should the Government Ban Certain Soda Sizes? In the spring of 2013 the mayor of New York City, Michael Bloomberg, put forth a measure to ban the sale of soft drink servings larger than 16 ounces. The measure failed, but the discussion about soft drink sizes, and whether they ought to be regulated by the government, continues. Do you think the government should ban certain soft drink sizes? Read the arguments, consider the critical-thinking questions, and decide for yourself.

yes

- This public health measure is beneficial because it could lower rates of diabetes and other diseases. One study suggests that drinking a 12-ounce soft drink daily can increase diabetes risk by 22 percent.[1] Another study associated the amount of soft drink consumption with an increased chance of asthma and/or COPD.[2]

- Larger portions not only provide more calories, but the large size of the container encourages people to drink more than is needed to quench their thirst.[3] A ban would reduce this effect.

- A recent study suggests that the soda ban would directly affect those who need it most—overweight people—with less impact on those in poverty.[4]

- Under current pricing strategies the more soda you buy, the cheaper each individual ounce, and consumers perceive that a larger soda is a better value than a small soda. This encourages consumers to buy more soda. A ban on larger sizes could reduce this problem.

no

- People ought to be allowed to decide for themselves. The government is overreaching into people's lives, and this law is "paternalistic."[5]

- Banning sizes of soda won't stop people from buying more soda—they could just buy two 16-ounce sodas.

- Government regulation could be unfair and discriminatory. In the case of New York City, supersizes were banned at restaurants, but the legislation did not apply to supermarkets or convenience stores.[6]

- A soda ban could backfire. A study has shown that selling soda in smaller packages prompts consumers to buy more servings, and drink more soda overall. Trying to limit soda consumption may cause consumers to drink more soda in defiance.[7]

- A government ban on soda sizes would cut into profit margins for soda sellers. The profit margin increases for the seller as the container gets bigger, because the cost of the large container and additional soda compared with a normal size is relatively small, yet sellers can charge more for the supersized soda.

what do you think?

1. Do you support the idea of banning certain soda sizes? **2.** Are you more likely to buy the amount of soda you want to drink right away, or do you go for the cheaper-per-ounce option and say to yourself that you'll save the rest of the bottle for later? **3.** Should the government discourage people from drinking sugary beverages, and if so, how should it go about doing so?

1 Carbohydrates Are Energy-Containing Nutrients

Carbohydrates are essential nutrients that are predominant in plant-based foods, and they make up the foundation of many diets around the world. You need carbohydrates on a daily basis because they are the most desirable source of energy for your body. Carbohydrates are divided into two categories or classifications based on the number of sugar units that are joined together. Simple carbohydrates, or sugars, include monosaccharides and disaccharides, and complex carbohydrates include polysaccharides.

Three monosaccharides are found in foods: glucose, fructose, and galactose. When two glucose units join together, the disaccharide maltose is created. When glucose and fructose pair up, the disaccharide sucrose, or table sugar, is formed. Galactose is joined with glucose to create lactose.

Starch, glycogen, and fiber are all polysaccharides. Starch is the storage form of glucose in plants, and glycogen is the storage form in your body. Fiber is nondigestible but important.

Monosaccharides

Fructose   Glucose   Galactose

Disaccharides

Sucrose (glucose and fructose)   Maltose (glucose and glucose)   Lactose (glucose and galactose)

Polysaccharides (starch)

Amylose (straight chain)

Amylopectin (branched)

2 Carbohydrates Are Digested in Your Mouth and Intestines

Although the digestion of carbohydrates starts in your mouth with the help of the enzyme amylase, which is in your saliva, most carbohydrate digestion occurs in the small intestine, facilitated by pancreatic amylase. Sucrose, maltose, and lactose are digested by small intestine enzymes into glucose, fructose, and galactose. Fiber continues down to the large intestine, where the majority of it is eliminated from your body in your stool.

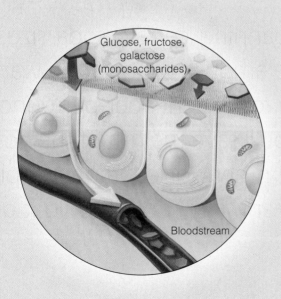

Glucose, fructose, galactose (monosaccharides)

Bloodstream

3 Hormones Help the Body Regulate Glucose

Your body uses carbohydrates, specifically glucose, for energy. To lower your blood glucose level, your pancreas releases the hormone insulin into the blood. Insulin helps direct the uptake of glucose by cells and also determines whether it will be used immediately as energy or stored for later use. Surplus glucose is stored in long chains of glycogen in a process called glycogenesis, which occurs only in your liver and muscle cells. Once glycogen stores are full, excess glucose is stored as fat. Your pancreas releases another hormone, glucagon, when the body needs to direct the release of glucose from the stored glycogen in your liver to help raise your blood glucose level. This breakdown of glycogen is called glycogenolysis.

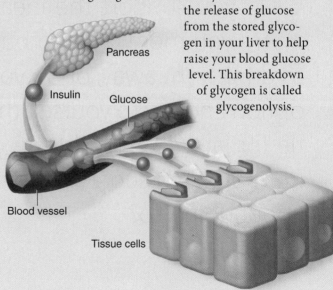

Pancreas

Insulin   Glucose

Blood vessel

Tissue cells

4 You Need to Consume Carbohydrates Daily

The latest Dietary Reference Intakes (DRIs) for carbohydrates recommend that adults and children consume a minimum of 130 grams daily. This is based on the estimated minimum amount of glucose your brain needs to function efficiently. A quick look at MyPlate shows that 130 grams is

less than the amount you would consume by eating the minimum recommended daily servings from the grain group (6 servings), vegetable group (3 servings), fruit group (2 servings), and dairy group (3 servings). The latest DRIs indicate that 45 to 65 percent of your total daily calories should come from carbohydrates. Adults should consume 21 to 38 grams of fiber daily and minimize their intake of added sugars.

5 There Is a Difference between Natural and Added Sugars

Your taste buds can't distinguish between naturally occurring sugars, which are found in foods such as fruit and dairy products, and added sugars, which are added by manufacturers to foods such as soft drinks. Foods that contain naturally occurring sugar tend to be nutrient dense and thus provide more nutrition per bite. In contrast, foods that contain a lot of added sugars tend to give little else. These sugar-laden foods are called empty calories.

6 Diabetes Is Considered an Epidemic

Individuals develop diabetes because they aren't producing enough insulin (type 1 diabetes) and/or they have developed insulin resistance, such that their cells do not respond to the insulin when it arrives (type 2 diabetes). Type 1 diabetes is an autoimmune disease and is the rarer of the two forms. Type 2 is the more common form and is seen in people who have become insulin resistant. Type 2 diabetes accounts for 90 to 95 percent of diagnoses of the disease.

Diabetes, especially if it is poorly managed, increases the likelihood of a multitude of dire effects such as nerve damage, leg and foot amputations, tooth loss, gum problems, kidney disease, and heart disease. Diabetes can also damage the tiny blood vessels in the retina of the eye, which can cause bleeding and cloudy vision, and eventually destroy the retina and cause blindness. Good nutrition and lifestyle habits play a key role in both the prevention and management of diabetes.

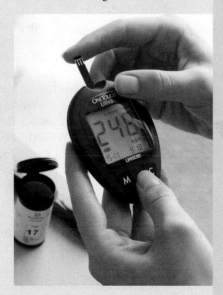

7 There Are Many Forms of Sugar Substitutes

Polyols, saccharin, aspartame, acesulfame-K, sucralose, rebaudioside A, tagalose, neotame, and monk fruit are all sugar substitutes currently deemed safe by the FDA. Americans are expressing a growing interest in sugar-free foods and beverages.

8 Fiber Has Many Health Benefits

Fiber has been shown to help lower your risk of developing constipation, diverticulosis, obesity, heart disease, cancer, and diabetes mellitus. Meals high in fiber are typically digested more slowly, which allows the absorption of the nutrients to be extended over a longer period of time. Foods high in fiber, such as whole grains, fruits, and vegetables, can add to satiation so that you need to eat fewer calories to feel full. Viscous, soluble fibers have been shown to help lower elevated blood cholesterol levels. A high blood cholesterol level can increase the risk of heart disease.

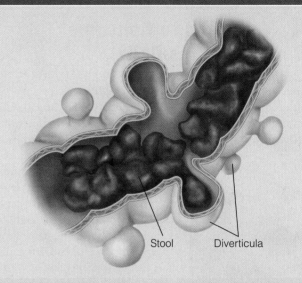

Stool Diverticula

Terms to Know

- glucose
- photosynthesis
- simple carbohydrates
- monosaccharides
- disaccharides
- complex carbohydrates
- polysaccharides
- fructose
- galactose
- maltose
- sucrose
- starch
- fiber
- glycogen
- hormones
- insulin
- glycogenesis
- glucagon
- glycogenolysis
- diabetes
- insulin resistance

MasteringNutrition™

Build your knowledge—and confidence—in the Study Area of MasteringNutrition with a variety of study tools.

Check Your Understanding

1. _____ is the storage form of glucose in your body.
   a. Glucagon
   b. Glycogen
   c. Gluconeogenesis
   d. Glucose

2. Sucrose is a
   a. monosaccharide.
   b. disaccharide.
   c. polysaccharide.
   d. starch.

3. The hormone that directs the breakdown of glycogen is
   a. galactose.
   b. glucagon.
   c. insulin.
   d. epinephrine.

4. The minimum amount of carbohydrates needed daily is
   a. 75 grams.
   b. 100 grams.
   c. 120 grams.
   d. 130 grams.

5. Which of the following can help someone who's lactose intolerant to enjoy dairy products?
   a. drinking Lactaid milk
   b. drinking milk on an empty stomach
   c. eating a large bowl of ice cream before going to bed
   d. having a milkshake for an afternoon snack

6. Reducing consumption of which item would have the biggest impact on decreasing the amount of added sugars that Americans consume?
   a. watermelon
   b. candy
   c. soda
   d. apples

7. Your blood cholesterol level is too high, so you would like to eat additional viscous, soluble high-fiber foods to help lower it. A good choice would be
   a. low-fat milk.
   b. chocolate chip cookies.
   c. orange juice.
   d. oatmeal.

8. Which of the following nutrients are added to enriched grains?
   a. folic acid, thiamin, B_{12}, niacin, and calcium
   b. folic acid, thiamin, riboflavin, B_{12}, and iron
   c. fiber, thiamin, riboflavin, niacin, and iron
   d. folic acid, thiamin, riboflavin, niacin, and iron

9. The small bulging pouches that are sometimes found along the intestinal lining are called
   a. diverticulosis.
   b. diverticulitis.
   c. diverticula.
   d. diabetes.

10. Which of the following can help reduce your risk of type 2 diabetes?
    a. playing computer games
    b. eating a high-fiber, plant-based diet
    c. watching TV
    d. eating a high-calorie, high-fat diet

Answers

1. (b) glycogen. Glycogen is stored in your liver and muscles and provides a ready-to-use form of glucose for your body. Glucagon is the hormone that directs the release of glucose from the stored glycogen. Gluconeogenesis is the creation of glucose from noncarbohydrate sources.

2. (b) Sucrose contains the two monosaccharides glucose and fructose, and is therefore a disaccharide. Starch contains many units of glucose linked together and is therefore a polysaccharide.

3. (b) When your blood glucose level drops too low, glucagon is released from your pancreas to direct the breakdown of glycogen in your liver to raise your blood level of glucose. Insulin is a hormone that directs the uptake of glucose by your cells. Galactose is a monosaccharide found in dairy foods.

4. (d) You should consume at least 130 grams of carbohydrates daily to supply your body, particularly your brain, with the glucose needed to function effectively.

5. (a) The Lactaid milk is pretreated to facilitate the breakdown of the lactose in the milk. Drinking milk on an empty stomach, eating a large bowl of ice cream before going to bed, and having a milkshake for an afternoon snack are all ways to consume a fair amount of lactose at one time and increase the symptoms of lactose intolerance.

6. (c) Sodas are the number-one source of added sugars in the American diet, so reducing the intake of these sugary beverages would go a long way in reducing the amount of added sugars that Americans consume. Reducing the amount of candy that Americans consume would also help reduce the added sugars in the diet but not as much as cutting back on soda. Watermelon and apples contain naturally occurring sugars.

7. (d) Oatmeal is rich in beta-glucan, a viscous fiber that can help lower your cholesterol when eaten as part of a heart-healthy diet. Though nutrient dense, the orange juice and milk do not contain fiber. Cookies won't help lower your cholesterol.

8. (d) These nutrients are added to enriched grains.

9. (c) Diverticula are a condition of diverticulosis. When these pouches become inflamed, diverticulitis occurs. Diabetes is a chronic disease that results from poor regulation of blood glucose.

10. (b) Unfortunately, if you want to try to prevent diabetes, playing sedentary computer games, watching TV, and eating a high-calorie, high-fat diet aren't healthy approaches. However, eating a high-fiber, plant-based diet, getting regular exercise, and maintaining a healthy weight are all part of the best approach, at present, to help reduce your risk of developing type 2 diabetes.

Web Resources

- For more on fiber, visit the American Heart Association at www.heart.org
- For more on diabetes, visit the National Diabetes Education Program (NDEP) at www.ndep.nih.gov
- For more on lactose intolerance, visit the National Institute of Diabetes and Digestive and Kidney Disease (NIDDK) at http://digestive.niddk.nih.gov

1. **False.** Many people who are lactose intolerant may still be able to enjoy some dairy products, especially if they are eaten with meals. In fact, dairy foods may be just what the doctor ordered. Turn to page 104 to learn why.

2. **True.** You need a *minimum* amount of carbohydrates daily to fuel your brain. See page 108 to find out how much you need to eat.

3. **True.** The average American consumes about half the amount of fiber that's recommended daily. Turn to page 109 to learn more about the potential problems associated with this shortfall.

4. **False.** Dark bread doesn't necessarily have more fiber than white bread. Learn why on page 110.

5. **False.** Calories, not carbs, are what you need to monitor to avoid weight gain. Turn to page 115 to find out why.

6. **False.** Eating sugar will not cause diabetes. Turn to page 120 to learn more.

7. **True.** The more sugar you eat, the more likely you are to have tooth decay. Turn to page 121 to find out why this is the case.

8. **False.** High fructose corn syrup doesn't automatically lead to weight gain. To find out why, turn to page 124.

9. **False.** Foods that contain sugar alcohols, such as sorbitol or other sugar substitutes can be labeled "sugar free," but they still provide calories. Turn to page 128 to learn more.

10. **False.** Though saccharin once bore the stigma of being a cancer causer, it's no longer thought to cause cancer in humans. Turn to page 128 to learn more about this turnaround.

Fats, Oils, and Other Lipids

hen you go shopping, what is on your grocery list? If you're like many Americans, you probably have the best intentions of filling your grocery cart with low-fat, nonfat, or cholesterol-free items to eat a more healthful diet. Even just saying the words *fat* or *cholesterol* brings up negative images of foods that we should avoid. The truth is, a small amount of dietary fat is essential to the body.

In this chapter, we will discuss the structure and functions of the different types of lipids, how they are handled in the body, and the amounts of each that should be consumed in a healthy diet. We will also explore the role of high-fat foods in the development of cardiovascular disease and other health conditions.

What Are Fats and Why Do You Need Them?

When you see the word *fat*, you may think of butter, mayonnaise, the cholesterol in meats and eggs, and even the fatty tissues in your own body. But technically speaking, these aren't all fats. Instead, they're examples of a broader category of substances known as **lipids**—compounds that contain carbon, oxygen, and hydrogen and which are **hydrophobic** (*hydro* = water, *phobic* = fearing), meaning they don't dissolve in water. If you were to drop lipids, such as butter or olive oil, into a glass of water, you would see them rise to the top and sit on the water's surface. This repelling of water enables lipids to play a unique role in foods and in your body.

To answer our original question, *fat* is the common name for just one type of lipid, known as a triglyceride. Because this is the type of lipid found most abundantly in foods, food labels and nutrition sources refer generally to this category as dietary *fat*—not dietary *lipid*—so fat is the term we'll use in this chapter.

Fats Serve Multiple Functions in Foods and in Your Body

Fats perform a variety of functions in cooking. They give a flaky texture to pie crusts and other baked goods, and they make meat tender and soups and puddings creamy. The flavors and aromas that fats provide can make your mouth water as you eye crispy fried chicken or smell baking cookies. Foods that are higher in fats contribute to satiety, that feeling of fullness you experience after eating.

In your body, fats are essential for energy storage and insulation. Two other types of lipids are also important as components of the membranes surrounding your cells and play a key role in transporting proteins in your blood.

The three types of lipids found in foods and in your body are triglycerides (*fats*), phospholipids, and sterols. Two of the three, triglycerides and phospholipids, are built from a basic unit called a fatty acid. So let's start our discussion of the structure of lipids with the fatty acids.

Fatty Acids Are Found in Triglycerides and Phospholipids

All **fatty acids** (**Figure 5.1**) consist of a chain of carbon and hydrogen atoms, with an acid group (COOH) at one end. There are more than 20 different fatty acids.

They can vary by (1) the length of the chain, (2) whether the carbons have a single or a double bond between them (C—C or C=C), and (3) the total number of double bonds. The way and where carbon bonds occur in different types of fatty acids is what makes some fatty acids healthier than others.

There are three main types of fatty acids:

➤ *Saturated fatty acids.* When each carbon in a fatty acid chain is bonded with two atoms of hydrogen, as we saw in Figure 5.1, the chain is considered *saturated* with hydrogen. It cannot hold any more. We therefore call such a fatty acid a **saturated fatty acid**. For example, stearic acid is a saturated fatty acid (**Figure 5.2a**). It has 18 carbons, all of which are bound, or saturated, with

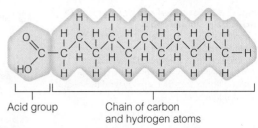

Acid group | Chain of carbon and hydrogen atoms

Figure 5.1 Structure of a Fatty Acid
Fatty acids are the building blocks of some lipids.

Figure 5.2 Saturated and Unsaturated Fatty Acids
Fatty acids differ by the length of the fatty acid chain, whether or not there are double bonds between the carbons, and (if there are double bonds) how many double bonds they contain.

a Stearic acid, a saturated fatty acid

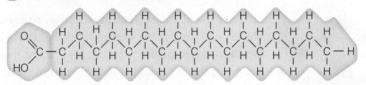

b Oleic acid, a monounsaturated fatty acid

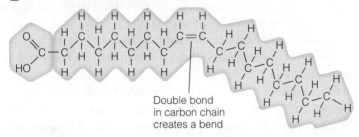

Double bond in carbon chain creates a bend

c Linoleic acid, a polyunsaturated, omega-6 fatty acid

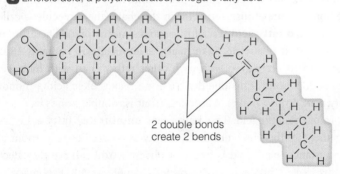

2 double bonds create 2 bends

d Alpha-linolenic acid, a polyunsaturated, omega-3 fatty acid

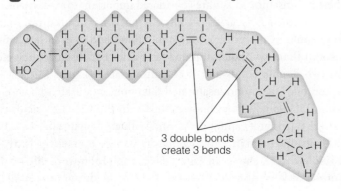

3 double bonds create 3 bends

lipids A category of carbon, hydrogen, and oxygen compounds that are insoluble in water.

hydrophobic Having an aversion to water.

fatty acid The basic unit of triglycerides and phospholipids.

saturated fatty acid A fatty acid that has all of its carbons bound with hydrogen.

Figure 5.3 Saturated and Unsaturated Fatty Acids Help Shape Foods
Saturated fatty acids are able to pack tightly together and are solid at room temperature. The double bonds in unsaturated fatty acids cause kinks in their shape and prevent them from packing tightly together, so they tend to be liquid at room temperature.

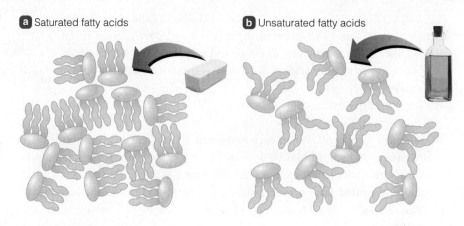

a Saturated fatty acids   **b** Unsaturated fatty acids

Cocoa butter melts at body temperature. This is why solid milk chocolate melts in your mouth.

saturated fats Fats that contain mostly saturated fatty acids.

monounsaturated fatty acid (MUFA) A fatty acid that has one double bond.

unsaturated fatty acid A fatty acid that has one or more double bonds between carbons.

unsaturated fats Fats that contain mostly unsaturated fatty acids.

polyunsaturated fatty acid (PUFA) A fatty acid with two or more double bonds.

essential fatty acids The two polyunsaturated fatty acids that the body cannot make and therefore must be eaten in foods: linoleic acid and alpha-linolenic acid.

linoleic acid A polyunsaturated essential fatty acid; part of the omega-6 fatty acid family.

alpha-linolenic acid A polyunsaturated essential fatty acid; part of the omega-3 fatty acid family.

hydrogen. Long fatty acids, such as stearic acid, are strongly attracted to one another, and are relatively straight, so they are able to pack tightly together in food, and thus become solid fats at room temperature. Stearic acid can be found in cocoa butter (in chocolate) and in the fatty part of meat. Shorter saturated fatty acids (with fewer than 12 carbons) have a weaker attraction to one another, and so do not pack tightly together. Because of this, foods that contain them are liquid at room temperature. Whole milk contains short-chain saturated fatty acids. Fats made up of mostly saturated fatty acids are called **saturated fats**. As you will learn later on in the chapter, saturated fats and other solid fats should be minimized in the diet, as they are not healthy for your heart.

➤ *Monounsaturated fatty acids (MUFAs).* Take a look at the fatty acid shown in Figure 5.2b. Do you notice that, at one place in the chain, two carbons are each bound to only one atom of hydrogen, and are joined twice to each other? This double carbon bond means that the carbons are not "saturated" with hydrogen atoms at that point in the chain. This makes the chain unsaturated. When a double bond occurs at just one point in the chain, the molecule is called a **monounsaturated fatty acid** (recall that *mono-* means one). The example shown in Figure 5.2b is oleic acid. Like stearic acid, oleic acid contains 18 carbons, but two of them are paired with each other rather than with hydrogen, so it has one double bond. This one double bond makes oleic acid a monounsaturated fatty acid. It also makes it crooked. That is, double bonds cause a kink in the chain of the fatty acid. This kink keeps **unsaturated fatty acids** from packing together tightly. Thus, unsaturated fatty acids are liquid at room temperature. For instance, oleic acid is found in olive oil. You can see the effect of straight versus kinked fatty acid chains on foods in **Figure 5.3**. Fats made up of mostly unsaturated fatty acids are called **unsaturated fats**. Whereas saturated fats are unhealthy, unsaturated fats are considered important to your health.

➤ *Polyunsaturated fatty acids (PUFAs).* A **polyunsaturated fatty acid** (*poly* = many) contains more than one double bond and is even less saturated with hydrogen than a monounsaturated fatty acid. For instance, linoleic acid contains two double bonds and is polyunsaturated (Figure 5.2c). It is found in soybean oil. Like monounsaturated fats, polyunsaturated fats are considered healthy. Incidentally, your body can make most of the fatty acids it needs, but there are two that it cannot make, and both are polyunsaturated. Because you must consume them in your diet, they're known as **essential fatty acids**. They are **linoleic acid**, shown in Figure 5.2c, and **alpha-linolenic acid**, shown in Figure 5.2d. We'll discuss these essential fatty acids in more detail later.

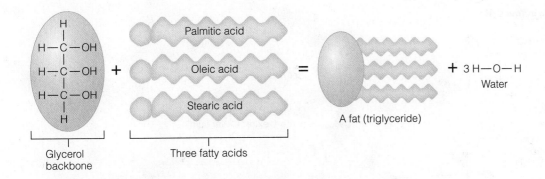

Triglycerides Contain Three Fatty Acid Chains

Triglycerides are the most common lipids found in foods and in your body. Each **triglyceride** compound is made up of three fatty acid chains (*tri* = three) connected to a **glycerol** "backbone." Glycerol is a compound containing carbon, hydrogen, and a type of alcohol. The three fatty acids join to the glycerol backbone to form the triglyceride (**Figure 5.4**). Any triglyceride can contain a variety of different fatty acids.

The more common name for triglycerides is **fat**, and this is the term we'll use throughout this chapter and the rest of the book. Most of the lipids that you eat and that are in your body are in the form of fat. Many fatty foods, such as butter, lard, and the fat in meats, are solid at room temperature so are often referred to as solid fats. **Oils** are fats that are liquid at room temperature.

Phospholipids Contain Phosphate

Like fats, **phospholipids** contain a glycerol backbone, but instead of being made up of three fatty acids, they contain two fatty acids and a phosphate group (a compound containing the mineral phosphorus) (**Figure 5.5**). The portion where the phosphate is attached to the glycerol is referred to as the head, which is *hydrophilic* (*philic* = loving), so it is able to attract water. In contrast, phospholipids' fatty acid tails are hydrophobic.

Phospholipids make up the phospholipid bilayer in cell membranes. Their water-loving heads face outward to the watery areas both outside and inside your cells, and their fat-loving tails line up with each other in the center, creating a phospholipid

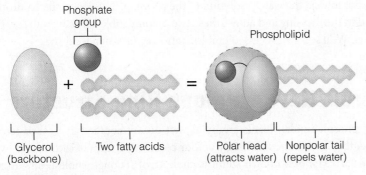

Figure 5.5 Structure of a Phospholipid
Phospholipids are similar to triglycerides but they have only two fatty acids and a phosphate group connected to the glycerol backbone. This configuration allows phospholipids, such as lecithin, to be attracted to both water and fat.

triglyceride Three fatty acids that are attached to a glycerol backbone.

glycerol The three-carbon backbone of a triglyceride.

fat The common name for triglycerides.

oils Fats that are liquid at room temperature.

phospholipids Lipids made up of two fatty acids and a phosphate group attached to a glycerol backbone.

Figure 5.6 Phospholipids' Role in Your Cell Membranes

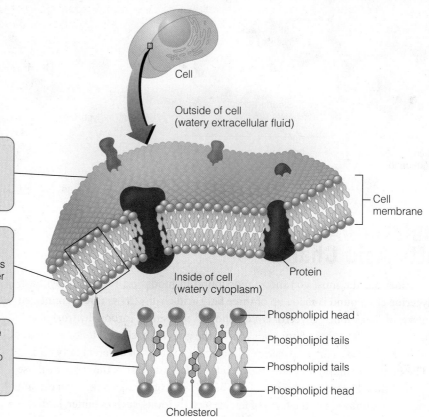

1 Because the phosphorus-containing head is polar, it attracts charged particles, such as water located both outside and inside your cells.

2 Its fatty acid–containing tail is nonpolar, so it mingles and lines up with other nonpolar molecules such as the fatty acid–containing ends of other phospholipids.

3 This creates a two-layer membrane that surrounds the cell and acts as a barrier, allowing certain substances to enter the cell but keeping others from leaving.

Cell

Outside of cell (watery extracellular fluid)

Cell membrane

Inside of cell (watery cytoplasm)

Protein

Phospholipid head
Phospholipid tails
Phospholipid tails
Phospholipid head

Cholesterol

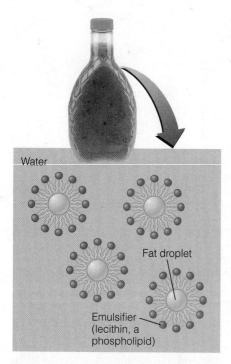

Water

Fat droplet

Emulsifier (lecithin, a phospholipid)

Figure 5.7 Keeping a Salad Dressing Blended
To prevent the fat from separating out in a salad dressing, an emulsifier is added. The emulsifier's fat-attracting tails surround the droplets of fat, whereas the water-attracting heads remain oriented toward the watery portion of the solution or dressing. This allows the fat droplet to stay suspended and blended in the dressing.

membrane that surrounds the cell and acts as a barrier (**Figure 5.6**). The cell membrane allows certain substances, such as water, to enter the cell but keeps others, like protein, from leaking out. You can visualize this phospholipid layer as being like a picket fence, acting as a barrier surrounding each cell.

The major phospholipid in your cell membranes is lecithin. Even though lecithin plays an important role in your body, you don't have to worry about eating large amounts of lecithin in foods. As with all phospholipids, your body is able to make all the lecithin it needs. Because of its unique water- and fat-loving attributes, lecithin is used in many foods as an **emulsifier**, which helps keep incompatible substances, such as water and oil, mixed together. For example, an emulsifier is sometimes added to commercially made salad dressings to prevent the fat from separating and rising to the top of the dressing (**Figure 5.7**). The emulsifier's nonpolar, fat-attracting tail surrounds the droplets of fat, which orients the polar, water-attracting head of the emulsifier toward the watery solution of the dressing. This keeps the fat droplet suspended in the dressing and allows these two incompatible substances to stay blended together. We'll see the process of emulsification again when we discuss how the body uses fat.

Sterols Have a Unique Ring Structure

Unlike phospholipids, **sterols** are lipids that do not contain glycerol or fatty acids. Instead, they are composed mainly of four connecting rings of carbon and hydrogen (**Figure 5.8**). The best known sterol is cholesterol. Though cholesterol's association with heart disease has blemished its reputation, it plays an important role in your cell membranes and is the **precursor** of some very important compounds in your body. As with lecithin, don't be concerned about meeting your daily need for this

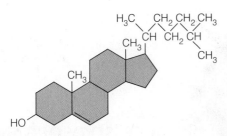

Figure 5.8 Structure of a Sterol
Rather than being made from fatty acids attached to a glycerol backbone, sterols have a carbon ring configuration with hydrogens and an oxygen attached. Cholesterol is the best-known sterol.

Lipid	Structure		Examples
Triglycerides	Glycerol	Fatty acids	Saturated fat Unsaturated fat *Trans* fat
Phospholipids	Phosphate head	Fatty acids	Lecithin
Sterols	HO		Cholesterol

Figure 5.9 Three Types of Lipids
The three types of lipids vary in structure. Triglycerides and phospholipids are built from fatty acids, whereas sterols are composed of carbon rings.

important substance through your diet, since your body manufactures all the cholesterol you need. **Figure 5.9** summarizes the structures of the three types of lipids.

The Take-Home Message Lipids are hydrophobic compounds made up of carbon, hydrogen, and oxygen. The three types of lipids are triglycerides, phospholipids, and sterols. Fatty acids, which consist of a carbon and hydrogen chain and an alcohol group, are the basic structural units of triglycerides and phospholipids. Triglycerides are formed from three fatty acids connected to a glycerol backbone and are the most prevalent lipids in your food and body. Phospholipids are made of two fatty acids and a phosphate-containing group attached to a glycerol backbone. Phospholipids are an important part of the structure of cell membranes. Cholesterol is an important sterol in your cell membranes and is the precursor to other essential compounds.

What Happens to the Fat You Eat?

As with all nutrients, the digestion of fat begins in your mouth (see **Figure 5.10** on page 148). Chewing mechanically breaks down the food—in this case, a slice of pizza. The enzyme lingual lipase in the mouth plays a minor role in breaking down some fat. Once food is swallowed, the stomach begins to breaks down fat further. Let's follow the fat in the cheese pizza through the rest of the GI tract.

You Digest Most Fat in Your Stomach and Small Intestine

In the stomach, fat mixes with gastric lipase, an enzyme that breaks down some of it into a fatty acid and a **diglyceride** (the remnant of fat digestion when only two fatty acids are left joined to the glycerol backbone). The majority of fat digestion occurs in your small intestine, where an enzyme released from your pancreas, pancreatic lipase, continues to break down the fat into two fatty acids and a **monoglyceride** (the remnant of fat digestion when only one fatty acid is left joined to the glycerol backbone).

Just as oil and water don't mix, fat can't mix with the watery fluids in your digestive tract. The fat globules tend to cluster together rather than disperse throughout

emulsifier A compound that keeps two incompatible substances, such as oil and water, mixed together.

sterol A lipid that contains four connecting rings of carbon and hydrogen.

precursor A substance that is converted into or leads to the formation of another substance.

diglyceride A glycerol with only two attached fatty acids.

monoglyceride A glycerol with only one attached fatty acid.

Most fat digestion occurs in the small intestine with the aid of bile and lipase enzymes. The absorbed digestive by-products are transported via chylomicrons into the lymphatic system.

ORGANS OF THE GI TRACT

MOUTH

Chewing begins the mechanical digestion of food. Solid fat melts with the warmth of the body. Lingual lipase in the saliva begins the chemical digestion of fats.

STOMACH

Peristalsis mixes and churns the fat-containing food with gastric juices. Gastric lipase breaks down some fats, creating diglycerides and free fatty acids.

SMALL INTESTINE

Bile secreted from the gallbladder through the common bile duct into the small intestine emulsifies fat into smaller globules.

Pancreatic lipase breaks down fats into monoglycerides, glycerol, and free fatty acids.

The by-products of fat digestion are packaged into micelles for transport through the cells of the intestinal wall.

As they are absorbed, the micelles separate into their component parts. Short-chain fatty acids enter the bloodstream directly. Long-chain fatty acids, cholesterol, phospholipids, and other remnants are repackaged into chylomicrons for transport into the lymphatic system.

ACCESSORY ORGANS

LIVER

Produces bile, which is stored in the gallbladder.

GALLBLADDER

Realeases bile into the small intestine through the common bile duct.

PANCREAS

Produces pancreatic lipase, which is secreted into the small intestine via the pancreatic duct.

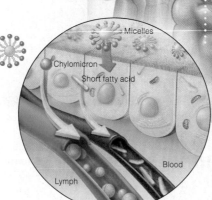

Micelles

Chylomicron

Short fatty acid

Blood

Lymph

the fluids. Mixing fats with watery fluids requires the addition of **bile**, which is made in your liver and stored in your gallbladder. When the fat from the pizza arrives in your intestines, your gallbladder releases bile. Bile contains bile acids that help to emulsify the fat into smaller globules within the watery digestive solution. This keeps the smaller fat globules dispersed throughout the fluids, and provides more surface area so that the pancreatic lipase can more easily break down the fat.

Monoglycerides and fatty acids are next packaged with lecithin, which is in the bile, and other substances to create **micelles** (small transport carriers). Once close to the mucosa of your small intestine, micelles travel into your intestinal cells.

The length of the fatty acid chain determines what happens next. Short-chain fatty acids will enter your bloodstream and go directly to your liver. The long-chain fatty acids can't enter your bloodstream directly. They enter your **lymph** and need transport carriers.

Lipoproteins Transport Fat through the Lymph and Blood

Long-chain fatty acids are reformulated into a fat within the cells of your intestinal wall as they are absorbed. These reformulated fats (as well as other lipids, such as cholesterol) are not soluble in your watery blood. They need to be packaged inside protein-containing carriers called **lipoproteins**. These capsule-shaped fat "carriers" have an outer shell high in protein and phospholipids and an inner compartment that carries the insoluble fat, as well as cholesterol, through your lymph and bloodstream. One example of a lipoprotein carrier that transports these lipids is a **chylomicron** (**Figure 5.11**).

Chylomicrons are too large to be absorbed directly into your bloodstream, so they travel through your lymph system first and then enter your blood. Once in the blood, the fat is broken down into fatty acids and glycerol with the help of the enzyme lipoprotein lipase, which is located in the walls of the capillaries. After the fat is removed from the chylomicrons, the remnants of these lipoproteins go to your liver to be dismantled.

The liver produces other lipoproteins with different roles in your body:

➤ **Very-low-density lipoprotein (VLDL)**
➤ **Low-density lipoprotein (LDL)**
➤ **High-density lipoprotein (HDL)**

Although all lipoproteins contain fat, phospholipids, cholesterol, and protein, the proportion of the protein in these substances differs in the various types. Protein is denser than fat, so the proportion of protein in the lipoproteins determines their overall density (see **Figure 5.12** on page 150).

For example, VLDLs are composed mostly of triglycerides and have very little protein, so they are considered to be of very low density. The LDLs, which are mostly made of cholesterol, have more protein than the VLDLs but less than HDLs, which have the highest density. The protein in the lipoproteins helps them to perform their functions in your body. For example, the high protein content in HDLs not only helps remove cholesterol from your cells, but also enables the carrier to expand and contract, depending on the amount of fat and cholesterol it is carrying.

Why is the proportion of protein in a lipoprotein carrier important? Each lipoprotein has a different role. The main role of the VLDLs is to deliver fat that is made in the liver to your tissues. Once the fat is delivered, the VLDL remnants are converted into LDLs. The LDLs deliver cholesterol to your cells and are often referred to as the "bad" cholesterol carriers because they deposit cholesterol in the walls of your arteries, which can lead to heart disease. To help you remember this, you may want to think of the "**L**" in **LDL** as being of "**L**ittle" health benefit.

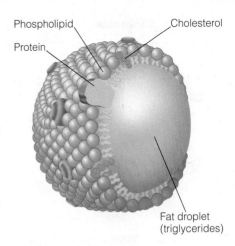

Figure 5.11 Chylomicron
Chylomicrons are one type of lipoprotein.

bile A substance produced by the liver, stored in the gallbladder, and secreted into the small intestine that emulsifies fat into smaller globules, allowing enzymes to break the fat down.

micelles Small transport carriers in the intestine that enable fatty acids and other compounds to be absorbed.

lymph Watery fluid that circulates through the body in lymph vessels and eventually enters the blood.

lipoproteins Capsule-shaped transport carriers that enable fat and cholesterol to travel through the lymph and blood.

chylomicron A type of lipoprotein that carries digested fat and other lipids through the lymph system into the blood.

very-low-density lipoprotein (VLDL) A lipoprotein that delivers fat made in the liver to the tissues. VLDL remnants are converted into LDLs.

low-density lipoprotein (LDL) A lipoprotein that deposits cholesterol in the walls of the arteries. Because this can lead to heart disease, LDL is referred to as the *bad* cholesterol carrier.

high-density lipoprotein (HDL) A lipoprotein that removes cholesterol from the tissues and delivers it to the liver to be used as part of bile and/or to be excreted from the body. Because of this, it is known as the *good* cholesterol carrier.

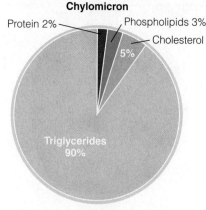

Chylomicron

Protein 2%

Phospholipids 3%

Cholesterol 5%

Triglycerides 90%

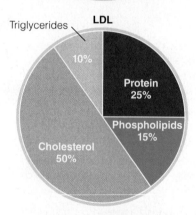

VLDL

Phospholipids

Protein 10%

18%

Triglycerides 60%

Cholesterol 12%

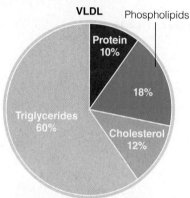

LDL

Triglycerides 10%

Protein 25%

Phospholipids 15%

Cholesterol 50%

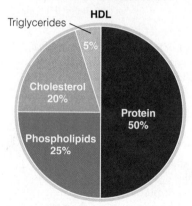

HDL

Triglycerides 5%

Cholesterol 20%

Protein 50%

Phospholipids 25%

Figure 5.12 Lipoproteins
The various types of lipoproteins and their composition.

The HDLs, as mentioned earlier, are mostly protein. They remove cholesterol from your cells and deliver it to your liver to be used to make bile or to be excreted from your body. For this reason, the HDLs are often referred to as the "good" cholesterol carriers, as they help remove cholesterol from your arteries. An easy way to remember this is to think of the "**H**" in **H**DL as referring to "**H**ealthy" (**Figure 5.13**).

The Take-Home Message The digestion of fat begins in your mouth, and with the help of enzymes and emulsifying bile acids, most of it is digested and then absorbed in your small intestine. Fat is generally packaged as part of a chylomicron lipoprotein carrier, and travels in the lymph before entering your bloodstream. The other lipoproteins are VLDLs, LDLs, and HDLs. The VLDLs are converted to the "bad" LDL cholesterol carriers, which can deposit cholesterol in the walls of your arteries. The "good" HDL cholesterol carriers remove cholesterol from your arteries and deliver it to your liver to be excreted from your body.

How Does Your Body Use Fat and Cholesterol?

Some people try to avoid fat in their diets, as they think it is unhealthy. This can actually be counterproductive, because fat plays many key roles in your body. Fat is an important source of energy and helps the absorption of some compounds. Fat also insulates your body and cushions your major organs. Some fats are essential for your good health. There are differences among the types of fat that you eat. Different fats can have different effects on your health, specifically your heart. Let's look at the roles that fats play in your body.

Fat Is Used as Energy

At 9 calories per gram, compared with 4 calories per gram for both carbohydrates and protein, fat is a major fuel source for your body. Your body has an *unlimited* ability to store excess energy (calories) as fat. In fact, your fat reserves have the capacity to enlarge as much as 1,000 times their original size, as more fat is added. If your cells fill to capacity, your body can add more fat cells.

Remember from Chapter 4 that your body only has a limited ability to store glucose, which is needed for the brain and red blood cells to function. When your blood glucose level begins to decline, the hormone glucagon promotes the release of glucose from the liver in order to supply the blood with glucose. Glucagon simultaneously promotes the release of fat from fat cells to provide additional energy for your body. Your heart, liver, and resting muscles prefer fat as their fuel source, which spares glucose to be used for your nervous system and red blood cells. In fact, fat is your main source of energy throughout the day. This fat stored in your fat cells provides a backup source of energy between meals. In a famine situation, some individuals could last months without eating, depending upon the extent of their fat stores and the availability of adequate fluids.

Fat Helps You Absorb Certain Compounds and Insulates the Body

Fat allows you to absorb the fat-soluble vitamins A, D, E, and K, as well as carotenoids, compounds that can have antioxidant properties in your body.[1] Consuming

Fat and cholesterol are transported in the body via several different lipoprotein compounds, such as chylomicrons, VLDLs, LDLs, and HDLs.

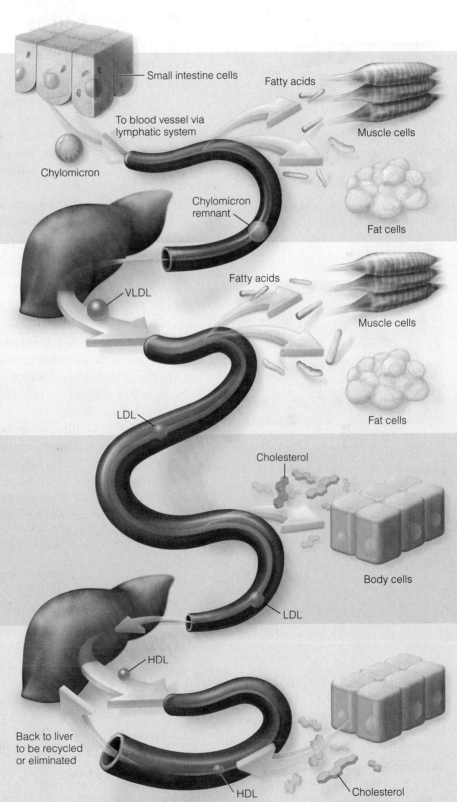

CHYLOMICRONS

Chylomicrons transport fat and cholesterol from a meal via the lymphatic system to your cells. Once in the blood, lipoprotein lipase helps break down fat. The remaining chylomicron remnant is dismantled in the liver.

VLDLs

VLDLs (very-low-density lipoproteins), produced mainly in the liver, transport fat to the cells. Lipoprotein lipase helps with the uptake of fatty acids into the cells, primarily those in muscle and fat tissue, transforming VLDLs to LDLs (low-density lipoproteins).

LDLs

Low-density lipoproteins release cholesterol into body cells. LDLs not taken up by cells degrade over time, releasing cholesterol that may then adhere to blood vessel walls.

HDLs

HDLs (high-density lipoproteins) produced by the liver circulate in the blood, picking up cholesterol from cells. The cholesterol is returned to the liver and excreted through the bile, removing it from the bloodstream.

Small intestine cells

Fatty acids

To blood vessel via lymphatic system

Muscle cells

Chylomicron

Chylomicron remnant

Fat cells

Fatty acids

VLDL

Muscle cells

LDL

Fat cells

Cholesterol

Body cells

LDL

HDL

Back to liver to be recycled or eliminated

HDL

Cholesterol

inadequate amounts of fat may impede your absorption of these fat-soluble vitamins and compounds. The fat that is located just under your skin helps to insulate your body and maintain your body temperature. Fat also acts as a protective cushion for your bones, organs, and nerves.

Essential Fatty Acids Help Keep Cells Healthy

Two polyunsaturated fatty acids, *linoleic acid* and *alpha-linolenic acid*, are essential, which means that your body can't make them; thus, you need to obtain them from your diet. Linoleic acid is also referred to as an *omega-6 fatty acid*, and alpha-linolenic acid is commonly called an *omega-3 fatty acid*. If this sounds like Greek to you, it should. The letters of the Greek alphabet help identify the placement of the carbons in fatty acids. Omega is the last letter of the Greek alphabet. Because the numbering of the carbons in a fatty acid starts from the acid end and is counted outward, the omega carbon is the *last* carbon of the fatty acid. In alpha-linolenic acid, the first double bond occurs at the third carbon from the omega end. Hence, it is referred to as an omega-3 fatty acid (refer again to Figure 5.2d).

Fatty fish, such as salmon, are an excellent source of omega-3 fatty acids.

The essential fatty acids help maintain healthy skin cells, nerves, and cell membranes. For example, a deficiency of linoleic acid can interfere with normal growth and result in inflammation of the skin. A deficiency in alpha-linolenic acid can affect the functioning of the brain and nervous system. Essential fatty acids are also necessary to make other substances your body needs. Linoleic acid is used to make another polyunsaturated fatty acid, called arachidonic acid (**Figure 5.14**). This fatty acid is important for your cells and for making **eicosanoids**, which are hormonelike substances. Among other roles, eicosanoids help with blood pressure, inflammation, and blood clotting.

A limited amount of alpha-linolenic acid can be converted to two other important omega-3 fatty acids: **eicosapentaenoic acid (EPA)** and **docosahexaenoic acid (DHA)**. EPA and DHA have been shown to reduce the risk of heart disease.[2] All fish contain EPA and DHA, although fatty fish such as salmon, herring, and sardines are especially rich sources. Cod-liver oil is abundant in EPA and DHA, but also in the fat-soluble vitamins A and D, which can both be toxic if consumed in high amounts. Eating fish is a safer way to obtain EPA and DHA, and it can also be very healthy for your heart, as discussed later in the chapter.

Some research suggests that a diet containing too much of the omega-6 fatty acids in comparison with omega-3 fatty acids may be unhealthy.[3] Consensus on this matter hasn't yet been reached.

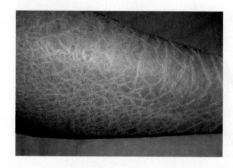

A deficiency of linoleic acid can interfere with normal growth and result in inflammation of the skin. Scaly skin can be a sign of inadequate amounts of alpha-linolenic acid.

eicosanoids Hormonelike substances in the body. Prostaglandins, thromboxanes, and leukotrienes are all eicosanoids.

eicosapentaenoic acid (EPA) and **docosahexaenoic acid (DHA)** Two omega-3 fatty acids that are heart healthy.

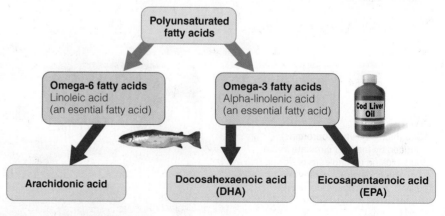

Figure 5.14 Essential Fatty Acids
Both linoleic acid (an omega-6 fatty acid) and alpha-linolenic acid (an omega-3 fatty acid) are essential fatty acids that you have to obtain from your diet. Other fatty acids can be made from these fatty acids.

Cholesterol Has Many Important Roles

Your body needs cholesterol both as a part of your cell membranes and as the precursor for vitamin D and bile acids. Cholesterol is also the precursor for the sex hormones such as estrogen and testosterone, which help to determine sexual characteristics.

The confusion over cholesterol persists. Though dietary cholesterol has been proclaimed as unhealthy, the cholesterol in your blood can be either "good" or "bad" cholesterol. How can one substance be both Dr. Jekyll and Mr. Hyde? Later in this chapter, we will look at the health effects of cholesterol, and try to clear up this confusion. During the discussion, keep in mind that the cholesterol in your diet isn't the only factor that determines the levels of cholesterol in your blood.

The Take-Home Message Fat contains 9 calories per gram and is an energy-dense source of fuel for your body. Fat cushions and protects your bones, organs, and nerves and insulates you to help maintain your body temperature. Fat also provides essential fatty acids and is needed for the absorption of fat-soluble vitamins and carotenoids. The essential fatty acids, linoleic acid (an omega-6 fatty acid) and alpha-linolenic acid (an omega-3 fatty acid), are necessary to keep cells healthy. Linoleic acid is necessary to make arachidonic acid and eicosanoids. A limited amount of alpha-linolenic acid can be converted to two other omega-3 fatty acids, EPA and DHA, which are also found in fish. Cholesterol is part of your cell membranes and is needed to make vitamin D, bile acids, and sex hormones.

How Much Fat Do You Need Each Day?

At first glance, it looks as though Americans' fat consumption has gone up and down over the last century. In the 1930s, Americans were consuming about 34 percent of their calories from fat; this number climbed to 42 percent in the mid-1960s. By 1984, fat consumption had declined to 36 percent of total calories, and current consumption is about 33 percent of calories.[4] However, while today's consumption levels are in line with the current recommendations, we can't break out the hot fudge sundaes just yet. Measuring fat consumption only as a percentage of total calories, and not including the type of fat, can be misleading. You will soon read that the amount of heart-unhealthy saturated fat that we are eating daily could use some adjusting.

But dietary fat is still essential for health. So, how much should you eat?

You Need to Consume a Specific Percentage of Your Daily Calories from Fat

The current AMDR (Acceptable Macronutrient Distribution Range) recommendation is that 20 to 35 percent of your daily calories should come from fat. For some individuals, especially sedentary, overweight folks, a very low-fat diet (providing less than 20 percent of daily calories from fat) that is consequently high in carbohydrates may cause an increase in fat in the blood and a lowering of the good HDL cholesterol—not exactly a healthy combination for the heart. For others, consuming more than 35 percent of their total daily calories from fat could perpetuate obesity, which is a risk factor for heart disease.[5]

Although consuming fat won't increase your weight unless you consistently consume more calories than you need, remember that dietary fat has more than twice the calories per gram of carbohydrates or protein. Therefore, eating too many fatty foods could perpetuate a weight-management problem. Numerous research studies have shown that reducing dietary fat can also reduce dietary calories, which can result in weight loss.[6] Consequently, controlling one's fat intake may help control one's weight.

According to the AMDR recommendation, if you need 2,000 calories daily to maintain your weight, you can consume between 44 and 78 grams of fat daily (Table 5.1). For your heart health, you should consume less than 10 percent (and ideally less than 7 percent) of your calories, or 16 to 22 grams, from saturated fats.

You Need to Consume a Specific Amount of Essential Fatty Acids Daily

To ensure that you consume enough linoleic acid and alpha-linolenic acid, a recommended amount has been set for each of these important nutrients. A minimum of 5 percent and up to 10 percent of the total calories in your diet should come from linoleic acid, and alpha-linolenic acid should make up 0.6 percent to 1.2 percent of your total calories.[7] These recommended amounts are based on the estimated daily caloric needs according to your gender and age. For example, men aged 19 to 50 need 17 grams of linoleic acid daily, and women aged 19 to 50 who aren't pregnant or lactating need 12 grams daily. For alpha-linolenic acid, men aged 14 to 70 need 1.6 grams daily, whereas women of the same age need 1.1 grams daily.

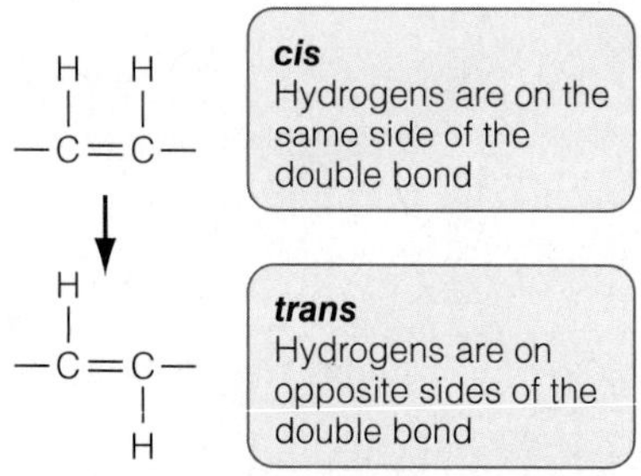

Vegetable oils are good sources of essential fatty acids.

cis
Hydrogens are on the same side of the double bond

trans
Hydrogens are on opposite sides of the double bond

Figure 5.15 Creating *Trans* Fatty Acids
Hydrogenating, or adding hydrogen to, an unsaturated fatty acid will create a more saturated fatty acid. This process will also cause some of the double bonds to twist from a *cis* position to a *trans* position. This creates a *trans* fatty acid.

hydrogenation Adding hydrogen to an unsaturated fatty acid to make it more saturated and solid at room temperature.

trans fatty acids Substances that result from the hydrogenating of an unsaturated fatty acid, causing a reconfiguring of some of its double bonds. A small amount of *trans* fatty acids occur naturally in animal foods.

trans fat Substance that contains mostly *trans* fatty acids.

Minimize Saturated and *Trans* Fats in Your Diet

While your diet should include essential fatty acids, some types of fats should be avoided. Solid fats—like butter, chicken fat, cream, coconut oil, palm kernel and palm oils, and partially hydrogenated oils—are major sources of heart-unhealthy saturated fat and hydrogenated oils are significant sources of *trans* fat in the diet (as mentioned in Chapter 2). These solid fats are often found in grain-based desserts, pizza, full-fat cheese, sausages, and franks.[8] In fact, the major source of saturated fat in the diets of Americans is full-fat cheese. Consuming too much saturated fat can lead to higher levels of the "bad" LDL cholesterol carrier (you'll learn more about how these lipoproteins affect heart disease risk later in the chapter).

The majority of *trans* fats in foods are created by food manufacturers through the process of **hydrogenation**. Hydrogenation involves heating an oil and exposing it to hydrogen gas, which causes some of the double bonds in the unsaturated fatty acid to become saturated with hydrogen. Typically, the hydrogens of a double bond are lined up in a *cis* (*cis* = same) configuration, that is, they are all on the same side of the carbon chain in the fatty acid. During hydrogenation, some hydrogens cross to the opposite side of the carbon chain, resulting in a *trans* (*trans* = cross) configuration (**Figure 5.15**). The newly configured fatty acid is now a synthetic ***trans* fatty acid**. These ***trans* fats** are actually worse for heart health than saturated fat because they not only raise the LDL cholesterol levels, but they also lower HDL cholesterol in the body.

Table 5.1

Capping Your Fat Intake

If You Need This Many Calories to Maintain Your Weight	You Should Eat No More Than This Much	
	Fat (grams) (20% to 35% of total calories)	Saturated Fat (grams) (<7 to 10% of total calories)
1,600	36–62	12–18
1,700	38–66	13–19
1,800	40–70	14–20
1,900	42–74	15–21
2,000	44–78	16–22
2,100	47–82	16–23
2,200	49–86	17–24
2,300	51–89	18–26
2,400	53–93	19–27
2,500	56–97	19–28
2,600	58–101	20–29
2,700	60–105	21–30
2,800	62–109	22–31

Sedentary women should consume approximately 1,600 calories daily. Teenage girls, active women, and many sedentary men need approximately 2,200 calories daily. Teenage boys, many active men, and some very active women need about 2,800 calories daily. To determine the number of calories you should be eating daily, turn to Table 2.1 in Chapter 2.

The percentage of calories from fat and the corresponding grams of fat can be calculated by multiplying your number of daily calories by 20 percent and 35 percent and then dividing those numbers by 9. (Fat provides 9 calories per gram.)

For example, if you consume 2,000 calories daily:

$$\underline{2,000} \times 0.20 \text{ (20 percent)} = \underline{400} \text{ calories} \div 9 = \underline{44} \text{ grams}$$

$$\underline{2,000} \times 0.35 \text{ (35 percent)} = \underline{700} \text{ calories} \div 9 = \underline{78} \text{ grams}$$

Your range of fat intake should be 44 to 78 grams daily.
To find the maximum grams of saturated fat that you should be consuming daily, repeat the process:

$$\underline{2,000} \times 0.07 \text{ (7 percent)} = \underline{140} \text{ calories} \div 9 = \underline{16} \text{ grams}$$

$$\underline{2,000} \times 0.10 \text{ (10 percent)} = \underline{200} \text{ calories} \div 9 = \underline{22} \text{ grams}$$

The total amount of saturated fat intake should be no more than 22 grams daily.

Commercially made peanut butter doesn't have any detectable levels of *trans* fatty acids. Even though partially hydrogenated oil is used as a stabilizer in many peanut butter brands, the amount is so small that it is insignificant.

Trans fats were initially used in many processed foods because they provide a richer texture, a longer shelf life, and better resistance to **rancidity** than unsaturated fats. After saturated fat fell out of favor in the 1980s, because of research that confirmed its association with heart disease, *trans* fats came into widespread commercial use. Everything from cookies, cakes, and crackers to fried chips and doughnuts used *trans* fats to maintain their texture and shelf life. *Trans* fats were also frequently used for frying at fast-food restaurants.

To make consumers more aware of *trans* fat, the FDA mandated in 2006 that most foods, and even some dietary supplements such as energy bars, list the grams of

rancidity The decomposition, or spoiling, of fats through oxidation.

Figure 5.16 Major Food Sources of Saturated and *Trans* Fats for Americans
Reducing the amount of food sources containing solid fats, such as cheese, pizza, grain-based desserts, and meat-containing dishes, will help you reduce saturated and *trans* fats in your diet.

Source: USDA and HHS. *Dietary Guidelines for Americans, 2010.* Available at www.health.gov/dietaryguidelines.

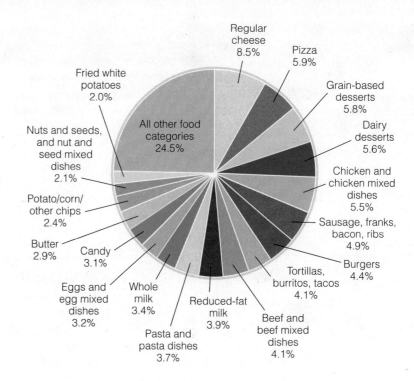

Regular cheese 8.5%
Pizza 5.9%
Grain-based desserts 5.8%
Dairy desserts 5.6%
Chicken and chicken mixed dishes 5.5%
Sausage, franks, bacon, ribs 4.9%
Burgers 4.4%
Tortillas, burritos, tacos 4.1%
Beef and beef mixed dishes 4.1%
Reduced-fat milk 3.9%
Pasta and pasta dishes 3.7%
Whole milk 3.4%
Eggs and egg mixed dishes 3.2%
Candy 3.1%
Butter 2.9%
Potato/corn/ other chips 2.4%
Nuts and seeds, and nut and seed mixed dishes 2.1%
Fried white potatoes 2.0%
All other food categories 24.5%

Table 5.2

How Much Cholesterol Is in Your Foods?

	Cholesterol (mg)
Liver, chicken, 3 oz	479
Breakfast biscuit with egg and sausage, 1	261
Shrimp, 3 oz, canned	214
Egg, 1 large	186
Lobster, cooked, 3 oz	124
Fast-food hamburger, large, double patty	122
Ice cream, soft serve, vanilla, ½ cup	78
Beef, ground, cooked, 3 oz	75
Turkey, light meat, cooked, 3 oz	68
Chicken or turkey, breast, cooked, 3 oz	72
Salmon, cooked, 3 oz	60
Egg noodles, 1 cup	46
Cheddar cheese, 1 oz	30
Frankfurter, beef, 1	28
Milk, whole, 1 cup	24
Butter, 1 tbs	10
Cheddar cheese, low fat, 1 oz	6
Milk, skim, 1 cup	5

Source: USDA National Nutrient Database for Standard Reference, Release 25. Available at www.ars.usda.gov. Accessed March 2013.

trans fats per serving on the Nutrition Facts panel on the food label. The label allows you to quickly add up the saturated and *trans* fats listed and makes it easier for you to monitor the amount of these fats that you consume.[9] Because of this labeling requirement, many food manufacturers reformulated their products to remove or reduce the amount of *trans* fats made with hydrogenation. In 2013, the FDA proposed a ban on the use of partially hydrogenated oils in foods to reduce the consumption of *trans* fat in the diets of Americans. Reducing the amount of food sources of solid fats in your diet will help you reduce your consumption of both saturated fats and *trans* fats (see **Figure 5.16**).

Minimize Cholesterol in Your Diet

As mentioned earlier, your body can make all the cholesterol it needs. Therefore, you do not need to consume it in your diet, and in fact, you should limit the amount of cholesterol you take in for the sake of your heart and arteries. Healthy individuals over the age of 2 are advised to limit their dietary cholesterol to less than 300 milligrams (mg) daily, on average. Adult males in the United States currently consume about 333 milligrams daily, whereas adult females eat slightly more than 224 milligrams of cholesterol daily, on average.[10] **Table 5.2** lists a variety of foods and their cholesterol content.

Keeping the types of lipids straight, and remembering how much of each to consume or avoid, can be a challenge. The following summary should help you remember what you have learned thus far:

➤ **DO** be sure to get enough of the two heart-healthy essential fatty acids, linoleic acid and alpha-linolenic acid, in your diet by consuming adequate amounts of polyunsaturated fats in your daily meals.

➤ **DO** choose mono- and polyunsaturated fats over saturated fats when possible, as these unsaturated fats are better for you. Saturated fats should be kept to less than 10 percent of your total calories, because they aren't good for your heart or your blood cholesterol levels.

How Much Fat Is in Your Diet?

Is your diet too overloaded with fat, and/or saturated fat? Use the diet analysis program, the Food Composition Table, and/or food labels to track your fat consumption for a day. How does your actual intake compare to the amount recommended for you in Table 5.1?

Food Log

	Food/Drink	Amount	Fat (g)	Saturated Fat (g)
Breakfast				
Snack				
Lunch				
Snack				
Dinner				
Snack				
Total				

➤ **DON'T** add *trans* fats to your diet. These are unhealthy for your heart and blood cholesterol levels and should be consumed as little as possible.

➤ **DON'T** worry about eating enough cholesterol, because your body makes all it needs.

When it comes to keeping track of your fat intake, counting grams of fat in your foods is the best strategy. Table 5.1 provided you with a healthy range of recommended fat intake based on your daily caloric needs. (To figure out your approximate daily caloric needs, see Chapter 2.) Use the Self-Assessment to estimate how much fat and saturated fat you consume daily.

The Take-Home Message You need to consume some fat in your diet, particularly the essential fatty acids, but you should limit other fats, like saturated fats and *trans* fats. Your fat intake should range from 20 to 35 percent of your total calories. To meet your essential fatty acid needs, 5 to 10 percent of your calories should come from linoleic acid and 0.6 to 1.2 percent of your daily calories should come from alpha-linolenic acid. No more than 10 percent of your fat intake should come from saturated fat, and *trans* fats should be limited in your diet. You do not need to eat cholesterol in foods, as your body makes all the cholesterol it needs.

Vegetables are a low-saturated-fat topping for pizza.

What Are the Best Food Sources of Fats?

Foods that contain unsaturated fats (both monounsaturated and polyunsaturated fats) are better for your health than foods high in saturated fat, cholesterol, and/or *trans* fat. So, where can you find the healthier fats in foods? Unsaturated fats

Figure 5.17 Food Sources of the Essential Fatty Acids

Many oils and nuts contain high amounts of the two essential fatty acids that you need to obtain in your diet.

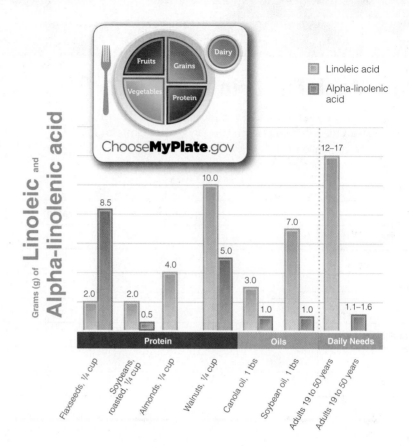

Linoleic and Alpha-linolenic acid

Grams (g) of

☐ Linoleic acid
☐ Alpha-linolenic acid

Protein | Oils | Daily Needs

Flaxseeds, ¼ cup — 2.0, 8.5
Soybeans, roasted, ¼ cup — 2.0, 0.5
Almonds, ¼ cup — 4.0
Walnuts, ¼ cup — 10.0, 5.0
Canola oil, 1 tbs — 3.0, 1.0
Soybean oil, 1 tbs — 7.0, 1.0
Adults 19 to 50 years — 12–17
Adults 19 to 50 years — 1.1–1.6

are abundant in vegetable oils, such as soybean, corn, and canola oils, as well as soybeans, walnuts, peanut butter, flaxseeds, and wheat germ. Vegetable oils, nuts, and flaxseeds are also good sources of the essential fatty acids. In fact, all the foods listed in **Figure 5.17** are excellent sources of both unsaturated fats and essential fatty acids.

Most saturated fat in the diet comes from animal foods, such as whole-milk dairy products like cheese, butter, and ice cream, fatty cuts of meat, and the skin on poultry. Choosing lean meats and dairy foods, skinless poultry, and oil-based spreads will help you minimize the saturated fat in your diet. Certain vegetable oils, such as coconut, palm, and palm kernel oils, are very high in saturated fat. Although food manufacturers now use these highly saturated tropical oils less often, they may still be found in foods such as candies, commercially made baked goods, and gourmet ice cream. Checking the ingredient label on food packages is the best way to find out if these oils are in the foods that you eat (**Figure 5.18**).

Because all fats and oils are a combination of fatty acids, however, it's not only impossible to eliminate saturated fat entirely from your diet, it is unhealthy for you to do so (see **Figure 5.19** on page 160). Extreme trimming of fats and oils could lead to the unnecessary elimination of certain foods, such as soybean and canola oils, lean meats, fish, poultry, and low-fat dairy foods, which could cause you to fall short of important nutrients such as essential fatty acids, protein, and calcium. Just remember to keep your dietary intake of saturated fat to less than 10 percent of your daily total calories.

The cheddar cheese on the top of a cheeseburger has more fat and saturated fat per ounce than the burger.

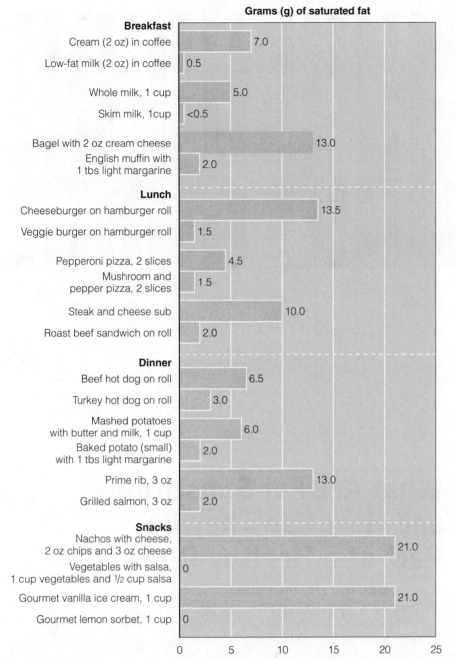

Grams (g) of saturated fat

Breakfast
- Cream (2 oz) in coffee — 7.0
- Low-fat milk (2 oz) in coffee — 0.5
- Whole milk, 1 cup — 5.0
- Skim milk, 1cup — <0.5
- Bagel with 2 oz cream cheese — 13.0
- English muffin with 1 tbs light margarine — 2.0

Lunch
- Cheeseburger on hamburger roll — 13.5
- Veggie burger on hamburger roll — 1.5
- Pepperoni pizza, 2 slices — 4.5
- Mushroom and pepper pizza, 2 slices — 1.5
- Steak and cheese sub — 10.0
- Roast beef sandwich on roll — 2.0

Dinner
- Beef hot dog on roll — 6.5
- Turkey hot dog on roll — 3.0
- Mashed potatoes with butter and milk, 1 cup — 6.0
- Baked potato (small) with 1 tbs light margarine — 2.0
- Prime rib, 3 oz — 13.0
- Grilled salmon, 3 oz — 2.0

Snacks
- Nachos with cheese, 2 oz chips and 3 oz cheese — 21.0
- Vegetables with salsa, 1 cup vegetables and 1/2 cup salsa — 0
- Gourmet vanilla ice cream, 1 cup — 21.0
- Gourmet lemon sorbet, 1 cup — 0

0   5   10   15   20   25

Figure 5.18 Where's the Saturated Fat in Your Foods?
Saturated fat is found in animal products, tropical oils, and hydrogenated foods. Choosing less-saturated-fat versions of some of your favorite foods at meals and snacks can dramatically lower the amount of "sat" fat you consume in your diet.

Americans on average consume about 11 percent of their daily calories from saturated fat, so it's likely that you need to reduce your intake.[11] You can use Figure 5.18 to make low-saturated-fat food choices at some of your meals and snacks.

The Take-Home Message Eating lean meats, skinless poultry, lean dairy products, and vegetable oils while limiting commercially prepared baked goods and snack items is a good strategy for overall good health. These foods will provide you with enough healthy unsaturated fats, with plenty of essential fatty acids, while limiting your intake of unhealthy, saturated fats.

Practical Nutrition **VIDEO**

Making Low Fat Choices

Do you know how much fat is in your ice cream? You may be surprised! Scan this QR code with your mobile device to access the video. You can also access the video in MasteringNutrition™.

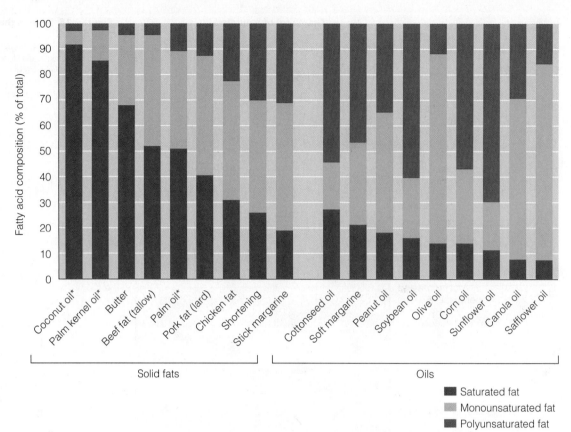

**Figure 5.19
Composition of
Various Fats**
Foods vary in their
composition of fat.

*Coconut oil, palm kernel
oil, and palm oil are called
oils because they come
from plants. However,
they are semi-solid at
room temperature due
to their high content of
short-chain saturated fatty
acids. They are considered
solid fats for nutritional
purposes.

Source: USDA and HHS.
*Dietary Guidelines for
Americans, 2010.* Avail-
able at www.health.gov/
dietaryguidelines.

What Are Fat Substitutes and How Can They Be Part of a Healthy Diet?

If you adore the taste and texture of creamy foods but don't adore the extra fat in your diet, you're not alone. According to a recent survey, over 55 percent of shoppers read the food label to find out how much fat, saturated fat, and *trans* fat is in the product.[12] Based on this information, three out of four shoppers say that they choose products that are lower in fat at least sometimes, if not always, when shopping.[13] Today, with few exceptions, you will probably find a lower-fat alternative for almost any high-fat food on the grocery store shelves. The keys to these products' containing less fat than their counterparts are **fat substitutes**.

Fat substitutes are designed to provide all the creamy properties of fat for fewer calories and total fat grams. Because fat has more than double the calories per gram of carbohydrates or protein, fat substitutes have the potential to reduce calories from fat by more than 50 percent without sacrificing taste and texture.

Fat Substitutes Can Be Carbohydrate, Protein, or Fat Based

No single substitute works in all foods and with all cooking preparations, so there are several types of fat substitutes. They fall into three categories depending on their primary ingredient:

fat substitutes Substances that replace added fat in foods by providing the creamy properties of fat for fewer calories and fewer total fat grams.

Table 5.3

The Lighter Side of Fat: Fat Substitutes

Name (trade names)	Calories per Gram	Properties	How It's Used
Carbohydrate Based			
Fibers from Grains (Beta-Trim)	1–4	Gelling, thickener	Baked goods, meats, spreads
Fibers, Cellulose (Avicel cellulose gel)	0	Water retention, texture, mouthfeel	Sauces, dairy products, frozen desserts, salad dressings
Gums (Slendid)	0	Thickener, texture, mouthfeel, water retention	Salad dressings, processed meats
Polydextrose (Litesse)	1	Water retention, adds bulk	Baked goods, dairy products, salad dressings, cookies, gum
Modified Food Starch (STA-SLIM)	1–4	Thickener, gelling, texture	Processed meats, salad dressings, frostings, fillings, frozen desserts
Protein Based			
Microparticulated Protein (Simplesse)	1–4	Mouthfeel	Dairy products, salad dressings, spreads
Fat Based			
Mono- or Diglycerides (Dur-Lo)	9*	Mouthfeel, moisture retention	Baked goods
Short-Chain Fatty Acids (Salatrim)	5	Mouthfeel	Confections, baked goods
Olestra (Olean)	0	Mouthfeel	Savory snacks

*Less of this fat substitute is needed to create the same effect as fat, so the calories are reduced in foods using this product.
Data from Calorie Control Council. 2013. Glossary of Fat Replacers. Available at www.caloriecontrol.org. Accessed March 2013; R. D. Mattes, "Fat Replacers," *Journal of the American Dietetic Association* 98 (1998): 463–468; J. Wylie-Rosett, "Fat Substitutes and Health: An Advisory from the Nutrition Committee of the American Heart Association," *Circulation* 105 (2002): 2800–2804.

➤ Carbohydrate-based substitutes
➤ Protein-based substitutes
➤ Fat-based substitutes[14]

Table 5.3 lists all three types of fat substitutes and their uses in foods.

The majority of fat substitutes are carbohydrate based and use plant polysaccharides such as fiber, starches, gums, and cellulose to help retain moisture and provide a fatlike texture.[15] For example, low-fat muffins might have fiber added to them to help retain the moisture that is lost when fat is reduced. Carbohydrate-based fat substitutes have been used for years and work well under heat preparations other than frying.

Protein-based fat substitutes are created from the protein in eggs and milk. The protein is heated and broken down into microscopic balls that tumble over each other when you eat them, providing a creamy mouthfeel that's similar to that of fat. Because these are protein based, they break down under high temperatures and lose their creamy properties. Therefore, they are not suitable for frying and baking.[16]

Fat-based substitutes are fats that have been modified either to provide the physical attributes of fat for fewer calories or to interfere with the absorption of fat.[17] Mono- and diglycerides are used as emulsifiers in products such as baked goods and icings to provide moistness and mouthfeel. Though these remnants of fat have the same number of calories per gram as fat, fewer of them are needed to create the same effect, so the total levels of calories and fat are reduced in the food product.[18] One fat substitute, olestra (also known as Olean), is a mixture of sucrose and long-chain fatty acids. Unlike fat, which contains three fatty acids connected to a glycerol backbone, olestra contains six to eight fatty acids connected to sucrose. The enzymes that normally break apart fatty acids from their glycerol backbones during digestion cannot disconnect the fatty acids in olestra. Instead, olestra moves through your gastrointestinal tract intact and unabsorbed. Thus, it doesn't provide calories. Olestra is very heat stable, so it can be used in baked and fried foods.

In 1996, the FDA approved olestra for use in salty snacks such as potato and corn chips. An ounce of potato chips made with olestra can trim half the calories and all the fat from regular chips. Because of its inability to be absorbed, there was concern about olestra's interference with the absorption of fat-soluble vitamins and carotenoids.[19] (Absorption of water-soluble vitamins is not affected by olestra.) Consequently, the FDA has mandated that fat-soluble vitamins be added to foods containing olestra to offset these losses.[20] Because olestra travels through your digestive tract untouched, there was also a concern that it may cause stomach cramps and loose stools. Though there have been anecdotal studies of individuals experiencing bouts of diarrhea and cramps after consuming olestra-containing products, controlled research studies don't seem to support this phenomenon.[21]

Reduced-Fat Products Aren't Calorie Free

Foods made with fat substitutes aren't calorie free.

The use of fat substitutes doesn't seem to be helping Americans curb their calories or weight, and one reason for this may be people's overeating of low-fat and fat-free foods. Another reason may be that many reduced-fat products have close to the same number of calories as their regular counterparts. Also, research indicates that snacking on fat-reduced products may reduce overall fat intake, but not the overall intake of calories in a day.[22] As with sugar substitutes, consumers need to recognize that using reduced-fat or fat-free products is not a blank check for eating unlimited amounts of those foods. The foods still contain calories, and overconsuming calories leads to weight gain.

Also, some fat-free foods, especially baked goods, may have a reduced fat content but added carbohydrates, which will add back some calories. Consequently, the savings in fat calories isn't always much of a savings in total calories (Table 5.4). Consumers should be careful not to assume that fat-free foods are healthy, because they often aren't. Jelly beans are fat free, but they don't provide the vitamins and minerals found in, for example, naturally fat-free green beans. Similarly, while choosing 4 ounces of fat-free chips will spare you half of the 600 calories found in the same amount of regular chips, those fat-free chips are also displacing 300 calories of more nutritious foods, such as fruits, vegetables, and whole grains, elsewhere in your diet. If you want chips, enjoy a handful rather than a large bag full, alongside your whole-grain sandwich and large salad at lunch.

Fats affect more than your weight and waistline. They also affect the health of your heart. The Health Connection feature "What Is Heart Disease and What Increases Your Risk?" on page 164 takes a closer look at how lipids in your diet can affect your risk for heart disease.

The Take-Home Message Fat substitutes are used in foods to provide the properties of fat for fewer calories and grams of fat. Fat substitutes can be carbohydrate based, protein based, or fat based. Though some fat substitutes provide fewer calories and fat grams than regular fat, others, such as olestra, aren't absorbed, so they are fat and calorie free. Reduced-fat or fat-free foods may help reduce the calories and fat in some foods, but shouldn't displace naturally low-fat and healthy foods such as fruits and vegetables.

Table 5.4

Fat Free Doesn't Equal Calorie Free

	Serving Size	Calories	Fat (g)	Carbohydrates (g)	Calories Saved
Fudgsicle Pop (Popsicle)	1 (1.65 fl oz)	60	1.5	12	
Fat-Free Fudgsicle Bar (Popsicle)	1 (1.75 fl oz)	60	0	13	0
Oatmeal Raisin Cookies	1 (28 g)	120	3.5	20	
Fat-Free Oatmeal Raisin Cookies (Archway)	1 (31 g)	110	0	25	10
Fig Newtons (Nabisco)	2 (31 g)	110	2	22	
Fat-Free Fig Newtons (Nabisco)	2 (29 g)	90	0	22	20

Source: Food manufacturers. Updated March 2013.

What Can You Do to Maintain Healthy Blood Cholesterol Levels?

Numerous research studies have shown that reducing the amount of LDL cholesterol in your blood will reduce your risk for heart disease.[23] Starting at age 20, you should have your blood tested at least once every five years to obtain your "lipoprotein profile." This profile shows the total cholesterol, LDL cholesterol, and HDL cholesterol levels in your blood. Table 5.5 provides the recommended goals for total cholesterol,

Table 5.5

What Your Cholesterol Level* Can Tell You

If Your Total Cholesterol Level Is	That Is Considered
<200	Fabulous! Keep up the good work!
200–239	Borderline high
≥240	High

If Your LDL Cholesterol Level Is	That Is Considered
<100	Fabulous! Congratulations!
100–129	Near or above optimal
130–159	Borderline high
160–189	High
190	Much too high!

If Your HDL Cholesterol Is	That Is Considered
≥60	Fabulous!
40–60	Good
<40	Too low

*All lipoprotein levels are measured in milligrams of cholesterol per deciliter of blood (mg/dl).

Source: National Cholesterol Education Program. Detection, Evaluation, and Treatment of High Blood Cholesterol in Adults (Adult Treatment Panel III). May 2001. National Institutes of Health Publication No. 01-3290.

What Is Heart Disease and What Increases Your Risk?

Cardiovascular disease (CVD) is a name that encompasses several disorders affecting the heart and blood vessels, including problems with heart valves, heart beat irregularities, infections, and other problems. But the most common type of CVD is *coronary heart disease*, which affects the blood vessels that serve the heart muscle, and can lead to a heart attack. That's the type we focus on in this chapter.

Heart disease has been the number-one killer of adults in the United States since 1918. Currently, one of every six deaths among Americans is caused by heart disease.[1] Let's look at how heart disease develops, and the types of lipids that can accelerate it.

Heart Disease Begins with a Buildup in the Arteries

Heart disease develops when the coronary arteries, the large blood vessels that supply oxygen and other nutrients to the heart, accumulate a buildup of substances such as fat and cholesterol along their walls. As the artery gets narrower, blood flow is impeded and less oxygen and nutrients are delivered to the heart. If the heart doesn't receive enough oxygen, chest pains can result. A narrowed artery also increases the likelihood that a blood clot can block the vessel, leading to a **heart attack**. If the artery leads to the brain, a **stroke** can occur. Approximately every 34 seconds, an adult will suffer a heart attack in the United States.[2]

The exact cause of the narrowed arteries, also known as **atherosclerosis** (*athero* = paste, *sclera* = hardness, *sis* = condition), is unknown, but researchers think it begins with an injury to the interior lining of an artery and subsequent inflammation in the injured area. High blood levels of cholesterol and fat, high blood pressure, diabetes, and smoking likely contribute to this injury.

Over time, LDLs and other substances are deposited along an injured artery wall. The LDLs seep beneath the vessel lining, become oxidized and attract macrophages (immune cells), which become enlarged with cholesterol-laden LDL and develop into foam cells. The foam cells build up along the wall of the artery, along with platelets (fragments of cells in the blood), calcium protein fibers, and other substances, into **plaque**. The plaque narrows the passageway of the artery (**Figure 1**).

heart attack Permanent damage to the heart muscle that results from a sudden lack of oxygen-rich blood.

stroke A condition caused by a lack of oxygen to the brain that could result in paralysis and possibly death.

atherosclerosis Narrowing of the coronary arteries due to buildup of debris along the artery walls.

plaque The hardened buildup of cholesterol-laden foam cells, platelets, cellular waste products, and calcium in the arteries that results in atherosclerosis.

Risk Factors for Heart Disease

Factors You Cannot Control	Factors You Can Control
Your age and gender	Type 2 diabetes mellitus
Your family history of heart disease	High blood pressure
Type 1 diabetes mellitus	Smoking
	Physical inactivity
	Excess weight
	A low HDL "good" cholesterol level
	A high LDL "bad" cholesterol level

What Are the Risk Factors for Heart Disease?

While the primary risk factor for heart disease is an elevated LDL cholesterol level, other risk factors also exist (see the table above). Some of these you can control, others you cannot.

Risk Factors You Can't Control

As your blood cholesterol increases, so does your risk of developing heart disease and experiencing a heart attack. Your blood cholesterol level tends to rise with age until it stabilizes around the age of 65. Your gender also plays a role. Up until menopause, which is around the age of 50, women tend to have a lower blood cholesterol level than men and a reduced risk of heart disease. After menopause, the blood cholesterol level in women tends to catch up and even surpass that of a man of the same age.[3] About one in eight American women between 45 and 64 years of age has heart disease, but this jumps to one out of every four women over the age of 65. The decrease in the level of the hormone estrogen in postmenopausal women plays a part in the increased risk of heart disease that occurs in older women.[4]

> One in every 30 American women dies each year of breast cancer, but one in every four female adult deaths is from heart disease.[5]

Because high blood cholesterol levels can be partly determined by your genes, such levels can sometimes run in families.[6] If your father or brother had early signs of heart disease before age 55, or your mother or sister had them before the age of 65, then you are at a greater risk of getting heart disease. Having diabetes also increases the risk of heart disease. Though the less common form of diabetes, type 1, is not preventable, the more prevalent form, type 2 diabetes, can be controlled.

Risk Factors You Can Control

Controlling diabetes can help dramatically lower the risk of heart disease for those with this condition. Type 2 diabetes can be managed

Plaque accumulation within coronary arteries narrows their interior and impedes the flow of oxygen-rich blood to the heart.

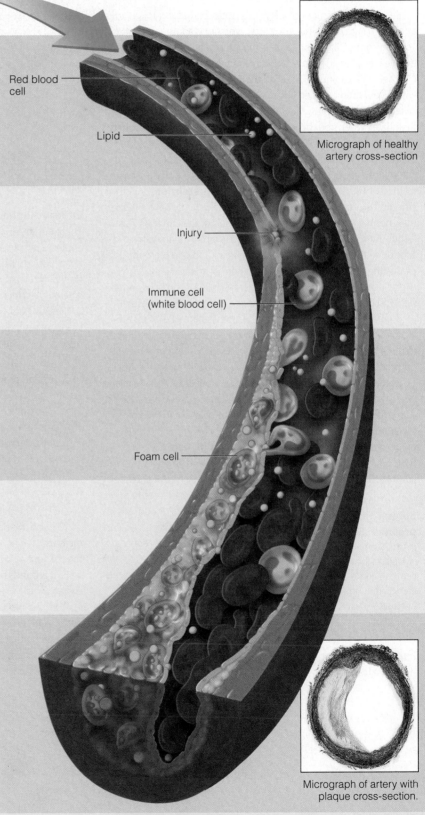

Red blood cell

Lipid

Micrograph of healthy artery cross-section

Injury

Immune cell (white blood cell)

Foam cell

Micrograph of artery with plaque cross-section.

HEALTHY ARTERY

Blood flows unobstructed through normal, healthy artery.

ARTERIAL INJURY

The artery's lining is injured, attracting immune cells, and prompting inflammation.

LIPIDS ACCUMULATE IN WALL

Lipids, particularly cholesterol-containing LDLs, seep beneath the wall lining. The LDLs become oxidized. Immune cells, attracted to the site, engulf the oxidized LDLs and are transformed into foam cells.

FATTY STREAK

The foam cells accumulate to form a fatty streak, which releases more toxic and inflammatory chemicals.

PLAQUE FORMATION

The foam cells, along with platelets, calcium, protein fibers, and other substances, form thick deposits of plaque, stiffening and narrowing the artery. Blood flow through the artery is reduced or obstructed.

and, as you read in the last chapter, possibly even prevented, through diet and lifestyle changes. Sometimes, the use of doctor-prescribed medication is also needed to control type 2 diabetes. Adults with diabetes are two to four times more likely to die of heart disease than adults without diabetes.[7]

Because chronic high blood pressure can damage or injure your arteries, maintaining a healthy blood pressure is another factor you can control. Blood pressure is the force of your blood against the walls of your arteries. A blood pressure reading consists of two numbers. The top number, called the *systolic pressure*, is the pressure within your arteries when your heart contracts. The bottom number, called the *diastolic pressure*, is the pressure in your arteries a moment later, when your heart is relaxed. A **normal blood pressure** is considered less than 120 millimeters of mercury (Hg) for the systolic pressure and less than 80 millimeters Hg for the diastolic pressure. You might hear this referred to as "120 over 80." A blood pressure reading of 140/90 or higher is considered **hypertension**, or high blood pressure. People with hypertension constantly have a higher-than-normal force pushing against the walls of their arteries. This is thought to damage the artery lining, prompt inflammation, and accelerate the buildup of plaque. Chronic high blood pressure also causes the heart to work harder than normal and can lead to an enlarged heart. (Chapter 8 contains a detailed discussion of hypertension and how a healthy diet can help lower high blood pressure.)

Smoking damages the walls of the arteries and accelerates atherosclerosis and heart disease. In fact, individuals who smoke are up to three times more likely to have heart disease and, compared with nonsmokers, their likelihood of experiencing a heart attack doubles.[8]

Because regular exercise can help lower your LDL cholesterol and raise your good HDL cholesterol, being inactive is a risk factor for heart disease. Whereas a high HDL cholesterol level can help protect you from heart disease, having an HDL level of less than 40 milligrams per deciliter (mg/dl) increases your risk of heart disease, as you don't have enough of this "good" cholesterol carrier in your body. In contrast, having a high level of HDL cholesterol, 60 mg/dl or higher, is considered a "negative" risk factor. In other words, there is so much of this "good" cholesterol in your body helping to protect against heart disease that it allows you to "erase" a risk factor from your list.

In addition to exercising regularly, losing excess weight and quitting smoking can help increase your HDL cholesterol. Exercise can also help you better manage your weight. Being overweight can raise your LDL cholesterol and increase your risk of heart disease. Whereas drinking modest amounts

normal blood pressure Less than 120 mm Hg (systolic—the top number) and less than 80 mm Hg (diastolic—the bottom number). Referred to as 120/80.

hypertension High blood pressure.

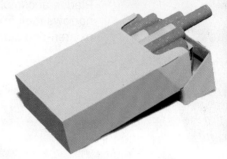

Over 20 percent of men and 16 percent of women 18 years of age and older smoke cigarettes.[9]

of alcohol has also been shown to raise HDL cholesterol, other problems can outweigh this benefit. In fact, for some individuals, drinking alcohol is not advised.[10]

Other Potential Risk Factors

There are some individuals who don't have an elevated level of LDL cholesterol in their blood, yet still experience a heart attack and heart disease, which points to other factors that must be affecting their heart health. These other potential risk factors are referred to as *emerging risk factors*.

Researchers are continually searching for clues or "markers" in the blood, other than cholesterol levels, that are signs of the presence of heart disease. Here are some:

➤ A high level of the amino acid homocysteine may injure arteries and promote the development of atherosclerosis.

➤ A high level of a protein called C-reactive protein can indicate that there is inflammation in the walls of the arteries, which can lead to plaque formation.[11]

➤ A lipid–protein compound called Lp(a) is being investigated for its role in promoting heart disease.

➤ Apolipoprotein B (ApoB) is a measure of the amount of "bad" LDL cholesterol in the blood. A high ApoB level indicates a higher risk for heart disease.

Though the name sounds mysterious, *syndrome X*, also called *metabolic syndrome*, refers to a cluster of many factors that increase the risk for heart disease. These include abdominal obesity (too much weight around the middle), insulin resistance, high blood pressure, elevated blood levels of triglycerides and the slower clearance of this fat from the blood, a low level of HDL cholesterol, smaller and more dense LDL cholesterol particles, the higher likelihood of forming and maintaining blood clots, too much insulin, and, possibly, too much glucose in the blood. Exercise and weight reduction can help reduce all of the risk factors associated with this syndrome.[12]

LDL cholesterol, and HDL cholesterol. The good news is that there are several diet and lifestyle changes you can make to help lower your LDL cholesterol level. The Examining the Evidence feature "The Mediterranean Diet: What Do People Living in the Mediterranean Do Differently?" on page 168 addresses one diet approach to heart-healthy eating.

Practical Nutrition VIDEO

Pizza Parlor Strategies

Even pizza can be a heart-healthy choice if you follow Joan's suggestions on how to top it. Scan this QR code with your mobile device to access the video. You can also access the video in MasteringNutrition™.

Minimize Saturated Fats, *Trans* Fats, and Cholesterol in Your Diet

In general, saturated fats raise your LDL cholesterol level, while unsaturated fats, when they replace saturated fats in your diet, will have a cholesterol-lowering effect. (Note that saturated fats in your diet will raise your blood cholesterol level more than cholesterol in your diet will.) Typically, the higher your consumption of saturated fats, the higher the LDL cholesterol levels in your blood.[24]

Americans consume about five times more saturated fat than *trans* fat. A food that is low in *trans* fats can still be heart unhealthy if it is high in saturated fat. For example, years ago, some consumers switched from using stick margarine, which is high in *trans* fat, to butter, thinking that butter was better for their blood cholesterol. As shown in **Figure 5.20**, although butter has less *trans* fat than stick margarine, if

a Butter is a rich source of saturated fatty acids and cholesterol. One tablespoon of butter contains 8 grams of saturated fat.

b Margarine doesn't contain cholesterol but it may contain *trans* fat formed during hydrogenation of vegetable oils.

c Use liquid fats over solid fats on your food and in cooking. The more liquid a fat is at room temperature, the less saturated fat and *trans* fat it contains.

Figure 5.20 Read Food Labels to Lower Saturated and *Trans* Fat Intake

The Mediterranean Diet: What Do People Living in the Mediterranean Do Differently?

The Mediterranean diet doesn't refer to the diet of a specific country but to the dietary patterns found in several areas of the Mediterranean region, specifically Crete (a Greek island), other areas of Greece, and southern Italy, circa 1960. Researchers were drawn to these areas because the adults living there had very low rates of chronic diseases, such as heart disease and cancer, and a very long life expectancy. For example, the natives of Greece had a rate of heart disease that was 90 percent lower than that of Americans at that time.[13] Ironically, the people in Crete, in particular, were less educated and affluent, and less likely to obtain good medical care than were Americans, so their health successes could not be explained by education level, financial status, or a superior health care system. Researchers found that compared with the diets of affluent Americans, the Cretans' diet was dramatically lower in foods from animal sources, such as meat, eggs, and dairy products, and higher in fat (mostly from olive oil and olives) and grains, fruits, and vegetables.

Research continues to support the benefits of a Mediterranean-style diet. Numerous studies indicate that adherence to a traditional Mediterranean diet is associated with greater longevity.[14] Adopting a Mediterranean-style diet has been shown to also help individuals who had experienced a heart attack reduce their risk of recurrent heart disease by 50 to 70 percent compared with those following a more classic low-saturated-fat, low-cholesterol diet.[15]

The Mediterranean Diet Pyramid shown here was designed to reflect these dietary patterns and lifestyle habits (see figure). Let's look a little closer at this pyramid, the dietary and lifestyle changes that augment it, and some potential changes that you can make in your diet and lifestyle to reap similar benefits.

The Mediterranean Lifestyle

First, notice that there are no portion recommendations in the Mediterranean Diet Pyramid. This purposeful omission portrays the relative importance and frequency of each grouping of foods as it contributes to the whole diet, rather than to a strict diet plan. It was designed to provide an overview of healthy food choices rather than dictate rigid amounts from each food group.[16]

Next, note that physical activity is front and center, at the base of this pyramid, reflecting the foundation for the Mediterranean way of life. This is an important concept, as the Mediterranean residents in the 1960s were very active and, not surprisingly, much leaner than Americans at that time. In addition to exercise, Mediterranean citizens enjoyed other lifestyle habits that have been known to promote good mental and physical health. They had a supportive community of family and friends, long relaxing family meals, and afternoon siestas (naps).[17] Exercising daily, resting, and relaxing

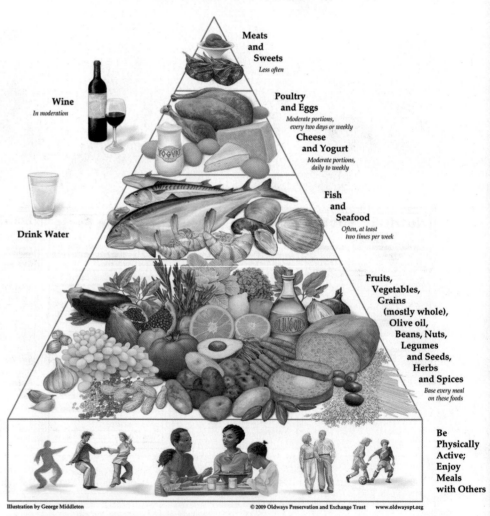

Mediterranean Diet Pyramid
A contemporary approach to delicious, healthy eating

Meats and Sweets
Less often

Wine
In moderation

Poultry and Eggs
Moderate portions, every two days or weekly

Cheese and Yogurt
Moderate portions, daily to weekly

Drink Water

Fish and Seafood
Often, at least two times per week

Fruits, Vegetables, Grains (mostly whole), Olive oil, Beans, Nuts, Legumes and Seeds, Herbs and Spices
Base every meal on these foods

Be Physically Active; Enjoy Meals with Others

Illustration by George Middleton   © 2009 Oldways Preservation and Exchange Trust   www.oldwayspt.org

The Healthy Mediterranean Diet Pyramid
A plant-based diet with minimal amounts of high-saturated-fat, high-sugar foods, coupled with daily physical activity, reflects the healthy habits of the Mediterranean lifestyle.

with family and friends is good health advice for all, no matter what food guidance system you follow.

A Diet of Well-Seasoned Plant Foods, Olive Oil, Fish, and Dairy

Plant-based foods such as whole grains, fruits, vegetables, legumes, and nuts are the focus of the Mediterranean diet. In fact, more than 60 percent of the calories of the Cretans' diets in the 1960s were supplied by these high-fiber, nutritionally dense plant foods. In traditional Mediterranean-style eating, a combination of plant foods, such as vegetables and legumes ladled over couscous or pasta, was the focus of the meal.[18] Fresh bread, without margarine or butter, often accompanied the meal, and fruit was served as dessert.

More than 75 percent of the fat in the diets of the Cretans was supplied by olives and olive oil.[19] As previously discussed, vegetable oils are low in saturated fat, and olive oil in particular is high in monounsaturated fat. Heart-healthy meals featuring fish and seafood should be enjoyed at least twice a week, following the example of the Mediterraneans.

Nonfat milk and yogurt, and low- or reduced-fat cheeses can be enjoyed on a daily basis when eating a Mediterranean-style diet. A small amount of grated Parmesan cheese sprinkled over vegetables and

a grain-based meal can provide a distinct Mediterranean flavor.

Occasional Poultry, Eggs, and Meat

Foods from animal sources were limited in the Cretan diet; local people consumed less than 2 ounces of meat and poultry daily. No more than four eggs were eaten weekly, which included those used in cooking and baking.[20] Following this trend, the Mediterranean Diet Pyramid suggests eating limited amounts of poultry and eggs weekly, but relegates red meat consumption to only occasionally.

Sweets, Water, and Wine

Historically, sweets were more prevalent during the holidays and fruit was the standard daily dessert.[21] Consequently, this pyramid recommends that consumption of honey- or sugar-based sweets remain modest. Water is recommended daily. The Cretans drank it all day long and with their meals. They also drank low to moderate amounts of wine, typically only with meals. Sometimes the wine was mixed with water, and many times women did not consume any alcohol. Though the pyramid depicts wine consumption on a daily basis, it is actually considered optional and based on personal preferences, family and medical history, and social situations.

How Does the Mediterranean Diet Pyramid Compare with MyPlate?

There are many similarities between the Mediterranean Diet Pyramid and MyPlate. Both emphasize the importance of regular physical activity, and both encourage a

plant-based diet rich in whole grains, fruits, and vegetables, and daily consumption of dairy products. Mediterranean-style eating encourages the use of olive oil, a fat source that is rich in heart-healthy, unsaturated fat, and fish and seafood. Vegetable oils are also encouraged on MyPlate, but more modestly. Whereas poultry, eggs, and meat are recommended more modestly in the Mediterranean Diet Pyramid than in MyPlate, both advise minimizing intake of sweets. Both tools can be used as a foundation for a healthy diet. The key is to stick to the recommendations.

What Do You Think?

1. What aspects of the Mediterranean Diet do you think contribute to heart health?
2. How are the lifestyle habits commonly associated with the Mediterranean Diet likely to impact heart health?
3. How does the Mediterranean Diet compare to your own currentt diet?

Dining Out with Your Heart In Mind

Having a yen for Mexican, Italian, Indian, or Chinese food but not sure what to order? Visit the Healthy Dining Finder interactive website to help you choose a restaurant with menu options than will please your palate and be healthy for your heart. Dinner is a click away at www.healthydiningfinder.com.

Eggs are an excellent source of protein, but egg yolks are high in cholesterol.

you combine both the saturated fat and *trans* fat in each spread, margarine would still be better for your blood cholesterol. Decreasing the *trans* fats in your diet at the expense of increasing the saturated fat won't be healthy for your heart. When it comes to lowering your LDL cholesterol level, you need to limit both types of fats in your diet.[25] For your heart's sake, cholesterol-raising saturated fat should contribute less than 10 percent of your daily calories (ideally, less than 7 percent) and *trans* fats should be as low as possible.[26]

Dietary cholesterol raises your LDL cholesterol level, although saturated fats and *trans* fats will raise it more.[27] The less cholesterol in your diet, the better for your heart. Dietary cholesterol is found in foods from animal sources, with egg yolks being a significant contributor in the diet.[28] Limiting the amount of these foods and choosing low-fat dairy products will cut down fat and trim dietary cholesterol.

The cholesterol in an egg is contained entirely in the yolk—the egg white is cholesterol free. Research now suggests that consuming up to an egg daily may not be associated with an increased risk of heart disease.[29] However, if you eat an egg yolk a day, you don't have a lot a leeway in your diet to keep your daily intake to no more than the 300 mg that is recommended.

Some shellfish, such as shrimp, are also high in cholesterol; however, these are very low in saturated fat and contain some heart-healthy omega-3 fatty acids. Lobster has more than 40 percent less cholesterol than shrimp and is also very low in total fat. Unfortunately, the high price of shrimp and lobster limits their consumption for many people.

Because cholesterol is not found in foods from plant sources, you won't find it in vegetables, fruits, pasta, nuts, peanut butter, or vegetable oils. The best way to minimize dietary cholesterol intake is to keep your portions of lean meat, skinless poultry, and fish to about 6 ounces daily; use only low-fat or nonfat dairy foods; use vegetable oils more often than butter; keep the consumption of baked goods to a minimum; and fill up on cholesterol-free fruits, vegetables, and whole grains.

Include Fish in Your Weekly Choices

Decades ago, researchers suggested that the Greenland Eskimos' regular consumption of fatty fish (approximately 14 ounces a day), which is rich in EPA and DHA, played a key role in their low incidences of death from heart disease.[30] Ongoing research continues to support the protective roles EPA and DHA may play in reducing the risk of heart disease and stroke.[31] These omega-3 fatty acids may prevent irregular heart beats, reduce atherosclerosis, mildly lower blood pressure, decrease the clustering or clumping of platelets, and lower the level of fat in the blood, to name a few protective actions.[32]

It is recommended that you consume at least two servings of fish (especially fatty fish such as salmon, sardines, or herring) per week, which is approximately 0.250 grams daily, to obtain these omega-3 fatty acids.[33] However, don't try to meet this quota at the fast-food drive-through. Fried fish that is commercially prepared tends to have few of these fatty acids and is often fried in unhealthy fat. Note some cautions regarding fish consumption in the Nutrition in the Real World feature "Mercury and Fish" on page 172.

Though consuming some omega-3 fatty acids is good, more may not be better. Because EPA and DHA interfere with blood clotting, consuming more than 3 grams, which typically only happens by taking supplements, can cause gastrointestinal discomfort, nausea, and the risk of excessive bleeding.[34] (Consuming large amounts of fish-oil supplements can also leave a less-than-appealing fishy aftertaste in your mouth.) Because of these potential adverse side effects, omega-3 fatty acid supplements (fish-oil supplements) should only be consumed with the advice and guidance of a doctor.[35]

While fish-oil supplements contain omega-3 fatty acids, excessive amounts can be unhealthy for some individuals.

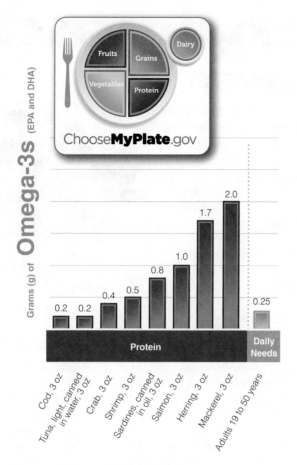

Figure 5.21 Food Sources of Omega-3 Fatty Acids
Several types of fish, particularly fatty fish, are high in the heart-healthy omega-3 fatty acids.

Americans are currently consuming only about 0.1 to 0.2 grams (as compared with the 0.25 grams recommended) of EPA and DHA daily.[36] **Figure 5.21** lists the omega-3 fatty acid content of some popular fish and seafood, and the Table Tips provide a few quick ways to add fish to your diet. Think of fish as food for your heart.

Eat Plenty of Plant Foods

In addition to fish, the AHA also recommends that you consume plant-based foods such as walnuts and flaxseeds, as well as soybean and canola oils, which are all high in alpha-linolenic acid.[37] As mentioned, some alpha-linolenic acid is converted in the body to these heart-healthy omega-3 fatty acids.

Eating more plant foods high in viscous, soluble fiber may be one of the easiest ways to decrease your LDL cholesterol level. In reviewing more than 65 studies, researchers found that each gram of viscous, soluble fiber consumed, in the range of 2 to 10 grams daily, from oatmeal, oat bran, legumes such as dried beans, psyllium, and/or pectin, lowered LDL cholesterol levels by more than 2.0 mg/dl on average.[38] Although the DRI for fiber ranges from consuming 20 to 38 grams daily, consuming about half of this amount, or 10 to 25 grams of viscous, soluble fiber, can help decrease high LDL cholesterol levels.[39] Increasing the soy in your diet may also help reduce the risk of heart disease.

Grind whole flaxseeds before eating them to best reap their nutritional benefits. Whole flaxseeds can pass through your gastrointestinal tract intact, keeping their essential fatty acids and vitamin E enclosed in the shell.

Mercury and Fish

Although the health benefits of eating fish are well established, not everyone should be eating unlimited amounts of *all* types of fish. In fact, pregnant and nursing women, women of childbearing age who may become pregnant, and young children should avoid certain types of seafood that may contain high amounts of methylmercury. This form of mercury can be harmful to the nervous systems of unborn children, especially during the first trimester of pregnancy, a time when women may not even realize that they are pregnant.[22]

Though mercury occurs naturally in nature, it is also a by-product of industrial processes and pollution. The airborne form of mercury accumulates on the surface of streams and oceans and is transformed by the bacteria in the water into the toxic form of methylmercury.[23] The fish absorb the methylmercury from the water, or get it by eating the organisms that live in the water. Because the ingested methylmercury accumulates over time, larger fish, such as swordfish, shark, king mackerel, and tilefish (golden bass or golden snapper), will have

the highest concentration of methylmercury, as they have a longer life span and feed on other, smaller fish. Women of childbearing age and young children should avoid eating these four types of fish.

However, eating fish, in particular the omega-3 fats from seafood, has been shown to *help* in the development of a fetus's nervous system.[24] Thus, pregnant women and women of childbearing age can eat up to 12 ounces weekly of other types of cooked fish, including shellfish, and should choose from a variety of fish to get these omega-3 fats in their diet. Luckily, the ten most popular types of seafood (canned *light* tuna, shrimp, pollock, salmon, cod, catfish, clams, flatfish, crabs, and scallops) contain only low amounts of methylmercury. Canned albacore (white) tuna has more mercury than the light variety, so should be limited to no more than 6 ounces weekly.[25] While the FDA regulates all commercial fish, the Environmental Protection Agency (EPA) oversees all freshwater fish caught recreationally, such as by family members and friends. This agency recommends that all women who are or may become

Large fish such as swordfish, shark, king mackerel, and tilefish are likely to contain high levels of methylmercury.

pregnant, nursing mothers, and young children should limit their consumption of freshwater fish to six ounces of cooked fish weekly for adults.[26] If you eat noncommercial fish from local waters, you should always check with your state or local health department for specific advice, as there could be additional fish consumption advisories based on your local waters. The EPA recommends that if you want to eat coastal and ocean fish that is caught recreationally, you should check with your local or state health department and follow the FDA advice referenced earlier.[27]

Spreads and soft-gel tablets containing plant sterols and stanols can be used as part of a heart-healthy diet to lower LDL cholesterol.

phytosterols Naturally occurring sterols found in plants. Phytosterols lower LDL cholesterol levels by competing with cholesterol for absorption in the intestinal tract.

Although all plant foods are cholesterol free, they do contain **phytosterols**, which are plant sterols similar to cholesterol that are found in the plant's cell membranes. Plant sterols can help lower LDL cholesterol levels by competing with cholesterol for absorption in the intestinal tract.[40] With less cholesterol being absorbed, there will be less in the blood. Plant sterols occur naturally in soybean oil, many fruits, vegetables, legumes, sesame seeds, nuts, cereals, and other plant foods.[41]

Research shows that consuming about 2 grams of plant stanols or sterols can lower LDL cholesterol by about 5 to 15 percent.[42] Products such as margarines, juices, snack items, and soft-gel tablets that contain plant sterols are now available.

Routinely Select Foods Rich in Antioxidants and Phytochemicals

You might think that a substance that starts with the prefix "anti" couldn't be good for you. However, the antioxidants vitamins C and E and beta-carotene appear to be "pro" heart health. Antioxidants may help LDL cholesterol become more resistant to oxidants, products of cell processes that may play a role in the progression of heart disease.[43] Antioxidants appear to protect LDL cholesterol from being oxidized by inhibiting the formation of oxidants, intercepting them once they are created, or helping to repair any injury to cells due to these substances. However, when there are more oxidants than antioxidant defense mechanisms occurring in the body, an imbalance occurs. This can cause adverse effects, such as heart disease.

Antioxidant-rich plant foods such as fruits and vegetables contain many other vitamins and minerals, which are not only healthy for your heart in their own right, but may also work with antioxidants. These foods are naturally low in saturated fat and *trans* fat and are cholesterol free, so they can displace heart-unhealthy foods in your diet. Plant foods are also full of fiber, particularly soluble fiber. For all of these reasons, your heart will benefit if you eat plant foods high in antioxidants at each meal.

Nuts are one type of food that is rich in antioxidants and fiber, and they can have a positive effect on LDL cholesterol levels for other reasons. Research involving healthy men showed that a diet with 20 percent of the calories coming from walnuts lowered LDL cholesterol by a little over 15 percent, and a study of more than 80,000 women showed that those who ate nuts frequently—an ounce of nuts at least five times a week—had an approximately 35 percent reduction in the risk of heart disease compared with women who hardly ever ate nuts.[44] The FDA now allows the food label on certain nuts and nut products to claim that the product potentially helps fight heart disease.[45]

The only downside to nuts is that they're high in calories. A mere ounce of nuts (about 24 almonds or 28 peanuts) can contribute a hefty 160 to 200 calories to your diet. Routinely sitting down with a jar of peanuts to eat while studying can quickly have you overconsuming calories. The Table Tips provide ideas on how to enjoy a modest amount of nuts in your diet.

There are other substances that may provide an extra boost to your heart health. Some research suggests that chocolate, due to its **flavonoid** content, may offer some antioxidant protection as well as potentially inhibiting platelet aggregation, which can perpetuate a blood clot.[46] However, keep in mind that the phytochemical, flavonoid, can vary among brands and that chocolate is a sweet that can contribute a hefty amount of calories if consumed in excess, which can lead to obesity, a risk factor for heart disease. When consumed in small amounts, as part of a healthy diet, flavonoid-rich chocolate will likely provide some minor heart-health benefits.[47]

Tea may also reduce your risk of heart disease. Research shows that consumption of tea is associated with a lower incidence of dying from heart disease.[48] Green tea in particular is not only high in catechins, which are antioxidants, but a review of 20 studies also showed that these substances may help reduce total and LDL cholesterol.[49] Drinking tea is good for your heart.

Table TIPS

Nuts about Nuts?

Have some mixed nuts as an afternoon snack. Though high in calories, they are an excellent source of antioxidants and fiber, have zero cholesterol, and are low in saturated fat.

Toss some nuts into your mealtime salad. Use less oil or salad dressing and more non-fat vinegar to adjust for the added calories.

Swap nuts for meat, like chicken or beef, in dishes such as stir-fries. A third of a cup of nuts is equal to an ounce of red meat or chicken.

Add a tablespoon of nuts to your morning cereal, and use skim rather than reduced-fat milk to offset some of the extra calories.

Add a tablespoon of chopped nuts to your afternoon yogurt.

Add a handful of peanuts to your air-popped popcorn the next time you need a snack.

Strive for Plenty of Exercise and Manage Your Weight

Routine exercise can help reduce LDL cholesterol levels, high blood pressure, insulin resistance, and excess weight, and improve HDL cholesterol levels.[50] To gain these health benefits, the current 2008 *Physical Activity Guidelines for Americans* recommend that adults should partake in 150 minutes (2 hours and 30 minutes) weekly of moderate-intensity activities such as walking briskly or 75 minutes (1 hour and 15 minutes) weekly of vigorous-intensity aerobic physical activity such as jogging, or a combination of the two.[51] Additional health benefits can be gained by increasing your physical activity above this level.[52]

Regular physical activity can also help accelerate weight loss. Losing excess weight can help not only to lower LDL cholesterol levels, high blood pressure, and the risk of developing type 2 diabetes, but also to raise HDL cholesterol levels. Hence, sedentary individuals should "move" and sedentary, overweight individuals should "move and

flavonoids Phytochemicals found in fruits, vegetables, tea, nuts, and seeds.

Table 5.6

To Decrease Excess LDL Cholesterol

Dietary Changes	Lifestyle Changes
Consume less saturated fat	Lose excess weight
Consume less *trans* fats	Exercise more
Consume less dietary cholesterol	
Consume more soluble fiber–rich foods	
Consume a more plant-based diet	

Table TIPS

Eating for a Healthy Heart

Choose only lean meats (round, sirloin, and tenderloin cuts) and skinless poultry and keep your portions of meat to about 6 ounces daily. Eat fish at least twice a week.

Use two egg whites in place of one whole egg when baking.

Use reduced-fat or nonfat dairy products, such as low-fat or skim milk, reduced-fat cheese, and low-fat or nonfat ice cream. Sprinkle cheese on top of your food rather than mixing it in so you use less. Be sure to keep ice cream servings small.

Substitute cooked beans for half the meat in chili, soups, and casseroles.

Use canola, olive, soybean, or corn oil, and *trans* fat–free margarine instead of butter or shortening.

lose" to lower their risk of heart disease. **Table 5.6** summarizes the diet and lifestyle changes you can make to reduce your LDL cholesterol and risk for heart disease.

A Word about the Protective Effects of Red Wine

Drinking alcohol in moderate amounts can reduce the risk of heart disease.[53] Alcohol can increase the level of the heart-protective HDL cholesterol. In fact, approximately 50 percent of alcohol's heart-protective effect is probably due to this positive effect on HDL cholesterol. Studies have also suggested that alcohol may decrease blood clotting by affecting the coagulation of platelets or by helping the blood to break up clots.[54]

Other studies have suggested that the antioxidants in wine as well as dark beer also contribute to the heart-protective aspects of alcohol.[55] Though some alcohol may be good, more is definitely not better. Drinking too much alcohol can increase the level of fat in your blood and lead to high blood pressure. Binge drinking, a common practice among young adults, is associated with an increased risk for heart disease and stroke.[56] We will talk more about alcohol consumption in younger individuals in Chapter 9.

The Whole Is Greater Than the Sum of Its Parts

When it comes to reducing the risk of heart disease, the whole diet may be greater than the sum of its parts. A study of more than 45 adults with elevated total and LDL cholesterol levels illustrated that a diet "portfolio" consisting of a diet low in saturated fat and cholesterol that was also high in soluble fiber, soy protein, plant sterols, and nuts lowered LDL cholesterol levels by almost 30 percent.[57] This impressive reduction was similar to that observed in the group that was given a cholesterol-lowering drug and limited *only* the saturated fat and cholesterol in their diet. The latter group's diet did not include the other items in the portfolio diet. Hence, a dietary portfolio approach to eating may be a viable way for individuals to lower high cholesterol levels and avoid taking medication that could have potential side effects.[58] The Table Tips on this page provide eating tips for a heart-healthy diet.

The Take-Home Message Limiting saturated fat, cholesterol, and *trans* fat, and increasing fish consumption, as well as consumption of antioxidant-rich fruits, vegetables, whole grains, and nuts, are associated with a reduction in the risk of heart disease. Regular exercise and weight loss can also help lower LDL cholesterol levels and raise HDL cholesterol levels. Drinking a moderate amount of alcohol may help reduce the risk of heart disease. Some individuals should avoid alcoholic beverages.

MADE over MADE better

Many Americans' diets are too high in fat and heart-unhealthy saturated fat. A few tweaks in your diet selections can help you keep your fat intake within a healthy range of 20 to 35 percent of your daily calories and your saturated fat intake to no more than 7 to 10 percent of your calories every day. Here are some typical fat-rich foods made over and made nutritionally better!

If you like this...	Try this to control your fat intake!

Mocha, 2% Milk, Whipped Cream
Serving size: 16 oz
Total Fat: 15 grams
Saturated Fat: 8 grams

Coffee, Brewed
Serving size: 16 oz
Total Fat: 0 grams
Saturated Fat: 0 grams

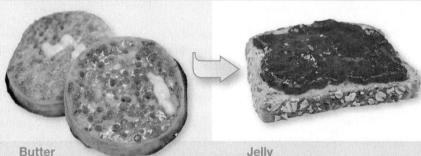

Butter
Serving size: 1 pat
Total Fat: 3.8 grams
Saturated Fat: 2.4 grams

Jelly
Serving size: 1 tbs
Total Fat: 0 grams
Saturated Fat: 0 grams

Cheddar Cheese
Serving size: 1.5 ounces
Total Fat: 14.1 grams
Saturated Fat: 9 grams

Reduced-fat Cheddar Cheese
Serving size: 2 ounces
Total Fat: 9 grams
Saturated Fat: 6 grams

Chocolate Ice Cream
Serving size: 1/2 cup
Total Fat: 14 grams
Saturated Fat: 9 grams

Low-fat Frozen Yogurt
Serving size: 1/2 cup
Total Fat: 1.5 grams
Saturated Fat: 1 gram

Source: Data from USDA National Nutrient Database for Standard Reference, www.nal.usda.gov.

Is Wild Salmon a Better Choice Than Farmed Salmon? Salmon is well known as an excellent source of omega-3 fatty acids. Both farmed and wild-caught salmon contain this essential nutrient; however, farmed salmon may also contain toxins such as methylmercury and polychlorinated biphenyls (PCBs).

Is the nutritional benefit of consuming high amounts of omega-3 fatty acids worth the risk of ingesting toxins? Should you avoid farmed salmon and eat only wild-caught salmon? After you've read the arguments for and against, answer the critical-thinking questions and decide for yourself.

yes

- Farmed salmon have much higher levels of toxic chemicals such as PCBs, dioxins, and certain pesticides than their wild-caught counterparts.[1] A review paper has found a possible link between PCBs and the development of type 2 diabetes mellitus.[2] The contamination source in farmed fish is fish oil and fishmeal in their feed. However, PCB levels vary greatly from farm to farm.

- There are some environmental concerns associated with farm-raised salmon. For instance, most salmon are farmed in open pens and cages in coastal waters. Waste from these farms is released directly into the ocean and can harm wild fish populations.[3]

- Salmon farms can be incubators of disease. One study found that reoccurring sea lice outbreaks killed up to 80 percent of young wild pink salmon whose migration paths crossed salmon farms.[4]

- Farmed salmon feed can contain high amounts of antibiotics and other chemicals, some of which are outlawed in the United States for threats to human and marine health.[5]

- It takes about 3 pounds of wild fish to grow 1 pound of farmed salmon. As global production increases, so does the environmental impact of farming salmon.[6]

no

- Farmed and wild salmon are both low in saturated fat and calories. Both are high in protein, and both are excellent sources of omega-3 fatty acids.[7]

- A study in 2004 found that farmed salmon had PCB levels 10 times as high as wild salmon,[8] but those levels were still very low[9]—well below those the Food and Drug Administration says are safe. And since then, PCB levels in farmed salmon have come down quite a bit.

- Researchers from the Harvard School of Public Health found that the benefits of eating oily fish outweighed the risk, even for the most sensitive parts of the population.[10]

- Most farm-raised salmon are Atlantic salmon and are readily available year-round. Wild populations of Atlantic salmon are generally at very low levels and their commercial harvest is limited.[11]

- Wild-caught salmon is often higher priced than farmed salmon.[12]

what do you think?

1. What is the most compelling argument for consuming wild rather than farm-raised salmon? Is this argument strong enough to influence your food choice? **2.** Do the benefits of eating farmed salmon outweigh the risks? **3.** How can consumers make the best choices when it comes to eating fish?

1 There Are Three Classifications of Lipids

Lipids refer to a category of carbon, oxygen, and hydrogen compounds that do not dissolve in water. There are three types of lipids: triglycerides, phospholipids, and sterols. A triglyceride, also known as a fat, contains three fatty acids joined to a glycerol backbone and is the most abundant type of lipid in your body and in foods. A fatty acid without any double bonds is called a saturated fatty acid. If one or more double bonds is present, it is called an unsaturated fatty acid. A saturated fat contains mostly saturated fatty acids and tends to be solid at room temperature. An unsaturated fat has mostly unsaturated fatty acids, is liquid at room temperature, and is also known as an oil.

Phospholipids contain two fatty acids at their tail end and have a phosphate-containing head. Their polar heads and nonpolar tails cause them to be attracted to both water and fat. Lecithin is the major phospholipid in your cell membranes. Lecithin is often used as an emulsifier in foods. Cholesterol is the major sterol in your body and in foods. Cholesterol is the precursor of vitamin D, bile acids, and sex hormones. Your body makes all the cholesterol it needs.

Lipid	Structure
Triglycerides	Glycerol — Fatty acids
Phospholipids	Phosphate head — Fatty acids
Sterols	HO

2 Fats Are Digested and Absorbed in the Small Intestine and Transported with the Help of Lipoproteins

The majority of fat in your diet is digested and absorbed in your small intestine with the help of bile acids and pancreatic lipase. The digested fat is predominantly packaged in protein- and phosphorus-containing lipoproteins called chylomicrons, which travel in your lymph to your bloodstream.

Other lipoproteins include the "bad" LDL cholesterol carrier and the "good" HDL cholesterol carrier. LDL deposits cholesterol along your artery walls and contributes to atherosclerosis. HDL removes cholesterol from arteries and brings it to the liver to be used or excreted from your body.

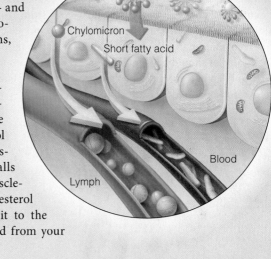

Micelles
Chylomicron
Short fatty acid
Blood
Lymph

3 Fat Plays Many Key Roles in the Body

In your body, fat is used as a protective cushion for your bones, organs, and nerves, in your cell membranes, and as insulation to maintain your body temperature. In food, fat provides texture and flavor, and contributes to satiety. Fat in food also aids in the absorption of fat-soluble vitamins.

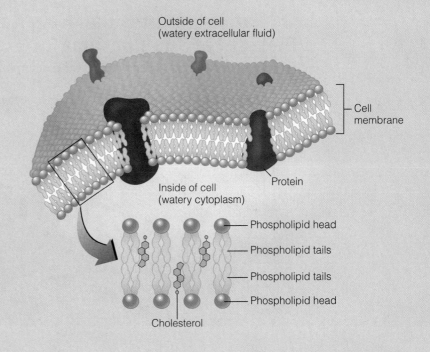

Outside of cell (watery extracellular fluid)
Cell membrane
Inside of cell (watery cytoplasm)
Protein
Phospholipid head
Phospholipid tails
Phospholipid tails
Phospholipid head
Cholesterol

4 Moderate Consumption of Dietary Fat Is Essential for Health

Your diet should contain 20 to 35 percent of calories coming from fat, with no more than 10 percent from saturated fat, and minimal amounts of *trans* fats. Because fat provides the essential fatty acids, linoleic acid and alpha-linolenic acid, a minimum of 5 percent and up to 10 percent of your total calories should be from linoleic acid, and 0.6 percent to 1.2 percent of total calories should be from alpha-linolenic acid.

5 The Best Food Sources of Fat Are Unsaturated Fats

Plant-based unsaturated fats are the best sources of fat and are abundant in vegetable oils, such as soybean, corn, and canola oils, as well as in soybeans, walnuts, peanut butter, and flaxseeds. Vegetables oils, nuts, and flaxseeds are good sources of essential fatty acids. A limited amount of alpha-linolenic acid can be converted to the omega-3 fatty acids, eicosapentaenoic acid (EPA) and docosahexaenoic acid (DHA), which have been shown to reduce the risk of heart disease and stroke. Because fish, especially fatty fish, are good sources of EPA and DHA, you should consume at least two servings of fish weekly. Most saturated fat in the diet comes from animal foods, including whole-milk dairy products such as cheese, butter, and ice cream, fatty cuts of meat, and the skin on poultry. The majority of *trans* fats in foods are created by food manufacturers through the process of hydrogenation. Reading food labels can help you lower your intake of both saturated and *trans* fats.

6 Fat Substitutes Can Help Reduce the Dietary Fat You Consume

Fat substitutes are designed to provide all the creamy properties of fat for fewer calories and total fat grams. Because fat has more than double the calories per gram of carbohydrates or protein, fat substitutes have the potential to reduce calories from fat.

7 Heart Disease Begins with a Buildup in the Arteries

Heart disease develops when the coronary arteries, the large blood vessels that supply oxygen and other nutrients to the heart, accumulate a buildup of LDLs and other substances along their walls. As the artery gets narrower, blood flow is impeded and less oxygen and nutrients are delivered to the heart; a blood clot could also block the narrowed artery, leading to a heart attack or stroke.

Heart disease is the leading cause of death in the United States. Risk factors that you can't control are your age, gender, family history of heart disease, and having type 1 diabetes. Risk factors that you can control include preventing and controlling type 2 diabetes, high blood pressure, smoking, physical inactivity, excess weight, a low HDL cholesterol level, and an elevated LDL cholesterol level.

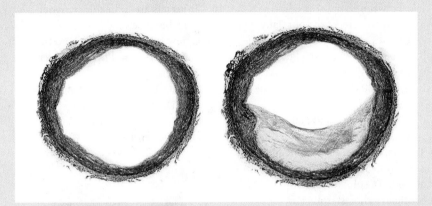

8 Diet Can Help Maintain Healthy Blood Cholesterol Levels

Eating a well-balanced plant-based diet that contains moderate amounts of heart-healthy unsaturated fat and less heart-unhealthy saturated fat is the best strategy to lower your LDL blood cholesterol level and your risk of heart disease. Commercially prepared baked goods, snack items, and fried foods should be limited so as to decrease *trans* fats. Your diet should contain no more than 300 milligrams of cholesterol daily, on average. Soluble fiber–containing foods such as oats, and plant sterols can also help lower your LDL cholesterol level. Exercising and losing excess weight can help lower your LDL cholesterol level and increase your HDL cholesterol level. The Mediterrean Diet Pyramid is a heart-healthy diet that can help you maintain healthy blood cholesterol levels.

Terms to Know

- lipids
- hydrophobic
- fatty acids
- saturated fatty acid
- unsaturated fatty acid
- monounsaturated fatty acid

- polyunsaturated fatty acid
- essential fatty acids
- linoleic acid
- alpha-linolenic acid
- glycerol
- triglyceride
- fat
- phospholipids

- sterols
- lipoprotein
- bile
- micelles
- chylomicron
- very low-density lipoproteins (VLDLs)
- low-density lipoproteins (LDLs)

- high-density lipoproteins (HDLs)
- hydrogenation
- *trans* fatty acids
- atherosclerosis
- plaque
- hypertension

Check Your Understanding

1. The primary lipid in your body is
   a. cholesterol.
   b. lecithin.
   c. triglycerides.
   d. chylomicrons.
2. Fat in foods is a source of
   a. flavor.
   b. carbohydrates.
   c. minerals.
   d. fiber.
3. The type of lipoprotein that carries absorbed fat and other lipids through your lymph system is called
   a. VLDL.
   b. LDL.
   c. bile acid.
   d. a chylomicron.
4. Donald has heart disease. To obtain heart-healthy omega-3 fatty acids, he should eat
   a. a tuna fish sandwich at lunch and a Burger King fish sandwich for dinner.
   b. shrimp for lunch and salmon for dinner.
   c. fish and chips for lunch and flounder at dinner.
   d. fried fish sticks at lunch and steamed lobster for dinner.

5. Which of following does *not* provide dietary cholesterol?
   a. steak
   b. skinless chicken
   c. low-fat milk
   d. margarine
6. You should keep your dietary fat intake between
   a. 8 and 10 percent of your daily calories.
   b. 20 and 35 percent of your daily calories.
   c. 35 and 40 percent of your daily calories.
   d. 300 milligrams and 500 milligrams daily.
7. The major dietary component that raises your LDL cholesterol is
   a. viscous, soluble fiber.
   b. dietary cholesterol.
   c. saturated fat.
   d. plant sterols.
8. Which of the following are good sources of the essential fatty acids linoleic acid and alpha-linolenic acid?
   a. bananas
   b. walnuts
   c. oatmeal
   d. chocolate

9. To raise your level of HDL cholesterol, you can
   a. increase the viscous, soluble fiber in your diet.
   b. increase the protein in your diet.
   c. drink more water.
   d. exercise more.
10. *Trans* fats are unhealthy for your heart because they
    a. lower LDL cholesterol levels.
    b. raise HDL and LDL cholesterol levels.
    c. raise LDL cholesterol and lower HDL cholesterol levels.
    d. have no effect on LDL cholesterol.

Answers

1. (c) The major lipid in your body is triglycerides, also known as fat. Cholesterol is another type of lipid but is not as abundant as fat. Lecithin is a phospholipid found in your cell membranes and is used as an emulsifier in some foods. Chylomicrons are lipoproteins that transport fat and other lipids to your liver.
2. (a) Fat provides flavor. It does not provide carbohydrates, minerals, or fiber.

3. (d) Chylomicrons enable insoluble fat as well as cholesterol and phospholipids to travel through the lymph system. Bile acids help emulsify fat in your GI tract. VLDLs and LDLs transport fat and other lipids through your blood.

4. (b) Though tuna fish is a wonderful way to enjoy fish at lunch, the commercially prepared fried fish sandwich, fish and chips, and fish sticks have little of the omega-3 fatty acids that would help Donald's heart. Shrimp and salmon are much better choices.

5. (d) Because dietary cholesterol can only be found in foods from animal sources, margarine, which is made from vegetable oils, is free of dietary cholesterol.

6. (b) Your daily fat intake should be between 20 and 35 percent of your daily calories.

7. (c) Whereas dietary cholesterol raises LDL cholesterol, saturated fat is the bigger culprit behind an elevated LDL cholesterol in the blood. Viscous, soluble fiber and plant sterols can help lower LDL cholesterol.

8. (b) Walnuts are a good source of essential fatty acids.

9. (d) Increasing your exercise can help increase your HDL cholesterol level. Increasing the soluble fiber, protein, or water in your diet does not affect your level of HDL cholesterol.

10. (c) *Trans* fats provide a double whammy for your heart because they raise the "bad" LDL cholesterol and lower the "good" HDL cholesterol in your body.

Web Resources

- National Heart, Lung, and Blood Institute at www.nhlbi.nih.gov
- American Heart Association at www.heart.org
- Centers for Disease Control and Prevention, at www.cdc.gov

1. **False.** Your body *does* need cholesterol for important functions. However, your body can manufacture it in sufficient amounts, so you don't need to eat any to meet your needs. See page 146.

2. **False.** However, don't start celebrating. We are still consuming too much fat from heart-unhealthy saturated fat in the diet. See page 153.

3. **False.** Whereas too much dietary fat may cause you to gain weight, eating too little isn't healthy either. A diet low in fat but high in added sugars may increase the level of fat in your blood. See page 153.

4. **False.** Red meat is not the major source of saturated fat in the diet. Turn to page 154 to find out what is.

5. **False.** Fat-free foods often have added carbohydrates, which add back calories. The savings in fat calories is usually not much of a savings in total calories. See page 162.

6. **False.** The HDL cholesterol in your body is healthy for you, and may protect against heart disease. Turn to page 166 to learn more.

7. **False.** Although stick margarines can contain heart-unhealthy *trans* fats, butter has more total cholesterol-raising fats than margarine, and so is ultimately less healthy. See page 167.

8. **False.** Because peanut butter doesn't come from an animal, it does not contain cholesterol. See page 170.

9. **False.** Consuming too much fish oil in supplement form can be unhealthy. See page 170.

10. **True.** The viscous, soluble fiber found in oatmeal and other foods can lower your blood cholesterol. See page 171.

6

Proteins and Amino Acids

True or False?

1. Your body can use protein as an **energy** source. Ⓣ Ⓕ p. 195

2. Proteins increase **satiety** after a meal. Ⓣ Ⓕ p. 195

3. You can **digest** the protein in pasta as easily as the protein in a chicken breast. Ⓣ Ⓕ p. 198

4. Soy is not as good a **source** of dietary protein as fish. Ⓣ Ⓕ p. 198

5. Approximately one-half of your daily **calories** should come from protein. Ⓣ Ⓕ p. 199

6. Most Americans are falling short of their protein **needs**. Ⓣ Ⓕ p. 199

7. Americans are eating **more** red meat than they were in the 1970s. Ⓣ Ⓕ p. 200

8. Protein **bars** are needed if you are very active. Ⓣ Ⓕ p. 202

9. Eating too much protein-rich food may increase your blood risk of **heart disease**. Ⓣ Ⓕ p. 205

10. **Vegetarian** athletes are at a competetive disadvantage compared with nonvegetarian competitors. Ⓣ Ⓕ p. 212

See page 221 for the answers.

183

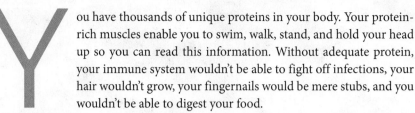

Chapter Objectives

After reading this chapter, you will be able to:

1. **Explain what proteins are and why they are important.**

2. **Describe how your body digests and absorbs proteins.**

3. **Describe the functions of protein in the body.**

4. **Determine your daily protein needs.**

5. **Identify healthy sources of protein in the diet.**

6. **Explain the health consequences of consuming too little or too much protein.**

7. **Describe the benefits and risks of a vegetarian diet.**

Y ou have thousands of unique proteins in your body. Your protein-rich muscles enable you to swim, walk, stand, and hold your head up so you can read this information. Without adequate protein, your immune system wouldn't be able to fight off infections, your hair wouldn't grow, your fingernails would be mere stubs, and you wouldn't be able to digest your food.

In this chapter we discuss the structure and roles of proteins and how they are digested, absorbed, and used by the body. We will also cover the health risks associated with consuming too much or too little protein and the pros and cons of different eating patterns, including vegetarian diets.

What Are Proteins and Why Are They Important?

Proteins are the predominant structural and functional materials in every cell, and you have thousands of unique proteins in your body. These diverse molecules play a role in virtually every cellular activity, from building, repairing, and maintaining cells to storage, transport, and utilization of the nutrients you eat. Hormones and enzymes, which control essential metabolic processes, are also made of proteins. In fact, proteins are involved in most of your body's functions and life processes, and without them, you wouldn't survive.[1]

We'll begin our discussion of proteins with a look at how they're structured. Specifically, we'll start by looking at the amino acids.

The Building Blocks of Proteins Are Amino Acids

All proteins consist of a chain of some combination of 20 unique **amino acids**, and they are classified according to the number of amino acids in the chain. If the chain contains fewer than 50 amino acids linked together, it is called a peptide. Two joined amino acids form a *dipeptide;* three joined amino acids form a *tripeptide;* and a *polypeptide* is more than 10 amino acids joined together. A chain with more than 50 amino acids is called a protein. Proteins typically contain between 100 and 10,000 amino acids in a sequence. For instance, the protein that forms the hemoglobin in red blood cells consists of close to 300 amino acids, as compared with collagen, which contains approximately 1,000 amino acids.

Amino acids are like numeric digits, in that their specific sequence will determine a specific function. Consider that telephone numbers, Social Security numbers, and bank PIN numbers are all made up of the same digits (0 to 9) arranged in different sequences of varying lengths. Each of these number combinations has a specific purpose. Similarly, amino acids can be linked together to make unique sequences of varying lengths, each with a specific function.

Anatomy of an Amino Acid

As illustrated in **Figure 6.1a,** each amino acid contains a central carbon (C) surrounded by four parts: an **acid group** (COOH) (which is why it is called an amino "acid"), an **amine group** (NH_2) that contains nitrogen, a hydrogen atom, and a unique **side chain**. Whereas all 20 nutritionally important amino acids contain the same four parts, it is the side chain that makes each amino acid different.

The side chain can be as simple as a single hydrogen atom, as in the amino acid glycine; or it can be a collection of atoms, as in aspartic acid and phenylalanine (see Figure 6.1b). (Do these last two amino acids sound familiar? Recall that they are the major components of the sugar substitute aspartame, which we discussed in Chapter 4.)

Now let's look at how amino acids are linked together to build proteins.

Peptide Bonds and Side Chains Determine a Protein's Shape and Function

Amino acids are joined to each other by **peptide bonds** to build proteins. A peptide bond is created when the acid group (COOH) of one amino acid is joined with the amine group (NH₂) of another amino acid (**Figure 6.2**). The unique nature of each amino acid side chain prevents a protein from remaining in an orderly straight line. Rather, each polypeptide folds into a precise three-dimensional shape, such as a coil, based on the interactions of its amino acid side chains with each other and the

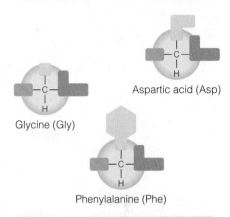

a **Amino acid structure.** All amino acids contain carbon, hydrogen, and oxygen, similar to carbohydrates and fat. They also contain a nitrogen-containing amine group and an acid group.

Glycine (Gly)

Aspartic acid (Asp)

Phenylalanine (Phe)

b **Different amino acids showing their unique side chains.** A unique side chain (shown in yellow) distinguishes the various amino acids.

Figure 6.1 The Structure of an Amino Acid

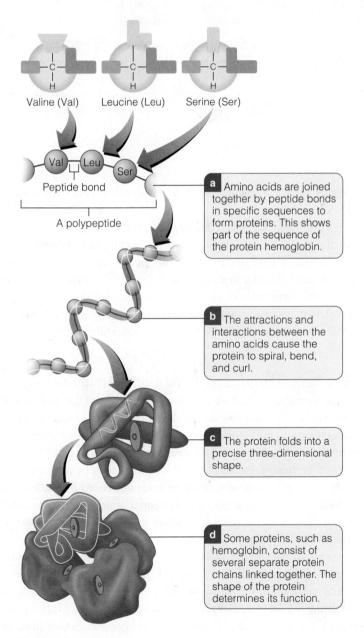

Valine (Val) Leucine (Leu) Serine (Ser)

Val Leu Ser

Peptide bond

A polypeptide

a Amino acids are joined together by peptide bonds in specific sequences to form proteins. This shows part of the sequence of the protein hemoglobin.

b The attractions and interactions between the amino acids cause the protein to spiral, bend, and curl.

c The protein folds into a precise three-dimensional shape.

d Some proteins, such as hemoglobin, consist of several separate protein chains linked together. The shape of the protein determines its function.

Figure 6.2 The Making of a Protein

proteins Compounds in your body that consist of numerous amino acids and are found in all living cells.

amino acids The building blocks of protein. Amino acids contain carbon, hydrogen, oxygen, and nitrogen. All amino acids are composed of an acid group, an amine group, and a unique side chain.

acid group The COOH group that is part of every amino acid; also called the *carboxyl group.*

amine group The nitrogen-containing part (NH₂) of an amino acid.

side chain The side group of an amino acid that provides it with its unique qualities; also referred to as the R group.

peptide bonds The bonds that connect amino acids, created when the acid group of one amino acid is joined with the nitrogen-containing amine group of another amino acid.

Table 6.1

The Mighty Twenty

Essential Amino Acids	Nonessential Amino Acids
Histidine (His)[a]	Alanine (Ala)
Isoleucine (Ile)	Arginine (Arg)[b]
Leucine (Leu)	Aspartic acid (Asp)
Lysine (Lys)	Asparagine (Asn)
Methionine (Met)	Cysteine (Cys)[b]
Phenylalanine (Phe)	Glutamic acid (Glu)
Threonine (Thr)	Glutamine (Gln)[b]
Tryptophan (Trp)	Glycine (Gly)[b]
Valine (Val)	Proline (Pro)[b]
	Serine (Ser)
	Tyrosine (Tyr)[b]

[a]Histidine was once thought to be essential only for infants. It is now known that small amounts are also needed for adults.
[b]These amino acids can be "conditionally essential" if there are either inadequate precursors or inadequate enzymes available to create them in the body. This can happen in certain illnesses and in premature infants.

environment. Some side chains are attracted to other side chains; some are neutral; and some repel each other.

Additionally, side chains can be *hydrophilic* ("water-loving") or *hydrophobic* ("water-fearing"), and this affects how they react with their environment. The hydrophobic side chains tend to cluster together in the interior of the protein, causing the protein to be globular in shape. The hydrophilic side chains assemble on the outside surface of the protein, closer to the watery environments of blood and other body fluids. The shape of a protein determines its function in your body. Therefore, anything that alters the bonds between the side chains will alter its shape and thus its function.

Essential, Nonessential, and Conditional Amino Acids

There are nine amino acids that your body cannot make and that you must therefore obtain from foods. These are the **essential amino acids**, and you can find them in foods such as meat and milk. It is *essential* that you obtain them from your diet.

The remaining 11 amino acids are **nonessential amino acids** because they can be synthesized, or created, in your body. It is *not essential* to consume them in the diet. Your body creates nonessential amino acids as needed by adding nitrogen to a carbon-containing structure. Some nonessential amino acids can also be made from other amino acids. This process occurs primarily in the liver. **Table 6.1** lists the 20 amino acids by their classification.

Some nonessential amino acids may become **conditionally essential** if the body cannot make them because of illness, or because the body lacks the necessary **precursors** or enzymes. In such situations, they are considered essential and must be consumed through food. An example of this is when premature infants are not able to make enough of the enzymes needed to create arginine, so they need to get this amino acid in their diet.[2]

essential amino acids The nine amino acids that the body cannot synthesize; they must be obtained through dietary sources.

nonessential amino acids The 11 amino acids that the body can synthesize.

conditionally essential amino acids Nonessential amino acids that become essential if the body cannot make them, such as during bouts of illness.

precursor A substance that is converted to another substance in the body.

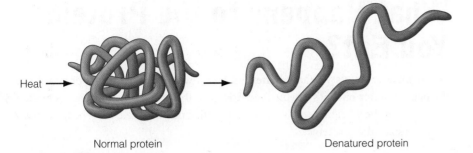

Heat → Normal protein → Denatured protein

Figure 6.3 Denaturing a Protein
A protein can be denatured, or unfolded, by exposure to heat, mechanical agitation, acids, bases, or salts. Any change in a protein's shape will alter its function.

Denaturation of Proteins Changes Their Shape

Proteins can be unfolded or *denatured* (**Figure 6.3**) by heat, acids, bases, salts, or mechanical agitation. **Denaturation** doesn't alter the primary structure of the protein (amino acids will still be in the same sequence), but it does change the shape. As mentioned earlier, changing the protein's shape will alter its function, sometimes permanently.

The protein found in eggs can be used to illustrate denaturation. When you apply heat to a raw egg, such as by frying it, the heat denatures the protein in both the yolk and the egg white. Heat disrupts the bonds between the amino acid side chains, causing the protein in the egg to uncoil. New bonds then form between the side chains, changing the shape and structure of the protein and the texture of the egg. As the egg cooks, it solidifies, illustrating the permanent change in the protein's shape and structure.

Similarly, mechanical agitation, such as beating egg whites when you prepare a meringue, can denature protein. Beating an egg white uncoils the protein, allowing the hydrophilic side chains to react with the water in the egg white, while the hydrophobic portions of the side chains form new bonds, trapping the air from the whipping. The stiffer the peaks of egg white, the more denatured the protein.[3]

Salts and acids can also denature proteins. For example, when you marinate a chicken breast or a steak before cooking, you might use salt (such as in soy sauce) or acid (such as wine or vinegar) to denature its protein. The end result is juicier, more tender meat.[4] During digestion, acidic stomach juices help denature and untangle proteins to reveal the peptide bonds. This allows digestive enzymes to break them apart.

Cooking denatures protein and will often improve the quality, structure, and texture of the protein-rich foods you eat. Raw eggs, meat, and poultry are basically inedible, but cooking these foods greatly increases their palatability.

The Take-Home Message
An amino acid is made up of carbon, oxygen, hydrogen, a nitrogen-containing amine group, and a unique side chain. There are 20 side chains and so 20 unique amino acids. Whereas all 20 amino acids are needed to make proteins, 11 of these can be synthesized in your body and are thus nonessential. The remaining nine amino acids are the essential amino acids that your body cannot synthesize. Essential amino acids must be obtained in your diet. Amino acids are joined together by peptide bonds to create proteins. The attractions and interactions between the side chains cause the protein to fold into a precise three-dimensional shape. The protein's shape determines its function. Heat, mechanical agitation, acids, bases, and salts can break, or denature, a protein and alter its shape and function.

denaturation The alteration of a protein's shape, which changes the structure and function of the protein.

What Happens to the Protein You Eat?

When you enjoy a tasty peanut butter sandwich, what happens to the protein from the peanut butter once it's in your body? How is the protein in the peanuts broken down so that the valuable amino acids can be efficiently digested, absorbed, and used to synthesize other proteins?

You Digest and Absorb Dietary Proteins in Your Stomach and Small Intestine

Protein digestion begins after chewed food enters your stomach (**Figure 6.4**). Stomach acids denature the protein strands, untangling their bonds. This allows the digestive enzyme pepsin, which is produced in your stomach lining and activated by its acidic environment, to begin breaking the proteins down and preparing them for absorption. Pepsin splits the protein into shorter polypeptide strands, and these strands are propelled into the small intestine.

In the small intestine, other enzymes further break down the strands into tripeptides and dipeptides, as well as some amino acids. The protein remnants are then absorbed into the cells of the small intestine lining, where the remaining tripeptides and dipeptides are broken down into single amino acids, which enter the blood and travel to the liver.

How the liver uses these amino acids depends on the needs of your body. For example, they might be used to make new proteins or, if necessary, as an energy source. They can also be converted to glucose if you are not getting enough carbohydrate in your diet. Some of these amino acids also travel back out to the blood to be picked up and used by your cells.

Your Body Degrades and Synthesizes Proteins

Your diet provides essential and nonessential amino acids. Your body stockpiles a limited amount of all these in **amino acid pools** in your blood and inside your cells. Because your body can't make the essential amino acids, the pools need to be constantly restocked.

Your body is also constantly degrading its proteins, that is, breaking them down into their component parts, to synthesize other needed proteins. Hence, amino acids are continually being removed from your amino acid pools to create proteins on demand. This process of continually degrading and synthesizing protein is called **protein turnover** (see **Figure 6.5** on page 190). In fact, more than 200 grams of protein are turned over daily. The proteins in your intestines and liver—two active areas in your body—account for as much as 50 percent of this turnover.[5] The cells that make up the lining of your intestines are continually being sloughed off and replaced. The proteins in these sloughed-off cells are degraded, and most of the resulting amino acids are absorbed and recycled in your body, although some are lost in your stool and urine. Proteins and amino acids are also lost daily through sloughed-off skin, hair, and nails. Replacements for these proteins must be synthesized, and the amino acid pools provide the building materials to do this. Some of the amino acids in the pools are used to synthesize nonprotein substances, including thyroid hormones and melanin, the pigment that gives color to dark skin and hair.

amino acid pools A limited supply of amino acids stored in your blood and cells and used to build new proteins.

protein turnover The continual process of degrading and synthesizing protein. When the daily amount of degraded protein is equivalent to the amount that is synthesized, you are in protein balance.

Protein digestion begins in the stomach with the aid of hydrochloric acid (HCl) and the enzyme pepsin. Other enzymes continue the digestion in the small intestine, breaking the protein down to single amino acids that are absorbed into the bloodstream.

ORGANS OF THE GI TRACT

ACCESSORY ORGANS

MOUTH

Mechanical digestion of protein begins with chewing, tearing, and mixing food with salivary juices to form a bolus.

STOMACH

Hydrochloric acid denatures protein and activates pepsinogen to form pepsin.

Pepsin breaks the polypeptide chain into smaller polypeptides.

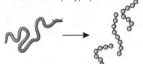

PANCREAS

Produces enzymes that are released into the small intestine via the pancreatic duct.

LIVER

Uses some amino acids to make new proteins or converts them to glucose. Most amino acids pass through the liver and return to the blood to be picked up and used by body cells.

SMALL INTESTINE

Enzymes continue to cleave peptide bonds, resulting in dipeptides, tripeptides, and single amino acids.

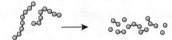

Enzymes in the lining of the small intestine finish the digestion to yield single amino acids, which can then be absorbed into the bloodstream and travel through the portal vein to the liver.

Amino acids

Intestinal cells

Blood

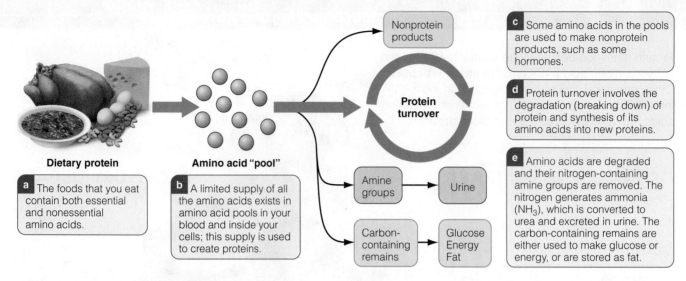

Figure 6.5 The Fate of Amino Acids in Your Body

Dietary protein

a The foods that you eat contain both essential and nonessential amino acids.

Amino acid "pool"

b A limited supply of all the amino acids exists in amino acid pools in your blood and inside your cells; this supply is used to create proteins.

Nonprotein products

Protein turnover

Amine groups → Urine

Carbon-containing remains → Glucose Energy Fat

c Some amino acids in the pools are used to make nonprotein products, such as some hormones.

d Protein turnover involves the degradation (breaking down) of protein and synthesis of its amino acids into new proteins.

e Amino acids are degraded and their nitrogen-containing amine groups are removed. The nitrogen generates ammonia (NH_3), which is converted to urea and excreted in urine. The carbon-containing remains are either used to make glucose or energy, or are stored as fat.

Amino acids are also broken down into their component parts for other uses or stored in another form. To begin the breakdown process, the amino acids lose their amine groups. The nitrogen in the amine groups forms ammonia (NH_2), which can be toxic to your cells in high amounts. Your liver converts the ammonia to **urea**, a waste product that is excreted in your urine via the kidneys.

The carbon-containing remnants of the amino acids are then converted to glucose, used as energy, or stored as fat, depending on the needs of your body. When your diet is too low in carbohydrates, the amino acids will be used to make glucose. When calories are inadequate, the amino acids can be sacrificed for energy. Surplus amino acids (beyond what is needed in the amino acid pools) from excess dietary protein can't be stored as protein in your body and so must be stored predominantly as fat. Hence, as you know from the last two chapters, *all* excess calories—whether from carbohydrates, proteins, or fats—will be stored as fat in your body.

Proteins don't have a mind of their own. How does your body know when to create or synthesize more proteins? Let's look at how proteins are synthesized in your body.

DNA Directs the Synthesis of New Proteins

Protein synthesis is directed by a molecule in the nucleus of your cells called **DNA** (**d**eoxyribo**n**ucleic **a**cid). DNA is the blueprint for every cell in your body.

Each DNA molecule carries the code to synthesize every protein that you need. However, your cells' protein-producing capabilities are specialized. For example, only cells in the pancreas make the hormone insulin, because no other cell in the body expresses the **gene** (a DNA segment that codes for a specific protein) to make insulin. Several hormones prompt DNA to synthesize proteins as needed.

As with any blueprint, DNA doesn't do the actual building or synthesizing; it only provides the instructions. DNA can't leave the nucleus of the cell, so it directs another important molecule within the cell, called **RNA** (**r**ibo**n**ucleic **a**cid), to carry out its instructions for building a protein. There are two specialized RNAs, called **messenger RNA (mRNA)** and **transfer RNA (tRNA)**, which perform very specific roles during protein synthesis. See **Figure 6.6** to view how protein synthesis takes place in a cell.

urea A nitrogen-containing waste product that is excreted in urine.

DNA The blueprint in cells that stores all genetic information. DNA remains in the nucleus of the cell and directs the synthesis of proteins.

gene A DNA segment that codes for a specific protein.

RNA A molecule that carries out the orders of DNA.

messenger RNA (mRNA) A type of RNA that copies the genetic information encoded in DNA and carries it out of the nucleus of the cell to synthesize the protein.

transfer RNA (tRNA) A type of RNA that collects the amino acids within the cell that are needed to make a specific protein.

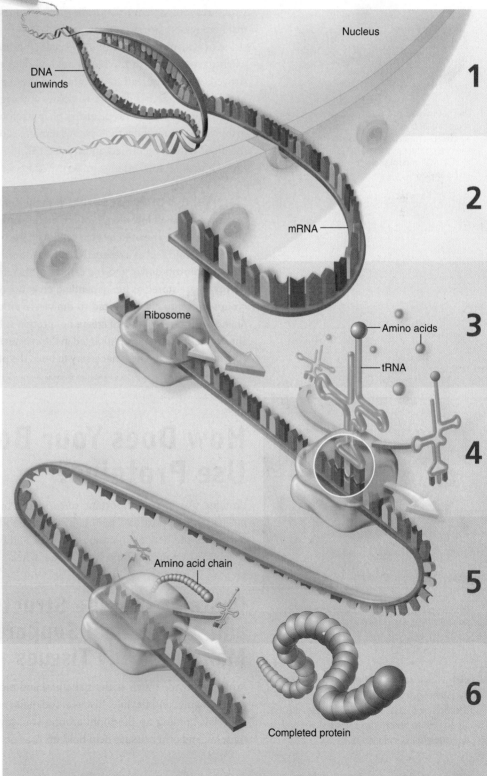

Protein synthesis is the process by which the DNA code within a cell's nucleus directs the cell's production of specific proteins.

Cell

Nucleus

Nucleus

1 In the nucleus, DNA unwinds to allow a copy of the code, called messenger RNA (mRNA) to be made.

DNA unwinds

1

2 The mRNA leaves the nucleus.

mRNA

2

3 The mRNA brings the coded information to the ribosome.

Ribosome

Amino acids

tRNA

3

4 The ribosome moves along the mRNA, reading the code. Transfer RNA (tRNA) brings specific amino acids to the ribosome based on the code.

4

5 The ribosome then builds a chain of amino acids (the protein) in the proper sequence, based on the code in the mRNA.

Amino acid chain

5

6 When all the appropriate amino acids are added and the protein is complete, the protein is released from the ribosome.

Completed protein

6

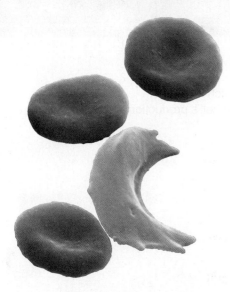

Red blood cells with normal hemoglobin, like the three similar ones, are smooth and round. A person with sickle-cell anemia has red blood cells like the one on the right; these cells are stiff and form a sickle (half-moon) shape when blood oxygen levels are low.

When abnormalities occur during protein synthesis, serious medical conditions may result. One such condition is **sickle-cell anemia**. The most common inherited blood disorder in the United States, sickle-cell anemia is caused by the abnormal formation of the protein hemoglobin. According to the National Institutes of Health (NIH), approximately one in 12 African-Americans and one in 100 Hispanics are carriers of the mutated gene that causes the disease.[6]

The mutation in the gene causes a change in the amino acid sequence in the hemoglobin molecule. In sickle-cell anemia, there is a displacement of just *one* amino acid, glutamine, with another amino acid, valine, in the polypeptide chains of hemoglobin. This causes the chains to stick to one another and form crescent-shaped structures rather than the normal globular ones. Whereas red blood cells with normal hemoglobin are smooth and round, those with this mutation are stiff and form a sickle or half-moon shape under certain conditions, such as after vigorous exercise, when oxygen levels in the blood are low. These abnormal sickle cells are easily destroyed, which can lead to anemia, and they can build up in blood vessels, causing painful blockages and damage to tissues and organs.

Another rare genetic disorder, phenylketonuria (PKU), is caused by the body's inability to properly degrade phenylalanine, causing a buildup of this amino acid in the blood. If not identified and treated early in life, PKU can cause mental retardation. To prevent this, infants are screened for PKU at birth.

The Take-Home Message With the help of gastric juices and enzymes in your stomach and small intestine, proteins are broken down into amino acids and absorbed into your blood to be used by your cells. A limited supply of amino acids exists in pools in your body, which act as a reservoir for the synthesis of proteins as needed. Surplus amino acids are broken down, and the carbon-containing remains can be used for glucose or energy, or are stored as fat, depending on your body's needs. The nitrogen in the amine groups is eventually converted to the waste product urea and excreted in your urine. Amino acids can be used to create nonprotein substances, including certain hormones. The synthesis of proteins is directed in the cell nucleus by DNA, which carries the code for the amino acid sequences necessary to build the proteins that you need.

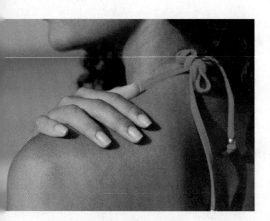

Proteins play an important role in keeping your skin healthy and your nails strong.

sickle-cell anemia A blood disorder caused by a genetic defect in the development of hemoglobin. Sickle-cell anemia causes the red blood cells to distort into a sickle shape and can damage organs and tissues.

How Does Your Body Use Proteins?

Proteins play many important roles in the body, from providing structural and mechanical support and maintaining your body's tissues to creating enzymes and hormones and helping maintain acid-base and fluid balance. They also transport nutrients, assist your immune system, and, when necessary, become a source of energy.

Proteins Provide Structural and Mechanical Support and Help Maintain Body Tissues

Proteins provide much of the structural and mechanical support that keeps you upright, moving, and flexible. Just as wood, nails, and plaster are the behind-the-scenes materials holding up the room around you, several fibrous proteins in your bones, muscles, and other tissues help hold up your body.

Collagen, the most abundant protein in your body, is found in all of your **connective tissues**, including the bones, tendons, and ligaments, that support and connect your joints and other body parts. This fibrous protein is also responsible for the elasticity in your skin and helps form scar tissue to repair injuries such as wounds. Two other proteins, actin and myosin, provide mechanical support by helping your muscles contract so you can run, walk, sit, and lie down.

The daily wear and tear on your body causes the breakdown of hundreds of grams of proteins each day. For example, the protein-rich cells of your skin are constantly sloughing off, and proteins help create a new layer of outer skin every 25 to 45 days.[7] Because your red blood cells have a short life span—only about 120 days—new red blood cells must continually be regenerated. The cells that line the inner surfaces of your organs, such as your lungs and intestines, are also constantly sloughed off, excreted, and replaced.

In addition to regular maintenance, extra protein is sometimes needed for "emergency repairs." Protein is essential in healing, and a person with extensive wounds, such as severe burns, may have dietary protein needs that are more than triple his or her normal needs.

Proteins Build Most Enzymes and Many Hormones

When your body needs a reaction to take place promptly, such as breaking down carbohydrates after a meal, it calls upon **enzymes**, biological **catalysts** that speed up reactions. Without enzymes, reactions would occur so slowly that you couldn't survive. Most enzymes are proteins, although some may also have a **coenzyme**, such as a vitamin, that aids in initiating a reaction.

Each of the thousands of enzymes in your body catalyzes a specific reaction. Some enzymes, such as digestive enzymes, break compounds apart. (Recall from Chapter 4 that the enzyme lactase is needed to break down the milk sugar lactose.) Other enzymes, such as those used to synthesize proteins, help compounds combine. Enzymes aren't changed, damaged, or used up in the process of speeding up a particular reaction. **Figure 6.7** shows how an enzyme breaks apart two compounds, yet isn't changed in the process. Thus, the enzyme is available to catalyze additional reactions.

While enzymes expedite reactions, hormones direct them. Many **hormones** are proteins that direct or signal an activity, often by turning on or shutting off enzymes. (Recall from Chapter 5 that some hormones can also be lipids.) Hormones are released from tissues and organs and travel to target cells in another part of your body to direct an activity. There are more than 70 trillion cells in your body, and all of these cells interact with at least one of more than 50 known hormones.[8]

Let's consider an example of one hormone in action. When your blood glucose level rises after a meal or snack, your pancreas (an organ) releases insulin (a hormone) into your blood, which in turn directs the uptake of glucose in your cells (the activity). If your blood glucose level drops too low, such as between meals, your pancreas (an organ) releases glucagon (a hormone), which promotes the release of glucose (the activity) from the glycogen stored in your liver, which in turn raises your blood glucose level.

Proteins Help Maintain Fluid Balance

Your body is made up predominantly of water, which is distributed throughout various body compartments. Proteins help ensure that all this water is dispersed evenly, keeping you in a state of **fluid balance**.

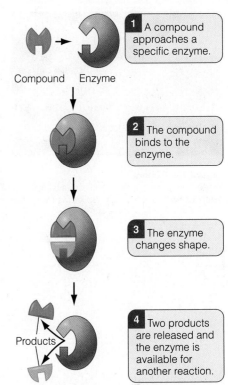

Figure 6.7 An Enzyme in Action
Enzymes speed up reactions in your body, yet they aren't changed, damaged, or used up in the process.

1 A compound approaches a specific enzyme.

2 The compound binds to the enzyme.

3 The enzyme changes shape.

4 Two products are released and the enzyme is available for another reaction.

Compound   Enzyme

Products

collagen A ropelike, fibrous protein that is the most abundant protein in your body.

connective tissue The most abundant tissue type in the body. Made up primarily of collagen, it supports and connects body parts as well as providing protection and insulation.

enzymes Substances that act as catalysts and speed up reactions.

catalysts Substances that aid and speed up reactions without being changed, damaged, or used up in the process.

coenzyme Substances, often vitamins, that are needed by enzymes to perform many chemical reactions in your body.

hormones Protein- or lipid-based chemical messengers that initiate or direct a specific physiological response. Insulin, glucagon, and estrogen are examples of hormones.

fluid balance The equal distribution of water throughout your body and within and between cells.

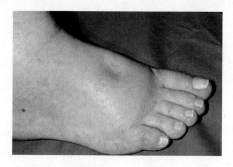

Figure 6.8 Edema
Inadequate protein in the blood can cause fluid retention within body tissue, also known as edema.

Normally, your blood pressure forces the nutrient- and oxygen-rich fluids out of your capillaries and into the spaces between your cells. Whereas fluids can flow easily in these spaces, proteins can't, because they are too big to cross the cell membranes. Proteins attract water, so the proteins remaining in the capillaries eventually draw the fluids back into the capillaries. Hence, protein plays an important role in the movement of fluids and in keeping the fluids balanced among these compartments. (Note: The mineral sodium also plays a major role in fluid balance.)

When fewer proteins are available to draw the fluid from between the cells back into the bloodstream, as during severe malnutrition, a fluid imbalance results. The spaces between the cell become bloated and the body tissue swells, a condition known as **edema** (**Figure 6.8**).

Proteins Help Maintain Acid-Base Balance

Proteins can alter the pH (the concentration of hydrogen ions) of your body fluids. Normally, your blood has a pH of about 7.4, and the fluid in your cells has a pH of about 7.0. Even a small change in the pH of your blood in either direction can be harmful or even fatal. With a blood pH below 7.35, a condition called acidosis sets in, which can result in a coma. A blood pH above 7.45, known as alkalosis, can result in convulsions.

Proteins act as **buffers** and minimize the changes in acid-base levels by picking up or donating hydrogen ions in the blood. Should your blood become too acidic, some of the amino acid side chains in the proteins will pick up excess hydrogen ions. Other side chains can donate hydrogen ions to your blood if it becomes too basic.

Proteins Transport Substances throughout the Body

Transport proteins shuttle oxygen, waste products, lipids, some vitamins, and sodium and potassium through your blood and into and out of cells through cell membranes. Hemoglobin acts as a transport protein that carries oxygen to cells from the lungs. Hemoglobin also picks up carbon dioxide waste products from cells for transport to your lungs to be exhaled from your body. Once in your blood, vitamin A travels to your liver and is bound to yet another protein to be transported to your cells.

Transport proteins in cell membranes form a "doorway" that allows substances such as sodium and potassium to pass in and out of cells (**Figure 6.9**). Substances that are not lipid-soluble or that are simply too big to pass through the lipid-rich membrane have to enter the cell through a protein channel.

Proteins Contribute to a Healthy Immune System

Your immune system works like an army to protect your body from foreign invaders, such as disease-causing bacteria and viruses. Specialized protein "soldiers" called **antibodies** eliminate these potentially harmful substances.

Once your body knows how to create antibodies against a specific invader, such as a virus, it stores that information and you have **immunity** to that pathogen. The next time the invader enters your body, you can respond very quickly (producing up to 2,000 precise antibodies per second!) to fight it. When this rapid immune response works efficiently, it prevents the virus or other invader from multiplying to levels high enough to make you sick.

edema The accumulation of excess fluid in the spaces surrounding your cells, which causes swelling of the body tissue.

buffers Substances that help maintain the proper pH in a solution by attracting or donating hydrogen ions.

transport proteins Proteins that carry lipids (fat and cholesterol), oxygen, waste products, and vitamins through the blood to various organs and tissues, or that serve as channels to allow substances to pass through cell membranes.

antibodies Proteins made by your body to bind to and neutralize foreign invaders, such as harmful bacteria, fungi, and viruses, as part of the body's immune response.

immunity The state of having built up antibodies to a particular foreign substance so that when particles of the substance enter the body, they are destroyed by the antibodies.

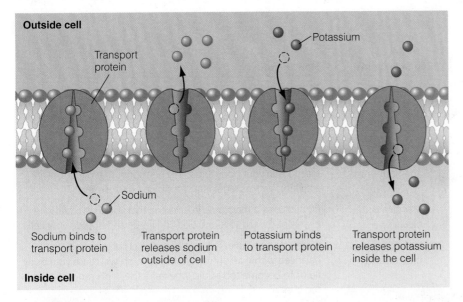

Outside cell

Potassium

Transport protein

Sodium

| Sodium binds to transport protein | Transport protein releases sodium outside of cell | Potassium binds to transport protein | Transport protein releases potassium inside the cell |

Inside cell

Figure 6.9 Proteins as Transport Channels
Transport proteins in cell membranes form a channel, or doorway, through which substances such as sodium and potassium can move from one side of the cell membrane to the other.

Sometimes, your body incorrectly perceives a nonthreatening substance as an invader and attacks it. This perceived invader is called an *allergen*. All food allergens contain proteins.[9] Individuals who react to these allergens are diagnosed with food allergies. You will learn more about food allergies in Chapter 15.

Proteins Can Provide Energy

Because proteins provide 4 calories per gram, they can be used as an energy source. However, the last thing you want to do is use this valuable nutrient, which plays so many important roles in your body, as a regular source of fuel, especially since carbohydrates and fats are far better suited for providing energy. When your diet contains adequate amounts of calories from carbohydrates and fat, proteins are used for their other important roles.

When your diet doesn't provide adequate amounts of calories—for example, in times of starvation—your body begins to break down its protein, mainly from muscles, into its amino acid components. The carbon skeletons of the amino acids are used for energy and for gluconeogenesis, the creation of glucose from noncarbohydrate sources. (Remember that your brain and nervous system need a minimum amount of glucose to function properly.) However, when proteins are used for energy, they create waste products that must be eliminated from your body, which is particularly burdensome for your liver and kidneys.

Protein Improves Satiety and Appetite Control

In addition to the structural and functional roles protein plays in the body, protein also helps increase satiety, the feeling of fullness, after a meal more than do either carbohydrate or fat.[10] Eating a meal that contains a good source of protein will leave you more satisfied than a meal containing the same amount of calories but with the majority of them coming from carbohydrate. Although the mechanism behind protein's effect on your appetite is not yet known, some research studies suggest that it

Table TIPS

Protein Power

Melt a slice of reduced-fat cheese between slices of a toasted whole-wheat English muffin for a protein-packed, portable breakfast.

Spread peanut butter on apple slices for a sweet, stick-with-you morning snack.

Add high-fiber, protein-rich chickpeas to your lunchtime salad.

Roast beef is the best-kept lunchtime secret. It's naturally lean and makes a mean sandwich filler.

Stuff a baked potato with cottage cheese, steamed broccoli, and a sprinkling of Parmesan cheese for a meal filled with protein and good nutrition.

Table 6.2

The Many Roles of Proteins

Role of Proteins	How It Works
1. Provide structural and mechanical support and maintenance	Proteins are your body's building materials, providing strength and flexibility to your tissues, tendons, ligaments, muscles, organs, bones, nails, hair, and skin. Proteins are needed for the ongoing maintenance of your body.
2. Build enzymes and hormones	Proteins are needed to make most enzymes that speed up reactions in your body and many hormones that direct specific activities, such as regulating your blood glucose level.
3. Maintain fluid balance	Proteins play a major role in ensuring that your body fluids are evenly dispersed in your blood and inside and outside your cells.
4. Maintain acid-base balance	Proteins act as buffers to help keep the pH of your body fluids balanced within a tight range. A drop in pH will cause your body fluids to become too acidic, whereas a rise in pH can make them too basic.
5. Transport substances	Proteins shuttle substances such as oxygen, waste products, and nutrients through your blood and into and out of your cells.
6. Affect antibodies and the immune response	Proteins create specialized antibodies that attack pathogens in your body that can make you sick.
7. Provide energy	Because proteins provide 4 calories per gram, they can be used as fuel or energy in your body.
8. Improves satiety	Protein increases satiety, which can help control your appetite and weight.

may be due to several factors, such as changes in appetite-suppressing hormones in the body, how the body metabolizes protein, and the levels of the amino acids in the blood.[11] Including protein in each meal can help control your appetite, which in turn can help you maintain a healthy weight.

Table 6.2 summarizes the many roles that proteins play in your body.

The Take-Home Message Proteins play many important roles in the body, including: (1) structural and mechanical support, (2) building enzymes and some hormones, (3) maintaining fluid balance, (4) maintaining acid-base balance, (5) transporting substances throughout the body, (6) providing antibodies for a strong immune system, (7) providing energy, and (8) promoting satiety.

How Much Protein Do You Need?

Healthy adults should consume enough dietary protein to replace the amount they use each day. Pregnant women, people recovering from surgery or an injury, and growing children need more protein to supply the necessary amino acids and nitrogen to build new tissue. **Nitrogen balance** studies have been used to determine how much protein individuals need to replace or build new tissue.

nitrogen balance The state in which an individual is consuming the same amount of nitrogen (from protein) in the diet as he or she is excreting in the urine.

Healthy Adults Should Be in Nitrogen Balance

A person's daily protein requirement can be estimated by using what we know about the structure of an amino acid. We know that 16 percent of every dietary protein molecule is nitrogen, and we also know that this nitrogen is retained by the body during protein synthesis. With this information, we can assess a person's protein status by measuring the amount of nitrogen consumed and subtracting the amount of nitrogen excreted. The goal is to achieve nitrogen balance.

If the nitrogen intake from dietary protein is equivalent to the amount of nitrogen excreted (mostly as urea) in the urine, then a person is in nitrogen balance. Such an individual is consuming a balanced diet with adequate amounts of protein and excreting an equally balanced amount of nitrogen. Healthy, nonpregnant adults are typically in nitrogen balance or equilibrium.

A body that retains more nitrogen than it excretes is in positive nitrogen balance. Rapidly growing babies, children, or teenagers are all in positive nitrogen balance because their bodies use nitrogen to build new tissues that aid growth, build muscles, and expand the supply of red blood cells. They therefore excrete less nitrogen in their urine. When your mother was pregnant with you, she was in positive nitrogen balance because she was building a robust baby.

Negative nitrogen balance occurs when the body excretes more nitrogen than is consumed due to some physical impairment, such as a serious injury, infection, malnutrition, or other trauma, where the body cannot synthesize protein as quickly as it's broken down. These situations all increase the body's need for both calories and protein. If the calories and protein in the diet are inadequate to cover the increased demands, then proteins from tissues are broken down to meet the body's needs. **Figure 6.10** lists some of the situations that lead to nitrogen balance or imbalance in the body.

While it is important to eat a sufficient quantity of protein to meet your needs, the quality of protein also matters.

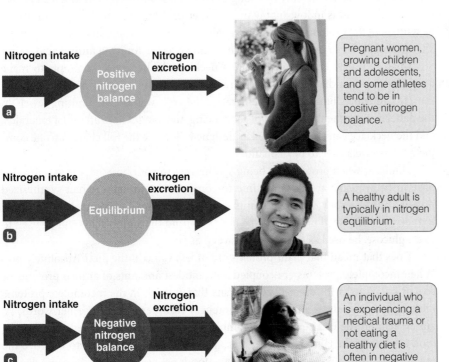

Figure 6.10 Nitrogen Balance and Imbalance

Nitrogen intake → Positive nitrogen balance → Nitrogen excretion
a Pregnant women, growing children and adolescents, and some athletes tend to be in positive nitrogen balance.

Nitrogen intake → Equilibrium → Nitrogen excretion
b A healthy adult is typically in nitrogen equilibrium.

Nitrogen intake → Negative nitrogen balance → Nitrogen excretion
c An individual who is experiencing a medical trauma or not eating a healthy diet is often in negative nitrogen balance.

Not All Protein Is Created Equal

A high-quality protein is digestible, contains all the essential amino acids, and provides sufficient protein to be used to synthesize the nonessential amino acids. **Protein quality** is determined by two factors: your body's ability to digest the protein (the protein's **digestibility**) and the types and amounts of amino acids (essential, nonessential, or both) that the protein contains.

Digestibility

The digestibility of proteins varies, depending on their source. In general, animal proteins are more digestible than plant proteins. Some of the plant proteins, especially when consumed raw, are protected by the plant's cell walls and cannot be broken down by the enzymes in your intestinal tract. Whereas 90 to 99 percent of the proteins from animal sources (cheese and other dairy foods, meat, poultry, and eggs) are digestible, only 70 to 90 percent of plant proteins, such as from chickpeas and other legumes, are typically digestible.[12]

Amino Acid Profile

The second factor that affects protein quality concerns the types and amounts of amino acids that the protein contains, or its **amino acid profile**. A protein that provides all nine of the essential amino acids, along with some of the 11 nonessential amino acids, is considered a **complete protein**. A protein that is low or deficient in one or more of the essential amino acids is considered an **incomplete protein**. A complete protein is considered of higher quality than an incomplete protein. Protein from animal sources, such as meat, fish, and poultry is typically complete protein, whereas protein from plant foods tends to be incomplete.

Two exceptions to this generalization are gelatin and soy. Gelatin, an animal protein, is not a complete protein because it is missing the amino acid tryptophan. Soy, a plant protein, has an amino acid profile that resembles the protein needs in your body, making it a complete protein.

Any protein chain is only as strong as its weakest amino acid link. If a single essential amino acid is in low supply in your diet, and thus in your body, your ability to synthesize the proteins that you need will be limited. The amino acid that is in the shortest supply in an incomplete protein is known as the **limiting amino acid**.

Imagine a jeweler trying to create a necklace. If the jeweler attempts to make a necklace using a diamond-ruby-emerald pattern with unlimited numbers of diamonds and rubies but only three emeralds, the emeralds are the limiting jewels in the pattern. After the third round of sequencing, the jeweler has run out of emeralds, and the necklace can't be completed as designed. Because the full chain can't be completed, the jewels have to be dismantled.

Similarly, when proteins are being synthesized in your body, all the amino acids have to be available at the same time to complete the protein. A half-synthesized protein can't wait for the needed amino acids to come along to complete the process. Rather, the unfinished protein will be degraded, and the amino acids will be used to make glucose, be used as energy, or be stored as fat.

Does that mean that plant proteins are of less value in the diet? Absolutely not. When incomplete proteins are coupled with modest amounts of animal proteins or soy, or combined with other plant proteins that are rich in the incomplete protein's limiting amino acids, the incomplete protein is **complemented**. In other words, its amino acid profile is upgraded to a complete protein. You don't have to eat the two food sources of the complementing plant proteins at the same meal to improve the quality of the protein source. As long as the foods are consumed in the same day, all the essential amino acids will be provided to meet your daily needs.

protein quality The measure of a protein's digestibility and how its amino acid pattern compares with your body's needs. Proteins that are more easily digested and have a complete set of amino acids are of higher quality.

digestibility A food's capacity to be broken down so that it can be absorbed.

amino acid profile The types and amounts of amino acids in a protein.

complete protein A protein that provides all the essential amino acids that your body needs, along with some nonessential amino acids. Soy protein and protein from animal sources, in general, are complete.

incomplete protein A protein that is low in one or more of the essential amino acids. Protein from plant sources tends to be incomplete.

limiting amino acid The amino acid that is in the shortest supply in an incomplete protein.

complemented proteins Incomplete proteins that are combined with modest amounts of animal or soy proteins or with other plant proteins that are rich in the limiting amino acids to create a complete protein.

Once the digestibility and the amino acid profile of a protein are known, the quality of a protein can be determined.

Protein Scoring

The **protein digestibility corrected amino acid score (PDCAAS)**, which is measured as a percentage, takes into account both the amino acid profile and digestibility of a protein to give a good indication of its quality. Milk protein, which is easily digested and meets essential amino acid requirements, has a PDCAAS of 100 percent. In comparison, chickpeas garner a PDCAAS of 87 percent, and wheat has a score of only 44 percent. If your only dietary source of protein is wheat, you are not meeting your essential amino acid needs.

The Food and Drug Administration (FDA) uses the PDCAAS to assess the quality of dietary proteins. On a food label, when protein is listed as a percentage of the daily value, this percentage is determined based on its PDCAAS.

Chickpeas are short of the limiting amino acid methionine. The addition of sesame seed paste, which has an abundance of methionine, completes the protein. Add garlic and lemon as seasonings for a completely delicious hummus.

You Can Determine Your Personal Protein Needs

There are two ways to determine protein intake in the diet. It can be measured as a percentage of total calories or as grams of protein eaten per day. The latest dietary recommendation, based on data from numerous nitrogen balance studies, is to consume from 10 to 35 percent of your total daily calories from protein. Currently, adults in the United States consume about 15 percent of their daily calories from protein, which falls within this range.[13]

The current recommendation for the grams of protein that you need daily is based on your age and your weight (**Table 6.3**). Adults age 19 and older should consume 0.8 gram (g) of protein for each kilogram (kg) of body weight. For example, a person who weighs 176 pounds (lb) would weigh 80 kg (176 lb ÷ 2.2 = 80 kg) and should consume 80 kg × 0.8 g, or 64 g of protein a day. A person who weighs 130 lb should consume approximately 47 g of protein daily (130 lb ÷ 2.2 = 59 kg × 0.8 g = 47 g). In the United States, men age 20 and older consume, on average, 99 grams of protein daily, while women of the same age consume, on average, 68 grams every day.[14] As you can see, Americans are typically meeting, and even exceeding, their dietary protein needs.

Even though most Americans consume more protein than they need, their percentage of daily calories contributed by protein (approximately 15 percent) falls

Table 6.3

Calculating Your Daily Protein Needs

If You Are	You Need
14–18 years old	0.85 g/kg
≥19 years old	0.80 g/kg

To calculate your needs, first convert your body weight from pounds (lb) to kilograms (kg) by dividing by 2.2, like this:

Your weight in pounds: _____ lb ÷ 2.2 = _____ kg

Then, multiply your weight in kilograms by 0.8 or 0.85:

Your weight in kilograms: _____ kg × 0.8 g = _____ g/day

Source: Institute of Medicine, *Dietary Reference Intakes for Energy, Carbohydrate, Fiber, Fat, Fatty Acids, Cholesterol, Protein, and Amino Acids* (Washington, D.C.: The National Academies Press, 2002).

protein digestibility corrected amino acid score (PDCAAS) A score measured as a percentage that takes into account both digestibility and amino acid profile and gives a good indication of the quality of a protein.

Practical Nutrition VIDEO

Healthy Snacks to Fuel Your Day

Snacks can be a great way to keep you going AND help you meet your daily protein needs. Scan this QR code with your mobile device to access the video. You can also access the video in MasteringNutrition™.

within the recommended range. This is because they consume an abundant amount of calories from carbohydrates and fats, which lowers the percentage of their total calories coming from protein.

An overweight individual's protein needs are not much greater than those of a healthy-weight person of similar height. This is because the Recommended Dietary Allowance (RDA) for dietary protein is based on a person's need to maintain protein-dependent tissues like lean muscle and organs and to perform protein-dependent body functions. Because most overweight people carry their extra body weight predominantly as fat, not muscle, they do not need to consume significantly more protein than normal-weight people.

The American College of Sports Medicine, the Academy of Nutrition and Dietetics, and other experts have advocated an increase of 50 to 100 percent more protein for competitive athletes participating in endurance exercise (marathon runners) or resistance exercise (weight lifters) to meet their needs.[15] However, because of their active lifestyles, athletes typically have a higher intake of food and thus already consume higher amounts of both calories and protein. Protein supplements are not needed. Now let's look at how you can meet your daily protein needs through a well-balanced diet.

The Take-Home Message Protein quality is determined by the protein's digestibility and by the types and amounts of amino acids (essential versus nonessential) it contains. Protein from animal foods is more easily digested than protein from plant foods. A complete protein, which is typically found in animal foods and soy, provides a complete set of the essential amino acids along with some nonessential amino acids. Plant proteins are typically incomplete, as they are missing one or more of the essential amino acids. Plant proteins can be complemented with protein from other plant sources or animal food sources to improve their protein quality. Adults should consume 0.8 gram of protein for each kilogram of body weight. In the United States, men, on average, consume nearly 100 grams of protein daily, while women, on average, are consuming 68 grams—in both cases, more than is needed.

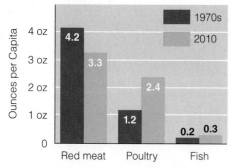

Figure 6.11 What Types of Proteins Are Americans Eating?
Americans' consumption of red meat has been declining, and they are eating more poultry and fish.

Economic Research Service (ERS), "Food Availability Per Capita Data System," 2010. Available at www.ers.usda.gov.

What Are the Best Food Sources of Protein?

Although some amount of protein is found in many foods, it is particularly abundant in meat, fish, poultry, and meat alternatives such as dried beans, peanut butter, nuts, and soy. Americans, on average, not only consume more than the recommended servings of the protein-rich foods in the meat and beans group, but also eat approximately 7 percent more than they did in the 1970s.[16] A 3-ounce serving of cooked meat, poultry, or fish, which is about the size of a woman's palm or a deck of cards, provides approximately 21 to 25 grams of protein, or about 7 grams per ounce, and is plenty of protein for one meal.

While red meat is still the most popular food in the meat and beans group, Americans' love of meat has declined over the last four decades. In contrast, Americans currently eat more than double the amount of poultry, and 50 percent more fish, than they did in 1970 (see **Figure 6.11**).[17] Dried beans such as kidney beans, pinto beans, and black beans not only provide an excellent source of protein, but are also a potent source of fiber (as you saw in Chapter 4). Dairy foods and eggs are also an excellent source of protein, and though grains and vegetables are less robust protein sources, as part of a varied, balanced diet they can aid significantly in meeting your daily needs.

Eating a wide variety of foods is the best approach to meeting your protein needs (**Figure 6.12**). A diet that consists of the recommended servings from the five food groups based on 1,600 calories, which is far less than most adults consume daily, will supply the protein needs for adult women and most adult men (see Table 6.4 on page 204). In fact, many people have already met their daily protein needs before they even sit down to dinner! How does your diet stack up when it comes to protein? Take the Self-Assessment on page 204 to find out.

Though most Americans are getting plenty of protein in their diets, there has recently been a boom in the consumption of high-protein energy bars. Are these a bargain? Do you need them? The Examining the Evidence feature "Protein Supplements: Are They Necessary?" on page 202 takes a look at this topic.

> More than half of the protein in an egg is in the white. In fact, two large egg whites provide 7 grams of protein, compared with only 6 grams in a large whole egg.

The Take-Home Message A well-balanced diet can easily meet your daily protein needs. Meat, fish, poultry, and meat alternatives such as dried beans, peanut butter, nuts, and soy are particularly abundant in protein. Dairy products and some vegetables can also be good sources.

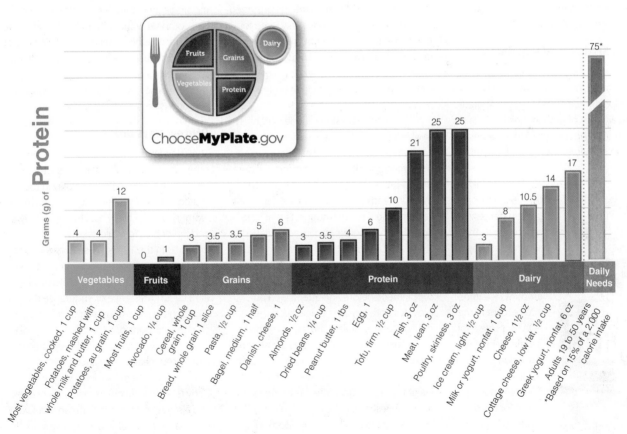

Figure 6.12 Food Sources of Protein
Food choices from the meat, poultry, fish, meat alternative, and milk groups are the most abundant sources of dietary protein. Grains and vegetables provide less protein per serving but as part of a varied, balanced diet can add significantly to meeting your daily needs.

USDA National Nutrient Database for Standard Reference (www.nal.usda.gov).

Protein Supplements: Are They Necessary?

The sale of protein supplements has sky-rocketed over the last decade, fueling an industry that now generates almost two billion dollars in the United States annually.[1] These products are enticing. They promise to give you an energy boost, help shed those unwanted pounds, build muscle, fight aging, and cure a host of health problems. With very few exceptions, purchasing and consuming these products is, at best, a waste of money, and at worst, exposure to potentially harmful heavy metals.

Protein supplement manufacturers use phrases such as "scientifically proven," "nutritious and time-saving snack or meal replacement," and "look years younger" as a promise to consumers. Unfortunately, dietary supplements do not go through a rigorous testing for screening or efficacy. So how do you know if these supplements contain what they say they contain, do what they say they do, and are safe? Is more protein always better? Let's examine the evidence.

Protein Shakes and Powder

Most protein shakes and powders use whey (concentrates, isolates, and hydrolysates), soy, or occasionally rice protein as a key ingredient. The amount of protein their label claims they contain ranges from 10 to 40 grams of protein per serving, along with added vitamins and minerals. Muscle Milk® lists 25 grams of protein per serving and suggests three servings per day for a total of 75 grams of protein. This amounts to almost 100 percent of the RDA for protein for a male weighting 176 pounds (RDA = 80 grams per day). This does not account for the other foods consumed during the day.

Do these products actually contain what is listed

on the label? Based on research conducted by ConsumerLab.com, 20 protein supplements tested did contain what the label claimed but two products were contaminated with lead (6 to 19 micrograms per day) and one product contained an additional 4 grams of sugar not accounted for on the label.[2] Other labs report arsenic, cadmium, lead, and mercury in 15 tested samples.[3] Chronic ingestion of these toxic metals can cause severe health consequences, including kidney and pulmonary damage, anemia, and osteoporosis. Exposure is avoidable because most consumers more than meet their daily protein requirements by choosing whole foods.

Protein intake does enhance muscle sythesis.[4] But athletes consume enough protein for muscle growth and repair in an average mixed diet. Whey protein used in protein supplements is abundant in milk and dairy products.[5] The additional protein consumed through powders and shakes not used for protein synthesis is either burned for energy or converted to a fatty acid and stored in the fat cells. In fact, excessive amounts of protein can be unhealthy and produce undesirable results.

The key to increasing muscle weight is a well-designed strength-training program combined with additional calories from all three macronutrients. These calories allow dietary protein to be used for muscle synthesis instead of energy. Another important key is timing. Research suggests that ingestion of protein before and immediately after a workout combined with a carbohydrate source improves muscle synthesis.[6] Choose a glass of nonfat milk, rather than a protein supplement, before and after a workout. Milk provides both key amino acids and the carbohydrate to stimulate muscle growth.

Protein shakes and powders are also marketed as meal replacers to those interested in losing weight. Whereas dieters may lose weight using a high-protein meal replacer, the same results can be obtained with a calorie-controlled meal of whole foods, without the risk. When it comes to losing weight, it's the total calories that count.

There are instances where protein shakes and supplements may be a nutritionally

sound approach. Older adults, who may have limited appetites and be less likely to consume adequate nutrients in foods, may benefit from ingesting a protein shake every day. However, these products should be used to *supplement* their meals, not replace them.

Amino Acid Supplements

Amino acid supplements, including those containing individual amino acids such as tryptophan and lysine, are marketed as remedies for a range of health issues, including pain, depression, insomnia, and certain infections. These supplements contain single amino acids often in amounts or combinations not found naturally in foods. Consuming single amino acids in unnatural doses can compete with other amino acids for absorption, possibly resulting in a deficiency of other amino acids. Further, overconsuming specific amino acids can lead to side effects such as nausea, light-headedness, vomiting, and drowsiness.

Protein Bars and Energy Bars

The sale of protein bars, energy bars, and other snack bars is a growing industry that generates over $6 billion annually in the United States.[7] There are bars advertised for women, bars for men, bars for the elderly, and junior bars for children. When they emerged in the 1980s, these bars were marketed as a portable snack or a quick meal in a cellophane wrapper to help athletes stay fueled for long-distance or endurance outings.

As you learned from the previous two chapters, all foods provide calories and therefore energy. Whether your calories come from a balanced meal or a "balanced bar," your body will either use them for fuel or store them as body fat if they are not immediately needed. You also just learned that you can meet your daily protein needs by making wise food choices. Given this knowledge, what advantage, if any, do you think protein bars provide?

If convenience and portability are the main attractions of protein bars, then consider another convenient and portable food, the peanut butter sandwich. It can be made in a snap, and since it doesn't have to be refrigerated, it can travel anywhere. The table lets you do some comparison shopping to see how a peanut butter sandwich stacks up to a protein bar.

From a price standpoint, a peanut butter sandwich is a bargain compared with bars that can cost more than $2.50 each, or ten times as much as the sandwich. While the calories and protein content of the sandwich are similar to that in many bars, the saturated fat and sugar contents are not. Some bars provide up to 7 grams of saturated fat, which is about one-third of the upper limit recommended for many adults daily. In contrast, the sandwich contains less saturated fat than all the bars listed. These bars can contain up to 7.5 teaspoons of sugar, so much of the "energy" in an energy bar is simply sugar. Because the peanut butter sandwich has lower amounts of sugar and a higher amount of fiber than almost all of the bars, it's actually the healthier food choice.

What Do You Think?

1. Do you think most people would benefit from consuming protein bars or shakes? Why or why not?
2. Are there any benefits of protein supplements that cannot be achieved by consuming protein-rich foods? If yes, what are they?
3. What role does marketing play in promoting protein shakes and supplements?

Bar Hopping

Product	Price ($)	Calories	Protein (g)	Total Carb. (g)	Total Fat (g)	Sat. Fat (g)	Sugar	Fiber (g)
Peanut butter (1 tbs) on 2 slices whole-wheat bread	**0.22**	**234**	**9**	**29**	**11**	**2**	**5%** (<1 tsp)	**5**
Balance, Chocolate Craze	$1.29	200	14	21	7	4	14% ½ (3.5 tsp)	2
Zone Perfect, Chocolate Peanut Butter	$1.29	210	14	24	7	4	15% ¾ (3.75 tsp)	3
PowerBar Protein Plus, Chocolate Brownie	$2.59	360	30	34	11	4.5	30% ½ (7.5 tsp)	0
Clif Luna, Nutz over Chocolate	$1.57	180	9	25	6	2.5	10% ½ (2.5 tsp)	4
Slim-fast Meal Options, Chocolate Fudge Brownie	$1.19	200	8	32	4	2.5	13% ¼ (3.25 tsp)	5
Clif Bar, Chocolate Brownie	$1.49	230	9	44	4.5	1.5	23% ¾ (5.75 tsp)	8
Larabar, Chocolate Chip Brownie	$1.59	200	4	31	9	2	23% ¾ (5.75 tsp)	4

Key: ✎ = 1 tsp sugar; 🌾 = 1 g fiber
Source: Manufacturers' labels.

self-Assessment

Do You Have a Protein-Friendly Diet?

Take this brief self-assessment to see if you have adequate amounts of protein-rich foods in your diet.

1. Do you eat at least 5 to 7 ounces of meat, fish, and/or poultry on most days of the week?
   Yes ☐ **No** ☐

2. Do you have at least 2 to 3 cups of milk, yogurt, soy milk, and/or soy yogurt daily?
   Yes ☐ **No** ☐

3. Do you enjoy at least 6 ounces of grains every day? (An ounce is considered 1 slice of bread, 1 cup of ready-to-eat cereal, or ½ cup of pasta or rice.)
   Yes ☐ **No** ☐

4. Do you eat at least 1 ounce of cheese or soy cheese daily?
   Yes ☐ **No** ☐

5. Do you eat at least 1 tablespoon of peanuts daily?
   Yes ☐ **No** ☐

6. Do you eat at least ½ cup of dried beans or peas, such as kidney beans or chickpeas, every day?
   Yes ☐ **No** ☐

7. Do you eat soy-based foods such as soy burgers and tofu daily?
   Yes ☐ **No** ☐

Answers

If you answered yes to at least the first three questions and are also meeting your calorie needs on a daily basis, you have a *very* protein-friendly diet! If you answered no to question 1 but yes to most of the other questions, you are also likely meeting your protein needs if your daily calories are adequate. If you have more no than yes answers, your diet may be in need of a protein makeover. Read on in the chapter to learn how you can easily add healthy sources of protein to your diet.

Table 6.4

It's Easy to Meet Your Daily Protein Needs

Food	Amount	Calories	Protein (g)	Vegetable Group (servings)	Fruit Group (servings)	Grain Group (servings)	Protein Group (oz)	Dairy Group (servings)	Oil Group (tsp)
Breakfast									
Bran flakes	2 cups	256	7.5			2			
Milk, nonfat	1 cup	83	8					1	
Orange juice	8 oz	117	2		1				
Lunch									
Turkey and cheese sandwich:									
Turkey breast	2 oz	69	11				2		
Cheese, low fat	2 oz	98	14					1	
Whole-wheat bread	2 slices	138	7			2			
Tossed salad	3 cups	66	15	1.5					
Italian dressing	1 tbs	35	0						3
Snack									
Yogurt, vanilla	8 oz	160	8					1	
Banana	1	105	1		1				
Dinner									
Chicken breast, skinless	3 oz	144	27				3		
Brown rice	1 cup	218	5			2			
Broccoli, cooked	1 cup	27	2	1					
Margarine	2 tsp	67	0						2
Totals		1,583	97	2.5	2	6	5	3	5

Note: A 140-pound adult needs 51 g of protein daily. A 180-pound adult needs 65 g of protein daily.

Source: U.S. Department of Agriculture, 2012. National Nutrient Database for Standard Reference, Release 25; MyPlate.gov.

What Happens If You Eat Too Much or Too Little Protein?

While protein is essential to health and normal body function, eating too much or too little can be unhealthy. Let's look at what happens to the human body when it gets too much or too little protein.

Eating Too Much Protein Can Be Unhealthy

Although consuming protein is a key to good health, eating more is clearly not necessarily eating better. In fact, a diet that is too high in protein is associated with the following risks:

➤ *Heart disease.* A high-protein diet may increase your risk for heart disease and dying prematurely from heart disease. Many foods rich in protein are also rich in heart-unhealthy saturated fats. Although lean meats and skinless poultry contain less saturated fat than some other cuts of meat, they are not completely free of saturated fat. Hence, a high protein intake can make a low saturated fat intake a challenge (see **Figure 6.13**). Lowering the saturated fat in your diet is important in lowering your risk for heart disease.

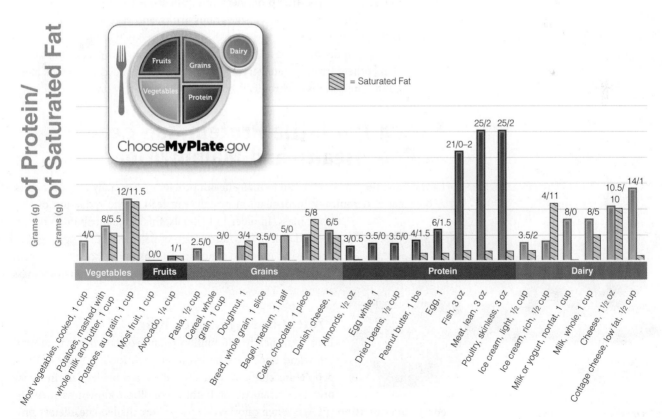

Figure 6.13 Where Are the Protein and Saturated Fat in Your Foods?
While many foods, in particular dairy foods and meats, can provide a hefty amount of protein, they can also provide a large amount of saturated fat. Choose nonfat and low-fat dairy foods and lean sources of meats and skinless poultry to enjoy your protein without consuming too much saturated fat.

- *Kidney stones.* A high-protein diet may also increase your risk for kidney stones, which commonly contain calcium. Kidney stones are one of the most common disorders of the urinary tract, sending more than 300,000 Americans to emergency rooms annually.[18]
- *Osteoporosis.* A high-protein diet may also increase your risk of osteoporosis (poor bone density). Although still a controversial issue, numerous research studies have shown that bones lose calcium when a person's diet is too high in protein. The loss seems to occur because calcium is taken from bone to act as a buffer, offsetting the acid generated when specific amino acids are broken down.[19] Other research has attempted to determine if calcium loss leads to osteoporosis when there is an adequate amount of calcium in a high-protein diet. If a higher dietary protein intake is coming from foods such as low-fat milk, yogurt, and cheese, it can add calcium to the diet.[20] Unfortunately, many American adults are falling short of their recommended calcium intake. If their diets are also high in protein, this isn't a healthy combination for their bones.
- *Cancer.* A high-protein diet may increase your risk for cancer; however, this relationship is also less than clear. While large amounts of meat, especially red and processed meats, may increase the risk for colon cancer, research doesn't necessarily support a connection between high amounts of total protein and increased colon cancer risk.[21]

One final health concern surrounding a high-protein diet is the displacement of other foods. If your diet is overloaded with protein-rich foods, such as meat, fish, and poultry, they will likely crowd out other nutrient- and fiber-rich foods. As you know, a diet that contains high fiber and a wide variety of nutrient-dense foods can help you reduce your risk for several chronic diseases, such as cancer, heart disease, diabetes, and stroke. If you fill up on meat and milk at meals, you might be short-changing yourself on foods, such as whole grains, fruits, and vegetables, that contain disease-fighting compounds.

While many individuals have the luxury of worrying about consuming too much protein, others are desperately trying to meet their daily needs. Let's look at the serious health implications of chronically eating too little dietary protein.

Eating Too Little Protein Can Lead to Poor Health and Malnutrition

Eating too little protein can lead to many health problems, especially in older adults. A diet that is chronically inadequate in protein can lead to the reduction of lean body mass. In older individuals, this can contribute to the increased risk of becoming frail, impairing wound healing, and decreasing immune function.[22] Consuming adequate protein throughout the day is important to preserving lean body mass as you age.

Almonds and other nuts are also good sources of protein. An ounce of almonds provides 6 grams of protein.

Protein-Energy Malnutrition

Every day, nearly 870 million people, or one in eight, around the world don't have access to enough food.[23] Many of these people are children, and their diets are inadequate in either protein or calories or both, a condition known as **protein-energy malnutrition (PEM)**. When calories and protein are inadequate, dietary protein is used for energy rather than reserved for its numerous other roles in the body.

protein-energy malnutrition (PEM)
A lack of sufficient dietary protein and/or calories.

Moreover, other important nutrients, such as vitamins and minerals, also tend to be in short supply, which further compounds PEM.

Many factors can lead to PEM, including poverty, poor food quality, insufficient food intake, unsanitary living conditions, ignorance regarding the proper feeding of children, and stopping lactation (nursing) too early. PEM can cause a child be become stunted (being too short for his or her age) and have a low body weight for his or her height and age.[24] Because they are growing, infants and children have higher nutritional needs for their size than adults. They are also dependent on others to provide them with food. For these reasons, PEM is more frequently seen in infants and children than in adults.

Because protein is needed for so many functions in the body, it isn't surprising that a chronic protein deficiency can lead to many health problems. For example, without adequate dietary protein, the cells in the lining of the gastrointestinal tract aren't adequately replaced when they are routinely sloughed off. The inability to regenerate these cells inhibits their function. Absorption of the little amount of food that may be available is reduced, and bacteria that normally stay in the intestines can get into the blood and poison it, causing septicemia. Malnourished individuals frequently have a compromised immune system, which can make fighting even a minor infection, such as a respiratory infection or diarrhea, impossible. Over 7.5 million children die annually due to malnutrition.[25]

While deficiencies of both calories and protein often occur simultaneously, sometimes one condition may be more prevalent than the other. A severe deficiency of protein is called **kwashiorkor**, whereas a severe deficiency of calories is called **marasmus**. A condition that is caused by a chronic deficiency of both calories and protein is called marasmic kwashiorkor.

Kwashiorkor

Kwashiorkor was first observed in the 1930s in tribes in West Africa: Often the first-born child became sick when a new sibling became part of the family. Typically, the newborn displaced the first child, usually around 18 months of age, from his or her lactating mother and her nutritionally balanced breast milk. The first child was then relegated to an inadequate and unbalanced diet high in carbohydrate-rich grains but severely deficient in protein. This sets the stage for serious medical complications.

A classic symptom of severe kwashiorkor is edema in the legs, feet, and stomach (see **Figure 6.14**). As we discussed earlier, protein plays an important role in maintaining fluid balance in the blood and around the cells. With protein deficiency, fluid accumulates in the spaces surrounding the cells, causing swelling. The body wastes away as the muscle proteins are broken down to generate the amino acids needed to synthesize other proteins. Consequently, muscle tone and strength diminish. Those with kwashiorkor often have skin that is dry and peeling. Rashes or lesions can also develop. Their hair is often brittle and can be easily pulled out. These children often appear pale, have facial expressions that display sadness and apathy, and cry easily. They are prone to infections, rapid heart beats, excess fluid in the lungs, pneumonia, septicemia, and water and electrolyte imbalances—all of which can be deadly.[26]

Marasmus and Marasmic Kwashiorkor

The bloating seen in kwashiorkor is the opposite of the frail, emaciated appearance of marasmus (**Figure 6.15**). Because they are not consuming enough calories, marasmic individuals are starving. They are often not even at 60 percent of their desirable body weight. Marasmic children's bodies use all available calories to stay alive; thus, growth

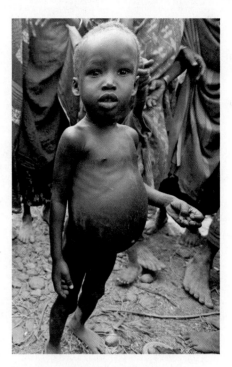

Figure 6.14 Kwashiorkor
The edema in this child's belly is a classic sign of kwashiorkor.

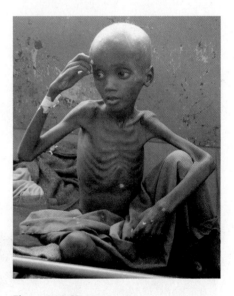

Figure 6.15 Marasmus
The emaciated appearance of this child is a sign (and symptom) of marasmus.

kwashiorkor A state of PEM where there is a severe deficiency of dietary protein.

marasmus A state of PEM where there is a severe deficiency of calories that perpetuates wasting; also called starvation.

is interrupted. These children are weakened and appear apathetic. Many can't stand without support. They look old beyond their years, as the loss of fat in the face—one of the last places that the body loses fat during starvation—causes the disappearance of a robust childlike appearance. Their hair is thin and dry and lacks the sheen seen in the hair of healthy children. Their body temperature and blood pressure are both low, and they are prone to dehydration, infections, and unnecessary blood clotting.[27]

Individuals with marasmic kwashiorkor have the worst of both conditions. They often have edema in their legs and arms, yet have a "skin and bones" appearance in other parts of the body. When these individuals are provided with medical and nutritional treatment, such as receiving adequate protein, the edema subsides and their clinical symptoms more closely resemble that of a person with marasmus.

Appropriate medical care and treatment can dramatically reduce the 20 to 30 percent mortality rate seen among children with severe PEM worldwide.[28] The treatment for PEM should be carefully and slowly implemented using a three-step approach. The first step addresses the life-threatening factors, such as severe dehydration and fluid and nutrient imbalances. The second step is to restore the individual's depleted tissues by gradually providing nutritionally dense calories and high-quality protein. The third step involves transitioning the person to foods and introducing physical activity. The only successful way to cure PEM is to eradicate it. The United Nation's has set a goal of reducing the percentage of undernourished people in the world to half of 1990 levels by 2015.[29]

The Take-Home Message A high-protein diet may play a role in increasing the risk of heart disease, kidney problems, and calcium loss from bone. Consuming too much protein from animal sources can increase the amount of heart-unhealthy saturated fat in your diet. Too many protein-rich foods in the diet can displace whole grains, fruits, and vegetables, which have been shown to help reduce many chronic diseases. A high-protein diet has also been shown to lead to loss of bone mass. PEM is caused by an inadequate amount of protein and/or calories in the diet. A severe deficiency of protein is called kwashiorkor; a deficiency of calories is called marasmus. These conditions can be improved with proper food and treatment.

How Do Vegetarians Meet Their Protein Needs?

What do spaghetti topped with marinara sauce, cheese pizza, and macaroni and cheese all have in common? These common, classic **vegetarian** meals all lack meat.

For many people, being a vegetarian is a lifestyle choice made for a particular reason. While some vegetarians avoid foods from animal sources for ethical, religious, or environmental reasons, others choose a vegetarian lifestyle because they believe it's better for their health.[30] An estimated 5 percent of Americans consider themselves vegetarians.[31]

Because vegetarians avoid meat, which is high in protein, they need to be sure to get adequate protein from other food sources. Vegetarians can meet their daily protein needs by consuming a varied plant-based diet that contains protein-rich meat alternatives such as soy, dried beans and other legumes, and nuts. Some vegetarians include protein-rich eggs, dairy foods, and fish as part of their diet. There are several types of vegetarians and associated ranges of acceptable foods. See **Table 6.5** for a description of vegetarian diets and the foods associated with each.

vegetarian A person who doesn't eat meat, fish, or poultry or (sometimes) foods made from these animal sources.

Table 6.5

The Many Types of Vegetarians

| Type | Dietary Patterns | |
	Does Eat	Doesn't Eat
Semivegetarian	Grains, vegetables, fruits, legumes, seeds, nuts, dairy foods, eggs	Meat, fish, and poultry, except on occasion
Pesco-vegetarian	Grains, vegetables, fruits, legumes, seeds, nuts, dairy foods, eggs, and fish	Meat and poultry
Lacto-ovo-vegetarian	Grains, vegetables, fruits, legumes, seeds, nuts, dairy foods, eggs	Meat, fish, and poultry
Lacto-vegetarian	Grains, vegetables, fruits, legumes, seeds, nuts, dairy foods	Meat, fish, poultry, and eggs
Ovo-vegetarian	Grains, vegetables, fruits, legumes, seeds, nuts, eggs	Meat, fish, poultry, dairy foods
Vegan	Grains, vegetables, fruits, legumes, seeds, nuts	Any animal foods, meat, fish, poultry, dairy foods, eggs

In the United States, the vegetarian food market continues to grow as manufacturers accommodate increased consumer demand with an array of new vegetarian products each year.[32] Many sit-down restaurants offer vegetarian entrées on their menus, and even some fast-food restaurants now offer veggie burgers. University food services are increasingly making vegetarian options available to meet growing student demand.

The Potential Benefits and Risks of a Vegetarian Diet

A plant-based diet can be rich in high-fiber whole grains, vegetables, fruits, legumes, and nuts and thus naturally lower in saturated fat and cholesterol. This type of diet contains the fundamentals for reducing the risk of the following diseases:

➤ *Heart disease.* Vegetarian food staples, such as soy, nuts, and soluble fiber–rich foods, such as beans and oats, have been shown to reduce blood cholesterol levels. Numerous studies have shown that a vegetarian diet is associated with a lower risk of dying from heart disease.[33]

➤ *High blood pressure.* Vegetarians tend to have lower blood pressure than meat eaters. Vegetarians tend to have a lower BMI (body mass index) as well as consume higher amounts of fruits and vegetables compared with nonvegetarians, both of which can play a role in lowering blood pressure.[34] High blood pressure is a risk factor not only for heart disease but also for stroke.

➤ *Type 2 diabetes.* You know from Chapter 4 that a plant-based diet can help reduce the risk for type 2 diabetes, so it shouldn't surprise you that vegetarians tend to have a lower risk for diabetes. Diabetes is also a risk for heart disease. For people with diabetes, consuming foods rich in fiber and low in saturated fat and cholesterol makes eating a vegetarian diet an attractive strategy to better manage this disease.[35]

> *Certain types of cancer.* Vegetarians tend to have a lower cancer rate compared with the general population. The latest World Cancer Research Fund Report advocates a plant-based diet that is high in nutrients and dietary fiber yet in low calorie-dense foods (highly processed foods with a lot of added sugars and fat as well as sugary beverages) to reduce the risk for cancer.[36]

> *Obesity.* A plant-based diet containing mostly fiber-rich whole grains and low-calorie, nutrient-rich vegetables and fruits tends to "fill you up before it fills you out," making you more likely to eat fewer calories overall. Hence, the plant-based foods of a vegetarian diet can be a healthy, satisfying strategy for those fighting the battle against obesity.

In addition to diet, other lifestyle habits such as not smoking, abstaining from alcohol and recreational drugs, and enjoying daily physical activity, which are all common among vegetarians, may also contribute to their lower risk of the above conditions.

The biggest risk of a vegetarian diet is in not consuming enough of the nutrients, such as protein and vitamin B_{12}, that are found in abundance in animal foods. Strictly avoiding meat, fish, poultry, and foods derived from animal sources can be *unhealthy* if you don't replace these foods with healthy, nutrient-dense, nonmeat alternatives. Also, vegetarian meals may not always be low in saturated fat if full-fat dairy products are heavily used. Planning is needed to be a healthy vegetarian.

How You Can Be a Healthy Vegetarian

To avoid nutrient deficiencies, vegetarians and vegans must consume adequate amounts of all nutrients by eating a wide variety of foods (see **Figure 6.16**). Some nutrients found in abundance in animal foods, including protein, iron, zinc, calcium, vitamin D, riboflavin (a B vitamin), vitamin B_{12}, vitamin A, and omega-3 fatty acids, are particularly important to monitor. The tips in **Table 6.6** can help you easily incorporate these nutrients in a vegetarian diet, and the Nutrition in the Real World feature

Figure 6.16 My Vegan Plate
Please see Table 6.6 for specific nutrients that could be missing in action in a vegetarian diet.

Source: The Vegetarian Resource Group, www.vrg.org.

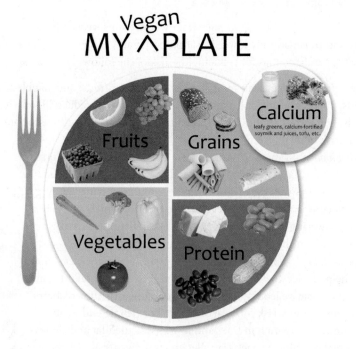

Table 6.6

Nutrients That Could Be MIA (Missing in Action) in a Vegetarian Diet

Vegetarians need to take care in planning a diet that meets all their nutritional needs. Here are the nutrients that a vegetarian diet could fall short of, some vegetarian food sources for these nutrients, and tips on how to enjoy these foods as part of a balanced diet.

Nutrient	Risks	Vegetarian Food Sources	Table Tips
Protein	A vegetarian's protein needs can be met by consuming a *variety* of plant foods. A combination of protein-rich soy foods, legumes, nuts, and/or seeds should be eaten daily.	Soybeans, soy burgers, tofu, tempeh, nuts, peanuts, peanut butter, legumes, sunflower seeds, milk, soy milk, yogurt, cheese	• Add nuts to your morning cereal. • Add beans to your salads, soups, and main entrées. • Have a soy burger for lunch. • Use tofu in stir-fries, rice and pasta dishes, and casseroles. • Snack on a soy milk and banana or berry shake.
Iron	The form of iron in plants is not as easily absorbed as the type in meat, milk, and poultry. Also, phytate in grains and rice and polyphenols in tea and coffee can inhibit iron absorption. The iron needs of vegetarians are about 1½ times higher than those of nonvegetarians. Vitamin C enhances the absorption of the iron in plant foods.	Iron-fortified cereals, enriched grains, pasta, bread, oatmeal, potatoes, wheat germ, cashews and other nuts, sunflower seeds, legumes, soybeans, tofu, bok choy, broccoli, mushrooms, dried fruits, raisins	• Make sure your morning cereal is iron fortified. • Add soybeans to your lunchtime salad. • Eat bread with your salad lunch or make a sandwich. • Pack a trail mix of dried fruits and nuts for a snack. • Add vitamin C–rich foods (broccoli, tomatoes, citrus fruits) to all your meals.
Zinc	The absorption of zinc is enhanced by animal protein. Eating a vegetarian diet means that you lose out on this benefit and are more likely to develop a deficiency. Phytate in grains also binds zinc, making it unavailable to your body. A vegan's zinc needs may be as much as 50 percent higher than a nonvegetarian's.	Soybeans, soy milk, tofu, tempeh, fortified soy burgers, legumes, nuts, sunflower seeds, wheat germ, fortified ready-to-eat cereals, mushrooms, low-fat or nonfat milk, yogurt, and cheese	• Douse your morning cereal with low-fat milk. • Add low-fat cheese and soybeans to your lunchtime salad. • Snack on sunflower seeds. • Top an afternoon yogurt with wheat germ. • Add soybeans to your dinner rice.
Calcium	Calcium is abundant in lean dairy foods such as nonfat or low-fat milk, yogurt, and cheese, so obtaining adequate amounts shouldn't be difficult if you consume these foods. Calcium-fortified soy milk and orange juice, as well as tofu, can provide about the same amount of calcium per serving as is found in dairy foods. Green vegetables can also provide calcium in the diet.	Low-fat or nonfat milk, yogurt, and cheese, fortified soy milk, soy yogurt, and soy cheese, calcium-fortified orange juice, legumes, sesame tahini, tofu processed with calcium, bok choy, broccoli, kale, collard greens, mustard greens, okra	• Add milk to your morning cereal and coffee. • Have at least one yogurt a day. • Have a glass of calcium-fortified orange juice with lunch. • Snack on low-fat cheese or yogurt in the afternoon. • Eat green vegetables often at dinner.

(continued)

Table 6.6 continued

Nutrients That Could Be MIA (Missing in Action) in a Vegetarian Diet

Nutrient	Risks	Vegetarian Food Sources	Table Tips
Vitamin D	Some vegetarians will need to consume vitamin D–fortified milk or soy products.	Low-fat or nonfat milk, egg yolk, fortified yogurt, soy milk, soy yogurt, ready-to-eat cereals; a vitamin supplement	• Have a glass of milk or soy milk at breakfast every day. • Make sure your morning cereal is vitamin D fortified. • Use fortified evaporated skim milk as a base for cream sauces. • Snack on fortified cereals. • Have a fortified yogurt each day.
Vitamin B$_{12}$	Animal foods are the only naturally occurring food source of B$_{12}$, so it is extremely important that vegetarians, especially strict vegans, look to fortified cereals and soy milk or a supplement to meet their daily needs.	Low-fat and nonfat milk, yogurt, or cheese, eggs, fortified soy milk, ready-to-eat cereals, soy burgers, egg substitutes; vitamin supplement	• Make sure your morning cereal is fortified with vitamin B$_{12}$. • Drink a cup of milk or fortified soy milk with your meals. • Top an afternoon yogurt snack with a fortified cereal. • Try an egg-substitute omelet for lunch. • Use fortified soy "meat" alternatives at dinner.
Vitamin A	Vitamin A is found only in animal foods. However, vegetarians can meet their needs by consuming the vitamin A precursor, beta-carotene.	Fortified low-fat or nonfat milk and soy milk, apricots, cantaloupe, mangoes, pumpkin, kale, spinach	• Enjoy a slice or bowl of cantaloupe in the morning. • Snack on dried apricots. • Add spinach to your lunchtime salad. • Drink a glass of fortified milk or soy milk with dinner. • Try mangoes for a sweet dessert.
Omega-3 fatty acids	If your vegetarian diet doesn't include fish, you may not be consuming enough of the essential omega-3 fatty acid called alpha-linolenic acid.	Fish, especially fatty fish such as salmon and sardines, walnuts, flaxseed and flaxseed oil, soybean and canola oil	• Add walnuts to baked breads and muffins. • Try canned salmon on top of your lunchtime salad. • Top your yogurt with ground flaxseeds. • Have fish regularly for dinner. • Cook with canola and flaxseed oil.

"The Joy of Soy" on page 214 gives an overview of the abundance of soy products available on the market. **Table 6.7** compares the nutrient composition of a traditional meat-based meal and a similar meal made solely from plant foods. Comparing these nutrient profiles may surprise you! Finally, when following a vegetarian diet, a vitamin and mineral supplement may be necessary.

Athletes Can Follow a Vegetarian Diet

Sports dietitians agree that athletes consuming a vegetarian diet can keep their competitive edge—with careful planning. Soy products, eggs, yogurt, cow's milk, cheese, and protein shakes can help a vegetarian athlete get needed amounts of protein, vitamin B$_{12}$, calcium, and vitamin D. Iron is a critical nutrient for athletes, because it carries oxygen to working muscles. Zinc is important to help tissues recover from the stress of training. Fortified foods can help increase the level of these minerals in

Table 6.7

How Does a Vegetarian Meal Compare?

Similar to meat meals, vegetarian meals can provide a robust amount of protein and iron with less heart-unhealthy saturated fat and cholesterol. While a tofu stir-fry doesn't provide as much zinc or vitamin B_{12} as meat, it is a fabulous source of calcium, a mineral many adults are falling short of.

	Beef Stir-Fry (per Serving)	vs.	Tofu Stir-Fry (per Serving)
Protein	38 grams		26 grams
Saturated Fat	3.3 grams		1.8 grams
Dietary Cholesterol	105 milligrams		0
Iron	3.9 milligrams		5.1 milligrams
Calcium	34 milligrams		450 milligrams
Zinc	6.8 milligrams		2.9 milligrams
Vitamin B_{12}	2.5 micrograms		0

a vegetarian diet, and a daily multivitamin/mineral supplement can provide added insurance. For athletes who don't consume fish, soy products, walnuts, flaxseeds, soybean oil, and canola oil provide omega-3 fatty acids. Vegetarian athletes should consult a registered dietitian nutritionist to plan a nutritionally complete diet.

The Take-Home Message Vegetarian diets can be a healthy eating style that may help reduce the risk of some chronic diseases. Some vegetarians abstain from all animal foods, while others may eat animal foods (such as eggs and dairy products) in limited amounts. All vegetarians must take care in planning a varied diet that meets their nutrient needs, especially for protein, iron, zinc, calcium, vitamin D, riboflavin (a B vitamin), vitamin B_{12}, vitamin A, and omega-3 fatty acids.

Practical Nutrition VIDEO

Getting the Nutrients You Need within Limitations

You don't need to eat meat in order to eat healthfully. Join Joan at the salad bar as she puts together a protein-packed, meat-free meal. Scan this QR code with your mobile device to access the video. You can also access the video in MasteringNutrition™.

The Joy of Soy

Soy has been used as a dietary staple for centuries in Asia. Soy consumption in the United States, in foods ranging from soy milk to soy bars, has been increasing in recent decades. From 1996 to 2011, the market for soy products grew from $1 billion to over $5 billion.[8] According to a survey conducted by the United Soybean Board, 80 percent of U.S. consumers perceive soy foods as being healthy.[9]

isoflavones Naturally occurring phytoestrogens, or weak plant estrogens, that function in a fashion similar to the hormone estrogen in the human body.

estrogen The hormone responsible for female sex characteristics.

Consumers choosing soy for its health benefits are doing so for its protein-rich, heart-healthy, and cholesterol-lowering properties.[10] Soy is a high-quality protein source that is low in saturated fat and that contains **isoflavones**, which are naturally occurring phytoestrogens (*phyto* = plant). These plant estrogens have a chemical structure similar to human **estrogen**. While they are considered weak estrogens (they have less than a thousandth of the potential activity of estrogen), they may interfere with or mimic some of estrogen's activities in certain cells in the body.[11] Although isoflavones can also be found in other plant foods, such as grains, vegetables, and legumes,

soybeans contain the largest amount found in food.

Eating soy protein as part of a heart-healthy diet may reduce the risk of heart disease by lowering cholesterol levels. Research suggests that soy protein can lower the "bad" LDL cholesterol by about 3 percent.[12] Soy protein may also help lower blood pressure.[13] High blood pressure is a risk factor for heart disease.

Some studies have suggested that isoflavones may also reduce the risk of certain cancers. Interest in soy as a cancer fighter was sparked after researchers observed that Asian countries had lower rates of breast cancer than Western countries, including

What's on the Soy Menu?

Tofu

➤ Cooked, puréed soybeans that are processed into a silken, soft, or firm texture; has a neutral flavor, which allows it to blend well

➤ Use the silken version in dips, soups, and cream pies. Use the firm variety in stir-fries or on salads, or marinate it and then bake or grill it.

Edamame

➤ Tender young soybeans; can be purchased fresh, frozen, or canned

➤ Use in salads, grain dishes, stir-fries, and casseroles.

Soy Flour

➤ Made from ground, roasted soybeans

➤ Use it in baked goods such as pancakes, muffins, and cookies. It can also substitute for eggs in baked goods:

Use 1 tbs soy flour combined with 1 tbs of water for each whole egg.

Soy Milk

➤ A soy beverage made from a mixture of ground soybeans and water

➤ Use it in place of cow's milk. Combine soy milk with ice and fruit in a blender for a soy shake.

the United States. Numerous studies suggest that the isoflavones in soy may help reduce the risk of cancer, as these weak estrogens may have anticancer functions in the body. One of the functions of isoflavones is that they compete with the hormone estrogen for its binding site on specific cells. The isoflavone latches onto the cell and blocks the binding of the hormone. Because estrogen may increase the risk of breast cancer, inhibiting or blocking the actions of estrogen may help reduce the risk.[14] This weak estrogen-like activity may also protect against other hormone-related cancers such as prostate and endometrium cancers.[15]

Timing may be an important part of the preventive role that soy plays in breast cancer. A study of Chinese women found that those who ate the most soy during their adolescent years had a reduced risk of breast cancer in adulthood. The early exposure to soy foods may be protective by stimulating the growth of cells in the breast, enhancing the rate at which the glands mature, and altering the tissues in a beneficial way.[16]

There was some concern that once the isoflavones are bound to the estrogen receptors, they can initiate the production of cancer cells, which can *raise* the risk of breast cancer.[17] However, research supports the safety of soy isoflavones when consumed as soy and soy products.[18]

According to the American Cancer Society, current research suggests that eating a moderate amount of soy foods is not harmful for breast cancer survivors, although less is known about the consumption of soy supplements.[19] A moderate amount is considered 1 to 2 standard servings of whole soy foods, such as soy milk, tofu, edamame, and soy nuts. A serving provides about 7 grams of protein and 25 milligrams of isoflavones.[20] Soy can be an inexpensive, heart-healthy protein source that may also help modestly lower your blood cholesterol, high blood pressure, and risk of certain cancers.

Tempeh

- ➤ Made from cooked whole soybeans that are condensed into a solid block
- ➤ Can be seasoned and used as a meat substitute

Soy Meat Analogs

- ➤ Products such as hot dogs, sausages, burgers, cold cuts, yogurts, and cheese that are made using soy
- ➤ Use as a meat substitute at meals and snacks.

Miso

- ➤ A flavorful paste of fermented soybeans used to season foods
- ➤ Use in soups, stews, and sauces.

Textured Soy Protein

- ➤ Created from defatted soy flour that has been compressed and dehydrated
- ➤ Use it as a meat substitute in foods such as meatballs, meatloaf, chili, tacos, and spaghetti sauce.

MADE over MADE better

Although protein is an important nutrient in your diet, you don't want to consume protein-rich sources at the expense of your heart. Your best bet is to choose leaner protein foods, as they contain less heart-unhealthy saturated fat.

Here are some typical protein-rich foods made over and made nutritionally better!

If you like this. . .	Try these healthier proteins!

Fried Chicken
3 oz = 246 calories
Protein: 19 grams
Fat: 15 grams
Saturated Fat: 4 grams

Roasted Chicken
3 oz = 147 calories
Protein: 26 grams
Total Fat: 4 grams
Saturated Fat: 1 gram

Hamburger
3 oz = 230 calories
Protein: 22 grams
Fat: 15 grams
Saturated Fat: 6 grams

Veggie Burger
3 oz = 119 calories
Protein: 12 grams
Fat: 4 grams
Saturated Fat: 1 gram

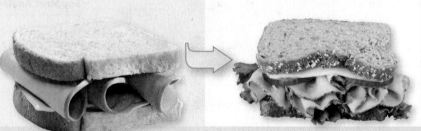

Bologna
3 oz = 261 calories
Protein: 12 grams
Fat: 24 grams
Saturated Fat: 10 grams

Turkey
3 oz = 72 calories
Protein: 13 grams
Fat: 1 gram
Saturated Fat: 0 grams

Fried Fish
3 oz = 195 calories
Protein: 15 grams
Fat: 11 grams
Saturated Fat: 3 grams

Grilled Fish
3 oz = 129 calories
Protein: 16 grams
Fat: 1 gram
Saturated Fat: 0 grams

Source: USDA National Nutrient Database for Standard Reference, 2012. www.nal.usda.gov.

Is the Paleo Diet a Good Choice for You? Named for the Paleolithic era, the Paleo Diet is supposed to imitate the diets of humans who lived before the advent of agriculture. Hence, it emphasizes foods that could be hunted and gathered: meats, fresh vegetables, and fruits. It frowns on cereal grains, refined sugars, dairy, and legumes, among other things. The diet has a large following of people who claim to have lost a lot of weight and to have improved their health by adhering to the diet.

Would the Paleo Diet be a good fit for you? After you've read the arguments for and against, answer the critical-thinking questions and decide for yourself.

yes

- The Paleo Diet consists of lots of plants, meat, and less grain.[1] The diet is a good fit for omnivores, and including lean meats and fresh vegetables is a good idea.[2]

- The diet avoids refined grains, which are bad for us—they cause a spike in blood sugar, are lower in fiber, and exclude some healthy nutrients.[3]

- The diet encourages consumption of non-starchy fresh fruits and vegetables as the main carbohydrate source.[4]

- This diet is an improvement over the average American's diet, given that it does not include refined sugar, processed foods, and added salt.[5]

no

- The diet is restrictive, which could make it difficult to stick to.[6]

- The diet excludes dairy and whole grains. This creates a risk of nutrient deficiency; moreover, research supports a recommendation that diets include a broad variety of foods to prevent metabolic syndrome.[7]

- Some varieties of the diet call for raw milk consumption. Without pasteurization, raw milk may contain *Salmonella*, *E. coli*, and *Campylobacter*, which can cause food-borne illness.[8]

- Humans have evolved genes to digest things that early humans couldn't digest, so the idea that our guts are exactly like cavemen's is disingenuous.[9]

what do you think?

1. Which side do you think has the more compelling argument? Why? **2.** Do you think that the Paleo Diet is a healthful diet choice? **3.** Do you think you could stick to the Paleo Diet?

1 Proteins Are Made of Amino Acids

Proteins are made of amino acids, which contain an acid group, an amine group, and a unique side chain. Each group is made of carbon, hydrogen, oxygen, and, in the case of the amine group, nitrogen. There are 20 unique side chains and therefore 20 unique amino acids. Amino acids are joined together by peptide bonds to form proteins.

The interactions between the amino acids cause individual proteins to fold into precise three-dimensional shapes. The shape of a protein determines its function. Heat, acids, bases, and salts denature these bonds and disrupt the shape and function of a protein.

Of the 20 amino acids, 9 are essential, so you need to obtain them through your diet. Your body can synthesize the remaining 11 amino acids, so they are nonessential.

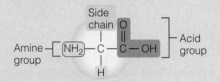

2 Your Body Digests, Absorbs, and Synthesizes Protein

With the help of stomach juices and intestinal enzymes, your body digests and breaks down proteins into amino acids to make them available for use. A limited amount of amino acids exists in pools in your body. The DNA in your cells directs the synthesis of proteins. Excess amino acids are also broken down and either stored in another form or used as energy, depending on your needs. The nitrogen is converted to the waste product urea and excreted in your urine.

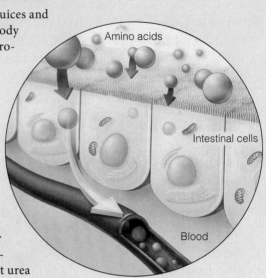

3 Protein Plays Many Roles in Your Body

Protein provides structural and mechanical support, supplies materials for ongoing maintenance, forms enzymes and hormones, maintains acid-base and fluid balance, transports nutrients, and aids your immune system. Protein can provide energy, be used to make glucose, and increase satiety at meals. Calories from excess protein will be stored as fat.

4 Protein Needs Are Determined by Nitrogen Balance in Your Body

Healthy adults are usually in a state of nitrogen balance, which means they excrete as much nitrogen as they consume. Pregnant and lactating women and growing children are in a state of positive nitrogen balance because they use additional nitrogen to grow new tissues. People who are malnourished or experiencing medical trauma may be in negative nitrogen balance.

Adults should consume 0.8 gram of protein for each kilogram of body weight. Protein quality is determined by the protein digestibility corrected amino acid score (PDCAAS), which is based on the protein's digestibility and its amino acid profile. Protein from animal foods is more easily digested than protein from plant foods. Proteins from animal foods and soy are typically complete proteins and provide all of the essential amino acids along with some nonessential amino acids. Plant proteins are typically incomplete, as they are missing one or more essential amino acids.

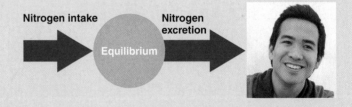

5 Protein Is Found in Many Foods

Protein is abundant in meat, fish, poultry, and meat alternatives such as dried beans, peanut butter, nuts, and soy. Dairy foods are also excellent sources of protein. Grains and vegetables are less robust protein sources. A varied, balanced diet can easily meet your daily protein needs.

6 Too Much or Too Little Protein Is Linked to Health Problems

Consuming too much protein from animal sources can increase the amount of heart-unhealthy saturated fat in your diet. A high-protein diet has been associated with the loss of calcium from the body, the development of kidney stones, and certain cancers. An excess of protein-rich foods in the diet can displace whole grains, fruits, and vegetables, and can be associated with excess saturated fat consumption, which may contribute to overweight or obesity.

Protein-energy malnutrition (PEM) is caused by an inadequate amount of protein and/or calories in the diet. Kwashiorkor is a severe deficiency of protein; marasmus is a severe deficiency of calories. A deficiency of both calories and protein is known as marasmic kwashiorkor.

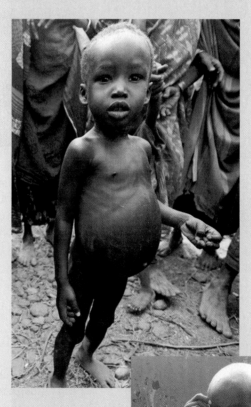

7 Vegetarian Diets Can Reduce the Risk of Certain Chronic Diseases and Conditions

A well-balanced, healthy vegetarian diet can help reduce the risk of heart disease, high blood pressure, type 2 diabetes, certains types of cancer, and obesity. Some vegetarians abstain from all animal foods, while others may eat a limited amount. All vegetarians must take care to eat a varied diet that meets all of their nutrient needs, especially for protein, iron, zinc, calcium, vitamin D, riboflavin, vitamin B_{12}, vitamin A, and omega-3 fatty acids.

Terms to Know

- amino acid
- acid group
- amine group
- side chain
- essential amino acid
- nonessential amino acid
- conditionally essential amino acid
- peptide bonds
- denaturation
- protein quality
- protein-energy malnutrition (PEM)
- amino acid pools
- protein turnover

- DNA
- gene
- RNA
- messenger RNA (mRNA)
- transfer RNA (tRNA)
- collagen
- enzymes
- catalysts
- hormones
- edema
- buffers
- transport proteins
- antibodies
- nitrogen balance

- digestibility
- amino acid profile
- complete protein
- incomplete protein
- limiting amino acid
- complemented protein
- protein digestibility corrected amino acid score (PDCAAS)
- kwashiorkor
- marasmus
- vegetarian
- isoflavones

MasteringNutrition™   Build your knowledge—and confidence—in the Study Area of MasteringNutrition with a variety of study tools.

Check Your Understanding

1. A protein's shape, and therefore its function in your body, is determined by the interactions of _____ with each other and their environment.
   a. the amino acids in the protein
   b. the water molecules in the protein
   c. the carbons in protein
   d. the peptide bonds in the protein

2. There are _____ essential amino acids that cannot be made by the body.
   a. 7
   b. 9
   c. 10
   d. 11

3. Which of the following will NOT denature a protein?
   a. grilling a chicken breast
   b. frying an egg
   c. marinating a steak in red wine
   d. refrigerating milk

4. Limited amounts of surplus amino acids are stored in your body in your
   a. muscles.
   b. fat stores.
   c. amino acid pools.
   d. stomach.

5. Protein plays many important roles in your body. Which role does it NOT play in your body?
   a. helping you fight the flu
   b. allowing you to walk, run, sit, and lie down
   c. helping you absorb fat-soluble vitamins in the diet
   d. transporting fat and cholesterol through your blood

6. Brendan is a 20-year-old male. How much protein does he need daily?
   a. 0.70 gram per kilogram body weight.
   b. 0.80 gram per kilogram body weight.
   c. 0.85 gram per kilogram body weight.
   d. 1.0 gram per kilogram body weight.

7. Protein is found abundantly in the
   a. dairy group and the fat group.
   b. protein group and the fruit group.
   c. fruit group and the dairy group.
   d. dairy group and the protein group.

8. Which of the following is a source of complete protein?
   a. kidney beans
   b. peanut butter
   c. soy milk
   d. pasta

9. Kwashiorkor is a type of PEM that develops when

   a. there is a severe deficiency of protein in the diet but an adequate amount of calories.
   b. there are inadequate amounts of both protein and calories in the diet.
   c. there is an inadequate amount of animal protein in the diet.
   d. there are adequate amounts of both protein and calories in the diet.

10. A lacto-ovo-vegetarian is coming to your house for dinner. You need to make a meal that she will enjoy. Which would NOT be an acceptable entrée?
    a. stir-fried tofu and vegetables over brown rice.
    b. a cheese and broccoli omelet.
    c. baked ziti with ricotta cheese, spinach, and tomato sauce.
    d. an anchovy pizza.

Answers

1. (a) The interactions of the amino acids with each other and with their environment determine the shape, and thus the function, of the proteins in your body.
2. (b) There are 9 essential amino acids that cannot be made in the body so you have to obtain these from foods.

3. (d) Heat and acids will denature proteins. Refrigeration does not alter the bonds between the amino acid side chains and so does not denature proteins.

4. (c) Limited amounts of all the amino acids exist in amino acid pools in your blood and inside your cells, not your stomach. Your muscles contain protein but don't store surplus amino acids. Your fat stores are the result of excess calories from carbohydrates, proteins, and/or fats.

5. (c) You need adequate amounts of protein to fight infections such as the flu, to provide structural and mechanical support when you're moving or lying down, and to transport substances such as fat and cholesterol through your blood. Protein does not help with the absorption of fat-soluble vitamins in your body.

6. (b) Individuals who are 19 years of age and older need 0.80 gram per kilogram body weight of protein daily.

7. (d) Both the dairy group and the protein foods group are full of protein-rich food sources. While there is some protein in vegetables, there is little in fruits. Fats do not contain protein.

8. (c) Soy foods such as soy milk provide all the essential amino acids that you need, along with some nonessential amino acids, and thus are a source of complete protein. Kidney beans, peanut butter, and pasta are missing adequate amounts of some essential amino acids.

9. (a) Kwashiorkor occurs when protein is deficient in the diet even though calories may be adequate. Marasmus occurs when calories are inadequate in a person's diet and thus he or she is starving. Protein from animal sources is not necessary because people can meet their protein needs from a combination of plant proteins, such as soy, legumes, grains, and vegetables, as part of a well-balanced diet.

10. (d) Because a lacto-ovo-vegetarian avoids meat, poultry, and fish, the anchovy (fish) pizza would not be an acceptable dinner option. However, because lacto-ovo-vegetarians eat a predominantly plant-based diet with dairy foods and eggs, the tofu stir-fry, cheese omelet, and baked ziti are all fine.

Web Resources

- For information on specific genetic disorders, including those that affect protein use in the body, visit the National Human Genome Research Institute at www.genome.gov
- For more information on vegetarian diets, visit the Vegetarian Research Group at www.vrg.org
- For more information on soy foods, visit the United Soy Board at www.unitedsoybean.org

1. **True.** However, burning proteins, rather than carbohydrates or fat, for energy is an inefficient way to use this precious nutrient. To learn why, turn to page 195.

2. **True.** Protein increases satiety, the feeling of fullness, after a meal more than either carbohydrates or fat. Turn to page 195 to learn more.

3. **False.** Although both pasta and chicken can contribute to your daily protein needs, the protein in poultry is more easily digested than the protein found in grains. Turn to page 198 to learn why.

4. **False.** Soy foods contain complete proteins, as do fish, so they are both good sources of protein. Turn to page 198 and find out more.

5. **False.** Proteins do play a vital role in your body, but a little can go a long way. For most healthy adults, less than one-fifth of their daily calories should come from dietary protein. For more on how to meet your protein needs, see page 199.

6. **False.** On average, most Americans are not only meeting their daily protein needs but are also surpassing them. Turn to page 199 to learn how.

7. **False.** Contrary to media headlines, Americans are eating less red meat than they were decades ago. To find out what they are eating more of, turn to page 200.

8. **False.** Even an extremely active person can easily meet his or her protein needs through a well-balanced diet. To learn more about protein bars, turn to page 202.

9. **True.** A high-protein diet is usually associated with high levels of artery-clogging saturated fat and low amounts of whole grains, fruits, and vegetables. This type of diet is not heart friendly and may raise your blood cholesterol. To learn more, turn to page 205.

10. **False.** Vegetarian athletes can keep their competitive edge if they are consuming a well-balanced vegetarian diet. Turn to page 212 to find out what that is.

7

Vitamins

True or False?

1. **Vitamins** provide your body with energy or the fuel that it needs to function. T F p. 224

2. Taking **water-soluble** vitamin supplements is never harmful because your body eliminates any excesses that you don't need. T F p. 225

3. Consuming too much **beta-carotene** from foods such as carrots, winter squash, and broccoli can cause vitamin A toxicity. T F p. 235

4. Too much vitamin E can interfere with **blood clotting**. T F p. 236

5. Vitamin K helps keep your **bones** healthy. T F p. 238

6. Because your body makes vitamin D with the help of **sunlight**, you don't have to worry about getting it from your diet. T F p. 240

7. Folate reduces the risk of certain **birth defects**. T F p. 251

8. Taking vitamin C supplements can help you ward off the **common cold**. T F p. 262

9. **Fortified foods** are a safe way to get your daily vitamins. T F p. 264

10. Everyone can meet their vitamin needs through food, so taking **supplements** is never necessary. T F p. 266

See page 277 for the answers.

223

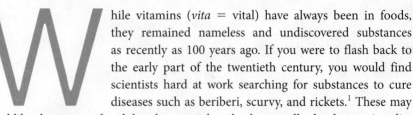

While vitamins (*vita* = vital) have always been in foods, they remained nameless and undiscovered substances as recently as 100 years ago. If you were to flash back to the early part of the twentieth century, you would find scientists hard at work searching for substances to cure diseases such as beriberi, scurvy, and rickets.[1] These may sound like the names of rock bands to you, but they're actually the devastating diseases caused by deficiencies of thiamin (for beriberi), vitamin C (for scurvy), and vitamin D (for rickets). Throughout the twentieth century, scientists received Nobel Prizes for their discoveries of the vitamins that cured these and other diseases. By the 1940s, the U.S. government mandated that specific vitamins be added to grains and milk to improve the nation's health by improving people's diet.

Now flash forward to the latter part of the twentieth century, when an improved diet meant that vitamin deficiencies became less of an issue for most Americans. Scientists shifted their focus from using vitamins to cure disease to using them to prevent disease. Today, research is being done to find out how vitamins affect and prevent everything from birth defects to heart disease and cancer.

What Are Vitamins?

Vitamins are organic compounds that you need in small amounts for growth, reproduction, and overall good health. Although they don't provide energy (calories) for your body, they are essential nutrients for your well-being. A deficiency of any one will cause physiological symptoms. There are 13 vitamins, and you get most of them by eating a variety of foods from each of the food groups (see **Figure 7.1**), though the vitamins D, K, niacin, and biotin can also be synthesized in your body or by microorganisms in the intestinal tract.

A chronic deficiency of any of the essential vitamins can cause a cascade of symptoms, from scaly skin to blindness. However, consuming too much of some vitamins can also cause adverse effects that can be as damaging as consuming too little. Balance is always your best bet when it comes to meeting your vitamin needs.

ChooseMyPlate.gov

Vegetables	Fruit	Grains	Protein	Dairy
Folate	Folate	Folic acid	Niacin	Riboflavin
Vitamin A	Vitamin C	Niacin	Thiamin	Vitamin A
Vitamin C	Vitamin A	Vitamin B_6	Vitamin B_6	Vitamin B_{12}
Vitamin E		Vitamin B_{12} (if fortified)	Vitamin B_{12}	Vitamin D
Vitamin K		Riboflavin		
		Thiamin		

Figure 7.1 Vitamins Found Widely in the Food Groups
Eating a wide variety of foods from all food groups will ensure that you meet your vitamin needs.

Vitamins Are Either Fat Soluble or Water Soluble

A vitamin is classified as either fat soluble or water soluble, depending on its chemical structure. Fat-soluble vitamins need dietary fat to be properly absorbed, whereas water-soluble vitamins are absorbed with water. Vitamins A, D, E, and K are fat soluble; the B vitamins and vitamin C are water soluble (**Figure 7.2**).

The fat-soluble vitamins are absorbed at the beginning of your small intestine (**Figure 7.3**). They are packaged with fatty acids and bile in micelles, small transport carriers that shuttle them close to the intestinal wall. Once there, the fat-soluble vitamins travel through the cells in the intestinal wall and are packaged with fat and other lipids in chylomicrons (one of the lipoprotein carriers discussed in Chapter 5). The vitamins then travel through your lymph system before they enter your bloodstream.

Fat-soluble vitamins are stored in your body and used as needed when your dietary intake falls short. Your liver is the main storage depot for vitamin A and to a lesser extent vitamins K and E, whereas vitamin D is mainly stored in your fat and muscle tissues. Because they are stored in the body, large quantities of some of the fat-soluble vitamins, particularly A and D, can build up to the point of toxicity, causing harmful symptoms and conditions.

Water-soluble vitamins are absorbed with water and enter your bloodstream directly (see Figure 7.3). Most water-soluble vitamins are absorbed in the upper portion of your small intestine, although vitamin B_{12} is absorbed in the lower part of your small intestine. Water-soluble vitamins are typically not stored in your body for long periods of time (vitamin B_{12} is the exception), and excess amounts are excreted, so it's important to consume adequate amounts of them every day. Note that even though most water-soluble vitamins aren't stored, dietary excesses can still be harmful. **Table 7.1** provides a summary of the two categories of vitamins.

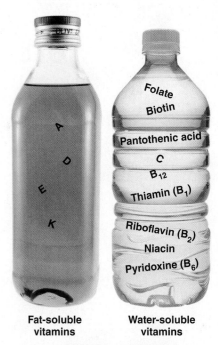

Figure 7.2 Categorizing the Vitamins: Fat Soluble and Water Soluble
Fat-soluble vitamins need dietary fat to be properly absorbed, whereas water-soluble vitamins are absorbed with water.

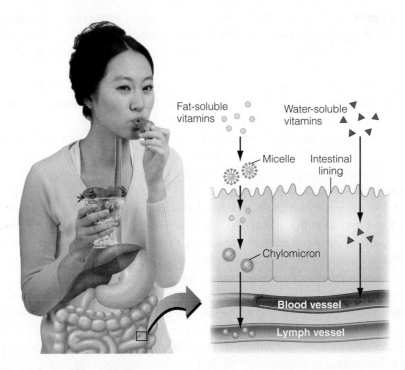

Figure 7.3 Absorbing Vitamins
Once in the small intestine, fat-soluble vitamins are packaged with fatty acids and bile in micelles that transport them into the intestinal wall. The fat-soluble vitamins travel through the cells in the intestinal wall and are packaged with fat and other lipids in chylomicrons. The chylomicrons travel through the lymph system and into the bloodstream. Water-soluble vitamins are absorbed directly into the bloodstream from the small intestine.

vitamins Non-energy-providing organic essential nutrients that your body needs in small amounts to grow, reproduce, and maintain good health.

Table 7.1

Fat-Soluble vs Water-Soluble Vitamins

	Fat Soluble: A, D, E, K	Water Soluble: Bs and C
Requirements	Needed in small amounts	Needed in small amounts
Absorption	Need fat to be absorbed. Absorbed in upper part of small intestine	Absorbed with water. Most absorbed in upper part of the small intestine. Vitamin B_{12} absorbed in the lower part of the small intestine
Transport through Body	Packed in micelles and chylomicrons in lymph	Enter bloodstream directly
Storage in Body	Stored in liver, fat, and muscle tissue	Not stored in body. Excess amounts excreted in the urine
Toxicity	Can be toxic in high doses	Low risk of toxicity, *but* excesses can be harmful
Major Food Sources	Fortified milk, oils	Fortified grains, whole fruits, vegetables, and some animal food sources

Some Vitamins Function as Antioxidants

Antioxidants (*anti* = against; *oxidants* = oxygen-containing substances) are a group of compounds that includes vitamins E and C, beta-carotene, the mineral selenium, and certain phytochemicals. Just as their name implies, antioxidants counteract **oxidation**, a harmful chemical reaction that takes place in your cells. During oxidation, oxygen-containing molecules called **free radicals** can damage cell structure, cell proteins, and even DNA.[2] Like prowling thieves, the unstable free radicals steal electrons from other molecules in order to stabilize themselves. The robbed molecule then itself becomes a free radical, and looks for another molecule to attack. This chain reaction, if not stopped, can significantly damage cells.

Free radicals are normal by-products of your body's metabolic reactions, which release energy from food. They can also result from exposure to chemicals in the environment (such as cigarette smoke and air pollution) and from the damaging effects of the sun's ultraviolet rays on unprotected skin.

Antioxidants are part of your body's natural defense system to harness free radicals and stop them from damaging cells (**Figure 7.4**). If free radicals accumulate faster than your body can neutralize them (a condition known as *oxidative stress*), their effects can contribute to various health problems, including heart disease, cancer, type 2 diabetes, arthritis, and Alzheimer's disease.[3]

Free radicals can also damage your eyes by contributing to age-related macular degeneration (AMD) and cataracts. **Age-related macular degeneration (AMD)** results from damage to the macula, a tiny area of the retina that is needed for central vision (the ability to see things that are directly in front of you). AMD can make activities such as reading, driving, and watching television difficult (compare **Figure 7.5a** with Figure 7.5b). It is a common eye condition among those who are 50 years of age and older and a leading cause of vision loss among older individuals.[4] A study conducted by the National Eye Institute (NEI) discovered that supplements

antioxidants Substances that neutralize free radicals. Vitamins A, C, and E and beta-carotene are antioxidants.

oxidation The process during which oxygen combines with other molecules.

free radicals Unstable oxygen-containing molecules that can damage the cells of the body and possibly contribute to the increased risk of chronic diseases.

age-related macular degeneration (AMD) A disease that affects the macula of the retina, causing blurry vision.

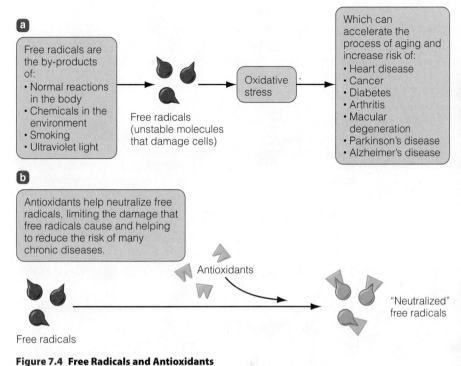

a

Free radicals are the by-products of:
- Normal reactions in the body
- Chemicals in the environment
- Smoking
- Ultraviolet light

Free radicals (unstable molecules that damage cells)

Oxidative stress

Which can accelerate the process of aging and increase risk of:
- Heart disease
- Cancer
- Diabetes
- Arthritis
- Macular degeneration
- Parkinson's disease
- Alzheimer's disease

b

Antioxidants help neutralize free radicals, limiting the damage that free radicals cause and helping to reduce the risk of many chronic diseases.

Antioxidants

"Neutralized" free radicals

Free radicals

Figure 7.4 Free Radicals and Antioxidants

a Normal vision and the ability to clearly see the world around you is often taken for granted.

b People with age-related macular degeneration (AMD) have difficulty seeing things directly in front of them.

c Cataracts cause vision to become cloudy.

Figure 7.5 Normal and Impaired Vision

Source: National Institutes of Health, National Eye Institute.

containing large amounts of antioxidants (vitamin C, vitamin E, and beta-carotene), with the minerals zinc and copper, are effective in reducing the risk for AMD, as well as the extent of vision loss.[5]

A **cataract** is a disorder in which the lens of the eye becomes cloudy, resulting in blurred vision (see Figure 7.5c). More than half of all Americans have experienced cataracts by the time they reach 80 years of age, and many undergo surgery to remove them.[6] The NIH recommends consuming antioxidant- and carotenoid-rich fruits and vegetables, such as leafy dark green vegetables and fish, for the health of your eyes.[7]

There is no question that diets high in antioxidant-rich fruits, vegetables, and whole grains are associated with a lower incidence of some diseases. However, these foods contain other compounds that may work with antioxidants to provide protection. For example, **phytochemicals** (*phyto* = plant), naturally occurring plant compounds that give fruits and vegetables their vibrant colors, have many beneficial functions in the body, such as acting as antioxidants, stimulating the immune system, and helping to prevent substances that cause cancer or helping cells stop the development of cancer.[8]

The big question that remains is if antioxidant *supplements* provide the same health protection as antioxidants consumed in foods. As you will soon read, too much of vitamins C and E, as well as beta-carotene supplements—all of which are antioxidants—can cause health problems. At this time, both the Academy of Nutrition and Dietetics and the *Dietary Guidelines for Americans* advocate that your nutrition needs should be met primarily through foods as part of a well-balanced diet.[9] Filling your plate with a colorful variety of antioxidant- and phytochemical-rich plant-based foods is currently one of the best-known strategies to fight chronic diseases. Table 7.2 provides you with a list of disease-fighting phytochemicals and their food sources.

cataract A common eye disorder that occurs when the lens of the eye becomes cloudy.

phytochemicals Naturally occurring substances in fruits, vegetables, and whole grains that protect against certain chronic diseases.

Table 7.2

The Phytochemical Color Guide

The National Cancer Institute recommends eating a variety of colorful fruits and vegetables daily to provide your body with valuable vitamins, minerals, fiber, and disease-fighting phytochemicals. Whole grains also have phytochemicals and have been added to this list.

Color	Phytochemical	Found In
Red	Anthocyanins	Apples, beets, cabbage, cherries, cranberries, red cabbage, red onion, red beans, peppers
	Lycopene	Tomatoes, watermelon, pink grapefruit
Yellow/Orange	Beta-carotene	Apricots, butternut squash, cantaloupe, carrots, mangoes, peaches, pumpkin, sweet potatoes
	Flavonoids	Apricots, clementines, grapefruits, lemons, papaya, pears, pineapple, yellow raisins
White	Alliums/allicin	Chives, garlic, leeks, onions, scallions
Green	Lutein, zeaxanthin	Broccoli, collard greens, honeydew melon, kale, kiwi, lettuce, mustard greens, peas, spinach
	Indoles	Arugula, broccoli, bok choy, brussels sprouts, cabbage, cauliflower, kale, Swiss chard, turnips
Blue/Purple	Anthocyanins	Blackberries, black currants, elderberries, purple grapes
	Phenolics	Eggplant, plums, prunes, raisins
Brown	Beta-gluton, lignans, phenols, plant sterols, phytoestrogens, saponins, tocotrienols	Barley, brown rice, oats, oatmeal, whole grains, whole-grain cereals, whole wheat

Salad Bar Savvy

A trip to your local salad bar can be a wonderful way to add vitamin-rich vegetables to your diet. However, some of the food choices at a salad bar may also be high in heart-unhealthy saturated fat. To learn how to build a heart-friendly, vitamin-rich salad at the salad bar, try the Build-a-Salad NutriTool in MasteringNutrition™.

Vitamins Differ in Bioavailability

Not all of the vitamins consumed in foods are available to be used in the body. In other words, they are not 100 percent bioavailable. The **bioavailability** of individual vitamins varies according to several factors, including the amount of the vitamin in the food; whether the food is cooked, raw, or refined; how efficiently the food is digested and absorbed; the individual's nutritional status; and whether or not the vitamin is natural or synthetic. In general, if the body needs more vitamins, a greater percentage will be absorbed. For example, a young child or pregnant woman will absorb more ingested vitamins than will a nonpregnant adult.

The bioavailability of fat-soluble vitamins is usually less than that of water-soluble vitamins because fat-soluble vitamins require bile salts and the formation of a micelle to be absorbed. Vitamins in plant foods are typically less bioavailable than those in animal foods because plant fiber can trap vitamins.

Vitamins were originally called *vitamines*. Casimir Funk, a chemist and early vitamin researcher, believed that vitamins were vital to life (he was correct) and were probably also a nitrogen-containing amine (he was incorrect). When later discoveries found that an amine wasn't present, the *e* was dropped from the word.

Vitamins Can Be Destroyed by Air, Water, or Heat

Water-soluble vitamins can be destroyed by exposure to air, water, or heat. In fact, vegetables and fruits begin to lose their vitamins almost immediately after being harvested, and some preparation and storage methods can accelerate vitamin loss. Although the fat-soluble vitamins tend to be more stable than water-soluble vitamins, some food preparation techniques can cause the loss of these vitamins as well.

Don't Expose Your Produce to Air

Air (oxygen) exposure can destroy the water-soluble vitamins and the fat-soluble vitamins A, E, and K. For this reason, fresh vegetables and fruits should be stored in airtight, covered containers and used soon after being purchased. Cutting vegetables and fruits increases the amount of surface exposed to air, so cut your produce close to the cooking and serving time to minimize vitamin loss.

A Little Water Is Enough

When you toss out the water that cooks your vegetables, you are also tossing out some water-soluble vitamins. Soaking foods will cause water-soluble vitamins to leach out of the food and into the liquid. To reduce vitamin loss, cook vegetables in a minimal amount of liquid—just enough to prevent the pot from scorching and to keep your vegetables crisp. Although cooking rice in water doesn't diminish its nutrient content (because the water is absorbed by the grain rather than discarded), washing rice before cooking it will wash away the B vitamins that were sprayed on during the enrichment process.[10]

Reduce Cooking Time

Heat, especially prolonged heat from cooking, will also destroy water-soluble vitamins, especially vitamin C. Because they are exposed to less heat, vegetables cooked by microwaving, steaming, or stir-frying can have approximately 1½ times more vitamin C after cooking than if they were boiled, which involves longer heat exposure.[11] The first three cooking methods are faster than boiling, reducing the length of time the food is in direct contact with the heat, and they all use less added water. (Stir-frying typically uses only oil.) Cooking vegetables until "just tender" is best, as it reduces the cooking time and heat exposure and preserves the vitamins. If you find yourself with a plate full of limp and soggy vegetables, this is a sure sign that vitamins have been lost.

Keep Your Food Cool

Whereas heat causes foods to lose vitamins, cooler temperatures help preserve them. For this reason, produce should be stored in your refrigerator rather than on a counter or in a pantry. A package of fresh spinach left at room temperature will lose more than half of its folate, a B vitamin, after four days. Keeping the spinach in the refrigerator delays that loss until eight days.[12] See the Table Tips for ways to preserve the vitamins in your foods.

Overconsumption of Some Vitamins Can Be Toxic

Vitamin **toxicity**, or *hypervitaminosis,* is very rare. This condition results from ingesting more of the vitamin than the body needs, to the point where tissues become saturated. The excess vitamin can damage cells, sometimes permanently. Vitamin toxicity does not occur by eating a normal balanced diet. It can result when individuals consume **megadose** levels of vitamin supplements, usually in the mistaken belief that "more is better." Many individuals, for example, overload on vitamin C tablets to ward off a cold, despite the fact that there is no evidence showing that vitamin C prevents the common cold, and despite the fact that too much vitamin C in the body can lead to unpleasant side effects.

To prevent excessive intake, the Dietary Reference Intakes include a tolerable upper intake level for most vitamins. Even though some vitamins lack sufficient evidence to establish a UL, there still may be risks in taking them in megadose amounts.

bioavailability The degree to which a nutrient is absorbed from foods and used in the body.

toxicity The accumulation of a substance to the level of being poisonous.

megadose A very large dose or amount.

Are You Getting Enough Fat-Soluble Vitamins in Your Diet?

Take this brief self-assessment to see if your diet contains enough food sources of the four fat-soluble vitamins.

1. Do you eat at least 1 cup of deep yellow or orange vegetables, such as carrots and sweet potatoes, or dark green vegetables, such as spinach, every day?
   Yes ☐ **No** ☐

2. Do you consume at least 2 glasses (8 ounces each) of milk daily?
   Yes ☐ **No** ☐

3. Do you eat a tablespoon of vegetable oil, such as corn or olive oil, daily? (Tip: Salad dressings, unless they are fat free, count!)
   Yes ☐ **No** ☐

4. Do you eat at least 1 cup of leafy green vegetables in your salad and/or put lettuce in your sandwich every day?
   Yes ☐ **No** ☐

Answers

If you answered yes to all four questions, you are on your way to acing your fat-soluble vitamin needs! If you answered no to any one of the questions, your diet needs some fine-tuning. Deep orange and dark green vegetables are excellent sources of vitamin A, and milk is an excellent choice for vitamin D. Vegetable oils provide vitamin E, and if you put them on top of your vitamin K–rich leafy green salad, you'll hit the vitamin jackpot.

Provitamins Can Be Converted to Vitamins by the Body

Provitamins are substances found in foods that are not in a form directly usable by the body, but that can be converted into an active form once they are absorbed. The best-known example of this is beta-carotene, which is split into two molecules of vitamin A in the small intestinal cell wall or in the liver cells. Vitamins found in foods that are already in the active form, called **preformed vitamins**, do not undergo conversion in the body.

Now that we've discussed the general characteristics of vitamins, let's review them individually. Before we begin our discussion of the fat-soluble vitamins, take the Self-Assessment to see if your diet is rich in foods containing these important nutrients.

The Take-Home Message Vitamins are essential nutrients needed in small amounts for growth, reproduction, and overall good health. All vitamins are either fat soluble or water soluble. The fat-soluble vitamins, A, D, E, and K, require fat for absorption and are stored in your body. For this reason, chronic dietary excesses of some fat-soluble vitamins can be toxic. The water-soluble B and C vitamins are absorbed with water. Excess water-soluble vitamins are excreted from your body, and surplus amounts generally aren't stored. Some vitamins, such as vitamins E and C, as well as the mineral selenium, flavonoids, and carotenoids, act as antioxidants because they help counteract the damaging effects of oxygen-containing molecules called free radicals. If free radicals accumulate faster than your body can neutralize them, their damaging effects can contribute to chronic diseases and conditions. Fruits, vegetables, and whole grains are robust sources of antioxidants. Many vitamins in foods can be destroyed or lost by exposure to air, water, and heat. The overconsumption of some vitamins can be toxic. Provitamins can be converted to vitamins in the body.

provitamins Substances found in foods that can be converted into an active vitamin form once they are absorbed.

preformed vitamins Vitamins that are found in active form in foods.

exploring
Vitamin A

What Is Vitamin A?

Vitamin A is actually a family of substances called **retinoids** that includes retinol, retinal, and retinoic acid. These are called **preformed vitamin A** because they are in a form that your body readily uses. **Retinol** is the most usable of the three forms and can be converted to both retinal and retinoic acid in your body.[13]

Preformed vitamin A is found only in foods from animal sources, such as liver and eggs, and is added to all processed milk. Plant food sources do not contain preformed vitamin A, but some do contain **provitamin A carotenoids**, which can be converted to retinol in your body. Carotenoids are the yellow-red pigments that give carrots, butternut squash, and cantaloupe their vibrant, deep orange color.

There are more than 600 different carotenoids, but only 3—beta-carotene (β-carotene), beta-cryptoxanthin (β-cryptoxanthin), and alpha-carotene (α-carotene)—can be converted to vitamin A. These three provide approximately 25 to 35 percent of the dietary vitamin A consumed by adults in the United States, with the majority of it coming from beta-carotene.[14] Other nutritionally significant carotenoids, including lycopene, lutein, and zeaxanthin, may function as antioxidants or provide health benefits, but cannot be converted to vitamin A.

The carotenoid lycopene, found in tomatoes and tomato products, functions as an antioxidant in the body.

Functions of Vitamin A

Vitamin A Is Essential for Vision

Rays of light are bouncing off this page. For you to read this sentence, your eyes receive this reflection of light and begin the process of translating the light into visible images. After light enters your eye through the cornea, it travels to the back of your eye to the macula (which is located in the retina and allows you to see fine details and things that are straight in front of you).

Vitamin A is a component of two light-sensitive proteins that are essential for vision. The two proteins, **rhodopsin** and **iodopsin**, are in the tips of light-absorbing cells in the retina called **rods** and **cones**, respectively.

As rhodopsin absorbs incoming light, the shape of vitamin A is altered, and it detaches from its protein (**Figure 7.6** on page 232). This causes a cascade of events that transmits visual messages through your optic nerve to your brain. This change in rhodopsin is called **bleaching**. Although the breakdown of iodopsin is similar, rhodopsin is more sensitive to light than iodopsin and is more likely to become bleached. After bleaching, the vitamin A returns to its original shape and becomes part of the protein again, regenerating the eye's light-absorbing capabilities. This regeneration process can take a few moments.

Have you ever been outside on a sunny day without sunglasses and then entered a dark building? Was it difficult for you initially to see the objects in the room? In this situation, your eyes needed an adjustment period because much of your rhodopsin had been bleached in the bright outdoor sun and your eyes needed to regenerate it once you were in the dark room. Luckily, there is a pool of vitamin A in your retina to immediately help with this regeneration.

Vitamin A Is Involved in Cell Differentiation, Reproduction, Bone Health, and Immunity

Vitamin A plays an important role in cell division and **cell differentiation**, the processes that determine what a cell becomes in your body.[15]

Vitamin A affects cell division by prompting gene expression, a process that uses genetic information to make the proteins needed to begin the process of cell division. As cells divide and cluster together, changes occur that cause them to become different from their initiating cells. This differentiation determines what they become in your body. When immature skin cells differentiate into mature skin cells, for example, vitamin A acts as a signal to turn on the genes to create the proteins needed to make healthy skin.

This role of vitamin A is one reason dermatologists prescribe retinoid-containing medicines, such as Retin-A or Accutane, to treat acne (see photo on page 233). Retin-A is a topical medication that works by enhancing the turnover of skin cells and inhibiting the formation of acne. Accutane is a medication taken orally that affects cell differentiation by manipulating the gene expression of acne-producing cells to alter their development in the skin.[16]

During the early stages of pregnancy, vitamin A signals cells to differentiate into tissues that form the baby's body. Vitamin A plays a particularly

retinoids The family or group of substances that include retinol, retinal, and retinoic acid.

preformed vitamin A The form of vitamin A that is readily used by the body.

retinol The most usable form of preformed vitamin A.

provitamin A carotenoids The family of compounds that includes beta-carotene that can be used to make vitamin A in the body.

rhodopsin A compound found in the rods of the eye that is needed for night vision.

iodopsin The compound found in the cones of the eye that is needed for color vision.

rods Light-absorbing cells responsible for black-and-white vision and night vision.

cones Light-absorbing cells responsible for color vision.

bleaching When light enters the eye and interacts with and changes rhodopsin.

cell differentiation The process that determines what a cell becomes in your body.

CONTINUED

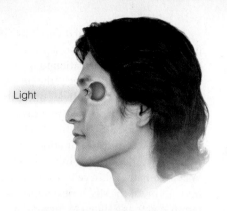

Light

Vitamin A is a component of two light-sensitive proteins, rhodopsin and iodopsin, that are essential for vision. Here we examine rhodopsin's role in vision. Although the breakdown of iodopsin is similar, rhodopsin is more sensitive to light than iodopsin and is more likely to become bleached.

EYE STRUCTURE

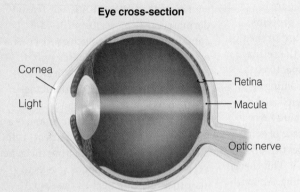

Eye cross-section

Cornea

Light

Retina

Macula

Optic nerve

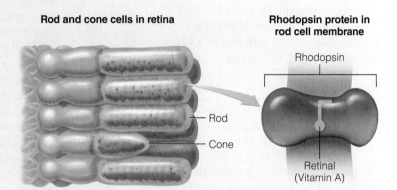

Rod and cone cells in retina

Rhodopsin protein in rod cell membrane

Rhodopsin

Rod

Cone

Retinal (Vitamin A)

1 After light enters your eye through the cornea, it travels to the back of your eye to the macula, which is located in the retina. The macula allows you to see fine details and things that are straight in front of you.

2 Inside the retina are two types of light-absorbing cells, rods and cones. Rods contain the protein rhodopsin, while cones contain the protein iodopsin.

EFFECT OF LIGHT ON RHODOPSIN

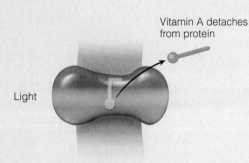

Vitamin A detaches from protein

Light

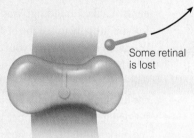

Some retinal is lost

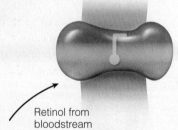

Retinol from bloodstream

1 As rhodopsin absorbs incoming light, the shape of vitamin A is altered, and it detaches from the rhodopsin.

2 This process, called bleaching, causes a cascade of events that transmits visual messages through your optic nerve to your brain. After bleaching, some retinal is lost.

3 Retinol from the blood is converted to retinal to replenish what is lost. The vitamin A returns to its original shape and becomes part of rhodopsin again, regenerating the eye's light-absorbing capabilities. This regeneration can take a few moments.

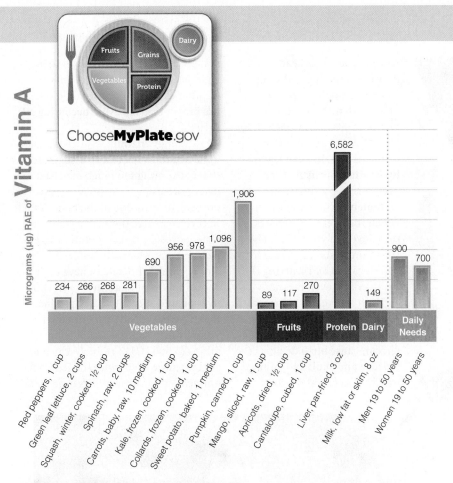

Figure 7.7 Vitamin A Content in Selected Foods

important role in the development of the limbs, heart, eyes, and ears.[17]

Vitamin A may help regulate the cells involved in bone growth through gene expression. Too much vitamin A, however, may negatively affect healthy bones.

Vitamin A is important for keeping your skin and the mucous membranes of your lungs, intestinal tract, and kidneys healthy and structurally sound. If these linings are weakened or damaged, bacteria and viruses can infiltrate your body and make you sick.

Vitamin A helps keep your skin, which acts as another barrier to infections, healthy to prevent harmful bacteria from entering your body. Vitamin A also works with your immune system to create white blood cells that fight pathogens that enter your bloodstream.

Daily Needs

Vitamin A in foods and supplements can be measured in two ways: in

microgroms (μg) of **retinol activity equivalents (RAE)** and in **international units (IU)**.

Because retinol is the most usable form of vitamin A and because provitamin A carotenoids can be converted to retinol, the preferred way to measure vitamin A in foods is its conversion to RAE. However, some vitamin supplements and food labels use the older measure, IU, on their products. (One RAE in micrograms is the equivalent of 3.3 IU.)

*Throughout this book, the amount of each nutrient that is needed daily is based on adults age 19 to 50. If you are younger than 19 or older than 50, your needs may be different. See the inside cover of this textbook for the specific amount of each nutrient you need daily based on your age and gender.

Adult females need 700 micrograms RAE of vitamin A daily, whereas adult males need 900 micrograms RAE daily.* This is the average amount needed to maintain adequate stores in your body to keep it healthy.[18]

A daily recommendation for beta-carotene hasn't been established, but the Institute of Medicine suggests consuming 3 to 6 milligrams of beta-carotene every day from foods.[19] (Beta-carotene is measured in milligrams.) You can obtain this easily by eating five or more servings of fruits and vegetables. This amount will provide about 50 percent of the recommended vitamin A intake.

Vegetarians who eat no animal foods, including vitamin A–rich milk and eggs, need to be especially conscientious about eating carotenoids and beta-carotene–rich foods to meet their daily vitamin A needs.

Food Sources

Organ meats (liver), milk, and eggs are the most popular sources of preformed vitamin A in the U.S. diet. Carrots, spinach, and sweet potatoes are American favorites for provitamin A carotenoids, including beta-carotene (**Figure 7.7**).

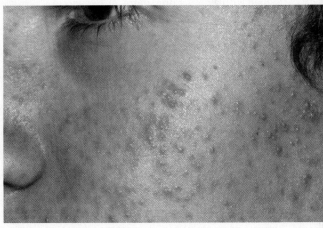

Vitamin A can aid in the treatment of acne.

retinol activity equivalents (RAE) The unit of measure used to describe the total amount of all forms of preformed vitamin A and provitamin A carotenoids in food.

international units (IU) A system of measurement of a biologically active ingredient such as a vitamin.

CONTINUED

nausea, vomiting, headaches, dizziness, and blurred vision.[21]

Chronic daily consumption of more than 30,000 micrograms of vitamin A (more than 300 times the amount that adults need daily) can lead to **hypervitaminosis A** (*hyper* = over, *osis* = condition), an extremely serious condition in which the liver accumulates toxic levels of vitamin A. Hypervitaminosis A can lead to deterioration and scarring of the liver and even death.[22]

High intake of preformed vitamin A during pregnancy, particularly in the first trimester, can cause birth defects in the face and skull and damage the child's central nervous system.[23] All women of childbearing age who are using retinoids for acne or other skin conditions should take the proper steps to avoid becoming pregnant.

Although vitamin A is needed for bone health, some research suggests that consuming too much may lead to **osteoporosis** (*osteo* = bone, *porosis* = porous), or thinning of the bone, which in turn increases the risk of fractures. Osteoporosis-related hip fractures appear to be prevalent in Swedes and Norwegians, who tend to have high consumption of vitamin A–rich cod-liver oil and specialty dairy products that have been heavily fortified with vitamin A.[24] As little as 1,500 micrograms (3,000 IU) of retinol, which is slightly more than twice the RDA recommended for women, has been shown

Similar to vitamin A and other fat-soluble vitamins, carotenoids are absorbed more efficiently when fat is present in your intestinal tract. Adding a reduced-fat or full-fat salad dressing to a salad can significantly increase the amount of carotenoids absorbed compared with a salad topped with a nonfat dressing.[20]

Too Much or Too Little

Because vitamin A is stored in your body, excessive amounts of preformed vitamin A can accumulate to toxic levels. The upper level for adults has been set at 3,000 micrograms of preformed vitamin A daily.

Overconsumption of preformed vitamin A is usually due to taking supplements and is less likely to occur from overeating vitamin A in foods. Consuming more than 15,000 micrograms of preformed vitamin A at one time or over a short period of time can lead to

hypervitaminosis A The serious condition in which the liver accumulates toxic levels of vitamin A.

osteoporosis A condition in which bones become brittle and porous.

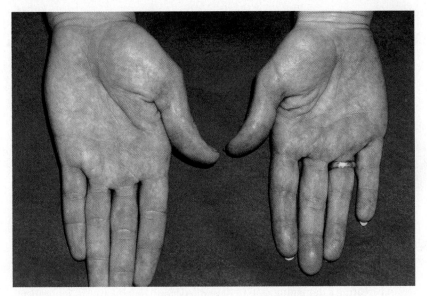

The hand on the right exhibits the orange-tinged skin characteristic of carotenodermia.

to be unhealthy for bones, although not all studies support this finding.[25]

The upper level applies *only* to preformed vitamin A from foods, fortified foods, and supplements. Provitamin A carotenoids in foods are not toxic and do not pose serious health problems. Your body has a built-in safeguard to prevent provitamin A carotenoids from contributing to vitamin A toxicity, birth defects, or bone damage. If you consume more carotenoids than you need to meet your vitamin A needs, your body will decrease their conversion to retinol. Extra amounts of carotenoids are stored in your liver and in the fat under your skin.[26]

Eating too many carotenoids can cause a nonthreatening condition called **carotenodermia** (*carotene* = carotene, *dermia* = skin) which results in orange-tinged skin, particularly on the palms of the hands and soles of the feet. Because these areas are cushioned with fat, they become more concentrated with the pigments and more visibly orange in

color (right hand in photo). Cutting back on carotenoid-rich foods will reverse carotenodermia.

Though a diet abundant in carotenoid-rich foods is not dangerous, carotenoid supplements may be. In a study of adult male smokers, those who consumed beta-carotene supplements were shown to have significantly higher rates of lung cancer than those who didn't take the supplements.[27] There is no known benefit associated with taking beta-carotene supplements. Eating a variety of fruits and vegetables is the safest and most healthful way to meet your vitamin A needs.

A chronic vitamin A deficiency can lead to an inability to regenerate rhodopsin, causing **night blindness**. Individuals with night blindness have difficulty seeing at dusk, because they can't adjust from daylight to dark, and may not be able to drive a car during this time of the day. If diagnosed early, night blindness can be reversed by taking vitamin A.

A prolonged vitamin A deficiency can also lead to dryness and permanent damage to the cornea, a condition called **xerophthalmia** (*xero* = dry, *ophthalm* = eye). Vitamin A deficiency is the number-one cause of preventable blindness in children.[28]

A deficiency of vitamin A is also associated with stunting, or reduction in the growth, of bones.

carotenodermia The presence of excess carotene in the blood resulting in an orange skin color, due to excessive intake of carotene-rich vegetables.

night blindness The inability to see in dim light or at night due to a deficiency of vitamin A.

xerophthalmia Permanent damage to the cornea causing blindness, due to a prolonged vitamin A deficiency.

What Is Vitamin E?

Vitamin E is sometimes referred to as a vitamin in need of a disease to cure. For almost 40 years after its discovery, scientists searched unsuccessfully for a curative role for vitamin E. They now have shifted their focus and begun valuing the vitamin's importance as an effective antioxidant.[29]

There are eight different forms of naturally occurring vitamin E, but one form, **alpha-tocopherol (α-tocopherol)**, is most active in your body. The synthetic form of vitamin E found in dietary supplements is only half as active as the natural form.[30]

Functions of Vitamin E

Vitamin E as an Antioxidant

Vitamin E's nutritional claim to fame is its role as a powerful antioxidant. This role is extremely important in protecting cell membranes and preventing oxidation of the "bad" LDL cholesterol carrier.

As you recall from Chapter 5, phospholipids (lipids that contain phosphorus and two fatty acids) are critical components of cell membranes. Many phospholipids contain unsaturated fatty acids, which are vulnerable to the damaging effects of free radicals. As an antioxidant, vitamin E neutralizes free radicals before they can harm cell membranes (see **Figure 7.8**).

When the bad LDL cholesterol carrier is oxidized, it contributes to the buildup of artery-clogging plaque. Antioxidants, including vitamin E, can help protect the LDL cholesterol carrier from being oxidized and reduce the buildup in the arteries, called atherosclerosis.[31]

Other Functions of Vitamin E

Vitamin E is an **anticoagulant** (*anti* = against, *coagulant* = causes clotting),

alpha-tocopherol (α-tocopherol) The most active form of vitamin E in the body.

anticoagulant A substance that interferes with blood coagulation.

hemorrhage Excessive loss of blood or bleeding.

which means that it inhibits platelets (fragments of cells used in blood clotting) from unnecessarily clumping together and creating a damaging clot in your bloodstream. Vitamin E also alters the stickiness of the cells that line your lymph and blood vessels. This decreases the ability of blood components to stick to these walls and clog these passageways.

However, research to date on the use of vitamin E to prevent heart disease is conflicting, and at this time, studies do not support the use of vitamin E supplements to protect against heart disease.[32]

Daily Needs

Adults need to consume 15 milligrams of vitamin E daily. Because alpha-tocopherol is the most active form of vitamin E in your body, your vitamin E needs are expressed in alpha-tocopherol equivalents.

Currently, American adults, on average, are consuming less than 9 milligrams of vitamin E daily, so are falling short of their dietary needs.[33]

Food Sources

Because vitamin E is fat soluble, vegetable oils, foods that contain these oils, nuts, and seeds are good sources (**Figure 7.9**). Some green leafy vegetables, avocado, and fortified cereals can also contribute to your daily needs.

Too Much or Too Little

There isn't any known risk of consuming too much vitamin E from natural food sources. However, overconsumption of the synthetic form that is found in supplements and/or fortified foods could pose risks.

Because vitamin E can act as an anticoagulant and interfere with blood clotting, excess amounts in your body increase the risk of **hemorrhage**. Because of this, the upper level from supplements

(T)(F)

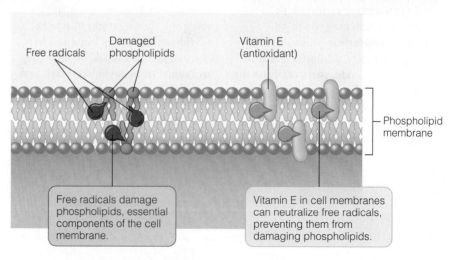

Free radicals

Damaged phospholipids

Vitamin E (antioxidant)

Phospholipid membrane

Free radicals damage phospholipids, essential components of the cell membrane.

Vitamin E in cell membranes can neutralize free radicals, preventing them from damaging phospholipids.

Figure 7.8 Vitamin E as an Antioxidant

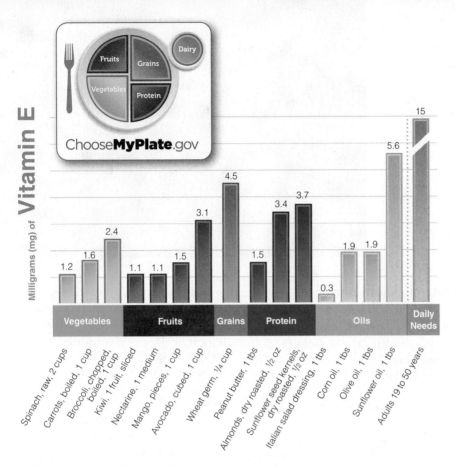

Vitamin E

Milligrams (mg) of Vitamin E

1.2	1.6	2.4
1.1	1.1	1.5
3.1	4.5	1.5
3.4	3.7	0.3
1.9	1.9	5.6
15		

Vegetables | Fruits | Grains | Protein | Oils | Daily Needs

- Spinach, raw, 2 cups
- Carrots, boiled, 1 cup
- Broccoli, chopped, boiled, 1 cup
- Kiwi, 1 fruit, sliced
- Nectarine, 1 medium
- Mango, pieces, 1 cup
- Avocado, cubed, 1 cup
- Wheat germ, 1/4 cup
- Peanut butter, 1 tbs
- Almonds, dry roasted, 1/2 oz
- Sunflower seed kernels, dry roasted, 1/2 oz
- Italian salad dressing, 1 tbs
- Corn oil, 1 tbs
- Olive oil, 1 tbs
- Sunflower oil, 1 tbs
- Adults 19 to 50 years

Figure 7.9 Vitamin E Content in Selected Foods

and/or fortified foods is 1,000 milligrams for adults. This applies only to healthy individuals consuming adequate amounts of vitamin K. (Vitamin K also plays a role in blood clotting. A deficiency of vitamin K can exacerbate the anticoagulant effects of vitamin E.) Individuals taking anticoagulant medication and vitamin E supplements should be monitored by their physician to avoid the serious situation in which the blood can't clot quickly enough to stop the bleeding from a wound.

Although the upper level of 1,000 milligrams was set to keep you safe, it may actually be too high. A study showed that those at risk of heart disease who took 400 IU (265 milligrams) or more of vitamin E daily for at least one year had an overall higher risk of dying during that time.[34] One theory is that too much vitamin E may disrupt the balance of other antioxidants in the body, causing more harm than good.

Individuals who can't absorb fat properly may fall short of their vitamin E needs. Though rare, a chronic deficiency can cause nerve problems, muscle weakness, and uncontrolled movement of body parts. Because vitamin E is an antioxidant and is found in the membranes of red blood cells, a deficiency can also increase the susceptibility of cell membranes to damage by free radicals.

exploring
Vitamin K

What Is Vitamin K?

There are two forms of vitamin K: **menaquinone** and **phylloquinone**. Menaquinone is synthesized by the bacteria that exist naturally in your intestinal tract. Phylloquinone is found in green plants, and is the primary source of vitamin K in your diet.

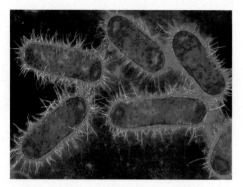

Bacteria in your GI tract synthesize one form of vitamin K.

Functions of Vitamin K
Vitamin K Is Essential for Blood Clotting

An easy way to remember vitamin K's major function is to associate the letter *K* with "klotting."

Vitamin K plays a major role in blood **coagulation**, or clotting. Blood clotting is a complex chain of events involving substances in your blood, many of which are proteins, called clotting factors. Vitamin K plays a role in synthesizing four of these **clotting factors**. Without vitamin K, a simple cut on your finger would cause uncontrollable bleeding.

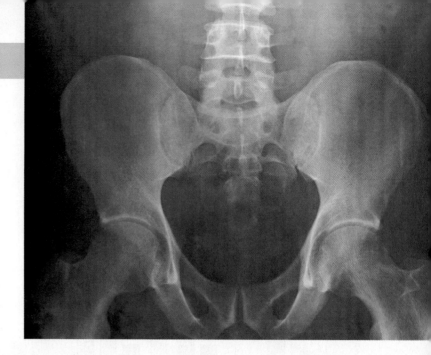

Vitamin K Is Important to Bone Health

Acting as a coenzyme, vitamin K aids an enzyme that alters the bone protein **osteocalcin**. Vitamin K enables osteocalcin to bind with the bone-strengthening mineral calcium.

Chronic inadequate amounts of dietary vitamin K may be a factor in osteoporosis. In a study of women over a ten-year period, researchers found that a low dietary intake of vitamin K was associated with an increased risk of hip fractures.[35] Research continues in the area of vitamin K and bone health.

Daily Needs

Currently, it is not known how much of the vitamin K made from bacteria in your intestinal tract truly contributes to meeting your daily needs. Because of this, it is hard to pinpoint the exact amount you need to consume daily in your foods. Therefore, the recommendation for dietary vitamin K is based on the current amount that is consumed, on average, by healthy Americans.[36]

Adult women need 90 micrograms of vitamin K per day, and men need 120 micrograms daily.

Food Sources

When it comes to meeting your vitamin K needs, think green. Vegetables like broccoli, spinach, salad greens, brussels sprouts, and cabbage are all rich in vitamin K (**Figure 7.10**). Vegetable oils and margarine are the second largest source of vitamin K in the diet.

menaquinone The form of vitamin K produced by bacteria in the colon.

phylloquinone The form of vitamin K found in green plants.

coagulation The process of blood clotting.

clotting factors Substances involved in the process of blood clotting.

osteocalcin The protein in bone that binds with bone-strengthening calcium.

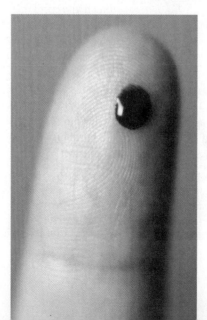

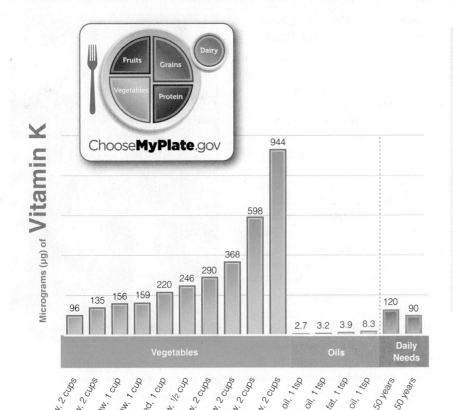

Figure 7.10 Vitamin K Content in Selected Foods

Vitamin K — Micrograms (µg) of

Values (µg):
- Romaine lettuce, raw, 2 cups: 96
- Green cabbage, raw, 2 cups: 135
- Brussels sprouts, raw, 1 cup: 156
- Coleslaw, 1 cup: 159
- Broccoli, cooked, 1 cup: 220
- Parsley, raw, ½ cup: 246
- Spinach, raw, 2 cups: 290
- Collards, raw, 2 cups: 368
- Swiss chard, raw, 2 cups: 598
- Kale, raw, 2 cups: 944

Oils:
- Olive oil, 1 tsp: 2.7
- Canola oil, 1 tsp: 3.2
- Margarine, regular, 80% fat, 1 tsp: 3.9
- Soybean oil, 1 tsp: 8.3

Daily Needs:
- Men 19 to 50 years: 120
- Women 19 to 50 years: 90

ChooseMyPlate.gov

Table TIPS

Getting Your Ks

Have a green salad daily.

Cook with soybean oil.

Add shredded cabbage to your salad, or top it with a scoop of coleslaw.

Add a tad of margarine to your steamed spinach. Both will provide some vitamin K.

Dunk raw broccoli florets in salad dressing for two sources of vitamin K.

A green salad with oil and vinegar dressing at lunch and ¾ cup broccoli at dinner will meet your vitamin K needs for the entire day.

Too Much or Too Little

There are no known adverse effects of consuming too much vitamin K from foods or supplements, so an upper intake level hasn't been set for healthy people.

Individuals taking anticoagulant (anticlotting) medications such as **warfarin** (also known as Coumadin) need to keep a consistent intake of vitamin K. This medication decreases the activity of vitamin K and prolongs the time it takes for blood to clot. If these individuals suddenly increase the vitamin K in their diets, the vitamin can override the effect of the drug, enabling the blood to clot too quickly. In contrast, a sudden decline in dietary vitamin K can enhance the effectiveness of the drug.[37]

A vitamin K deficiency severe enough to affect blood clotting is extremely rare in healthy individuals.[38] People with illnesses affecting absorption of fat in the intestinal tract, which is necessary to absorb fat-soluble vitamin K, may be at risk of not meeting their vitamin K needs.

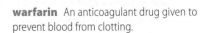

warfarin An anticoagulant drug given to prevent blood from clotting.

exploring
Vitamin D

What Is Vitamin D?

Vitamin D is called the "sunshine vitamin" because it is made in your body with the help of **ultraviolet (UV) rays** from sunlight.[39] Many individuals do not obtain enough sun exposure, so they must meet their needs through their diets.

Whether from food or sunlight, vitamin D enters your body in an inactive form. The ultraviolet rays of the sun convert a cholesterol-containing compound in your skin to previtamin D, which is then converted to an inactive form of vitamin D in your blood. The vitamin D in your foods is also in this inactive form.

This inactive form travels in your blood to your liver, where it is changed into a circulating form of vitamin D and is released back into your blood. Once in your kidneys, it is converted to an active form of vitamin D.

Functions of Vitamin D
Vitamin D Helps Bone Health by Regulating Calcium and Phosphorus

Once in an active form, vitamin D acts as a hormone and regulates two important bone minerals, calcium and phosphorus. Vitamin D stimulates the absorption of calcium and phosphorus in the intestinal tract, helping to keep the levels of these minerals within a healthy range in your blood. Because of its role in regulating these minerals, vitamin D helps to build and maintain your bones.

Although phosphorus deficiency is very rare, dietary calcium deficiencies do occur, causing blood levels of calcium to drop. When this happens, vitamin D and **parathyroid hormone** cause calcium to leave your bones to maintain the necessary levels in your blood. Vitamin D then signals your kidneys to decrease the amount of calcium excreted in the urine. All of these actions help to regulate the amount of calcium in your blood.

ultraviolet (UV) rays The rays from sunlight that cause the production of vitamin D in the skin.

parathyroid hormone (PTH) The hormone secreted from the parathyroid glands that activates vitamin D formation in the kidney.

Vitamin D May Prevent Some Cancers and Other Conditions

The role of vitamin D in preventing cancer has produced interesting but mixed research results. Some research studies suggest that vitamin D may help protect against breast, colon, and prostate cancers.[40] Unfortunately, other studies suggest that some individuals with excessive blood levels of vitamin D may be at higher risk for prostate, breast, pancreas, and espohagus cancers.[41]

Because of this discrepancy, further research is needed to determine whether vitamin D could play a protective role in certain cancers, how much would be protective, and most importantly, if excessive amounts may be detrimental.[42]

Exciting research is also emerging as to the role that vitamin D may play in preventing or treating diabetes, heart disease, high blood pressure, and autoimmunue disorders such as multiple sclerosis, as well as other conditions.[43]

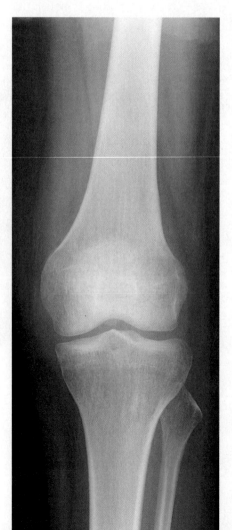

Until more is known to confirm the association of vitamin D and these numerous medical conditions, your daily needs are based on the amount needed for healthy bones.

Daily Needs

Most individuals can synthesize some of their needed vitamin D with adequate exposure to the sun. However, during the winter months in areas above latitudes of approximately 40 degrees north (Boston, Toronto, Salt Lake City) and below approximately 40 degrees south (Melbourne, Australia), sun exposure is not strong, and vitamin D synthesis in the skin is dramatically reduced.

Individuals with darker skin, such as African-Americans, have a higher amount of the skin pigment melanin, which reduces vitamin D production from sunlight. These individuals need a longer period of sun exposure, compared with a person who has less melanin, to derive the same amount of vitamin D. The amounts of cloud cover, smog, and air pollution can all reduce the amount of vitamin D produced in the skin. Although the use of sunscreen with a sun protective factor (SPF) of 8 or more can also block the body's ability to synthesize vitamin D, individuals

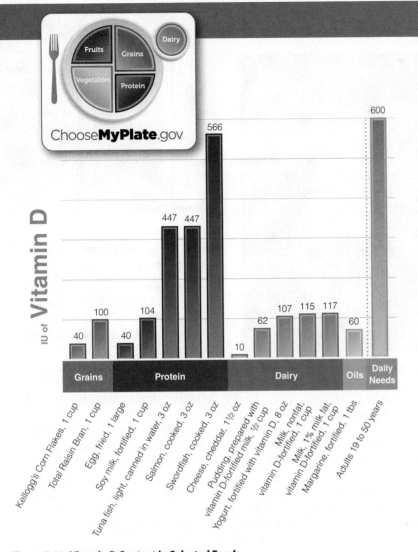

Figure 7.11 Vitamin D Content in Selected Foods

cereals, juice, and yogurt, very few foods provide ample amounts of vitamin D (**Figure 7.11**). With this scarcity of naturally occurring vitamin D–rich sources, it isn't surprising that many Americans are not meeting their daily dietary vitamin D needs.[46]

Too Much or Too Little

Consuming too much vitamin D can cause loss of appetite, weight loss, irregular heart beats, and increased urination. The upper level for vitamin D has been set at 4,000 IU (100 micrograms), which is five to six times higher than the daily recommendation.

As with the other fat-soluble vitamins, excess amounts of vitamin D are stored in the fat cells, and an accumulation can reach toxic levels, causing **hypervitaminosis D**. This condition causes overabsorption of calcium from the intestines as well as calcium loss from bones. When both of these symptoms occur, blood calcium levels can become dangerously high.

A chronically high amount of calcium in the blood, or **hypercalcemia** (*hyper* = over, *calc* = calcium, *emia* = blood), can cause damaging calcium deposits in the tissues of your kidneys, lungs, blood vessels, and heart.[47]

The good news is that it is highly unlikely that you will get hypervitaminosis D from foods, even fortified foods. The only exception is fish oils, specifically cod-liver oil, which provides 1,360 IU of vitamin D per tablespoon. Luckily, the less-than-pleasant taste of this oil is a safeguard against overconsumption. A more likely culprit behind hypervitaminosis D is the overuse of vitamin D supplements.

Sun worshippers don't have to worry about getting hypervitaminosis D from the sun (although they should be concerned about the risk of skin cancer). Overexposing the skin to UV rays will eventually destroy the inactive form of

typically do not apply enough of it, cover all of their skin, or reapply it during the day, so some synthesis likely occurs.[44]

Because of these variables involving sun exposure, your daily vitamin D needs are based on the amount you would need to eat in foods and are not based on the synthesis of vitamin D in your skin from sunlight.

Based on the important roles that vitamin D plays in your body, it is currently recommended that adults age 19 to 70 consume 15 micrograms, or 600 IU, of vitamin D daily. This is a

significant increase from previously recommended daily amounts. Also, based on revised Dietary Reference Intakes, adults over the age of 70 should incorporate 20 micrograms, or 800 IU, into their daily consumption.[45]

When you are reading labels to assess the amount of vitamin D in your foods, keep in mind that the Daily Value (DV) on the Nutrition Facts panel is set at 400 IU, less than the current amount recommended for adults.

Food Sources

One of the easiest ways to get your vitamin D from food is to drink fortified milk, which provides 100 IU, or 2.5 micrograms, of vitamin D per cup. Other than fatty fish (such as sardines and salmon) and fortified milk, breakfast

hypervitaminosis D A condition resulting from excessive amounts of vitamin D in the body.

hypercalcemia A chronically high amount of calcium in the blood.

Exploring Vitamin D **241**

Vitamin D

vitamin D in the skin, causing the body to shut down production of vitamin D.

Rickets on the Rise

Rickets is a vitamin D deficiency disease that occurs in children. The bones of children with rickets aren't adequately mineralized with calcium and phosphorus, and this causes them to weaken. Because of their "soft bones," these children develop bowed legs, as they are unable to hold up their own body weight when they are standing upright.[48]

Since milk became fortified with vitamin D in the 1930s, rickets has been considered a rare disease among children in the United States. However, the disease has once again become a public health concern. In the late 1990s, a review of hospital records in Georgia suggested that as many as five out of every 1 million children between 6 months and 5 years of age were hospitalized with rickets associated with a vitamin D deficiency.[49] This probably underestimates the prevalence of rickets in the state, as only hospitalized children were investigated. Similarly, more than 20 percent of more than 300 adolescents at a Boston-based hospital clinic were recently found to be deficient in vitamin D.[50]

Changes in the diets and lifestyles of children provide clues as to why rickets is on the rise in America. One factor may be the increased consumption of soft drinks. A U.S. Department of Agriculture (USDA) report found that the number of children who drank soft drinks, in and outside of school, has more than doubled over a 20-year period.[51] This displacement of milk (a good source of vitamin D) with soft drinks (a poor source) is causing many children to come up short in their vitamin D intake.

Increased concern over skin cancer may be another factor. Skin cancer is the most common form of cancer in the United States, and childhood sun

rickets A vitamin D deficiency in children, resulting in soft bones.

osteomalacia The adult equivalent of rickets, causing muscle and bone weakness, and pain.

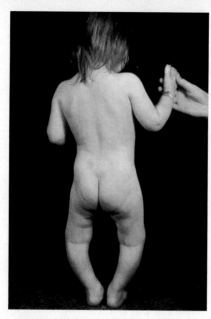

A child with rickets.

exposure appears to increase the risk of skin cancer in later years. Because of this, organizations such as the Centers for Disease Control and the American Cancer Society have run campaigns that recommend limiting exposure to ultraviolet light. People are encouraged to use sunscreen, wear protective clothing when outdoors, and minimize activities in the sun. The American Association of Pediatricians also recommends that infants younger than 6 months not be exposed to direct sunlight and that children use sunscreen before going outside.[52] With less exposure to UV light, many children aren't able to synthesize vitamin D in adequate amounts to meet their needs, thereby increasing their risk of developing rickets. The increased use of child day-care facilities, which may limit outdoor activities during the day, may also play a role in this increased prevalence of rickets.[53]

Finally, air pollution reduces the ultraviolet rays of the sun by as much as 60 percent—another factor limiting the production of vitamin D in the skin. In fact, children living in an industrial, polluted region of India were shown to have less vitamin D in their blood than children living in a less polluted area of the country.[54]

Other Vitamin D Deficiency Disorders

Osteomalacia is the adult equivalent of rickets and can cause muscle and bone weakness and pain. The bones can't mineralize properly because there isn't enough calcium and phosphorus available in the blood.[55] Although there may be adequate amounts of these minerals in the diet, the deficiency of vitamin D hampers their absorption.

Vitamin D deficiency and its subsequent effect on decreased calcium absorption can lead to osteoporosis, a condition in which the bones can mineralize properly, but there isn't enough calcium in the diet to maximize the bone density, or mass.

Table TIPS

Dynamite Ways to Get Vitamin D

Use low-fat milk, not cream, in your hot or iced coffee.

Buy vitamin D–fortified yogurts and have one daily as a snack. Top it with a vitamin D–fortified cereal for another boost of D.

Start your morning with cereal, and douse it with plenty of low-fat or skim milk.

Flake canned salmon over your lunchtime salad.

Make instant hot cocoa with hot milk rather than water.

Are You Getting Enough Water-Soluble Vitamins in Your Diet?

Take this brief self-assessment to see if your diet is rich in the water-soluble B vitamins and vitamin C.

1. Do you eat at least 1 cup of a ready-to-eat cereal or hot cereal every day?
   Yes ☐ **No** ☐

2. Do you enjoy a citrus fruit or fruit juice, such as an orange, a grapefruit, or orange juice, every day?
   Yes ☐ **No** ☐

3. Do you have at least one slice of bread, a bagel, or a muffin daily?
   Yes ☐ **No** ☐

4. Do you have at least a cup of vegetables throughout your day?
   Yes ☐ **No** ☐

5. Do you consume at least ½ cup of pasta daily?
   Yes ☐ **No** ☐

Answers

Yes answers to all of these questions make you a vitamin superstar! Rice, pasta, cereals, and bread and bread products are all excellent sources of B vitamins. Citrus fruits are a ringer for vitamin C. In fact, all vegetables can contribute to meeting your daily vitamin C needs. If you answered no more than yes, read on to learn how to add more Bs and C to your diet.

The B Vitamins and Vitamin C Are Water Soluble

There are nine water-soluble vitamins, and eight of them belong to the vitamin B complex. When initially discovered in the early 1900s, the "water-soluble B" was thought to be one vitamin. After years of research, it became apparent that this was not a single substance but rather many vitamins—thiamin, riboflavin, niacin, vitamin B_6, folate, vitamin B_{12}, pantothenic acid, and biotin—known collectively as the B vitamins. The ninth water-soluble vitamin is vitamin C.

Water-soluble vitamins are different from fat-soluble vitamins in that they dissolve in water, are generally not stored in the body, and are often excreted through the urine. Consumers who take large amounts of water-soluble vitamins in an attempt to "beef up" their vitamin stores literally end up flushing their vitamins, and their money, down the toilet. Because excess amounts are not stored, most water-soluble vitamins are not toxic. However, routine intakes of excessive amounts can be harmful. Underconsuming the water-soluble vitamins can lead to deficiency symptoms, and because many B vitamins are found in similar food sources, an individual experiencing a deficiency of one B vitamin is likely also deficient in others.

Water-soluble vitamins serve numerous similar functions in the body. The B vitamins share a common role as **coenzymes** (see **Figure 7.12**), helping numerous enzymes produce reactions in your cells. Although vitamins don't provide calories and thus aren't sources of energy, you need many of the B vitamins to use the three energy-yielding nutrients (carbohydrates, proteins, and fat). Each vitamin has other important functions in your body. Vitamin C plays important roles in the immune system and in bone health, in addition to its other functions. Take the Self-Assessment to see if you are consuming foods that are rich in the B vitamins and vitamin C.

The Take-Home Message There are nine water-soluble vitamins: eight B-complex vitamins and vitamin C. All water-soluble vitamins dissolve in water, are generally not stored in the body, and are excreted through the urine. The B-complex vitamins function as coenzymes in energy production and have roles in other important functions. Vitamin C acts as an antioxidant and is necessary for immune system health and bone health.

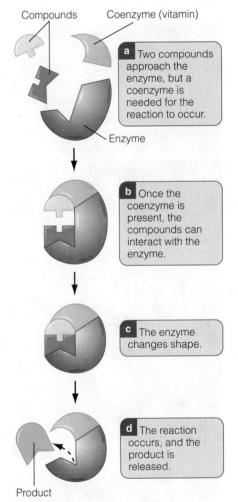

Compounds   Coenzyme (vitamin)

a Two compounds approach the enzyme, but a coenzyme is needed for the reaction to occur.

Enzyme

b Once the coenzyme is present, the compounds can interact with the enzyme.

c The enzyme changes shape.

d The reaction occurs, and the product is released.

Product

Figure 7.12 How B Vitamins Function as Coenzymes

coenzymes Substances needed by enzymes to perform many chemical reactions in your body. Many vitamins act as coenzymes.

exploring
Thiamin (B₁)

What Is Thiamin?

Thiamin, or vitamin B_1, was the first B vitamin to be discovered. The path to its discovery began in the 1890s in East Asia. A Dutch doctor, Christiann Eijkman, noticed that chickens and pigeons that ate polished rice (rice with the nutrient- and thiamin-rich outer layer and germ stripped away) developed **polyneuritis** (*poly* = many, *neur* = nerves, *itis* = inflammation). This debilitating nerve condition resulted in the birds not being able to fly or stand up. Eijkman noted that polyneuritis was also a symptom of beriberi, a similar disease that had been observed in humans.

When Eijkman changed the birds' diet to unpolished rice, with the outer layer and germ intact, the birds were cured.[56] Though Eijkman realized that the unpolished rice eliminated the symptoms, he didn't know why. Finally, in 1911, Casimir Funk identified thiamin as the curative factor in the unpolished rice.

Functions of Thiamin

Thiamin plays a role in the transmission of nerve impulses and so helps keep nerves healthy and functioning properly.

You also need thiamin for the metabolism of carbohydrates and certain amino acids. Thiamin also plays a role in breaking down alcohol in the body.

Daily Needs

The RDA for thiamin for adults is 1.1 milligrams for women and 1.2 milligrams for men. Currently, adult American men consume close to 2 milligrams of thiamin daily, whereas women, on average, eat approximately 1.4 milligrams daily, so both groups are meeting their daily needs.[57]

Food Sources

Enriched and whole-grain foods, such as bread and bread products, ready-to-eat cereals, pasta, and rice, and combined foods, such as sandwiches, are the biggest contributors of thiamin in the American diet (**Figure 7.13**). A medium-sized bowl of ready-to-eat cereal in the morning and a sandwich at lunch will just about meet your daily thiamin requirement.

Pork is the richest source of naturally occurring thiamin.

Too Much or Too Little

There are no known toxicity symptoms from consuming too much thiamin from food or supplements, so no upper level has been set.

The disease that occurs in humans who are deficient in thiamin is **beriberi**. There are two types of beriberi. Wet beriberi affects the cardiovascular system, so symptoms often include a rapid heartbeat, shortness of breath, and edema (swelling) in a person's calves and feet. Dry beriberi affects the nervous system, so symptoms may include difficulty in walking, tingling and loss of feeling in the hands and feet, confusion, and problems with coordination.[58] The populations of poor countries with an inadequate food supply rely heavily on refined grains that are not enriched (recall that enriched grains have the B vitamins thiamin,

polyneuritis Inflammation of the peripheral nerves.

beriberi A thiamin deficiency that can affect the cardiovascular and nervous systems and results in weakness in the body.

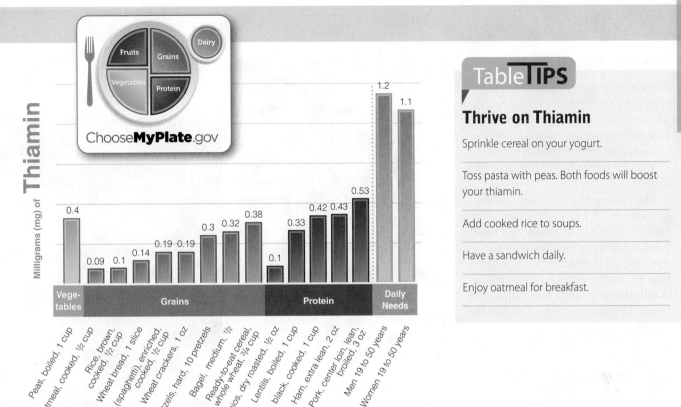

Figure 7.13 **Thiamin Content in Selected Foods**

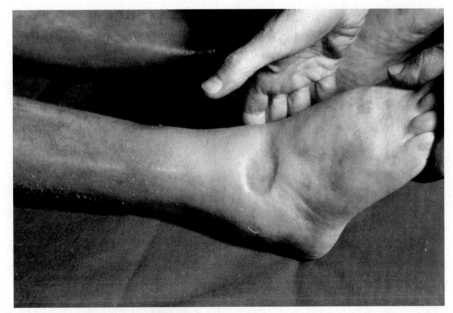

Edema is one of the symptoms of beriberi.

Table TIPS

Thrive on Thiamin

Sprinkle cereal on your yogurt.

Toss pasta with peas. Both foods will boost your thiamin.

Add cooked rice to soups.

Have a sandwich daily.

Enjoy oatmeal for breakfast.

riboflavin, niacin, and folic acid, as well as the mineral iron, added to them). These people are more susceptible to a thiamin deficiency and the side effects of beriberi.

In the United States, widespread use of enriched grains means that instances of beriberi are rare. Americans, however, are not completely immune to thiamin deficiencies. Those who chronically abuse alcohol tend to have a poor diet that is probably deficient in thiamin. Alcohol consumption also interferes with the absorption of the small amounts of thiamin that may be in the diet, accelerating its loss from the body. Alcoholics may find themselves battling a thiamin deficiency that can cause beriberi, and chronic alcohol abuse can lead to an advanced form of thiamin deficiency called **Wernicke-Korsakoff syndrome**. The syndrome is a progressively damaging brain disorder that can cause mental confusion and memory loss, loss of muscle coordination, leg tremors, abnormal eye movements, and hallucinations. Although some of these symptoms can be reversed after the person is medically treated with thiamin, some of the memory loss may be permanent.[59]

Wernicke-Korsakoff syndrome A progressively damaging brain disorder due to chronic thiamin deficiency.

Riboflavin (B₂)

What Is Riboflavin?

Riboflavin, also known as vitamin B_2, is a light-sensitive B vitamin that is abundant in milk. One of the reasons that milk is packaged in opaque bottles or cardboard containers is to prevent its riboflavin content from being destroyed by light.

Not so long ago, milk made its way to a household not via the grocery store cooler, but by way of a daily visit from a milkman in the early hours of the morning. At each delivery, the milkman placed the clear glass milk bottles inside a covered "milk box" outside the home. The milk box helped protect the light-sensitive riboflavin in the milk from being destroyed by the morning sunlight. Sunlight destroys riboflavin quickly. In fact, just 30 minutes of midday summer sun will destroy more than 30 percent of the riboflavin in glass-bottled milk.[60]

A breakfast of cereal and milk and a lunchtime pita sandwich and yogurt will meet your riboflavin needs for the day.

Functions of Riboflavin

Your body needs riboflavin to turn the carbohydrates, proteins, and fats that you eat into energy, and to keep the cells in your body healthy. Riboflavin also enhances the functions of other B vitamins, such as niacin and B_{12}.

Too Much or Too Little

Your body has a limited ability to absorb riboflavin, so excessive amounts are excreted in urine. No upper level for riboflavin has been determined. However, because riboflavin is a bright yellow compound, consuming large

Daily Needs

You need to consume a little over 1 milligram of riboflavin daily to be healthy. Adult males should consume 1.3 milligrams and females, 1.1 milligrams of riboflavin, every day. Americans, on average, typically exceed their daily needs.[61]

Food Sources

Milk and yogurt are the most popular sources of riboflavin in the diets of American adults, followed by enriched cereals and grains (**Figure 7.14**).

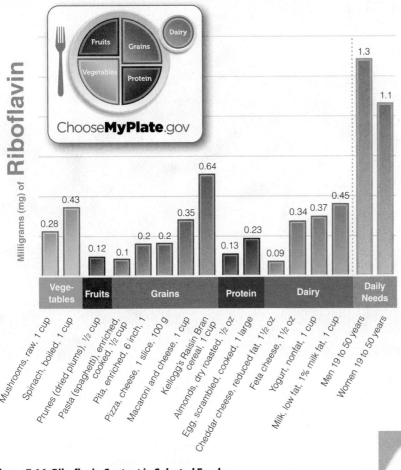

Milligrams (mg) of **Riboflavin**

ChooseMyPlate.gov

| Vege-tables | Fruits | Grains | Protein | Dairy | Daily Needs |

0.28, 0.43, 0.12, 0.1, 0.2, 0.2, 0.35, 0.64, 0.13, 0.23, 0.09, 0.34, 0.37, 0.45, 1.3, 1.1

Mushrooms, raw, 1 cup · Spinach, boiled, 1 cup · Prunes (dried plums), ½ cup · Pasta (spaghetti), enriched, cooked, ½ cup · Pita, enriched, 6 inch, 1 · Pizza, cheese, 1 slice, 100 g · Macaroni and cheese, 1 cup · Kellogg's Raisin Bran cereal, 1 cup · Almonds, dry roasted, ½ oz · Egg, scrambled, cooked, 1 large · Cheddar cheese, reduced fat, 1½ oz · Feta cheese, 1½ oz · Yogurt, nonfat, 1 cup · Milk, low fat, 1% milk fat, 1 cup · Men 19 to 50 years · Women 19 to 50 years

Figure 7.14 Riboflavin Content in Selected Foods

Table TIPS

Rally Your Riboflavin

Have a glass of milk with your meals.

A yogurt snack is a riboflavin snack.

Add spinach to your salad for a riboflavin bonus.

Enriched pasta will enrich your meal with riboflavin.

Macaroni and cheese provides a double source of riboflavin from the pasta and the cheese.

amounts through supplements will turn urine as yellow as a school bus. While this isn't dangerous to your health, it isn't beneficial either, so you should skip the supplements and pour yourself a glass of milk instead.

If you don't consume enough of this B vitamin, the cells in the tissues that line your throat, mouth, tongue, and lips will be the first to signal a deficiency. Your throat would be sore, the inside of your mouth would swell, your tongue would be inflamed and look purplish red, and your lips would be dry, cracked, and scaly. Deficiencies are rarely seen in healthy individuals who eat a balanced diet.

An inflamed tongue (glossitis) is one symptom of a riboflavin deficiency.

exploring
Niacin (B₃)

What Is Niacin?

Niacin, or vitamin B_3, is the generic term for **nicotinic acid** and **nicotinamide**, which are the two active forms of niacin that are derived from foods.

Functions of Niacin

Niacin Is Needed to Use the Energy in Your Food

Niacin is another nutrient your body needs in order to use carbohydrates, proteins, and fats. Without niacin, you wouldn't be able to create energy from the foods that you eat. Niacin is also needed to synthesize fat and cholesterol.

Other Functions of Niacin

Niacin is needed to keep your skin cells healthy and your digestive system functioning properly.

Niacin has been shown to lower the total amount of cholesterol in the blood and the "bad" LDL cholesterol carrier. It can also lower high levels of fat (triglycerides) in the blood and simultaneously raise the level of the "good" HDL cholesterol carrier. The nicotinic acid form of niacin is sometimes prescribed by physicians for patients with high blood cholesterol levels. When niacin is used to treat high blood cholesterol, it is considered a drug. The amount prescribed by a physician is often more than 50 times the upper level for niacin. Note that you should *never* consume high amounts of niacin unless a physician is monitoring you.

nicotinic acid One of the two active forms of niacin that are derived from foods.

nicotinamide One of the two active forms of niacin that are derived from foods.

tryptophan An amino acid that can be converted to niacin in the body.

niacin equivalents (NE) A measurement that reflects the amount of niacin and tryptophan in foods that can be used to synthesize niacin.

flushing A reddish coloring of the face, arms, and chest.

Daily Needs

The recommended daily amount for adults is 14 milligrams for women and 16 milligrams for men, an amount set to prevent the deficiency disease pellagra. American adults, on average, far exceed their daily niacin needs.[62]

Niacin is found in many foods, but it can also be synthesized in the body from the amino acid **tryptophan**. For this reason, your daily niacin needs are measured in **niacin equivalents (NE)**. It is estimated that 60 milligrams of tryptophan can be converted to 1 milligram of niacin or 1 milligram NE.

Food Sources

Niacin is found in meat, fish, poultry, enriched whole-grain breads and bread products, and fortified cereals (**Figure 7.15**). Protein-rich foods, particularly animal foods such as meat, are good sources of tryptophan and thus of niacin. However, if you are falling short of both your dietary protein and niacin, tryptophan will first be used to make protein in your body, at the expense of your niacin needs.[63]

As with thiamin, your niacin needs are probably met after you eat your breakfast and lunch, especially since similar foods contain both vitamins.

Too Much or Too Little

As with most water-soluble vitamins, there isn't any known danger from consuming too much niacin from foods such as meat and enriched grains. However, overconsuming niacin by taking supplements or eating too many overly fortified foods can cause **flushing**, a reddish coloring of the face, arms, and chest. Too much niacin consumption can also cause nausea and vomiting, be toxic to your liver, and raise your blood glucose levels.

The upper level for niacin for adults is 35 milligrams to prevent flushing, the first side effect to be observed when too much niacin is consumed. This upper level applies only to healthy individuals.

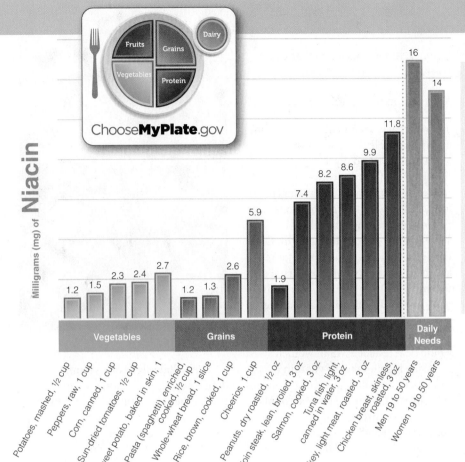

Figure 7.15 Niacin Content in Selected Foods

Nail Your Niacin

Have a serving of enriched cereal in the morning.

Dip niacin-rich peppers in hummus.

Enjoy a lean chicken breast at dinner.

Snack on peanuts.

Put tuna fish flakes on your salad.

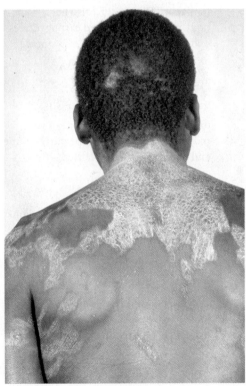

Inflamed skin (dermatitis) can result from pellagra.

pellagra The disease caused by a deficiency of niacin in the body.

dermatitis Inflammation or irritation of the skin.

dementia Loss of memory along with confusion and disorientation.

It may be too high for those with certain medical conditions, such as diabetes mellitus and liver disease.[64]

Too little niacin in the diet can result in the deficiency disease called **pellagra**. In the early 1900s, pellagra was widespread among the poor living in the southern United States, where people relied on corn—a poor source of niacin—as a dietary staple. The symptoms of pellagra—**dermatitis** (inflammation or irritation of the skin), **dementia** (loss of memory along with confusion and disorientation), and **d**iarrhea—led to its being known as the disease of the three Ds. A fourth D, **d**eath, was often associated with the disease.

Once other cereal grains were available, pellagra disappeared as a widespread disease in the United States. The niacin in the grains was later identified as the curative factor for pellagra. Although no longer common in the United States, pellagra does occur among individuals who abuse alcohol and have a very poor diet.

exploring
Vitamin B₆

What Is Vitamin B₆?

Vitamin B₆ is a collective name for several related compounds, including **pyridoxine**, the major form found in plant foods and the form used in supplements and fortified foods.[65] Two other forms, pyridoxal and pyridoxamine, are found in animal food sources such as chicken and meat.

Functions of Vitamin B₆

Vitamin B₆ Is an Active Coenzyme

Vitamin B₆ acts as a coenzyme with more than 100 enzymes involved in the metabolism of proteins. It is needed to create nonessential amino acids and to convert the amino acid tryptophan to niacin.[66] Vitamin B₆ also helps your body metabolize fats and carbohydrates and break down glycogen, the storage form of glucose.

Other Functions of B₆

Vitamin B₆ is needed to make the oxygen-carrying hemoglobin in your red blood cells and to keep your immune and nervous systems healthy.[67]

Daily Needs

Adult women need 1.3 to 1.5 milligrams and men need 1.3 to 1.7 milligrams of vitamin B₆ daily, depending on their age.

Food Sources

Because vitamin B₆ is found in so many foods, including ready-to-eat cereals, meat, fish, poultry, many vegetables and fruits, nuts, peanut butter, and other

pyridoxine The major form of vitamin B₆ found in plants foods, supplements, and fortified foods.

premenstrual syndrome (PMS) A variety of symptoms such as moodiness, irritability, bloating, and anxiety that some women may experience during the menstrual cycle.

anemia A condition in which your blood has a lower than normal number of red blood cells than it should to be healthy.

legumes, Americans on average easily meet their daily needs (**Figure 7.16**).

Too Much or Too Little

To protect against potential nerve damage, the upper level for vitamin B₆ is set at 100 milligrams daily for adults over the age of 19. Luckily, it would be extremely difficult to take in a dangerous level of vitamin B₆ from food alone.

However, taking vitamin B₆ in supplement form can be harmful. Over the years, vitamin B₆ has been touted to aid the symptoms of **premenstrual syndrome (PMS)**, which include moodiness, irritability, bloating, and anxiety. However, more research is needed to determine if vitamin B₆ supplements would help reduce PMS in women.

While high intakes of vitamin B₆ from foods do not appear to be problematic, chronically taking large amounts of vitamin B₆ through supplements has been associated with a variety of ill effects, including nerve damage, losing control of bodily movements, and gastrointestinal issues such as nausea and heartburn. Typically these symptoms subside once supplement consumption stops.[68]

The telltale signs of a vitamin B₆ deficiency are a sore tongue, inflammation of the skin, depression, confusion, and possibly **anemia**.

Those who consume too much alcohol are more likely to fall short of their needs. Not only does alcohol cause your body to lose vitamin B₆, but those suffering from alcoholism are likely to have an unbalanced diet, with little variety.

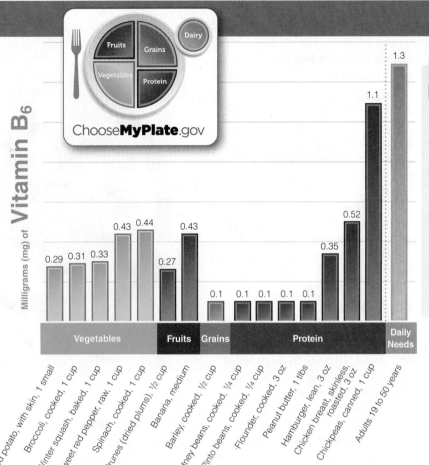

Figure 7.16 Vitamin B₆ Content in Selected Foods

Table**TIPS**

Beam with B₆

Have a stuffed baked potato with steamed broccoli and grilled chicken for lunch.

Grab a banana for a midmorning snack.

Add cooked barley to your soup.

Snack on prunes.

Add kidney beans to your chili or salad.

---

exploring
Folate

What Is Folate?

There are two forms of the vitamin folate: the naturally occurring folate in foods and the synthetic form, **folic acid**, which is added to foods (such as ready-to-eat cereals and grains) and found in supplements. (A very small amount of folic acid can occur naturally in foods. But, for practical purposes here, *folic acid* refers to the synthetic variety.)

Functions of Folate
Folate Is Vital for DNA Synthesis

Folate is vital to making the DNA in your cells. If the synthesis of DNA is disrupted, your body's ability to create and maintain new cells is impaired.[69]

For this reason, folate plays many important roles, from maintaining healthy blood cells and preventing birth defects to possibly fighting cancer. Folate also helps your body use amino acids and is needed to help red blood cells divide and increase in adequate numbers.

Folate Prevents Birth Defects

Folate plays an extremely important role during pregnancy, particularly in the first few weeks after conception, often before the mother knows she is pregnant. Folate is needed to create new cells so that the baby can grow and develop. A deficiency during pregnancy can result in birth defects called **neural tube defects**. The neural tube forms the baby's spine, brain, and skull. If the neural tube

folic acid The form of folate used in vitamin supplements and fortification of foods.

neural tube defects Any major birth defect of the central nervous system, including the brain, caused by failure of the neural tube to properly close during fetal development.

CONTINUED ▶

Folate

doesn't develop properly, two common birth defects, **anencephaly** and **spina bifida**, can occur. In anencephaly, the brain doesn't completely form, so the baby can't move, hear, think, or function. An infant with anencephaly dies soon after birth. In spina bifida (see photo), the baby's spinal cord and backbone aren't properly developed, causing physical disabilities, such as the inability to walk.[70] Folic acid reduces the risk of these birth defects by 50 to 60 percent if consumed at least the month prior to conception and during the early part of pregnancy.[71]

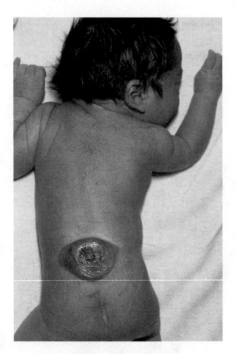

Infant with spina bifida.

anencephaly A neural tube defect that results in the absence of major parts of the brain and spinal cord.

spina bifida A serious birth defect in which the spinal cord is malformed and lacks the protective membrane coat.

dietary folate equivalents (DFE) A measurement used to express the amount of folate in a food or supplement.

Folate Reduces Some Cancer Risks

Inadequate amounts of folate in the body can disrupt the cell's DNA, potentially triggering the development of cancer. While research has shown that an adequate intake of folate may help reduce the risk of certain cancers, specifically colon cancer, some studies suggest that folate supplements may actually increase the risk of prostate cancer.[72] This suggests that while some may be good, more (through supplements) may not be better.

Daily Needs

Your body absorbs the synthetic folic acid more easily than it absorbs naturally occurring folate. In fact, synthetic folic acid is absorbed 1.7 times more efficiently than most folate that is found naturally in foods.[73] Because of this, your folate needs are measured in **dietary folate equivalents (DFE)**. Most adults should consume 400 micrograms DFE of folate daily.

While the foods in your diet analysis program database list the micrograms of folate as DFE, the Nutrition Facts panel on the food label doesn't make this distinction. To convert the micrograms of folic acid found on the food labels of foods with folic acid added, such as enriched pasta, rice, cereals, and bread, to dietary folate equivalents, multiply the amount listed on the label by 1.7:

$$100 \ \mu g \times 1.7 = 170 \ \mu g \ DFE$$

Women who are planning to become pregnant should consume 400 micrograms of synthetic folic acid daily from fortified foods or supplements, along with a diet high in naturally occurring folate. Women with a family history of neural tube defects should, under the guidance of their physicians, take even larger amounts.[74] Because 50 percent of pregnancies in the United States are unplanned, any woman who may become pregnant is advised to follow these same recommendations.

Food Sources

Since 1998, the FDA has mandated that folic acid be added to all enriched grains and cereal products. This enrichment program has reduced the incidence of neural tube defects by 25 to 30 percent.[75] Enriched pasta, rice, breads and cereals, legumes (dried peas and beans), leafy green vegetables (spinach, lettuce, collards), broccoli, asparagus, and orange juice are all good sources of this vitamin (**Figure 7.17**).

Too Much or Too Little

There isn't any danger in consuming excessive amounts of naturally occurring folate in foods. However, consuming too much folic acid, either through supplements or fortified foods, can be harmful for individuals who are deficient in vitamin B_{12}. A vitamin B_{12} deficiency can cause anemia and, more dangerous, crippling and irreversible nerve damage. Too much folate in the diet masks the symptoms of B_{12}-deficiency anemia. Though the folate can correct anemia, the nerve damage due to the vitamin B_{12} deficiency persists. This delays a proper diagnosis and corrective therapy with vitamin B_{12}. By the time the person is given

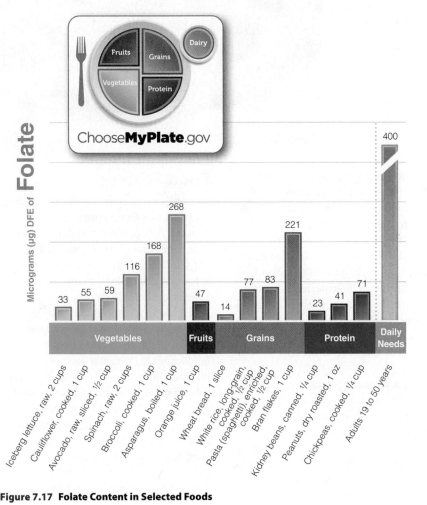

Figure 7.17 Folate Content in Selected Foods

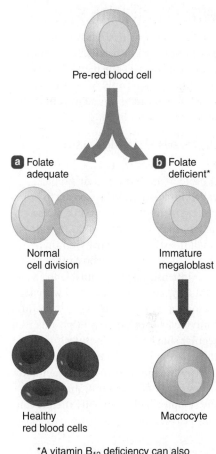

Pre-red blood cell

a Folate adequate

b Folate deficient*

Normal cell division

Immature megaloblast

Healthy red blood cells

Macrocyte

*A vitamin B$_{12}$ deficiency can also cause the formation of macrocytes.

Figure 7.18 Altered Red Blood Cells with Folate Deficiency

TableTIPS

Fulfill Your Folate Needs

Have a bowl of cereal in the morning.

Add chickpeas to your salad.

Enjoy a tossed salad with your lunch.

Add fresh spinach leaves to your sandwich.

Have a handful of crackers as a late afternoon snack.

the vitamin B$_{12}$, irreversible nerve damage may have occurred. While, as you read, low folate intake may be associated with increased cancer risk, studies suggest that folate consumption double the DRI or even higher may also increase the risk of cancer.[76]

A folate deficiency can also result in abnormally large and immature blood cells known as **megaloblasts** (*megalo = large*). These megaloblasts develop into abnormally large red blood cells, or **macrocytes**, that have a diminished oxygen-carrying capacity. Eventually, **macrocytic anemia** causes a person to feel tired, weak, and irritable and to experience shortness of breath. Because

folate acts with vitamin B$_{12}$ to produce healthy red blood cells, a deficiency of either vitamin can lead to macrocytic anemia (**Figure 7.18**).

An upper level of 1,000 micrograms has been set for folic acid from enriched and fortified foods and supplements to safeguard those who may be unknowingly deficient in vitamin B$_{12}$.

megaloblasts Large, immature red blood cells.

macrocytes Abnormally large cells such as red blood cells.

macrocytic anemia A form of anemia characterized by large, immature red blood cells, due to a vitamin B$_{12}$ deficiency.

exploring
Vitamin B$_{12}$

What Is Vitamin B$_{12}$?

The family of compounds referred to as vitamin B$_{12}$ is also called cobalamin because it contains the metal cobalt.[77] Vitamin B$_{12}$ is the only water-soluble vitamin that can be stored in your body, primarily in your liver.

B$_{12}$ Needs Intrinsic Factor to Be Absorbed

A protein produced in your stomach called **intrinsic factor** is needed to promote vitamin B$_{12}$ absorption. Intrinsic factor binds with vitamin B$_{12}$ in your small intestine, where the vitamin is absorbed. Individuals who cannot produce intrinsic factor are unable to absorb vitamin B$_{12}$ and are diagnosed with **pernicious anemia** (*pernicious* = harmful). Individuals with this condition are given regular shots of vitamin B$_{12}$, which inject the vitamin directly into the blood, bypassing the intestine. Because your body stores plenty of vitamin B$_{12}$ in the liver, the symptoms of pernicious anemia can take years to develop.

Functions of Vitamin B$_{12}$
Vitamin B$_{12}$ Is Vital for Healthy Nerves and Red Blood Cells

Your body needs vitamin B$_{12}$ to use certain fatty acids and amino acids and to make the DNA in your cells. Vitamin B$_{12}$ is also needed for healthy nerves and tissues. Like folate, vitamin B$_{12}$ plays an important role in keeping your cells, particularly your red blood cells, healthy.[78]

Daily Needs

Adults need 2.4 micrograms of vitamin B$_{12}$ daily. American adults, on average, consume more than 4 micrograms daily.

The body's ability to absorb naturally occurring vitamin B$_{12}$ from foods diminishes with age. This decline appears to be due to a reduction in the acidic juices in the stomach, which are needed to break the bonds that bind the B$_{12}$ to the proteins in food. If the bonds aren't broken, the vitamin can't be released. Up to 30 percent of individuals over the age of 50 experience this decline in acidic juices in their stomachs. Not surprisingly, the pernicious anemia associated with a vitamin B$_{12}$ deficiency occurs in about 1 to 2 percent of older adults.[79]

With less acid present, the bacteria normally found in the intestines aren't properly destroyed and so tend to overgrow. This abundance of bacteria feed on vitamin B$_{12}$, diminishing the amount of the vitamin that may be available. Luckily, the synthetic form of vitamin B$_{12}$ that is used in fortified foods and supplements isn't bound to a protein, so it doesn't depend on your stomach secretions to be absorbed. (Synthetic vitamin B$_{12}$ still needs intrinsic factor to be absorbed.)

Because the synthetic variety is a more reliable source, individuals over the age of 50 should meet their vitamin B$_{12}$ needs primarily from fortified foods or a supplement.[80]

Food Sources

Naturally occurring vitamin B$_{12}$ is found only in foods from animal sources, such as meat, fish, poultry, and dairy products. (See **Figure 7.19**.) A varied diet that includes the minimum recommended servings of these food groups will easily meet your daily needs.

Synthetic vitamin B$_{12}$ is found in fortified soy milk and some ready-to-eat cereals, which are ideal sources for older adults and strict vegetarians, who avoid all foods from animal sources. If you are relying solely on fortified foods to meet your vitamin B$_{12}$ needs, continually check the labels on these products to make sure they haven't unexpectedly been reformulated to exclude the vitamin.

Too Much or Too Little

At present, there are no known risks of consuming too much vitamin B$_{12}$ from foods, fortified foods, or supplements, and no upper level has been set. There is also no known benefit from taking B$_{12}$ supplements if your diet contains foods from animal sources and/or fortified foods.

intrinsic factor (IF) A protein secreted by the stomach that helps in the absorption of vitamin B$_{12}$.

pernicious anemia A form of anemia characterized by large, immature red blood cells, due to a lack of intrinsic factor.

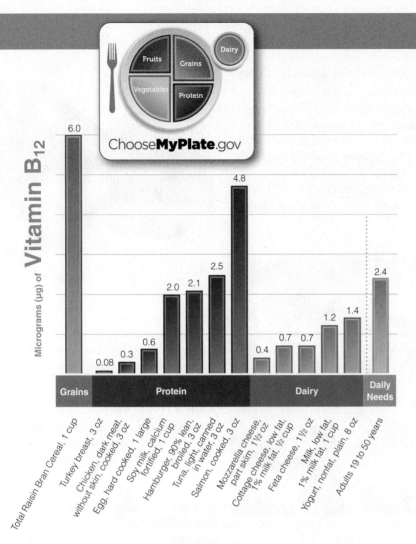

Figure 7.19 Vitamin B₁₂ Content in Selected Foods

Chart: Microgams (μg) of Vitamin B₁₂

Grains:
- Total Raisin Bran Cereal, 1 cup: 6.0

Protein:
- Turkey breast, 3 oz: 0.08
- Chicken, dark meat, without skin, cooked, 3 oz: 0.3
- Egg, hard cooked, 1 large: 0.6
- Soy milk, calcium fortified, 1 cup: 2.0
- Hamburger, 90% lean, broiled, 3 oz: 2.1
- Tuna, light, canned in water, 3 oz: 2.5
- Salmon, cooked, 3 oz: 4.8

Dairy:
- Mozzarella cheese, part skim, 1½ oz: 0.4
- Cottage cheese, low fat, 1% milk fat, ½ cup: 0.7
- Feta cheese, 1½ oz: 0.7
- Milk, low fat, 1% milk fat, 1 cup: 1.2
- Yogurt, nonfat, plain, 8 oz: 1.4

Daily Needs:
- Adults 19 to 50 years: 2.4

TableTIPS

Boost Your B₁₂

Enjoy heart-healthy fish at least twice a week.

Sprinkle your steamed vegetables with reduced-fat shredded cheese.

Drink milk or fortified soy milk.

Try a cottage cheese-and-fruit snack in the afternoon.

Enjoy a grilled chicken breast on a bun for lunch.

A Vitamin B₁₂ Deficiency Can Cause Macrocytic Anemia

Because vitamin B₁₂ and folate work closely together to make healthy red blood cells, a vitamin B₁₂ deficiency can cause macrocytic anemia, the same type of anemia caused by a folate deficiency. In macrocytic anemia due to a vitamin B₁₂ deficiency, there is enough folate available for red blood cells to divide, but the folate can't be utilized properly because there isn't enough vitamin B₁₂ available. In fact, the true cause of macrocytic anemia is more likely a B₁₂ deficiency than a folate deficiency.

Because pernicious anemia (caused by a lack of intrinsic factor) is a type of macrocytic anemia, its initial symptoms are the same as those seen in

folate deficiency: fatigue and shortness of breath.

Vitamin B₁₂ is needed to protect nerve cells, including those in your brain and spine, so one long-term consequence of pernicious anemia is nerve damage marked by tingling and numbness in the arms and legs and the inability to maintain balance. If diagnosed early enough, these symptoms can be reversed with treatments of vitamin B₁₂.

exploring
Vitamin C

What Is Vitamin C?

You don't have to go out of your way to ensure that your dog's daily chow contains enough vitamin C. Dogs and many other animals possess an enzyme that can synthesize vitamin C from glucose. Humans, however, lack the necessary enzyme for this conversion, and have to rely on food to meet their daily vitamin C needs.[81]

Functions of Vitamin C

Vitamin C Acts as a Coenzyme

Vitamin C, also known as **ascorbic acid**, acts as a coenzyme that is needed to synthesize and use certain amino acids. In particular, vitamin C is needed to make collagen, the most abundant protein in your body. Collagen is plentiful in your connective tissue, which supports and connects all your body parts, so this protein is needed for healthy bones, teeth, skin, and blood vessels.[82] Thus, a vitamin C–deficient diet would affect your entire body.

Vitamin C contributes to healthy, glowing skin by facilitating the production of collagen.

ascorbic acid The active form of vitamin C.

Vitamin C Acts as an Antioxidant

Like beta-carotene and vitamin E, vitamin C acts an antioxidant that may help reduce the risk of chronic diseases such as heart disease and cancer. It also helps you absorb the iron in plant foods such as grains and cereals and break down histamine, the component behind the inflammation seen in many allergic reactions.[83]

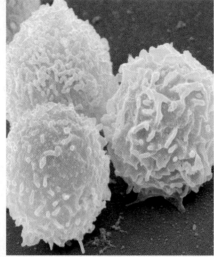

White blood cells.

Vitamin C Boosts Your Immune System

Vitamin C helps keep your immune system healthy by enabling your body to make white blood cells, like the ones shown in the photo. These blood cells fight infections, and this immune-boosting role has fostered the belief that high doses of vitamin C can cure the common cold. (The Examining the Evidence feature "Gesundheit! Myths and Facts about the Common Cold" on pages 262–263 takes a look at this theory.)

Daily Needs

Women need to consume 75 milligrams of vitamin C daily, and men need to consume 90 milligrams daily to meet their needs.

Smoking accelerates the breakdown and elimination of vitamin C from the

body, so smokers need to consume an additional 35 milligrams of vitamin C every day to make up for these losses.[84]

Food Sources

Most Americans can meet their vitamin C needs by consuming fruits and vegetables. One serving of either orange or grapefruit juice will just about meet an adult's daily needs. Tomatoes, peppers, potatoes, broccoli, oranges, and cantaloupe are also excellent sources (**Figure 7.20**).

Too Much or Too Little

Though excessive amounts of vitamin C aren't known to be toxic, consuming more than 3,000 milligrams daily through the use of supplements has been shown to cause nausea, stomach cramps, and diarrhea.

The upper level for vitamin C for adults is set at 2,000 milligrams to avoid the intestinal discomfort that excessive amounts of the vitamin can cause. Too much vitamin C can also lead to the formation of kidney stones in individuals with a history of kidney disease.

Because vitamin C helps to absorb the form of iron found in plant

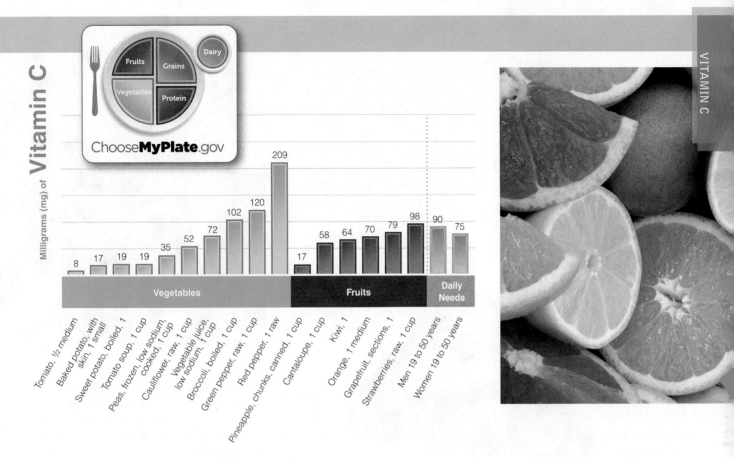

Vitamin C

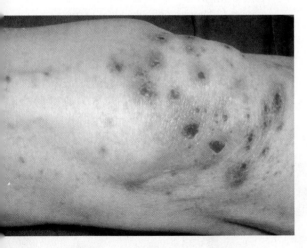

Figure 7.20 Vitamin C Content in Selected Foods

Vitamin C–deficiency can cause skin hemorrhages.

foods, those with a rare disorder called **hemochromatosis** (*hemo* = blood; *chroma* = color; *osis* = condition), which causes the body to store too much iron, should avoid excessive amounts of vitamin C. Iron toxicity is extremely dangerous and can damage many organs in your body, including the liver and heart.

For centuries, **scurvy**, the disease of a vitamin C deficiency, was the affliction of sailors on long voyages. After many weeks at sea, sailors would run out of vitamin C–rich produce and then develop the telltale signs of scurvy: swollen and bleeding gums, a rough rash on the skin, coiled or curly arm hairs, and wounds that wouldn't heal. Because vitamin C is needed for healthy blood vessels, a deficiency also often causes purple-colored spots, a sign of skin hemorrhages, to appear on the skin and in mucus membranes of the body such as the lining of the mouth.

In 1753, a British naval surgeon discovered that orange and lemon juice prevented scurvy. Decades later, the British government added lemon or lime juice to their standard rations for sailors to thwart scurvy. In 1919, vitamin C was discovered as the curative factor in these juices.[85]

TableTIPS

Juicy Ways to Get Vitamin C

Have at least one citrus fruit (such as an orange or grapefruit) daily.

Put sliced tomatoes on your sandwich.

Enjoy a fruit cup for dessert.

Drink low-sodium vegetable juice for an afternoon refresher.

Add strawberries to your low-fat frozen yogurt.

hemochromatosis A blood disorder characterized by the retention of an excessive amount of iron.

scurvy A disease caused by a deficiency of vitamin C and characterized by bleeding gums and a skin rash.

Pantothenic Acid and Biotin

What Are Pantothenic Acid and Biotin?

Pantothenic acid and biotin are B vitamins.

Functions of Pantothenic Acid and Biotin

Pantothenic acid and biotin aid in the metabolism of the nutrients that provide you with energy: carbohydrates, proteins, and fats.

Daily Needs

Adults need 5 milligrams of pantothenic acid and 30 micrograms of biotin daily.

Food Sources

Both pantothenic acid and biotin are widely available in foods, including whole grains and whole-grain cereals,

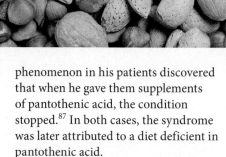

nuts and legumes, broccoli, peanut butter, meat, milk, and eggs. Most Americans easily meet their needs.[86]

Biotin deficiency is so rare that an accurate list of the amount in foods is hard to find. In addition to its abundance in foods, biotin can be synthesized by the bacteria in your intestinal tract, providing yet another avenue to meet your needs.

Eating a healthy diet to meet all of your other B vitamin needs will ensure that you meet your needs for pantothenic acid and biotin.

Too Much or Too Little

Like many of the other B vitamins, there are no known adverse effects from consuming too much pantothenic acid or biotin. An upper level has not been determined for either of these vitamins.

Although a pantothenic acid deficiency is rare, if you do fall short of your needs, your symptoms might include fatigue, nausea, vomiting, numbness, muscle cramps, and difficulties walking.

During World War II, prisoners of war in Asia experienced a "burning feet" syndrome. The symptoms ranged from heat sensations and tingling on the soles of their feet to a painful burning intense enough to disrupt sleep. Their diet consisted predominantly of nutrient-poor polished rice. A doctor in India who was studying an identical

phenomenon in his patients discovered that when he gave them supplements of pantothenic acid, the condition stopped.[87] In both cases, the syndrome was later attributed to a diet deficient in pantothenic acid.

Consuming inadequate amounts of biotin can cause hair loss, skin rash, and feelings of depression, fatigue, and nausea.[88] Though deficiencies are rare, they can occur if you eat a lot of raw egg whites. The protein avidin, found in egg whites, binds with biotin and blocks it from being absorbed in your intestine. Cooking the egg denatures and inactivates the protein, eliminating the problem.[89]

Are There Other Important Vitamin-Like Nutrients?

Choline Is an Essential Nutrient

Choline is an essential nutrient that your body needs for healthy cells and nerves and the transportation of lipids in your body, but it is not classified as a vitamin. Although your body can synthesize it, it does not make enough to meet your daily needs.[90] To be safe, the current dietary recommendation of 425 milligrams for women and 550 milligrams for men is based on the amount needed to protect the liver.

Although choline is widely available in foods, especially milk, liver, eggs, wheat germ, and peanuts, Americans' diets appear to be falling short of this nutrient. Too much choline from supplements can cause sweating and vomiting as well as **hypotension** (*hypo* = low), or low blood pressure. Too much choline can also cause a person to emit an unpleasant fishy odor as the body tries to get rid of the excess. The upper level of 3,500 milligrams for choline has been set to prevent your blood pressure from dropping too low and to keep you from smelling like a fish.

Carnitine, Lipoic Acid, and Inositol Are Vitamin-Like Substances

Certain vitamin-like substances are needed for overall health and important body functions, but they are not considered essential nutrients because your body can synthesize them in adequate amounts without consuming them in foods, and deficiency symptoms are not known to occur in humans.

Carnitine (*carnus* = flesh) is needed to properly utilize fat. It is abundant in foods from animal sources, such as meat and dairy products. Although there is no research to support the claim, carnitine supplements are sometimes promoted to help athletes improve their performance.[91]

Similar to many B vitamins, **lipoic acid** helps your cells generate energy, and it was in fact initially thought to be a vitamin.[92] Lipoic acid is also being studied for its potential role as an antioxidant that could help reduce the risk of certain chronic diseases, such as diabetes mellitus and cataracts.

Lastly, **inositol** is needed to keep cell membranes healthy. Inositol can be found in foods from plant sources. As with the other important vitamin-like substances, healthy individuals can synthesize enough inositol to meet their needs, so supplements are not necessary.

Table 7.3 on pages 260–261 provides you with a quick guide to your vitamin needs.

│ The Take-Home Message Choline, carnitine, lipoic acid, and inositol are vitamin-like substances. Choline is an essential nutrient that is needed for healthy cells and nerves. Americans' diets may be falling short of choline. Carnitine, lipoic acid, and inositol are needed for important body functions and overall health, but are not essential nutrients. Your body can synthesize these substances in adequate amounts, and there are no known deficiency symptoms.

choline A vitamin-like substance needed for healthy cells and nerves.

hypotension Low blood pressure.

carnitine A vitamin-like substance needed to properly utilize fat.

lipoic acid A vitamin-like substance that your body needs for energy production; it may also act as an antioxidant.

inositol A vitamin-like substance synthesized in your body that helps to keep your cells and their membranes healthy.

Table 7.3

Vitamins at a Glance

	Major Functions	Adult DRI, Age 19 to 50 Years	Food Sources	Toxicity Symptoms/UL	Deficiency Symptoms/ Conditions
Fat-Soluble Vitamins					
Vitamin A	Vision, cell differentiation, reproduction, bone health, immune function	700–900 µg RAE/ day	Beef liver, fortified dairy products	Compromised bone health, birth defects during pregnancy UL: 3,000 µg RAE/day of preformed vitamin A	Night blindness, xerophthalmia, stunting of bones
Beta-carotene	Provitamin A carotenoid, antioxidant		Sweet potatoes, carrots, winter squash, cantaloupe	Carotenodermia	
Vitamin D	Calcium balance, bone health, cell differentiation, immune system	15 µg (600 IU)/day	Fatty fish (salmon, tuna, sardines) Fortified foods (dairy products, orange juice, cereals)	Hypercalcemia UL: 100 µg (4,000 IU)/day	Rickets and osteomalacia
Vitamin E	Antioxidant, health of cell membranes, heart health	15 mg alpha-tocopherol/ day	Vegetable and seed oils, nuts, seeds, fortified cereals, green leafy vegetables	Interference with blood clotting and increased risk of hemorrhage UL: 1,000 mg AT/day from supplements and/or fortified foods	Nerve problems, muscle weakness, and uncontrolled movement of body parts
Vitamin K	Blood clotting, bone health	90–120 µg/day	Green leafy vegetables, soybeans, canola and soybean oils, beef liver	None known	Excessive bleeding
Water-Soluble Vitamins					
Thiamin (B₁)	Coenzyme, needed for nerve function and energy metabolism	1.1–1.2 mg/day	Pork Enriched and fortified foods, whole grains	None known	Beriberi, Wernicke-Korsakoff syndrome
Riboflavin (B₂)	Coenzyme in energy metabolism, enhances function of other B vitamins	1.1–1.3 mg/day	Milk, enriched and fortified grains, whole grains	Can turn urine bright yellow	Sore throat, inflammation of the mouth, tongue, and lips
Niacin (B₃)	Coenzyme in energy metabolism, needed to synthesize fat and cholesterol	14–16 mg/day	Lean meats, fish, poultry, enriched and fortified grains and cereals, whole grains, corn, sweet potatoes	Flushing, nausea, vomiting, toxic to liver, may raise blood glucose levels UL: 35 mg/day	Pellagra, characterized by dermatitis, diarrhea, and dementia

(continued)

Table 7.3 continued

Vitamins at a Glance

	Major Functions	Adult DRI, Age 19 to 50 Years	Food Sources	Toxicity Symptoms/UL	Deficiency Symptoms/ Conditions
Water-Soluble Vitamins					
Vitamin B$_6$	Coenzyme in energy metabolism, hemoglobin, healthy immune and nervous systems, homocysteine metabolism	1.3–1.7 mg/day	Fortified cereals, meat, fish, poultry, many vegetables and fruits, nuts, peanut butter, and other legumes	Nerve damage, tingling in hands and feet UL: 100 mg/day	Sore tongue, inflammation of skin, depression, possible anemia, confusion
Folate	DNA and red blood cell formation, prevention of specific birth defects, homocysteine metabolism	400 µg DFE/day	Dark green leafy vegetables, enriched pasta, rice, breads and cereals, legumes, orange juice, asparagus, spinach	Masks vitamin B$_{12}$ deficiency UL: 1,000 µg/day from supplements and/or fortified foods	Macrocytic anemia
Vitamin B$_{12}$	Synthesis of new cells, especially red blood cells, healthy nerves and tissues Activates folate	2.4 µg/day	Animal products, including lean meats, fish, poultry, eggs, cheese, fortified foods	None known	Pernicious anemia, macrocytic anemia, nerve damage as indicated by tingling and numbness in the hands and feet
Vitamin C	Collagen formation, antioxidant, enhanced iron absorption, healthy immune system	75–90 mg/day (an additional 35 mg if a smoker)	Citrus fruit, tomatoes, peppers, potatoes, broccoli, cantaloupe	Nausea, diarrhea, stomach cramps UL: 2,000 mg/ day	Scurvy; characterized by bleeding gums, skin hemorrhages, coiled or curly arm hairs
Biotin and Pantothenic Acid	Aid in the metabolism of the energy nutrients	Pantothenic acid: 5 mg/day Biotin: 30 µg/day	Both are widespread in foods	No known adverse effects UL has not been set	For pantothenic acid: fatigue, nausea, vomiting, numbness, muscle cramps, and difficulty walking For biotin: hair loss, skin rash, depression, fatigue, nausea

Gesundheit! Myths and Facts about the Common Cold

You probably know the symptoms well. Your nose runs like a leaky faucet and turns beet red from constant wiping. Your head seems stuffed with cotton, and it feels like someone is playing bongo drums under your scalp. Between coughing and sneezing, you can't get the rest you need to relieve what feels like constant fatigue. The diagnosis? At least one of the more than 200 varieties of cold virus

has invaded your body, and you have a cold that could last as long as two weeks.

You're never alone if you have a case of the common cold—Americans will suffer a billion of them this year alone.[1] Students miss more than 22 million school days every year battling the common cold.[2]

The Truth about Catching a Cold

Contrary to popular belief, you can't catch a cold from being outside on a cold day without a coat or hat. Rather, the only way to catch a cold is to come into contact with a cold virus. Contact can be direct, such as when you hug or shake hands with someone who is carrying the virus; or indirect, such as when you touch an object like a keyboard or telephone contaminated with a cold virus. The next time you touch your nose or rub your eyes, you transfer these germs from your hands into your body. You can also catch a cold virus by inhaling virus-carrying droplets from a cough or sneeze of someone with the cold.

The increased frequency of colds during the fall and winter is likely due to people spending more time indoors in the close quarters of classrooms, dorm rooms, and the workplace, which makes the sharing of germs easier. The low humidity of the winter air can also cause the inside of your nose to

be drier and more permeable to the invasion of these viruses.

Vitamin C and the Common Cold

In the 1970s, a scientist named Linus Pauling theorized that consuming at least 1,000 milligrams of vitamin C daily would prevent the common cold. The latest extensive review of almost 30 controlled studies involving over 11,000 individuals who consumed 200 milligrams or more of vitamin C daily suggests that the regular ingestion of a supplement doesn't prevent healthy individuals from getting a cold.[3] However, this research did show that individuals who are involved in

How Should You Get Your Vitamins?

Store vitamin B–rich whole-wheat flour in an airtight container in your refrigerator or freezer. Because whole-wheat flour contains the germ of the wheat kernel, which is rich in unsaturated fatty acids, it is more susceptible to becoming rancid than refined white flour.

Natural food sources, like fruits and vegetables, have long been advocated as an excellent way to get your vitamins. With advances in fortified foods and supplements, new options became available for meeting your nutrient needs. Let's look next at the pros and cons of each of these.

Foods Are Still the Best Way to Meet Your Vitamin Needs

Because foods provide more than just vitamins (many are also rich in disease-fighting phytochemicals, antioxidants, short periods of heavy physical stress, such as marathon runners and skiers, may gain some protection against the common cold when routinely taking a supplement. Some research also suggests that regularly consuming vitamin C may reduce the severity of symptoms and decrease the duration of a cold should you catch it.[4] While it is very individualized, the reduction is only about a day *annually*, and the jury is still out on the amount needed to reap this very small benefit.

Other Cold Remedies: The Jury Is Still Out

Recently, other dietary substances, such as the herb *Echinacea* and the mineral zinc, have emerged as popular treatment strategies for the common cold. *Echinacea* had been used centuries ago by some Native American populations to treat coughs and sore throats. A study of over 700 individuals, published in the *Annals of Internal Medicine*, failed to prove that the herb, *Echinacea*, prevented getting a cold compared with those getting a placebo or no treatment.[5] Results are mixed as to whether the herb can reduce the duration or the severity of cold symptoms. A major issue with using *Echinacea* is that the available supplements on the market vary greatly between the nine different species of the herb as well as the various parts of the plant used in the product.

Zinc may be helpful. In a review of 15 controlled trials, zinc lozenges or syrup were shown to help reduce the duration and severity of colds in healthy people, when consumed within the first 24 hours of the first sign of a cold.[6] But there is a catch. Those taking zinc lozenges may experience nausea and a bad aftertaste in their mouth. More research is needed to determine the correct dosage and usage for the general population, especially those with chronic illnesses. You will learn more about zinc and its role in the immune system in Chapter 8.

What You Can Do

One of the best ways to reduce your chances of catching a cold is to wash your hands frequently with soap and water. This will lower the likelihood of germs being transmitted from your hands to your mouth, nose, or eyes. When soap and water aren't available, gel sanitizers or disposable alcohol-containing hand wipes can be an effective alternative. Covering your mouth and nose when you cough or sneeze and then immediately washing your hands will help you keep from contaminating the people around you.

Finally, the National Institute of Allergy and Infectious Diseases recommends the following steps if you do get a cold:

- Get plenty of rest.
- Drink plenty of fluids. (Chicken soup and juices are considered fluids.)
- Gargle with warm salt water or use ice chips, throat lozenges, or sprays for a sore throat.
- Dab petroleum jelly on a raw nose to relieve irritation.
- Use a decongestant or saline nasal spray to help relieve nasal symptoms.
- Take aspirin* or acetaminophen (Tylenol) for headache or fever.

What Do You Think?

1. Given your knowledge of the functions of vitamin C in the body, why do you think it has been theorized that vitamin C may combat colds?
2. Many people have anecdotal accounts of vitamin C or other supplements preventing or helping them recover from a cold. Why are these accounts not considered scientific evidence?
3. How do folk remedies like the use of vitamin C or echinacea for colds come about, and why do you think so many people trust them?

*The American Academy of Pediatrics recommends that children and teenagers avoid consuming aspirin or medicine containing aspirin when they have a viral illness, such as the common cold, as it can lead to a rare but serious illness called Reye's syndrome. This syndrome can cause brain damage or death.

and fiber), they are the best way to meet your vitamin needs. The substances and nutrients in foods all work together to keep you healthy. For example, the fat in your salad dressing helps you absorb the carotenoids in the carrots in your salad. The vitamin C–rich tomatoes on your sandwich help you absorb the iron in the wheat bread. The whole is indeed greater than the sum of its parts when it comes to eating a balanced diet to meet your vitamin needs.

The *Dietary Guidelines for Americans* recommend eating a wide variety of foods from each food group with ample amounts of vitamin-rich fruits, vegetables, whole grains, and lean dairy foods. Table 7.4 on page 264 shows the estimated intake of each nutrient that a 2,000-calorie diet based on the *Dietary Guidelines* will provide. As you can see from the table, it may be challenging to get enough of vitamins E and D to meet your needs.[93] Refer to the Table Tips for these vitamins on pages 237 and 242 for more suggestions on meeting your vitamin needs for the day.

If you are falling short of some vitamins in your diet, fortified foods can help make up the difference.

Practical Nutrition VIDEO

When Is a Fruit Smoothie Not a Healthy Smoothie?

Pre-made fruit smoothies may not be as healthy as you think! Scan this QR code with your mobile device to access the video. You can also access the video in MasteringNutrition™.

Table 7.4

You Can Meet Your Vitamin Needs with Healthy Food Choices

Nutrient	USDA Food Intake Pattern, 2,000 Calories	Institute of Medicine Recommendations RDA/AI*
Vitamin A, μg RAE	851	700–900
Vitamin D, IU	258	600
Vitamin E, mg AT	8.3	15
Vitamin K, μg	140	90–120
Thiamin, mg	1.8	1.1–1.2
Riboflavin, mg	2.2	1.1–1.3
Niacin, mg	23	14–16
Vitamin B_6, mg	2.3	1.3–1.7
Folate, μg DFE	628	400
Vitamin B_{12}, μg	6.5	2.4
Vitamin C, mg	126	75–90
Choline, mg	340	425–550

Note: RDA = Recommended Dietary Allowance; AI = Adequate Intakes; RAE = retinol activity equivalents; AT = α-tocopherol; mg = milligrams; μg = micrograms.

*The recommended intake level for adult men or women, age 19 to 50 years old, is stated.

Source: U.S. Department of Agriculture. 2010. Report of the Dietary Guidelines Advisory Committee on the Dietary Guidelines for Americans, 2010. Available at www.cnpp.usda.gov; Institute of Medicine. 2011. Dietary Reference Intakes for Calcium and Vitamin D. Available at www.iom.edu.

Fortified foods can give your diet a vitamin boost.

fortified foods Foods with added nutrients.

Fortified Foods Can Provide Additional Nutrients, but at a Price

When you pour your morning glass of orange juice, you know that you are getting a significant splash of vitamin C. However, depending on the brand of orange juice, you may also be meeting your vitamin E and vitamin D needs—two nutrients that are not (and never have been) naturally found in oranges. Welcome to the world of fortified foods.

Fortified foods—that is, foods that have nutrients added to them—can be a valuable option for individuals whose diets fall short of some nutrients. For instance, someone who doesn't drink milk, such as a strict vegetarian or an individual who is lactose intolerant, would benefit from drinking vitamin D- and calcium-fortified soy milk. Older adults who are inactive, and thus have lower calorie needs, may choose fortified foods to add nutrients, such as vitamins B_{12} and E, to their limited dietary selections. Women in their childbearing years may look to folic acid–fortified cereals to help them meet their daily needs of this B vitamin.

Fortified foods can do a disservice in the diet if they displace other vitamin- and mineral-rich foods. For example, a sugary orange drink that has vitamin C added to it should not replace vitamin C–rich orange juice. Although the vitamin C content of the two beverages may be the same, the orange-flavored drink doesn't compare well to the juice when it comes to providing other nutrients and phytochemicals. As you can see from **Figure 7.21**, the orange drink is basically orange-flavored water sweetened with 7 teaspoons of sugar and enriched with vitamin C.

A diet containing numerous fortified foods can put you at risk of overconsuming some nutrients. If a heavily fortified food, like some cereals, snack bars, and

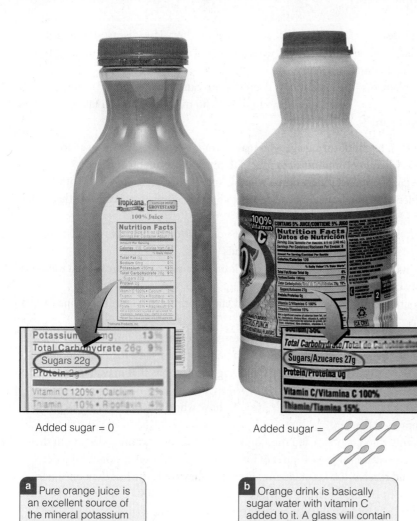

Added sugar = 0

Added sugar =

a Pure orange juice is an excellent source of the mineral potassium and doesn't contain any added sugar.

b Orange drink is basically sugar water with vitamin C added to it. A glass will contain the equivalent of 7 teaspoons of added sugar.

= 1 tsp of added sugar

beverages, claims to contain "100% of the vitamins needed daily," then eating several servings of the food or a combination of several fortified foods is similar to taking several multivitamin supplements. You are more likely to overconsume vitamins from fortified foods than from whole foods.

Vitamin Supplements Are Not a Substitute for Healthy Eating

Americans spend more than $12 million on vitamin- and mineral-containing supplements annually, including more than $5 billion on multivitamin/mineral supplements.[94] The aging of the population appears to be one of the forces driving this increase in the use of supplements—older people may use vitamins and minerals in an attempt to mitigate ongoing medical issues.[95]

Vitamin supplements are called supplements for a reason: A vitamin pill or a combined multivitamin and mineral pill may be used to *supplement* your diet. Supplements should never be used to replace a healthy diet. A consistent diet of nonnutritious foods followed by a daily supplement won't transform your

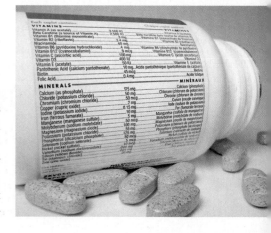

less-than-desirable eating habits into a healthy diet. The disease-fighting phytochemicals, fiber, and other substances that your body needs are all missing from a bottle of supplements.

Supplements are useful for people who cannot meet their nutrient needs through a regular, varied diet. Among those who may benefit from taking a dietary supplement are:[96]

> Women of childbearing age who may become pregnant, as they need to consume adequate amounts of folic acid to prevent certain birth defects
> Pregnant and lactating women who can't meet their nutrient needs with foods
> Older individuals, who need adequate amounts of vitamin D and synthetic vitamin B_{12}
> Individuals who do not drink enough milk and/or do not have adequate sun exposure to meet their vitamin D needs
> Individuals on low-calorie diets that limit the amount of vitamins and minerals they can consume through food
> Strict vegetarians, who have limited dietary options for vitamins B_{12} and D and other nutrients
> Individuals with food allergies or lactose intolerance that limit food choices
> Individuals who abuse alcohol, have a poor appetite, have medical conditions such as intestinal disorders, or are taking medications that may increase their need of certain vitamins
> Individuals who are food insecure and those who are eliminating food groups from their diet
> Infants who are breast-fed should receive 400 IU of vitamin D daily until they are consuming at least 1 quart of formula daily. Children age one and older should receive 400 IU of vitamin D daily if they consume less than one quart of milk per day. Adolescents who consume less than 400 IU of vitamin D daily from their diet would also benefit from a supplement.

Always talk to your health care professional or a registered dietitian nutritionist (RDN) before taking a vitamin or mineral supplement to make sure it is appropriate based on your medical history, especially if you are taking prescription medications. Supplements can interact or interfere with certain medications. If you regularly eat many fortified foods, the addition of a supplement could cause you to overconsume some nutrients. A meeting with an RDN for a diet "checkup" can help you decide if a supplement is needed.

See Table 7.5 for a brief consideration of the pros and cons of relying on foods, supplements, and fortified foods to meet your vitamin needs.

Who's Minding the Vitamin Store?

Dietary supplements, a category that includes vitamins, minerals, and herbs, are regulated less stringently by the Food and Drug Administration (FDA) than are drugs. In 1994, Congress passed the Dietary Supplement Health and Education Act, which shifted the responsibility for determining the quality, effectiveness, and safety of dietary supplements from the FDA to the manufacturers. Unlike drugs, dietary supplements do not require FDA approval before they can be marketed to the public, unless they contain a new ingredient that hadn't been used prior to 1994. Recall from Chapter 2 that supplement manufacturers are legally permitted to make structure/function claims on the labels of dietary supplements. The FDA cannot remove a supplement from the marketplace unless it has been shown to be unsafe or harmful to the consumer.[97]

The FDA is trying to tighten its regulation of dietary supplements to better safeguard the public against harmful products and misleading claims. One way it plans

Practical Nutrition VIDEO

Do You Need a Supplement to Meet Your Vitamin C Needs?

For most people and most nutrients, consuming a healthy, varied diet trumps taking supplements. Let Joan show you how. Scan this QR code with your mobile device to access the video. You can also access the video in MasteringNutrition™.

Table 7.5

Foods, Fortified Foods, and Supplements

There are a variety of ways to meet your vitamin needs. Consider the pros and cons to find out the best combination for you.

Foods

Pros: Sources of other nutrients and energy; can supply phytochemicals, antioxidants, and fiber; delicious and satisfying
Cons: Need to shop for and prepare meals; need to plan for in diet

Fortified Foods

Pros: Easy to obtain a specific nutrient; can be delicious and satisfying
Cons: Often more expensive than regular variety; risk of overconsumption of nutrients; can displace a more nutrient-dense food

Supplements

Pros: Easy to obtain; no planning or preparation involved
Cons: Can be expensive; risk of overconsumption of nutrients; lack of antioxidants, phytochemicals, and fiber found naturally in foods; not satisfying

to do this is to improve the criteria that it uses to make enforcement decisions about dietary supplements. The FDA has improved its process for evaluating potential safety concerns and adverse reports that may arise from a variety of sources, including consumers, media reports, consumer groups, and experts.

An option exists to help consumers choose among dietary supplements. The **U.S. Pharmacopoeia (USP)** is a nonprofit organization that sets standards for dietary supplements.[98] Although it does *not* endorse or validate health claims that the supplement manufacturers make, it sets standards for the identity, strength, quality, and purity of dietary supplements. Supplement manufacturers can voluntarily submit their products to the USP's staff of scientists for review. USP verifies supplements through a comprehensive testing and evaluation process and awards its USP Verified Mark only after rigorous facility audits, product documentation reviews, and product testing have been completed and approved.

What's a Consumer to Do?

With hundreds of bottles of vitamin and mineral supplements available on the store shelves, you could get dizzy trying to find one that's right for you. The best place to start when picking a supplement is to carefully read the label. The FDA has strict

U.S. Pharmacopeia (USP) A nonprofit organization that sets purity and reliability standards for dietary supplements.

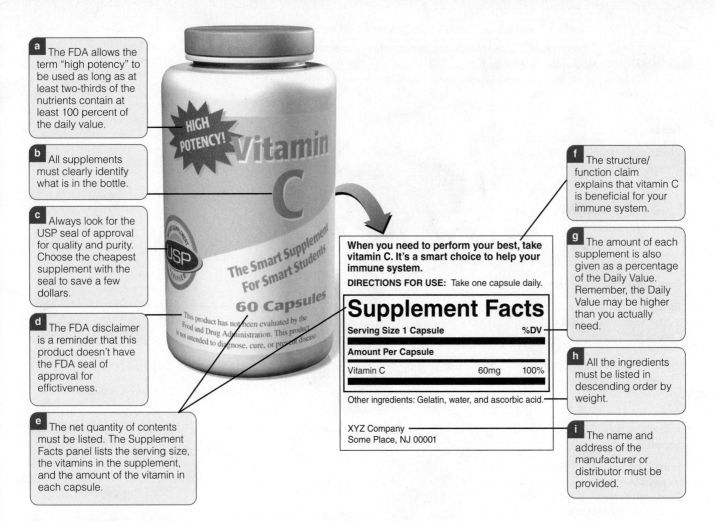

a The FDA allows the term "high potency" to be used as long as at least two-thirds of the nutrients contain at least 100 percent of the daily value.

b All supplements must clearly identify what is in the bottle.

c Always look for the USP seal of approval for quality and purity. Choose the cheapest supplement with the seal to save a few dollars.

d The FDA disclaimer is a reminder that this product doesn't have the FDA seal of approval for effectiveness.

e The net quantity of contents must be listed. The Supplement Facts panel lists the serving size, the vitamins in the supplement, and the amount of the vitamin in each capsule.

f The structure/function claim explains that vitamin C is beneficial for your immune system.

g The amount of each supplement is also given as a percentage of the Daily Value. Remember, the Daily Value may be higher than you actually need.

h All the ingredients must be listed in descending order by weight.

i The name and address of the manufacturer or distributor must be provided.

When you need to perform your best, take vitamin C. It's a smart choice to help your immune system.

DIRECTIONS FOR USE: Take one capsule daily.

Supplement Facts

Serving Size 1 Capsule		%DV
Amount Per Capsule		
Vitamin C	60mg	100%

Other ingredients: Gelatin, water, and ascorbic acid.

XYZ Company
Some Place, NJ 00001

Figure 7.22 Supplement Smarts
The FDA has strict guidelines for the information that must appear on any supplement label.

guidelines for the information that must appear on any supplement label. For example, the term "high potency" can be used only if at least two-thirds of the nutrients in the supplement contain at least 100 percent of the daily value (**Figure 7.22**). The label must also clearly identify the contents of the bottle. While a supplement may have the USP seal of approval for quality and purity, it doesn't have the FDA's approval, even if it makes a claim. Supplements must contain a panel that lists the serving size, the number of tablets in the bottle, the amount of the vitamin in each capsule, and the percentage of the Daily Value. All the ingredients must also be listed.

The Take-Home Message A well-balanced diet that provides adequate calories can meet most individuals' daily vitamin needs. Fortified foods, as part of a healthy diet, can provide extra nutrients for those whose diets fall short. A vitamin supplement is another option for individuals unable to meet their daily vitamin needs. The consumer needs to take care when selecting a dietary supplement and should seek advice and guidance from a qualified health professional.

MADE over MADE better

Including vegetables in your diet is a good step in the right direction, but sometimes there are improvements that can be made to increase the vitamin content and/or improve the nutritional quality of your meals and snacks.

Here are some typical vitamin-rich foods made over and made nutritionally better!

Creamed Spinach
1 cup: 180 calories
Vitamin A: 600 micrograms RAE

Steamed Spinach
1 cup: 54 calories
Vitamin A: 4,437 micrograms RAE

Fried, Breaded Onion Rings
10 rings: 244 calories
Vitamin C: 0.8 milligrams

Sautéed Onions
1 onion: 115 calories
Vitamin C: 1.6 milligrams

Cheese & Bacon Stuffed Baked Potato
1 loaded potato: 451 calories
Folate: 30 micrograms

Baked Potato
1 plain potato: 161 calories
Folate: 49 micrograms

Milk Chocolate Bar with Almonds
1.5 ounce bar: 216 calories
Vitamin E: 1.3 milligrams

Almonds, Raw
1 ounce: 169 calories
Vitamin E: 1.3 milligrams

Is Sun Exposure Necessary to Ensure Adequate Vitamin D Intake? Vitamin D is essential for optimal function of all cells and tissues, so having adequate amounts in the body is essential to overall health. Although vitamin D is added to some foods, notably milk, some researchers contend that it is best produced by the body after exposure to sunlight. This exposure, however, leads to increased risk of skin cancer.

Is synthesizing vitamin D in the skin after sun exposure preferable to consuming it in foods or supplements? After you've read the arguments for each side, read the critical-thinking questions and decide for yourself.

yes

- Obtaining sufficient vitamin D from natural food sources alone can be difficult.[1]

- Taking vitamin D supplements carries the risk of consuming too much and experiencing toxicity symptoms.[2]

- Controlled exposure to sunlight eliminates the risk of toxicity because your body produces only a limited amount of vitamin D from sun exposure.[3]

- Epidemiologic research suggests that low blood levels of vitamin D are associated with higher risk of some internal cancers, including cancers of the colon, breast, and prostate.[4] Vitamin D deficiency is also associated with osteoporosis, heart disease, and autoimmune diseases.[5] Given the potential health risks of vitamin D deficiency, and the difficulty in obtaining adequate vitamin D without sun exposure, sensible exposure of skin to the sun may result in a net health benefit.[6]

no

- Each year in the United States, doctors diagnose more than 3.5 million skin cancers—more than all other cancers combined.[7] There is no scientifically proven safe amount of ultraviolet exposure to increase your vitamin D without increasing your skin cancer risk.[8]

- The American Academy of Dermatology advises that appropriate measures, including the use of sunscreen, hats, and protective clothing, be taken whenever one is exposed to the sun.[9]

- Even the modest amount of recommended exposure—exposing the arms and legs or hands, arms, and face to the sun for 5 to 15 minutes, two to three times per week, between 10 a.m. and 3 p.m. without sunscreen protection—would result in damage to the skin and increase the risk of skin cancer.[10,11]

- Dietary supplements can be tailored to individual needs, and do not result in skin cancer.

what do you think?

1. Which argument is more compelling—that some sun exposure is necessary for adequate vitamin D synthesis, or that all unprotected sun exposure should be avoided because of the risk of skin cancer? **2.** Should kids be exposed to sunlight, or should they be given vitamin D via supplements? **3.** What is the best way to increase your vitamin D intake?

1 Vitamins Are Essential Nutrients Needed by Your Body to Grow, Reproduce, and Maintain Good Health

A vitamin is either fat soluble or water soluble, depending on how it is absorbed and handled in your body. The fat-soluble vitamins A, D, E, and K are stored in your body and require fat for absorption. They can accumulate to the point of toxicity if your intake is excessive. The water-soluble B vitamins and vitamin C are absorbed with water and typically aren't stored for extended periods. Excess amounts of water-soluble vitamins do not accumulate to toxic levels, but can be harmful if you routinely consume too much.

Antioxidants, such as vitamins E and C and beta caro-tene, neutralize harmful oxygen-containing molecules called free radicals that can damage cells. Free radicals can contribute to chronic diseases such as cancer and heart disease and accelerate the aging process. They also contribute to age-related macular degeneration and cataracts, two common eye disorders. Diets abundant in antioxidant-rich fruits, vegetables, and whole grains are associated with a lower incidence of many diseases.

Vitamins are found naturally in foods, added to fortified foods, or are available in a pill form through dietary supplements. Food preparation techniques can cause the loss of vitamins, particularly from fruits and vegetables. To preserve the vitamins in your produce, limit its exposure to air, keep it cool, use less water in cooking it, and reduce cooking time.

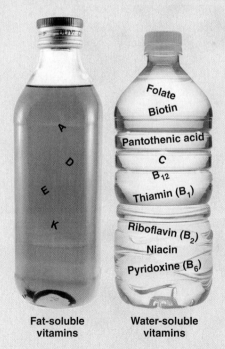

Fat-soluble vitamins   **Water-soluble vitamins**

2 Vitamin A

Vitamin A refers to a family of retinoids, which are needed for strong vision, reproduction, and healthy fetal development. Carotenoids are yellow-reddish pigments that give some fruits and vegetables their vibrant yellow-red color. The carotenoid beta-carotene is a common provitamin that can be converted to vitamin A in your body. Two other carotenoids, lutein and zeaxanthin, are being investigated for their potential role in eye health. The carotenoid lycopene acts as an antioxidant in the body. Preformed vitamin A is found in milk, organ meats, and eggs, whereas carrots, spinach, and sweet potatoes are good sources for provitamin A carotenoids. Toxic amounts of preformed vitamin A can compromise bone health and cause birth defects during pregnancy. Deficiencies of vitamin A can result in vision problems.

3 Vitamin E

Vitamin E is an antioxidant that protects your cells' membranes. Vitamin E plays an important role in helping prevent the "bad" LDL cholesterol carrier from being oxidized. High levels of artery-clogging, oxidized LDL cholesterol are a risk factor for heart disease. Vegetable oils, avocados, nuts, and seeds are good sources of vitamin E.

Green leafy vegetables and fortified cereals also contribute to your daily intake. The recommended intake for vitamin E is presented in alpha-tocopherol equivalents. Excessive amounts of vitamin E from supplements may cause hemorrhage. Too little vitamin E, although rare, may result in nerve problems, muscle weakness, and increased susceptibility to free radical damage.

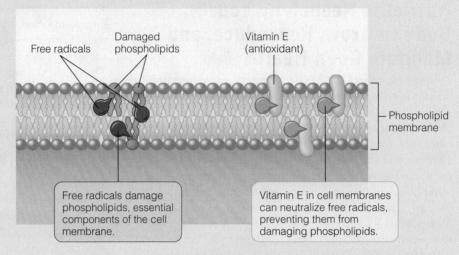

Free radicals   Damaged phospholipids   Vitamin E (antioxidant)

Phospholipid membrane

Free radicals damage phospholipids, essential components of the cell membrane.

Vitamin E in cell membranes can neutralize free radicals, preventing them from damaging phospholipids.

4 Vitamin K

Vitamin K helps your blood to clot and helps synthesize proteins that keep bones healthy. Dietary sources of vitamin K include leafy greens, vegetable oils, and margarine. While there are no known toxicity problems, a deficiency of vitamin K may result in hemorrhage and bone fractures. Individuals taking anticoagulant medications need to carefully monitor their vitamin K intake.

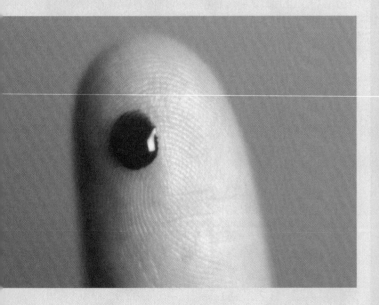

5 Vitamin D

Vitamin D is necessary for absorption of calcium and phosphorus. Although vitamin D can be made in your body with the help of ultraviolet rays from the sun, some individuals are not exposed to enough sunlight to meet their needs. Milk and fortified yogurts are excellent sources of vitamin D. Consuming too much vitamin D can cause loss of appetite, nausea, vomiting, and constipation. A deficiency of vitamin D can cause rickets in children and osteomalacia in adults.

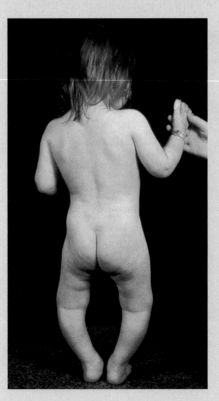

6 Water-Soluble Vitamins Act as Coenzymes in Metabolic Processes

The B-complex vitamins thiamin, riboflavin, niacin, vitamin B$_6$, vitamin B$_{12}$, pantothenic acid, and biotin function as coenzymes in the conversion of carbohydrates, proteins, and fats to energy; in fatty acid, cholesterol, and protein synthesis; and in glycogenolysis and gluconeogenesis. Vitamins catalyze enzyme activity when they bind to the active site of an enzyme. Water-soluble vitamins also act as antioxidants (vitamin C), nerve function (thiamin), DNA synthesis (folate), and red blood cell formation (vitamin B$_{12}$).

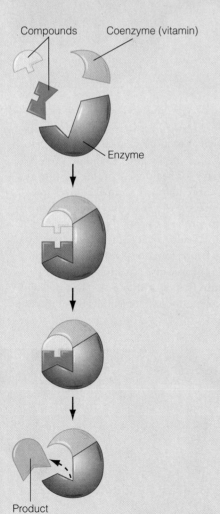

Compounds   Coenzyme (vitamin)

Enzyme

Product

7 Thiamin

Thiamin is needed for nerve function and energy metabolism. The best sources of thiamin are lean pork, enriched and whole-grain foods, ready-to-eat cereals, pasta, rice, and nuts. There are no known toxicity problems for thiamin, but a deficiency can result in beriberi. Chronic alcohol abuse can lead to an advanced form of thiamin deficiency called Wernicke-Korsakoff syndrome.

8 Riboflavin

Riboflavin is important for energy metabolism and healthy cells. Milk and yogurt are the most popular sources of riboflavin. Excess amounts are excreted in urine and there are no known toxicity symptoms. A deficiency in riboflavin results in symptoms such as a sore throat, a swelling in the inside of the mouth, an inflamed tongue, and dry and scaly lips.

9 Niacin

Niacin is needed for the body to use the energy in your food. In larger doses, niacin has been shown to lower blood cholesterol levels. When it is used to treat high blood cholesterol levels, it is considered a drug. Niacin is found in a variety of foods, including meat, fish, poultry, fortified cereals, and enriched breads. There is no danger of consuming too much niacin through foods, although overconsumption of niacin supplements can cause flushing. A deficiency of niacin results in pellagra.

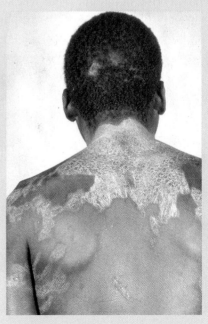

10 Vitamin B₆

Vitamin B$_6$ also known as pyridoxine, acts as a coenzyme for over 100 enzymes. Vitamin B$_6$ is also a key player in red blood cell synthesis, and in keeping the immune and nervous systems healthy. Vitamin B$_6$ is found in meat, fish, poultry, legumes, bananas, and fortified cereals. Consuming excessive amounts from supplements may cause neurological damage. A deficiency of vitamin B$_6$ can result in anemia, depression, and inflammation of the skin. Drinking too much alcohol can deplete the body of vitamin B$_6$.

11 Folate

Folate is vital for DNA synthesis and critical in cell division. Folate is naturally found in foods but is more easily absorbed as the synthetic form, folic acid. Folic acid is found mostly in fortified foods and supplements. Folate is found in leafy green vegetables, enriched pasta, rice, breads, and cereals. Consuming too much folate can obscure a vitamin B$_{12}$ deficiency. A deficiency of folate results in macrocytic anemia. Babies born to mothers who are deficient in folate have a higher risk of neural tube defects such as anencephaly and spina bifida.

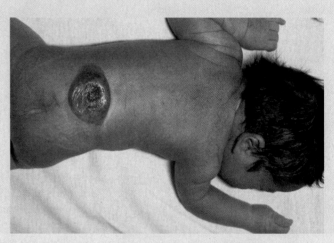

12 Vitamin B₁₂

Vitamin B$_{12}$ is a family of compounds also referred to as cobalamin. Vitamin B$_{12}$ is vital for healthy nerves and red blood cells. It requires the aid of intrinsic factor from the stomach to be properly absorbed. Vitamin B$_{12}$ is found naturally in animal foods, and the synthetic form is used in fortified soy milk and some cereals. There are no known toxicity risks of consuming too much vitamin B$_{12}$. A deficiency of vitamin B$_{12}$ causes macrocytic anemia and nerve damage.

13 Vitamin C

Vitamin C, also known as ascorbic acid, assists in the formation of collagen. Collagen, the most abundant protein in the body, is necessary for healthy bones, teeth, skin, and blood vessels. As an antioxidant, vitamin C reduces free radical damage and supports a healthy immune system. Vitamin C also improves the absorption of nonheme iron. Vitamin C is found in a wide variety of fruits and vegetables, including citrus fruits, tomatoes, potatoes, and broccoli. Excessive amounts can cause intestinal discomfort. A deficiency of vitamin C results in scurvy. The regular ingestion of a supplement doesn't prevent healthy individuals from getting a cold.

14 Pantothenic Acid and Biotin

Pantothenic acid and biotin are both B vitamins that aid in metabolism. Pantothenic acid and biotin are found in a wide variety of foods, including whole-grain cereals, nuts and legumes, peanut butter, milk, meat, and eggs. There are no known adverse effects from consuming too much pantothenic acid and biotin from foods, and deficiencies are rare.

Deficiencies of biotin can occur when large amounts of raw eggs are consumed. Avidin in raw egg whites binds biotin in the intestinal tract and prevents it from being absorbed.

15 Other Vitamin-Like Compounds Are Not Essential

Choline is a conditionally essential nutrient that the body needs for healthy cells and nerves. Carnitine, lipoic acid, and inositol are vitamin-like compounds that are used for important body functions and overall health. They are not considered essential because they can be synthesized in sufficient amounts in the body.

16 Fortified Foods and Supplements Can Provide Vitamins

Fortified foods and vitamin supplements can help individuals with inadequate diets to meet their nutrient needs. However, supplements should never replace a healthy diet. The U.S. Pharmacopoeia (USP) seal on a supplement label indicates that the supplement has been tested and meets the USP's criteria for purity and accuracy.

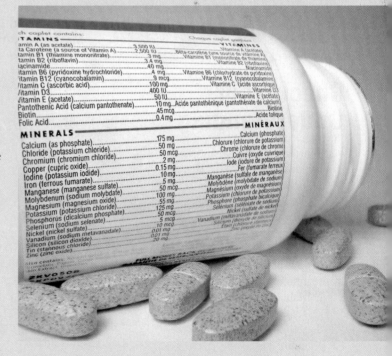

Terms to Know

- vitamins
- antioxidants
- oxidation
- free radicals
- phytochemicals
- bioavailability
- toxicity
- provitamins
- preformed vitamins
- retinoids
- retinol
- retinal
- retinoic acid
- carotenoids
- retinol activity equivalents (RAE)
- international units (IU)
- alpha-tocopherol
- anticoagulant
- hemorrhage
- menaquinone
- phylloquinone
- coagulation
- ultraviolet (UV) rays
- parathyroid hormone
- rickets
- osteomalacia
- osteoporosis

- coenzymes
- beriberi
- Wernicke-Korsakoff syndrome
- nicotinic acid
- nicotinamide
- tryptophan
- niacin equivalents (NE)
- pellagra
- pyridoxine
- pyridoxal
- pyridoxamine
- anemia
- folate
- folic acid
- spina bifida
- dietary folate equivalents (DFE)
- macrocytic anemia
- intrinsic factor
- pernicious anemia
- ascorbic acid
- hemochromatosis
- scurvy
- fortified foods
- age-related macular degeneration (AMD)
- cataract
- megadose
- preformed vitamin A
- rhodopsin
- iodopsin

- rods
- cones
- bleaching
- cell differentiation
- hypervitaminosis A
- carotenodermia
- night blindness
- xerophthalmia
- clotting factors
- osteocalcin
- warfarin
- hypervitaminosis D
- hypercalcemia
- polyneuritis
- flushing
- dermatitis
- dementia
- premenstrual syndrome (PMS)
- neural tube defects
- anencephaly
- megaloblasts
- macrocytes
- choline
- hypotension
- carnitine
- lipoic acid
- inositol
- U.S. Pharmacopeia (USP)

MasteringNutrition™

Build your knowledge—and confidence—in the Study Area of MasteringNutrition with a variety of study tools.

Check Your Understanding

1. Which of the following is a water-soluble vitamin?
   a. vitamin A
   b. vitamin E
   c. vitamin C
   d. vitamin K
2. The most usable form of vitamin A in your body is
   a. retinol.
   b. retinal.
   c. retinoic acid.
   d. retinoids.
3. Vitamin D is
   a. a carbohydrate.
   b. made in your body with the help of sunscreen.
   c. found in fortified milk.
   d. water soluble.
4. You are enjoying a salad bar lunch (good choice!). You want to top your greens with vitamin E–rich foods. You could choose
   a. olive oil.
   b. pickles.
   c. tomatoes.
   d. vinegar.
5. A deficiency of thiamin can cause
   a. rickets.
   b. beriberi.
   c. scurvy.
   d. osteomalacia.
6. Which of the following is considered an antioxidant?
   a. vitamin D
   b. vitamin K
   c. beta-carotene
   d. vitamin A
7. Adam Craig is 55 years old. Which of the following might his body have difficulty absorbing?
   a. the vitamin B_{12} in a piece of steak
   b. the vitamin B_6 in liver
   c. the folate in spinach
   d. the riboflavin in milk
8. You are enjoying a breakfast of raisin bran cereal in skim milk accompanied by a glass of orange juice. The vitamin C in the orange juice will enhance the absorption of
   a. the calcium in the milk.
   b. the vitamin D in fortified milk.
   c. the iron in the cereal.
   d. the fiber in the cereal.

9. Folic acid can help reduce the risk of
   a. acne.
   b. neural tube defects.
   c. night blindness.
   d. pellagra.
10. Which of the following statements is NOT correct? The USP seal on the vitamin label means that the dietary supplement has been tested and shown to
   a. contain the amount of the substance that is stated on the label.
   b. be of good quality.
   c. be free of any contaminants.
   d. meet your daily needs of that vitamin.

Answers

1. (c) Vitamin C is water soluble, whereas vitamins A, E, and K are fat soluble.
2. (a) Retinol is the most usable form of vitamin A in your body. Retinoids include all three forms of preformed vitamin A: retinol, retinal, and retinoic acid.
3. (c) Vitamin D is a hormone that can be obtained by drinking fortified milk. It can be made in your body with the help of adequate exposure to the sun's ultraviolet rays.
4. (a) Go for the olive oil for a good source of fat-soluble vitamin E.
5. (b) A chronic deficiency of thiamin can cause beriberi. A vitamin D deficiency can cause rickets in children and osteomalacia in adults. Scurvy is the result of a vitamin C deficiency.
6. (c) Beta-carotene functions as an antioxidant in your body.
7. (a) Approximately 10 to 30 percent of adults over the age of 50 have reduced secretions of acidic stomach juices, which affects the absorption of the vitamin B_{12} that is found naturally in food. The other B vitamins should be readily absorbed regardless of Adam's age.
8. (c) Vitamin C will help your body absorb the iron in grain products and cereals. Vitamin C does not affect the absorption of calcium, vitamin D, or fiber. However, the vitamin D in the milk will help you absorb the mineral calcium.
9. (b) If consumed prior to and during the first several weeks of pregnancy, adequate amounts of folic acid can reduce the risk of neural tube defects, including spina bifida and anencephaly. Vitamin A–containing medication may be used to treat acne. Vitamin A can also help prevent night blindness. Consuming adequate amounts of niacin prevents pellagra.
10. (d) Manufacturers of dietary supplements can voluntarily have their products tested for the strength, quality, and purity of the supplement. It does not confirm that it will meet your daily need for the vitamin.

Web Resources

- To learn more about fulfilling your needs for fruits and vegetables, visit www.fruitsandveggiesmorematters.org
- For more information on the disease-fighting capabilities of fruits and vegetables, visit www.fruitsandveggiesmatter.gov
- To find out the latest recommendations for vitamins, see the dietary supplements fact sheets in the Health Information section at http://ods.od.nih.gov

1. **False.** Although vitamins perform numerous functions in your body, they don't provide energy, as do carbohydrates, proteins, and fats. To find out more, turn to page 224.
2. **False.** Routinely taking an excess of many vitamins, including many water-soluble vitamins, can be harmful. To find out more, turn to page 225.
3. **False.** Deep orange vegetables and some green vegetables are good sources of the vitamin A precursor beta-carotene, which is converted to vitamin A in your body. While an excess of beta-carotene will not cause vitamin A toxicity, it could make your skin change color. To find out more, turn to page 235.
4. **True.** Consuming excessive amounts of vitamin E supplements can interfere with blood clotting. To learn more, turn to page 236.
5. **True.** Vitamin K helps a protein in your bones bind with the bone-strengthening mineral calcium. To learn about other functions of vitamin K, turn to page 238.
6. **False.** Many people are unable to meet their vitamin D needs through sunlight exposure alone. To find out if you are at risk, turn to page 240.
7. **True.** Folate can lower the risk of some birth defects during pregnancy. However, timing is everything. To find out when a pregnant woman needs to be taking this B vitamin, turn to page 251.
8. **False.** There is no clear evidence that taking megadoses of vitamin C, such as from supplements, protects you from the common cold. To find out what role it does play in combating colds, turn to page 262.
9. **False.** Fortified foods are not always a safe way to meet your vitamin needs. To find out why, turn to page 264.
10. **False.** While foods are an excellent source of vitamins, some individuals may need extra vitamin support from a supplement. To find out who would benefit from a supplement, turn to page 266.

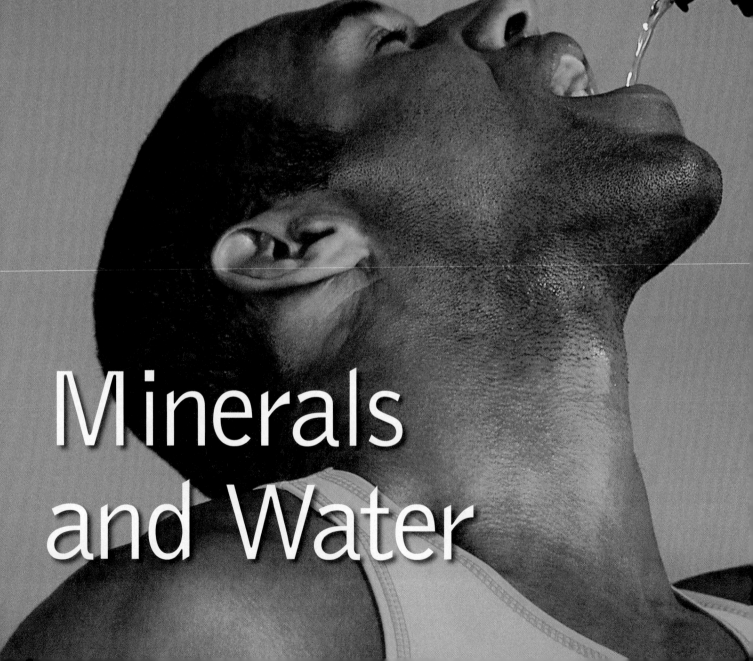

8

Minerals
and Water

True or False?

1. Vitamin waters are **healthier** for you than plain water. Ⓣ Ⓕ p. 289

2. Your morning mug of **coffee** counts toward fulfilling your daily water needs. Ⓣ Ⓕ p. 290

3. Most of your dietary **sodium** comes from the salt that you shake on your foods. Ⓣ Ⓕ p. 294

4. Magnesium can help lower your **blood pressure**. Ⓣ Ⓕ p. 297

5. A serving of **milk** will provide about one-third of an adult's daily calcium needs. Ⓣ Ⓕ p. 300

6. Meat is the major source of **iron** in the American diet. Ⓣ Ⓕ p. 310

7. **Zinc** can fight the common cold. Ⓣ Ⓕ p. 313

8. Fluoride has been added to most **bottled water**. Ⓣ Ⓕ p. 318

9. Chromium can help you build bigger muscles and **stay lean** when you are lifting weights. Ⓣ Ⓕ p. 319

10. **Kosher salt** is a good source of iodine. Ⓣ Ⓕ p. 321

See page 335 for the answers.

You could survive for weeks without food, but only a few days without water. Water is needed for chemical reactions that take place in your cells, and essential for maintaining the fluid balance inside your body. Minerals also participate in fluid balance, along with performing many other structural and functional roles in the body. In this chapter we will explore these vital nutrients.

Why Is Water So Important?

The average healthy adult is about 60 percent water, which makes water the most abundant substance in your body. However, individuals vary in the exact amount of water they carry, because factors such as age, gender, and the body's amount of fat and muscle tissue affect body water (**Figure 8.1**). Muscle tissue is approximately 75 percent water, whereas fat tissue is up to 20 percent water.[1] Generally, men have a higher percentage of muscle mass and a lower percentage of fat tissue than women of the same age, so they have more body water. For the same reason, muscular athletes have a higher percentage of body water than do sedentary individuals.

You learned in Chapter 6 that fluid balance refers to the equal distribution of fluid among several compartments in your body. The fluid inside your cells is in the **intracellular fluid compartment**, whereas the fluid in the space outside your cells is in the **extracellular fluid compartment**. The extracellular fluids are further broken down into (1) **interstitial fluids**, which are in the space immediately outside your cells, and (2) the fluids in your blood (see **Figure 8.2**). The interstitial fluids act as an area of exchange between your blood fluids and your cells.

Maintaining the equal distribution of all this body fluid is crucial to health, and water and dissolved minerals play key roles. The minerals important in fluid balance are called **electrolytes** (*electro* = electricity, *lytes* = soluble). They include sodium, potassium, phosphate, magnesium, calcium, and chloride. Water in your body is drawn into and out of your cells by the "pull" of electrolytes. When cells have more electrolytes than the fluid outside them, water flows in, and vice versa.

Water Is the Universal Solvent

Water is a wonderful **solvent**, a liquid in which substances dissolve. In fact, water is commonly known as the universal solvent. As a solvent, water is part of the medium in which molecules come in contact with each other. This contact between molecules allows chemical reactions to take place. For example, the combining of specific amino acids to synthesize a protein occurs in the watery medium inside your cells.

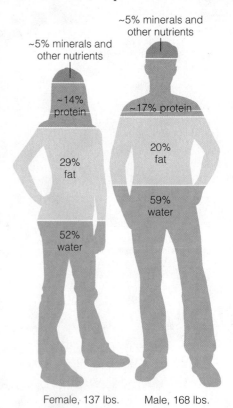

~5% minerals and other nutrients

~14% protein

29% fat

52% water

~5% minerals and other nutrients

~17% protein

20% fat

59% water

Female, 137 lbs.   Male, 168 lbs.

Figure 8.1 Your Body Is Mostly Water

Water Is a Transport Medium

The water in blood and lymph helps transport substances throughout your body. Did you know that only about 45 percent of your blood is red blood cells? Most of the rest is water. As part of blood, water helps transport oxygen, nutrients, and other important substances to your cells. It also helps transport waste products away from cells to be excreted in urine and stool. Like the fluid in blood, lymph fluid is almost entirely water. Lymph transports proteins back to the bloodstream, and it is important in the absorption of fats. Lymph also transports wastes and microbes through "cleaning stations" called *lymph nodes,* where defensive cells consume these harmful substances before the lymph returns to the blood.

Water Helps Maintain Body Temperature

The water in your blood is like the coolant that runs through a car. They both absorb, carry, and ultimately release heat in order to keep a running machine from overheating. In a car, the coolant absorbs the heat from a running engine and carries it to the radiator for release. In your body, the water in your circulating blood absorbs the heat from your internal core—the center of your body, where your most important organs are located—and carries it to the skin for release (**Figure 8.3**). Water works so well as a coolant in both your car and your body because it has a

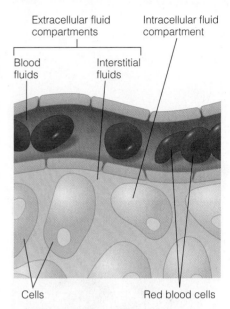

Figure 8.2 Water as Part of Body Fluids
Water is a key component of the fluid compartments both inside and outside cells.

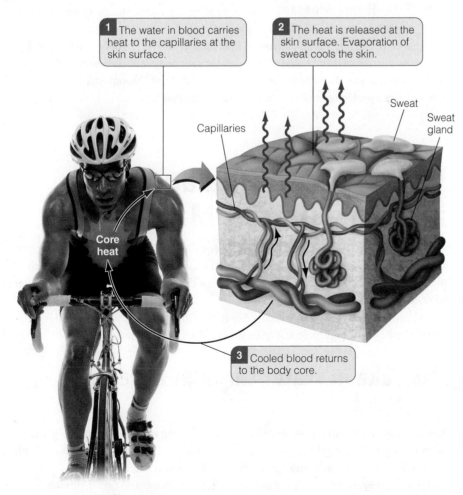

1 The water in blood carries heat to the capillaries at the skin surface.

2 The heat is released at the skin surface. Evaporation of sweat cools the skin.

3 Cooled blood returns to the body core.

Figure 8.3 Water Helps Regulate Your Body Temperature

intracellular fluid compartment The fluid located inside your cells.

extracellular fluid compartment The fluid located outside your cells. Interstitial fluids and fluids in the blood are extracellular fluids.

interstitial fluids Fluids located between cells.

electrolytes Charged ions that conduct an electrical current in a solvent such as water. Sodium, potassium, and chloride are examples of electrolytes in the body.

solvent A liquid that acts as a medium in which substances dissolve. Water is considered the universal solvent.

unique ability to absorb and release a tremendous amount of heat. Like a car, your body sometimes gets overheated. For instance, if you were to go jogging on a hot summer day, the enormous amount of internal heat that would be generated would probably overwhelm the heat-absorbing capacity of your body's water. The increasing heat would break apart the molecules of water on your skin, transforming them from a liquid (sweat) to a vapor. The evaporation of sweat from your skin would release the heat and cool you down, enabling you to maintain a safe body temperature. When you are cold, less blood flows to your body surface, so that your core stays warm. That's why your hands, feet, and face can become so cool to the touch on a cold day.

Water Is a Lubricant and a Protective Cushion

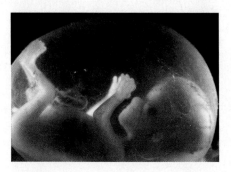

A developing fetus is cushioned in a sac of watery amniotic fluid to protect it from physical harm during pregnancy.

Water, combined with other molecules, acts as a lubricant for your joints, helping to promote easy, reduced-friction movement. The water in tears lubricates your eyes and helps flush out dust and other debris. Water is also part of the saliva that moistens your mouth and foods and the mucus that lubricates your intestinal tract. Water is the main part of the fluid that surrounds certain organs, including your brain; thus, it acts as a cushion to protect them from injury during a fall or other trauma. During pregnancy, a developing fetus is surrounded by a sac of watery amniotic fluid, which helps protect it from physical harm.

The Take-Home Message Your body is mostly water. Muscle tissue has more water than does fat tissue. The water inside your body cells is balanced by the water outside your cells. Electrolytes help maintain fluid balance. Water is a universal solvent that helps transport oxygen and nutrients throughout your body. It also absorbs and releases heat to regulate your body temperature, acts as a lubricant through saliva and mucus, and provides a protective cushion for your brain and other organs.

What Is Water Balance and How Do You Maintain It?

When the amount of water you consume is equal to the amount you lose daily, you are in **water balance**. When you are not in water balance—that is, having too much or too little water in your system—health problems can occur. Thus, maintaining water balance is very important.

There are several ways in which water is lost from your body and several mechanisms that help you replenish those losses. Let's look at this next.

You Take in Water through Beverages and Food

water balance The state whereby an equal amount of water is lost and replenished daily in the body.

The first aspect of being in water balance is consuming enough water. You get most of your daily water from beverages such as tap or bottled water, milk, juices, and soft drinks. You also get some water from the foods that you eat, although much less in comparison (**Figure 8.4**). Even the driest foods, like oatmeal and bread, provide some water. A small amount of water is also generated during metabolism.

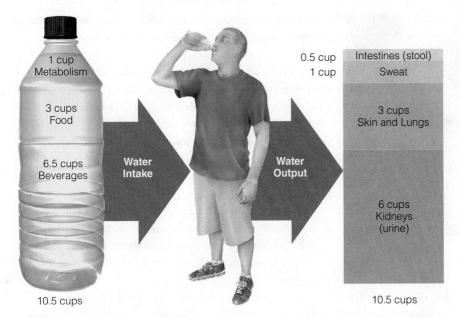

You Lose Water through Your Kidneys, Large Intestine, Lungs, and Skin

The other aspect of water balance is excreting excess water so that you don't have too much in your body. You normally lose water daily through these four routes:

➤ Via your kidneys in the form of urine
➤ Via intestinal fluids in your stool (unless you are experiencing diarrhea, the amount of water lost in stool is normally small)
➤ Via the water that evaporates when you exhale
➤ Via your skin when you release the heat produced in your body core

The water that evaporates when you exhale and the water lost through your skin when you release the heat generated during normal reactions is called **insensible water loss**, as it occurs without your noticing it. An individual living in a moderate or temperate climate and doing little physical activity loses between one-half and one quart of water daily through insensible water loss.[2]

Insensible water loss doesn't include the water lost in sweat. Sweating is your body's way of releasing a higher than normal amount of heat. The amount of water lost during sweating varies greatly and depends upon many environmental factors, such as the temperature, the humidity, the wind, the sun's intensity, clothing worn, and the amount of physical activity you are doing.[3] For example, if you jump rope in the noontime sun on a summer day wearing a winter coat, you'll soon be losing a lot of water as sweat. In contrast, little or no sweat will leave your body if you sit under a shady tree on a dry, cool day wearing shorts and a light tee shirt.

Losing Too Much Water Can Cause Dehydration

Dehydration is a state in which you've lost too much, or aren't taking in enough, water. Dehydration can result from not drinking enough fluids and/or from conditions that result in too much water (and sodium) being lost from the body, such as diarrhea, vomiting, high fever, or the use of **diuretics**. If dehydration persists, a person can experience

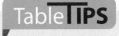

Bottoms Up

Drink low-fat or skim milk with each meal to add calcium as you meet your fluid needs.

Freeze grapes for a juicy and refreshing snack.

Add a vegetable soup to your lunch for a fluid-packed meal.

Cool down with a sweet treat by spooning slightly thawed frozen strawberries onto low-fat vanilla ice cream.

Add zip to your water by adding a slice of fresh lemon or lime.

insensible water loss The water that is lost from the body daily through exhalation from the lungs and evaporation off the skin.

dehydration The state whereby there is too little water in the body due to too much water being lost, too little being consumed, or a combination of both.

diuretics Substances such as alcohol and some medications that cause the body to lose water.

Water is vital for many body functions, but it isn't stored in the body, so it's important to take in enough water every day.

weight loss, fever, dizziness, and confusion, as well as impaired physical coordination, and, in extreme situations, death.[4]

Your Thirst Mechanism Signals Dehydration

Have you ever been outside for a while on a hot day and noticed that your mouth was as dry as the Sahara Desert? The dry mouth is part of your **thirst mechanism**, and is your body's way of telling you to find a water source—you are on the road to dehydration. The thirst mechanism plays an important role in helping you avoid dehydration and restore the water balance in your body.

The dry mouth that makes you thirsty when you are dehydrated is due to the increased concentration of electrolytes in your blood. As the concentration of these minerals increases, less water is available to your salivary glands to make saliva.[5] Thus, your mouth feels very dry.

When you are dehydrated, the fluid volume in your blood decreases, resulting in a higher concentration of sodium in the blood. To restore balance, the fluid inside your cells will move through the membrane to the outside of the cell and into your blood to balance the concentration of sodium between these compartments. This movement of water across the cell membrane is called **osmosis** (see **Figure 8.5**).

Your brain detects the increased concentration of sodium in your blood and triggers your thirst mechanism, reminding you to drink fluids. Your brain will also trigger the secretion of **antidiuretic hormone (ADH)** from the pituitary gland. ADH causes your kidneys to decrease further loss of water and thus concentrate your urine.[6] These mechanisms work together to keep your body in water balance.

Other Ways to Tell If You Are Dehydrated

Just quenching your thirst will not typically provide enough fluids to remedy dehydration. This isn't a concern for moderately active individuals eating a balanced

thirst mechanism Various bodily reactions caused by dehydration that signal you to drink fluids.

osmosis The movement of a solvent, such as water, from an area of lower concentration of solutes across a membrane to an area of higher concentration of solutes. It balances the concentration of solutes between the compartments.

antidiuretic hormone (ADH) A hormone that directs the kidneys to concentrate urine and reduce urine production in order to reduce water loss from the body.

1. A selectively permeable filter is placed in a glass of pure water.

2. Salt is added to the water on one side of the filter.

3. Drawn by the high concentration of electrolytes, pure water flows to the "salt water" side of the filter.

Figure 8.5 A Simple Demonstration of Osmosis

diet, as fluids from beverages and food throughout the day will eventually restore water balance.[7] However, older adults, and individuals who are very physically active and/or who have physically vigorous jobs, such as firefighters, are at higher risk of dehydration because they don't take in enough fluid, or they lose body water copiously through sweating. These individuals need to take additional steps to ensure that they are properly hydrated.

One way to monitor hydration is the cornerstone method, which involves measuring body weight before and after long bouts of intense physical activity or labor and noting any changes. If a person weighs less after an activity than before, the weight change is due to loss of body water, and that water must be replenished. (Alternatively, if a weight gain is noted, overhydration is likely, and you need to drink less before your next activity.)

Urine color can also be used to assess hydration. When you are dehydrated, you produce less urine due to the release of ADH. The urine you do produce is more concentrated, as it contains a higher proportion of compounds to the smaller volume of water. This causes the urine to be darker in color.[8] The National Athletic Trainers Association has created a chart to help individuals assess if they are drinking enough fluids to offset the amount of water lost through sweating (see **Figure 8.6**).[9] If you are very physically active and the color of your urine darkens during the day, to the point where it resembles the shade of a "yield" sign or darker, you likely need to increase the amount of fluids in your diet. (Note: Other factors, such as consuming excessive amounts of the B vitamin, riboflavin, and certain medications can also affect the color of urine.)

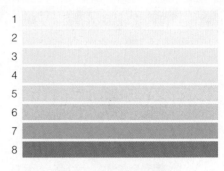

Figure 8.6 Urine Color Can Signal Dehydration
If you collect your urine in a cup and it looks like the color of 1 through 3 on the chart, you are well hydrated. If it resembles color 7 or is darker, you are dehydrated and need to drink more fluids.

Consuming Too Much Water Can Cause Hyponatremia

For healthy individuals who consume a balanced diet, it's hard to consume too much water, because the body will just produce more urine to eliminate the excess. However, some individuals, particularly soldiers during military training and athletes who participate in endurance events such as marathons, have experienced water toxicity in certain circumstances.[10]

In April 2002, 28-year-old Cynthia Lucero was running the Boston Marathon. About five miles from the finish line, Lucero began to feel wobbly and mentioned to a friend that she felt dehydrated even though she had been consuming fluids throughout her run. She suddenly collapsed and was taken to a nearby hospital. She died the next day, not of dehydration, but of overhydration. In January 2007, 28-year-old Jennifer Strange collapsed after competing in a California radio contest to see who could drink the most water without using the restroom. She was found dead in her home a few hours after completing the contest.[11] The cause of death for both of these individuals was swelling of the brain brought on by **hyponatremia** (*hypo* = under, *natrium* = sodium, *emia* = blood), caused by overconsumption of fluids. In both cases, drinking too much fluid diluted the blood to the point where sodium levels were too low, which in turn resulted in the swelling of body tissues (see **Figure 8.7** on page 286). When swelling occurs in the brain, the person can experience symptoms similar to those of dehydration—confusion and disorientation.[12] Mistakenly treating these symptoms by consuming more fluids will only make matters worse.

Even though dehydration is more common and a bigger challenge to physically active individuals than overhydration, the seriousness of overhydration has prompted the USA Track & Field association to revise its hydration guidelines for long-distance and marathon runners to avoid hyponatremia. Chapter 11 will provide these guidelines and show you how to calculate how much fluid you need during exercise.

hyponatremia A condition of too little sodium in the blood.

The health of our body's cells depends on maintaining the proper balance of fluids and electrolytes on both sides of the cell membrane, both at rest and during exercise. Let's examine how this balance can be altered under various conditions of exercise and fluid intake.

MODERATE EXERCISE

When you are appropriately hydrated, engaged in moderate exercise, and not too hot, the concentration of electrolytes is likely to be the same on both sides of cell membranes. You will be in fluid balance.

Concentration of electrolytes about equal inside and outside cell

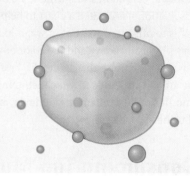

STRENUOUS EXERCISE WITH RAPID AND HIGH WATER INTAKE

If a person drinks a great deal of water quickly during intense, prolonged exercise, the extracellular fluid becomes diluted. This results in the concentration of electrolytes being greater inside the cells, which causes water to enter the cells, making them swell. Drinking moderate amounts of water or sports drinks more slowly will replace lost fluids and restore fluid balance.

Lower concentration of electrolytes outside

H_2O

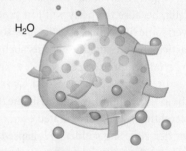

Higher concentration of electrolytes inside

STRENUOUS EXERCISE WITH INADEQUATE FLUID INTAKE

If a person does not consume adequate amounts of fluid during strenuous exercise of long duration, the concentration of electrolytes becomes greater outside the cells, drawing water away from the inside of the cells and making them shrink. Consuming sports drinks will replace lost fluids and electrolytes.

Higher concentration of electrolytes outside

H_2O

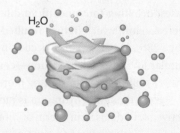

Lower concentration of electrolytes inside

self-Assessment

Do You Consume Enough Water?

Do you think you are consuming enough fluids each day? Answer these questions to find out.

1. Do you drink a glass (8 ounces) of orange juice or other juices in the morning?
   Yes ☐ **No** ☐
2. Do you have at least two cups (16 ounces) of coffee or tea daily?
   Yes ☐ **No** ☐
3. Do you drink at least 2 cups (16 ounces) of water daily?
   Yes ☐ **No** ☐

4. Do you drink 1 to 3 cups (8 to 24 ounces) of milk daily?
   Yes ☐ **No** ☐
5. Do you consume at least 5 servings of fruits and vegetables daily?
   Yes ☐ **No** ☐

Answers

If you answered yes to at least four questions, it's likely that you are easily meeting your daily water needs.

The Take-Home Message You lose water daily through your kidneys, intestinal tract, lungs, and skin. If you lose more water than you take in, you will become dehydrated. Your thirst mechanism reminds you to drink fluids and helps restore water balance. Although rare, overconsumption of fluids can lead to an electrolyte imbalance (hyponatremia) and can be fatal.

How Much Water Do You Need and What Are the Best Sources?

Your daily water requirements may be different from those of your grandparents, parents, siblings, and even the classmate sitting next to you. The amount of water a person needs depends on his or her physical activity, environmental factors such as air temperature, and diet. (Recall from Chapter 4 that increasing the fiber in your diet should be accompanied by an increase in water consumption.)

The current recommendation for the amount of water you should consume daily is based on the reported total water intake (from both beverages and food) of healthy Americans. Currently, healthy female adults consume about 12 cups, whereas men consume about 16 cups of water daily.[13] About 80 percent of this intake is from beverages. Therefore, adult women should ingest about 9 cups (~80 percent of 12 cups) and adult males approximately 13 cups (~80 percent of 16 cups) of beverages daily.[14] People who are very active will have higher water requirements because they lose more water by sweating. Complete the Self-Assessment to see if you are meeting your daily fluid needs.

If you think that sounds like a lot, keep in mind that a well-balanced, 2,200-calorie diet that includes beverages at all meals and snacks will provide about 12 cups of water.[15] Drinking water (either from the tap or from a bottle), milk, and juices throughout the day can help you meet your needs. The Nutrition in the Real World feature "Tap Water or Bottled Water: Is Bottled Better?" on pages 288–289 discusses the differences and similarities between tap water and bottled water.

Practical Nutrition VIDEO

Are Enhanced Waters Necessary?

Bottled water gets fancier all the time as new "enhanced waters" hit the shelves. You may buy these products for their added vitamins and minerals, but are they really a nutritional bargain? Scan this QR code with your mobile device to access the video. You can also access the video in MasteringNutrition™.

Tap Water or Bottled Water: Is Bottled Better?

What items do you *have* to have when you walk out the door in the morning? Your keys? Your student ID? Your wallet? What about a bottle of water? Would you never leave home without it? Are you one of the many individuals who drink *only* bottled water because you think it is superior to tap water? If you are, you're certainly not alone. But is bottled water really better or safer for you than tap water?

Although many individuals drink bottled water thinking that it is "pure," consuming 100 percent *pure* water is impossible. Whether you fill your reusable water bottle from the tap or purchase bottled water, the water will contain some impurities. However, this does not mean that the water is unsafe for most individuals to drink. (Note that individuals with a weakened immune system, such as those with HIV/AIDS, undergoing chemotherapy, and/or taking steroids, should speak with their health care provider prior to drinking any water. These individuals may need to take precautions such as boiling their water—no matter the source—before consuming it.[1])

The source of any water will vary from faucet to faucet and bottle to bottle, so it is virtually impossible to make a direct comparison. There are some basic points to understand about each type, though. Let's look at how tap and bottled water compare in terms of regulation, cost, and safety.

Turn on the Tap

Most Americans obtain their drinking water from a community water system. The source of this municipal water can be underground wells or springs, or rivers, lakes, or reservoirs. Regardless of the source, all municipal water is sent to a treatment plant where any dirt and debris are filtered out, bacteria are killed, and other contaminants are removed. The Environmental Protection Agency (EPA) oversees the safety of public drinking water with national standards that set limits for more than 80 contaminants, either naturally occurring ones, such as bacteria, or man-made ones, such as chemicals, that may find their way into your drinking water. Hundreds of billions of dollars have been invested in

A Well of Sources for Bottled Water

Water can be classified according to its source or how it is treated prior to bottling.

Mineral water	Water derived from an underground source that contains a specific amount of naturally occurring minerals and trace elements. The minerals and elements cannot be added to the water after bottling.
Spring water	Water that is obtained from underground water that flows naturally to the surface. The water is collected at the spring or at the site of the well purposefully drilled to obtain this water.
Sparkling water	Spring water that has carbon dioxide gas added to supply "bubbles" before bottling. Also sold as seltzer water or club soda. *Note:* This is technically considered a soft drink and does not have to adhere to FDA bottled water regulations.
Distilled water	Water that has been boiled and processed to remove most, but not all, contaminants.
Flavored water	Water that has a flavor such as lemon or lime added. It may also contain added sugars and calories.
Vitamin or enhanced waters	Water that has vitamins, protein, herbs, and/or caffeine added to it. Such water may also contain added sugars and calories.

Source: Environmental Protection Agency. 2005. Water Health Series: Bottled Water. Available at www.epa.gov. Accessed May 2013; U.S. Government Accounting Office. 2009. Bottled Water: FDA Safety and Consumer Protections Are Often Less Stringent Than Comparable EPA Protections for Tap Water. Available at www.gao.gov. Accessed May 2013.

these treatment systems to ensure that the public water is safe to drink.[2]

Each year, the water supplier in your community must provide you with an annual report about the quality and source of your tap water. In fact, many of these regional reports can be accessed online at www.epa.gov. Even with these precautions, some individuals, who may not like the taste of their tap water or have health concerns, use an in-home water treatment device to further filter their water. Filter devices can range from a less costly pitcher (see photo) or device mounted on the kitchen faucet to a more costly, larger system that treats all the water that enters the home. Depending upon the device, it can filter contaminants such as bacteria, viruses, lead, nitrates, and pesticides. Whatever the device used, it is important that it be maintained regularly to ensure that it is working effectively.

You may have heard the terms "hard" or "soft" water used to describe tap water. The "hardness" refers to the amount of metals—specifically, calcium and magnesium—in the water. The higher the amount, the harder the water. There aren't any health concerns from drinking hard water. In fact, there may be a benefit, as hard water may contribute small amounts of these minerals to your daily diet. Whether your water is hard or soft is less important than meeting your daily needs for enough water.

Another benefit of consuming tap water is that many municipalities add fluoride to their water. About 74 percent of Americans who drink from public systems have fluoride in their water (see the map on page 317).[3] Fluoridation of public water has had a positive impact on the nation's dental health, reducing the incidence of dental caries.

Lastly, tap water costs less than a penny a gallon, making it a very affordable way to stay hydrated.

Bottling Boom

Bottled water is second only to carbonated soft drinks in popularity among Americans. Bottled water that is sold through interstate commerce is regulated by the FDA. Thus, as with other food products, manufacturers must adhere to specific FDA regulations, such as standards of identity. In other words, if the label on the bottle states that it is "spring water," the manufacturer must derive the water from a very specific source (see the table on page 288). Interestingly, some bottled water may actually be from a municipal water source. The bottled water must also adhere to a standard of quality set forth by the FDA, which specifies the maximum amount of contaminants that can be in the water for it still to be considered safe for consumption. The FDA sets its standards for bottled water based on the EPA's standards for public drinking water. However, water that is bottled and sold in the same state is not regulated by the FDA. Water that is bottled and sold within the same state is under the jurisdiction of the state.[4]

The price of bottled water can be hefty, ranging from $1 to $4 a gallon. If you pay $1.50 per bottle and buy two bottles daily, you will be shelling out more than $20 a week and $80 monthly buying bottled water. Over the course of a nine-month term at college, you would be spending more than $750 on a beverage that you can get free from the campus water fountain. Finally, many bottled waters are not fluoridated, so bottled water drinkers may be losing out on this important cavity fighter if this is their predominant source of drinking water.[5]

Another costly bottled beverage option is the newer "designer" drinks such as vitamin waters and enhanced waters. Although bottled plain water has become increasingly popular in the past few decades, it seems to be losing ground to these new types of waters. These drinks often advertise health benefits beyond just keeping you hydrated. Sold under brand names such as Vitamin Water, they are often enhanced or fortified with additional compounds such as vitamins, sugar, and caffeine, as well as calories, though most Americans typically consume enough or even too much of these in their diet. These designer waters can cost more than $2.50 for a 20-ounce bottle, more than $10 a gallon!

Keep in mind that reusing the bottles from bottled water is not advised. The plastic containers cannot withstand repeated washing and the plastic can actually break down, causing chemicals to leach into the water. Sturdier water bottles that are designed for reuse must be thoroughly cleaned with hot soapy water after each use to kill germs.

The bottom line is that both tap water and bottled water can be safe to drink. Your choice is likely to come down to personal preference and costs. Consider your choice carefully using the table below.

Bottled vs. Tap Water: A Summary

Bottled Water	Tap Water
Cost to Consumers	
➤ About $1.00–$4.00 per gallon (plain water)	➤ About $0.003 per gallon
➤ Designer waters can cost more than $10 per gallon and may contain added sugar and calories	
Safety	
➤ Generally safe	➤ Municipal water is regulated by EPA, state, and local regulations
➤ Some bottled water is not tested for contaminants	
➤ Only bottled water sold across state lines is regulated by the FDA; bottled water not sold across state lines is regulated by state and local guidelines	➤ EPA guidelines require that the public have access to water quality reports and be notified if water quality is outside established bounds
Benefits to Consumers	
➤ Packaging of bottled water may make it more convenient than tap water	➤ Available at the faucet
➤ May taste better than tap water	➤ Often contains fluoride, which helps to prevent tooth decay
	➤ Doesn't contain any added sugar or calories

Figure 8.8 Water Content of Foods
Approximately 20 percent of the water you consume comes from foods. Fruits, vegetables, and cooked grains all contain a high percentage of water by weight.

Source: A. Grandjean and S. Campbell, *Hydration: Fluids for Life* (Washington, D.C.: ILSI Press, 2004). Available at www.ilsi.org.

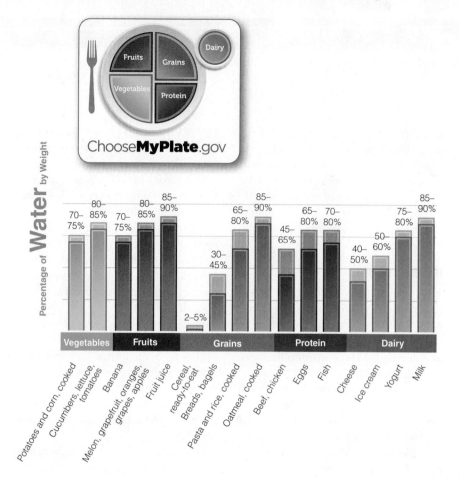

The remaining 20 percent of your water can come from foods. All foods contain some water. Cooked hot cereals and many fruits and vegetables are robust sources of water (see **Figure 8.8**).

Contrary to popular belief, beverages like caffeinated coffee, tea, and soft drinks will contribute to your daily water needs. Caffeine is a diuretic, so it causes water to be excreted, but the water loss it causes is short lived. In other words, the caffeine doesn't cause a significant loss of body water over the course of a day compared with noncaffeinated beverages. In fact, research suggests that individuals who routinely consume caffeinated beverages actually develop a tolerance to its diuretic effect and experience less water loss over time.[16]

Even though caffeinated beverages can count as a water source, this doesn't mean you should start guzzling caffeinated colas and other soft drinks. Their high calorie and sugar contents can quickly have you drinking your way into a very unbalanced, high-calorie diet. These soft drinks also contain acids that can contribute to erosion of tooth enamel. See **Figure 8.9** for a list of the healthiest fluids to drink to meet your daily water needs.

The Take-Home Message Adult women should ingest about 9 cups of water daily, whereas adult men should drink about 13 cups daily. Those who are very active will need more water to avoid dehydration. Foods and beverages, even caffeinated beverages, contribute to your daily water needs.

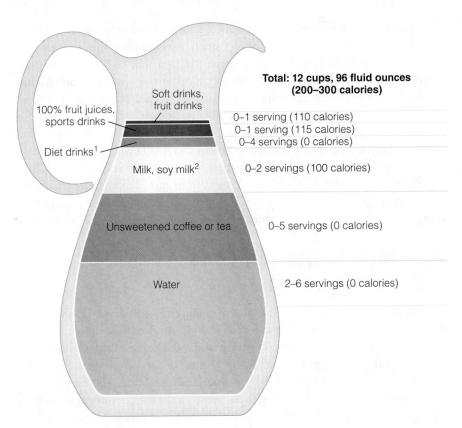

Figure 8.9 **The Best Way to Meet Your Daily Water Needs**

Total: 12 cups, 96 fluid ounces (200–300 calories)

100% fruit juices, sports drinks

Soft drinks, fruit drinks — 0–1 serving (110 calories)

Diet drinks[1] — 0–1 serving (115 calories)

0–4 servings (0 calories)

Milk, soy milk[2] — 0–2 servings (100 calories)

Unsweetened coffee or tea — 0–5 servings (0 calories)

Water — 2–6 servings (0 calories)

[1] Includes diet soft drinks and tea or coffee with sugar substitutes.
[2] Includes fat-free or 1% milk and unsweetened fortified soy milk.

What Are Minerals and Why Do You Need Them?

What do a cast-iron skillet, the salt on an icy road, and the copper plumbing pipes in some houses all have in common? They're made from some of the same **minerals** that play essential roles in your body. From iron to sodium to copper, these rocky substances occur as part of the earthen world around you and are necessary for your day-to-day functioning. You already read that electrolytes (minerals that are charged ions in your body fluids) help maintain fluid balance. Minerals can also be part of enzymes, work with your immune system, and play an invaluable role in structural growth. They help chemical reactions take place in your cells, help your muscles contract, and keep your heart beating. Your body needs these **inorganic** elements in relatively small amounts. Like vitamins, minerals don't provide calories, so they aren't a source of energy themselves, but they work with other nutrients to enable your body to function properly.

Bioavailability Affects Mineral Absorption

Minerals are found in both plant and animal foods, but the best food sources, as you will soon see, tend to be vegetables, legumes, milk, and meats. Absorption of minerals from your foods can vary depending upon their **bioavailability**. The mineral content of plants reflects the soil in which they are grown, as plants must derive nutrients from the soil through their roots. Some minerals compete with each other for absorption in your intestinal tract, and too much of one can cause an imbalance of another. For example, too much zinc in your diet can decrease the absorption of copper. Minerals

minerals Inorganic elements essential to the nutrition of humans.

inorganic Not containing carbon and not formed by living things.

bioavailability The degree to which a nutrient from foods is available for absorption by the body.

are also sometimes bound to other substances and your body cannot absorb them (they are eliminated from your body in your stool). An example of this is the calcium in spinach. Spinach is technically high in calcium, but is a poor source of this nutrient because it contains oxalates, which bind with the calcium and render most of it unavailable for absorption. Recall from Chapter 6 that phytates, compounds in fibrous plant foods, can bind to both iron and zinc and inhibit their absorption. This is why the DRI for both zinc and iron is increased for vegans, who consume only plant-based foods. Similarly, the polyphenols in tea and coffee can inhibit your body's absorption of iron, reducing its bioavailability. In contrast, vitamin C will enhance the absorption of iron that is found in plant foods. Protein from animal foods will enhance the absorption of zinc and iron, and (as you read in Chapter 7) vitamin D enhances the absorption of calcium. All these factors affect the bioavailability of these nutrients.

You Need Major Minerals in Larger Amounts

Minerals are categorized into two groups, depending on how much of them you need. The **major minerals**, known also as *macrominerals,* are needed in amounts greater than 100 milligrams per day, and the **trace minerals**, known also as *microminerals,* are needed in amounts less than 20 milligrams per day. The major minerals are major because you need more of them in your body, and thus, you need more of them in your diet (**Figure 8.10**).[17] Your daily needs for the major minerals range from hundreds of milligrams daily to more than a thousand. The major minerals include sodium, chloride, potassium, calcium, phosphorus, magnesium, and sulfur.

Many of these minerals work closely together to perform major body functions. For example, the sodium and chloride located mainly outside your cells, and the potassium, calcium, magnesium, and sulfur, which are mostly inside your cells, all play a key role in maintaining fluid balance. Calcium, phosphorus, and magnesium work together to strengthen your bones and teeth.

major minerals Minerals needed from your diet and in your body in amounts greater than 100 milligrams per day. These include sodium, chloride, potassium, calcium, phosphorus, magnesium, and sulfur. Also called *macrominerals.*

trace minerals Minerals needed from your diet and in your body in small amounts, less than 20 milligrams daily. These include iron, zinc, selenium, fluoride, chromium, copper, manganese, and molybdenum. Also called *microminerals.*

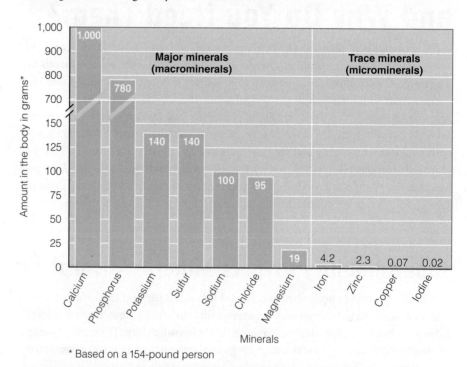

* Based on a 154-pound person

Figure 8.10 The Amounts of the Different Minerals in Your Body
The major minerals are present in larger amounts than the trace minerals. However, all are equally important to your health.

The Trace Minerals Are Needed in Small Amounts

The trace minerals—iron, zinc, selenium, fluoride, chromium, copper, iodine, manganese, and molybdenum—are needed in much smaller amounts, less than 20 milligrams daily, compared with the major minerals.[18] However, don't assume that this diminishes their importance. Trace minerals play essential roles that are as important as those of the major minerals. Some (chromium, iodine) help certain hormones, such as insulin and thyroid hormones, function. They are indispensable for maintaining healthy red blood cells (iron) and protecting your teeth (fluoride), and can be cofactors (iron, zinc, copper, manganese, and molybdenum) that work with enzymes to ensure that numerous critical reactions occur.

Overconsumption of Minerals Can Be Toxic

As with many other nutrients, consuming large amounts of some minerals, particularly the trace minerals, including iron and copper, can have toxic effects. In fact, for some minerals such as magnesium, there isn't a huge difference between the amount that is recommended daily for good health and the excessive amount that can cause gastrointestinal problems such as diarrhea and cramps. The good news is that foods alone rarely provide excessive amounts of any of the minerals; toxicities are usually the result of the use of supplements. This is one more reason why you should try to eat a wide variety of foods to meet your daily needs. **Figure 8.11** gives examples of minerals that are often obtained by following the MyPlate plan. In the following pages, we will look at each of the major and trace minerals closely, considering their functions, recommended intake, food sources, and the possible health consequences of over- or underconsumption.

Figure 8.11 Minerals Are Found Widely in MyPlate
Eating a variety of foods from all food groups is the best strategy to meet your daily mineral needs.

Vegetables	Fruits	Grains	Protein	Dairy
Potassium	Potassium	Sodium	Sodium	Potassium
Calcium	Calcium	Phosphorus	Phosphorus	Calcium
Magnesium	(fortified juice)	Magnesium	Magnesium	Phosphorus
Chromium	Manganese	Iron	Iron	
Manganese	Boron	Zinc	Copper	
		Selenium	Zinc	
		Chromium	Selenium	
		Manganese		

exploring
Sodium

What Are Sodium and Salt?

Sodium is an electrolyte in your body. Most sodium in your body is in your blood and in the fluid surrounding your cells. About 90 percent of the sodium you consume is in the form of sodium chloride, commonly known as table salt.

Functions of Sodium

Sodium's chief role is regulation of fluid balance. Sodium also plays an important role in transporting substances such as amino acids across cell membranes.

Salt is frequently added to foods to enhance flavor and as a preservative. It is also used to reduce the growth of bacteria and mold in many bread products and deli meats. Sodium phosphate, sodium carbonate, and sodium bicarbonate (baking soda) are food additives and preservatives that perform similar functions in foods. Monosodium glutamate (MSG) is a common additive in Asian cuisines that is used to intensify the flavor of foods.

Sodium Balance in Your Body

Physiological processes maintain the amount of sodium in your body at a certain level. When your body needs more sodium, your kidneys reduce the amount that is excreted in your urine. Likewise, when you take in too much sodium, you excrete the excess. For example, when you eat salty pretzels or potato chips, your kidneys will excrete the extra sodium you take in from these snacks.

Smaller amounts of sodium are lost in your stool and through daily perspiration. The amount of sodium lost through perspiration depends upon the rate at which you are sweating, the amount of sodium you have consumed (the more sodium in your diet, the higher the loss), and the intensity of

heat in the environment. As you get acclimated to environmental heat, less sodium will be lost over time in your sweat.[19] This built-in protective mechanism helps to prevent the loss of too much sodium from your body.

Daily Needs

The penny shown below is covered with about 180 milligrams of sodium. This is

the bare minimum you need daily. It is based on the amount of sodium needed by individuals who live in temperate climates and those who have become acclimated to hotter environments.[20]

Planning a balanced diet with such a small amount of sodium is virtually impossible, so the recommended sodium intake for adults up to 51 years of age is set at 1,500 milligrams daily. This sodium recommendation allows you to eat a variety of foods from all the food groups so that you can meet your other nutrient needs. It also covers any sodium that is lost in sweat by moderately active individuals, or those who are not acclimated to the environmental temperature. Those who are very physically active and/or not acclimated to heat will likely need to consume a higher amount of sodium. This can easily be obtained in the diet.

Americans currently consume more than double the recommended amount, or more than 3,400 milligrams of sodium daily, on average (**Figure 8.12**).

Food Sources

Sodium is so widely available in foods that you don't have to go out of your way to meet your needs (**Figure 8.13**).

About 10 percent of Americans' consumption of sodium is from foods in which it occurs naturally, such as fruits, vegetables, milk, meat, fish, poultry, and legumes.[21] Another 5 to 10 percent gets added during cooking and to season foods at the table.

Processed foods contribute a hefty 75 percent of the sodium in the diet of Americans.[22] Comparing the amount of sodium in a fresh tomato (6 milligrams) with the amount found in a cup of canned tomatoes (355 milligrams) aptly illustrates just how much more sodium is found in processed foods.

Because the majority of your sodium comes from processed foods, and a fair amount comes from the salt that you add to your foods, cutting back on these two sources is the best way to lower your intake. When you buy processed

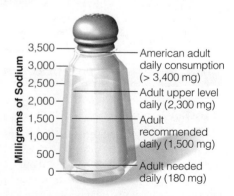

Figure 8.12 Recommended Intake of Sodium

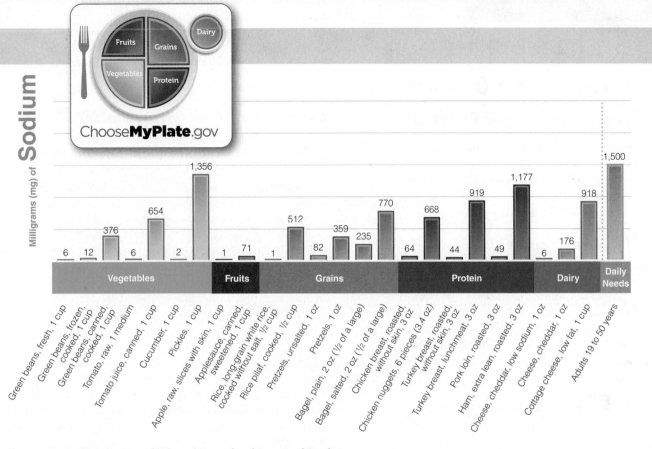

Milligrams (mg) of Sodium

ChooseMyPlate.gov

	Vegetables	Fruits	Grains	Protein	Dairy	Daily Needs

Values shown: 6, 12, 376, 6, 654, 2, 1,356, 1, 71, 1, 82, 512, 359, 235, 770, 64, 668, 44, 919, 49, 1,177, 6, 176, 918, 1,500

Food items: Green beans, fresh, 1 cup; Green beans, frozen, cooked, 1 cup; Green beans, canned, cooked, 1 cup; Tomato, raw, 1 medium; Tomato juice, canned, 1 cup; Cucumber, 1 cup; Pickles, 1 cup; Apple, raw, slices with skin, 1 cup; Applesauce, canned, sweetened, 1 cup; Rice, long-grain white rice, cooked without salt, ½ cup; Rice pilaf, cooked, ½ cup; Pretzels, unsalted, 1 oz; Pretzels, 1 oz; Bagel, plain, 2 oz (½ of a large); Bagel, salted, 2 oz (½ of a large); Chicken breast, roasted, without skin, 3 oz; Chicken nuggets, 6 pieces (3.4 oz); Turkey breast, roasted, without skin, 3 oz; Turkey breast, lunchmeat, 3 oz; Pork loin, roasted, 3 oz; Ham, extra lean, roasted, 3 oz; Cheese, cheddar, low sodium, 1 oz; Cheese, cheddar, 1 oz; Cottage cheese, low fat, 1 cup; Adults 19 to 50 years

Figure 8.13 Sodium Content of Selected Natural and Processed Foods
While sodium is naturally occurring in many foods, processing adds a tremendous amount, as you can see by the pairing of items within each food group (e.g., compare 2 mg of sodium in 1 cup of cucumbers to 1,356 mg of sodium in 1 cup of pickles).

foods, look for the terms "low sodium," "reduced sodium," or "sodium free" on the labels. Further, bypass the salt shaker at the table and season foods with black pepper, Tabasco sauce, lemon juice, or a no-salt seasoning blend.

Too Much or Too Little

There is a direct relationship between sodium and blood pressure in many people. In general, as a person's intake of sodium increases, so does his or her blood pressure. Blood pressure that becomes too high, known as hypertension, increases the risk for heart disease, stroke, and kidney disease (see the Health Connection feature "You and Your Blood Pressure" on pages 296–297). Unfortunately, many Americans will develop hypertension sometime during their lives. Researchers estimate that if Americans reduced their sodium intake by 40 percent over the next ten years, over 275,000 deaths from cardiovascular disease could be prevented.[23] To help reduce

the risk of high blood pressure, the upper level for adults for daily sodium intake is set at 2,300 milligrams. Many Americans exceed this upper limit daily.

Sodium deficiency is rare in healthy individuals consuming a balanced diet.

Practical Nutrition VIDEO

Sodium: What You Need Compared to What You Consume

Even if you never pick up a salt shaker, you may be far exceeding your daily sodium needs. Scan this QR code with your mobile device to access the video. You can also access the video in MasteringNutrition™.

TableTIPS

Shake Your Salt Habit

When buying canned soups, look for the reduced-sodium or low-sodium versions.

Keep your portions of deli meats to no more than 3 ounces and build a "meaty" sandwich by adding naturally low-sodium vegetables. Remember to skip the high-sodium pickles!

Nibble on low-sodium dried fruits (apricots, raisins) and unsalted walnut pieces.

Skip the salty French fries and potato chips and enjoy the sodium-free baked potato at dinner.

Use olive oil and balsamic vinegar for a salad dressing with less sodium than is in bottled dressings. Or, dilute regular salad dressing with an equal portion of vinegar to cut the sodium.

SODIUM

You and Your Blood Pressure

High blood pressure, or **hypertension**, is an increasing problem in the United States. In fact, if you were sitting in a room with two other adults, there is a good chance that one of you would have high blood pressure. High blood pressure increases the risk of heart disease, stroke, and kidney damage.[6]

What Is Blood Pressure?

Your blood pressure is a measure of the force your blood exerts against the walls of your arteries. With every beat, your heart pumps blood into your arteries, and thus to all the areas in your body. Blood pressure is highest at the moment of the heart beat. This is known as your **systolic pressure**. Pressure is lower when your heart is at rest between beats. This is called your **diastolic pressure**. Your blood pressure is expressed using these two measurements: systolic pressure/diastolic pressure. Blood pressure of less than 120/80 mm Hg (millimeters of mercury) is considered normal. Your blood pressure rises naturally as you age, which is believed to be due in part to the increased stiffness of the arteries.[7] However, if it rises too much, serious medical problems may occur.

Why Is Hypertension a Silent Killer?

Hypertension happens gradually. As blood pressure begins to rise above normal—that is, systolic is 120 or above and diastolic is 80 or above—it is classified as prehypertension. Many individuals with prehypertension will develop hypertension if they don't lower their blood pressure. A blood pressure of 140/90 mm Hg or above is classified as high blood pressure or hypertension.

Hypertension is referred to as the "silent killer" because there aren't any outward symptoms that your pressure is dangerously elevated; people can have it for years without knowing it. The only way to be sure you don't have it is to have your blood pressure checked regularly.

Individuals with chronic high blood pressure have a higher than normal force pounding against the walls of their arteries, which makes the walls thicker and stiffer, and contributes to atherosclerosis. The heart becomes enlarged and weakened, as it has to work harder to pump enough oxygen- and nutrient-laden blood throughout the body. This can lead to fatigue, shortness of breath, and possibly heart attack. Hypertension can also damage the arteries leading to the brain and kidneys, which increases the risk of stroke and kidney disease.[8]

hypertension High blood pressure.

systolic pressure The force of your blood against the artery walls when your heart beats.

diastolic pressure The pressure of your blood against the artery walls when the heart is at rest between beats.

Can You Control Your Hypertension?

There are factors that increase the chances of developing hypertension, some of which you can control and others you cannot.

Your family history, the aging process, and your race all affect the likelihood that you will develop high blood pressure. These are the risk factors that you can't control. If your parents, siblings, and/or grandparents have or had hypertension, you are at a higher risk of developing it yourself. Typically, the risk of hypertension increases with age. It is more likely to occur after the age of 35 for men, and women generally experience it after menopause. Hypertension is more prevalent in African-Americans, and tends to occur earlier and be more severe than in Caucasians.[9]

The good news is that there are more risk factors that you *can* control than those that you can't. You can change several dietary and lifestyle habits to help reduce your risk (see the table on the next page). Among these are your weight and your physical activity level. Individuals who are obese are twice as likely to have hypertension as those at a healthy weight. Even a modest weight loss can have an impact. Losing as little as 10 pounds can reduce a person's blood pressure, and may actually prevent hypertension in overweight individuals even if they haven't yet reached a healthy weight. Additional weight loss can have an even more dramatic effect on blood pressure. Regular physical activity can lower blood pressure even if weight loss hasn't occurred.[10]

You can also control your alcohol consumption, which affects your risk of developing high blood pressure. Studies have shown that

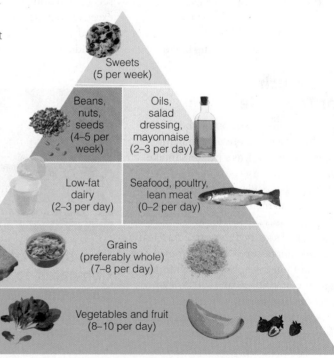

The DASH diet, which is rich in whole grains, fruits, vegetables, and low-fat dairy foods, can help lower blood pressure.

drinkers who consumed 3 to 6 drinks daily and then reduced their alcohol consumption by 67 percent, on average, were able to reduce their systolic pressure by more than 3 mm Hg and their diastolic pressure by 2 mm Hg.[11] Less drinking and more physical activity is the name of the game when it comes to keeping high blood pressure at bay.

Lastly, eating a balanced diet is a proven strategy to lower your blood pressure. A large research study, called the DASH (Dietary Approaches to Stop Hypertension) study, followed individuals on three different diets. One diet was a typical American diet: low in fruits, vegetables, and dairy products and high in fat, saturated fat, and cholesterol. A second was rich in just fruits and vegetables, and a third, the DASH diet, was a balanced diet that was lower in fat, saturated fat, cholesterol, and sweets, and high in whole grains, fruits, vegetables, and low-fat dairy products (see the figure on page 296).

The individuals in the study who followed the DASH diet experienced a significant reduction in blood pressure compared with those who followed the other two diets. Because the sodium content of all three diets was the same, about 3,000 milligrams, which is the approximate amount that Americans consume daily, on average, the blood pressure lowering effect was attributed to some other substance, or a combination of nutrients working together. For example, due to its abundance of fruits and vegetables, the DASH diet provides healthy doses of potassium and magnesium, and because of its numerous servings of dairy foods, it is also rich in calcium. Dietary potassium, magnesium, and calcium can all play a role in lowering blood pressure.[12]

A follow-up to the DASH study, called the DASH-Sodium study, went one step further and investigated whether reducing the amount of

Calculating Your Risk for Hypertension

Would you like to find out *your* risk for developing high blood pressure and learn how lifestyle changes can affect your personal risk? Visit the American Heart Association website at www.americanheart.org and search for the "High Blood Pressure Health Risk Calculator."

dietary sodium in each of the three diets could also help lower blood pressure. Not surprisingly, it did. We know that, in general, as a person's sodium intake increases, so does the blood pressure. Although this study showed that reducing dietary sodium from about 3,300 milligrams to 2,400 milligrams daily lowered blood pressure, the biggest reduction occurred when sodium intake was limited to only 1,500 milligrams daily. Most importantly, the overall best diet combination for lowering blood pressure was the DASH diet plus consuming only 1,500 milligrams of sodium daily.[13] The *Dietary Guidelines for Americans, 2010* recommend that Americans should reduce their sodium to less than 2,300 milligrams daily. Other populations should reduce their sodium even further, to 1,500 milligrams daily; this lower recommendation applies to about half of the U.S. population, including children and those looking to fight hypertension (see Chapter 2 for more on the *Dietary Guidelines*).[14]

Take Charge of Your Blood Pressure!

Diet and lifestyle changes help reduce blood pressure and help prevent hypertension.

If You	By	Your Systolic Blood Pressure* May Be Reduced by
Reduce your sodium intake	Keeping dietary sodium consumption to less than 2,400 mg daily	8–14 mm Hg
Lose excess weight	Modifying your diet and exercise to reach and maintain a normal, healthy body weight	5–20 mm Hg for every 22 lbs of weight loss
Stay physically active	Partaking in 30 minutes of aerobic activity (e.g., brisk walking) on most days of the week	4–9 mm Hg
Drink alcohol only in moderation	Limiting consumption to no more than 2 drinks daily for men and 1 drink daily for women	2–4 mm Hg
Follow the DASH diet	Consuming this diet, which is abundant in fruits and vegetables and low-fat dairy products	8–14 mm Hg

*Controlling the systolic pressure is more difficult than controlling the diastolic pressure, especially for individuals 50 years of age and older. Therefore, it is the primary focus for lowering blood pressure. Typically, as systolic pressure goes down with diet and lifestyle changes, the diastolic pressure will follow.
Source: Adapted from A. V. Chobanian, et al., The Seventh Report of the Joint National Committee on Prevention, Detection, Evaluation, and Treatment of High Blood Pressure, *Journal of the American Medical Association* 289 (2003): 2560–2572.

exploring
Potassium

What Is Potassium?

Potassium is an important mineral with numerous functions in your body. Luckily, it is also found in numerous foods, so it's not difficult to meet your needs for it.

Functions of Potassium

Potassium Is Needed for Fluid Balance and as a Blood Buffer

More than 95 percent of the potassium in your body is inside your cells, with the remainder in the fluids outside your cells, including your blood. As with other electrolytes, potassium helps maintain fluid balance and keeps your blood pH and acid-base balance correct.

Potassium Is Needed for Muscle Contraction and Nerve Impulse Conduction

Potassium plays a role in the contraction of your muscles, including your heart, and the conduction of nerve impulses. Because of this, a dramatic increase of potassium in your body can lead to irregular heart beats or heart attack, whereas dangerously low levels could cause paralysis. Thus, potassium is tightly controlled and balanced in your body with the help of your kidneys.

Potassium Can Help Lower High Blood Pressure

A diet with plentiful potassium has been shown to help lower blood pressure, especially in salt-sensitive individuals who respond more intensely to sodium's blood pressure–raising capabilities. Potassium causes the kidneys to excrete excess sodium from the body, and keeping sodium levels low can help lower blood pressure. The DASH diet is abundant in foods with potassium.

kidney stone A solid mass formed in the kidneys from dietary minerals.

hyperkalemia Abnormally high levels of potassium in the blood.

hypokalemia Abnormally low levels of potassium in the blood.

Potassium Aids in Bone Health and Reduces Kidney Stones

Because potassium plays a buffering role in your blood, it helps keep the bone-strengthening minerals, calcium and phosphorus, from being lost from the bones and kidneys. Numerous studies suggest that having adequate amounts of potassium in your diet helps increase the density, and thus the strength, of your bones.[24]

Potassium also helps reduce the risk of **kidney stones** by causing the body to excrete citrate,[25] a compound that binds with calcium to form kidney stones, shown in **Figure 8.14**.

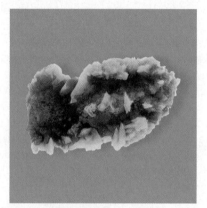

Figure 8.14 Kidney Stone

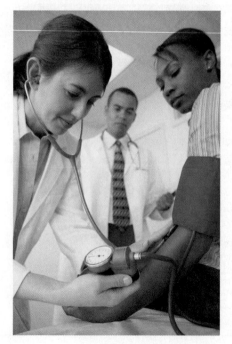

Daily Needs

Adults should consume 4,700 milligrams of potassium daily. This amount is recommended to help reduce the risk of high blood pressure. Potassium can also help lower the risk of developing kidney stones and preserve bone health.

Because Americans fall short of their servings of fruits, vegetables, and lean dairy, they are also falling short of their daily potassium needs. Adult females are consuming only about 2,400 milligrams of potassium daily, and adult males are consuming only about 3,170 milligrams daily, on average.[26]

Food Sources

The *Dietary Guidelines for Americans, 2010* recommend consuming an abundance of fruits and vegetables so as to meet your potassium needs. A diet rich in at least 4½ cups of fruits and vegetables, especially leafy greens, which is the *minimum* amount you should be consuming daily, can help you meet your potassium needs. Dairy foods, nuts, and legumes are also good sources (**Figure 8.15**).

Too Much or Too Little

There isn't any known danger from consuming too much potassium that occurs naturally in foods. These excesses will be excreted in your urine. However, consuming too much from supplements or salt substitutes (the sodium in some salt substitutes is replaced with potassium) can cause **hyperkalemia** (*hyper* = too much, *kalemia* = potassium in the blood) for some individuals.

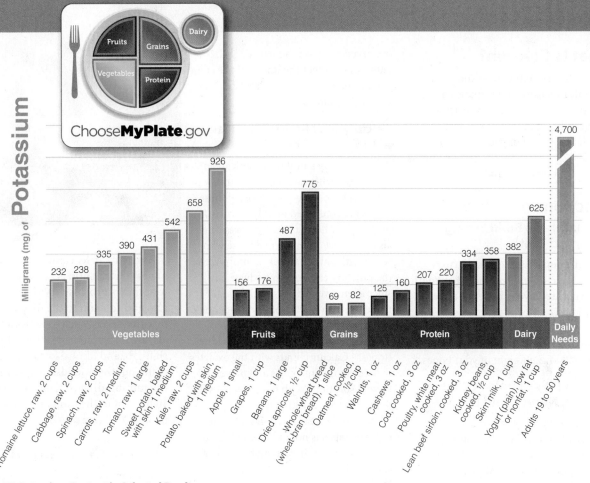

Figure 8.15 **Potassium Content in Selected Foods**

Hyperkalemia can cause irregular heart beats, damage the heart, and be life-threatening.[27]

Those at a higher risk for hyperkalemia include individuals with impaired kidneys, such as people with type 1 diabetes mellitus, those with kidney disease, and individuals taking medications for heart disease or diuretics that cause the kidneys to block the excretion of potassium. These individuals may also need to consume less than the recommended amount of potassium daily, as advised by their health care professional.

Although a deficiency of dietary potassium is rare, too little potassium can cause **hypokalemia** (*hypo* = too little, *kalemia* = potassium in the blood). This may occur during bouts of vomiting and/or diarrhea. It has been seen in individuals who have anorexia nervosa and/or bulimia nervosa. Hypokalemia can cause muscle weakness, cramps, and, in severe situations, irregular heart beats and paralysis.[28]

Individuals who consume high-protein diets that contain few fruits and vegetables may be depriving themselves of the buffering actions of potassium.[29] The breakdown of excessive amounts of dietary protein causes the formation of acids that are balanced by the buffering action of potassium. A diet too low in fruits and vegetables is setting the stage for an imbalance of acids and bases in the blood and the increased risk of kidney stones, loss of bone mass, and high blood pressure.

TableTIPS

Potassium Power!

Slice a banana on your oatmeal at breakfast to begin the day with a potassium boost.

Add leafy greens to all your sandwiches. Spinach in particular is a potassium dynamo!

Add a spoonful of walnuts to your mid-morning yogurt for a one-two (nuts and dairy) potassium punch.

Have bean soup with your lunchtime sandwich for a warm way to enjoy your potassium.

Baked regular or sweet potatoes are potassium powerhouses on your dinner plate.

Calcium

CALCIUM

What Is Calcium?

Calcium is one of the most abundant minerals in nature and is found in everything from pearls to seashells to eggshells. Calcium is also the most abundant mineral in your body. More than 99 percent of your body's calcium is located in your bones and teeth.

Functions of Calcium

Calcium Helps Build Strong Bones and Teeth

Calcium couples with phosphorus to form *hydroxyapatite*, providing strength and structure in your bones and the enamel on your teeth. Adequate dietary calcium is needed to build and maintain bone mass. Calcium makes up almost 40 percent of the weight of your bones.[30]

Calcium Plays a Role in Your Muscles, Nerves, and Blood

The remaining 1 percent of calcium is in your blood, in the fluids that surround your cells, in your muscles, and in other tissues. Calcium is needed for muscle contraction, and to help your nervous system transmit messages. Calcium is also involved in the dilation and contraction of blood vessels, and it helps your blood clot. Finally, calcium is necessary for the secretion of some hormones and enzymes. It must be maintained at a constant level for your body to function properly.[31]

Calcium May Help Lower High Blood Pressure

Studies have shown that a heart-healthy diet rich in calcium, potassium, magnesium, fruits, vegetables, and low-fat dairy products can help lower blood pressure.[32] One example of such a diet, the DASH diet, contains three servings of lean dairy foods, the minimum amount of servings recommended to obtain this protective effect[33] (see the Health Connection feature "You and Your Blood Pressure" on page 296).

Calcium May Help Prevent Colon Cancer

A diet with plenty of calcium has been shown to help reduce the risk of developing benign tumors in the colon that

may eventually lead to cancer.[34] Calcium may protect the lining of the colon from damaging bile acids and cancer-promoting substances.

Calcium May Reduce the Risk of Kidney Stones

Approximately a million American adults visit their health care providers annually with kidney stones.[35] Most of these stones are composed mainly of calcium oxalate.[36] Although health professionals in the past often warned those who suffer with kidney stones to minimize their dietary calcium, this advice has since been reversed. Research has shown that a balanced diet, along with adequate amounts of *dietary* calcium, may actually reduce the risk of developing kidney stones.[37] Calcium binds with the oxalates in foods in the intestines and prevents their absorption. With fewer oxalates filtering through the kidneys, fewer stones are formed. Research involving calcium supplements has not indicated the same protective effect. In fact, high intake of calcium supplements, not food sources, has been shown to increase the risk of kidney stones[38] (see the section on Too Much or Too Little). The current upper levels set for calcium are based on research related to risk for increased kidney stones.[39]

Daily Needs

Adults age 19 to 50 need 1,000 milligrams of calcium daily. Women older than 50, and men age 70 and beyond, should increase their daily intake to 1,200 mg.[40] Most women and many older males do not meet their daily calcium needs.[41]

Food Sources

Milk, yogurt, and cheese are the major sources of calcium in the American diet (**Figure 8.16**). Each serving from the dairy group will provide approximately 300 milligrams of calcium. (Choose nonfat, low- or reduced-fat, or skim milk versions to reduce the amount of saturated fat in these foods.) Although three servings of dairy foods will just about meet many adults' daily needs, American adults consume only about 1½ servings of dairy daily, on average.[42]

Broccoli, kale, canned salmon with bones (the calcium is in the bones), and tofu that is processed with calcium can also add calcium to the diet. Calcium-fortified foods, such as juices and cereals, are also excellent sources. Spinach, rhubarb, and okra also contain calcium, but these foods are also high in calcium-binding oxalates, so less than 10 percent of the mineral is absorbed in the body (**Figure 8.17**).

Too Much or Too Little

The upper level for calcium has been set at 2,500 milligrams daily for adults age 19 to 50, and at 2,000 milligrams for those age 51 and beyond, to avoid kidney stones. Too much dietary calcium can also cause constipation and interfere with the absorption of other minerals, such as iron, zinc, magnesium, and phosphorus. **Hypercalcemia**, or having abnormally high blood levels of calcium, can potentially impair kidney function and lead to calcium deposits in the body.

If your diet is low in calcium, calcium leaves your bones in order to maintain a constant level in your blood. A chronic

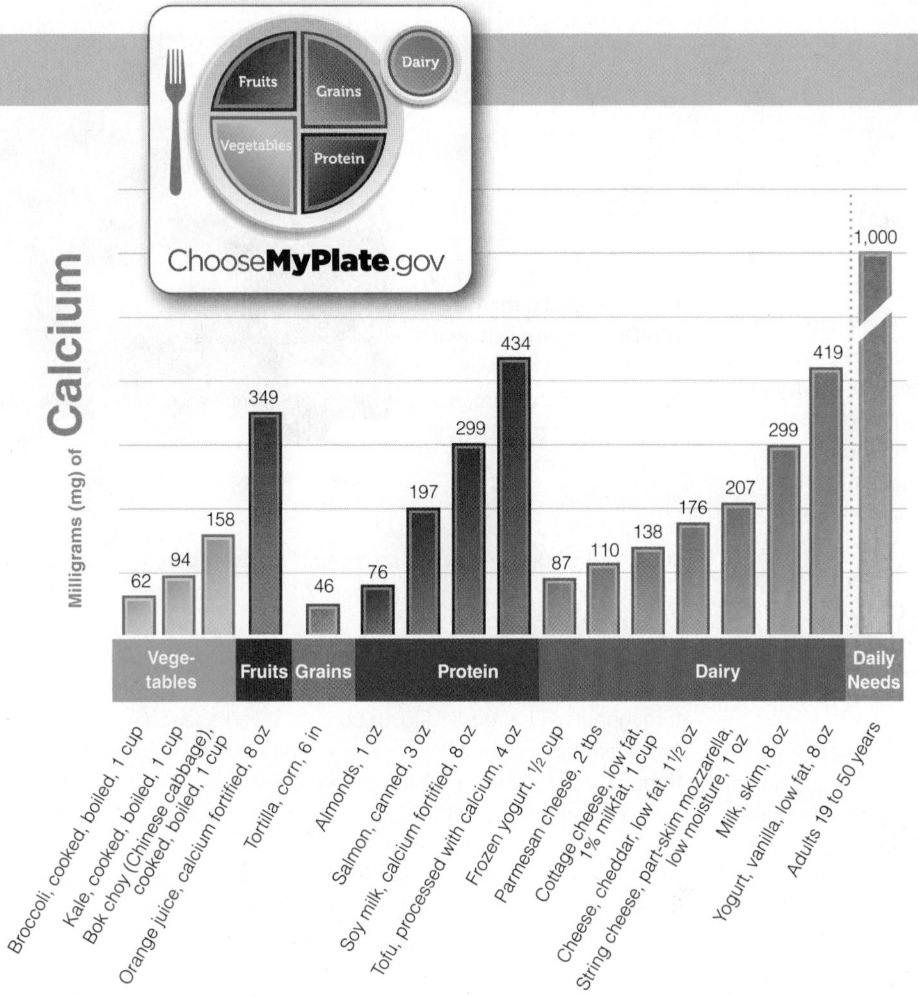

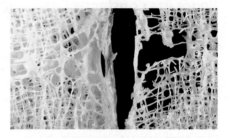

Calcium

ChooseMyPlate.gov

Milligrams (mg) of **Calcium**

Bar chart values: 62, 94, 158, 46, 76, 197, 299, 434, 87, 110, 138, 176, 207, 299, 419, 1,000

Categories: Vegetables | Fruits | Grains | Protein | Dairy | Daily Needs

Labels:
- Broccoli, cooked, boiled, 1 cup
- Kale, cooked, boiled, 1 cup
- Bok choy (Chinese cabbage), cooked, boiled, 1 cup
- Orange juice, calcium fortified, 8 oz
- Tortilla, corn, 6 in
- Almonds, 1 oz
- Salmon, canned, 3 oz
- Soy milk, calcium fortified, 8 oz
- Tofu, processed with calcium, 4 oz
- Frozen yogurt, 1/2 cup
- Parmesan cheese, 2 tbs
- Cottage cheese, low fat, 1% milkfat, 1 cup
- Cheese, cheddar, low fat, 1½ oz
- String cheese, part-skim mozzarella, low moisture, 1 oz
- Milk, skim, 8 oz
- Yogurt, vanilla, low fat, 8 oz
- Adults 19 to 50 years

Figure 8.16 Calcium Content in Selected Foods

Figure 8.18 Healthy Bone (left) vs Weakened Bone (right)

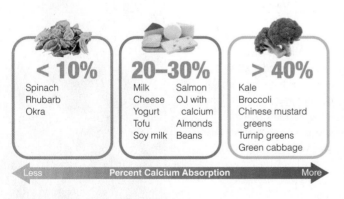

< 10%
Spinach
Rhubarb
Okra

20–30%
Milk   Salmon
Cheese   OJ with
Yogurt   calcium
Tofu   Almonds
Soy milk   Beans

> 40%
Kale
Broccoli
Chinese mustard greens
Turnip greens
Green cabbage

Less ← **Percent Calcium Absorption** → More

Figure 8.17 Bioavailability of Calcium

deficiency of dietary calcium can lead to less dense, weakened, and brittle bones and increased risk for osteoporosis and bone fractures (**Figure 8.18**). See the Health Connection feature "Osteoporosis: Not Just Your Grandmother's Problem" on pages 302–303 for more about the importance of forming and maintaining healthy bone.

Calcium Supplements

Some individuals are advised by their health care provider to take a calcium supplement. The calcium in supplements is part of a compound, typically either calcium carbonate or calcium citrate. Calcium carbonate tends to be the form of calcium most commonly purchased. It is most effective when consumed with a meal, as the acidic juices in your stomach help with its absorption.[43] Calcium citrate can be taken any time throughout the day, as it doesn't need the help of acidic juices to be absorbed.

Regardless of the form, all calcium, whether from supplements or from fortified or naturally occurring foods, should be consumed in doses of 500 milligrams or less, as this is the maximum that your body can absorb efficiently at one time.[44]

Calcium from unrefined oyster shell, bone meal, or dolomite (a rock rich in calcium) may also contain lead and other toxic metals. Supplements from these sources should state on the label that they are "purified" or carry the USP symbol to ensure purity. Because calcium can interfere with and reduce the absorption of iron, a calcium supplement shouldn't be taken along with an iron supplement.

Be cautious about adding a calcium supplement to your diet if you are already consuming plenty of dairy foods and/or calcium-fortified foods.

hypercalcemia Abnormally high levels of calcium in the blood.

health

CONNECTION

CALCIUM

Osteoporosis: Not Just Your Grandmother's Problem

If you are fortunate enough to have elders, such as grandparents, in your life, you may have heard them comment that they are "shrinking" as they age. Of course, they aren't really shrinking, but they may be losing height as the tissues supporting their spine lose mass and elasticity and the joint capsules between the bones (or vertebrae) of the spine lose their cushion of fluid. This is normal. In many older adults, however, the vertebrae themselves lose mass and begin to collapse, so that it becomes more difficult for the spine to hold the weight of the head and upper body. This leads to a gradual curvature of the spine, which affects their posture (**Figure 1**). As older individuals begin to hunch over, they can lose as much as a foot in height.[15]

Bones Are Constantly Changing

Bones are a dynamic, living tissue. Older layers of bones are constantly removed, and new bone is constantly added. In fact, your entire skeleton is replaced with new bone about every decade. During childhood and adolescence, more bone is added than is removed, as the bones grow in length and mass. Although growth of bone length typically ceases during the teenage years, bone mass will continue to accumulate into the early years of young adulthood (**Figure 2**). **Peak bone mass**, which is the genetically determined maximum amount of bone mass an individual can build up, typically occurs when a person is in his or her 20s. Some additional bone mass can be added when an individual is in his or her 30s. After peak bone mass is reached, the loss of bone mass begins to slowly exceed the rate at which new bone is added.[16]

peak bone mass The genetically determined maximum amount of bone mass an individual can build up.

osteoporosis A condition in which the bones are less dense, increasing the risk of fractures.

bone mineral density (BMD) The amount of minerals, in particular calcium, per volume in an individual's bone.

osteopenia A condition in which bone mineral density is lower than normal but not low enough to be classified as osteoporosis.

As bones lose mass, they become porous, and **osteoporosis** (*osteo* = bone, *porosis* = porous) can develop. The weakened, fragile bones are prone to fractures. A minor stumble while walking can result in a broken ankle, rib cage, or arm bone as the result of an ensuing fall. Shopping for groceries, showering, dressing, and even brushing one's teeth become challenges for many older people with osteoporosis.

Hip fractures can be devastating because they often render a person immobile, which quickly affects quality of life. Feelings of helplessness and depression often ensue. Individuals with hip fractures are never able to regain the quality of life they had prior to the injury, and an elderly person is up to four times more likely to die within three months of a hip fracture.[17] It is estimated that by the year 2020, one out of every two Americans over age 50 will either have or be at risk for hip fractures due to osteoporosis, and even more will be at risk for fractures of other bones.[18]

Adults can have a bone test done by their doctors to assess how their **bone mineral density (BMD)** compares with that of a healthy 30-year-old. BMD refers to the amount of minerals, in particular calcium, per volume in an individual's bone. The denser the bones, the stronger the bones. A low test score indicates **osteopenia** (*penia* = poverty), which signals low bone mass. A very low test score indicates osteoporosis.

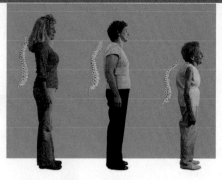

Figure 1 Weak bones cause the spine to collapse over time.

Ironically, though osteoporosis is often thought of as a condition of the elderly, it has its roots in childhood and must be prevented throughout adulthood. Saving up bone mass is like saving money for retirement. The more you save when you are young and preserve throughout your adulthood, the more you will have for your later years. Conversely, if you don't save enough early in life, you may end up with little to fall back on when you need it later.

It's never too late to try to reduce your risk of osteoporosis. To take a look at the risk factors involved, see the Self-Assessment.

After you have completed the Self-Assessment, look at the skeleton. If it has mostly shaded areas, you have fewer risk factors for osteoporosis; the less shaded the skeleton, the more risk factors you have, and the higher your risk of developing osteoporosis. Many of these risk factors can be reduced by a healthy diet and lifestyle.

Although you cannot control the first five risk factors (your gender, ethnicity, age, body type, and family history), you can control the remaining six risk factors. If your sex hormone levels are lower than they should be and/or if you are taking medications that may increase your risk of osteoporosis, talk to your doctor. Quitting smoking, exercising regularly, and limiting or avoiding alcohol will help reduce your risk. Lastly, make sure that you consume adequate amounts of vitamin D (Chapter 7) and calcium (see Exploring Calcium on page 300). If you can't meet your calcium needs through food, a supplement may be necessary.

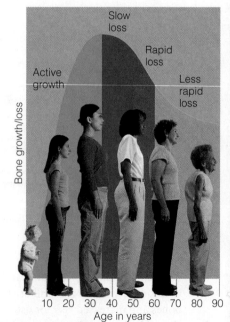

Figure 2 In your early years, more bone mass is added than lost in your body. In their mid-30s, women begin to slowly lose bone mass until menopause, when the rate of loss is accelerated for several years. Bone loss continues after age 60 but at a slower rate. Bone loss also occurs in men as they age.

self-Assessment

Are You at Risk for Osteoporosis?

Answer the following questions to determine how many risk factors you have for osteoporosis. Shade in each part of the skeleton based on your answers.

1. *Gender:* Are you female?
   Yes ☐ **No** ☐ (If you answered no, shade in the left arm of the skeleton.)
   Females are at higher risk for osteoporosis than males because they have smaller bones, and thus less bone mass. Also, bone mass is lost at a faster rate right after menopause due to the decline of estrogen in women's bodies. However, men can suffer from osteoporosis and can experience it at a fairly young age.[19]

2. *Ethnicity:* Are you a Caucasian or Asian-American female?
   Yes ☐ **No** ☐ (If no, shade in the right arm of the skeleton.)
   Caucasian and Asian women typically have lower bone mass than other women.

3. *Age:* Are you over 30 years of age?
   Yes ☐ **No** ☐ (If no, shade in the left hand of the skeleton.)
   You begin to lose bone mass after about age 30, which increases your risk of osteoporosis and fractures.

4. *Body Type:* Are you a small-boned or petite woman?
   Yes ☐ **No** ☐ (If no, shade in the right hand of the skeleton.)
   Thin women have lower bone mass and increased risk of fractures. A higher body weight puts more weight-bearing, mechanical stress on bones, helping them to stay healthy. A healthy body weight also means you'll have some padding should a fall occur. Also, since most of the estrogen produced in menopausal women's bodies is formed in fat tissue, thinner women have less bone-protecting estrogen.[20]

5. *Family History of Fractures:* Have your parents or grandparents ever experienced any bone fractures in their golden years?
   Yes ☐ **No** ☐ (If no, shade in the left leg of the skeleton.)
   A family history of bone fractures in your relatives' later years increases your risk of osteoporosis.

6. *Level of Sex Hormones:* Are you a premenopausal woman who has stopped menstruating, a menopausal woman, or a male with low testosterone levels?
   Yes ☐ **No** ☐ (If no, shade in the right leg of the skeleton.)
   Women with amenorrhea (the absence of menstrual periods) experience hormonal imbalances, especially if they are at a dangerously low body weight.[21] Menopausal women, or men with low levels of sex hormones, which are protective against bone loss, are also at a higher risk.

7. *Medications:* Are you taking certain medications such as glucocorticoids (prednisone), antiseizure medications (phenytoin), aluminum-containing antacids, and/or excessive amounts of thyroid replacement hormones?
   Yes ☐ **No** ☐ (If no, shade in the torso of the skeleton.)
   The long-term use of glucocorticoids, antiseizure medicines, certain antacids, or too much thyroid hormone–replacing medication can lead to a loss of bone mass and increase the risk of fractures.[22] Certain cancer treatments can also cause bone loss. Though you shouldn't stop taking any prescribed medications, you should speak to your doctor regarding your bone health.

8. *Smoking:* Do you smoke?
   Yes ☐ **No** ☐ (If no, shade in the left foot of the skeleton.)
   Smokers absorb less calcium than do nonsmokers. Women smokers have lower levels of estrogen in their bodies and begin menopause earlier than do nonsmokers.

9. *Physical Activity:* Do you spend less than 30 minutes exercising daily?
   Yes ☐ **No** ☐ (If no, shade in the left hip of the skeleton.)
   Regular physical activity contributes to higher peak bone mass in a person's early years, and strength and weight-bearing activities such as walking, hiking, and tennis help maintain bone mass during adulthood. These activities cause you to work against gravity, which helps strengthen your bones. Regular exercise also helps you maintain healthy muscles and improves your coordination and balance, which can help prevent falls.[23]

10. *Alcohol:* Do you consume more than one alcoholic drink a day if you are a woman or consume more than two alcoholic drinks daily if you are a man?
    Yes ☐ **No** ☐ (If no, shade in the right hip of the skeleton.)
    Heavy consumption of alcohol can reduce bone mass by inhibiting the formation of new bone, preventing the activation of vitamin D, and increasing the loss of calcium. It can also increase the risk of stumbling and falling.[24]

11. *Inadequate Amounts of Calcium and Vitamin D:* Do you consume less than 3 cups daily of milk or yogurt that has been fortified with vitamin D?
    Yes ☐ **No** ☐ (If no, shade in the right foot of the skeleton.)
    Because calcium is needed to build and maintain bone mass, and vitamin D is needed for your body to absorb this mineral, having inadequate amounts of either or both of these nutrients increases your risk of low bone mass, bone loss, and bone fractures.

exploring
Phosphorus

What Is Phosphorus?

Phosphorus is the second most abundant mineral in your body. The majority of phosphorus—about 85 percent—is in your bones. The remainder is in your cells and fluids outside your cells, including your blood.

Functions of Phosphorus

Phosphorus Is Needed for Bones and Teeth and Is an Important Component of Cells

As mentioned, phosphorus combines with calcium to form hydroxyapatite, the strengthening material found in bones and teeth.

Phosphorus is part of phospholipids, which give your cell membranes their structure (**Figure 8.19**). Phospholipids act as a barrier to keep specific substances out of the cells, while letting others in.

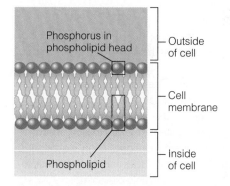

Figure 8.19 Phosphorus in Phospholipids Phosphorus makes up part of the phospholipids found in cell membranes.

Phosphorus Is Needed during Metabolism

Phosphorus helps your body store the energy generated from the metabolism of carbohydrates, protein, and fat for later use. Your body can draw upon these stores as needed.

hyperphosphatemia Abnormally high levels of phosphorus in the blood.

Phosphorus Acts as a Buffer and Is Part of the DNA and RNA of Every Cell

If your blood becomes too acidic or too basic, phosphorus can act as a buffer to help return your blood pH to normal. Your blood pH must stay within a very narrow range to prevent damage to your tissues.

Phosphorus is part of your DNA and RNA. The instructions for your genes are coded in your DNA and transcribed in your RNA to make the proteins needed in your body.

Daily Needs

Adults, both male and female, need 700 milligrams of phosphorus daily. Americans, on average, consume more than 1,000 milligrams of phosphorus daily.[45]

Food Sources

A balanced, varied diet will easily meet your phosphorus needs. Foods from animal sources such as meat, fish, poultry, and dairy products are excellent sources of phosphorus (**Figure 8.20**). Phosphorus is also part of many food additives.

Too Much or Too Little

Typically, consuming too much dietary phosphorus and its subsequent effect, **hyperphosphatemia**, is an issue only

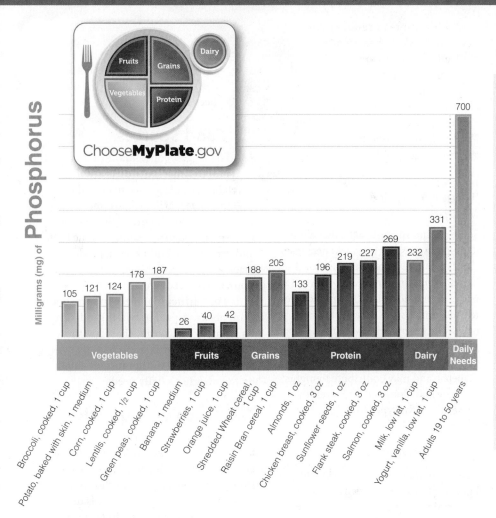

Figure 8.20 **Phosphorus Content of Selected Foods**

for individuals with kidney problems who cannot excrete excess phosphorus.

Constantly high phosphorus intake and low calcium intake can cause the loss of calcium from your bones and a subsequent decrease in bone mass. Loss of bone mass increases the risk of osteoporosis. Hyperphosphatemia can also lead to calcification of tissues in the body. To protect against this, the upper level for phosphorus has been set at 4,000 milligrams daily for adults age 19 to 50 and 3,000 milligrams for those 50 years of age and older.

Too little phosphorus in the diet can cause its level in your blood to drop dangerously low and result in muscle weakness, bone pain, rickets, confusion, and, at the extreme, death. Because phosphorus is so abundant in the diet, a deficiency is rare. In fact, a person would have to be in a state of near starvation before experiencing a phosphorus deficiency.[46]

---

exploring
Magnesium

MAGNESIUM

What Is Magnesium?

Magnesium is another abundant mineral in your body. While about half of the magnesium is in your bones, most of the remaining magnesium is inside the cells. A mere 1 percent is found in your blood and, like calcium, this amount must be maintained at a constant level.

Functions of Magnesium

Magnesium Is Needed for Metabolism and to Maintain Healthy Muscles, Nerves, Bones, and Heart

Magnesium helps more than 300 enzymes produce reactions inside your cells. It is needed for the metabolism of carbohydrates, proteins, and fats. Magnesium is used during the synthesis of protein and to help your muscles and nerves function properly. It is also needed to help you maintain healthy bones and a regular heart beat.[47]

Magnesium May Help Lower High Blood Pressure

Studies have shown that magnesium may help regulate blood pressure and that a plant-based diet abundant in fruits and vegetables, which are rich in magnesium as well as other minerals, can lower blood pressure.[48]

The blood-pressure-lowering DASH diet, which has been clinically proven to lower blood pressure, is rich in magnesium as well as calcium and potassium (see the Health Connection feature "You and Your Blood Pressure" on page 296).[49]

Magnesium May Help Reduce the Risk of Diabetes Mellitus

Some studies suggest that a diet abundant in magnesium may help decrease the risk of type 2 diabetes mellitus. Low blood levels of magnesium, which often occur in individuals with type 2 diabetes, may impair the release of insulin, one of the hormones that regulate blood glucose. This may lead to elevated blood glucose levels in those with preexisting diabetes, and may contribute to higher than normal blood glucose levels in those at risk for type 2 diabetes.[50]

Daily Needs

Adult females age 19 to 30 need 310 milligrams of magnesium, whereas men of the same age need 400 milligrams daily. Females age 31 and over need 320 milligrams; men of this age need 420 milligrams of magnesium daily.

Currently, many Americans fall short of their magnesium needs. Women consume only about 85 percent of their needs, or about 265 milligrams daily, on average. Men consume approximately 350 milligrams daily, on average, which is only about 80 percent of the amount recommended daily.[51] Because older adults tend to consume fewer calories, and thus less dietary magnesium, elders are at an even higher risk of falling short of their needs.

Food Sources

The biggest contributors of magnesium to Americans' diets are vegetables, whole grains, nuts, and fruits (**Figure 8.21**). Milk, yogurt, meat, and eggs are also good sources. Because the majority of the magnesium is in the bran and germ of the grain kernel, products made with refined grains, such as white flour, are poor sources.

It's not difficult to meet your magnesium needs. A peanut butter sandwich on whole-wheat bread, chased with a glass of low-fat milk and a banana, will provide over 200 milligrams, or about half of an adult's daily needs.

Too Much or Too Little

There isn't any known risk in consuming too much magnesium from food sources. However, consuming large amounts from supplements has been shown to cause intestinal problems such as diarrhea, cramps, and nausea. In fact, some laxatives purposefully contain magnesium because of its known purgative effect. Because of the potential for distress to the intestinal system, the upper level for magnesium from supplements,

Milligrams (mg) of **Magnesium**

Romaine lettuce, 2 cups	12
Spinach, fresh, 2 cups	47
Pineapple, diced, 1 cup	20
Banana, 1 medium	32
Oatmeal, 1/2 cup	30
Wheat germ, 2 tbs (approx. 1/8 cup)	34
Brown rice, cooked, 1/2 cup	43
Kidney beans, cooked, 1/2 cup	19
Chickpeas, cooked, 1/2 cup	20
Edamame, 1/2 cup	49
Peanut butter, 2 tbs	49
Almonds, 1 oz	80
Milk, low fat, 1 cup	27
Yogurt, low fat, strawberry, 1 cup	30
Men 19 to 30 years	400
Men 31 to 50 years	420
Women 19 to 30 years	310
Women 31 to 50 years	320

Groups: Vegetables, Fruits, Grains, Protein, Dairy, Daily Needs

Figure 8.21 Magnesium Content of Selected Foods

not foods, is set at 350 milligrams for adults. This level is to prevent diarrhea, the first symptom that typically arises when too much magnesium is consumed.[52] As mentioned earlier in this chapter, the difference between consuming enough and getting too much magnesium is rather narrow. Look to food to meet your magnesium needs rather than supplements, which can quickly cause you to consume too much.

Even though many Americans don't meet their magnesium needs, deficiencies are rare in healthy individuals because the kidneys compensate for low magnesium intake by excreting less of it. However, some medications may cause magnesium deficiency. Certain diuretics can cause the body to lose too much magnesium, and some antibiotics, such as tetracycline, can inhibit the absorption of magnesium, both of which can lead to a deficiency. Individuals with poorly controlled diabetes or who abuse alcohol can experience excessive losses of magnesium in the urine, which could also cause a deficiency. A severe magnesium deficiency can cause muscle weakness, seizures, fatigue, depression, and irregular heart beats.

Table TIPS

Magnificent Magnesium

Sprinkle chopped almonds over your morning whole-grain cereal for two crunchy sources of magnesium.

Add baby spinach to your salad.

Add rinsed, canned beans to salsa for a veggie dip with a magnesium punch.

Spread peanut butter on whole-wheat crackers for a satisfying afternoon snack.

Try precooked brown rice for an easy way to add whole grains to your dinner!

exploring
Chloride

What Is Chloride?

Chloride is a form of chlorine, an element you've surely smelled in bleach. Chlorine is a powerful disinfectant that if inhaled or ingested can be poisonous.

Fortunately, most of the chlorine in your body is in the nontoxic form of chloride (Cl^-). Chloride is part of hydrochloric acid, a strong acid in your stomach that enhances protein digestion and kills harmful bacteria that may be consumed with your foods.

Functions of Chloride

Chloride Helps Maintain Fluid Balance and Acid-Base Balance

Sodium and chloride are the major electrolytes outside your cells and in your blood. They help maintain fluid balance between these two compartments. Chloride also acts as a buffer to help keep your blood at a normal pH.

Daily Needs

Adults age 19 to 50 should consume 2,300 milligrams of chloride a day.

Food Sources

Sodium chloride, which is 60 percent chloride, is the main source of chloride in your diet, so the food sources for it are the same as those for sodium (**Figure 8.22**).

Because Americans consume plenty of salt, it is estimated that they are consuming, on average, 3,400 milligrams to just over 7,000 milligrams of dietary chloride daily.

Too Much or Too Little

Because sodium chloride is the major source of chloride in the diet, the upper level for adults for chloride is set at 3,600 milligrams to coincide with the upper level for sodium.[53]

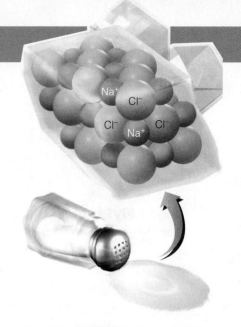

Figure 8.22 Table Salt Is Composed of Sodium and Chloride

A chloride deficiency rarely occurs in healthy individuals. Individuals who experience significant bouts of vomiting and diarrhea may become deficient as chloride is lost from the body.

exploring
Sulfur

What Is Sulfur?

Sulfur is typically found in your body as part of other compounds. For example, sulfur is part of the vitamins thiamin, biotin, and pantothenic acid.

Functions of Sulfur

Sulfur Helps Shape Some Amino Acids

The amino acids methionine, cystine, and cysteine all contain sulfur. The sulfur part of these amino acids helps give some proteins their three-dimensional shape. This enables these proteins to perform effectively as enzymes and hormones.[54]

Sulfites Are Preservatives

Sulfur-based substances called *sulfites* are often used as a preservative by food manufacturers. They help prevent food

spoilage and discoloration. (We discuss sulfites further in Chapter 13.)

Food Sources

Foods that contain the amino acids mentioned above are the major dietary sources of sulfur. A varied diet that contains meat, poultry, fish, eggs, legumes, dairy foods, fruits, and vegetables will provide sulfur.

Daily Needs and Too Much or Too Little

There isn't any recommendation for the amount of sulfur to be consumed daily, nor are there any known toxicity or deficiency symptoms. Most people get plenty of sulfur in their diet.

Iron

What Is Iron?

Iron is the most abundant mineral on Earth, and the most abundant trace mineral in your body. A 130-pound female has more than 2,300 milligrams of iron in her body—about the weight of a dime—whereas a 165-pound male will have 4,000 milligrams of iron in his body—slightly less than the weight of two dimes.

As a key component of blood, iron is highly valuable to the body and is treated accordingly. For the most part, iron is not excreted in the urine or stool, so once absorbed very little of it leaves the body. Approximately 95 percent of your iron is recycled and reused.[55] Whereas some iron is shed in hair, skin, and sloughed-off intestinal cells, most iron loss is due to bleeding.

Iron Occurs in Two Forms: Heme and Nonheme

Foods from animal sources, such as meat, poultry, and fish, provide heme iron in your diet. Heme iron (**Figure 8.23**) is part of the protein **hemoglobin** in your red blood cells and the protein **myoglobin** in your muscles. Heme iron is easily absorbed by your body.

Plant foods such as grains and vegetables are the main sources of nonheme iron in your diet. Nonheme iron is not as easily absorbed as heme iron. This is because other compounds in foods, such as phytates in legumes, rice, and grains, the polyphenols in tea, and the protein in soy products, all inhibit its absorption.

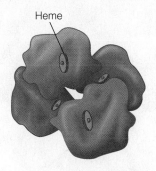

Heme

Figure 8.23 Hemoglobin Contains Heme Iron

In general, your body absorbs only about 10 to 15 percent of the iron you eat. However, if your body stores are low, the amount you absorb from foods will increase. You can enhance your nonheme iron absorption by eating a food that's high in vitamin C along with iron-rich foods. Vitamin C and the acids in your stomach change the configuration of nonheme iron, which improves its absorption. As little as 25 milligrams of vitamin C—the amount in about one-quarter cup of orange juice—can double the amount of nonheme iron you absorb from your meal, and 50 milligrams of vitamin C can increase the amount absorbed about sixfold.[56] Keep this in mind when you make your next peanut butter-on-whole-wheat sandwich and have an orange for dessert.

Another way to enhance nonheme iron absorption from foods is to eat meat, fish, or poultry at the same meal as the nonheme iron–containing food. The peptides in these animal-derived foods are thought to be the enhancing factors. The meat in your next turkey sandwich will help enhance the absorption of the nonheme iron in the whole-wheat bread.

Functions of Iron

Hemoglobin and Myoglobin Transport Oxygen

Approximately two-thirds of the iron in your body is in hemoglobin, the oxygen-carrying transport protein in your red blood cells. The iron-containing heme group binds with oxygen from your lungs and is transported to your tissues for their use. Hemoglobin also picks up carbon dioxide waste products from your cells and brings them to your lungs to be exhaled from your body. Similarly, iron is part of the myoglobin that transports and stores oxygen in your muscles.

Iron Is Needed for Brain Function

Iron helps enzymes that are involved in the synthesis of neurotransmitters in your brain, which send messages to the rest of your body. A deficiency of iron in children can reduce their ability to learn and retain information. Studies have shown that children with iron-deficiency anemia in their early years can have persistent, decreased cognitive ability during their later school years.[57]

Daily Needs

Adult females, age 19 to 50, need 18 milligrams daily to cover the iron lost during menstruation. During pregnancy, a woman's iron needs increase

hemoglobin The oxygen-carrying, heme-containing protein found in red blood cells.

myoglobin The oxygen-carrying, heme-containing protein found in muscle cells.

CONTINUED

Iron

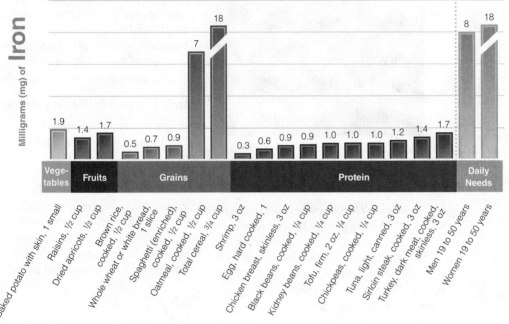

Figure 8.24 Iron Content of Selected Foods

to 27 milligrams per day to support her growing fetus. After a woman stops menstruating, usually around age 50, her daily iron needs drop to 8 milligrams because she is no longer losing blood monthly.

Adult males need 8 milligrams of dietary iron daily. These recommendations for women and men take into account a typical American diet, which includes both heme and nonheme iron sources.

Adult men consume more than twice their recommended iron needs—more than 17 milligrams, on average, daily.[58] Adult premenopausal women consume only about 70 percent of their daily need, or approximately 13 to 14 milligrams, on average.[59] Postmenopausal women consume approximately 13 milligrams of iron daily, so, like men, they are meeting their needs.

The iron needs of vegetarians are 1.8 times higher than those of nonvegetarians due to components in plant foods that inhibit iron absorption.[60]

Food Sources (T/F)

About half of Americans' dietary iron intake comes from iron-enriched bread and other grain foods such as cereals (**Figure 8.24**). Heme iron in meat, fish, and poultry contributes only 12 percent of the dietary iron needs of males and females. Cooking foods in iron pans and skillets can increase their nonheme iron content, as foods absorb iron from the pan.[61]

Too Much or Too Little

Consuming too much iron from supplements can cause constipation, nausea, vomiting, and diarrhea. The upper level for iron for adults is set at 45 milligrams daily, as this level is slightly less than the amount known to cause these intestinal symptoms. This upper level doesn't apply to individuals with liver disease or other diseases, such as hemochromatosis, which can affect iron stores in the body. It is too high for these individuals.

In the United States, the accidental consumption of supplements containing iron is a leading cause of poisoning deaths in children under age 6. Ingestion of as little as 200 milligrams of iron has been shown to be fatal. Children who swallow iron supplements can experience symptoms such as nausea, vomiting, and diarrhea within minutes. Intestinal bleeding can also occur, which can lead to shock, coma, and even death. The FDA has mandated that a warning statement about the risk of iron poisoning in small children be put on every iron supplement label.[62]

Excessive storing of iron in the body over several years is called iron overload and, if undetected, can damage a person's tissues and organs, including the heart, kidneys, liver, and nervous system. **Hemochromatosis**, a genetic disorder in which individuals absorb too much dietary iron, can cause iron overload. Though this condition is congenital, its symptoms often aren't manifested until adulthood. If not diagnosed and treated early enough, organ damage can occur. These individuals need to avoid iron supplements throughout their lives, as well as large amounts of vitamin C supplements, which enhance iron absorption.

Iron overload from consuming too much dietary iron has occurred in South Africans and Zimbabwean natives who consume large amounts of beer.[63] The iron content in the particular beer that they drink is high: 80 milligrams per liter. However, these individuals may also have a genetic disorder that contributes to excessive iron storage in the body. It is not known if excessive amounts of dietary iron alone in healthy individuals could cause iron overload.

The jury is still out about the role of iron in heart disease. Some studies suggest that iron can stimulate free radical production in the body, which can damage the arteries leading to the heart. Though this association is not definite, unless you are medically diagnosed with iron deficiency, it doesn't make any sense to consume excessive amounts of iron.

Iron deficiency is the most common nutritional disorder in the world. If your diet is deficient in iron, your body stores will be slowly depleted so as to keep your blood hemoglobin in a normal range. **Iron-deficiency anemia** occurs when your stores are so depleted that your hemoglobin levels decrease (**Figure 8.25**). This will diminish the

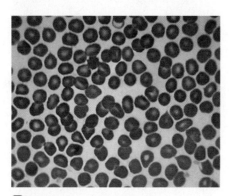

a Normal red blood cells

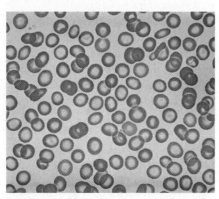

b Red blood cells affected by anemia

Figure 8.25 Normal and Anemic Red Blood Cells
Red blood cells affected by anemia are small and pale in color compared with normal red blood cells due to lower heme concentration.

Table TIPS

Ironing Out Your Iron Needs

Enjoy an iron-enriched whole-grain cereal along with a glass of vitamin C–rich orange juice to boost the nonheme iron absorption from your bowl of cereal.

Add plenty of salsa (vitamin C) to your bean burritos to enhance the absorption of the nonheme iron in both the beans and the flour tortilla.

Stuff a cooked baked potato (nonheme iron, vitamin C) with shredded cooked chicken (heme iron) and broccoli (vitamin C) and top it with melted low-fat cheese for a delicious dinner.

Eat a small box of raisins (nonheme iron) and a clementine or tangerine (vitamin C) as a sweet, iron-rich afternoon snack.

Add chickpeas (nonheme iron) to your salad greens (vitamin C). Don't forget the tomato wedges for another source of iron-enhancing vitamin C.

delivery of oxygen through the body, causing fatigue and weakness. Premenopausal females, menstruating women and teenage girls (especially those with heavy blood losses), pregnant women (because of their increased iron needs), preterm and low-birth-weight infants, and older infants and toddlers are at risk of developing iron-deficiency anemia because they often fall short of the recommended dietary amounts.[64] (This is discussed further in Chapters 14 and 15.)

hemochromatosis A genetic disorder that causes the body to store excessive amounts of iron.

iron-deficiency anemia An anemia caused by low hemoglobin levels due to insufficient dietary intake and absorption of iron.

Copper

What Is Copper?

Copper may bring to mind ancient tools, great sculptures, or American pennies (although pennies are no longer made of solid copper), but it is also associated with several key body functions.

Functions of Copper

Copper is part of many enzymes and proteins. It is important for iron absorption and transfer and the synthesis of hemoglobin and red blood cells. Copper helps generate energy in your cells, synthesize melanin (the dark pigment found in skin), and link the proteins collagen and elastin together in connective tissue. It works with enzymes to protect your cells from free radicals. Copper also plays an important role in blood clotting and in maintaining a healthy immune system.[65]

Daily Needs

Both adult women and men need 900 micrograms of copper daily. American women consume 1,200 micrograms, whereas men consume 1,500 micrograms daily, on average.

Food Sources

Organ meats such as liver, seafood, nuts, and seeds are abundant in copper (**Figure 8.26**). Bran cereals, whole-grain products, and cocoa are also good sources. Whereas potatoes, milk, and chicken are low in copper, they are consumed in such abundant amounts that they contribute a fair amount of copper to Americans' diets.

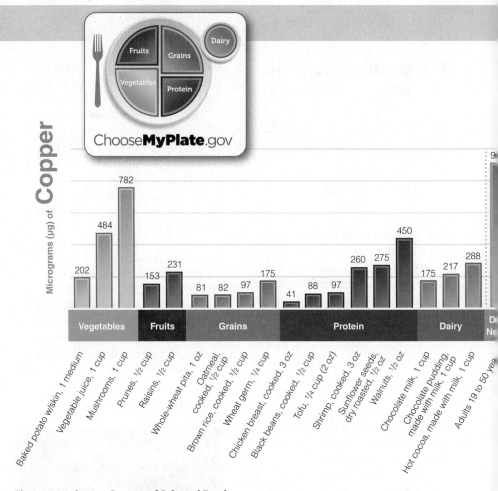

Figure 8.26 Copper Content of Selected Foods

Too Much or Too Little

Too much copper can cause stomach pains and cramps, nausea, diarrhea, vomiting, and even liver damage. The upper level for copper for adults is set at 10,000 micrograms daily.

Copper deficiency is rare in the United States. It has occurred in premature babies fed milk formulas, malnourished infants fed cow's milk, and individuals given intravenous feedings that lacked adequate amounts of copper.

Table TIPS

Counting Your Copper

Make your hot cocoa with milk, rather than water, for two sources (cocoa and milk) of copper in your mug.

Mix raisins with your brown rice at dinner.

Top chocolate pudding with a sprinkling of crushed walnuts for a dessert that is both sweet and crunchy.

Choose sunflower seeds for an afternoon snack.

Ladle black beans and salsa into a whole-wheat pita. Top with reduced-fat cheddar cheese. Zap it in the microwave for a Mexican lunch with a copper kick.

What Is Zinc?

Zinc is found in almost every cell of your body. It is involved in the function of more than 100 enzymes, including those used for protein synthesis. As important as it is, it was not considered an essential nutrient until 1974.

Functions of Zinc

Zinc Is Needed for DNA Synthesis and Growth and Development

Zinc plays a role in the structure of both RNA and DNA in your cells and in gene expression. Zinc is needed for adequate growth in developing infants and throughout the adolescent years.[66]

Zinc Helps Keep Your Immune System Healthy and Helps Wounds Heal

Zinc is needed for production of white blood cells, so it helps keep your immune system healthy. It helps reduce the inflammation that can accompany skin wounds. Zinc also helps in wound healing by being part of enzymes and proteins that repair and enhance the proliferation of skin cells.[67]

Zinc Brings Out the Best in Your Taste Buds

One lick of a chocolate ice cream cone or a forkful of cherry cheesecake will make you appreciate the role that zinc plays in taste acuity, which is the ability to savor the flavors of your foods. A deficiency of zinc has been shown to alter taste perceptions.[68]

Zinc and the Common Cold

A recent review of 15 randomly controlled studies of healthy individuals has shown promise that zinc can affect the common cold. In these studies, those who consumed zinc lozenges or syrup within 24 hours of the onset of the first sniffle or sneeze appeared to somewhat benefit from a reduction in the duration and severity of a cold. These were healthy individuals so it is too early to say if these results would occur in people with chronic illnesses or a compromised immune system. Also, those who took zinc lozenges were more likely to experience (T/F) side effects such as nausea. More studies are needed to determine if zinc could be safely used in the general population to treat the common cold, and to determine a safe dose and appropriate duration without adverse effects.[69]

Recent research suggests that zinc lozenges and nasal gels may help reduce the severity and duration of cold symptoms.

Zinc May Help Fight AMD

Research studies do support the assertion that zinc may play a role in reducing the risk of age-related macular degeneration (AMD), a condition that hampers central vision. Zinc may work with an enzyme in your eyes that's needed to properly utilize vitamin A for vision. Zinc may also help mobilize vitamin A from the liver to ensure adequate blood levels of this vitamin. Supplements that contain antioxidants along with zinc have been shown to reduce the risk of AMD.[70] (See the section on antioxidants in Chapter 7.)

Daily Needs

Adult males need 11 milligrams of zinc, whereas women need 8 milligrams daily. American adults, on average, are meeting their daily zinc needs. Men are consuming approximately 14 milligrams and women are consuming 10 milligrams of zinc daily, on average.

Vegetarians, especially strict vegetarians, can have as much as a 50 percent higher need for zinc. Phytates in grains and legumes, which are staples of vegan diets, can bind with zinc, reducing its absorption in the intestinal tract.

Food Sources

Red meat, some seafood, and whole grains are excellent sources of zinc (**Figure 8.27**). Because zinc is found in the germ and bran portion of the grain, refined grains stripped of these components have as much as 80 percent less zinc than whole grains.

CONTINUED

Zinc

ZINC

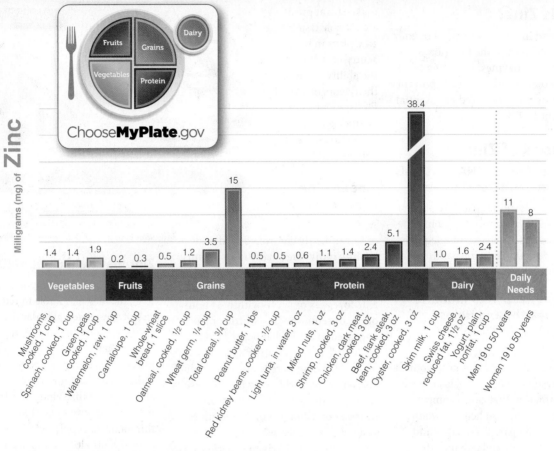

Figure 8.27 Zinc Content of Selected Foods

Milligrams (mg) of **Zinc**

Food	mg
Mushrooms, cooked, 1 cup	1.4
Spinach, cooked, 1 cup	1.4
Green peas, cooked, 1 cup	1.9
Watermelon, raw, 1 cup	0.2
Cantaloupe, 1 cup	0.3
Whole-wheat bread, 1 slice	0.5
Oatmeal, cooked, 1/2 cup	1.2
Wheat germ, 1/4 cup	3.5
Total cereal, 3/4 cup	15
Peanut butter, 1 tbs	0.5
Red kidney beans, cooked, 1/2 cup	0.5
Light tuna, in water, 3 oz	0.6
Mixed nuts, 1 oz	1.1
Shrimp, cooked, 3 oz	1.4
Chicken, dark meat, cooked, 3 oz	2.4
Beef, flank steak, lean, cooked, 3 oz	5.1
Oyster, cooked, 3 oz	38.4
Skim milk, 1 cup	1.0
Swiss cheese, reduced fat, 1 1/2 oz	1.6
Yogurt, plain, nonfat, 1 cup	2.4
Men 19 to 50 years (Daily Needs)	11
Women 19 to 50 years (Daily Needs)	8

Too Much or Too Little

The upper level for zinc in food and/ or supplements for adults is set at 40 milligrams daily. Consuming too much zinc, as little as 50 milligrams, can cause stomach pains, nausea, vomiting, and diarrhea. Approximately 60 milligrams of zinc daily has been shown to lower the level of copper in your body by competing with this mineral for absorption in the intestinal tract. This is an excellent example of how the overconsumption of one mineral can compromise the benefits of another.

Excessive amounts, such as 300 milligrams of zinc daily, have been shown to suppress the immune system and lower blood levels of HDL ("good") cholesterol.[71]

A deficiency of zinc can cause hair loss, loss of appetite, impaired taste of foods, diarrhea, and delayed sexual maturation, as well as impotence and skin rashes.

Because zinc is needed during development, a deficiency can slow and impair growth. Classic studies of groups of people in the Middle East showed that people who consumed a diet mainly of unleavened bread, which is high in zinc-binding phytates, experienced impaired growth and dwarfism.[72]

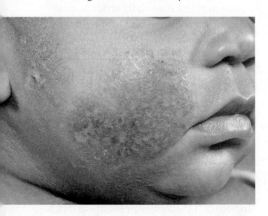

Skin rash is one of the symptoms of zinc deficiency.

Table TIPS

Zapping Your Zinc Needs!

Enjoy a tuna fish sandwich on whole-wheat bread at lunch for a double serving (fish and bread) of zinc.

Add kidney beans to your cup of soup. (These beans are often at cafeteria salad bars, so add a spoonful to your soup-and-salad lunch.)

Pack a small handful of mixed nuts and raisins in a zip-closed bag for a snack on the run.

Top your breakfast yogurt with cereal for two servings of zinc in one bowl!

Add cooked green peas to casseroles, stews, soups, and salads.

Selenium

What Is Selenium?

The mineral selenium is often incorporated into a class of proteins called selenoproteins, many of which are enzymes. Selenoproteins have important functions in your body.

Functions of Selenium

Selenium Is Needed by Your Thyroid

Selenium-containing enzymes help regulate thyroid hormones in your body.

Selenium Plays an Antioxidant Role

Selenoproteins can also function as antioxidants that protect your cells from free radicals. (See the section on antioxidants in Chapter 7.) As you recall, free radicals are natural by-products of metabolism and can also result from exposure to chemicals in the environment. If free radicals accumulate faster than your body can neutralize them, their damaging effects can contribute to chronic diseases, such as heart disease.[73]

Selenium May Help Fight Cancer

Research studies have suggested that deaths from cancers, such as lung, colon, and prostate cancers, are lower in groups of people that consume more selenium. Selenium's antioxidant capabilities, and its ability to potentially slow the growth of tumors, are thought to be the mechanism behind its anticancer effects.

The FDA now allows a Qualified Health Claim on food labels and dietary supplements stating that "selenium may reduce the risk of certain cancers but the evidence is limited and not conclusive to date."[74]

Daily Needs

Both adult females and males need 55 micrograms of selenium daily. American adults are more than meeting their needs—they consume about 94 micrograms to 134 micrograms daily, on average.

Food Sources

Meat, seafood, pasta, grains, dairy foods, and fruits and vegetables can all contribute to dietary selenium (**Figure 8.28**). However, the amount of selenium in the foods you eat depends upon the soil where the plants were grown and the animals grazed. For example, wheat grown in selenium-rich soil can have more than ten times as much selenium as an identical wheat grown in selenium-poor soil.

CONTINUED

Selenium

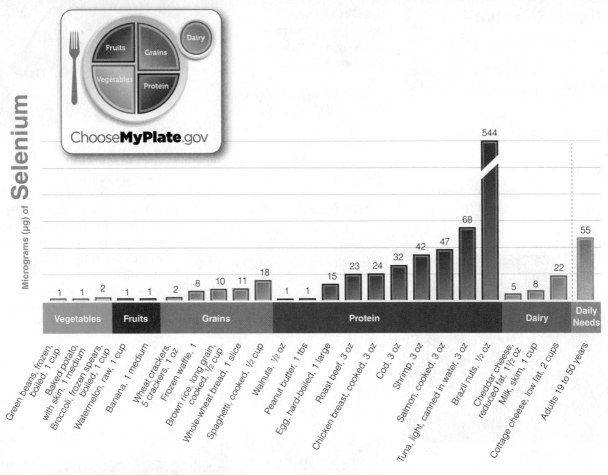

Figure 8.28 Selenium Content of Selected Foods

Too Much or Too Little

Too much selenium can cause toxicity and a condition called **selenosis**. A person with selenosis will have brittle nails and hair, both of which may fall out. Other symptoms include stomach and intestinal discomfort, a skin rash, garlicky breath, fatigue, and damage to the nervous system. The upper level for selenium for adults is set at

selenosis The presence of toxic levels of selenium.

Keshan disease A disease related to a deficiency of selenium.

400 micrograms per day to prevent the loss and brittleness of nails and hair, which is the most common symptom of selenosis.

Though rare in the United States, a selenium deficiency can cause **Keshan disease**, which damages the heart. This disease typically only occurs in children who live in rural areas that have selenium-poor soil. However, some researchers speculate that selenium deficiency alone may not cause Keshan disease; the selenium-deficient individual may also be exposed to a virus, which, together with the selenium deficiency, leads to the damaged heart.[75]

TableTIPS

Seeking Out Selenium

Top a toasted whole-wheat bagel with a slice of reduced-fat cheddar cheese.

Spread peanut butter on whole-wheat crackers and top with a slice of banana.

Top your dinner pasta with broccoli for a selenium-smart meal.

Zap sliced apples, sprinkled with a little apple juice and cinnamon, in the microwave and top with vanilla yogurt.

Spoon a serving of low-fat cottage cheese into a bowl and top with canned sliced pears and walnuts.

What Is Fluoride?

Fluoride is the safe ion form of fluorine, a poisonous gas. Calcium fluoride is the form that is found in your bones and teeth.

Functions of Fluoride

Fluoride Protects against Dental Caries

The best known function of fluoride is its role in keeping teeth healthy. Your teeth have an outer layer called enamel (**Figure 8.29**), which can become eroded over time by acids and result in dental caries. The acids are produced by the bacteria in your mouth when they feast on the carbohydrates that you eat. Continual exposure of your teeth to these acids can cause erosion and create a cavity.

Fluoride from food, beverages, and dental products, such as toothpaste, helps protect your teeth in several ways. It helps to repair the enamel that has already started to erode, and it interferes with the ability of the bacteria to metabolize carbohydrates, thus reducing the amount of acid they produce. Finally, fluoride provides a protective barrier between your tooth and the destructive acids. As a component of saliva, it provides a continual fluoride bath to your teeth's surfaces.[76]

Consuming adequate amounts of fluoride is extremely important during infancy and childhood, when teeth

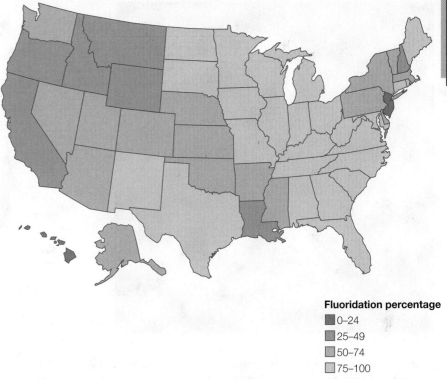

Fluoridation percentage
- 0–24
- 25–49
- 50–74
- 75–100

Figure 8.30 Percentage of Americans Living in Communities with a Fluoridated Water Supply, by State, 2006

Source: National Center for Chronic Disease Prevention and Health Promotion, Oral Health Branch. 2013. Oral Health Maps. Available at www.cdc.gov. Accessed July 2013.

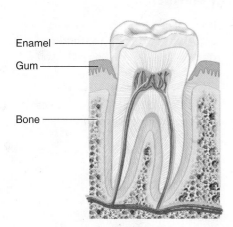

Enamel
Gum
Bone

Figure 8.29 Structure of a Tooth

are developing, and for maintenance of healthy teeth throughout your life.

Fluoride in Drinking Water Has Improved the Nation's Dental Health

In the 1930s, scientists noticed lower rates of dental caries among individuals whose community water systems contained significant amounts of fluoride. Studies confirmed that the fluoride was the protective factor in the water that helped fight dental decay. Since 1945, most communities have fluoridated their water, and today, almost 74 percent of Americans live in communities that have a fluoridated water supply (**Figure 8.30**).

The increase in access to fluoridated water is one of the major reasons why there has been a decline in dental caries in the United States, and fluoridation of water is considered one of the ten greatest public health advances of the twentieth century.[77]

To find out if your community water is fluoridated and how much fluoride is added, visit the Centers for Disease Control and Prevention's website, My Water's Fluoride, at http://apps.nccd.cdc.gov/MWF/Index.asp.

Daily Needs

Adult men should consume 3.8 milligrams and women 3.1 milligrams of fluoride daily to meet their needs. If the tap water in your community is fluoridated at 0.7 milligram/liter, you would have to consume more than 15 cups of water daily, through either beverages or cooking, to meet your fluoride needs (1 liter = 4.2 cups). The toothpaste that you use to brush your teeth can also be a source of fluoride.

Food Sources

Foods in general are not a good source of fluoride. The best sources are fluoridated water and beverages and foods

CONTINUED

Fluoride

made with this water, such as coffee, tea, and soups. Another source of fluoride can be juices made from concentrate using fluoridated tap water.

If you shy away from tap water and drink and cook predominantly with bottled water, you may be robbing yourself of some cavity protection. Most bottled waters sold in the United States have less than the optimal amount of fluoride. It is difficult to determine the fluoride content of many bottled waters because currently, the amount of fluoride in bottled water has to be listed on the label only if fluoride has been specifically added. Check the label to see if your bottled water contains added fluoride. For more information about the differences between bottled and tap water, and their advantages and disadvantages, see the Nutrition in the Real World feature "Tap Water or Bottled Water: Is Bottled Better?" on page 288.

Too Much or Too Little

Because of fluoride's protective qualities, too little exposure to or consumption of fluoride increases the risk of dental caries.

fluorosis A condition caused by excess amounts of fluoride, resulting in mottling of the teeth.

Having some fluoride is important for healthy teeth, but too much can cause **fluorosis**, a condition whereby the teeth become pitted and develop white patches or stains on the surface, which can become brownish as the disease progresses. Fluorosis creates teeth that are extremely resistant to caries but cosmetically unappealing (see photo).

Fluorosis occurs when teeth are forming, so only infants and children up to 8 years of age are at risk. Once teeth break through the gums, fluorosis can't occur. Fluorosis results from overfluoridation of water, the misuse of dietary fluoride supplements, or excessive use of dental products that contain fluoride.[78]

Skeletal fluorosis can occur in bones when a person consumes at least 10 milligrams of fluoride daily for 10 or more years. This is a rare situation

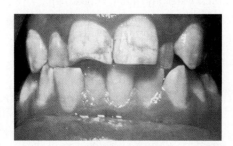

Teeth pitted by fluorosis

that occurs when water is mistakenly overfluoridated. This can cause bone concentrations of fluoride that are up to five times higher than normal and result in stiffness or pain in joints, osteoporosis, and calcification of the ligaments.[79]

The upper level for adults has been set at 10 milligrams to reduce the risk of fluorosis in the bones. (Note, however, that the upper level for infants and children is much lower, to prevent fluorosis in teeth. See the inside cover of the textbook for this upper level.)

Table TIPS

Fabulous Ways to Get Fluoride

Pour orange juice into ice cube trays and pop a couple of frozen cubes into a glass of tap water for a refreshing and flavorful beverage.

Use tap water when making coffee, tea, or juice from concentrate, and for food preparation.

Brew a mug of flavored decaffeinated tea, such as French vanilla or gingerbread, to keep you warm while you're hitting the books.

exploring
Chromium

What Is Chromium?

The most recent mineral to be found necessary in humans, chromium, was identified as an essential mineral in 1977, although researchers have had an interest in chromium and its roles in the metabolism of glucose since the 1950s.

Functions of Chromium

Chromium Helps Insulin in Your Body

The main function of this mineral is to increase insulin's effectiveness in cells. The hormone insulin plays an important role in the metabolism and storage of carbohydrates, fats, and protein in your body. Individuals who were intravenously fed a chromium-free diet experienced high blood levels of glucose, weight loss, and nerve problems—all telltale signs of uncontrolled diabetes and poor blood glucose control. The problems were corrected when chromium was provided.[80]

Chromium May Reduce Prediabetes

Because it works with insulin, some researchers think that chromium may help individuals who have diabetes mellitus or prediabetes (glucose intolerance) improve their blood glucose control. There has yet to be a large research study in the United States that confirms this theory.

One small study suggests that a chromium supplement may reduce the risk of insulin resistance, and therefore,

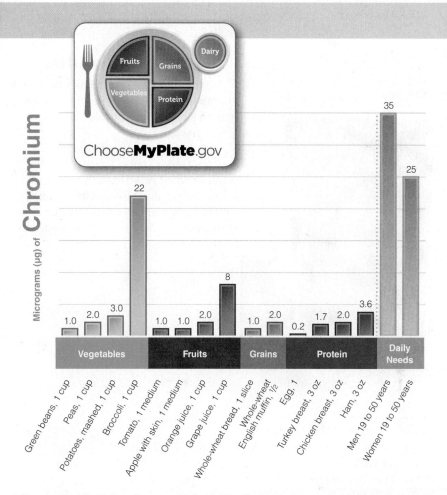

Figure 8.31 **Chromium Content of Selected Foods**

favorably affect the handling of glucose in the body.[81] Improving the body's sensitivity to insulin and maintaining a normal blood glucose level can possibly lower the incidence of type 2 diabetes in individuals at risk.

Based on this one study, the FDA has allowed a Qualified Health Claim on chromium supplements. However, the supplement label must state that the evidence regarding the relationship between chromium supplements and either insulin resistance or type 2 diabetes is not certain at this time.[82]

Chromium Does Not Help Build Muscle Mass

Although advertisements have sometimes touted chromium supplements as an aid to losing weight and building lean muscle, the research doesn't support the claim. A review of more than 20 research studies didn't find any benefits from

taking up to 1,000 micrograms of chromium daily.[83] If you are trying to become lean and mean, taking chromium supplements isn't going to help.

Daily Needs

Adult men age 19 to 50 need 30 to 35 micrograms of chromium daily, whereas women of the same age need 20 to 25 micrograms daily, on average, depending upon their age. It is estimated that American men consume 39 to 54 micrograms of chromium from foods, and women consume 23 to 29 micrograms, on average, daily.[84]

Food Sources

Grains are good sources of chromium. Meat, eggs, and poultry and some fruits and vegetables can also provide chromium, whereas dairy foods are low in the mineral (**Figure 8.31**).

CONTINUED

Chromium

Too Much or Too Little

As yet, there is no known risk from consuming excessive amounts of chromium from food or supplements, so no upper level has been set.

A chromium deficiency is very rare in the United States. The jury is still out on whether individuals with diabetes who did not have a chromium deficiency would benefit by taking a supplement. More research is needed in this area.[85]

Table TIPS

Cram in the Chromium

Toast a whole-wheat English muffin and top it with a slice of lean ham for a meaty, chromium-laden breakfast.

Add broccoli florets to your salad for a chromium-packed lunch.

Try an afternoon glass of cold grape juice for a refreshing break. Add an apple for a double dose of chromium.

Combine mashed potatoes and peas for a sweet and starchy addition to your dinner plate and your chromium count.

Slice tomatoes on your sandwich for a chromium-rich lunch.

exploring

Iodine

What Is Iodine?

Like the fluoridation of community drinking water, the iodization of salt was a significant advance for public health in the United States. Prior to the 1920s, many Americans suffered from the iodine-deficiency disease, goiter. Once salt manufacturers began adding iodine to their product, incidence of the disease dropped. Today, rates of the disease are very low in the United States, though not in other parts of the world.

Functions of Iodine

Iodine is an essential mineral for your thyroid, a butterfly-shaped gland located in your neck (**Figure 8.32**). The thyroid needs iodine to make some essential hormones. In fact, approximately 60 percent of your thyroid hormones are comprised of iodine.

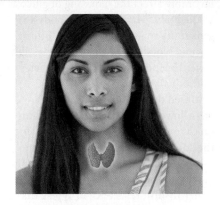

Figure 8.32 Location of Thyroid Gland

Thyroid hormones affect the majority of your cells, regulate your metabolic rate, and help your heart, nerves, muscles, and intestines function properly. Children need thyroid hormones for normal bone growth and brain development.[86]

Daily Needs

Adult men and women need 150 micrograms of iodine daily to meet their needs. Americans currently consume 230 micrograms to 410 micrograms of iodine daily, on average, depending upon their age and gender.

Food Sources

The amount of iodine that occurs naturally in foods is typically low, approximately 3 to 75 micrograms in a serving, and is influenced by the amount of iodine in the soil, water, and fertilizers used to grow foods (**Figure 8.33**).

Fish can provide higher amounts of iodine, as they concentrate it from seawater. Iodized salt provides 400 micrograms of iodine per teaspoon. Note that

Iodine

not all salt has added iodine. Kosher salt, for example, has no additives, including iodine. Processed foods that use iodized salt or iodine-containing preservatives are also a source.

Too Much or Too Little

Consuming too much iodine can challenge the thyroid, impairing its function and reducing the synthesis and release of thyroid hormones. Because of this, the upper level for adults for iodine is 1,100 micrograms.

An early sign of iodine deficiency is **goiter**, which is an enlarged thyroid gland. An iodine-deficient thyroid has to work harder to make the thyroid hormones, causing it to become enlarged.[87]

A deficiency of iodine during the early stages of fetal development can damage the brain of the developing baby, causing mental retardation. Inadequate iodine during this critical time can cause lower IQ scores. Depending upon the severity of the iodine deficiency, **cretinism**, also known as *congenital hypothyroidism* can occur. Individuals with cretinism can experience abnormal sexual development, mental retardation, and dwarfism.

Early detection of an iodine deficiency and treatment in children is critical to avoiding irreversible damage.

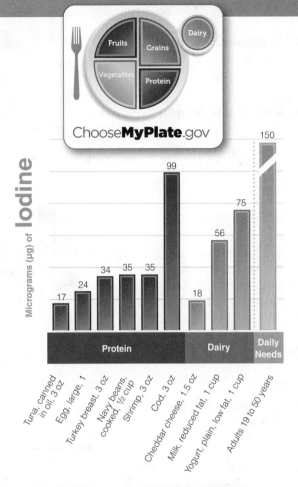

ChooseMyPlate.gov

Microgram (μg) of **Iodine**

Food	μg
Tuna, canned in oil, 3 oz	17
Egg, large, 1	24
Turkey breast, 3 oz	34
Navy beans, cooked, ½ cup	35
Shrimp, 3 oz	35
Cod, 3 oz	99
Cheddar cheese, 1.5 oz	18
Milk, reduced fat, 1 cup	56
Yogurt, plain, low fat, 1 cup	75
Adults 19 to 50 years	150

Protein — Dairy — Daily Needs

Figure 8.33 Iodine Content of Selected Foods

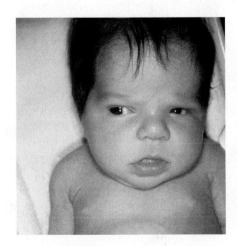

Cretinism can result in a child born to a mother who was iodine deficient during early pregnancy.

Goiter is an enlarged thyroid gland caused by an iodine deficiency.

goiter Enlargement of the thyroid gland, mostly due to iodine deficiency.

cretinism A condition caused by a deficiency of thyroid hormone during prenatal development, resulting in abnormal mental and physical development in children. It is also known as *congenital hypothyroidism*.

exploring
Manganese

What Is Manganese?

Manganese is either part of, or activates, many enzymes in your body.

Functions of Manganese

This mineral is involved in the metabolism of carbohydrates, fats, and amino acids. Manganese is needed for the formation of bone.

Daily Needs

Adult women need 1.8 milligrams, whereas men need 2.3 milligrams, of manganese daily. Americans are easily meeting their manganese needs. Adult women consume more than 2 milligrams of manganese daily, and adult men consume more than 2.8 milligrams daily, on average, from the foods in their diet.[88]

Food Sources

When it comes to meeting your manganese needs, look to whole grains, nuts, legumes, tea, vegetables, and fruits such as pineapples, strawberries, and bananas (**Figure 8.34**). A teaspoon of ground cinnamon provides just under 0.5 milligram of manganese.

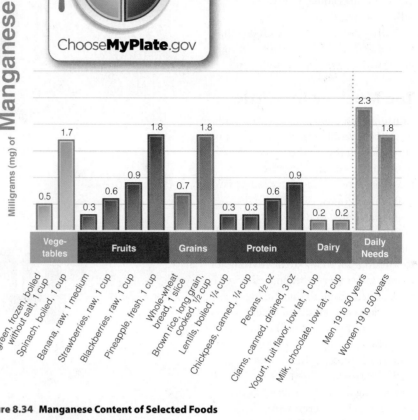

Figure 8.34 Manganese Content of Selected Foods

Too Much or Too Little

Manganese toxicity, which has occurred in miners who have inhaled manganese dust, can cause damage to the nervous system and symptoms that resemble Parkinson's disease.[89] A study of individuals who drank water with high levels of manganese showed that they also experienced Parkinson's disease–like symptoms.

To protect against this toxicity, the upper level has been set at 11 milligrams daily.

A deficiency of manganese is rare in healthy individuals who have a balanced diet. Individuals fed a manganese-deficient diet developed a rash and scaly skin.

Table TIPS

Managing Your Manganese

Sprinkle your whole-wheat toast with a dusting of cinnamon to spice up your morning.

Combine cooked brown rice, canned and rinsed lentils, and chickpeas for a dinner in a snap.

Spoon vanilla yogurt over canned crushed pineapple and sliced bananas for a tropical treat.

exploring
Molybdenum

What Is Molybdenum?

Molybdenum is part of several enzymes involved in the breakdown of certain amino acids and other compounds.

Daily Needs

Adult men and women need to consume 45 micrograms of molybdenum daily. American women currently consume 76 micrograms and men consume

109 micrograms of molybdenum daily, on average.

Food Sources

Legumes are excellent sources of molybdenum. Grains and nuts are also good sources.[90]

Too Much or Too Little

There is limited research on the adverse effects of too much dietary molybdenum in humans. In animal studies, too much can cause reproductive problems. Because of this finding in animals, the upper level for molybdenum in humans has been set at 2 milligrams for adults.

A deficiency of molybdenum has not been seen in healthy individuals. However, a deficiency was observed in an individual who was fed intravenously for years and developed symptoms that included rapid heart beats, headaches, and night blindness.

Other Minerals: Arsenic, Boron, Nickel, Silicon, and Vanadium

A few other minerals exist in your body, but their nutritional importance in humans has not yet been established. These minerals include arsenic, boron, nickel, silicon, and vanadium. Although limited research suggests that these may have a function in animals, there isn't enough data to confirm an essential role in humans.[91]

Table 8.1 on page 324 summarizes these minerals, their potential role in animal health, their food sources, and the levels of deficiency and toxicity, if known, in humans.

Table 8.1

Additional Minerals

Mineral	Potential Role and Deficiency Symptoms	Food Sources	Potential Toxicity
Arsenic	May be needed in the metabolism of a specific amino acid in rats. A deficiency may impair growth and reproduction in animals.	Dairy products, meat, poultry, fish, grains, and cereal products	No known adverse effect in humans from the organic form of arsenic found in foods. The inorganic form is poisonous to humans.
Boron	A deficiency may be associated with reproductive abnormalities in certain fish and frogs, which suggests a possible role in normal development in animals.	Grape juice, legumes, potatoes, pecans, peanut butter, apples, and milk	No known adverse effect from boron in food. Some research suggests that high amounts of boron may cause reproductive and developmental problems in animals. Because of this, the upper limit for human adults has been set at 20 mg daily, which is more than 10 times the amount American adults consume daily, on average.
Nickel	May be needed by specific enzymes in the body. It is considered an essential mineral in animals.	Grains and grain products, vegetables, legumes, nuts, and chocolate	No known toxicity of nickel in humans when consuming a normal diet. In rats, high exposure to nickel salts can cause toxicity, with symptoms such as lethargy, irregular breathing, and lower than normal weight gain. Because of this, the upper limit for adults is set at 1 mg daily for nickel salts.
Silicon	May be needed for bone formation in animals.	Grains, grain products, and vegetables	No known risk of silicon toxicity in humans from food sources.
Vanadium	In animals, vanadium has insulin-like actions and a deficiency increases the risk of abortion.	Mushrooms, shellfish, parsley, and black pepper	No known risk of toxicity in humans from vanadium in foods. Too much has been shown to cause kidney damage in animals. Vanadium can be purchased as supplements. Because of the known toxicity in animals, the upper limit for adults is set at 1.8 mg daily.

Source: Institute of Medicine. *Dietary Reference Intakes: Vitamin A, Vitamin K, Arsenic, Boron, Chromium, Copper, Iodine, Iron, Manganese, Molybdenum, Nickel, Silicon, Vanadium, and Zinc.* (Washington, D.C.: The National Academies Press, 2001). Available at www.nap.edu.

Putting Together All the Major Nutrients

Table 8.2 on page 325 and Table 8.3 on page 326 provide you with a summary of all the minerals and your needs.

Currently Americans, on average, meet many of their nutrient needs. As Table 8.4 on page 327 shows, however, our diets could still use a little fine-tuning to meet all of the recommendations for a healthy diet. Consuming a wide variety of foods from all the food groups, with an emphasis on whole grains, whole fruits, and vegetables along with adequate amounts of lean dairy and meat, poultry, and plenty of fluids, is the best diet prescription to meet your needs for carbohydrates, protein, fat, vitamins,

Table 8.2

Minerals at a Glance: Major Minerals

Major Minerals	Major Functions	Adult DRI, 19 to 50 years	Food Sources	Excessive/Toxicity Symptoms/UL	Deficiency Symptoms/ Conditions
Sodium	Major electrolyte outside the cell; helps regulate body water and blood pressure	1,500 mg/day	Processed foods, table salt, meat, seafood, milk, cheese, eggs	Hypertension UL: 2,300 mg/day	Rare in individuals consuming a healthy diet
Potassium	Major mineral inside the cell, needed for muscle contraction and nerve impulses; regulates body water and blood pressure	4,700 mg/day	Potatoes, melons, citrus fruits, most fruits and vegetables, meat, milk, legumes	Hyperkalemia	Hypokalemia
Calcium	Formation of bones and teeth, muscle contraction and relaxation, blood clotting, heart and nerve function	1,000 mg/day	Milk and dairy products, leafy greens, broccoli, salmon, sardines, tofu	Hypercalcemia UL: 2,500 mg/day	Osteoporosis
Phosphorus	Formation of bones and teeth	700 mg/day	Meat, fish, poultry, eggs, dairy, cereals	Hyperphosphatemia UL: 4,000 mg/day	Muscle weakness, bone pain, rickets, confusion, and death
Magnesium	Participates in muscle contraction and nerve conduction	310 to 420 mg/day	Meat, seafood, nuts, legumes, dairy, whole grains	Large intakes from supplements can cause diarrhea, cramps, and nausea	Rare
Chloride	Helps maintain fluid and acid-base balance	2,300 mg/day	Found as sodium chloride in foods	UL: 3,600 mg/day	Rare
Sulfur	A part of other compounds in body; helps give some amino acids their three-dimensional shape	None	Meats, fish, poultry, eggs, dairy foods, fruits, vegetables	None	None

minerals, and water. The Table Tips in this and the preceding chapters can help you with your diet fine-tuning.

The Take-Home Message Minerals are essential nutrients needed in relatively small amounts to enable your body to function properly. All minerals are inorganic elements. The body's absorption of minerals from foods varies, depending on their bioavailability. The seven major minerals are needed in amounts greater than 100 milligrams per day, and the nine trace minerals are needed in amounts less than 20 milligrams per day. Several minerals, particularly the trace minerals, can be toxic if consumed in high amounts.

Table 8.3

Minerals at a Glance: Trace Minerals

Trace Minerals	Major Functions	Adult DRI, 19 to 50 years	Food Sources	Excessive/Toxicity Symptoms/UL	Deficiency Symptoms/Conditions
Iron	As a major component of hemoglobin and myoglobin, helps transport oxygen throughout the body; enhances brain function	8 to 18 mg/day	Meat, fish, poultry, enriched and fortified breads and cereals	Vomiting, nausea, diarrhea, constipation, organ damage including the kidney and liver UL: 45 mg/day	Fatigue, iron-deficiency anemia, growth retardation in infants
Copper	A component of several enzymes; involved in iron transport; needed for healthy connective tissue enzymes; role in blood clotting and a healthy immune system	900 µg/day	Organ meats, nuts, seeds, cocoa, whole grains, legumes, and shellfish	Vomiting, abdominal pain, nausea, diarrhea, liver damage UL: 10,000 µg/day	Impaired growth and development
Zinc	Cofactor for several enzymes; DNA and RNA synthesis; needed for a healthy immune system, wound healing, and taste acuity	8 to 11 mg/day	Meat, poultry, seafood, whole grains	Nausea, vomiting, cramps, diarrhea, impaired immune function UL: 40 mg/day	Skin rash and hair loss, diarrhea, loss of taste and smell
Selenium	A component of enzymes; antioxidant	55 µg/day	Meat, seafood, fish, eggs, whole grains	Selenosis, brittle hair and nails, skin rash, garlic breath odor, fatigue UL: 400 µg/day	Keshan disease
Fluoride	Makes teeth stronger	3.1 to 3.8 mg/day	Fluoridated water, tea	Fluorosis in teeth and skeletal fluorosis UL: 10 mg/day	Increased susceptibility to dental caries
Chromium	Improves insulin response	20 to 35 µg/day	Pork, egg yolks, whole grains, nuts	Unconfirmed toxicity effects	Potential increase of insulin resistance
Iodine	Component of a thyroid hormone	150 µg/day	Iodized salt, seafood, dairy products	Impaired functioning of thyroid UL: 1,100 µg/day	Goiter, cretinism
Manganese	Cofactor involved in metabolism	1.8 to 2.3 mg/day	Beans, oats, nuts, tea	Abnormal central nervous system effects UL: 11 mg/day	Deficiency rare; rash and scaly skin
Molybdenum	Cofactor for a variety of enzymes	45 µg/day	Legumes, nuts, leafy vegetables, dairy, cereals	Unknown in humans UL: 2 mg/day	Unknown in humans

Table 8.4

Putting It All Together: Making Better Choices

American Adults Typically Consume Enough:	But Could Fine-Tune Their Dietary Choices to Include More:
Saturated fat	Unsaturated fat in place of saturated fat
Carbohydrates	Fiber-rich foods and fewer added sugars
Vitamins A, E, and K	Vitamin D if not exposed to adequate sunlight
B vitamins and vitamin C	Synthetic folic acid (premenopausal women only) Synthetic vitamin B_{12} (individuals 51+ years, vegans)
Sodium, phosphorus, zinc, selenium, chromium, copper, iodine, manganese, molybdenum	Potassium, calcium, magnesium, iron (premenopausal women, vegans), zinc (vegans), fluoride (if not consuming fluoridated water)
Fluids with added sugar	Fluids (water)

Fresh fruits and vegetables can be natural sources of multiple nutrients. Jicama (shown here) can add potassium, calcium, folate, and phosphorus to an afternoon snack.

MADE over MADE better

Snacks can be a great way to give your diet a mineral boost. Bananas, for example, are packed with potassium, raisins are naturally high in iron, peanuts are rich in magnesium, and cheese is a ringer for calcium. However, depending upon how these foods are processed, they may be higher in calories, fat, and saturated fat than you bargained for.

Here are some typical mineral-rich snacks made over and made nutritionally better!

If you like this. . .   Try this healthy alternative!

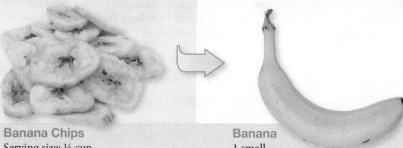

Banana Chips
Serving size: ½ cup
Calories: 300
Fat: 14 grams
Saturated Fat: 12 grams

Banana
1 small
Calories: 90
Fat: < 0.5 grams
Saturated Fat: 0 grams

Yogurt-Covered Raisins
Serving size: ½ cup
Calories: 280
Fat: 12 grams
Saturated Fat: 9 grams

Raisins
Serving size: ½ cup
Calories: 123
Fat: 0 grams
Saturated Fat: 0 grams

Trail Mix
Serving size: ½ cup
Calories: 300
Fat: 20 grams
Saturated Fat: 4 grams

Peanuts in Shell
Serving size: ½ cup
Calories: 170
Fat: 13 grams
Saturated Fat: 2 grams

Cheddar Cheese
Serving size: 1 ounce
Calories: 120
Fat: 10 grams
Saturated Fat: 6 grams

String Cheese
Serving size: 1 ounce
Calories: 80
Fat: 6 grams
Saturated Fat: 3 grams

Source: USDA National Nutrient Database for Standard Reference.

Is Fluoridation of the Water Supply a Good Thing?

About 204 million people received fluoridated water through their municipal water supply in 2010.[1] "Optimally fluoridated" water has been shown to reduce tooth decay.[2] But over-consuming fluoride can result in toxicity symptoms, and some groups oppose the addition of fluoride to drinking water. Do the benefits of fluoridated water outweigh the drawbacks? Read the arguments on both sides of the issue and decide for yourself.

yes

- Tooth decay is one of the most common childhood diseases: It is five times more common than asthma and seven times more common than hay fever in children aged 5 to 17. Considering that every $1 spent on fluoridation per community saves $38 in dental costs, fluoridated water is the most efficient way to prevent this disease.[3]

- Water fluoridation is effective in reducing dental decay by 20 to 40 percent, even now, in an era where other sources of fluoride, such as toothpaste, are widely available.[4]

- Fluoridation of the public water supply benefits Americans of all ages and socioeconomic status.[5]

- In 1960, the town of Antigo, Wisconsin stopped fluoridating its water after 11 years of doing so. By 1965, second-graders in the town had 200 percent more tooth decay than second-graders in 1960, fourth-graders had 70 percent more, and sixth-graders 90 percent more.[6]

- The EPA and the U.S. Department of Health and Human Services continue to strive to find the optimal fluoride recommendation. In 2011, they recommended lowering the levels of fluoride in drinking water to 0.7 mg/L, based on studies by the National Research Council.[7]

no

- Chronic, high-level exposure to fluoride can lead to skeletal fluorosis, which can result in changes to bone structure and hardened ligaments. Ingesting a large amount of fluoride, while rare, causes abdominal pain, nausea, and vomiting, with possible seizures and muscle spasms.[8]

- In children, overconsumption of fluoride can lead to dental fluorosis, which leads to staining and/or pitting of the teeth.

- The Environmental Protection Agency, which officially neither opposes nor endorses fluoridated drinking water, reports that drinking water with more than 4 milligrams of fluoride per liter can lead to skeletal fluorosis, and sets a Maximum Contaminant Level (MCL) of 4.0 milligrams of fluoride per liter.[9] In 2011, the EPA established a Secondary Maximum Contaminant Level (SMCL) of 2 mg/L to protect against moderate dental fluorosis in children.[10]

- Some environmental organizations oppose mandatory fluoridation, and would like the MCL level lowered, because of fluoride's impact on aquatic life and ecosystems, and human health.[11]

- In a 2006 scientific review, the National Research Council concluded that the MCL of 4 mg/L should be lowered because of the risk to children of dental and skeletal fluorosis.[12]

what do you think?

1. Which side do you think has the more compelling argument? Why? **2.** Does the public benefit (lower rates of tooth decay) outweigh the rights of individual choice? Why or why not? **3.** Do you think that you would consume adequate amounts of fluoride if it weren't added to your drinking water?

VISUAL Chapter Summary

1 Water Is an Important Nutrient in the Diet

Water is the universal solvent that helps transport oxygen, nutrients, and other substances throughout your body and that carries waste products away from your cells. It helps regulate body temperature and cushion organs. Combined with other substances to form saliva and mucus, it acts as a lubricant in your mouth and intestines.

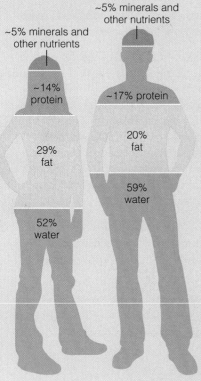

~5% minerals and other nutrients

~5% minerals and other nutrients

~14% protein

~17% protein

29% fat

20% fat

52% water

59% water

Female, 137 lbs.   Male, 168 lbs.

2 Water Balance Is Maintained through the Food and Beverages You Consume and the Amount You Excrete

When the amount of water consumed in foods and beverages is equal to the amount excreted, the body is in water balance. You lose water through your kidneys, large intestines, lungs, and skin. Consuming too little will cause dehydration, whereas consuming excessive amounts could cause hyponatremia.

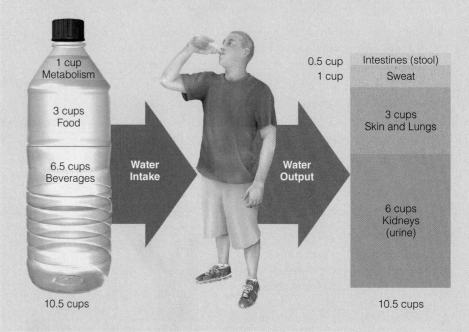

1 cup Metabolism

3 cups Food

6.5 cups Beverages

Water Intake

Water Output

10.5 cups

0.5 cup Intestines (stool)
1 cup Sweat

3 cups Skin and Lungs

6 cups Kidneys (urine)

10.5 cups

3 You Need to Consume Water Daily to Meet Your Needs

Adult women should consume 9 cups of water, and adult men should drink approximately 13 cups of water, daily. Caffeinated beverages, juices, and milk can all count toward meeting your water needs. Many foods are also a good source of water.

4 Minerals Are Essential Micronutrients That Play Many Roles in the Body

Many minerals are part of enzymes. Minerals help maintain fluid and acid-base balance; play a role in nerve transmission and muscle contractions; help strengthen bones, teeth, and the immune system; and are involved in growth. Minerals are found in both plant and animal foods, but often vary in bioavailability due to binding agents (oxalates, phytates) or competition with other minerals for absorption in the intestinal tract.

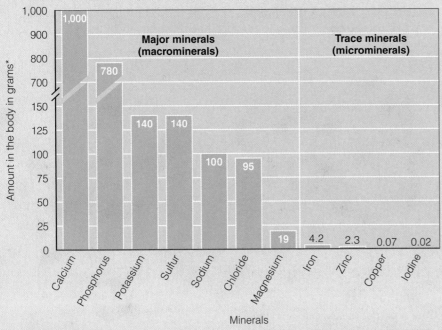

* Based on a 154-pound person

5 Sodium

Sodium plays an important role in balancing the fluid between your blood and cells. Americans currently consume more than double the sodium recommended daily, predominantly as sodium chloride (table salt). Processed foods are the major source of sodium chloride in the diet. Consuming too much sodium can contribute to hypertension. Reducing dietary sodium and following the DASH diet, which is abundant in foods rich in potassium, magnesium, and calcium, can help lower blood pressure. Losing excess weight, being physically active, and limiting alcohol can also lower blood pressure.

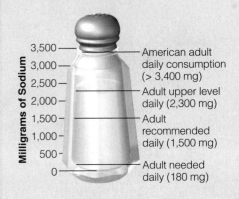

6 Potassium

Potassium helps keep your heart, muscles, nerves, and bones healthy. It can help lower high blood pressure by causing the kidneys to excrete excess sodium, and it may help prevent kidney stones. It also is involved in the maintenance of fluid balance and acid-base balance in the blood. The current recommendations to increase the fruits and vegetables in your diet will help you meet your potassium needs. Too much potassium from supplements results in hyperkalemia, whereas too little causes hypokalemia.

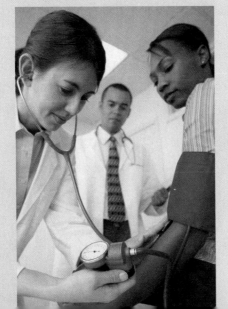

7 Calcium

Calcium, along with phosphorus, forms hydroxyapatite, which provides strength and structure for bones and teeth. Dairy foods are a good source of calcium. A diet adequate in protein, vitamin K, calcium, and vitamin D, along with regular physical activity, is needed to build and maintain healthy bones. Consuming too much calcium causes hypercalcemia and may cause kidney stones or constipation. Osteoporosis is a condition caused by frail bones. A chronic deficiency of dietary calcium and/or vitamin D, excess alcohol consumption, and smoking can all increase the risk of osteoporosis.

8 Phosphorus

Phosphorus is a major component of bones, teeth, and cell membranes. It is needed during metabolism, acts as an acid-base buffer, and is part of your DNA and RNA. Meat, fish, poultry, and dairy products are good sources of phosphorus. Consuming too much can result in hyperphosphatemia. Too little phosphorus in the diet can result in muscle weakness, bone pain, and confusion.

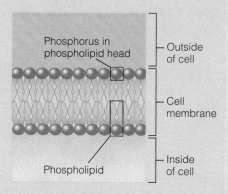

Phosphorus in phospholipid head — Outside of cell

— Cell membrane

Phospholipid — Inside of cell

9 Magnesium

Magnesium is needed for metabolism and to maintain healthy muscles, nerves, bones, and heart. Magnesium is abundant in leafy green vegetables, almonds, and legumes. Too much magnesium from taking supplements can cause intestinal problems such as diarrhea, cramps, and nausea. Deficiencies are rare but the use of some medications can result in magnesium deficiency.

10 Chloride

Chloride works with sodium to maintain fluid balance as well as acid-base balance in the body. Table salt accounts for almost all the chloride you consume. Chloride toxicity is rare but hyperchloremia can occur due to extreme dehydration. Deficiencies are also rare and are generally caused by extreme vomiting and diarrhea, resulting in hypochloremia.

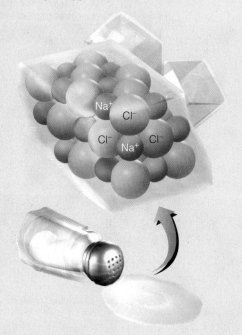

11 Sulfur

In the body, sulfur provides shape to amino acids. Sulfites are used as a preservative in processed foods. The best food sources of sulfur are meats, chicken, and fish. It can also be found in fruits and vegetables. There are no known toxicity or deficiency symptoms.

12 Iron

Iron is part of the oxygen-carrying transport proteins—hemoglobin in your red blood cells and myoglobin in your muscles. Heme iron is found in meat, poultry, and fish. Nonheme iron is found in plant foods, such as grains and vegetables. Nonheme iron is the predominant source of the iron in your diet but isn't absorbed as readily as heme iron. Too much iron from supplements can cause constipation, nausea, vomiting, and diarrhea. A deficiency of iron in children can reduce their ability to learn and retain information. Iron-deficiency anemia can cause fatigue and weakness.

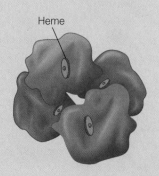

Heme

13 Copper

Copper is part of many enzymes and proteins that are involved in the absorption and transfer of iron and the synthesis of hemoglobin and red blood cells. Other enzymes containing copper are involved in energy production and protecting cells from free radicals. Copper is found in a variety of foods, especially seafood, nuts, and seeds. Too much copper can cause stomach pains, nausea, diarrhea, vomiting, and even liver damage. A copper deficiency is rare in the United States.

14 Zinc

More than 100 enzymes in your cells need zinc to function properly. Zinc plays a role in the structure of both RNA and DNA, in your taste acuity, and in helping fight age-related macular degeneration (AMD). Meat, fish, and whole grains are good sources of zinc. Too much zinc can cause intestinal problems, nausea, and vomiting, and can lower the HDL cholesterol in the body. A deficiency can cause hair loss, loss of appetite, impaired taste of foods, diarrhea, skin rashes, and delayed sexual maturation.

17 Chromium

Chromium helps the hormone insulin function, but has not been proven to enhance weight loss or build muscle mass during exercise. It may reduce insulin resistance and help lower the risk of type 2 diabetes. Grains, meat, eggs, poultry, and some fruits and vegetables are good sources of chromium. A chromium deficiency is very rare in the United States.

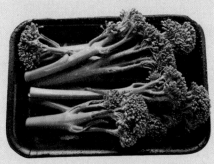

15 Selenium

Selenium acts as an antioxidant in your body and may help fight cancer. It is also a component of enzymes that help regulate thyroid hormones. All food groups contribute selenium, including nuts, meat, and seafood. Too much selenium can cause selenosis, the symptoms of which include brittle teeth and fingernails, garlic odor in the breath, gastrointestinal problems, and damage to the nervous system. A deficiency of selenium can lead to Keshan disease, which damages the heart.

18 Iodine

Iodine is essential to make thyroid hormones, which affect the majority of the cells and help regulate metabolic rate. Children need iodine for normal growth and development. Iodine is found mostly in iodized salt, seafood, and foods processed using iodized salt or iodine-containing perservatives. A deficiency of iodine during pregnancy can cause mental retardation and cretinism in the child. A deficiency of iodine during adulthood causes goiter, which is an enlarged thyroid gland.

16 Fluoride

Fluoride helps maintain the structure of bones and teeth and helps prevent dental caries. The primary dietary source of fluoride is a fluoridated water supply and the consumption of foods and beverages prepared using fluoridated water. In children, consumption of too much fluoride during tooth development can result in fluorosis. In adults, too much fluoride can cause skeletal fluorosis, which results in joint stiffness or pain, osteoporosis, and calcification of the ligaments.

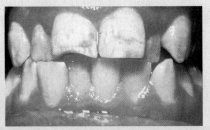

19 Manganese

Manganese assists enzymes involved in metabolism, and functions in the formation of bone. Manganese is found in legumes, nuts, fruits, and whole grains. A deficiency of manganese causes a rash and scaly skin. Manganese is generally not toxic except due to environmental contamination, osteoporosis, and calcification of the ligaments.

20 Molybdenum

Molybdenum also is a part of several enzymes involved in the breakdown of amino acids and other compounds. Molybdenum is found in legumes, whole grains, and nuts. A deficiency of molybdenum causes cardiovascular problems and headaches. Molybdenum does not appear to be toxic in humans, but in animal studies excess amounts of it can cause reproductive problems.

Terms to Know

- intracellular fluid
- extracellular fluid
- interstitial fluids
- electrolytes
- water balance
- dehydration
- diuretics

- osmosis
- hyponatremia
- inorganic
- solvent
- insensible water loss
- thirst mechanism
- antidiuretic hormone (ADH)
- minerals

- bioavailability
- major minerals
- trace minerals
- hypertension
- systolic pressure
- diastolic pressure
- kidney stones
- hypokalemia
- hyperkalemia

- hypercalcemia
- osteoporosis
- peak bone mass
- osteopenia
- bone mineral density (BMD)
- hyperphosphatemia
- hemoglobin
- myoglobin

- iron-deficiency anemia
- selenosis
- hemochromatosis
- Keshan disease
- fluorosis
- goiter
- cretinism

MasteringNutrition™   Build your knowledge—and confidence—in the Study Area of MasteringNutrition with a variety of study tools.

Check Your Understanding

1. The most abundant substance in your body is
   a. magnesium.
   b. iron.
   c. sodium.
   d. water.
2. All bottled water is regulated by the FDA.
   a. true
   b. false
3. In your body, minerals cannot
   a. help maintain fluid balance.
   b. be part of enzymes.
   c. work with your immune system.
   d. help absorb vitamin C.
4. The daily recommendation for dietary sodium intake for adults up to age 51 is
   a. 3,400 milligrams.
   b. 2,300 milligrams.
   c. 1,500 milligrams.
   d. 180 milligrams.
5. Which are NOT good sources of potassium?
   a. fruits and vegetables
   b. healthy unsaturated oils

   c. dairy and protein
   d. vegetables and grains
6. Which of the following can decrease the risk for hypertension?
   a. a family history of high blood pressure
   b. consuming excessive amounts of alcohol
   c. being inactive
   d. consuming fruits and vegetables
7. One cup of skim milk, 8 ounces of low-fat yogurt, and 1½ ounces of reduced-fat cheddar cheese *each* provide
   a. 100 milligrams of calcium.
   b. 200 milligrams of calcium.
   c. 300 milligrams of calcium.
   d. 400 milligrams of calcium.
8. You are having pasta for dinner. You want to enhance your absorption of the nonheme iron in the pasta. To do that, you could top your spaghetti with
   a. butter.
   b. olive oil.
   c. tomato sauce.
   d. nothing; eat it plain.

9. Chromium increases the effectiveness of
   a. thyroid hormones.
   b. the hormone insulin.
   c. antidiuretic hormone (ADH).
   d. hemoglobin.
10. Fluoride will help strengthen and repair the enamel on your teeth. What other mineral strengthens your teeth?
    a. chloride
    b. phosphorus
    c. sulfur
    d. zinc

Answers

1. (d) Your body is about 60 percent water. Water bathes the trillions of cells in your body and is part of the fluid inside your cells where reactions take place. Iron, though part of hemoglobin, is a trace mineral, so you only have small amounts in your body. Both magnesium and sodium are major minerals used in your body but are not as abundant as water.

2. (b) False. The FDA only regulates bottled water that is sold through interstate commerce. Bottled water that is manufactured and sold within the same state is not regulated by the FDA.

3. (d) Although you need only small amounts of minerals in your diet, they play enormously important roles in your body, such as helping to maintain fluid balance, being part of enzymes, and working with your immune system to keep you healthy. Unfortunately, they can't help absorb vitamin C.

4. (c) The daily recommended amount of sodium for adults up to age 51 is 1,500 milligrams. The upper level for sodium daily is 2,300 milligrams, whereas the absolute minimum that should be consumed is 180 milligrams per day. Unfortunately, Americans far exceed these recommendations and consume more than 3,400 milligrams of sodium daily, on average.

5. (b) While oils are a heart healthy way to get some fat in your diet, they are not a good source of potassium. The good news is that fruits, vegetables, protein, and dairy products are good sources of this mineral.

6. (d) Eating fruits and vegetables can decrease your risk of hypertension. A family history of hypertension, consuming excessive amounts of alcohol, and being inactive can all increase your risk.

7. (c) Each of these servings of dairy foods provides 300 milligrams of calcium. Consuming the recommended three servings of lean dairy products daily will just about meet the amount of calcium recommended daily (1,000 milligrams) for many adults.

8. (c) Ladle the tomato sauce on your pasta—the vitamin C in it can enhance nonheme iron absorption. Though the butter and olive oil will give your spaghetti flavor, they won't help you absorb iron.

9. (b) Chromium increases insulin's effectiveness in your cells. Iodine is needed to make thyroid hormones, and ADH is the hormone that directs kidneys to minimize water loss and concentrate urine.

10. (b) Phosphorus, along with calcium, forms hydroxyapatite, which is the strengthening material found in your teeth. Chloride is one of the electrolytes in your blood that helps maintain fluid and acid-base balance. Sulfur plays an important role as part of many compounds in your body, such as certain amino acids. Zinc helps with wound healing and maintaining a healthy immune system.

Web Resources

- To learn more about the safety of your local water supply, visit the EPA's website at www.epa.gov
- For more on the DASH diet, visit DASH for Health at www.dashforhealth.com
- For more on osteoporosis, visit the National Osteoporosis Foundation at www.nof.org
- For more on high blood pressure, visit www.nhlbi.nih.gov

1. **False.** Vitamin waters contain additional calories that you may not need. To improve your fluid intake, plain water is just as healthy and much cheaper. Turn to page 289 to learn more about these waters.

2. **True.** Your mug of java does contribute to meeting your daily water needs, even though it may contain caffeine, a diuretic. Turn to page 290 to find out why.

3. **False.** Although seasoning your food with salt adds sodium, it is not the major culprit in sodium overload. Turn to page 294 to find out what is.

4. **True.** Magnesium, along with calcium and potassium, is part of a diet that has been shown to substantially lower blood pressure. To find out more, turn to page 297.

5. **True.** In fact, the recommended three servings of dairy foods, including milk, yogurt, and/or cheese, will almost nail your calcium needs for the day. Unfortunately, most Americans' diets fall short in regard to this food group. To find out how to meet your needs, turn to page 300.

6. **False.** Although meat, fish, and poultry are fabulous sources of iron, they are not the main sources in Americans' diets. Turn to page 310 to find out what contributes the most iron to our diets.

7. **True.** Taking a zinc lozenge may help reduce the severity and duration of a common cold but there is a catch. Turn to page 313 to find out what the side effects can be.

8. **False.** Most bottled water sold in the United States does not contain fluoride. Turn to page 318 to find out why this could be bad news for your teeth.

9. **False.** Dream on. Turn to page 319 to learn the truth.

10. **False.** Kosher salt doesn't contain iodine. Turn to page 321 to find foods that are good sources of this mineral.

9

Alcohol

True or False?

1. A **shot** of whiskey contains more alcohol than a can of beer. ⒯⒡ p. 339

2. Red wine contains **phytochemicals** that are good for your heart. ⒯⒡ p. 340

3. If you passed out from heavy drinking, your **blood alcohol level** would stabilize and gradually return to normal. ⒯⒡ p. 342

4. Women feel the **effects** of alcohol sooner than men. ⒯⒡ p. 344

5. Drinking a Bloody Mary (tomato juice and vodka) will help with a **hangover**. ⒯⒡ p. 347

6. Drinking alcohol will improve **sexual function**. ⒯⒡ p. 347

7. **Alcohol** provides 7 calories per gram. ⒯⒡ p. 347

8. **Binge drinking** is considered drinking 7 or more drinks in a very short time. ⒯⒡ p. 353

9. Some states in the United States have lowered the **legal** drinking age to 18. ⒯⒡ p. 356

10. Alcoholism can be **cured** through counseling. ⒯⒡ p. 356

See page 363 for the answers.

After reading this chapter, you will be able to:

1. **Explain what alcohol is and how it is made.**

2. **Explain why people drink alcohol.**

3. **Describe how alcohol is absorbed and metabolized in the body.**

4. **List the harmful effects of alcohol in the body.**

5. **Describe the difference between alcohol abuse and alcoholism.**

I n this chapter, we discuss the nature of alcohol, including its various forms, how it is digested and absorbed in the body, and its potential short-term and long-term health effects. We also explore alcohol use and abuse, and steps you can take if you suspect that you or someone close to you is abusing alcohol.

What Is Alcohol and How Is It Made?

Your body doesn't need alcohol to survive. Therefore, alcohol is not an essential nutrient. You don't gain any nutrition from drinking it, other than calories. Ounce for ounce, it can cost 100 times more than bottled water. It's legally sold in the United States, but supposedly off limits to those who aren't adults, even though teenagers often feel under social pressure to consume it. Some medical reports say that in moderation, it can be good for you, while others tell you that drinking too much of it can kill you.

A bottle of beer, a glass of wine, or a rum and cola are all drinks that might come to mind when we consider the term **alcohol**. Technically, these beverages aren't alcohol by themselves, but they all contain a type of alcohol called **ethanol**.

Ethanol is one of three similar compounds in the chemical category of alcohol. The other two compounds, methanol (used in antifreeze) and isopropanol (used in rubbing alcohol), are both poisonous when ingested. Ethanol is considered safe for consumption, but it is not harmless. Consuming excessive amounts of ethanol can be toxic and damage your body. Too much can even kill you.

Ethanol is made through the **fermentation** of yeast and the natural sugars in grains (glucose and maltose) and fruits (fructose and glucose). The yeast breaks down the sugar into ethanol and carbon dioxide. The carbon dioxide evaporates, leaving an alcohol-containing beverage. Grapes provide the sugar for making wine, whereas the starch from grains provides the sugar when producing beer.

Liquors, such as rum, scotch, and whiskey, are made through a process called **distillation** and are more accurately called distilled spirits.[1] In this process, an alcoholic beverage is heated, causing the ethanol to vaporize. The vapor is collected, cooled, and condensed into a very concentrated liquid called liquor.

Although ethanol is the scientific name for the alcohol found in beverages, we will use the more common term *alcohol* throughout this chapter.

The Take-Home Message Ethanol is the type of alcohol consumed in alcoholic beverages. Alcoholic beverages are made by the processes of fermentation or distillation. Alcohol is not an essential nutrient because your body does not need it to survive.

Why Do People Drink Alcohol?

People around the world drink alcohol in many different forms and for many different reasons. The sake (rice wine) of Japan is used during tea and Shinto ceremonies, while the dark beer of the Irish is consumed by many pub patrons celebrating their favorite sport. The vodka of Russia and the chardonnay of Napa Valley are consumed in the pursuit of relaxation and pleasure. Globally, wine is part of many religious traditions, including the Catholic Mass and the Jewish Sabbath, and in some cultures, it's the beverage of choice during the main meal of the day. For parts of human history, wine and beer were safer to drink than water, which was often polluted.

In the United States, more than half of adults consume at least one alcoholic beverage per month.[2] Americans drink alcohol for many of the same reasons people in other parts of the world do. We use it to relax, celebrate, and socialize. We have also found that it may provide health benefits. Let's explore these motives for drinking alcohol more closely.

People Drink to Relax, Celebrate, and Socialize

Alcohol is a drug that alters your conscious mind. Within minutes of sipping an alcoholic beverage, a person will feel more relaxed. After a few more sips, a mild, pleasant euphoria sets in and inhibitions begin to loosen. By the end of the first or second drink, a person will often feel more outgoing, happy, and social. This anxiety-reducing, upbeat initial effect is why people seek out and continue to drink alcohol.[3]

Having a drink with another person symbolizes social bonding. When it comes to mingling with others or celebrating a special occasion, whether it's with friends, co-workers, or even strangers, pubs and parties are common gathering spots, and alcoholic drinks are commonly served. This is considered **social drinking**, which is defined as drinking patterns that are considered acceptable by society.[4] Social drinking is not the same as moderate drinking (see the next section), as consuming too much alcohol, even in socially acceptable situations, can be harmful, even if it is only done on the weekends. Later in this chapter we discuss binge drinking, which often occurs in social settings.

Moderate Alcohol Consumption May Have Health Benefits

Some people drink alcohol because of its health benefits. That's right. Some studies have suggested that moderate alcohol consumption may reduce the risk of heart disease, and the risk of dying in general, for middle-aged and older adults.[5] **Moderate alcohol consumption** is defined as an average daily consumption of up to one drink per day for women and up to two drinks per day for men, as well as no more than three drinks in any single day for women and no more than four drinks in a single day for men.

A standard drink is any one of the following:

➤ One 12-ounce serving of beer
➤ One 1.5-ounce shot of liquor
➤ One 5-ounce glass of wine

Ⓣ/Ⓕ Each of these contains about half an ounce of alcohol (**Figure 9.1**).

On November 17, 1991, the television news show *60 Minutes* aired a segment called "The French Paradox," touting the benefits of modest amounts of red wine to help reduce the risk of heart disease. The French Paradox is so called because the people of France have lower rates of heart disease even though their saturated fat intake mimics that of Americans. They also drink more red wine than Americans do, which is thought to be the differentiating factor. (However, the French also consume fewer *trans* fats and have a less stressful lifestyle and better developed social networks, which can also contribute to their impressively lower risk of heart disease.) In the four weeks after the segment was aired, sales of red wine increased by about 45 percent.[6] Suddenly,

Beer is made from the fermentation of yeast and the natural sugars from grains.

Figure 9.1 What Is a Standard Drink?
One standard drink of beer (12 ounces), wine (5 ounces), or liquor (1½ ounces) contains the same amount of alcohol.

alcohol A chemical class of substances that include ethanol, methanol, and isopropanol.

ethanol The type of alcohol in alcoholic beverages such as wine, beer, and liquor.

fermentation The process by which yeast converts sugars in grains or fruits into ethanol and carbon dioxide.

distillation The evaporation and then collection of a liquid by condensation.

social drinking Drinking patterns that are considered acceptable by society.

moderate alcohol consumption An average consumption of up to one drink per day for women and up to two drinks per day for men, as well as no more than three drinks in any single day for women and no more than four drinks in a single day for men.

12 oz
(1 drink)

16 oz
(1⅓ drink)

5 oz
(1 drink)

8 oz
(1½ drink)

Figure 9.2 When a Drink Is More Than a Drink . . .
Depending on the size, one drink may actually be the equivalent of 1⅓ to 2 drinks or more.

instead of thinking that "an apple a day keeps the doctor away," people were hoping that "a drink a day keeps the cardiologist at bay." Were these people on the right track?

Red wine contains resveratrol, a flavonoid and type of phytochemical, which acts as an antioxidant. (Dark beer also contains flavonoids.) Antioxidants help prevent the "bad" LDL cholesterol from becoming oxidized, which leads to its accumulation in the artery wall and atherosclerosis. Flavonoids help inhibit the stickiness of platelets in the blood. Alcohol also helps inhibit the stickiness of platelets in the blood, just like flavonoids, but also increases the level of heart-protective "good" HDL cholesterol. Because of these potential heart-healthy attributes, alcohol and red wine have been in the media limelight since the 1990s.

There isn't enough evidence to support the theory that wine, whether red, white, or rosé, has any health superiority over beer and distilled spirits. In fact, some studies comparing various alcohol sources have found that the majority of heart-protective effects are attributable to the alcohol content regardless of the source.[7] In other words, a beer, a glass of cabernet, or a shot of scotch all appear to have similar heart-protective effects. When it comes to the health benefits of alcohol, the source is unlikely to make much of a difference.

Before you crack open a beer to celebrate though, be aware that the people who gain the health benefits from moderate alcohol consumption are women age 55 and older and men age 45 and older. Alcohol consumption by younger people has not been shown to provide many—if any—health benefits. In fact, drinking alcohol during your younger years increases the risk of injuries and violent, traumatic deaths, which offsets any possible health benefits from the alcohol.[8]

All individuals who choose to drink alcohol need to stick to moderate drinking, and even then they need to carefully monitor their intake. Moderate drinkers need to watch out for (1) the size of their drinks and (2) the frequency of their drinking. As mentioned earlier, a standard drink contains about 0.5 ounce of alcohol. If your 8-ounce wine glass gets filled to the brim, or you chug an oversized mug of beer, you could consume close to two standard drinks in one glass or mug (**Figure 9.2**). A 750-milliliter bottle of wine contains five, 5-ounce glasses of wine. If you split a bottle with a friend, you are consuming the equivalent of 2½ standard drinks. One rum and cola can provide the equivalent of more than 2½ alcoholic drinks. Another important point to remember is that abstaining from drinking through the week and then having seven drinks on a single Friday night does not count as moderate drinking. When it comes to alcohol, no "banking" is allowed.

The Take-Home Message People drink alcohol to relax, celebrate, and socialize. Moderate alcohol consumption, which means 1 to 2 drinks per day for men and 1 drink per day for women, may provide health benefits in some older adults. While the flavonoids in red wine and dark beer are thought to be beneficial compounds, the alcohol itself may also provide protective benefits, such as increasing "good" HDL cholesterol levels. Individuals who choose to drink alcohol need to do so in moderation and monitor both the size of their drinks and the frequency of their drinking.

What Happens to Alcohol in the Body?

Your body treats alcohol differently from any other substance. Unlike the other energy-containing nutrients, such as carbohydrates and fats, your body cannot store alcohol. Because alcohol is a toxin, the body quickly works to metabolize and eliminate it.

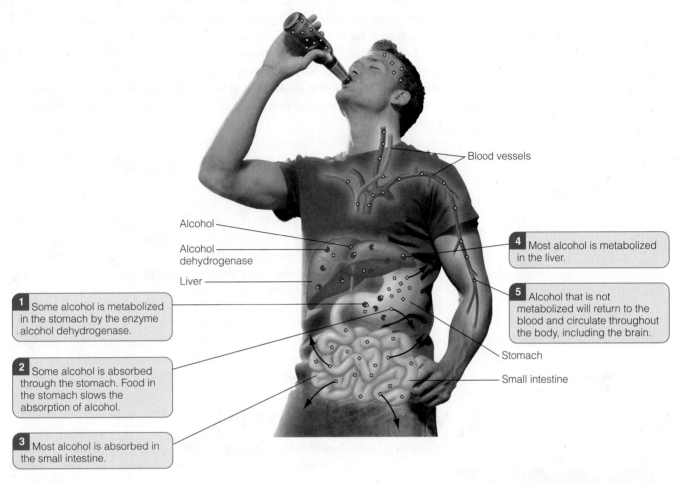

Blood vessels

Alcohol

Alcohol
dehydrogenase

Liver

4 Most alcohol is metabolized in the liver.

5 Alcohol that is not metabolized will return to the blood and circulate throughout the body, including the brain.

1 Some alcohol is metabolized in the stomach by the enzyme alcohol dehydrogenase.

2 Some alcohol is absorbed through the stomach. Food in the stomach slows the absorption of alcohol.

3 Most alcohol is absorbed in the small intestine.

Stomach

Small intestine

Figure 9.3 The Metabolism of Alcohol

Many factors, including your gender, your body type, the amount of food in your stomach, and the amount of alcohol you drink, will affect how quickly you absorb and metabolize it.[9] Alcohol travels through the body in the blood, and is distributed throughout the watery tissues, including the brain. Let's follow a swallow of beer through your digestive system and see how it's handled along the way (**Figure 9.3**).

You Absorb Alcohol in Your Stomach and Small Intestine

Within seconds of the first sip of the beer, about 20 percent of the alcohol will be directly absorbed through the stomach and into your blood. Some alcohol is also metabolized in the stomach by an enzyme called **alcohol dehydrogenase** before it is absorbed. The majority of alcohol, about 80 percent, is absorbed in the small intestine.

The amount and type of food in the stomach determine how long alcohol lingers there before entering the small intestine. If your swallow of beer chases a bacon cheeseburger and fries, the alcohol will take longer to leave the stomach than if the beer was consumed without food after a period of fasting. One study showed that an alcoholic drink consumed after a meal was absorbed about three times more slowly than if it was consumed on an empty stomach.[10] This is why you should always try to avoid drinking alcohol on an empty stomach. Fat also slows down the departure of

Light beer has about the same amount of alcohol as regular beer.

alcohol dehydrogenase One of the alcohol-metabolizing enzymes found in the stomach and the liver.

food from the stomach, so a large amount of fat in the food, as in this burger meal, will help delay the arrival of the alcohol into the small intestine.

Keep in mind, however, that though a stomach full of high-fat food will delay the arrival of alcohol in the small intestine, the alcohol will still eventually arrive there. If a person drinks several glasses of beer with dinner, the alcohol will be absorbed once the stomach starts emptying. Intoxication could be an unexpected post-dinner surprise.

You Metabolize Alcohol Primarily in Your Liver

Once in your blood, alcohol travels to the liver, where the majority of it is metabolized. Enzymes in the liver, most importantly alcohol dehydrogenase, convert the alcohol to **acetaldehyde**, which is eventually metabolized to carbon dioxide and water.[11] A healthy liver can metabolize about one alcoholic drink in about 1½ to 2 hours. Regardless of the amount consumed, the metabolism of alcohol occurs at a steady rate in your body.

There is a second enzyme system in the liver that metabolizes alcohol: the **microsomal ethanol-oxidizing system (MEOS)**. Individuals who consume a lot of alcohol will have a somewhat more active MEOS because this system is revved up when chronically high levels of alcohol are present in the liver.

Alcohol Circulates in Your Blood

If your liver cannot handle the amount of alcohol all at once, the extra alcohol reenters the blood and is distributed in the watery tissues in your body. Your **blood alcohol concentration (BAC)** is the amount of alcohol in your blood, measured in grams of alcohol per deciliter of blood, usually expressed as a percentage.[12] **Table 9.1** gives you a ballpark idea of how your BAC is affected by the number of alcoholic beverages you consume. As you can see, the more you drink, the higher your BAC. Because alcohol infiltrates your brain, as your BAC increases so does your level of mental impairment and intoxication.

Though the liver will eventually metabolize most of the alcohol that is consumed, a small amount will leave your body intact through your breath and urine. Because the amount of alcohol in your breath correlates with the amount of alcohol in your blood, a Breathalyzer test can be used to measure your BAC. Police officers often use this device when they suspect that a person has consumed too much alcohol.

A Breathalyzer is used to measure a person's blood alcohol concentration (BAC).

acetaldehyde An intermediary by-product of the breakdown of ethanol in the liver.

microsomal ethanol-oxidizing system (MEOS) The other major enzyme system in the liver that metabolizes alcohol.

blood alcohol concentration (BAC) The measurement of the amount of alcohol in your blood. BAC is measured in grams of alcohol per deciliter of blood, usually expressed as a percentage.

The Effects of Alcohol on Your Brain

Alcohol is a *depressant,* a substance that slows the transmission of nerve impulses. Your brain is very sensitive to the depressant effect of alcohol. For instance, alcohol slows down your reaction time to stimuli (such as a car coming toward you on the road), confuses your thoughts, impairs your judgment, and induces sleepiness. The more you drink, the more areas of the brain are affected. **Table 9.2** and **Figure 9.4** on page 344 show how increasing BAC levels affect specific areas of the brain, and how body movements and behaviors are affected. (*Note:* A person's BAC can continue to rise even after unconsciousness.) If enough alcohol has been consumed, the activities of the brain stem, which controls breathing and heart rate, can be suppressed, and ultimately cause death. Excessive amounts of alcohol can cause "brain shrinkage," which can impair memory and learning as well as coordination and balance. Heavy

Table 9.1

Blood Alcohol Concentration Tables

For Women
Body Weight in Pounds

Drinks per Hour	100	120	140	160	180	200
1	0.05	0.04	0.03	0.03	0.03	0.02
2	0.09	0.08	0.07	0.06	0.05	0.05
3	0.14	0.11	0.10	0.09	0.08	0.07
4	0.18	0.15	0.13	0.11	0.10	0.09
5	0.23	0.19	0.16	0.14	0.13	0.11
6	0.27	0.23	0.19	0.17	0.15	0.14
7	0.32	0.27	0.23	0.20	0.18	0.16
8	0.36	0.30	0.26	0.23	0.20	0.18
9	0.41	0.34	0.29	0.26	0.23	0.20
10	0.45	0.38	0.32	0.28	0.25	0.23

For Men
Body Weight in Pounds

Drinks per Hour	100	120	140	160	180	200
1	0.04	0.03	0.03	0.02	0.02	0.02
2	0.08	0.06	0.05	0.05	0.04	0.04
3	0.11	0.09	0.08	0.07	0.06	0.06
4	0.15	0.12	0.11	0.09	0.08	0.08
5	0.19	0.16	0.13	0.12	0.11	0.09
6	0.23	0.19	0.16	0.14	0.13	0.11
7	0.26	0.22	0.19	0.16	0.15	0.13
8	0.30	0.25	0.21	0.19	0.17	0.15
9	0.34	0.28	0.24	0.21	0.19	0.17
10	0.38	0.31	0.27	0.23	0.21	0.19

Tables are adapted from those of the Pennsylvania Liquor Control Board, Harrisburg.

Notes: The darkly shaded areas indicate legal intoxication.

Blood alcohol concentrations are expressed as percent, meaning grams of alcohol per 10 milliliters (per deciliter) of blood.

drinking also reduces blood flow to the brain, which can similarly impair balance and coordination, such as for walking.[13]

Because alcohol is a depressant, it can be very unhealthy, and even dangerous, to mix it with a stimulant, such as the high amounts of caffeine found in energy drinks. In a study of more than 4,000 college students, research found that those who consumed alcohol mixed with caffeinated energy drinks were twice as likely to be injured, require medical attention, ride with an intoxicated driver, and either take sexual advantage of someone or be the victim of sexual aggressiveness.[14] Because energy drinks can reduce the symptoms of alcohol intoxication, such as tiredness, individuals may continue drinking to the point where the BAC increases to dangerous levels, affecting both the body's mental and physical functions.[15]

Mixing alcohol with caffeinated energy drinks can have dangerous consequences.

Table 9.2

Progressive Effects of Alcohol

Blood Alcohol Concentration	Changes in Feelings and Personality	Brain Regions Affected	Impaired Functions (continuum)
0.01–0.05	Relaxation, sense of well-being, loss of inhibition	Cerebral cortex	Alertness; judgment
0.06–0.10	Pleasure, numbing of feelings, nausea, sleepiness, emotional arousal	Cerebral cortex and forebrain	Coordination (especially fine motor skills); visual tracking
0.11–0.20	Mood swings, anger, sadness, mania	Cerebral cortex, forebrain, and cerebellum	Reasoning and depth perception; appropriate social behavior
0.21–0.30	Aggression, reduced sensations, depression, stupor	Cerebral cortex, forebrain, cerebellum, and brain stem	Speech; balance; temperature regulation
0.31–0.40	Unconsciousness, coma, death possible	Entire brain	Bladder control; breathing
0.41 and greater	Death		Heart rate

Source: National Institute on Alcohol Abuse and Alcoholism. 2003. Understanding Alcohol: Investigations into Biology and Behavior. Available at http://science.education.nih.gov. Accessed June 2013.

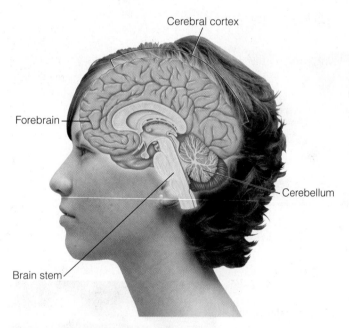

Figure 9.4 The Brain and Alcohol
As you consume more alcohol, additional areas of your brain are affected. Your cerebral cortex is affected first, followed by your forebrain, cerebellum, and brain stem. The greater the alcohol intake, the greater the physical and behavioral changes in your body.

Women Are More Susceptible to the Effects of Alcohol Than Men

In essence, every alcoholic beverage that a male consumes is equivalent to about 1⅓ alcoholic beverages for a woman. Two factors contribute to women's greater susceptibility to alcohol:

➤ Women have about 20 to 30 percent less alcohol dehydrogenase in their stomachs than men, so more alcohol will enter the blood immediately through women's stomachs.[16]

➤ Women generally have less muscle mass, and thus less body water, than men. (Recall from Chapter 8 that muscle tissue has a higher percentage of water than fat.) Because alcohol mixes in water, people with more muscle are able to distribute more of the alcohol throughout their body than people who have more fat.

Because of these factors, women will feel alcohol's effects sooner than men. Women take note: It's dangerous to try to keep up, drink for drink, with male companions. You will begin to feel the effects of alcohol long before a man will.

Finally, people of Asian descent also need to be aware of a potential lower tolerance to alcohol. About 50 percent of Asians (both men and women) experience "alcohol flush," a reddish skin reaction that occurs because of an enzyme deficiency. Symptoms include facial flushing, nausea, and rapid heart beat, and one study has shown that people who experience this condition, particularly East Asians, are at higher risk of esophageal cancer.[17]

The Take-Home Message Alcohol is absorbed in the stomach and small intestine and is metabolized primarily in the liver. Your sex, body type, the amount of food in your stomach, and the quantity of alcohol consumed will affect the rate of absorption and metabolism in your body. The blood alcohol concentration (BAC) is the measurement of alcohol in your blood. Alcohol is a central nervous system depressant. Because your brain is sensitive to alcohol, alcohol affects your behavior. Because of having less alcohol dehydrogenase in the stomach and less body water, women will feel the effects of the same amount of alcohol before men will.

How Can Alcohol Be Harmful?

Although alcohol is often advertised in magazines, billboards, and television commercials as a trendy and sexy way to relax and socialize (see the Examining the Evidence feature "Alcohol and Advertising" on page 346), it can cause a number of problems for those who abuse it. Some of these problems merely cause temporary discomfort, but other long-term effects can be extremely damaging to health.

Alcohol Can Disrupt Sleep and Cause Hangovers

Many people wrongly think that a drink before bed will help them sleep better, but it will actually have the opposite effect. Whereas having a drink within an hour before bed may help you to fall asleep sooner, it will disrupt your sleep cycle, potentially causing you to awaken in the middle of the night, and making returning to sleep a challenge. As a result, you will likely feel tired the next morning, and you may find it harder to pay attention to what you are learning in class.[18] Even a moderate amount of alcohol consumed at dinner—or even late in the afternoon during happy hour—can disrupt that night's sleep.

If you have a bad night's sleep, it's a bad idea to drink alcohol the next day. Studies have shown that a night of sleep disruption followed by even small amounts of alcohol the next day reduces the reaction time and alertness in individuals performing a simulated driving test. Being tired and then drinking alcohol exacerbates alcohol's sedating effect.[19]

A **hangover** is your body's way of saying, "don't do that to me again." After a bout of heavy drinking, individuals can experience hangover symptoms ranging from a pounding headache, fatigue, nausea, and increased thirst to a rapid heart beat, tremors, sweating, dizziness, depression, anxiety, and irritability. A hangover begins within hours of your last drink, as your BAC begins to drop. The symptoms will appear in full force once all the alcohol is gone from your blood, and these symptoms can linger for up to an additional 24 hours.[20] In other words, a few hours of excessive alcohol consumption on a Saturday night can not only ruin your entire Sunday but even disrupt part of your Monday morning.

There are several ways that alcohol contributes to the symptoms of a hangover. Alcohol is a diuretic, so it can cause dehydration, and thus, electrolyte imbalances. It inhibits the release of antidiuretic hormone from your pituitary gland, which in turn causes your kidneys to excrete water, as well as electrolytes, in your urine. Vomiting and sweating during or after excessive drinking will further contribute to dehydration and electrolyte loss. Dehydration also increases your thirst and can make you feel

eLearn

How Much Alcohol Is Too Much?

If you drink alcohol, take the short, ten-question survey based on the World Health Organization's Alcohol Use Disorders Identification Test (AUDIT), which will help you analyze your current drinking habits and provide information on what to do if you drink too much. To access the survey, go to www.alcoholscreening.org.

Practical Nutrition **VIDEO**

Step Up to the Bar

Joan has some flavorful "mocktail" ideas that will help you avoid dehydration and a hangover. Scan this QR code with your mobile device to access the video. You can also access the video in **Mastering**Nutrition™.

hangover A collective term for the unpleasant symptoms, such as a headache and dizziness, that occur after drinking an excessive amount of alcohol.

Alcohol and Advertising

Advertising for alcoholic beverages is pervasive and persuasive. You need only drive down a major highway or turn on your television to see billboards and commercials for a beer or liquor brand. In some media, including popular magazines like *Rolling Stone* and *Sports Illustrated*, alcohol ads can outnumber non–alcohol ads by almost 3 to 1.[1]

Companies that make alcoholic beverages pay large sums of money to create and show these ads for one reason: They work. Studies have shown that advertisements for alcoholic beverages are associated with an increase in drinking among adolescents.[2] Many ads tend to emphasize sexual and social stereotypes. When targeted to underage drinkers, this type of message has been shown to increase adolescents' desire to emulate those portrayed in the advertisements.[3]

Alcohol ads should be viewed with caution, as the messages in them are often misleading and in some cases blatantly false. Let's take a look at the messages and realities in a typical alcohol advertisement that might appear in a magazine.

What Do You Think?

1. Do advertisements for alcoholic beverages in trendy magazines, television commercials, and on the Internet motivate adolescents to drink?
2. Should advertisements for alcoholic beverages be banned in media outlets that attract a younger audience?
3. Should advertisements for alcohol geared to underage drinkers also state the dangers of consuming it?

This Photo Says: "Drinking Enables Me to Feel More Masculine and in Charge"
Reality: Alcohol will increase fantasies of being more masculine, strong, and powerful. However, excessive alcohol consumption causes a reduction in male sex hormones along with changes that include breast development and testicle shrinkage.

This Photo Says: "Drinking Helps Me Relax and Be Happy"
Reality: While initially you may feel relaxed, consuming a few drinks will actually make you feel anxious and depressed.

This Photo Says: "Drinking Makes Me Feel More Feminine"
Reality: As with males, too much alcohol will interfere with a woman's sex hormones and cause sexual, menstrual, and infertility problems.

This Photo Says: "Drinking Makes Me VERY Sexy"
Reality: Alcohol will actually *reduce* sexual arousal. The more alcohol consumed, the worse the problem. Chronic drinking will decrease the level of sexual hormones in the body and sexual desire.

This Photo Says: "Drinking With Friends and Co-Workers Means that I Am Successful"
Reality: Anyone can obtain and drink alcohol. It isn't a beverage tied to social class.

lightheaded, dizzy, and weak. Increased acid production in the stomach and secretions from the pancreas and intestines can cause stomach pain, nausea, and vomiting.

Lastly, alcoholic beverages often contain compounds called **congeners**, which enhance their taste and appearance but may contribute to hangover symptoms. Congeners can be produced during the fermentation process or be added during production of the alcoholic beverages. The large number of congeners in red wine can cause headaches in some people.[21]

Forget the old wives' tale of consuming an alcoholic beverage to "cure" a hangover. Drinking more alcohol, even if it is mixed with tomato or orange juice, during a hangover only prolongs the recovery time. In fact, time is the only true remedy for hangover symptoms. Whereas aspirin and other nonsteroidal anti-inflammatory medications, such as ibuprofen, can ease a headache, these medications can also contribute to stomachache and nausea. Taking acetaminophen (Tylenol) during and after alcohol consumption, when the alcohol is being metabolized, has been shown to intensify this pain reliever's toxicity to the liver and may cause liver damage in some cases.[22] The best strategy for dealing with a hangover is to avoid it by limiting the amount of alcohol consumed.

Coffee will not sober you up. An intoxicated person who drinks coffee will end up being a stimulated drunk. It takes time to sober up because your liver has to metabolize all the alcohol that you consumed.

Alcohol Can Interact with Hormones

Many individuals who overindulge in alcohol tend not to eat enough while they are drinking, which causes their body's glucose stores to become depleted and their blood glucose levels to fall. Typically, the hormones insulin and glucagon would automatically be released to make glucose, but alcohol interferes with this process. Because the brain needs glucose to function properly, a low blood glucose level can contribute to the feelings of fatigue, weakness, mood changes, irritability, and anxiety often experienced during a hangover.

In addition to the hormones that regulate your blood glucose level, alcohol can interfere with other hormones. Alcohol can also increase estrogen levels in women, which may increase the risk of breast cancer.[23] Drinking alcohol can affect reproductive hormones and is associated with both male and female sexual dysfunction, and alcohol abuse has been associated with infertility.[24]

Alcohol May Lead to Overnutrition and Malnutrition

At 7 calories per gram, alcohol provides fewer calories than fat (9 calories per gram) but more than either carbohydrates or protein (4 calories per gram each). However, unless you are drinking a straight shot of liquor, your alcoholic beverages will contain additional calories (see **Table 9.3** on the next page). For example, a rum and cola contains the calories from both the rum and the cola, making the drink more than three times as high in calories as the rum itself. Depending on the mixers and ingredients added to your beverage, the calorie count in your drink can escalate to that of a meal. A mudslide, for example, made with vodka, Irish cream, coffee liqueur, ice cream, and cream, should be ordered from the dessert menu and served with a spoon.

If you consistently add extra calories from alcoholic beverages—or any food or beverage source—to a diet that is already meeting your daily calorie needs, you will gain weight. Excessive consumption of alcohol has also been shown to increase fat and weight around the stomach. Though this is usually referred to as a "beer" belly, extra calories from any type of alcoholic beverage can contribute to a paunch.

congeners Compounds in alcohol that enhance the taste but may contribute to hangover symptoms.

Table 9.3

Calories in Selected Alcoholic Drinks

Beer
Serving size: 12 oz
Alcohol serving: 1
Calories per drink: 150

Light Beer

Serving size: 12 oz
Alcohol serving: 1
Calories per drink: 110

Distilled Spirits (e.g., whiskey, vodka, gin, rum)

Serving size: 1.5 oz
Alcohol serving: 1
Calories per drink: 100

Wine (white or red)

Serving size: 5 oz
Alcohol serving: 1
Calories per drink: 100–105

Cosmopolitan

Serving size: 2.5 oz
Alcohol servings: 1.7
Calories per drink: 131

Mudslide

Serving size: 12 oz
Alcohol servings: 4
Calories per drink: 820

Bloody Mary

Serving size: 5.5 oz
Alcohol serving: 1
Calories per drink: 97

Margarita

Serving size: 6.3 oz
Alcohol servings: 3
Calories per drink: 327

Rum and Cola

Serving size: 12 oz
Alcohol servings: 2.7
Calories per drink: 361

Note: Alcohol servings are per beverage.

If high-calorie "bar foods" are consumed with the drinks, the calories can add up rapidly (**Figure 9.5**).

Compensating for calories in alcoholic beverages by cutting out more nutritious foods will cause you to fall short of your nutrient needs. If you drink a daily glass of beer instead of an equal amount of low-fat milk, your waist may not suffer, but your bones could. You will rob yourself of an excellent source of calcium and vitamin D that the milk, but not the beer, provides. A chronic substitution of excessive amounts of alcohol for nutritious foods in the diet can lead to malnutrition.

Dinner 1

5 12-oz beers

1,719 total calories

8 BBQ chicken wings

1 handful goldfish crackers

1 large serving nachos with cheese

Total fat (g)	51	
Saturated fat (g)	16	
Cholesterol (mg)	154	

Dinner 2

724 total calories

2 oz whole-wheat dinner roll
4 tsp soft margarine

1 cup fat-free milk

4 oz grilled chicken breast
3/4 cup mashed potatoes
1 1/2 cup steamed carrots

28	Total fat (g)	
8	Saturated fat (g)	
89	Cholesterol (mg)	

Figure 9.5 Too Much Alcohol Costs You Good Nutrition
A dinner of several alcoholic beverages and bar foods not only adds calories, fat, and saturated fat to your diet, but also displaces healthier foods that would provide better nutrition.

Individuals who drink excessively often eat diets inadequate in nutrients, especially vitamins and minerals. Often, they drink too much and don't eat enough. Those who consume more than 30 percent of their daily calories from alcohol tend to consume less protein, fiber, vitamins A, C, D, riboflavin, and thiamin, and the minerals calcium and iron.[25] This isn't surprising once you consider that if a person consuming 2,000 calories daily devotes 600 (30 percent) of these calories to alcohol, there would only be 1,400 calories left to meet all of his or her nutrient needs. When you're routinely limited to a diet of 1,400 calories daily, you're bound to have nutrient deficiencies.

Excessive alcohol consumption can also affect how the body handles the essential nutrients it actually gets. Routinely drinking too much alcohol can interfere with the absorption and/or use of protein, zinc, magnesium, the B vitamins thiamin, folate, and B_{12}, and the fat-soluble vitamins A, D, E, and K. As you have read in previous chapters, a chronic deficiency of nutrients can cause a cascade of ill health conditions and diseases. In particular, a thiamin deficiency can affect brain function, including memory loss, and increase the risk of Wernicke-Korsakoff syndrome, which includes mental confusion and uncontrolled muscle movement (see Chapter 7).

Alcohol Can Harm Your Digestive Organs, Heart, and Liver

Chronically drinking too much alcohol can lead to an inflamed esophagus. Alcohol inhibits the ability of the esophagus to contract. This enables the acid juices in the stomach to flow back up into the esophagus, causing inflammation. Chronic inflammation can be a stepping-stone to esophageal cancer. If you smoke when you drink, your chances of developing esophageal cancer, as well as mouth and throat cancer, are even higher.[26] Individuals who are heavy drinkers also have increased incidences of **gastritis** (*gastr* = stomach, *itis* = inflammation) and stomach ulcers.[27]

Excessive amounts of alcohol can also affect the beating and rhythm of the heart, which likely plays a role in the sudden deaths of some individuals who abuse alcohol.[28] It can damage heart tissue and increase the risk of hypertension. Hypertension is a risk factor for both heart disease and stroke.

Alcohol can also damage your liver and cause **alcoholic liver disease** (**Figure 9.6**). The disease develops in three stages, although some stages can occur simultaneously. The first stage of the disease is **fatty liver**, which can result from just a weekend or a few days of excessive drinking. Because alcohol metabolism takes top priority in the liver, the metabolism of other nutrients, including fats, will take a back seat to alcohol. Thus, the liver isn't able to metabolize all the fat that arrives in the liver, causing a buildup in this organ. Simultaneously, the liver uses some of the by-products of alcohol metabolism to make even more fat. The net effect is a liver that has cells that are full of fat.[29] A fatty liver can reverse itself *if* the alcohol consumption is stopped.

If the drinking doesn't stop, the second stage of liver disease, **alcoholic hepatitis**, can develop. In alcoholic hepatitis, the liver basically becomes irritated by various by-products of alcohol metabolism. Some by-products, namely acetaldehyde, are toxic to the liver. Free radicals, another by-product of alcohol metabolism, react with the proteins, lipids, and DNA in your cells, causing damage. Nausea, vomiting, fever, jaundice, and loss of appetite are signs of alcoholic hepatitis. Chronic, excessive amounts of alcohol may also impair your immune system, which can contribute to liver damage and increase the susceptibility to pneumonia and other infectious diseases.

Heavy drinking can also cause the increased passage of destructive **endotoxin**, which is released from bacteria in your intestines into your blood. Once endotoxin arrives in your liver, it can cause the release of substances called *cytokines* that further damage healthy liver cells and perpetuate scarring.[30]

As bouts of heavy drinking continue, chronic inflammation further injures the liver cells and can cause scarring. **Cirrhosis** is the third and final stage of alcoholic

gastritis Inflammation of the stomach.

alcoholic liver disease A degenerative liver condition that occurs in three stages: (1) fatty liver, (2) alcoholic hepatitis, and (3) cirrhosis.

fatty liver Stage 1 of alcoholic liver disease.

alcoholic hepatitis Stage 2 of alcoholic liver disease; due to chronic inflammation.

endotoxin A damaging product produced by intestinal bacteria that travels in the blood to the liver and initiates the release of cytokines that damage liver cells, leading to scarring.

cirrhosis Stage 3 of alcoholic liver disease in which liver cells die, causing severe scarring.

a **Normal liver**

b **Fatty liver**
A fatty liver can occur after just a few days of overconsumption.

c **Cirrhosis**
By the cirrhosis stage, permanent damage is done and scar tissue has developed.

Figure 9.6 Alcoholic Liver Disease

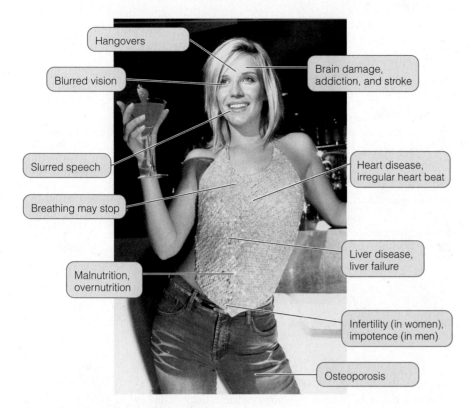

Figure 9.7 Effects of Alcohol on the Body

liver disease. In cirrhosis, the cells of the liver die and form scar tissue, which prevents this organ from performing critical metabolic roles, such as filtering toxins and waste products in the blood and out of the body. If these toxins and waste products build up, it can lead to mental confusion, nausea, tremors or shakiness, and even coma.

As many as 70 percent of individuals with alcoholic hepatitis end up developing cirrhosis.[31] Unfortunately, cirrhosis is among the 15 leading causes of deaths among Americans.[32] **Figure 9.7** summarizes the many harmful effects of excessive drinking.

Alcohol Can Put a Healthy Pregnancy at Risk

More than 30 years ago, Drs. David Smith and Kenneth Jones noticed an interesting trait among children in their clinic at the University of Washington School of Medicine. Some children looked alike even though they weren't related. Many had facial abnormalities such as eyes with very small openings and thin upper lips (**Figure 9.8** on the next page). These children also weren't physically growing as normally as other children their age, and they seemed to have some mental and behavioral difficulties, such as reduced attention span and memory, and learning disabilities. The scientists discovered that these children were all born to women who drank alcohol during their pregnancy. The doctors coined the term "fetal alcohol syndrome" (FAS) to describe these physical, mental, and behavioral abnormalities.[33]

When a pregnant woman drinks, she is never drinking alone—her fetus becomes her drinking partner. Because the baby is developing, the alcohol isn't broken down as quickly as in the mother's body. The baby's BAC can become higher and stay higher longer than the mother's, causing serious damage to its central nervous system, particularly the brain. FAS is the leading cause of mental retardation and birth defects in the United States. Children with FAS often have problems in school and interacting

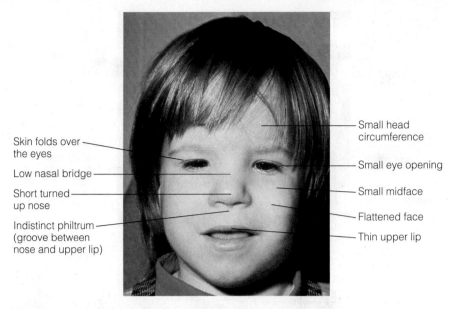

Skin folds over the eyes

Low nasal bridge

Short turned up nose

Indistinct philtrum (groove between nose and upper lip)

Small head circumference

Small eye opening

Small midface

Flattened face

Thin upper lip

Figure 9.8 Fetal Alcohol Syndrome
Children born with fetal alcohol syndrome often have facial abnormalities.

What Are Those Drinks Costing You?

Did you ever consider how much you're spending on alcohol in a given year? Use the Alcohol Cost Calculator in the Calculators section of www.collegedrinkingprevention.gov to see how quickly a few drinks will add up.

fetal alcohol spectrum disorders (FASDs) A range of conditions that can occur in children who are exposed to alcohol in utero. Fetal alcohol syndrome (FAS) is the most severe of the FASDs; children with FAS will display physical, mental, and behavioral abnormalities.

alcohol abuse The continuation of alcohol consumption even though this behavior has created social, legal, and/or health problems.

alcoholism Chronic disease with genetic, psychological, and environmental components; also referred to as *alcohol dependence*. Alcoholics crave alcohol, can't control their intake, and develop a higher tolerance for it. Alcoholics also exhibit a dependency on alcohol, as abstaining from drinking will cause withdrawal symptoms.

socially with others, poor coordination, low IQ, and problems with everyday living. It is estimated that 10 percent of women consume alcohol during pregnancy.[34]

Recently a newer term, **fetal alcohol spectrum disorders (FASDs)**, which includes FAS, has been adopted by major health organizations to describe a wide range of conditions that can occur in children exposed to alcohol prenatally. For example, not all children exposed to alcohol during pregnancy may experience *all* of the physical, mental, and behavioral abnormalities seen in FAS, which is the severe end of the FASDs. However, no matter the degree of abnormalities, FASDs are permanent. The only proven, safe amount of alcohol a pregnant woman can consume is *none*. Women should avoid alcohol if they think they are, or could become, pregnant.

The Take-Home Message Excessive drinking can disrupt your sleep, cause hangovers, and add extra calories to your diet, which can lead to weight gain. Drinking too much alcohol can also cause hormone imbalances; lead to malnutrition; harm your digestive organs, heart, and liver; and cause irreversible damage to a developing fetus during pregnancy. Individuals with alcoholic liver disease can experience a fatty liver and deterioration of the liver that develops into alcohol-related hepatitis and cirrhosis.

What Are Alcohol Abuse and Alcoholism?

When people choose not to drink alcohol responsibly, they often end up abusing alcohol, or suffering from a full-blown addiction. **Alcohol abuse** begins when a person allows alcohol to interfere with his or her life. He may have to call in sick to work or school due to a hangover, or he may have blank spots in his memory due to intoxication.[35] At the extreme end of the spectrum is the disease of **alcoholism**. By the time a person is addicted to alcohol, she is no longer in control of her drinking habits and is at serious risk of suffering long-term health damage.

Let's take a closer look at both of these categories of alcohol dysfunction.

Binge Drinking, Drinking and Driving, and Underage Drinking Are Forms of Alcohol Abuse

When people continue to consume alcohol even though the behavior has created social, legal, and/or health problems for them, they are abusing alcohol. Binge drinking and drunk driving are situations in which alcohol is being abused. Because 21 is the legal drinking age in the United States, anyone under this age who consumes alcohol is abusing it.

Binge Drinking

Binge drinking occurs when a male consumes 5 or more drinks or when a woman consumes 4 or more drinks in a very short time. It is estimated that more than 38 million American adults binge drink.[36]

College students who binge drink are more likely to miss classes, have hangovers, and experience unintentional injuries, such as falling, motor vehicle accidents, and drowning, and may even die (**Figure 9.9**).[37] Research also indicates that binge drinkers engage in more unplanned sexual activity and fail to use safe-sex strategies more frequently than nonbinge drinkers.[38] Sexual aggression and assaults on campus increase when drinking enters the picture. Alcohol is involved in thousands of reported sexual assaults and rapes on college campuses. Victims are often too drunk to consent to or refuse the actions of the other person.

Binge drinking is associated with many other health problems, such as hypertension, heart attack, sexually transmitted infections, suicide, homicide, and child abuse.[39] Binge drinking can also cause **blackouts**, which are periods of time that a person cannot remember, even though he or she may have been conscious. A research study of more than 700 college students found that more than half of them had blacked out at least once in their lives, and many found out after the fact that they had taken part in activities such as vandalism, unprotected sex, and driving a motor vehicle during the blackout period.[40]

College students many times have exaggerated perceptions of the amount of alcohol their peers consume. Many college-aged binge drinkers think that everyone is drinking all the time, but this isn't always the case. Those who think binge drinking is just a normal part of the college experience often have a circle of like-minded buddies who reinforce their misperceptions.

Drinking in groups is also associated with an increased intake of alcohol. Joining a fraternity or sorority tends to increase alcohol consumption among college students and frequenting frat parties raises the bar as to what is the normal amount and frequency of alcohol consumption during college life.[41] The Health Connection feature "Smashed: Story of a Drunken Girlhood" on page 354 describes the true story of Koren Zailckas and her struggles with alcohol abuse during college. The Self-Assessment on page 355 will help you recognize some red flags of alcohol abuse.

Binge drinking can lead to **alcohol poisoning**, which can have devastating results. Bradley was a junior at Michigan State University. At midnight on the eve of Brad's twenty-first birthday, he and a group of friends went to a bar to celebrate his birthday. A birthday tradition around campus was to "drink your age" in shots of liquor. Brad not only drank 21 shots but gulped down another three for a grand total of 24 shots in less than two hours. On the way out of the bar, Brad passed out. His friend brought him home and put him in his bed to "sleep it off." Unfortunately, because he had drunk an enormous amount of alcohol, his BAC level continued to rise to a lethal level, even though he was unconscious and no longer taking in alcohol. Brad stopped breathing and died before the sun came up on his twenty-first birthday.[42]

Number of college students, 18–24, per year

| Deaths | Sexual assaults | Injuries | Assaults |
| 1,825 | 97,000 | 599,000 | 696,000 |

Figure 9.9 Consequences of College Binge Drinking
Alcohol use by college students results in numerous assaults, injuries, and deaths each year.

Source: National Institute on Alcohol Abuse and Alcoholism. 2012. College Drinking. Available at http://pubs.niaaa.nih.gov. Accessed June 2013.

binge drinking The consumption of 5 or more alcoholic drinks by men, or 4 or more drinks by women, in a very short time.

blackouts Periods of time when an intoxicated person cannot recall part or all of an event.

alcohol poisoning When the BAC rises to such an extreme level that a person's central nervous system is affected and his or her breathing and heart rate are interrupted.

Smashed: Story of a Drunken Girlhood

Koren Zailckas was a shy, insecure girl raised in an upscale town in the Boston suburbs. She started drinking at the age of 14, and almost from her first sip, there was no turning back. During a socially awkward adolescence, Koren found it difficult to be at ease around other people, particularly girls her own age. When she drank, she became assertive and friendly. She bonded with other girls and met tons of guys. Throughout her high school and college years, alcohol was her crutch and best pal.

Koren didn't think of herself as an alcoholic, but she was a binge drinker. She drank herself into her first blackout with a thermos full of vodka at the age of 16. She woke up in her bedroom wearing a hospital Johnny and a pink plastic bracelet on her wrist. The bracelet was compliments of her local hospital emergency room. The Johnny had replaced her vomit-covered clothes from the night before. Her stomach had been pumped. Her parents had carried her from the back seat of the family car to her bedroom in the middle of the night. They were devastated.

As a freshman entering college, Koren used beer and liquor to make friends and be accepted. She pledged a sorority for the sisterhood and booze. She frequently drank herself into a state of numbness and allowed sorority sisters and male friends to make many of her decisions. She was often the last girl to leave the party because she was too drunk to know that she should have left an hour before.

After college graduation, Koren continued her drunken lifestyle in New York City. She worked hard during the day and drank hard at night. One morning she woke up in a strange bed, in a strange condo, next to a stranger from the cab ride the night before. For Koren, this was rock bottom. She realized that her chronic drinking was a magnet for like-minded people who similarly abused alcohol and were as damaged in life as she. But she wanted a good life. She wanted sound friendships and self-confidence, and she recognized that she wasn't going to achieve these goals with alcohol. At that moment, she decided to get help.

Through guidance from an addiction counselor and her own drive to quit drinking, Koren stopped her destructive behavior and began surrounding herself with a healthier circle of friends. Today, she is sober, and has a new lease on life.

You can read more about Koren's struggles and triumphs in her best-selling book, *Smashed* (Penguin, 2006).

Table 9.4	
The CAGE Screening Tool	
C	Have you ever felt that you should **c**ut down on your drinking?
A	Have people **a**nnoyed you by criticizing your drinking?
G	Have you ever felt **g**uilty about your drinking?
E	Have you ever had a drink first thing in the morning (**e**ye opener) to steady your nerves of get rid of a hangover?

Source: National Institute on Alcohol Abuse and Alcoholism. 2005. Screening for Alcohol Use and Alcohol-Related Problems. Available at http://pubs.niaaa.nih.gov. Accessed June 2013.

Chronic drinking can lead to **alcohol tolerance**, which occurs over time as the body adjusts to long-term alcohol use. As the brain becomes less sensitive to alcohol, more is needed to get the same intoxicating effect.[43] People who've developed an alcohol tolerance should not think they can drink more without damaging the body. The harmful effects that you read about in the previous section still occur.

Many health professionals use a four-question screening tool called CAGE to assess if their patients have a problem controlling their alcohol consumption (**Table 9.4**). If a person is experiencing two or more of the responses, this is a sign that alcohol abuse may be a problem for that individual.

Drinking and Driving

If you have spent any time behind a steering wheel, you know that you can't *just* drive. You have to drive defensively. Driving involves multitasking. You need to keep the car within your lane, stay within the speed limit, make constant quick decisions, and, of course, maneuver the car based on these decisions. Alcohol intake impairs all of these skills. It is illegal to drive in the United States with a BAC of 0.08 (some states in the United States have set their legal limit even lower), but the level of alcohol in

Red Flags for Alcohol Abuse

Complete the following self-assessment to see if you may be at increased risk for alcohol abuse.

1. Do you fail to fulfill major work, school, or home responsibilities because of your consumption of alcohol?
   Yes ☐ **No** ☐
2. Do you drink in situations that are potentially dangerous, such as while driving a car or operating heavy machinery?
   Yes ☐ **No** ☐
3. Do you experience repeated alcohol-related legal problems, such as being arrested for driving while intoxicated?
   Yes ☐ **No** ☐
4. Do you have relationship problems that are caused or made worse by alcohol?
   Yes ☐ **No** ☐
5. Do you try to hide your alcohol consumption from family or friends because you know they will tell you to stop?
   Yes ☐ **No** ☐

Answers

If you answered yes to any of these questions, you should speak with your health care provider for insight and guidance.

Source: Adapted from National Institute on Alcohol Abuse and Alcoholism. 2003. Understanding Alcohol: Investigations into Biology and Behavior. Available at http:// science.education.nih.gov. Accessed June 2013; U.S. Department of Health and Human Services. 1997. Ninth Special Report of the U.S. Congress on Alcohol and Health. Bethesda, MD: National Institute on Alcohol Abuse and Alcoholism.

---

the blood doesn't have to get that high to impair your driving. As we saw in Table 9.1, even the lowest level of BAC, the level that occurs after one alcoholic beverage, will impair alertness, judgment, and coordination. In 2011, almost 10,000 people died in alcohol-related, driving-impaired automobile accidents, accounting for 31 percent of total traffic fatalities that year.[44]

The latest data regarding the alcohol intake of Americans shows that adults admitted to driving while alcohol impaired over 110 million times in 2010 and that 1.4 million Americans were arrested for driving under the influence (DUI) of alcohol.[45] Legal penalties for DUI can be severe, ranging from stiff fines and loss of license to jail time in some states.

People who ride with drunk drivers put themselves at high risk of being involved in an accident. To educate the public about the risks of drinking and driving, the Ad Council and the United States Department of Transportation launched a campaign in the early 1980s to promote the Designated Driver Program. The concept of the program was to designate a sober driver at social gatherings to ensure that people who choose to drink have a safe ride home. The "Friends Don't Let Friends Drive Drunk" tagline has been instrumental in reducing the annual number of alcohol-related automobile fatalities since its inception in 1983. Unfortunately, many people think they can still drive safely as long as they consume "only a few" drinks. But because even one alcoholic beverage can affect the skills needed when driving, the only sober driver is one who completely abstains from drinking alcohol.

Another campaign, entitled "Buzzed Driving Is Drunk Driving," has been launched to reinforce the concept that the designated driver shouldn't be the least drunk member of the group, but rather the one who hasn't consumed any alcohol.

The "It's Only Another Beer" Black and Tan

8 oz. pilsner lager
8 oz. stout lager
1 frosty mug
1 icy road
1 pick-up truck
1 10-hour day
1 tired worker
A few rounds with the guys

Mix ingredients.
Add 1 totalled vehicle.

Never underestimate 'just a few.'
Buzzed driving is drunk driving.

Ad Council.org

U.S. Department of Transportation

"Buzzed driving is drunk driving" was a successful ad campaign that underscored the dangers of drinking and driving.

alcohol tolerance When the body adjusts to long-term alcohol use by becoming less sensitive to the alcohol. You need to consume more alcohol in order to get the same effect.

Drinking and driving can be deadly.

Underage Drinking

By age 15, more than 50 percent of adolescents in the United States have consumed alcohol.[46] In fact, individuals aged 12 through 20 drink 11 percent of all of the alcohol that is consumed in the United States.[47] Even more importantly, about 90 percent of the alcohol consumed by this age group is consumed by binge drinking.[48] Underage drinking not only increases the risk of violence, injuries, and other health risks, as discussed earlier, but alcohol consumption at this age can also interfere with brain development and lead to permanent cognitive and memory damage in teenagers.

Underage drinking, coupled with driving, is a disaster waiting to happen. Adolescent drivers are inexperienced behind the wheel to begin with, so it isn't surprising that automobile accidents are the number-one cause of death of young people between the ages of 15 and 20.[49] Those between the ages of 16 and 20 are 17 times more likely to die in an automobile accident when they have a BAC of 0.08 than when they have not been drinking.[50] In fact, this is why the minimum legal drinking age in the United States is 21. Studies conducted between 1970 and 1975, when several states had lowered the legal drinking age to under 21, showed that the rate of motor vehicle crashes and fatalities increased among teenagers.[51] Since 1984, all states have adopted 21 as the minimum legal drinking age and prohibited the sale of alcohol to underage individuals.

As the price of alcohol goes up, the number of people involved in fatal traffic accidents goes down.[52]

There is another danger in consuming alcohol at a young age. The earlier in life a person starts drinking, the higher the chances that alcohol will become a problem later in life. A person who starts drinking at age 15 is five times more likely to develop alcohol dependency or abuse later in life than an individual who doesn't start drinking until after the age of 21.[53]

Alcoholism Is a Disease

Individuals who suffer from alcoholism exhibit four classic symptoms:

1. they crave alcohol;
2. they continue to drink alcohol even though it causes repeated physical, psychological, or social problems;
3. they can't control or limit their intake once they start drinking; and
4. they have developed a dependency on alcohol.

An alcoholic's craving, loss of control, and physical dependency distinguish him or her as an "alcoholic" rather than a person who abuses alcohol but doesn't have these three other characteristics.[54]

Because the disease runs in families, research has shown that children of alcoholics are about four times more likely to develop alcohol-related problems than those who do not have parents with alcoholism.[55] However, this genetic risk alone does not destine a person to become an alcoholic. The risk for alcoholism is also influenced by the individual's environment. A person's home life, the drinking habits of his or her family and friends, social pressures, and access to alcohol will all affect whether he or she develops the disease. There is no cure for alcoholism. However, it can be treated using a physical and psychological approach. The physical symptoms, such as the severe craving for alcohol, can be treated with medication that helps reduce the craving. Psychologically, self-help therapies and support groups can be invaluable to an alcoholic on the road to recovery. Because alcoholics can't limit their consumption once they start drinking, reducing the amount of alcohol consumed will not work for them. They must eliminate alcohol entirely from their lifestyle to have a successful recovery.

Alcoholics Anonymous (AA), the first support group devoted to helping those who suffer with alcoholism, was created in 1935 by Bill Wilson, a stockbroker, and Dr. Robert Smith, a surgeon, who together declared themselves hopeless drunks. They founded AA to help themselves and others stay sober. With more than 100,000 groups worldwide, AA is a global fellowship of men and women with various backgrounds, lifestyles, and educational levels who meet, bond, and support each other, with the sole purpose of remaining sober. AA's 12 steps for recovery and supportive group meetings help individuals maintain sobriety.[56]

If you are interested in learning more about AA or finding a group in your area, look in your local telephone directory or online at www.alcoholics-anonymous.org. Everyone is welcomed at their meetings, including family members, friends, and coworkers.

Alcohol abusers and alcoholics should avoid alcohol. But they're not the only ones. According to the latest *Dietary Guidelines for Americans*, the following people should also abstain from alcohol:[57]

➤ Women of childbearing age who may become pregnant
➤ Pregnant women
➤ Children and adolescents
➤ Those taking medications that can interact with alcohol, which include prescription and over-the-counter medications
➤ Those with specific medical conditions, such as liver disease
➤ Those engaging in activities that require attention, skill, or coordination, such as driving or operating machinery
➤ Those who cannot restrict their alcohol intake

For these individuals, abstinence is the best option, as even modest amounts of alcohol can have detrimental health effects.

The Take-Home Message Individuals who abuse alcohol by binge drinking, drinking and driving, and underage drinking are putting themselves and others at risk of injuries, violence, and even death. Alcoholism is a disease that can't be cured, but it can be treated with medical help and psychological support. People who are addicted to alcohol need to abstain from drinking it entirely. Other individuals who need to avoid alcohol include pregnant and lactating women; women who may become pregnant; anyone who is under the legal drinking age; those with specific medical conditions or taking certain medications; people who operate heavy machinery; those who plan to drive, operate machinery, or take part in activities (such as swimming or climbing a ladder) in which impaired judgment could provoke an injury; and those who cannot control their intake.

Table**TIPS**

Keeping Your Drinking to a Moderate Amount

Never drink on an empty stomach. The alcohol will be absorbed too quickly, which will impair your judgment and lower your willpower to decline the next drink.

Make your first—and even your second—drink at a party a tall glass of water. This will allow you to pace yourself and eliminate the chance that you will guzzle your first alcoholic drink because you are thirsty. Also, have a glass of water before you have a second alcoholic drink. By the time you drink all this water, it will be time to go home.

Drink fun nonalcoholic drinks. Try a Virgin Mary (a Bloody Mary without the vodka), a tame margarita (use the mix and don't add the tequila), or a Tom Collins without the gin (club soda, lemon, and sugar).

Be an alcohol snob. Rather than consume excessive amounts of cheap beer or jug wine at parties, just have one better quality microbrewed beer or a glass of nice wine. Don't drink a lot of junk; drink a little of the good stuff.

Become the standing Designated Driver among your friends and make your passengers reimburse you for the cost of the gasoline. You'll be everyone's best friend and have the money to buy the good stuff to drink when you're off duty.

MADE over MADE better

Trendy "mocktails" are increasing in popularity. These nonalcoholic beverages can be a caloric bargain in comparison with traditional cocktails.

Here are some typical cocktails made over and made nutritionally better!

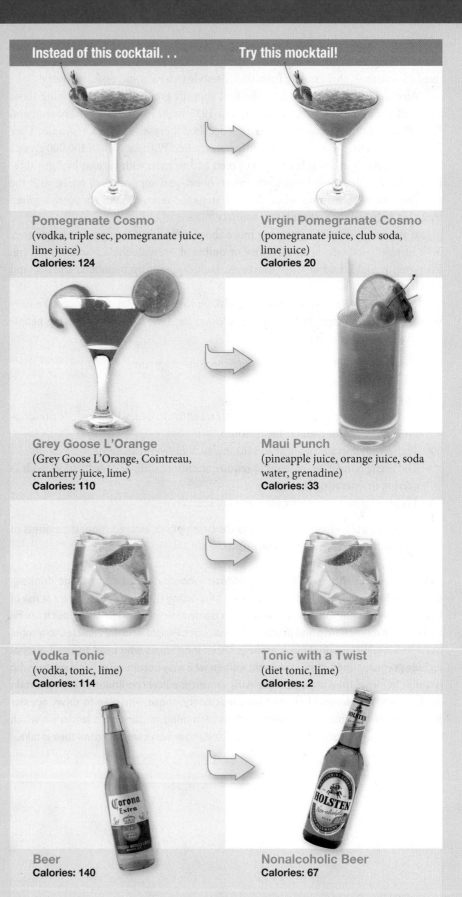

Instead of this cocktail. . .   **Try this mocktail!**

Pomegranate Cosmo
(vodka, triple sec, pomegranate juice, lime juice)
Calories: 124

Virgin Pomegranate Cosmo
(pomegranate juice, club soda, lime juice)
Calories 20

Grey Goose L'Orange
(Grey Goose L'Orange, Cointreau, cranberry juice, lime)
Calories: 110

Maui Punch
(pineapple juice, orange juice, soda water, grenadine)
Calories: 33

Vodka Tonic
(vodka, tonic, lime)
Calories: 114

Tonic with a Twist
(diet tonic, lime)
Calories: 2

Beer
Calories: 140

Nonalcoholic Beer
Calories: 67

Do the Health Benefits of Drinking Alcohol Outweigh the Risks?

Do the Health Benefits of Drinking Alcohol Outweigh the Risks? Many people have heard about the supposed health benefits of moderate alcohol consumption, but the potential negative health effects of drinking alcohol in excess—alcoholism, cirrhosis, and behavioral issues—are still very big problems in the United States.

Should young adults drink alcohol for its health benefits? Or do the risks associated with alcohol consumption outweigh those benefits? After you've read the arguments for and against, answer the critical thinking questions and decide for yourself.

yes

- There is evidence that moderate alcohol consumption reduces the risk of heart attack and stroke.[1]

- Moderate alcohol consumption may also lead to fewer gallstones, fewer kidney stones, and improved cognitive function in the elderly.[2]

- People who drink alcohol in moderation have been shown to have greater longevity than those who abstain or those who abuse alcohol.[3]

- One review of several studies concludes that moderate use of alcohol may reduce the risk of type 2 diabetes.[4]

- Beer and wine can provide some nutrients, including soluble fiber, vitamins, anti-oxidants, and minerals.[5]

no

- Alcohol consumption is disproportionately risky for college students, for whom binge drinking is often an issue.[6]

- It is estimated that each year, among college students aged 18–24, 1,825 die from alcohol-related unintentional injuries, including motor vehicle crashes, 599,000 are unintentionally injured under the influence of alcohol, 696,000 are assaulted by another student who has been drinking, 97,000 are victims of alcohol-related sexual assault or date rape, and 3,360,000 drive under the influence of alcohol.[7]

- Because the brain is not fully developed until the early twenties, underage consumption of alcohol can compromise the development of the brain.[8]

- People who start drinking at an early age are more likely to become addicted.[9]

what do you think?

1. Are the benefits of alcohol consumption worth the risks? **2.** How are those risks different for you and your peers as opposed to the general population? **3.** Why do you think overconsumption of alcohol is so prevalent among college students? **4.** Aside from abstaining from alcohol entirely, how can some of the potential risks associated with drinking be avoided?

1 Alcohol Is a Nonessential Nutrient That Is Made through Fermentation or Distillation

Ethanol is the type of alcohol found in alcoholic beverages. While it provides calories, you don't need to consume alcoholic beverages to maintain good health. Alcoholic beverages are made via the processes of fermentation (turning sugars into alcohol and carbon dioxide; examples include beer and wine) or distillation (causing alcohol to vaporize and then collecting and condensing the vapor; examples include distilled spirits).

2 People Drink Alcohol For Many Reasons

Alcohol produces an initial euphoric, pleasurable state of mind. Drinking alcohol in moderation may help reduce the risk of heart disease in older adults. For adults who choose to drink, moderate alcohol consumption is considered up to one drink for women daily and up to two drinks a day for men. A standard drink is 12 ounces of beer, 5 ounces of wine, or 1.5 ounces of liquor.

3 Your Body Works to Metabolize Alcohol As Soon As You Drink It

About 20 percent of the alcohol you drink is absorbed in the stomach. The rest is absorbed in the small intestine. Alcohol dehydrogenase begins to metabolize some of the alcohol in the stomach before it reaches your blood. Alcohol mixes with water and is distributed in the watery tissues of the body. Women have less body water and less alcohol dehydrogenase in their stomachs than men. Both of these factors cause women to feel the narcotic effects of alcohol sooner than men do.

The majority of the alcohol you consume is metabolized in your liver. Some alcohol is lost from your body in your breath and urine. Your liver can only metabolize about one standard drink in about 1½ to 2 hours. As you drink more alcohol, your BAC goes up, as does your level of impairment and intoxication.

Whereas alcohol is often thought of as a stimulant, it is actually a central nervous system depressant. Your brain is sensitive to the effects of alcohol, and depending on the amount you consume, alcohol can cause numerous mental, behavioral, and physical changes in your body. Your alertness, judgment, and coordination will initially be affected. As you drink more alcohol, your vision, speech, reasoning, and balance will be altered. An excessive amount of alcohol can interfere with your breathing and heart rate.

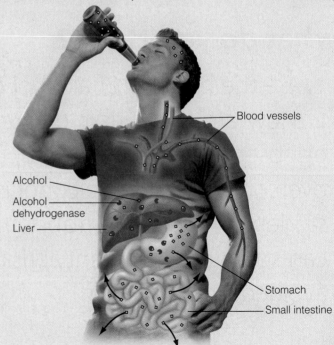

Blood vessels

Alcohol

Alcohol dehydrogenase

Liver

Stomach

Small intestine

4 Alcohol Can Have Short-Term and Long-Term Effects on the Body and Brain

Alcohol can have short-term effects on your body such as disrupting your sleep, causing hangovers, interfering with hormones, adding excess calories, and displacing healthier food choices from your diet. Chronically consuming excessive amounts of alcohol can harm your digestive organs, heart, and liver. It can also do long-term damage to the brain. The three stages of alcoholic liver disease are fatty liver, alcoholic hepatitis, and cirrhosis. Liver disease is one of the 15 leading causes of deaths among Americans. Maternal alcohol consumption can put a fetus at risk for fetal alcohol spectrum disorders.

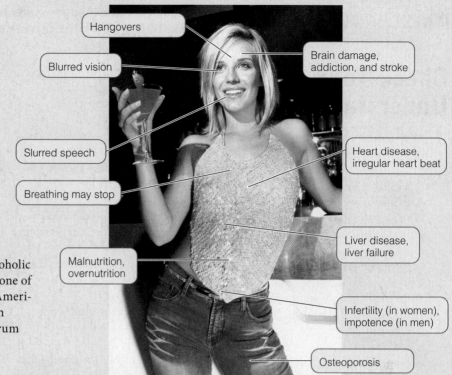

Hangovers

Blurred vision

Brain damage, addiction, and stroke

Slurred speech

Breathing may stop

Heart disease, irregular heart beat

Malnutrition, overnutrition

Liver disease, liver failure

Infertility (in women), impotence (in men)

Osteoporosis

5 Alcohol Abuse and Alcoholism Negatively Affect One's Life and Health

Alcohol abuse occurs when people continue to consume alcohol even though this behavior negatively affects their lives. Binge drinking, underage drinking, and drinking and driving are examples of alcohol abuse. Individuals who binge drink, many of whom are also underage, are at risk for blackouts and alcohol poisoning. Individuals who chronically drink alcohol often develop alcohol tolerance, which occurs when the brain becomes less sensitive to alcohol. Because alcohol affects alertness and judgment, the only safe amount of alcohol to consume when driving is none.

Alcoholism, also called alcohol dependence, is a disease characterized by four symptoms: a craving for alcohol, a higher tolerance for alcohol, the inability to control or limit one's intake, and a physical dependence on it. Genetics plays a role in increasing certain people's risk of developing alcoholism. Though alcoholism can't be cured, it can be treated with medical and psychological support and the avoidance of alcohol.

Alcohol should also be avoided by women of childbearing age who may become pregnant, or who are pregnant or lactating; anyone under the age of 21; those engaging in activities that require attention, skill, or coordination, such as driving or operating machinery; those taking certain medications or with specific medical conditions; and those who cannot restrict or limit their intake of alcohol.

Terms to Know

- alcohol
- ethanol
- fermentation
- distillation
- social drinking
- moderate alcohol consumption
- alcohol dehydrogenase
- blood alcohol concentration (BAC)
- hangover
- congeners
- gastritis
- alcoholic liver disease
- fatty liver
- alcoholic hepatitis
- cirrhosis
- alcohol abuse
- alcoholism
- binge drinking
- fetal alcohol spectrum disorders (FASDs)
- blackouts
- alcohol poisoning
- alcohol tolerance

Check Your Understanding

1. Alcohol provides
   a. 9 calories per gram.
   b. 7 calories per gram.
   c. 4 calories per gram.
   d. 0 calories per gram.
2. Which of the following is NOT considered a standard drink?
   a. a 12-ounce can of beer
   b. a 7-ounce glass of red wine
   c. a shot (1.5 ounces) of liquor
   d. a 5-ounce glass of white wine
3. The major site of alcohol metabolism in your body is your
   a. kidneys.
   b. lungs.
   c. liver.
   d. stomach.
4. Which of the following factors affect(s) your rate of absorption and the metabolism of alcohol?
   a. whether you're male or female
   b. the place where you are drinking
   c. the time of day you drink
   d. the individuals you are drinking with
5. Blood alcohol concentration (BAC) is the
   a. minimum amount of alcohol needed in your blood daily.
   b. amount of alcohol in your blood, measured in grams of alcohol per deciliter of blood.
   c. number of drinks you consumed in an hour.
   d. grams of alcohol per liter of beverage.
6. The *best* cure for a hangover is
   a. chicken soup.
   b. a light beer.
   c. time and abstinence.
   d. taking acetaminophen (Tylenol).
7. The first stage in alcoholic liver disease is
   a. malnutrition.
   b. a fatty liver.
   c. cirrhosis.
   d. alcoholic hepatitis.

8. The four characteristics of alcoholism are (1) a craving for alcohol, (2) the development of a higher tolerance for alcohol, (3) the inability to control or limit the intake of alcohol, and (4) _____.
   a. the inability to keep a stable job
   b. the inability to maintain social relationships
   c. the tendency to become violent
   d. the development of a dependency on alcohol
9. Of the following list, who shouldn't drink alcohol?
   a. your pregnant aunt
   b. your high-school–aged brother
   c. your uncle who has a stomach ulcer
   d. your father while he is riding the lawn mower
   e. all of the above
10. Drinking 4 to 5 alcoholic beverages on one occasion in a very short time is called
    a. alcoholism.
    b. drunk driving.
    c. blackout.
    d. binge drinking.

Answers

1. (b) Alcohol serves up 7 calories per gram, which is less than fat at 9 calories per gram, and more than carbohydrates and protein, which each provide 4 calories per gram. Alcohol isn't an essential nutrient—your body doesn't need it to survive—and it's not calorie free.
2. (b) Five ounces of wine is considered a standard drink, so a 7-ounce glass of red wine is the equivalent of almost 1.5 drinks.
3. (c) Most alcohol in the body is metabolized in the liver. A small amount of alcohol is lost in your urine (kidneys) and in your breath (your lungs). Some alcohol is also metabolized in your stomach, though substantially less than in your liver.

4. (a) Your gender will affect the rate of absorption and the metabolism of alcohol. Women have less of the enzyme alcohol dehydrogenase in their stomachs, which means they metabolize less alcohol in the stomach and more alcohol will be absorbed into the blood. They also tend to have less body water, so the concentration of alcohol in their systems is higher. The time of day and the place where you drink do not have any effect on the absorption and metabolism of alcohol. Your drinking partners also won't alter the absorption and metabolism of alcohol. Of course, they could influence the *amount* of alcohol you consume.
5. (b) Your BAC is the concentration of alcohol in your blood. It is measured in grams of alcohol per deciliter of blood. Your body doesn't need a minimum intake of alcohol daily. The number of drinks that you consume in an hour will affect your BAC; the more you drink, the higher the concentration of alcohol in your blood. BAC has nothing to do with the concentration of alcohol in a drink.
6. (c) The best cure is to stop drinking and let your body have the time it needs to recover from consuming too much alcohol. Neither chicken soup nor coffee nor any other food or beverage will cure the fatigue and other ill effects of drinking too much alcohol. Taking acetaminophen is not recommended, as its toxicity to your liver is enhanced if it is consumed while alcohol is being metabolized. The worst thing you can do for a hangover is to have another alcoholic beverage.
7. (b) The first stage of alcoholic liver disease is a fatty liver. Alcoholic hepatitis is the second stage, followed by cirrhosis. Some people who have alcoholic liver disease are also malnourished.

8. (d) The last characteristic of alcoholism is the development of a dependency on alcohol, such that a withdrawal will cause symptoms in the body. Although alcoholism can have financial consequences such as job instability, interfere with personal relationships, and increase the risk of violence, not all individuals with alcoholism have these experiences.

9. (e) All pregnant women should avoid alcohol, as drinking during pregnancy will increase the risk of fetal alcohol spectrum disorders (FASDs). Unless your brother is 21 years old, he shouldn't be drinking alcohol. Because alcohol causes gastritis, your uncle would benefit from avoiding alcohol. Your father should wait until he has finished mowing the lawn before having a drink, as this chore involves operating machinery that requires attention, skill, and coordination.

10. (d) Consuming that much alcohol in a very short time is considered binge drinking. Binge drinking can lead to alcoholism. Individuals who binge drink may experience blackouts or may drive while drunk.

Web Resources

- For more information about drinking at college, visit www.collegedrinkingprevention.gov
- For more information about alcohol and your health, visit the National Institute on Alcohol Abuse and Alcoholism (NIAAA) at www.niaaa.nih.gov
- For more information about alcohol consumption and its consequences, visit the Centers for Disease Control and Prevention's Alcohol and Public Health section, at www.cdc.gov

1. **False.** A straight shot of liquor may look and taste more potent than a can of beer, but it isn't. To learn more, turn to page 339.

2. **True.** Red wine does contain heart-healthy compounds. To find out more about them, turn to page 340.

3. **False.** The alcohol in your stomach and small intestine would continue to be absorbed, your blood alcohol concentration would continue to rise, and you could die from alcohol poisoning. See page 342 for more.

4. **True.** Women respond more quickly to the narcotic effects of alcohol than do men. To find out why, turn to page 344.

5. **False.** Drinking more alcohol isn't going to take away the ill effects of a hangover. To find out what will, turn to page 347.

6. **False.** Alcohol can interfere with your sex hormones and may impair your sexual function. To find out more, turn to page 347.

7. **True.** However, not all alcoholic beverages contain equal amounts of calories. For an eye-opener as to the amount of calories in some common alcoholic drinks, turn to page 347.

8. **False.** Binge drinking is considered the consumption of 5 or more alcoholic drinks by men, or 4 or more drinks by women, in a very short time. To find out more, turn to page 353.

9. **False.** Decades ago, some states lowered their legal drinking age, but today you have to be 21 to legally purchase and consume alcohol anywhere in the United States. Turn to page 356 to learn more.

10. **False.** Although counseling is an important component of alcoholism recovery, it will not cure it. Page 356 explains why.

10

Weight Management and Energy Balance

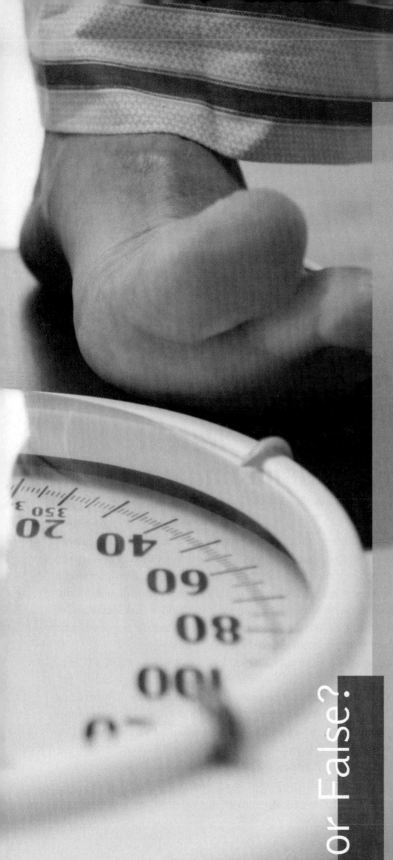

True or False?

1. Overweight people often have less restful **sleep** compared to people who are at a healthy weight. (T)(F)   p. 367

2. Being **skinny** is always healthy. (T)(F)   p. 367

3. One of the best ways to tell if you are at a healthy weight is to compare yourself to **celebrities**. (T)(F)   p. 368

4. Fat around the **hips** is as unhealthy as fat stored around the waist. (T)(F)   p. 370

5. The number of **calories** you burn daily is affected by your body size. (T)(F)   p. 374

6. Your body weight is affected by your genes and your **environment**. (T)(F)   p. 379

7. Eating **more vegetables** and fruits can help you lose weight. (T)(F)   p. 383

8. The nutrient that has the most effect on **satiety** is fat. (T)(F)   p. 386

9. **Disordered eating** and eating disorders are the same thing. (T)(F)   p. 396

10. Eating disorders can be **fatal**. (T)(F)   p. 399

See page 411 for the answers.

1. Explain the concept of a healthy weight, and differentiate between the conditions of underweight, overweight, and obesity.

2. Define and identify how to determine if you know you are at a healthy weight.

3. Explain what energy balance is, what determines your daily energy needs, and what are the effects of energy imbalance.

4. Explain the factors that affect body weight.

5. Explain how to lose weight healthfully.

6. Describe a basic plan for healthy weight maintenance.

7. Describe how to gain weight healthfully.

8. Define disordered eating and discuss the warning signs and treatment options for eating disorders.

Flip through a magazine, watch a little television, or spend some time online, and before long you'll find someone talking about weight loss. You may be used to so much coverage of weight management, but it hasn't always been that way. In the early 1960s, fewer than 32 percent of Americans were overweight, so weight didn't receive much media attention. Today, the majority of Americans are overweight, so it's a much hotter topic.[1] In fact, obesity is one of the most frequently covered health stories in the media.[2]

Americans currently spend more than $60 billion—the highest amount ever—on everything from over-the-counter diet pills to books, magazines, online support groups, and commercial dieting centers to help shed excess weight.[3] Unfortunately, these programs usually aren't successful, and the U.S. health care system bears more than $145 billion in costs of treating the medical complications associated with being overweight.[4] No matter what you personally weigh, some of your tax dollars are supporting these costs. Despite spending so much money on the battle of the bulge, we are not winning the war for weight control.

What is causing this trend, and how unhealthy is it? What does it mean to manage your weight, and what are the best strategies for doing so? Lastly, should we strive to be thin at all costs—or can this be equally unhealthy?

Let's try to figure this all out.

What Is a Healthy Weight and Why Is Maintaining It Important?

A **healthy weight** is considered a body weight that doesn't increase your risk of developing weight-related health problems or diseases. Rather than a single number, it's a range of weight that is appropriate for your gender, height, and muscle mass, a weight at which you feel energetic and fit. A healthy weight is also a *realistic* weight, one that you can maintain naturally through consuming a nourishing diet and engaging in regular physical activity. As the U.S. Centers for Disease Control and Prevention (CDC) puts it, a healthy weight is not a diet; it's a healthy lifestyle![5]

Weight management, then, means maintaining your weight within a healthy range. Either extreme—being very overweight or very underweight—can be unhealthy, a red flag for undernutrition of some nutrients, overnutrition of others, and impending health problems. Being **overweight**, or weighing 10 to 15 pounds more than your healthy weight, tends to be a stepping stone to **obesity**. A person with 25 to 40 or more pounds of weight above his or her healthy weight is considered obese. With more than 69 percent of Americans overweight and close to 36 percent of those obese, the American Medical Association now recognizes obesity as a disease.[6]

In addition to potentially leading to obesity, being overweight can increase your risk of numerous other health problems, including:

➤ Hypertension and stroke
➤ Heart disease
➤ Gallbladder disease
➤ Type 2 diabetes
➤ Osteoarthritis
➤ Some cancers
➤ Sleep apnea

Generally, as a person's weight increases, so does his or her blood pressure. Overweight individuals can experience increased retention of sodium, which causes both increased blood volume and resistance in the blood vessels. This and additional demands on the heart all likely contribute to high blood pressure.[7] High blood pressure increases the risk of stroke and heart disease. Overweight people also tend to have high blood levels of both fat and the "bad" LDL cholesterol, and less of the "good" HDL cholesterol, which is an unhealthy combination for the heart. High blood cholesterol levels increase the risk for gallstones and gallbladder disease. They are also more likely to contribute to an enlarged gallbladder, impeding its function.

More than 80 percent of those with type 2 diabetes are overweight. Excess weight causes the body's cells to become insulin resistant. Over time, this resistance causes the pancreas to work harder to produce more insulin and can eventually cause the pancreas to stop producing it altogether. Incidences of cancers of the colon, uterus, and breast (in postmenopausal women) are also higher. Excess weight means extra stress on joints, especially in the knees, hips, and lower back, and contributes to osteoarthritis. Sleep apnea, a condition in which breathing stops for brief periods during sleep, disrupts a person's ability to obtain a restful slumber. The fat stored around the neck, as well as fat-induced inflammation in that area, may contribute to a smaller airway and interfere with breathing.[8]

Although being overweight can lead to many unhealthy conditions and diseases, the good news is that losing as little as 5 to 10 percent of a person's body weight can produce health benefits such as lower blood pressure, cholesterol, and glucose levels in the body.[9]

While overweight and obesity are currently far more prevalent among Americans, being **underweight** is also of concern, especially among teens and young adults, because of the potential negative health effects that are associated with it. Being underweight means that a person doesn't have enough weight on his or her body for his or her height. For some, being very slender is their natural, healthy body shape, but for others, it's a sign of malnutrition. Excessive calorie restriction and/or physical activity, emotional stress, or an underlying medical condition such as cancer or an intestinal disorder can often cause someone to be underweight.[10] Young adults who are underweight often face health challenges, including nutrient deficiencies, electrolyte imbalance, low energy levels, and decreased concentration. Over time, more serious health effects can arise, such as heart complications that can be fatal. For older adults (those over age 65), being undernourished means an increased risk for low body protein and fat stores and a depressed immune system, which makes it more difficult to fight infections. Injuries, wounds, and illnesses that would normally abate in healthy individuals can cause serious medical complications, including death, for older individuals.[11]

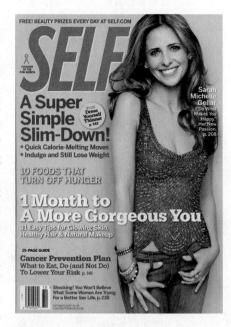

Weight management is such a hot topic in the United States that it is frequently covered by the mainstream media.

American people aren't the only ones getting bigger—American pets are also putting on pounds. According to the National Academy of Sciences, there has been an epidemic of obesity among pet dogs and cats.

healthy weight A body weight in relationship to your height that doesn't increase the risk of developing any weight-related health problems or diseases.

weight management Maintaining your weight within a healthy range.

overweight Carrying extra weight on your body in relation to your height. Clinically defined as having a body mass index (BMI) of 25 to 29.9.

obesity Carrying an excessive amount of body fat above the level of being overweight. Clinically defined as having a body mass index (BMI) of 30 or higher.

underweight Weighing less than is healthy for your height. Clinically defined as having a body mass index (BMI) below 18.5.

The Take-Home Message A healthy weight is a body weight that doesn't increase your risk of developing weight-related health problems or diseases. It's realistic for your build and can be attained with a nourishing diet and regular exercise. Weight management means maintaining a healthy weight to reduce your risk for specific health problems. Being overweight, obese, or underweight can be unhealthy.

How Do You Know If You're at a Healthy Weight?

Over the years, varying body shapes have trended in and out of the media spotlight. In the 1980s, fashion models were 8 percent thinner than the average woman. Today, the typical cover girl is more than 20 percent thinner. The male physique is being held to a similarly unattainable standard. Witness the change from scrawny to beefy in toy action figures over the years.[12] Although models, celebrities, and dolls may reflect the "in" look, they don't necessarily correlate with good health, nor should they be your reference for the body weight that *you* should strive to obtain.

So, how can you determine if your body weight is within a healthy range? Following are a few methods that can be helpful.

BMI Measurements Can Provide a General Guideline

One of the most common and inexpensive ways to assess a healthy weight is to measure **body mass index (BMI)**. BMI is a calculation of weight in relationship to height using the following formula:

$$BMI = \frac{\text{weight (pounds)} \times 703}{\text{height squared (inches}^2)}$$

Here's how to interpret your BMI:

➤ *Underweight.* If your BMI falls in the first part of the graph (shaded orange in **Figure 10.1**), it is below 18.5 and you are considered underweight. Although people who are underweight are at reduced risk for the chronic diseases associated with obesity, they are at increased risk for infection, and their overall risk of mortality is higher than for people of healthy weight.

➤ *Healthy weight.* If your BMI falls between 18.5 and 24.9 (the green part of the graph), it is considered healthy.

Over the years, the idealized model look has gone from curvy to stick thin to sporty and back to waiflike again. Today, superslender women are the norm in magazines and movies.

The male physique depicted in popular action figures in the 1970s, like Luke Skywalker and Han Solo from *Star Wars*, was more realistic than the bulked-up versions of the late 1990s.

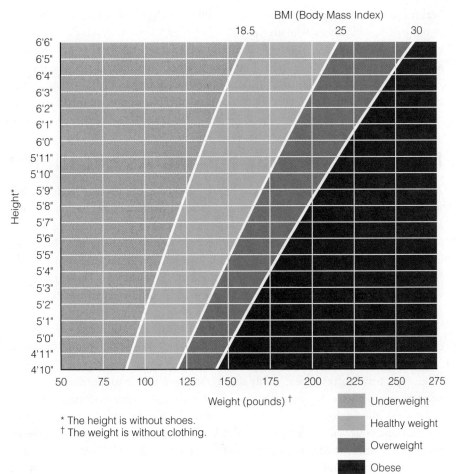

BMI (Body Mass Index)

Height*

Weight (pounds) †

* The height is without shoes.
† The weight is without clothing.

Underweight
Healthy weight
Overweight
Obese

➤ *Overweight.* If your BMI falls between 25 and 29.9 (the blue area of the graph), you are considered overweight. As the amount you are overweight increases, so does your risk of dying from certain chronic diseases, although research shows that the risk is modest until a person reaches a BMI of closer to 30.

➤ *Obese.* If your BMI is 30 or over (the purple part of the graph), you are considered obese. Obese individuals have a 50 to 100 percent higher risk of dying prematurely, compared with those at a healthy weight.[13]

BMI is used as a screening tool to identify potential weight problems and should not be used as a diagnostic tool for specific medical conditions. Also, because BMI is not a direct measure of percentage body fat, it may not be accurate for everyone. This is particularly true for athletes. Many athletes have a BMI that should put them in the "unhealthy" category, but they aren't unhealthy because their body weight is predominantly muscle, not fat. For example, Tom Brady, the New England Patriots quarterback, and Peyton Manning, the quarterback for the Denver Broncos, both have a BMI of 27. They are not "overfat" and unhealthy, and their muscular weight does not increase their health risk. Therefore, athletes and other people with a high percentage of muscle mass may have a BMI over 25 yet still be healthy, as they have a low percentage of body fat. Many young, athletic adults may also have BMI results similar to those of these professional athletes, but once again, they are not considered "unhealthy" or at risk for other health conditions because of their muscular physique.

In contrast, a person may be in a healthy weight range, but may have been steadily losing weight due to an unbalanced diet or poor health. This chronic weight loss is a loss of muscle mass and the depletion of nutrient stores in the body, which increases

body mass index (BMI) A calculation of your weight in relationship to your height. A BMI between 18.5 and 24.9 is considered healthy.

Determining Your BMI

Want to know your exact BMI based on your height and weight? Use the BMI calculator at www.nhlbisupport.com.

health risks even though the BMI seems healthy. Lastly, because height is factored into the BMI, individuals who are very short—under 5 feet—may have a high BMI, but, similarly to athletes, may not be unhealthy.[14] In general, BMI is best used to assess overweight and obesity for populations rather than individuals. If someone is classified as underweight, overweight, or obese according to BMI, further assessments by a health care provider will determine health risks or present medical conditions associated with weight.

Measure Your Body Fat and Its Location

According to the American College of Sports Medicine, the average healthy adult male between the ages of 20 and 49 carries 16 to 21 percent of his weight as body fat. The average woman of the same age range carries 22 to 26 percent of her weight as body fat. There are several techniques you can use to measure total body fat, including skinfold thickness measurements, bioelectrical impedance, dual-energy X-ray absorptiometry, underwater weighing, and air displacement. These tests must be conducted by trained technicians and some of them can be expensive. **Table 10.1** describes the ways to measure body fat.

How much fat you carry isn't the only determinant of health risk—where you carry it also matters. **Central obesity**, that is, carrying excess fat around the waist (sometimes referred to as an "apple" body shape) versus carrying it around the buttocks, hips, and thighs (a "pear" body shape), has been shown to increase the risk of heart disease, diabetes, and hypertension.[15] Central obesity is due to storing too much **visceral fat** (the fat that surrounds organs in your chest and stomach and above your hips) around your waist (see **Figure 10.2**). (Another type of fat, called **subcutaneous fat**, is the fat sandwiched between your skin and your muscles.) On average, men tend to be apple shaped and women more pear shaped, because of the female hormone estrogen. This hormone is made by the ovaries and is responsible for prompting ovulation every menstrual cycle. The presence of estrogen causes more fat to be stored in the lower body than the abdomen, resulting in women of childbearing age being more pear shaped. However, keep in mind that women being more likely to have a

central obesity An excess storage of visceral fat in the abdominal area, which increases the risk of heart disease, diabetes, and hypertension.

visceral fat The fat stored in the abdominal area.

subcutaneous fat The fat located under the skin.

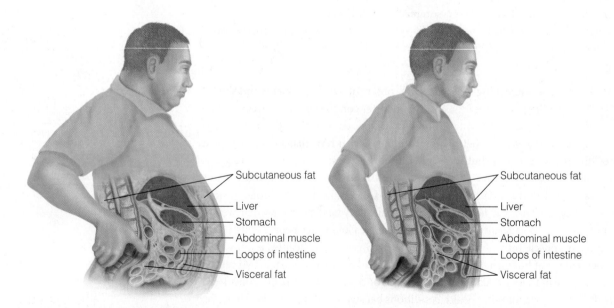

Figure 10.2 Visceral and Subcutaneous Fat Storage in the Body
Visceral fat stored around the waist is more likely to lead to health problems than subcutaneous fat stored elsewhere in the body.

Table 10.1

Ways to Measure Percentage of Body Fat

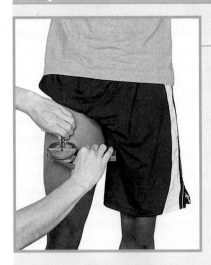

Skinfold Thickness Measurements

How It Is Done: Calipers are used to measure the thickness of fat that is located just under the skin in the arm, in the back, on the upper thigh, and in the waist area. From these measurements, percent body fat can be determined.
Cost: $

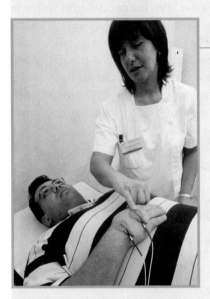

Bioelectrical Impedance

How It Is Done: An electric current flows through the body and its resistance is measured. Lean tissue is highly conductive and less resistant than fat mass. Based on the current flow, the volume of lean tissue can be estimated. From this information, the percentage of body fat can be determined.
Cost: $

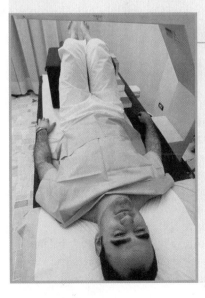

Dual-Energy X-Ray Absorptiometry (DXA)

How It Is Done An X-ray is used to measure bone, fat, and lean tissue. The type of tissue that the X-ray passes through will absorb different amounts of energy. The amount of energy lost will allow the percentage of body fat to be determined.
Cost: $$$

Underwater Weighing

How It Is Done A person is weighed on land and also suspended in a water tank. This is done to determine the density of the body. Fat is less dense and weighs less than muscle mass and will be reflected as such when the person is weighed in the water. The difference of a person's weight in water and on land is then used to calculate the percentage of body fat.
Cost: $$

Air Displacement Using a BodPod

How It Is Done A person's body volume is determined by measuring air displacement from a chamber. The person sits in a special chamber (called the BodPod) and the air displacement in the chamber is measured. From this measurement, the percentage of body fat can be estimated.
Cost: $$$

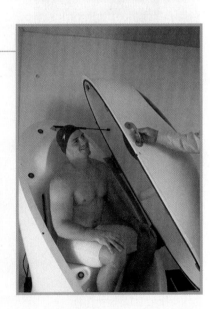

$ = very affordable
$$ = less affordable
$$$ = expensive

Figure 10.3 Waist Measurement
Your waist circumference should be measured around your bare abdomen just above your hip bone.

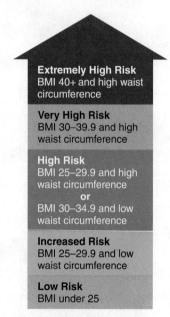

Extremely High Risk
BMI 40+ and high waist circumference

Very High Risk
BMI 30–39.9 and high waist circumference

High Risk
BMI 25–29.9 and high waist circumference
or
BMI 30–34.9 and low waist circumference

Increased Risk
BMI 25–29.9 and low waist circumference

Low Risk
BMI under 25

Figure 10.4 How at Risk Are You?
Considering both your BMI and your waist circumference can give you a good idea of your level of risk for health problems.

energy balance The state at which energy (calorie) intake and energy (calorie) output in the body are equal.

energy excess Consuming more energy than is expended. Also called *positive energy balance*.

energy deficit Expending more energy than is consumed. Also called *negative energy balance*.

pear shape is a generalization, not an absolute. People of both genders can be of either shape and develop health risks associated with it.

Because visceral fat is located near the liver, it is believed that fatty acids released from the fat storage area travel to the liver and can lead to insulin resistance, high levels of fat, low levels of the good HDL cholesterol, and high levels of LDL cholesterol in the blood, which all increase the risk of heart disease and diabetes. Insulin resistance also increases the risk for hypertension.[16] Men, postmenopausal women, and obese people tend to have more visceral fat than young adults and lean individuals.

Measuring a person's waist circumference can quickly reveal whether he or she is at risk. (**Figure 10.3** shows how to make this measurement accurately.) A woman with a waist measurement of more than 35 inches or a man with a belly that's more than 40 inches around is at a higher health risk than people with slimmer middles. Carrying extra fat around your waist can increase health risks even if you are not overweight. In other words, a person who may be at a healthy weight according to BMI, but who has excess fat around the middle, is at a higher health risk. A person who has both a BMI ≥ 25 and a large waist circumference is considered at a higher risk for health problems than if he or she only had a high BMI (**Figure 10.4**).

The Take-Home Message Body mass index (BMI) is a calculation of weight in relationship to height and can be used to assess if weight increases health risks. It is not a direct measure of body fat and may be inaccurate for people who are muscular or who are frail due to illness. Skinfold thickness measurements using calipers, bioelectrical impedance, dual-energy X-ray absorptiometry, underwater weighing, and air displacement are all techniques that can be used to measure the percentage of body fat. Individuals with central obesity, who carry excess fat around the middle, have an increased risk of several chronic diseases, regardless of BMI.

What Is Energy Balance and What Determines Energy Needs?

To maintain your weight, you need to make sure that you don't consume more calories than you expend daily. Spending as many calories as you take in is the concept behind energy balance.

Energy Balance Is Calories in versus Calories Out

Energy balance is the state at which your energy intake and your energy expenditure, both measured in calories, are equal (**Figure 10.5**). When you consume more calories than you expend, you have **energy excess** and are in *positive energy balance*. Routinely eating more calories than you expend will cause the storage of fat and weight gain. When your calorie intake falls short of your needs, you have an **energy deficit** and are in *negative energy balance*. Imbalances that occur over a long time period, such as weeks and months, are what change body weight.

You can determine whether you are in positive or negative energy balance by comparing the number of calories you take in to the number of calories you expend on a given day. Figuring out how many calories you take in is fairly straightforward.

Energy balance is the relationship between the food we eat and the energy we expend each day. Finding the proper balance between energy intake and energy expenditure allows us to maintain a healthy body weight.

ENERGY INTAKE = ENERGY EXPENDITURE = WEIGHT MAINTENANCE

ENERGY BALANCE

When the calories you consume meet your needs, you are in energy balance. Your weight will be stable.

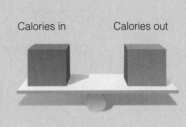
Calories in Calories out

ENERGY INTAKE < ENERGY EXPENDITURE = WEIGHT LOSS

ENERGY DEFICIT

When you consume fewer calories than you expend, your body will draw upon your stored energy to meet its needs. You will lose weight.

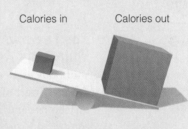
Calories in Calories out

ENERGY INTAKE > ENERGY EXPENDITURE = WEIGHT GAIN

ENERGY EXCESS

When you take in more calories than you need, the surplus calories will be stored as fat. You will gain weight.

Calories in Calories out

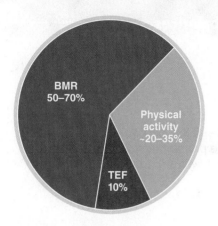

Figure 10.6 The Three Components of Energy Needs
The "calories out" side of the energy balance equation includes your basal metabolic rate (BMR), the thermic effect of food (TEF), and the energy you use to fuel physical activity.

An Estimated Energy Requirement Online Tool

To calculate a more precise EER, you need to record all of your daily physical activity. Visit the interactive tracker tool at www.ChooseMyPlate.gov and enter your gender, height, weight, age, and all the activities you do in a 24-hour period. The Tracker will then calculate your EER.

basal metabolism The amount of energy the body expends to meet its basic physiological needs. Also referred to as *basal metabolic rate (BMR)*.

lean body mass The body mass once the fat mass has been subtracted. It contains mostly muscle but also organs and fluids.

thermic effect of food (TEF) The amount of calories the body uses to digest, absorb, metabolize, and store food.

You can use the food label or a diet analysis program (like the one available with this book) to find out how many calories are in the foods and beverages you eat and drink.

You can also use the grams of macronutrients in foods to calculate the number of total calories they contain. Recall from Chapter 1 that carbohydrates and protein each contain 4 calories/gram and fat contains 9 calories/gram. (Note that alcohol, at 7 calories/gram, can also contribute calories.) Multiplying the number of grams of carbohydrates, protein, or fat by the calories per gram and then adding up these numbers will provide the total amount of calories in the food.

Calculating the number of calories you expend daily is a little more complicated.

Energy Needs Are Different for Everyone

Energy needs are unique to every individual, and your energy needs are different from those of your 80-year-old grandparents, your 50-year-old parents, and your marathon-running roommate. Your energy needs are comprised of your basal metabolism, the thermic effect of food (TEF), and the calories needed to fuel your physical activities. (See **Figure 10.6**.)

Your BMR Is the Minimum Amount of Energy You Need to Function

Even when you're not at the gym or sprinting to class, your body is using energy. Pumping your blood, expanding your lungs, and using your brain all require energy every moment of your life. **Basal metabolism** is the amount of energy expended to meet the basic physiological needs that enable your organs and cells to function. Also referred to as your *basal metabolic rate (BMR)*, it is the minimum energy needed to keep you alive.

Approximately 60 percent of your daily energy need is determined by your BMR. The factor that most affects your BMR, **lean body mass**, accounts for about 70 percent of your BMR. Age, gender, body size, genes, ethnicity, emotional and physical stress, thyroid hormone, nutritional state, and environmental temperature, as well as your caffeine and nicotine intake, affect your BMR. **Table 10.2** explains each of these factors.

The Thermic Effect of Food Is the Energy Your Body Needs to Process Food

Your body uses energy to extract the calories from the foods that you consume. The **thermic effect of food (TEF)** is the amount of calories you expend to digest, absorb, metabolize, and store your food. Approximately 10 percent of calories in the food consumed is used for TEF. In other words, if you eat a 100-calorie cookie, about 10 calories will be used to metabolize the cookie. The TEF varies by the type of food you eat. Protein and carbohydrate have a higher TEF than dietary fat. This is because your body requires more energy to digest, absorb, and metabolize amino acids, starches, and sugar into stored body fat than to metabolize dietary fat into body fat.

Physical Activity Will Increase Your Energy Needs

If you are very physically active, you're going to need more energy than someone who is sedentary. For sedentary people, the amount of energy expended in physical activity is less than half of their BMR. For very physically active individuals, such as athletes, it can be as much as double their BMR. The more physical activity you routinely incorporate into your day, the more calories you will need to eat to meet your energy needs. The amount of energy expended during physical activity goes beyond the activity itself. Exercise causes a small increase in energy expenditure for some time after the activity has stopped.[17]

Table 10.2

Factors That Affect Your Basal Metabolic Rate

Factor	Explanation
Lean body mass	Lean body mass, which is mostly muscle mass, is more metabolically active than fat tissue, so more calories are needed to maintain it. Athletes who have a large percentage of lean body mass due to their increased muscle mass will have a higher BMR than individuals who aren't athletic.
Age	For adults, BMR declines about 1 to 2 percent per decade after the early adult years, but it increases by 15 percent during pregnancy. For children, BMR increases during times of rapid growth such as infancy and adolescence.
Gender	Women have less lean body mass, and typically have a higher percentage of body fat than men. This results in women having up to a 10 percent lower BMR. Women also tend to have a smaller body size.
Body size	Larger individuals will have a higher BMR due to increased surface area compared with smaller individuals. More surface area means more heat lost from the body, which causes the metabolism rate to increase to maintain the body's temperature.
Genes	Research suggests that genes may affect BMR, as individuals within families have similar metabolic rates.
Ethnicity	African-Americans have BMRs that are about 10 percent lower than that of Caucasians.
Stress	Hormones such as epinephrine, which are released during emotional stress, increase BMR. Physiological stress on the body caused by injury, fever, burns, and infections also causes the release of hormones that raise BMR. Heat lost from the body through wounds, as well as the response of the immune system during infection, increase BMR.
Hormones	An increase in thyroid hormone increases BMR, whereas too little of this hormone lowers BMR. Hormone fluctuations during a woman's menstrual cycle lower BMR during the phase before ovulation.
Starvation	Both starvation and fasting for more than about 48 hours lower BMR.
Environmental temperature	Being very cold or very hot can increase BMR, but the change is minimal if you make adjustments in your clothing or in the temperature of your surroundings.
Caffeine	Caffeine can raise BMR, but only slightly, when consumed regularly in moderate amounts.
Drugs	Nicotine may increase BMR.* Drugs such as amphetamines and ephedrine increase BMR.

*Note: Smoking is not a weight-management strategy. Some people may think that replacing snacks with cigarettes helps them stay slim, but the health risks associated with smoking, such as lung cancer, heart disease, and stroke, make it a foolish habit. Anyone concerned about weight gain when quitting smoking can minimize the chances of this with exercise (plus, you'll be able to run farther and faster with your cleaner lungs!).

Source: Institute of Medicine, *Dietary Reference Intakes for Energy, Carbohydrate, Fiber, Fat, Fatty Acids, Cholesterol, Protein, and Amino Acids*. 2002. Available at www.iom.edu.

Calculating Your Energy Needs

Recall Table 2.1 from Chapter 2, which helped you estimate your energy needs. This table was derived from the DRIs' **estimated energy requirement (EER)**. The estimated energy requirement is the average calorie intake that is estimated to maintain energy balance based on a person's gender, age, height, body weight, and level of physical activity. (Physical activity levels are separated into categories ranging from sedentary to very active.) While Table 2.1 used a reference height and weight for each age grouping, you can calculate your own EER using your specific height and weight with the Self-Assessment "What's Your Estimated Energy Requirement (EER)?" on page 376.

Energy Imbalances over Time Can Lead to Changes in Body Weight

The handful of cheese curls that Pam eats every night while watching television is adding about 100 more calories than she needs daily. After three months, she's gained a little over two pounds. Bryan, in contrast, is so busy juggling studying with tennis

estimated energy requirement (EER)
The amount of daily energy needed to maintain a healthy body weight and meet energy (calorie) needs based on age, gender, height, weight, and activity level.

self-Assessment

What's Your Estimated Energy Requirement (EER)?

Calculating your EER is a two-step process.

1. First, complete the information below.
   a. My age is _____.
   b. My physical activity during the day based on the chart below is

Physical Activity	Male	Female
Sedentary (no exercise)	1.00	1.00
Low active (walks about 2 miles daily at 3–4 mph)	1.11	1.12
Active (walks about 7 miles daily at 3–4 mph)	1.25	1.27
Very active (walks about 17 miles daily at 3–4 mph)	1.48	1.45

   c. My weight in pounds is _____ divided by 2.2 = _____ kg.
   d. My height in inches is _____ divided by 39.4 = _____ meters.

2. Using your answers from each part of step 1, complete the following calculation based on your gender and age.

Males, 19+ years old, use this calculation:

$$662 - (9.53 \times \underset{a}{\underline{\quad}}) + \underset{b}{\underline{\quad}} \times [(15.91 \times \underset{c}{\underline{\quad}}) + (539.6 \times \underset{d}{\underline{\quad}})] = \underset{EER}{\underline{\quad}}$$

Females, 19+ years old, use this calculation:

$$354 - (6.91 \times \underset{a}{\underline{\quad}}) + \underset{b}{\underline{\quad}} \times [(9.36 \times \underset{c}{\underline{\quad}}) + (726 \times \underset{d}{\underline{\quad}})] = \underset{EER}{\underline{\quad}}$$

---

practice that he consumes about 50 calories fewer daily than he expends. After four months, he has dropped about 1½ pounds from his already light frame. Over time, a chronic energy imbalance results in a change in body weight. Let's look at what is happening inside your body when an energy imbalance occurs.

Reducing Calories Can Lead to Weight Loss

Consuming fewer calories than you need daily will cause your body to draw upon its energy stores to overcome the deficit. In Chapter 4, you learned that when you don't eat for a period of time, glycogen and fat are used as fuel sources to meet your body's glucose and energy needs until your next meal or snack. Amino acids from the breakdown of body protein, particularly muscle, can also be used to make glucose.

In prolonged fasting, all of the glycogen in your liver is depleted. The breakdown of body fat contributes to your energy needs, while the breakdown of muscle provides materials to meet your glucose needs. Ketone bodies are also generated through the incomplete breakdown of fat, and these are used as an energy source. People starting at a healthy weight can't live much beyond 60 days of fasting, as their fat stores, as well as about one-third of their lean tissue mass, will be depleted by this time.[18]

> Your body contains about 35 billion fat cells, which can expand to accommodate a surplus of calories.

Excess Calories Can Lead to Weight Gain

Eating more calories than you need, regardless of the foods they come from, will result in your body storing the excess as fat. Recall from Chapters 4 and 6 that you have limited capacity to store glucose as glycogen and you can't store extra protein. However, you have unlimited capacity to store fat.

Although the relationship between eating too many calories and gaining weight appears straightforward, this isn't necessarily the case. The causes of overweight and obesity and the ability to prevent them can be complex, as there is more to eating than just nourishing the body. Let's look at this next.

The Take-Home Message Energy balance is the relationship between your energy intake and your energy expenditure, which are both measured in calories. Your basal metabolism, the thermic effect of food (TEF), and your physical activities all determine your daily energy needs. When you don't eat enough calories to meet your needs, your glycogen and fat stores, as well as muscle mass, will be broken down for fuel. A chronic deficit of calories will produce weight loss. When you chronically consume more calories than you need, the excess will be stored as fat, and weight gain will occur.

What Factors Are Likely to Affect Body Weight?

Numerous factors influence weight management, starting with what and how often you eat. Physiology, genetics, and your environment also play a role. Let's look at how each of these can affect your body weight.

Hunger and Appetite Affect What You Eat

Recall from Chapter 3 that there is a difference between your physiological need for food (or hunger) and the psychological factors that prompt you to eat (your appetite). Hunger is the physical need for nourishment that drives you to consume food. Once you start eating, hunger will subside as the feeling of **satiation** begins to set in. Satiation will determine how long and how much you eat. **Satiety** is the sensation that you feel when you have had enough to eat. Satiety determines the length of time between eating episodes.[19] An increase in satiety will delay the start of your next meal or snack.

Your appetite is affected by hunger, as well as environmental factors, like seeing or smelling something that you think will taste good, your social setting, your stress level, and so forth. Hunger, in turn, is affected by many physiological mechanisms, as well as genetics. Both hunger and appetite ultimately affect what you eat.

Hunger is stimulated by circulating hormones and signals from your intestinal tract.

Physiological Mechanisms Help Regulate Hunger

Being sleep deprived can increase your appetite by lowering the levels of leptin and increasing the amount of ghrelin in your body.

Various physiologic feedback mechanisms involving the mouth, stomach, intestines, and brain all work together to increase or decrease your hunger. For example, many hormones play a role. When your stomach is empty, the hormone **ghrelin**, which is produced mainly in the stomach, signals your brain that you need to take in food. Your body produces more ghrelin during fasting (such as between meals) in order to stimulate hunger, and it produces less after food is consumed. Another hormone, **leptin**, which is produced in fat tissue, helps regulate your body fat by affecting hunger. As your fat stores increase, leptin signals the brain to decrease your level of hunger and food intake.

Once food enters your mouth, sensory signals are sent to the brain to tell you whether or not to continue eating. The feedback mechanism is very much affected by your prior experience of tasting that food.[20] For example, a spoonful of your favorite ice cream is a pleasant stimulus, and your brain would encourage you to keep eating it. However, if you took a sip of sour milk, this stimulus would be unacceptable to the brain, especially if the last time you drank sour milk it made you sick. Your brain will instruct you to spit out the sour milk so that you don't swallow it.

satiation The feeling during eating that determines how long and how much you eat.

satiety The sensation that you feel when you have had enough to eat. It determines how long you will go between meals and/or snacks.

ghrelin A hormone produced mainly in the stomach that increases hunger.

leptin A hormone produced in fat tissue that helps regulate body fat by signaling the reduction of food intake in the brain and interfering with the storage of fat in the cells.

Once food is in your stomach, other factors, such as the size of the meal, come into play. After you eat a large meal, your stomach becomes distended. This will signal the brain to decrease your hunger, and you will stop eating. A distended stomach also causes the release of **cholecystokinin**, a hormone that is associated with the feeling of satiation. Cholecystokinin will also decrease your hunger.[21]

When the food reaches your small intestine, the nutrients, protein, fatty acids, and monosaccharides all stimulate feedback to the brain to decrease your hunger. Once these nutrients are absorbed, the hormone insulin is released, which also causes the brain to decrease your hunger.[22]

Changes in your food intake can also cause changes in your hunger cues. If you suddenly decrease the size of your meals, you may feel an initial increase in hunger. If you continue eating smaller meals, your stomach adapts to the reduced quantity and the feelings of extreme hunger will diminish over time. After a while, a larger meal can make you feel extremely full and uncomfortable because your stomach has gotten used to smaller meals.[23] People sometimes refer to this effect as the "shrinking" of the stomach, but the organ itself does not get smaller.

In a perfect world, all these physiologic mechanisms, when recognized and responded to appropriately, would keep you in perfect energy balance. When you are hungry, you eat, and when you are satiated, you stop. The reality, however, is that many people override these mechanisms and end up in energy imbalance. Factors like genetics and the environment also affect how much energy you consume and expend.

Genetics Partially Determine Body Weight

Genetics has such a strong influence on your body weight that if your mother and father are overweight (BMI ≥ 25), your risk of becoming obese approximately doubles, and your risk triples if they are obese (BMI ≥ 30). If your parents are severely obese (BMI > 40), your risk increases fivefold.[24] Studies on separated identical twins raised in different home environments confirm this, as both twins showed similar weight gain and body fat distribution.[25]

Research suggests that genetic differences in the level or the functioning of some hormones can influence a person's body weight and appetite. For example, genetically high levels of ghrelin may cause some people to overeat and become obese.[26] Individuals who are genetically prone to being leptin deficient become massively obese, yet when they are given leptin, their appetite decreases and their weight falls to within a healthy range.[27] Ironically, many obese people have adequate amounts of leptin but the brain has developed a resistance to it, rendering its appetite control ineffective.[28] For these individuals, other mechanisms are coming into play that prevent leptin from functioning as a regulator of their appetite.

Genetics may also affect how calories are expended in the body by affecting **thermogenesis** (*thermo* = heat, *genesis* = origin), which is the production of heat in body cells. Genes may cause different rates of **nonexercise-associated thermogenesis (NEAT)**, which is the energy you expend during fidgeting, standing, chewing gum, getting up and turning off the television, and other nonexercise movement throughout the day. When some individuals overeat, they are able to rev up their NEAT to expend some of the excess calories and are thus better able to manage their energy balance.[29] Many overweight individuals don't appear to have this compensatory mechanism.

Some researchers have described a genetic "set point" that determines body weight. This theory holds that the body fights to remain at a specific body weight

People who share genes will often have similar body weights.

cholecystokinin A hormone released when the stomach is distended. It is associated with the feeling of satiation.

thermogenesis The production of heat in body cells.

nonexercise-associated thermogenesis (NEAT) The energy expenditure that occurs during nonexercise movements, such as fidgeting, standing, and chewing gum.

and opposes attempts at weight loss. The body may even enable very easy weight gain in order to get back to this "set point" when weight is lost. In other words, a person's weight remains fairly constant because the body "has a mind of its own." Given that the weight of Americans has disproportionately increased over the last few decades relative to previous decades, this theory either isn't true or the set point can be overridden.[30]

Research also suggests that people with a genetic propensity to become overweight experience greater challenges to preventing obesity in an environment that is conducive to gaining weight. This relationship is referred to as a **gene–environment interaction**. To explain how these two entities interact with each other, researchers have used the analogy that genes load the gun but an obesity-promoting environment pulls the trigger.[31] For instance, if a person's lifestyle stays the same, his or her weight should remain fairly stable. However, if the environment shifts to make it easier to gain weight, the body will also shift, but it will shift upward. This means that an environment in which people can easily and cheaply obtain endless amounts of energy-dense food may be one of the biggest culprits in the current obesity epidemic. In one study, rats, which should genetically be able to maintain a healthy body weight, were shown to overeat and become fat when they had access to unlimited fatty foods and sweets.[32]

The same effect has been observed in human populations. For instance, Pima Indians of the southwestern United States have a high rate of obesity. Research comparing Pimas in Mexico with Pimas living in Arizona suggested that the environment promoted weight gain in this weight-susceptible population. The traditional Mexican Pimas whom the researchers studied lived an active lifestyle and ate a diet rich in complex carbohydrates and lower in animal fats than that of the "Americanized" Pimas in Arizona, who had a more sedentary lifestyle and fatty diet. The overweight Mexican Pimas, on average, had a BMI of about 25, compared with the obese Arizona Pimas, who had, on average, a BMI of over 33.[33] The traditional Pimas had a better chance of avoiding obesity because they lived in a healthier environment. As this study suggests, even if you have a genetic predisposition to being overweight, it's not a done deal. If you are determined to make healthy dietary choices and engage in regular physical activity, you can "outsmart" your genes.

Environmental Factors Can Increase Appetite and Decrease Physical Activity

How many times have you eaten a satisfying meal before going to the movies, but bought a bucket of popcorn at the theater anyway? You didn't buy the popcorn because you were hungry. You just couldn't resist the buttery smell and the allure of munching during the film. Environmental factors don't just affect people who are genetically prone to being overweight—anyone can fall prey to an environment that encourages eating! In fact, there are many stimuli in the environment that can drive your appetite. In addition to aromas and certain venues such as movie theaters, events such as holidays and sporting events, people such as your friends and family, and even the convenience of obtaining food can all encourage you to eat even when you're not hungry.

Over the past few decades, the environment around us has changed in ways that have made it easier for many of us to incur an energy imbalance and a propensity to gain weight. Take the Self-Assessment "Does Your Environment Affect Your Energy Balance?" on page 380 to reflect upon how your environment may influence the lifestyle decisions that you make throughout your day.

Let's look at some environmental issues that are feeding Americans' energy imbalance.

Practical Nutrition VIDEO

Coffee Shop Strategies

Is stopping at a coffee shop part of your daily morning routine? If so, a few small changes to what you order could make a big difference to your waist line! Scan this QR code with your mobile device to access the video. You can also access the video in MasteringNutrition™.

gene–environment interaction The interaction of genetics and the environment that increases the risk of obesity in some people.

Does Your Environment Affect Your Energy Balance?

1. Do you eat out at least once a day?
   Yes ☐ **No** ☐

2. Do you often buy snacks at convenience stores, coffee shops, vending machines, sandwich shops, or other eateries?
   Yes ☐ **No** ☐

3. Do you buy the largest portions of fast foods or snacks because you think you're getting more for your money?
   Yes ☐ **No** ☐

4. When you order pizza, do you have it delivered?
   Yes ☐ **No** ☐

5. Do you drive around the parking lot to get the closest parking space to the entrance?
   Yes ☐ **No** ☐

6. Do you get off at the subway or bus stop that is nearest to your destination?
   Yes ☐ **No** ☐

7. Do you take the elevator when stairs are available in a building?
   Yes ☐ **No** ☐

8. Do you e-mail or call your friends and neighbors rather than walk next door to talk to them in person?
   Yes ☐ **No** ☐

Answers

All of the habits listed above contribute to an obesity-promoting environment. If you answered yes to more than half, you should think about how you can improve your lifestyle habits.

We Work More and Cook Less

One reason Americans are getting larger is that they often don't eat at home. Research shows that adults today spend more time traveling to work and devote more of their daily hours to work than in previous decades.[34] This longer workday means there is less time to devote to everyday activities, such as food preparation. In fact, the amount of time devoted to food preparation has declined by over 40 percent since 1965.[35]

Today, 32 percent of Americans' daily calories come from ready-to-eat foods that are prepared outside the home, and this is having an effect on the quality of their diets.[36] Research shows that when compared with foods made at home, foods that are obtained away from home, from establishments such as sit-down restaurants and fast-food outlets, contain more total fat, saturated fat, sodium, and cholesterol but less calcium, fiber, and iron. Not surprisingly, the food choices at these establishments are less likely to contain whole grains, fruit, and lean dairy foods.[37] Cooking less in the home and obtaining ready-to-eat foods outside the home isn't a formula that is healthy for the diets of Americans.

Dining out frequently is also associated with a higher BMI. Research suggests that there is a strong association between the consumption of one or more fast-food meals a week and obesity.[38] The top three foods selected when eating out, especially among college-aged diners, are energy-dense french fries, hamburgers, and pizza. Less-energy-dense, waist-friendly vegetables, fruits, and salads don't even make the top five choices on the list among college-aged diners. For many people, dining out often is harming their diet by making energy-dense foods too readily available and displacing less-energy-dense vegetables and fruits.

We Eat More (and More)

In the United States food is easy to get, there's a lot to choose from, and portion sizes are generous. All of these factors are associated with consuming too many calories.[39]

Years ago, people went to a bookstore for the sole purpose of buying a book. Now they go to a bookstore to sip a mocha latte and nibble on biscotti while they ponder which book to buy. Americans can grab breakfast at a hamburger drive-through, lunch at a fast-food court, a sub sandwich at many gas stations, and a three-course

Research has shown that women who dine out five or more times weekly consume close to 300 calories more on dining-out days than do women who eat at home.

meal of nachos, pizza, and ice cream at a movie theater. At any given moment of your day, you can probably easily find a bundle of calories to consume.

This access to a variety of foods is problematic for weight-conscious individuals. While the appeal of a food diminishes as it continues to be eaten (that is, the first bite will taste the best, but each subsequent bite loses some of that initial pleasure), having a variety of foods available allows the eater to move on to another food once boredom sets in.[40] The more good-tasting foods that are available, the more a person will eat. For example, during that three-course meal at the movie theater, once you're tired of the nachos, you can move on to the pizza, and when that loses its appeal, you can dig into the ice cream. If the pizza and ice cream weren't available, you would have stopped after the nachos and consumed fewer calories.

Over time, the portion sizes of many foods, such as french fries and sodas, have doubled, if not tripled, compared with the portions listed on food labels. Because the larger portions often cost only slightly more than the regular size, they are perceived as bargains by the consumer. Research shows that people tend to eat more of a food, and thus more calories, when larger portions are served.[41]

Portion sizes of french fries have more than doubled from the past. Choose the smaller size to reduce the ingestion of calories.

When serving yourself at home, the size of the serving bowl or package of food influences the amount of the food you put on your plate. Serving yourself from a large bowl or package has been shown to increase the serving size by more than 20 percent.[42] This means that you are more likely to scoop out (and eat) a bigger serving of ice cream from a half-gallon container than from a pint container. To make matters worse, most people don't compensate for these extra calories by reducing the portions at the next meal.[43]

The size of the average dinner plate has increased by more than 20 percent since 1960. The larger the plate, the more food it will hold, and the more food you will likely consume.

We Sit More and Move Less

Americans not only have more food choices and calories available to them in the food supply to choose from daily—about 600 calories more daily since 1970—but they are also expending fewer calories during their day.[44] The resulting increase in "calories in" and decrease in "calories out" is a recipe for an energy imbalance and weight gain. Compared with years past, Americans are expending less energy both at work and during their leisure time.

When your great-grandparents went to work in the morning, chances are good they headed out to the fields or off to the factory. Your parents and older siblings, though, are more likely to go to an office and sit in front of a computer, and you yourself probably sit at a desk for much of your day. This shift in work from jobs that required manual labor to jobs that are more sedentary has been shown to increase the risk of becoming overweight or obese.[45] One study found that men who sit for more than 6 hours during their workday are at higher risk of being overweight than those who sit for less than an hour daily.[46] Technology in the workplace now allows us to communicate with everyone without having to leave our desks. This means that people no longer have to get up and walk to see the colleague down the hall or the client across town. Researchers estimate that a 145-pound person expends 3.9 calories for each minute of walking, compared with 1.8 calories per minute sitting. Thus, walking 10 minutes during each workday to communicate in person with coworkers would expend 10,000 calories annually, yet only about 5,000 calories would be expended if the person spent those daily 10 minutes sitting in the office sending e-mails or calling colleagues on the phone.[47]

Labor-saving devices have also affected energy expenditure outside of work. Driving short distances is now the norm, while walking and biking have decreased over the years.[48] Dishes aren't washed by hand but are stacked in a dishwasher.[49] The labor saved by these devices adds up, and the cumulative daily savings of energy expenditure can be more than 100 calories.[50] As technology continues to advance and

Increased amounts of "screen time" are contributing to decreased amounts of physical activity.

allows you to become more energy efficient in your work and lifestyle habits, you need to offset this conservation of energy with *planned* physical activity at another time of the day.

More than half of Americans do not accumulate the recommended minimum 150 minutes (2 hours and 30 minutes) weekly of moderate-intensity aerobic activity such as brisk walking.[51] In fact, more than 20 percent of Americans report no leisure-time physical activity daily, due partly to the fact that leisure and social activities have become more sedentary.[52] Unfortunately, Americans are spending more than 41 hours weekly viewing their televisions, computers, and mobile phones.[53] Young adults in particular have increased their "screen time," due in part to a growing trend for watching videos on handheld mobile devices.[54]

We are moving less during both work and play. With less energy being expended, weight gain is becoming easier and the need for weight loss even greater. Combine this with an environment that is conducive to eating and with the genetic makeup of many Americans, and it's not difficult to see why many people are becoming overweight or obese (**Figure 10.7**). Many Americans have to begin making conscious diet and lifestyle changes that will help them lose weight, or at the very least, prevent further weight gain.

Let's look at what is a realistic amount of weight to lose and how to do it healthfully.

The Take-Home Message Your appetite is your desire to eat and is affected by hunger, satiation, and satiety. It is influenced by your physiology, your genes, and your environment. Physiological mechanisms, such as hormones, signal your brain to increase your hunger when you are hungry and decrease it after you have eaten. Genetics can make it more difficult for some individuals to manage their weight. The current environment—which provides easy access to a variety of excessive amounts of energy-dense foods and at the same time decreases energy expenditure—encourages obesity.

Less in-home food preparation
More dining out

Larger portion sizes
More energy-dense foods

Higher calorie intake

Lack of physical activity

Weight gain
Higher BMI

Figure 10.7 Environmental and Lifestyle Factors of Weight Gain
This flowchart shows how eating out more often leads to consuming larger portion sizes of energy-dense foods, which leads to intake of excess calories. Combine this with less physical activity and the result is weight gain and a higher BMI.

How Can You Lose Weight Healthfully?

According to the National Institutes of Health, overweight individuals should aim to lose about 10 percent of their body weight over a six-month period.[55] This means that the goal for an overweight 180-pound person should be to shed 18 pounds over six months, about 3 pounds a month, or ¾ pound weekly. Because a person must have an energy deficit of approximately 3,500 calories over time to lose a pound of fat, a deficit of 250 to 500 calories daily will result in a weight loss of about ½ to 1 pound weekly. This is a healthy rate of weight loss that you can sustain. Although fad diets promise dramatic weight loss "overnight," don't be fooled. These plans are not based on legitimate science, and some can endanger your health. We'll talk more about fad diets in the Examining the Evidence feature "Evaluating Popular Diets" on page 384.

Although there is no single diet approach that has been universally embraced, many health experts agree that a person needs to adjust three areas of life for successful, long-term weight loss (**Figure 10.8**):

➤ Diet
➤ Physical activity
➤ Behavior modification

Let's start with the diet.

Physical activity

Healthy diet

Behavior modification

Figure 10.8 Three Pieces of the Long-Term Weight-Loss Puzzle
Diet, physical activity, and behavior modification are all necessary for long-term weight management.

Eat Smart, Because Calories Count

When it comes to losing weight, you need to remember two important words: *calories count*—no matter where they come from. Because an energy imbalance of too many calories in and not enough calories out causes weight gain, reversing the imbalance will cause the opposite. That is, taking in fewer calories and burning off more will result in weight loss. However, cutting back too drastically on calories often results in a failed weight-loss attempt. If a person skips meals or isn't satiated at each meal because of skimpy portions, the person will experience hunger between meals and be more inclined to snack on energy-dense foods. Thus, a key strategy during the weight-loss process is for the person to eat a healthy, balanced diet that is not only lower in calories, but is also *satisfying*. One way you can add heft and satiation to your lower-calorie meals is by including higher-volume foods.

Eat More Vegetables, Fruit, and Fiber

People tend to eat the same amount of food regardless of its energy density—that is, the amount of calories in the meal.[56] In other words, you need a certain volume of food in order to feel full. As you learned in Chapter 4, it is very easy to overeat energy-dense, low-volume foods such as candy, which can easily fill you *out* before they fill you *up*. You'll overeat them before you become satiated. The reverse of this— eating high-volume, low-energy-density foods that fill you up before they fill you out—can help in weight management. High-volume foods include fruits and vegetables, which are bulked up because of their water content, and whole grains, which contain a lot of fiber. These foods are also low in fat (which contains 9 calories/gram) and high in carbohydrate (which contains only 4 calories/gram.) Research shows that these foods are associated with increased satiety and reduced feelings of hunger and calorie intake.[57]

Practical Nutrition **VIDEO**

What Does 100 Calories Look Like?

Every calorie counts! Let Joan show you how much more food you can get per calorie when you make high-volume, low-energy-density choices. Scan this QR code with your mobile device to access the video. You can also access the video in MasteringNutrition™.

Evaluating Popular Diets

Americans spend over $61 billion annually on weight-loss programs, products, and pills and are more than willing to keep reaching into their wallets for the next quick diet fix.[1] Though it may seem that there is a new fad diet around every corner, many of these diets have actually been around for years.

The low-carbohydrate, high-protein, and high-fat diets of the 1970s (Dr. Atkins' Diet Revolution) were replaced by the very high-carbohydrate and very low-fat diets of the 1980s (Pritikin diets), which continued into the early 1990s (Dr. Ornish's diet). These diets led the way to the more carbohydrate-restricted, moderate protein and fat diets of the late 1990s (the Zone diet), only to flip back to the low-carbohydrate, high-protein and high-fat diets in the early part of 2000s (Dr. Atkins' New Diet Revolution, South Beach). In the later part of the last decade, portion sizes and an emphasis on increasing whole grains, fruits, and vegetables in the diet became the talk of the diet scene. The table on the next page summarizes the main types of popular diet plans and the differences among them.

After decades of clashing diet books and plans, does one emerge as the clear winner in the battle of the bulge? The answer is no. Researchers who analyzed close to 200 weight-loss studies using a variety of these diets concluded that it's the calories, not the composition of the diet, that count when it comes to losing weight.[2] In fact, a study comparing the Atkins, Ornish, Weight Watchers, and Zone diets showed that no matter what diet the individuals followed, they all lost about the same amount of weight, on average, by the end of one year.[3] Whereas each of these diets provides a different percentage of carbohydrates, protein, and fat, they all had one important thing in common: They all reduced calories.

A very interesting point emerged from this study: People who were most diligent about adhering to the diet—no matter which one—experienced the most weight loss.[4] However, more than 20 percent of the dieters quit just two months into the study, and more than 40 percent of them dropped out after one year. The highest dropout rates occurred among followers of the Atkins or Ornish diets. The researchers speculate that the rigidity of these extreme diets may have caused the higher dropout rates. Thus, the problem with many fad diets is that people give up on them long before they meet their weight-loss goals. A fad diet doesn't fix anything in the long term. If it did, there wouldn't be new (or recycled) fad diets continually appearing on the market. Some extreme diets may also be unhealthy in the long term. In fact, the high dropout rate for some fad diets has probably protected many individuals from serious ill health effects and long-term nutrient deficiencies.

Red Flags for Diet Hype

Marketers often make sensational claims about fad diets and weight-loss products. These red flags can often tell you if a diet is questionable.

⚑ It's the Carbs, Not the Calories, That Make You Fat!

Some fad diet ads claim that you can eat as much protein and fat as you want as long as you keep away from the carbs. These diets claim that your consumption of pasta, breads, rice, and many fruits and vegetables should be limited, but fatty meats such as ribs, salami, bologna, and poultry with skin, as well as butter, bacon, and cheeses should be on the menu often.

The Truth behind the Hype

Diets that severely limit carbohydrates (< 130 grams daily) eliminate so many foods, as well as sweets and treats, that it is impossible for a person not to consume at least 500 fewer calories daily. This will theoretically produce about one pound of weight loss per week.[5] When you curtail the carbohydrates, you likely will also be cutting back on fat.[6] When you stop eating the bagel (carbs), you'll also eliminate the cream cheese (fat) you slather on each half. Also, the monotonous nature of these diets causes people to become bored with eating, so they stop. Because the bread, mashed potatoes, and corn are off limits at dinner, the dieter is limited to fatty steak and not much else. Most people can only eat so much of this before it loses its appeal, so they're likely to stop eating sooner. As always, putting down the fork will cut calorie consumption.

Buyer Beware

A diet high in saturated fat and low in fiber and phytochemicals because it is low in whole grains, fruits, and vegetables is a recipe for heart disease, cancer, constipation, elevated blood cholesterol levels, and deficiencies in many vitamins and minerals, such as vitamins A, E, and B_6, folate, calcium, iron, zinc, and potassium.[7] So each time you follow a diet low in whole grains, fruits, and vegetables and high in animal fats, you are robbing your body of the protection of plant foods and overfeeding it the wrong type of fat. The high protein content of these diets may also cause the loss of calcium, and thus increase the risk of osteoporosis, as well as kidney stones.

⚑ Lose Seven Pounds in One Week!

Many diets guarantee rapid weight loss. This may happen on a low-carbohydrate diet—but only during the first few days, and only temporarily.

The Truth behind the Hype

The 4- to 7-pound weight loss during the first week of low-carbohydrate dieting is due to loss of body water that results from two

Distinguishing Among Popular Diets

Dietary Approach	Weight Loss Claim	What You Eat	Pros	Cons	Examples
Very low calorie diet (VLCD)	Severely limiting calories burns fat and reduces body weight	400 to 800 calories per day; liquid meals containing vitamins, electrolytes, minerals, and essential fatty acids; high in protein (up to 125 g/day)	Quick weight loss of 15–20% in 12–16 weeks; improves glycemic control in type 2 diabetics, reduced hypertension and hyperlipidemia	Numerous side effects: fatigue, hypotension, headaches, dizziness, constipation, and gallstones in long-term use; loss of lean body tissue; regain 50% of weight lost in one year	➤ Medifast ➤ Cabbage Soup ➤ Cookie Diet
Balanced, reduced calorie	Moderate reduction of calories promotes weight loss at a healthy rate	1,200 to 1,800 calories per day; balanced 45–65% carbohydrate, 20–30% fat, and 10–35% protein; wide variety of foods; portions are controlled	Average weight loss of 1 to 2 pounds per week; approach balances reduced food intake by portion sizes and exercise, which helps maintain lean body mass; incorporates behavior modification	Low adherence rates; some programs require prepackaged foods	➤ Jenny Craig ➤ Weight Watchers ➤ Nutri-System ➤ The Biggest Loser
Restricted carbohydrate, high protein	Insulin promotes fat storage; low glycemic foods are more satisfying, which limits total food intake	< 20% carbohydrate, 55–65% fat, 25–30% protein; less than 100 g carbohydrate per day; excludes most fruits, grains, starchy vegetables, and legumes; allows meat, limited dairy, and fats	Hunger is controlled, weight loss, improved glycemic control; may improve HDL and triglycerides	Reduced glycogen, loss of lean body tissue and electrolytes; side effects include fatigue, headaches, dizziness, and constipation; nutritional deficiencies	➤ Dr. Atkins ➤ South Beach ➤ Belly Fat Cure ➤ Wheat Belly Diet
High carbohydrate, low fat	When fat is restricted, fewer calories are consumed	> 65% carbohydrate, > 20% fat, 10–20% protein; low-energy-dense plant foods: fruits, vegetables, whole grains; low or void of animal foods; limited nuts and seeds	Significant weight loss due to low calorie intake; allows you to eat more	Low adherence rates; limited food options; may have poor nutrient absorption due to low fat intake and high fiber	➤ Ornish ➤ Pritikin ➤ Pasta Diet

physiological processes. First, because the reduced amount of carbohydrates can't support the body's need for glucose, the stored glycogen in the liver and muscle will be broken down. Each gram of glycogen removed from storage causes the loss of 2 grams of water with it. Because you store about 500 grams of glycogen in your body, you can expect to lose approximately 2 pounds of water weight during the first week of a low-carbohydrate diet. Secondly, the ketone bodies generated by the breakdown of fat are lost from the body through the kidneys. This will also cause the body to lose sodium. As you know from Chapter 8, where sodium goes, water follows. Therefore, the ketone bodies that cause you to lose sodium will also cause you to lose water.[8]

Buyer Beware

Though water weight may be lost during the first week, the rate of weight loss after that will be determined by the energy imbalance in the body, as in any calorie-reducing diet. As soon as carbohydrates are added back to the diet, the body will retain water and some water weight will come back on. When it comes to shedding

CONTINUED ➤

weight, quick loss usually means quick regain.

🏳 Celebrity-Endorsed Miracle Weight-Loss Products with a Money-Back Guarantee!

Just because a celebrity actor or model tries to sell you a product doesn't mean that the product is valid. It just means that the celebrity is being paid to do what he or she does best: act.

The Truth behind the Hype

No cream, shake, or potion will magically melt away body fat, and many marketers who claim that their products do this end up paying millions of dollars in fines to the Federal Trade Commission (FTC) for public deception.[9]

Buyer Beware

Forget about getting your money back. The FTC has received numerous complaints from dissatisfied customers who have unsuccessfully tried to get a refund. The more miraculous the claim, the more

likely you are to lose (money, that is, not weight).

🏳 Naturally Occurring Plants, Herbs, and Other Substances Will Help You Lose Weight without Risk!

"Natural" substances, such as glucomannan, guar gum, chitosan, green tea extracts, and bitter orange are not necessarily safer or more effective for weight loss.

The Truth behind the Hype

Glucomannan is a compound found in the root of the starchy konjac plant, and guar gum is a type of dietary fiber found in a specific bean. Both are ineffective in weight loss. Chitosan is produced from a substance found in shellfish. Though the claim is that these substances decrease the absorption of fat in the body, research doesn't back up the claim. While green tea extracts have been marketed to help with weight loss there isn't research evidence to support the hype. In fact, there have been reports of liver problems in people taking concentrated green tea extracts.[10] Bitter orange is a plant that is touted as a

substitute for ephedra (see the medications listed in the Health Connection feature "Extreme Measures for Extreme Obesity" on page 393), yet the research is not definitive on its ability to stimulate weight loss.

Buyer Beware

Guar gum has been shown to cause diarrhea, flatulence, and gastrointestinal disturbances. Chitosan may cause nausea and flatulence.[11] Bitter orange can increase blood pressure and interfere with the metabolism of other drugs in the body.[12] Naturally occurring substances are not necessarily safe to consume, and there's no evidence that they help you lose weight.

What Do You Think?

1. How can you best evaluate new diet products, programs, and books?
2. What marketing ploys have you noticed in advertisements for diet products and programs?
3. Why do you think some of the popular diet plans seem to contradict each other?

Table TIPS

Eat More to Weigh Less

Eat more whole fruit and drink less juice at breakfast for more fiber and bulk.

Make the vegetable portions on your dinner plate twice the size of your meat portion.

Have a side salad with low-fat dressing with your lunchtime sandwich instead of a snack bag of chips.

Order your next pizza with less pepperoni and more peppers, onions, and tomatoes.

Cook up a whole-wheat-blend pasta instead of enriched pasta for your next Italian dinner. The fiber will help you feel full sooner. Ladle on plenty of tomato sauce and don't forget the big tossed salad as the appetizer.

In fact, consuming a large, high-volume, low-energy-density salad before a meal can reduce the calories eaten at that meal by more than 10 percent.[58] Adding vegetables to sandwiches and soups will increase both the volume of food consumed and meal satisfaction and help displace higher-calorie items (**Figure 10.9**). If you are full after eating a sandwich loaded with vegetables, you'll eat less from the bag of energy-dense chips. This is important because you don't need to eliminate chips from your diet if you enjoy them. Any food—from chocolate to chips—can be modest in calories if you eat modest amounts. Table 10.3 provides examples of low-, moderate-, and high-energy-density foods. See the Table Tips for ways to increase the volume of foods you consume, while decreasing your overall caloric intake.

Fiber also contributes to the bulk of vegetables and fruits and their ability to prolong satiety.[59] Overweight individuals have been shown to consume less dietary fiber and fruit than normal-weight people.[60] For these reasons, high-fiber foods, such as vegetables, fruit, and whole grains, are a key part of a weight-loss diet.

Include Some Protein and Fat in Your Meals

Of all the dietary substances that increase satiety, protein will have the most dramatic effect. Even though the mechanism is unknown, this is likely one of the reasons why high-protein diets tend to reduce hunger and can help in weight loss.[61] Because fat slows the movement of food out of the stomach into the intestines, it can also prolong satiety. Therefore, including some lean protein and fat in all meals and even with snacks can help increase satiety between meals.

Change low-volume...

³/₄ cup chicken broth: **29** calories
¹/₂ cup chicken (white meat): **106** calories
1 cup noodle: **212** calories

347 total calories

2 slices whole-wheat bread: **138** calories
4 oz ham: **125** calories
2 oz American cheese: **213** calories

476 total calories

...to high volume

³/₄ cup chicken broth: **29** calories
¹/₂ cup chicken (white meat): **106** calories
¹/₂ cup noodles: **106** calories
¹/₂ cup mixed vegetables: **59** calories

300 total calories

2 slices whole-wheat bread: **138** calories
2 oz ham: **63** calories
1 oz American cheese: **106** calories
2 slices tomato: **7** calories
2 leaves Romaine lettuce: **10** calories

324 total calories

Figure 10.9 Adding Volume to Your Meals Aids Weight Loss
Adding high-volume foods like fruits and vegetables to your sandwiches, soups, and meals can add to satiety and displace higher-calorie foods, two factors that can help in weight management.

Table 10.3
The Energy Density of Foods

Low

These foods provide 0.7 to 1.5 calories per gram and are high in water and fiber. Examples include most vegetables and fruits—tomatoes, cantaloupe, strawberries, broccoli, cauliflower—as well as broth-based soups, fat-free yogurt, and cottage cheese.

Medium

These foods have 1.5 to 4 calories per gram and contain less water. They include bagels, hard-cooked eggs, dried fruits, lean sirloin steak, hummus, whole-wheat bread, and part-skim mozzarella cheese.

High

These foods provide 4 to 9 calories per gram, are low in moisture, and include chips, cookies, crackers, cakes, pastries, butter, oil, and bacon.

Source: Adapted from the Centers for Disease Control and Prevention, "Can Eating Fruits and Vegetables Help People to Manage Their Weight?" 2011. Available at www.cdc.gov. Accessed July 2013.

The next time you want to chat with your dorm mate, skip the text message and go knock on his door.

Don't go to the closest coffee shop for your morning latte. Walk to the java joint that is a few blocks farther away.

Take a five-minute walk at least twice a day. A little jolt of exercise can help break the monotony of studying and work off some stress.

Accomplish two goals at once by scrubbing down your dorm room or apartment. A 150-pound person will burn about 4 calories for every minute spent cleaning. Scrub for 30 minutes and you could work off about 120 calories.

Offer to walk your neighbor's pet daily.

However, you don't want to add high-saturated-fat foods such as whole milk and/or whole-milk cheese, fatty cuts of meat, and butter, because eating these foods to feel full will come at the expense of your heart. It would be better to add lean meat, skinless chicken, fish, nuts, and oils, which are kinder to a person's waist and heart. (Note: Unsaturated fat still contains 9 calories per gram, so excessive amounts of nuts and oils, even though these are heart healthy, can quickly add excess calories to the diet.)

Look at the difference between the foods shown in **Figure 10.10**. The snack and dinner on the left are low in volume, but high in calories. The foods on the right are high in volume but have almost 500 fewer calories combined! These higher-volume foods will be more satisfying for fewer calories.

Use MyPlate as a Weight-Loss Guide

Meals that contain a high volume of fruits and vegetables, whole grains, some lean protein, and modest amounts of fat are a smart combination for weight loss, so a diet that contains all the five food groups can be used to lose weight. Most importantly, this type of diet is well balanced and will meet your daily nutrient needs.

Reducing caloric intake a little at a time can add up to healthy weight loss. A 180-pound, overweight person who consumes 2,800 calories daily can reduce his or her intake to 2,400 to 2,600 calories for a calorie deficit of 200–400 calories per day. He or she will then lose 5–10 pounds in about three months. Small changes, like switching from full-fat to nonfat dairy products or replacing the afternoon soda with a glass of water, will contribute to this calorie reduction. Following the recommendations at ChooseMyPlate.gov to eat a variety of foods, but replacing higher-calorie foods with lower-calorie options within each food group, results in a satisfying diet while losing weight.

If this person added some extra physical activity, he or she could further increase that daily calorie deficit. Let's now look at the other side of the energy equation: energy expenditure.

Move to Lose

Research shows that regular physical activity is associated with a healthier body weight. Some individuals may need to devote 45 minutes or more to participation in moderate-intensity activities daily to prevent overweight or to aid in weight loss for those who need to lose weight.[62] Moderately intense physical activity would be the equivalent of walking 3.5 miles per hour (**Table 10.4**). Regular physical activity can also displace sedentary activity such as watching television, which often leads to mindless snacking on energy-dense foods.[63] Going for a walk and expending calories rather than watching television while snacking on a bag of chips will provide caloric benefits beyond the exercise alone.

A way to assess if you are incorporating enough physical activity into your day is to count your steps (such as with a pedometer). Research suggests that accumulating 10,000 steps daily, which is the equivalent of walking 5 miles, can help reduce the risk of becoming overweight.[64] Americans, on average, accumulate only 900 to 3,000 steps daily.[65] To reach 10,000 steps, a conscious effort is needed by most people to keep moving. See the Table Tips for some ideas for fun ways to expend more energy during the day.

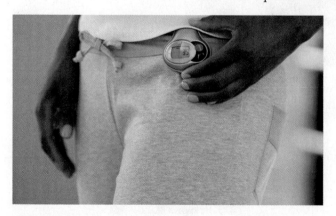

Wearing a pedometer, like the one shown here, can help you track your steps. Remember to aim for 10,000 steps per day.

Low-volume, high-calorie

16 oz Dunkin Donuts Coffee Coolata® with cream: **350** calories

460 total calories

Dunkin Donuts chocolate chunk cookie: **110** calories

Pizza Hut Pepperoni Lover's® Pizza 2 slices, large pizza: **570** calories

890 total calories

Cheese breadstick **320** calories

High-volume, low-calorie

Pop Secret Snack popcorn, 94% fat free, butter: **110** calories

180 total calories

16 oz Dunkin Donuts Hot Latte Lite made with skim milk: **70** calories

Pizza Hut Veggie Lover's® Pizza 3 slices, large pizza: **610** calories

676 total calories

1 cup Romaine lettuce: **8** calories
½ cup cherry tomatoes: **13** calories
½ cup sliced cucumbers: **7** calories
1 tbs light ranch dressing: **38** calories

Figure 10.10 The Volume of Food You Eat Affects Satiety
Low-volume, high-calorie foods can be much less satisfying than higher-volume, lower-calorie foods.

Table 10.4
Calories Used during Activities

Moderate Physical Activity	Approximate Calories/ Hour for a 154-lb Person*	Vigorous Physical Activity	Approximate Calories/ Hour for a 154-lb Person*
Hiking	370	Running/jogging (5 mph)	590
Light gardening/yard work	330	Bicycling (> 10 mph)	590
Dancing	330	Swimming (slow freestyle laps)	510
Golf (walking and carrying clubs)	330	Aerobics	480
Bicycling (< 10 mph)	290	Walking (4.5 mph)	460
Walking (3.5 mph)	280	Heavy yard work (chopping wood)	440
Weight lifting (general light workout)	220	Weight lifting (vigorous effort)	440
Stretching	180	Basketball (vigorous)	440

*Note: Calories burned per hour will be higher for persons who weigh more than 154 lbs (70 kg) and lower for persons who weigh less.
Source: Adapted from Centers for Disease Control and Prevention, "Physical Activity for a Healthy Weight" 2,011. Available at www.cdc.gov. Accessed July 2013.

Break Bad Habits

Have you ever heard about the "freshman 15"? If you have, you may be relieved to find out that a 15-pound weight gain is not inevitable for college freshmen. In fact, research to support the "freshman 15" is rather slim. Some research has found that weight gain didn't occur at all or didn't occur in the majority of the students during the first semester (the length of the study) or the entire first year.[66] Other studies found that students gained less than 5 pounds, on average, and one of these studies showed that certain behaviors such as snacking in the evening, consumption of junk foods, and the number of meals eaten on weekends were associated with weight gain.[67]

However, if students get in the habit of skipping breakfast, hitting the vending machine for a midmorning snack, and mindlessly munching late at night, they may find weight management during their freshman year to be an uphill struggle and would benefit from some behavior modification.

Behavior modification focuses on changing the behaviors that contribute to weight gain or impede weight loss. Several behavior modification techniques can be used to identify and change poor eating behaviors. These techniques include self-monitoring the behaviors by keeping a food log, controlling environmental cues that trigger eating when not hungry, and learning how to better manage stress.

Do you really know when, why, and what you eat? Understanding the habits and emotions that drive your eating patterns can help you change your less-than-healthy eating behaviors. In a 12-month study of over 120 overweight/obese women, journaling in a food log was found to be one of the key strategies that helped the women not only meet their weight-loss goal of losing 10 percent of their body weight by 6 months but also to maintain the weight loss at 12 months.[68] In fact, the women in the study who consistently keep food logs lost about 6 pounds more than those who didn't journal.

> The average weight gain between Thanksgiving and New Year's Day is about a pound. But many people don't lose this extra weight and add to it every year.

Keeping a food log is a great way to track the kinds of foods you eat during the day, when and where you eat them, your moods, and hunger ratings. You can use this information to minimize or eliminate the eating behaviors that interfere with weight management.

A typical day's log might be similar to the one in **Figure 10.11** and is a good way to uncover habits that are common to people who struggle with their weight. For example, a study of overweight women who typically skipped breakfast showed that once they started consuming cereal for breakfast, they indulged in less impulsive snacking.[69] Eating a bowl of high-fiber whole-grain cereal (approximately 200 calories) will likely appease a person's morning hunger and help bypass an 11 a.m. vending machine snack such as a package of 270-calorie cookies and a 210-calorie sports drink. This one behavior change would not only save 280 calories in the morning, but also reduce the calories from added sugars in the diet and add more nutrition to the day. Similarly, adding a less-energy-dense salad at lunch could help increase satiety and lessen the desire to eat a couple of the cookies.

Because studying for exams can be anxiety inducing for students and cause them to munch even though they aren't hungry, they should think twice about studying in their dorm rooms or other areas where they are surrounded by snacks. Rather, studying at the campus library, an environment where eating is typically prohibited, would be a better bet. Exercising before or after studying would also be a healthier way for students to relieve stress rather than eating their way through a bag of snacks.

Changing behaviors that have become unhealthy habits is another important piece of improving weight management. Individuals who eat "out of habit" and in

behavior modification Changing behaviors to improve health. Identifying and altering eating patterns that contribute to weight gain or impede weight loss is behavior modification.

Food Log

For: Hannah

Date: Monday, September 6

Food and drink	Time eaten	What I ate/ Where I ate it	Hunger level*	Mood †
Breakfast		Skipped it	3	G
Snack	11 a.m.	Oreo cookies, PowerAde from vending machine during morning class.	5	E
Lunch	1:30 p.m.	Ham and cheese sandwich, 2 large M&M cookies in student union cafeteria.	4	B
Snack				
Dinner	6:30 p.m.	Hamburger, french fries, salad at kitchen table	4	F
Snack	7 p.m. to 10 p.m.	Large bag of tortilla chips and entire bag of Pepperidge Farm Milano cookies while studying at kitchen table	1	I

*Hunger levels (1–5): 1 = not hungry; 5 = super hungry

† **Moods:**
A = Happy; B = Content; C = Bored; D = Depressed; E = Rushed; F = Stressed;
G = Tired; H = Lonely; I = Anxious; J = Angry

Figure 10.11 Food Log
Keeping track of when, where, and what you eat, as well as why you ate it, can yield some surprising information. Do you think you sometimes eat out of boredom or stress, rather than because you're hungry?

Table TIPS

Adopt Some Healthy Habits

Don't eat out of boredom; go for a jog instead. If we ate only when hungry, we would probably be a lot leaner.

Food shop with a full stomach and a grocery list. Walking around aimlessly while hungry means you are more likely to grab items on a whim.

When you feel wound up or stressed, lace up those sneakers and go for a walk.

The next time you pass a difficult course, or get that long-awaited raise, reward yourself with something other than food. Instead of a celebratory dinner, buy a new book or some music, or spend time with friends.

Declare a vending machine–free day at least once a week and stop the impulsive snacking. On that day, pack two pieces of fruit as satisfying snacks.

response to their emotions need to replace this unnecessary eating to better manage their weight. The Table Tips lists some healthy behaviors that can easily be incorporated into your life.

The Take-Home Message For successful, long-term weight loss, people need to reduce their daily calorie intake, increase their physical activity, and change their behavior. Adding low-energy-dense, high-volume vegetables, fruit, and fiber along with some lean protein and healthy oils to the diet can help in satiety and reduce unplanned snacking. Incorporating physical activity daily can help with weight loss. Changing unhealthy habits by restructuring the environment to minimize or eliminate the eating behaviors that interfere with weight loss can also help shed extra pounds.

How Can You Maintain Weight Loss?

You, or someone you know, may be familiar with the typical fad diet experience: the triumphant rush associated with the dropping of 10 pounds, the disappointment that sets in when 15 pounds is regained, then a new round of hope when 10 of them are re-shed. This fluctuation is known as **weight cycling**, and some research suggests

weight cycling The repeated gain and loss of body weight.

that it can lead to problems such as hypertension, gallbladder disease, and elevated blood cholesterol levels, not to mention depression and feelings of frustration.[70] The good news is that research does not show that fat mass increases nor is muscle mass lost after weight cycling. Rather, it appears that individuals just regain the weight that was lost and end up with the same amount of fat and muscle mass as they did before dieting.[71]

Research suggests that weight cycling may not be as common as previously thought. Studies have shown that people who lose weight are able to keep it off for at least 5 years.[72] These people were successful because they maintained their physical activity habits and positive behavior changes after they reached their weight goal. They commonly limited the intake of fatty foods, monitored their calorie intake, consumed breakfast, and ate nearly five times a day, on average. (For many people, eating smaller meals allows them to avoid becoming ravenous and overeating at the next meal.) The majority of them weighed themselves weekly and maintained a high level of daily physical activity, expending the energy equivalent of walking four miles a day.[73] This suggests that weight loss can be maintained as long as the individual doesn't abandon the healthy habits that promoted the weight loss and revert to the unhealthy habits that caused the excess weight in the first place.

Physical activity can also help those who've lost weight close the "energy gap." After weight loss, a person will have lower overall energy needs, as there is less body weight to maintain. The **energy gap** is the difference in daily calories that are needed for weight maintenance before and after weight loss.[74] Researchers have estimated that the energy gap is about 8 calories per pound of lost weight.[75]

For example, someone who lost 30 pounds would need approximately 240 fewer calories a day to maintain the new, lower body weight. This person can eat 240 fewer calories, expend this amount of calories through added physical activity, or do a combination of both. Because the environment we live in seems to encourage eating more than discourage it, researchers feel that increasing daily physical activity is likely the easier way to close the energy gap and help maintain the weight loss.[76] *Adding* something (physical activity) to your lifestyle is often easier than *removing* something (calories). Regular physical activity may help prevent weight gain as you age.[77] Some individuals are candidates for extreme treatment to help them shed their unhealthy excess weight. The Health Connection feature "Extreme Measures for Extreme Obesity" discusses treatment options for those with BMIs of greater than 40.

| The Take-Home Message People who lose weight are most likely to keep it off if they maintain the positive diet and lifestyle habits that helped them lose the weight. Eating less and/or exercising more will help close the energy gap after weight loss.

How Can You Gain Weight Healthfully?

For people who are underweight, weight gain can be as challenging and frustrating as losing weight is for an overweight individual. The major difference is that the thin person rarely gets sympathy from others. Like overweight individuals, those who are underweight experience an energy imbalance. In their case, however, they consume fewer calories than they expend.

People who want to gain weight need to do the opposite of those who are trying to lose weight. Whereas waist watchers hunt for the lower-calorie foods, individuals

energy gap The difference between the numbers of calories needed to maintain weight before and after weight loss.

Extreme Measures for Extreme Obesity

People with a BMI greater than 40 fall into the category of **extreme obesity**. They are at such a high risk for conditions such as heart disease and stroke, and even of dying, that an aggressive weight-loss treatment is necessary. Treatments that go beyond eating less and exercising more, such as a very low-calorie diet, medications, and/or surgery, are often recommended. Let's look at each of these options.

A Very Low-Calorie Diet

On her television show in 1988, a very petite Oprah Winfrey beamed with joy after having lost 67 pounds using a **very low-calorie diet**. Oprah achieved her weight loss by consuming a liquid protein diet, or *protein-sparing modified fast*. Such protein-rich diets provide fewer than 800 calories daily, are very low in or devoid of carbohydrates, and have minimal amounts of fat. They are designed to help individuals at high risk of disease drop a substantial amount of weight in a short amount of time. However, they are not a long-term solution. After consuming the diet for 12 to 16 weeks, the dieter is switched over to a well-balanced, low-calorie diet.

Very low-calorie diets have to be supplemented with vitamins and minerals and must be supervised by a medical doctor, as they can cause dangerous electrolyte imbalances as well as gallstones, constipation, fatigue, hair loss, and other side effects. The National Institutes of Health doesn't recommend very low-calorie diets because well-balanced low-calorie diets are just as effective in producing a similar amount of weight loss after one year and are less dangerous.[13]

In the 1980s Oprah Winfrey reached her goal weight by consuming a very low-calorie, liquid-protein diet. She has since regained and lost the weight several times, and often publicly discusses the challenges of maintaining a stable, healthy weight.

After all that effort, Oprah ultimately regretted her very low-calorie diet. "I had literally starved myself for four months—not a morsel of food—to get into a pair of size 10 Calvin Klein jeans," claims Oprah. "Two hours after that show, I started eating to celebrate—of course, within two days those jeans no longer fit!"[14] In 2005, Oprah reached her goal weight of 160 pounds and was convinced she knew how to maintain her new weight. Two years later her life started to become "unbalanced," which resulted in weight gain once again. By 2009, she had regained 40 pounds, putting her back up to the 200-pound mark.

Medication

Some prescription medications can help a person lose weight. The drugs either suppress the appetite or inhibit the absorption of fat in the intestinal tract. For example, the drug sibutramine (trade name Meridia) reduces hunger and increases thermogenesis, which increases energy expenditure. The drug can also increase a person's heart rate and blood pressure. Therefore, it may not be appropriate for those who have hypertension, which tends to occur often in overweight individuals. In fact, because all drugs have side effects, their use must be monitored by a doctor.

Orlistat (trade name Xenical; recall that this drug is discussed in Chapter 3) inhibits an intestinal enzyme that is needed to break down fat. If it isn't broken down, the fat (and calories) will not be absorbed by the body. Up to about one-third of the dietary fat will be blocked and expelled in the stool. Orlistat has to be taken at each meal and should accompany a diet that provides no more than about 30 percent of its calories from fat. Because fat is lost in the stool, the drug can cause oily and more frequent stools, flatulence, and oily discharge.[15] Ironically, these side effects may help an individual adhere to a low-fat diet, as these effects are more pronounced if a high-fat meal is consumed. Today, a reduced-strength version of orlistat (trade name Alli) is approved for over-the-counter sale to adults 18 years and older. It is intended to be used in conjunction with a low-fat, low-calorie meal and regular exercise to treat obesity, and can have the same unpleasant side effects as the full-strength version. Because of the recent reports of rare, but serious, cases of liver damage in individuals using Xenical and Alli, both of these drugs must now carry warnings on their labels.

The newest weight-loss drugs that have been approved by the FDA are Belviq and Qsymia. Belviq works by affecting a part of the brain that regulates hunger. Qsymia is a combination of two drugs, phentermine, an appetite suppressant, and topiramate, used to treat epilepsy and migraines. Both drugs should be consumed in conjunction with a healthy diet and routine exercise program and have been shown in studies to help individuals lose from 3 to 9 percent of their body weight compared with those who were given a placebo.[16]

Sometimes the side effects of weight-loss medications can be so serious that the medication must be withdrawn from the market. For instance, the FDA has prohibited the sale of supplements that contain ephedra (also called Ma huang), the plant source for ephedrine.[17] Ephedrine has been shown to cause chest pains, palpitations, hypertension, and an accelerated heart rate. In 2003, baseball player Steve Bechler died at age 23 after taking a weight-loss supplement containing ephedrine during spring training. Ephedrine was determined to have contributed to his death.

extreme obesity Having a BMI > 40.

very low-calorie diet A diet of fewer than 800 calories per day and high in protein.

CONTINUED

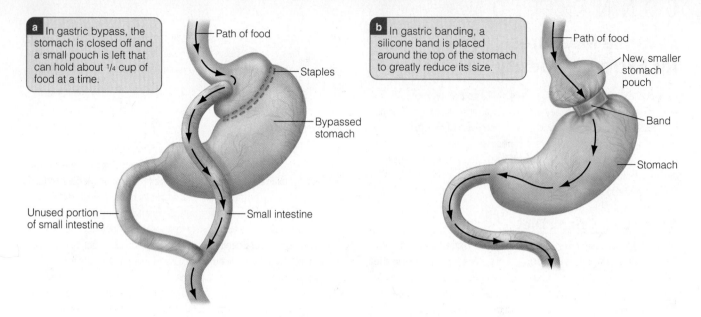

a In gastric bypass, the stomach is closed off and a small pouch is left that can hold about ¼ cup of food at a time.

- Path of food
- Staples
- Bypassed stomach
- Unused portion of small intestine
- Small intestine

b In gastric banding, a silicone band is placed around the top of the stomach to greatly reduce its size.

- Path of food
- New, smaller stomach pouch
- Band
- Stomach

Bariatric surgeries such as gastric bypass and gastric banding restrict food intake and promote malabsorption.

Whereas individuals who take prescription medications to lose weight have been shown to lose as much as 20 pounds, these drugs should be coupled with, and can't replace, a lower-calorie diet, regular physical activity, and behavior modification for long-term weight loss.

Surgery

In 1998, approximately 13,000 obese patients went under the knife to reduce the size of their stomachs. Twelve years later, in 2010, an estimated 160,000 people in the United Stated had **bariatric surgery**.[18] In one version of this surgery, **gastric bypass surgery**, the majority of the stomach is stapled shut. This reduces the size of the stomach so that it holds about ¼ cup of fluid. Food consumed leaves the small stomach pouch through a surgically added intestinal loop that bypasses the original stomach and attaches directly to the small intestine. After the surgery, these individuals need to consume small, frequent meals because the stomach pouch can only expand to a maximum of about 5 ounces, the size of a woman's fist. Individuals not only eat less because of their smaller stomachs, but have higher levels of satiety and lower levels of hunger after the surgery. This effect on their appetite may be associated with lower levels of the hormone ghrelin due to the loss of stomach area after the surgery.[19]

Because both the majority of the stomach and the upper part of the small intestine are bypassed after the surgery, individuals can experience deficiencies of vitamin B_{12}, iron, and calcium. (Vitamin B_{12} needs intrinsic factor from the stomach to be absorbed, which is missing after surgery. Iron and calcium are typically absorbed in the upper part of the small intestine, which is now bypassed.) Supplements must be given because of these deficiencies.

A type of bariatric surgery that's becoming more popular is **gastric banding**, in which a silicone band is placed around the top of the stomach to create a small pouch with a very narrow opening at the bottom for the food to pass through. This delays the emptying of the stomach contents so that a person will feel fuller longer. The doctor can adjust the opening of the pouch by inflating or deflating the band.

bariatric surgery Surgical procedures that reduce the functional volume of the stomach so that less food is eaten. Such surgeries are sometimes used to treat extreme obesity.

gastric bypass surgery A type of bariatric surgery that reduces the functional volume of the stomach to minimize the amount of food eaten.

gastric banding A type of bariatric surgery that uses a silicone band to reduce the size of the stomach so that less food is needed to feel full.

Al Roker, NBC's *Today Show* weather man, lost approximately 140 pounds after gastric bypass surgery.

Liposuction is a surgical procedure that removes subcutaneous fat. Unlike gastric banding or bypass surgeries, liposuction is purely cosmetic and does not result in health benefits.

Although dramatic amounts of weight loss can occur and research has shown that incidences of hypertension, diabetes, high blood cholesterol levels, and sleep apnea have been reduced among people who've had the surgery, there are also risks involved. Less than 1 percent of those undergoing bariatric surgery experience complications such as gallstones and less than 0.1 percent die from the surgery.[20] After surgery, individuals need to be monitored long term by medical and nutrition professionals to ensure that they remain healthy and meet their nutritional needs.

Another type of surgery, **liposuction**, is less about health and more about physical appearance. During this procedure, a doctor removes subcutaneous fat from the abdomen, hips, or thighs (and sometimes other areas of the body) by suctioning it out with a penlike instrument. People often undergo liposuction to get rid of **cellulite**, which isn't a medical term, but refers to the fat cells that give the skin a dimpled appearance. Complications such as infections, scars, and swelling can arise after liposuction. Fat can also reappear at the site where it was removed, so the results of liposuction may not be permanent.

The Bottom Line

Very low-calorie diets, medications, and surgery may be viable options for those with extreme obesity, but they are not without risks. For those who are overweight, the safest route to a healthy weight is to make incremental diet and lifestyle changes to take in fewer calories and expend more calories. Of course, the best overall strategy for weight management is to avoid becoming overweight in the first place.

liposuction The surgical removal of subcutaneous fat with a penlike instrument. Usually performed on the abdomen, hips, and thighs, and/or other areas of the body.

cellulite A nonmedical term that refers to fat cells under the skin that give it a ripplelike appearance. Contrary to popular belief, cellulite is no different from other fat in the body.

seeking to gain weight should make each bite more energy dense. These individuals need to add at least 500 calories to their daily energy intake. This will enable them to add about a pound of extra body weight weekly.

Of course, someone who wants to gain weight should not just load up on high-fat, high-calorie foods. The quality of the extra calories is very important. Snacking on an extra 500 calories of jelly beans will add 500 calories of sugar and little nutrition. Rather, these individuals should make energy-dense, nutritious choices from a variety of foods within each food group. For example, instead of eating a slice of toast in the morning, they should choose a waffle. Adding coleslaw rather than cabbage will increase the calories in a salad-bar lunch more than tenfold. **Figure 10.12** on page 396 contrasts more- and less-energy-dense foods within each food group. Eating snacks during the day will also add calories. The Table Tips provides easy and portable snack ideas.

Regular exercise and resistance training will stimulate muscle growth and help avoid excess fat storage. Remember that it takes time to gain weight and build sufficient muscle mass. Be patient and continue to choose healthy foods until you reach your goal weight.

The Take-Home Message People who want to gain weight need to add energy-dense foods to their diet so that they take in more energy than they expend. Adding nutrient-dense snacks between meals is an easy way to increase the number of calories consumed daily.

Table TIPS

Healthy Snacks for Healthy Weight Gain

For healthy snacks that travel well and don't need refrigeration, try this: Stash an 8-ounce can or box of 100 percent fruit juice (about 100 calories) in your bag along with one of the 150-calorie snacks listed below for a quick 250-calorie snack (food and juice combined) between meals.

Graham crackers, 5 crackers (2 ½ inches square)

Mixed nuts, 1 oz

Fig bars, 2-oz package

Pudding, individual serving sizes, 4 oz

Peanut butter on whole-wheat crackers (1 tbs peanut butter on 6 crackers)

Figure 10.12 More- and Less-Energy-Dense Food Choices, by Food Group
Choosing more energy-dense, but still nutritious, foods can help those who are underweight gain weight.

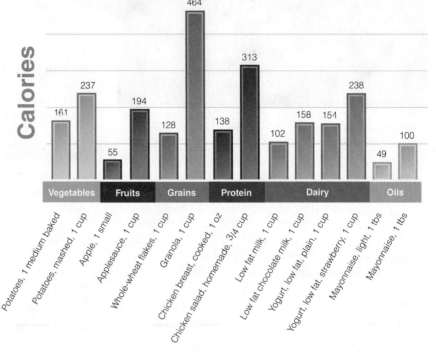

What Is Disordered Eating and What Are the Warning Signs?

Attaining a healthy weight, whether it means gaining or losing a few pounds, is a worthwhile goal that can result in lowered risk of disease and a more productive life. However, it's important to reach and maintain a healthy weight in a positive way. Patterns of eating that involve severe calorie restriction, purging, or other abnormal behaviors can be severely damaging to health. Whereas disordered eating and eating disorders are diagnosed as psychological disorders rather than nutrition-related issues, it's important to be aware of them and recognize their symptoms.

The term **disordered eating** is used to describe a variety of eating patterns considered abnormal and potentially harmful. Refusing to eat, compulsive eating, binge eating, restrictive eating, vomiting after eating, and abusing diet pills, laxatives, or diuretics are all examples of disordered eating behaviors. **Eating disorders**, in contrast, are diagnosed by meeting specific criteria that include disordered eating behaviors as well as other factors (see Table 10.5). It is possible for someone to engage in disordered eating patterns without having a clinically diagnosed eating disorder.

There are three main types of eating disorders that someone could develop, including anorexia nervosa, bulimia nervosa, and binge eating disorder. In the United States, approximately 20 million women and 10 million men struggle with eating

disordered eating Abnormal and potentially harmful eating behaviors that do not meet specific criteria for an eating disorder.

eating disorders The term used to describe psychological illnesses that involve specific abnormal eating behaviors, such as anorexia nervosa (self-starvation), bulimia nervosa (bingeing and purging), and binge eating disorder.

Table 10.5

Diagnostic Criteria for Eating Disorders

Eating Disorder	Diagnostic Criteria
Anorexia Nervosa	• Restriction of energy intake relative to requirements leading to a significantly low body weight in the context of age, sex, developmental trajectory, and physical health • Intense fear of gaining weight or becoming fat, even though underweight • Disturbance in the way one's body weight or shape is experienced, undue influence of body weight or shape on self-evaluation, or denial of the seriousness of the current low body weight

Bulimia Nervosa	• Recurrent episodes of binge eating, which is characterized by BOTH of the following:
	  ➤ Eating in a discrete amount of time (within a 2-hour period) large amounts of food
	  ➤ Sense of lack of control over eating during an episode
	• Recurrent inappropriate compensatory behavior in order to prevent weight gain (purging)
	• The binge eating and compensatory behaviors both occur, on average, at least once per week for three months.
	• Self-evaluation is unduly influenced by body shape and weight.
	• The disturbance does not occur exclusively during episodes of anorexia nervosa.

Binge Eating Disorder	• Recurrent episodes of binge eating. An episode of binge eating is characterized by both of the following:
	  ➤ Eating, in a discrete period of time, an amount of food that is definitely larger than most people would eat in a similar period of time under similar circumstances
	  ➤ A sense of lack of control over eating during the episode (for example, a feeling that one cannot stop eating or control what or how much one is eating)
	• The binge eating episodes are associated with three (or more) of the following:
	  ➤ Eating much more rapidly than normal
	  ➤ Eating until feeling uncomfortably full
	  ➤ Eating large amounts of food when not feeling physically hungry
	  ➤ Eating alone because of feeling embarrassed by how much one is eating
	  ➤ Feeling disgusted with oneself, depressed, or very guilty afterward
	• Marked distress regarding binge eating is present.
	• The binge eating occurs, on average, at least once a week for three months.
	• The binge eating is not associated with the recurrent use of inappropriate compensatory behavior (for example, purging) and does not occur exclusively during the course of anorexia nervosa, bulimia nervosa, or avoidant/restrictive food intake disorder.

Feeding or Eating Disorders Not Elsewhere Classified	• Disordered eating behaviors that do not meet the criteria for anorexia nervosa, bulimia nervosa, or binge eating disorder, including orthorexia and night eating syndrome.

Source: The Alliance for Eating Disorders Awareness. 2013. Available at www.allianceforeatingdisorders.com. Accessed July 2013.

disorders at some time in their life.[78] Adolescent and young adult females in predominantly white upper-middle- and middle-class families are the population with highest prevalence. However, eating disorders and disordered eating among males, minorities, and other age groups are increasing.[79] In fact, about 10 percent of all cases of anorexia nervosa and bulimia nervosa occur in men. And this may be an underestimate, as many men, as well as women, feel ashamed or embarrassed and may hide their problem. The prevalence of eating disorders among both males and females is probably higher than reported. Anyone can develop one of these conditions regardless of gender, age, race, ethnicity, or social status.

No Single Factor Causes Eating Disorders

Although there is typically no one cause of disordered eating and eating disorders, there are certain factors that may increase one's risk for developing these conditions. Current research suggests that eating disorders are prompted by a complex network of sociocultural, genetic, and preexisting psychological factors (**Figure 10.13**).

Figure 10.13 Factors That Contribute to Eating Disorders

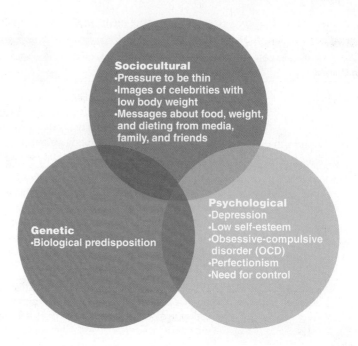

Sociocultural
- Pressure to be thin
- Images of celebrities with low body weight
- Messages about food, weight, and dieting from media, family, and friends

Genetic
- Biological predisposition

Psychological
- Depression
- Low self-esteem
- Obsessive-compulsive disorder (OCD)
- Perfectionism
- Need for control

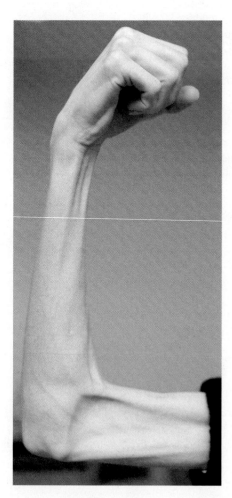

Although the highest rates of disordered eating patterns occur among females, males are not immune. Adolescents in particular can feel pressure to achieve a certain body image.

Sociocultural Factors

Some researchers theorize that the higher prevalence of eating disorders in females is due in part to the greater societal pressure they experience to be thin and have a "perfect" figure.[80] Thinness is too often associated with beauty, success, and happiness in our society, as evidenced by images in magazines and on billboards of fashion models and celebrities with abnormally low body weights. Even the average BMI of Miss America winners has decreased from 22 to 16.9 in the past 80 years, while BMIs of girls and women has increased.[81] Many females don't realize that nearly all media images have been digitally enhanced and do not depict the people as they appear in real life. Instead, they come to believe that extreme thinness is both possible and desirable and that they cannot be beautiful, successful, or happy unless they achieve it. Some may feel such extreme body dissatisfaction that they try to lose weight at any cost, including engaging in disordered eating behaviors.

Men also experience societal pressure to have a specific look, often focusing on muscle mass and looking "cut." They, too, can be influenced by images of professional athletes, body builders, celebrities, and models in advertising, and some may strive to achieve the same look through extreme, unhealthy behaviors.

Genetic Factors

Researchers have not found a gene or genes that promote eating disorders; however, they theorize that a combination of genetic predisposition and environmental factors can increase an individual's risk. Certainly, eating disorders have been observed to "run in families." For example, an adolescent female has a greatly increased risk of developing an eating disorder if she has a sibling with an eating disorder, even if she does not live with that sibling.[82]

Psychological Factors

Depression and anxiety are common in people with an eating disorder,[83] as is obsessive-compulsive disorder (OCD),[84] a psychiatric illness characterized by intrusive thoughts that something bad will happen if a certain behavior is not repeated in a certain way. Not only women but men diagnosed with eating disorders have higher rates of other psychiatric illness, compared with men who do not have eating disorders.[85] Alcohol and other substance abuse disorders are four times more common in people with eating disorders than in the general population.[86]

A personality trait that can contribute to eating disorders is perfectionism, as an inability to reach unrealistic standards (such as in school or in athletic competition) can lead to a sense of failure and lowered self-worth. Many people who struggle with eating disorders are trying to gain some control in their lives. When external factors feel out of control, the person with an eating disorder gets a sense of security from being able to control food intake and body weight. Other common psychological factors include lack of self-esteem, high family expectations, and family dysfunction.

The most common eating disorders are anorexia nervosa, bulimia nervosa, and binge eating disorder. Let's take a look at each type of disorder and the characteristics that make each one unique.

Societal pressure to be thin can cause people to feel fat when they look in the mirror regardless of their body weight. Dissatisfaction with one's body can lead to disordered eating behaviors.

Anorexia Nervosa Results from Severe Calorie Restriction

Anorexia nervosa is a serious, potentially life-threatening eating disorder that is characterized by self-starvation and excessive weight loss. People who suffer from anorexia nervosa have an intense fear of gaining weight or being fat. This fear causes them to control their food intake by restricting the amount they consume, resulting in significant weight loss.

People with anorexia nervosa have a distorted sense of body image and usually see themselves as fat even though they are underweight (you can read more about the concept of body image in the Nutrition in the Real World feature, "A Closer Look at Body Image" on page 400). This misperception of body size contributes to the behavior of restricting food intake in order to lose (more) weight. For instance, someone with anorexia nervosa might eat only a piece of fruit and a small container of yogurt during an entire day. They may also have a fear of eating certain foods, such as those that contain fat and sugar. They believe that these foods (and possibly others) will make them fat, regardless of how much they eat. Some may also exercise excessively as a means of controlling their weight.

There are numerous health consequences that can occur with anorexia nervosa, and some can be fatal.[87] A recent study that reviewed nearly fifty years of research found that anorexia nervosa has the highest mortality rate of any psychiatric disorder.[88] One of the most serious health effects is an electrolyte imbalance, specifically low blood potassium, which can also occur if someone with anorexia nervosa engages in episodes of purging. An electrolyte imbalance can lead to an irregular heart rhythm and possibly heart failure, which can be fatal. Because someone with anorexia nervosa is not getting enough calories, the body begins to slow or shut down some processes in an effort to conserve energy for its most vital functions. The person may experience a decrease in heart rate and blood pressure, overall weakness and fatigue, and hair loss. The digestive process also slows down, which often results in constipation, bloating, and delayed gastric emptying.

Someone who's lost an extreme amount of body fat may experience a drop in body temperature and feel cold even when it is hot outside. In an effort to regulate body temperature, this person's body may begin to grow **lanugo** (downy hair), particularly on the face and arms. Dehydration, iron deficiency, menstrual disturbances, and osteoporosis are also negative health effects caused by anorexia nervosa.

Bulimia Nervosa Involves Cycles of Binge Eating and Purging

Bulimia nervosa is another type of eating disorder that can be life-threatening. During times of binge eating, the person lacks control over eating and consumes larger than normal amounts of food in a short period of time. Following the binge, the

lanugo Very fine, soft hair on the face and arms of people with anorexia nervosa.

A Closer Look at Body Image

What Is Body Image?

Body image refers to the way that you perceive and what you believe about your physical appearance, whether you are looking in the mirror or picturing yourself in your mind.[21] Most people think of body image as being about body weight and shape, but it actually refers to any physical attribute such as skin color, hair texture, or height.

Body image can be further defined as having positive or negative characteristics. People with a positive body image view themselves as they truly are (no distortion) and overall feel comfortable and confident in and about their body. They engage in healthy eating and exercise behaviors and don't spend a lot of time worrying about weight, dieting, or changing their looks using extreme measures. They accept their body and don't define their self-worth based on physical appearances.[22] In contrast, those with a negative body image often have distorted views of the way they look and may view their shape as larger than they actually are. This is especially true of people with anorexia nervosa. Additionally, they may feel ashamed, uncomfortable, or self-conscious about their physical appearance and spend a large amount of time focusing on their weight or aspects of their looks that they perceive as unattractive. They often believe that only others are attractive.[23] A negative body image can contribute to the development or continuation of unhealthy behaviors, like eating disorders, in many individuals.

What Is Body Dysmorphic Disorder?

Body dysmorphic disorder (BDD) is a mental illness in which a person's preoccupation with minor or imaginary physical flaws causes significant distress or impairment in work, school, or other areas of functioning. BDD is estimated to affect slightly more than 2 percent of the U.S. population and

body dysmorphic disorder A mental illness in which a person is excessively concerned about and preoccupied by a perceived defect in his or her body.

Both men and women can experience issues with body image.

frequently occurs along with other psychiatric disorders, such as obsessive-compulsive disorder, anorexia nervosa, and clinical depression.[24]

Muscle dysmorphia, also referred to as "bigorexia" or "reverse anorexia," is a specific type of BDD that typically occurs in males who have a well-defined muscular build but view themselves as being small or weak.[25] Symptoms of muscle dysmorphia include extreme exercise (especially weight lifting) and attention to diet, anxiety when missing a workout, constant mirror checking, use of anabolic steroids to enhance muscle mass, and neglecting family, friends, or work in order to exercise. Media influence on men and their muscle mass and size is thought to be a major contributing factor in the increasing prevalence of muscle dysmorphia. Anyone with these symptoms should seek professional help and treatment, as they can get worse over time.

How Can You Attain a Positive Body Image?

Many factors can influence your body image, including family, friends, peers, media, and culture. We live in a society where certain images are labeled "ideal," yet are not achievable by most. Nonetheless, we strive to get the "perfect" body through any means necessary. Comparing our bodies to those of friends, models, and celebrities that we view as more attractive only leads to lowered self-esteem and feeling "not good enough."

The following are strategies to help you attain a positive body image:[26]

➤ Know and accept what determines your physical characteristics (genetics, stage of life, nutritional intake, activity levels).

➤ Avoid dieting and eat normally by responding to hunger and fullness cues.

➤ Avoid comparing yourself to others, especially models and celebrities, based on weight, shape, or size.

➤ Recognize that you are a whole person and not just individual parts.

➤ Respect yourself and others based on the qualities of character and accomplishments, rather than appearance.

person counters the binge with some type of **purging**. Many people assume that bulimics purge only by vomiting, but self-induced vomiting is just one form. Purging can be described as any behavior that assists in "getting rid" of food to prevent weight gain or to promote weight loss. This can include excessive exercise; abuse of diet pills, laxatives, or diuretics; and strict dieting or fasting.

Most of the health consequences that occur with bulimia nervosa are associated with self-induced vomiting, such as tears in the esophagus, swollen parotid glands, tooth decay and gum disease (due to stomach acid in the mouth), and broken blood vessels in the eyes (due to pressure from vomiting). Electrolyte imbalance may occur with bulimia nervosa and can be fatal, just as with anorexia nervosa. People with bulimia nervosa may also experience dehydration and constipation due to frequent episodes of binge eating and purging.[89]

Laxative abuse can also cause serious medical complications depending on the type, amount, and length of time the person has used them. Laxatives used repeatedly can cause constipation, dehydration due to fluid loss in the intestines, electrolyte imbalances, fluid retention, bloody stools, and impaired bowel function.

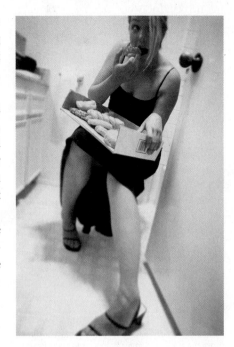

People with binge eating disorder often eat in secret.

Binge Eating Disorder Involves Compulsive Overeating

Binge eating disorder is characterized by recurrent episodes of binge eating without purging. People who have binge eating disorder eat without regard to physiological cues. They may eat for emotional reasons, and feel out of control while eating. The overeating results in physical and psychological discomfort. Many people who struggle with this type of eating disorder will often eat in secret and feel ashamed about their behaviors.

The health effects of binge eating disorder are commonly those that are associated with obesity, because most people who struggle with binge eating disorder are of normal or heavier-than-average weight. Health effects may include high blood pressure, high cholesterol levels, heart disease, type 2 diabetes, and gallbladder disease.[90]

Other Disordered Eating Behaviors Can Be Harmful

In addition to anorexia nervosa, bulimia nervosa, and binge eating disorder, there are other abnormal eating behaviors that can be harmful and require treatment. These include orthorexia, night eating syndrome, and pica.

Orthorexia is defined as an obsession with "healthy or righteous eating" and often begins with someone's simple desire to live a healthy lifestyle. Someone with orthorexia fixates on defining the "right" foods, and will spend just as much time and energy thinking about food as someone with anorexia nervosa or bulimia nervosa. While this person may not obsess about calories, they think about the overall health benefits and how the food was processed, prepared, etc. Various factors can contribute to this obsession for healthy foods, including hearing something negative about a food or food group, which then leads to completely eliminating the food or foods from their diet. Be aware that the restrictive nature of orthorexia has the potential to develop into anorexia nervosa.

Night eating syndrome is a unique combination of disordered eating, a sleep disorder, and a mood disorder.[91] Someone with this syndrome consumes the majority of daily calories after the evening meal, as well as wakes up during the night, possibly even several times, to eat. In addition, the person typically does not have an appetite during the morning hours and consumes very little throughout the day. One study

purging Measures taken to prevent weight gain or to lose weight after consuming food; examples include self-induced vomiting, laxatives, diuretics (water pills), excessive exercise, and/or fasting.

People with night eating syndrome may consume more than half their day's calories between 8 p.m. and 6 a.m.

found that people with night eating syndrome consume 56 percent of their 24-hour calorie intake between the hours of 8:00 p.m. and 6:00 a.m. This study also found that people with night eating syndrome generally do not binge eat with each awakening; rather, they eat smaller portions of food on several occasions throughout the night.[92]

Pica refers to a strong, persistent desire to eat, lick, or chew nonnutritive substances, such as clay, dirt, or chalk, for a period of at least 1 month. Consuming nonfood substances can cause serious medical complications such as intestinal obstruction, intestinal perforation, infections, or lead poisoning.

Because orthorexia, night eating syndrome, and pica do not meet the diagnostic criteria for anorexia nervosa, bulimia nervosa, or binge eating disorder, but still require treatment, they fall into the diagnostic category of "Feeding and Eating Disorders Not Elsewhere Classified." Other behaviors in this category include purging without binging, restrictive eating by people who are in a normal weight range despite having significant weight loss, binging and purging but not frequently enough to meet criteria for bulimia, and chewing and spitting out food instead of swallowing it.

There Are Some Common Signs of Disordered Eating

There are both physical and behavioral warning signs of eating disorders and disordered eating (Table 10.6). Hair loss is very common among people with anorexia nervosa and bulimia nervosa, as the body does not receive adequate nutrients for hair maintenance and growth. You may also notice significant weight changes, such as sudden weight loss in anorexia nervosa, and sudden weight gain in bulimia nervosa or binge eating disorder. *Russell's sign,* which is scar tissue on the knuckles of fingers

Table 10.6
Warning Signs for Eating Disorders

Symptom	Explanation/Example
Weight is below 85% of ideal body weight	Refusal to accept and maintain body weight (even if it is within normal range)
Exercising excessively	Often exercise daily for long periods of time to burn calories and prevent weight gain. May skip work or class to exercise.
Preoccupation with food, weight, and diet	Constantly worry about amount and type of food eaten. May weigh themselves daily or several times per day.
Distorted body image	Do not see themselves as they truly are. May comment on being fat even if underweight.
Refusing to eat	Will avoid food in order to lose weight or prevent weight gain. May avoid only certain foods, such as those with fat and sugar.
Diet pill use or laxative use	Evidence of pill bottles, boxes, or packaging
Changes in mood	May become more withdrawn, depressed, or anxious, especially around food
Hair loss	Hair becomes thinner and falls out in large quantities.
Avoiding eating around others	Want to eat alone. Make excuses to avoid eating with others.

used to induce vomiting, is one indicator of bulimia nervosa. This is caused by scraping the knuckles when removing the fingers from the mouth during purging.

People with disordered eating often avoid social situations because they know food will be present and do not feel comfortable eating around others. Preoccupation with food and body weight is also present among people with eating disorders, such as weighing several times each day or obsessively counting calories. They may also deny unusual eating behaviors if confronted about them.

What Can You Do If You Suspect a Friend Has an Eating Disorder?

You may know someone with an eating disorder, but do not know how to help them, or you may be concerned about your own eating patterns (see the Self-Assessment "Are You at Risk for an Eating Disorder?"). Learning about eating disorders will help you understand why a friend or loved one can have destructive eating behaviors and be seemingly unaware of the damage, pain, or danger they can cause. Knowing the warning signs can also help you identify disordered eating behaviors that could progress into more serious eating disorders.

If you are concerned about someone, find a good time and place to gently express your concerns without criticism or judgment. Realize that you may be rejected or your friend may deny the problem. Be supportive and let them know that you are available if they want to talk to you at another time. Unfortunately, there are many things that you cannot do to help a loved one or friend get better. You cannot force an anorexic to eat, keep a bulimic from purging, or make a binge eater stop overeating. It is up to the individual to decide when he or she is ready to deal with the issues in life that led to the eating disorder.

The best thing you can do is learn to listen to your friend or loved one. Find out about resources in your area for treating eating disorders so that you can refer someone there when that person is ready to get help. Some Web-based resources are listed on page 411.

Eating Disorders Can Be Treated

The most effective treatment for eating disorders is a multidisciplinary team approach including psychological, medical, and nutrition professionals. All members of the team must be knowledgeable and experienced with eating disorders because it is a complex area that some health care professionals do not feel comfortable treating. A psychologist can help the person deal with emotional and other psychological issues that may be contributing to the eating disorder. Anyone who struggles with an eating disorder should be closely monitored by a physician or other medical professional, as some eating disorders can be life-threatening. A registered dietitian can help someone with an eating disorder establish normal eating behaviors.

Some nutritional approaches to eating disorders include identifying binge triggers, safe and unsafe foods, and hunger and fullness cues. Food journals are often helpful to identify eating patterns, food choices, moods, eating disorder triggers, eating cues, and timing of meals and snacks. Meal plans are also used in some instances to ensure intake of adequate calories and nutrients among those with anorexia nervosa, and to help avoid overeating among those with bulimia nervosa or binge eating disorder.

Many people recover from eating disorders and do not struggle with them for the rest of their lives. When treatment is sought in the early stages, there is a better chance that the person will recover fully and have a shorter recovery process than someone who begins treatment after many years.[93] Some people continue to have the desire to engage in disordered eating behaviors; however, they are able to refrain from actually doing these behaviors. Unfortunately, some individuals may never fully recover from an eating disorder. Caregivers must recognize that recovery is a process that often takes years; it is not a quick fix.

│ The Take-Home Message Disordered eating is characterized by an abnormal eating pattern. Eating disorders include disordered eating behaviors and other specific criteria. Eating disorders are prompted by a complex network of factors, including sociocultural, genetic, and preexisting psychological factors. The most common eating disorders include anorexia nervosa, bulimia nervosa, and binge eating disorder. Eating disorders are most effectively treated with a multidisciplinary team of psychologists, physicians, and registered dietitians. A full recovery takes time but is possible, especially if the disorder is treated in the early stages.

MADE over MADE better

Eating on the run doesn't have to ruin your health. Many eateries are now offering a wide range of options for the health-conscious consumer—if you make the right selection. Try these options the next time you're eating on the fly!

If you like this. . .	Try this instead!

Double Chocolaty Chip Blended Beverage
Calories: 410
Fat: 20 grams
Saturated Fat: 12 grams

Iced Coffee with Skim Milk
Calories: 110
Fat: 0 grams
Saturated Fat: 0 grams

Dunkin' Donuts Coffee Cake Muffin
Calories: 660
Fat: 26 grams
Saturated Fat: 7 grams

Dunkin' Donuts Multigrain Bagel
Calories: 390
Fat: 8 grams
Saturated Fat: 0.5 grams

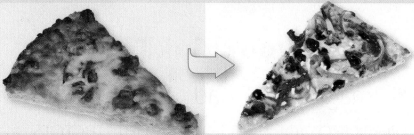

Taco Bell Grilled Stuffed Beef Burrito
Calories: 700
Fat: 30 grams
Saturated Fat: 10 grams

Fresco Burrito Supreme®— Steak
Calories: 330
Fat: 8 grams
Saturated Fat: 3 grams

Pizza Hut Meat Lovers Pan Pizza
Calories: 480 (1 slice)
Fat: 28 grams
Saturated Fat: 10 grams

Pizza Hut Veggie Lovers Thin Crust Pizza
Calories: 410 (1 slice)
Fat: 9 grams
Saturated Fat: 4 grams

Source: USDA National Nutrient Database for Standard Reference.

Is Gastric Bypass Surgery a Healthy Weight-Loss Measure for Obese Adolescents?
Gastric bypass surgery is the most commonly performed bariatric surgery in the United States.[1] By changing the digestive system, it limits the amount of food a person can eat.[2] In recent years, this type of surgery has been increasingly performed on adults, and scientists expect the number of surgeries for adolescents to increase as well.[3]

Is this type of surgery a healthy weight-loss measure for young people? Or are the risks too great? Take a close look at the arguments for both sides and see what you think.

yes

- In the past 30 years, the rate of obesity among children has more than doubled, and the rate of obesity among adolescents has tripled, leaving children and teens at greater risk for a host of diseases, including cardiovascular disease and diabetes, at earlier ages.[4]

- Childhood obesity can also lead to depression and increased tendency toward risk-taking behaviors.[5]

- As with adults, gastric bypass surgery does have risks, and as a result is not for everyone. Only severely obese children and teens, with a BMI in the 95th percentile and with other medical complications as a result of obesity, should be considered, and then only after all other weight-loss measures have failed.[6]

- One study has shown that surgery could actually reverse the effects of type 2 diabetes in obese adolescents.[7]

- As gastric banding becomes more commonly used among adolescents, outcomes are even better. One study found that 24 of 25 adolescent patients who underwent gastric banding lost more than 50 percent of their excess weight.[8]

no

- Because of the drastically reduced amount of food their bodies are taking in, adolescents who have undergone gastric bypass surgery are at a heightened risk of nutritional deficiencies, especially iron, which is normally absorbed through the duodenum, a section of the digestive tract that is bypassed in the surgery.[9]

- Whereas young people tend to dramatically shed excess weight during the first year after surgery, as with adults, the weight loss tends to slow over time; their BMI tends to level off in the second year at a point that remains above normal.[10]

- Some researchers fear that as weight-loss surgery for teenagers becomes more popular, some doctors—because they are either tempted by a potentially lucrative market or motivated by a sincere desire to help—will operate on patients who should not have the surgery.[11]

- More research is needed on the long-term outcomes of bariatric surgery in adolescents. Some patients are likely to have later complications that are not yet apparent.[12]

- Adolescents are at risk for bone loss after bariatric surgery, according to a case review of 61 patients.[13]

what do you think?

1. Imagine you had an obese child whom doctors recommended for surgery. What factors would you consider in deciding whether or not your child should have it? **2.** Do you think rates of gastric surgery among adolescents are likely to increase or decrease in the future? Explain your answer.

VISUAL Chapter Summary

1 A Healthy Body Weight Is Healthy for You

A healthy body weight is considered a body weight that doesn't increase the risk of developing any weight-related health problems. Being very underweight increases the risk of nutritional deficiencies and related health problems. Being overweight increases the risk of chronic diseases such as heart disease, cancer, and type 2 diabetes.

2 Your BMI Can Help You Determine If You Are at a Healthy Weight

To assess if you are at a healthy weight, you can consider your BMI (body mass index), which is your weight in relationship to your height. A BMI of 18.5 to 24.9 is considered healthy. A BMI of 25 up to 29.9 is considered overweight. A BMI of 30 or higher is considered obese. As your BMI increases above 25, so does your risk of dying from many chronic diseases. However, some individuals, such as athletes, may have a high BMI but their weight doesn't put them at a health risk because they are not overfat. In contrast, some individuals who have unintentionally lost weight may have a healthy BMI but be at nutritional risk. In general, BMI is best used to assess overweight and obesity for populations rather than individuals. Excess weight around the middle, measured by your waist circumference, could put you at a higher health risk, regardless of your BMI.

Extremely High Risk
BMI 40+ and high waist circumference

Very High Risk
BMI 30–39.9 and high waist circumference

High Risk
BMI 25–29.9 and high waist circumference
or
BMI 30–34.9 and low waist circumference

Increased Risk
BMI 25–29.9 and low waist circumference

Low Risk
BMI under 25

3 Energy Balance Is Achieved When Energy (Calories) In Equals Energy (Calories) Out

Body weight remains constant when energy (calorie) intake equals energy (calorie) expenditure. When you consume more energy (calories) than you expend, you have an energy excess, or positive energy balance, and weight gain occurs. When your calories fall short of your needs and/or you expend more energy, you have an energy deficit, or negative energy balance, and you will lose weight. Your basal metabolic rate (BMR), the thermic effect of food (TEF), and your physical activities all factor into your daily energy (calorie) needs. Your BMR is influenced mainly by your lean body mass, but also by your age, gender, body size, genes, ethnicity, emotional and physical stress, thyroid hormone, nutritional state, and environmental temperature. Your caffeine intake and use of nicotine can also affect your BMR.

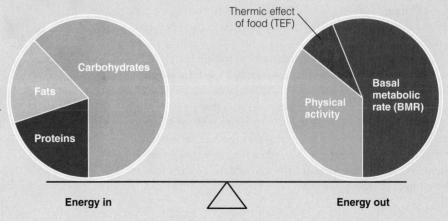

Thermic effect of food (TEF)

Carbohydrates

Fats

Proteins

Physical activity

Basal metabolic rate (BMR)

Energy in

Energy out

4 Many Factors Affect Your Body Weight

Appetite is your psychological desire for food and is affected by hunger, satiety, and satiation, as well as your emotions and your environment. Hunger prompts you to eat, and it will subside as the feeling of satiation sets in after you start eating. Satiety is the feeling you experience when you have had enough to eat and determines the length of time between meals or snacks. Physiological mechanisms such as hormones, sensory signals, and a distended stomach, as well as the size of the meal and the nutrients in your foods, all influence your appetite. Genetics and your environment also play a role in your appetite and weight. If your parents were overweight, you are at a higher risk of developing obesity. An environment that enables easy access to a variety of large portions of foods, and encourages you to be sedentary, will also promote obesity.

5 Losing Weight Healthfully Involves Diet, Physical Activity, and Behavior Modification

Losing 10 percent of your body weight over a six-month period is considered a reasonable rate of weight loss. Losing weight rapidly can cause a person to fall short of meeting nutrient needs. Many fad diets promise quick results but can be unhealthy for the long term.

Eating more low-energy-density, high-volume foods, such as vegetables and fruit, can help you lose weight because you will feel full for fewer calories. Fiber also promotes satiation. Because protein has the most dramatic effect on satiety, eating high-protein lean meats, chicken, and fish at meals can help reduce hunger between meals. Because fat slows the movement of food out of the stomach into the intestines, it can also prolong satiety.

Changing the eating behaviors that contribute to weight gain or impede weight loss is necessary for long-term weight-loss success. Self-monitoring of these behaviors by keeping a food record, controlling environmental cues that trigger eating when not hungry, and learning how to better manage stress are all behavior modification techniques that can be used by individuals who eat out of habit and in response to their environment. Routine physical activity can add to the daily energy deficit needed for weight loss.

HEALTHY WEIGHT

Physical activity

Healthy diet

Behavior modification

6 Maintaining Weight Loss Involves a Lifetime of Healthy Habits

Weight cycling is the repeated gain and loss of body weight. Individuals who lose weight often experience an "energy gap" due to their lower overall energy needs because there is less body weight to maintain. In order to account for the energy gap and successfully maintain their new weight, individuals who have lost weight must continue to eat a healthy diet, follow healthy habits, and maintain a high level of physical activity.

7 Consuming a Healthy Diet Is Important When Trying to Gain Weight

Individuals who are trying to gain weight should consume a healthy diet that is calorie and nutrient rich and exercise to build muscle mass. Consuming larger portions at mealtimes and energy-dense snacks between meals can help with weight gain.

8 Disordered Eating Describes a Variety of Abnormal Eating Patterns

Disordered eating includes restrictive eating, binge eating, vomiting after eating, and abusing laxatives or diet pills. Eating disorders are diagnosed by meeting specific criteria that include disordered eating behaviors.

Anorexia nervosa is characterized by self-starvation and excessive weight loss. Bulimia nervosa involves repeated cycles of binge eating and purging. Binge eating disorders are characterized by binge eating without purging. Orthorexia is an obsession with "healthy or righteous eating." Night eating syndrome is described as excessive calorie intake in the evening and waking up during the night to eat. Pica is a compulsion to eat nonnutritive substances.

Numerous health consequences can occur with eating disorders, such as hair loss, digestive problems, electrolyte imbalances, changes in heart rate and blood pressure, dehydration, and nutrient deficiencies. The most effective treatment for eating disorders involves a multidisciplinary team approach including psychological, nutrition, and medical professionals.

Terms to Know

- healthy weight
- overweight
- obesity
- underweight
- body mass index (BMI)
- energy balance
- energy excess
- energy deficit
- basal metabolic rate (BMR)
- thermic effect of food (TEF)
- estimated energy requirement (EER)
- satiety
- behavior modification
- disordered eating
- eating disorders

Check Your Understanding

1. Which one of the following is NOT influenced by being overweight?
   a. heart disease
   b. osteoarthritis
   c. gallbladder disease
   d. hair loss

2. Kyle has a BMI of 27. He is considered
   a. underweight.
   b. overweight.
   c. at a healthy weight.
   d. obese.

3. Central obesity refers to
   a. the accumulation of excess fat in your hips and thighs.
   b. the accumulation of excess fat in your stomach area.
   c. the accumulation of excess fat in your arms and legs.
   d. the accumulation of excess fat in your ankles and feet.

4. Your basal metabolic rate (BMR) refers to
   a. the amount of energy you expend during physical activity.
   b. the amount of energy you expend digesting your food.
   c. the amount of energy (calories) that you consume daily.
   d. the amount of energy expended to meet your basic physiological needs.

5. You just ate a large plate of pasta and tomato sauce, so your stomach is full and distended. Which hormone is released because of the distention of your stomach?
   a. cholecystokinin
   b. insulin
   c. thyroid hormone
   d. leptin

6. Which of the following can increase your risk of becoming overweight?
   a. having a parent who is obese
   b. consuming more meals at home than dining out

   c. reducing the amount of "screen time" during the day
   d. decreasing your portion sizes

7. Which are examples of low-energy-density, high-volume foods that can aid in weight loss?
   a. raw vegetables and salsa
   b. jelly beans
   c. olive oil
   d. ice cream

8. Research suggests that accumulating _____ daily, which is the equivalent of walking 5 miles, can help reduce the risk of becoming overweight.
   a. 1,000 steps
   b. 5,000 steps
   c. 7,500 steps
   d. 10,000 steps

9. Which of the following is NOT a form of purging in bulimia nervosa?
   a. self-induced vomiting
   b. fasting
   c. exercise
   d. sleeping

10. Lanugo, or downy hair growth, is common in what type of eating disorder?
    a. anorexia nervosa
    b. bulimia nervosa
    c. binge eating disorder
    d. night eating syndrome

Answers

1. (d) Hair loss. Being overweight increases your risk of all these diseases and conditions, as well as type 2 diabetes, some cancers, and sleep apnea.

2. (b) Because Kyle's BMI falls between 25 and 29.9, he is considered overweight. If his BMI was under 18.5, he would be underweight, whereas a BMI of 18.5 to 24.9 would put him in the healthy weight category. A BMI of 30 and higher is considered obese.

3. (b) Central obesity refers to the accumulation of excess fat in the stomach area and can

be determined by measuring a person's waist circumference. Central obesity increases the risk of heart disease, diabetes, and hypertension.

4. (d) Your BMR refers to the bare minimum amount of energy (calories) your body expends to keep your blood circulating and lungs breathing so that you can stay alive. The amount of energy or calories that you expend during physical activity is not factored into your BMR. The energy that you expend digesting, absorbing, and processing food is called the thermic effect of food (TEF) and is also not part of your BMR. The amount of energy or calories that you consume daily doesn't factor into your BMR.

5. (a) A distended stomach causes the release of cholecystokinin, which is associated with the feeling of satiation and the ending of eating. Insulin will be released once this carbohydrate-heavy meal is digested and absorbed into the blood. Thyroid hormone affects your BMR and is not associated with your stomach being distended, and leptin is secreted from fat cells and decreases hunger.

6. (a) Having a parent who is obese can increase your risk of becoming overweight. Consuming more meals at home, reducing your "screen time" and decreasing your portion sizes can all help you reduce your risk of becoming overweight.

7. (a) Vegetables, including the salsa, are low-energy-density, high-volume foods. These foods will increase satiation, contain few calories per bite, and can displace more energy-dense foods in the diet, all of which can help promote weight loss. The jelly beans, olive oil, and ice cream are all very energy dense.

8. (d) Accumulating 10,000 steps daily can help reduce the risk of becoming overweight.
9. (d) Sleeping is not considered a form of purging. However, self-induced vomiting, fasting, and exercise are all forms of purging, as they assist in "getting rid" of food.
10. (a) Lanugo grows typically on the face and arms of people with anorexia nervosa as a way of regulating body temperature.

Web Resources

- For more on overweight and obesity, visit the Centers for Disease Control and Prevention at www.cdc.gov
- For more information on weight control and physical activity, visit the Weight-control Information Network (WIN) at http://win.niddk.nih.gov
- For more weight-loss shopping tips, recipes, and menu makeovers, visit the USDA's Weight Management website at www.nutrition.gov
- For more on eating disorders, visit the National Eating Disorders Association at www.nationaleatingdisorders.org

1. **True.** Overweight people can suffer from a condition called sleep apnea. To find out what this is and why being overweight contributes to it, turn to page 367.

2. **False.** Being underweight due to a poor diet can have serious health risks. Turn to page 367 to find out why.

3. **False.** Celebrities and models in magazine photos may reflect social trends, but they often don't reflect a healthy body weight. Turn to page 368 to find out more.

4. **False.** Fat around the belly puts a person at a higher health risk than fat stored on the hips and thighs. To find out why, turn to page 370.

5. **True.** But this isn't the only factor. Turn to page 374 to find out the others.

6. **True.** To find out why and how these factors interact with each other, turn to page 379.

7. **True.** Surprising as it may be, eating *more* of certain foods can help you lose weight. To find out why, turn to page 383.

8. **False.** Whereas fat makes food stay in the stomach longer, which slows its digestion and absorption, it isn't the nutrient that provides the greatest level of satiety. You may be surprised to learn what is. Turn to page 386 to find out.

9. **False.** Technically, disordered eating describes abnormal eating behaviors, whereas eating disorders are clinically diagnosed illnesses. Turn to page 396 to learn more about these behaviors and illnesses.

10. **True.** Some eating disorders can be life-threatening. Turn to page 399 to learn about the health effects of eating disorders.

11

Nutrition and Fitness

True or False?

1. Physical **activity** and exercise are technically the same. ⓉⒻ p. 414

2. As little as **60 minutes** of physical activity per week is enough to provide health benefits. ⓉⒻ p. 419

3. Energy for exercise is derived from both anaerobic and **aerobic** metabolic pathways. ⓉⒻ p. 422

4. Eating a **high-carbohydrate** meal before an exercise session will always result in improved energy and performance. ⓉⒻ p. 425

5. Athletes should eat immediately after **training**. ⓉⒻ p. 432

6. Vitamins and minerals are not as important to **exercise** as are carbohydrate, protein, and fat. ⓉⒻ p. 433

7. Many **athletes** are at risk for iron deficiency. ⓉⒻ p. 434

8. Everyone who exercises should consume **sports drinks**. ⓉⒻ p. 437

9. **Thirst** is the best indicator for monitoring fluid needs. ⓉⒻ p. 438

10. The National Collegiate Athletic Association (NCAA) classifies **caffeine** as a banned substance when consumed in high amounts. ⓉⒻ p. 441

See page 451 for the answers.

After reading this chapter, you will be able to:

1. **List and describe the five basic components of fitness.**

2. **Describe the FITT principle and how to use it to create a fitness program.**

3. **Describe the roles of carbohydrate, fat, and protein during physical activity.**

4. **List optimal food sources before, during, and after exercise.**

5. **Describe the importance of vitamins and minerals for physical fitness.**

6. **Explain the relationship between fluid intake and fitness.**

7. **List and describe ergogenic aids that claim to improve athletic performance and physical fitness.**

Whether you are a competitive athlete or strive to stay "in shape," your eating habits are just as important to your fitness and performance as the exercise itself. Your body is like a car: It requires fuel to make it move and proper maintenance to keep it in good working condition. If you are driving a car in a race, you will make sure that you have enough gas to make it through the competition. Similar to gas in a car, nutrients from food provide the energy needed to move the body, especially during exercise. The more you move, the more energy is needed. Nutrients are necessary to help the body recover after exercise so that you receive the benefits of the activity and have energy to repeat the activity. Fueling your body with the proper balance of nutrients is essential to achieving optimal fitness levels and optimal athletic performance.

What Is Physical Fitness and Why Is It Important?

Physical fitness is simply defined as good health or physical condition, primarily as the result of exercise and proper nutrition. Some people think of exercise and physical activity as the same thing, but this isn't technically the case. **Physical activity** refers to body movement that results in expending calories. Activities such as gardening, walking the dog, and playing with children can all be regarded as physical activity. **Exercise** is defined as formalized training or structured activity, like step aerobics, running, or weight lifting. For the purpose of this chapter, though, the terms *exercise* and *physical activity* are used interchangeably.

Being physically active and consuming a healthy diet are the two most important components of overall health and fitness. You will not achieve optimal fitness if you ignore either of these areas.

Physical Fitness Has Five Basic Components

The five basic components of fitness include cardiorespiratory endurance, muscular strength, muscular endurance, flexibility, and body composition. Most strength training programs blend muscular strength and muscular endurance, which is generally referred to as *muscular fitness*. To be physically fit, one must consider all five variables.

Cardiorespiratory endurance is the ability to sustain cardiorespiratory exercise, such as running and biking, for an extended length of time. This requires that the body's cardiovascular and respiratory systems provide enough oxygen and energy to the working muscles without becoming overly fatigued or exhausted. Someone who can run a leisurely mile without being too out of breath to talk has good cardiorespiratory endurance. Someone who is out of breath after climbing one flight of stairs, in contrast, does not.

Muscle strength is the ability to produce force for a brief period of time, while **muscle endurance** is the ability to exert force over a long period of time without fatigue. Increasing muscle strength and muscle endurance is best achieved with **strength training**. You probably associate muscle strength with bodybuilders or weight lifters, and it's true that these people train to be particularly strong. However, other athletes, such as cheerleaders and ballet dancers, also work hard to strengthen their muscles. Consider the strength it takes to lift another person above your head. If you could hold the person up for several minutes, that would show exceptional muscle endurance.

Flexibility is the range of motion around a joint and is improved with stretching. Athletic performance and joint and muscular function are all enhanced with improved flexibility, which also reduces the likelihood of injury. A gymnast exhibits high flexibility when performing stunts and dance routines. In contrast, someone with low flexibility might not be able to bend over and touch his toes from a standing or sitting position.

Finally, **body composition** is the proportion of muscle, fat, water, and other tissues in the body. Together, these tissues make up your total body weight. Your body composition can change without your total body weight changing, due to the fact that muscle takes up less space (per pound) than does body fat. This is why you can lose inches on your body without losing pounds of weight when you increase your lean muscle mass and decrease body fat.

Running is a great way to improve cardiorespiratory endurance.

Physical Fitness Provides Numerous Benefits

We have long heard that eating a balanced diet and exercising regularly maintains good health. We also know that even modest amounts of exercise will provide health benefits, and the more you exercise, the more fit you'll be. However, despite knowing the benefits that exercise brings, more than half of the adults living in the United States do not meet the recommendations for regular physical activity.[1]

So, how does physical activity improve and maintain good health? One of the most obvious ways is that it helps you achieve or maintain a healthy body weight, which in turn helps reduce the risk of developing chronic diseases like type 2 diabetes mellitus and heart disease. In addition, being physically fit can improve overall health in other ways, like helping you get restful sleep and reducing stress. **Table 11.1** on the next page lists some of the numerous health benefits that result from being physically active on a regular basis. You have to be cautious, however, not to overexercise and increase your risk of injury.

To improve the health of American adults and children through regular physical activity, the U.S. Department of Health and Human Services developed the *2008 Physical Activity Guidelines for Americans*. This publication gives information and guidance on the types and amounts of physical activity that provide substantial health benefits for Americans age 6 and older. The recommendations are based on a review of scientific research on the benefits of physical activity, and conclude with the main idea that regular physical activity over time can produce long-term health benefits.[11]

The Take-Home Message Physical fitness is the state of being in good physical condition through proper nutrition and regular physical activity. The five components of physical fitness are cardiorespiratory endurance, muscle strength, muscle endurance, flexibility, and body composition. To achieve optimal fitness, all five components must be considered. The numerous health benefits of physical activity include higher likelihood of a healthy body weight, as well as reduced risk of several chronic diseases, including type 2 diabetes, heart disease, and cancer; improved body composition, bone health, immune function, and mental well-being; more restful sleep; and reduced stress.

physical fitness The ability to perform physical activities requiring cardiorespiratory endurance, muscle endurance, and strength and/or flexibility; physical fitness is acquired through physical activity and adequate nutrition.

physical activity Voluntary movement that results in energy expenditure (burning calories).

exercise Any type of structured or planned physical activity.

cardiorespiratory endurance The body's ability to sustain prolonged exercise.

muscle strength The greatest amount of force exerted by a muscle at one time.

muscle endurance The ability of a muscle to produce prolonged effort.

strength training Exercising with weights or other resistance to build, strengthen, and tone muscle to improve or maintain overall fitness; also called *resistance training*.

flexibility A joint's ability to move freely through a full and normal range of motion.

body composition The relative proportion of muscle, fat, water, and other tissues in the body.

Table 11.1

The Benefits of Physical Fitness

Reduced Risk of Heart Disease

How It Works: Research has shown that moderate physical activity lowers blood pressure.[2] In addition, exercise is positively associated with high-density lipoprotein (HDL) cholesterol.[3]

Improved Body Composition

How It Works: Exercise helps burn excess stored body fat and builds muscle, resulting in a leaner body mass. Individuals with moderate cardiorespiratory fitness have less total fat and abdominal fat compared with people with low cardiorespiratory fitness.[4]

Reduced Risk of Type 2 Diabetes

How It Works: Exercise helps control blood glucose levels by increasing insulin sensitivity.[5] This not only reduces risk for type 2 diabetes, but also improves blood glucose control for those who have been diagnosed with type 2 diabetes.

Reduced Risk of Some Forms of Cancer

How It Works: Increased physical activity has been associated with a reduced risk of colon, breast, endometrial, and lung cancers. This reduced risk is likely the result of a reduction in overall body weight and other hormonal and metabolic mechanisms.[6]

What Does a Physical Fitness Program Look Like?

Physical fitness programs are generally based on the five components of fitness, and include aerobic exercise, resistance training, and stretching. A successful fitness program should be tailored to meet the needs of the individual and performed consistently so that any gains in physical fitness are not lost. It is also important to incorporate activities that are enjoyable so that they become a regular part of your lifestyle. If you dislike jogging, for example, you won't be likely to consistently work a daily run into your schedule.

Cardiorespiratory Exercise Can Improve Cardiorespiratory Endurance and Body Composition

Between birth and old age, you will walk about 70,000 miles. Walking is one of the best activities you can do to improve cardiovascular health and maintain a healthy weight. Plus, it can be done anywhere!

Cardiorespiratory exercise usually involves continuous activities that use large muscle groups, such as high-impact aerobics, stair climbing, and brisk walking. This type of exercise is predominantly aerobic because it uses oxygen. During cardiorespiratory exercise, your heart beats faster and more oxygen-carrying blood is delivered to your tissues. How does this work? As you begin to exercise, your body requires more oxygen to break down nutrients for energy, so it increases blood flow (volume) to the working muscles. It accomplishes this by increasing your heart rate and

Improved Bone Health

How It Works: Bone density has been shown to improve with weight-bearing exercise and resistance training, thereby reducing the risk for osteoporosis.[7]

Improved Mental Well-Being

How It Works: Regular exercise protects against the onset of depression and anxiety disorders, reduces symptoms in people diagnosed with depression and anxiety, delays the incidence of dementia, and overall enhances mental well-being.[9]

Improved Immune System

How It Works: Regular moderate exercise can enhance the immune system by increasing immunoglobulins in the body. Immunoglobulins function like antibodies, protecting against colds and other infectious diseases.[8]

Improved Sleep

How It Works: People who engage in regular exercise often have better quality of sleep due to anxiety reduction, antidepressant effect, and changes in body temperature that promote sleep.[10]

stroke volume. Your body also redistributes blood from your internal organs to maximize the volume of blood that is delivered to the muscles during exercise.

Your level of cardiorespiratory fitness can be measured by the maximum amount of oxygen your muscles can consume during exercise, or **VO$_2$max**. People who are more physically fit have a higher VO$_2$max and can exercise at a higher intensity without fatigue than someone who is not as fit.

Cardiorespiratory exercise provides the most benefits to your cardiovascular system (heart, blood, and blood vessels), which improves your cardiorespiratory endurance. In addition, it reduces stress and lowers your risk of heart disease by maintaining normal cholesterol levels, heart rate, and blood pressure. Cardiorespiratory exercise also helps you maintain a healthy weight and improve your body composition by burning excess calories, leading to a reduction of body fat.

Strength Training Can Improve Muscle Strength, Muscle Endurance, and Body Composition

Strength (or resistance) training has long been associated with gaining muscle mass, strength, and endurance. Maintaining adequate muscle mass and strength is important for everyone. Just because you engage in resistance training does not mean that you will develop large, bulky muscles. Many females, as well as males, use resistance training to tone and define their muscles to improve their physical appearance and body composition.

To increase muscle strength, you should perform a low number of repetitions using heavy weights or other resistance. If you want to increase muscle endurance, you should perform a high number of repetitions using lighter resistance. However,

Resistance training improves muscle strength and endurance.

stroke volume The amount of blood pumped by the heart with each heart beat.

VO$_2$max The maximum amount of oxygen (ml) a person uses in one minute per kilogram of body weight.

heavier resistance can also be used to improve muscle endurance by allowing short rest intervals between repetition sets.

Rest periods between sets of an exercise and between workouts are important so that you do not overwork your muscles and increase your risk of muscle strains or other injury. If you don't allow time for your muscles to rest, your muscles may break down and not recover, leading to a loss of muscle mass. The amount of rest depends on your fitness goals and level of **conditioning**. If increasing strength is your goal, you should allow long rest periods of 2 to 3 minutes between sets. If increasing muscle endurance is your goal, shorter rest periods of 30 seconds or less are recommended.

Between workouts, the general guideline to reduce the risk of injury is to allow 48 hours between sets that use the same muscle groups. However, strength training can be done daily as long as different muscles are used on consecutive days.

Stretching Can Improve Flexibility

When you think about your flexibility, you are likely considering how far you can stretch in a particular way without feeling pain or discomfort. Improving flexibility can improve balance, posture, and circulation of blood and nutrients throughout your body. The most common exercise used to improve flexibility is stretching.

There are several types of stretching. The most common form is *static stretching*, which consists of relaxing a muscle, then extending it to a point of mild discomfort for about 10 to 30 seconds, and then relaxing it again. You can use static stretching exercises to stretch one muscle at a time, or you can stretch more than one muscle or muscle group simultaneously.

A form of stretching used by many professional athletes as a pre-event warm-up is *dynamic stretching*, which stretches muscles while moving, for example, by performing arm swings, kicks, or lunges. A form of exercise called *yoga* incorporates aspects of both static and dynamic stretching, and individuals who perform yoga on a regular basis can significantly improve their flexibility. Note that when you perform these stretches for the first time, you'll need to consult a qualified trainer, coach, or physician on proper techniques to reduce your risk of injury.

Another form of stretching, called *ballistic stretching*, involves a repetitive, bouncing motion while you are stretching. Some believe that ballistic stretching increases your risk for pulling a muscle; therefore, it is less favored than static and dynamic stretching. Other, less common forms of stretching are types that involve a partner or machine to create the force needed to stretch the muscle, and controlled stretches that use momentum to create the force needed to extend the muscle.

Recommendations about stretching often conflict and the research to sort it out is limited. Some researchers have concluded that stretching before exercise does not prevent muscle soreness after exercise, nor does it prevent acute sports injuries.[12] However, stretching afterward has been shown to relax and reduce tension on muscles that were just exercised.[13]

Improving your flexibility can help you reduce muscle soreness and lower your risk of injury.

The FITT Principle Can Help You Design a Fitness Program

One easy way to design a successful physical fitness program is to follow the FITT principle. FITT is an acronym for frequency, intensity, time, and type. Let's take a closer look at each of these components:

➤ **Frequency** is how often you do the activity, such as the number of times per week.

conditioning The process of improving physical fitness through repeated activity.

Table 11.2

Target Heart Rate

Age	Percent of Maximum Heart Rate*			
	55%	65%	85%	95%
20	106	126	164	184
25	105	124	162	181
30	103	121	159	177
35	101	119	156	174
40	99	117	153	171
45	97	115	150	168
50	95	113	147	165

*Maximum heart rate (HRmax) can be estimated using the following equation:

$$206.9 - (\text{age in years} \times 0.67) = \text{estimated HRmax.}$$

➤ Intensity refers to the degree of difficulty at which you perform the activity. Common terms used to describe **intensity** are low, moderate, and vigorous (high). One measure of intensity for cardiorespiratory exercise is the **rating of perceived exertion (RPE)**, in which the person performing the activity self-assesses the level of intensity. The RPE is based on your current level of fitness and your perception of how hard you are working. The scale ranges from 1 (rest) to 10 (maximal exertion). A range of 5 to 7 on the RPE scale (somewhat hard to hard) is recommended for most adults to achieve fitness. A more precise method of measuring intensity is using your **target heart rate**. (See **Table 11.2**.) Your target heart rate is the range (given in percentages of maximum heart rate) that your heart rate should fall within to ensure that you are training aerobically. A target heart rate of 55 percent to 64 percent of maximum heart rate is considered low intensity, 65 percent to 84 percent of maximum heart rate is defined as moderate intensity, and 85 percent to 95 percent is considered high intensity. For strength training, intensity is referred to as **repetition maximum (RM)**. For example, 1 RM is the maximum amount of weight that can be lifted one time; 10 RM is the maximum amount of weight that can be lifted ten times.

➤ Time, or **duration**, is how long you performed the activity, such as a 30-minute run.

➤ Type means the specific activity that you are doing, such as step aerobics or cycling.

The frequency, intensity, time (duration), and type of exercise that are right for you depend partly on what goal you are trying to achieve. For some health benefits, the *2008 Physical Activity Guidelines* state that as little as 60 minutes a week of moderate-intensity activity, such as brisk walking or dancing, will help you achieve that goal. However, adults who wish to see substantial health benefits, including a reduced risk of many chronic diseases, need a total amount of 150 minutes (2 hours and 30 minutes) of moderate-intensity aerobic activity per week. Additionally, resistance training, such as by lifting weights, at a moderate or high intensity, should be performed two or more days per week. Anyone who wants to maintain body weight and prevent gradual weight gain should participate in approximately 60 minutes of moderate- to vigorous-intensity activity on most days of the week while not consuming excess calories. Those wishing to lose weight need to participate in at least 60 to 90 minutes of daily moderate-intensity physical activity and make calorie adjustments to their diet. You can use the Physical Activity Pyramid to help you become more physically active or improve your current level of fitness (**Figure 11.1** on the next page). People with diabetes, high blood pressure, and other types of heart disease should consult with a health care provider

eLearn

Small Steps for Big Gains

You have numerous opportunities every day to be physically active. Go to www.choosemyplate.gov/physical-activity to see how you can incorporate little changes into your daily routine to attain the health benefits of physical activity.

intensity The level of difficulty of an activity.

rating of perceived exertion (RPE) A subjective measure of the intensity level of an activity using a numerical scale.

target heart rate A heart rate in beats per minute (expressed as a percentage of maximum heart rate) achieved during exercise that indicates the intensity of the exercise.

repetition maximum (RM) The maximum amount of weight that can be lifted for a specified number of repetitions.

duration The length of time of performing an activity.

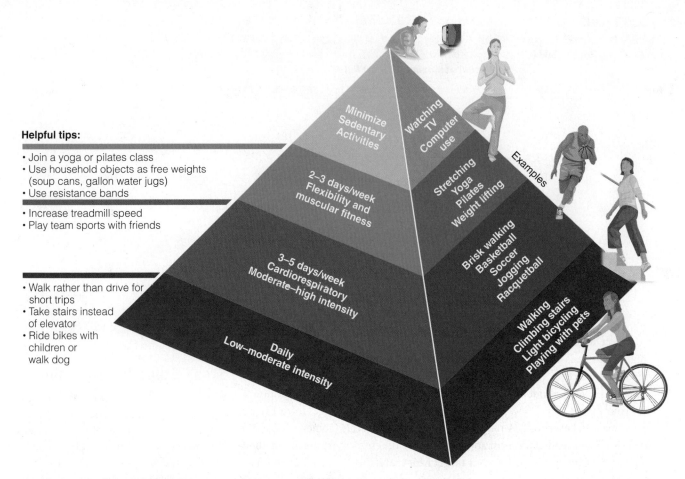

Helpful tips:

- Join a yoga or pilates class
- Use household objects as free weights (soup cans, gallon water jugs)
- Use resistance bands

- Increase treadmill speed
- Play team sports with friends

- Walk rather than drive for short trips
- Take stairs instead of elevator
- Ride bikes with children or walk dog

Within the pyramid:

Minimize Sedentary Activities

Watching TV Computer use

2–3 days/week Flexibility and muscular fitness

Stretching Yoga Pilates Weight lifting

Examples

3–5 days/week Cardiorespiratory Moderate–high intensity

Brisk walking Basketball Soccer Jogging Racquetball

Daily Low–moderate intensity

Walking Climbing stairs Light bicycling Playing with pets

Figure 11.1 Physical Activity Pyramid
Participating in a variety of activities, such as those shown in this Physical Activity Pyramid, will have you on your way to physical fitness.

Do you feel like you don't have a 30-minute block of time to exercise? The good news is that you don't have to do an activity for 30 consecutive minutes to get health benefits. You can break this time up into three 10-minute bouts of activity and still receive the same benefits as if you were to do it all at one time.[14]

before participating in any exercise program, especially one to be performed at a vigorous intensity.

The key to being physically active is to find activities that you enjoy so that you continue to do them on a regular basis. If you don't like jogging, you don't have to do it! Just find other activities that you like. Maybe you enjoy playing basketball, going for a walk, or hiking. It doesn't really matter what the activity is, as long as you take pleasure in what you are doing and do it regularly.

You can use the FITT approach to meet the American College of Sports Medicine's guidelines for cardiorespiratory endurance, muscular fitness, and flexibility for healthy adults, which are summarized in **Table 11.3**. For example, for your FITT program, you may want to jog three days a week for 30 minutes on Tuesday, Thursday, and Friday to attain your cardiorespiratory fitness. On Monday and Wednesday, you may want to lift weights for muscular fitness and make sure that you incorporate stretching throughout the week to improve your flexibility.

The Progressive Overload Principle Can Help Improve Fitness over Time

During conditioning, the body gradually adapts to the activities that are being performed. Over time, if the activity is kept exactly the same, the body doesn't have

Table 11.3

Using FITT to Improve Fitness

	Cardiorespiratory Fitness	Muscular Fitness	Flexibility
Frequency	3–5 days per week	2–3 days per week	2–3 days per week
Intensity	64–95% of maximum heart rate	60–80% of 1 RM	To the point of feeling tightness or slight discomfort
Time	20–60 minutes per day (150 minutes per week), continuous or intermittent (minimum of 10-minute bouts)	8–10 different exercises performed in 2–4 sets, 8–12 repetitions	2–4 repetitions for each muscle group; hold static stretch for 10–30 seconds
Type	Brisk walking, jogging, biking, step aerobics	Free weights, machines with stacked weights, resistance bands	Stretching, yoga

Source: Data from American College of Sports Medicine, "Position Stand: Quantity and Quality of Exercise for Developing and Maintaining Cardiorespiratory, Musculoskeletal, and Neuromotor Fitness in Apparently Healthy Adults: Guidance for Prescribing Exercise," *Medicine & Science in Sports & Exercise* 43 no. 7 (2011).

to work as hard and fitness levels will plateau as a result. To continue to improve your fitness level, you must challenge your body by using the **progressive overload principle**. Modifying one or more of the FITT principles so that you gradually increase exercise demands on the body will improve fitness. For example, if you are trying to improve cardiorespiratory endurance, you might gradually increase the duration of a run. To increase muscle strength, you may gradually increase the amount of weight being lifted.

As your body responds to the work that it is being asked to do, physical fitness will be attained. Muscles will increase in size, endurance, and strength and you will notice increased cardiorespiratory endurance and improved flexibility. However, if conditioning is executed improperly or nutrient intake is inadequate for physical activity, muscles can lose mass, endurance, and strength, and cardiorespiratory fitness levels will suffer.

The Take-Home Message Cardiorespiratory exercise improves cardiorespiratory endurance and body composition. Strength training can improve muscle strength and endurance as well as body composition. Flexibility can be enhanced by stretching. An effective training program can be designed using the FITT principle, which stands for frequency, intensity, time, and type of activity. Most people should aim for 60 minutes of moderate activity per week for some health benefits; greater amounts of exercise are needed for substantial health benefits, weight management, and physical fitness improvement. Applying the progressive overload principle to workouts will help you achieve optimal fitness levels.

How Are Carbohydrate, Fat, and Protein Used during Exercise?

In addition to regular physical activity, you need the right foods and fluids in order to be physically fit. When you eat and drink, you meet your nutrient needs for physical activity in two ways: (1) You supply the energy, particularly from carbohydrate and

progressive overload principle A gradual increase in exercise demands resulting from modifications to the frequency, intensity, time, or type of activity.

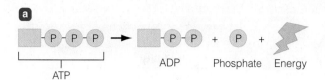

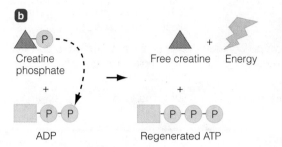

Figure 11.2 Energy Metabolism
During anaerobic metabolism, energy is derived from the breakdown of ATP and creatine phosphate. (**a**) Energy is released when one phosphate group is removed from ATP, leaving ADP. (**b**) Creatine phosphate directly provides energy when the phosphate group is removed from creatine, as well as donates the phosphate group to ADP, regenerating ATP, thereby facilitating energy production as described in (a).

fat, that your body needs for the activity; and (2) you provide the nutrients, particularly carbohydrate and protein, that will help you recover properly so that you can repeat the activity.

We mentioned earlier in the chapter that much energy production during cardiorespiratory exercise is **aerobic** because it uses oxygen. But during the first few seconds of exercise, energy production occurs under **anaerobic** conditions, or without oxygen. For the anaerobic production of energy, the body relies heavily on two high-energy molecules in muscle cells:

➤ **Adenosine triphosphate (ATP)** is a compound composed of a molecule called adenosine attached to a "tail" of three phosphates (*tri* = three). When one of these phosphates is removed from ATP, energy is released as a by-product (**Figure 11.2**). The remaining compound is called adenosine diphosphate (ADP), because it contains only two phosphates (*di* = two). The amount of ATP (energy) in cells is limited, so its breakdown can support only a few seconds of intense exercise.

➤ **Creatine phosphate** is a compound containing the molecule creatine attached to a single phosphate. Your body produces creatine with the help of the liver and kidneys and then stores it in skeletal muscle and other tissues. Your body also gets some creatine from foods, including meat and fish. Direct energy is produced when the phosphate is split off from the creatine, and indirect energy is produced when the phosphate is donated to ADP, thereby regenerating ATP. The amount of creatine that can be stored in the muscles is very limited and becomes depleted after about 10 seconds of high-intensity activity.

As you continue exercising, you will breathe more heavily and take in an increased amount of oxygen. At this point your body begins to rely more on aerobic energy production because the amount of ATP needed to support your activity cannot be generated fast enough by anaerobic energy production to meet the energy demands. To supply your body with the energy it needs, you begin to oxidize carbohydrate (glucose), fat (fatty acids), and, to a minimal extent, protein (amino acids) to produce energy in the form of ATP.

Your body relies on carbohydrate, fat, and protein for energy during exercise, but the type and amount of energy that is used depends highly on the intensity and duration of the exercise, your nutritional status, and your level of physical fitness. Carbohydrate and fat contribute most of the energy needed for activity (**Figure 11.3**), while protein is best used to promote muscle growth and recovery. The following section discusses the roles of carbohydrate, fat, and protein during exercise.

Carbohydrate Is the Primary Energy Source during High-Intensity Exercise

During exercise, you obtain energy from carbohydrate through blood glucose and stored glycogen in the muscles and the liver. In an average-sized man, about 525 grams of glycogen are stored in the muscle, 100 grams of glycogen are stored in the liver, and 25 grams of glucose are in the blood.

The total amount of energy stored as carbohydrate in the body is about 2,600 calories (650 grams multiplied by 4 calories per gram), of which 2,000 calories can be used. This is enough energy to perform about 2 hours of moderate exercise, and then glycogen stores are almost completely depleted.

Depending on the duration and intensity of the activity, our bodies may use ATP-CP, carbohydrate, or fat in various combinations to fuel muscular work. Keep in mind that the amounts and sources shown below can vary based on the person's fitness level and health, how well fed the person is before the activity, and environmental temperatures and conditions.

SPRINT START (0–3 seconds)
A short, intense burst of activity like sprinting is fueled by ATP and creatine phosphate (CP) under anaerobic conditions.

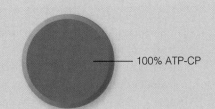

100% ATP-CP

100-M DASH (10–12 seconds)
ATP and CP provide energy for about 10 seconds of quick, intense activity, after which energy is provided as ATP from the breakdown of carbohydrates.

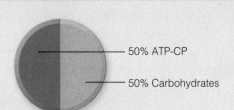

50% ATP-CP

50% Carbohydrates

1500-M RACE (4–6 minutes)
Energy derived from ATP and CP is small and would be exhausted after about 10 seconds of the race. At this point, most of the energy is derived from aerobic metabolism of primarily carbohydrates.

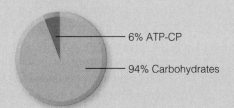

6% ATP-CP

94% Carbohydrates

10-KM RACE (30–40 minutes)
During moderately intense activities such as a 10-kilometer race, ATP is provided by fat and carbohydrate metabolism. As the intensity increases, so does the utilization of carbohydrates for energy.

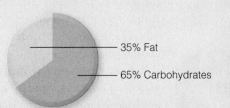

35% Fat

65% Carbohydrates

MARATHON (2.5–3 hours)
During endurance events such as marathons, ATP is primarily derived from carbohydrates, and to a lesser extent fat. A very small amount of energy is provided by the breakdown of amino acids to form glucose.

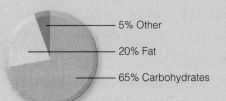

5% Other

20% Fat

65% Carbohydrates

DAY-LONG HIKE (5.5–7 hours)
The primary energy source for events lasting several hours at low intensity is fat (free fatty acids in the bloodstream which derive from triglycerides stored in fat cells). Carbohydrates contribute a small percentage of energy needs.

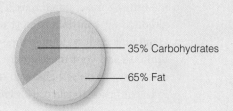

35% Carbohydrates

65% Fat

Glucose derived from stored muscle glycogen is the preferred carbohydrate source for energy during exercise. However, liver glycogen stores are just as important to your body during activity. Glycogen stored by the liver can be converted into glucose and delivered to the bloodstream in order to maintain normal blood glucose levels, both during times of activity and while you are at rest.

While muscle glycogen provides energy for the muscles during activity, blood glucose is the energy source for your brain. If you are not supplying your brain with the energy it needs, you may feel a lack of coordination or a lack of concentration—two things you especially *don't* want to experience during exercise or a sport competition.

Intensity Affects How Much Glucose and Glycogen You Use

Your muscles will use carbohydrates for energy no matter how intense the exercise. However, the *amount* of carbohydrate used is affected by intensity, as well as your level of fitness, initial muscle glycogen stores, and whether you're consuming carbohydrates during exercise. Research shows that as the intensity of exercise increases, so does the use of glucose and glycogen for energy.[15] At very high intensities (85 percent of VO_2max), most of the energy is supplied by carbohydrates in the form of muscle glycogen. During exercise of moderate intensity (65 percent of VO_2max), carbohydrate (in the form of blood glucose and muscle glycogen) contributes to approximately half to two-thirds of the energy needed, with the remainder coming from fat (more on this in a later section). Although carbohydrates are not the main energy source during exercise of low intensity (25 percent of VO_2max), they still provide some energy for the working muscles from glucose in the bloodstream. Additionally, if carbohydrates are consumed before or during exercise, the use of carbohydrates as an energy source would be greater, even at lower intensities.

When glucose is broken down at a very high rate and there is not enough oxygen, the muscles produce a by-product called **lactate**. Lactate is continuously produced and removed from the body at all times, even at rest. When produced at a low rate, the muscles can effectively clear lactate from the blood and use it directly as an energy source or convert it to glucose (which can also be used for energy). For example, during low-intensity exercise, the body is able to oxidize the lactate that is produced by the muscles for energy and therefore it does not accumulate in the working muscle tissue. This makes it an important fuel source for exercise. The body also shuttles excess lactate to other tissues, such as the brain, heart, and liver, to prevent excessive accumulation.

As exercise intensity increases, the body relies more heavily on breaking down glucose as an energy source, which occurs at a faster rate, and less oxygen becomes available. As a result, more lactate is formed and begins to accumulate in the muscles faster than it can be used for energy or shuttled elsewhere in the body. This can potentially negatively affect exercise performance due to a reduction in pH in the muscle cells, thereby causing fatigue. The good news is that the ability of the muscles to effectively use and shuttle lactate to other tissues improves with training.

Duration Affects How Much Glucose and Glycogen You Use

In addition to intensity, the duration of exercise also affects the source and amount of carbohydrate that you use to fuel physical activity. At the start of low- to moderate-intensity exercise, stored muscle glycogen is the main carbohydrate source of energy, although fat contributes most of the total energy at lower intensities. After about 20 minutes, as low- to moderate-intensity exercise continues, muscle glycogen stores diminish and your muscles rely more on fat for fuel (more on this in a later discussion). As your muscle glycogen stores diminish, the liver also contributes its glycogen to be converted to glucose for energy and to prevent hypoglycemia.

A pre-exercise meal must contain adequate amounts of carbohydrate.

lactate A by-product of rapid glucose metabolism.

Remember that your body will always use glycogen for energy during exercise, and if the intensity and duration of the exercise last long enough, muscle and liver glycogen stores become depleted and the activity that you are doing can no longer be sustained. Many endurance runners refer to this as "hitting the wall" or "bonking."

Conditioning Affects How Much Glucose and Glycogen You Use

Research has shown that the amount of glycogen that muscles can hold can be affected by training.[16] When your muscles are well trained, they have the ability to store 20 to 50 percent more glycogen than untrained muscles. More stored glycogen means more fuel for your working muscles, which means you can exercise for a longer period of time and increase your endurance. Just eating a high-carbohydrate meal before an exercise session or athletic competition will not increase your muscles' ability to store glycogen or optimize your performance. You need to train your muscles *and* eat a high-carbohydrate diet regularly to improve endurance.

How Much Carbohydrate Do I Need for Exercise?

Most adults should be getting 45 to 55 percent of their daily energy intake from carbohydrates. Glycogen stores are continuously being depleted and replenished. If you exercise often, eating carbohydrate-rich foods on a regular basis is important to provide your muscles with adequate glycogen. When glycogen stores are inadequate, the muscles have only a limited amount of energy available to support activity, which has been shown to reduce performance and promote fatigue.[17] Keep in mind that the glycogen storage capacity of both the muscles and the liver is limited. Once your muscles and liver have stored all of the glycogen possible, any excess glucose will be converted into fatty acids and stored in the form of body fat.

The best types of carbohydrates to eat during and/or immediately after exercise are simple carbohydrates such as sports drinks, bars, and gels, bananas, bagels, or corn flakes because they are quickly absorbed and enter the bloodstream, and therefore can be used immediately for energy (glucose) or to replenish glycogen stores. Complex carbohydrates like whole grains, rice, pasta, oatmeal, and corn are ideal a couple of hours before exercise because they take longer to digest than simple carbohydrates and enter the bloodstream much more slowly, thereby providing a sustained source of energy. Remember, however, that complex carbohydrates are generally high in fiber, and too much fiber can cause bloating, gas, and diarrhea.

You will learn more about timing your nutrient intake in a later section of this chapter. Carbohydrate recommendations for athletes range from 5 to 12 grams per kilogram of body weight per day. Table 11.4 shows the amount of carbohydrate needed for different durations and intensities of physical activity.[18] **Carbohydrate loading** is one training strategy that athletes use to build up muscle glycogen stores before a competition (see the Nutrition in the Real World feature "Carbohydrate Loading" on the next page).

Fat Is the Primary Energy Source during Low-Intensity Exercise

Fat supplies nearly all of the energy required during prolonged low-intensity activity. Even at rest, your body uses fat as its main energy source. Unlike glycogen, fat does not contain water, so the amount of energy stored in the form of body fat is far greater, and more concentrated, than the amount of energy that is stored as glycogen.

Fat is supplied as an energy source during exercise in two forms: fatty acids in the bloodstream (derived from food and triglycerides released from fat stores) and fatty acids in muscle tissue (also in the form of triglycerides). When the body uses stored

Table 11.4

Carbohydrate Needs for Activity and Recovery

Duration/Intensity of Activity (per Day)	Grams Carbohydrate/ Kg Body Weight (per Day)
60 to 90 minutes moderate intensity	5–7
1 to 3 hours moderate to high intensity	7–12
4 to 6+ hours extreme endurance	10–13

Source: Data from L. Burke, B. Kiens, and J. Ivy. "Carbohydrate and Fat for Training and Recovery," *Journal of Sports Science* 22 (2004): 15–30.

carbohydrate loading A diet and training strategy that maximizes glycogen stores in the body before an endurance event.

Carbohydrate Loading

The goal of carbohydrate loading before an endurance event is to maximize the storage capacity of muscle glycogen. Increasing the amount of stored muscle glycogen can improve an athlete's endurance performance by giving the energy to fuel activity at an optimal pace for a longer period of time.

Not all athletes or physically active people will have improved performance with carbohydrate loading. The people who are likely to benefit the most from this strategy are those who participate in endurance events or exercise that lasts more than 90 minutes. Examples of endurance events include marathons, triathlons, cross-country skiing, and long-distance cycling and swimming. If you exercise or train for less than 90 minutes, you should follow the standard recommendations for carbohydrate intake for athletes to ensure that you have adequate muscle glycogen stores. Research has also shown that women are less likely than men to have improved performance with carbohydrate loading because women oxidize significantly more fat and less carbohydrate and protein compared with men during endurance exercise.[1] Additionally, recall that when the muscles store more glycogen, they also hold more water (3 grams per 1 gram of glycogen). This additional water causes an increase in weight and potential decrease in flexibility, therefore making this method less desirable for some athletes.

So how do athletes start carbohydrate loading? When this concept was first recognized by athletes, they began by training very hard for three to four days in addition to eating a low-carbohydrate diet (less than 5 to 10 percent of total calories). This period was called the depletion phase and was thought to be necessary to increase glycogen stores during the next phase, called the loading phase. The loading phase involved

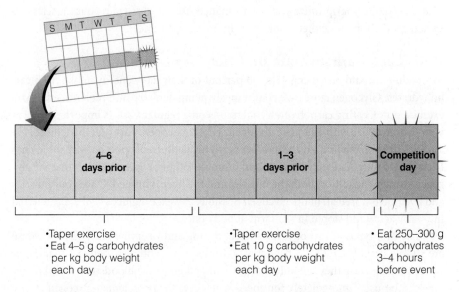

•Taper exercise
• Eat 4–5 g carbohydrates per kg body weight each day

•Taper exercise
• Eat 10 g carbohydrates per kg body weight each day

• Eat 250–300 g carbohydrates 3–4 hours before event

Carbohydrate loading involves tapering exercise and gradually increasing carbohydrate intake the week before a competitive endurance event. On the day of the competition, a high-carb meal is eaten 3 to 4 hours before the event begins.

fat for energy, it is broken down into fatty acids and then supplied to the muscles via the bloodstream, where it is converted into energy (ATP). Muscle triglycerides are directly oxidized to provide energy to the working muscles in which they are stored.

Intensity, Duration, and Training Affect How Much Fat You Use

For low-intensity exercise, your body uses mostly fat for energy in the form of free fatty acids in the blood rather than fatty acids stored in muscles. Oxidation of fat from fat (adipose) tissue typically occurs after 15 to 20 minutes of aerobic exercise. When exercising at a low intensity for a period of up to 2 hours, fatty acids in the bloodstream that are used for energy are replaced by fatty acids from adipose tissue to sustain energy levels. During moderate exercise, approximately one-third to half of the energy needed is supplied by fat and the rest is supplied by carbohydrates. For moderate-intensity exercise lasting up to 3 hours, your body begins to use equal amounts of fatty acids derived from muscle triglycerides and fatty acids in the bloodstream (derived from adipose tissue). This, in turn, results in an increase in total fat oxidation compared with a lower intensity at which muscle triglycerides are not significantly used. At high levels of activity, fatty acids cannot be converted into energy fast enough to meet the demand; therefore, fat use decreases and carbohydrates three to four days of minimal or no training while eating a diet high in carbohydrates. This resulted in higher muscle glycogen stores and better endurance performance.

Many people found the depletion phase hard to endure and would often experience irritability, hypoglycemia, and fatigue. In fact, today, many endurance athletes have modified this training strategy to exclude the depletion phase. Research has shown that depleting muscle glycogen stores is not necessary to increase the amount of stored muscle glycogen. However, there will be greater increases in muscle glycogen by initially depleting muscle glycogen stores.[2]

To begin a modified carbohydrate loading regimen, you should taper your exercise about seven days prior to the event by doing a little bit less activity each day. This is often the hardest recommendation to follow because many athletes feel that they will be out of shape if they stop training before competition. But tapering your exercise is necessary to increase muscle glycogen; otherwise, you will continue to burn glycogen for fuel rather than storing it to be used for energy during the upcoming event. One study showed that you can decrease your training by 70 percent of your normal training schedule about one

week prior to an endurance event without negatively affecting your performance.[3]

In addition to tapering your exercise, you should eat a high-carbohydrate diet that provides about 4 to 5 grams of carbohydrate per kilogram of body weight for the first three to four days. During the last three days of tapering exercise, increase your intake of carbohydrates to 10 grams per kilogram of body weight. Lastly, a meal that is high in carbohydrate (providing about 250 to 300 grams of carbohydrate), moderate in protein, and low in fat should be consumed

about 3 to 4 hours prior to the start of the event to further maximize glycogen stores.

Despite the emphasis on carbohydrates, you do not want to compromise your intake of protein and fat by eating too much carbohydrate. Remember to include at least 0.8 grams of protein per kilogram of body weight (some athletes may require more protein) in your training diet, as well as about 20 to 25 percent of calories coming from fat, preferably unsaturated fats. Below is a sample one-day menu that is high in carbohydrate, adequate in protein, and low in fat.

Breakfast	Lunch	Dinner	Snack
1 cup orange juice	2 slices oatmeal bread	3 cups spaghetti (6 ounces uncooked)	1 cup vanilla yogurt
½ cup Grape-Nuts			
1 medium banana	3 oz turkey breast with lettuce, tomato	1 cup tomato sauce	6 fig bars
1 cup 2% milk	8 oz apple juice	2 oz ground turkey	
1 English muffin	1 cup frozen yogurt	¼ loaf multigrain bread (4 ounces)	
1 tbs jelly			
750 calories	750 calories	1,300 calories	500 calories
85% carbohydrates	65% carbohydrates	70% carbohydrates	80% carbohydrates
Total: 3,300 calories: 75% carbohydrates (610 g), 15% protein (125 g), 10% fat (40 g)			

Source: Data from N. Clark, *Nancy Clark's Sports Nutrition Guidebook*, 3rd ed. (Champaign, IL: Human Kinetics, 2003).

become the preferred energy source. Also note that your body requires more oxygen to convert fat into energy compared with carbohydrate, which creates more stress for the cardiovascular system.

Your level of training can affect how much fat your body will use for energy. Muscles that are well trained will burn more fat than muscles that are not as well trained. This is thought to be caused by an increase in enzymes that are necessary to burn fat for energy. As a result, well-trained muscles use less glycogen for energy and more fat, thereby having the potential to increase endurance by "saving" your glycogen stores for later energy use. So, if you are trying to lose weight and body fat, should you reduce the intensity of your workout? The Examining the Evidence feature "The Truth about the Fat-Burning Zone" on the next page addresses this question.

How Much Fat Do I Need for Exercise?

Dietary recommendations for fat intake are generally the same for active people as for the average adult population, with 20 to 35 percent of calories coming from fat.[19] Recall from Chapter 5 that high intakes of saturated and *trans* fats have been linked to high blood cholesterol levels and heart disease. Physically active people sometimes assume that because they're in shape, they don't have to worry about these

The Truth about the Fat-Burning Zone

Many people recognize the importance of exercise, especially of the cardiovascular system, for weight loss. They head off to the gym and jump on an exercise machine to start their workout. Once on the machine, they hook up to a device that monitors their heart rate, which lets them know if they are in the "fat-burning" zone (65 to 73 percent of one's maximum heart rate) or the "cardio" zone (more than 73 percent of one's maximum heart rate). Because most people seek to lose body fat, they exercise in the fat-burning zone, believing that this is the most effective way to lose weight. After all, it is true that the body will burn more fat at lower intensities and will burn more carbohydrate as the intensity increases. So, is staying in the fat-burning zone the best advice to follow if you are trying to lose weight? The simple answer is no. Let's look at some calculations to better understand why.

If you are trying to lose weight, you need to burn more calories than you consume. Working out is an excellent way to do this, but you need to be aware of how many calories you are burning, and aim to work off as many as possible. In the fat-burning zone at 65 percent of maximum heart rate, a moderately fit person will burn an average of 220 calories during 30 minutes of exercise. Also at this same intensity, fat supplies about 50 percent of the total calories burned for energy. This means that the person is burning an average of 110 fat calories (50 percent of 220). As the intensity increases to about

85 percent of maximum heart rate, this same person burns an average of 330 calories during 30 minutes of exercise, with fat supplying only about 33 percent of the total calories burned. Guess what? The person still burns the same number of fat calories (33 percent of 330, or 110), but is burning more total calories (330 calories) at a higher intensity, which will help meet the weight-loss goal sooner than exercising at a lower intensity (burning 220 calories). The bottom line is, you don't need to stay in the fat-burning zone to effectively lose body fat. You just need to burn calories so that there is an overall calorie deficit.

If you prefer not to exercise at a high intensity, there is an advantage to exercising at a lower intensity. If you have time for a long workout, you can probably exercise at a lower intensity for a longer period of time without getting tired. In other words, if you are jogging at 6 mph (high intensity) you may get tired after you cover 3 miles. However, if you are walking briskly at 4 mph (lower intensity), you may be able to cover 4 miles because you aren't as fatigued. Walking the extra 30 minutes and covering that extra mile will allow you to expend more overall calories during your workout (330 calories for 30 minutes of jogging versus 440 calories for 60 minutes of walking). But if you have a busy lifestyle and feel pressed for time to exercise, don't be afraid to go out of the fat-burning zone to get the most out of your workout and effectively lose weight!

Exercising in the "fat-burning" zone or the "cardio" zone are both effective methods to burn calories and reduce body weight.

What Do You Think?

1. What are some examples of exercises that would keep you in the fat-burning zone and in the cardio zone?

2. Have you or someone that you know stayed in the fat-burning zone to lose weight?

3. Knowing what you know now, would you still exercise in the fat-burning zone to lose weight?

diseases. While it is true that physical activity grants some protection against heart disease, athletes and other fit people can also have high cholesterol, heart attacks, and strokes. Everyone, regardless of activity level, should limit saturated fat to no more than 10 percent of total calories, while consuming 10 percent of total calories from monounsaturated fat and 10 percent of total calories from polyunsaturated fat.[20]

Some athletes, such as endurance runners and those in sports in which low body weight is important, like gymnasts and figure skaters, may feel they can benefit from a very low-fat diet (less than 20 percent). Though consuming too much dietary fat is a concern, you don't want to limit your fat intake too much. When you consume less than adequate amounts of fat, you are more likely at risk for consuming inadequate calories, essential fatty acids, and fat-soluble vitamins, which can negatively affect exercise performance.[21]

Protein Is Primarily Needed to Build and Repair Muscle

Amino acids obtained from protein are the main nutrients needed to promote muscle growth and recovery. Muscle damage is one of the most significant physiological effects of exercise, especially in weight or strength training. You need to supply your muscles with protein so that this muscle damage does not result in decreased muscle mass and strength. Not all muscle damage is bad, however. It can stimulate remodeling of the muscle cells, which increases muscle strength and mass.

The Body Can Use Protein for Energy

Your body prefers to use carbohydrate and fat as its main energy sources during exercise (refer again to Figure 11.3). Small amounts of protein are used for energy, but greater amounts are used when calorie intake and carbohydrate stores are insufficient. When needed, proteins can be broken down into amino acids and oxidized to provide energy directly to the working muscles in the form of ATP. Excess protein that is not used by your body for its normal functions is converted into glycogen or fatty acids, which can provide energy at a later time.

Muscle protein can also be an energy source by being broken down into amino acids that are then released into the bloodstream. These amino acids are carried to the liver, where they get converted into glucose, which supplies the working muscles with energy. If the body has to use a significant amount of protein for energy, including muscle protein, that protein is not available to build and repair tissues. If this occurs too often, a loss of muscle mass will likely result.

How Much Protein Do I Need for Exercise?

Many athletes and exercisers assume that they need substantially more protein than nonexercisers need. It is true that those who are fit and physically active need more protein than those who are sedentary, but those needs are not significantly higher. Recall from Chapter 6 that the RDA for protein for most healthy adults is 0.8 gram per kilogram of body weight per day, and most people, including athletes, far exceed this.

People who are recreational exercisers can meet their needs for protein with a balanced diet. The increased protein needs of competitive and elite athletes, as well as bodybuilders, can also be met with a balanced diet. Endurance athletes are advised to consume 1.2 to 1.4 grams of protein per kilogram of body weight per day. People who primarily participate in resistance and strength activities may need to consume as much as 1.2 to 1.7 grams of protein per kilogram of body weight per day.[22]

Total Calorie Needs Depend on the Type and Schedule of Exercise

Your daily calorie needs depend on the type of exercise (such as swimming, volleyball, or tennis) you choose and your training schedule. Playing an hour of Frisbee with your friends will use a little over 200 calories (based on a 150-pound person). Compare that with an hour of downhill skiing, which will burn over 500 calories. When eight-time Olympic gold medal champion swimmer Michael Phelps is training, he needs to consume more than 10,000 calories daily to fuel his activities and maintain his weight. However, if the average jogger were to adopt this eating pattern, he would quickly gain a lot of body fat. The best way to determine if you are consuming enough calories is to monitor your weight. If your weight doesn't decrease, you are consuming enough calories. If your weight *increases*, and it's not due to an increase in muscle mass, you are consuming too many calories.

Unfortunately, some female athletes in certain "lean-build" sports are under pressure to maintain a low weight that's not conducive to good health. This pressure can contribute to a complex condition known as the **female athlete triad**, as discussed in the Health Connection feature "What Is the Female Athlete Triad?"

The Take-Home Message Carbohydrate and fat are the primary sources of fuel during exercise. Carbohydrates provide energy in the form of blood glucose and muscle and liver glycogen, and are the main energy source during high-intensity exercise. Fat is the main energy source during low-intensity exercise. Carbohydrate and fat contribute equally as energy sources during moderate-intensity exercise. Protein provides amino acids that are necessary to promote muscle growth and repair muscle damage caused by exercise.

How Does the Timing of Meals Affect Fitness and Athletic Performance?

Timing the foods that you eat around exercise has a significant impact on energy levels and recovery time. As you learned in Chapter 6, inadequate calorie intake leads to muscles being broken down for energy. This in turn can lead to loss of muscle mass and strength, and lack of energy, which can negatively affect exercise performance.

During exercise, especially weight training, muscles are under a great deal of stress, which can result in overstretching and tearing of proteins and potential inflammation. After exercise, the body is in a catabolic (breaking down) state: Muscle and liver glycogen stores are low or depleted, muscle protein is broken down, and the immune system is suppressed. Therefore, supplying the body with the nutrients needed to reverse this catabolic state into an anabolic (building up) state is crucial and necessary for optimal fitness.

Optimal Foods before Exercise

You need to eat before exercise or a competition so that you have enough energy for optimal performance. However, one of the most important considerations about eating before exercise is allowing sufficient time for the food to be digested so that it doesn't negatively affect your performance. In general, larger meals (making you feel quite full) may take 3 to 4 hours to digest, whereas smaller meals (making you feel satisfied but not overly full) may take only 2 to 3 hours to digest. If you are drinking a liquid supplement or having a small snack, you should allow about 30 minutes to 1 hour for digestion. These are general guidelines and may not apply to everyone, so be sure that you experiment with your own eating and exercise schedule well before a workout or competition so that you know how long you need to wait before starting your activity.

You just learned that carbohydrates are one of the main sources of energy during exercise. Thus, your pre-exercise meal should contain adequate amounts of carbohydrate so that you maximize muscle and liver glycogen stores and maintain normal blood glucose levels. In general, your pre-exercise meal should contain 1 to 4.5 grams of carbohydrate per kilogram of body weight and be consumed 1 to 4 hours prior to exercise.

Consuming carbohydrate immediately before exercise (about 15 to 30 minutes prior to the start) provides an advantage because it gives your muscles an immediate

Crackers can be consumed before and during endurance exercise to supply an easily digestible source of carbohydrate and help prevent early fatigue.

female athlete triad A syndrome of the three interrelated conditions occurring in some physically active females: low energy availability, menstrual dysfunction, and low bone density.

health
CONNECTION

What Is the Female Athlete Triad?

Christy Henrich joined the U.S. gymnastics team in 1986 weighing 95 pounds at 4 feet, 11 inches tall. Christy soon succeeded as a gymnast, but after a judge told her she needed to lose weight, she developed anorexia nervosa. Sadly, her weight plummeted to 47 pounds, and she died from multiple organ failure at the age of 22.

The anorexia that Christy battled is one part of the *female athlete triad*, a syndrome of interrelated conditions existing on a continuum of severity: low energy availability, menstrual dysfunction, and low bone mineral density. Female athletes are often pressured to reach or maintain an unrealistically low body weight and/or level of body fat. This pressure contributes to the development of disordered eating, which helps to initiate the triad. Of major concern with this disorder is that it not only reduces the performance of the athlete, but may have serious medical and psychological consequences later in life.

The major components of the triad are discussed here.

Low Energy Availability/Disordered Eating

Athletes wishing to lose weight or maintain a low body weight may restrict their energy intake or develop abnormal eating behaviors. At the most extreme, an athlete with disordered eating may fulfill the diagnostic criteria for anorexia nervosa or bulimia nervosa. However, disordered eating occurs on a continuum and is not always so pronounced. Many athletes mistakenly believe that losing weight by any method enhances performance, and that disordered eating is harmless. Disordered eating is most common

Female athletes for whom body size or appearance is an issue, such as dancers, gymnasts, and skaters, are often particularly vulnerable to the female athlete triad.

among athletes in sports where appearance is important, such as figure skating, gymnastics, and ballet, but can occur in athletes in all types of sports. It is also possible for athletes who do not exhibit disorded eating patterns to unintentionally take in fewer calories than they need. They may appear to be eating a healthy diet—one that would be adequate for a sedentary individual—but their caloric needs are higher due to their level of physical activity.

Menstrual Dysfunction/Amenorrhea

The failure to consume enough energy to compensate for the "energy cost" of the exercise can lead to disruption of the menstrual cycle. At its most extreme and recognizable, this results in amenorrhea, the absence of three or more consecutive menstrual cycles. Unfortunately, many females welcome the convenience of not menstruating and do not report it.

Low Bone Mineral Density/Osteoporosis

Energy deficiency and decreased estrogen levels due to menstrual dysfunction contribute to bone loss and low bone mineral density. At its most extreme this causes premature osteoporosis, putting the athlete at risk for stress fractures, hip and vertebral fractures, and the loss of bone mass, which may be irreplaceable.

Signs and Treatment

All individuals, including friends, teachers, and coaches, involved with these athletes should be aware of the warning signs because the triad components are very often not recognized, not reported, or are denied. Warning signs include menstrual changes, weight changes, disordered eating patterns, cardiac arrythmia, depression, or stress fractures. Those working with such athletes should provide a training environment in which athletes are not pressured to lose weight, and should be able to recommend appropriate nutritional, medical, and/or psychological resources if needed. Treatment of an athlete with this disorder is multidisciplinary, and needs to involve cooperation among the athlete's physician, dietitian, psychologist, coach or trainer, family, and friends.

---

source of energy (glucose) and spares your glycogen stores so that you can exercise for a longer period or at a higher intensity without becoming tired as quickly.[23] Carbohydrate intake prior to the start of exercise can also help reduce muscle damage by causing the release of insulin, which promotes muscle protein synthesis.

Just as your body needs a continuous supply of carbohydrate, it also needs moderate amounts of protein throughout the day. Timing your protein intake around activity will have a significant impact on muscle preservation, growth, and recovery.

The consumption of foods with both protein *and* carbohydrate before exercise, such as fruit and yogurt, benefits the body by causing a greater increase in muscle glycogen synthesis than consuming carbohydrate alone. With more glycogen in your muscles, you can increase endurance. Another benefit of consuming both protein and carbohydrate before exercise is that it results in greater protein synthesis after the exercise is over compared with either protein or carbohydrate alone.[24] The making of new proteins, including muscles, is necessary for optimal fitness and muscle preservation, repair, and growth.

Foods with a higher fat content take longer to digest than foods that are higher in carbohydrate and protein. For this reason, high-fat foods should generally be avoided several hours before exercise. If you eat high-fat foods before exercise, you may feel sluggish or have stomach discomfort, which can impair your performance. Of course this is a general guideline, and not all active people have difficulty during exercise if they consume higher-fat foods before starting to exercise.

Optimal Foods during Exercise

For exercise lasting longer than 1 hour, carbohydrate intake should begin shortly after the start of exercise and continue at 15- to 20-minute intervals throughout. For long-lasting endurance activities, a total of 30 to 60 grams of carbohydrate should be consumed per hour to prevent early fatigue. Sports drinks and gels are one way to take in carbohydrate immediately before and/or during activity, but foods such as crackers and sports bars are also commonly eaten.

The best types of carbohydrate to consume during exercise are glucose, sucrose, and maltodextrin because they are absorbed by the body more quickly than other carbohydrates. Fructose, the sugar found in fruit and fruit juice, should generally be avoided because it may cause gastrointestinal problems or stomach discomfort.

Many sports drinks and gels contain only carbohydrate and electrolytes; others also contain protein. For endurance athletes, consuming both carbohydrate and protein during exercise has been shown to improve net protein balance at rest as well as during exercise and postexercise recovery.[25] This will, in turn, have an effect on muscle maintenance and growth.

Optimal Foods after Exercise

What you eat after exercise will affect how fast you recover, which may affect how soon you're ready for your next workout or training session. This is especially important for competitive athletes who train more than once per day. Some people who load up on high-fat foods after a workout or competition experience fatigue that may result in less-than-optimal performance during the next workout.

The best postexercise meal is consumed quickly and contains both carbohydrate and protein. The muscles are most receptive to storing new glycogen within the first 30 to 45 minutes after you have finished exercising, so this is a crucial time period in which to provide the body with carbohydrate.[26] Research shows that consuming carbohydrate immediately after exercise also results in a more positive body protein balance.[27] In addition, protein intake immediately after exercise rather than several hours later results in greater muscle protein synthesis. Finally, the consumption of protein with carbohydrate causes an even greater increase in glycogen synthesis than carbohydrate or protein alone.[28] In short, both nutrients should be consumed soon after exercise.

What is the best way to get these two nutrients? Studies have shown that consumption of carbohydrate and protein in a ratio of approximately 3:1 (in grams) is ideal to promote muscle glycogen synthesis, protein synthesis, and faster recovery time.[29] Whey protein (such as in milk) is the preferred protein source because it is rapidly absorbed and contains all of the essential amino acids that your body needs.

Low-fat chocolate milk is a low-cost option for providing the whey protein and carbohydrate that help with muscle and glycogen synthesis after exercise.

You can use commercial shakes and drinks, but they can be expensive. A cheaper alternative is low-fat chocolate milk, which will provide you with adequate amounts of carbohydrate and protein to assist in recovery after exercise.[30] If you consume a liquid supplement or small snack after exercise, this should be followed by a high-carbohydrate, moderate-protein, low-fat meal within the next 2 hours. An old-fashioned peanut butter and jelly sandwich or a slice of cheese pizza are inexpensive and can help you recover after exercise too.

If you are a competitive athlete, always experiment with timing your nutrient intake and consuming new foods and beverages during practice, not on the day of competition. You don't want to be unpleasantly surprised to find that a particular food doesn't agree with you a few hours before an important race or other event.

In addition to consuming adequate protein and carbohydrate, drinking adequate fluids is important for exercise performance and recovery. You will learn more about hydration in a later section of this chapter.

The Take-Home Message Consuming the right balance of nutrients at the right time can improve exercise performance and recovery time. Higher fat foods should generally be avoided before exercise, while carbohydrate and protein are important for energy and recovery before, during, and after exercise.

What Vitamins and Minerals Are Important for Fitness?

In addition to several other important functions, vitamins and minerals play a major role in the metabolism of carbohydrate, fat, and protein for energy during exercise. Some also act as antioxidants and help protect cells from the oxidative stress that can occur with exercise.

Antioxidants Can Help Protect Cells from Damage Caused by Exercise

Your muscles use more oxygen during exercise than while you are at rest. As a result, your body increases its production of free radicals that damage cells, especially during intense, prolonged exercise. Antioxidants, such as vitamins E and C, are known to protect cells from the damage of free radicals. Vitamin C also assists in the production of collagen, which provides most of the structure of connective tissues like bone, tendons, and ligaments. This, in turn, can affect your likelihood of developing strains, sprains, and fractures that may occur as a result of exercise.

Research has not proven that supplementation with vitamins E or C improves athletic performance, nor that it decreases oxidative stress in highly trained athletes.[31] Therefore, you do not need to consume more than the RDA of these vitamins, but you do need to be sure to consume adequate amounts from foods like nuts, vegetable oils, broccoli, and citrus fruits to meet your needs.

Some Minerals Can Be of Concern in Highly Active People

You learned in Chapter 8 that minerals have important roles in normal body functions and health. Minerals are also essential to physical fitness and athletic performance.

Though active people do not need more minerals than less active individuals, there are two minerals they must be careful to consume in adequate amounts.

Iron

Iron is important to exercise because it is necessary for energy metabolism and transporting oxygen throughout the body and within muscle cells. Iron is a structural component of hemoglobin and myoglobin, two proteins that carry and store oxygen in the blood and muscle, respectively. If iron levels are low, hemoglobin levels can also fall, diminishing the blood's ability to carry oxygen to the cells. If this occurs during exercise, you will experience early fatigue. (You can also feel tired if iron levels are low and you are not exercising.) Iron supplementation can improve aerobic performance for people with depleted iron stores.[32]

Many athletes and physically fit people are prone to iron-deficiency anemia. Although iron-deficiency anemia can occur in both females and males, female athletes are at a greater risk. Long-distance runners, as well as athletes in sports where they must "make weight," have also been noted to be at higher risk for iron-deficiency anemia. Athletes in other sports such as basketball, tennis, softball, and swimming also have been shown to have suboptimal iron status.[33]

Low iron levels can be a result of poor dietary intake or increased iron losses. Women can lose a lot of iron during menstruation, depending on their iron status and menstrual blood flow. Iron is also lost in sweat, but not in amounts significant enough to lead to iron deficiency.

Another effect of exercise on iron is intravascular hemolysis (*hemo* = blood, *lysis* = breaking down), which is the bursting of red blood cells. This happens when you are running and your feet repeatedly hit the ground (a hard surface), causing red blood cells to burst and release iron. This iron is recycled by the body and not lost, and therefore does not typically contribute to iron deficiency.

Some people experience decreased levels of hemoglobin because of training, especially when the training is quite strenuous. During exercise your blood volume increases, which in turn causes lower concentrations of hemoglobin in the blood. This is often referred to as sports anemia, or pseudoanemia, and is not the same as iron-deficiency anemia. Iron-deficiency anemia typically has to be treated with iron supplementation. Sports anemia can be corrected on its own because the body can adapt to training and produce more red blood cells, which restores normal hemoglobin levels.

Whether you exercise or not, you can maintain your iron status by consuming adequate amounts of iron-rich foods, and supplements if necessary. However, many female athletes do not consume enough iron to meet their needs, which often leads to low iron levels. Vegetarian athletes are especially susceptible to iron deficiency and need to plan their diets appropriately so they consume adequate amounts of foods plentiful in iron.

Kidney beans, steak, and iron-fortified bread and cereal are good sources of iron. Female and vegetarian athletes are at higher risk of iron deficiency.

Calcium

Most people know about the importance of calcium to maintain bone health, but athletes are particularly susceptible to broken bones and fractures. Therefore, they need to consume enough calcium in their diets to reduce their risk of sustaining these types of injuries. Calcium affects both skeletal and heart muscle contraction, and hormone and neurotransmitter activity during exercise. It also assists in blood clotting when you have a cut or other minor hemorrhage, which may occur during exercise or competition.

Many people may not be aware that calcium is lost in sweat, and the more you sweat the more calcium you lose. One study concluded that bone loss is related to dietary calcium, and that exercise can increase bone mineral content (the mass of all minerals in bone) only when calcium intake is sufficient to compensate for what is lost through sweating.[34]

Calcium supplements are not recommended unless your intake from food and beverages is inadequate and you are not meeting your daily needs. Choosing foods that are high in calcium, including fortified foods, can ensure that athletes meet their needs for calcium.

Vitamin and Mineral Supplements Are Generally Not Necessary

Active people generally do not need more vitamins than sedentary people, because vitamins can be used repeatedly in metabolic reactions. Many athletes mistakenly believe that vitamins and minerals themselves supply energy, and often consume extra vitamins and minerals so that they can perform better. In fact, studies have shown that multivitamin and mineral supplements are the supplements most commonly used by college athletes.[35] As you know by now, vitamins and minerals themselves don't provide energy. But can taking these supplements improve athletic performance for other reasons? The answer is: not unless you are experiencing a deficiency. For people who consume enough vitamins and minerals in their diet, taking more than the RDA will not result in improved performance during exercise.[36]

Everyone, not just athletes, should obtain vitamins and minerals through nutrient-dense foods before considering the use of supplements. Eating a wide variety of foods that meets your calorie needs will likely provide your body with plenty of vitamins and minerals. Thus, it is probably a waste of money to use vitamin and mineral supplements.

The Take-Home Message Athletes need to pay special attention to their intakes of certain vitamins and minerals. Antioxidants such as vitamins E and C are not needed in excessive amounts, as they have not been proven to reduce oxidative damage to cells from exercise. Iron is important because of its role in transporting oxygen in blood and muscle, and deficiency is prevalent among athletes, especially females and vegetarians. Calcium intake is important for bone health and muscle contraction. Adequate amounts of all nutrients can be consumed in foods, so supplements are not usually necessary.

Eating calcium-rich foods daily assists with bone health, muscle contraction, and blood clotting.

How Does Fluid Intake Affect Fitness?

As basic as it sounds, water is one of the most important nutrients during physical activity. When you drink too little fluid, or you lose too much fluid and electrolytes through sweating, this causes physiological changes that can negatively affect exercise performance and health. You may experience early fatigue or weakness when your body doesn't have sufficient amounts of water. Consuming adequate fluids on a regular basis, as well as monitoring fluid losses during physical activity, are key to maintaining optimal performance and preventing **dehydration** and electrolyte imbalance.

Fluid and Electrolyte Balance and Body Temperature Are Affected by Exercise

You learned in Chapter 8 that water and some electrolytes are necessary to maintain the fluid balance in your body. When you are physically active, your body will lose more water via sweat and exhalation of water vapor than when you are less active, so you need to replace water lost during exercise to maintain normal fluid balance.

Staying hydrated during physical activity is important to maintain electrolyte balance and help regulate body temperature.

dehydration Loss of water in the body as a result of inadequate fluid intake or excess fluid loss, such as through sweating.

In 1965, an assistant coach for the University of Florida Gators football team, along with the team physicians, determined that fluids and electrolytes lost by the players through sweat were not being replaced, which negatively affected their performance. In a lab, they formulated a beverage that would adequately replace these components and called it "Gatorade." Soon after, the team starting winning and other universities began ordering batches of the sports beverage for their players.[37]

Sodium and chloride are the two primary electrolytes that are lost in sweat. Potassium is also lost in sweat, but to a lesser extent than sodium and chloride. An electrolyte imbalance can cause heat cramps, as well as nausea, lowered blood pressure, and edema in the hands and feet, all of which can hinder your performance. When electrolyte losses are within the range of normal daily dietary intake, they can easily be recovered by consuming a balanced meal within 24 hours after exercise. Electrolytes can also be replaced by beverages that contain them, such as sports drinks, if food is not available.

The sweat you produce during exercise releases heat and helps keep your body temperature normal. The amount of fluid lost through sweating depends on the type, intensity, and duration of exercise and varies from person to person. Some people sweat heavily, while others may sweat very little. Regardless of how much you sweat, it is important that you don't allow your body to lose too much fluid without replacing it with water or other beverages.

Exercising in hot, humid weather results in more fluid lost in breathing in addition to sweating, which will increase your body's need for fluids. However, if the air outside is very humid (that is, it contains a lot of water), sweat may not evaporate off the skin, and the body won't cool down. This can cause heat to build up in your body, placing you at risk for heat exhaustion or heat stroke. One significant warning sign of heat stroke is if you are *not* sweating when you should be. This happens when you are extremely dehydrated and cannot produce sweat, which prevents the release of heat and causes your body temperature to rise. Other warnings signs of heat exhaustion and heat stroke are shown in Table 11.5.

You Need Fluids before, during, and after Exercise

Many active people are aware that it's important to stay hydrated during exercise, but your need for water doesn't begin with your first sit-up or lap around the track. Meeting your fluid needs before and after activity is also important to maintain fluid and electrolyte balance and optimize performance.

Consuming adequate fluid every day is important for everyone, from sedentary individuals to competitive athletes. Recall from Chapter 8 that most healthy adult

Table 11.5

Warning Signs of Heat Exhaustion and Heat Stroke

Heat Exhaustion	Heat Stroke
Profuse sweating	Extremely high body temperature (above 103°F [39.4°C], measured orally)
Fatigue	
Thirst	Red, hot, and dry skin (no sweating)
Muscle cramps	Rapid, strong pulse
Headache	Rapid, shallow breathing
Dizziness or light-headedness	Throbbing headache
Weakness	Dizziness
Nausea and vomiting	Nausea
Cool, moist skin	Extreme confusion
	Unconsciousness

women need approximately 9 cups of beverages daily, while most healthy adult men need about 13 cups. This is a general guideline to follow for adequate hydration. Another way to determine your estimated daily fluid needs is to divide your body weight by 2. This tells you the number of ounces of fluid you need (8 ounces = 1 cup) on a daily basis, not including the additional needs associated with exercising.

For active individuals, pre-exercise hydration is essential to replace sweat losses. As you learned in Chapter 8, you can determine your fluid needs during exercise by weighing yourself both before and after an activity. Because the amount of weight that is lost is mainly due to losses in body water, you should consume 16 to 24 fluid ounces (about 2 to 3 cups) of fluid for every pound of body weight lost.[38] The American College of Sports Medicine (ACSM) has specific recommendations for how much fluid to drink before and during exercise. See **Table 11.6** for these recommendations.

Some Beverages Are Better than Others

Beverages like tea, coffee, soft drinks, fruit juice, and, of course, water contribute to your daily fluid needs. But what is the best type of fluid for preventing dehydration prior to and during activity? What about for rehydrating your body after activity? For these purposes, not all beverages are equal.

Sports drinks are popular in the fitness world and are often marketed as tasty beverages to all groups of people, not just athletes. They typically contain 6 to 8 percent carbohydrate as well as sodium and potassium, two electrolytes that are critical in muscle contraction and maintaining fluid balance. One purpose of sports drinks is to replace fluid and electrolytes that are lost through sweating. These drinks have been shown to be superior to water for rehydration, mostly because their flavor causes people to drink more than they would of just plain water.[39]

Sports drinks also provide additional carbohydrate to prevent glycogen depletion. This is beneficial if you engage in long endurance events or exercise when glycogen stores may be running low. When you consume a sports drink during exercise, you provide your body with glucose to be used as an immediate energy source and prevent further decline in muscle glycogen stores.

(T)(F) However, not everyone actually needs sports drinks in order to stay adequately hydrated, and at about 60 calories per 8-ounce cup, they can be a source of unwanted extra calories. For exercise that lasts less than 60 minutes, water is sufficient to replace fluids lost through sweating

Sports drinks can replace electrolytes and fluids lost during exercise.

Table 11.6	
ACSM Hydration Recommendations	
When?	**How Much Fluid?**
4 hours before exercise	16–20 fl oz (2–2½ cups)
10 to 15 minutes before exercise	8–12 fl oz (1–1½ cups)
At 15- to 20-minute intervals when exercising less than 60 minutes	3–8 fl oz (⅜–1 cup)
At 15- to 20-minute intervals when exercising more than 60 minutes	3–8 fl oz (⅜–1 cup) sports beverage (5–8 percent carbohydrate with electrolytes)
After exercise for every pound of body weight lost	20–24 fl oz (2½–3 cups)

Source: Table from SELECTING AND EFFECTIVELY USING HYDRATION FOR FITNESS, by Michael. R. Simpson, and Tom Howard. Reprinted with permission of the American College of Sports Medicine. Copyright © 2011 American College of Sports Medicine. This brochure is a product of ACSM's Consumer Information Committee.

For most people, water will provide adequate hydration before, during, and after exercise, and it's lower in both calories and cost than sports drinks.

and food consumption following exercise will adequately replace electrolytes. A sports drink is most appropriate when physical activity lasts longer than 60 minutes.[40]

Other beverages may be suboptimal for hydration during physical activity. Fruit juice and juice drinks contain a larger concentration of carbohydrate and do not hydrate the body as quickly as beverages with a lower concentration of carbohydrates (like sports drinks). Carbonated drinks contain a large amount of water; however, the air bubbles from the carbonation can cause stomach bloating and may limit the amount of fluid consumed.

Though alcohol may seem like an unlikely choice for rehydration, some people may drink alcoholic beverages, such as beer, in order to quench thirst. But because alcohol is a diuretic, it can actually contribute to dehydration. Alcohol during athletic performance can also impair your judgment and reasoning, which can lead to injuries not only for you, but for those around you.

Another diuretic, the caffeine found in coffee and some soft drinks, should only be consumed in moderate amounts, because excessive intake can cause increased heart rate, nausea, vomiting, excessive urination, restlessness, anxiety, and difficulty sleeping. Moderate caffeine intake is about 250 milligrams (the amount found in about three cups of coffee) per day.[41]

Consuming Too Little or Too Much Fluid Can Be Harmful

As your body loses fluid through sweating and exhalation during physical activity, it will let you know that you need to replace these fluids by sending a signal of thirst. However, by the time you're thirsty, you may already be dehydrated. **Figure 11.4** shows the effect of dehydration on exercise performance. As you can see from the figure, thirst is not a good indicator of fluid needs for most athletes and physically active people.

Figure 11.4 Effects of Dehydration on Exercise Performance
Failing to stay hydrated during exercise or competition can result in fatigue and cramps and, in extreme cases, heat exhaustion. Because the thirst mechanism doesn't kick in until after dehydration has begun, replacing fluids throughout physical activity is important.

Source: Based on E. Burke and J. Berning, *Training Nutrition* (Travers City, MI: Cooper Publishing Group, 1996).

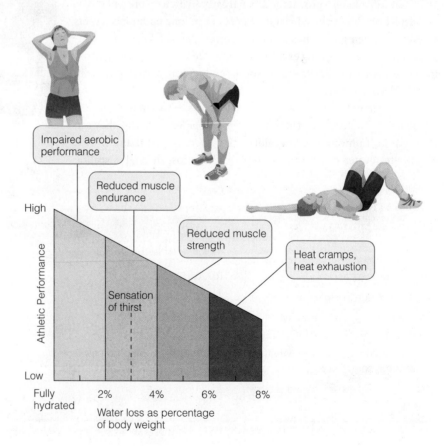

Knowing the warning signs of dehydration so that you can respond by drinking adequate fluids will help prevent health consequences and impaired exercise performance.

If you become dehydrated over a short period of time, such as during a single exercise session or sport competition, **acute dehydration** may set in. Acute dehydration most commonly occurs if you are not adequately hydrated before beginning a hard exercise session, especially if you have been sick, if it is extremely hot and humid, or if the temperature is significantly different from what you are used to. To prevent acute dehydration, follow a regimented hydration schedule using water or sports drinks to hydrate before, during, and after exercise sessions and/or competition.

Chronic dehydration refers to when you are not adequately hydrated over an extended period of time, such as during several sport practices or games. The most common warning signs of chronic dehydration include fatigue, muscle soreness, poor recovery from a workout, headaches, and nausea. If your urine is very dark and you do not need to go to the bathroom every 3 or 4 hours, then you could be experiencing chronic dehydration. As with acute dehydration, following a regimented hydration schedule throughout the day will help prevent chronic dehydration.

When speaking of hydration and physical activity, we are usually concerned about consuming *enough* fluids so that we do not become dehydrated. As you recall from Chapter 8, consuming too much fluid can also be harmful. Taking in too much water without sufficient electrolytes can result in **hyponatremia**. Symptoms of severe hyponatremia may include rapid weight gain, bloated stomach, nausea, vomiting, swollen hands and feet, headache, dizziness, confusion, disorientation, and lack of coordination. Hyponatremia is more likely to occur in those who participate in endurance sports or prolonged exercise periods (greater than 4 hours), in which fluid and sodium loss is more likely.

Drinking as much fluid as possible and "staying ahead of thirst" has been the recommendation for hydration among long-distance runners for quite some time. Due to the growing concern about overhydration and hyponatremia, USA Track & Field (USATF) provides guidelines on hydration in order to lower the risk of hyponatremia among long-distance runners. USATF recommends consuming 100 percent of fluids lost due to sweat while exercising, and to be sensitive to the onset of thirst as the signal to drink, rather than "staying ahead of thirst."[42]

If you are a distance runner, take the Self-Assessment on the next page to determine your fluid needs during long-distance races.[43] Keep in mind that you should perform this hydration test well before a competition or event, and perform the test again if your level of fitness improves or if the climate changes from when you initially determined your fluid needs.

The Take-Home Message Being adequately hydrated before, during, and after exercise is important to sustain fluid and electrolyte balance and a normal body temperature. Inadequate hydration can impair performance. Water is the preferred beverage for hydration, but sports drinks can be beneficial during moderate- or vigorous-intensity exercise that lasts longer than 60 minutes. Too little fluid intake can result in acute or chronic dehydration, while consuming too much water can lead to hyponatremia.

Can Dietary Supplements Contribute to Fitness?

Competitive athletes are always looking for an edge, and many turn to supplements in the hope of improving their performance. The pill and powder manufacturers may claim that their products enhance immunity, boost metabolism, improve memory,

acute dehydration Dehydration starting after a short period of time.

chronic dehydration Dehydration over a long period of time.

hyponatremia Dangerously low levels of sodium in the blood.

Calculating Your Fluid Needs for Endurance Exercise

The next time you take a 1-hour training run, use the following process to determine your fluid needs.

1. Make sure that you are properly hydrated before the workout. Your urine should be clear.
2. Do a warm-up run to the point where you start to sweat, then stop. Urinate if necessary.
3. Weigh yourself on an accurate scale.
4. Run for one hour at an intensity similar to your targeted race.
5. Drink a measured amount of a beverage of your choice during the run to quench your thirst. Be sure to keep track of how much you drink.
6. Do not urinate during the run.
7. After you have finished the run, weigh yourself again on the same scale you used in Step 3.

8. Calculate your fluid needs using the following formula:
   a. Enter your body weight from Step 3 in pounds _____
   b. Enter your body weight from Step 7 in pounds − _____
   c. Subtract b from a = _____
   × 15.3
   d. Convert the pounds of weight in c to fluid ounces by multiplying by 15.3 _____
   e. Enter the amount of fluid you consumed during the run in ounces + _____
   f. Add e to d = _____

   The final figure is the number of ounces of fluid that you must consume per hour to remain well hydrated.

Source: Adapted from "USA Track & Field Self-Testing Program for Optimal Hydration for Distance Running" by Douglas Casa, from USA Track and Field website. Copyright © 2003 by Douglas Casa. Reprinted with permission.

---

or provide some other physical advancement. Because dietary supplements are not strictly regulated by the Food and Drug Administration, their manufacturers do not have to prove the purity, quality, safety, or efficacy of any of their products or claims. As a result, many athletes risk their health and, in some cases, eligibility for competition by taking supplements that can be ineffective, dangerous, or contain banned substances. Proper nutrition and exercise should be first and foremost in any training regimen. Once these requirements have been met, then supplementation can be considered to improve health and overall fitness. Meeting with a sports dietitian will help you determine if you need supplements and what risks you might be taking by consuming them.

Dietary Supplements and Ergogenic Aids May Improve Performance, but Can Have Side Effects

The term **ergogenic aid** describes any substance, including dietary supplements, used to improve athletic performance. Although the makers of dietary supplements do not have to prove their effectiveness, researchers have examined several supplements and their effects on athletic performance. Studies have indicated that some dietary supplements have a positive effect on performance, while others do not. Further, some ergogenic aids cause serious side effects. Let's take a closer look at some of the most popular dietary supplements and ergogenic aids in the fitness industry.

Creatine

Creatine is one of the best-known dietary supplements in the fitness industry today. In the early 1990s, research revealed that creatine supplementation increased creatine stores in the muscles (in the form of creatine phosphate), which increased the amount of ATP generated and improved performance during high-intensity, short-duration exercise.[44]

However, the data on whether creatine enhances performance are mixed. Studies have shown that creatine supplementation does improve athletic performance in high-intensity, short-duration activities such as weight training, when the body relies

Athletes sometimes take supplements, such as creatine or caffeine, to enhance their athletic performance. Supplements are not strictly regulated by the FDA, so their quality and effectiveness can vary widely.

ergogenic aid A substance, such as a dietary supplement, used to enhance athletic performance.

on anaerobic energy metabolism. Creatine supplementation has also been shown to increase muscle strength and muscle mass. But research yields mixed results as to whether creatine supplementation improves sprint-running performance, with some studies showing improvement and others showing no benefit.[45]

To date, creatine has not been found to have negative effects on blood pressure, or kidney or liver function among healthy people.[46] Still, anyone considering taking creatine supplements should check with a health care provider first.

Caffeine

Caffeine used to be known mostly in the context of its negative effect on hydration (recall that caffeine is a diuretic). Today, caffeine has gained popularity as an ergogenic aid among athletes, trainers, and coaches. Caffeine may decrease perception of effort by stimulating the central nervous system, directly affect the breakdown of muscle glycogen, and increase the availability of fatty acids during exercise, therefore sparing glycogen stores. Studies on the effects of caffeine on exercise have shown that caffeine does enhance athletic performance, mostly during endurance events.[47] However, research has not proven that caffeine provides any benefit during short-duration activities, such as sprinting.[48] Caffeine is considered a banned substance by some athletic associations when consumed in high amounts. For example, the National Collegiate Athletic Association (NCAA) classifies caffeine as a banned substance when urine concentrations exceed 15 micrograms per milliliter. For most people, this would be the equivalent of drinking four or five cups of coffee within one hour.

Anabolic Steroids

Anabolic steroids (*anabolic* = to stimulate growth) are testosterone-based substances designed to mimic the bodybuilding traits of testosterone. There are two primary effects of anabolic steroids. The anabolic effect, which is the one users are seeking, results in the promotion of protein growth and muscle development, which leads to bigger muscles and greater strength. Most athletes want to be stronger and will often turn to anabolic steroids to build up muscle to a level that's not naturally possible.

Anabolic steroids are sometimes used by athletes seeking to bulk up. Because they are testosterone based, they can have undesirable effects on the body for both men and women.

The other, undesirable, effect of anabolic steroids is the androgenic effect (*andro* = testosterone promoting). Taking in testosterone causes the body to decrease its own production of the hormone, leading to a hormone imbalance. In men, this can cause shrinkage of the testicles, decreased sperm production, impotence, painful urination, severe acne (especially on the back), and changes in hair growth (an increase in facial hair and a decrease in hair on the head). Men may also experience psychiatric side effects such as extreme mood swings and aggressiveness, which can lead to violence.

Women who use anabolic steroids also experience androgenic effects. Just as with men using anabolic steroids, women experience severe acne, increased facial and body hair, and loss of hair on the head. Additionally, women may experience a lower voice, increased aggressiveness, amenorrhea, and increased sex drive.

Although anabolic steroids can increase muscle mass and strength, their use among collegiate and professional athletes is prohibited by most governing agencies. Abusing anabolic steroids, to improve performance or physical appearance, can lead to severe health consequences such as liver and kidney tumors, liver cancer, high blood pressure, trembling, and increases in LDL cholesterol.

Growth Hormone

Growth hormone has been promoted with claims that it will increase muscle mass and strength and decrease body fat, thereby improving performance. Some competitive athletes use growth hormone instead of anabolic steroids to build muscles because they believe it is less likely to be detected through current testing methods.

The man on the right, who is more than eight feet tall, has acromegaly caused by a tumor on his pituitary gland. Growth hormone abuse can also cause acromegaly in specific tissues, bones, or organs of the body.

Growth hormone is naturally produced by the pituitary gland to stimulate growth in children. Synthetic, or man-made, growth hormone was originally created for children with growth hormone deficiency to enable them to grow to their full height. It targets numerous tissues, including bones, skeletal muscle, fat cells, immune cells, and liver cells. Growth hormone increases protein synthesis by increasing amino acid transport across cell membranes, causing an increase in muscle mass but not strength. This increased muscle mass but not strength could actually impair performance by reducing one's power, speed, and endurance.

Growth hormone also decreases glycogen synthesis and the use of glucose for energy, causing an increase in fat breakdown and the use of fatty acids for energy. This, in turn, can improve body composition by decreasing body fat. For these reasons, many people assume they can improve their performance with the use of growth hormone.

Little research exists on the effectiveness of growth hormone on improving fitness and athletic performance, and the results of studies that have been done are mixed. Growth hormone has been shown to reduce body fat and increase fat-free mass in well-trained adults.[49] However, other studies show that it does not improve muscle strength or lean body mass in healthy adult athletes or the elderly.[50] It also appears to have no positive effect on cardiovascular performance in adults with growth hormone deficiency.[51]

Abuse of growth hormone can have serious health effects, including the development of diabetes, atherosclerosis (hardening of the arteries), and hypertension. Excess growth hormone can also cause **acromegaly**, a condition in which tissues, bones, and internal organs grow abnormally large.

Erythropoietin and Blood Doping

Erythropoietin is a hormone produced by the kidneys when there is a decrease in blood oxygen levels. The hormone travels to the bone marrow and stimulates the formation of red blood cells, which carry oxygen to tissues. Synthetic versions of erythropoietin are used as ergogenic aids by athletes because increasing the number of red blood cells increases the oxygen-carrying capacity of the blood. This results in the athlete's being able to train at a higher intensity without becoming fatigued as quickly,[52] thereby having the potential to improve performance and overall physical fitness. Despite its popularity among competitive athletes, synthetic erythropoietin is a banned substance in most athletic organizations.

Before synthetic erythropoietin was discovered, the most common way to increase the oxygen-carrying capacity of the blood was blood doping. Blood doping, or red blood cell reinfusion, involves removing 250 to 500 milliliters (about 0.5 to 1 pint) of an athlete's own blood, extracting the red blood cells, and storing them for a few weeks prior to competition, during which time the athlete's body produces more red blood cells. The stored red blood cells are reinfused as the competition day approaches, so that the athlete has a higher than normal number of blood cells in his or her body. This results in an increase in the amount of oxygen in the blood, which can increase aerobic endurance.

Synthetic erythropoietin and blood doping can be dangerous because they increase blood viscosity (thickness). If the blood becomes too thick, it moves slowly and can clog capillaries. If this occurs in the brain, it can result in a stroke. If there is a blood clot in the heart, it can cause a heart attack. Both of these can be life-threatening. Erythropoietin may also cause sudden death during sleep, which is believed to have been a contributing factor in numerous deaths among professional European cyclists.

In 2012, U.S. cyclist Lance Armstrong shocked the sports world after he admitted to using performance-enhancing drugs including steroids, erythropoietin, and growth hormones. Consequently, he received a lifetime ban from sports from the U.S.

acromegaly A condition caused by excess growth hormone in which tissues, bones, and internal organs grow abnormally large.

Anti-Doping Agency and was stripped of all seven Tour de France titles, in addition to having a tarnished image and lack of respect from other athletes, sports organizations, and devoted fans.

Table 11.7 summarizes the supplements that are often used to enhance athletic performance.

Table 11.7
The Truth about Supplements and Ergogenic Aids

Supplement/Ergogenic Aid	Belief or Claim	Evidence/Potential Side Effects
Multivitamin/mineral (most common among college athletes)	Improves overall health and performance; provides energy	Will improve health and performance only when deficiencies exist. Avoid multivitamin/mineral supplements containing more than 100% RDA of contents. Vitamins and minerals do not directly supply energy, but assist with the breakdown of carbohydrate, fat, and protein to use for energy.
Creatine	Increases muscle mass and strength; makes athlete faster and stronger	Mixed results in clinical trials. Has been shown to increase muscle mass and strength and improve performance in high-intensity, short-duration exercise by increasing ATP. Mixed results in improving performance in exercise of longer duration. No negative effects seen in healthy individuals.
Caffeine	Improves endurance	Has been shown to improve endurance in some athletes, but no improvement shown in short-duration activities. NCAA lists caffeine as a banned substance when urine concentrations exceed 15 mcg/ml.
Anabolic steroids	Increase muscle mass, size, and strength	Have been shown to increase muscle mass, size, and strength, but also contribute many negative side effects such as hormone imbalance, changes in hair growth, shrinkage of testicles and decreased sperm count in men, and psychiatric effects like extreme mood swings and aggressiveness. Steroids are illegal in the United States unless prescribed by a physician.
Growth hormone	Increases muscle mass and strength, decreases body fat	Mixed results in clinical trials regarding improved athletic performance. May improve body composition in well-trained adults, but not others. Can have negative side effects such as acromegaly, and the development of diabetes, atherosclerosis, and hypertension. NCAA lists GH as a banned substance.
Erythropoietin	Improves cardiorespiratory fitness and endurance	Has been shown to improve cardiorespiratory fitness and endurance in athletes, but can be dangerous by increasing blood thickness and possibly forming blood clots. Has been linked to sudden death during sleep among European cyclists. NCAA lists erythropoietin as a banned substance.

Sports Bars, Shakes, and Meal Replacers May Provide Benefits

Sports bars and shakes are not considered dietary supplements because they are more like food and contain one or more macronutrients.

The main energy source in most sports bars and shakes is carbohydrate, with protein and fat contributing smaller amounts of energy. The ratio of the macronutrients in these foods varies depending on the purpose. Bars and shakes that are intended to provide energy for and recovery from exercise have a greater proportion of energy supplied by carbohydrates. Those that are promoted for muscle protein synthesis typically contain more protein than carbohydrate and fat. Bars and shakes that are high in protein are often used by vegetarians and some athletes who may think that they need additional sources of protein in their diet. Most bars and shakes also contain a variety of vitamins and minerals. Of course, these vitamins and minerals may not be necessary if you are consuming balanced meals regularly or taking a daily multivitamin. Table 11.8 separates fact from fiction when it comes to using protein supplements to bulk up.

If you're a supremely busy person, these products may be a convenient alternative to meals or snacks prepared at home. However, keep in mind that these items are

Table 11.8

Bulking Up on Protein to Bulk Up?

Probably one of the biggest dietary misconceptions related to fitness is that to bulk up your muscles, you need to bulk up the protein or amino acids in your diet. Although athletes need more dietary protein than less active folks, their diets are likely supplying more than enough to build muscle. Expensive protein supplements are not only unnecessary, but may actually provide undesirable results. The following chart will help you separate fact from fiction:

Fact	Fiction
You need weight-resistance training to build muscle mass. The purpose of resistance training is to stress the muscle tissue so it increases its bulk. This is the only process that will result in increased muscle strength.	**Protein intake is more important than weight-resistance training to build muscle.** This is pure fiction, as regularly scheduled weight-resistance exercises are a key component to building muscle. No matter how much protein you consume, you won't build muscle without proper training.
Consuming adequate daily calories, especially from carbohydrates and fat, are vital to building muscle. A diet adequate in all three nutrients—carbohydrates, fat, and protein—is a muscle must! You need adequate carbohydrates and fats to fuel your workouts so that your dietary protein will be preserved to build and repair your muscles.	**There isn't any downside to eating a lot of protein.** Excessive amounts of protein, beyond your daily calorie needs, will be stored as body fat. Also, excessive protein burdens the kidneys to excrete the excess nitrogen as urea in urine.
The best recovery snack after your workout is one that will supply both carbohydrates and protein. Carbohydrates are needed for post-workout recovery to replenish your glycogen stores. Protein is also needed to aid in muscle repair and growth. Peanut butter on crackers with a glass of milk, yogurt and fruit, or chocolate milk all make excellent post-workout snacks.	**The protein and amino acids in supplements are more easily used by the body.** Your body doesn't distinguish between sources of protein and amino acids, but your wallet does. A supplement can cost more than $25 for 12 servings. Whole foods not only provide all three nutrients needed to build muscle, but they are also less expensive than overpriced supplements.
For best results, your recovery snack or meal should occur within 30-45 minutes of your workout. It's a fact!	**It doesn't matter when you eat after your workout.** Wrong again. Timing is everything, and waiting too long will diminish the body's ability to use the newly consumed carbohydrate and protein for glycogen replacement and muscle repair.

Source: Based on "Eating for Recovery" by Sports, Cardiovascular, and Wellness Nutrition (SCAN) - a dietetic practice group of the Academy of Nutrition and Dietetics, from NUTRITION FACT SHEET, Issue 1, April 2009; "Gaining Weight and Building Muscle" by SCAN, from NUTRITION FACT SHEET, Issue 8, January 2010; and "Nutrition for Muscle Mass" by R. Skinner, from Gatorade Sports Science Institute website, 2008..

self-Assessment

Are You Meeting Your Fitness Recommendations and Eating for Exercise?

Now that you know how to plan an effective fitness strategy and eat for optimal fitness and performance, think about your current dietary and exercise habits. Take this brief assessment to find out if your daily habits are as healthful as they could be:

1. Do you participate in 30 minutes of moderately intense physical activity most days of the week?
   Yes ☐ **No** ☐

2. Do you participate in weight training 2 to 3 times per week?
   Yes ☐ **No** ☐

3. Do you drink 6 to 12 ounces of fluid every 15 to 20 minutes during exercise?
   Yes ☐ **No** ☐

4. Do you drink a sports beverage after moderate- or high-intensity exercise lasting longer than 1 hour?
   Yes ☐ **No** ☐

5. Do you consume carbohydrate and protein within 30 to 45 minutes after stopping exercise?
   Yes ☐ **No** ☐

Answers

If you answered yes to all of the questions, you are well on your way to optimal fitness. Participating in regular exercise, including aerobic exercise and strength training, helps you maintain optimal health and improves your level of fitness. Eating and drinking adequate nutrients also improves fitness. If you answered no to any of the questions, review this chapter to learn more on fitness and eating for exercise.

No Oven Needed Energy Bars

Ingredients:

5 Tablespoons natural peanut butter

6 scoops chocolate whey protein (~130 grams protein)

1 cup dry oats

1 cup non-fat dry milk

1 teaspoon vanilla

1/2 cup water

Directions:

Spray an 8x8 inch baking dish with non-stick cooking spray. Mix oats, whey protein, and non-fat dry milk in a bowl. Stir in peanut butter (mixture will look crumbly and dry). Add water and vanilla to mixture and stir until it forms a dough. Spray a clean spatula with non-stick cooking spray and use it to spread dough in baking dish. Refrigerate for a few hours, then cut into squares. Wrap bars individually in plastic wrap and keep in refrigerator until you are ready to eat them!

Figure 11.5 "No Oven Needed" Energy Bars Try this recipe as an inexpensive alternative to commercial energy bars.

often expensive. An energy bar may be trendy and easy to stash in your book bag, but an old-fashioned peanut butter sandwich on whole-grain bread would cost less and be just as easy to carry. Alternatively, you could even make your own energy bars for much less than it costs to buy them (see **Figure 11.5**).

The Take-Home Message Dietary supplements and ergogenic aids, such as creatine, caffeine, anabolic steroids, growth hormone, erythropoietin, and blood doping, may enhance performance, but can have serious health effects. Sports bars and shakes are convenient sources of energy, but are more expensive than whole foods and should only be included as a minor part of an overall healthy diet.

Practical Nutrition **VIDEO**

Energy Bars: Are They Needed?

Energy bars can seem like the most simple choice for food on-the-go. But are they really the best option for fuelling your active lifestyle? Scan this QR code with your mobile device to access the video. You can also access the video in MasteringNutrition™.

MADE over MADE better

Many athletes choose quick, convenient foods that are often processed, high in refined sugars, and low in protein. Making a few small changes in your diet can result in big gains in your physical fitness. Here are some typical foods consumed by athletes made over to provide more balanced nutrients and fuel the body for exercise.

Pop Tarts
2 pastries = 360 calories
Fat: 2 grams
Carbohydrates: 76 grams
Protein: 4 grams

Whole-Wheat Bagel with Peanut Butter
1 bagel with 1 tbs peanut butter = 345 calories
Fat: 10 grams
Carbohydrates: 54 grams
Protein: 16 grams

Potato Chips
1 oz = 160 calories
Fat: 10 grams
Carbohydrates: 15 grams
Protein: 2 grams

Trail Mix (dried fruit and nuts)
1 oz = 140 calories
Fat: 10 grams
Carbohydrates: 10 grams
Protein: 5 grams

Ramen Noodles
1 package = 380 calories
Fat: 14 grams
Carbohydrates: 26 grams
Protein: 4 grams

Baked Potato Topped with Beans
1 large potato with 1/2 cup beans = 380 calories
Fat: 0.5 gram
Carbohydrates: 83 grams
Protein: 14 grams

Soda (cola)
12 oz = 140 calories
Fat: 0 grams
Carbohydrates: 65 grams
Protein: 0 grams

Low-Fat Chocolate Milk
12 oz = 270 calories
Fat: 4 grams
Carbohydrates: 44 grams
Protein: 17 grams

Should Caffeine Be Limited as a Controlled Substance in Athletics? Caffeine was removed from the World Anti-Doping Agency's (WADA's) Prohibited List in 2004. Its use by competitors as part of a normal diet or specifically for performance enhancement is not prohibited.[1] The National Collegiate Athletic Association (NCAA), however, does not allow concentrations exceeding 15 micrograms per milliliter in urine.[2] In recent years, the WADA has reopened the discussion about caffeine over concerns about competitors using caffeine to enhance performance. What do you think? Should certain levels of caffeine be banned in all athletics?

Read the arguments, then consider the critical-thinking questions and decide for yourself.

yes

- Caffeine has been shown to impact performance in endurance events such as cycling and running, and use of the substance could give some competitors an unfair advantage over others.[3]

- Limiting caffeine would help to deter competitors from the vicious cycle of using uppers to compete, and downers to sleep.[4]

- Caffeine impacts different bodies to different extents. Some people react poorly to it, while others gain alertness and energy.[5] If one person gets more boost out of the same amount of caffeine, that person would have an unfair advantage.

- Excessive caffeine consumption can cause harm,[6] particularly in situations where athletes are dehydrated and attempt to rehydrate with energy drinks.[7]

no

- Caffeine is a legal substance. Athletes should be allowed to use the caffeine in coffee or in other beverages to get a boost to their workout, much as they strategically use their diet to get a boost from carbo-loading.[8]

- Given that 80 percent of adults in the United States consume caffeine every day—2 cups for the average adult[9]—it is inconsistent to ban athletes from consuming it.

- Because each person reacts to caffeine to a different extent,[10] there is no way to determine a fair limit.

- Caffeine is not currently regulated by the FDA,[11] and caffeine amounts are not routinely listed on beverage cans,[12] nor is it always possible to tell how much caffeine is in a cup of coffee, so it would be difficult for athletes to monitor their dosage in order to comply with regulations.

what do you think?

1. Should the use of caffeine be banned in athletics? **2.** Do you consume caffeine, and have you used it to benefit your athletic performance? **3.** How does the use of caffeine compare with the use of steroids, or alternatively, to the consumption of chocolate milk after a workout? **4.** Do you think caffeine could be a "gateway drug" to use of stronger drugs for athletic improvement?

1 Physical Fitness Includes Five Components for Health

Physical fitness is defined as good health or physical condition, especially as the result of exercise and proper nutrition. There are five basic components of physical fitness: cardiorespiratory endurance, muscle strength, muscle endurance, flexibility, and body composition.

2 A Successful Physical Fitness Program Uses FITT Principles

Fitness programs generally incorporate exercises that are based on the five components of fitness, and include aerobic activities, resistance training, and stretching. A successful fitness program should be tailored to meet the needs of the individual and performed consistently so that any gains in physical fitness are not lost. FITT is an acronym for frequency, intensity, time and type of activity.

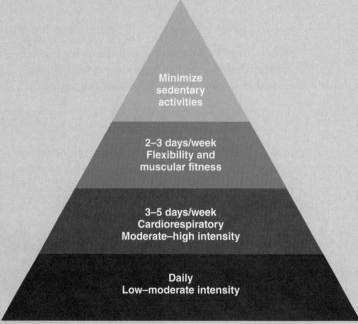

Minimize sedentary activities

2–3 days/week Flexibility and muscular fitness

3–5 days/week Cardiorespiratory Moderate–high intensity

Daily Low–moderate intensity

3 Carbohydrate, Fat, and Protein Fuel Exercise

Carbohydrate, fat, and protein are all used by the body during exercise. The source of energy needed to fuel exercise depends on the intensity and duration of the activity, and an individual's current level of fitness. The body relies heavily on anaerobic energy from ATP and creatine phosphate during the first few seconds of exercise. As exercise continues, the body relies on aerobic production of ATP mainly from carbohydrate and fat, obtained from blood glucose and stored glycogen, and fatty acids stored in mucle tissue and free fatty acids in the blood derived from fat tissue. Fat supplies nearly all of the energy required during rest and low- to moderate-intensity activity. Protein primarily functions to maintain, build, and repair tissues, including muscle tissue. As long as the diet is adequate in total calories, carbohydrate, and fat, only small amounts of protein are used for energy during exercise.

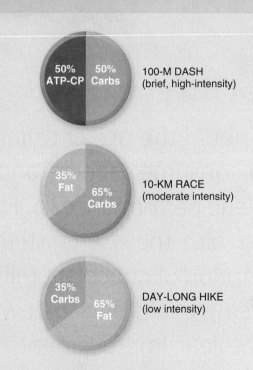

50% ATP-CP 50% Carbs 100-M DASH (brief, high-intensity)

35% Fat 65% Carbs 10-KM RACE (moderate intensity)

35% Carbs 65% Fat DAY-LONG HIKE (low intensity)

4 The Timing of Meals Affects Fitness Performance

The timing of meals before, during, and after exercise impacts energy levels and recovery time. Consuming both carbohydrate and protein 1 to 4 hours before exercise produces a greater increase in muscle glycogen synthesis, promotes greater endurance, and results in greater protein synthesis after exercise is over. Consuming carbohydrate 15 to 30 minutes prior to the start of exercise give muscles an immediate source of energy, spares glycogen stores, and protects muscles from damage. Within the first 30 to 45 minutes after exercise, carbohydrate helps replenish glycogen stores and stimulates muscle protein synthesis, with protein intake immediately following exercise resulting in greater protein synthesis.

5 Vitamins and Minerals Assist in Energy Metabolism

Vitamins and minerals assist in energy metabolism and are necessary for fitness. Athletes do not have greater needs for vitamins and minerals than do nonathletes, and intakes of vitamins and minerals above the RDA do not improve athletic performance. Supplements containing vitamins and minerals are not necessary when adequate amounts are obtained through consuming a variety of foods. Female and vegetarian athletes are at greater risk of developing iron deficiency and should consume iron-rich foods regularly. Athletes also need to be sure their calcium intake is adequate to help reduce their risk of bone fractures during physical activity.

6 Fluid Intake Affects Fitness and Performance

Being adequately hydrated before, during, and after exercise helps maintain fluid and electrolyte balance and normal body temperature. Water is the best fluid for hydration during exercise, though sports drinks can be beneficial for moderate- to vigorous-intensity exercise. Dehydration and overhydration should both be avoided because they can be harmful to health.

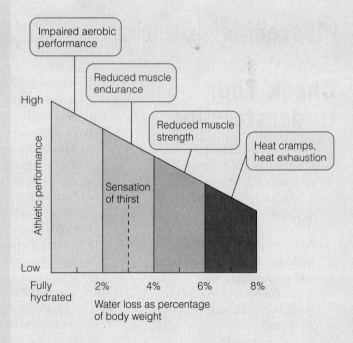

7 Some Dietary Supplements Can Contribute to Fitness

Dietary supplements are not strictly regulated for their safety and efficacy; those who choose to use them may be placing their health at risk. Some dietary supplements, such as creatine and caffeine, are used as ergogenic aids to improve athletic performance. Creatine has been shown to increase both muscle strength and mass. Caffeine has been shown to improve endurance performance, but has not shown any benefit in activities of short duration. Anabolic steroids can increase muscle mass and strength, but will also cause undesirable androgenic side effects for both men and women. Growth hormone may increase muscle mass and decrease body fat, but also has serious health effects. Synthetic erythropoietin and blood doping can improve endurance, but can also thicken the blood, which may lead to a stroke, heart attack, or death.

Terms to Know

- physical fitness
- cardiorespiratory endurance
- muscle strength
- muscle endurance
- strength training
- flexibility
- body composition
- stroke volume
- VO$_2$max
- intensity
- repetition maximum (RM)
- rating of perceived exertion (RPE)
- duration
- progressive overload principle
- aerobic
- anaerobic
- adenosine triphosphate (ATP)
- creatine phosphate
- dehydration
- hyponatremia
- female athlete triad
- ergogenic aid

MasteringNutrition™ Build your knowledge—and confidence—in the Study Area of MasteringNutrition with a variety of study tools.

Check Your Understanding

1. Which of the following is *not* a component of physical fitness?
   a. muscle strength
   b. cardiorespiratory endurance
   c. stress
   d. body composition

2. If you are able to do 100 consecutive push-ups without taking a break, you are exhibiting great
   a. cardiorespiratory endurance.
   b. muscle endurance.
   c. flexibility.
   d. muscle strength.

3. Energy derived from anaerobic conditions (without oxygen) comes from what two molecules in muscle cells?
   a. ATP and creatine phosphate
   b. creatine phosphate and lactate

   c. ATP and lactate
   d. ATP and ADP

4. During low-intensity activity, your body obtains most of its energy from
   a. muscle glycogen.
   b. liver glycogen.
   c. muscle protein.
   d. fatty acids.

5. Under what conditions will the body use significant amounts of protein for energy during exercise?
   a. inadequate calorie and fluid intake
   b. inadequate carbohydrate and protein stores
   c. inadequate protein stores and fluid intake
   d. inadequate calorie intake and carbohydrate stores

6. A pre-game meal should be
   a. high in carbohydrate, low in fat.
   b. high in carbohydrate and high in fat.

   c. low in carbohydrate, high in fat.
   d. low in protein, high in fat.

7. A condition that occurs when too much water is consumed or too much sodium is lost in sweating, resulting in abnormally low levels of sodium in the blood, is called
   a. acute dehydration.
   b. chronic dehydration.
   c. hyponatremia.
   d. hyperglycemia

8. A commercial sports drink might be beneficial after 60 minutes or more of exercise because it
   a. provides electrolytes and carbohydrates, and contributes to hydration.
   b. is marketed to everyone, not just athletes.
   c. typically contains 12 to 16 percent carbohydrate.
   d. tastes good so you will drink more.

9. An appropriate exercise recovery beverage would be
   a. a soft drink.
   b. coffee.
   c. low-fat chocolate milk.
   d. orange juice.
10. Acromegaly can be caused by abuse of which ergogenic aid?
   a. creatine
   b. growth hormone
   c. anabolic steroids
   d. erythropoietin

Answers

1. (c) Muscle strength, cardiorespiratory endurance, and body composition, along with muscle endurance and flexibility, are the five basic components of physical fitness. Stress is not a component of physical fitness.
2. (b) Performing 100 consecutive push-ups without resting shows great muscle endurance because you are able to exert the force needed to push yourself up over a long period of time without getting tired.
3. (a) The body relies on two high-energy molecueles, ATP and creatine phosphate, for energy during anaerobic exercise.
4. (d) Fatty acids are the main source of energy during low-intensity activity. As the intensity increases, the body will use fewer fatty acids and more glycogen for energy.
5. (d) The body will use larger amounts of protein for energy if overall calorie intake is inadequate and if carbohydrate stores are low.
6. (a) A meal before a game or workout should be high in carbohydrate to maximize glycogen stores and low in fat to prevent feelings of fatigue or discomfort.
7. (c) Hyponatremia occurs when blood levels of sodium become abnormally low as a result of drinking too much water or not replacing sodium lost through sweating. Long-distance runners are at higher risk for developing hyponatremia.

8. (a) Sports drinks supply fluids to rehydrate the body during and after exercise, electrolytes to replace those lost during sweating, and carbohydrate, which acts as an immediate source of energy that can potentially improve performance.
9. (c) Low-fat chocolate milk is a good exercise recovery beverage because it contains an appropriate ratio of carbohydrate and protein that is necessary for optimal recovery. Soft drinks, coffee, and orange juice will provide your body with fluids, but lack other nutrients that are ideal for recovery after exercise.
10. (b) Abusing growth hormone causes acromegaly, a disease in which tissues, bones, and internal organs grow abnormally large in size.

Web Resources

- The President's Council on Physical Fitness and Sports, www.fitness.gov
- Let's Move, www.letsmove.gov
- American Council on Exercise, www.acefitness.org
- American College of Sports Medicine, www.acsm.org
- Academy of Nutrition and Dietetics, www.eatright.org
- Sports, Cardiovascular, and Wellness Nutritionists: A Dietetics Practice Group of the Academy of Nutrition and Dietetics, www.scandpg.org
- Gatorade Sports Science Institute, www.gssiweb.org
- For information on independent testing and product reviews about dietary supplements, visit www.ConsumerLab.com

Answers to True or False?

1. **False.** Physical activity refers to general body movement such as walking the dog, while exercise is defined as formalized training or structured activity like weight lifting. Refer to page 414 for more information.
2. **True.** You don't have to be an Olympian to enjoy the health benefits of exercise. With as little as 60 minutes per week, you can burn more calories and lower your risk of certain diseases. Turn to page 419 for more information.
3. **True.** Energy is produced anaerobically during the first few seconds of exercise, and aerobically as exercise continues beyond several seconds. Turn to page 422 to learn about energy sources during exercise.
4. **False.** It is necessary to eat a high-carbohydrate diet on a regular basis to improve athletic performance, not just before exercise or competition. Turn to page 425 to learn more.
5. **True.** Consumption of nutrients immediately after stopping exercise will improve recovery. Find out more on page 432.
6. **False.** Vitamins and minerals have important roles in exercise, including assisting in the metabolism of carbohydrate, fat, and protein for energy. Turn to page 433 to learn more about the roles of vitamins and minerals during exercise.
7. **True.** Female and vegetarian athletes are at higher risk for iron deficiency. Turn to page 434 to find out why this is the case.
8. **False.** Sports drinks are generally beneficial only when you exercise for longer than one hour. Find out more about fluid needs during exercise on page 437.
9. **False.** Once you feel the sensation of thirst, you are already experiencing dehydration. Turn to page 438 to learn more about proper hydration during exercise.
10. **True.** You may be surprised to learn that just a few cups of coffee can supply excessive amounts of caffeine. To learn more, turn to page 441.

12

Consumerism:
From Farm to Table

1. Food **advertising** probably has little effect on what foods you buy and consume. T/F p. 454

2. The **ingredients** used to make your favorite food came from a farm. T/F p. 455

3. Most farms in the United States are small family **farms**. T/F p. 456

4. Most of the **corn** grown in the United States is used to feed animals, not humans. T/F p. 459

5. Eating **locally** grown food can help reduce energy costs. T/F p. 464

6. The FDA requires special labels for products produced from the milk of cows treated with synthetic **hormones**. T/F p. 470

7. The majority of soybeans grown in the United States to produce soybean oil and other products are **genetically modified**. T/F p. 475

8. Food **policy** recently influenced farmers to grow different varieties of grain. T/F p. 478

9. All organic foods certified by the USDA are 100 percent **pesticide** free. T/F p. 481

10. **Organic** foods are more nutritious than nonorganic foods. T/F p. 481

See page 487 for the answers.

True or False?

453

Chapter Objectives

After reading this chapter, you will be able to:

1. **Describe how food advertising and marketing affect your food choices.**

2. **Recognize where your food comes from.**

3. **Describe how the resources used to grow and harvest food affect the environment.**

4. **Describe the benefits and risks of using hormones, antibiotics, and pesticides in food production.**

5. **Describe the benefits and risks of using biotechnology in agriculture.**

6. **Explain how food policy affects the foods that are available to you to buy and consume.**

7. **Recognize how label terms can help you know how food was produced.**

The fact that we buy food, whether at the dining hall, mini mart, grocery store, or a restaurant, makes us all **food consumers**. As such, we command a great deal of influence on the **food industry**, which is a global, $4 *trillion*-a-year business.[1] We literally speak with our food dollars. The foods we choose to buy, where we choose to buy them, and how often we make these purchases are decisions that are tremendously important to the people who grow, process, market, distribute, and sell our food products. Although you may think that you are in the "driver's seat" when choosing the foods you eat, this isn't entirely the case. In fact, there are many outside factors that influence the foods that you have access to and end up purchasing.

How Do Advertising and Marketing Influence Your Food Choices?

Every year, vast amounts of money are spent by food companies to persuade you to buy their products. Whether they are advertised on television, radio, magazines, or the Internet, or placed in movies, these products' manufacturers spend more than $10 billion annually to promote them. Much of the promotion is for nutritionally dubious products. In fact, more than $7 million is spent on the marketing of breakfast cereals, candy, and gum. Another $500 million is spent on advertising carbonated soft drinks.[2] You can probably think of an ad campaign you've seen recently for a particular brand of soda or fast-food chain. In comparison, when was the last time you saw an advertisement for broccoli? Have you *ever* seen an ad for broccoli?

A growing trend in food advertising is to market heavily to college-aged and young adults by targeting college campuses and social venues that are popular with this age group. For example, one marketing strategy for Red Bull, a caffeinated energy drink, was to give away free samples on college campuses, at sports events, and in trendy clubs and bars. And it worked like a charm. Within three years of rolling out this product in the United States, Red Bull sparked a booming trend in energy beverage consumption. In 2008, Red Bull enjoyed $1 billion in sales.[3] Why did this advertising and marketing strategy work? Red Bull astutely identified where the members of its target audience hang out, and then the beverage company hung out with them.

More recently, Red Bull has followed its target audience online to social media sites, including Facebook, MySpace, and Twitter.[4] Facebook users can "like" Red Bull, and those on Twitter can "follow" the drink's tweets. While you may

Red Bull uses strategies that help it target college-aged, young-adult consumers.

Figure 12.1 From Farm to Consumer
Many individuals make it easier for you to obtain the foods you consume and enjoy.

1 **Farm:** Trees, bushes, plants, and animals produce the raw materials that eventually end up on your plate.

think you are immune to the influence of these techniques, companies like Red Bull put a lot of thought and effort into keeping you excited about their brand, and they do it because they think it works. Wherever you, and your wallet, go, they will follow.

In contrast, advertising for fruits and vegetables is almost nonexistent, which is a shame because healthy foods can be successfully marketed. When the dairy industry noted a decline in milk consumption among Americans in the early 1990s, it launched the *Got Milk?* ad campaign, which featured celebrities wearing milk mustaches. This campaign strove to make drinking milk sexy, and it worked. Milk sales increased by nearly 1.5 billion pounds, the equivalent of about 45 million pounds of milk being sold for each ad dollar spent.[5]

2 **Food Processor:** Food processors clean and sort the raw food products. The food is then either ready for shipping (in the case of whole foods like fruits, vegetables, and grains), or processed with heat, salt, or sugar, or combined with other ingredients to convert it into a packaged food.

The Take-Home Message The food industry spends large amounts of money on marketing and advertising its products, often to target audiences. The most heavily advertised foods are often the least nutritious.

3 **Distributor:** Once processed, foods are transported via truck, ship, or train from the plant to a retail outlet, where consumers can buy them.

Where Does Your Food Come From?

4 **Seller:** While people buy food from several sources, including, family farms, restaurants, farmers' markets, and convenience stores, most food shopping takes place at the grocery store.

Most people don't think too much about where their food comes from before it appears on the supermarket shelf. Have you ever considered where the ingredients in your morning cereal and orange juice, for example, originate? Unless you're growing wheat and oranges and keeping a cow in your backyard, you're depending on the work of numerous individuals, from the farmer to the food distributor, to transform raw milk and stalks of wheat into the foods that you have available to you. No matter what you're eating, in some form or another, it started out on a farm (see **Figure 12.1**).[6]

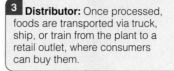

5 **Consumer:** You, the consumer, are the final step in the process.

Much of Your Food Comes from Small, Family-Run American Farms

In the United States, a **farm** is considered an establishment that produces and sells at least $1,000 of agricultural products annually. By this definition, there are just over 2 million farms in the United States, and they're largely concentrated in the Midwest,

food consumers Individuals who make decisions about which foods to buy.

food industry The collective efforts of various businesses that provide food to consumers.

farm An establishment that produces and sells at least $1,000 of agricultural products annually.

Figure 12.2 The Location and Number of Farms in the United States, 2007

Source: United States Department of Agriculture, "2007 Census of Agriculture." 2009. Available at www.agcensus.usda.gov.

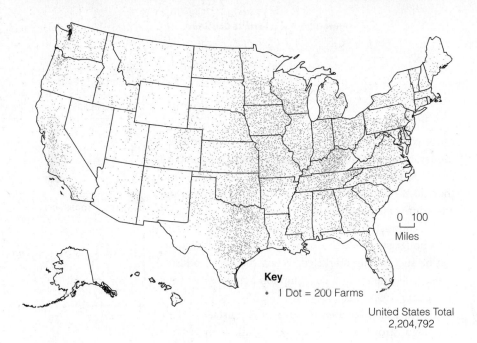

0 100
Miles

Key

• I Dot = 200 Farms

United States Total
2,204,792

Great Plains, and California (**Figure 12.2**). Although 2 million may sound like a lot of farms, it's actually many fewer than in the past. In 1935, there were more than 6.5 million farms feeding approximately 127 million Americans.[7] Currently, fewer than 960,000 hard-working Americans—less than 1 percent of the population—are producing food to feed the country's 300 million people. This lopsided scenario, with fewer farms but more people, has forced farmers to become more efficient in the ways they produce food. We will read more about this later in the chapter.

You probably think that to feed all these people, farms must be mammoth, but most (87 percent) American farms are actually small farms (see **Table 12.1**). Further, more than 95 percent of U.S. farms, both large and small, are owned and operated by

Nearly all the food that you consume originates on a farm.

families. However, these families are not necessarily passing the business on to the next generation, and the age of the average farmer is increasing.[8]

Challenges of Farming

While running a family farm may sound like a desirable career path—after all, you'd spend much of your time outside and, if you're working for your family, would probably enjoy a flexible schedule—the challenges farmers face are actually quite steep. High costs, a demand for low food prices, competition, and a dependence on the cooperation of Mother Nature can all derail a farmer's bottom line. In fact, less than one in four farms generates gross revenues (this is revenue before expenses) of more than $50,000 per year.[9] Because land, equipment, facilities, fuel, and fertilizer are all expensive (a combine used for harvest, for example, can cost upwards of $200,000), farmers must depend on a hearty yield to cover their costs and make a profit.[10]

Approximately 40 percent of famers in the United States are 55 years old or older.

Fortunately, technology and machinery allow today's farmers to produce more food on less land. Whereas a farmer in the 1930s could expect to harvest about 100 bushels (1 bushel is equal to 32 quarts) of corn daily, current farmers can harvest as much as 900 bushels of corn every hour.[11] But again, the machines that allow them to do this are very expensive. Thus, farmers are caught in this cycle of having to continually invest in new machines and technology to ensure a hearty crop in order to make enough money to pay for the expense of farming.

Some farmers use computers and the Internet to farm more efficiently. Known as **precision agriculture** or *satellite farming*, these farmers use a Global Positioning System (similar to the GPS in a car) along with other technologies to help collect and evaluate data on the soil, pests, and disease at specific field locations. The farmers then enter that information into a computer and, based on the findings, adjust their farming practices accordingly to optimize returns while preserving natural resources. For example, information gained by practicing precision agriculture may allow a farmer to use less water and/or less fertilizer in specific areas of a field.[12]

The consumer is also squeezing the farmer's bottom line, as there is a limit to what people are willing to spend for food. In the 1930s, Americans spent 25 percent of their disposable income on food. Today, Americans allocate less than 10 percent of their earnings to what they eat.[13] Once again, farmers are forced to produce large volumes in order to keep foods affordable for consumers, cover their expenses, and still make a profit.[14]

Table 12.1

Types of Farms in the United States

Farm Type	Number of Farms	Percent of Total Farms
Small Family Farms		
(annual sales less than $250,000)	1,925,799	87.3
Large Farms		
(annual sales greater than $250,000)	278,993	12.7
Non-family	91,177	4.1
Family	187,816	8.6
Total farms in the United States	2,204,792	100

Source: United States Environmental Protection Agency, "Ag 101: Demographics." Updated April 2013. Available at www.epa.gov. Accessed June 2013.

precision agriculture A cost-efficient, precise farming method that uses new technologies to collect data about variations in field soil to better manage the use of appropriate seeds, fertilizer, water, and pesticides for the growing of crops with less waste. Also known as *satellite farming*.

Modern machinery has helped farmers increase yields.

To try to offset their rising costs, many farmers take advantage of government-sponsored financial subsidies paid to farmers for growing select **commodity crops**, such as corn and soybeans. The government subsidy program has helped to manage and ensure the supply of these crops over time. However, because not all crops are subsidized, farmers may opt to grow subsidized commodity crops over other specialty crops such as fruits and vegetables. To obtain these government-sponsored subsidies farmers must grow the approved crops in accordance with conservation plans that protect the environment.[15] Unfortunately, even with this support, there has been a trend toward larger farms, which are sometimes owned by giant corporations, producing large amounts of agricultural products in America. This can make it more difficult for small farms, especially those that specialize in non–commodity crops such as fruits and vegetables, to stay in business.[16]

The Role of Agribusiness

All farming, large and small, is part of a wider field known as **agribusiness**—the blending of agricultural and business entities that affect how food, as well as the clothes in your closet and the furnishings in your home, are developed, processed, distributed, and purchased in the United States. The food component of agribusiness includes not only food production but also agricultural chemicals; agricultural finance, legal support and trade; farm management, environmental considerations; and land development. In essence, it involves all of the major elements needed in the efficient meshing of agriculture and the food business.[17]

The agribusiness sector employs approximately 16 million Americans, or about 5 percent of the U.S. population.[18] *Food-processing companies*, which take raw fruits, vegetables, grains, meats, and dairy products and convert them into edible food, comprise a large segment of those employed in agriculture (**Figure 12.3**). While agribusiness is "big business" because it employs many individuals, this doesn't mean

commodity crops Crop products such as corn and soybeans that can be used for commerce.

agribusiness The businesses collectively associated with the production, processing, and distribution of agricultural products, including food.

Corn Belt The parts of the United States where corn is grown in abundance. This includes Iowa, Indiana, most of Illinois, and parts of Kansas, Missouri, Nebraska, South Dakota, Minnesota, Ohio, and Wisconsin.

Figure 12.3 The Location and Number of Food- and Beverage-Processing Facilities, 2007
Food- and beverage-processing facilities employ many of the 16 million people who work in the American agriculture sector.

Source: United States Environmental Protection Agency, "Location of U.S. Facilities." Available at www.epa.gov. Accessed May 2010.

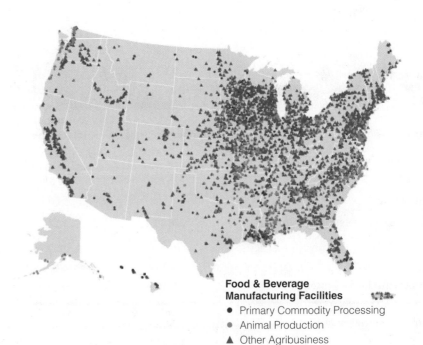

Food & Beverage Manufacturing Facilities
- ● Primary Commodity Processing
- ● Animal Production
- ▲ Other Agribusiness

that it consists only of enormous conglomerates. In fact, two-thirds of the more than 20,000 processing operations in the United States have fewer than 20 employees.[19]

Crops Grown for Food

The top three agricultural food crops grown in the United States are corn, soybeans, and wheat (see **Table 12.2**). The United States is the largest producer of corn in the world, with 10 billion bushels harvested on more than 400,000 farms spread out over 84 million acres, primarily located in the **Corn Belt** (**Figure 12.4**). Most of that corn, however, isn't consumed as cornflakes, corn syrup, cornmeal, high-fructose corn syrup, or other human food products. Rather, about 80 percent ends up as feed for livestock, poultry, and fish.

Fifty percent of the world's soybean production occurs on just over 290,000 U.S. farms (see Figure 12.4). In addition to products like tofu, soy sauce, and edamame, soy is used to produce soybean oil, the number-one oil consumed by Americans. More than 30 million tons of soybean meal (the part of the soybean left after the oil is extracted) are used to feed livestock annually.[20]

The United States produces about 10 percent of the world's wheat, which is harvested from more than 160,000 farms clustered in the Great Plains from Texas to Montana (see Figure 12.4). More than 70 percent of this wheat is used for food products, such as bread and cereal; about 22 percent is used for animal feed; and the rest is left for seeds to replenish the crops.[21]

As you can tell from these statistics, most of the staple crops grown in the United States are used not to feed humans, but to feed animals that will themselves later enter

Table 12.2
Major Agricultural Crops Produced in the United States, 2011

Crop	Harvested Area (millions of acres)
Corn (grain)	84.0
Soybeans	73.8
Hay	55.7
Wheat	45.7
Cotton	9.5
Sorghum (grain)	3.9
Rice	2.6

Source: United States Environmental Protection Agency, "Ag 101: Crop Systems." Updated March 2013. Available at www.epa.gov/oecaagct/ag101/cropsystems.html. Accessed June 2013.

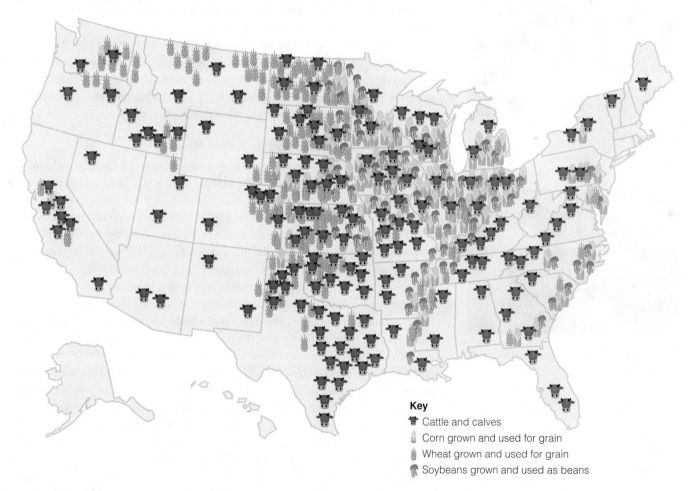

Key

- 🐄 Cattle and calves
- Corn grown and used for grain
- Wheat grown and used for grain
- Soybeans grown and used as beans

Figure 12.4 Major U.S. Centers of Cattle, Corn, Wheat, and Soybean Production

Source: Data from United States Department of Agriculture, "2007 Census of Agriculture." 2009. Available at www.agcensus.usda.gov.

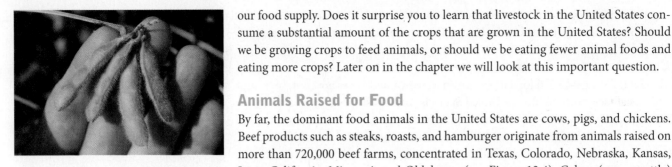

Soy is used to make numerous food products, including soybean oil, which is the number-one oil used by Americans.

our food supply. Does it surprise you to learn that livestock in the United States consume a substantial amount of the crops that are grown in the United States? Should we be growing crops to feed animals, or should we be eating fewer animal foods and eating more crops? Later on in the chapter we will look at this important question.

Animals Raised for Food

By far, the dominant food animals in the United States are cows, pigs, and chickens. Beef products such as steaks, roasts, and hamburger originate from animals raised on more than 720,000 beef farms, concentrated in Texas, Colorado, Nebraska, Kansas, Iowa, California, Missouri, and Oklahoma (see Figure 12.4). Calves (young cattle) typically graze on croplands after harvest or in open grass pasturelands until they reach a certain weight. They are then confined to **feedlots**, where they are fed roughage (hay and inedible plant parts such as cornstalks) and grains (such as corn, soybeans, and wheat) as a complete feed or meal, so that they will grow to 1,000 pounds or more before being slaughtered.[22]

Some pork by-products have medical applications: insulin for managing diabetes used to be extracted from pig pancreases, and pig heart valves have been used for heart surgery in humans.

There are about 60,200 U.S. pig farms, concentrated in the Corn Belt and in North Carolina, producing pork products such as bacon, pork chops, and ham. Unlike their ancestors, most of today's hogs are raised indoors to protect them from weather, predators, and the spread of disease. They're also leaner and meatier than ever, with a 250-pound animal producing 150 pounds of pork.[23] However, the reduced price that you are used to paying for pork has forced smaller pork farmers out of business. They can't compete with larger-scale farms to produce the volume of product necessary to make a profit.

Americans eat more poultry than either beef or pork.

If you enjoy eggs with your bacon, you can thank the more than 145,000 poultry farms located in the Corn Belt, North Carolina, and the southern United States that focus on poultry and egg production.[24] Americans eat more poultry products than either beef or pork.[25] As with pork, raising poultry indoors has increased production and reduced labor, and thus has resulted in lower poultry and egg prices.

Exporting Foods: The Good and Bad News

In addition to producing enough food to feed Americans, U.S. farmers help feed the world. An estimated 30 percent of the income from a U.S. farm is derived from trading with other countries.[26] Since the mid-1940s, the United States has exported more agricultural products than it has imported.[27] In 2013, agricultural exports were predicted to top $139.5 billion, an increase of $3.7 billion from the previous year.[28] Grains (corn, soybeans, and wheat) and oilseeds (seeds used to make oils such as corn oil and soybean oil) are the most popular exports from the United States.

Many countries do not produce enough food and need to import food from the United States to meet their needs.

We are also exporting many of our unhealthy eating habits, including the consumption of large amounts of high-calorie, high-fat, processed foods, many of which are made primarily from corn, soybeans, and wheat. According to the Economic Research Service, the globalization of the food industry has caused the "Americanization" of many food cultures around the world. As the income of individuals in countries such as Mexico, Poland, Brazil, and China has increased, so has their desire for an American-like diet. As these more-affluent individuals shift their food choices from native grains and other carbohydrate-rich staples to more expensive meats, dairy foods, confectionery products, soft drinks, convenience foods, and fast foods,[29] they experience the same shift in body weight as we are seeing in the United States. That is, they also experience a growing problem with obesity.

Globesity, or the rapidly growing incidence of obesity worldwide, is becoming a global threat. For example, in the late 1980s, less than 10 percent of Mexicans were overweight. Currently, more than 65 percent of citizens in Mexico are overweight or

feedlot A facility where cattle are fed grain and other foods before being slaughtered.

globesity A blend of the words *global* and *obesity*, coined by the World Health Organization, which refers to the worldwide obesity epidemic.

obese, which, not coincidentally, is similar to the 69.2 percent of citizens of the United States who are also overweight.[30] It is now estimated that more than 115 million people worldwide suffer health problems related to being overweight and obese.[31]

Food Production Outside the United States

So, if we are exporting so much food and we are producing plenty of food here at home, does that mean we don't import foods from other countries? In a word, no. The next time you are in a supermarket, look beyond the colorful fruits and vegetables in the produce aisle, and read the signs posted alongside these foods. It's not uncommon for those juicy green grapes to be from Chile, the vibrant red peppers from Mexico, the fresh shrimp from Canada, and the nuts from Costa Rica. You may feel as though you are traveling around the world rather than around the grocery aisles.

Americans' plates are filled with more imported foods than ever before. In fact, most fish and shellfish eaten in the United States is now imported from other countries, including China and Thailand, and about 39 percent of the fruit and nuts that we buy originate outside the United States (see **Figure 12.5**). The United States currently imports close to $2 billion worth of bananas annually from Guatemala, Ecuador, Costa Rica, Colombia, and Honduras.[32] Vegetable imports have doubled, and importation of fruits, juices, and nuts has increased by 20 percent from decades ago.[33] The majority of our coffee comes from Colombia and Brazil. All told, approximately 17 percent of your food comes from outside the United States.[34]

Importing Foods: The Good and Bad News

Why do we get so much of our food from other countries? Two primary reasons are our demand for a diverse array of products year round, regardless of U.S. growing seasons, and our demand for cheap food.

Americans have lost their patience for waiting. Even with a foot of snow on the ground, Northerners in the United States still want to wake up to fresh cantaloupe for breakfast, so retailers have the fruit shipped in from Mexico. The novelty of waiting until the summer to enjoy melons is, well, a novelty.

Also, as already mentioned, farming in the United States is an expensive endeavor. This opens the door to the outsourcing of agricultural production to poorer, developing nations that have lower overhead costs, and hence, can provide cheaper food to the consumer.[35] Although this outsourcing can provide jobs and income for developing countries (good news), you will learn in the next section that there are environmental costs (bad news) of shipping these foods long distances to the United States and ultimately to your plate.

In addition to the environmental costs, the other downside to importing foods is the potential for contamination. There have been reports of imported foods containing excessive amounts of pesticides and foodborne pathogens compared with similar domestic products.[36] This increased risk of contamination places an increased burden on the FDA, the agency that polices the safety of the domestic food supply. Because of the tremendous

Other countries are "Americanizing" their local culture's diet with sugary and/or high-fat foods that add little nutrition to the diet.

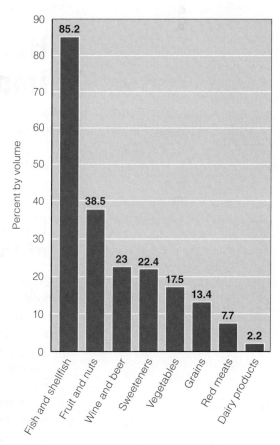

Figure 12.5 Percent of Selected Foods and Beverages Consumed in the United States That Are Imported, by Volume
America is importing foods such as seafood now more than ever before.

Source: Data from USDA, Economic Research Service, "Import Share of Consumption." 2009. Available at http://ers.usda.gov. Accessed August 2013.

volume of imports, the FDA only inspects about 1 percent of all food products brought into the United States.[37] The FDA can't inspect everything, but it takes a targeted and risk-based approach. In the past, the FDA has had to block contaminated farm-raised fish imported from China because the fish contained additives that have been shown to cause cancer in animals.[38] The globalization of the food supply is going to require that uniform, global food-safety standards be developed and implemented to keep imported foods safe.[39] This will entail an enormous, unified effort among many countries.

Let's now look at how all of this modernization and globalization affect the environment.

| **The Take-Home Message** The majority of the food that you consume originates on a farm. Most farms in the United States are small and family operated. Agribusiness is a blending of agriculture and business and affects how foods are developed, processed, distributed, and purchased. The major crops grown in the United States are corn, soybeans, and wheat, and the major animals raised for food are cows, pigs, and chickens. Many of the crops grown in the United States are used to feed the animals that are raised for food. Some of the foods you consume are grown in the United States but a good portion is likely imported from other countries. Many countries rely on the United States for part of their food supply. There are pros and cons to both the import and export of foods.

How Does Food Production Impact the Environment?

All agriculture affects the environment in some way.[40] From the water required for irrigation to the fuel needed to run the tractors to the animal wastes produced in feedlots, the processes of growing, harvesting, slaughtering, transporting, and processing food products require the use, depletion, and potential contamination of natural resources.

Food Production Requires the Use of Internal and External Resources

Numerous natural resources are used when growing crops and raising animals for food. Both natural and man-made by-products that are produced during these processes can affect the environment. Natural resources are used "internally" to produce foods and "externally" to move these food products from the farm to the consumer. **Table 12.3** describes several of the challenges associated with using internal resources, including land and water, to produce food, and various strategies that can be employed to protect the environment.

External resources, or those not used in the actual growing of the food, also contribute to the environmental costs of food production. For example, the use of fossil fuels to harvest, process, and transport food contributes to the release of carbon dioxide gas emissions. The carbon dioxide and other gases released when fossil fuels are burned for energy are referred to as **greenhouse gases**, as these gases absorb and trap the heat in the air and re-radiate that heat downward. It is estimated that global temperatures could increase by 35 to 39 degrees Fahrenheit by 2100 due to these greenhouse gases, and this may have consequences on the temperature of the earth and agriculture around the globe.[41] The carbon emissions associated with the transport of

greenhouse gases Gases that absorb and "trap" the heat in the air and re-radiate that heat downward.

Table 12.3

Environmental Effects of Food Production

	The Challenge	How Can We Minimize the Environmental Impact?
Land overuse	Excessive use of farming equipment, overtilling, and livestock overgrazing can all damage soil.	Proper land management, including crop rotation, and conservation methods of tilling can help preserve the land and replenish soil nutrients.
Soil erosion	Wind and rain can cause nutrient-rich topsoil to be blown and washed away. When fertile topsoil is lost, crop yield declines.	Proper crop covering and shielding from wind as well as proper tillage of the soil can dramatically reduce erosion.
Water depletion	Irrigation accounts for 80 percent of water consumption in the United States; hence, excessive irrigation can deplete naturally occurring groundwater.	Precision farming and the conscious reduction of overwatering can help preserve water.
Water runoff	After a rainfall (or watering of crops), the water runoff from farms can spread pesticides from crops and pathogens in animal manure to other fields, surface water, and downfield rivers and streams, contaminating these ecosystems.	Basins can be installed to collect the runoff water to prevent this contamination prior to discharge to streams and rivers.
Nitrate production	The production of nitrates from the nitrogen in manure can pollute surface water and groundwater that is used as drinking water.	Proper collection, stockpiling, and disposal of manure to minimize the leaching of nitrates into runoff and groundwater, as proposed in the latest EPA regulations, will help concentrated animal feeding operations to safely manage manure.
Airborne emissions	Emissions of ammonia and nitrogen in manure are released into the air. The ammonia released from these airborne emissions can settle on water surfaces, killing fish and encouraging the growth of toxic algae, both of which disrupt the natural ecosystem.	The proper handling of manure mitigates this problem.

Source: A. H. Harmon and B. L. Gerald, "Position of the American Dietetic Association: Food and Nutrition Professionals Can Implement Practices to Conserve Natural Resources and Support Ecological Sustainability," *Journal of the American Dietetic Association* 107 (2007): 1033–1043; U.S. Department of Agriculture, Economic Research Service, "Irrigation and Water Use." 2004. Available at www.ers.usda.gov. Accessed January 2010; U.S. Environmental Protection Agency, "Ag 101: Crop Production." 2009. Available at www.epa.gov. Accessed January 2010; U.S. Environmental Protection Agency, "Ag 101: Beef Production." 2009. Available at www.epa.gov. Accessed January 2010.

food from farm to supermarket are substantial, and you use additional fuel to drive to the supermarket and to prepare your food at home. Depending on where you live and shop, the lettuce, orange, or cantaloupe that you buy could easily have traveled 1,500 or more miles to reach you. The Leopold Center for Agriculture compiled data from the USDA and found that the average mileage for produce to travel to a Chicago market was just over 1,500 miles, which is more than a 20 percent increase from that observed in the early 1980s (see **Figure 12.6** on the next page).[42] A study conducted in Iowa showed that produce imported into the United States from different countries used 4 to 17 times more fuel and released 5 to 17 times more carbon dioxide gas emissions than produce that was locally produced.[43]

Natural resources aside, these fuel costs are also factored into the price of the food, so they affect your financial resources as well. An estimated 12 percent of your food dollars go toward the cost of getting the food from the farm to your plate. Consequently, as the price of oil increases, the price that you pay for your food will also increase.[44] Thus, the farther your food has to travel, the more resources will be used, which not only has a negative effect on the environment, but is also a drain on your wallet. Because of these and other reasons, many people are trying to buy more of their food from locally grown sources.

Figure 12.6 How Far Did Your Food Travel?
You might be surprised to learn just how far some of your food travels to get to your local supermarket.

Source: Data from "Food, Fuel, and Freeways: An Iowa Perspective on How Far Food Travels, Fuel Usage, and Greenhouse Gas Emissions" from Iowa State University Leopold Center for Sustainable Agriculture website, 2002.

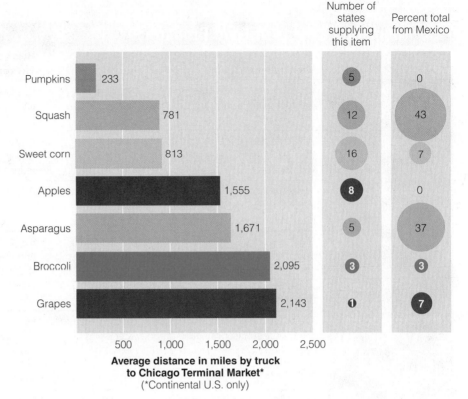

	Average distance in miles by truck to Chicago Terminal Market* (*Continental U.S. only)	Number of states supplying this item	Percent total from Mexico
Pumpkins	233	5	0
Squash	781	12	43
Sweet corn	813	16	7
Apples	1,555	8	0
Asparagus	1,671	5	37
Broccoli	2,095	3	3
Grapes	2,143	1	7

Locally Grown Food Requires Fewer External Resources

Depending on where you live it may be difficult for you to be a **locavore** and consume only locally grown food 100 percent of the time. For example, while people living in Vermont, a state in the United States with a cold climate much of the year, have access to fresh dairy foods year round, fruits and vegetables are hard to find under a foot of snow in the dead of winter. Many locavores try to eat foods grown locally and then supplement their meals with foods from the supermarket if needed.

> The Oxford American Dictionary declared the word *locavore* the 2007 Word of the Year!

The movement for "eating locally" has gained momentum for numerous reasons. Among these is that most people perceive locally grown foods as tasting better. A locally grown summer tomato, for example, is usually much more flavorful than one that has been shipped in a refrigerated truck for 1,500 miles. Similarly, a New England Macintosh apple tastes much better picked off a tree at the height of apple season than after sitting in a cold-storage room for three months. As previously discussed, eating locally also has environmental benefits, because the less your food travels, the less energy is being used to get it to you.

Small farms often provide foods to people living in those communities in different ways, including **community-supported agriculture (CSA)**, farmers markets, and contracts through local grocery stores. Produce is often picked at the peak of ripeness, and sold without having to be processed or packaged. While fuel and environmental costs are lower for locally grown food compared with food that has to travel long distances from farm to consumers, these costs depend on the type of food and the type of transportation used. **Table 12.4** shows the distance traveled for the ingredients in a meal that was obtained locally or from conventional sources. For

locavore A person who eats locally grown food whenever possible.

community-supported agriculture (CSA) An arrangement whereby individuals pay a fee to support a local farm, and in exchange receive a weekly or biweekly box of fresh produce from the farm.

Table 12.4

Food Miles in a Meal

Food Item	Local Source	Distance Traveled from Local Source	Conventional Source	Distance Traveled through Conventional Channels
Chuck roast	Local grass-fed beef farm	75 miles	Colorado	675 miles
Potatoes	Farmers' market	10–15 miles	Idaho	1,300 miles
Carrots	Backyard garden	40 feet	California	1,700 miles
Green beans	Backyard garden	40 feet	California	1,700 miles

example, a meal consisting of foods obtained at a local supermarket can travel as much as 60 times the miles as the same meal made from locally grown foods.

Many large supermarkets now sell locally grown produce. This combining of locally grown foods with conventionally grown foods allows the consumer to do "one-stop shopping" rather than having to drive to the farmers' markets, farm stands, and CSA pick-ups in addition to the supermarket. Corporate America is also making it easier to eat locally. It is becoming more common for some large corporations and industrial complexes to host weekly farmers' markets on their premises and for restaurants to feature menu items from locally grown products.[45] The USDA recently awarded more than $5 million in grants to support local food connections between farmers and consumers, even in large cities, with its "Know Your Farmer, Know Your Food" initiative.[46]

One way that you can reduce your "food miles" and eat more locally is to start a home garden. Home gardening can greatly reduce food miles to mere food "steps." The Nutrition in the Real World feature "You as a Sustainable Farmer" on the next page shows you how to grow your own vegetables even if you don't have a backyard by using container gardening methods.

Some individuals wrongfully assume that locally grown food is the same as sustainably grown food. A *sustainable diet* contains foods that meet your nutrient and health needs but can be sustained for a long time without negatively impacting the environment.[47] Buying food from small local farms doesn't guarantee that the foods were grown in a sustainable way, nor does being from a distant farm mean that those farmers didn't practice sustainable agriculture. The Nutrition in the Real World feature "What Is a Sustainable Food System?" on page 467 looks at the issue of sustainable diets and how farms, both small and large, are implementing sustainable farming practices.

Farmers' markets provide fresh, local produce to consumers.

The Take-Home Message Numerous natural resources are used when growing crops and raising animals for food. Natural resources are used internally to produce foods and externally to move these food products from the farm to the consumer. By-products that are produced during food production and processing can affect the environment. Locally grown foods use fewer external resources.

You as a Sustainable Farmer: Growing Vegetables in a Container

You might think you need a yard, a hoe, and a shovel to have a garden, but this isn't necessarily the case. Edible plants can grow in all kinds of environments and containers, and for those living in dorms or apartments, a sunny window sill, a balcony, or your front step will provide enough space to create your own garden. All you need are a container, potting soil, water, a plant, and sun. In fact, there are even advantages to growing plants in containers rather than in the ground. There won't be any weeds to pull, and you'll have fewer pests to damage your plants. Your garden is also transportable so you can move it if you need to.

Here's what you need to get started:[1]

The Container

Most any container, such as a ceramic pot, planter box, one- to five-gallon tubs, or even the plastic trash container under your desk, will do. The size of the container will depend on what you want to grow (see table). Drainage is key to growing a hearty plant. So, your container must have two important elements: 1) ¼-inch drilled holes, evenly spaced along the bottom of the container, and 2) an inch-thick layer of coarse gravel, pebbles, or broken pieces of a clay pot in the bottom of the container. This layer will allow excess water to drain from the plant.

The Potting Mixture

In place of soil, potting mixtures, which may be a combination of several compounds such as sawdust, peat moss, and vermiculite (a mineral that puffs up when exposed to heat such as from the sun), can be purchased at most garden centers, many hardware stores, and even on the Internet. The amount of potting mixture that you need will depend on the type of vegetables you want to grow and the size of your container.

The Plant

Many of the vegetables that grow in a backyard garden will also sprout quite nicely in a container garden. The table provides a list of the easier-to-grow vegetables for first-time gardeners that are ideal for containers. Transplants (small plants that you transfer to

the container) can be purchased at garden centers, farmers' markets, local farm stands, and even some supermarkets. When these transplants become available in your area, it is time to begin your vegetable garden.

Fertilizing

Because the rejuvenating, nutrient-rich soil of a backyard is missing in a container garden, you will need to routinely fertilize your plants. You can purchase a powdered fertilizer at your local supermarket, garden center, or hardware store and dilute it with water as directed on the package. Pour this diluted nourishment around the plant once a week or every other week.

Watering

Container plants tend to dry out more quickly than plants grown in outdoor gardens. Depending on the plant, you may need to water daily. Avoid waiting until the soil is completely dried out. Pour enough water so that some liquid will drain out the bottom of the container. (Put a foil pan under your plant if you are growing it inside your home to catch any excess water.) Avoid overwatering, which can be as damaging to a grown plant as underwatering. If your plant becomes waterlogged, the roots won't be able to "breathe" and receive the oxygen the plant needs to grow. You'll end up with root rot, and the plant may not survive.

Growing plants in a container garden can provide healthy, nutritious vegetables for your dinner table.

Harvesting

The best part of gardening of any type is getting to harvest and eat what you grew. Plants like cabbage, cucumbers, green beans, and lettuce take about six weeks to mature before they are ready to harvest and eat. Tomatoes and peppers take about three months.

Vegetables: From Plant to Plate

Vegetable	Minimum Container Size	Number of Plants	Amount of Sunlight	Approximate Number of Days to Harvest
Cabbage	1 gallon	1 plant	Partial shade	48–53
Cucumbers	1 gallon	2 plants	Full sun	46–66
Green beans	1 gallon	2–3 plants	Full sun	37–58
Lettuce	1 gallon	4–6 plants	Partial shade	41–56
Peppers	2 gallon	2 plants	Full sun	82–112
Tomatoes	3 gallon	1 plant	Full sun	84–124

Source: Adapted from S. Cotner and J. Masabni, "Vegetable Gardening in Containers," AgriLife Extension, Texas A&M System (March 2009). Available at http://repository.tamu.edu. Accessed June 2013; Iowa State University Extension, "Container Vegetable Gardening." (2005). Available at www.extension.iastate.edu. Accessed June 2013.

What Is a Sustainable Food System?

"Eat Green" or "Eat Sustainably"? If you have seen these phrases in the media lately and are not sure what they mean, you're among friends. According to a recent survey, only one in five Americans reports giving a lot of thought to whether or not the food they purchase is produced in a sustainable way.[2] In that same survey, 17 percent of Americans reported being influenced to purchase a food because it is advertised as being "green" or "eco friendly."

According to the USDA, a **sustainable food system** is one that 1) satisfies human food needs; 2) enhances environmental quality and natural resources; 3) makes the most efficient use of nonrenewable resources; 4) sustains the economic viability of farmers; and 5) enhances the quality of life for farmers and the society in which they live.[3] The prevailing industrial agriculture system has delivered enormous gains in the yield of product, but at what cost? America's industrialized agriculture system is using topsoil, fossil fuel, and water—all precious

natural resources—at unsustainable rates. Many food systems are currently degrading the environment, reducing **biodiversity**, and polluting the air and water.[4] Striving for more sustainable food systems is our best shot at making sure future generations will have access to the food needed to sustain life and health.

The Academy of Nutrition and Dietetics (formerly the American Dietetic Association) developed a model that provides a useful way to think about the factors that contribute to a sustainable food system (see **Figure 1**).[5] Sustainability involves every sector of the food system, from farmer to consumer, and is influenced by many factors. For example, economics, social expectations, and political forces may influence what crops farmers grow and what resources are used to grow them. Any factor that leads to the abuse or unnecessary waste of inputs, especially nonrenewable natural resources, may prevent sustainability. Many of the current practices involving the use of soil, energy, and

water in industrial agriculture provide cause for concern.

Concerns about the Use of Soil

More than 99 percent of the food you eat is produced on land, compared to less than one percent that comes from the sea. All land crops are dependent upon the thin layer of topsoil that sits atop the earth's crust.[6] Topsoil is regenerated from decaying plants, microorganisms, and animals and provides the oxygen and nutrients needed to support the growth of hearty plants. Plants in turn contribute to the health of the topsoil by providing nutrients back to the soil and roots that help prevent the erosion of topsoil by wind and water. **Figure 2** on the next page shows the complex relationships between plants and they soil they grow in.

Problems arise when the topsoil can't be regenerated and/or is less fertile. When this happens plants cannot grow, the web is severed, and nourishment for all—the animals, microorganisms, and *you*—suffers.[7] Unfortunately, the natural process of regenerating *one inch* of nutrient-rich topsoil takes more than 500 years.[8] Improper agricultural practices that facilitate soil erosion faster than it can be regenerated may disrupt the entire web and food system.[9] For example, overgrazing of land by animals leads to topsoil erosion. This is a growing problem in areas of the world like parts of Africa.

Concerns about Energy Use

Research suggests that almost 16 percent of the total energy consumption in the United States is used in the production, processing, transport, and preparation of our food.[10] As you have read, the use of fossil fuel is costly and the release of carbon dioxide from the burning of it harms the environment. Sustainable food systems use as little fossil fuel in the production and transport of food as possible, which is why eating local foods is one way to support sustainable food systems. Purchasing

Figure 1 Sustainable Food Systems Model

Source: "Sustainable Food System Model" from "Healthy Land, Healthy People: Building a Better Understanding of Sustainable Food Systems for Food and Nutrition Professionals" Copyright © 2007 Alison Harmon, PhD, RD and the ADA Sustainable Food System Task Force, 2007 Academy of Nutrition and Dietetics. Reprinted with permission.

sustainable food system A system that conserves the natural resources and can be maintained indefinitely.

biodiversity Having a wide variety of plant and animal species within an environment.

CONTINUED

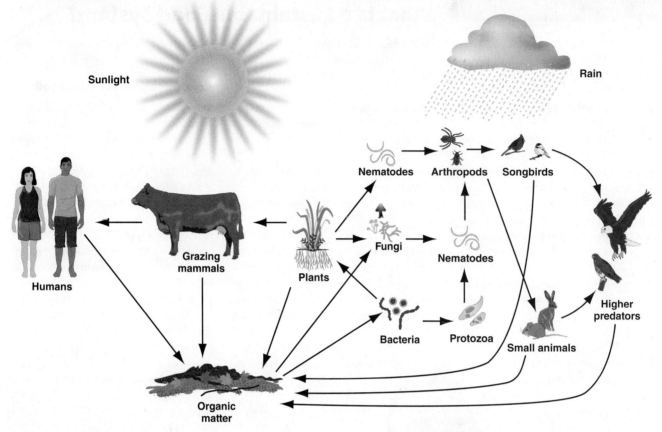

Sunlight

Rain

Nematodes Arthropods Songbirds

Fungi

Nematodes

Grazing
mammals

Plants

Humans

Bacteria Protozoa Small animals

Higher
predators

Organic
matter

Figure 2 The Soil Food Web

Source: Adapted from Bureau of Land Management, "The Soil Food Web." Available at www.blm.gov. Accessed May 2010.

and using energy-efficient refrigerators and ovens is another thing that consumers can do to help reduce the amount of energy needed to store and prepare foods.

Producing chemical fertilizers and pesticides for crops also requires large amounts of fossil fuels.[11] Avoiding these chemicals and using natural fertilizers, such as animal manure, not only cuts the use of fossil fuel, but also can make soil more fertile.[12] Research also shows that crop rotation and other aspects of organic farming result in less soil erosion than nonorganic methods.[13]

Concerns about Water Use

According to the EPA, since the 1950s, the population in America has nearly doubled while our water consumption has more than tripled.[14] Americans, on average, use 100 gallons—about 1,600 full glasses—of water per person each day.[15]

Water shortages in many places are due to the use of ground and surface water for irrigation without consideration of the natural

ecosystem. All plants and animals, including humans, need water to survive, so the potential for water shortage is not only a danger to the environment but also to your health. Conserving water now to ensure a healthy supply in the future makes sense. There are several steps you and/or your family can take to conserve water. Installing water-efficient appliances, including washing machines and dishwashers, helps cut down on water used for daily chores. If all households installed water-efficient appliances, the United States would save more than 3 trillion gallons annually.[16] Low-flow toilets and showerheads can also help save water, as can turning off the tap while washing dishes or brushing your teeth. When it comes to individual water conservation, think of saving water "one gallon at a time."

Being a More Sustainable Food Consumer

If each American set a goal to incorporate three "greener" habits in his or her daily life

over the next year, the reduction in natural resources could be dramatic. Here's an interesting example. Did you know that more energy (as well as land and water) is required to produce a meat-based diet than to produce a plant-based diet?[17] Every pound of animal protein generated from livestock requires approximately 6 pounds of plant protein in the form of feed.[18] Much of the feed fed to animals has to be transported long distances and contributes to energy costs of raising the animal that provides the meat. Choosing to eat less meat, or eating meat from organically and locally grown animals, can also help to support sustainable food systems.

The "How Sustainable Is Your Food Shopping?" Self-Assessment can help you determine if the foods that you purchase were made in a sustainable way. Think about these questions as you plan, shop for, and prepare your next meal and consider following some of the suggestions in the "Go Green" table.

How Sustainable Is Your Food Shopping?

Use the following checklist to assess a food or beverage product before you purchase it. Check the box next to each statement that is true of the product you are considering. The more check marks, the greater contribution the food product makes to a sustainable food system.

❏ The producer or farmer who grew the food is known.

❏ The location where the food originated is known.

❏ The food traveled the least distance possible.

❏ The food is fresh, seasonal, and grown without harming soil, water, or air quality.

❏ The food was raised humanely without synthetic hormones or antibiotics.

❏ The process used to produce the food conserves genetic biodiversity and ecological integrity.

❏ The farm workers, processors, or food-service workers earned a fair wage, worked in safe conditions, and were not exploited in the making of this food.

❏ The nutritional value of the food is maintained and it is free of artificial ingredients.

❏ There were no or low environmental impacts as a result of processing and transporting the food.

❏ The food packaging is minimal, made from renewable resources, and is recyclable.

❏ The label on the food product directs you to find more information. Product labeling is transparent.

❏ The name and any claims of the food product are specific, meaningful, and logical.

❏ The food product has a legitimate and reputable third-party seal or certification.

❏ The local, national, and global implications of this food product are known.

Source: Adapted from Angie Tagtow, MS, RD, LD, "Shades of Green: Looking at the Food System with a Critical Eye" in "Healthy Land, Healthy Food & Healthy Eaters" by A. Tagtow and A. Harmon. Available at University of Wyoming website, 2009. Copyright © 2009 Angie Tagtow and Alison Harmon. Adapted with permission from the author.

Go Green

What You Can Do	How You Can Do It
Purchase locally grown, seasonal foods when possible	Visit the Natural Resources Defense Council for an interactive guide to the seasonal foods available in your area at www.nrdc.org.
Waste not, want not	Don't buy excessive amounts of food at one time. If you can't eat the food that you purchased before it goes bad, consider donating it to a food pantry and/or shelter. Your excess is someone else's dinner.
Eat more plant protein	Go meatless at least one meal a week. For delicious meatless ideas, visit www.meatlessmonday.com.
Plant your own garden	For the ultimate reduction in food miles, plant your produce in your backyard or in containers. To help you develop a green thumb, visit the National Gardening Association's Food Gardening Guide, the ultimate source for information on growing your favorite vegetables, fruits, and herbs, at www.garden.org.
Buy from local farm stands, farmers' markets, and community-supported agriculture (CSA) farms	Shop at local farmers' markets and roadside farm stands to find just-picked fruits and veggies (which will be at their peak nutritional value) for minimal food miles. You can also join a CSA to enjoy weekly or monthly boxes of farm-fresh produce delivered to your doorstep or a local pick-up site. Find local farmers' markets and community-supported farms in your area at http://ams.usda.gov and www.localharvest.org.
Conserve water in your home	➤ Only run the dishwasher when it is full. ➤ Recycle cooled cooking water to water your plants and garden. ➤ Defrost food in your refrigerator rather than under running water. ➤ Scrape rather than rinse your plates before putting them in the dishwasher. Visit the EPA's WaterSense for more ways to conserve water at www.epa.gov.
Conserve energy in your home	➤ Use pots with lids for a shorter cooking time. ➤ Turn off an electric stovetop before the food is cooked and let the residual heat finish the dish.
Buy foods with less packaging	➤ To reduce the waste you throw in the garbage, buy foods in bulk, with less packaging. ➤ Use reusable cloth bags to carry your food home from the market or grocery store. ➤ Recycle food containers. For more tips, visit CalRecycle at www.calrecycle.ca.gov.

What Are the Benefits and Risks of Using Hormones, Antibiotics, and Pesticides in Food Production?

Sometimes farmers use hormones, antibiotics, and pesticides to try to improve the yield of their crops and livestock. Even though these methods are beneficial because they allow farmers to produce more food on less land, introducing these compounds into the food supply may be cause for some concern.

Hormones

Scientists and dairy farmers have known for years that cows injected with a naturally occurring bovine **growth hormone**, also known as bovine somatotropin, produce more milk. Cows injected with a synthetic version of this hormone, **recombinant bovine somatotropin (rbST)**, can produce more milk than untreated cows. The FDA has reviewed the use of rbST in the United States and found no evidence that milk

Cows being raised for beef are often confined to feedlots, where they may be treated with antibiotics to prevent disease transmission, or hormones to facilitate greater weight gain.

from cows treated with rbST is significantly different than milk from cows not treated with rbST nor that it poses any long-term health threat to humans.[48] Other consumer groups, including Health Canada (the FDA equivalent in Canada) continue to question the long-term safety of the use of rbST in the food supply. There is some concern that milk from cows treated with rbST may contain higher amounts of other hormones as well and the consequences of humans consuming milk with these higher amounts of hormones is unknown.[49] Currently, the FDA does not require that manufacturers include information about whether or not cows that produced the milk in their products were treated with rbST. Other hormones are sometimes used to increase the amount of weight that cattle gain and the amount of meat that they produce.[50] An additional concern is that the runoff from sewage sludge containing these hormones can reach surface waters and may interfere with the reproductive cycle of wildlife.[51]

Antibiotics

Antibiotics, whether injected into food-producing animals or given via feed, are used for three purposes: (1) to treat animals that are sick; (2) to preventively treat animals that may be at risk of being sick (for example, if one animal becomes ill, the entire herd may be given antibiotics); and (3) to promote growth by keeping the gut and intestines healthy. When antibiotics are used for the first two purposes, they are used for a relatively short period of time. This isn't true when antibiotics are used for the third purpose. Low-dose antibiotics are sometimes put in animal feed, because animals that consume this feed gain more weight than animals fed antibiotic-free feed.

Pathogenic bacteria such as *Campylobacter*, *E. coli* O157:H7, and *Salmonella* are commonly found in the gastrointestinal tracts of animals without making them sick. However, when animals are chronically given antibiotics, **antibiotic-resistant bacteria** strains can sometimes grow in their intestinal tracts. If a human contracts

growth hormone A protein-based hormone that stimulates cell growth and reproduction in humans and animals.

recombinant bovine somatotropin (rbST) A synthetically made hormone identical to a cow's natural growth hormone, somatotropin, that stimulates milk production. Also known as rbGH (recombinant bovine growth hormone).

antibiotics Drugs that kill or slow the growth of bacteria.

antibiotic-resistant bacteria Bacteria that have developed a resistance to an antibiotic such that they are no longer affected by antibiotic medication.

a foodborne illness from this animal food source, treatment with the same antibiotic that was used in the feed, which killed the bacteria in the past, may no longer be effective. One example of this occurred as follows: In the late 1980s, the antibiotic fluoroquinolone was successfully used to treat *Campylobacter,* which is commonly found in chickens. In 1995, this antibiotic began to be used regularly in poultry. Shortly after, doctors began seeing patients with *Campylobacter*-induced foodborne illness whose infections were resistant to treatments with fluoroquinolone.[52]

The National Antimicrobial Resistance Monitoring System–Enteric Bacteria (NARMS) has been established, which is a joint effort between the Food and Drug Administration's Center for Veterinary Medicine (FDA CVM), the U.S. Department of Agriculture (USDA), and the Centers for Disease Control and Prevention (CDC), to monitor this important issue of preventing antibiotic-resistant bacteria strains in animals and humans.[53] The Center for Veterinary Medicine has developed guidelines for the judicious use of antibiotics in food-producing animals in order to minimize the development of antibiotic-resistant bacteria.[54] The National Organic Program prohibits the use of antibiotics in organic-certified livestock.[55] The risk of finding antibiotic-resistant bacteria was found to be 33 percent higher in livestock grown with conventional methods than in organically grown livestock.[56]

Pesticides

You have probably been handling **pesticides** for years and not even realizing it. If you use a disinfectant to control the mold in your shower, bug spray to ward off flesh biters on muggy summer nights, or a flea collar to keep your pet itch free, you're making use of chemicals that destroy or mitigate pests. These chemicals are collectively known as pesticides. Whereas pesticides can cause harm if consumed in high enough quantities, some more so than others, they are needed to control disease-causing organisms and pests that threaten or affect the food supply. By using pesticides on agricultural crops, food plants can flourish and produce a hearty bounty. This enables farmers to offer affordable crops to consumers.

Types of Pesticides

Several different types of pests can diminish or destroy crop yields, including insects, microorganisms (bacteria, viruses), fungi (mold), and rodents (rats and mice). Pesticides used to kill weeds are called **herbicides**, whereas those used on microorganisms are **antimicrobials**. **Fungicides** are used to destroy fungi.

Pesticides can be chemically or biologically based. Biologically based pesticides, such as **biopesticides** and sex pheromones, use materials from animals, plants, bacteria, and some minerals. Biopesticides are less toxic than chemically based pesticides, generally affect only the targeted pest, and often decompose relatively quickly, minimizing the potential for environmental pollution. For example, baking soda (sodium bicarbonate) can be diluted with water and sprayed onto plants to inhibit the growth of fungi without any known risk to humans or birds. The most commonly used biopesticides are strains of the bacterium *Bacillus thuringiensis*, or *Bt*, which kills developing insects.[57] Insect **sex pheromones** can be used to interfere with the mating of certain pests. Scented extracts from plants can also be used to lure and then trap insects. Biopesticides are typically safer than chemical pesticides; however, for biopesticides to be effective the user must understand exactly which pests are the problem.[58]

Chemically based **organophosphates** make up about half of all the insecticides used in the United States and are used on fruits, nuts, vegetables, corn, wheat, and other crops, as well as on commercial and residential lawns and plants.[59] These pesticides affect the nervous systems of the pests they destroy, but also affect other animals and even humans. The EPA (Environmental Protection Agency) banned residential

pesticides Substances that kill or repel pests such as insects, weeds, microorganisms, rodents, or fungi.

herbicides Substances that are used to kill and control weeds.

antimicrobials Substances or a combination of substances, such as disinfectants and sanitizers, that control the spread of bacteria and viruses on nonliving surfaces or objects.

fungicides Chemicals used to kill mold.

biopesticides Substances used to kill pests that are derived from natural materials such as animals, plants, bacteria, and certain minerals.

sex pheromones Naturally occurring chemicals secreted by one organism to attract another; used as a biopesticide to control pests by interfering with their mating.

organophosphates A group of synthetic pesticides that adversely affect the nervous systems of pests.

Farmers use pesticides on food crops to diminish the damage from pests.

use of most organophosphates, but some are still used in agriculture for the production of fruits and vegetables. Organophosphates degrade relatively quickly when exposed to light and oxygen, but small quantities can still be detected in the U.S. food supply. All pesticides, including organophosphates, are continually re-reviewed by the EPA to ensure their safety.

Risks and Regulation of Pesticides

The problem with pesticides, especially chemically based pesticides, is that they can cause unintended harm to animals, the environment, and even humans. The American bald eagle almost became extinct due to a now-banned pesticide that was ingested by the eagles.[60] Research has shown that some pesticides, depending upon their level of toxicity and how much is consumed, may cause serious health problems, such as cancer, birth defects, and nerve damage, in humans.[61] Infants and young children are especially susceptible to the ill effects of organophosphates as their internal organs are continuing to develop.[62]

To prevent potential harm to consumers, pesticide use is heavily regulated in the United States. Though some pesticides continue to be allowed by the National Organic Program, the risk for pesticide contamination is 30 percent lower for organically grown produce compared with conventionally grown produce. However, there is little difference in the risk of going over the maximum allowed limits between organic and conventional methods methods.[63] The EPA evaluates all food pesticides with a four-part **risk assessment** to ensure that they can be used with "a reasonable certainty of no harm." The risk assessment process includes the following:

1. *Hazard identification* identifies the potential hazards or ill effects that may develop after exposure to a specific pesticide in animals.
2. *Dose-response assessment* determines the dose at which these ill effects occur in animals and then uses this information to identify a potentially equal dose in humans.
3. *Exposure assessment* determines all the ways that a person could typically be exposed to that pesticide. Exposure could occur orally when you eat food or drink water, or by inhalation or absorption through your skin when you are using household disinfectants or gardening pesticides around your home.
4. *Risk characterization* uses the information obtained in the first three steps to determine the overall risk of the pesticide.[64]

Because there are potential differences between the effects of a pesticide on animals and its effect on humans, as well as differences among humans, the EPA builds in a margin of safety when determining the health risk. An extra tenfold safety factor is added (unless there is evidence that a lesser margin of safety is adequate) to protect the most vulnerable groups, such as infants and children, who could be exposed to the pesticide. Before a pesticide can be registered by the EPA, the manufacturer must submit it to more than 100 health and environmental tests, at a cost of over $150 million, and it takes approximately nine years before being approved.[65] Thus, much effort goes into ensuring that the foods you eat are safe, yet affordable, in order for you to reap their health benefits and minimize any known risks. **Figure 12.7** shows what you can do to reduce the pesticides on the foods that you consume.

The EPA also conducts environmental risk assessments to make sure that a pesticide doesn't pose any risk to wildlife and the environment. If it does, or is even thought to hurt the environment, acceptable levels are determined to prevent any known harm.[66]

Alternatives to Pesticides

Rather than use pesticides, some growers, including those certified as organic farmers, use an approach called **integrated pest management (IPM)** to manage pests in

risk assessment The process of determining the potential human health risks posed by exposure to substances such as pesticides.

integrated pest management (IPM) Alternative to pesticides that uses the most economical and the least harmful methods of pest control to minimize risk to consumers, crops, and the environment.

Figure 12.7 Reducing Pesticides in Food

Wash: Thoroughly wash and scrub all fresh fruits and vegetables with a vegetable brush with sturdy surfaces under running water to dislodge bacteria and some of the pesticide residue. Running water is more effective for this purpose than soaking the fruit and vegetables.

Peel and trim: Peeling fruits and vegetables and tossing the outer leaves of leafy vegetables helps reduce pesticides. Trimming the visible fat from meat and the fatty skin from poultry and fish helps reduce some of the pesticide residue that remains in the fatty tissue of the animal.

Eat a variety of foods: Eating a variety of foods reduces your chances of being overexposed to any particular pesticide.

their crops. The goal of this approach is to use the most economical methods to control pests while causing the least risk of harm to the consumer, the crops, or the environment. The IPM method includes preventive measures, such as rotating crops and choosing pest-resistant strains of crops, to reduce the likelihood of attracting pests. When these measures aren't adequate to control pests, biologically based alternatives, such as biopesticides or the introduction of natural predators (specific insects that eat the unwanted pests), may be used to curtail an infestation. If all these methods don't control the spread of the pests, targeted spraying of chemically based pesticides is then considered.[67] Note that foods grown using IPM methods typically aren't labeled, so the consumer can't easily spot them in the supermarket.

The Take-Home Message Hormones, antibiotics, and pesticides are used to increase food production, but may impact the environment and human health. Cows treated with synthetic growth hormone produce more milk than untreated cows. The FDA says milk from cows treated with synthetic hormone is safe, but some question its long-term safety for humans. Animals treated chronically with antibiotics may grow to be larger than untreated animals, but may develop antibiotic-resistant strains of bacteria that may be passed on to humans through foodborne illness. Pesticides control the growth of disease-causing organisms and pests that threaten the food supply. The FDA, USDA, and EPA tightly regulate the use of pesticides, but some pose risks to humans if consumed at high doses.

What Are the Risks and Benefits of Using Biotechnology in Agriculture?

Another strategy of the food industry to maximize food production is the use of **biotechnology**. Although this sounds like a high-tech term, humans have actually been manipulating the genes of food products for generations. In years past, they did

biotechnology The application of biological techniques to living cells, which alters their genetic makeup.

The apples of today are larger and sweeter than their ancestors, thanks to hundreds of years of selective breeding.

this through selective breeding. In fact, the fresh apples that you eat today look nothing like their small, sour Asian ancestors. Because apples have been intentionally grown (or cultivated) by humans for thousands of years, apple farmers have had plenty of time to crossbreed different versions of the tree to produce more desirable offspring. For example, if one tree produced large, fleshy apples with thinner skins, and another produced smaller, sour apples with thicker skins, an ancient apple farmer might have bred the two in the hope of producing a tree with large, fleshy, hardy fruit. This process is a form of selective **plant breeding**.

Historically, farmers have crossbred plants by trial and error, hoping for the best results and using the best offspring to further breed more desirable plants. Farmers in the United States and around the world routinely use selectively bred plants to create bigger and better produce and disease-resistant crops, and to increase crop yields. In fact, you would be hard pressed to find many fruits and vegetables today that aren't a product of genetic modification through this type of selective plant breeding. In the past two centuries, as scientists learned more about DNA and its workings, and how to manipulate it, the process of genetic modification has become faster and more controlled.

Genetic Engineering

Today's versions of bioengineered foods include new techniques, such as **genetic engineering (GE)**, to alter the genetic makeup of an organism. In this type of bioengineering, the exact gene or genes from the DNA of a plant cell are isolated and inserted into the DNA of another cell to create the genetically modified product (**Figure 12.8**).

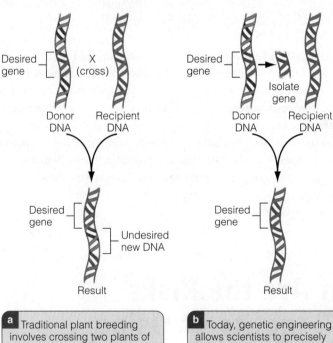

a Traditional plant breeding involves crossing two plants of the same species to produce DNA with more desirable traits. The process is imprecise, however, and achieving the desired result could take years.

b Today, genetic engineering allows scientists to precisely manipulate the DNA from plants and impart desirable qualities from one plant to its offspring much more quickly.

Figure 12.8 Plant Breeding versus Genetic Engineering

plant breeding A type of biotechnology in which two plants are crossbred to produce offspring with desired traits from both.

genetic engineering (GE) A biological technique that isolates and manipulates the genes of organisms to produce a targeted, modified product.

This cutting and splicing of genes into the DNA of another cell is called *recombinant DNA* (rDNA) technology. Organisms that have been genetically engineered to contain both original and foreign genes are called **genetically modified organisms (GMOs)**. These GMOs are used to grow GE plants that produce GE foods.

Genetically modified crops were first grown in the early 1990s, and by 2007, 140 million acres of bioengineered crops, including corn, cotton, canola, and soybeans, had been planted in the United States. In fact, 85 percent of the soybeans grown in the United States in 2004 were genetically modified.[68] Bioengineered crops are being cultivated in 23 countries worldwide.[69] While some individuals and groups have expressed concern about the use of genetically modified foods (sometimes calling them "frankenfoods"), proponents believe that GMOs can be good for the environment, help feed countries that have an inadequate food supply, improve the quality and quantity of foods available all year round, and create new uses for plants in industries such as pharmaceuticals and manufacturing. In the words of former President Jimmy Carter, "Responsible biotechnology is not the enemy; starvation is."[70]

The original purpose of using biotechnology in plants was to reduce the amount of pesticides used on food crops. For example, the bacterium *Bacillus thuringiensis*, mentioned previously and found naturally in soil, produces a toxin that is poisonous to certain pests but not to humans or other animals. When the gene for this toxin is inserted into a crop plant, the plant becomes resistant to these pests. Some corn crops in the United States contain the *Bt* gene, which makes them resistant to some insect pests. The use of biotechnology to reduce the use of pesticides is working—the total amount of pesticides has declined by 2.5 million pounds by using bioengineered crops.[71]

First-generation bioengineered products were also created to improve a crop's tolerance to herbicides. With an herbicide-resistant version of a desired crop, a farmer can spray herbicide over a field to kill a variety of weeds without harming the crop. Approximately 93 percent of soybeans grown in the United States in 2013 were varieties that had been genetically modified to be herbicide resistant.[72]

Bt corn has been genetically engineered to produce a protein that is toxic to the larva of the European corn borer, the most damaging insect pest of corn in North America.

The second-generation bioengineered products were designed to provide consumers with added nutritional value as well as other attributes, such as increasing the crop's shelf life. For example, "golden" rice contains foreign gene segments that encode the rice grain to make beta-carotene and to stockpile extra iron. This "super" rice, if planted by farmers and accepted by consumers in Southeast Asia, could help eliminate the epidemic of vitamin A and iron deficiency in children there.[73] Bioengineered, high-oleic-acid oil is less prone to becoming rancid, and thus is more stable when used for frying foods.[74]

Third-generation bioengineered products hold promise in the pharmaceutical, environmental, and industrial arenas. In fact, the first such bioengineered product created for commercial use was human insulin (needed by diabetics) produced by genetically engineered *E. coli*. Other examples are delivering vaccinations for the hepatitis B virus in potatoes and lettuce.[75]

Concerns and Regulations Associated with GE Foods

While many professional organizations, such as the American Medical Association, the National Academy of Sciences, the World Health Organization, and the Society

genetically modified organisms (GMOs) Organisms that have been genetically engineered to contain both original and foreign genes.

of Toxicology, have all supported agricultural and biotechnology, some opponents of bioengineered foods fear that biotechnology can cause the creation of "Frankenstein" foods.[76] Though bioengineering in agriculture is tightly regulated, there are many unanswered questions regarding the development of GMOs. For example, in many cases we are not aware of how GMOs may change or impact the natural environment or ecological balance of the ecosystems in which they are allowed to grow. Other concerns have arisen about the production of plant toxins, the introduction of new allergens into the human food chain, changes in the nutrient content and creation of new substances in foods, the production of unsafe animal feed, and horizontal transfer of genes to humans as they consume these products. **Table 12.5** lists some of the concerns and regulatory safeguards that are in place to address these issues. In addition, some people have ethical and religious concerns about introducing GMOs into the U.S. food supply.

Bioengineered foods in the United States are regulated by the same three government agencies that regulate pesticides: the FDA, USDA, and EPA. The FDA's role is to ensure that foods are safe to eat, and the USDA's role is to ensure that the plants are safe to grow. The EPA's role is to ensure that foods will not negatively affect the environment, for example, that the gene for any pesticide, such as that for *Bt* toxin, inserted into a plant is safe and won't hurt the environment. Though these agencies work together to ensure the safety of these foods, the FDA has the overall authority to remove any food that doesn't meet the same high safety standards that are set for its conventionally grown equivalent.[77] Currently, labeling of GMO foods is not mandated by the FDA because the FDA says that in most cases there is little scientific evidence that GE foods are different in nutritional content than conventional foods. This continues to be a current topic of controversy. The FDA does require labeling if the food is significantly different than the conventional food in the nutrients it provides, if it introduces an allergen that consumers may not expect, or if it contains a toxicant. Though not mandated to do so, some companies choose to include information about genetic engineering on their food labels.

Table 12.5

Concerns and Regulations for GE Foods

Concern	FDA Regulation
Undesirable genetic modification	To avoid the creation of undesirable products, all genes used must not have prior evidence of encoding any harmful substances. The genes must also be stably inserted into the plant in order to avoid any rearranging of genetic information that would produce an undesirable substance.
Introduction of allergens	GE foods must be monitored for food allergens. Protein encoded from common allergen food sources (such as milk, eggs, fish, tree nuts, and legumes) should be presumed to be allergens and should be labeled as such on the GE food.
Excessive level of toxins	GE foods should not contain natural toxins at levels that are higher than those found naturally in plants.
Changes in nutrients	All GE foods should be monitored to assess unintentional changes in the nutrient levels in the plants and their ability to be utilized in the human body as compared with their conventional counterparts.
Creation of new substances	If the genes that are introduced into plants encode substances that are different in structure and function than those normally found in foods, these substances would have to be approved by the FDA, as would any other food additive. However, if these substances are GRAS (generally recognized as safe) or "substantially equivalent" to substances that already exist in foods, they do not require premarket approval from the FDA.
Unsafe animal feeds	Because a single plant type may be the predominant food source in an animal feed, all GE animal feeds must meet the same strict safety standards that are in place for food that is grown for humans.

Source: FDA, "Policy for Food Developed by Biotechnology," 1995. Available at http://vm.cfsan.fda.gov; J. H. Maryanski, "Bioengineered Foods: Will They Cause Allergic Reactions?" 1997. Center for Food Safety and Applied Nutrition. Available at www.cfsan.fda.gov; FDA, "Plant Biotechnology for Food and Feed. FDA's Biotechnology Policy." 2009. Available at www.fda.gov. Accessed January 2010; C. Bruh, "Position of the American Dietetic Association: Agricultural and Food Biotechnology." *Journal of the American Dietetic Association* 106 (2006): 285–293.

The public seems to be warming up to bioengineered foods because of their health benefits and improved quality. In a survey of 1,000 Americans, almost 50 percent of them stated that they would likely purchase bioengineered foods if the food provided less unhealthy saturated fat and *trans* fats as well as fewer pesticides, yet only 23 percent knew that bioengineered foods have already entered the United States.[78]

The Take-Home Message Both plant breeding and genetic engineering are types of biotechnology that alter the genetic makeup of an organism's cells to create a new plant with more desirable traits. Genetically modified corn and soybeans are more resistant to pests and have been grown in the United States since the early 1990s. Genetic modification of plants has also led to the development of rice that is a good source of beta-carotene and vegetables that deliver a vaccination. Some consumers worry that genetically modified plants may alter the natural environment or ecological balance of the food system in unpredictable ways.

How Does Food Policy Affect the Foods Available to You to Buy and Consume?

Farmers and food companies aren't the only ones responsible for keeping food safe, healthy, available, and sustainable. Several government agencies, including the USDA, FDA, the Environmental Protection Agency (EPA), and the Federal Trade Commission (FTC), regulate the food industry and set national food and nutrition policy (see Table 12.6). These policies have a dramatic effect on the foods available to you

Table 12.6

Who Oversees the Food Supply?

Agency	Responsible for
United States Department of Agriculture (USDA)	Monitoring agriculture and food production and ensuring safe and accurately labeled meat, poultry, and eggs. The USDA enforces tolerances for pesticide residues in meat, poultry, and eggs set forth by the EPA.
Food and Drug Administration (FDA)	Overseeing domestic and imported foods except for meat and poultry products. Ensuring that these foods are safe, sanitary, nutritious, wholesome, and honestly and adequately labeled. Overseeing food-processing plants and approval and surveillance of food-animal drugs, feed additives, and all food additives. FDA enforces tolerances for pesticide residues that are set by the EPA.
Environmental Protection Agency (EPA)	Protecting you and the environment from harmful pesticides. EPA is responsible for the safe use of pesticides and fertilizers, as well as food-plant detergents and sanitizers on foods and in the environment. It establishes the safe tolerances for pesticide residues in or on food commodities and animal feed.
Animal and Plant Health Inspection Service (APHIS)	Protecting against plant and animal pests and disease
National Marine Fisheries Service (NMFS)	Overseeing a voluntary seafood inspection for quality and a grading program
Centers for Disease Control and Prevention (CDC)	Surveillance and investigation of human and animal diseases
Federal Trade Commission (FTC)	Regulating food advertising
Department of Health and Human Services (DHHS)	Protecting the health of and providing essential human services to Americans, including those who are less able

Source: Data from Committee to Ensure Safe Food from Production to Consumption, Institute of Medicine, and National Research Council, "Ensuring Safe Food: From Production to Consumption." Washington, D.C., The National Academies Press (1998).

Food policy can drive the food industry. The recommendation for Americans to consume more whole grains caused food manufacturers to increase their production of whole-grain products.

to purchase and consume. Sometimes policy drives the production of healthier foods and sometimes it doesn't.

Food Policy Can Help Encourage Food Producers to Create Healthier Products

In 2005, the Department of Health and Human Services (DHHS) and USDA's *Dietary Guidelines for Americans* not only encouraged the public to eat more whole grains, but for the first time in history made a specific recommendation that at least half of daily grain servings should come from whole grains. This policy released a tidal wave of reaction in the food industry. Manufacturers quickly scrambled to increase the production of good-tasting whole-grain products to keep up with consumer demand. In 2006, soon after the release of the *Dietary Guidelines*, whole-grain bread sales increased more than 200 percent.[79] This increased demand caused a change in crop production at the farm level, as farmers switched from growing crops such as red winter wheat to a different variety that can be used in processed whole-grain food products.[80] In essence, the farmers had to catch up to the demands of consumers.

Interestingly, this industry shift of offering more whole-grain products to the consumer also had an impact on the American diet. The availability of a slew of newly reformulated whole-grain products enabled even the less motivated, less health-conscious consumers to more easily incorporate this recommendation into their lives. Americans increased their whole-grain consumption by 20 percent from 2005 to 2008, but most people still get far fewer whole grains than recommended.[81]

In fact, according to a report published by the Whole Grain Council, only 11 percent of the grains that Americans eat are whole grains.[82] Nevertheless, it appears that food consumers may have increased whole grains in their diet without even realizing it, as their favorite reformulated products continued to taste good.[83] This is an example of how food policy and food production can work together to make it easier for the food consumer to consume healthy foods.

Food Policy Can Lead to Relabeling and Reformulating without Providing a Healthier Food Product

Unfortunately, changes in nutrition and food policy can also sometimes result in less-than-healthy consequences. For example, the food labeling policy on *trans* fats caused some manufacturers to reformulate their products in ways that did not benefit the consumer. In 2003, based on the research documenting the heart-unhealthy attributes of *trans* fat, the FDA issued a policy for the mandatory labeling of *trans* fats on the Nutrition Facts panel of food labels. Major food manufacturers, such as Kraft, Campbell's, and Frito-Lay, reformulated some of their cookies, crackers, chips, and bakery items to remove *trans* fat. While some of these products were reformulated to replace the *trans* fats with healthy vegetable oils, others were reformulated using heart-unhealthy saturated fats, such as butter and palm oil.[84] As a result, the products ended up containing little or no *trans* fat, but often containing other varieties of unhealthy fats. Also, the removal of the *trans* fats from the cookies, crackers, chips, and other bakery items enabled manufacturers to boast "0 grams *trans* fats" on the food label (as long as the product contains < 0.5 gram of *trans* fat per serving). This kind of labeling can lead to a "halo effect" on these foods, leaving consumers with the impression that these no-*trans*-fat foods are good for them because they contain no *trans* fats, and they need not worry about the consequences of eating them. In reality, these foods may or may not be foods that contribute to a healthy and balanced diet.[85]

Let's face it, when you take the *trans* fats out of the doughnut, you are still left with a doughnut. The doughnut didn't magically morph into an apple. No matter what type of fat is in the bakery item, few Americans have room in their diets for a lot of cookies or pastries, especially when they displace much-needed fruit or vegetables.

What Are the Politics of the Food Industry?

The intersection of food policy (set by various government agencies) and the interests of the food industry (made up of hundreds of companies that produce, distribute, and sell food) can often yield interesting results. The National School Lunch Program, which you will learn more about in Chapter 15, is one example. This program supplies American children with reduced-price, nutritionally regulated lunches via the standard school cafeteria. Who supplies the schools with the massive amounts of food needed for this nationwide program? The answer is the federal government, the nation's biggest food consumer.

Government Programs Are Food Consumers

In addition to the $8 billion the government provides to help cover the costs of the meals for the National School Lunch Program, about $1 billion in free food commodities, including poultry, eggs, fruits, vegetables, peanut butter, and dairy products, also make their way to school cafeterias. School districts can request these commodities to help keep the cost of the school lunch at an affordable rate. Where do these commodities come from? They are the surplus, unsold foods grown and raised on our U.S. farms. The government buys these foods from the farmers and gives them to schools.[86]

In addition to the National School Lunch Program, other U.S. programs, such as the Summer Food Service Program, the Emergency Food Assistance Program, and the Child and Adult Care Food Program, all have access to these commodities.[87] In 2008, the U.S. Congress passed a Farm Bill, which, among other things, reauthorized the distribution of surplus commodities to these special nutrition projects. The advantage of this arrangement is twofold: The government provides a market for farmers' surplus foods while ensuring that American citizens get fed.

Food Lobbyists Exert Influence

Food companies and other members of the food industry often voice their preferences to government agencies and politicians via individuals known as *lobbyists*. A lobbyist is paid to meet with and persuade politicians to vote on pending legislation in a direction that would favor the interests of the party the lobbyist represents. All lobbyists must be registered, make the parties that they represent publicly known, and report how they are funded.[88]

Sometimes research can prompt food companies and businesses to spring food lobbyists into action. In 2009, a report published in the *New England Journal of Medicine* by a group of prominent researchers claimed that the consumption of sugar-sweetened beverages was linked to an increased risk of obesity, diabetes, and heart disease among Americans. The researchers' solution: to tax these beverages to dissuade consumption.[89] They also recommended that monies generated from the tax could be used to support childhood nutrition and obesity prevention programs, and fund health care in general. The makers of these sweetened beverages, supermarket companies, fast-food restaurants, and other organizations with a vested interest in maintaining high sales of sugary beverages such as the National Corn Growers Association (whose products create high-fructose corn syrup, the main sweetener found in soft drinks), spent more than $20 million on lobbying efforts to convince Congress to block this not-so-sweet proposal.[90] Will sweetened beverages be taxed? Only time will tell. But you can be sure that businesses that will be impacted by this tax aren't going to leave Washington, D.C., without a fight.

The Take-Home Message Several government agencies, including the FDA, USDA, and EPA, regulate the food industry and set national food and nutrition policy. The U.S. government is also a food consumer, and it purchases large amounts of surplus commodities that are used in various national food and nutrition programs. Large food companies often hire lobbyists to persuade politicians about food policy.

The term "natural," when used on the packaging of meat and poultry, indicates that no artificial ingredients were added and that the product is minimally processed.

How Do You Know How Foods Were Produced?

As you just read, many factors, including decisions made by farmers, food companies, grocery stores, and government agencies, will affect the foods that are available to you. At the end of the day, though, you get to choose which food products to buy and consume. Knowing and understanding the terms found on food labels or posted near foods can help you select the healthiest, most environmentally friendly options.

Label Terms Provide Information about How Foods Were Produced

Both the FDA and the USDA are the consumer watchdogs for food labeling, and labeling of animal food products is essential when it comes to determining how the animals were fed, raised, and treated. The label terms for meat and poultry are determined and defined by the USDA. The following list includes terms often found on prepackaged meat products:[91]

➤ *Certified.* Indicates that the USDA has evaluated a meat product for class, grade, or other quality characteristics (for example, "Certified Angus Beef").
➤ *Fresh Poultry.* Poultry that has never had an internal temperature below 26°F.
➤ *Free Range.* Producers must demonstrate that the animal has been allowed access to the outdoors.
➤ *Kosher.* Meat and poultry products that were prepared under the supervision of a rabbi.
➤ *Natural.* The food contains no artificial ingredient or added color and is only minimally processed; that is, using processes that do not fundamentally alter the raw product. The label must explain the use of the term natural (such as "no added colorings or artificial ingredients").
➤ *No Hormones (pork or poultry).* Hormones are not allowed in raising hogs or poultry. Therefore, the claim "no hormones added" cannot be used on the labels of pork or poultry unless it is followed by the statement, "Federal regulations prohibit the use of hormones."
➤ *No Hormones (beef).* The phrase "no hormones administered" may be approved for use on the label of beef products if no hormones were used in raising the animals.
➤ *No Antibiotics.* May be used on labels for meat or poultry products if the animals were raised without antibiotics.

In addition to these common terms, the use of the term "organic" is appearing on increasing numbers of products on supermarket shelves.

Understand the Meaning of the Term *Organic*

As more consumers become concerned about how their food is grown and raised, the popularity of **organic** foods has increased, with sales rising from $11 billion in 2004 to an estimated $27 billion in 2012, which is more than double the annual growth rate for all food sales.[92] In fact, a broader segment of the U.S. population is buying organic foods and organic food options are becoming more and more prevalent even in mainstream supermarkets and warehouse- or club-style stores. More than one-third of Americans buy organic products at least monthly.[93]

This growing interest in organic foods prompted the USDA to develop National Organic Standards (NOS) in 2002. The NOS provide specific criteria that food producers must meet during production, handling, and processing to label their products organic. As a result of these standards, you can be confident that if the food is labeled as organic, it was produced and handled using specific guidelines and certified by a USDA-accredited inspector.[94]

Organic farming involves growing crops without the use of *some* synthetic pesticides, synthetic fertilizers, bioengineering, or irradiation. Contrary to popular belief, organic foods are not necessarily free of all pesticides. Organically grown crops may come into contact with chemicals due to drift from wind and rainwater. Also, though organic farmers use IPM, and grow more disease- and pest-resistant plants, sometimes synthetic pesticides and biopesticides may still be needed. The National Organic Program has created the National List of Allowed and Prohibited Substances that identifies substances that can and cannot be used in organic crop production. According to the list, several synthetic pesticides, such as insecticidal soaps, are allowed, while some natural substances, such as ash from the burning of manure, cannot be used in organic farming.[95] For animal food products, only antibiotic-free or growth hormone–free animals can be used to produce organic meat, poultry, eggs, and dairy foods.[96]

You can identify organically produced foods in your supermarket by looking for the USDA Organic seal (**Figure 12.9**). Foods that display this seal or otherwise state that they are organic must contain at least 95 percent organic ingredients. However, organic food producers can choose whether or not to display this seal, so it may not be on all such products. There are other label claims and standards for foods that are 100 percent organic, or that use organic ingredients. **Table 12.7** on the next page describes the standards that organic label claims must meet.

There is little scientific evidence supporting the idea that organic foods are nutritionally superior to those grown in a conventional manner.[97] However, organically grown food is less likely to have detectable levels of pesticides or antibiotics (for animal food products) than conventionally grown food.[98] Studies have shown that organic farming can help the environment by reducing pesticide use, energy use, and greenhouse emissions, and by increasing biodiversity in fields.[99] Unfortunately, organic foods tend to cost more than those that are conventionally grown. For example, organic produce can cost anywhere from 5 to 70 percent more than conventional foods. The price isn't likely to decline any time soon, as the demand for organic food is currently higher than the supply. Another issue to consider when choosing organic foods is where they were grown. The USDA currently has trade arrangements with India, Israel, Japan, and New Zealand to allow organic foods from these countries to enter the U.S. market.[100] Keep in mind that if your organic food has to travel from New Zealand, the food miles that it travels may negate some of the environmental benefits described earlier.[101] Finally, organic foods are not always healthy foods. There are plenty of processed foods that contain high amounts of salt, sugar, and fat that are made with some organic ingredients, and therefore bear the organic label.

Figure 12.9 The USDA Organic Seal
Foods that are labeled or advertised with the USDA Organic seal must contain at least 95 percent organic ingredients.

organic Being free of chemical-based pesticides, synthetic fertilizers, irradiation, and bioengineering. A USDA-accredited certifying inspector must certify organic foods.

Table 12.7

Various Levels of Organic

If the label says "100% Organic"

Then: The food must be composed entirely of organic ingredients. *Note:* These foods cannot contain sulfites and must declare the certifying agent. The USDA Organic seal may be displayed.

If the label says "Made with Organic Ingredients"

Then: The food contains at least 70 percent organic ingredients.

If the label says "Organic" and/or displays the USDA Organic seal

Then: The food contains at least 95 percent organic ingredients.

If the label says nothing about organic claims

Then: The food contains less than 70 percent organic ingredients.

The Take-Home Message Food labels provide information that help consumers know how their food was produced. Foods labeled as organic certified are grown without the use of some synthetic pesticides, synthetic fertilizers, bioengineering, or irradiation. Organically produced animal foods are produced without antibiotics or hormones. The National Organic Standards provide specific criteria and guidelines for the production, handling, processing, and labeling of organic foods, as well as mandatory certification by an accredited inspector. Organic foods usually cost more than conventionally grown foods, and there is little scientific evidence that they are more nutritious than conventionally grown foods, though they may have lower levels of pesticides and antibiotics than do conventionally grown foods.

POINTS OF VIEW

Are Large Scale Organics Truly Organic? More and more people are seeking out and purchasing organic foods, and the increasing demand for organic products has motivated numerous large retailers to stock and sell these items. But is organic food from large chain stores the same as organic food from your local farmers' market? Does the production of organic food on a large scale defeat the purpose? Take a look at both sides of the issue and decide for yourself.

yes

- According to federal legislation, all foods that carry the USDA Organic label must meet strict standards that are set and enforced by the USDA.[1]

- Consumers now have more choice when it comes to organic products. Market growth in the organic sector averaged 17 percent a year between 1995 and 2006, dramatically increasing the number of organic food products flowing along the supply chain.[2]

- Organic foods are usually more expensive than their nonorganic counterparts, and national retailers can use their large-scale buying power to make such products more affordable to more people. For example, an informal survey of organic milk at Denver area grocery stores found that Wal-Mart's label was 8 percent to 35 percent cheaper than other brands.[3]

- Hundreds of thousands of pounds of agricultural chemicals are *not* being used because of the large shifts to organic production.[4]

- Interest in organic food has also led to growth in small cooperative farms and farmers' markets, and more interest in buying local.[5] As this trend continues, it will hopefully yield improved dietary habits as well as environmental benefits.

no

- Large-scale retailers may sometimes misuse the organic label. Wal-Mart's store brand organic milk, for example, comes from Aurora Dairy in Boulder, Colorado. In 2007, federal investigators found that Aurora had "willfully" violated 14 tenets of the organic standards, including confining their cattle to feedlots, instead of grazing, and bringing thousands of illegal conventional cows into their organic operation.[6]

- Taking organic large scale means making it more industrial. Big supermarket chains find it easier, and therefore more profitable, to buy from big farms selling lots of one thing (monoculture). This trend comes at the expense of small farmers and of some of the founding principles of organic farming, including its commitment to polyculture and to social and economic sustainability.[7]

- Not all organic foods are healthy foods. Processed foods like tortilla chips and cookies may be labeled organic, but they are still nutritionally dubious.[8]

- Organic foods, or the resources needed to produce them, are often shipped in from overseas, where they are produced more cheaply. This threatens the business of small, local, organic producers who may not be able to compete on price.[9]

what do you think?

1. Has the large-scale growth of the organic food industry been helpful or harmful to consumers in general? What about to the environment? **2.** Does the term "organic" mean the same thing today that it did a decade ago? **3.** What is the likely difference between an organic food purchased at a farmers' market and one purchased at a large grocery store?

1 Food Advertising and Marketing Affects Your Food Choices

The food industry spends large amounts of money on marketing and advertising its products, often to target audiences. The most heavily advertised foods are often the least nutritious.

2 Whole Foods and Ingredients Used to Make Processed Foods Come from Farms

Only 2 percent of the American public are farmers and most farms in the United States are small and family operated. Farming is a type of agribusiness, a sector that encompasses how foods are developed, processed, distributed, and purchased. The major crops grown in the United States are corn, soybeans, and wheat, and the major animals raised for food are cows, pigs, and chickens. Many of the crops grown in the United States are used to feed the animals that are raised for food. The United States participates in both the import and export of foods.

3 Resources Used to Grow and Harvest Food Affect the Environment

Many natural resources are used when growing crops and raising animals for food. Natural resources (such as land and water) are used internally to produce foods and externally to move these food products from the farm to the consumer (such as fossil fuels and other forms of energy). By-products that are produced during food processing can negatively affect the environment. Locally grown foods use fewer external resources to reach consumers than do non–locally grown foods.

4 Food Additives, Chemical Enhancers, and Pesticides Play a Role in Food Production and Safety

Hormones, antibiotics, and pesticides are used to increase the yield of animal foods and crops. The FDA, USDA, and EPA regulate the use of these products but some people have concerns over the long-term safety for humans when products from animals and plants treated with these products are consumed by humans. In addition, contamination of water supplies by these products may harm the environment.

5 Biotechnology Is Used to Alter the Genetic Makeup of Plants

Genetically modified corn and soybeans, developed using a type of biotechnology known as bioengineering, have been grown in the United States for several years. Biotechnology may lead to the development of plants that have more desirable traits than the original, such as rice that is a good source of beta-carotene. Some consumers worry that genetically modified plants may alter the natural environment or ecological balance of the food system in unpredictable ways.

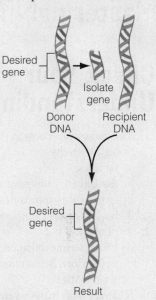

Desired gene

Isolate gene

Donor DNA   Recipient DNA

Desired gene

Result

6 Food Policy Affects the Foods That Are Available to You to Buy and Consume

Several government agencies, including the FDA, USDA, and EPA, regulate the food industry and set national food and nutrition policy. The U.S. government is also a food consumer, and it purchases large amounts of surplus commodities that are used in various national food and nutrition programs. Large food companies often hire lobbyists to persuade politicians about food policy.

7 Label Terms Can Help You Know How Food Was Produced

Foods labeled as organic certified are grown without the use of some synthetic pesticides, synthetic fertilizers, bioengineering, or irradiation. Organically produced animal foods are produced without antibiotics or hormones. Organic foods usually cost more than conventionally grown foods, and there is little scientific evidence that they are more nutritious than conventionally grown foods, though they may have lower levels of pesticides and antibiotics than do conventionally grown foods.

Terms to Know

- food consumers
- food industry
- farm
- agribusiness
- locavore
- community-supported agriculture (CSA)
- sustainable food system
- growth hormone
- recombinant bovine somatotropin (rbST)
- antibiotics
- pesticides
- integrated pest management (IPM)
- biotechnology
- genetic engineering (GE)
- genetically modified organisms (GMOs)
- organic

MasteringNutrition™   Build your knowledge—and confidence—in the Study Area of MasteringNutrition with a variety of study tools.

Check Your Understanding

1. The majority of farms in the United States are run by
   a. families.
   b. the United States government.
   c. large private companies.
   d. large overseas companies.
2. Agribusiness is
   a. a food business that occurs only in the Corn Belt section of the United States.
   b. a very large business entity.
   c. the combination of agricultural and business entities that impacts how foods are developed, processed, distributed, and purchased.
   d. only comprised of large conglomerates.
3. Most of the corn grown in the United States is _____.
   a. used in the National School Lunch Program
   b. used to feed animals
   c. used to make high-fructose corn syrup
   d. sold to local markets and eaten by Americans
4. Farmers may receive subsidies for growing which of the following products?
   a. corn
   b. carrots
   c. watermelon
   d. strawberries

5. Americans eat more _____ than any other animal food.
   a. poultry
   b. beef
   c. pork
   d. soy
6. Which of the following is an example of a challenge that can deplete internal natural resource(s) in the production of food?
   a. fossil fuel used to transport food from the farm to consumers
   b. soil erosion
   c. carbon dioxide gas emission from trucks transporting food from the farm to the supermarket
   d. the amount of money it takes to purchase food by the consumer
7. A sustainable diet is
   a. a diet that can sustain your life.
   b. a diet that is financially sustainable.
   c. a diet that contains foods that meet your nutrient and health needs and can be sustained for a long time without negatively impacting the environment for future generations.
   d. a diet that a family can sustain.
8. A food lobbyist works for
   a. the government.
   b. the interests of all food consumers.
   c. a food company or organization that has a vested interest in the outcome of food policy.
   d. only those in health care.

9. You are in the supermarket shopping for cereal and find a package of raisin bran that bears the USDA Organic seal. You can be assured that in this cereal
   a. 100 percent of the ingredients are certified organic.
   b. only ingredients that were grown without the use of any pesticide, even if some of the ingredients are not organic certified, are used.
   c. at least 95 percent of the ingredients are certified organic.
   d. at least 50 percent of the ingredients are certified organic.
10. The process of applying biological techniques to a living cell in order to alter its DNA and create a desired trait is called
    a. biology.
    b. biotechnology.
    c. bioterrorism.
    d. biochemistry.

Answers

1. (a) The majority of farms in the United States are family farms.
2. (c) Agribusiness refers to the entire industry of agricultural and business entities that produce most of our food supply. Small farms and small food companies are part of agribusiness, as are large corporate farms and food company conglomerates.

3. (b) Eighty percent of the corn grown in the United States is used to feed animals, not humans.
4. (a) U.S. farmers may be eligible to receive subsidies (that is, money) from the government when they grow specific crops such as corn, wheat, and soybeans. Farmers that grow a variety of fruits and vegetables are typically not eligible for government subsidies.
5. (a) Poultry is the predominant type of animal food consumed by Americans. Soy is a plant food.
6. (b) Soil erosion depletes internal natural resources that are needed to produce food. Carbon emission from trucks that transport food is considered an external natural resource.
7. (c) A sustainable diet is a healthy diet for you and for future generations.
8. (c) While it would be nice to think that a food lobbyist works for the interests of all food consumers, in reality the lobbyist works for a company or organization that has an interest in the outcome of food policy. A lobbyist's job is to persuade government officials to vote in a direction favorable to the companies or organizations the lobbyist represents.

9. (c) Only foods made with at least 95 percent organic ingredients can display the USDA Organic seal. If a product is made with at least 70 percent organic ingredients, an organic statement can be made, but the seal cannot be displayed. Some pesticides may be used to grow organic ingredients.
10. (b) Biotechnology, through either plant breeding or bioengineering, can alter a cell's genetic makeup to create a desirable trait and genetically modified product.

Web Resources

- Looking to help the environment? Pick five easy changes you can make that are environmentally friendly, by visiting "Pick Five for the Environment" at www.epa.gov
- For more on living green, visit "Learn the Issues" at www.epa.gov
- To help you pick environmental products while shopping, visit "While Shopping" at www.epa.gov
- For help in finding local farms, visit www.localharvest.org

1. **False.** Although you may think you are indifferent to food advertising, it likely has a significant impact on your food decisions. See page 454.

2. **True.** Would you be surprised to learn that food doesn't originate in your grocer's freezer? Go to page 455 to read where it really comes from.

3. **True.** Small family farms comprise the majority of farms in the United States. Learn more on page 456.

4. **True.** Although corn is the number-one food crop grown by American farmers, the majority is used to feed animals and not humans. Find out more about factors that impact what plants and animals U.S. farmers grow on page 459.

5. **True.** Food that's produced locally will require less fossil fuel for distribution and transport than food that's shipped a great distance. To find out more, turn to page 464.

6. **False.** The U.S. government currently does *not* require label information to indicate whether or not animals were treated with synthetic hormones. Turn to page 470 to learn more about this interesting point of controversy.

7. **True.** Genetically engineered forms of corn and soybeans have been the mainstay in the United States since the 1990s. Find out more about bioengineering on page 475.

8. **True.** Food policy may influence the products that farmers grow. This was the case for whole grains. Learn more about this story on page 478.

9. **False.** Organic foods are not necessarily pesticide free. To learn more, turn to page 481.

10. **False.** Although organic foods do have some advantages when it comes to preserving the environment and introducing fewer pesticides and antibiotics into the food supply, there is little scientific evidence that they are more nutritious than foods that were grown using traditional methods. Learn more on page 481.

13

Food Safety and Technology

True or False?

1. The most common type of **virus** that causes foodborne illness is *Salmonella*. ⓉⒻ p. 491

2. Foods that smell bad will give you **foodborne illness** if you consume them. ⓉⒻ p. 491

3. Washing your hands for 10 seconds under **running water** is necessary to reduce your chances of getting foodborne illness. ⓉⒻ p. 500

4. Grilled chicken that is pink in the middle is never **safe** to eat. ⓉⒻ p. 502

5. The **temperature** for your refrigerator should be set at 40°F or below. ⓉⒻ p. 503

6. Freezing foods kills **bacteria**. ⓉⒻ p. 503

7. **Leftovers** that have been stored in the fridge for a week will still be safe to eat. ⓉⒻ p. 504

8. Food **irradiation** makes food radioactive. ⓉⒻ p. 510

9. As long as the **expiration date** hasn't passed, packaged food is always safe to eat. ⓉⒻ p. 511

10. *E. coli* is considered a bacterium that could be used for **bioterrorism**. ⓉⒻ p. 517

See page 521 for the answers.

After reading this chapter, you will be able to:

1. Name the pathogens and other agents that cause foodborne illness.

2. Identify the four Cs that can prevent foodborne illness.

3. Discuss how the food supply is protected in the United States.

4. Explain the role that food additives play in food production.

5. Explain what are toxins and chemical agents in the food supply.

6. Explain how food can play a role in bioterrorism.

Although the United States enjoys one of the safest food supplies in the world, millions of Americans still suffer annually from some type of **foodborne illness**. In fact, cases of foodborne illness cause about 76 million illnesses, 325,000 hospitalizations, and 5,000 deaths per year, and the medical costs and lost wages associated with just one type of illness, that due to the bacterium *Salmonella,* are estimated to top $1 billion per year.[1] These illnesses often result in distressing gastrointestinal symptoms such as cramps, diarrhea, and vomiting.

Efforts to prevent foodborne illnesses have led to the development of extensive **food safety** practices and guidelines. Several government agencies work together to ensure the safety of foods from the farm to the table. Food safety is also the practice of minimizing your risk of contaminating foods as you store and prepare them in your kitchen. There are several strategies consumers can use to make sure the foods they eat and serve are safe. We'll find out more about all of these in this chapter.

What Causes Foodborne Illness?

Most people do not question the safety of the foods they eat until there is a national food-safety recall or they experience firsthand the effects of foodborne illness. A classic example of emerging public awareness occurred in 1906 with the publication of *The Jungle,* by Upton Sinclair. The descriptions of the unsanitary conditions in the Chicago meat-packing plants,[2] which among other atrocities included rodent droppings and body parts making their way into consumer-bound meat products, horrified the public. Meat sales plummeted as a result of consumer fear about eating contaminated foods. Due to the enormous public health risks associated with these unsanitary practices, President Theodore Roosevelt incited the United States Congress to pass the Meat Inspection Act.[3] The act demanded a continuous inspection of all meat-processing plants by the United States Department of Agriculture.[4] Other improvements in food safety, such as pasteurization of milk, safe canning, and disinfection of water supplies, conquered the common foodborne illnesses of the era. Before long, these food-safety precautions resulted in positive effects on the nation's health. By 1920, instances of one foodborne illness, typhoid fever, had declined by about two-thirds, and by the 1950s it had virtually disappeared in the United States.[5]

Today, advances in production and distribution, new food sources, and the growing volume of food imports continue to present challenges to maintaining a safe food supply. Prior to the advent of convenience foods like bagged lettuce, a contaminated head of lettuce might have affected only one family. Now, however, contaminated lettuce may be processed with thousands of other heads and placed into bags that end up in thousands of homes. This could lead to large outbreaks, making the source difficult to pinpoint.[6] Prevention of such outbreaks remains a public health priority for governmental agencies.

Even with stringent regulations in place, however, bouts of foodborne illness still happen. Let's take a look at the causes of foodborne illness.

Foodborne Illnesses Are Often Caused by Pathogens

To contract a foodborne illness, you must eat foods or beverages that contain one or more harmful agents. The agents can be disease-causing microbes, also known as

pathogens, such as viruses, bacteria, parasites, fungal agents, or prions. Pathogens can be found in the stool or droppings of infected humans and/or animals. Drinking water that has been contaminated with infected droppings, or putting anything in your mouth (such as food or your hands) that has been in contact with fecal matter, are common ways to become infected. This route of transmission is known as **fecal-to-oral transmission**, and this is why people should always wash their hands after using the bathroom and before preparing foods. Eating raw or undercooked meat, poultry, or fish from an infected animal can also expose you to pathogens.

Pathogenic viruses and bacteria are the most common causes of foodborne illness in the United States. Parasites, fungi, and prions are less common causes. Let's begin with the various viruses that can make you sick.

Viruses

The term **virus** denotes a microscopic infectious agent that contains chromosomes that carry genetic information (DNA or RNA) for their own replication. Viruses must have a living **host**, such as a plant or an animal, to survive. When an individual eats a contaminated plant or animal as food, the pathogen can invade the cells of the stomach and intestinal walls. The virus can then cause the cells' genetic material to start producing more viruses, ultimately leading to illness.[7]

The most common type of virus that causes foodborne illness is the **norovirus**. In fact, norovirus is the most common cause of foodborne illness in the United States (see **Table 13.1**).[9] Norovirus are named after the original strain of the virus, Norwalk virus, which was the cause of **gastroenteritis** (*gastro* = stomach, *entero* = intestines, *itis* = inflammation), or the "stomach flu," in a school in Norwalk, Ohio, in 1968.[8] (Note: The stomach flu is not the same as influenza (flu), which is a respiratory illness caused by the influenza virus.)

Another foodborne virus, hepatitis A, caused a multistate outbreak among young concertgoers in 2003.[10] The concerts were often multiday events at campgrounds that had less than optimal sanitary conditions. The unofficial food vendors were the attendees themselves. Many of the concert attendees traveled from concert to concert. This type of living environment, in which people are living, cooking, and eating in unsanitary conditions, practicing poor hand washing and hygiene, and traveling from state to state, can create a breeding ground for an outbreak. Approximately 300 attendees had to be vaccinated against hepatitis A.

Bacteria

If you were to swab your kitchen sink right now and look at the results under a microscope, you would find that there are about 16 million **bacteria** living on each square centimeter (less than half an inch) of your sink. Whereas viruses need a host to survive, bacteria can flourish on both living and nonliving surfaces. They live on your computer mouse, keyboard, body, clothing, and in every room of your house. In fact, there are hundreds of different types of bacteria on your skin alone.[11] The majority of bacteria around you are harmless, and some are even essential, such as the ones in your intestine that synthesize biotin and vitamin K. Bacteria are also used to make some of the foods we enjoy, like yogurt, cheese, and buttermilk.

A few bacteria are harmful, however, and can cause food spoilage or illness. The bacteria that cause food spoilage are not the same as those that cause foodborne illness. Food spoilage bacteria cause the deterioration of the quality of food. For example, a carton of sour milk and that forgotten Chinese takeout in the back of your refrigerator have gone "bad" because of food spoilage bacteria. Though most individuals will not become seriously ill after eating spoiled foods, these items can cause nausea and shouldn't be eaten. (Luckily, the less-than-pleasant odor of sour milk or spoiled food usually leads to it being thrown away.) In contrast to spoiled foods,

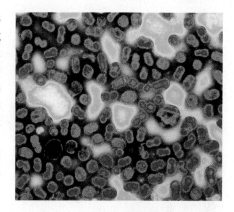

Viruses, such as the hepatitis A virus shown here, need a host to survive and multiply.

foodborne illness Sickness caused by consuming contaminated food or beverages. Also known as foodborne disease or food poisoning.

food safety Guidelines and procedures that help keep foods free from contaminants.

pathogens Collective term for disease-causing microorganisms (microbes). Includes viruses, bacteria, and parasites. The most common source of foodborne illness.

fecal-to-oral transmission The spread of pathogens by putting something in the mouth that has been in contact with infected stool. Poor hygiene, such as not washing hands after using the bathroom, can lead to this type of contamination.

virus A microscopic organism that carries genetic information for its own replication; can infect a host and cause illness.

host A living plant or animal (including a human) that a virus or parasite infects for the sake of reproducing.

norovirus The most common type of virus that causes foodborne illness. Noroviruses can cause gastroenteritis, or the "stomach flu." Also known as Norwalk-like viruses.

gastroenteritis Inflammation of the stomach and intestines.

bacteria Single-celled microorganisms without an organized nucleus. Some are benign or beneficial to humans, while others can cause disease.

Table 13.1

Pathogens That Cause Foodborne Illness

Microbe	Where You Find It	How You Can Get It	What You May Experience	Treatment
Viruses				
Norovirus	In the stool or vomit of infected individuals	Fecal-to-oral transmission; eating ready-to-eat foods or drinking liquids contaminated by an infected person; eating contaminated shellfish; touching contaminated objects and then putting hands in mouth	Watery diarrhea, nausea, vomiting, flulike symptoms; possible fever. Can appear 12 to 48 hours after onset and last 12 to 60 hours. Typically not serious	Symptoms usually abate without treatment; fluid replacement may be necessary to treat dehydration due to vomiting and/or diarrhea.
Hepatitis A (HAV)	In the stool of infected individuals	Fecal-to-oral transmission; eating raw produce irrigated with contaminated water; eating raw or undercooked foods that have not been properly reheated; drinking contaminated water	Diarrhea, vomiting, muscle aches, jaundice, inflammation of the liver that can appear 30 days after incubation. Can last 2 weeks to 6 months	Treatment of symptoms only. Vaccination is the most effective means of preventing HAV transmission among persons at risk for infection.
Bacteria				
Campylobacter jejuni	Intestinal tracts of animals and birds, raw milk, untreated water, and sewage	Drinking contaminated water or raw milk; eating raw or undercooked meat, poultry, or shellfish	Fever, headache, and muscle pain followed by diarrhea (sometimes bloody), abdominal pain, and nausea. Appears 2 to 5 days after eating; may last 2 to 10 days. Guillain-Barré syndrome may occur.	Almost all persons infected with *Campylobacter* recover without any specific treatment. Patients should drink extra fluids as long as the diarrhea lasts. In more severe cases, antibiotics such as erythromycin and quinolones can shorten the duration of symptoms if given early in the illness.
Clostridium botulinum	Widely distributed in nature in soil, water, on plants, and in the intestinal tracts of animals and fish. Grows only in environments with little or no oxygen	Eating improperly canned foods, garlic in oil, vacuum-packaged and tightly wrapped food	Bacteria produce a toxin that causes illness by affecting the nervous system. Symptoms usually appear after 18 to 36 hours. May experience double vision, droopy eyelids, trouble speaking and swallowing, and difficulty breathing. Fatal if not treated immediately.	The respiratory failure and paralysis that occur with severe botulism may require a patient to be on a breathing machine (ventilator) for weeks, plus intensive medical and nursing care. After several weeks, the paralysis slowly improves. If diagnosed early, foodborne and wound botulism can be treated with a botulinum antitoxin.
Clostridium perfringens	Soil, dust, sewage, and intestinal tracts of animals and humans. Grows only in environments with little or no oxygen.	Called "the cafeteria germ" because many outbreaks result from eating food left for long periods in steam tables at improper temperatures or at room temperature. Bacteria are destroyed by cooking, but some spores may survive.	Diarrhea and gas pains may appear 8 to 24 hours after eating; usually last about 1 day, but less severe symptoms may persist for 1 to 2 weeks.	Supportive care; avoid dehydration

Table 13.1 continued

Pathogens That Cause Foodborne Illness

Microbe	Where You Find It	How You Can Get It	What You May Experience	Treatment
Bacteria *continued*				
Escherichia coli O157:H7	Intestinal tracts of some mammals, raw milk, unchlorinated water; one of several strains of *E. coli* that can cause human illness	Drinking contaminated water, unpasteurized apple juice or cider, or raw milk, or eating raw or rare ground beef or uncooked fruits and vegetables	Diarrhea or bloody diarrhea, abdominal cramps, nausea, and weakness Can begin 2 to 5 days after food is eaten, lasting about 8 days Small children and elderly adults may develop hemolytic uremic syndrome (HUS) that causes acute kidney failure. A similar illness, thrombotic thrombocytopenic purpura (TTP), may occur in adults.	Supportive care and avoidance of dehydration Antibiotics should not be used to treat this infection. There is no evidence that treatment with antibiotics is helpful, and taking antibiotics may increase the risk of HUS.
Enterotoxigenic *Escherichia coli* (major cause of traveler's diarrhea)	Intestinal tracts of some mammals and unpasteurized dairy products More common in developing countries	Fecal-to-oral transmission Consuming stool-contaminated water and foods from unsanitary water supplies and food establishments	Diarrhea, nausea, vomiting, stomach cramping, bloating, fever, and weakness	Traveler's diarrhea often resolves without specific treatment; however, oral rehydration is often beneficial to replace lost fluids and electrolytes.
Listeria monocytogenes	Intestinal tracts of humans and animals, milk, soil, leafy vegetables; can grow slowly at refrigerator temperatures	Eating ready-to-eat foods such as hot dogs, luncheon meats, cold cuts, fermented or dry sausage, other deli-style meat and poultry, or soft cheeses; drinking unpasteurized milk	Fever, nausea, vomiting, headache, aches; may take hours to up to 3 months to become ill; may later develop more serious illness in high-risk individuals	When infection occurs during pregnancy, antibiotics given promptly to the pregnant woman can often prevent infection of the fetus or newborn. Babies with listeriosis receive the same antibiotics as adults. Even with prompt treatment, some infections result in infant death.
Salmonella (more than 2,500 types)	Intestinal tracts and feces of animals; *Salmonella enteritidis* in eggs	Eating raw or undercooked eggs, poultry, and meat, raw milk and dairy products, and seafood Can also be spread by infected food handlers	Stomach pain, diarrhea, nausea, chills, fever, and headache usually appear 6 to 72 hours after eating; may last 4 to 7 days.	Supportive care and plenty of fluids. Antibiotics are not usually necessary unless the infection spreads from the intestines.

CONTINUED ▶

Table 13.1 continued

Pathogens That Cause Foodborne Illness

Microbe	Where You Find It	How You Can Get It	What You May Experience	Treatment
Bacteria *continued*				
Shigella (more than 30 types)	Human intestinal tract; rarely found in other animals	Fecal-to-oral transmission by consuming contaminated food and water. Most outbreaks result from eating food, especially salads, prepared and handled by workers with poor personal hygiene.	Disease referred to as "shigellosis" or bacillary dysentery. Diarrhea containing blood and mucus, fever, abdominal cramps, chills, and vomiting begins 8 to 50 hours from ingestion of bacteria; typically resolves in 5 to 7 days.	Persons with mild infections usually recover quickly without antibiotic treatment. However, an appropriate antibiotic may be needed.
Staphylococcus aureus	On human skin and the mucous membranes of the mouth	Consuming foods that were contaminated by being improperly handled. Bacteria multiply rapidly at room temperature.	Severe nausea, abdominal cramps, vomiting, and diarrhea occur 1 to 6 hours after eating; recovery within 1 to 2 days.	The best treatments are rest and plenty of fluids.
Parasites				
Cryptosporidium parvum	In the intestines of humans and animals	Fecal-to-oral transmission; drinking contaminated water, eating contaminated vegetables and fruits	Stomach pains, diarrhea, cramps, fever, and vomiting. Usually goes away without medical intervention in 2 days to 2 weeks.	Adequate fluids are necessary to avoid dehydration. For individuals with weakened immune systems, cryptosporidiosis can be serious, long-lasting, and sometimes fatal.
Cyclospora cayetanensis	Human stool	Fecal-to-oral transmission. Drinking contaminated water, eating contaminated produce	Diarrhea, loss of appetite, bloating, cramps, fatigue	Can be treated with antibiotics
Giardia duodenalis	In the intestines of humans and animals	Fecal-to-oral transmission. Drinking contaminated water, eating contaminated produce	Diarrhea, stomach pains, flatulence	Several prescription drugs are available to treat *Giardia* infection. Although *Giardia* can infect all people, young children and pregnant women might be more susceptible to dehydration resulting from diarrhea and should, therefore, drink plenty of fluids while ill.
Toxoplasma gondii	Develops in cats and passed on through their feces	Fecal to oral transmission. Can also get it from eating raw or uncooked meat and seafood	In pregnant women, can cause miscarriages, and birth defects.	Can be treated with sulfur drugs
Trichinella spiralis	In undercooked or raw meats containing *Trichinella* worms	Eating raw or undercooked contaminated meat, usually pork or game meats	Nausea, vomiting, diarrhea, fever, aching joints and muscles	Safe and effective prescription drugs are available to treat trichinellosis.

Source: Data from the Food and Drug Administration, "Bad Bug Book," 2012. Available at www.fda.gov. Accessed July 2013; Centers for Disease Control and Prevention (CDC), "Diagnosis and Management of Foodborne Illness: A Primer for Physicians," 2004. Available at www.cdc.gov. Accessed July 2013.

health

CONNECTION

The Lowdown on *Listeria*

Listeriosis, the illness caused by the bacterium *Listeria monocytogenes,* seriously affects approximately 1,600 Americans annually, with 14 percent of cases being in pregnant women and 58 percent of cases being in people age 65 or over.[1] In nonpregnant people under 65 years old, 74 percent of cases occur in people with a comprised immune system. *Listeria* can reach the fetus through the placenta, be transmitted to the newborn, and lead to severe problems in the fetus or newborn such as premature delivery, miscarriage, or stillbirth.[2] Older adults and those with a weakened immune system are also at risk for becoming very sick or even dying. Listeriosis is the third leading cause of death from food poisoning in the United States.[3]

Animals can harbor *Listeria,* which leads to contamination of meat and dairy foods. Produce such as cantaloupes and celery can also be contaminated with *Listeria*. Pasteurization will kill *Listeria*, so unpasteurized soft cheeses, such as Camembert, Brie, and blue cheeses, carry a higher risk of containing *Listeria*. Compared with hard cheeses such as Parmesan, these soft cheeses are less acidic and contain more moisture, two conditions that enhance bacterial growth. Even though cooking can also destroy *Listeria*, the lower cooking temperature used during the processing of soft cheeses isn't high enough to destroy this bacterium. Because contamination can occur after processing, many outbreaks have been associated with foods such as hot dogs, deli-style luncheon meats, salami, and paté. *Listeria* can also continue to multiply at refrigerated temperatures.

The following tips can help pregnant women and other higher risk individuals reduce their likelihood of contracting listeriosis:[4]

- ➤ Reheat ready-to-eat luncheon meats, cold cuts, fermented and dry sausage, deli-style meat and poultry products, and hot dogs until they are steamy hot (165°F if you are using a thermometer) to kill any existing bacteria before you eat them. Pregnant women should avoid cold luncheon meats.
- ➤ Don't allow the fluid from hot dog packages to drip on other foods, utensils, and food preparation surfaces. Always wash your hands after handling hot dogs, luncheon meats, and deli meats.

- ➤ Wash your hands with hot, soapy water after touching these types of ready-to-eat foods, or any foods, for that matter. Thoroughly wash cutting boards, dishes, and utensils to avoid cross-contamination.
- ➤ Avoid soft cheeses such as feta, Brie, Camembert, blue-veined (blue) cheese, and Mexican-style cheeses unless they are made with pasteurized milk. (Read the ingredients list to see if pasteurized milk was used.)
- ➤ Avoid unpasteurized milk and foods made from unpasteurized milk.
- ➤ Avoid refrigerated smoked seafood such as smoked salmon (lox or nova style), trout, whitefish, cod, tuna, or mackerel unless they are used in a cooked entrée such as in a heated casserole. You can safely eat canned fish and shelf-stable smoked seafood.
- ➤ Avoid refrigerated paté or meat spreads. You can safely eat canned or shelf-stable varieties.
- ➤ Eat precooked or ready-to-eat perishable items before the expiration date on the food label.
- ➤ Rinse raw produce thoroughly under running tap water before eating, cutting, or cooking. Even if the produce will be peeled, it should be washed first. Scrub firm produce items such as melons with a clean produce brush before cutting into them.

contaminated foods that contain bacterial pathogens may look and smell perfectly fine. Pathogenic bacteria can cause illness in several ways: 1) by directly invading the intestinal wall and multiplying; 2) by producing an infection via a toxin that is absorbed into your blood; or 3) by invading deeper body tissues.[12]

The most common bacteria that cause foodborne illness are *Campylobacter, Escherichia coli (E. coli)* O157:H7, and *Salmonella* (see Table 13.1). Another bacterium, *Listeria monocytogenes*, a less prevalent cause of foodborne illness, is still of concern for individuals most likely to get foodborne illness, especially pregnant women and newborns (see the Health Connection feature "The Lowdown on *Listeria*").

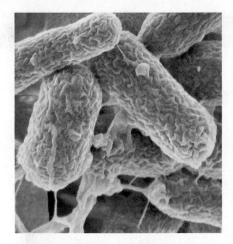

E. coli O157:H7 is the strain of E. coli bacteria that causes the most foodborne illness.

Campylobacter is one of the most common causes of bacteria-related diarrhea in the United States.[13] It is estimated that 1.3 million people are infected annually in the United States.[14] It is found mostly in contaminated water, raw milk, and raw meat products, particularly poultry. Some individuals may develop a rare nerve disease called **Guillain-Barré syndrome** after contracting a *Campylobacter* infection, which causes a person's immune system to attack the body's own nerves and results in temporary paralysis.[15]

Though most strains of *E. coli* are harmless, *E. coli* O157:H7 is estimated to cause more than 90,000 cases of foodborne illness[16] in the United States annually. Contaminated cattle have been the culprits behind most cases of foodborne illness caused by *E. coli* O157:H7. Because bacteria live in the gastrointestinal tract of healthy cattle, they can easily come into contact with the meat of the animal during the slaughtering process. Proper cooking can destroy these bacteria. In people at highest risk for foodborne illness (the very young and the elderly), *E. coli* O157:H7 can cause **hemolytic uremic syndrome** (HUS; *hemo* = blood, *lyti* = destroyed, *uremic* = too much urea in blood), which results in the destruction of red blood cells and damage to and eventual failure of the kidneys.[17]

Another type of *E. coli*, called enterotoxigenic (*entero* = intestines, *toxi* = toxin, *genic* = forming) *E. coli*, is a common cause of **traveler's diarrhea**. Each year, up to 50 percent of international travelers have their trips interrupted by unpleasant intestinal side effects. Traveler's diarrhea is primarily caused by consuming contaminated food or water. People visiting countries where proper sanitation is in question, including some developing countries in Latin America, Africa, the Middle East, and Asia, are at a higher risk of contracting it.[18] See the Table Tips for suggestions on how to avoid traveler's diarrhea.

Reptiles (lizards, snakes, and turtles) often carry *Salmonella*. You should always wash your hands after touching a reptile, and keep reptiles away from small children.

There are several types of *Salmonella* bacteria. *Salmonella enteritidis* is one of the most common varieties found in the United States. An estimated 40,000 incidences of *Salmonella*-related foodborne illness occur annually, and about 400 individuals die yearly due to this bacterium.[19] *S. enteritidis* is most commonly found in raw eggs, so foods that contain raw eggs, such as the dressing on homemade Caesar salad, raw cookie dough, or cake batter, can potentially cause illness.

Parasites

Parasites are microscopic animals that take their nourishment from hosts. They can be found in food and water and are often transmitted through the fecal-to-oral route.[20] The most common parasitic illness outbreaks in the United States have been caused by just a few types: *Crytosporidium parvum, Cyclospora cayatenensis, Giardia duodenalis, Toxoplasma gondii,* and *Trichinella spiralis.*[21]

Crytosporidium parvum, Cyclospora cayatenensis, and *Giardia duodenalis* can be found in contaminated water or food sources, and individuals can also get infected by the fecal-to-oral route. *Toxoplasma gondii* is the third leading cause of death from foodborne illness. It develops in cats and is passed on through their feces. Cleaning a cat's litter box but not washing your hands could cause fecal-to-oral transmission. *Trichinella spiralis* is an intestinal worm whose larvae (hatched eggs) can travel from the digestive tract to the muscles of the body. *Trichinella spiralis* is typically transmitted by eating undercooked or raw pork or wild game. Refer to Table 13.1 for a summary of these parasites and the foodborne illnesses they cause. Consuming undercooked or raw fish can also cause foodborne illness; see the Nutrition in the Real World feature "Sushi: A Cautionary Tale" on page 498.

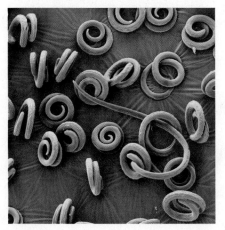

The parasitic roundworm *Trichinella spiralis.*

Prions

Prions are an extremely rare but deadly infectious agent. **Bovine spongiform encephalopathy (BSE)** is a slow, degenerative, and deadly disease caused by an unusual protein called a prion that attacks the central nervous system of cattle. Cattle can become infected by consuming feed that is contaminated with BSE.[22] Individuals who are exposed to BSE by eating beef from infected cattle experience neurological symptoms and damage.

Meat and bone meal given to young calves and cattle that was rendered from contaminated tissues, such as the brain or spinal cord of infected bovines, is the primary source of BSE.[23] In 1986, BSE was first observed in the United Kingdom, where the majority of cases have occurred worldwide.[24] Since then, the FDA has banned the use of contaminated meat and bone meal as feed for all animals, including cattle and sheep, as this type of feed has been identified as a major route of BSE transmission.[25] Also, meat and meat products from animals that were given animal feed that contains animal protein derived from countries that are at risk for BSE cannot be imported into the United States.[26] In addition, the United States Department of Agriculture has established an ongoing BSE Surveillance Program to monitor cattle in the United States.[27]

All of these measures have played a part in limiting the incidences of BSE in the United States to only four cases to date.[28] The contaminant that causes BSE in animals is thought to cause a similar disease, called *variant Creutzfeldt-Jakob Disease (vCJD)*, in humans. vCJD causes a degenerative, fatal brain disorder in humans. Luckily, no one has acquired vCJD from cattle in the United States.[29]

Chemical Agents and Toxins Can Also Cause Illness

Foodborne illnesses can also be caused by **toxins** and chemical agents that occur naturally in foods, such as those found in certain fungi (including poisonous mushrooms) and some fish. Chemical agents, such as antibiotics and pesticides that are intentionally added to foods, can also cause foodborne illness. We'll discuss specific toxins and chemicals later in the chapter.

Some People Are at Higher Risk for Foodborne Illness

Some individuals are at greater risk of developing foodborne illness than others. Older adults, young children, and those with a compromised immune system are more susceptible to the adverse effects of foodborne illness.

In older adults, the age-related deterioration of the immune system increases the risk for foodborne illness. Also, because less acidic gastric juice is produced in the stomach as you age, fewer foodborne pathogens are destroyed during digestion, resulting in greater risk of gastrointestinal infections and their complications. In fact, the elderly are at higher risk of dying of gastroenteritis, which is a severe complication of foodborne illness.[30]

Young children, because of their underdeveloped immune systems, are also more vulnerable to foodborne illness. Children are also smaller and weigh less than adults, and can become sickened by exposure to a smaller quantity of pathogens. Also, their reduced production of stomach acids impedes their ability to destroy harmful bacteria that may be in foods.[31]

Table TIPS

Don't Let Bad Bugs Ruin Your Trip

If you are traveling abroad, look up the country you're visiting on the Travelers' Health website at www.cdc.gov/travel to find out about any *specific* health advisories for that area.

Do not eat raw or undercooked meat or seafood.

Do not consume raw fruits and vegetables unless you peel them. Thoroughly cooked fruits and vegetables should be safe to eat.

Do not consume foods or beverages from street vendors or restaurants that appear to be unsanitary.

Do not drink tap water or use ice made from tap water unless it has been boiled first or treated with iodine or chlorine.

Do not consume unpasteurized milk or other unpasteurized dairy foods.

Source: Data from Centers for Disease Control, "Travelers' Diarrhea." Available at www.cdc.gov.

Guillain-Barré syndrome A condition that can result from a *Campylobacter* infection. It causes the immune system to attack the body's own nerves and can lead to temporary paralysis.

hemolytic uremic syndrome A rare condition caused by *E. coli* O157:H7 that results in the destruction of red blood cells and kidney failure.

traveler's diarrhea A pathogen-induced intestinal disorder experienced by some travelers who visit areas with unsanitary conditions.

parasites Organisms that live on or in another organism, obtaining nourishment from it.

prions Misfolded proteins that can act as disease agents. An abnormal prion protein is the cause of mad cow disease.

bovine spongiform encephalopathy (BSE) A slow, degenerative, and deadly disease that attacks the central nervous system of cattle. Also known as *mad cow disease*.

toxins Poisons produced by living organisms.

Sushi: A Cautionary Tale

Are you looking for a delicious meal that's typically low in calories, high in nutrients, and a good source of omega-3 fatty acids? Well, then, sushi may be for you! But before we declare sushi the next great superfood, we need a reality check. When improperly handled, some types of sushi can be a significant harbor for organisms that cause foodborne illness.

Sushi is a traditional Japanese food that contains vinegared rice, seaweed (*nori*), vegetables (such as cucumber, radish, or avocado), and seafood (for example, tuna, yellowtail, salmon, squid, octopus, shrimp, eel, or roe, among many others). Some types

sushi A Japanese dish of cooked, vinegared rice served with fish or other seafood, vegetables, and/or seaweed.

sashimi A type of sushi that primarily consists of raw seafood, sliced into thin pieces and served with a dipping sauce (soy sauce with wasabi paste) or other condiments (such as fresh ginger).

of sushi are made with vegetables and rice only, or use cooked fish or other seafood, and therefore create less risk of harm. However, sushi that specifically contains raw fish, including the type of sushi known as **sashimi**, carries a greater potential risk.

Raw-fish versions of sushi can sometimes carry illness-inducing parasites, including nematodes (roundworms), tapeworms, and flukes, in the flesh or organs of the fish.[5] These parasites can be killed with heat (by cooking) or cold (by freezing). However, freezing will not kill other pathogens, such as bacteria, so using cooked seafood would more effectively reduce the risk of foodborne illness.[6]

If you make your own sushi at home, make sure that you buy high-quality seafood that is very fresh. Store it in your refrigerator at 40°F or less and eat it promptly. Always wash your hands thoroughly before and after handling it to avoid cross-contamination. Remember that even the rice that has come

into contact with sushi or sashimi can make you sick if you don't keep it refrigerated. When dining out, frequent only restaurants that are reputable and have a chef who has been trained to safely prepare raw seafood.

Pregnant women, young children, and older adults are more susceptible to foodborne illness and should avoid raw seafood—as should anyone with a compromised immune system, including those being treated for cancer, AIDS, diabetes, or kidney disease.[7]

Any condition that weakens a person's immune system can increase his or her risk of contracting foodborne illness. This applies to individuals with HIV, AIDS, cancer, and diabetes.[32] The hormonal shifts seen during pregnancy can affect a pregnant woman's immune system, making her more vulnerable to certain foodborne illnesses such as listeriosis. Often in cases of foodborne illness in pregnancy, the mother is mildly sick, but the risk to the fetus can be great and often can lead to death of the baby.

Individuals in institutional settings (such as nursing homes, hospitals, and schools), where groups of people eat foods from the same source, are also at higher risk of foodborne illness. Improper handling of foods and poor hygiene practices of food-service workers are often the cause of foodborne disease outbreaks in institutional settings. Luckily, there are many ways to reduce your risk of contracting such an illness.

The Take-Home Message Foodborne illness is frequently caused by consuming pathogens in contaminated food or drinks. Viruses and bacteria are the most common causes in the United States, though parasites, prions, and fungal agents can cause some foodborne illness as well. Natural toxins and chemical agents can also cause illness. Certain populations, including the elderly, children, and those with compromised immune systems, are at higher risk of contracting foodborne illness.

Figure 13.1 A Bulk Recipe for Bacteria

A Bulk Recipe for Bacteria

Ingredients:
1. Nutrients (such as those contained in raw meat)
2. Moisture
3. Proper pH
4. Temperature (from 40°F–140°F)
5. Time (over 2 hours)

Directions:
Remove raw meat [nutrients] from the refrigerator. Let the juicy meat [moisture, proper pH] sit on your counter at room temperature (70°F) for more than 2 hours [time]. Watch the meat turn colors—the bacteria are having a field day multiplying.

Serving size:
Makes millions of bacteria, so don't eat or even handle the meat once it's been out for a while. Toss it immediately.

What Can You Do to Prevent Foodborne Illness?

Because foods may harbor some contamination even when you bring them home from the store, the best way to fight foodborne illness is to take action in your kitchen to kill any disease-causing microbes and to prevent them from flourishing. Bacteria, for instance, thrive and multiply in an environment with the following characteristics (see **Figure 13.1**):

➤ *Adequate nutrients.* Protein- and nutrient-rich animal foods, such as raw and undercooked meat, poultry, seafood, eggs, and unpasteurized milk, are the most common havens for bacterial growth.
➤ *Moisture.* Bacteria thrive in moist environments, such as in raw chicken that is sitting in its own juices.[33]
➤ *A change in pH.* Over time, a food's pH may change and allow for the growth of bacteria.[34]
➤ *The correct temperature.* Bacteria multiply most abundantly between the temperatures of about 40°F and 140°F.
➤ *Time.*

Perishable food, such as raw meat, left at room temperature for an extended period can become a feast for bacterial growth.

You can reduce your risk for foodborne illness by practicing proper food-handling and -storage strategies. They're easy to remember as the "four *Cs*" of food safety: cleaning, combating cross-contamination, cooking, and chilling (**Figure 13.2**). Let's look at each of these four steps individually.

Figure 13.2 Fight BAC!
The Fight BAC! symbol sums up the four Cs of keeping food safe in your kitchen: clean, combat cross-contamination (separate raw meats from ready-to-eat foods), cook thoroughly, and chill to a cold enough temperature.

Source: Copyright ©2010 Partnership for Food Safety Education. Reprinted with permission.

cross-contaminate Transfer pathogens from a food, utensil, cutting board, kitchen surface, and/or hands to another food.

Clean Your Hands and Produce

You were probably taught as a child to wash your hands before eating, and guess what? Your parents were right. Hand washing is one of the most important strategies for preventing foodborne illness. In fact, research suggests that nearly 50 percent of all cases of food poisoning can be prevented if everyone correctly washed their hands.[35] However, washing your hands *correctly* is where many people fall short. In a recent study, researchers watched and collected data on over 3,700 individuals who used the bathroom in bars, restaurants, and other public establishments. Their results showed that about 15 percent of the men didn't wash their hands at all, compared with 7 percent of women.[36] When the men did wash their hands, only 50 percent of them used soap, compared with 79 percent of women. Washing your hands *correctly* means wetting them under cleaning running water, adding soap, rubbing your hands together to make lather, scrubbing, rinsing, and then air drying your hands or drying them with a *clean* towel. This whole procedure should take at least 20 seconds.

In addition to your hands, anything that touches your food, such as knives, utensils, and countertops, should be thoroughly cleaned between each use. Cutting boards should be placed in the dishwasher or scrubbed with hot soapy water and rinsed after each use. Nonporous cutting boards made of plastic, marble, and tempered glass are typically easier to keep clean than the more porous wood cutting boards or wooden surfaces. Cracks in a cutting board can become a hideaway for microbes, so try to keep only unbroken boards on hand. You can routinely sanitize your cutting board by flooding it in your sink in a solution of one teaspoon bleach in one quart of water. Let the board sit in the sanitizing liquid for a few minutes to kill the microbes, then rinse it thoroughly.

A moist sponge that contains food scraps and has been left at room temperature is an ideal environment for bacteria. Sponges and dishcloths should be washed often in the hot cycle of your washing machine, preferably with bleach in addition to the soap. Sponges can also be put in your dishwasher or microwave.

Fruits and vegetables should be thoroughly washed under cold running tap water before eating. This will help remove any dirt or microbes on their surfaces. Produce with a firm surface can be scrubbed with a vegetable brush. The Table Tips summarize the cleaning strategies you should apply when preparing food.

You should also keep your refrigerator clean. Research shows that many Americans, especially young adults, neglect to properly clean their refrigerators adequately and often enough.[37] Interestingly, research has shown that the vegetable drawer was found to harbor more bacteria than the meat drawer.[38] The interior of your refrigerator should be cleaned weekly with hot, soapy water and then thoroughly rinsed. Toss out leftovers and perishable foods that are no longer safe to eat.[39]

Combat Cross-Contamination

Produce, especially if it's going to be eaten raw, should never come in contact with raw meat, poultry, or fish during the food preparation process. If these items do come in contact, they could **cross-contaminate** each other, meaning that microbes from one could move to the other and vice versa. Microbe-containing raw meat, poultry, and fish should be kept separate from ready-to-eat foods during food preparation, and stored separately in your refrigerator. You should even keep these products apart on the trip home from the grocery store.

Marinades that are used to tenderize and flavor meats, poultry, or fish shouldn't be used as a serving sauce unless they have been boiled for several minutes to kill any pathogens; instead of reusing, set aside an amount for sauces before marinating.

The knife and cutting board used to cut and prepare raw meat, poultry, or fish shouldn't be used to slice vegetables or bread unless both have been thoroughly cleaned. Your best bet is to use separate cutting boards for meat and nonmeat foods to avoid cross-contamination. Keep one board for slicing raw meats, poultry, and fish, and use another one for cutting fresh produce, breads, rolls, and other ready-to-eat foods. All plates and bowls that have contained raw meats, poultry, and fish should be thoroughly washed before they are reused. For example, at a barbecue, the plate that held the raw hamburgers should *never* be used to serve the cooked burgers unless it has been thoroughly washed between each use. In addition, the tongs that you use to handle the raw meat should be either cleaned or exchanged for a clean pair as the meat cooks.

Soiled dish towels shouldn't be used to dry clean dishes or utensils. A towel that was used to wipe up raw meat juices from a counter or your hands can transfer any microbes from the juices to your clean dishes or utensils. You could easily coat those clean surfaces with a layer of germs. Dishes and utensils should air-dry for the least contamination. **Figure 13.3** illustrates more ways to combat cross-contamination when you prepare food.

Packaging materials like zip-close bags, egg cartons, and takeout containers should be thrown away after use. Even if you clean them, pathogens can cling to these items and contaminate other foods.

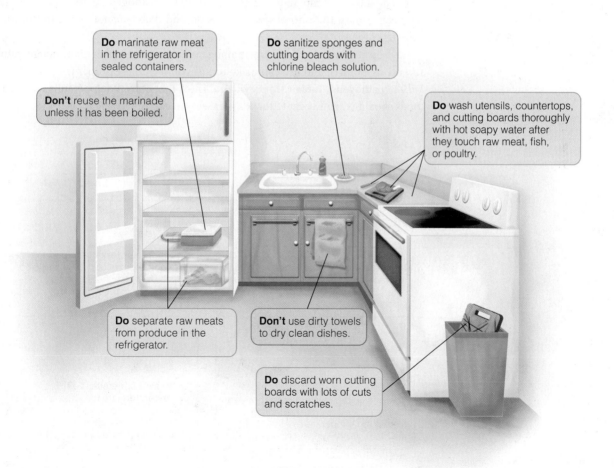

Do marinate raw meat in the refrigerator in sealed containers.

Don't reuse the marinade unless it has been boiled.

Do sanitize sponges and cutting boards with chlorine bleach solution.

Do wash utensils, countertops, and cutting boards thoroughly with hot soapy water after they touch raw meat, fish, or poultry.

Do separate raw meats from produce in the refrigerator.

Don't use dirty towels to dry clean dishes.

Do discard worn cutting boards with lots of cuts and scratches.

Figure 13.3 The Do's and Don'ts of Cross-Contamination

Figure 13.4 Color Is Not Always an Indicator of Whether Meat Is Thoroughly Cooked
A hamburger needs to reach an internal temperature of 160°F to ensure that all foodborne pathogens are killed. Can you tell which of these two hamburgers is safe to eat? (If you answered "a," you're right!)

Cook Foods Thoroughly

Though you may assume that brown meat is cooked meat, this is often not the case. Look at the two hamburger patties in **Figure 13.4**. Which one do you think looks safe to eat? The answer may surprise you. The patty on the bottom looks as though it is more thoroughly cooked than the patty on the top, but it's actually not. Color is not always a proper indication that meat is safe to eat; some lean varieties of beef can remain pink even though they have reached an internal temperature of 160°F, high enough to kill any potential pathogens.

The color of beef is largely determined by *myoglobin*, a protein that provides the purplish-red pigment in meat (and poultry). Whereas meat typically turns from pink to brown during cooking, if it starts out brown, this color change won't occur. Thus, the burger could look "done" when it may still be raw in places. Research has shown that hamburgers can look "well done" while having reached an internal temperature of only approximately 135°F.[40]

Poultry can also remain pink after thorough cooking. Gases in your oven can cause a chemical reaction in the poultry that will give the meat a pink tinge. Because younger birds have thin skins, the gases can react with their flesh more easily and make the meat look pinker than that of older birds. Also, if nitrates and nitrites are added as a preservative, these can give poultry a pink tinge (see the discussion of food additives later in the chapter).[41]

With so many variables in fresh meat and poultry, color is not a reliable indicator that food is safe to eat. The only way to determine if your food has reached an appropriate internal temperature, high enough to kill pathogens, is to use a food thermometer. **Figure 13.5** shows several types of food thermometers you can use when cooking.

When it comes to foodborne pathogens, always remember that though eating raw meats, poultry, and fish can make you *ill*, cooking to the proper temperature will *kill* the pathogens. **Table 13.2** provides a list of the internal temperatures that your foods should reach to ensure that they are safe to eat.

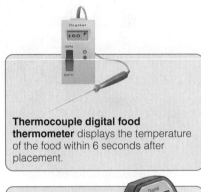

Thermocouple digital food thermometer displays the temperature of the food within 6 seconds after placement.

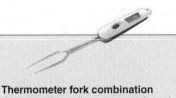

Thermometer fork combination thermometers allow you to stab and check. A device that measures the temperature in the food is located in the tines of the fork.

Thermistor digital food thermometers take approximately 10 seconds to display the temperature of the food on the dial.

Oven-safe bimetallic-coil thermometers are most useful when cooking thick foods such as roasts and turkeys. They are unique, as they can stay in the food during cooking.

danger zone The range of temperatures (between 40°F and 140°F) at which foodborne bacteria multiply most rapidly. Room temperature falls within the danger zone.

Figure 13.5 Food Thermometers
There are several types of food thermometers you can use to tell if your food is safe to eat. The thermometer should be inserted at least ½ inch deep into the food. It should be washed thoroughly after each use, before it is inserted back into food.

Table 13.2

Cook It Until It's Done!

If You Are Cooking This Food	The Food Thermometer Should Reach (°F)*
Ground Meat and Meat Mixtures	
Beef, pork, veal, lamb	160
Turkey, chicken	165
Fresh Beef, Veal, Lamb	145**
Poultry	
Chicken, turkey, whole or parts	165
Duck and goose	165
Fresh Pork	145**
Ham, raw	145**
Ham, precooked (to reheat)	140
Eggs and Egg Dishes	
Eggs	Cook until yolk and white are firm
Egg dishes	160
Leftovers and Casseroles	165

Source: Adapted from "Food Safety Information: Kitchen Thermometers" from USDA's Food Safety and Inspection Service website, 2013.

*The thermometer should be placed in the thickest part of the food item.

**Meat should rest for 3 minutes before consumption to ensure that pathogens are destroyed.

Chill Foods at a Low Enough Temperature

Just as cooking foods to a high enough temperature to kill pathogens is essential, chilling foods at a low enough temperature to inhibit pathogenic growth is also important. Foodborne bacteria multiply most rapidly in temperatures between 40°F and 140°F (or 5°C to 60°C), a range known as the **danger zone**. To keep foods out of the danger zone, make sure that you keep hot foods *hot*, above 140°F, and cold foods *cold*, 40°F or below (**Figure 13.6**). In other words, the lasagna on a buffet table should be sitting on a hot plate or other heat source that keeps its temperature above 140°F, while the potato salad should be sitting on ice that will keep it chilled and at 40°F or below at all times.

Cold temperatures will slow down microbes' ability to multiply to dangerous levels. (The only exception to this is *Listeria*, which can multiply at refrigerator temperatures.) Because of this, the temperature in your refrigerator should be set at or below 40°F. The only way to know if the temperature in your refrigerator or freezer is low enough is to use a thermometer.

The temperature for the freezer should be set at 0°F or below. Food will stay safe in the freezer indefinitely, though its quality may deteriorate. (For example, freezer burn may occur if frozen food is not tightly wrapped and gets exposed to air. Freezer burn causes food to dry out and taste less pleasant, but it isn't harmful.) Most microbes become dormant and are unable to multiply when they are frozen, but they aren't destroyed. In fact, once the frozen foods are defrosted, many microbes can "thaw out" and thrive if given the proper conditions.

Perishables such as raw meat and poultry shouldn't be left out at room temperature (a temperature within the danger zone) for more than two hours. If the air temperature is above 90°F, foods shouldn't be left out for more than one hour.[42] Leftovers

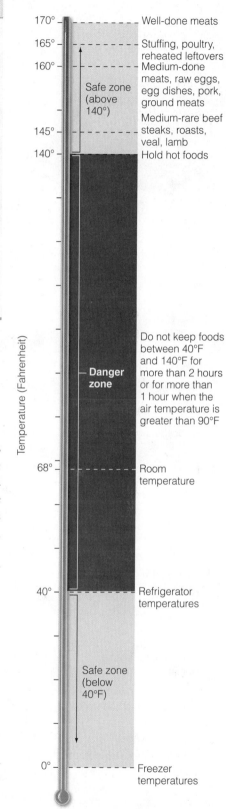

Figure 13.6 The Danger Zone
Bacteria multiply rapidly in the "danger zone," between temperatures of 40°F and 140°F.

should be refrigerated within two hours of being served. Large roasts and pots of soup or stews should be divided into smaller batches in order to cool down more quickly in the refrigerator. If these items have been left in the danger zone for too long or have been mishandled, bacteria can not only grow, but can also produce toxins that are heat resistant. These toxins won't be destroyed even if the food is cooked to a proper internal temperature, and could make you sick if consumed.[43]

Raw eggs and other perishables should not be stored in your refrigerator door, as temperature swings there are more likely. Store perishables in the back of the refrigerator, for a colder and more constant temperature.

Even stored at a proper temperature, foods shouldn't remain in the refrigerator for more than a few days. The rule of thumb is that leftovers can be in the refrigerator at 40°F or below for no more than four days. Here's an easy way to remember this: After *four* days in the refrigerator, leftovers are ready *for* disposal. Raw meats and poultry can be kept for a maximum of two days in the refrigerator. Table 13.3 provides a listing of the storage times for various foods. If you are unsure about the safety of a food, remember this: *When in doubt, throw it out.*

Table 13.3
Keeping It Cool!

Follow these guidelines to keep your perishable foods safe.

Preparation	Type or Description	Refrigerate (40°F)	Freeze (0°F)*
Beef, Lamb, Pork, Veal			
Fresh beef, lamb, veal, and pork	Ground, hamburger, stew meat, variety meat (tongue, liver, heart, kidney, chitterlings)	1–2 days	3–4 months
	Chops, roasts, steaks	3–5 days	4–12 months
	Chops, prestuffed	1 day	Does not freeze well
Leftovers	Including casseroles	3–4 days	2–3 months
Corned beef	In pouch, with pickling juices	5–7 days	Drained, 1 month
Bacon	Bacon	7 days	1 month
Ham (Precooked)			
Fully cooked	Slices	3–4 days	1–2 months
	Half	3–5 days	1–2 months
	Whole	7 days	1–2 months
Canned labeled "keep refrigerated"	Opened	3–5 days	1–2 months
	Unopened	6–9 months	Do not freeze
Vacuum sealed	Unopened, fully cooked, vacuum sealed, dated	"Use by" date	1–2 months
	Unopened, fully cooked, vacuum sealed, undated	2 weeks	1–2 months
Chicken, Turkey, Other Poultry			
Fresh	Chicken breast, prestuffed	1 day	Does not freeze well
	Ground, patties, giblets	1–2 days	3–4 months
	Pieces	1–2 days	9 months
	Whole	1–2 days	1 year

Table 13.3 continued

Keeping It Cool!

Preparation	Type or Description	Refrigerate (40°F)	Freeze (0°F)*
Leftovers	Casseroles	3–4 days	4–6 months
	Chicken nuggets, patties	1–2 days	1–3 months
	Pieces, plain or fried	3–4 days	4 months
	Pieces in broth or gravy	3–4 days	6 months
Eggs			
Fresh	In shell	3–5 weeks	Do not freeze
	Yolk, whites	2–4 days	1 year
Leftovers	Casserole, quiche, omelet	3–4 days	2 months
	Hard-cooked	1 week	Does not freeze well
Opened	Liquid pasteurized eggs, egg substitutes	3 days	Does not freeze well
Unopened	Liquid pasteurized eggs, egg substitutes	10 days	1 year
Sausages, Lunch Meats			
Hard sausage	Jerky sticks, pepperoni	2–3 weeks	1–2 months
Raw sausage	Beef, chicken, pork, turkey	1–2 days	1–2 months
Smoked sausage	Breakfast links, patties	7 days	1–2 months
Lunch meat	Deli-sliced or store-prepared	3–5 days	1–2 months
Opened	Hot dogs	1 week	1–2 months
	Lunch meat—vacuum packed, sliced	3–5 days	1–2 months
	Summer sausage labeled "keep refrigerated"	3 weeks	1–2 months
Unopened	Hot dogs	2 weeks	1–2 months
	Lunch meat—vacuum packed, sliced	2 weeks	1–2 months
	Summer sausage labeled "keep refrigerated"	3 months	1–2 months
Seafood			
Fresh	Fish	1–2 days	3–8 months
	Shellfish	1–2 days	3–12 months
Leftovers	Fish and shellfish	3–4 days	3 months
Miscellaneous			
Frozen dinners and entrées	"Keep frozen"	Unsafe to thaw	3–4 months
Mayonnaise	Commercial, "refrigerate after opening"	2 months	Do not freeze
Other leftovers	Gravy and meat broth	3–4 days	2–3 months
	Pizza	3–4 days	1–2 months
	Soups and stews	3–4 days	2–3 months
	Stuffing	3–4 days	1 month
Salads	Egg, chicken, ham, macaroni, tuna (store-prepared, homemade)	3–5 days	Does not freeze well

Source: USDA Food Safety and Inspection Service, "Cold Storage Chart" from "Keep Food Safe! Food Safety Basics," 2013.
Available at www.fsis.usda.gov. Accessed July 2013.
* Because freezing at 0°F keeps food safe indefinitely, recommended storage times are for quality only.

How Do Your Food-Safety Habits Stack Up?

Take the following quiz to find out.

How Often Do You	Always	Sometimes	Never
Wash your hands before preparing food?			
Scrub your fruits and vegetables under cold, running water before eating them?			
Use an insulated pouch and an ice pack to transport your perishable lunches and snacks?			
Wash your hands after using the bathroom?			
Throw out refrigerated leftovers after four days?			
Chop raw vegetables on a clean chopping board rather than the one you just used for raw meat, fish, or poultry?			
Use a thermometer to determine if the meat or poultry is done cooking?			

Answers

If you answered "Always" to all of the above, you are a food-safety superstar. If you didn't, there's more you can do to reduce your chances of contracting a foodborne illness. This chapter will help!

---

eLearn

Test Your Food-Safety Smarts in the Kitchen

Click your way through this interactive quiz to test your food-safety smarts in the kitchen: www.homefoodsafety.org/quiz.

Practical Nutrition VIDEO

Food Safety with Picnics

Now that you know how to practice food safety in the kitchen, let's take it on the road! Joan shows you how to pack a picnic without bringing along unwanted pathogens. Scan this QR code with your mobile device to access the video. You can also access the video in MasteringNutrition™.

Now that you've read about how cleaning, cooking, chilling, and avoiding cross-contamination can help keep your foods safe, think about how many of these strategies you use in your own kitchen. The Self-Assessment will help you identify areas in which you may need to improve your food-safety habits.

The Take-Home Message Proper food-handling and food-storage strategies, particularly cleaning, combating cross-contamination, cooking, and chilling, can help reduce your risk of foodborne illness. Anything that comes in contact with your foods, including your hands, should be thoroughly washed. You should always wash produce before eating it, and separate raw meats, poultry, and fish, plus any utensils that touch them, from ready-to-eat foods to prevent cross-contamination. A food thermometer is the only accurate way to tell if your cooked food is safe to eat. Perishables should be properly and promptly chilled to minimize the growth of bacteria.

Who Protects Your Food and How Do They Do It?

Foods don't originate in the grocery store. Whether in a bag, box, or bin, nearly every food you buy starts life on a farm. Keeping food safe from the time it's harvested until you buy it is the responsibility of farmers, food manufacturers, and several government agencies. In this section, we'll look at the regulations, food preservation techniques, product dating, and irradiation that are done during various steps between the farm and the table. We'll start by looking at the government agencies that keep an eye on the food supply.

Several Government Agencies Police the Food Supply

Today, several federal agencies share responsibility for food safety in the United States.[44] Table 13.4 lists these agencies and summarizes the roles they each play in safeguarding your foods. This shared responsibility has paid off. There has been a 24 percent decline in foodborne illness since 1996.[45] Much of this decline can be attributed to the **Food Safety Initiative (FSI)**, which was begun in 1997. The FSI coordinates the research, inspection, outbreak response, and educational activities of the various government agencies. The goal of the FSI is to make sure that government agencies work collaboratively.[46]

One FSI program is FoodNet, a combined effort among the Centers for Disease Control and Prevention (CDC), the United States Department of Agriculture (USDA), the Food and Drug Administration (FDA), and other health departments to conduct ongoing active monitoring of specific foodborne illnesses when they arise in the United States. Improved reporting and monitoring systems, as well as outbreak investigations, have helped to quickly identify and trace the causes of foodborne illness.

PulseNet, another foodborne disease watchdog, is a network of government and public health laboratories that specializes in detecting foodborne diseases using **DNA fingerprinting**. Finding similar strains of a bacterium in both a person and a food suggests a common source and potential connection.[47] Once these patterns are determined, they are entered into an electronic database at a local or state health department, maintaining an ongoing collection of DNA fingerprints. These patterns are also sent to the CDC's central computer. If similar patterns emerge at the same time in different states, this could indicate a potential outbreak. Once a suspicious foodborne illness outbreak is reported, several government agencies work together to contain the disease.

The *E. coli* O157:H7 outbreak in spinach that occurred in the fall of 2006 provides one example of how these multiple agencies work together to identify and contain an outbreak. First, the CDC alerted the FDA of an outbreak of illness due to *E. coli* O157:H7 that spanned 26 states in the United States. PulseNet used DNA fingerprinting to determine that the strain of *E. coli* was the same in all those infected. The suspected food was bagged raw spinach grown in California. The CDC issued an official health alert about the outbreak, and the FDA advised consumers to stop eating raw spinach. Before it was over, more than 200 people were infected, and more than half of them were hospitalized. Three individuals died and 31 developed hemolytic uremic syndrome from the infection. However, the swift, coordinated action of these

The FDA, CDC, and USDA worked together to combat an outbreak of *E. coli* O157:H7 in 2006 that was traced to bagged prewashed spinach.

Table 13.4
Who's Policing the Food Supply?

Agency	Responsible for
USDA Food Safety and Inspection Service (FSIS)	Ensuring safe and accurately labeled meat, poultry, and eggs
Food and Drug Administration (FDA)	Ensuring the safety of all other foods besides meat, poultry, and eggs
Environmental Protection Agency (EPA)	Protecting you and the environment from harmful pesticides
Animal and Plant Health Inspection Service (APHIS)	Protecting against plant and animal pests and disease

Source: Data from Food and Drug Administration and the U.S. Department of Agriculture, "A Description of the U.S. Food Safety System," 2000. Available at www.fsis.usda. Accessed July 2013.

Food Safety Initiative (FSI) The program that coordinates the research, surveillance, inspection, outbreak response, and educational activities of the various government agencies that work together to safeguard food.

DNA fingerprinting A technique in which DNA "gene patterns" (or "fingerprints") are detected and analyzed. Used in food safety to distinguish between different strains of a bacterium.

1 **Farm: Use good agricultural practices.** Farmers grow, harvest, sort, pack, and store their crops in ways that help reduce food safety hazards.

2 **Processing: Monitor at critical control points.** During processing, HACCP measures are implemented.

3 **Transportation: Use clean vehicles and maintain the proper temperature.** Food is kept at a proper temperature during transportation to reduce the growth of foodborne microbes.

4 **Retail: Follow the Food Code guidelines.** Retail outlets, including restaurants, grocery stores, and institutions (such as hospitals), use the Food Code guidelines to reduce the risk of foodborne illness.

5 **Consumer: Always follow the four Cs of food safety (clean, combat cross-contamination, cook, chill).** The consumer uses the four Cs to reduce the risk of foodborne illness.

Figure 13.7 The Farm-to-Table Continuum
Every step in the farm-to-table continuum plays an important role in reducing microbes and the spread of foodborne illness.

federal and state agencies helped curtail the outbreak and kept it from being much worse.[48] Investigators from the FDA, CDC, and USDA worked with the state of California to conclude that the infected spinach came from one grower and most likely occurred because of cross-contamination of infected water and animals with the produce in the field. The same strain of *E. coli* was found in a nearby stream and in the feces of cattle on a neighboring farm.

The FDA and USDA have also adopted a food-safety program called Hazard Analysis and Critical Control Points (HACCP) (pronounced "hassip") that is used to identify and control foodborne hazards that may occur in all the stages of the food production process.[49] HACCP procedures are in place for food manufacturers and transporters to help safeguard food. Manufacturers also apply food preservation techniques to some foods to make them safer when you buy them. These techniques will be discussed in the next section.

Once the food arrives at retail and food-service establishments such as grocery stores and restaurants, these outlets use the Food Code, a reference document published by the FDA. The Food Code provides practical, science-based guidance, including HACCP guidelines, and provisions to help purveyors minimize foodborne illness.[50] The FDA updates the Food Code periodically to keep pace with emerging science, and states use the FDA Food Code to present their food codes and laws. The Partnership for Food Safety Education (PFSE) is a program designed to educate the public about safe food handling after purchase.

From the farmer to the consumer, everyone involved in the production and preparation of food plays a role in making sure the food we eat is safe. The **farm-to-table continuum** is a visual tool that shows how farmers, food manufacturers, transporters of food, retailers, and you, the consumer, can help ensure a safe food supply. **Figure 13.7** shows the steps in this continuum.

In addition to government efforts to help prevent foodborne illness, food manufacturers also work to safeguard food. Food processing, preservation techniques, and irradiation help destroy contaminants and/or maintain a food's color and freshness, and product dating can help you know when a food is past its prime and should be tossed.

Food Manufacturers Use Preservation Techniques to Destroy Contaminants

One way to control foodborne hazards is to use **food preservation** methods. Pickling (adding an acidic substance such as vinegar to the food), salting, drying, heating, freezing, and newer techniques such as irradiation and the use of food additives are all methods of food preservation. You use some of these yourself when you cook (apply heat to) or freeze (apply cold to) foods. Pickling, drying, and canning (a form of heating) have been in use for centuries, though today they're more often done by food manufacturers than home cooks.

Pasteurization is a technique that involves heating foods and liquids to a high enough temperature to kill pathogens. The process kills *E. coli* O157:H7 as well as other bacteria. In addition to dairy foods, most juices sold in supermarkets in the United State are pasteurized. Juices that aren't pasteurized must display a warning on the label.[51] Another method of pasteurization is ultra-high temperature (UHT) pasteurization, which is often used to aseptically package juice and some milks in "boxes." These are shelf stable until opened, which saves manufacturers (and you) a lot of money because the products don't have to be shipped and stored under expensive refrigeration. Once they are opened, they do have to be refrigerated.

Pasteurizing milk and dairy foods improves their quality and helps them stay fresh longer. Though raw (unpasteurized) milk and cheese are sometimes touted as being more healthful, this is an unfounded claim and can be dangerous, as raw milk can contain *Salmonella*, *E. coli* O157:H7, and *Listeria monocytogenes*.

Canning goes a step beyond pasteurization by packing food in airtight containers after heating it to a temperature high enough to kill most bacteria. Though this preserves the safety of most foods, botulism is one illness that can still result from improperly canned foods. The bacterium *Clostridium botulinum* can survive environments without air, such as sealed cans, and creates **spores** that are not destroyed at normal cooking temperatures; a temperature higher than boiling (212°F) is needed to kill these spores.[52] **Retort canning** has eliminated botulism from commercially canned foods. Because of the success of retort canning, the very rare cases of botulism typically result from products that have been home canned. This is a great reason to make sure you are using modern canning methods at home. If you have an old recipe from Grandma, you need to modify Grandma's instructions to make the product safe.

Many people were initially resistant to the processes of pasteurization and canning because they thought the techniques would promote the use of inferior ingredients. The federal government helped address such fears by putting formal food grading processes in place to reassure consumers that only quality foods would be used. Both of these preservation methods are now widely used and generally regarded as effective to thwart foodborne illness.

Two newer preservation methods used to keep foods fresh are MAP and HPP. **Modified atmosphere packaging (MAP)** is a process during which the manufacturer changes the composition of the air surrounding the food in a package. Usually, the amount of oxygen is reduced, which delays the decay of packaged fruits and vegetables. MAP is used in such foods to extend their shelf life and preserve their quality.[53] **High-pressure processing (HPP)** is a newer method in which foods are exposed to pulses of high pressure, which destroys microorganisms. If bacterial spores are present on the food, heat may also have to be applied along with the HPP. Foods such as jams, fruit juices, ham, rice cakes, guacamole, and pourable salad dressing can be treated with HPP.[54]

Irradiation

Another method of food preservation that manufacturers and growers use to keep food safe is **irradiation**. After foods have been packaged by a manufacturer, they may undergo irradiation, at either the manufacturing plant or another facility. During this

farm-to-table continuum Illustrates the roles that farmers, food manufacturers, food transporters, retailers, and consumers play in ensuring that the food supply, from the farm to the plate, remains safe.

food preservation The treatment of foods to reduce deterioration and spoilage, and help prevent the multiplication of pathogens that can cause foodborne illness.

pasteurization The process of heating liquids or food at high temperatures to destroy foodborne pathogens.

canning The process of heating food to a temperature high enough to kill bacteria and then packing the food in airtight containers.

spores Hardy reproductive structures that are produced by certain bacteria. Some bacterial spores can survive boiling temperature (212°F).

retort canning The process of subjecting already-canned foods to an additional high-temperature heat source to destroy potential pathogens.

modified atmosphere packaging (MAP) A food preservation technique that changes the composition of the air surrounding the food in a package to extend the food's shelf life.

high-pressure processing (HPP) A method used to pasteurize foods by exposing the items to pulses of high pressure, which destroys the microorganisms that are present.

irradiation A process in which foods are placed in a shielded chamber, called an irradiator, and subjected to a radiant energy source. This kills specific pathogens in food by breaking up the cells' DNA.

process, foods are subjected to a radiant energy source. This level of energy damages the harmful organisms, either killing them all or greatly reducing their numbers, thus reducing the risk of foodborne disease.[55] Irritation also destroys the bacteria that cause food spoilage.[56] This will allow foods to have a longer shelf life.[57] Foods that have been irradiated are not radioactive and don't undergo any harmful or dangerous chemical changes.[58]

The temperature of the food isn't significantly raised during irradiation, which helps prevent nutrient losses.[59] Irradiation destroys bacteria such as *Campylobacter*, *E. coli* O157:H7, and *Salmonella* and helps control insects and parasites. It does not destroy viruses such as norovirus and hepatitis A, however, because the higher radiation levels needed to destroy the DNA of these smaller microbes have not yet been approved by the FDA.[60]

Food irradiation has been studied and tested for more than 50 years and remains the most researched food-related technology ever approved in the United States.[61] Irradiation has been used for years to sterilize surgical instruments and implants. Hospitals have used irradiation to destroy disease-promoting microbes in foods served to patients with cancer and others who have weakened immune systems.

Foods that are irradiated must bear the "radura" logo, along with the phrase "treated by irradiation" or "treated with radiation" on the package (**Figure 13.8**).[62] A label is not required if a minor ingredient, such as a spice, has been irradiated and used in the product. Foods that are currently approved for irradiation in the United States include:[63]

> ➤ Fruits and vegetables
> ➤ Herbs and spices
> ➤ Fresh meat, pork, and poultry
> ➤ Wheat flour
> ➤ White potatoes
> ➤ Molluscan shellfish (oysters, clams, mussels, scallops)
> ➤ Alfalfa sprouts
> ➤ Shell eggs

Though irradiation has many advantages, it doesn't guarantee that a food is safe, and some foods should still not be eaten raw, even if they have been irradiated. Steak tartare (a dish that contains raw ground beef) isn't a safe menu option even if it is made with irradiated ground beef, because the beef could be recontaminated after irradiation. Proper food-handling, preparation, and cooking techniques must still be used for foods that have been irradiated.

Product Dating Can Help You Determine Peak Quality

Although food product dating isn't federally mandated, except for infant formula and some baby foods, more than 20 states in the United States require some form of food product dating. There are two types of food product dating: closed dating and open dating. **Closed (or "coded") dating** refers to the packing numbers used by manufacturers that are often found on nonperishable, shelf-stable foods, such as cans of soup and fruit (see **Figure 13.9**). This type of dating is used by the manufacturer to keep track of product inventory, rotate stock, and identify products that may be involved in a recall.[64]

Open dating is typically found on perishable items such as meat, poultry, eggs, and dairy foods, and is more useful for the consumer. Open dating must contain a calendar date that includes at least a month and day. (If the product is shelf stable or frozen and a calendar date is used, the year must also be included in the date.) You

Figure 13.8 The International Radura Symbol
The radura symbol must appear on all irradiated foods.

Source: U.S. Food and Drug Administration.

closed or **"coded" dating** Refers to the packing numbers that are decodable only by manufacturers and are often found on nonperishable, shelf-stable foods.

open dating Typically found on perishable items such as meat, poultry, eggs, and dairy foods; must contain a calendar date.

can use open dating to help you decide when to buy and consume a product while it is at its peak quality. Note: This date does not refer to food safety, but to the *quality* of the food. For example, a carton of yogurt that has been mishandled and not refrigerated for several hours may be unsafe to eat even though the date on the container hasn't passed.

When open dating is used, there must be a phrase next to the date that tells you how to interpret it. If there is "Sell By" next to the date, you should purchase the product on or before that date. If there is "Best if Used By" or "Use By" next to it, this refers to the date by which you should consume the product in order to enjoy it at its best.[65] If you don't plan to consume a product by its Use By date, you can freeze it; once frozen, the Use By date doesn't apply.

The Take-Home Message Several government agencies share responsibility for food safety in the United States. HACCP is a food safety program used to identify and control hazards that may occur in any part of the food system. Manufacturers may use other techniques such as pasteurization, canning, and irradiation to preserve food and destroy contamination.

a Closed food product dating refers to the coded packing numbers that you often see on nonperishable foods such as canned soups.

b Open food product dating must contain a calendar date and is used on perishable food items along with information on how to use the date.

Figure 13.9 Closed and Open Food Product Dating

What Are Food Additives and How Are They Used?

Food manufacturers use **food additives** for numerous reasons, including to increase the shelf life of products, enrich nutrient content, and improve the flavor and texture of foods. Commonly used additives include preservatives (such as antioxidants and sulfites), nutrients, and flavor enhancers (such as MSG).

Preservatives Prevent Spoilage and Increase Shelf Life

Most additives are *preservatives* that are added to foods to prevent spoilage (usually by destroying microbes) and increase shelf life. The most common antimicrobial preservatives are salt and sugar. Salt has been used for centuries, particularly in meat and fish, to create a dry environment in which bacteria cannot multiply. Sugar is used for the same preserving effect in products such as canned and frozen fruits and condiments.

Nitrites and **nitrates** are salts that are added to foods to prevent microbial growth and are used in cured meats such as hot dogs and ham to prevent the growth of *Clostridium botulinum*. They are also the chemicals that give these foods their pink color. The use of these salts has been controversial due to the fact that they form **carcinogenic** nitrosamines in the digestive tract of animals.

The addition of antioxidants to foods can prevent an off taste or off color in a product that's vulnerable to damage by oxidation. Currently two vitamins have been

food additives Substances added to food that affect its quality, flavor, freshness, and/or safety.

nitrates (nitrites) Substances that can be added to foods to function as a preservative and to give meats such as hot dogs and luncheon meats a pink color.

carcinogenic Cancer-causing.

approved for use as food additives due to their actions as antioxidants: vitamin E and vitamin C. Vitamin E is added to oils and cereals to prevent the fats in them from becoming rancid, and vitamin C is often added to cut fruit to prevent premature browning. Butylated hydroxyanisole (BHA) and butylated hydroxytoluene (BHT) are two chemical antioxidants that are also used as preservatives.

Sulfites are a group of antioxidants that are used as preservatives to help prevent the oxidation and browning of some foods and to inhibit the growth of microbes.[66] Sulfites are often found in dried fruits and vegetables, packaged and prepared potatoes, wine, beer, bottled lemon and lime juice, and pickled foods.

For most people, sulfites pose no risk, but there are people who experience adverse reactions. Individuals who are sensitive to sulfites may experience symptoms ranging from chest tightness and difficulty breathing to hives.[67] People at highest risk for negative reactions include people who suffer from asthma and others who are sensitive to sulfites. Due to the risk of adverse reactions in people who are sulfite sensitive, the FDA has prohibited the use of sulfites on fruits and vegetables that are served raw, such as in a salad bar, or are advertised as "fresh." Foods that contain sulfite additives or ingredients treated with sulfites must declare "added sulfites" in the ingredients listing on the label. Food sold in bulk, such as dried fruit treated with sulfites, must display the ingredients on a sign near the food. Because sulfites destroy the B vitamin thiamin, the FDA prohibits their use in foods that are good sources of the vitamin.[68]

Dried fruits often have sulfur dioxide or other sulfites added to them to preserve color and flavor. People with sulfite sensitivity should avoid products containing these additives.

Some Additives Enhance Texture and Consistency

Food additives can improve food quality in a number of ways. Gums and pectins are used to improve consistency and texture and are added to thicken yogurts and puddings. Emulsifiers improve the stability, consistency, and homogeneity of products like mayonnaise and ice cream. Lecithin is an example of an emulsifier that is added to some salad dressing. Leavening agents are added to breads to incorporate gases that cause them to rise. Anti-caking agents prevent products like powdered sugar that are crystalline in nature from absorbing moisture and lumping. Humectants such as propylene glycol are added to increase moisture in products so that they stay fresh.

Some Additives Improve Nutrient Content

Additives can be used to enhance a product's nutrition content, such as when refined grains are enriched with added B vitamins and iron. In some cases, such additions are mandated. This was the case in 1996 when the FDA published regulations requiring the addition of folic acid to enriched breads, cereal, and other grain products in order to help decrease the risk of neural tube defects in newborns.

Color and Flavor Enhancers Improve the Appeal of Foods

Additives can be used to enhance the color of foods. Two main categories make up the FDA's list of permitted colors. "Certifiable" color additives are man-made and are derived primarily from petroleum and coal sources. You can recognize these types of additives by the prefixes FD&C, D&C, or Ext. An example is FD&C Yellow, which is often found in cereals and baked goods. The second main category of color additives

sulfites Preservatives used to help prevent foods from turning brown and to inhibit the growth of microbes. Often used in wine and dried fruit products.

includes those obtained largely from plant, animal, or mineral sources. Examples include caramel color and grape color extract. Reactions to color additives are rare, though FD&C Yellow No. 5 may cause itching and hives in some people. This additive is found in beverages, desserts, and processed vegetables and is required to be listed on food labels. **Table 13.5** provides a list of commonly used additives and their functions in foods.

MSG Is a Common Flavor Enhancer

Monosodium glutamate (MSG) is often used as a flavor enhancer in Asian foods, canned vegetables and soups, and processed meats. Consumers can buy it in a form that is similar in texture to salt; although it doesn't have a strong taste of its own, it enhances sweet, salty, sour, and bitter tastes in other foods. Because of its long history of safe use, MSG is **generally recognized as safe (GRAS)**. However, the FDA has received numerous consumer complaints that it can cause symptoms such as headaches and nausea, along with concerns that it can contribute to Alzheimer's disease, brain tumors, and nerve cell damage.[69]

After an extensive review, the FDA confirmed that MSG is safe to consume in the amounts typically used in processed foods and cooking (a typical meal that contains MSG has less than 0.5 gram). However, when consumed in large quantities such as 3 or more grams at a time, it may cause short-term reactions in people who are sensitive to it.[70] These reactions, which are called the **MSG symptom complex**, can include numbness, burning sensation, facial pressure or tightness, chest pain, rapid heart beat, and drowsiness. In addition, people with asthma may have difficulty breathing after consuming MSG. For these reasons, the FDA requires that all foods containing MSG declare this ingredient on the food label.

Table 13.5

Commonly Used Food Additives

Additive(s)	Function(s)	Where You'll Find Them
Alginates, carrageenan, glyceride, guar gum, lecithin, mono- and diglycerides, methyl cellulose, pectin, sodium aluminosilicate	Impart/maintain desired consistency	Baked goods, cake mixes, coconut, ice cream, processed cheese, salad dressings, table salt
Ascorbic acid (vitamin C), calcium carbonate, folic acid, thiamine (B_1), iron, niacin, pyridoxine (B_6), riboflavin (B_2), vitamins A and D, zinc oxide	Improve/maintain nutritive value	Biscuits, bread, breakfast cereals, desserts, flour, gelatin, iodized margarine, milk, pasta, salt
Ascorbic acid, benzoates, butylated hydroxyanisole (BHA), butylated hydroxytoluene (BHT), citric acid, propionic acid and its salts, sodium nitrite	Maintain palatability and wholesomeness	Bread, cake mixes, cheese, crackers, frozen and dried fruit, lard, margarine, meat, potato chips
Citric acid, fumaric acid, lactic acid, phosphoric acid, sodium bicarbonate, tartrates, yeast	Produce light texture and control acidity/alkalinity	Butter, cakes, cookies, chocolates, crackers, quick breads, soft drinks
Annatto, aspartame, caramel, cloves, FD&C Red No. 40, FD&C Blue No. 1, fructose, ginger, limonene, MSG, saccharin, turmeric	Enhance flavor or provide desired color	Baked goods, cheeses, confections, gum, spice cake, gingerbread, jams, soft drinks, soup, yogurt

Source: FDA, "Food Additives," 2010. Available at www.fda.gov.

monosodium glutamate (MSG) A flavor enhancer.

generally recognized as safe (GRAS) Describes a substance that is believed to be safe to consume based on a long history of use by humans or a substantial amount of research that documents its safety.

MSG symptom complex A series of reactions such as numbness, burning sensation, facial pressure or tightness, chest pain, rapid heart beat, and drowsiness that can occur in some individuals after they consume MSG.

Food Additives Are Closely Regulated by the FDA

Food additives are under strict regulation by the FDA, with consumer safety a top priority. The Federal Food, Drug and Cosmetic Act of 1938 gave the FDA authority to regulate food and food ingredients, including the use of food additives. The 1958 Food Additives Amendment further mandated that manufacturers document the safety of a food additive and obtain FDA approval before using it in a food.[71]

Two categories of food additives were exempted from this amendment. The first category includes substances that were known to be safe before 1958 and were given **prior-sanctioned** status. For example, because nitrates were used to preserve meats before 1958, they have prior-sanctioned status, but *only* for their use in meats. They cannot be used in other foods, such as vegetables, without FDA approval.[72] The second category includes substances that have a long history of being safe for consumption, such as salt, sugar, and spices, or have extensive research documenting that they are safe to consume, such as vitamins. These additives are exempt from FDA approval because they are "generally recognized as safe" (GRAS).[73]

The FDA continually monitors both prior-sanctioned additives and those with GRAS status to ensure that current research continues to support their safety. To remain on the GRAS list, an additive must not have been found to be cancer causing in animals or humans. The 1958 Food Additives Amendment also included the *DeLaney Clause,* which was created to protect consumers from additives found to cause cancer. The clause states that no substances that have been shown to cause cancer in animals or humans at any dosage may be added to foods. However, with the present increases in technology and the ability to detect substances at very low levels, the clause is considered outdated. To address this issue, the FDA deems additives safe if lifetime use presents no more than a one-in-a-million risk of cancer in human beings. If an additive is suddenly called into question, the FDA can prohibit its use or require that the food manufacturer conduct additional studies to ensure its safety.[74] Even with these safeguards in place, some additives, such as MSG and sulfites, may cause adverse reactions in some people and should be avoided by those who are sensitive to them.

Some Food Additives Are Unintentional

The food additives already discussed are all *intentional food additives* used to improve the quality of food products. However, *unintentional food additives* may sometimes be added indirectly to a food. For example, very small amounts of substances used during packaging or processing may inadvertently end up in the food. The safety of packaging must therefore be determined by manufacturers to ensure that packing substances aren't harmful to the consumer. Unintentional additives may also include chemicals from processing, and *dioxins* used during the manufacture of bleached paper such as coffee filters. Dioxins can accumulate in the food chain and cause cancer in animals. The FDA monitors the level of dioxins in food that you consume and in the feed that animals consume.[75]

The Take-Home Message Food additives are often used by manufacturers to preserve foods, enhance their color or flavor, or add to their nutrient content. Some additives, such as MSG and sulfites, may cause unpleasant symptoms in sensitive individuals, but all additives are strictly regulated by the FDA. All intentional food additives must be listed on food labels. Some additives may be added unintentionally during processing or cause adverse reactions in sensitive individuals.

prior-sanctioned Having previous approval.

What Are Toxins and Chemical Agents?

In addition to pathogens, naturally occurring toxins can contaminate foods, and chemicals can accumulate in foods. In this section we'll discuss some of these toxins.

Toxins Occur Naturally

Toxins frequently occur in nature to help a plant or animal fend off predators or capture its meals. In many cases, toxins in food animals exist in amounts too small to harm humans, but there are instances in which the toxins found in plant and animal foods can make a person ill, or worse.

Marine Toxins

Although there are numerous reasons to include fish and seafood in your diet (recall their omega-3 fatty acid and low saturated fat content from Chapter 5), you should be aware of the risks involved. Some seafood, such as some of the raw fish used in sushi, can contain pathogens, and some can harbor naturally occurring **marine toxins**. Thorough cooking will kill many harmful bacteria and viruses found in seafood, but it won't destroy any of the marine toxins.

Spoiled finfish, such as tuna and mackerel, can cause **scombrotoxic fish poisoning**, in which the spoilage bacteria break down proteins in the fish and generate histamine. Other by-products are created that block the breakdown of histamine. Consuming fish that contain large amounts of histamine can cause symptoms such as diarrhea, flushing, sweating, and vomiting within 2 minutes to 2 hours.[76]

Eating large, predatory reef fish, such as barracuda and grouper, can sometimes result in **ciguatera poisoning**, which is caused by ciguatoxins. These toxins originate in microscopic sea organisms called *dinoflagellates*, which are then eaten by small tropical fish. As larger fish eat the smaller fish, the toxins **bioaccumulate** and become more concentrated in the larger fish.[77] **Figure 13.10** shows how these toxins can accumulate in the food chain. In addition to experiencing various gastrointestinal discomforts, individuals infected with ciguatera may have temperature sensation reversal in the mouth when they eat.[78] To them, ice cream feels hot and hot coffee feels cold.

Warning signs like this one are often posted when local waters have been found to contain high amounts of pollutants. Fish caught in such waters should never be eaten.

marine toxins Chemicals that occur naturally and contaminate some fish.

scombrotoxic fish poisoning A condition caused by consuming spoiled fish that contain large amounts of histamines.

ciguatera poisoning A condition caused by marine toxins produced by *dinoflagellates* (microscopic sea organisms).

bioaccumulate When a substance or chemical builds up in an organism over time, so that the concentration of the chemical is higher than would be found naturally in the environment.

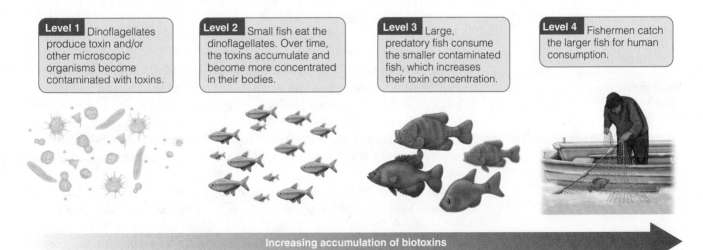

Level 1 Dinoflagellates produce toxin and/or other microscopic organisms become contaminated with toxins.

Level 2 Small fish eat the dinoflagellates. Over time, the toxins accumulate and become more concentrated in their bodies.

Level 3 Large, predatory fish consume the smaller contaminated fish, which increases their toxin concentration.

Level 4 Fishermen catch the larger fish for human consumption.

Increasing accumulation of biotoxins

Figure 13.10 Bioaccumulation of Toxins

Certain shellfish, such as mussels, clams, scallops, oysters, crabs, and lobsters, that typically live in the coastal waters of New England and the Pacific states can be contaminated with **neurotoxins** (*neuro* = nerve, *toxin* = toxic). Neurotoxins are also produced by dinoflagellates, and the particular reddish-brown-colored dinoflagellates that contain them can become so abundant that the ocean appears to have red streaks, also known as "red tides." Eating contaminated shellfish can lead to **paralytic shellfish poisoning**. Symptoms include mild numbness or tingling in the face, arms, and legs, as well as headaches and dizziness. Muscle paralysis, inability to breathe, and, in severe cases, death could result.[79]

Toxins in Other Foods

Many plant foods naturally contain toxins in small amounts, so though they're generally safe to eat, consuming them in very large amounts could be harmful. Potatoes that have been exposed to light and turned green, for example, contain increased amounts of solanine, a toxin that can cause fever, diarrhea, paralysis, and shock. (Luckily, peeling potatoes usually removes the green layer and the potato can be safely eaten. If it tastes bitter, however, throw it out.) Wild lima beans contain high amounts of cyanogenic glycosides, which can be converted to the poison cyanide. (The variety of lima beans sold commercially have minimal, nonthreatening amounts of this substance, so are safe to eat.) Cassava also contains cyanogenic glycosides and has been known to cause cyanide poisoning in people who eat large amounts of this root vegetable. Raw soybeans contain amylase inhibitors, which are inactivated when cooked or fermented.[80]

Other foods contain toxins that are harmful even in trace amounts, and so should be avoided altogether. Certain wild mushrooms, for example, are poisonous; they contain toxins that can cause nausea, vomiting, liver damage, and death.

Contamination Is Sometimes Due to Pollution

One person's trash can become another person's illness. Although industrial and household chemicals have useful purposes, if traces of these substances end up in the food supply, they can have negative health effects. Two pollutants of concern are PCBs and methylmercury.

Polychlorinated biphenyls (PCBs) are chemicals that occur in the food supply due to industrial pollution. A few decades ago, these chemicals were used as coolants and lubricants because they are good insulators and don't burn easily. They were banned in 1977 due to concerns about their toxicity.[81] For example, they may be responsible for promoting cancer in humans. Although PCBs are no longer manufactured in the United States, they can still make their way into the environment through hazardous waste sites, the burning of wastes, and the improper disposal of consumer products, such as old television sets and other electrical fixtures and devices.[82] PCBs have been shown to contaminate the sediments in rivers and lakes. Because PCBs don't break down over time, they bioaccumulate in small organisms and fish. In fact, PCBs are the major chemical risk associated with eating fish.[83]

Mercury occurs in nature, but it is also a by-product of industrial pollution. An airborne form of mercury can accumulate on the surface of streams and oceans and be transformed by the bacteria in the water into the toxic form of methylmercury. As fish either absorb the methylmercury from the water or eat smaller fish that contain methylmercury, they can bioaccumulate the substance to high levels.

neurotoxins Toxins that affect the nerves and can cause symptoms including mild numbness or tingling in the face, arms, and legs, as well as headaches and dizziness. Severe cases could result in death.

paralytic shellfish poisoning A condition caused by consuming shellfish contaminated with neurotoxins.

polychlorinated biphenyls (PCBs) Synthetic chemicals that have been shown to cause cancer and other adverse effects on the immune, reproductive, nervous, and endocrine systems in animals. PCBs may cause cancer in humans.

The Take-Home Message Toxins can occur naturally in foods and can cause harm to humans. Marine toxins can occur in certain varieties of spoiled fish and bioaccumulate in fish that feed on toxin-containing sea organisms. Chemicals can also get into the food supply as a result of environmental contamination. Polychlorinated biphenyls (PCBs) and methylmercury have been shown to bioaccumulate in fish.

What Is Bioterrorism and How Can You Protect Yourself?

Food and water supplies are potential targets for **bioterrorism**. Agents such as the bacterium that causes anthrax and the virus that causes smallpox are examples of possible bioterrorist weapons. Until recently, scenarios of human-caused outbreaks of these diseases were thought to exist only in Hollywood movies. Today, Americans face the real threat of someone using plant or animal food supplies, or drinking water sources, to cause harm.[84]

Food can be the primary agent of bioterrorism by being contaminated with a biological or chemical toxin. In fact, the CDC lists several foodborne pathogens, such as botulism, *Salmonella*, *E. coli* O157:H7, and *Shigella* as potential bioterrorism agents.[85]

Food and water can also be used as secondary agents of bioterrorism by disrupting the availability of adequate safe amounts of these necessities and by limiting the fuel needed to safely cook and refrigerate perishable foods. Several years ago, London police arrested individuals involved in a plot to add poison to the food served at a British military base.[86] Tainted foods, or even the threat of such contamination, could cause a mandatory or self-imposed avoidance of a particular category of food and/or eating establishment and contribute to social disarray.[87]

To combat these threats, governmental agencies have made bioterrorism a national priority. Under the direction of the Department of Homeland Security, numerous local, state, and federal agencies, such as the Federal Emergency Management Agency (FEMA), FDA, and USDA, work together at each stage of the food continuum—from the farm to the table—to protect your foods.

As a consumer, you also play an important role in **food biosecurity**, and there are strategies you can employ if you should come into contact with suspicious-looking food items. Although food tampering is rare in the United States, a watchful consumer can spot it and avoid it. The Table Tips list ways you can identify food items that may have been tampered with, and where to report suspicious items if you find them.

The Take-Home Message Food and water can be primary agents of bioterrorism by being contaminated with a biological or chemical toxin. These necessities can also be used as secondary agents if a terrorist act disrupts their availability, or limits access to the fuel needed to safely cook and refrigerate perishable foods. If you come into contact with a tampered food, you should report the suspicious items to the appropriate authorities.

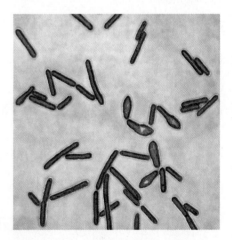

Clostridium botulinum, the bacterium that causes the deadly disease botulism, is classified by the CDC as a "Category A" biological agent posing the highest risk to national security.

bioterrorism The use of a biological or chemical agent to frighten, threaten, coerce, injure, and/or kill individuals.

food biosecurity Protecting the food supply from bioterrorist attacks.

Are Plastics Safe for Our Food? You may have heard warnings to avoid plastic containers because they can break down when exposed to heat (for example, during microwaving) and release chemicals, such as bisphenol A (BPA) and phthalates, that can leach into food.[1] How valid is this concern, particularly for infants and small children? Is it safe to eat food or drink beverages that are stored in, or consumed from, plastic containers? Take a look at the evidence on both sides of the issue, consider the questions posed, and decide for yourself.

yes

- Bisphenol A has been in use in plastic bottles and in metal can linings since the 1960s.[2]

- The FDA's current stance on BPA, based upon hundreds of studies, is that "BPA is safe at the very low levels that occur in some foods."[3]

- As chemical analysis techniques become more sophisticated, they can find one part per trillion. Chemicals found in such trace amounts are not necessarily harmful.[4]

no

- While claiming that BPA is safe, the FDA supports efforts to make BPA-free baby bottles and recommends the development of BPA-free can liners.[5]

- The U.S. National Toxicology Program and the National Institutes of Health found that there is "some concern" about the effects of BPA on infants and children. Both had lower levels of concern for other groups and concluded that more research is needed to determine just what the risks of BPA exposure might be.[6]

- Prenatal exposure to phthalates has been associated with behavioral disorders in children.[7]

what do you think?

1. Which side do you think has the more compelling argument? Why? **2.** Do you think warnings to avoid plastic food and beverage containers are justified? Why or why not? **3.** Are there other concerns aside from potential BPA contamination that should be considered when using plastic containers to store or prepare food?

1 Pathogens Are the Primary Cause of Foodborne Illness

Pathogens, which include viruses, bacteria, and parasites, as well as fungal agents and prions, all can cause foodborne illness. Noroviruses are the single largest cause of foodborne illness. The most common bacteria that cause foodborne illness are *Campylobacter, E. coli* O157:H7, and *Salmonella*.

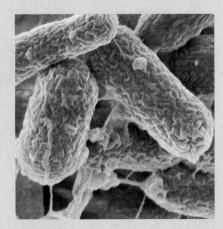

3 Many Agencies Work Together to Keep Food Safe

Through the coordinated effort of the Food Safety Initiative, numerous United States government agencies work together to safeguard America's food supply against foodborne illness. Food manufacturers use preservation techniques such as pasteurization and irradiation to destroy contaminants. Food product dating can help you enjoy your foods at peak quality.

2 Practicing the Four Cs Can Prevent Foodborne Illness

Proper food-handling techniques during four critical steps—**c**leaning, **c**ombating cross-contamination, **c**ooking, and **c**hilling—can help reduce your risk of foodborne illness. Washing your hands and cleaning produce before eating it is important to prevent foodbornes illness. Separate cutting boards should be used for meat and nonmeat foods, and utensils and serving dishes that touch raw meat should not be used to handle cooked meat. The only way to tell if a meat product has been thoroughly cooked is to check its internal temperature with a meat thermometer. When serving foods, hot foods should be kept hot and cold foods should be kept cold. Leftovers should be divided and refrigerated quickly (within 1 to 2 hours), and frozen foods should never be thawed at room temperature. Refrigerators should always be set at 40°F or below and freezers should always be set at 0°F or below.

4 Food Additives Can Help Keep Your Foods Safe and Healthy

Food additives are used as preservatives, antioxidants, flavoring, coloring, and leavening agents. They are also used to maintain a food's consistency and to add nutrients. The FDA must approve most additives before they can be used in foods, and all additives must be listed on the food label. Some additives are exempted from obtaining FDA approval by having attained GRAS or prior-sanctioned status based on their long history of safe consumption.

5 Toxins and Chemical Agents Can Contaminate Foods

In addition to pathogens, toxins and chemical agents can also cause foodborne illness. Naturally occurring toxins include marine toxins and toxins that can occur naturally in foods. Chemical agents such as polychlorinated biphenyls can occur as a by-product of industrial pollution.

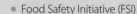
Increasing accumulation of biotoxins

6 Food and Water Supplies Are Potential Targets for Bioterrorism

The Department of Homeland Security coordinates the efforts of numerous local, state, and federal agencies to protect the United States, which includes safeguarding your food and water supply. Although food tampering is rare in the United States, a watchful consumer can play a role in spotting it and avoiding it.

Terms to Know

- foodborne illness
- food safety
- pathogens
- virus

- norovirus
- gastroenteritis
- bacteria
- parasites
- toxins
- cross-contaminate

- Food Safety Initiative (FSI)
- pasteurization
- irradiation
- closed or "coded" dating
- open dating
- food additives

- GRAS (generally recognized as safe)
- bioaccumulate
- polychlorinated biphenyls (PCBs)
- bioterrorism

MasteringNutrition™ Build your knowledge—and confidence—in the Study Area of MasteringNutrition with a variety of study tools.

Check Your Understanding

1. Which of the following is NOT a potential cause of foodborne illness?
   a. parasites
   b. viruses
   c. bacteria
   d. food additives
   e. naturally occurring chemicals and toxins

2. Which group is at greatest risk of contracting a foodborne illness?

   a. a 70-year-old grandmother, a toddler, and a teenage boy
   b. a 35-year-old basketball coach, a 70-year-old grandmother, and a 45-year-old professor
   c. a 70-year-old grandmother, a toddler, and a middle-aged woman who has diabetes
   d. a 45-year-old professor, a middle-aged woman who has diabetes, and a teenage boy

3. Which of the following U.S. government agencies is NOT involved in policing the food supply?

   a. the Internal Revenue Service (IRS)
   b. the Food and Drug Administration (FDA)
   c. the Centers for Disease Control and Prevention (CDC)
   d. the United States Department of Agriculture (USDA)

4. The "Best Used By" date on the food container refers to the date by which
   a. you should consume the product so that you don't get sick.
   b. you should consume the product to get your money's worth.

c. you should purchase the product.

d. to consume the product to enjoy it at its best quality.

5. For bacteria to multiply, they need nutrients, moisture, the correct temperature, and
   a. sunlight and the proper pH.
   b. the proper pH and plenty of time.
   c. heat and plenty of time.
   d. water and heat.
   e. water and sunlight.

6. The danger zone temperature range at which bacteria will multiply most rapidly is
   a. 40°F to 140°F.
   b. 45°F to 140°F.
   c. 40°F to 145°F.
   d. 50°F to 150°F.
   e. 50°F to 140°F.

7. The four critical steps in the food-handling process that you need to take to help prevent foodborne illness are
   a. cutting, cleaning, chopping, and chilling.
   b. cleaning, combating cross-contamination, cutting, and chilling.
   c. clearing, combating cross-contamination, cutting, and chilling.
   d. cleaning, combating cross-contamination, cooking, and chilling.
   e. cooking, combating cross-contamination, cutting, and chilling.

8. Though most bacteria will grow more slowly in a refrigerator set at 40°F and below, one of the following does not. Which one?
   a. *E. coli* O157:H7
   b. *Salmonella*
   c. Norwalk virus
   d. *Campylobacter*
   e. *Listeria*

9. Two intentional food additives that some people are sensitive to are
   a. *Salmonella* and antioxidants.
   b. heat and lemon juice.
   c. sulfites and MSG.
   d. dioxins and MSG.

10. Which of following is NOT a function of food additives?
    a. adding neurotoxins to foods
    b. preventing spoilage
    c. increasing the shelf life of a food
    d. enhancing the flavor of foods

Answers

1. (d) Parasites, viruses, bacteria, and naturally occurring toxins and chemicals can cause foodborne illness. Food additives do not. In fact, they are either approved by the FDA prior to use or have GRAS or prior-sanctioned status based on a history of safe consumption.

2. (c) Older adults, children, and individuals with a compromised immune system, such as those with diabetes, are at a higher risk of contracting foodborne illness.

3. (a) The IRS. The FDA, CDC, and USDA all play important roles in keeping the food supply safe.

4. (d) The "Best Used By" dated on the food container refers to the date by which to consume the product to enjoy it at its best quality.

5. (b) In addition to nutrients, moisture, and the correct temperature, bacteria also need the proper pH and plenty of time (2 hours or more) to multiply to potentially dangerous levels.

6. (a) The danger zone is 40°F to 140°F.

7. (d) To prevent foodborne illness, it's important to employ proper food-handling strategies when cleaning, combating cross-contamination, cooking, and chilling the foods in your meal.

8. (e) *Listeria* can multiply at temperatures of 40°F or below.

9. (c) Sulfites and MSG are fine for most people but can cause unpleasant symptoms in people who are sensitive to them.

10. (a) Food additives help prevent spoilage, increase the shelf life of the product, and can enhance the flavor of foods.

Web Resources

- For food safety education, visit www.fightbac.org
- For food safety tips for college students, visit www.fsis.usda.gov
- For foodborne illness fact sheets, visit www.foodsafety.gov

Answers to True or False?

1. **False.** *Salmonella* is a bacterium, not a virus. To find out the most common virus that causes foodborn illness, turn to page 491.

2. **False.** An off smell in food is more likely a sign of food spoilage rather than containing a pathogen that could cause foodborne illness. Unfortunately, a food that contains a disease-causing pathogen could smell perfectly fine. Turn to page 491 to find out more.

3. **False.** Running your hands under water for 10 seconds is not the correct way to wash your hands to reduce your risk of getting sick. To find out the correct method, turn to page 500.

4. **False.** It's not the color but rather the internal temperature of the chicken that will determine if it is safe to eat. Turn to page 502 to learn why color should not be used to determine if your food is safe to eat.

5. **True.** To be effective at keeping food safe, the temperature in your refrigerator should be 40°F or below. To find out why, turn to page 503.

6. **False.** Freezing doesn't kill bacteria, but only puts them in a dormant state. Find out what happens once the food is thawed on page 503.

7. **False.** Leftovers should be thrown out if they're not consumed within 3 to 5 days. To find out more about safe food storage, turn to page 504.

8. **False.** Irradiated food is treated with gamma rays that interrupt DNA and make cells unable to reproduce, thus killing harmful pathogens. It does not make foods radioactive. Learn more on page 510.

9. **False.** Package dates refer to food quality, not safety. To find out why consuming a food before the expiration date can't guarantee that the item is safe to eat, turn to page 511.

10. **True.** *E. coli* as well as other pathogens can be used in bioterrorism. To learn more, turn to page 517.

Life Cycle Nutrition:

Pregnancy through Infancy

True or False?

1. A **father's** health has no impact on the health of a developing fetus. Ⓣ Ⓕ p. 524

2. Women who are **obese** may have more trouble becoming pregnant than women who are normal weight or only somewhat overweight. Ⓣ Ⓕ p. 525

3. **Morning sickness** only happens before noon during the first trimester. Ⓣ Ⓕ p. 528

4. Drinking red wine is healthy during **pregnancy**. Ⓣ Ⓕ p. 532

5. Pregnant women shouldn't **exercise**. Ⓣ Ⓕ p. 534

6. Infant **formula** is better for babies than breast milk. Ⓣ Ⓕ p. 538

7. Chubby **babies** should be put on diets. Ⓣ Ⓕ p. 547

8. Infants never need dietary **supplements**. Ⓣ Ⓕ p. 547

9. Commercial baby food is always less healthy than **homemade**. Ⓣ Ⓕ p. 549

10. Raw carrots are a **safe food** for infants to help meet their need for vitamin A. Ⓣ Ⓕ p. 550

See page 559 for the answers.

When a woman is pregnant, her body facilitates the division, growth, and specialization of millions of new cells in her developing child. The raw materials for this rapid growth are provided by the nutrients she consumes in foods. Her diet, then, must not only maintain her own health, but also foster and maintain the health of her baby.

In this chapter, we will explore the specific nutrient requirements that a pregnant woman needs to ensure a healthy pregnancy. We'll also explore the diet and lifestyle factors in both the mother and father that can help ensure successful conception and healthy fetal development, as well as the nutritional needs and concerns of infants in their first year of life.

What Nutrients and Behaviors Are Important before Attempting a Healthy Pregnancy?

You're probably aware of at least a few things that women shouldn't do during pregnancy to support the baby's health. For instance, you probably know that pregnant women shouldn't smoke cigarettes or drink alcohol. But it might surprise you to learn that, even before a couple attempt to get pregnant, they should both adopt some healthy behaviors, including several by the father-to-be. Let's review these now.

A Man's Diet and Lifestyle Affect the Health of His Sperm

The moment when a sperm fertilizes an egg is called **conception**. For conception to occur, the male's sperm has to be plentiful and motile—capable of "swimming" to the waiting egg. Thus, men who hope to father a child should take note: Their lifestyle and dietary habits may affect the number and motility of their sperm. Smoking cigarettes, abusing alcohol and drugs, and obesity have been associated with decreased production and function of sperm.[1] Stopping smoking, striving for a healthy body weight, drinking in moderation, and abstaining from drugs are all beneficial behaviors that promote conception.

As part of a healthy eating plan, an adequate intake of zinc and folate has been associated with the production of healthy sperm. In addition, antioxidants, such as vitamins E and C and carotenoids, may help protect sperm from damage by free radicals.[2] Men should make sure to eat a balanced diet that contains adequate amounts of fruits and vegetables (which provide antioxidants, vitamins, minerals, and folate), as well as whole grains and healthy protein foods, such as lean meats, nuts, low-fat dairy foods, and legumes.[3]

Women Need to Adopt a Healthy Lifestyle before Conception

If you have ever run a marathon or know someone who has, you know that a tremendous amount of effort and diligence goes into training for the event. Your commitment doesn't begin on the day of the race, but as far as a year in advance. In fact, the more time and effort the runner puts into preparing for the race, the better the results are likely to be.

Ask any woman who has had a baby and she will tell you that planning, carrying, and delivering a healthy child was the marathon of her life. The commitment to change not-so-healthy behaviors is an extremely important part of prepregnancy preparation.

Let's look at the specific nutritional and lifestyle adjustments a woman needs to make to improve her chances of conceiving a healthy baby.

Attain a Healthy Weight

(T|F) Women who want to get pregnant should strive for the healthiest weight possible *before* conception. Women who begin pregnancy at a healthy weight are likely to conceive more easily, have an uncomplicated pregnancy,[4] and may have an easier time with breast-feeding.[5] Underweight women and overweight women may have a harder time getting pregnant, possibly because of irregular menstrual cycles. When they do become pregnant, they are at increased risk for a variety of health problems, some of which can affect the baby.

Get Adequate Folic Acid

Folic acid is the synthetic form of the B vitamin, folate. Folate and folic acid are needed to create new cells and help the baby grow and develop properly throughout pregnancy. During the first month after conception, consuming adequate folic acid plays a particularly important role in reducing the risk for neural tube defects (NTDs) in infants. NTDs, which include spina bifida, occur very early in pregnancy—when a woman may not know she is pregnant. For this reason, health experts recommend that all women who are capable of becoming pregnant should consume 400 micrograms of folic acid every day from dietary supplements, fortified foods, or both.

conception The moment when a sperm fertilizes an egg.

Table 14.1

Fishing for a Healthy Baby

Pregnant and nursing women and women of childbearing age who may become pregnant should follow these guidelines for eating seafood:

Do Not Eat	Limit	Enjoy

• Shark
• Swordfish
• King mackerel
• Tilefish (golden bass or golden snapper)
	• Albacore (white) tuna to no more than 6 oz weekly
	• Locally caught fish from nearby lakes, rivers, and coastal areas. Check local advisories regarding its safety before consuming it. If no advice is available, eat up to 6 oz weekly. Don't consume any other fish during that week.
		Up to 12 oz weekly of fish with low levels of methylmercury, such as:
		  • Canned light tuna
		  • Cod
		  • Catfish
		  • Crab
		  • Pollock
		  • Salmon
		  • Scallops
		  • Shrimp

Source: Data from Food and Drug Administration. 2004. What You Need to Know About Mercury in Fish and Shellfish: EPA and FDA Advice for Women Who Might Become Pregnant, Women Who Are Pregnant, and Nursing Mothers. Available at www.fda.gov. Accessed March 2013.

Table 14.2

A Jolt of Caffeine

Beverage	Caffeine (mg)
Coffee, brewed, drip (8 oz)	85
"Energy" drinks (8 oz)	80
Espresso (1 oz)	40
Tea, brewed (8 oz)	40
Tea, iced (8 oz)	25
Soft drinks (8 oz)	24
Hot cocoa (8 oz)	6
Milk chocolate (1 oz)	6
Chocolate milk (8 oz)	5
Coffee, brewed, decaffeinated (8 oz)	3

Source: Data from National Toxicology Program, Department of Health and Human Services, http://ntp-server.niehs.nih.gov; the International Food Information Council (IFIC), www.ific.org.

Moderate Fish and Caffeine Consumption

The Food and Drug Administration (FDA) recommends that women of childbearing age who may become pregnant avoid certain fish that may contain high amounts of the toxin *methylmercury*. Methylmercury builds up in a woman's body and may be passed on to an unborn child during pregnancy. Methylmercury can harm the nervous system of a developing fetus, especially during the first trimester of pregnancy. All fish contain some methylmercury, but larger fish accumulate more of it in their bodies. Table 14.1 summarizes the seafood consumption guidelines for women of childbearing age.

Caffeine consumption may affect a woman's fertility. Some research suggests that consuming 500 milligrams or more of caffeine daily may delay conception, but there is no definitive evidence that caffeine interferes with getting pregnant. To be safe, women who are trying to conceive should consume fewer than 200 milligrams of caffeine per day.[6] This means limiting brewed coffee and energy drinks to no more than about 12 ounces a day—or better yet, switching to decaffeinated versions of these drinks. See Table 14.2 for other common sources of caffeine in the diet.

Avoid Cigarettes and Other Toxic Substances

Cigarette smoking increases the risk of infertility, prolonging the time to conception.[7] If a female smoker is able to conceive, she'll face the difficulty of needing to quit smoking along with the many other challenges of pregnancy. The risks of maternal smoking are discussed later in this chapter.

Alcohol can affect a baby within weeks of conception, before a woman is aware that she is pregnant. For this reason, the office of the Surgeon General has recommended that all women who may become pregnant abstain from alcohol.[8]

Smoking marijuana can reduce fertility in both men and women. Women who use marijuana should speak with their health care provider about how to stop. They can also access the National Drug and Alcohol Treatment Referral Routing Service through the National Institute on Alcohol Abuse and Alcoholism at www.niaaa.nih.gov.

Now that you've learned which health habits are important to establish before trying to become parents, the next step is to learn what is needed for a healthy pregnancy.

The Take-Home Message Good nutrition and healthy lifestyle habits are important for both men and women before conception. Smoking cigarettes, alcohol abuse, and obesity are associated with the decreased production and function of sperm. Conception is easier for women when they are at a healthy weight. Women should consume adequate amounts of folic acid prior to getting pregnant and throughout their pregnancy. Women should also avoid consuming fish that may contain high amounts of methylmercury and should consume caffeine only in moderation. They should not smoke cigarettes, drink alcohol, or use illicit drugs.

What Nutrients and Behaviors Are Important in the First Trimester?

When a woman is pregnant, her diet must maintain her health, and foster the health and growth of her baby. She is truly eating for two. To help you appreciate the increased nutrient needs during pregnancy, let's examine how a pregnancy begins and how the developing child obtains nutrients from the mother.

During the First Trimester, the Fertilized Egg Develops into a Fetus

A full-term pregnancy is approximately 40 weeks long and is divided into three **trimesters**. The moment of conception marks the beginning of the first trimester. During the first few days of this 13-week period, the fertilized egg travels down the fallopian tube to embed itself in the lining of the woman's uterus (**Figure 14.1**). This enables the developing **embryo** to obtain nutrients via the **placenta**, an organ of common tissue between the mother and the growing embryo that develops in the mother's uterus (**Figure 14.2** on the next page). The placenta is attached to the growing baby via the **umbilical cord**. After the eighth week of pregnancy, the developing embryo is called a **fetus**. As the fetus develops, the mother's diet and lifestyle habits are critical in supporting and nurturing it.

By the end of the first trimester, the baby's liver is already forming red blood cells, the heart is pumping blood, the limbs are taking shape, and the brain is growing rapidly. In spite of all the activity taking place, the fetus weighs just ½ ounce and

Virtual Stages of Pregnancy

For a summary of the developments during each stage of pregnancy, visit the pregnancy page at www.womenshealth.gov.

trimesters The three time periods of pregnancy.

embryo Term that refers to a fertilized egg during the third through the eighth week of pregnancy.

placenta The organ that allows nutrients, oxygen, and waste products to be exchanged between a mother and fetus.

umbilical cord Cord connecting the fetus to the placenta that allows the transfer of nutrients and waste products between the mother and the fetus.

fetus A developing embryo that is at least 8 weeks old.

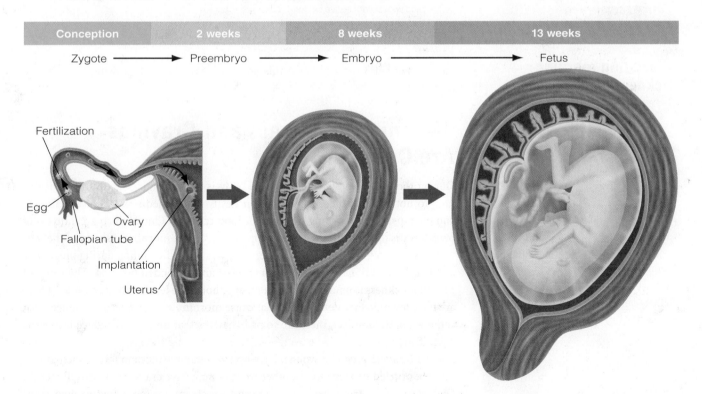

Figure 14.1 Fetal Development in the First Trimester
An embryo embeds itself into the uterine wall shortly after conception. After eight weeks, it is called a fetus.

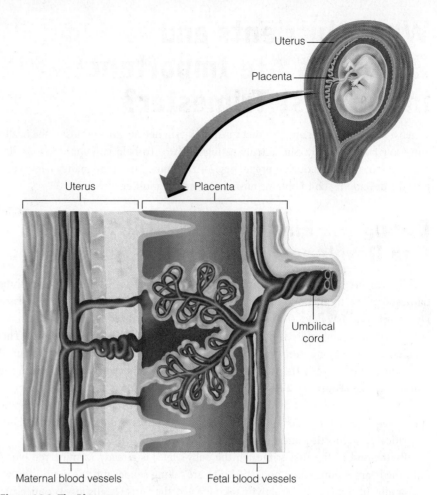

Figure 14.2 The Placenta
The placenta is the site of common tissue between the mother and the developing fetus where nutrients, oxygen, and waste products are exchanged.

measures about 3 inches long at this point. It has a lot more growing to do before being born.

"Morning" Sickness and Cravings Are Common

During the first trimester, the mother's body is also changing rapidly. She's beginning to notice some breast tenderness, a newly heightened sense of taste or smell, and perhaps some "morning sickness" or food cravings. One of the biggest myths of pregnancy is that morning sickness happens only in the morning. Ask any of the estimated 80 percent of women who experience nausea and vomiting during pregnancy and many will tell you that they wish their symptoms ended by noon. The cause of morning sickness is unknown, but fluctuating hormone levels may play a role.[9] There are no known dietary deficiencies that cause morning sickness, or diet changes that can prevent it. However, there are some behaviors that might help reduce it (see the Table Tips).

While some pregnant women develop an aversion to certain foods, such as coffee, tea, or fried or spicy foods, other women may have cravings for specific foods. Chocolate, citrus fruits, pickles, chips, and ice cream are foods that women commonly want when they are pregnant.[10] Sometimes women even crave and consume

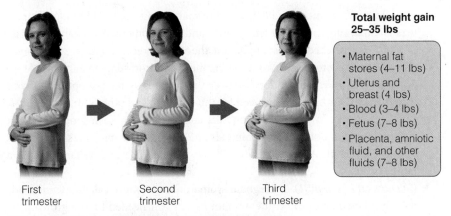

Total weight gain
25–35 lbs

- Maternal fat stores (4–11 lbs)
- Uterus and breast (4 lbs)
- Blood (3–4 lbs)
- Fetus (7–8 lbs)
- Placenta, amniotic fluid, and other fluids (7–8 lbs)

First trimester

Second trimester

Third trimester

Figure 14.3 Components of Weight Gain during Pregnancy
Women who begin pregnancy at a healthy weight should gain between 25 and 35 pounds.

nonfood substances, such as cornstarch, clay, dirt, or baking soda, a condition called *pica*. Experts are uncertain why pica occurs, but it may signal iron and zinc deficiencies in the diet. Women with the urge to eat nonfood items and large amounts of foods such as raw flour or cornstarch should tell their doctor immediately.[11]

Adequate Weight Gain Supports the Baby's Growth

Women who begin their pregnancies at a healthy weight are generally advised to gain 25 to 35 pounds (women having twins should gain between 37 and 54 pounds). This is the approximate amount of weight needed to support the growth of the baby (**Figure 14.3**). The amount of weight an individual woman gains should be enough to ensure a healthy 6.5- to 8.5-pound baby, but not so much that she increases her risk for complications during delivery (see Table 14.3). Gaining excess weight will also make it more difficult to lose the weight once the baby is born, increases the likelihood of the mother's remaining overweight many years after childbirth, and also increases the risk that the baby will be obese later in life. While women may gain between 1 and 4.5 pounds during the first trimester, health experts do not suggest increasing calories during the first trimester.[12] However, pregnant women have an increased need for certain nutrients after conception.

The Need for Certain Nutrients Increases

From the moment of conception, a pregnant woman needs certain vitamins and minerals in higher quantities. Luckily, her body adjusts somewhat to help make this happen, by increasing absorption of certain nutrients and slowing down digestion to allow for the increased absorption of others. Many of the increased nutrient requirements can be met easily through a healthy diet. However, the greater need for certain nutrients, including folate/folic acid, may not be achieved through food or increased absorption, and women who don't eat a balanced diet may not get enough iron, zinc, copper, calcium, and vitamin D.

Let's examine these specific nutrients individually:

➤ *Folate/Folic acid.* If a woman is conscientious about consuming 400 micrograms of folic acid every day prior to conception and continues to take a dietary supplement and/or consume folic acid–fortified grains, in addition to eating foods rich in folate, she should be able to meet her increased needs for this vitamin. Foods high in folate include green leafy vegetables, legumes, and citrus fruits and juices.

Table 14.3

Recommended Weight Gain during Pregnancy

Body Mass Index (BMI) Prior to Conception	Recommended Weight Gain for a Single Baby* (in Pounds)
<18.5	28–40
18.5–24.9	25–35
25.0–29.9	15–25
>30.0	11–20

Note: *Suggested weight gain is higher for multiple fetuses.
Source: WEIGHT GAIN DURING PREGNANCY, by Institute of Medicine. Copyright © 2009. Reprinted with permission from the National Academy of Sciences, Courtesy of the National Academies Press, Washington, D.C.

➤ *Iron.* Pregnant women need extra iron to make additional red blood cells, prevent anemia, and provide for fetal growth and development. Although meat, fish, poultry, and enriched grains supply iron, the amount recommended during pregnancy is unlikely to be met from food alone, so an iron supplement is needed.[13] Many women take prescription and over-the-counter prenatal supplements with iron to help them satisfy their need for this mineral, and other nutrients.

➤ *Zinc and copper.* Women who don't eat enough nutrient-rich foods may lack zinc and copper. Both of these minerals are key to a growing baby's cell growth and development. A multivitamin pill can help fill in small dietary gaps in a mother's diet.

➤ *Calcium and vitamin D.* A pregnant woman absorbs more calcium from foods during pregnancy to offset the amount of calcium needed by the growing fetus, but she still needs to meet her own daily needs for calcium, as well as for vitamin D, to preserve bone mass and prevent osteoporosis later in life. One way to ensure an adequate calcium and vitamin D intake is to drink milk and fortified orange juice, which are nutrient rich, rather than soda, juice beverages, and sports drinks, which are low in nutrients other than calories.

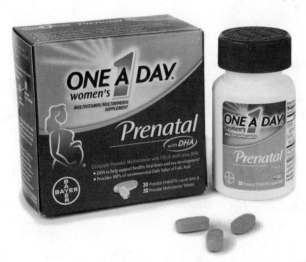

Prenatal supplements can help pregnant women meet their increased needs for iron, folic acid, and other essential nutrients.

Other nutrients are also of concern during pregnancy, especially if the mother is a vegetarian or a vegan, who eats no animal products.

Pregnant women who avoid seafood may not get enough of an omega-3 fat called docosahexaenoic acid (DHA). DHA is found in high concentrations in the brain and in the retina. The fetus accrues DHA rapidly during the second half of pregnancy, and during the first two years of life.[14]

Choline, an essential nutrient, is important during pregnancy and breast-feeding. Choline is needed for healthy cells to divide and grow, especially in the brain.[15] Observational studies suggest choline may help to prevent neural tube defects, which occur in the first month of pregnancy.[16]

Vitamin B_{12} is necessary for healthy nerve and red blood cells and for the production of nucleic acids. Vitamin B_{12} is found naturally only in animal foods. Vegans and others who consume few or no animal foods may be at risk of vitamin B_{12} deficiency, and should make sure that they are getting adequate vitamin B_{12} from fortified foods or a dietary supplement, or both.

While it's important that pregnant women meet their nutrient needs, it is equally important that they not consume too much of some nutrients. Too much preformed vitamin A, found in dietary supplements and in certain foods, can be toxic and increase the risk for birth defects, especially when taken during the first trimester, a time when women may not realize they are pregnant. The Institute of Medicine recommends no more than 3,000 IU of vitamin A daily for pregnant women.[17]

Although vitamin and mineral supplements (multivitamins) are not suitable substitutes for a healthy diet at any time during the reproductive years, they are useful for filling nutrient gaps for nutrients that could affect pregnancy. Most prenatal supplements, including the over-the-counter variety that don't require a prescription, have higher levels of folic acid, iron, zinc, and calcium than regular supplements and may be a suitable choice for women who are at risk for not meeting their nutrient needs, including teens, women carrying multiple fetuses, older women, and women who did not eat an adequate diet before pregnancy or are not eating well during pregnancy.

To assist women in having healthy pregnancies, the USDA has created a program that personalizes dietary recommendations during pregnancy and lactation

ChooseMyPlate.gov

Vegetables	Fruits	Grains	Protein	Dairy	Oils
2.5 cups	2 cups	6 oz eq	5.5 oz eq	3 cups	6 tsp

Nutrient	Recommended DRI for Nonpregnant Women Age 19–50 Years	Recommended Nutrient Intake during Pregnancy
Protein	46 g	71 g
Carbohydrates (minimum)	130 g	175 g
Dietary folate equivalents	400 µg	600 µg*
Thiamin	1.1 mg	1.4 mg
Riboflavin	1.3 mg	1.4 mg
Niacin equivalents	14 mg	18 mg
Vitamin B_6	1.3–1.5 mg	1.9 mg
Vitamin B_{12}	2.4 µg	2.6 µg
Vitamin C	75 mg	85 mg
Vitamin E	15 mg	19 mg
Vitamin A	700 µg	770 µg
Vitamin D	15 µg	15 µg
Calcium	1,000 mg	1,000 mg
Magnesium	310–320 mg	350–360 mg
Copper	900 µg	1,000 µg
Iron	18 mg	27 mg†
Phosphorus	700 mg	700 mg
Zinc	8 mg	11 mg
Calories	**2,000–2,200‡**	**§**

* Dietary supplements and/or fortified foods are recommended.
† Dietary supplements are usually needed to meet iron needs.
‡ Varies depending upon activity level and weight.
§ Add 340 calories/day in second trimester; 450 calories/day in third trimester.

(available at www.choosemyplate.gov).[18] The site includes menu-planning tools that can be used to show how much and what women need to eat and provides links to additional topics and advice.

Figure 14.4 compares the nutrient needs of nonpregnant and pregnant women.

Pregnancy Increases the Risk for Foodborne Illness

During pregnancy, a woman's immune system is weakened and the fetus's immune system is undeveloped, both of which set the stage for potential difficulties in fighting off pathogens that can cross the placenta. The bacterium *Listeria monocytogenes,* for example, may cause miscarriages, premature labor, low birth weight, developmental problems, and even infant death. Meat and dairy foods are most likely to be contaminated, but a variety of foods may contain *Listeria.* Pasteurization kills *Listeria,* which is why soft cheeses made from unpasteurized milk, such as Camembert, Brie, and blue cheeses, may be contaminated. Deli-style luncheon meats, salami, paté and other

Food that may carry pathogens, such as sashimi and other undercooked animal foods, should be avoided by pregnant women for their own safety and the safety of the fetus.

meat spreads, and smoked seafood may also harbor the bacteria. Pregnant women should avoid foods known to cause *Listeria* infection.

Raw meats and fish are more likely to carry pathogens and should be avoided during pregnancy. Sushi and sashimi, for example, contain raw fish, which are more likely to contain parasites or bacteria. Pregnant women should also avoid raw and undercooked meat, shellfish, and poultry; unpasteurized juice; and raw sprouts, such as bean sprouts.

Pregnant Women Should Avoid Many Other Substances

We noted earlier that smoking decreases the chance that a woman will conceive. When a woman continues smoking during pregnancy, her infant may weigh less than it should at delivery, and has an increased risk of being born too soon or dying soon after birth. Prenatal exposure to cigarette smoke can also increase the risk for sudden infant death syndrome (SIDS)—the unexplained death of an infant less than 1 year of age—and may stunt the infant's growth. Even secondhand smoke can affect the health of a mom-to-be and her infant. Exposure to passive smoke can affect the infant's ability to grow properly.[19] Thus, pregnant women and new mothers should avoid secondhand smoke whenever possible.

The term fetal alcohol spectrum disorders (FASDs) describes the problems that arise in infants whose mothers consume alcohol during pregnancy. The most severe effect of prenatal alcohol intake is fetal alcohol syndrome (FAS) in the baby, which you read about in Chapter 9. Children exposed to even low levels of alcohol during pregnancy can experience learning and behavioral disabilities later in life. Because there is no known safe level of alcohol consumption, pregnant women need to abstain completely to eliminate the chance of doing irreversible harm to the baby.

When used during pregnancy, illicit drugs, including marijuana, heroin, and prescription painkillers, can increase the risk for miscarriage, preterm labor, a **low birth weight baby**, and birth defects.[20] After birth, the baby may experience drug withdrawal symptoms, such as excessive crying, trembling, and seizures, as well as long-term problems, such as heart defects and behavioral and learning problems.

Pregnant women should restrict their intake of caffeine, which can be passed on to the fetus. Some research suggests that intakes greater than 200 milligrams (found in about 16 ounces of home-brewed coffee) daily may increase the risk for miscarriage. There is no conclusive evidence about how much caffeine during pregnancy is safe, but health experts advise pregnant women to limit their daily caffeine intake to 200 milligrams.[21]

The Importance of Critical Periods

The early part of pregnancy is when the main body systems and major organs are forming. Cells multiply, differentiate, and establish functional tissues and organs during various **critical periods** in the first trimester of pregnancy. During these times of rapid cellular activity, the embryo and the fetus are highly vulnerable to nutritional deficiencies, toxins, and other potentially harmful factors. It's also when the risk for spontaneous termination, also called miscarriage, is the greatest.

The harm that results from the influence of toxins, such as alcohol, or a nutrient deficiency, such as inadequate folic acid, during a critical developmental period is often irreversible, and can affect health decades later (see **Figure 14.5**). For example, persons conceived during famines not only have a higher incidence of heart disease, but also an earlier onset of the condition. Inadequate fetal growth may have later,

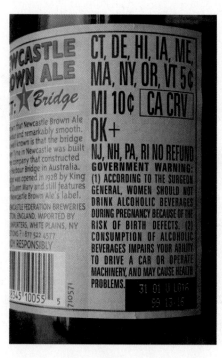

As with smoking, drinking alcohol during pregnancy exposes the fetus to potentially toxic substances.

low birth weight baby A baby weighing less than 5½ pounds at birth.

critical periods Developmental stages during which cells and tissues rapidly grow and differentiate to form body structures.

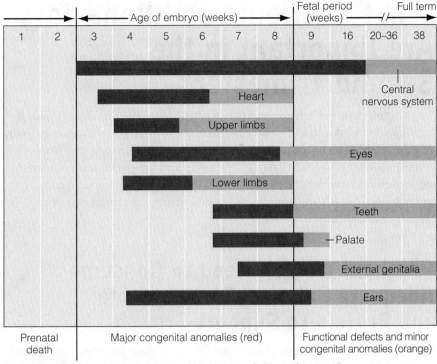

Figure 14.5 Critical Periods of Development

*Red indicates highly sensitive periods when teratogens may induce major anomalies.

Figure 14.5 Critical Periods of Development
The damage caused by toxins or lack of nutrients during pregnancy can vary according to the stage of fetal development. Damage done during critical periods may be irreversible.

long-term effects on hypertension, glucose tolerance, and lipid metabolism, and inadequate intakes of calories, fat, protein, and a variety of vitamins and minerals may contribute to the heart disease risk and time of onset.[22] Poor iron intake in early pregnancy, when the central nervous system is starting to form, may cause poor cognitive development.[23]

There is growing evidence that maternal nutrition can alter how genes are expressed during critical periods of gestation to permanently alter development.[24] This phenomenon is part of an emerging area of research into "fetal programming." The relationship between maternal nutrition and metabolic fetal programming is supported by studies showing that inadequate nutrient intakes during pregnancy may predispose the child to metabolic diseases in adulthood.[25] A mother's diet may even impact future generations.

The Take-Home Message A pregnancy is divided into trimesters. During the first trimester, the fertilized egg develops into an embryo and eventually into a fetus. The placenta is the site of common tissue between the fetus and the mother, and is attached to the baby via the umbilical cord. Many women experience morning sickness, food cravings, and food aversions during the first trimester. Women who begin pregnancy at a healthy weight should gain 25 to 35 pounds during pregnancy. The need for several nutrients, including folate, iron, and zinc, increase during pregnancy. Pregnant women should avoid excess amounts of preformed vitamin A. They also need to avoid foods known to contain pathogens. Caffeine intake should be limited to no more than 200 milligrams daily. Tobacco, alcohol, and illicit drugs should be avoided throughout pregnancy but particularly in the first trimester. Potentially harmful toxins and other substances can cause irreversible damage to the fetus, especially during critical growth periods.

What Nutrients and Behaviors Are Important in the Second Trimester?

For many pregnant women, the nausea and fatigue of the first trimester subside during the second trimester, and appetite begins to improve. The baby is growing rapidly, and the mother's body is changing to accommodate this growth. The fetus is just under 2 pounds and measures about 13 inches long by the end of this trimester. During the second trimester, the mother should focus on consuming adequate calories and nutrients, participating in regular physical activity, and awareness of potential pregnancy complications.

Pregnant Women Need to Consume Adequate Calories, Carbohydrate, and Protein to Support Growth

Health experts advise pregnant women who begin their pregnancy at a healthy weight to consume 340 calories more a day during the second trimester than they did when not pregnant, and to gain about 1 pound per week. Pregnant women should choose nutrient-rich foods to get the additional calories they need. For example, a whole-wheat English muffin topped with peanut butter and paired with baby carrots supplies about 340 calories while providing complex carbohydrates, healthy fat, protein, fiber, iron and zinc—nutrients that a woman needs more of during pregnancy (**Figure 14.6**).

Pregnant women require a minimum of 175 grams of carbohydrates per day (versus 130 grams for nonpregnant women) to provide the amount of glucose mom needs, and to foster the growth and development of the embryo and fetus. Protein needs increase by about 35 percent, to about 71 grams daily, during the second and third trimesters, as you can see from Figure 14.4 on page 531. Women typically meet higher protein needs with a balanced diet.

1 whole-wheat English muffin
2 tbs peanut butter
5 baby carrots

340 total calories

Figure 14.6 Adding Calories and Nutrients The extra calorie needs and most increased nutrient needs of the second and third trimesters can be met with nutrient-rich foods.

Exercise Is Important for Pregnant Women

Exercise during pregnancy is beneficial for improving the possibility of gaining weight within the targeted ranges.[26] It also helps to decrease minor aches and pains, lessen constipation, improve energy level, reduce stress, improve the quality of sleep, and reduce the risk for gestational diabetes.[27]

Healthy pregnant women should get at least 150 minutes (2 hours and 30 minutes) of moderate-intensity aerobic activity, such as brisk walking, each week. It's best to spread exercise over a 7-day period. Pregnant women who are healthy and already participate in vigorous-intensity aerobic activity, such as running, can continue provided they remain healthy and discuss adjustments in exercise with their health care provider as their pregnancy progresses.[28] Some forms of exercise are considered dangerous during pregnancy, however (**Table 14.4**). Pregnant women should check with their health care providers before exercising to see what type, and how much, is appropriate. See the Table Tips for more on exercising while pregnant.

Table 14.4

Safe and Unsafe Exercises during Pregnancy

Safe Activities	Unsafe Activities (Contact Sports and High-Impact Activities)
Walking	Hockey (field and ice)
Stationary cycling	Basketball
Low-impact aerobics	Football
Swimming	Soccer
Dancing	Gymnastics
	Horseback riding
	Skating
	Skiing (snow and water)
	Vigorous racquet sports
	Weight lifting

Source: Adapted from "Exercise During Pregnancy" by T. Wang and B. Apgar, from AMERICAN FAMILY PHYSICIAN, 1998, Volume 57. Copyright © 1998 by American Academy of Family Physicians. Adapted with permission.

Potential Complications: Gestational Diabetes and Hypertension

Sometimes a pregnant woman develops high blood glucose levels and is diagnosed with **gestational diabetes** (*gestation* = pregnancy-related). This type of diabetes occurs in an estimated 18 percent of pregnancies in the United States, typically toward the end of the second trimester and in the early part of the third trimester.[29]

Though the cause of gestational diabetes is unknown, hormones from the placenta appear to lead to insulin resistance in the mother, which in turn causes hyperglycemia. Extra blood glucose crosses the placenta, stimulating the baby's pancreas to make more insulin, which leads to the storage of excess glucose as fat on the baby's body and can result in **macrosomia** (*macro* = large, *somia* = body), or a larger-than-normal baby. Large babies have an increased risk of shoulder injury during delivery, and are more often born by cesarean delivery. Gestational diabetes also increases the risk of the baby developing **jaundice**, breathing problems, and birth defects. Because the baby produces extra insulin during pregnancy, this hormone is elevated after birth when the baby no longer has high levels of blood glucose, causing a rapid drop in blood glucose levels, which may lead to hypoglycemia.[30]

Certain factors can increase a woman's risk for gestational diabetes:

➤ Being overweight or obese
➤ Being over 25 years old
➤ Having a history of higher-than-normal blood glucose levels
➤ Having a family history of diabetes
➤ Being of Hispanic/Latina, African-American, American Indian, Alaska Native, Asian American, or Pacific Islander descent
➤ Having any of the following in a previous pregnancy: gestational diabetes, stillbirth, miscarriage, or large baby (weighing more than 9 pounds)
➤ Having polycystic ovary syndrome (PCOS) or another condition linked to problems with insulin

Table TIPS

Exercising while Pregnant

Consult your health care provider before beginning an exercise program.

Begin slowly to avoid excessive fatigue and shortness of breath.

Exercise in the early morning or in the evening to avoid becoming overheated.

Drink plenty of fluids to stay hydrated.

Avoid any activity that involves lying on your back or puts you at risk for falling and other injuries to your abdomen.

Report any problems or unusual symptoms such as chest pains, contractions, dizziness, headaches, calf swelling, blurred vision, vaginal discharge or bleeding, and/or abdominal pain immediately to your health care provider.

Source: Adapted from The National Women's Health Information Center, U.S. Department of Health and Human Services, "Healthy Pregnancy: Have a Fit Pregnancy," 2006. Centers for Disease Control and Prevention. 2011. Physical Activity, Healthy Pregnant or Postpartum Women. Available at www.cdc.gov. Accessed March 2013.

gestational diabetes Diabetes that occurs in women during pregnancy.

macrosomia A large baby, weighing more than 8 pounds, 13 oz.

jaundice A yellowish coloring of the skin due to the presence of bile pigments in the blood.

Walking is one form of exercise that is safe for most pregnant women. Regular exercise may help a pregnant woman maintain healthy blood glucose levels.

➤ Having ever had problems with insulin or blood glucose, such as insulin resistance, glucose intolerance, or prediabetes

➤ Having high blood pressure, high cholesterol, and/or heart disease

According to the National Institute of Child Health and Human Development, if a woman has two or more of these risk factors, she is at high risk for developing gestational diabetes, and should contact her physician to be tested for the condition as soon as she knows she is pregnant. If she has one risk factor, she is at an average risk, and should be tested for gestational diabetes between 24 and 28 weeks of her pregnancy. If she has no risk factors, she may not need testing for the condition.[31] Eating healthfully, gaining the appropriate pregnancy weight, and engaging in regular physical activity can help reduce the risk of developing diabetes during pregnancy.

Hypertension (high blood pressure) during pregnancy can damage the woman's kidneys and other organs and increase the risk for low birth weight and preterm delivery. **Pregnancy-induced hypertension** includes *gestational hypertension*, *preeclampsia*, and *eclampsia*, which vary in medical severity. Gestational hypertension is more likely to occur halfway through pregnancy and signal preeclampsia. Preeclampsia occurs when the pregnant woman has hypertension and her urine contains protein, which is a sign of damage to her kidneys. The cause of preeclampsia is not known. Preeclampsia is dangerous to the baby because it increases the risk of low birth weight babies and babies who are delivered early, and stillbirth. Women with hypertension prior to pregnancy or who developed it during a prior pregnancy, those who are obese, are under the age of 20 or over the age of 40, are carrying more than one baby, or have diabetes, kidney disease, rheumatoid arthritis, lupus, or scleroderma are at higher risk of developing preeclampsia. If left untreated, preeclampsia can lead to eclampsia, which can cause seizures in the mother and is a major cause of death of women during pregnancy.[32] The only cure for preeclampsia and eclampsia is to deliver the baby. However, delivery too early (before 32 weeks) is unsafe for the baby. Women are often confined to bed rest, managed with medications, and even hospitalized to treat preeclampsia until the baby can be safely born. Calcium supplements had been proposed to prevent preeclampsia, but research doesn't support that they reduce the risk, especially if the mother's diet is adequate in calcium. Some research suggests that antioxidants, specifically vitamins C and E, may reduce the risk, but more research is needed.[33]

The Take-Home Message Pregnant women who begin pregnancy at a healthy weight need to consume about an additional 340 calories daily during the second trimester. A varied selection of nutrient-rich foods will help women meet most nutrient needs. Exercise can provide numerous benefits during pregnancy. Some women develop gestational diabetes and pregnancy-induced high blood pressure and need to be monitored closely by a health care professional to help manage these pregnancy complications.

pregnancy-induced hypertension A category of hypertension that includes *gestational hypertension* (occurs in pregnancy in a woman without a prior history of high blood pressure), *preeclampsia* (hypertension, severe edema, and protein loss occur), and *eclampsia* (can result in seizures; may be extremely dangerous for mother and baby).

What Nutrients and Behaviors Are Important in the Third Trimester?

At the end of the third trimester, the baby will weigh about 7 pounds, although healthy birth weights vary. Many pregnant women who conceived at a healthy weight should be taking in 450 more calories each day than before pregnancy in order to gain about one pound per week.[34] A banana, whole-wheat English muffin with peanut butter, and baby carrots supply about 450 calories.

As the growing baby exerts pressure on her intestines and stomach, and hormonal changes slow the movement of food through the gastrointestinal (GI) tract, she may experience heartburn. To minimize heartburn, pregnant women should eat frequent, small meals and avoid foods that may irritate the esophagus, such as spicy or highly seasoned foods. They should also avoid lying down after meals and elevate their heads during sleep.

The slower movement of food through the GI tract and a tendency toward less physical activity are factors that contribute to constipation, which, like heartburn, is common near the end of pregnancy. The large amount of iron in prenatal supplements can also contribute to constipation. Eating more fiber-rich foods, along with drinking plenty of fluids, can help prevent and manage constipation.

Pregnancy also makes a woman more prone to hemorrhoids, in part because the growing uterus puts pressure on the pelvic veins and the large vein on the right side of the body that receives blood from the lower limbs. The increased pressure can slow the return of blood from the lower half of the body, which causes the veins below the uterus to become swollen. Straining to have a bowel movement because of constipation is also a cause of hemorrhoids.

The Take-Home Message During the third trimester, women who begin pregnancy at a healthy weight need to eat 450 calories more per day than when not pregnant and should continue gaining about a pound per week. Heartburn and constipation commonly occur during the third trimester. Eating smaller meals and consuming more fiber can help.

What Special Concerns Might Younger or Older Mothers-to-Be Face?

Pregnancy and childbirth place demands on the body of a mother-to-be no matter what her age, but women who become pregnant during their teenage years face particular challenges. Women over the age of 35 also face some additional challenges.

A teenage girl's body is still growing, so she has higher nutrient needs than does an adult woman. In addition, teenage girls, like many adolescents, are more likely to eat on the run, skip meals, eat less-nutrient-dense snacks, and consume inadequate amounts of whole grains, fruits, vegetables, and lean dairy products. Pair this lower-nutrient diet to the increased needs of pregnancy, and these young girls are likely to fall short of many of their nutrient requirements, especially iron, folic acid, calcium, and potentially even calories. In some cases, a teenage girl may delay prenatal care because she is in denial of the pregnancy or fears telling others. She may also restrict her calorie intake to avoid weight gain as she attempts to hide her pregnancy.

Teenage mothers are also more likely to develop pregnancy-induced hypertension and deliver preterm and low birth weight babies, putting the baby at risk for health problems. They are more likely to engage in unhealthy lifestyle habits such as smoking, drinking alcohol, and taking illicit drugs, all of which can compromise the baby's health, as well as the mother's.[35]

Women who delay pregnancy until their 30s or beyond may also face additional challenges. Fertility typically begins to decline starting in a woman's early 30s, so

Due to additional steps taken to ensure pregnancy, older mothers more often deliver multiples—twins, triplets, or quads—than do younger women.

conception may take longer. Women are not only at higher risk of having diabetes and high blood pressure after the age of 35, but also are at a greater risk of developing these conditions during pregnancy. Older mothers are also more physiologically likely to conceive multiples. Multiples are more likely to be born preterm, and, as a result, are at greater risk for low birth weight and medical complications.

Older mothers should try to achieve a healthy body weight prior to conception, avoid smoking, eat a balanced diet before and during pregnancy, and, like all potential mothers, consume adequate amounts of folic acid. Women over the age of 35 who may conceive should work closely with their doctors to manage health conditions, such as high blood pressure, to the best of their ability. As with all pregnant women, they should limit their caffeine intake and avoid alcohol and illicit drugs.

Regardless of age, as her due date draws near, an expectant mother needs to decide how to nourish her newborn after delivery: Should she breast-feed or use infant formula? Let's look at both of these options next.

The Take-Home Message Teens who become pregnant are at higher risk of developing hypertension and delivering a premature and low birth weight baby. Because a teen is still growing, she may have a harder time satisfying her own nutrient needs and her baby's unless she is diligent about eating a well-balanced diet. Women over age 35 may have more difficulty conceiving and are at higher risk for high blood pressure and diabetes during pregnancy.

What Is Breast-Feeding and Why Is It Beneficial?

A woman who has just given birth will begin a period of **lactation**; that is, her body will produce milk to nourish her new infant. Milk production is initially driven by hormonal changes following the delivery of the placenta and is subsequently stimulated by the infant's suckling at the mother's nipple. Signals sent from the nipple to the hypothalamus in the mother's brain prompt the pituitary gland to release two hormones: prolactin and oxytocin. Prolactin causes milk to be produced in the breast, while oxytocin causes the milk to be released in a **let-down response**, so the infant can receive it through the nipple (see **Figure 14.7**).[36]

The old adage "breast is best" when it comes to nourishing an infant is still true. The American Academy of Pediatrics recommends exclusive breast-feeding for the first six months of the baby's life for most women.[37] Through **breast-feeding**, or nursing, mothers provide food that is uniquely tailored to meet their infant's nutritional needs in an easily digestible form. Breast-feeding also provides many other advantages for both the mother and the baby.

Newborn babies may eat as often as 12 times a day!

Breast-Feeding Provides Physical, Emotional, and Financial Benefits for Mothers

Breast-feeding provides short- and long-term benefits for both mother and child. During infancy, breast-feeding can be cheaper, safer, and more convenient than infant formula. The long-term health and emotional benefits of breast-feeding can last for years after infancy.

lactation The production of milk in a woman's body after childbirth, and the period during which it occurs.

let-down response The release of milk from the mother's breast to feed the baby.

breast-feeding The act of feeding an infant milk from a woman's breast.

Hypothalamus

2 Hypothalamus stimulates the release of prolactin and oxytocin

Pituitary

1 Sucking stimulates nerve that sends signal to mother's hypothalamus

3 Prolactin triggers milk production and oxytocin triggers the let-down response

Figure 14.7 The Let-Down Response

Breast-Feeding Helps with Pregnancy Recovery and Reduces the Risk of Some Chronic Diseases

In addition to stimulating the release of breast milk, the hormone oxytocin stimulates contractions in the uterus, which helps the organ return to its prepregnancy size and shape. Breast-feeding also reduces blood loss in the mother after delivery, and may help some women return to their prepregnancy weight.[38]

Breast-feeding, especially if it is done exclusively (not in combination with formula-feeding), can also help delay the return of the menstrual cycle, which may decrease fertility. However, this does not mean that women who breast-feed their newborns should assume they won't get pregnant. They still need to take precautions if they wish to avoid pregnancy.

Observational studies suggest that the longer women breast-feed, the lower the risk for premenopausal breast cancer and ovarian cancer. Breast-feeding may also reduce a woman's risk of hip fractures later in life, as well as her risk of type 2 diabetes.[39]

Breast Milk Is Less Expensive and More Convenient than Formula

Making breast milk costs significantly less than using infant formula to nourish a baby. Feeding a baby infant formula may cost $2,000 or more, depending on the form, during the first year of life. The cost associated with the extra food required to promote breast-feeding, estimated at a minimum of $300 yearly, is significantly less than infant formula.[40]

There are other costs associated with formula-feeding beyond the price of the product. For example, there are substantial environmental costs of dealing with the millions of formula containers and hundreds of thousands of pounds of paper packaging and waste that are disposed of in landfills each year, as well as costs associated with the energy needed to properly clean the feeding bottles. Health care costs are higher, too. One study concluded that if 90 percent of mothers breast-fed their children exclusively for the first six months of life, the United States would save $13 billion dollars a year, the majority of it in medical costs.[41] For the family, the environment, and for society as a whole, breast-feeding is relatively less expensive all around than formula-feeding.

Finally, feeding from the breast is more convenient than bottle-feeding because the milk is always sterile and at the right temperature, and there isn't any need to prepare bottles. The mother also doesn't need to prepare the milk before feeding, and there is less cleanup involved.

Breast-Feeding Promotes Bonding

The close interaction between mother and child during nursing promotes a unique bonding experience. The physical contact helps the baby feel safe, secure, and emotionally attached to the mother.

Breast-Feeding Provides Nutritional and Health Benefits for Infants

There are more than 200 compounds in breast milk that benefit infants. Numerous research studies have indicated that breast-feeding provides nutritional and health advantages that can last years beyond infancy.

Breast Milk Is Best for an Infant's Unique Nutritional Needs

The nutritional composition of breast milk changes as the infant grows. Right after birth, a new mother produces a carotenoid-rich, yellowish fluid called **colostrum** that has little fat but a lot of protein, vitamin A, and minerals. Colostrum also contains antibodies that help protect the infant from infections, particularly in the digestive tract.

Four to seven days after birth, breast milk production begins in earnest. Breast milk is high in lactose, fat, and B vitamins, and lower in fat-soluble vitamins, sodium, and other minerals. These nutrients are balanced to enhance their absorption. Breast milk is relatively low in protein so as not to stress the infant's immature kidneys with excessive amounts of nitrogenous waste products from protein digestion. The protein is also mostly in the form of alpha-lactalbumin, which is easier for the infant to digest. The nutrient composition of breast milk continues to change as the baby grows and his or her needs change.[42]

Breast-Feeding Protects Against Infections, Allergies, and Chronic Diseases and May Enhance Brain Development

Breast milk provides the infant with a disease-fighting boost as his or her immune system matures. Research supports that breast-feeding decreases the risk and severity of diarrhea and other intestinal disorders, respiratory infections, meningitis, ear infections, and urinary tract infections.[43] One protein in breast milk, lactoferrin, protects the infant against infection from a variety of bacteria, and viruses. Breast milk also contains the antioxidants, hormones, enzymes, and growth factors that help a child's immune system to grow and develop properly.[44]

Breast-feeding, especially if continued beyond six months, may help reduce the risk of childhood obesity. The reason for this isn't clear, but could be associated with

colostrum The fluid that is expressed from the mother's breast after birth and before the development of breast milk.

the tendency of breast-fed infants to gain less weight during the first year of life than formula-fed infants. The lower weight gain may be due to breast-fed infants having more control over when they start and stop eating than their bottle-fed counterparts.[45] Babies at the breast may be allowed by their mothers to rely more on their internal cues to eat until they are full, and then stop eating, which may influence food intake later in life.

Lastly, breast milk may help infants with their intellectual development. The breast milk of mothers that consume an adequate diet provides two unsaturated fatty acids, docosahexaenoic acid (DHA) and arachidonic acid (AA), which are important for the development of the central nervous system, particularly the brain (see Chapter 5). The levels of these fatty acids vary in the mother's diet, and, therefore, in her breast milk. Research suggests that breast-fed infants may have greater cognitive function, measured by IQ and academic success in school through adolescence, than formula-fed babies, which may be due in part to DHA and AA.[46] DHA and AA are added in varying amounts to nearly all infant formula sold in the United States.

The breast-fed infant doesn't always need to consume breast milk directly from the breast. Milk can be pumped, or expressed, with a breast pump, refrigerated, and fed to the baby in a bottle by another caregiver at any time. This allows the mother to work outside the home or enjoy a few hours "off duty." The Nutrition in the Real World feature "Breast-Feeding at Work Can Work" addresses the challenges faced by nursing mothers who work outside the home. Fresh expressed breast milk should be refrigerated within 3-6 hours and used within 3 days, or stored in the freezer for up to six months.

Women can express breast milk using a breast pump and store the milk in the refrigerator or freezer for later use.

The Take-Home Message Breast-feeding provides numerous benefits for women and babies. It may help mothers return to their prepregnancy weight faster and reduce the risk of certain cancers, osteoporosis, and type 2 diabetes. Breast-feeding is the least expensive and most convenient way to nourish an infant, and helps the mother and baby to bond. Human milk is rich in nutrients, antibodies, and other compounds not available in formula that can protect the baby against infections, allergies, and chronic diseases, and may enhance the child's cognitive development. Women are advised to breast-feed exclusively for the first six months, and then breast-feed to supplement solid food through the rest of the first year.

Breast milk should be stored in the back of the freezer, where there is less temperature fluctuation and it is less likely to defrost. Premature defrosting increases the risk of harmful bacteria multiplying.

What Are the Best Dietary and Lifestyle Habits for a Breast-Feeding Mother?

During the first six months of breast-feeding, the mother produces about 24 ounces of breast milk daily and about 16 ounces a day during the second six months of breast-feeding. During this period, her body needs additional amounts of fluid and nutrients.

To meet her increased fluid needs, a breast-feeding woman should drink about 13 cups of water and beverages daily. It takes 500 calories a day to produce milk during the first six months of lactation. A combination of energy liberated from stored fat, and calories from food, provide the necessary fuel to make milk. Approximately 170 calories are mobilized daily from fat that was stored during pregnancy. A nursing woman who began her pregnancy at a healthy weight and gained a healthy amount

nutrition
IN THE Real World

Breast-Feeding at Work Can Work

For many women, the decision to breast-feed their infants is an easy one. The bigger challenge is how to juggle breast-feeding with returning to work or school.

Women often feel uncomfortable about breast-feeding outside the home, especially in the workplace, and it's no wonder. Most companies don't offer support for working mothers, even though employer support for breast-feeding can extend the duration that a mother nurses her baby, which benefits both mother and child.[1] Sometimes, women have to choose between breast-feeding and a paycheck. But the attitude toward supporting breast-feeding mothers in the workplace is improving, albeit slowly. For example, in 1998, the state of Minnesota mandated that its companies aid and support breast-feeding moms. From 1998 to 2002, the percentage of women still breast-feeding at six months more than doubled within the state.[2] Forty-five states, the District of

Columbia, and the Virgin Islands have laws that specifically allow women to breast-feed in any public or private location, and 24 states, the District of Columbia, and Puerto Rico have laws related to breast-feeding in the workplace.[3]

Women who return to work while lactating require minimal worksite resources to accommodate their breast-feeding efforts. First, they need adequate break times and access to a private, comfortable room with an electrical outlet in order to pump their breast milk. They need a sink for cleaning their hands and the pumping equipment, and a refrigerator that runs at 40°F or below for storing expressed milk.

Worksite support of breast-feeding women is not only healthy for the infant but, in many ways, better for the corporate bottom line. Lactation support programs at work help to lower medical costs and health insurance costs for breast-feeding women and their infants, and promote employee

morale and loyalty to the company.[4] It is estimated that each $1 invested in a corporate breast-feeding program saves the company $2 to $3.[5]

Practical Nutrition VIDEO

Take Care When Eating Fish

In many ways, nursing mothers are still "eating for two" so they need to be careful not to consume toxins. Joan spells out the guidelines for safe consumption of fish to avoid excess methylmercury. Scan this QR code with your mobile device to access the video. You can also access the video in MasteringNutrition™.

of pregnancy weight needs just 330 more calories from food every day than when she was not pregnant.[47] Overweight and obese women and women who gained too much weight during pregnancy may not need to consume additional calories when breast-feeding, but need to eat a nutrient-rich diet.[48]

During the second six months of breast-feeding, fewer calories (theoretically) are available from stored body fat, so a lactating woman at a healthy weight prior to pregnancy needs to consume about 400 extra calories daily to meet her needs.[49] Although a breast-feeding woman's dietary carbohydrate, vitamin, and mineral requirements increase slightly, a well-balanced diet similar to the one she consumed during pregnancy will meet her needs. Lactating women who avoid or underconsume animal foods should make sure that they consume adequate amounts of vitamin B_{12}, iron, and zinc from dietary supplements, fortified foods, or a combination.

Anything that goes into a breast-feeding mother's body can potentially pass into her breast milk, and ultimately to her baby. Illicit drugs, such as cocaine, heroin, and marijuana, for example, can be transferred to a breast-fed infant and cause harm. Methylmercury, which a mother can overconsume if she doesn't avoid certain fish, can also be harmful, so nursing mothers should adhere to the FDA's guidelines about fish to minimize the infant's exposure, and her own, to methylmercury (see Table 14.1 on page 526).

A small amount of caffeine is transferred into breast milk, but caffeine consumption is generally considered safe for breast-feeding women. Coffee should be limited to no more than three cups daily, and possibly less, depending on how your child reacts, because caffeine can interfere with the baby's sleep and cause crankiness.[50]

Alcohol is transferred to breast milk, and is capable of slowing infant growth. It also inhibits milk production, and milk availability to the baby. An occasional drink when lactating probably presents little risk to a nursing child, but mothers should discuss alcohol consumption with their health care provider. The nicotine from cigarette smoking passes into breast milk and has been linked to decreased milk production and decreased weight gain in nursing infants.[51]

Breast milk can also reflect the foods a mother eats, and babies may become fussy if the mother has consumed certain spicy or gassy foods, such as garlic, beans, and broccoli. The mother can stop eating the food, wait a few days, and then try it again in her diet. If the infant reacts the same way, it's best to stop eating that food while nursing. If the mother's diet becomes too restrictive, she needs to consult with a registered dietitian to tailor a diet that works to nourish her body and her baby's.

The Take-Home Message A nursing mother who began her pregnancy at a healthy weight and gained the recommended pregnancy pounds needs to consume about 330 calories more daily during the first six months of lactation than she did when not pregnant and an extra 400 calories daily during the second six months. She needs to increase her fluid and nutrient intake to help her body produce breast milk. Anything a woman consumes can be passed on to her baby in breast milk, so nursing mothers should avoid all illicit drugs, caffeine, and smoking, and speak with their doctor about the use of alcohol.

When Is Infant Formula a Healthy Alternative to Breast Milk?

If the infant isn't going to be breast-fed, the only other healthy option is infant formula. For some women, the choice is a personal preference. For others, breast-feeding may not be possible due to illness or other circumstances, and formula-feeding is necessary.

Some Women May Not Be Able to Breast-Feed

Women who are infected with HIV (human immunodeficiency virus), the virus that causes AIDS (acquired immune deficiency syndrome), should not breast-feed, as this virus can be transmitted to the child through breast milk. Women who have AIDS, human T-cell leukemia, active tuberculosis, are receiving chemotherapy and/or radiation, or use illicit drugs such as marijuana and cocaine should not breast-feed either. (*Note:* For HIV-infected women living in countries where there is inadequate food, an unsafe food supply, and/or frequent incidences of nutritional deficiencies and infectious diseases, the benefits of providing the infant with nutrient- and immune-rich breast milk may outweigh the risks of HIV infection for the baby.) An infant born with a genetic disorder called galactosemia can't metabolize lactose and shouldn't be breast-fed.[52] Lastly, any woman taking prescription or over-the-counter medications should check with her health care provider to ensure that they are safe to consume while breast-feeding.

Infant formula is available in several forms and varies in cost and ingredients. Infant formula is highly regulated by the FDA, so any formula on the market in the United States is considered safe.

Formula Can Be a Healthy Alternative to Breast-Feeding

The best alternative to breast-feeding is to feed an infant with a commercially made formula. Cow's milk should not be used to feed infants because it can't meet a baby's nutritional needs. Cow's milk is more difficult for the infant to digest, and even the full-fat variety is too low in total fat and the essential fatty acid linoleic acid, and too high in sodium and potassium. Also, the iron in cow's milk is poorly absorbed, and to make matters worse, cow's milk can cause intestinal blood loss in infants, which will cause iron loss and, possibly, anemia.[53]

Infant formula is developed to be as similar as possible to breast milk (see Table 14.5), and formula-fed infants grow and develop normally. The FDA regulates all infant formulas sold in the United States and has set specific requirements for the nutrients that the formula must contain.

Infant formula is typically made from cow's milk that has been altered to improve its nutrient content and digestibility. Soy protein–based formulas are free of cow's protein and lactose and can be used for infants who can't tolerate cow's milk protein–based formula or who are vegetarians. **Hypoallergenic infant formulas** are available for infants who can't consume cow's milk or soy formulas. The AAP and the American Academy of Family Physicians recommend that all formula-fed infants consume iron-fortified formulas to reduce the risk of iron deficiency.[54]

Formula can be purchased as powder, as a concentrated liquid, or as the ready-to-use variety. Powdered formula is the least expensive form and the ready-to-use form tends to be the most expensive. Care should be taken to mix the powdered or concentrated liquid with the correct amount of water so the formula will not be too diluted or too concentrated. (Water does not need to be treated by boiling first unless the infant's immune system is compromised.)

If the infant doesn't finish the bottle, the formula should be discarded, rather than saved for another feeding. The bacteria in the infant's mouth can contaminate the formula and multiply to levels that could be harmful even if the formula is reheated. Reheating of infant formula can destroy some of the heat-sensitive nutrients. Also, formula should not be left out at room temperature for more than two hours, as any bacteria present can multiply to unhealthy levels.

hypoallergenic infant formulas Specially developed formulas for infants who have food allergies and cannot tolerate regular formula.

Table 14.5

Nutritional Similarities between Infant Formula and Breast Milk

Nutrient	Amount in Breast Milk	Amount in Formula
Protein (g/100 ml)	1.1	1.8
Fat (g/100 ml)	4	4.8
Carbohydrate (g/100 ml)	7	7.3
Sodium (mg/100 ml)	1.3	0.7
Calcium (mg/100 ml)	22	53
Phosphorus (mg/100)	14	38
Iron (mg/100 ml)	0.03	0.1
Zinc (mg/100 ml)	3.2	5.1
Vitamin D (IU/100 ml)	4	41

Note that infants should not be allowed to sleep with a bottle containing milk, formula, or other sugary liquids (such as fruit juice, soda, or other sweetened drinks), as this practice can potentially lead to ear infections and to **early childhood caries** (see **Figure 14.8**). Liquids from bottles tend to pool in the mouth during sleep. The normal bacteria in the mouth change the sugar to an acid, which gradually dissolves the immature enamel and allows tooth decay to occur. The American Academy of Pediatric Dentistry recommends avoiding putting infants to sleep with bottles filled with sugar-containing beverages, among other strategies for reducing early childhood caries.[55]

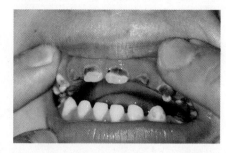

Figure 14.8 Early Childhood Caries When infants are given a bottle shortly before sleep, the sugary beverage can pool in the mouth and dissolve developing tooth enamel, causing early childhood dental caries.

| **The Take-Home Message** If a woman doesn't breast-feed, commercial iron-fortified infant formula is the only other healthy option. Cow's milk should not be offered before age 1, as it is too high in protein and some minerals and too low in calories and fat. Powdered and concentrated infant formulas must be mixed carefully so they are not too diluted or concentrated for the baby's digestive system. Infants should never be given a bottle as they are put down to sleep, as this can lead to tooth decay and ear infections.

What Are the Nutrient Needs of an Infant and Why Are They So High?

Whereas parents and caregivers can be confident that breast milk and commercial formulas are meeting their infants' unique nutritional needs, they would benefit from knowing exactly what those nutrient needs are, and what causes them to be so high. Let's explore these topics next.

Infants Grow at an Accelerated Rate

During a child's **infancy**, or first year of life, he experiences a tremendous amount of growth. In fact, an infant doubles his birth weight by about 6 months of age, and triples it by the age of 12 months. Length will double around the end of the first year as well. Let's try to imagine the physical growth of an infant in adult terms. On January first, you weigh 100 pounds. Around the month of June, you have grown to 200 pounds. By New Year's Eve, you would weigh 300 pounds! You would have to eat an enormous amount of food every day to actually make this happen. For an infant, though, this is a normal growth rate.

Infants are doing much more than just getting heavier and longer. Intellectual and social developments are also under way. As time goes by, infant communication skills go beyond crying, and at around three months of age a baby usually starts to smile. Preferences also become clearer: for particular people (such as the mom), for specific activities (getting kisses or being held), and for certain foods (such as mashed bananas).

An infant should reach certain stages of physical development within a distinct time frame. If an infant is not growing in the expected fashion, this may be a sign that something is wrong. Parents, caregivers, and health care providers need to be alert to infants who miss the mark, and then look more deeply into the situation. The child may not be receiving sufficient nutrition. Perhaps an infant has a poor appetite, and the new mom has no idea that the child should be eating more frequently. Maybe an infant is having some digestive problems, and the new day care provider does not mention the frequency of dirty diapers.

early childhood caries Tooth decay from prolonged contact with formula, milk, fruit juice, or other carbohydrate-rich liquid offered to an infant in a bottle.

infancy The age range from birth to 12 months.

Of course, optimal infant nutrition is sometimes hindered by circumstance. In less developed countries where poverty is the norm and food is scarce, problems such as protein-energy malnutrition (see Chapter 6) are common. Even in developed countries, such as the United States, there are problems with poor infant nutrition that may affect growth. For example, iron-deficiency anemia (see Chapter 8) sometimes occurs in infants when caregivers substitute juice or cow's milk for adequate amounts of breast milk or iron-fortified formula. Breast-fed infants who don't begin to consume iron-fortified foods, such as puréed meats and fortified cereals, at around 6 months may have low iron levels in their blood, which may result in iron deficiency and iron-deficiency anemia.

Monitoring Infant Growth

An infant who does not receive adequate nutrition (whether in terms of quantity or quality) may have difficulty reaching developmental **milestones** (**Figure 14.9**). Think of developmental milestones as checkpoints, which can be physical, social, or intellectual. While most parents do not know the specific nutrient needs of their infant, it's important that the infant attain the specific milestones at the appropriate time. This assures parents that they are providing the right amount and type of nourishment.

If a child doesn't reach the appropriate milestones, he or she may eventually develop a condition called failure to thrive (FTT). A child with FTT is delayed in physical growth or size or does not gain enough weight. Poor appetite, an unbalanced diet, or a medical problem that has not yet been diagnosed can all be causes of FTT. Sometimes, FTT results from inappropriate care or neglect. Caregivers and health care providers need to be aware of the signs of this condition and watch for those signs in their children and patients.

In addition to milestones, parents and health care providers use **growth charts** to track physical development progress. Typically, measures of head circumference, length, weight, and weight for length are used to assess growth. These measures are taken at each "well-check" visit to the health care provider, about once a month for the first year. The information obtained from the measurements is plotted on the growth

milestones Objectives or significant events that occur during development.

growth charts Series of percentile curves that illustrate the distribution of selected body measurements in U.S. children.

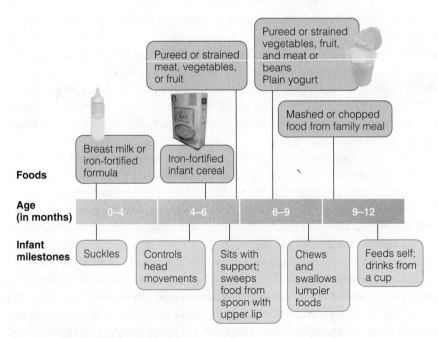

Figure 14.9 Foods for Baby's First Year
During the first year after birth, as developmental milestones are being met, an infant's diet will progress from breast milk or infant formula to age-appropriate versions of family meals.

chart, placing the child into a **percentile**. Percentiles rank the infant with regard to other infants of the same age in a reference group. For example, a four-month-old who is in the 25th percentile for weight for age weighs less than 75 percent of the four-month-olds and weighs the same as or more than 25 percent (see **Figure 14.10**).[56]

Infants Have Higher Nutrient Needs

Because they are growing rapidly, infants have a greater need for many nutrients, based on weight, including calories. For example, a 6-month-old boy requires about 82 calories for every kilogram (kg).[57] A 35-year-old adult sedentary male who weighs 154 pounds needs about 34 calories per kilogram to maintain his weight.[58] As infants grow, their needs for carbohydrate and protein increase. Fat is a concentrated source of energy and should not be limited during infancy, and neither should overall calories. Doing so may restrict a child's physical and mental development.

Several nutrients in particular are important for an infant's health and well-being. As you recall from Chapter 7, all infants should receive an injection of vitamin K at birth to ensure that their blood clots properly. Vitamin K is produced by the bacteria in the gut. Infants are born with a sterile gut, so giving vitamin K at birth provides the infant with the vitamin K he needs until he is able to produce his own.[59]

The amount of vitamin D in breast milk is not enough to prevent rickets, so infants should receive 400 IU of vitamin D drops daily starting within the first few days of life. (Fortified infant formula contains adequate levels of vitamin D.) Once they reach age 1, children should drink vitamin D–fortified milk with meals and snacks. Even though vitamin D is produced in the body in response to strong ultraviolet rays from the sun, experts warn against exposing a child under the age of 6 months because of the risk for sunburn, which can lead to skin cancer in the future.[60]

Term infants are born with a six-month supply of iron. Iron-rich foods, such as fortified cereals and puréed meats, should be introduced to the infant's diet at about 6 months to provide adequate iron for growth and development.

Vitamin B$_{12}$ is found naturally only in animal foods. Breast-feeding women who avoid animal foods or eat insufficient amounts of animal foods rich in vitamin B$_{12}$ need to supplement their diets with vitamin B$_{12}$ supplements, fortified foods, or both to supply the infant with the vitamin B$_{12}$ she needs.

Infant formula is relatively low in fluoride. If the water used to make a child's infant formula is not fluoridated, she may need a fluoride supplement. However, before giving a child supplements, parents should check the fluoride levels in their water and speak with their pediatrician about the best course of action.[61]

Water (or, more correctly, fluid) needs generally are met with breast milk or formula. Extra fluid is only necessary to replenish stores following episodes of diarrhea, fever, or vomiting when the body loses fluid and electrolytes. Parents do not need to offer infants fluids other than breast milk or infant formula before the age of 6 months, as doing so may prevent the baby from being hungry for these nutrient-rich beverages.[62]

The Take-Home Message Infants grow at a dramatic rate during the first year of life. Caregivers and health care providers can monitor infant growth by making sure the child achieves appropriate developmental milestones and by using growth charts. Nutrient needs during the first year of life are substantial, and dietary supplements and fortified foods may be needed in some circumstances.

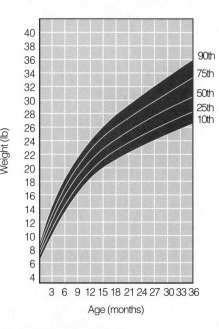

Figure 14.10 Growth Chart
Growth charts can help determine if a child is growing at a healthy rate for his or her age.

"Colic" is characterized by an infant's chronic, inconsolable crying, often for long periods of time. Though the cause of colic is not known, some possible nutrition-related contributors include an immature digestive tract, cow's milk allergies or intolerance, food backup into the esophagus, increased intestinal gas, or the breast-feeding mother's diet.

percentile The most commonly used clinical indicator to assess the size and growth patterns of children in the United States. An individual child is ranked according to the percentage of the reference population he equals or exceeds.

When Are Solid Foods Safe?

Often, proud parents can hardly wait to show off how their baby is eating "real food." It is an exciting time, because eating **solid foods** represents maturing skills in the baby. Children typically start eating solid foods around 6 months of age.[63] However, parents should not suddenly decide to serve their baby steak or other foods that are difficult to chew and digest! The infant must be nutritionally, physiologically, and physically ready to eat solid foods. Let's take a look at what we mean by this.

Solid Foods May Be Introduced Once Certain Milestones Are Met

Infants must be developmentally ready for solid foods before parents introduce them into a child's diet. At about 6 months old, an infant has depleted his or her stored iron and will need to begin consuming iron from solid foods, such as puréed meats and fortified infant formula. Also, common sense tells us that as babies get bigger in size, they need more nutrients. Thus, an older, larger infant has higher nutrient needs than a younger, smaller one. Introducing solid foods will help to meet the infant's nutrient needs and help her develop feeding skills.

The infant also needs to be physiologically ready; that is, his body systems must be able to process solid foods. At birth, and in early infancy, the GI tract and digestive organs cannot process solid foods.

These next questions are very specific to the individual child. Is the infant physically ready for solid foods? Has he or she met the necessary developmental milestones? To determine this, caretakers need to answer the following questions:

➤ Has the infant doubled his birth weight to at least 13 pounds?
➤ Has the infant's **tongue-thrust reflex** faded? This is a reflex infants have to protect against choking. The tongue automatically pushes outward when a substance is placed on it. The reflex fades at around 4 to 6 months of age.
➤ Does the infant have head and neck control? Without control, the infant is at greater risk for choking on solids.
➤ Have the infant's swallowing skills matured enough?
➤ Is the infant able to sit with support?
➤ Does the infant have the ability to turn his or her head to indicate "I'm full!"?

All of these questions should be answered with a "Yes" to know that it is safe and realistic to begin offering solid foods. If not, parents and caregivers would be wise to wait until the infant does develop these skills.[64] Still nervous about feeding an infant? See the Nutrition in the Real World feature "Feeding the Baby" for more information.

Solid Foods Should Be Introduced Gradually

Phasing in solid foods should take place over a period of several months. The food should initially be served puréed; eventually it can be served mashed so that the texture is soft, as the infant's chewing and swallowing skills are sharpened with practice and develop as she gets older. Puréed meat or fortified infant rice cereal are healthy first foods. Many parents choose infant cereal. Diluting infant cereal with breast milk or formula so there is a familiar taste mixed in with the new taste helps to promote the infant's acceptance of the new food. Whole milk shouldn't be given to an infant until after one year of age.

solid foods Foods other than breast milk or formula given to an infant, usually around 6 months of age.

tongue-thrust reflex A forceful protrusion of the tongue in response to an oral stimulus, such as a spoon.

Feeding the Baby

New parents are often nervous when it comes to feeding their newborns. They may wonder if their baby is eating too much or too little, or swallowing too much air, and, if they are bottle-feeding, they may be worried about nipple confusion or other concerns they have heard about from well-meaning friends and relatives. The good news is that most parents can relax when it comes to feeding baby, as Mother Nature has built in numerous mechanisms to help babies

healthfully consume the amount of food they need.

For example, infants are equipped with several reflexes that help them take in adequate amounts of breast milk (or infant formula) or solid foods and avoid choking. Among these reflexes are:

➤ Rooting reflex—When a baby's mouth, lips, cheek, or chin are touched by an object, such as a nipple, the head and mouth turn toward it.
➤ Suck/swallow reflex—After opening the mouth when a baby's lips and mouth area are touched, suckling movements begin and the tongue moves to the back of the mouth for swallowing.
➤ Tongue-thrust reflex—When the lips are touched, the baby's tongue moves forward in the mouth.
➤ Gag reflex—When an object such as a spoon or solid is placed in the mouth, it is pushed back out by the tongue.

Note that a baby should be fed when he indicates that he is hungry, rather than on a set schedule. Newborns may need to eat as often as every ½ hour to 2 hours, whereas older infants, who have larger stomachs, may taper off to 3 to 4 hours between feedings. Some cues that a baby is hungry include waking and tossing, sucking on a fist, crying or fussing, and looking like he is going to cry.

Caregivers should respond early to the signs of hunger rather than waiting until the baby is crying. Infants are usually very clear about when they are ready to stop feeding, and use several techniques to communicate this to a caregiver. For example, they may spit out the nipple, close their lips, and decrease the rate of suckling.

When feeding an infant from a bottle, the baby should be gently and slowly positioned for feeding. The baby should be held upright in the cradle of the arm with the head higher than the rest of the body, to avoid choking. The bottle should be held and not propped during feeding because propping can cause choking or baby bottle tooth decay, and deprives the baby of human contact. To expel any excess swallowed air and alleviate potential gassiness, a baby needs to be burped after she eats. The best way to burp a baby is to gently pat or rub her back while she is resting on the caregiver's shoulder or sitting on the lap.

All babies develop at their own rate and each individual baby's developmental readiness should be used to determine which foods should be fed, what texture the foods should be, and what feeding styles should be used.

Source: USDA. 2002. Feeding Infants: A Guide for Use in Child Nutrition Programs. Available at www.fns.usda.gov.

Eating solid foods is new for infants, and they don't always accept certain foods on the first try. Rather than deciding that the infant does not like sweet potatoes because he spits it out upon the first taste, parents and caregivers should offer a given food more than once, over several days, to give the infant the opportunity to accept the food. After several days of feeding the infant a single food, proceed with other foods, such as puréed meats, fruits and vegetables, and barley or oat cereals.

Many parents wonder if they should feed their child homemade baby food for the sake of safety and better nutrition. It's good to know that commercially made baby foods are of high quality and often comparable to homemade. The choice is really up to the parent or caregiver. One benefit of homemade food that everyone might agree upon is the financial savings—there are no added costs for fancy packaging and labels. (See "Two Points of View" at the end of this chapter for more on this topic.)

Refer again to Figure 14.9 on page 546 for suggested foods for a baby's first year of life.

Some Foods Are Dangerous and Should Be Avoided

In spite of all the new skills an infant develops during the first year, becoming stronger, smarter, and more independent, parents and caregivers still need to "baby the baby" when it comes to eating. Many foods are just not appropriate for a baby. For example, some foods, like hot dog rounds or raw carrots, present a choking hazard for young infants and should be cut into very small pieces or avoided altogether. Because infants have few teeth, foods should be soft in texture so they do not require excessive chewing, and ideally should easily "melt" in the mouth, like a cracker. No matter what they are eating, infants should always be supervised.

Solid foods like fortified infant rice cereal and oatmeal can be introduced between 4 and 6 months of age.

Once an infant is ready for solids, foods should be introduced gradually to make sure the child isn't allergic or intolerant. It's best to introduce one new single-ingredient food at a time, and wait for three to five days to see if the baby is allergic.[65] If she develops hives or a rash, or starts sneezing or vomiting, food may be the culprit. Allergic reactions may also include a very mild tingling sensation in the mouth or swelling of the tongue and the throat, difficulty breathing, diarrhea, a drop in blood pressure, and loss of consciousness or death.

In the past, medical experts and organizations such as the AAP have advised against introducing so-called highly allergenic foods, such as eggs, peanuts, and peanut products, to infants until a child's first birthday, or well after. However, there is no convincing evidence for delaying the introduction of specific highly allergenic foods. In fact, there is evidence that delaying the introduction of solid foods may actually increase the risk of food allergy, not reduce it.[66] The Health Connection feature on the next page provides more information about how food allergies develop.

Some foods, including raw and undercooked meat, seafood, and eggs, are so dangerous as to be potentially fatal. Honey may contain the bacterium *Clostridium botulinum*, which can lead to a fatal disease called **botulism**. Though some cultures and families have used honey-dipped pacifiers to calm infants for generations, this is a dangerous practice. Infants with botulism become lethargic, feed poorly, and suffer from constipation. They will have a weak cry and poor muscle tone. Untreated symptoms may cause paralysis of the arms, legs, trunk, and respiratory muscles. The resulting respiratory failure is what makes this food potentially deadly. An infant's immune system is not developed enough to fight off botulism, but honey does not present problems for older children and adults, who have adequate amounts of intestinal microorganisms that compete with botulism and inhibit its growth in the intestines.[67]

Parents and caregivers also need to consider the amount of salt, sugar, and butter in their infants' foods. Bland food is fine for infants. At this stage of the life cycle, infants can learn to find the natural flavors in whole foods satisfying, without added sugar or salt.

botulism A rare but serious paralytic illness caused by the bacterium *Clostridium botulinum*. Infant botulism is caused by consuming the spores of the bacteria, which then grow in the intestines and release toxins. It can be fatal.

The Take-Home Message An infant must be physically, physiologically, and nutritionally ready before being introduced to solid foods. Solid foods should be introduced gradually and cautiously. Parents and caregivers must educate themselves about foods that are appropriate and those that are not in order to keep the infant safe and healthy.

A Taste Could Be Dangerous: Food Allergies

A **food allergy** is an abnormal physical reaction of the immune system in response to the consumption of a particular food allergen. **Food allergens** are proteins that are not broken down during cooking or by the gastric juices and enzymes in the body during digestion. Because they are not degraded, they enter the body intact, and can cause an adverse immune reaction if the allergen is perceived as a foreign invader.

A food allergy reaction occurs in two stages, the "sensitization stage" followed by the actual response or "allergic reaction stage." In the first stage (see **Figure 1**), the food allergens don't provoke a reaction, but rather introduce themselves to the person's immune system. In response, the immune system creates an army of antibodies that enter the blood and stand ready for the next time the allergen appears. The antibodies

food allergy An abnormal reaction by the immune system to a particular food.

food allergens Proteins not broken down by cooking or digestion that enter the body intact, causing an adverse immune response.

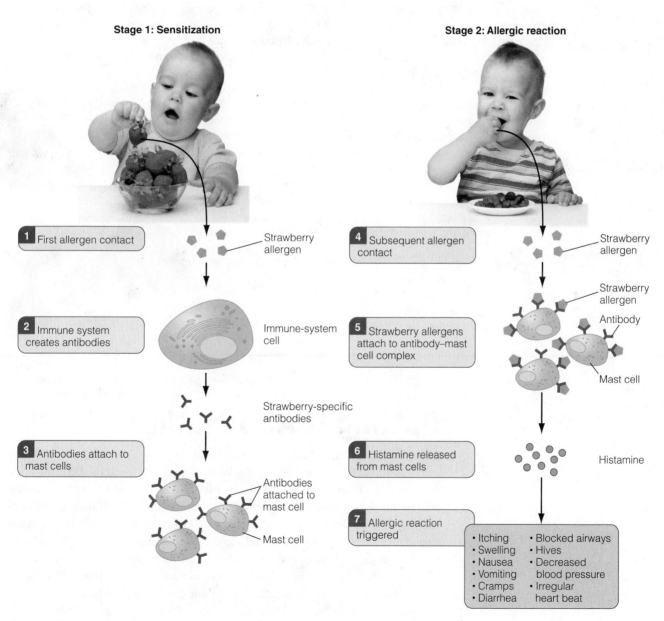

Stage 1: Sensitization

1 First allergen contact

Strawberry allergen

2 Immune system creates antibodies

Immune-system cell

Strawberry-specific antibodies

3 Antibodies attach to mast cells

Antibodies attached to mast cell

Mast cell

Stage 2: Allergic reaction

4 Subsequent allergen contact

Strawberry allergen

Strawberry allergen

Antibody

5 Strawberry allergens attach to antibody–mast cell complex

Mast cell

6 Histamine released from mast cells

Histamine

7 Allergic reaction triggered

- Itching
- Swelling
- Nausea
- Vomiting
- Cramps
- Diarrhea
- Blocked airways
- Hives
- Decreased blood pressure
- Irregular heart beat

Figure 1 Immune Response to a Food Allergy

CONTINUED ▶

attach to **mast cells**, setting the stage for a potential future allergic reaction.

The second stage, the reaction stage, occurs when a person eats the food allergens for the second and subsequent times. After they are consumed, the food allergens come in contact with the mast cells. The mast cells release chemicals, including histamine, that trigger reactions in the body. The areas in the body that manifest a food allergy reaction are the areas where mast cells are prevalent. In very sensitive individuals, a minute exposure of a food allergen—1/4,000 of a peanut, for example—can trigger an allergic reaction.

mast cells Cells in connective tissue to which antibodies attach, setting the stage for potential future allergic reactions.

anaphylactic reactions Severe, life-threatening reactions that cause constriction of the airways in the lungs, which inhibits the ability to breathe.

food intolerance Adverse reaction to a food that does not involve an immune response. Lactose intolerance is one example.

Reactions can appear as quickly as a few minutes after eating the food. In fact, itchiness in the mouth may occur as soon as the food touches the tongue. After the food reaches the stomach and begins to be digested, vomiting and/or diarrhea may result. When they enter the blood, the food allergens can cause a drop in blood pressure. When the allergens are near the skin, hives can develop, and as the allergens make their way to the lungs, asthma can ensue.

Individuals with allergies, or their caretakers, often carry a syringe injector of epinephrine (adrenaline) to be administered when severe reactions occur, to help treat these symptoms. Epinephrine constricts blood vessels, relaxes the muscles in the lungs to help with breathing, and decreases swelling and hives.

Eggs, milk, and peanuts are the most common sources of food allergens in children. In adults, shellfish, peanuts, tree nuts, fish, wheat, soy, and eggs are the most common sources of food allergens. These foods together cause 90 percent of all reactions to food allergens. Some children will outgrow their reaction to milk, eggs, or soy, but they generally do not outgrow a peanut allergy.[6] People who develop food allergies as adults usually will have that allergy for life.

In the United States, food allergies are the cause of 2,000 admittances to the hospital, approximately 30,000 **anaphylactic** (*ana* = without, no, *phylaxis* = protection) **reactions** (severe, life-threatening allergic reactions), and almost 200 deaths annually.[7] According to the Centers for Disease Control and Prevention, from 2004 to 2006, 9,500 hospital discharges a year carried a diagnosis related to food allergy.[8] Most of these visits to health care facilities were no doubt the result of an anaphylactic reaction. Anaphylactic reactions can cause vomiting and constriction or narrowing of the airways in the lungs, which inhibits breathing.

The symptoms of a **food intolerance** may mimic a food allergy, but they are different responses. A food intolerance does not involve the immune system. Recall from Chapter 4 that one common food intolerance, lactose intolerance, is caused by inadequate amounts of the enzyme lactase in the body.

Proper food labeling can help reduce the risks associated with food allergy. The FDA requires that virtually all food ingredients be listed on the food label, and that the food label state whether the product contains protein from any of the major foods known to cause an allergic reaction: milk, egg, fish, shellfish, tree nuts, peanuts, soybeans, or wheat.[9]

Putting It All Together

Pregnancy, lactation, and infancy are periods of the life cycle during which women and babies have unique nutrient needs. Women need to refer to the DRIs for pregnancy and lactation (listed on the inside cover of this textbook) to make sure they consume adequate kilocalories, protein, iron, and folate for both their own health and that of their developing baby. Babies have high nutrient and kilocalorie needs during their first year to sustain their rapid growth and development. **Figure 14.11** summarizes the nutritional and lifestyle guidelines for babies and their parents. The lifestyle habits mentioned in earlier chapters—like smoking and drinking too much alcohol—that have been shown to lead to chronic diseases such as heart disease, cancer, and cirrhosis are also unhealthy during pregnancy and lactation. Both men and women should adopt healthier lifestyles before pregnancy in order to increase the likelihood of having a healthy baby.

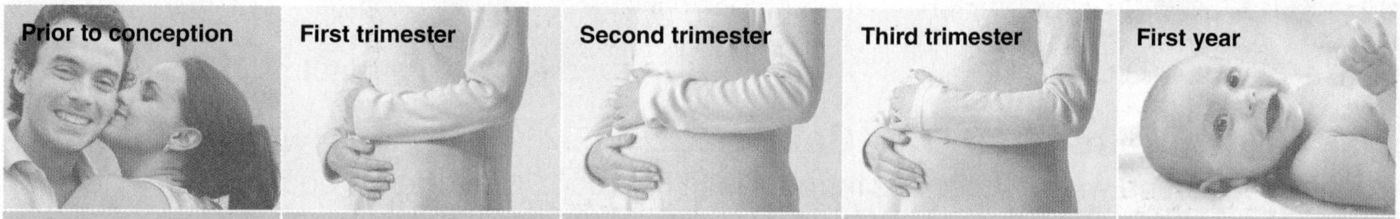

Prior to conception	First trimester	Second trimester	Third trimester	First year

Father
- Stop smoking
- Limit alcohol
- Maintain a healthy weight
- Consume a balanced diet

Mother				
• Consume a balanced diet • Maintain a healthy weight • Add folic acid to diet • Limit caffeine • Avoid certain fish with high levels of methylmercury • Avoid alcohol, herbs, illicit drugs, and smoking • Exercise regularly	• Consume a balanced diet • Continue getting folic acid • Take an iron-rich supplement • Limit caffeine • Avoid too much vitamin A • Avoid foodborne illness • Continue exercising	• Consume a balanced diet with adequate calories for growth • Continue exercising	• Consume a balanced diet with adequate calories for growth • Eat frequent small meals if more comfortable • Choose high-fiber foods • Drink plenty of fluids • Continue nonimpact exercises	• Consume a balanced diet with adequate calories and fluids for breast-feeding • Nursing mothers should avoid illicit drugs, smoking, and alcohol • Limit caffeine • Avoid certain fish with high levels of methylmercury

Baby				
				• Supplement diet with vitamins K and D and sources of iron or iron-fortified foods • Avoid common food allergens, honey, and herbal tea • Consume breast milk or formula as primary source of calories • Do not start drinking cow's milk until after this year • Introduce solid foods gradually and one at a time • Avoid too much fiber and excessive amounts of juice

Figure 14.11 Summary of Nutritional Guidelines
Nutritional guidelines for both parents and infants are shown above.

Should Parents Make Their Own Baby Food? Many anxious parents worry about the foods they feed their babies, and when it comes to introducing solid foods, they often struggle with the question of whether to make their own baby food, buy organic versions of commercially produced products, or purchase regular, nonorganic (and usually less expensive) baby foods.

What concerns do parents have when it comes to commercially made baby food, and are those concerns valid? What other options are available? Are there advantages other than nutrition to making homemade baby food, or buying only organic products? Read through the arguments on both sides of the issue, and then consider the critical thinking questions to decide for yourself!

yes

- Homemade baby foods may be more nutrient rich. Commercial baby foods often contain more water, starch, and sugar than homemade baby foods. The addition of these additives dilutes the nutrient content of commercial foods.[1]

- Commercially made baby foods are often processed with high heat during jarring, which can destroy some of the vitamins and other nutrients.[2]

- The average baby in the United States will consume 600 jars of baby food. Parents who use processed baby food spend an average of $300 during their infant's first year of life. On average, baby food prepared at home can cost as little as $55 in the first year.[3]

- Providing babies with homemade baby food made of fresh fruits and vegetables can help instill taste and preference for these healthy food choices. Babies will get used to the fresher tastes, and be less interested in the tastes of highly processed foods later on in life.[4]

no

- Pesticide levels in commercial baby foods are tightly regulated by U.S. law, which mandates a safety factor that is ten times the levels known to be safe.[5]

- Homemade baby foods may spoil more quickly and require refrigeration, which will take up room in the fridge or freezer if a lot of servings are made ahead of time. Prepackaged baby foods don't have to be refrigerated until they've been opened.[6]

- In preparing homemade food, adults may season it to their own tastes, adding enough salt or sugar to raise pediatric concerns.[7]

- Certain vegetables, particularly spinach, beets, and carrots, may contain high levels of nitrates, which can be harmful to young babies. There seems to be little or no risk of nitrate poisoning from commercially prepared infant foods in the United States. However, reports of nitrate poisoning from home-prepared vegetable foods for infants indicate that this does occur.[8]

what do you think?

1. Which side has the overall stronger argument? Why? **2.** Why might parents need to choose commercially prepared food over homemade food? **3.** Do you think making homemade baby food is worth the extra time and effort? Why or why not?

1 Nutrient Intake and Healthy Behaviors Impact Fertility

Both the father and the mother should make healthy diet and lifestyle changes if needed prior to pregnancy. For healthy sperm, men should stop smoking, abstain from alcohol or drink only in moderation, strive for a healthy body weight, and consume a well-balanced diet with adequate amounts of fruits and vegetables, whole grains, lean meats, low-fat dairy foods, and legumes. Prior to pregnancy, women should also abstain from alcohol, smoking, and caffeine, and strive for a healthy weight. In addition, women should consume adequate amounts of folic acid prior to conception to reduce the risk of neural tube defects.

2 Specific Nutrients and Behaviors Are Important during the First Trimester

Healthy women who begin pregnancy at a healthy weight should gain 25 to 35 pounds during pregnancy. A woman's needs for many nutrients, including folate, iron, zinc, copper, and calcium, increase up to 50 percent during pregnancy. Care should be taken to avoid consuming too much preformed vitamin A, which can cause birth defects.

Exercise during pregnancy can help improve sleep, lower the risk of hypertension and diabetes, prevent backaches, help relieve constipation, shorten labor, reduce stress and depression, and possibly allow women to return more quickly to their prepregnancy weight after delivery.

Awareness of food safety is also important, as bacteria such as *Listeria monocytogenes* may cause miscarriages, premature labor, delivery of a low birth weight infant, developmental problems, or even infant death. Pregnant women should abstain from alcohol, herbal teas and herbal supplements, and illicit drugs, as these can all harm fetal growth and development. They should avoid fish that contain high amounts of methylmercury and consume caffeine only in moderation.

3 Additional Carbohydrates and Protein Are Important during the Second Trimester

Many pregnant women find that the nausea and fatigue of the first trimester diminish during the second trimester, and appetite begins to increase. The mother's calorie needs also increase. A pregnant woman should consume an additional 340 calories daily during the second trimester and should gain around a pound per week. Pregnant women need about 175 grams of carbohydrate and 71 grams of protein. These needs can be met with a balanced diet. Sometimes a woman develops gestational diabetes and/or hypertension during pregnancy. Gestational diabetes increases the risk of delivering a larger-than-normal baby who may also be at risk for developing jaundice, breathing problems, and birth defects. Pregnancy-induced hypertension includes gestational hypertension, preeclampsia, and eclampsia, each progressively more medically serious. The risk of gestational diabetes and hypertension can be reduced during the second trimester with a healthy diet, daily exercise, and managing body weight.

1 whole-wheat English muffin
2 tbs peanut butter
5 baby carrots

340 total calories

4 Healthy Eating Behaviors and Weight Gain Are Important Considerations during the Third Trimester

By the end of the last trimester, a pregnant woman should be taking in an extra 450 calories daily and continue to gain about 1 pound per week. The slower movement of food through the GI tract can contribute to heartburn and constipation. Reduced physical activity and iron supplementation can also contribute to constipation. To minimize heartburn, pregnant women should eat smaller but frequent meals, eliminate spicy foods that may irritate the esophagus, and avoid lying down immediately after meals. Exercise and consuming fiber-rich foods, along with plenty of fluids, can help prevent or alleviate constipation.

Total weight gain 25–35 lbs

- Maternal fat stores (4–11 lbs)
- Uterus and breast (4 lbs)
- Blood (3–4 lbs)
- Fetus (7–8 lbs)
- Placenta, amniotic fluid, and other fluids (7–8 lbs)

5 Younger and Older Mothers-to-Be Face Special Challenges

Women younger or older than the physically optimal childbearing age range of 20 to 35 may face additional challenges during pregnancy. Teenage mothers-to-be are at risk for pregnancy-induced hypertension, iron-deficiency anemia, and delivering premature and low birth weight babies. Older mothers-to-be are at risk of developing diabetes and high blood pressure. Their infants are more likely to have Down syndrome or other disabilities. Older women who use fertility-enhancing techniques are also more likely to give birth to multiples, which carries other increased risks including premature birth, labor difficulties, and low birth weight.

6 Breast-Feeding Benefits Both Mother and Child

Breast-feeding is the gold standard for feeding an infant. It provides physical, emotional, convenience, and financial benefits for the mother and nutritional and health benefits for the infant. Breast milk is rich in nutrients, antibodies, and other compounds that provide the infant with a disease-fighting boost until the baby's own immune system matures. Because of all the benefits, women are encouraged to exclusively breast-feed for the first six months. Breast-feeding women can also express their breast milk with a pump and store it for later use, allowing for more flexibility in their schedules.

7 Breast-Feeding Mothers Have Increased Nutrient Needs

Breast-feeding mothers who began pregnancy at a healthy weight need to consume 330 to 400 extra calories daily to produce breast milk, and a breast-feeding woman should drink about 13 cups of water and beverages daily. Anything that goes into a breast-feeding mother's body can potentially pass into her breast milk, so she should limit caffeine consumption and discuss alcohol and medication intake with her health care provider. Breast-feeding mothers should also be careful to avoid overconsumption of fish that may contain methylmercury.

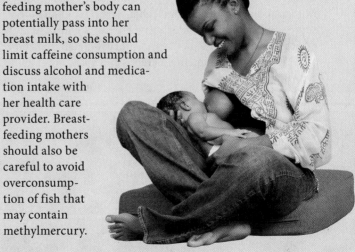

8 Formula Can Be a Healthy Alternative to Breast Milk

If an infant isn't breast-fed, the only healthy alternative is commercially made formula. Commercially made formulas are modified from soy or cow's milk, and patterned after human breast milk. For some women, formula-feeding is a personal preference. For others it is necessary, as breast-feeding may not be possible due to illness or other circumstances. Tooth decay and ear infections can be prevented by avoiding bedtime bottle feedings when infants are placed in bed with a bottle.

9 Infants Have Specific Nutrient Needs

An infant doubles his or her birth weight by around 6 months of age, and triples it by 12 months. With proper nutrition, an infant should reach certain stages of physical development within a distinct time frame. Poor infant nutrition (whether in quality or quantity) will likely prevent ideal growth and the ability of the child to reach milestones on time. All infants should receive a vitamin K injection at birth, and breast-fed infants need vitamin D supplements until 1 year of age. Infants older than 6 months need to begin taking in iron through food sources, as their stored iron supply is depleted around this time.

10 Solid Foods Should Be Introduced Gradually after Certain Milestones Are Reached

Infants need to be nutritionally, physiologically, and physically ready before they begin eating solid foods. Foods should be introduced gradually and one at a time to monitor possible allergies or intolerances. Certain foods can be dangerous and should be avoided. Parents and caregivers should avoid adding heavy seasoning (such as sugar or salt) and offering excess amounts of fruit juice (which can lead to overconsumption of calories) to an infant's diet.

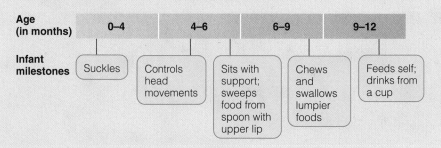

Age (in months)	0–4	4–6	6–9	9–12
Infant milestones	Suckles	Controls head movements	Sits with support; sweeps food from spoon with upper lip	Chews and swallows lumpier foods	Feeds self; drinks from a cup

Terms to Know

- trimesters
- embryo
- placenta
- fetus
- gestational diabetes
- pregnancy-induced hypertension
- lactation
- breast-feeding
- let-down response
- colostrum
- early childhood caries
- milestones
- food allergy

Check Your Understanding

1. To prevent neural tube birth defects, a woman should take 400 micrograms of folic acid
   a. during the first trimester.
   b. during the second trimester.
   c. throughout her childbearing years, if she's capable of conceiving.
   d. during the last trimester.

2. The production and function of sperm may decrease because of
   a. inadequate sleep.
   b. stress.
   c. obesity.
   d. dehydration.

3. A low birth weight baby is a baby who is born weighing
   a. more than 5½ pounds.
   b. less than 5½ pounds.
   c. more than 6 pounds.
   d. less than 7 pounds.

4. Two potential complications of pregnancy that must be closely monitored by a health care provider are
   a. cravings and morning sickness.
   b. gestational diabetes and preeclampsia.
   c. weight gain and exercise.
   d. constipation and heartburn.

5. A woman who begins pregnancy at a healthy weight should gain _____ pounds during pregnancy.
   a. 20 to 30 pounds
   b. 15 to 25 pounds
   c. 50 to 60 pounds
   d. 25 to 35 pounds

6. During pregnancy a woman's need for many nutrients increases. Which mineral requirement is unlikely to be met through her diet alone?
   a. iron
   b. potassium
   c. sodium
   d. calcium

7. During the second trimester of pregnancy, a woman who begins pregnancy at a healthy weight should increase her daily calorie intake by
   a. 450 calories a day.
   b. 340 calories a day.
   c. 500 calories a day.
   d. No increase is needed.

8. Breast-feeding cannot
   a. help women reduce their risk of breast cancer.
   b. reduce women's risk of type 2 diabetes.
   c. prevent pregnancy.
   d. decrease the risk of the baby developing respiratory and ear infections.

9. Andy is a healthy 3-month-old baby boy who is being breast-fed by his mother. Which of the following nutrients should be added to his diet in supplement form?
   a. vitamin D
   b. potassium
   c. vitamin C
   d. omega-3 fats

10. Six-month-old Cathy is ready to take on solid foods. One healthy and safe first food that could be introduced in her diet is
    a. chopped meat.
    b. ready-to-eat crunchy cereal.
    c. iron-fortified rice cereal.
    d. scrambled eggs.

Answers

1. (c) To reduce the risk of these birth defects, folic acid should be consumed prior to conception and continue during the early weeks of pregnancy. Waiting until pregnancy occurs may be too late to help prevent birth defects during the first trimester. Because pregnancy increases the need for this vitamin, the mother should continue to make sure that folate intake is adequate throughout her pregnancy.

2. (c) Obesity is associated with the decreased production and functioning of sperm; smoking, alcohol abuse, and using illicit drugs negatively affect sperm health, too. Antioxidants, in particular vitamins E and C and carotenoids, may help protect sperm.

3. (b) A baby born weighing less than 5½ pounds is considered a low birth weight baby.

4. (b) Gestational diabetes and preeclampsia are both potentially life-threatening complications that can be brought on by pregnancy and should be closely monitored by a physician. Cravings, morning sickness, constipation, and heartburn can all occur during pregnancy, but are not considered serious unless they are severe. Weight gain and exercise are not complications of pregnancy.

5. (d) A woman at a healthy weight before pregnancy should gain 25 to 35 pounds during pregnancy.

6. (a) Because a pregnant woman's increased iron needs cannot be easily met through the diet, she will likely need a supplement. She can get the potassium, sodium, and calcium she needs through a well-balanced diet.

7. (b) A pregnant woman at a healthy weight before pregnancy needs 340 more calories than her pre-pregnancy energy needs every day during the second trimester. During the third trimester, she needs an extra 450 calories every day. She doesn't require additional daily calories during the first trimester, but does have additional nutrient needs, so she should be sure to eat nutrient-rich foods.

8. (c) Breast-feeding provides health advantages to both the mother and the baby. Breast-feeding reduces the risk of breast cancer and diabetes in the mother and the incidences of respiratory and ear infections in the baby. Breast-feeding cannot be relied upon to prevent pregnancy, however.

9. (a) Although breast milk is an ideal food for baby Andy, it doesn't contain enough vitamin D, so Andy should receive daily drops in his diet. He doesn't need to be supplemented with vitamin C, potassium, or omega-3 fats.

10. (c) Iron-fortified rice cereal is a good choice and is unlikely to cause an allergic reaction. If Cathy tolerates the rice cereal well, oatmeal could be the next grain added to her diet, or she could try puréed meats, which are rich in iron.

Web Resources

- For more information on breast-feeding, visit the La Leche League International website at www.llli.org
- For more food safety guidance for during pregnancy and after the baby is born, visit the FDA's Center for Food Safety and Applied Nutrition website at www.fda.gov
- For more on infant nutrition, visit the USDA's Food and Nutrition Center website at www.nal.usda.gov
- For more information on children and their dietary needs, visit the American Academy of Pediatrics' consumer website at www.healthychildren.org
- For more information on food allergies, visit the Food Allergy and Anaphylaxis Network at www.foodallergy.org

1. **False.** Fathers-to-be need to eat a healthy diet and avoid certain substances to help produce a healthy baby. Turn to page 524 to find out why this is the case.

2. **True.** Obese women may have more difficulty conceiving, possibly because of irregular menstrual cycles. Turn to page 525 to find out more.

3. **False.** Though it's called morning sickness, nausea can happen at any time of day, and sometimes occurs after the first trimester. To learn more about conditions during pregnancy, turn to page 528.

4. **False.** Any type of alcohol, including red wine, can harm a growing embryo and fetus. To find out what other substances can be harmful during pregnancy, turn to page 532.

5. **False.** Physical activity can be good for women expecting a baby, though some activities should be avoided. To find out which activities are safe, turn to page 534.

6. **False.** Infant formula is a healthy alternative, but breast milk is best for a baby. Turn to page 538 to find out why.

7. **False.** Infants should never be put on a weight-loss diet. Babies need calories and fat to support their rapid growth and development. To find out more about the demands of infant growth, turn to page 547.

8. **False.** Most infants receive an injection of vitamin K at birth, and there are other nutrients that infants may need to supplement their diet. Find out why this is the case on page 547.

9. **False.** Although there's probably nothing as delicious and fresh as homemade, most brands of jarred baby foods are just as healthy. Read more about commercially made versus homemade baby foods on page 549.

10. **False.** Although they're a good source of vitamin A and other nutrients, raw carrots are a potential choking hazard for an infant. For more on potentially dangerous foods, turn to page 550.

15

Life Cycle Nutrition:

Toddlers through the Later Years

See page 593 for the answers.

True or False?

1. **Toddlers** don't grow as quickly as infants do. ⓉⒻ p. 562

2. Young children who fill up on low-iron foods, such as milk and juice, may have an **iron deficiency**. ⓉⒻ p. 564

3. Once a child **refuses** a food, there is no point in offering it again. ⓉⒻ p. 565

4. Young children often get "**stuck**" on particular foods. ⓉⒻ p. 566

5. The increase in childhood obesity is due entirely to **fast food** intake. ⓉⒻ p. 567

6. Lunches served under the National School Lunch Program must meet certain nutritional **standards**. ⓉⒻ p. 572

7. As long as teens drink **diet soda**, there's no need to be concerned about the negative health effects of carbonated soft drinks. ⓉⒻ p. 574

8. Older adults don't need as many **calories** daily as they did when they were younger. ⓉⒻ p. 576

9. **Food insecurity** among elders is a nonissue in the United States. ⓉⒻ p. 585

10. **Alcohol abuse** is extremely rare among older adults. ⓉⒻ p. 588

1. Describe young children's nutrient needs, and discuss some of the nutrition-related issues they face.

2. Describe school-aged children's nutrient needs, and discuss some of the nutrition-related issues they face, including childhood obesity.

3. Describe adolescents' nutrient needs, and discuss some of the nutrition-related issues they face, including disordered eating.

4. Summarize the nutrient needs of older adults, and discuss some of the nutrition-related health concerns common to old age.

5. Describe the social, economic, and psychological factors that can affect the health of older Americans.

Toddlers live busy lives. The world is full of interesting things to explore and do, so sitting down at a table to eat isn't high on their list of priorities. In addition, their stomachs are still small, so a few bites of fruit, a handful of cereal, and a cup of milk may be enough to satisfy them before they are squirming in their seats, looking for the next adventure.

Just when parents think they've got a handle on good nutrition and eating habits for their toddlers, they find the toddler is no more and they have a young child heading off to kindergarten. During the elementary school years, providing healthy nutrition for a child begins to change dramatically and parents need to develop a whole new set of skills and knowledge. And so it goes through adolescence. As children grow, their nutritional needs change, sometimes because of physical changes and sometimes because of social and emotional changes. In the first part of this chapter, we'll explore the unique nutrition needs of toddlers, preschoolers, school-aged children, and adolescents as they grow and change.

The adult years between the ages of 20 and 65 are a period of homeostasis and optimally functioning body systems for most people. After about age 65, body functions begin to slow and older adulthood begins. The experience of aging is unique for everyone, and changes in functions do not occur at the same rate or to the same degree in any two people. Although the risk of disease and disability increases with age, poor health is not inevitable. In the latter part of this chapter we'll discuss the physical, economic, and emotional aspects of aging, and the nutrient needs of older adults. We'll also examine the most common dietary challenges older adults face, and ways to minimize health risks and promote a healthier older age.

What Are the Issues Associated with Feeding Young Children?

For the purposes of explaining growth, development, and nutritional needs, very young children may be categorized into two distinct groups: **toddlers** (1- to 3-year-olds) and **preschoolers** (aged 3 to 5 years). Toddlers and preschoolers develop relatively rapidly, but their growth rates have slowed significantly compared with infancy. For example, during the second year of life, average weight gain is about 3 to 5 pounds, and the average height or gain in length is about 3 to 5 inches.[1] Children 2 years and older gain between 4½ to 6½ pounds and 2½ to 3½ inches in height every year.[2] It's important to note that each child grows at her or his own pace, and that growth statistics serve as guidelines.

As a result of this slower growth, toddlers and preschoolers have smaller appetites and lower calorie needs relative to the needs of infants. Parents and other caregivers may become concerned about this change, and think that their child is not eating enough to grow and develop properly. However, as long as parents and pediatricians monitor growth and stay alert for decreased energy levels, diarrhea, nausea, vomiting, changes in the quality of the child's hair, skin, or nails, or other changes in health, it is likely that the child's diet is sufficient.

Young Children Need to Eat Frequent, Small Meals with Nutrient-Rich Foods

Toddlers tend to be extremely active. They also have smaller stomachs than older children, and may eat less at mealtimes. The key to ensuring that a toddler consumes

Table 15.1

Calorie Needs for Children and Adolescents

Age	Gender	Activity Level*		
		Sedentary	Moderately Active	Active
2–3 years	Male and Female	1,000–1,200	1,000–1,400	1,000–1,400
4–8 years	Female	1,200–1,400	1,400–1,600	1,400–1,800
4–8 years	Male	1,200–1,400	1,400–1,600	1,600–2,000
9–13 years	Female	1,400–1,600	1,600–2,000	1,800–2,200
9–13 years	Male	1,600–2,000	1,800–2,200	2,000–2,600
14–18 years	Female	1,800	2,000	2,400
14–18 years	Male	2,000–2,400	2,400–2,800	2,800–3,200

*Based on Estimated Energy Requirements (EER) equations, using reference heights (average) and reference weights (healthy) for each age/gender group. For children and adolescents, reference height and weight are based on median height and weight for ages up to 18 years. EER equations are from the Institute of Medicine. Dietary Reference Intakes for Energy, Carbohydrate, Fiber, Fat, Fatty Acids, Cholesterol, Protein, and Amino Acids. Washington (DC): The National Academies Press; 2002.

Source: Adapted from *Dietary Guidelines for Americans, 2010*. www.cnpp.usda.gov. Accessed May 2013.

adequate calories, protein, vitamins, minerals, and other nutrients is to offer him nutrient-rich foods at every meal and snack. Generally speaking, toddlers aged 2 to 3 require 1,000 to 1,400 calories per day (see **Table 15.1**). Meals and snacks should consist of small portions of protein-rich foods, such as lean meat, eggs, poultry, dairy products, beans, fruits, vegetables, and whole grains, rather than more processed, lower-nutrient foods such as chicken nuggets, prepared macaroni and cheese, french fries, sugary drinks, cookies, and crackers. (You can use MyPlate's Daily Food Plans for Preschoolers and Kids, discussed later in this chapter, for specific daily eating plans for young children.)

Parents and other caregivers should be mindful not only about what they serve young children, but how much, and should avoid encouraging toddlers and preschoolers to eat more than they want at meals and snacks. Using child-sized plates and cups is one way to help ensure proper portion sizes. Caregivers should tailor portion sizes to each child's individual needs, and pay attention to a child's cues about wanting less, or more, food.

By about 15 months, children are typically able to feed themselves and should be drinking from a cup. Between the first and second year, a child goes from holding a spoon to developing the fine motor skills needed to scoop the food and bring the spoon to her mouth. Younger children should always be offered a spoon at mealtimes to improve their feeding skills.

Allowing a child to self-feed is often messy and time-consuming, but it's important to his development and ability to regulate his own food intake. Choking and inhaling food is a top concern with toddlers and other young children, and close supervision is necessary. The American Academy of Pediatrics recommends parents and other caregivers avoid offering foods to children under age 4 that are easily lodged in the airway, including nuts, raw carrots, popcorn, peanuts and peanut butter, seeds, marshmallows, raisins and other dried fruit, chunks of meat or cheese, chewing gum, and round candy. Hot dogs are the leading cause of fatal food-related choking in children, but they, and other potentially problematic foods, such as whole grapes and string cheese, are less risky when cut into small pieces.[3] Children should always sit while eating to reduce the likelihood of food becoming lodged in the windpipe during a trip or fall. Children should not be allowed to eat while riding in the car because should the child begin choking, it may be difficult for the driver to pull over and assist the child.[4]

Tasty Treats for Toddlers

Serve toddlers these and other nutrient-rich foods, cut into small, bite-sized pieces. Always supervise young children when they are eating.

Peeled, fresh, ripe fruit such as pears, bananas, peaches, and plums

Mini whole-grain bagel, not toasted

Muffins made with whole grains

Unsweetened applesauce

Yogurt with bananas

toddlers Children aged 1 to 3 years old.

preschoolers Children aged 3 to 5 years old.

Using child-sized dishes at mealtimes can help caregivers monitor portion sizes.

Table**TIPS**

Kid-Friendly, Iron-Rich Foods

For children age 4 and older, stir raisins into prepared, iron-fortified cereal, or provide a small box of raisins as a snack.

Add kale and spinach to fruit smoothies made with fruit and milk.

Tote a baggie of an enriched breakfast cereal on car trips and errands for an iron-rich snack.

Serve fortified grains, such as pasta and rolls, with lean meat, such as meatballs, for additional iron.

Toss iron-fortified rice or other grains with veggies for a nutrient-rich side dish.

Children who attend day care may receive a substantial portion of their daily food in that setting. In some cases, day-care providers may offer menu items or snacks that are superior to what is given at home. Every state, with the exception of Idaho (which doesn't license child-care centers) requires that licensed child-care centers meet minimum standards for nutrition. The National Resource Center for Health and Safety in Child Care and Early Education website (http://nrckids.org) posts all child-care regulations for each state. Parents should know what is being offered at the day-care site and provide alternative foods for their child when necessary. This is particularly important for children with food allergies or food intolerances. Parents should ask day-care providers to alert them about special occasions, such as birthday parties, so they can bring in a treat for their own child if their child is allergic to certain foods. Even if children do not have special dietary concerns, parents have the right to be firm about what their child eats.

Young Children Have Special Nutrient Needs

The following nutrients are of special concern in the diets of young children:

➤ *Calcium.* Young children need calcium to develop healthy bones. Children between 1 and 3 years of age should consume 500 milligrams of calcium per day, and children aged 4 to 8 need 800 milligrams.[5] Milk and other dairy products, and calcium-added foods help children meet their calcium requirements. Eight ounces of milk, fortified soy beverage, or fortified orange juice each provide about 300 milligrams of calcium.[6]

➤ *Iron.* Children aged 1 to 3 need 7 milligrams of iron daily; those aged 4 to 8 require 10 milligrams.[7] Young children are prone to iron deficiency. Iron deficiency during infancy and early childhood can interfere with a child's cognition, behavior, and overall development, and have lasting effects.[8] In the United States, an estimated 14 percent of children aged 1 to 2 years old, and 4 percent of children aged 3 to 4 years old, experience iron deficiency.[9] Parents and caregivers should offer iron-rich foods, including lean meats and poultry, and fortified grains such as breakfast cereal, to children on a daily basis and avoid allowing children to fill up on iron-poor foods, such as juice and milk. (See the Table Tips for more ideas for iron-rich foods).

➤ *Vitamin D.* To build healthy bones, children over age 1 need 600 IU of vitamin D daily.[10] Children who don't consume 32 ounces of vitamin D–enriched milk daily or the equivalent from other foods need dietary supplements to achieve their vitamin D goals.[11]

➤ *Fiber.* The recommended daily intake for fiber is 19 grams for children aged 1 to 3 and 25 grams for 4- to 8-year-olds.[12] Like adults, toddlers need fiber to promote bowel regularity and prevent constipation. A balanced diet that contains whole fruits, vegetables, and whole grains helps a young child to meet his daily fiber needs.

➤ *Fluid.* Water is the single largest constituent of the human body. Every chemical reaction that supports life takes place in a watery medium. Children aged 1 to 3 need about 4 cups of fluid a day, including water. Children 3 to 5 need about 5 cups of fluid. Milk and juice count toward daily fluid intake, and fruits and vegetables also supply fluid.[13] Caregivers need to monitor a child's beverage intake and provide water, milk, and no more than 6 ounces of 100% fruit juice daily, while avoiding soda and sugary drinks.[14]

Picky Eating and Food Jags Are Common in Small Children

According to Ellyn Satter, an expert on child feeding and nutrition, there is a division of responsibility when it comes to control of feeding. The adult is responsible for the type of food children are offered to eat, as well as when and where children eat. The child, however, is responsible for whether he or she eats, and how much.[15]

Food and power struggles can occur when adults think that their job is not only to provide the food but also to make sure that the child eats all of it. Often, parents encourage their children to "clean their plates," even though the children show signs that they are finished eating. Children are good self-regulators; they tend to obey signals from their body that tell them when to eat and when to stop. Encouraging a young child to overeat may result in overweight in childhood and later in life.

As young children grow and develop, they begin to feed themselves independently on a more regular basis. They also become more opinionated about their food preferences, especially when confronted with foods they've never tried before. For example, a child's first encounter with cooked mashed peas may result in the peas ending up on the floor. That doesn't mean that peas should be permanently off the menu, however. Children may need to be exposed to a food repeatedly (10 times or more) before accepting it. Health experts recommend a varied diet for people of all ages, and caregivers should keep offering an array of nutritious choices to children, even when they don't accept new foods right away. Children will often adapt to the foods available to them.

Young children have more taste buds than adults, so food may taste stronger to them, which may be one reason for narrow food preferences. Though it's true that toddlers often demonstrate **picky eating**, parents should not give up on encouraging them to try and accept new foods.

Parents who eat a varied diet tend to have children who do the same, and eating meals together reinforces healthy eating habits.[16] Children often mimic adults' healthy—and unhealthy—eating behaviors. A mother who drinks diet soda for dinner instead of milk, or a father who insists that his 3-year-old eat asparagus but never puts it on his own plate, sends confusing messages about good nutrition. Involving children, even young ones, in food shopping, menu planning, and meal and snack preparation encourages them to enjoy a variety of foods (see **Table 15.2**).

Having kids help in the kitchen is one way to get them excited about trying new foods and eating healthy meals.

When five-year-old girls (many of whom had dieting mothers) were asked, "What do people do when they are on a diet?" their responses included, "Eat more good things," "Can't eat any more snacks; smoke instead," and "Cook for the kids but don't eat the food they make." Caretakers should model healthy eating habits for all in view.[17]

Table 15.2	
Food Skills of Young Children	
Age	**Developmental Feeding Skill**
1–2	Child uses the big muscles of the arm and can tear and snap vegetables, help scrub, drink from a cup, and help feed self.
3	Child uses the medium muscles of the hand and can help pour, mix, shake, and spread foods. Child can crack nuts with supervision and feed self independently.
4	Child uses the small muscles of the fingers and can peel, juice, crack raw eggs, and use all utensils and napkins.
5	Child uses eye-hand coordination and can measure, cut with supervision, grind, and grate.

Source: A. Hertzler, "Preschoolers' Food Handling Skills and Motor Development," *Journal of Nutrition Education* 21 (1989): 100B–100C.

picky eating Unwillingness to try unfamiliar foods.

Food jags, such as wanting to eat only one food (like macaroni and cheese), or avoiding certain foods, are common among toddlers.

food jags When a child will only eat the same food meal after meal.

school-aged children Children between the ages of 6 and 11.

While so-called "picky eating" is characterized by avoiding new foods, **food jags** are characterized by a child's tendency to favor certain foods to the exclusion of others. Did your parents ever mention that when you were small, all you wanted to eat was macaroni and cheese or peanut butter and jelly sandwiches on white bread? This behavior of getting "stuck" on a small selection of foods is quite common and normal in young children. It's important to note that food jags are usually temporary. A child who only wants to eat pretzels and oranges, or refuses to eat anything green, will likely emerge from the phase within a few days or weeks.

If a parent or other caregiver senses that the food jag is not going away in a reasonable amount of time, the child's eating pattern may pose a health threat. At that point, it is helpful to pay careful attention to what the child is eating as well as what he or she is avoiding. Is the child really "eating only crackers all day long," or is the parent forgetting that the child also drinks milk and eats chicken, green beans, and orange slices when they are offered? A parent or caregiver can keep a food diary of what the child eats and drinks for a few days to help identify any major problems. Sharing concerns (and the food diary) with the child's health care provider and asking for advice may prevent serious nutrient deficiencies in the long run.

Raising a Vegetarian Child

Young children can grow and develop normally on a vegetarian diet, as long as their eating pattern includes adequate calcium, iron, zinc, and other nutrients they may be missing by avoiding animal foods. Like any eating style, vegetarian diets should provide adequate servings of whole grains, vegetables, fruit, and lean protein sources, such as low-fat dairy foods, eggs, beans, and soy products. A vegetarian diet may be high in fiber, which can be so filling for children that they don't include a variety of foods that provide the nutrients they need. Children who completely avoid animal foods or eat inadequate servings of animal foods require vitamin B_{12} from dietary supplements, fortified foods, or both, because vitamin B_{12} is found naturally only in animal foods.

The Take-Home Message Toddlers grow at a slower rate than infants, and have reduced appetites. Caregivers need to be sure that toddlers get adequate amounts of calcium, iron, vitamin D, and fiber. Caregivers also need to monitor a child's beverage intake and provide water, milk, and 100% juice while avoiding soda and sugary drinks. Adults should be sure to offer children appropriate portion sizes. Toddlers and preschoolers will stop eating when full and shouldn't be forced to clean their plates. Caregivers should be good role models when it comes to getting children to try new foods, which may need to be offered 10 times or more before they are accepted. Food jags are normal and usually temporary. Young children can grow and thrive on vegetarian diets as long as the diets are carefully planned.

What Are the Nutritional Needs and Issues of School-Aged Children?

School-aged children, those between the ages of 6 and 11, have plenty of growing to do and they, like their younger counterparts, require a high-quality diet to maximize growth and development. (See Table 15.1 on page 563 for the range of calorie needs for children in this age group.) School-aged children have a more rigid schedule than younger children and they may not eat as often throughout the day as toddlers and preschoolers.

At this point in the life cycle, children are learning habits that they will probably have for life, so encouraging a healthy lifestyle is essential. Parents and caregivers should capitalize on their role-model status, as children are heavily influenced by their parents and other adult caregivers. Although school-aged children, even the younger ones, have developed skills such as tying their own shoes or buckling their own seat belts, parents and caregivers continue to be in charge of a child's diet.

While most children develop normally, some have developmental disabilities that may affect their eating patterns. The Examining the Evidence feature "Nutrition and Developmental Disabilities" on the next page explores the possible interconnections of nutrition and developmental disabilities. Children who have health issues may have special dietary concerns. For example, children with autism often become especially fixated on eating certain foods and may be reluctant to try new foods. Overcoming eating issues generally requires intervention and support from health professionals, such as registered dietitians, who work with children with special needs.

High Obesity Rates in School-Aged Children

Childhood obesity has more than doubled in children and tripled in adolescents in the past 30 years.[18] (See **Figure 15.1**.) Eighteen percent of children aged 6 to 11 were considered obese as of 2010.[19] Several factors contribute to the excess calories and inadequate activity that lead to **childhood overweight and obesity**.

Children Are Overeating

Children are taking in excess calories from several sources, including sugary soda and other sugar-added drinks, candy, chips, and baked goods such as cookies. Food seems to be everywhere, including in places where it was previously unavailable, such as gas stations, hardware stores, and bookshops, making it easier to overeat. Portion sizes, at home and in restaurants, are bigger than they were decades ago. For example, bagels were typically 3 inches in diameter and about 140 calories 20 years ago. Today, they measure about twice that and supply 350 calories.[20] American children, on the whole, eat more than the recommended solid fat, added sugar, and sodium, and fewer whole

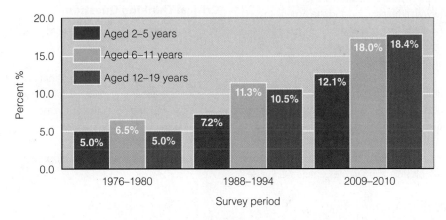

Figure 15.1 Increase in Obesity among U.S. Children and Adolescents

Note: Childhood obesity is defined as a BMI greater than or equal to the gender- and weight-specific 95th percentile from the CDC 2000 Growth Charts.
Data from NCHS Health E-Stat: Prevalence of Obesity among Children and Adolescents: United States Trends 1963–1965 through 2009–2010. Available at www.cdc.gov. Accessed June 2013.

childhood overweight and obesity
Excess body fat in children.

Nutrition and Developmental Disabilities

An estimated 3 to 7 percent of children in the United States have **attention deficit/hyperactivity disorder (ADHD)**, also called attention deficit disorder, or ADD. ADHD is a condition in which children have trouble paying attention, are impulsive, and are overly physically active. ADHD symptoms often appear in early childhood.[1] ADHD affects the child who has it, and, depending on its severity, ADHD may also cause difficulty for the entire family. ADHD is often treated with medication and behavioral therapy, and parents of children with the condition may wonder whether diet, particularly the amount of sugar and food additives a child consumes, also plays a role in managing ADHD.

Research suggest that the behavior of some children with ADHD improves with the avoidance of certain foods and food additives. In the early 1970s Dr. Benjamin Feingold, an allergist, promoted the idea that some foods triggered ADHD. Feingold's hypothesis generated interest among parents and controversy among health professionals. In 1982, the National Institutes of Health convened a panel to review the research on diet and hyperactivity, and concluded that food additives and some foods aggravated hyperactivity in some children.[2] The popularity of the so-called Feingold Diet persists today, but it doesn't work for every child. See more about the Feingold diet at www.feingold.org.

attention deficit/hyperactivity disorder (ADHD) Previously designated as attention deficit disorder (ADD). A condition in which an individual may be easily distracted, may have difficulty listening, following directions, and focusing and sustaining attention, and/or may have inconsistent performance in school.

autism spectrum disorder (ASD) Collective term for a group of brain disorders that make it difficult or impossible for a person to communicate and relate to others and may also be characterized by repetitive activities.

Sugar has also been targeted for worsening behavioral problems. High-sugar foods elevate blood glucose levels, especially when eaten alone, and may cause temporary hyperactivity in children. However, there is little evidence that solidifies a direct relationship between sugar and ADHD.[3] According to the American Academy of Pediatrics, although one early study did reveal a link between high sugar consumption and hyperactive behavior, there was no evidence that one caused the other or that the behavior problems were not due to different parenting styles or other factors.[4] While sugar consumption has not been shown to cause or enhance ADHD-related behavior, it's a good idea for parents to limit added sugars and provide a balanced diet, which is a healthy strategy for all children.

Identifying and eliminating foods that may exacerbate ADHD can be challenging, especially because children don't eat the same foods every day, and limiting their diets to "special" foods draws attention to children. Parents of children with ADHD may want to consult with a registered dietitian nutritionist to help their child with nutritional issues, such as underweight due to side effects of certain prescription medications used to treat ADHD that cause decreased appetite and lead to weight loss. Disruptive mealtimes may also be a concern from a nutritional standpoint because the child may not eat the amount of food he needs to grow and develop properly. Organizations such as the National Institute of Mental Health (www.nimh.nih.gov) and the American Academy of Child and Adolescent Psychiatry (www.aacap.org) provide information for families with children who have ADHD.

Autism is another developmental condition that is actually a group of developmental brain disorders, collectively called **autism spectrum disorder (ASD)**. "Spectrum" refers to the wide range of symptoms, skills, and levels of impairment, or disability, that children with ASD may exhibit. According to the Centers for Disease Control, 1 in 50 U.S. children aged 6 to 17 had diagnosed ASD per parental reports during the period of 2011 to 2012, up from 1 in 86 for the same age group in 2007.[5]

ASD symptoms often appear within the first three years of life, and ASD may result in impaired communication and social interaction, and repetitive behaviors. The symptoms and severity of autism vary greatly. There is no cure for ASD. Effective treatment includes intensive behavioral therapy during the toddler and preschool years to improve cognition and language skills.[6]

Parents of children with ASD may seek out alternative therapies, including specialized diets, to help their children. Several diet strategies have been suggested as possible treatments for reducing the behaviors associated with autism. Some researchers speculate that autism may also involve the gastrointestinal tract and the immune system, but the evidence is not conclusive. One of the most popular diets eliminates gluten (a protein found in most grains, including wheat) as well as casein (a milk protein). Other dietary interventions include restricting food allergens; including probiotics in the diet; following a yeast-free diet; and supplementing the diet with vitamin A, vitamin C, vitamin B_6, magnesium, folic acid, vitamin B_{12}, and omega-3 fatty acids.[7] More research is needed to determine the efficacy of dietary interventions, and parents of autistic children are encouraged to work with a registered dietitian nutritionist with expertise in this field.

Critical Thinking Questions

1. How can developmental disorders affect the nutritional status of young children?

2. What are some possible explanations for the apparent increase in diagnoses of ADHD and ASD in recent years?

3. Why is it difficult for researchers to determine whether there is a relationship between nutrition and developmental disorders?

grains, fruits, vegetables, and lower-fat dairy products, than they should. Such gaps in a child's eating pattern are the reason why many kids don't get enough calcium, vitamin D, potassium, and fiber.[21]

Children Are Not Getting Enough Physical Activity

Children fail to get the suggested amount of daily physical activity to help them grow and develop properly and to balance the calories they consume from foods and beverages. The following are two factors contributing to the decreased level of physical activity among children in America in recent years:

➤ *Increased screen time.* Research shows that 8- to 18-year-olds devote an average of 7 ½ hours daily to entertainment media, including television, computer time, video games, and movies.[22] The American Academy of Pediatrics recommends limiting combined screen time from television, DVDs, computers, and video games to 2 hours per day for preschool-aged children. School-aged children and teens should engage with entertainment media, such as TV and video games, for no more than 1 or 2 hours per day, and that should be high-quality content.[23]

➤ *Inadequate physical activity.* Children and teens require at least 60 minutes of physical activity every day; most are not reaching the suggested level for exercise, however. One recent study found that 42 percent of children and only 8 percent of adolescents engaged in moderate- to vigorous-intensity activity on 5 of the past 7 days for at least 60 minutes each day.[24] Schools are an ideal setting to provide physical activity, as a typical school day lasts about 7 hours for many kids. Yet academic achievement is often emphasized over exercise at school. For example, just six states (Illinois, Hawaii, Massachusetts, Mississippi, New York, and Vermont) require physical education in every grade, K–12.[25] In addition, loss of recess may be used as punishment for students, further limiting their daily physical activity. Valuing physical activity as a family helps reduce the risk of children becoming overweight and obese. Families should be encouraged to be active together and separately, and parents should model healthy lifestyle habits that include regular exercise to encourage children to behave the same way.

Obesity Contributes to Type 2 Diabetes

Overweight and obesity in children is linked to several chronic conditions, including type 2 diabetes. Type 2 diabetes, historically seen in adulthood, is on the rise in U.S. children and teens, and obesity is often associated with a diagnosis of the condition.[26] Prediabetes, which is characterized as a fasting blood glucose level of ≥ 100 mg/dL to < 126 mg/dL, is considered a marker for type 2 diabetes. An estimated 16 percent of 16- to 19-year-olds in the United States have prediabetes, and overweight teens have a significantly higher chance of prediabetes.[27]

Early intervention and constant attention to healthy lifestyle factors, such as eating a balanced diet with adequate calories, and regular physical activity, are necessary for children affected by type 2 diabetes or by prediabetes. The sooner the family learns what the child should eat and how to manage the other aspects of the disease, the better off the child will be immediately and in the long run. In fact, the entire family should consider eating in the same healthy fashion as the child, because managing type 2 diabetes involves dietary moderation, variety, and balance. Physical activity is also a major part of managing diabetes, and everyone benefits from regular exercise. Taking a family walk or bike ride after dinner and enjoying weekend games of basketball or tennis instead of watching TV or playing sedentary video games are excellent ways to teach the importance of physical activity. Tackling any health issue as a family provides support for the child and increases the chance of controlling the effects of the condition. Children with type 2 diabetes, prediabetes, or weight-control issues

We Can!

Want to learn more about programs that help families battle obesity? Visit the National Heart, Lung, and Blood Institute at www.nhlbi.nih.gov to learn about the We Can! program (Ways to Enhance Children's Activity & Nutrition) from the National Institutes of Health, which helps parents and caregivers prevent overweight and obesity in children.

should work with a registered dietitian nutritionist to determine the best eating plan for growth and development.

Daily Food Plans For Kids Help Guide Food Choices

Most parents are not nutrition experts, and the idea of trying to meet a child's nutrient needs every day may be overwhelming and confusing. Consumer-friendly Daily Food Plans available at ChooseMyPlate.gov help parents and other caregivers make good food choices for children. The 10 Tips Nutrition Education Series (see **Figure 15.2**), also available at ChooseMyPlate.gov in English and Spanish, are useful tip sheets that address a number of important nutrition topics.

ChooseMyPlate.gov encourages children and adults to:

➤ *Eat foods from every food group every day.* Including an array of foods provides children and adults with the nutrients they need. See Table 15.3 for ideas to help school-aged children get the fruits and vegetables they need every day.

➤ *Choose healthier foods from each group.* While all foods fit into a balanced diet, some foods are healthier than others, such as whole grains versus refined white grains, and low-fat dairy foods rather than higher-fat versions.

➤ *Make the right choices for you.* ChooseMyPlate.gov provides eating advice for healthy people over the age of 2.

Cut back on kid's sweet treats

1 Serve small portions
2 Offer healthy drinks
3 Use the check-out lane that does not display candy
4 Choose not to offer sweets as rewards
5 Make fruit the everyday dessert
6 Make food fun
7 Encourage kids to invent new snacks
8 Play detective in the cereal aisle
9 Make treats "treats," not everyday foods
10 If kids don't eat their meal, they don't need sweet "extras"

Be a healthy role model for children

1 Show by example
2 Go food shopping together
3 Get creative in the kitchen
4 Offer the same foods for everyone
5 Reward with attention, not food
6 Focus on each other at the table
7 Listen to your child
8 Limit screen time
9 Encourage physical activity
10 Be a good food role model

Figure 15.2 Tips for Helping Children Eat Healthfully from ChooseMyPlate.gov

Source: Adapted from USDA, 10 Tips Nutrition Education Series. 2011. Available at www.choosemyplate.gov.

Table 15.3

TASTE: More Matters: Include Fruit and Vegetables in Meals and Snacks

T: Try something new	Add shredded carrots to casseroles, chili, lasagna, meatloaf, soups, and stews. Purée a can of drained legumes (chickpeas, black beans, etc.) and add to sauces, soups, and stews. Drop berries into cereal, yogurt, and pancake batter. Make fruit and vegetable smoothies. Enjoy bean and vegetable burritos. Use leftover veggies in salads, or add them to a can of soup. Keep grab-and-go snacks handy, such as snack-sized boxes of raisins, dried fruit, trail mix, and frozen 100% fruit juice bars. Cherry tomatoes and carrot sticks with hummus make a great pairing.
A: All forms of fruits and veggies count!	Consider fresh, frozen, 100% juice, canned, and dried. Cook fruits and veggies in different ways, including steamed, slow-cooked, sautéed, stir-fried, grilled, roasted, and microwaved.
S: Shop smart	Fresh produce in season is more affordable. Look for specials. Clean and cut up produce so it's ready to use. At a restaurant, substitute vegetables such as a baked potato for rice or french fries.
T: Turn it into a family activity	Make fruit or vegetable kabobs with older kids. Add vegetables to homemade pizza. Take kids to farmer's markets.
E: Explore the bountiful variety	Use salad bars or buffets to try new flavors. When grocery shopping, encourage kids to choose a new produce item for meals and snacks.

➤ *Take healthy eating one step at a time.* Start with one positive change that's easy to make, and wait until that new behavior becomes second nature. Add another change to your eating pattern when you're ready.

➤ *Use healthy fats.* Fats are not an official MyPlate food group, but they are part of a balanced diet for children and adults. Healthy fats, such as olive oil and canola oil, tub margarine, and the fat in avocados, nuts, and nut butters are encouraged.

➤ *Be physically active on a regular basis.* Physical activity balances calories consumed and helps to promote a healthy weight.

The Importance of Breakfast

It's difficult to overstate the importance of a nutritious morning meal for school-aged children, or for anyone, for that matter. Breakfast can positively benefit mental function (especially memory), academic performance, school attendance rates, psychosocial function, and mood. If a child is hungry during the midmorning hours, it may affect her ability to learn. Breakfast literally "breaks the fast" of going without eating for 10 to 12 hours overnight. That's why the morning meal improves blood glucose levels, which supports a child's energy levels and comprehension. Studies conducted by the USDA on the School Breakfast Program have found that children who received a school breakfast performed better on standardized tests than children who did not eat breakfast.[28]

Research has also shown that eating breakfast may be associated with healthier body weight and a higher-quality diet in children and adolescents. Nutrients missed at breakfast, including calcium, fiber, and certain vitamins and minerals, are rarely made

Stir low-sugar ready-to-eat whole-grain cereal into a single-serving container of low-fat yogurt; add banana slices, berries, or dried fruit to make it even more nutritious.

Sprinkle reduced-fat cheese on a corn tortilla and melt it in the oven or microwave. Add some salsa and corn and roll it up into a portable tortilla tube.

Spread a thin layer of peanut butter or sunflower seed butter on a toasted whole-wheat waffle, and pair it with a travel cup of low-fat or fat-free milk.

up for during the rest of the day. The 2010 *Dietary Guidelines for Americans* (DGA) concluded that moderate evidence suggests that children who skip breakfast are at increased risk of overweight and obesity, and that the evidence is even stronger for adolescents. The DGA also concluded that moderate evidence supports a link between eating breakfast and the consumption of certain nutrients in children and teens.

Optimally, children should eat breakfast at home before school. Low-sugar, fortified cereal with milk and fruit or 100% fruit juice is a quick and nutritious choice that provides several nutrients, including fiber. Fortified cereals are good or excellent sources of vitamins and minerals including iron, folic acid, zinc, and B vitamins. Many fortified cereals also contain added vitamin A, thiamin, niacin, calcium, phosphorus, and magnesium. If children don't have time to eat breakfast at home, and aren't receiving breakfast at school, parents and other caregivers can also provide quick, nutritious morning meals that can be eaten on the way to school. See the Table Tips for some on-the-go breakfast ideas.

School Lunch Contributes to a Child's Nutritional Status

The National School Lunch Program (NSLP) is a federally assisted meal program that provides nutritionally balanced, low-cost or free lunches. In 2011, the NSLP fed more than 31 million children lunch each school day. NSLP meals must meet nutrition standards based on the latest *Dietary Guidelines for Americans*. While school lunches must meet federal meal requirements, decisions about what foods to serve and how they are prepared are made by local school food authorities.[29]

A school food-service director's job is important. For some children, school lunch is the healthiest meal—and perhaps the only significant meal—they eat all day. Imagine that you are a school food-service director. On the one hand, you are running a business. You need to make enough money to pay your employees and meet your expenses. To help control the cost of school lunches, the USDA donates certain foods to schools, which helps to keep the price of meals down. In order to receive food donations, food-service directors must adhere to USDA regulations for NSLP meals. That means the food-service director must meet strict nutritional guidelines for meals determined by the USDA while satisfying young customers, who have an array of food preferences. As a director, you may also face competition from nearby fast-food restaurants, convenience stores, and vending machines vying for your customers' food dollars. School food-service directors must satisfy several different groups of people, so they have a lot to consider when deciding what to serve.

School food-service directors may also face competition from foods in their own cafeteria. Many schools also sell foods separate from these NSLP meals—as à la carte offerings in school cafeterias or in school stores, snack bars, or vending machines—that are not subject to federal nutritional requirements. These foods are called "competitive foods" because they compete with school meals, and they may be lower in nutrients and higher in calories than cafeteria food.[30]

When children do not choose a school lunch, it's up to the parents and other caregivers to provide lunch. Children who don't buy a school meal need a suitable substitute. Simply giving a child money may result in unhealthy food choices for lunch, which will shortchange him of about one-third of his nutrition for the day. It makes more sense for parents and kids to use the

The National School Lunch Program provides breakfast and noontime meals for millions of school-aged children.

Daily Food Plans at ChooseMyPlate.gov as a guide for healthier brown-bag lunches. A lunch that the child has helped to plan has a better chance of being eaten. Without the child's input, the "healthy lunch" may end up being swapped for unhealthy foods, or worse, tossed in the trash. The Table Tips provide some useful ideas to improve the likelihood that a child will eat his or her packed lunch.

The Take-Home Message Increasing obesity rates are contributing to rising rates of type 2 diabetes in children. Parents and caregivers need to be sure children limit their intake of low-nutrient foods and get enough physical activity. Daily Food Plans available at ChooseMyPlate.gov address the nutritional needs of preschool and school-aged children. Children who eat breakfast tend to have better concentration in class and better overall dietary habits, among other benefits, than those who do not eat breakfast. School meals provide nourishment for children. For children who don't eat school lunches, parents and caregivers need to provide a healthy alternative.

What Are the Nutritional Needs and Issues of Adolescents?

Adolescence is the stage of the life cycle between the start of puberty and adulthood. Adolescence is a time of transformation that includes the following physical and psychological changes:

➤ *Hormonal changes.* Hormones are responsible for the development of secondary sex characteristics, such as pubic hair, and a lower speaking voice in boys. Girls experience breast development and their first menstrual period (called *menarche*). Adolescents may also experience acne.

➤ *Physical changes.* During adolescence, children get taller and heavier. Lean muscle mass and body fat stores increase, and bones become longer and thicker. For example, by age 18, teens have accrued about 92 percent of their peak bone mass, which is important because peak bone mass is linked to risk of bone fracture later in life.[31] An adolescent's rapid rate of growth must be supported with a balanced eating plan that includes adequate amounts of protein, calcium, vitamin D, and iron. As with younger age groups, the rate of obesity is increasing among adolescents, and approximately 18 percent are now considered obese.[32]

➤ *Emotional changes.* Some nutrition-related issues that arise during adolescence may be related to a child's emotional growth. Adolescents experience a strong desire for independence and individuality, and may want to make their own food choices, which may differ from what is typically served at home.

Peer Pressure and Other Factors Influence Teen Eating Behaviors

Parents and other caregivers have the most control over what children eat when they are young. As children get older, however, their peers become increasingly influential when it comes to food choices. Fitting in is very important to teens, including when eating with their friends; if a soft drink and a burger is what everyone else is eating, then a teen may be less likely to opt for a salad and a bottle of water. Young people may notice what, when, and how their peers eat and base their own eating decisions on how others in their group behave.

Teen eating habits are often influenced by peers and social settings.

adolescence The developmental period between childhood and early adulthood.

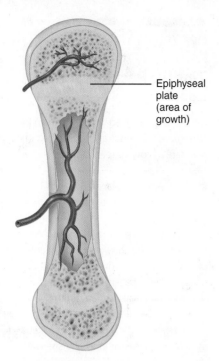

Epiphyseal
plate
(area of
growth)

Figure 15.3 Epiphyseal Plate in Long Bone
Adolescent bone growth takes place along the epiphyseal plate. Once the plates close, lengthening of the bone stops.

Some teens may defy authority or express their individuality by adopting different dietary eating choices than their parents, such as insisting on organically grown foods or adopting a vegan diet. They may also choose to smoke cigarettes, use illicit drugs, and drink alcohol as a result of influence from peers, the media, and adult role models. Teens who struggle with their body image may skip breakfast and other meals in an effort at weight control.

A teen's busy schedule may also influence his or her diet. Snacking—eating between meals—is typically part of an adolescent's eating style, and is useful when kids don't have the time for a full meal. However, snacks should be regarded as nutritious mini-meals, and not meal wreckers. For the most part, teens should avoid high-calorie foods that offer little in the way of nutrition, such as soda, sports drinks and energy drinks, cookies, chips, and candy, and reserve these foods for treats. Excess calories as fast food or other lower-cost convenience foods may increase the risk for overweight and obesity in teens, and certainly affects the quality of their eating plans.

Adolescents Need Calcium and Vitamin D for Bone Growth

Adolescents experience rapid bone growth. Most of the growth occurs in the **epiphyseal plate** (**Figure 15.3**), the area of tissue near the end of the long bones in children and adolescents.[33] **Bone mineral density (BMD)** increases through early adulthood, and **peak bone mass** may not be reached until age 30.

More than 99 percent of total body calcium resides in the skeleton. Vitamin D promotes calcium absorption. During rapid periods of bone growth, such as adolescence, inadequate intakes of calcium and vitamin D can result in low peak bone mass and increase fracture risk now and decades later.

Adolescents require 600 IU of vitamin D daily from foods, dietary supplements, or a combination, and 1,300 milligrams of calcium daily.[34] Generally speaking, teenagers don't consume enough calcium and vitamin D. One reason for this trend is teens' increased preference for soft drinks, which are nearly devoid of calcium and vitamin D, over milk and other beverages, such as fortified soy beverages and fortified orange juice, that provide calcium and vitamin D. Consumption of sugar drinks is highest among people aged 12 to 19 (see **Figure 15.4**). Sodas and other sugar-sweetened

epiphyseal plate The growth plate of the bone. In puberty, growth in this area leads to increases in height.

bone mineral density (BMD) The amount of minerals, in particular calcium, per volume in an individual's bone.

peak bone mass The genetically determined maximum amount of bone mass an individual can build up.

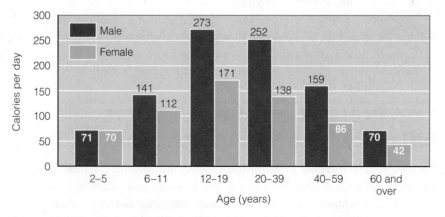

Figure 15.4 Daily Calorie Intake from Sugar Drinks, United States, 2005–2008
The rate of consumption of sugar drinks increases among both males and females until ages 12–19 years and then decreases with age.

Source: C. L. Ogden, B. K. Kit, M. D. Carroll, and S. Park, "Consumption of Sugar Drinks in the United States, 2005–2008." *NCHS Data Brief no. 71* (Hyattsville, MD: National Center for Health Statistics, 2011).

beverages, such as energy drinks and sports drinks, may taste good and be popular with teens, but the beverages lack the nutrients that are crucial for developing bones.

Teenage Girls Need More Iron

Compared with earlier in their childhood, adolescents need additional iron to support muscle growth and increased blood volume, and teen girls need more iron than boys to offset blood loss in menstruation. Many adolescent girls, especially those who restrict their calorie intake, have an inadequate iron intake. An estimated 9 percent of girls aged 12 to 19 have iron deficiency or iron-deficiency anemia.[35] Teens who limit their intake of fortified grains, such as breakfast cereal, and of lean meats, poultry, and seafood, may fail to meet iron needs unless they take a dietary supplement.

Adolescents: At Risk for Disordered Eating

Disordered eating, such as anorexia nervosa, bulimia, and binging, and other behaviors, including excessive exercising, typically emerge during adolescence. Disordered eating has emotional as well as physical consequences. Teens who don't eat enough or eat and then purge run the risk of severe nutrient deficiencies that affect their energy level and their health in the short term and the long run. Adolescents who are struggling with body image should seek help from a licensed mental health professional who specializes in disordered eating.

The Take-Home Message Adolescents face hormonal, physical, and emotional changes. They typically want to have control over their food and lifestyle decisions, and peers and the media exert a tremendous amount of influence on eating habits. Calcium, vitamin D, and iron intakes are particularly important during adolescence to ensure adequate bone and muscle growth and to prevent deficiencies. Increased consumption of soft drinks and decreased milk consumption can compromise bone health. Adolescents are sometimes at risk of developing disordered eating patterns due to poor body image, emotional issues, and peer pressure. Because many adolescents live in the "here and now," they may not realize the long-term health consequences of the poor diet and lifestyle habits they adopt during their teenage years.

What Are the Nutritional Needs of Older Adults?

If you were born in the United States around 1900, you would have been lucky to see your fiftieth birthday, as the average **life expectancy** at the time was 47 years. When it comes to life span, things have changed considerably since 1900.

Those born at the tail end of the so-called baby boom generation, between 1946 and 1964, are expected to be the fastest growing segment of the population in years to come (**Figure 15.5** on the next page). The number of people age 65 or older is expected to increase to an estimated 71 million in 2030, and the number of people over the age of 80 years is expected to increase to 19.5 million in 2030.[36]

Advances in medical research, health care, and public health policy are among the factors that have contributed to Americans' living longer. For example, the infectious and deadly diseases of the early 20th century, such as tuberculosis, pneumonia,

People are living longer today than in previous decades.

life expectancy The number of years that a person will live.

Figure 15.5 Aging of the Baby Boomers
The number of older adults in the United States is expected to increase dramatically over the next several decades.

Source: Federal Interagency Forum on Aging-Related Statistics, www.agingstats.gov.

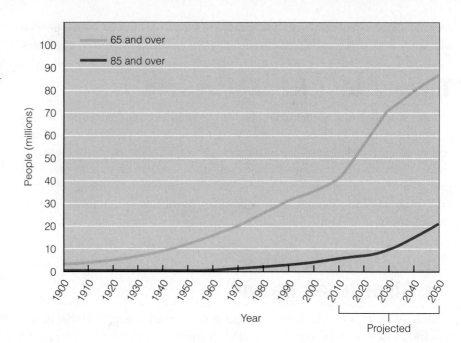

polio, mumps, and measles, have been dramatically reduced, thanks to widespread efforts to vaccinate children, as well as improved medical treatment for infectious diseases and other conditions, such as chronic illness. Public education campaigns that emphasize healthy lifestyle habits to prevent and manage conditions such as high blood pressure and elevated blood cholesterol levels to reduce the risk of heart disease, stroke, and certain cancers have also contributed to people living longer.

Good nutrition plays a key role in healthy aging. Seniors require a balanced eating plan with adequate amounts of protein, carbohydrate, and healthy fats. Caloric needs tend to decline with advancing age, but with the exception of a few vitamins and minerals, other nutrient needs do not decrease, which makes it even more important for older adults to choose nutrient-rich foods every day.

Older Adults Need Fewer Calories, Not Less Nutrition

The body's metabolic rate declines with age, and generally speaking, older adults require fewer calories as time goes on. The decline in calorie needs is often a result of lean tissue loss, primarily muscle mass, and less physical activity. For example, a 70-year-old moderately active man needs about 400 fewer calories—about the amount in a turkey sandwich—than his 40-year-old counterpart. By the age of 80, a sedentary female requires only about 1,600 calories a day, which is 600 fewer calories than she did when she was a moderately active 20-year-old.[37]

Protein intake tends to decline with age because people eat less food, and the oldest of the old have the lowest protein consumption. Adequate protein is necessary throughout the life cycle to support good health by providing amino acids to build cells and repair tissues, among other functions. As you get older, it's important to provide the body with the protein it needs to repair and produce lean tissue and to make bone tissue, too.

Though calorie needs may be reduced, the needs for vitamins, minerals, fiber, and other nutrients are not, and some nutrient requirements increase. **Figure 15.6** addresses the unique nutritional needs of older Americans. Foods rich in phytonutrients, such as fruits, vegetables, and whole grains, are as important as ever because phytonutrients play a role in reducing the risk of conditions that are more common in the aged, including certain cancers, heart disease, cataracts, and age-related macular degeneration.

Older Adults Need Adequate Fiber and Fluid

Adults of all ages need adequate fiber throughout the day. Fiber requirements are based on calorie needs, so adults may eat less fiber as they age. Recall from Chapter 4 that fiber may help reduce the risk of diverticulosis, heart disease, type 2 diabetes mellitus, obesity, and certain cancers, which are typically more common later in life.

Fluid works with fiber to help prevent constipation. Consuming adequate fluid is important to prevent dehydration that may cause a lack of energy and may be confused with dementia. An older person's thirst mechanism also becomes blunted to the point where he doesn't detect that his body needs fluid, which can increase dehydration risk.

People in their 70s, 80s, and 90s may take diuretics, which prevent excess fluid buildup in the body. Diuretics may cause frequent urination and people who take them may drink less fluid to avoid frequent trips to the bathroom, which may contribute to inadequate hydration. Dehydration can also lead to constipation, another common condition in older adults, as the stool becomes hard and compacted in the colon.

As with most adults, there is little room for low-nutrient drinks, such as soda, and alcoholic beverages in an older adult's diet. Water and milk are the best beverages for meeting fluid needs and avoiding dehydration. Table 15.4 summarizes some dietary needs of older adults.

MyPlate for Older Adults

Illustration by Betsy Hayes ©2011 Tufts University   http://now.tufts.edu/articles/eat-well-age-well

Figure 15.6 Older Adults Benefit from Good Nutrition and Physical Activity
Older adults need to focus on nutrient-dense foods that contain adequate fiber, calcium, vitamin B_{12}, and vitamin D. With a declining metabolic rate, they require fewer calories. Food choices should emphasize complex carbohydrates, lean protein foods, and healthy fats. They also need to ensure adequate fluid intake and regular participation in physical activity.

Source: Copyright 2011 Tufts University. For details about MyPlate for Older Adults, please see http://nutrition.tufts.edu/research/myplate-older-adults.

Table 15.4

Dietary Needs of Older Adults

What Older Adults Need	Why Older Adults Need It	How They Can Get It
Nutrient-rich food	Lower metabolic rate reduces daily calorie needs and makes higher quality food even more necessary to supply nutrients.	Choose foods in each food group that are low in added sugar, fat, and sodium.
Adequate protein	Provides the amino acids to preserve lean tissue and bones	Include protein-rich foods, such as dairy, eggs, seafood, and chicken, at every meal and snack.
Adequate fiber	Reduced calorie intake decreases fiber intake.	Choose whole-wheat bread, cereals, and grains such as brown rice, vegetables, and whole fruit.
Adequate fluid	Decreased ability of kidneys to concentrate urine and a blunted thirst mechanism, which can increase risk of dehydration	Drink milk or water with and between meals.
Vitamin D–rich foods	Decreased ability to make the active form of vitamin D, which decreases the absorption of calcium and phosphorus and increases the risk of osteoporosis	Choose vitamin D–fortified milk, yogurt, and cereals. Add a vitamin D supplement if needed.
Synthetic vitamin B_{12}	Reduced production of stomach acid that releases naturally occurring vitamin B_{12} from foods. Synthetic vitamin B_{12} does not require stomach acid.	Choose vitamin B_{12}–fortified cereals, breads, and soy milk. Add a dietary supplement if needed.
Adequate iron-rich foods	Necessary for strong immune system and transportation of oxygen to cells and tissues	Choose lean meat, fish, and poultry. Enjoy enriched grains and cereals along with vitamin C–rich foods (e.g., citrus fruits) to enhance iron absorption.
Adequate calcium	To help prevent the loss of bone mass with age	Consume 3 servings of dairy foods daily. Add a dietary supplement if necessary.

Older Adults Should Monitor Their Micronutrients

Appropriate intakes of certain micronutrients become a concern as we age, including the following:

➤ *Vitamin A.* Although the recommended daily amount of vitamin A doesn't change for people over the age of 50, too much preformed vitamin A (derived from animal sources), which is stored in the body, may increase the risk for osteoporosis and fractures. Older adults should be cautious when choosing supplements and fortified foods so as to prevent overconsuming this form of vitamin A. However, beta-carotene and other carotenoid precursors of vitamin A, found in dietary supplements and in brightly colored fruits and vegetables, do not pose a threat to health and are considered beneficial.

➤ *Vitamin D.* The skin's ability to make vitamin D from sunlight declines with age. Further, the intestines and kidneys lose some ability to absorb and convert vitamin D into its active form. Vitamin D needs are age dependent. The suggested daily intake for vitamin D in the diet increases from 600 IU daily to 800 IU daily for those age 70 and older.[38]

➤ *Vitamin B_{12}.* Health experts estimate that a significant number of people over the age of 50 have trouble absorbing the naturally occurring form of vitamin B_{12}, which is found only in animal products. As you age, the stomach secretes less hydrochloric acid, which functions to separate vitamin B_{12} from the proteins in foods of animal origin, such as eggs, meat, and milk. To combat this change in body chemistry, people over age 50 should consume the majority of their vitamin B_{12} in the synthetic form, found in fortified foods and dietary supplements. Synthetic vitamin B_{12} does not require hydrochloric acid to benefit the body.[39]

- *Iron.* Iron deficiency is uncommon among adult men and postmenopausal women who are not losing blood on a regular basis. However, iron deficiency can occur in older adults who do not consume adequate iron-rich foods, and those with chronic malabsorption, intestinal blood loss, or other ongoing conditions including kidney disease, cancer, and arthritis.[40]

- *Zinc.* Zinc is found in lean meat, poultry, fortified cereals, dairy foods, and legumes (dried beans and peas). A zinc deficiency may affect the immune system, as well as the sense of taste, which could reduce a person's intake of nutritious foods. Data from the National Health and Nutrition Examination Study (NHANES) III indicate that adults age 60 years or older from food-insufficient families had lower intakes of zinc and several other nutrients and were more likely to have zinc intakes below 50 percent of the RDA on a given day than those from food-sufficient families.[41]

- *Calcium.* Calcium absorption declines with age, and suggested intakes change with time. After age 50, experts suggest women consume 1,200 milligrams of calcium daily, up from the recommended 1,000 milligrams; men need 1,000 milligrams daily until age 70, and then should take in 1,200 milligrams of calcium daily after that.[42] Three daily servings of dairy, such as milk, yogurt, and cheese, or fortified foods such as orange juice and soy beverages, as part of a balanced diet supplies nearly all the calcium older people require. However, many adults, especially older Americans, are calcium deficient, increasing their risk for bone disease. People who do not get the recommended daily calcium may need supplements to make up the difference between what they need and what they consume from foods.

- *Sodium.* The 2010 *Dietary Guidelines for Americans* recommends that everyone over the age of 50 reduce their daily sodium intake to 1,500 milligrams or less to help reduce the risk of high blood pressure, which is more common with advancing age. Keeping blood pressure in the normal range reduces an individual's risk of cardiovascular disease, congestive heart failure, and kidney disease. People who have high blood pressure, or who have diabetes or chronic kidney disease, may need to make further modifications in their sodium intake.[43]

The Take-Home Message Life expectancy has increased in the last century due to improved research and health care, as well as dietary and lifestyle changes. Older adults need fewer calories but not less nutrition as they age. Nutrient-rich food selections are important to meet their fiber, fluid, vitamin, mineral, and phytonutrient needs.

What Additional Challenges Do Older Adults Face?

Many adults live productive, happy lives well into their 80s. But many seniors may not. Certain physical and emotional changes that accompany old age can make eating and exercise a challenge; such changes can include health conditions such as heart disease, cancer, and arthritis.

Eating Right for Health and to Prevent and Manage Chronic Disease

Eating right is important in every stage of the life cycle, especially in older adults. Compounds, such as fiber, vitamins, and minerals, in whole and lightly processed foods help to prevent age-related diseases including certain cancers, heart disease, osteoporosis, cataracts, and age-related macular degeneration. The antioxidants found in plant products also help protect the body against free radicals, which damage cells, including those in the brain. Preliminary research suggests that, along with a healthy lifestyle, a diet rich in antioxidants may reduce the risk of cognitive problems, such as those seen in dementia, including Alzheimer's disease.

The majority of older Americans are not eating the healthiest diet possible. When the diets of Americans 65 years of age and older were assessed to see if they adhered to recommendations, many fell short. On average, people age 65 and older consumed too much sodium, saturated fat, and calories from added sugars and alcohol. They also lacked adequate servings from several food groups including dairy, fruits, vegetables, and whole grains.[44]

Whereas heart disease is the leading cause of death in the United States, many people are concerned with getting cancer. The Health Connection feature "Fighting Cancer with a Healthy Lifestyle" provides more information about the ways that good nutrition can potentially help reduce the risk.

A varied, plant-based diet with plenty of phytonutrients, fiber, and essential nutrients is the best diet defense against the conditions and chronic diseases associated with aging.

Heart Disease and Stroke

Cardiovascular disease, which includes stroke, is more common with age. The most common cardiovascular disease is coronary heart disease, caused by a buildup of plaque that restricts the flow of blood to the heart; it is the number-one cause of death in the United States.[45] An ischemic stroke results from a clot, which may be the result of a piece of plaque that's been dislodged from a diseased blood vessel.

Millions of elderly people are living with coronary heart disease. They may also have diabetes and hypertension, adding to their risk for heart attack and stroke. Adults of any age who have coronary heart disease should be following a heart-healthy diet that limits saturated and *trans* fats, cholesterol, and sodium, and includes protein from plant sources, whole grains, lean meat, seafood, and low-fat dairy.

Type 2 Diabetes

The body's ability to maintain a normal blood level of glucose diminishes with age. The decline is typically gradual. If not corrected through lifestyle changes, medication, or both, prolonged elevated blood glucose concentrations can result in type 2 diabetes. Most people who have type 2 diabetes are overweight. Being overweight can trigger insulin resistance, which occurs when the body's cells are resistant to the effects of insulin, resulting in elevated blood glucose levels that can damage the eyes, kidneys, and heart, and the circulatory system.[46]

Hypertension

It's common for seniors to have hypertension, which is considered blood pressure above 120/80, and most are on medication to control it. The majority of high blood pressure is primary, or essential, hypertension, which probably cannot be cured but can be controlled. If left untreated or if poorly controlled, hypertension can result in heart attack, stroke, and kidney failure. Obesity, a high-sodium diet, and excessive alcohol use are among the major risk factors for hypertension. Some people can reduce their blood pressure by losing weight and being more active, and cutting down on alcohol and sodium.[47]

Arthritis

For people with **arthritis** (*arthr* = joint, *itis* = inflammation), simple activities, including getting out of bed, opening a jar, or climbing stairs, can be challenging. Arthritis causes painful and often debilitating swelling in the joints that restricts mobility.

arthritis Inflammation in the joints that can cause pain, stiffness, and swelling.

health

CONNECTION

Fighting Cancer with a Healthy Lifestyle

Cancer is the term used to identify a group of more than 100 diseases that are all characterized by the uncontrolled growth and spread of abnormal cells. Most of the time, the body quickly repairs or destroys a cell whose DNA has been altered or damaged, making it unable to reproduce and cause problems (see **Figure 1a**). Cancer begins when the body cannot halt the growth of abnormal cells, which then multiply and form tumors (Figure 1b), or, in the case of leukemia, a blood cancer, spur the growth of problematic cells in the bloodstream. Sometimes cells break off from the tumor and spread to other parts of the body.

Half of all men and one-third of all women in the United States will develop cancer during their lifetimes. Age increases cancer risk because it often takes many years for tumors to develop. The most common cancer among men is prostate cancer and, in women, breast cancer (men make up a small percentage of breast cancer cases). The second most common cancer in both men and women is lung cancer.[8]

Cancer risk increases with age, but decades of healthy habits reduce the chances for cancer.

Carcinogens Are Thought to Cause Most Cancers

All cancers involve the malfunction of genes that control cell growth and division, but only about 5 percent of cancers are strongly hereditary.[9] Most cases of cancer are not the result of inherited genes but of damage to DNA from carcinogens, a.k.a. cancer starters, that include:

➤ *Tobacco.* At least 69 chemicals in tobacco are known carcinogens. Cigarette smoking is the primary cause of lung cancer, and about 3,000 lung cancer deaths occur each year among adult nonsmokers in the United States as a result of exposure to secondhand smoke.[10] However, lung cancer also can occur in people who have never smoked and in those who never had prolonged exposure to secondhand smoke.

➤ *Radiation.* Excessive exposure to UV radiation, from sunlight and from tanning beds, is associated with an increased risk for skin cancer, and frequent exposure to other types of radiation—for instance, from X-rays—has long been associated with an increased risk for certain types of cancer.

➤ *Industrial chemicals.* Certain metals (such as nickel), some pesticides, and some chemical compounds (such as benzene) can act as carcinogens. People who are exposed to certain chemicals, including those who use them for work, are at the greatest risk for DNA damage from industrial chemicals.

➤ *Cancer-causing agents in foods and beverages.* Chemicals formed as a result of cooking meat, poultry, and fish at high temperatures, heterocyclic amines (HCAs) and polycyclic aromatic hydrocarbons (PAHs), have caused cancer in animal studies, but their effects in humans are unclear.[11] Molds, which may be present in cereals and legumes, are to be avoided, as is excessive alcohol intake.[12]

You Can Reduce Your Risk for Cancer with a Healthy Diet

Some compounds, found largely in fruits and vegetables, can help reduce your risk for numerous cancers:

➤ Certain *phytonutrients* can help reduce cancer risk. For example, the phytochemical lycopene, abundant in tomatoes and tomato products, is thought to help prevent certain cancers, including prostate cancer.

➤ *Antioxidants,* including carotenoids, the vitamins C and E, and the mineral selenium, neutralize free radicals, which can damage cellular DNA. They may also help prevent cancer from spreading to nearby tissues.

➤ *Retinoids* (vitamin A), *vitamin D,* and *folate* can stop the development of cancer by inhibiting the progression of damaged cells.

cancer A group of diseases characterized by the uncontrolled growth and spread of abnormal cells.

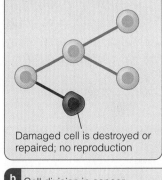

a Normal cell division

Damaged cell is destroyed or repaired; no reproduction

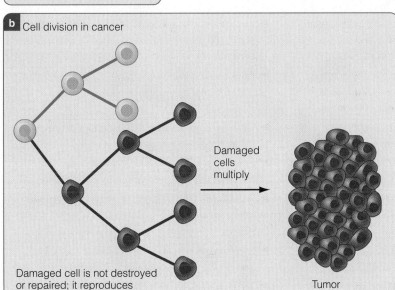

b Cell division in cancer

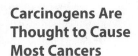
Damaged cells multiply

Damaged cell is not destroyed or repaired; it reproduces

Tumor

Figure 1 Cancer Occurs When Abnormal Cells Reproduce

CONTINUED ➤

> *Omega-3 fatty acids,* found in fatty fish and some oils, may help reduce cancer cell growth.

> *Fiber* helps dilute waste products, which may contain cancer-promoting agents, in your intestinal tract and quickly move these out of your body. Also, the healthy bacteria that live in your colon feast on dietary fiber, creating a by-product that may also help in the fight against cancer, especially colorectal cancer.

Avoid Foods and Beverages That May Increase Your Risk for Cancer

Some foods and beverages, when consumed in excessive amounts, may increase your risk:

> A diet high in red and/or processed meats can increase your risk for cancer. *Nitrites,* which are commonly used to preserve

processed meats such as ham and bacon, can react with the amino acids in the meat or in your stomach to form potential cancer-promoting compounds called nitrosamines and nitroamides.

> *Alcohol,* especially when consumed in excess, can increase the risk for cancer of the mouth, pharynx, larynx, and esophagus, as well as breast cancer in women and colorectal cancer in men. The more you drink, the higher your risk.

> High *salt* consumption can damage the lining of the stomach, paving the way for stomach cancer.

> Excess body *weight* contributes to as many as 1 out of 5 cancer-related deaths.[13]

The best strategy to reduce your risk for cancer is to follow the cancer-fighting recommendations listed in the table below.

Recommendations for Preventing Cancer

Recommendation	What to Do	How to Do It
1. Achieve and maintain a healthy weight, including during the teen years and young adulthood.	> Maintain a BMI between 21 and 23.* > Avoid weight gain, especially around your middle, as you age.	> Your pants are your best predictor of weight gain. If they begin to feel snug, assess your diet and your BMI. Is your diet heavy on the junk food? > See recommendation 3. > Review Chapters 10 and 11 for strategies to obtain and maintain a healthy BMI.
2. Be physically active as a part of everyday life.	> Incorporate at least 30 to 60 minutes of physical activity into your day. > Reduce the amount of screen time (TV, DVDs, computer, video games) spent daily.	> Set a timer at your computer and get up and move for at least 5 minutes every hour. > Watch one less TV show or play one less computer game daily. Spend that time cleaning, doing laundry, or running errands.
3. Limit consumption of energy-dense foods. Avoid sugary drinks.	> Cut back on sweets and treats that are energy (calorie) dense and serve up little nutrition besides calories. > Don't drink your calories by guzzling sodas, sports and energy drinks, fruit juices, or sweetened coffee beverages.	> If you want to snack on goodies, eat no more than about 100 calories of the item. That's typically one cookie or a small handful of chips or candy. > Drink one less sweetened beverage and one more glass of water daily.
4. Eat mostly foods of plant origin.	> Eat at least 5 cups of a variety of colorful fruits and veggies for phytochemicals, fiber, and nutrients. > At least half of your daily grain choices should be whole grains. > Eat dried peas and beans (legumes) as often as you can.	> Eat at least one salad with a minimum of three different colored veggies daily. > Choose only whole-grain cereals, such as raisin bran, oatmeal, and shredded wheat, in the morning. > Add legumes to the daily salad that you are now going to be eating.
5. Limit intake of red meat and avoid processed meat.	> Limit beef, lamb, and pork to no more than 18 ounces a week. > Avoid processed meats, such as ham, bacon, salami, hot dogs, and sausages.	> Eat red meat only at lunch in a sandwich, as the portion size will be only about 3 ounces. > Try veggie or turkey sausages.

Recommendations for Preventing Cancer *continued*

Recommendation	What to Do	How to Do It
6. Limit alcoholic drinks.	If you choose to drink, ➤ Women should consume no more than one alcoholic drink daily. ➤ Men should consume no more than two alcoholic drinks daily.	➤ Make a glass of water the first drink, rather than alcohol, when you are socializing. ➤ Alternate alcoholic beverages with nonalcoholic drinks to pace your evening. Make the nonalcoholic drink twice as big as the one containing the booze.
7. Limit salt consumption.	➤ Avoid salt and salt-preserved or salty foods. ➤ Limit sodium to no more than 2,400 mg daily.	➤ Remove the salt from your salt shaker and fill it with a no-salt seasoning blend, such as Mrs. Dash, to accompany the pepper shaker.
8. Aim to meet nutritional needs through diet alone.	➤ Look to food, not supplements, to fight cancer. ➤ Eat at least three meals a day to increase the variety and all the potential cancer-fighting compounds in food.	➤ Don't skip meals. ➤ Eat at least three pieces of fruit daily. Use a stoplight as your guide. Choose one fruit from each of the following colors: 1. **red** (apple, watermelon, red grapes) 2. **yellow** (banana, pineapple, citrus fruit) 3. **green** (green grapes, Granny Smith apples, kiwi)

Other Recommendations

- If you are pregnant, plan to breast-feed exclusively for up to six months and continue with complementary breast-feeding afterward to reduce your risk for breast cancer. Being breast-fed may also protect your child from becoming overweight.
- Cancer survivors should obtain nutritional recommendations from an appropriately trained professional, such as a registered dietitian, and should eat a healthy diet, maintain a healthy weight, and be as physically active as they are able.

Data adapted from the World Cancer Research Fund/American Institute for Cancer Research (AICR), *Food, Nutrition, Physical Activity, and the Prevention of Cancer: A Global Perspective* (Washington, D.C.: AICR, 2007).
*See Chapter 10 to determine your BMI.

Osteoarthritis is the most common form of the condition and often occurs in older people. As the population ages, the number of people with osteoarthritis will grow. By 2030, a projected 67 million people will have arthritis.[48] Osteoarthritis occurs when the cartilage, which covers the ends of the bones at the joints, wears down, causing bones to rub together. Friction between the bones causes swelling, loss of motion, and pain. Osteoarthritis commonly occurs in the fingers, neck, lower back, knees, and hips, which can interfere with the normal activities of daily living. Exercises that increase flexibility, keep joints limber, and improve the range of motion can help with osteoarthritis. Losing excess weight will also help relieve some of the stress at the hip and knee joints that bear most of the weight of the body.

Dietary supplements, such as glucosamine sulfate, may help ease osteoarthritis. Glucosamine is present in tendons, ligaments, cartilage, and the fluid that surrounds and cushions joints. Taking glucosamine supplements, particularly glucosamine sulfate, may help to prevent the breakdown of cartilage and fluid, or may increase the body's production of both of these protective substances, although results vary. Several studies have suggested that chondroitin, especially when combined with glucosamine, may be effective for treating the pain, swelling, and stiffness of knee osteoarthritis in people who have mild pain. Chondroitin is a compound that the body produces naturally as a major component of cartilage, and is thought to help keep cartilage healthy and support joint health by allowing cartilage to absorb and retain

Exercise for Life!

Want to learn more about how to help an older relative or friend stay active and healthy? Visit www.asaging.org and search for "Physical Activity" to find information about how to increase physical activity in older people's lives.

Severe arthritis can make everyday activities, like writing, typing, and handling objects, a challenge.

water and by blocking enzymes that destroy cartilage, as well as providing the raw material for building new cartilage.[49]

People with osteoarthritis should speak with their health care provider to assess the benefits of taking either or both of these supplements. For safety's sake, they should also discuss their use of all dietary supplements, including herbs, with a health care provider prior to consuming them. The Nutrition in the Real World feature "Drug, Food, and Drug-Herb Interactions" on page 586 discusses the potentially harmful interactions between certain herbs, nutrients, and drugs.

Rheumatoid arthritis (RA), the second most common form of arthritis, affects an estimated 1.3 million U.S. adults. In rheumatoid arthritis the immune system attacks the tissues of the joints, leading to pain, inflammation, and joint damage and malformation. RA often begins in middle age and occurs with increased frequency in older people.[50]

With the exception of the omega-3 fatty acids in seafood and olive oil and other unsaturated fats, there is no scientific evidence that any specific food or nutrient helps or harms people with rheumatoid arthritis. A balanced diet with adequate calories, protein, and calcium is most beneficial. The omega-3 fatty acids in fish have anti-inflammatory effects and may help reduce the stiffness and joint tenderness characteristic of rheumatoid arthritis.[51] The current recommendation to eat at least two fish meals weekly to protect against heart disease may also be helpful to arthritis sufferers.

Alzheimer's Disease

Although it's normal for older adults to experience some cognitive changes, such as taking longer to learn new information, more drastic changes are cause for concern. Some adults begin to forget where they live, become increasingly disoriented, have difficulty speaking, and may become emotionally unstable. These individuals may be experiencing **dementia**, which is the loss of cognitive functioning—thinking, remembering, and reasoning—and behavioral abilities, to such an extent that it interferes with a person's daily life and activities.

Alzheimer's disease (AD), an irreversible, progressive brain disease that slowly destroys memory and thinking skills, and eventually even the ability to carry out the simplest of daily tasks, is the most common form of dementia. Estimates vary, but experts suggest that as many as 5.1 million Americans may have Alzheimer's disease.[52]

Experts don't know how Alzheimer's disease begins, but it seems likely that damage to the brain starts a decade or more before problems become apparent in older adults. Some research suggests a connection between the risk for AD and heart disease, stroke, high blood pressure, diabetes, and obesity, but the evidence is preliminary. A nutritious diet, regular physical activity, social engagement, and mentally stimulating activities, such as reading and doing challenging puzzles, help people stay healthy as they age. New research suggests the possibility that these and other factors also might help to reduce the risk of Alzheimer's disease and other forms of cognitive decline.[53]

Depending on the stage of dementia, older adults may need part- or full-time supervision, and may not be allowed to take walks or to drive alone. However, accompanying an elder during any of these activities is a great way for both of you to get some exercise. While those with dementia experience mental deterioration, they should not be allowed to also experience physical deterioration.

Economic and Emotional Conditions Can Affect Nutritional Health

Staying active while managing chronic conditions is a common challenge for older adults, who may also be coping with food insecurity, depression, grief, or drug and alcohol abuse.

dementia A disorder of the brain that interferes with a person's memory, learning, and mental stability.

Alzheimer's disease (AD) A type of dementia.

Are You at Nutritional Risk?

Circle the number in the right column for the statements that apply to you (or someone you know if you are taking the assessment for a friend or relative). Add up the circled numbers to determine your score.

I have an illness or condition that has made me change the kind and/or amount of food I eat.	2
I eat fewer than two meals per day.	3
I eat few fruits or vegetables or milk products.	2
I have three or more drinks of beer, liquor, or wine almost every day.	2
I have tooth or mouth problems that make it hard for me to eat.	2
I don't always have enough money to buy food.	4
I eat alone most of the time.	1
I take three or more different prescribed or over-the-counter drugs a day.	1
Without wanting to, I have lost or gained 10 pounds in the last six months.	2
I am not always physically able to shop, cook, and/or feed myself.	2
Total =	___

Answers

If your score is

0–2: Good! Your diet and lifestyle don't appear to put you at risk of not meeting your nutritional needs.

3–5: You are at moderate nutritional risk. Your local office on aging, senior citizens' center, or health department can help you improve your nutritional health.

6 or over: You are at high nutritional risk. Bring this checklist the next time you see your doctor, dietitian, or other qualified health or social service professional. Ask for help to improve your nutritional health.

Source: American Academy of Family Physicians, Academy of Nutrition and Dietetics, and National Council on Aging, Inc. 2002. The Nutrition Screening Initiative is available at www.aafp.org. Accessed July 2010.

Food Insecurity

Between his medical and pharmaceutical costs and basic living expenses, Joe Powers exhausts his entire Social Security check by the twentieth day of each month. For the 10 days until he gets his next check, Joe is relegated to a stark menu of lower-cost foods such as oatmeal and eggs. His limited diet deprives him of the calories and other nutrients he needs until his next Social Security check arrives.

(T/F) Joe is not alone. He is experiencing **food insecurity**, which means he does not have access at all times to enough food for an active, healthy life.[54] Research has shown that elders who consistently experience food insecurity not only have more than double the risk of not meeting their daily nutritional needs, but also tend to be in only fair to poor health.

Limited finances aren't always the cause of food insecurity. Some elders may be able to afford food but lack the physical means to obtain it, prepare it, or, because of health issues such as tooth loss, consume it. A quick and easy assessment of an older adult's diet can help determine whether he or she is at risk for food insecurity (see the Self-Assessment).

To help prevent food insecurity in seniors, Congress passed the Older Americans Act in 1965 to provide support and services, including nutritious meals and nutrition education, to those age 60 and older to help them maintain good health, an adequate quality of life, and an acceptable level of independence.[55]

Congregate meals are one type of service available to elders as a result of the Older Americans Act. Nutritious hot meals are served at specified sites in the community, such as churches, synagogues, and senior centers, helping older adults meet their nutrient needs and offering opportunities for socializing. Often, transportation to these meals is also available in the community.

Homebound elders can receive home meal delivery as part of the Meals On Wheels program. The Meals On Wheels Association of America is the largest

Programs such as Meals On Wheels provide hot meals to elderly adults who cannot leave their homes.

food insecurity The chronic lack of sufficient resources to nutritiously feed oneself.

congregate meals Meals served at churches, synagogues, or other community sites where older adults can receive a nutritious meal and socialize.

Drug, Food, and Drug-Herb Interactions

Seventy-nine-year-old Donald David uses a seven-day plastic pill box to remind him to take his four daily prescriptions. Because Donald takes pills for heart disease, high blood pressure, and diabetes, his local pharmacist works with him to make sure that the drugs do not interact with each other in a way that could harm his health. The pharmacist also reminds Donald that he needs to keep his dietary vitamin K intake at an even keel, as major fluctuations in blood levels of vitamin K affect his blood thinner medication, and he warns Donald about taking certain herbs that could also interfere with this, and other, drugs.

Donald is lucky to have a pharmacist to remind him how drugs, food, and herbs can interact and produce unhealthy effects. Some older adults aren't so lucky. Older adults who take prescription and nonprescription medications on a daily basis may use more than one pharmacy or order medications online or through the mail, and they may lack guidance about drugs and dietary supplements. In addition, there's little research assessing all the potential interactions between prescription drugs, food, and herbal remedies. When patients are not fully informed about the potential interactions between their diets and their medication

or herbal supplements, the results may be dangerous.

Food can interact with medications in several ways. For example, it can delay or increase the absorption of a drug. Calcium, for instance, can bind with tetracycline (an antibiotic), decreasing its absorption. For this reason, this drug shouldn't be taken with milk or calcium-fortified foods.[14]

Drugs can also interfere with the metabolism of certain substances in foods. The compound tyramine, which is abundant in aged cheese, smoked fish, yogurt, and red wine, is metabolized by an enzyme called monoamine oxidase. Certain medications called monoamine oxidase inhibitors, sometimes prescribed to treat depression, prevent tyramine from being properly metabolized. High levels of tyramine in the blood can result in dangerously high blood pressure.

Herbs can also interact with medications. Herbs are regulated as food and not as drugs under the Dietary Supplement Health and Education Act of 1994. This act allowed manufacturers to be exempt from premarket safety and efficacy testing. Many people falsely assume that herbal remedies are safe because they are natural; however, dangerous interactions can occur when they

Daily pill containers like this one are often used by the elderly to remind them to take various medications.

are combined with prescription medications. For example, ginkgo biloba can interfere with blood clotting and shouldn't be consumed with the blood-thinning drug Coumadin (warfarin), or with aspirin, which also thins the blood. Consuming ginkgo with either or both of these medications can increase the risk of bleeding as well as hemorraghic stroke.[15]

The best way to avoid interactions is to make sure a health care provider and/or a pharmacist is aware of all the prescribed and over-the-counter medications, herbs, and dietary supplements that a person takes. See the accompanying table for a list of potential interactions.

Potential Interactions of Medications, Herbs, Nutrients, and Foods

Herb/Nutrient/Food	Purported Use	Potential Side Effects	Drug Interactions
Astragalus	Enhance and support the immune system	Not well known	Medications that suppress immunity
Black cohosh	Reduce hot flashes and other menopausal symptoms	Possible headache, stomach discomfort, rash, possible liver dysfunction	Risk of interactions appears to be small
Calcium	Prevent osteoporosis	Constipation; calcium deposits in body	Decreases the absorption of antibiotics, bisphosphates, digoxin, high blood pressure medications, medications used to regulate heart beat, and more
Coenzyme Q10	Treatment of heart and blood vessel conditions	Mild stomach upset, decreased appetite, nausea, diarrhea, rash, low blood pressure	Decreased efficiency of some cancer medications; enhanced effect of drugs to lower blood pressure; decreases warfarin (anticoagulant) effectiveness
Dong quai root	Relieve menstrual and menopausal symptoms	Excessive bleeding. Skin sensitivity. May be carcinogenic with long-term use.	Enhances the blood-thinning effects of aspirin and anticoagulants as well as garlic and ginkgo biloba

Potential Interactions of Medications, Herbs, Nutrients, and Foods *continued*

Herb/ Nutrient/Food	Purported Use	Potential Side Effects	Drug Interactions
Echinacea	Treat the common cold	Fever, nausea, vomiting, stomach pain. Allergic reaction if also allergic to ragweed and other plants.	Decreased effectiveness of immune-suppressing medications and drugs that are changed by the body
Fish oil	Reduce triglycerides and blood pressure; eye conditions; decrease inflammation	Excessive bleeding, fishy aftertaste in mouth, and allergic reaction in those with fish allergy	Enhances effectiveness of anticoagulant drugs such as warfarin and aspirin, and certain blood pressure drugs
Garlic, garlic supplements	Lower blood pressure and blood cholesterol levels	Possible stomach and intestinal discomfort	Do not take with drugs used to treat tuberculosis and certain HIV/AIDs drugs. Avoid with anticoagulant medication, such as warfarin.
Ginkgo biloba	Reduce memory loss, dementia	Possible stomach and intestinal discomfort	Blood-thinning drugs and aspirin. Enhances the blood-thinning actions of vitamin E and garlic.
Ginseng	Stress reduction, enhance immunity, stimulant	Diarrhea, itchiness, insomnia, headache, nervousness, rapid heart rate	May enhance drugs used to reduce blood glucose levels in type 2 diabetes. Do not combine with the anticoagulant warfarin. Enhances the blood-thinning actions of vitamin E, garlic, and ginkgo biloba.
Grapefruit, grapefruit juice	Source of vitamin C and phytonutrients	None known	Enhances effect of certain heart medications (calcium channel blocking agents), corticosteroids, immunosuppressants
Hawthorn	Congestive heart failure	Rare, but may cause stomach upset, headache, dizziness	Not much evidence, but may interact with certain heart medications
Licorice	Various disorders, including infections	Fatigue, headache, high blood pressure, weakness, among others	May reduce effectiveness of anticoagulant drugs such as warfarin
Milk thistle	Liver disorders	Allergic reactions in people who are allergic to ragweed and other plants; may lower blood glucose levels. Some gastrointestinal discomfort.	Medications that lower blood glucose levels
Kava kava	Reduce anxiety, stress, insomnia	Liver damage; long-term use may result in scaly, yellowed skin; drowsiness.	Increases effectiveness of antianxiety drugs and sedatives
Saw palmetto	Treatment for benign prostatic hyperplasia	Stomach upset	Anticoagulants, birth control pills
St. John's wort	Reduce depression, anxiety, fatigue	Stomach upset, dry mouth, dizziness, headache, skin tingling	Must avoid with many medications. Alert pharmacist and doctor about St. John's wort use.
Vitamin E	Possibly preventing the risk of heart disease and Alzheimer's disease	Excessive amounts can interfere with blood clotting, causing bruising and bleeding. Also, nausea, diarrhea, stomach cramps, fatigue, rash.	Certain immunosuppressive drugs; anticoagulants, such as warfarin; statins used to lower cholesterol; and large amounts of niacin
Yohimbine	Erectile dysfunction and sexual dysfunction in women	Increases blood pressure, heart rate, headache, anxiety, stomach upset, sleeplessness	Do not combine with monoamine oxidase (MAO) inhibitors, as effect is additive. Interacts with high blood pressure medications, and certain drugs used to treat mental illness.

organization in the United States providing meals to the homes of older adults who need them. Find out more about Meals On Wheels at www.mowaa.org.

Young people and others in the community can help make sure that older adults are aware of these meal programs and that they take advantage of the services available to them. Consider "adopting" an older adult in your neighborhood or a family member and, if need be, help him or her locate meal program services. Visit First.gov for Seniors at www.seniors.gov to locate these, and other, resources for seniors.

Depression and Grief

When Laura lost her husband at the age of 78, she stopped cooking dinner and took to opening a can of chicken soup for most of her evening meals. Her energy level dropped dramatically after his death, and on many days, she didn't even bother to get out of her pajamas. Like many elders who lose relatives and friends, Laura became depressed.

The loss of significant others and friends as well as chronic pain and concerns about their own health can add to feelings of sadness and isolation. Depression can interfere with an elder's motivation to eat, be physically active, and socialize—all of which can impact a person's mental and physical health. The risk of depression in older people increases with other illnesses and when their mobility and function is increasingly limited. Estimates of major depression in seniors range from less than 1 percent to about 5 percent, but rises to 13.5 percent in elderly people who require home health care and to 11.5 percent in elderly hospital patients.[56]

Alcohol Abuse

An elderly person's increased alcohol consumption could be a sign of depression and grief. Chronic health problems, loss of friends and loved ones, and financial stress could make alcohol an appealing sedative to temporarily ease psychological pain. However, heavy drinking can worsen depression, which can lead to more drinking. Also, because alcohol impairs one's judgment and interferes with coordination and reaction time, elders who have been drinking are at a higher risk for stumbling, falling, and fracturing bones. Anyone of any age can abuse alcohol, and drinking too much is not uncommon in the elderly. (T)(F)

The National Institute on Alcohol Abuse and Alcoholism recommends that people over age 65 limit their alcohol intake to seven drinks a week and no more than three drinks on any one day. People with certain health problems and those taking medications may need to drink less or avoid alcohol completely.[57] Alcohol may interact with prescription or over-the-counter medications, intensifying or diminishing their effects. For example, alcohol increases the effectiveness of medication taken to prevent blood clots.

Alcohol abuse in elders may be mistaken as the forgetfulness and disorientation associated with normal aging. **Figure 15.7** lists the red flags from the National Institute of Aging that may signal alcohol abuse in an older adult.

Red Flags for Alcohol Abuse in Older Adults

- Drinks to calm nerves, reduce stress or depression, or forget his or her troubles.
- Gulps drinks.
- Frequently has more than one drink a day.
- Lies about or tries to hide his or her drinking habits.
- Hurts self or others when drinking.
- Needs increased amounts of alcohol to get high.
- Feels irritable, resentful, or unreasonable when not drinking.
- Has medical, social, or financial worries caused by drinking.

Figure 15.7 Red Flags for Alcohol Abuse in Older Adults

Source: National Institute on Aging, "Alcohol Use and Abuse." Available at www.niaPublications.org. Accessed July 2010.

Staying Physically Active

Joan loves to ski downhill and cross-country and has been attending exercise classes six days a week for the past decade—a rather active schedule for a 76-year-old. Robert, age 78, attends weekly fitness classes and plays tennis a few times a week.

Physical activity is not an option for older adults; it's a necessity. Regular physical activity can help lower the risk of heart disease, colon and breast cancer, diabetes, hypertension, osteoporosis, arthritis, and obesity. Exercise helps maintain healthy bones, muscles, and joints, and reduces anxiety, stress, and depression. It improves sleep, flexibility, and range of motion, and can help postpone the decline in cognitive ability that naturally occurs in aging. Elders in good physical shape are also able to live independently longer, reducing the need for assistance with everyday activities, such as food shopping and housework.

Despite the many health benefits of being physically active, older people don't always get the recommended amount of exercise they need. The 2008 *Physical Activity Guidelines for Americans* suggests that adults over the age of 65 get at least 150 minutes (2 hours and 30 minutes) a week of moderate-intensity or 75 minutes (1 hour and 15 minutes) of vigorous-intensity aerobic physical activity, or the equivalent combination of moderate and vigorous activity. Older adults should also do muscle-strengthening activities on two or more days a week. When seniors are unable to get the suggested amount of exercise, they should be as physically active as their abilities and conditions allow.[58]

While regular physical activities that raise the heart rate and challenge the muscles are highly beneficial, it's important to be active all day long and to avoid sitting for long periods. Activities such as working in the garden, mowing the lawn, raking leaves, and dancing all provide health benefits.

The Take-Home Message Older adults should consume a balanced diet to meet their nturient needs and help prevent many of the chronic diseases associated with aging. Seniors also benefit from regular physical activity, and should do what they can in the way of exercise. Arthritis, Alzheimer's disease, food insecurity, depression, and alcohol abuse can challenge the abilities of older adults to maintain healthy diets and lifestyles.

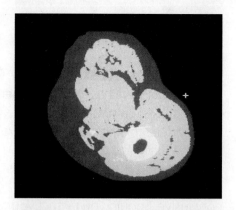

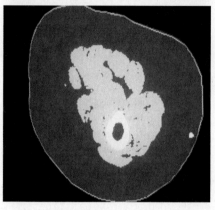

Although the cross sections of the thigh are similar in size, note the greatly reduced muscle area (in yellow) and increased fat area (in red) of the older, sedentary adult in the bottom image compared with that of a younger, more active adult. Most people lose a significant amount of muscle as they age, which could be prevented by engaging in regular physical activity.

Should You Restrict Your Caloric Intake to Increase Your Life Span? The Japanese island of Okinawa has the largest percentage of people aged 100 and older in the world, and the Okinawans have a strong cultural tradition of eating until they are only 80 percent full.[1] Some animals—monkeys, rats, and spiders, for example—also live longer when their caloric intake is reduced, laboratory studies have shown.[2] Believing that it will prolong their life, some people have begun to follow a calorie-restricted (CR) diet, reducing their caloric intake by as much as 30 percent of the daily recommended intake. This way of eating is difficult to maintain, and evidence about the impact of caloric restriction from researchers is not conclusive. Should you restrict your caloric intake, with an eye to extending your life span? After you've read the arguments for and against, answer the critical-thinking questions, and decide for yourself.

yes   no

- Even if you don't increase your life span, calorie restriction can improve your *health span*—the amount of time you are healthy in your life. Risk factors for atherosclerosis and diabetes are reduced in humans on calorie restriction.[3]

- Underfed rats can live up to 50 percent longer than rats on an unlimited diet.[4] Studies of other animals, including a 2009 study of monkeys, have also shown increased life span with a CR diet.[5]

- In human subjects, CR has been shown to lower cholesterol, fasting glucose, and blood pressure.[6]

- While the Okinawans' cultural rule to eat until you are only 80 percent full could be a key to their longevity, other factors, such as their varied, mostly vegetarian diet, an active lifestyle, and island living, rather simple calorie restriction, may play an important role.[7]

- In a recent study completed on monkeys, the rhesus monkeys on restricted diets aged just as quickly as their counterparts who were not restricted.[8]

- Side effects reported by people who follow a CR diet include constant, low-level hunger, a drop in core body temperature, and reduced sex drive.[9]

what do you think?

1. Which side do you think has the more compelling argument? Why? **2.** Do you think the benefits of a calorie-restricted diet outweigh the risks? **3.** Are you likely to alter your habits based on the evidence provided?

1 The Needs of Toddlers and Preschoolers Are Met with Small, Nutrient-Dense Meals

Toddlers and preschoolers grow and develop at a slower rate than infants. Children require small, frequent, nutrient-rich meals and snacks to fuel their busy lifestyles. Young children may be picky eaters and go on food jags, but these behaviors are normal and usually temporary. Caregivers may need to offer a new food up to 10 times before the child accepts it.

2 The Nutritional Needs of School-Aged Children Can Be Guided by MyPlate

Young children and teens are prone to iron deficiency. Children of all ages need adequate calcium and vitamin D for bone growth, and fiber and fluid to prevent constipation. Milk, water, and diluted 100% fruit juices are better beverage choices than sweetened beverages. Obesity and type 2 diabetes are occurring more frequently in children and teens. Poor dietary choices and insufficient exercise are two of the key culprits of this problem. Parents and caregivers must provide healthy foods and encourage physical activity to combat a child's likelihood of developing these conditions.

3 Nutritional Needs of Adolescents Are Based on Hormonal and Physical Changes

Calcium, vitamin D, and iron intakes are particularly important during adolescence to ensure adequate bone and muscle growth and to prevent deficiencies. Adolescents are sometimes at risk of developing disordered eating patterns due to poor body image, emotional issues, and peer pressure. Because many adolescents live in the "here and now," they may not realize the long-term health consequences of the poor diet and lifestyle habits they adopt during their teenage years.

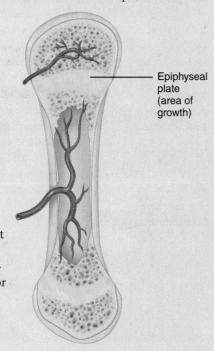

Epiphyseal plate (area of growth)

4 Nutrient Needs Change along with the Physical and Cognitive Changes That Are Part of the Aging Process

Metabolism slows with age, so older adults need fewer calories than their younger counterparts. Staying physically active is important during a person's later years, though sometimes this is challenging due to the fact that many older people are managing at least one chronic condition, such as arthritis, dementia, or heart disease. Older adults need to be sure to consume adequate protein, fiber, fluid, vitamins D and B_{12}, and the minerals iron, calcium, and zinc. Prescription medications, over-the-counter medications, and herbal remedies can affect nutrient absorption, or otherwise interact with nutrients.

5 Socioeconomic and Psychological Issues Can Affect the Nutritional Health of Older Adults

Older adults sometimes suffer from food insecurity, due to decreased mobility, financial hardship, or health conditions such as tooth loss. Social programs can help ensure the proper nourishment of homebound adults by providing meals in the community. Alcohol abuse may be an issue with older adults and may affect how they deal with daily life and manage chronic conditions.

Terms to Know

- toddlers
- preschoolers
- picky eating
- food jags
- school-aged children
- adolescence
- bone mineral density (BMD)
- peak bone mass
- life expectancy
- arthritis
- dementia
- food insecurity
- congregate meals

MasteringNutrition™   Build your knowledge—and confidence—in the Study Area of MasteringNutrition with a variety of study tools.

Check Your Understanding

1. Because they are still growing but have diminished appetites (compared with infants), toddlers and preschoolers should
   a. consume large meals.
   b. consume nutrient-dense foods.
   c. consume foods high in fat.
   d. consume foods high in sugar.
2. One of the key messages for children at ChooseMyPlate.gov is to
   a. drink water instead of milk.
   b. choose healthier foods from each food group.
   c. choose only whole grains.
   d. avoid all high-fat foods.
3. Breakfast is important for school-aged children because
   a. it improves alertness and ability to concentrate throughout the day.
   b. it helps them slow down in the morning.
   c. it gives them energy for after-school activities.
   d. it prevents adult obesity.

4. There appears to be a relationship between the rise in childhood obesity and the increase in
   a. childhood cancers.
   b. ADHD.
   c. type 2 diabetes in children.
   d. childhood cavities.
5. The National School Lunch Program
   a. doesn't hold schools to nutritional standards for meals.
   b. is a mandatory requirement for all public schools.
   c. often serves balanced meals at a reduced cost.
   d. is run by the Centers for Disease Control.
6. Which mineral supports healthy bone development and is particularly important during adolescence?
   a. calcium
   b. iron
   c. vitamin D
   d. copper
7. Teen boys and girls are at risk for a deficiency of which of the following?
   a. fat
   b. vitamin C
   c. iron
   d. vitamin A

8. Which of the following two nutrient needs increase with age?
   a. water and lead
   b. calcium and vitamin D
   c. protein and lipids
   d. vitamin K and biotin
9. Which of the following probably has the most influence on older adults' ability to consume a nutritious diet?
   a. eating three meals a day
   b. working outside the home
   c. television-watching habits
   d. living on a fixed income
10. Congregate meals are
   a. meals delivered to the homes of older adults who are homebound.
   b. frozen meals that adults can purchase at the supermarket.
   c. hot meals that are served at a site in the community, such as at churches and synagogues.
   d. meals made at home and eaten with friends.

Answers

1. (b) Toddlers need to eat nutrient-dense foods in order to obtain all the nutrients they need. Their smaller appetites mean they aren't likely to eat large meals, and foods high in fat and sugar may add significant calories without contributing many nutrients.

2. (b) The ChooseMyPlate.gov website encourages healthy food choices from a variety of food groups for children on a daily basis.

3. (a) School-aged children who eat breakfast have been shown to perform better in school and to have higher rates of physical activity and lower rates of obesity. Breakfast doesn't have to be eaten at the table, as caregivers can provide "to go" foods for children if they are in a hurry.

4. (c) Rates of type 2 diabetes among children have risen along with rates of overweight and obesity.

5. (c) The cost of National School Lunch Program meals are kept relatively low, as the USDA provides a certain amount of food free of charge to schools that participate. The Food and Nutrition Service, part of the USDA, provides guidelines that direct the minimum amounts of some nutrients, and the maximum amounts of calories and saturated fat, that school lunches provide.

6. (a) Adolescents need adequate amounts of calcium to support their growing bones. Vitamin D is not a mineral, but is also very important for bone growth.

7. (c) Teenagers are growing at a rapid rate and they require adequate iron to make muscle mass. Teen girls need to replace monthly losses of iron caused by menstruation.

8. (b) The need for both vitamin D and calcium is increased in older adults. Lead is a toxin and should never be consumed. Vitamin K and biotin are necessary for health, but you don't need them in higher amounts as you age.

9. (d) Older adults who may have a limited income may not be able to purchase adequate amounts of healthy foods to meet their nutrient needs. Dental problems, including ill-fitting dentures and tooth loss, may limit their food choices based on their inability to chew certain nutritious foods such as meat. Excessive alcohol in the diet displaces nutritious foods, and alcohol use increases the risk of falls and injuries.

10. (c) Congregate meals allow older adults in a community to meet and eat hot meals together. Older adults who are homebound can request that a healthy meal be delivered to their home. A variety of frozen meals can be purchased at the grocery store by adults of all ages.

Web Resources

- For more information on nutrition during the younger years, visit the Adolescent and School Health section at www.cdc.gov
- For more information on children's and teens' health, visit www.kidshealth.org
- For more about ADHD, search www.nimh.nih.gov
- For more about the USDA's National School Lunch Program, visit the Child Nutrition section at www.fns.usda.gov
- For more health information for older adults, visit the Aging section at www.cdc.gov
- For more information on herbs, visit the National Center for Complementary and Alternative Medicine, National Institutes of Health, at http://nccam.nih.gov

Answers to True or False?

1. **True.** Between the ages of 1 and 4, small children are extremely active and may not be interested in eating at mealtime. Turn to page 562 to find out how to make sure children get the nutrients they need.

2. **True.** In small children, iron deficiency is often caused by a limited diet that relies too heavily on milk or other iron-poor food sources. Read more about this condition on page 564.

3. **False.** Parents and caregivers may need to offer foods several times before a child accepts the food. This topic is covered in more detail on page 565.

4. **True.** Young children often go on food "jags" or may get hooked on particular foods and eat only those items. Learn more about these short-term habits and how to cope with them on page 566.

5. **False.** Fast food is only part of the problem. Too little exercise and too much screen time also contribute. Read more about the obesity epidemic among children on page 567.

6. **True.** Meals served as part of the National School Lunch Program must meet specific requirements established by the USDA. Details are found on page 572.

7. **False.** Sugary sodas and diet soda are nutritionally empty beverages. Turn to page 574 to find which beverages will help adolescents achieve healthy adult bodies.

8. **True.** Because a person's metabolism slows naturally with age, older adults need fewer calories than their younger counterparts. Learn more about the altered energy and nutrient needs associated with aging on page 576.

9. **False.** Financial circumstances or reduced mobility can cause older adults to experience food insecurity. Turn to page 585 to find out how this happens.

10. **False.** Older adults sometimes turn to alcohol to deal with discomfort, loneliness, or boredom. Find out more on page 588.

16

Hunger at Home and Abroad

True or False?

1. **Food insecurity** in the developing world is primarily due to poverty. T/F *p. 598*

2. No hard-working American goes to bed **hungry**. T/F *p. 599*

3. People who are **obese** don't experience food insecurity. T/F *p. 600*

4. Not enough food is produced in the **world** to feed everyone. T/F *p. 601*

5. **Children** are at a higher risk for food insecurity than are adults. T/F *p. 604*

6. Older adults who are financially secure can still sometimes experience low food security and **undernutrition**. T/F *p. 604*

7. Consuming **inadequate** nutrients won't affect mental development. T/F *p. 606*

8. Agricultural advances can help increase food **production**. T/F *p. 608*

9. **Fortifying** foods doesn't alter their nutritional content. T/F *p. 610*

10. The only thing you can do to alleviate hunger is give **money** to charities. T/F *p. 611*

See page 615 for the answers.

Chapter Objectives

After reading this chapter, you will be able to:

1. **Define food insecurity, food security, and hunger, and summarize the extent of food insecurity in the United States and worldwide.**

2. **Explain some of the causes of food insecurity in the United States.**

3. **Explain some of the causes of food insecurity worldwide.**

4. **List populations at highest risk for experiencing undernutrition.**

5. **Describe the effects of chronic malnutrition.**

6. **Describe some of the strategies currently in use to reduce food insecurity.**

e all know what "I'm hungry" feels like. After a long day working, a grumbling or gnawing in the stomach, a feeling of fatigue, or maybe light-headedness are all signs that tell us we need to eat. How many of us, however, know what it is like to be hungry day in and day out, never to feel truly full, or to lose weight though we don't want to?

Who are the people in the United States and the rest of the world who are hungry? What are the effects of chronic hunger? And, once we understand the causes and scope of this problem, what can we do about it? Can one person's actions really help people who are hungry? In this chapter, we'll explore the conditions of hunger and malnutrition, their causes and effects, and potential solutions in the United States and around the world.

What Are Food Insecurity, Food Security, and Hunger?

The U.S. Department of Agriculture (USDA) describes an American household as *food secure* if it has access at all times to enough food for an active, healthy life for all household members.[1] In contrast, a household is *food insecure* when any of its members do not have the resources they need to get adequate amounts of nutritious food. People who experience **food insecurity** may be at risk for undernutrition due to insufficient calories and nutrients in the diet. (You can see the range of definitions for high to very low food security in **Table 16.1**).

Many People Experience Food Insecurity in the U.S. and Worldwide

Because the United States is one of the wealthiest countries in the world, it may not seem likely that some of its citizens would be unable to buy an adequate supply of healthy foods. However, food insecurity in the United States is a major problem: In 2011, 14.9 percent of American households—about 17.9 million households—were food insecure at least some time during the year. Food-insecure households (those with low and very low food security) had difficulty at some time during the year

Table 16.1

Ranges of Food Security

Level of Food Security	Description of Conditions in the Household
High food security	No reported indications of food-access problems or limitations
Marginal food security	One or two reported indications—typically of anxiety over food sufficiency or shortage of food in the house. Little or no indication of changes in diets or food intake.
Low food security	Reports of reduced quality, variety, or desirability of diet. Little or no indication of reduced food intake.
Very low food security	Reports of multiple indications of disrupted eating patterns and reduced food intake

Adapted from USDA Economic Research Service. 2012. Food Security in the U.S. Available at www.ers.usda.gov. Accessed April 2013.

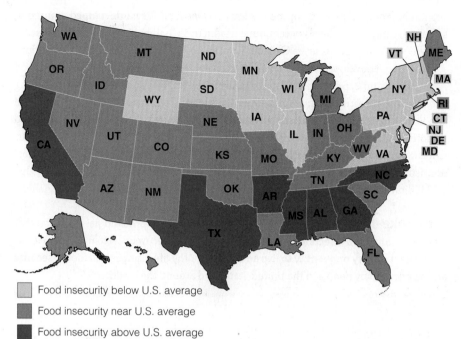

Figure 16.1 Prevalence of Food Insecurity in the United States
Although some areas of the United States have higher rates of food insecurity, these conditions can happen anywhere. In this map, data for three years, 2009–2011, was combined to provide more reliable statistics at the state level.

Source: USDA Economic Research Service. Updated 2012. Food Security in the U.S.: Key Statistics and Graphics. Available at www.ers.usda.gov. Accessed May 2013.

Food insecurity below U.S. average

Food insecurity near U.S. average

Food insecurity above U.S. average

providing enough food for all their members due to a lack of resources.[2] **Figure 16.1** illustrates the prevalence of food insecurity in the United States.

> Enough food is available to provide at least 4.3 pounds of food per person per day worldwide.

Also in 2011, 12.1 million adults lived in households with very low food security. In 2011, 845,000 children lived in households with very low food security among children. However, according to the USDA, children are usually protected from substantial reductions in food intake even in households with very low food security.[3]

Food insecurity is a household-level economic and social condition of limited access to food, while **hunger** is an individual-level physiological condition that may result from food insecurity.[4] People who have very low food security are at significant risk for hunger. Prolonged hunger can lead to **starvation**, a state in which the body breaks down its own tissues for fuel. As shown in **Figure 16.2**, you can think of these states—from food security to starvation and death—as occurring along a continuum.

The number of Americans who experience food insecurity might surprise you, but it is much lower than the number of food insecure people in many other countries of the world. While the United States is a **developed country** (also called a *more developed country*) with a high rate of industrial capacity, technological sophistication, and

food insecurity The inability to satisfy basic food needs due to lack of financial resources or other problems. The USDA further defines food insecurity as falling into the categories of either *low food security* or *very low food security*.

hunger Physical discomfort that results from the lack of food associated with food insecurity.

starvation To suffer severely from lack of food; a state in which the body breaks down its own tissue for fuel.

developed country A nation advanced in industrial capability, technological sophistication, and economic productivity; also called *most developed country*.

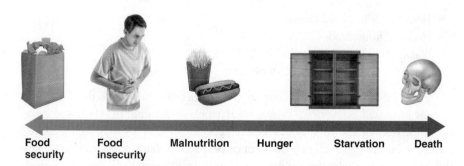

| Food security | Food insecurity | Malnutrition | Hunger | Starvation | Death |

Figure 16.2 Spectrum of Food Security
Food insecurity and hunger are points along the continuum between being food secure and dying from starvation.

economic productivity, **developing** (or *less developed*) and **least developed countries**, by contrast, have lower levels of economic productivity, and higher rates of food insecurity and very low food security. Canada, Australia, and most western European nations are considered developed countries, while many of the countries in South America and Asia—for example, Brazil, China, India, and Saudi Arabia—are considered developing nations. The majority of the world's least developed countries are located in central and western Africa. Worldwide, the Food and Agriculture Organization of the United Nations (FAO) estimates that between 2010 and 2012, 12 percent of the world's population were hungry.[5] In developing countries, such as those in southern Asia, under-nourishment has increased to 35 percent.[6] As of 2013, the World Bank estimated that 1.22 billion poor people in developing countries lived on $1.25 a day or less in 2010.[7]

The Take-Home Message Hunger is an individual physiologial condition that may result from food insecurity. Food insecurity is the limited or uncertain access to foods of sufficient quality or quantity to live an active, healthy life. Hunger and food insecurity are experienced by people in the United States and around the world.

In the United States, poor single parents and their children can experience food insecurity due to unemployment, low wages, or other circumstances that lead to financial hardship.

developing country A nation having a relatively low level of industrial capability, technological sophistication, or economic productivity; also called *less developed country*.

least developed country A nation having a low level of economic productivity and technological sophistication within the contemporary range of possibility.

poverty Lacking the means to provide for material or comfort needs.

What Causes Food Insecurity in the United States?

In developed countries, food insecurity typically results from factors affecting individuals, such as **poverty** or poor health. In developing and least developed countries, regional problems, such as discrimination, armed conflict, natural disasters, and population overgrowth, can be as significant as individual hardships. Let's take a closer look at these factors, beginning with those contributing to food insecurity in the United States.

In the United States, Food Insecurity Is Often Caused by Poverty

Poverty levels in the United States are defined according to strict guidelines. A family of four is considered impoverished if its annual income is at or below $23,283.[8] The U.S. Census Bureau reports that in 2011, 46.2 million people (15 percent) lived in poverty in 2011, a rate unchanged from the 2010 poverty rate.[9] In 2011, 21.9 percent of children under 18 (16.1 million) lived in poverty.[10]

According to the U.S. Census Bureau, those at greater than average risk of experiencing poverty and food insecurity are people living in the following households:[11]

> ➤ Households headed by a single woman (36.8 percent)
> ➤ Hispanic households (26.2 percent)
> ➤ Black, non-Hispanic households (25.1 percent)
> ➤ Households with children (20.6 percent)

These circumstances contribute to poverty because they have disadvantages, such as increased exposure to crime, fewer employment opportunities, and lower wages for women and minorities. For example, single mothers may feel "trapped," with very few options to explore different career paths, because of obligations to their children. Also, arranging for childcare can prompt additional stress and drain an already tight budget. Single mothers are more likely to experience times without adequate amounts of food than are families headed by a married couple.[12]

You may be surprised to learn that steady employment does not guarantee that an individual or a family won't experience food insecurity. People can be steadily employed in a low-wage full-time job, in a series of seasonal jobs, or in several part-time jobs and still experience food insecurity. In fact, in 2003, about 7.4 million Americans were classified among the **working poor**. In these households, once the monthly expenses are paid, there is often too little money available to feed everyone adequately (see **Figure 16.3**). Additionally, even people with excellent jobs may experience food insecurity if they are laid off.

People living in poverty often try to shop for "value." For example, they may opt for cheap fast food rather than cooking for themselves. However, buying nutritious food at the grocery store and using it to make healthy sandwiches, salads, and snacks is often actually cheaper than a daily trip through the drive-through (see **Table 16.2**).

Health Problems Contribute to Food Insecurity among Americans

A variety of health issues can also set the stage for food insecurity:

➤ *Chronic illness.* Adults who are chronically ill are less likely to earn a steady income and therefore are at risk of having a poor diet. Chronic illness in an elderly person can reduce mobility, making it difficult to get to a grocery store or to prepare nourishing meals.

➤ *Disability.* Many adults who are disabled lead highly productive lives, but others are limited to low-skilled, low-wage jobs. Some cannot work at all and must depend on disability income, which may not provide adequate money for nourishing food. Similar to chronic illness, disability can make it difficult for a person to shop for food and prepare meals.

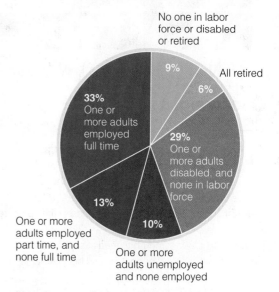

Figure 16.3 Employment Status of Food-Insecure Households
Almost half of households with the greatest difficulty putting adequate food on the table include an employed adult.

Source: USDA Economic Research Service, "Economic Information Bulletin," 2009. www.ers.usda.gov. Accessed June 2010.

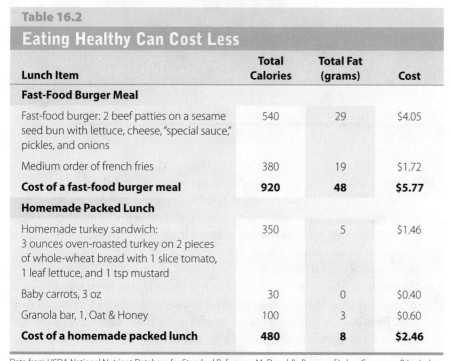

Table 16.2

Eating Healthy Can Cost Less

Lunch Item	Total Calories	Total Fat (grams)	Cost
Fast-Food Burger Meal			
Fast-food burger: 2 beef patties on a sesame seed bun with lettuce, cheese, "special sauce," pickles, and onions	540	29	$4.05
Medium order of french fries	380	19	$1.72
Cost of a fast-food burger meal	**920**	**48**	**$5.77**
Homemade Packed Lunch			
Homemade turkey sandwich: 3 ounces oven-roasted turkey on 2 pieces of whole-wheat bread with 1 slice tomato, 1 leaf lettuce, and 1 tsp mustard	350	5	$1.46
Baby carrots, 3 oz	30	0	$0.40
Granola bar, 1, Oat & Honey	100	3	$0.60
Cost of a homemade packed lunch	**480**	**8**	**$2.46**

Data from USDA National Nutrient Database for Standard Reference; McDonald's; Bureau of Labor Consumer Price Index. Accessed February 2010.

working poor Individuals or families who are steadily employed but still experience poverty due to low wages or high dependent expenses.

health
CONNECTION

Overweight and Undernourished

Tia, a mother of two school-aged children, works full-time for minimum wage at a fast-food restaurant, and is considered one of the "working poor." She has difficulty making ends meet, especially during the winter months, when the cost of heating her one-bedroom apartment cuts into her monthly food budget. Tia eats breakfast and lunch at her job. She purposely fills up on french fries before she leaves work so that she can skip dinner without feeling hungry. With one less mouth to feed at supper, she can stretch her limited household food budget to feed her children and husband. Not surprisingly, Tia is obese.

According to the CDC, adults in situations similar to Tia's are at risk for being overweight. Non-Hispanic black women with low income have the greatest likelihood of being obese.[1] But they aren't alone. In 2007–2008, more than one-third of adults in the United States were obese. And obesity "now affects 17 percent of all children and adolescents in the United States."[2] Among men, "obesity prevalence is generally similar at all income levels, with a tendency to be slightly higher at higher income levels."[3]

These high rates of overweight and obesity are thought to result from an interaction of several contributing factors, including cultural factors that influence diet and exercise behaviors.[4] Other factors include lack of access to healthy food in communities where supermarkets are not available (the so-called "food deserts"); lack of safe areas in which to exercise or for children to play; lack of access to basic health care; poor housing; low-wage work and long working hours; advertising of less-healthy foods; and increased stress that can lead to central adiposity and emotional eating.

What do you think Tia can do to improve the nutritional status of herself and her family? What government or community programs are most likely to help? What other steps could be taken to address the problems of limited access to healthier, nutrient-dense foods and adequate physical activity?

People in poor, urban areas often find themselves in "food deserts," with little access to the fresh, healthy food found in supermarkets, and easy access to fast foods and snack foods like those found in drive-through restaurants and liquor or convenience stores.

> *Substance abuse.* Drug and alcohol abuse are common causes of food insecurity, in part because of the challenge these problems create in maintaining steady employment. Many people who abuse substances become unable to keep up their mortgage or rent, and they descend into homelessness. In fact, an estimated 85 percent of all homeless men and women in urban areas abuse substances and/or have a mental illness.

> *Mental illness.* Many mentally ill people, often including the **homeless**, are forced to rely on charity, church meals, or public assistance programs for most of their food. Even people with homes and jobs who suffer from mental illness can lose interest in eating or have decreased ability to prepare meals. For example, clinical depression among mothers, particularly those in low-income families, has been associated with food insecurity in households.[13]

homeless Individuals who are either "crashing" with friends or family members, or residing on the street or in their automobiles.

Are You at Risk for Food Insecurity?

Take this quiz to find out if you are at risk for food insecurity and/or hunger.

In the past 12 months:

1. Have you ever run out of money to buy food?
   Yes ☐ **No** ☐

2. Have you ever eaten less than you felt you should because there was not enough money to buy food or enough food to eat?
   Yes ☐ **No** ☐

3. Have you ever completely depleted your food supply because there was not enough money to buy replacement groceries?
   Yes ☐ **No** ☐

4. Have you ever gone to bed hungry because there was not enough food to eat?
   Yes ☐ **No** ☐

5. Have you ever skipped meals because there was not enough money to buy food?
   Yes ☐ **No** ☐

6. Have you ever relied on a limited number of foods to feed yourself because you were running out of money to buy food?
   Yes ☐ **No** ☐

Answers

If there are zero "yes" replies, you are food secure. If there are one to three "yes" replies, you are at risk for food insecurity. If there are four or more "yes" replies, you are classified as "hungry."

Source: Adapted from The Community Childhood Hunger Identification Project Survey, July 1995; R. E. Kleinman, et al., "Hunger in Children in the United States: Potential Behavioral and Emotional Correlates," *PEDIATRICS* 101 (1998): 3–10.

Now that you've learned about the factors contributing to food insecurity in the United States, you may be wondering whether you're at risk. If so, take the Self-Assessment to find out.

The Take-Home Message The causes of food insecurity in the United States include individual hardships, such as poverty, unemployment, and health problems. Food insecurity and hunger are particularly prevalent in households headed by a single mother, minority households, households with children, those living in inner cities, and among those with unstable or seasonal professions.

What Causes Food Insecurity and Poverty Around the Globe?

(T|F) Worldwide, food insecurity persists despite the fact that global food production exceeds the needs of the world's population. This sobering reality tells us that agricultural production is not the problem, and increasing it is not the sole solution. So, what causes global hunger?

Discrimination and Inequality Promote Poverty

Racial, gender, and ethnic discrimination can contribute to reduced employment, lower educational achievement, and fewer business opportunities. Vulnerable groups include women, the elderly, people with disabilities, refugees, orphans, migrant workers, and people who are illiterate. In many countries, such as Sudan, Afghanistan, Angola, and Ethiopia, discrimination exists at both the national and local levels. For example, at the national level, control over land and other assets is often unequal.

Many hunger relief programs work to provide food aid to needy nations. However, successfully delivering the food to those who need it is often challenging.

Thanks to agricultural advances, the world's farmers can grow plenty of food. However, distribution problems and other factors keep some people from getting enough to stave off hunger.

At the local or household level, access to food is influenced by factors such as gender, control over income, education, birth order, and age.[14] Much of the inequity is due to educational disparities between boys and girls. Two-thirds of the almost 900 million illiterate adults in the world are women. Thus, it's not surprising that worldwide, 70 percent of the 1.2 billion people who live in extreme poverty are female.[15]

Political Sanctions and Armed Conflicts

One government or country may try to force political change on another using **political sanctions**, such as boycotts and trade embargoes. Sometimes the goal of sanctions is to postpone or replace possible military action. Other goals include restoring democracy, condemning the abuse of human rights, and punishing groups that protect terrorists or international criminals. Although the goals of the sanctions may be noble, the "indiscriminate economic impact and negative humanitarian consequences"—such as shortages in food, fuel, or medicine—often harm innocent people, instead of influencing a country's leaders.[16] Agricultural embargoes create food shortages by decreasing access to agricultural supplies, fuel, or crops. As with sanctions, embargoes more often hurt the average citizen than affect government authorities.

> Eighty percent of people who experience hunger around the world make their living from the land, and 50 percent are actually farmers.

War, armed conflict, and civil unrest may cause **famine** because of the disruption to agriculture, food distribution, and normal community activities. During wars and regional conflicts, governments often divert money from nutrition programs and food distribution efforts and redirect it toward weapons and military support. Conflicts cause increases in hunger and overwhelm the humanitarian safety network. Political turbulence can compromise food distribution programs.[17] People may be displaced, lose most of their possessions and their jobs, and then be unable to find local jobs because they are foreign workers.

Crop Failure, Natural Disasters, and Wasteful Agricultural Practices

Natural disasters, such as drought, floods, crop diseases, and insect infestations, can occur in any country, on any continent. However, the impact of natural disasters is much greater on least developed countries than on developed countries. There are several reasons for this, including the population's inability to relocate away from disaster-prone areas and people's inability to make their homes and farms less vulnerable to destructive natural forces. Additionally, the local economy and infrastructure tend to be less stable in least developed areas, so a natural disaster can quickly become devastating.[18] (See the Nutrition in the Real World feature "Natural Disasters and Food Insecurity" for a closer examination of efforts conducted to feed the hungry in the wake of severe natural disasters.)

> Because of water's essential role in growing crops, water and food security are closely linked.

Drought is the leading cause of severe food shortages in developing and least developed countries. Lack of water can lead to famine and undernutrition. However, floods can also destroy food crops, and are major causes of food shortages.

Wasteful agricultural practices also threaten limited resources. The depletion of natural resources through practices such as overcropping, overgrazing of livestock, aggressive timber harvesting, and the misuse of fertilizers, pesticides, and water may increase the yield of food in the short term at the cost of long-term sustainability.[19]

political sanctions Boycotts or trade embargoes used by one country or international group to apply political pressure on another.

famine A severe shortage of food caused by crop destruction due to weather problems or poor agricultural practices so that the food supply is destroyed or severely diminished. Famine can also be caused by pestilence or war.

Natural Disasters and Food Insecurity: A Dire Combination

Natural disasters, including earthquakes, hurricanes, tsunamis, and floods, can be disastrous no matter where they occur, but when they strike a country or region that's particularly ill-prepared or impoverished, the impact can be devastating.

In 2008, 231 worldwide natural disasters, including one major (7.9) earthquake in the Sichuan province of China, killed almost 236,000 people and cost an estimated $181 billion.[5] In February 2010, a sizable (7.0) earthquake rocked the small, impoverished nation of Haiti, where more than 2 million people—over half the population—were already food insecure or undernourished. The earthquake resulted in more than 200,000 deaths, 300,000 injuries, and a million people being left homeless.[6] As people's homes and possessions were destroyed, they were often left wandering and destitute. They were afraid to reenter damaged housing for fear of aftershocks or further collapse. Those who sustained injuries were often untreated for days, without food and water, as relief workers struggled to find and rescue them.

Those lucky individuals who escaped the initial encounter were faced with a second crisis: shortages of food, clean water, and shelter. Aid workers rushed in with supplies, such as nutritious biscuits and bottled water, only to find that remote sites were largely inaccessible due to difficult terrain, extensive damage, or lack of infrastructure. Thus, widespread food insecurity developed. While some farmers were still producing food, damage to infrastructure such as roads and bridges prevented many of them from reaching markets with it. The food that did end up in the marketplace was often too expensive even for those who had a bit of money.[7]

The distribution of high-energy, nutritious biscuits was a lifeline in the first days after the 2010 disaster in Haiti.

As the situation stabilized and people returned home or left the cities to find shelter with families or friends in rural areas, the long-term consequences of the disaster began to be addressed. In the case of Haiti, 62 percent of the country's population lives in rural areas, and 80 percent relies on agriculture for its livelihood, including small-scale production in the form of backyard gardening and small animal rearing in urban areas.[8] International relief efforts therefore focused on:[9]

- ➤ Rapidly restoring food production through input distribution and technical support to small-scale urban and rural farmers in time for the planting season
- ➤ Reestablishing the livelihoods of about 1 million people living in urban and rural areas that were directly or indirectly hit by the earthquake, by supporting field-based and backyard food production, and providing assistance for small-scale agricultural and livestock production, including seeds, fertilizers, seedlings, and small animals
- ➤ Rehabilitating basic rural infrastructure in the affected areas, such as rural roads, irrigation facilities, food storage, and farm infrastructure, for about 1 million people

These efforts were not cheap, and the international relief community relied heavily on monetary and other assistance from nations, organizations, and charities to facilitate the repair and rebuilding necessary to restore a basic quality of life.

Lack of irrigation also contributes to crop failures and low yields. The proper use of irrigation can increase crop yield by 100 to 400 percent. Surprisingly, only 17 percent of the world's land is irrigated, yet this small amount disproportionately produces 40 percent of the world's food.[20]

As the world's population continues to grow, demands on limited resources for food production will increase.

Population Overgrowth

The human population is growing by about 200,000 people a day, and the projected world population for 2025 is 8 billion people.[21] By 2050, the United Nations estimates, the world population will reach 8 to 12 billion people. Most of this growth is occurring in developing and least developed countries. Whenever rapid population growth occurs in areas that are strained for food production, the resulting **overpopulation** can take a toll on the local people's nutritional status.

The Take-Home Message Factors that give rise to hunger and food insecurity around the world include poverty, discrimination, political sanctions, military conflicts, crop failures, natural disasters, wasteful agricultural practices, and overpopulation.

Who Is at Increased Risk for Undernutrition?

Hunger and food insecurity usually result in **undernutrition**, in which a person's nutrient or energy needs are not being met by his or her diet. Some people are particularly susceptible to experiencing undernutrition because they have high nutrient needs or because they have a reduced ability to process nutrients. The following populations are at increased risk for undernutrition:

> *Pregnant and lactating women.* Pregnant women need extra calories and nutrients—in particular, protein, vitamins, and minerals—to support their own health and their growing baby. Many inadequately nourished pregnant women give birth to undernourished infants. Lactating women need even more calories than pregnant women if they are to maintain a healthy weight and produce adequate, nourishing breast milk. The global recommendation is for women to nurse their babies for the first six months and to continue nursing with supplemental foods into the second year of life or beyond.[22]

> *Infants and children.* Infants are vulnerable to undernutrition because they are growing rapidly, have high nutrient requirements (per unit of body weight), and may be breast-fed by mothers who are undernourished themselves. Because they are dependent on their caregivers to give them adequate breast milk, formula, or foods, they are particularly vulnerable to neglect. From 6 to 12 months of age, as an infant transitions from breast milk to a diet of breast milk plus solid foods, inadequate feeding can lead to diminished growth and the potential for severe undernutrition during the second year of life.[23] The risk for undernutrition continues into childhood if the family experiences food shortages or chronic disease. For example, AIDS can result in the death, and loss of income, of one or both parents. An estimated 16 million children worldwide have become orphaned by AIDS.[24]

> *The critically ill.* Liver and kidney disease can impair the body's ability to process and use some nutrients. Loss of appetite, as seen in some cancer patients and most people with AIDS, can reduce patients' ability to eat, and complicate their treatment.

> *Older adults.* Older adults are at increased risk for undernutrition because of a decreased sense of taste and smell, dental problems, immobility, malabsorption, or chronic illnesses.[25] In addition, loneliness, isolation, confusion, or depression can diminish appetite or cause a person to lose interest in cooking and eating.

overpopulation When a region has more people than its natural resources can support.

undernutrition A state of inadequate nutrition whereby a person's nutrient and/or energy needs are not being met through the diet.

The Take-Home Message Pregnant and lactating women, infants and children, and the ill and elderly are particularly vulnerable to the effects of undernutrition.

What Are the Effects of Chronic Malnutrition?

Once people move along the continuum from food insecurity and undernutrition to **malnutrition** and hunger, it can be extremely difficult to recover. That's because lack of food can lead to physical problems that interfere with a person's ability to earn an adequate income, a situation that leads to continued poverty and lack of adequate food (**Figure 16.4**).

In general, whenever the body experiences fasting, famine, serious disease, or severe malnutrition, it attempts to conserve energy and preserve body tissues. Over an extended period of fasting, however, the body breaks down stored fat, then muscle tissue and internal organs as sources of energy. In prolonged starvation, adults can lose up to 50 percent of their body weight. The greatest amount of organ deterioration occurs in the intestinal tract and the liver. The loss is moderate in the heart and kidneys, and the least damage occurs in the brain and nervous system.[26]

Let's look at some individual effects of chronic malnutrition.

Children Suffer Impaired Growth and Development

When children do not receive the nutrients they need to grow and develop properly, they are likely to experience both physical and mental problems, including insufficient weight gain, improper muscle development, lowered resistance to infection, **growth stunting**, and impaired brain development (**Figure 16.5**).[27] Their bodies

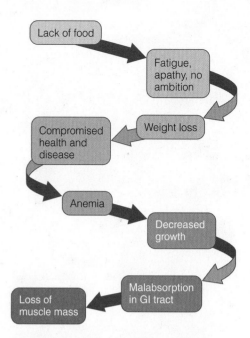

Figure 16.4 Downward Spiral of Poverty and Hunger
Lack of food can lead to numerous other symptoms that compound the problem of hunger.

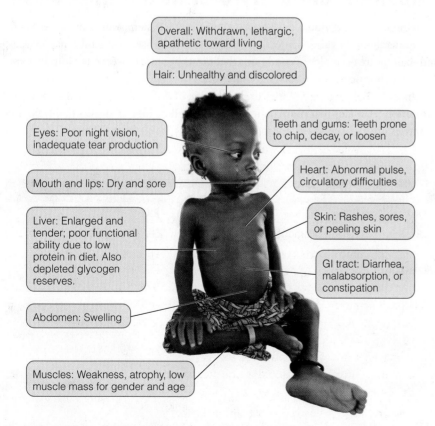

Figure 16.5 Effects of Undernutrition
As hunger persists, physical symptoms set in and lead to further complications.

malnutrition The long-term outcome of consuming a diet that contains an imbalance of nutrients.

growth stunting Impaired growth and development primarily manifested in early childhood and including malnutrition during fetal development. Once growth stunting occurs, it is usually permanent.

attempt to adapt to a lack of food by decreasing physical and intellectual growth. Children are more likely to show behavioral, emotional, and academic problems if they come from families that experience hunger and food insufficiency rather than families that do not report hunger experiences.[28] In particular, long-term undernutrition can slow behavioral and cognitive development, interfere with learning, impact reproductive health, and undermine future work productivity.[29]

If hunger persists or occurs at early, crucial times of brain development, cognitive development is impaired.[30] This could result in permanent lower intelligence and hindered learning ability. As a result, undernourished children may have a difficult time completing their basic elementary education. Research demonstrates that underweight and malnourished children perform poorly in school.[31] This is particularly unfortunate because school performance has a measurable impact on earning ability later in life.

Even if children are healthy enough to regularly attend school, hunger and malnutrition impair learning ability. In one study, children with enough iron scored higher in math than children with iron deficiency.[32] Malnourished children also seem to be fatigued, inattentive, and unresponsive to their learning environment. An isolated child who does not respond to or interact with others tends to be neglected by peers, teachers, and adult caregivers.

In 2011 an estimated 165 million children globally experienced stunted growth because of deficiencies in protein and other nutrients. About 26 percent of children under 5 years of age living in developing countries are physically stunted (decreased height for age). Globally in 2011, 52 million children under age 5 had moderate or severe **wasting** (having decreased weight for age).[33] Growth stunting has also been associated with long-term detrimental effects on physical work capacity and fertility.[34]

Impaired Immunity Can Result in Disease

A malnourished individual has a weakened immune system, which increases his or her vulnerability to various infections. Fever, parasitic disease, pneumonia, measles, and malaria are examples of conditions that occur because of weakened immune systems and chronic malnutrition (see Table 16.3).

In 2011, 6.9 million children under the age of 5 died.[35] The World Health Organization estimates that more than one-third of all childhood deaths in developing countries are associated with chronic hunger and malnutrition. The most common

Table 16.3

Common Illnesses in Malnourished Children

Disease/Condition	Cause	Effect
Diarrhea	Pathogenic infections	Severe dehydration
Acute respiratory infection	Virus or bacteria	Pneumonia, bronchitis, colds, fast breathing, coughing, and fever
Malaria	Parasite (transmitted by a mosquito)	Fever, weakness, sweating, shivering, shaking, nausea, liver failure, infected red blood cells, kidney failure or bleeding in the kidneys
Measles	Respiratory illness caused by a highly contagious virus, from airborne droplets (coughing/sneezing)	Pneumonia, brain inflammation, infection, diarrhea, and seizures

wasting The diminishment of muscle and fat tissue caused by extremely low energy intake from too little food. It is sometimes referred to as acute malnutrition.

Table 16.4

Most Common Vitamin and Mineral Deficiencies among the Malnourished

Vitamin or Mineral	Effects	Incidence
Vitamin A	Eye disease; blindness	Vitamin A deficiency is the leading cause of preventable blindness in children in developing countries.
Iron	Iron-deficiency anemia	Most common nutrtional disorder worldwide—affects over 30% of the world population. Half of pregnant women in developing countries are estimated to be anemic.
Iodine	Goiter, cretinism	Iodine-deficiency disorder is a serious public health threat for 2 billion people worldwide. According to UNICEF, only about two-thirds of households have access to iodized salt.
Folic acid	Macrocytic anemia	Folic acid deficiency is common among women of reproductive age; individuals with limited diets and reduced vegetable consumption; individuals who abuse alcohol; and obese individuals.
Vitamin B_{12}	Pernicious anemia	B_{12} deficiency is common among elderly men and women (>50 years of age); African-American adults; individuals who have malabsorption syndromes; and persons who practice extreme vegetarianism.

Data from World Health Organization. 2010. Micronutrients. Available at www.who.int.

causes of death in post-neonatal children (that is, those who survive birth and the first 28 days of life) are pneumonia or other acute respiratory infection, diarrhea, malaria, and measles, all of which have malnutrition as an underlying contributing factor.[36]

Diarrhea—caused by viruses, parasites, and other harmful microorganisms—can result in severe dehydration (loss of fluids and electrolytes). The gastrointestinal infections that cause diarrhea kill around 2.2 million people globally each year, mostly children in developing countries. The use of contaminated water is a major cause of diarrhea.[37]

Children experiencing malnutrition are especially vulnerable to respiratory problems.[38] Viruses or bacteria in the respiratory tract can cause acute respiratory infection. Pneumonia, the most serious respiratory infection, is the leading killer of children worldwide, and, when caused by bacteria, can be successfully treated with oral antibiotics. Malaria is carried by parasite-infected mosquitoes. Vitamin and mineral deficiencies and their resulting diseases are serious concerns for people living in developing countries and in the United States. For example, approximately 40 percent of the world's children under age 5 lack sufficient vitamin A, which makes them more susceptible to impaired vision and blindness, malaria, and diarrhea.[39] Iron and iodine deficiencies are also major world health issues that cause severe health problems. These micronutrient deficiencies are referred to as "hidden hunger." Table 16.4 lists the most common vitamin and mineral deficiencies observed in those who are malnourished.

Infant and Child Mortality Rates Increase

As mentioned, malnutrition is part of a vicious cycle that passes hunger from one generation to the next. Unfortunately, many young women experience undernutrition during their own infancy and childhood. Girls who were low birth weight babies, premature, or were undernourished and ill during the first five years of life may be physically stunted and less able to support a healthy pregnancy when they become adults. The infants born to malnourished women are more likely to be malnourished, experience chronic illness, and have an increased risk of premature death.

What Can Be Done to Reduce Food Insecurity?

Everyone—from children to adults—can help eradicate hunger.

Global hunger harms all of us. When citizens of your community experience hunger, you are likely to see increased disease incidence, low ambition, poverty, and general apathy among the individuals affected. Additionally, from a humanitarian perspective, the painful physical symptoms of hunger are unacceptable when you consider that a surplus of food is grown each year.

At the local level, individuals, families, churches, and community relief agencies seek out and assist people who have insufficient resources. From providing free food and meals to education and job training, there are numerous ways such organizations can help alleviate hunger. Similarly, corporations and governments can help solve the hunger problem by providing food aid and creating economic opportunity to help people improve their lives. See **Table 16.5** for examples of programs that help combat hunger in the United States.

In addition to the human (person-to-person) help provided by people and organizations, technology also plays a role in alleviating malnutrition. As research and development provide new ways to pack more nutrition into food crops, hunger may be reduced. Enriched crops ultimately benefit hungry people by providing some of the common nutrients (iron, vitamin A, and iodine) that are in low supply in current crops.

Better Land Management and Proper Sanitation

Proper land management and appropriate crop selection can help increase agricultural production. For example, productive land is frequently used for nonconsumable crops, such as tobacco or flowers, for sale to industrialized nations. Raising edible, nutritious plants such as high-protein beans, vegetables, grains, seeds, nuts, or fruit instead of planting export crops like tea, coffee, and cocoa, or raising animal feed for livestock, would help eliminate hunger.[40]

Food security and land access are directly related, even if the land is not irrigated or of the highest quality. Farmers who own the land they farm may be more likely to make better farming decisions regarding irrigation, crop rotation, land fallowing (plowed, but unplanted, land), and appropriate soil management. Land ownership, and in particular female land ownership, is part of a long-term solution to a very complex problem. At this time, available data suggests that less than a quarter of land in developing countries is operated, let alone owned, by women.[41]

Better land and water management and appropriate crop selection can help eliminate hunger.

Table 16.5

Food Assistance Programs in the United States

Program	Eligibility	Description	Prevalence
Supplemental Nutrition Assistance Program (SNAP), (formerly the Food Stamp Program)	Low income (for a family of four, the net monthly income cannot exceed $1,921)	Individuals who are eligible for food stamps are issued a debit card to purchase specified foods, such as fruit, vegetables, cereals, meats, and dairy products, at their local authorized supermarket. (Items such as alcohol, tobacco, nonfood items, vitamins and medicines, and hot foods are not covered.)	In 2012, more than 46.6 million people per month in the United States
Special Supplemental Nutrition Program for Women, Infants and Children (WIC)	At-risk low-income pregnant and lactating women, infants, and children less than 5 years old	The program provides nutritious, culturally appropriate food, including tortillas, brown rice, soy-based beverages, and a wide choice of fruits and vegetables, to supplement the diet. There are even some organic forms of WIC-eligible foods. The program also emphasizes nutrition education and offers referrals to health care professionals.	8.9 million women, infants, and children per month in 2012
National School Lunch Program	Children with families with incomes at or below 130% of the poverty level are eligible for free meals and those with incomes between 130% and 185% of the poverty level are eligible for reduced-price meals	Eligible children receive free or reduced-price lunches each year. A subsidized breakfast is sometimes also available at schools.	More than 31.8 million American children in 2011
Summer Food Service Program	Available to communities based on income data	Federal program that combines a meal or feeding program with a summer activity program for children	Almost 2 million children at 31,000 sites
Child and Adult Care Food Program	Available to communities based on income data	Program provides nutritious meals to low-income children and senior adults who receive day care or adult care outside the home. There are income guidelines and specific menu requirements for program participation.	3.3 million children and 120,000 adults receive meals and snacks each day as part of this program
Congregate Meals for the Elderly and Meals on Wheels	Age 60 or over	The programs provide meals at a community site or delivered to the home.	More than one million meals per day served at sites across the country

Data from USDA, Food and Nutrition Service. 2012. www.fns.usda.gov; Meals on Wheels Association of America. 2013. www.mowaa.org.

Most people think providing food is the primary means of reducing hunger, but safe water is equally important. According to the World Health Organization, "a significant proportion of diarrheal disease can be prevented through safe drinking water and adequate sanitation and hygiene."[42] More than 2.5 billion people (40 percent of the world's population) lack basic sanitation facilities, and 780 million people lack access to safe water.[43] The consequences of unsanitary conditions are enormous. Thousands of children become ill or die each month from dehydration-related diseases, and adult workers are less productive when they are ill themselves or caring for family members. Entire communities are often at risk for health problems from drinking contaminated water.

Some innovative solutions are being proposed to alleviate the world's water problems. For example, in Kenya, Latin America, and India, some villagers let the

Access to clean drinking water is just as important as adequate nutrition for human health.

sun purify the water supply. They pour water into clear plastic jugs, then place the jugs in the sun for 6 hours. The combination of heat and UV radiation destroys common waterborne bacteria such as cholera, typhoid, and dysentery. This solution, called SODIS, for Solar Disinfection, is available, inexpensive, and accessible in many countries with a warm climate.[44]

Other water sanitation solutions are more complex. They include chlorination of water, irrigation technology, river diversion projects, piped water systems, and community wells. Sustained economic development for a country or a community depends on a reliable, sanitary water supply.

Fortification of Foods

Food fortification can help alleviate micronutrient deficiencies. Ⓣ Ⓕ Because they are the most commonly deficient (see Table 16.4), iodine, iron, and vitamin A are the three nutrients most often added to foods. For food fortification to work, the foods chosen to carry these extra nutrients must be a staple in the community's food supply (and therefore eaten often) and consistently available. The food should also be shelf stable and affordable. Rice, cereals, flours, salt, and even sugar are examples of foods that can be successfully fortified.

Because food fortification is inexpensive, yet enormously beneficial, fortification programs are being developed and implemented worldwide. Countries across the globe, both developed and developing, have programs to fortify foods such as salt, flour, oil, sugar, and soy sauce with iron, iodine, and vitamin A.[45]

Education Is Key

Education plays an important role in ensuring food security (see **Figure 16.6**). Educated people are more likely to have increased economic and career opportunities, and less likely to fall into the trap of poverty. Literacy and education also build self-esteem and self-confidence, two qualities that help people overcome life's challenges.

Education also reduces poverty in other ways. For example, one study found that societies with a more educated population enjoyed:[46]

➤ Higher earning potential
➤ Improved sanitation
➤ More small businesses/rural enterprises
➤ Lower rates of infant mortality and improved child welfare
➤ Higher likelihood of technological advancement

The curriculum and format for international education are somewhat different in the developing world than in the developed world. International education that aims to improve rates of food security ought to focus on literacy, technical knowledge, agricultural skills, horticulture, health education, and the development of natural resources. Agricultural education and increased agricultural production in developing countries help create jobs, which increases income, which then lifts people out of poverty.[47]

Meanwhile, education related to reducing food insecurity in the developed world should focus on land management, improved crop yields, boosting nutrient levels within crops, and continued development of drought-resistant and insect-repelling plants.

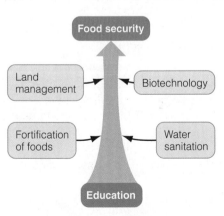

Figure 16.6 Factors in Food Security

nutrition IN THE Real World

Food Insecurity among Us— and How You Can Help!

Food insecurity may be closer than you think. In fact, you may have friends, relatives, or neighbors who've experienced hunger sometime in their lives.

Feeding America, formerly called Second Harvest, is the nation's leading domestic hunger-relief charity. It is a national network of individuals, local food banks, and offices, as well as corporate and government partners, that helps distribute excess and donated food and grocery items annually to those who are hungry. Its mission is to feed America's hungry through a network of more than 200 member food banks and to continue the fight to end food insecurity in this country.

Feeding America collects surplus food from national food companies and other large donors and stores it in a centralized location. The food is then moved to local food pantries in order to reach those who need it.

When it comes to fighting hunger in America, everyone needs to pitch in. You can help your needy neighbors in three ways: give funds, give food, and/or give time. Funds can be donated online at www .feedingamerica.org. Every dollar donated can provide seven meals for those in need. You can also donate food by hosting a food drive. Finally, you can volunteer your time by helping out in your local community, perhaps tutoring children at a local afterschool feeding program, repackaging donated food, stocking shelves at a local food pantry, or transporting food to the hungry.

To find out where you can help, visit the Feeding America website and search for opportunities using the Volunteer Match service.

You Can Help Reduce Food Insecurity

(TF) Hunger can seem like an overwhelming problem, but there are specific things an individual person (you!) can do to help. If you have the funds, you can certainly give money or food to organizations that will distribute your offerings where they are needed. Just as important, and possibly more satisfying, is the idea of giving time. Contact a local food bank to ask how you can help with gathering and distributing food to those in need. For further tips on how you can contribute to reducing food insecurity, see the Nutrition in the Real World feature "Food Insecurity among Us— and How You Can Help!"

The Take-Home Message Eradicating hunger benefits everyone, and local charities and community groups, including faith-based organizations, as well as corporations and governments, can provide aid and organize programs to alleviate hunger. Education of the world's population is also important, along with proper land management and proper crop selection.

Practical Nutrition VIDEO

Does It Cost More to Eat Healthy?

Having limited funds shouldn't have to mean poor nutrition. Sometimes the healthiest foods are among the least expensive. Let Joan show you how to stretch your food dollar for nutritional value. Scan this QR code with your mobile device to access the video. You can also access the video in MasteringNutrition™.

Food vs Cash: Which Is More Effective for Alleviating Hunger? As discussed in this chapter, food insecurity and hunger are major issues both in the United States and around the world. Numerous government agencies and nonprofit organizations attempt to remedy food insecurity with both food and monetary aid. However, experts differ as to which of these strategies is more effective.

Is the disbursement of food aid effective for alleviating hunger? Are cash payments more likely to be misused or abused? Read the two sets of arguments presented below, and then answer the questions to draw your own conclusions.

food aid

- Food aid has clearly had a significant role in reducing the loss of life during food emergencies in such countries as Ethiopia, Sudan, Somalia, Afghanistan, Rwanda, and Haiti.[1]

- Giving people money instead of food can upset local economies, fuel conflicts, and exclude the most needy.[2] For example, cash transfers can cause local food prices to rise, which can cause additional hardship for those who don't directly receive food aid.[3]

- Cash can be physically risky for those handling the money, and may disadvantage women who are less able to keep control of it.[4] In contrast, food aid that's given to women and children tends to be consumed by women and children.

- Food aid may be less vulnerable to corruption. Bags of maize cannot easily be swapped for cigarettes or beer, and stories of food being turned into fleets of Mercedes Benzes are few and far between.[5]

- Cash is not useful when there is no food to buy. Refugees fleeing war and living in camps or earthquake victims living amid rubble are better benefited by receiving food directly.[6]

monetary aid

- Cash aid has larger positive effects on household welfare, and benefits extended family members and not just the direct recipients of aid.[7]

- In cases where food is locally available, monetary donations are more cost effective than food donations, because the cost of shipping food internationally usually exceeds the cost of purchasing food locally.[8]

- Flooding a market with food aid can drive down the price for local farmers and therefore provide a disincentive to local food production.[9]

- In the case of emergency food aid, it often arrives too late, it fails to be properly and efficiently distributed to the neediest regions and groups, and/or it often consists of the wrong commodities.[10]

- In the United States, political considerations can influence which types of food are sent and which companies provide it. U.S. law mandates that all food aid be grown by American farmers. More than half the $700 million in food provided through USAid in 2004 came from just four large food corporations.[11]

what do you think?

1. What are the underlying causes of food insecurity in many countries around the world? **2.** Which approach do you think is likely to yield greater benefits—food aid or monetary aid? **3.** Why is food aid currently the preferred method of the U.S. government? Is this likely to change?

1 Chronic Hunger Is Prevalent throughout the World

Food security is the access by all people at all times to enough food for an active, healthy life. Food insecurity is the inability to secure adequate amounts of nutritious foods to meet one's need due to lack of available resources. Hunger describes a feeling of discomfort or weakness caused by lack of food, coupled with the desire to eat. In the United States, about 14.9 percent of American households were food insecure at least some time in 2011. And the FAO estimates that between 2010 and 2012, 12 percent of world's population was hungry.

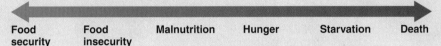

| Food security | Food insecurity | Malnutrition | Hunger | Starvation | Death |

2 Food Insecurity in the United States Is Often Related to Poverty and Health Problems

In the United States, food insecurity often occurs among people in disadvantaged circumstances in rural areas, inner cities, and suburbs. Causes include poverty, disease or disability, lack of education, and inadequate wages. Mental illness and/or drug and alcohol abuse sometimes lead to homelessness, which in turn often results in hunger.

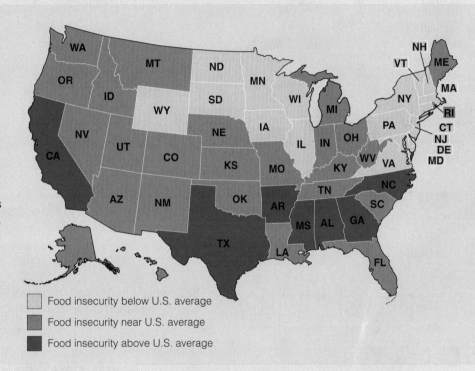

Food insecurity below U.S. average
Food insecurity near U.S. average
Food insecurity above U.S. average

3 Worldwide Food Insecurity Has Multiple Causes

Food insecurity and hunger are more prevalent in developing countries and least developed countries than in developed countries. In these nations, food insecurity may arise out of poverty or poor health, in addition to other risks, such as discrimination, armed conflict, natural disasters, poor agricultural practices, and population overgrowth.

4 Pregnant and Lactating Women, Children, the Ill, and Older Adults Are at the Highest Risk for Undernutrition

Pregnant and lactating women have higher calorie and nutrient needs. If they are improperly nourished, their infants may be, too. Infants and children in general have high nutrient needs because they are growing rapidly. They are dependent on their caregivers for food, making them more susceptible to undernutrition. Chronically ill people may have malabsorption problems. Older adults may be at risk for undernutrition because of higher needs for several micronutrients, decreased senses of smell and taste, chronic illness, compromised immunity, and lack of mobility.

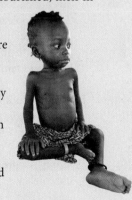

5 Chronic Malnutrition Damages Your Health

Effects of chronic malnutrition include stunted growth, wasting, impaired immune function, infections, anemia, and nutrient deficiencies. A nutrient deficiency can lead to serious, permanent health damage, or even death, in both children and adults.

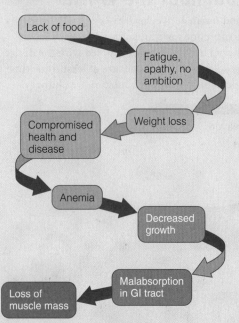

6 Providing Greater Food Resources Can Reduce Hunger

Community and faith-based organizations can help ease hunger by providing free food and assistance programs to help people overcome poverty and food insecurity. Corporations and governments can invest in biotechnologies and education programs that provide more nutrient-dense foods and increase economic opportunity. Food assistance programs like Supplemental Nutrition Assistance Program (SNAP), WIC, and the National School Lunch Program, among others, provide assistance to those who experience food insecurity in the United States.

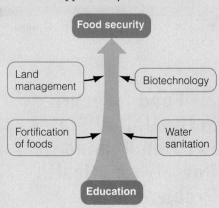

Terms to Know

- hunger
- food insecurity
- starvation
- developed country
- developing
- least developed countries
- poverty
- working poor
- homeless
- political sanctions
- famine
- overpopulation
- undernutrition
- malnutrition
- growth stunting
- wasting

MasteringNutrition™

Build your knowledge—and confidence—in the Study Area of MasteringNutrition with a variety of study tools.

Check Your Understanding

1. Food insecurity exists because
   a. not enough food is produced in the world to feed everyone adequately.
   b. food distribution is uneven, and some people do not have access to enough food.
   c. some people choose not to eat.
   d. people feel insecure about whether their food is safe.

2. What causes famine?
   a. poverty
   b. lack of education and economic opportunity
   c. war, natural disaster, or civil unrest
   d. using inappropriate farm machinery

3. In which one of the following countries is food insecurity most prevalent?
   a. Canada
   b. Argentina
   c. Germany
   d. Haiti

4. What is the general term for the common condition where micronutrients are consistently deficient in the diet?
   a. malaria
   b. hidden hunger
   c. diarrhea
   d. dehydration

5. Which of the following groups are especially vulnerable to food insecurity–related illness?
   a. infants and young children
   b. adolescents
   c. adult men
   d. adult women

6. Which of the following is a nutritional risk factor for older adults?
   a. increased metabolic rate
   b. rapid cell growth and turnover
   c. decreased sense of taste and smell
   d. increased energy needs

7. A lack of which micronutrient has been implicated in causing blindness in children?
   a. vitamin K
   b. vitamin A
   c. iodine
   d. iron

8. Who are the "working poor"?
   a. all individuals classified as low income by the United States Department of Labor
   b. all individuals who fall outside the middle-class range of income
   c. individuals who are employed but have incomes that fall below the poverty line
   d. all minimum-wage workers

9. Which nutrients are most likely to be used to fortify food?
   a. vitamins D, E, and K
   b. sodium, potassium, and chloride
   c. magnesium, phosphorus, and sulfur
   d. iron, iodine, and vitamin A
10. Which of the following programs serves the greatest number of people in the United States?
   a. Meals on Wheels
   b. Supplemental Nutrition Assistance Program
   c. Feeding America
   d. the National School Lunch program

Answers

1. (b) Although enough food is produced to feed everyone in the world, the distribution of the world's food supply is uneven, and people in some parts of the world do not have access to, or cannot afford, adequate food. Everyone needs to eat to survive.
2. (c) Famine is an extreme situation in which food crops cannot be produced because of war, civil unrest, or a natural disaster. Poverty and lack of education are factors that can lead to individual hunger, but don't generally cause crop failure.
3. (d) In this group of nations, Haiti experiences the most drastic levels of food insecurity, but all of these countries have some number of people who are food insecure.
4. (b) Hidden hunger refers to vitamin A, iron, or iodine deficiency. This condition affects more than 2 billion people in the world.
5. (a) Infants and young children have immature immune systems, making them more susceptible to illness related to undernutrition. Adolescents and adults have mature immune systems that are stronger and better functioning.
6. (c) Older adults sometimes lose interest in food or have a diminished appetite because they cannot enjoy food's smells or tastes. Older people have a decreased basal metabolic rate and experience slower cell growth and decreased energy requirements.
7. (b) Vitamin A is implicated in preventable blindness. Deficiency in vitamin K can lead to excessive bleeding; deficiency in iodine can cause goiter and cretinism; and deficiency in iron can result in iron-deficiency anemia.
8. (c) The working poor includes individuals who are employed 27 or more weeks of each year, yet still have incomes below the official poverty line.
9. (d) Iron, iodine, and vitamin A are frequently used to fortify food because deficiencies of them are linked to many common and serious illnesses. The other nutrients listed are important, but are not generally incorporated into food fortification programs.
10. (b) All of these programs feed millions of people, but the program with the greatest number assisted is the Supplemental Nutrition Assistance Program (SNAP).

Web Resources

- For more on the state of food insecurity and hunger in the United States and around the world, visit the Bread for the World Institute at www.bread.org
- To learn more about one organization that is fighting global poverty, visit CARE at www.care.org
- To find out how the Food and Agriculture Organization of the United Nations leads international efforts to defeat hunger, visit www.fao.org
- To learn more about the efforts of the Global Health Council, visit the National Council for International Health website at www.globalhealth.org
- To learn more about an international children's group, visit the UNICEF website at www.unicef.org
- For more about the World Health Organization, visit www.who.int/en

1. **True.** Poverty does play a significant role in food insecurity around the world. Additional factors like war, overpopulation, and disease can also affect people's access to sufficient food. Find out more on page 598.
2. **False.** Despite living in a wealthy nation, many people in the United States grapple with food insecurity. Turn to page 599 to find out why.
3. **False.** An overweight or obese individual can also experience a chronic shortage of food. To learn more, turn to page 600.
4. **False.** The world's farmers grow enough food to nourish every man, woman, and child on the planet. The challenge lies in distributing their products evenly. Learn more on page 601.
5. **True.** Children are dependent on the adults around them for adequate food, and therefore are susceptible to food insecurity. Children are also more prone to long-term consequences of nutrient deficiencies. Find out more on page 604.
6. **True.** Older adults may have sufficient funds for food, but may experience food insecurity due to mobility issues or emotional problems. Learn more on page 604.
7. **False.** Poor nutrition can negatively affect mental development, as well as physical development. Turn to page 606 to learn more.
8. **True.** Advances in agricultural processes do increase the amount of food grown per acre of farmland. Find out more on page 608.
9. **False.** Fortifying foods improves their nutritional value and can provide numerous nutrients that some populations wouldn't otherwise obtain. Learn which foods are being fortified on page 610.
10. **False.** You can also help the hungry by volunteering your time, hosting a food drive, or making a food donation to your local food bank. Learn more on page 611.

Appendices

Calculation and Conversion Aids

Commonly Used Metric Units

millimeter (mm) : one-thousandth of a meter (0.001)
centimeter (cm) : one-hundredth of a meter (0.01)
kilometer (km)   : one-thousand times a meter (1,000)
kilogram (kg)   : one-thousand times a gram (1,000)
milligram (mg)   : one-thousandth of a gram (0.001)
microgram (µg)   : one-millionth of a gram (0.000001)
milliliter (ml) : one-thousandth of a liter (0.001)

Conversion Factors

Use the following table to convert U.S. measurements to metric equivalents:

Original Unit	Multiply By	To Get
ounces avdp	28.3495	grams
ounces	0.0625	pounds
pounds	0.4536	kilograms
pounds	16	ounces
grams	0.0353	ounces
grams	0.0022	pounds
kilograms	2.2046	pounds
liters	1.8162	pints (dry)
liters	2.1134	pints (liquid)
liters	0.9081	quarts (dry)
liters	1.0567	quarts (liquid)
liters	0.2642	gallons (U.S.)
pints (dry)	0.5506	liters
pints (liquid)	0.4732	liters
quarts (dry)	1.1012	liters
quarts (liquid)	0.9463	liters
gallons (U.S.)	3.7854	liters
millimeters	0.0394	inches
centimeters	0.3937	inches
centimeters	0.0328	feet
inches	25.4000	millimeters
inches	2.5400	centimeters
inches	0.0254	meters
feet	0.3048	meters
meters	3.2808	feet
meters	1.0936	yards
cubic feet	0.0283	cubic meters
cubic meters	35.3147	cubic feet
cubic meters	1.3079	cubic yards
cubic yards	0.7646	cubic meters

International Units

Some vitamin supplements may report vitamin content as International Units (IU).

To convert IU to:

➤ Micrograms of vitamin D (cholecalciferol), multiply the IU value by 0.025.
➤ Milligrams of vitamin E (alpha-tocopherol), multiply the IU value by 0.67 if vitamin E is from natural sources. Multiply the IU value by 0.45 if vitamin E is from synthetic sources.
➤ Vitamin A: 1 IU = 0.3 µg retinol or 0.3 µg RAE or 0.6 µg beta-carotene

Retinol Activity Equivalents

Retinol activity equivalents (RAE) are a standardized unit of measure for vitamin A. RAE account for the various differences in bioavailability from sources of vitamin A. Many supplements will report vitamin A content in IU, as shown above, or in retinol equivalents (RE).

1 µg RAE = 1 µg retinol
            12 µg beta-carotene

To calculate RAE from the RE value of vitamin carotenoids in foods, divide RE by 2. Divide the amount of beta-carotene by 12 to convert to RAE.

For vitamin A supplements and foods fortified with vitamin A, 1 RE = 1 RAE.

Folate

Folate is measured as dietary folate equivalents (DFE). DFE account for the different factors affecting bioavailability of folate sources.

1 µg DFE = 1 µg food folate
            0.6 µg folate from fortified foods
            0.5 µg folate supplement taken on an empty stomach
            0.6 µg folate as a supplement consumed with a meal

To convert micrograms of synthetic folate, such as that found in supplements or fortified foods, to DFE:

$$\text{µg synthetic folate} \times 1.7 = \text{µg DFE}$$

For naturally occurring food folate, such as spinach, each microgram of folate equals 1 microgram DFE:

$$\text{µg folate} = \text{µg DFE}$$

Niacin

Niacin is measured as niacin equivalents (mg NE). NE reflects the amount of preformed niacin in foods or the amount that can be formed from a food's content of the amino acid niacin.

To calculate mg NE from a meal:

If you know the tryptophan and preformed niacin in a meal: (tryptophan $\times$ 1,000 $\div$ 60) + preformed niacin = mg NE

If you know the total amount of protein in a meal but not the tryptophan content: (0.011 $\times$ g of protein) $\times$ 1,000 $\div$ 60 + preformed niacin = mg NE

Length: U.S. and Metric Equivalents

¼ inch	= 0.6 centimeters
1 inch	= 2.5 centimeters
1 foot	= 0.3048 meter
	30.48 centimeters
1 yard	= 0.9144 meter
1 millimeter	= 0.03937 inch
1 centimeter	= 0.3937 inch
1 decimeter	= 3.937 inches
1 meter	= 39.37 inches
	1.094 yards
1 micrometer	= 0.00003937 inch

Weights and Measures

Food Measurement Equivalencies from U.S. to Metric

Capacity

⅕ teaspoon	= 1 milliliter
¼ teaspoon	= 1.23 milliliters
½ teaspoon	= 2.5 milliliters
1 teaspoon	= 5 milliliters
1 tablespoon	= 15 milliliters
1 fluid ounce	= 30 milliliters
¼ cup	= 59 milliliters
⅓ cup	= 79 milliliters
½ cup	= 118 milliliters
1 cup	= 237 milliliters
1 pint (2 cups)	= 473 milliliters
1 quart (4 cups)	= 0.95 liter
1 liter (1.06 quarts)	= 1,000 milliliters
1 gallon (4 quarts)	= 3.79 liters

Weight

0.035 ounce	= 1 gram
1 ounce	= 28 grams
¼ pound (4 ounces)	= 113 grams
1 pound (16 ounces)	= 454 grams
2.2 pounds (35 ounces)	= 1 kilogram

U.S. Food Measurement Equivalents

3 teaspoons	= 1 tablespoon
½ tablespoon	= 1½ teaspoons
2 tablespoons	= ⅛ cup
4 tablespoons	= ¼ cup
5 tablespoons + 1 teaspoon	= ⅓ cup
8 tablespoons	= ½ cup
10 tablespoons + 2 teaspoons	= ⅔ cup
12 tablespoons	= ¾ cup
16 tablespoons	= 1 cup
2 cups	= 1 pint
4 cups	= 1 quart
2 pints	= 1 quart
4 quarts	= 1 gallon

Volumes and Capacities

1 cup	= 8 fluid ounces
	½ liquid pint
1 milliliter	= 0.061 cubic inch
1 liter	= 1.057 liquid quarts
	0.908 dry quart
	61.024 cubic inches
1 U.S. gallon	= 231 cubic inches
	3.785 liters
	0.833 British gallon
	128 U.S. fluid ounces
1 British Imperial gallon	= 277.42 cubic inches
	1.201 U.S. gallons
	4.546 liters
	160 British fluid ounces
1 U.S. ounce, liquid or fluid	= 1.805 cubic inches
	29.574 milliliters
	1.041 British fluid ounces
1 pint, dry	= 33.600 cubic inches
	0.551 liter
1 pint, liquid	= 28.875 cubic inches
	0.473 liter
1 U.S. quart, dry	= 67.201 cubic inches
	1.101 liters
1 U.S. quart, liquid	= 57.75 cubic inches
	0.946 liter
1 British quart	= 69.355 cubic inches
	1.032 U.S. quarts, dry
	1.201 U.S. quarts, liquid

Energy Units

$$1 \text{ kilocalorie (kcal)} = 4.2 \text{ kilojoules}$$
$$1 \text{ megajoule (MJ)} = 239 \text{ kilocalories}$$
$$1 \text{ kilojoule (kJ)} = 0.24 \text{ kcal}$$
$$1 \text{ gram carbohydrate} = 4 \text{ kcals}$$
$$1 \text{ gram fat} = 9 \text{ kcals}$$
$$1 \text{ gram protein} = 4 \text{ kcals}$$

Temperature Standards

	°Fahrenheit	°Celsius
Body temperature	98.6°	37°
Comfortable room temperature	65–75°	18–24°
Boiling point of water	212°	100°
Freezing point of water	32°	0°

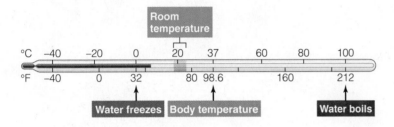

Temperature Scales

To Convert Fahrenheit to Celsius

[(°F − 32) × 5]/9

1. Subtract 32 from °F
2. Multiply (°F – 32) by 5, then divide by 9

To Convert Celsius to Fahrenheit

[(°C × 9)/5] + 32

1. Multiply °C by 9, then divide by 5
2. Add 32 to (°C × 9/5)

U.S. Exchange Lists for Meal Planning

Adapted from "Choose Your Foods: Exchange Lists For Diabetes" Copyright © 2008 the Academy of Nutrition and Dietetics (formerly the American Dietetic Association) and American Diabetes Association. Reprinted with permission.

Starch List

1 starch choice = 15 g carbohydrate, 0–3 g protein, 0–1 g fat, and 80 cal

Icon Key

☺ = More than 3 g of dietary fiber per serving.

! = Extra fat, or prepared with added fat. (Count as 1 starch + 1 fat.)

▮ = 480 mg or more of sodium per serving.

Food	Serving Size
Bread	
Bagel, 4 oz	¼ (1 oz)
! Biscuit, 2½" across	1
Bread	
☺ reduced-calorie	2 slices (1½ oz)
white, whole-grain, pumpernickel, rye, unfrosted raisin	1 slice (1 oz)
Chapatti, small, 6" across	1
! Cornbread, 1¾" cube	1 (1½ oz)
English muffin	½
Hot dog bun or hamburger bun	½ (1 oz)
Naan, 8" by 2"	¼
Pancake, 4" across, ¼" thick	1
Pita, 6" across	½
Roll, plain small	1 (1 oz)
! Stuffing, bread	⅓ cup
! Taco shell, 5" across	2
Tortilla	
Corn, 6" across	1
Flour, 6" across	1
Flour, 10" across	⅓ tortilla
! Waffle, 4"-square or 4" across	1
Cereals and Grains	
Barley, cooked	⅓ cup
Bran, dry	
☺ oat	¼ c
☺ wheat	½ c
☺ Bulgur (cooked)	½ c
Cereals	½ c
☺ bran	½ c
cooked (oats, oatmeal)	½ c
puffed	1½ c
shredded wheat, plain	½ c
sugar-coated	½ c
unsweetened, ready-to-eat	¾ c
Couscous	⅓ c
Granola	
low-fat	¼ c
! regular	¼ c

Food	Serving Size
Grits, cooked	½ c
Kasha	½ c
Millet, cooked	⅓ c
Muesli	¼ c
Pasta, cooked	⅓ c
Polenta, cooked	⅓ c
Quinoa, cooked	⅓ c
Rice, white or brown, cooked	⅓ c
Tabbouleh (tabouli), prepared	½ c
Wheat germ, dry	3 tbs
Wild rice, cooked	½ c
Starchy Vegetables	
Cassava	⅓ c
Corn	½ c
on cob, large	½ cob (5 oz)
☺ Hominy, canned	¾ c
☺ Mixed vegetables with corn, peas, or pasta	1 c
☺ Parsnips	½ c
☺ Peas, green	½ c
Plantain, ripe	⅓ c
Potato	
baked with skin	¼ large (3 oz)
boiled, all kinds	½ c or ½ medium (3 oz)
! mashed, with milk and fat	½ c
French fried (oven-baked)	1 cup (2 oz)
☺ Pumpkin, canned, no sugar added	1 c
Spaghetti/pasta sauce	½ c
☺ Squash, winter (acorn, butternut)	1 c
☺ Succotash	½ c
Yam, sweet potato, plain	½ c
Crackers and Snacks	
Animal crackers	8
Crackers	
! round-butter type	6
saltine-type	6
! sandwich-style, cheese or peanut butter filling	3
! whole-wheat regular	2–5 (¾ oz)
☺ whole-wheat lower fat or crispbreads	2–5 (¾ oz)

Food	Serving Size	Food	Serving Size
Graham crackers, 2½" square 3		Snack chips	
Matzoh ....¾ oz		fat-free or baked (tortilla, potato),	
Melba toast, about 2" by 4" piece ....4 pieces		baked pita chips.....................15–20 (¾ oz)	
Oyster crackers 20		! regular (tortilla, potato)............9–13 (¾ oz)	

Crackers and Snacks

Food	Serving Size
Popcorn...3 c
!☺ with butter.................................3 c
☺ no fat added ....3 c
☺ lower fat ....3 c
Pretzels..¾ oz
Rice cakes, 4" across 2

Beans, Peas, and Lentils
(Count as 1 starch + 1 lean meat)

Food	Serving Size
☺ Baked beans ....⅓ c
☺ Beans, cooked (black, garbanzo, kidney, lima, navy, pinto, white)..............½ c
☺ Lentils, cooked (brown, green, yellow) ....½ c
☺ Peas, cooked (black-eyed, split) ....½ c
▮ ☺ Refried beans, canned ....½ c

Fruit List

1 fruit choice = 15 g carbohydrate, 0 g protein, 0 g fat, and 60 cal

Weight includes skin, core, seeds, and rind.

Icon Key

☺ = More than 3 g of dietary fiber per serving.

! = Extra fat, or prepared with added fat.

▮ = 480 mg or more of sodium per serving.

Food	Serving Size	Food	Serving Size
Apples		Grapes, small .... 17 (3 oz)	
unpeeled, small ....1 (4 oz)		Honeydew melon .... 1 slice or 1 c cubed (10 oz)	
dried...........................4 rings		☺ Kiwi .... 1 (3½ oz)	
Applesauce, unsweetened...........½ c		Mandarin oranges, canned .... ¾ c	
Apricots		Mango, small..................... ½ fruit (5½ oz) or ½ c	
canned ....½ c		Nectarine, small .... 1 (5 oz)	
dried...........................8 halves		☺ Orange, small .... 1 (6½ oz)	
☺ fresh ....4 whole (5½ oz)		Papaya .... ½ fruit or 1 c cubed (8 oz)	
Banana, extra small ....1 (4 oz)		Peaches	
☺ Blackberries ....¾ c		canned........................ ½ c	
Blueberries........................¾ c		fresh, medium................. 1 (6 oz)	
Cantaloupe, small ....⅓ melon or 1 c cubed (11 oz)		Pears	
Cherries		canned........................ ½ c	
sweet, canned ....½ c		fresh, large .... ½ (4 oz)	
sweet, fresh ....12 (3 oz)		Pineapple	
Dates 3		canned .... ½ c	
Dried fruits (blueberries, cherries, cranberries, mixed fruit, raisins) ....2 tbs		fresh .... ¾ c	
Figs		Plums	
dried...........................1½		canned .... ½ c	
☺ fresh ....1½ large or 2 medium (3½ oz)		dried (prunes) 3	
Fruit cocktail ....½ c		small .... 2 (5 oz)	
Grapefruit		☺ Raspberries...................... 1 c	
large ....½ (11 oz)		☺ Strawberries..................... 1¼ c whole berries	
sections, canned ....¾ c		☺ Tangerines, small .... 2 (8 oz)	
		Watermelon .... 1 slice or 1¼ c cubes (13½ oz)	

Food	Serving Size	Food	Serving Size
Fruit Juice		Orange juice	½ c
Apple juice/cider	½ c	Pineapple juice	½ c
Fruit juice blends, 100% juice	⅓ c	Prune juice	⅓ c
Grape juice	⅓ c		
Grapefruit juice	½ c		

Milk and Yogurts

1 milk choice = 12 g carbohydrate and 8 g protein

Food	Serving Size	Count As
Fat-Free or Low-Fat (1%)		
(0–3 g fat per serving, 100 calories per serving)		
Milk, buttermilk, acidophilus milk, Lactaid	1 c	1 fat-free milk
Evaporated milk	½ c	1 fat-free milk
Yogurt, plain or flavored with an artificial sweetener	¾ c (6 oz)	1 fat-free milk
Reduced-Fat (2%)		
(5 g fat per serving, 120 calories per serving)		
Milk, acidophilus milk, kefir, Lactaid	1 c	1 reduced-fat milk
Yogurt, plain	¾ c (6 oz)	1 reduced-fat milk
Whole		
(8 g fat per serving, 160 calories per serving)		
Milk, buttermilk, goat's milk	1 c	1 whole milk
Evaporated milk	½ c	1 whole milk
Yogurt, plain	8 oz	1 whole milk
Dairy-Like Foods		
Chocolate milk		
fat-free	1 c	1 fat-free milk + 1 carbohydrate
whole	1 c	1 whole milk + 1 carbohydrate
Eggnog, whole milk	½ c	1 carbohydrate + 2 fats
Rice drink		
flavored, low-fat	1 c	2 carbohydrates
plain, fat-free	1 c	1 carbohydrate
Smoothies, flavored, regular	10 oz	1 fat-free milk + 2½ carbohydrates
Soy milk		
light	1 c	1 carbohydrate + ½ fat
regular, plain	1 c	1 carbohydrate + 1 fat
Yogurt		
and juice blends	1 c	1 fat-free milk + 1 carbohydrate
low carbohydrate (less than 6 g carbohydrate per choice)	¾ c (6 oz)	½ fat-free milk
with fruit, low-fat	¾ c (6 oz)	1 fat-free milk + 1 carbohydrate

Sweets, Desserts, and Other Carbohydrates List

1 other carbohydrate choice = 15 g carbohydrate and variable protein, fat, and calories.

Icon Key

▮ = 480 mg or more of sodium per serving.

Food	Serving Size	Count As
Beverages, Soda, and Energy/Sports Drinks		
Cranberry juice cocktail	½ c	1 carbohydrate
Energy drink	1 can (8.3 oz)	2 carbohydrates
Fruit drink or lemonade	1 c (8 oz)	2 carbohydrates
Hot chocolate		
regular	1 envelope added to 8 oz water	1 carbohydrate + 1 fat
sugar-free or light	1 envelope added to 8 oz water	1 carbohydrate
Soft drink (soda), regular	1 can (12 oz)	2½ carbohydrates
Sports drink	1 cup (8 oz)	1 carbohydrate
Brownies, Cake, Cookies, Gelatin, Pie, and Pudding		
Brownie, small, unfrosted	1¼" square ⅞", high (about 1 oz)	1 carbohydrate + 1 fat
Cake		
angel food, unfrosted	1½ of cake (about 2 oz)	2 carbohydrates
frosted	2" square (about 2 oz)	2 carbohydrates + 1 fat
unfrosted	2" square (about 2 oz)	1 carbohydrate + 1 fat
Cookies		
chocolate chip	2 cookies (2¼" across)	1 carbohydrate + 2 fats
gingersnap	3 cookies	1 carbohydrate
sandwich, with creme filling	2 small (about ⅔ oz)	1 carbohydrate + 1 fat
sugar-free	3 small or 1 large (¾ oz–1 oz)	1 carbohydrate + 1–2 fats
vanilla wafer	5 cookies	1 carbohydrate + 1 fat
Cupcake, frosted	1 small (about 1¾ oz)	2 carbohydrates + 1–1½ fats
Fruit cobbler	½ c (3½ oz)	3 carbohydrates + 1 fat
Gelatin, regular	½ c	1 carbohydrate
Pie		
commercially prepared fruit, 2 crusts	⅙ of 8" pie	3 carbohydrates + 2 fats
pumpkin or custard	⅛ of 8" pie	1½ carbohydrates + 1½ fats
Pudding		
regular (made with reduced-fat milk)	½ c	2 carbohydrates
sugar-free, or sugar-free and fat-free (made with fat-free milk)	½ c	1 carbohydrate
Candy, Spreads, Sweets, Sweeteners, Syrups, and Toppings		
Candy bar, chocolate/peanut	2 "fun size" bars (1 oz)	1½ carbohydrates + 1½ fats
Candy, hard	3 pieces	1 carbohydrate
Chocolate "kisses"	5 pieces	1 carbohydrate + 1 fat
Coffee creamer		
dry, flavored	4 tsp	½ carbohydrate + ½ fat
liquid, flavored	2 tbs	1 carbohydrate

Food	Serving Size	Count As
Fruit snacks, chewy (pureed fruit concentrate)	1 roll (¾ oz)	1 carbohydrate
Fruit spreads, 100% fruit	1½ tbs	1 carbohydrate
Honey	1 tbs	1 carbohydrate
Jam or jelly, regular	1 tbs	1 carbohydrate
Sugar	1 tbs	1 carbohydrate
Syrup		
chocolate	2 tbs	2 carbohydrates
light (pancake type)	2 tbs	1 carbohydrate
regular (pancake type)	1 tbs	1 carbohydrate

Condiments and Sauces

Food	Serving Size	Count As
Barbeque sauce	3 tbs	1 carbohydrate
Cranberry sauce, jellied	¼ c	1½ carbohydrates
Gravy, canned or bottled	½ c	½ carbohydrate + ½ fat
Salad dressing, fat-free, low-fat, cream-based	3 tbs	1 carbohydrate
Sweet and sour sauce	3 tbs	1 carbohydrate

Doughnuts, Muffins, Pastries, and Sweet Breads

Food	Serving Size	Count As
Banana nut bread	1" slice (1 oz)	2 carbohydrates + 1 fat
Doughnut		
cake, plain	1 medium, (1½ oz)	1½ carbohydrates + 2 fats
yeast type, glazed	3¾" across (2 oz)	2 carbohydrates + 2 fats
Muffin (4 oz)	¼ muffin (1 oz)	1 carbohydrate + ½ fat
Sweet roll or Danish	1 (2½ oz)	2½ carbohydrates + 2 fats

Frozen Bars, Frozen Dessert, Frozen Yogurt, and Ice Cream

Food	Serving Size	Count As
Frozen pops	1	½ carbohydrate
Fruit juice bars, frozen, 100% juice	1 bar (3 oz)	1 carbohydrate
Ice cream		
fat-free	½ c	1½ carbohydrates
light	½ c	1 carbohydrate + 1 fat
no sugar added	½ c	1 carbohydrate + 1 fat
regular	½ c	1 carbohydrate + 2 fats
Sherbet, sorbet	½ c	2 carbohydrates
Yogurt, frozen		
fat-free	⅓ c	1 carbohydrate
regular	½ c	1 carbohydrate + 0–1 fat

Granola Bars, Meal Replacement Bars/Shakes, and Trail Mix

Food	Serving Size	Count As
Granola or snack bar, regular or low-fat	1 bar (1 oz)	1½ carbohydrates
Meal replacement bar	1 bar (1⅓ oz)	1½ carbohydrates + 0–1 fat
Meal replacement bar	1 bar (2 oz)	2 carbohydrates + 1 fat
Meal replacement shake, reduced-calorie	1 can (10–11 oz)	1½ carbohydrates + 0–1 fat
Trail mix		
candy/nut-based	1 oz	1 carbohydrates + 2 fats
dried-fruit-based	1 oz	1 carbohydrate + 1 fat

Nonstarchy Vegetable List

1 vegetable choice = 5 g carbohydrate, 2 g protein, 0 g fat, 25 cal

Icon Key

☺ = More than 3 g of dietary fiber per serving.

▮ = 480 mg or more of sodium per serving.

Amaranth or Chinese spinach
Artichoke
Artichoke hearts
Asparagus
Baby corn
Bamboo shoots
Beans (green, wax, Italian)
Bean sprouts
Beets
▮ Borscht
Broccoli
☺ Brussels sprouts
Cabbage (green, bok choy, Chinese)
☺ Carrots
Cauliflower
Celery
☺ Chayote
Coleslaw, packaged, no dressing
Cucumber
Eggplant
Gourds (bitter, bottle, luffa, bitter melon)
Green onions or scallions
Greens (collard, kale, mustard, turnip)
Hearts of palm
Jicama

Kohlrabi
Leeks
Mixed vegetables (without corn, peas, or pasta)
Mung bean sprouts
Mushrooms, all kinds, fresh
Okra
Onions
Oriental radish or daikon
Pea pods
☺ Peppers (all varieties)
Radishes
Rutabaga
▮ Sauerkraut
Soybean sprouts
Spinach
Squash (summer, crookneck, zucchini)
Sugar pea snaps
☺ Swiss chard
Tomato
Tomatoes, canned
▮ Tomato sauce
▮ Tomato/vegetable juice
Turnips
Water chestnuts
Yard-long beans

Meat and Meat Substitutes List

Icon Key

! = Extra fat, or prepared with added fat. (Add an additional fat choice to this food.)

▮ = 480 mg or more of sodium per serving (based on the sodium content of a typical 3 oz serving of meat, unless 1 or 2 is the normal serving size).

Food	Amount	Food	Amount
Lean Meats and Meat Substitutes		*Fish, fresh or frozen, plain:* catfish, cod, flounder, haddock, halibut, orange roughy, salmon, tilapia, trout, tuna	1 oz
(1 lean meat choice = 7 g protein, 0–3 g fat, 45 calories)		▮ *Fish, smoked:* herring or salmon (lox)	1 oz
Beef: Select or Choice grades trimmed of fat: ground round, roast (chuck, rib, rump), round, sirloin, steak (cubed, flank, porterhouse, T-bone), tenderloin	1 oz	*Game:* buffalo, ostrich, rabbit, venison	1 oz
▮ Beef jerky	1 oz	▮ Hot dog with 3 g of fat or less per oz (8 dogs per 14 oz package) (*Note: May be high in carbohydrate.*)	1
Cheeses with 3 g of fat or less per oz	1 oz	*Lamb:* chop, leg, or roast	1 oz
Cottage cheese	¼ cup	*Organ meats:* heart, kidney, liver (*Note: May be high in cholesterol*)	1 oz
Egg substitutes, plain	¼ cup	Oysters, fresh or frozen	6 medium
Egg whites	2		

Pork, lean

    ▮ Canadian bacon . . . . .1 oz

    rib or loin chop/roast, ham, tenderloin . . . . .1 oz

Poultry without skin: Cornish hen, chicken,

    domestic duck or goose (well drained

    of fat), turkey . . . . .1 oz

Processed sandwich meats with 3 g of

    fat or less per oz: chipped beef, deli

    thin-sliced meats, turkey ham, turkey

    kielbasa, turkey pastrami. . . . . .1 oz

Salmon, canned. . . . . .1 oz

Sardines, canned . . . . .2 medium

▮ Sausage with 3 g or less fat per oz . . . . .1 oz

Shellfish: clams, crab, imitation shellfish,

    lobster, scallops, shrimp .1 oz

Tuna, canned in water or oil, drained. . . . . .1 oz

Veal: Lean chop, roast . . . . .1 oz

Medium-Fat Meat and Meat Substitutes

(1 medium-fat meat choice = 7 g protein, 4–7 g fat,
and 130 calories)

Beef: corned beef, ground beef, meatloaf,

    Prime grades trimmed of fat (prime rib),

    short ribs, tongue . . . . .1 oz

Cheeses with 4–7 g of fat per oz: feta,

    mozzarella, pasteurized processed

    cheese spread, reduced-fat

    cheeses, string . . . . .1 oz

Egg (*Note:* High in cholesterol, limit

    to 3 per week.) 1

Fish, any fried product. . . . . .1 oz

Lamb: ground, rib roast. . . . . .1 oz

Pork: cutlet, shoulder roast. . . . . .1 oz

Poultry: chicken with skin; dove, pheasant,

    wild duck, or goose; fried chicken;

    ground turkey. . . . . .1 oz

Ricotta cheese . . . . .2 oz or ¼ c

▮ Sausage with 4–7 g fat per oz . . . . .1 oz

Veal: Cutlet (no breading). . . . . .1 oz

High-Fat Meat and Meat Substitutes[a]

(1 high-fat meat choice = 7 g protein, 8+ g fat, 150 calories)

Bacon

    ▮ pork . . . . .2 slices (16 slices

        per lb or 1 oz

        each, before

        cooking)

    ▮ turkey . . . . .3 slices (½ oz

        each before

        cooking)

Cheese, regular: American, bleu, brie,

    cheddar, hard goat, Monterey Jack,

    queso, Swiss. . . . . .1 oz

▮! *Hot dog:* beef, pork, or combination

    (10 per lb-sized package) .1

▮ *Hot dog:* turkey or chicken (10 per

    lb-sized package). 1

Pork: ground, sausage, spareribs . . . . .1 oz

Processed sandwich meats with 8 g of fat or

    more per oz: bologna, pastrami,

    hard salami. . . . . .1 oz

▮ *Sausage with 8 g of fat or more per oz:*

    bratwurst, chorizo, Italian, knockwurst,

    Polish, smoked, summer .1 oz

[a]These foods are high in saturated fat, cholesterol, and calories, and may raise blood cholesterol levels if eaten on a regular basis. Try to eat 3 or fewer servings from this group per week.

Plant-Based Proteins

Because carbohydrate and fat content varies among plant-based proteins, you should read the food label.

Icon Key

☺ =More than 3 g of dietary fiber per serving; 7g protein; calories vary.

▮ = 480 mg or more of sodium per serving (based on the sodium content of a typical 3-oz serving of meat, unless 1 or 2 oz is the normal serving size).

	Food	Amount	Count As
	"Bacon" strips, soy-based	3 strips	1 medium-fat meat
☺	Baked beans	⅓ c	1 starch + 1 lean meat
☺	*Beans, cooked:* black, garbanzo, kidney, lima, navy, pinto, white	½ c	1 starch + 1 lean meat
☺	"Beef" or "sausage" crumbles, soy-based	2 oz	½ carbohydrate + 1 lean meat
	"Chicken" nuggets, soy-based	2 nuggets (1½ oz)	½ carbohydrate + 1 medium-fat meat
☺	Edamame.	½ c	½ carbohydrate + 1 lean meat
	Falafel (spiced chickpea and wheat patties)	3 patties (about 2 inches across)	1 carbohydrate + 1 high-fat meat
	Hot dog, soy-based.	1 (1½ oz)	½ carbohydrate + 1 lean meat
☺	Hummus.	⅓ c	1 carbohydrate + 1 high-fat meat

☺ Lentils, brown, green, or yellow	½ c	1 carbohydrate + 1 lean meat
☺ Meatless burger, soy-based	3 oz	½ carbohydrate + 2 lean meats
☺ Meatless burger, vegetable- and starch-based	1 patty (about 2½ oz)	1 carbohydrate + 2 lean meats
Nut spreads: almond butter, cashew butter, peanut butter, soy nut butter	1 tbs	1 high-fat meat
☺ *Peas, cooked:* black-eyed and split peas	½ c	1 starch + 1 lean meat
▮☺ Refried beans, canned	½ c	1 starch + 1 lean meat
"Sausage" patties, soy-based	1 (1½ oz)	1 medium-fat meat
Soy nuts, unsalted	¾ oz	½ carbohydrate + 1 medium-fat meat
Tempeh	¼ cup	1 medium-fat meat
Tofu	4 oz (½ cup)	1 medium-fat meat
Tofu, light	4 oz (½ cup)	1 lean meat

Fat List

1 fat choice = 5 g fat, 45 cal

Icon Key

▮ = 480 mg or more of sodium per serving.

Food	Serving Size	Food	Serving Size
Unsaturated Fats—Monounsaturated Fats		**Oil:** corn, cottonseed, flaxseed, grape seed, safflower, soybean, sunflower	1 tsp
Avocado, medium	2 tbs (1 oz)	**Oil:** made from soybean and canola oil—Enova	1 tsp
Nut butters (trans fat-free): almond butter, cashew butter, peanut butter (smooth or crunchy)	1½ tsp	Plant stanol esters	
Nuts		light	1 tbs
almonds	6 nuts	regular	2 tsp
Brazil	2 nuts	Salad dressing	
cashews	6 nuts	▮ reduced-fat (*Note: May be high in carbohydrate.*)	2 tbs
filberts (hazelnuts)	5 nuts	▮ regular	1 tbs
macadamia	3 nuts	Seeds	1 tbs
mixed (50% peanuts)	6 nuts	flaxseed, whole	1 tbs
peanuts	10 nuts	pumpkin, sunflower	1 tbs
pecans	4 halves	sesame seeds	1 tbs
pistachios	16 nuts	Tahini or sesame paste	2 tsp
Oil: canola, olive, peanut	1 tsp	**Saturated Fats**	
Olives		Bacon, cooked, regular or turkey	1 slice
black (ripe)	8 large	Butter	
green, stuffed	10 large	reduced-fat	1 tbs
Polyunsaturated Fats		stick	1 tsp
Margarine: lower-fat spread (30% to 50% vegetable oil, *trans* fat-free)	1 tbs	whipped	2 tsp
Margarine: stick, tub (*trans* fat-free), or squeeze (*trans* fat-free)	1 tsp	Butter blends made with oil	
Mayonnaise		reduced-fat or light	1 tbs
reduced-fat	1 tbs	regular	1½ tsp
regular	1 tsp	Chitterlings, boiled	2 tbs (½ oz)
Mayonnaise-style salad dressing		Coconut, sweetened, shredded	2 tbs
reduced-fat	1 tbs	Coconut milk	
regular	2 tsp	light	⅓ c
Nuts		regular	1½ tbs
Pignolia (pine nuts)	1 tbs	Cream	
walnuts, English	4 halves	half and half	2 tbs
		heavy	1 tbs

light..................................1½ tbs	*Oil:* coconut, palm, palm kernel............1 tsp
whipped..........................2 tbs	Salt pork...............................¼ oz
whipped, pressurized...............¼ c	Shortening, solid.........................1 tsp
Cream cheese	Sour cream
reduced-fat.........................1½ tbs (¾ oz)	reduced-fat or light..................3 tbs
regular.............................1 tbs (½ oz)	regular...............................2 tbs
Lard......................................1 tsp	

Free Foods List

A *free food* is any food or drink that has less than 20 calories and 5 g or less of carbohydrate per serving. Foods with a serving size listed should be limited to three servings per day. Foods listed without a serving size can be eaten as often as you like.

Icon Key

▮ = 480 mg or more of sodium per serving.

Food	Serving Size	Food	Serving Size
Low Carbohydrate Foods		Salad dressing	
Cabbage, raw......................½ c		fat-free or low-fat....................1 tbs
Candy, hard (regular or sugar-free)..............1 piece		fat-free, Italian.......................2 tbs
Carrots, cauliflower, or green beans, cooked........¼ c		Sour cream, fat-free, reduced-fat...............1 tbs
Cranberries, sweetened with sugar substitute......½ c		Whipped topping	
Cucumber, sliced......................½ c		light or fat-free.......................2 tbs
Gelatin		regular...............................1 tbs
dessert, sugar-free		**Condiments**	
unflavored		Barbecue sauce.........................2 tsp
Gum		Catsup (ketchup).........................1 tbs
Jam or jelly, light or no sugar added...............2 tsp		Honey mustard..........................1 tbs
Rhubarb, sweetened with sugar substitute..........½ c		Horseradish	
Salad greens		Lemon juice	
Sugar substitutes (artificial sweeteners)		Miso.................................1½ tsp
Syrup, sugar-free.....................2 tbs		Mustard	
Modified Fat Foods with Carbohydrate		Parmesan cheese, freshly grated..............1 tbs
Cream cheese, fat-free.....................1 tbs (½ oz)		Pickle relish...............................1 tbs
Creamers		Pickles	
nondairy, liquid.......................1 tbs		▮ dill.................................1½ medium
nondairy, powdered....................2 tsp		sweet, bread and butter..................2 slices
Margarine spread		sweet, gherkin..........................¾ oz
fat-free.............................1 tbs		Salsa.................................¼ c
reduced-fat.........................1 tsp		▮ Soy sauce, regular or light...................1 tbs
Mayonnaise		Sweet and sour sauce......................2 tsp
fat-free.............................1 tbs		Sweet chili sauce.........................2 tsp
reduced-fat.........................1 tsp		Taco sauce..............................1 tbs
Mayonnaise-style salad dressing		Vinegar	
fat-free.............................1 tbs		Yogurt, any type.........................2 tbs
reduced-fat.........................1 tsp			

Drinks/Mixes

Any food on this list—without serving size listed—can be consumed in any moderate amount.

Icon Key

▮ = 480 mg or more of sodium per serving.

▮Bouillon, broth, consommé

Bouillon or broth, low sodium

Carbonated or mineral water

Club soda

Cocoa powder, unsweetened (1 tbs)

Coffee, unsweetened or with sugar substitute

Diet soft drinks, sugar-free

Drink mixes, sugar-free

Tea, unsweetened or with sugar substitute

Tonic water, diet

Water

Water, flavored, carbohydrate free

Seasonings

Any food on this list can be consumed in any moderate amount.

Flavoring extracts (for example, vanilla, almond, peppermint)

Garlic

Herbs, fresh or dried

Nonstick cooking spray

Pimento

Spices

Hot pepper sauce

Wine, used in cooking

Worcestershire sauce

Combination Foods List

Icon Key

☺ = More than 3 g of dietary fiber per serving.

▮ = 600 mg or more of sodium per serving (for combination food main dishes/meals).

Food	Serving Size	Count As
Entrées		
▮Casserole type (tuna noodle, lasagna, spaghetti with meatballs, chili with beans, macaroni and cheese)	1 c (8 oz)	2 carbohydrates + 2 medium-fat meats
▮Stews (beef/other meats and vegetables)	1 c (8 oz)	1 carbohydrate + 1 medium-fat meat + 0–3 fats
Tuna salad or chicken salad	½ c (3½ oz)	½ carbohydrate + 2 lean meats + 1 fat
Frozen Meals/Entrées		
▮☺ Burrito (beef and bean)	1 (5 oz)	3 carbohydrates + 1 lean meat + 2 fats
▮Dinner-type meal	generally 14–17 oz	3 carbohydrates + 3 medium-fat meats + 3 fats
▮Entrée or meal with less than 340 calories	about 8–11 oz	2–3 carbohydrates + 1–2 lean meats
Pizza		
▮cheese/vegetarian thin crust	¼ of 12" (4½ to 5 oz)	2 carbohydrates + 2 medium-fat meats
▮meat topping, thin crust	¼ of 12" (5 oz)	2 carbohydrates + 2 medium-fat meats, + 1½ fats
▮Pocket sandwich	1 (4½ oz)	3 carbohydrates + 1 lean meat + 1–2 fats
▮Pot pie	1 (7 oz)	2½ carbohydrates + 1 medium-fat meat + 3 fats
Salads (Deli-Style)		
Coleslaw	½ c	1 carbohydrate + 1½ fats
Macaroni/pasta salad	½ c	2 carbohydrates + 3 fats
▮Potato salad	½ c	1½ carbohydrates + 1–2 fats
Soups		
▮Bean, lentil, or split pea	1 cup	1 carbohydrate + 1 lean meat
▮Chowder (made with milk)	1 c (8 oz)	1 carbohydrate + 1 lean meat + 1½ fats
▮Cream (made with water)	1 c (8 oz)	1 carbohydrate + 1 fat

Food	Serving Size	Exchanges per Serving
▮Instant	6 oz prepared	1 carbohydrate
▮ with beans or lentils	8 oz prepared	2½ carbohydrates + 1 lean meat
▮Miso soup	1 c	½ carbohydrate + 1 fat
▮Oriental noodle	1 c	2 carbohydrates + 2 fats
Rice (congee)	1 c	1 carbohydrate
▮Tomato (made with water)	1 c (8 oz)	1 carbohydrate
▮Vegetable beef, chicken noodle, or other broth-type	1 c (8 oz)	1 carbohydrate

Fast Foods List[a]

Icon Key

☺ = More than 3 g of dietary fiber per serving.

! = Extra fat, or prepared with added fat.

▮ = 600 mg or more sodium per serving (for fast food main dishes/meals).

Food	Serving Size	Exchanges per Serving
Breakfast Sandwiches		
▮ Egg, cheese, meat, English muffin	1 sandwich	2 carbohydrates + 2 medium-fat meats
▮ Sausage biscuit sandwich	1 sandwich	2 carbohydrates + 2 high-fat meats + 3½ fats
Main Dishes/Entrees		
▮☺ Burrito (beef and beans)	1 (about 8 oz)	3 carbohydrates + 3 medium-fat meats + 3 fats
▮ Chicken breast, breaded and fried	1 (about 5 oz)	1 carbohydrate + 4 medium-fat meats
Chicken drumstick, breaded and fried	1 (about 2 oz)	2 medium-fat meats
▮ Chicken nuggets	6 (about 3½ oz)	1 carbohydrate + 2 medium-fat meats + 1 fat
▮ Chicken thigh, breaded and fried	1 (about 4 oz)	½ carbohydrate + 3 medium-fat meats + 1½ fats
▮ Chicken wings, hot	6 (5 oz)	5 medium-fat meats + 1½ fats
Oriental		
▮ Beef/chicken/shrimp with vegetables in sauce	1 c (about 5 oz)	1 carbohydrate + 1 lean meat + 1 fat
▮ Egg roll, meat	1 (about 3 oz)	1 carbohydrate + 1 lean meat + 1 fat
Fried rice, meatless	½ c	1½ carbohydrates + 1½ fats
▮ Meat and sweet sauce (orange chicken)	1 c	3 carbohydrates + 3 medium-fat meats + 2 fats
▮☺ Noodles and vegetables in sauce (chow mein, lo mein)	1 c	2 carbohydrates + 1 fat
Pizza		
▮ Cheese, pepperoni, regular crust	⅛ of 14" (about 4 oz)	2½ carbohydrates + 1 medium-fat meat + 1½ fats
▮ Cheese/vegetarian, thin crust	¼ of 12" (about 6 oz)	2½ carbohydrates + 2 medium-fat meats + 1½ fats
Sandwiches		
▮ Chicken sandwich, grilled	1	3 carbohydrates + 4 lean meats
▮ Chicken sandwich, crispy	1	3½ carbohydrates + 3 medium-fat meats + 1 fat
Fish sandwich with tartar sauce	1	2½ carbohydrates + 2 medium-fat meats + 2 fats
Hamburger		
▮ large with cheese	1	2½ carbohydrates + 4 medium-fat meats + 1 fat
regular	1	2 carbohydrates + 1 medium-fat meat + 1 fat
▮ Hot dog with bun	1	1 carbohydrate + 1 high-fat meat + 1 fat
Submarine sandwich		
▮ less than 6 grams fat	6" sub	3 carbohydrates + 2 lean meats
▮ regular	6" sub	3½ carbohydrates + 2 medium-fat meats + 1 fat
Taco, hard or soft shell (meat and cheese)	1 small	1 carbohydrate + 1 medium-fat meat + 1½ fats

[a]The choices in the Fast Foods list are not specific fast food meals or items, but are estimates based on popular foods. You can get specific nutrition information for almost every fast food or restaurant chain. Ask the restaurant or check its website for nutrition information about your favorite fast foods.

Salads

▌☺ Salad, main dish (grilled chicken type,
no dressing or croutons) .... Salad .... 1 carbohydrate + 4 lean meats

Salad, side, no dressing or cheese .... Small (about 5 oz) .... 1 vegetable

Sides/Appetizers

▌ French fries, restaurant style .... Small .... 3 carbohydrates + 3 fats

Medium .... 4 carbohydrates + 4 fats

Large .... 5 carbohydrates + 6 fats

▌ Nachos with cheese .... Small (about 4½ oz) .... 2½ carbohydrates + 4 fats

▌ Onion rings .... 1 serving (about 3 oz) .... 2½ carbohydrates + 3 fats

Desserts

Milkshake, any flavor .... 12 oz .... 6 carbohydrates + 2 fats

Soft-serve ice cream cone .... 1 small .... 2½ carbohydrates + 1 fat

Alcohol List

In general, 1 alcohol choice (½ oz absolute alcohol) has about 100 calories.

Alcoholic Beverage	Serving Size	Count As
Beer		
light (4.2%)	12 fl. oz.	1 alcohol equivalent + ½ carbohydrate
regular (4.9%)	12 fl. oz.	1 alcohol equivalent + 1 carbohydrate
Distilled spirits: vodka, rum, gin, whiskey, 80 or 86 proof	1½ fl. oz.	1 alcohol equivalent
Liqueur, coffee (53 proof)	1 fl. oz.	1 alcohol equivalent + 1 carbohydrate
Sake	1 fl. oz.	½ alcohol equivalent
Wine		
dessert (sherry)	3½ fl. oz.	1 alcohol equivalent + 1 carbohydrate
dry, red or white (10%)	5 fl. oz.	1 alcohol equivalent

Academic Journals

*International Journal of Sport Nutrition
and Exercise Metabolism*
www.humankinetics.com/IJSNEM

Journal of Nutrition
http://jn.nutrition.org/

Nutrition Research
www.journals.elsevierhealth.com/periodicals/NTR

Nutrition
www.journals.elsevierhealth.com/periodicals/NUT

Nutrition Reviews
http://onlinelibrary.wiley.com/journal/10.1111/
(ISSN)1753-4887

Obesity
http://onlinelibrary.wiley.com/journal/10.1002/
(ISSN)1930-739X

International Journal of Obesity
www.nature.com/ijo

Journal of the American Medical Association
http://jama.ama-assn.org

New England Journal of Medicine
http://content.nejm.org

American Journal of Clinical Nutrition
www.ajcn.org

Journal of the Academy of Nutrition and Dietetics
www.adajournal.org

Aging

Administration on Aging
www.aoa.gov

American Association of Retired Persons (AARP)
www.aarp.org

National Council on Aging
www.ncoa.org

International Osteoporosis Foundation
www.iofbonehealth.org

National Institute on Aging
www.nia.nih.gov

*Osteoporosis and Related Bone Diseases National
Resource Center*
www.osteo.org

American Geriatrics Society
www.americangeriatrics.org

National Osteoporosis Foundation
www.nof.org

Alcohol and Drug Abuse

National Institute on Drug Abuse
www.nida.nih.gov

*National Institute on Alcohol Abuse
and Alcoholism*
www.niaaa.nih.gov

Alcoholics Anonymous
www.alcoholics-anonymous.org

Narcotics Anonymous
www.na.org

National Council on Alcoholism and Drug Dependence
www.ncadd.org

Substance Abuse and Mental Health Services Administration
www.samhsa.gov

Canadian Government

Health Canada
www.hc-sc.gc.ca

Agricultural and Agri-Food Canada
www.agr.gc.ca

Canadian Food Inspection Agency
www.inspection.gc.ca/english/toce.shtml

Canadian Institute for Health Information
www.cihi.ca

Canadian Public Health Association
www.cpha.ca

Canadian Nutrition and Professional Organizations

Dietitians of Canada, Canadian Dietetic Association
www.dietitians.ca

Canadian Diabetes Association
www.diabetes.ca

National Eating Disorder Information Centre
www.nedic.ca

Canadian Paediatric Society
www.cps.ca

Disordered Eating/ Eating Disorders

American Psychiatric Association
www.psych.org

Klarman Eating Disorders Center at McLean Hospital
www.mclean.harvard.edu/patient/child/edc.php

National Institute of Mental Health
www.nimh.nih.gov

National Association of Anorexia Nervosa and Associated Disorders (ANAD)
www.anad.org

National Eating Disorders Association
www.nationaleatingdisorders.org

Eating Disorder Referral and Information Center
www.edreferral.com

Overeaters Anonymous
www.oa.org

Exercise, Physical Activity, and Sports

American College of Sports Medicine (ACSM)
www.acsm.org

American Physical Therapy Association (APTA)
www.apta.org

Gatorade Sports Science Institute (GSSI)
www.gssiweb.com

National Coalition for Promoting Physical Activity (NCPPA)
www.ncppa.org

Sports, Cardiovascular, and Wellness Nutrition (SCAN)
www.scandpg.org

President's Council on Fitness, Sports & Nutrition
www.fitness.gov

American Council on Exercise
www.acefitness.org

IDEA Health & Fitness Association
www.ideafit.com

Food Safety

Food Marketing Institute
www.fmi.org

Agency for Toxic Substances and Disease Registry (ATSDR)
www.atsdr.cdc.gov

Food Allergy Research & Education
www.foodallergy.org

Foodsafety.gov
www.foodsafety.gov

The USDA Food Safety and Inspection Service
www.fsis.usda.gov

Consumer Reports
www.consumerreports.org

Center for Science in the Public Interest: Food Safety
www.cspinet.org/foodsafety/index.html

Center for Food Safety and Applied Nutrition
www.fda.gov/Food

Food Safety Project
www.extension.iastate.edu/foodsafety

Organic Consumers Association
www.organicconsumers.org

Infancy and Childhood

Administration for Children and Families
www.acf.hhs.gov

American Academy of Pediatrics
www.aap.org

Kidshealth: The Nemours Foundation
www.kidshealth.org

National Center for Education in Maternal and Child Health
www.ncemch.org

Birth Defects Research for Children, Inc.
www.birthdefects.org

USDA/ARS Children's Nutrition Research Center
at Baylor College of Medicine
www.kidsnutrition.org

Centers for Disease Control—Healthy Youth
www.cdc.gov/healthyyouth

International Agencies

UNICEF
www.unicef.org

World Health Organization
www.who.int/en

The Stockholm Convention on Persistent
Organic Pollutants
www.pops.int

Food and Agricultural Organization of the United Nations
www.fao.org

International Food Information Council Foundation
www.ific.org

Pregnancy and Lactation

San Diego County Breastfeeding Coalition
www.breastfeeding.org

National Alliance for Breastfeeding Advocacy
www.naba-breastfeeding.org

American Congress of Obstetricians and Gynecologists
www.acog.org

La Leche League
www.lalecheleague.org

National Organization on Fetal Alcohol Syndrome
www.nofas.org

March of Dimes Birth Defects Foundation
http://modimes.org

Professional Nutrition Organizations

Academy of Nutrition and Dietetics (AND)
www.eatright.org

American Dental Association
www.ada.org

American Heart Association
www.americanheart.org

The American Society for Nutrition (ASN)
www.nutrition.org

Dietitians in Integrative and Functional Medicine
www.complementarynutrition.org

The Institute for Functional Medicine
www.functionalmedicine.org

The Society for Nutrition Education and Behavior
www.sneb.org

American College of Nutrition
www.americancollegeofnutrition.org

The Obesity Society
www.obesity.org

American Council on Science and Health
www.acsh.org

American Diabetes Association
www.diabetes.org

Institute of Food Technologists
www.ift.org

ILSI Human Nutrition Institute
www.ilsi.org

Trade Organizations

American Meat Institute
www.meatami.com

National Dairy Council
www.nationaldairycouncil.org

United Fresh Produce Association
www.uffva.org

U.S.A. Rice Federation
www.usarice.com

U.S. Government

The USDA
Agricultural Marketing Service
www.ams.usda.gov

U.S. Department of Health and Human Services
www.hhs.gov

Food and Drug Administration (FDA)
www.fda.gov

Environmental Protection Agency
www.epa.gov

Federal Trade Commission
www.ftc.gov

Office of Dietary Supplements
National Institutes of Health
http://dietary-supplements.info.nih.gov

Nutrient Data Laboratory
Beltsville Human Nutrition Research Center,
Agricultural Research Service
www.ars.usda.gov/nutrientdata

National Digestive Diseases Information Clearinghouse
http://digestive.niddk.nih.gov

National Cancer Institute
www.cancer.gov

National Eye Institute
www.nei.nih.gov

National Heart, Lung, and Blood Institute
www.nhlbi.nih.gov/index.htm

National Institute of Diabetes and Digestive
and Kidney Diseases
www.niddk.nih.gov

National Center for Complementary
and Alternative Medicine
http://nccam.nih.gov

U.S. Department of Agriculture (USDA)
www.usda.gov

Centers for Disease Control and Prevention (CDC)
www.cdc.gov

National Institutes of Health (NIH)
www.nih.gov

Food and Nutrition Information Center
Agricultural Research Service, USDA
www.nal.usda.gov/fnic

National Institute of Allergy and Infectious Diseases
www.niaid.nih.gov

Weight and Health Management

The Vegetarian Resource Group
www.vrg.org

The Obesity Society
www.obesity.org

Anemia Lifeline
www.anemia.com

The Arc
www.thearc.org

Bottled Water Web
www.bottledwaterweb.com

Food and Nutrition
Institute of Medicine
www.iom.edu/Global/Topics/Food-Nutrition.aspx

The Calorie Control Council
www.caloriecontrol.org

TOPS (Take Off Pounds Sensibly)
www.tops.org

Shape Up America!
www.shapeup.org

World Hunger

Friedman School of Nutrition Science and Policy
http://nutrition.tufts.edu

Freedom from Hunger
www.freefromhunger.org

Oxfam International
www.oxfam.org

WorldWatch Institute
www.worldwatch.org

The Hunger Project
www.thp.org

U.S. Agency for International Development
www.usaid.gov

Feeding America
www.feedingamerica.org

Food First
www.foodfirst.org

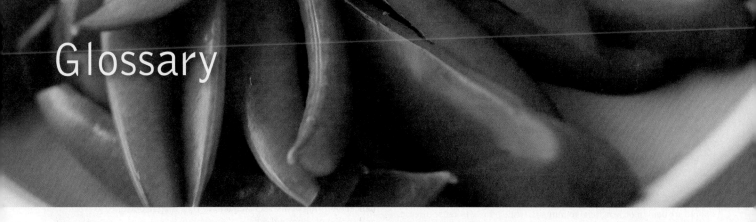

Glossary

A

absorption The process by which digested nutrients move into the tissues where they can be transported and used by the body's cells.

Acceptable Macronutrient Distribution Range (AMDR) A healthy range of intakes for the energy-containing nutrients—carbohydrates, proteins, and fats—in your diet, designed to meet your nutrient needs and help reduce the risk of chronic diseases.

acetaldehyde An intermediary by-product of the breakdown of ethanol in the liver.

acid group The COOH group that is part of every amino acid; also called the *carboxyl group*.

acromegaly A condition caused by excess growth hormone in which tissues, bones, and internal organs grow abnormally large.

active transport The process of absorbing nutrients across the intestinal cell membrane with the help of a carrier molecule and energy.

acute dehydration Dehydration starting after a short period of time.

added sugars Sugars that are added to processed foods and sweets.

adenosine triphosphate (ATP) A compound that is broken down to produce energy for working muscles and other tissues.

Adequate Intake (AI) The *approximate* amount of a nutrient that groups of similar individuals are consuming to maintain good health.

adolescence The developmental period between childhood and early adulthood.

aerobic With oxygen.

age-related macular degeneration (AMD) A disease that affects the macula of the retina, causing blurry vision.

agribusiness The businesses collectively associated with the production, processing, and distribution of agricultural products, including food.

alcohol A chemical class of substances that include ethanol, methanol, and isopropanol.

alcohol abuse The continuation of alcohol consumption even though this behavior has created social, legal, and/or health problems.

alcohol dehydrogenase One of the alcohol-metabolizing enzymes found in the stomach and the liver.

alcohol poisoning When the BAC rises to such an extreme level that a person's central nervous system is affected and his or her breathing and heart rate are interrupted.

alcohol tolerance When the body adjusts to long-term alcohol use by becoming less sensitive to the alcohol. You need to consume more alcohol in order to get the same effect.

alcoholic hepatitis Stage 2 of alcoholic liver disease; due to chronic inflammation.

alcoholic liver disease A degenerative liver condition that occurs in three stages: (1) fatty liver, (2) alcoholic hepatitis, and (3) cirrhosis.

alcoholism Chronic disease with genetic, psychological, and environmental components; also referred to as *alcohol dependence*.

Alcoholics crave alcohol, can't control their intake, and develop a higher tolerance for it. Alcoholics also exhibit a dependency on alcohol, as abstaining from drinking will cause withdrawal symptoms.

alpha-linolenic acid A polyunsaturated essential fatty acid; part of the omega-3 fatty acid family.

alpha-tocopherol (α-tocopherol) The most active form of vitamin E in the body.

Alzheimer's disease (AD) A type of dementia.

amine group The nitrogen-containing part (NH_2) of an amino acid.

amino acid pools A limited supply of amino acids stored in your blood and cells and used to build new proteins.

amino acid profile The types and amounts of amino acids in a protein.

amino acids The building blocks of protein. Amino acids contain carbon, hydrogen, oxygen, and nitrogen. All amino acids are composed of an acid group, an amine group, and a unique side chain.

anaerobic Without oxygen.

anaphylactic reactions Severe, life-threatening reactions that cause constriction of the airways in the lungs, which inhibits the ability to breathe.

anemia A condition in which your blood has a lower than normal number of red blood cells than it should to be healthy.

anencephaly A neural tube defect that results in the absence of major parts of the brain and spinal cord.

antibiotic-resistant bacteria Bacteria that have developed a resistance to an antibiotic such that they are no longer affected by antibiotic medication.

antibiotics Drugs that kill or slow the growth of bacteria.

antibodies Proteins made by your body to bind to and neutralize foreign invaders, such as harmful bacteria, fungi, and viruses, as part of the body's immune response.

anticoagulant A substance that interferes with blood coagulation.

antidiuretic hormone (ADH) A hormone that directs the kidneys to concentrate urine and reduce urine production in order to reduce water loss from the body.

antimicrobials Substances or a combination of substances, such as disinfectants and sanitizers, that control the spread of bacteria and viruses on nonliving surfaces or objects.

antioxidants Substances that neutralize free radicals. Vitamins A, C, and E and beta-carotene are antioxidants.

anus The opening at the end of the rectum where waste is eliminated from the body.

arthritis Inflammation in the joints that can cause pain, stiffness, and swelling.

ascorbic acid The active form of vitamin C.

atherosclerosis Narrowing of the coronary arteries due to buildup of debris along the artery walls.

attention deficit/hyperactivity disorder (ADHD) Previously designated as attention deficit disorder (ADD). A condition in which an individual may be easily distracted, may have difficulty listening, following directions, and focusing and sustaining attention, and/or may have inconsistent performance in school.

autism spectrum disorder (ASD) Collective term for a group of brain disorders that make it difficult or impossible for a person to communicate and relate to others and may also be characterized by repetitive activities.

B

bacteria Single-celled microorganisms without an organized nucleus. Some are benign or beneficial to humans, while other can cause disease.

bariatric surgery Surgical procedures that reduce the functional volume of the stomach so that less food is eaten. Such surgeries are sometimes used to treat extreme obesity.

basal metabolism The amount of energy the body expends to meet its basic physiological needs. Also referred to as *basal metabolic rate (BMR)*.

behavior modification Changing behaviors to improve health. Identifying and altering eating patterns that contribute to weight gain or impede weight loss is behavior modification.

beriberi A thiamin deficiency that can affect the cardiovascular and nervous systems and results in weakness in the body.

bile A yellowish-green fluid made in the liver and concentrated and stored in the gallbladder. It helps emulsify fat and prepare it for digestion.

binge drinking The consumption of 5 or more alcoholic drinks by men, or 4 or more drinks by women, in a very short time.

bioaccumulate When a substance or chemical builds up in an organism over time, so that the concentration of the chemical is higher than would be found naturally in the environment.

bioavailability The degree to which a nutrient is available to be absorbed from foods and used in the body.

biodiversity Having a wide variety of plant and animal species within an environment.

biopesticides Substances used to kill pests that are derived from natural materials such as animals, plants, bacteria, and certain minerals.

biotechnology The application of biological techniques to living cells, which alters their genetic makeup.

bioterrorism The use of a biological or chemical agent to frighten, threaten, coerce, injure, and/or kill individuals.

blackouts Periods of time when an intoxicated person cannot recall part or all of an event.

bleaching When light enters the eye and interacts with and changes rhodopsin.

blood alcohol concentration (BAC) The measurement of the amount of alcohol in your blood. BAC is measured in grams of alcohol per deciliter of blood, usually expressed as a percentage.

body composition The relative proportion of muscle, fat, water, and other tissues in the body.

body dysmorphic disorder A mental illness in which a person is excessively concerned about and preoccupied by a perceived defect in his or her body.

body mass index (BMI) A calculation of your weight in relationship to your height. A BMI between 18.5 and 24.9 is considered healthy.

bolus Chewed mass of food.

bone mineral density (BMD) The amount of minerals, in particular calcium, per volume in an individual's bone.

botulism A rare but serious paralytic illness caused by the bacterium *Clostridium botulinum*. Infant botulism is caused by consuming the spores of the bacteria, which then grow in the intestines and release toxins. It can be fatal.

bovine spongiform encephalopathy (BSE) A slow, degenerative, and deadly disease that attacks the central nervous system of cattle. Also known as *mad cow disease*.

bran The indigestible outer shell of the grain kernel.

breast-feeding The act of feeding an infant milk from a woman's breast.

buffers Substances that help maintain the proper pH in a solution by attracting or donating hydrogen ions.

C

cancer A group of diseases characterized by the uncontrolled growth and spread of abnormal cells.

canning The process of heating food to a temperature high enough to kill bacteria and then packing the food in airtight containers.

carbohydrate loading A diet and training strategy that maximizes glycogen stores in the body before an endurance event.

carcinogenic Cancer-causing.

cardiorespiratory endurance The body's ability to sustain prolonged exercise.

carnitine A vitamin-like substance needed to properly utilize fat.

carotenodermia The presence of excess carotene in the blood resulting in an orange skin color, due to excessive intake of carotene-rich vegetables.

catalysts Substances that aid and speed up reactions without being changed, damaged, or used up in the process.

cataract A common eye disorder that occurs when the lens of the eye becomes cloudy.

celiac disease An autoimmune disease of the small intestine that involves the inability to digest the protein gluten.

cell differentiation The process that determines what a cell becomes in your body.

cellulite A nonmedical term that refers to fat cells under the skin that give it a ripplelike appearance. Contrary to popular belief, cellulite is no different from other fat in the body.

central obesity An excess storage of visceral fat in the abdominal area, which increases the risk of heart disease, diabetes, and hypertension.

chemical digestion Breaking down food with enzymes or digestive juices.

childhood overweight and obesity Excess body fat in children.

chlorophyll The green pigment in plants that absorbs energy from sunlight to begin the process of photosynthesis.

cholecystokinin A hormone released when the stomach is distended. It is associated with the feeling of satiation.

choline A vitamin-like substance needed for healthy cells and nerves.

chronic dehydration Dehydration over a long period of time.

chylomicron A type of lipoprotein that carries digested fat and other lipids through the lymph system into the blood.

chyme The semiliquid, partially digested food mass that leaves the stomach and enters the small intestine.

ciguatera poisoning A condition caused by marine toxins produced by *dinoflagellates* (microscopic sea organisms).

cirrhosis Stage 3 of alcoholic liver disease in which liver cells die, causing severe scarring.

closed or "coded" dating Refers to the packing numbers that are decodable only by manufacturers and are often found on nonperishable, shelf-stable foods.

clotting factors Substances involved in the process of blood clotting.

coagulation The process of blood clotting.

coenzyme Substances, often vitamins, that are needed by enzymes to perform many chemical reactions in your body.

collagen A ropelike, fibrous protein that is the most abundant protein in your body.

colostrum The fluid that is expressed from the mother's breast after birth and before the development of breast milk.

commodity crops Crop products such as corn and soybeans that can be used for commerce.

community-supported agriculture (CSA) An arrangement whereby individuals pay a fee to support a local farm, and in exchange receive a weekly or biweekly box of fresh produce from the farm.

complemented proteins Incomplete proteins that are combined with modest amounts of animal or soy proteins or with other plant proteins that are rich in the limiting amino acids to create a complete protein.

complete protein A protein that provides all the essential amino acids that your body needs, along with some nonessential amino acids. Soy protein and protein from animal sources, in general, are complete.

complex carbohydrates A category of carbohydrates that contain many sugar units combined. A polysaccharide is a complex carbohydrate.

conception The moment when a sperm fertilizes an egg.

conditionally essential amino acids Nonessential amino acids that become essential if the body cannot make them, such as during bouts of illness.

conditioning The process of improving physical fitness through repeated activity.

cones Light-absorbing cells responsible for color vision.

congeners Compounds in alcohol that enhance the taste but may contribute to hangover symptoms.

congregate meals Meals served at churches, synagogues, or other community sites where older adults can receive a nutritious meal and socialize.

connective tissue The most abundant tissue type in the body. Made up primarily of collagen, it supports and connects body parts as well as providing protection and insulation.

consensus The opinion of a group of experts based on a collection of information.

constipation Difficulty in passing stools.

control group The group given a placebo.

Corn Belt The parts of the United States where corn is grown in abundance. This includes Iowa, Indiana, most of Illinois, and parts of Kansas, Missouri, Nebraska, South Dakota, Minnesota, Ohio, and Wisconsin.

creatine phosphate A compound stored in the muscles that is broken down to replenish ATP stores.

cretinism A condition caused by a deficiency of thyroid hormone during prenatal development, resulting in abnormal mental and physical development in children. It is also known as *congenital hypothyroidism.*

critical periods Developmental stages during which cells and tissues rapidly grow and differentiate to form body structures.

Crohn's disease An inflammatory bowel disease involving inflammation and swelling of the intestines.

cross-contaminate Transfer pathogens from a food, utensil, cutting board, kitchen surface, and/or hands to another food.

D

Daily Values (DVs) Established reference levels of nutrients, based on a 2,000-calorie diet, that are used on food labels.

danger zone The range of temperatures (between 40°F and 140°F) at which foodborne bacteria multiply most rapidly. Room temperature falls within the danger zone.

dehydration Loss of water in the body as a result of inadequate fluid intake or excess fluid loss, such as through sweating.

dementia A disorder of the brain that interferes with a person's memory, learning, and mental stability.

denaturation The alteration of a protein's shape, which changes the structure and function of the protein.

dental caries The decay or erosion of teeth.

deoxyribonucleic acid (DNA) Genetic material within cells that directs the synthesis of proteins in the body.

dermatitis Inflammation or irritation of the skin.

developed country A nation advanced in industrial capability, technological sophistication, and economic productivity; also called *most developed country.*

developing country A nation having a relatively low level of industrial capability, technological sophistication, or economic productivity; also called *less developed country.*

diabetes mellitus A medical condition whereby an individual either doesn't have enough insulin or is resistant to the insulin available, causing the blood glucose level to rise.

diarrhea Frequent, loose, watery stools.

diastolic pressure The pressure of your blood against the artery walls when the heart is at rest between beats.

dietary fiber Nondigestible polysaccharides found naturally in foods.

dietary folate equivalents (DFE) A measurement used to express the amount of folate in a food or supplement.

Dietary Guidelines for Americans Guidelines published every five years that provide dietary and lifestyle advice to individuals aged 2 and older to maintain good health and prevent chronic diseases.

Dietary Reference Intakes (DRIs) Reference values for the essential nutrients needed to maintain good health, to prevent chronic diseases, and to avoid unhealthy excesses.

digestibility A food's capacity to be broken down so that it can be absorbed.

digestive process The breakdown of foods into absorbable components using mechanical and chemical means.

diglyceride A glycerol with only two attached fatty acids.

disaccharide Two sugar units combined. There are three disaccharides: sucrose, lactose, and maltose.

disordered eating Abnormal and potentially harmful eating behaviors that do not meet specific criteria for an eating disorder.

distillation The evaporation and then collection of a liquid by condensation.

diuretics Substances such as alcohol and some medications that cause the body to lose water.

diverticula Small bulges at weak spots in the colon wall.

diverticulitis Infection of the diverticula.

diverticulosis The existence of diverticula in the lining of the intestine.

DNA The blueprint in cells that stores all genetic information. DNA remains in the nucleus of the cell and directs the synthesis of proteins.

DNA fingerprinting A technique in which DNA "gene patterns" (or "fingerprints") are detected and analyzed. Used in food safety to distinguish between different strains of a bacterium.

double-blind placebo-controlled study When the scientists and subjects in a research experiment can't distinguish between the treatments given to the subjects and don't know which group of subjects received which treatment.

duration The length of time of performing an activity.

dysphagia Difficult swallowing.

E

early childhood caries Tooth decay from prolonged contact with formula, milk, fruit juice, or other carbohydrate-rich liquid offered to an infant in a bottle.

early childhood tooth decay The decay of baby teeth in children due to continual exposure to fermentable sugary liquids.

eating disorders The term used to describe psychological illnesses that involve specific abnormal eating behaviors, such as anorexia nervosa (self-starvation), bulimia nervosa (bingeing and purging), and binge eating disorder.

edema The accumulation of excess fluid in the spaces surrounding your cells, which causes swelling of the body tissue.

eicosanoids Hormonelike substances in the body. Prostaglandins, thromboxanes, and leukotrienes are all eicosanoids.

eicosapentaenoic acid (EPA) and docosahexaenoic acid (DHA) Two omega-3 fatty acids that are heart healthy.

electrolytes Charged ions that conduct an electrical current in a solvent such as water. Sodium, potassium, and chloride are examples of electrolytes in the body.

embryo Term that refers to a fertilized egg during the third through the eighth week of pregnancy.

empty calories Calories that come with little nutrition. Jelly beans are an example of a food that provides lots of calories from sugar but few nutrients.

emulsifier A compound that keeps two incompatible substances, such as oil and water, mixed together.

endosperm The starchy part of the grain kernel.

endotoxin A damaging product produced by intestinal bacteria that travels in the blood to the liver and initiates the release of cytokines that damage liver cells, leading to scarring.

energy balance The state at which energy (calorie) intake and energy (calorie) output in the body are equal.

energy deficit Expending more energy than is consumed. Also called *negative energy balance.*

energy density A measurement of the calories in a food compared with the weight (grams) or volume of the food.

energy excess Consuming more energy than is expended. Also called *positive energy balance.*

energy gap The difference between the numbers of calories needed to maintain weight before and after weight loss.

enriched grains Refined grain foods that have folic acid, thiamin, niacin, riboflavin, and iron added.

enzymes Substances that produce chemical changes, catalyze chemical reactions, and speed up chemical reactions.

epidemiological research Research that looks at populations of people; it is often observational.

epiglottis Flap of tissue that protects the trachea while swallowing.

epiphyseal plate The growth plate of the bone. In puberty, growth in this area leads to increases in height.

ergogenic aid A substance, such as a dietary supplement, used to enhance athletic performance.

esophagus Tube that extends from the throat to the stomach.

essential amino acids The nine amino acids that the body cannot synthesize; they must be obtained through dietary sources.

essential fatty acids The two polyunsaturated fatty acids that the body cannot make and therefore must be eaten in foods: linoleic acid and alpha-linolenic acid.

Estimated Average Requirement (EAR) The average amount of a nutrient that is known to meet the needs of 50 percent of the individuals in a similar age and gender group.

Estimated Energy Requirement (EER) The amount of daily energy needed to maintain a healthy body weight and meet energy (calorie) needs based on age, gender, height, weight, and activity level.

estrogen The hormone responsible for female sex characteristics.

ethanol The type of alcohol in alcoholic beverages such as wine, beer, and liquor.

Exchange Lists for Meal Planning A grouping of foods, in specific portions, according to their carbohydrate, protein, and fat composition to ensure that each food in the group contributes a similar amount of calories per serving.

exercise Any type of structured or planned physical activity.

experimental group The group given a specific treatment.

experimental research Research involving at least two groups of subjects.

extracellular fluid compartment The fluid located outside your cells. Interstitial fluids and fluids in the blood are extracellular fluids.

extreme obesity Having a BMI > 40.

F

facilitated diffusion The process of absorbing nutrients across the intestinal cell membrane with the help of a carrier molecule.

famine A severe shortage of food caused by crop destruction due to weather problems or poor agricultural practices so that the food supply is destroyed or severely diminished. Famine can also be caused by pestilence or war.

farm An establishment that produces and sells at least $1,000 of agricultural products annually.

farm-to-table continuum Illustrates the roles that farmers, food manufacturers, food transporters, retailers, and consumers play in ensuring that the food supply, from the farm to the plate, remains safe.

fat The common name for triglycerides.

fat substitutes Substances that replace added fat in foods by providing the creamy properties of fat for fewer calories and fewer total fat grams.

fatty acid The basic unit of triglycerides and phospholipids.

fatty liver Stage 1 of alcoholic liver disease.

fecal-to-oral transmission The spread of pathogens by putting something in the mouth that has been in contact with infected stool. Poor hygiene, such as not washing hands after using the bathroom, can lead to this type of contamination.

feedlot A facility where cattle are fed grain and other foods before being slaughtered.

female athlete triad A syndrome of the three interrelated conditions occurring in some physically active females: low energy availability, menstrual dysfunction, and low bone density.

fermentation The process by which yeast converts sugars in grains or fruits into ethanol and carbon dioxide.

fetal alcohol spectrum disorders (FASDs) A range of conditions that can occur in children who are exposed to alcohol in utero. Fetal alcohol syndrome (FAS) is the most severe of the FASDs; children with FAS will display physical, mental, and behavioral abnormalities.

fetus A developing embryo that is at least 8 weeks old.

fiber The portion of plant foods that isn't digested in the small intestine.

flatulence Production of excessive gas in the stomach or the intestines.

flavonoids Phytochemicals found in fruits, vegetables, tea, nuts, and seeds.

flexibility A joint's ability to move freely through a full and normal range of motion.

fluid balance The equal distribution of water throughout your body and within and between cells.

fluorosis A condition caused by excess amounts of fluoride, resulting in mottling of the teeth.

flushing A reddish coloring of the face, arms, and chest.

folic acid The form of folate used in vitamin supplements and fortification of foods.

food additives Substances added to food that affect its quality, flavor, freshness, and/or safety.

food allergens Proteins not broken down by cooking or digestion that enter the body intact, causing an adverse immune response.

food allergy An abnormal reaction by the immune system to a particular food.

food biosecurity Protecting the food supply from bioterrorist attacks.

food consumers Individuals who make decisions about which foods to buy.

food guidance systems Visual diagrams that provide a variety of food recommendations to help create a well-balanced diet.

food industry The collective efforts of various businesses that provide food to consumers.

food insecurity The inability to satisfy basic food needs due to lack of financial resources or other problems. The USDA further defines food insecurity as falling into the categories of either *low food security* or *very low food security*.

food intolerance Adverse reaction to a food that does not involve an immune response. Lactose intolerance is one example.

food jags When a child will only eat the same food meal after meal.

food preservation The treatment of foods to reduce deterioration and spoilage, and help prevent the multiplication of pathogens that can cause foodborne illness.

food safety Guidelines and procedures that help keep foods free from contaminants.

Food Safety Initiative (FSI) The program that coordinates the research, surveillance, inspection, outbreak response, and educational activities of the various government agencies that work together to safeguard food.

foodborne illness Sickness caused by consuming contaminated food or beverages. Also known as *foodborne disease* or *food poisoning*.

fortified foods Foods with added nutrients.

free radicals Unstable oxygen-containing molecules that can damage the cells of the body and possibly contribute to the increased risk of chronic diseases.

fructose The sweetest of the monosaccharides; also known as *fruit sugar*.

functional fiber The nondigestible polysaccharides that are added to foods because of a specific desired effect on health.

functional foods Foods that have a positive effect on health beyond providing basic nutrients.

fungicides Chemicals used to kill mold.

G

galactose A monosaccharide that links with glucose to create the sugar found in dairy foods.

gallbladder A pear-shaped organ located behind the liver. The gallbladder stores bile produced by the liver and secretes the bile through the bile duct into the small intestine.

gallstones Small, hard, crystalline structures formed in the gallbladder or bile duct due to abnormally thick bile.

gastric banding A type of bariatric surgery that uses a silicone band to reduce the size of the stomach so that less food is needed to feel full.

gastric bypass surgery A type of bariatric surgery that reduces the functional volume of the stomach to minimize the amount of food eaten.

gastrin A digestive hormone produced in the stomach that stimulates digestive activities and increases motility and emptying.

gastritis Inflammation of the stomach.

gastroenteritis Formal term for "stomach flu." Caused by a virus or bacteria and results in inflammation of the stomach and/or intestines.

gastroesophageal reflux disease (GERD) The backward flow of stomach contents past the lower esophageal sphincter into the esophagus.

gastrointestinal (GI) tract Body area containing the organs of the digestive tract. It extends from the mouth to the anus.

gene A DNA segment that codes for a specific protein.

gene expression The processing of genetic information to create a specific protein.

gene–environment interaction The interaction of genetics and the environment that increases the risk of obesity in some people.

generally recognized as safe (GRAS) Describes a substance that is believed to be safe to consume based on a long history of use by humans or a substantial amount of research that documents its safety.

genetic engineering (GE) A biological technique that isolates and manipulates the genes of organisms to produce a targeted, modified product.

genetically modified organisms (GMOs) Organisms that have been genetically engineered to contain both original and foreign genes.

germ In grains, the seed of the grain kernel.

gestational diabetes Diabetes that occurs in women during pregnancy.

ghrelin A hormone produced mainly in the stomach that increases hunger.

globesity A blend of the words *global* and *obesity*, coined by the World Health Organization, which refers to the worldwide obesity epidemic.

glucagon The hormone that directs glycogenolysis and gluconeogenesis to increase glucose in the blood. Glucagon is produced in and released from the pancreas.

gluconeogenesis The creation of glucose from noncarbohydrate sources, predominantly protein.

glucose The most abundant sugar in foods and the primary energy source for your body.

gluten intolerance A sensitivity to the protein gluten, which is found in wheat and other grains. Symptoms include stomachaches, diarrhea, bloating, and tiredness.

glycerol The three-carbon backbone of a triglyceride.

glycogen The storage form of glucose in humans and animals.

glycogenesis The process of converting excess glucose into glycogen in your liver and muscle.

glycogenolysis The breakdown of glycogen to release glucose.

goiter Enlargement of the thyroid gland, mostly due to iodine deficiency.

greenhouse gases Gases that absorb and "trap" the heat in the air and re-radiate that heat downward.

growth charts Series of percentile curves that illustrate the distribution of selected body measurements in U.S. children.

growth hormone A protein-based hormone that stimulates cell growth and reproduction in humans and animals.

growth stunting Impaired growth and development primarily manifested in early childhood and including malnutrition during fetal development. Once growth stunting occurs, it is usually permanent.

Guillain-Barré syndrome A condition that can result from a *Campylobacter* infection. It causes the immune system to attack the body's own nerves and can lead to temporary paralysis.

H

hangover A collective term for the unpleasant symptoms, such as a headache and dizziness, that occur after drinking an excessive amount of alcohol.

health claims Claims on the label that describe a relationship between a food or dietary compound and a disease or health-related condition.

Healthy People 2020 A set of disease prevention and health promotion objectives for Americans to meet during the second decade of the new millennium.

healthy weight A body weight in relationship to your height that doesn't increase the risk of developing any weight-related health problems or diseases.

heart attack Permanent damage to the heart muscle that results from a sudden lack of oxygen-rich blood.

heartburn A burning sensation originating in the esophagus. Heartburn is usually caused by the reflux of gastric contents from the stomach into the esophagus. Chronic heartburn can lead to gastroesophageal reflux disease (GERD).

hemochromatosis A blood disorder characterized by the retention of an excessive amount of iron.

hemoglobin The oxygen-carrying, heme-containing protein found in red blood cells.

hemolytic uremic syndrome A rare condition caused by *E. coli* O157:H7 that results in the destruction of red blood cells and kidney failure.

hemorrhage Excessive loss of blood or bleeding.

hemorrhoids Swelling in the veins of the rectum and anus.

herbicides Substances that are used to kill and control weeds.

high-density lipoprotein (HDL) A lipoprotein that removes cholesterol from the tissues and delivers it to the liver to be used as part of bile and/or to be excreted from the body. Because of this, it is known as the *good* cholesterol carrier.

high-pressure processing (HPP) A method used to pasteurize foods by exposing the items to pulses of high pressure, which destroys the microorganisms that are present.

homeless Individuals who are either "crashing" with friends or family members, or residing on the street or in their automobiles.

hormones Protein- or lipid-based chemical substances that act as "messengers" in the body to initiate or direct actions or processes. Insulin, glucagon, and estrogen are examples of hormones.

host A living plant or animal (including a human) that a virus or parasite infects for the sake of reproducing.

Human Genome Project A project sponsored by the United States government to determine the complete set and sequencing of DNA in human cells and identify all human genes.

hunger Physical discomfort that results from the lack of food associated with food insecurity.

hydrochloric acid (HCl) A powerful acid made in the stomach that has digestive functions. It also helps to kill microorganisms and lowers the pH in the stomach.

hydrogenation Adding hydrogen to an unsaturated fatty acid to make it more saturated and solid at room temperature.

hydrophobic Having an aversion to water.

hypercalcemia A chronically high amount of calcium in the blood.

hyperkalemia Abnormally high levels of potassium in the blood.

hyperphosphatemia Abnormally high levels of phosphorus in the blood.

hypertension High blood pressure.

hypervitaminosis A The serious condition in which the liver accumulates toxic levels of vitamin A.

hypervitaminosis D A condition resulting from excessive amounts of vitamin D in the body.

hypoallergenic infant formulas Specially developed formulas for infants who have food allergies and cannot tolerate regular formula.

hypoglycemia A blood glucose level that drops to lower than 70 mg/dl. Hunger, shakiness, dizziness, perspiration, and light-headedness are some signs of hypoglycemia.

hypokalemia Abnormally low levels of potassium in the blood.

hyponatremia Dangerously low levels of sodium in the blood.

hypotension Low blood pressure.

hypothesis An idea generated by scientists based on their observations.

I

ileocecal sphincter Gateway between the end of the small intestine and the beginning of the large intestine. The sphincter prevents backflow of fecal contents from the large intestine into the small intestine.

immunity The state of having built up antibodies to a particular foreign substance so that when particles of the substance enter the body, they are destroyed by the antibodies.

incomplete protein A protein that is low in one or more of the essential amino acids. Protein from plant sources tends to be incomplete.

infancy The age range from birth to 12 months.

inorganic Not containing carbon and not formed by living things. Inorganic compounds include minerals, water, and salts.

inositol A vitamin-like substance synthesized in your body that helps to keep your cells and their membranes healthy.

insensible water loss The water that is lost from the body daily through exhalation from the lungs and evaporation off the skin.

insoluble fiber A type of fiber that doesn't dissolve in water and is not fermented by intestinal bacteria.

insulin The hormone, produced in and released from the pancreas, that facilitates the movement of glucose from the blood into cells.

insulin resistance The inability of cells to respond to insulin.

integrated pest management (IPM) Alternative to pesticides that uses the most economical and the least harmful methods of pest control to minimize risk to consumers, crops, and the environment.

intensity The level of difficulty of an activity.

international units (IU) A system of measurement of a biologically active ingredient such as a vitamin.

interstitial fluids Fluids located between cells.

intracellular fluid compartment The fluid located inside your cells.

intrinsic factor (IF) A protein secreted by the stomach that helps in the absorption of vitamin B_{12}.

iodopsin The compound found in the cones of the eye that is needed for color vision.

iron-deficiency anemia An anemia caused by low hemoglobin levels due to insufficient dietary intake and absorption of iron.

irradiation A process in which foods are placed in a shielded chamber, called an irradiator, and subjected to a radiant energy source. This kills specific pathogens in food by breaking up the cells' DNA.

irritable bowel syndrome (IBS) A functional disorder that involves changes in colon rhythm.

isoflavones Naturally occurring phytoestrogens, or weak plant estrogens, that function in a fashion similar to the hormone estrogen in the human body.

J

jaundice A yellowish coloring of the skin due to the presence of bile pigments in the blood.

K

Keshan disease A disease related to a deficiency of selenium.

ketoacidosis The buildup of ketone bodies to dangerous levels, which can result in coma or death.

ketone bodies The by-products of the incomplete breakdown of fat.

ketosis The condition of increased ketone bodies in the blood.

kidney stones A solid mass formed in the kidneys from dietary minerals.

kilocalories The measurement of energy in foods. Commonly referred to as *calories.*

kwashiorkor A state of PEM where there is a severe deficiency of dietary protein.

L

laboratory experiment A scientific experiment conducted in a laboratory. Some laboratory experiments involve animals.

lactate A by-product of rapid glucose metabolism.

lactation The production of milk in a woman's body after childbirth, and the period during which it occurs.

lactose A disaccharide composed of glucose and galactose; also known as milk sugar.

lactose intolerant When maldigestion of lactose results in symptoms such as nausea, cramps, bloating, flatulence, and diarrhea.

lactose maldigestion The inability to digest lactose in foods due to low levels of the enzyme lactase.

lanugo Very fine, soft hair on the face and arms of people with anorexia nervosa.

large intestine Final organ of the GI tract. It consists of the cecum, appendix, colon, and rectum.

lean body mass The body mass once the fat mass has been subtracted. It contains mostly muscle but also organs and fluids.

least developed country A nation having a low level of economic productivity and technological sophistication within the contemporary range of possibility.

leptin A hormone produced in fat tissue that helps regulate body fat by signaling the reduction of food intake in the brain and interfering with the storage of fat in the cells.

let-down response The release of milk from the mother's breast to feed the baby.

licensed dietitian nutritionist (LDN) An individual who has met specified educational and experience criteria deemed necessary by a state licensing board to be considered an expert in the field of nutrition. An RDN would meet all the qualifications to be an LDN.

life expectancy The number of years that a person will live.

limiting amino acid The amino acid that is in the shortest supply in an incomplete protein.

linoleic acid A polyunsaturated essential fatty acid; part of the omega-6 fatty acid family.

lipids A category of carbon, hydrogen, and oxygen compounds that are insoluble in water.

lipoic acid A vitamin-like substance that your body needs for energy production; it may also act as an antioxidant.

lipoproteins Capsule-shaped transport carriers that enable fat and cholesterol to travel through the lymph and blood.

liposuction The surgical removal of subcutaneous fat with a penlike instrument. Usually performed on the abdomen, hips, and thighs, and/or other areas of the body.

liver The largest gland of the body. It aids in digestive activity and is responsible for metabolism of nutrients, detoxification of alcohol, and some nutrient storage.

locavore A person who eats locally grown food whenever possible.

low birth weight baby A baby weighing less than 5 ½ pounds at birth.

low-density lipoprotein (LDL) A lipoprotein that deposits cholesterol in the walls of the arteries. Because this can lead to heart disease, LDL is referred to as the *bad* cholesterol carrier.

lower esophageal sphincter (LES) A circular band of muscle between the esophagus and the stomach that opens and closes to allow food to enter the stomach.

lumen The interior of the digestive tract, through which food passes.

lymph Watery fluid that circulates through the body in lymph vessels and eventually enters the blood.

M

macrocytes Abnormally large cells such as red blood cells.

macrocytic anemia A form of anemia characterized by large, immature red blood cells, due to a vitamin B_{12} deficiency.

macronutrients The energy-containing essential nutrients that you need in higher amounts: carbohydrates, lipids (fats), and proteins.

macrosomia A large baby, weighing more than 8 pounds, 13 oz.

major minerals Minerals needed from your diet and in your body in amounts greater than 100 milligrams per day. These include sodium, chloride, potassium, calcium, phosphorus, magnesium, and sulfur. Also called *macrominerals.*

malnourished The long-term outcome of consuming a diet that doesn't meet nutrient needs.

malnutrition The long-term outcome of consuming a diet that contains an imbalance of nutrients.

maltose A disaccharide composed of two glucose units joined together.

marasmus A state of PEM where there is a severe deficiency of calories that perpetuates wasting; also called *starvation.*

marine toxins Chemicals that occur naturally and contaminate some fish.

mast cells Cells in connective tissue to which antibodies attach, setting the stage for potential future allergic reactions.

mechanical digestion Breaking food down through chewing and grinding, or moving it through the GI tract with peristalsis.

medical nutrition therapy The integration of nutrition counseling and dietary changes based on an individual's medical and health needs to treat a patient's medical condition.

megadose A very large dose or amount.

megaloblasts Large, immature red blood cells.

menaquinone The form of vitamin K produced by bacteria in the colon.

messenger RNA (mRNA) A type of RNA that copies the genetic information encoded in DNA and carries it out of the nucleus of the cell to synthesize the protein.

metabolism The numerous reactions that occur within the cell. The calories in foods are converted to energy in the cells of the body.

micelles Small transport carriers in the intestine that enable fatty acids and other compounds to be absorbed.

micronutrients Essential nutrients that you need in smaller amounts: vitamins and minerals.

microsomal ethanol-oxidizing system (MEOS) The other major enzyme system in the liver that metabolizes alcohol.

microvilli Tiny projections on the villi in the small intestine that increase the surface area even more.

milestones Objectives or significant events that occur during development.

minerals Inorganic elements essential to the nutrition of humans.

moderate alcohol consumption An average consumption of up to one drink per day for women and up to two drinks per day for men, as well as no more than three drinks in any single day for women and no more than four drinks in a single day for men.

modified atmosphere packaging (MAP) A food preservation technique that changes the composition of the air surrounding the food in a package to extend the food's shelf life.

monoglyceride A glycerol with only one attached fatty acid.

monosaccharide One sugar unit. There are three monosaccharides: glucose, fructose, and galactose.

monosodium glutamate (MSG) A flavor enhancer.

monounsaturated fatty acid (MUFA) A fatty acid that has one double bond.

MSG symptom complex A series of reactions such as numbness, burning sensation, facial pressure or tightness, chest pain, rapid heart beat, and drowsiness that can occur in some individuals after they consume MSG.

mucus Viscous, slippery secretions found in saliva and other digestive juices.

muscle endurance The ability of a muscle to produce prolonged effort.

muscle strength The greatest amount of force exerted by a muscle at one time.

myoglobin The oxygen-carrying, heme-containing protein found in muscle cells.

MyPlate A tool that depicts five food groups using the familiar mealtime visual of a place setting. It is part of a USDA Web-based initiative to provide consumer information with a food guidance system to help you build a healthy diet based on the current *Dietary Guidelines for Americans*.

N

naturally occurring sugars Sugars such as fructose and lactose that are found naturally in fruit and dairy foods.

neural tube defects Any major birth defect of the central nervous system, including the brain, caused by failure of the neural tube to properly close during fetal development.

neurotoxins Toxins that affect the nerves and can cause symptoms including mild numbness or tingling in the face, arms, and legs, as well as headaches and dizziness. Severe cases could result in death.

niacin equivalents (NE) A measurement that reflects the amount of niacin and tryptophan in foods that can be used to synthesize niacin.

nicotinamide One of the two active forms of niacin that are derived from foods.

nicotinic acid One of the two active forms of niacin that are derived from foods.

night blindness The inability to see in dim light or at night due to a deficiency of vitamin A.

nitrates (nitrites) Substances that can be added to foods to function as a preservative and to give meats such as hot dogs and luncheon meats a pink color.

nitrogen balance The state in which an individual is consuming the same amount of nitrogen (from protein) in the diet as he or she is excreting in the urine.

nonessential amino acids The 11 amino acids that the body can synthesize.

nonexercise-associated thermogenesis (NEAT) The energy expenditure that occurs during nonexercise movements, such as fidgeting, standing, and chewing gum.

normal blood pressure Less than 120 mm Hg (systolic—the top number) and less than 80 mm Hg (diastolic—the bottom number). Referred to as 120/80.

norovirus The most common type of virus that causes foodborne illness. Noroviruses can cause gastroenteritis, or the "stomach flu." Also known as *Norwalk-like viruses*.

nutrient content claims Claims on the label that describe the level or amount of a nutrient in a food product.

nutrient density The amount of nutrients per calorie in a given food. Nutrient-dense foods provide more nutrients per calorie than less nutrient-dense foods.

nutrients Compounds in foods that sustain your body processes. There are six classes of nutrients: carbohydrates, fats (lipids), proteins, vitamins, minerals, and water.

nutrition The science that studies how the nutrients and compounds in foods that you eat nourish and affect your body functions and health.

Nutrition Facts panel The area on the food label that provides a uniform listing of specific nutrients obtained in one serving of the food.

nutritional genomics A field of study that researches the relationship between nutrition and genomics (the study of genes and gene expression).

nutritionist A generic term with no recognized legal or professional meaning. Some people may call themselves nutritionists without having any credible training in nutrition.

O

obesity Carrying an excessive amount of body fat above the level of being overweight. Clinically defined as having a body mass index (BMI) of 30 or higher.

observational research Research that involves looking at factors in two or more groups of subjects to see if there is a relationship to certain outcomes.

oils Fats that are liquid at room temperature.

open dating Typically found on perishable items such as meat, poultry, eggs, and dairy foods; must contain a calendar date.

organic Describes compounds that contain carbon. Also used to describe foods that are free of chemical-based pesticides, synthetic fertilizers, irradiation, and bioengineering. A USDA-accredited certifying inspector must certify organic foods.

organophosphates A group of synthetic pesticides that adversely affect the nervous systems of pests.

osmosis The movement of a solvent, such as water, from an area of lower concentration of solutes across a membrane to an area of higher concentration of solutes. It balances the concentration of solutes between the compartments.

osteocalcin The protein in bone that binds with bone-strengthening calcium.

osteomalacia The adult equivalent of rickets, causing muscle and bone weakness, and pain.

osteopenia A condition in which bone mineral density is lower than normal but not low enough to be classified as osteoporosis.

osteoporosis A condition in which the bones are less dense, increasing the risk of fractures.

overnutrition A state of excess nutrients and calories in the diet.

overpopulation When a region has more people than its natural resources can support.

overweight Carrying extra weight on your body in relation to your height. Clinically defined as having a body mass index (BMI) of 25 to 29.9.

oxidation The process during which oxygen combines with other molecules.

P

pancreas Accessory organ of digestion that produces hormones and enzymes. It's connected to the duodenum via the bile duct.

paralytic shellfish poisoning A condition caused by consuming shellfish contaminated with neurotoxins.

parasites Organisms that live on or in another organism, obtaining nourishment from it.

parathyroid hormone (PTH) The hormone secreted from the parathyroid glands that activates vitamin D formation in the kidney.

passive diffusion The process of absorbing nutrients across the intestinal cell membrane from a high concentration to a low concentration.

pasteurization The process of heating liquids or food at high temperatures to destroy foodborne pathogens.

pathogens Collective term for disease-causing microorganisms (microbes). Includes viruses, bacteria, and parasites. The most common source of foodborne illness.

peak bone mass The genetically determined maximum amount of bone mass an individual can build up.

peer-reviewed journal A research journal in which fellow scientists (peers) review studies to assess if they are accurate and sound before they are published.

pellagra The disease caused by a deficiency of niacin in the body.

pendular movement A constrictive wave that involves both forward and reverse movements of chyme and enhances nutrient absorption.

pepsin A digestive enzyme produced in the stomach that breaks down protein.

peptic ulcers Sores, erosions, or breaks in the mucosal lining of the stomach.

peptide bonds The bonds that connect amino acids, created when the acid group of one amino acid is joined with the nitrogen-containing amine group of another amino acid.

percentile The most commonly used clinical indicator to assess the size and growth patterns of children in the United States. An individual child is ranked according to the percentage of the reference population he equals or exceeds.

peristalsis The forward, rhythmic motion that moves food through the digestive system. Peristalsis is a form of mechanical digestion because it influences motion, but it does not add chemical secretions.

pernicious anemia A form of anemia characterized by large, immature red blood cells, due to a lack of intrinsic factor.

pesticides Substances that kill or repel pests such as insects, weeds, microorganisms, rodents, or fungi.

pharynx The throat. Passageway for the respiratory (air) and digestive tracts (food and beverages).

phospholipids Lipids made up of two fatty acids and a phosphate group attached to a glycerol backbone.

photosynthesis A process by which green plants create carbohydrates using the energy from sunlight.

phylloquinone The form of vitamin K found in green plants.

physical activity Voluntary movement that results in energy expenditure (burning calories).

physical fitness The ability to perform physical activities requiring cardiorespiratory endurance, muscle endurance, and strength and/or flexibility; physical fitness is acquired through physical activity and adequate nutrition.

phytochemicals Plant chemicals that have been shown to reduce the risk of certain diseases such as cancer and heart disease. Beta-carotene is a phytochemical.

phytosterols Naturally occurring sterols found in plants. Phytosterols lower LDL cholesterol levels by competing with cholesterol for absorption in the intestinal tract.

picky eating Unwillingness to try unfamiliar foods.

placebo A sugar pill that has no impact on the individual's health when ingested.

placenta The organ that allows nutrients, oxygen, and waste products to be exchanged between a mother and fetus.

plant breeding A type of biotechnology in which two plants are crossbred to produce offspring with desired traits from both.

plaque The hardened buildup of cholesterol-laden foam cells, platelets, cellular waste products, and calcium in the arteries that results in atherosclerosis.

political sanctions Boycotts or trade embargoes used by one country or international group to apply political pressure on another.

polychlorinated biphenyls (PCBs) Synthetic chemicals that have been shown to cause cancer and other adverse effects on the immune, reproductive, nervous, and endocrine systems in animals. PCBs may cause cancer in humans.

polyneuritis Inflammation of the peripheral nerves.

polysaccharide Many sugar units combined. Starch, glycogen, and fiber are all polysaccharides.

polyunsaturated fatty acid (PUFA) A fatty acid with two or more double bonds.

poverty Lacking the means to provide for material or comfort needs.

precision agriculture A cost-efficient, precise farming method that uses new technologies to collect data about variations in field soil to better manage the use of appropriate seeds, fertilizer, water, and pesticides for the growing of crops with less waste. Also known as *satellite farming*.

precursor A substance that is converted into or leads to the formation of another substance.

preformed vitamin A The form of vitamin A that is readily used by the body.

preformed vitamins Vitamins that are found in active form in foods.

pregnancy-induced hypertension A category of hypertension that includes *gestational hypertension* (occurs in pregnancy in a woman without a prior history of high blood pressure), *preeclampsia* (hypertension, severe edema, and protein loss occur), and *eclampsia* (can result in seizures; may be extremely dangerous for mother and baby).

premenstrual syndrome (PMS) A variety of symptoms such as moodiness, irritability, bloating, and anxiety that some women may experience during the menstrual cycle.

preschoolers Children aged 3 to 5 years old.

prions Misfolded proteins that can act as disease agents. An abnormal prion protein is the cause of mad cow disease.

prior-sanctioned Having previous approval.

progressive overload principle A gradual increase in exercise demands resulting from modifications to the frequency, intensity, time, or type of activity.

proportionality The relationship of one entity to another. Vegetables and fruits should be consumed in a higher proportion than dairy and protein foods in the diet.

protein digestibility corrected amino acid score (PDCAAS) A score measured as a percentage that takes into account both digestibility and amino acid profile and gives a good indication of the quality of a protein.

protein quality The measure of a protein's digestibility and how its amino acid pattern compares with your body's needs. Proteins that are more easily digested and have a complete set of amino acids are of higher quality.

protein turnover The continual process of degrading and synthesizing protein. When the daily amount of degraded protein is equivalent to the amount that is synthesized, you are in protein balance.

protein-energy malnutrition (PEM) A lack of sufficient dietary protein and/or calories.

proteins Compounds in your body that consist of numerous amino acids and are found in all living cells.

provitamin A carotenoids The family of compounds that includes beta-carotene that can be used to make vitamin A in the body.

provitamins Substances found in foods that can be converted into an active vitamin form once they are absorbed.

public health nutritionist An individual who may have an undergraduate degree in nutrition but isn't an RDN.

purging Measures taken to prevent weight gain or to lose weight after consuming food; examples include self-induced vomiting, laxatives, diuretics (water pills), excessive exercise, and/or fasting.

pyloric sphincter Sphincter in the bottom of the stomach that separates the pylorus from the duodenum of the small intestine.

pyridoxine The major form of vitamin B_6 found in plants foods, supplements, and fortified foods.

R

rancidity The decomposition, or spoiling, of fats through oxidation.

rating of perceived exertion (RPE) A subjective measure of the intensity level of an activity using a numerical scale.

recombinant bovine somatotropin (rbST) A synthetically made hormone identical to a cow's natural growth hormone, somatotropin, that stimulates milk production. Also known as *rbGH (recombinant bovine growth hormone)*.

Recommended Dietary Allowance (RDA) The average amount of a nutrient that meets the needs of 97 to 98 percent of individuals in a similar age and gender group. The RDA is higher than the EAR.

rectum The lowest part of the large intestine, continuous with the sigmoid colon and the anus.

refined grains Grain foods that are made with only the endosperm of the kernel. The bran and germ are not included.

registered dietitian nutritionist (RDN) A health professional who has completed at least a bachelor's degree in nutrition from an accredited university or college in the United States, completed a supervised practice, and passed an exam administered by the Academy of Nutrition and Dietetics (AND).

remineralization The repairing of teeth by adding back the minerals lost during tooth decay. Saliva can help remineralize teeth.

repetition maximum (RM) The maximum amount of weight that can be lifted for a specified number of repetitions.

retinoids The family or group of substances that include retinol, retinal, and retinoic acid.

retinol The most usable form of preformed vitamin A.

retinol activity equivalents (RAE) The unit of measure used to describe the total amount of all forms of preformed vitamin A and provitamin A carotenoids in food.

retort canning The process of subjecting already-canned foods to an additional high-temperature heat source to destroy potential pathogens.

rhodopsin A compound found in the rods of the eye that is needed for night vision.

rickets A vitamin D deficiency in children, resulting in soft bones.

risk assessment The process of determining the potential human health risks posed by exposure to substances such as pesticides.

RNA A molecule that carries out the orders of DNA.

rods Light-absorbing cells responsible for black-and-white vision and night vision.

S

saliva Watery fluid secreted by the salivary glands in the mouth. Saliva moistens food and makes it easier to swallow.

sashimi A type of sushi that primarily consists of raw seafood, sliced into thin pieces and served with a dipping sauce (soy sauce with wasabi paste) or other condiments (such as fresh ginger).

satiation The feeling during eating that determines how long and how much you eat.

satiety The sensation that you feel when you have had enough to eat. It determines how long you will go between meals and/or snacks.

saturated fats Fats that contain mostly saturated fatty acids.

saturated fatty acid A fatty acid that has all of its carbons bound with hydrogen.

school-aged children Children between the ages of 6 and 11.

scientific method A stepwise process used by scientists to generate sound research findings.

scombrotoxic fish poisoning A condition caused by consuming spoiled fish that contain large amounts of histamines.

scurvy A disease caused by a deficiency of vitamin C and characterized by bleeding gums and a skin rash.

segmentation A "sloshing" motion that thoroughly mixes chyme with the chemical secretions of the intestine.

selenosis The presence of toxic levels of selenium.

sex pheromones Naturally occurring chemicals secreted by one organism to attract another; used as a biopesticide to control pests by interfering with their mating.

sickle-cell anemia A blood disorder caused by a genetic defect in the development of hemoglobin. Sickle-cell anemia causes the red blood cells to distort into a sickle shape and can damage organs and tissues.

side chain The side group of an amino acid that provides it with its unique qualities; also referred to as the *R group*.

simple carbohydrates A category of carbohydrates that contain a single sugar unit or two sugar units combined. Monosaccharides and disaccharides are simple carbohydrates.

small intestine Comprised of the duodenum, jejunum, and ileum, the small intestine is the longest part of the GI tract. Most of the digestion and absorption of food occurs in the small intestine.

social drinking Drinking patterns that are considered acceptable by society.

solid foods Foods other than breast milk or formula given to an infant, usually around 6 months of age.

soluble fiber A type of fiber that dissolves in water and is fermented by intestinal bacteria. Many soluble fibers are viscous and have gummy or thickening properties.

solvent A liquid that acts as a medium in which substances dissolve. Water is considered the universal solvent.

spina bifida A serious birth defect in which the spinal cord is malformed and lacks the protective membrane coat.

spores Hardy reproductive structures that are produced by certain bacteria. Some bacterial spores can survive boiling temperature (212°F).

starch The storage form of glucose in plants.

starvation To suffer severely from lack of food; a state in which the body breaks down its own tissue for fuel.

sterol A lipid that contains four connecting rings of carbon and hydrogen.

stomach Digestive organ that holds food after it's moved down the esophagus and before it is propelled into the small intestine.

stool (feces) Waste products that are stored in the large intestine and then excreted from the body. Consists mostly of bacteria, sloughed-off gastrointestinal cells, inorganic matter, water, unabsorbed nutrients, food residue, undigested fibers, fatty acids, mucus, and remnants of digestive fluids.

strength training Exercising with weights or other resistance to build, strengthen, and tone muscle to improve or maintain overall fitness; also called *resistance training*.

stroke A condition caused by a lack of oxygen to the brain that could result in paralysis and possibly death.

stroke volume The amount of blood pumped by the heart with each heart beat.

structure/function claims Claims on the label that describe how a nutrient or dietary compound affects the structure or function of the human body.

subcutaneous fat The fat located under the skin.

sucrose A disaccharide composed of glucose and fructose; also known as table sugar.

sugar substitutes Alternatives to table sugar that sweeten foods for fewer calories.

sulfites Preservatives used to help prevent foods from turning brown and to inhibit the growth of microbes. Often used in wine and dried fruit products.

sushi A Japanese dish of cooked, vinegared rice served with fish or other seafood, vegetables, and/or seaweed.

sustainable food system A system that conserves the natural resources and can be maintained indefinitely.

systolic pressure The force of your blood against the artery walls when your heart beats.

T

target heart rate A heart rate in beats per minute (expressed as a percentage of maximum heart rate) achieved during exercise that indicates the intensity of the exercise.

thermic effect of food (TEF) The amount of calories the body uses to digest, absorb, metabolize, and store food.

thermogenesis The production of heat in body cells.

thirst mechanism Various bodily reactions caused by dehydration that signal you to drink fluids.

toddlers Children aged 1 to 3 years old.

Tolerable Upper Intake Level (UL) The highest amount of a nutrient that can be consumed daily without harm in a similar age and gender group of individuals.

tongue-thrust reflex A forceful protrusion of the tongue in response to an oral stimulus, such as a spoon.

toxicity The level at which exposure to a substance becomes harmful.

toxins Poisons produced by living organisms.

trace minerals Minerals needed from your diet and in your body in small amounts, less than 20 milligrams daily. These include iron, zinc, selenium, fluoride, chromium, copper, manganese, and molybdenum. Also called *microminerals*.

trans **fat** Substance that contains mostly *trans* fatty acids.

trans **fatty acids** Substances that result from the hydrogenating of an unsaturated fatty acid, causing a reconfiguring of some of its double bonds. A small amount of *trans* fatty acids occur naturally in animal foods.

transfer RNA (tRNA) A type of RNA that collects the amino acids within the cell that are needed to make a specific protein.

transport proteins Proteins that carry lipids (fat and cholesterol), oxygen, waste products, and vitamins through the blood to various organs and tissues, or that serve as channels to allow substances to pass through cell membranes.

traveler's diarrhea A pathogen-induced intestinal disorder experienced by some travelers who visit areas with unsanitary conditions.

triglyceride Three fatty acids that are attached to a glycerol backbone.

trimesters The three time periods of pregnancy.

tryptophan An amino acid that can be converted to niacin in the body.

type 1 diabetes Autoimmune form of diabetes in which the pancreas does not produce insulin.

type 2 diabetes Form of diabetes characterized by insulin resistance.

U

U.S. Pharmacopeia (USP) A nonprofit organization that sets purity and reliability standards for dietary supplements.

ultraviolet (UV) rays The rays from sunlight that cause the production of vitamin D in the skin.

umbilical cord Cord connecting the fetus to the placenta that allows the transfer of nutrients and waste products between the mother and the fetus.

undernutrition A state of inadequate nutrition whereby a person's nutrient and/or calorie needs aren't met through the diet.

underweight Weighing less than is healthy for your height. Clinically defined as having a body mass index (BMI) below 18.5.

unsaturated fats Fats that contain mostly unsaturated fatty acids.

unsaturated fatty acid A fatty acid that has one or more double bonds between carbons.

urea A nitrogen-containing waste product that is excreted in urine.

V

vegetarian A person who doesn't eat meat, fish, or poultry or (sometimes) foods made from these animal sources.

very low-calorie diet A diet of fewer than 800 calories per day and high in protein.

very-low-density lipoprotein (VLDL) A lipoprotein that delivers fat made in the liver to the tissues. VLDL remnants are converted into LDLs.

villi Projections on the walls of the small intestine that increase the surface area over which nutrients can be absorbed.

virus A microscopic organism that carries genetic information for its own replication; can infect a host and cause illness.

visceral fat The fat stored in the abdominal area.

vitamins Non-energy-providing organic essential nutrients that your body needs in small amounts to grow, reproduce, and maintain good health.

VO₂max The maximum amount of oxygen (ml) a person uses in one minute per kilogram of body weight.

W

warfarin An anticoagulant drug given to prevent blood from clotting.

wasting The diminishment of muscle and fat tissue caused by extremely low energy intake from too little food. It is sometimes referred to as acute malnutrition.

water balance The state whereby an equal amount of water is lost and replenished daily in the body.

weight cycling The repeated gain and loss of body weight.

weight management Maintaining your weight within a healthy range.

Wernicke-Korsakoff syndrome A progressively damaging brain disorder due to chronic thiamin deficiency.

whole grains Grain foods that are made with the entire edible grain kernel: the bran, the endosperm, and the germ.

working poor Individuals or families who are steadily employed but still experience poverty due to low wages or high dependent expenses.

X

xerophthalmia Permanent damage to the cornea causing blindness, due to a prolonged vitamin A deficiency.

Z

zoochemicals Compounds in animal food products that are beneficial to human health. Omega-3 fatty acids are an example of zoochemicals.

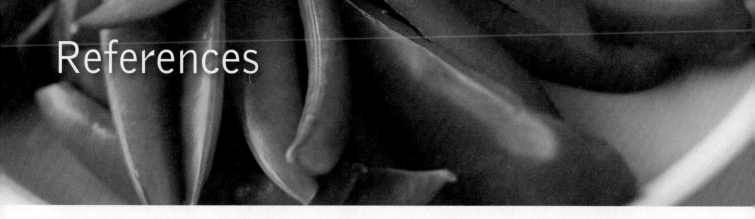

References

Chapter 1

1. Freeland-Graves, J., and S. Nitzke. 2013. Position Paper of the Academy of Nutrition and Dietetics: Total Diet Approach to Healthy Eating. *Journal of the Academy of Nutrition and Dietetics* 113: 307–317.
2. National Turkey Federation. 2011. Turkey Facts and Trivia. Available at www.eatturkey.com. Accessed February 2013.
3. Freeland-Graves, J. 2013.
4. National Restaurant Association. 2011. Pizza Is King of Super Bowl Takeout. Available at www.restaurant.org. Accessed February 2013.
5. Mintel International Group. 2005. Cinemas and Movie Theaters-United States, Mintel Reports-USA, Leisure-USA. Available at www.reports.mintel.com. Accessed March 2006.
6. United States Department of Agriculture, Economic Research Service. 2013. Food Security in the U.S.: Key Statistics and Graphics. Available at www.ers.usda.gov. Accessed September 2013.
7. Freeland-Graves, J. 2013.; Carlson, A., and Frazao, E. 2012. Are Healthy Foods Really More Expensive? It Depends How You Measure the Price. Available at www.ers.usda.gov. Accessed February 2013.
8. Freeland-Graves, J. 2013.
9. Specialty Coffee Association. 2012. Specialty Coffee in the USA 2008–2009. Available at www.scaa.org. Accessed November 2012.
10. Mintel International Group. 2012. Breakfast Foods-US; Mintel International Group. 2012. Fruit Juice and Juice Drinks-US. Available at www.reports.mintel.com. Accessed February 2013.
11. Centers for Disease Control. 2013. Leading Causes of Death in the United States, Preliminary Data for 2011. Available at www.cdc.gov.
12. U.S. Department of Agriculture, U.S. Department of Health and Human Services. 2010. *Dietary Guidelines for Americans, 2010.* 7th ed. Washington, D.C.: U.S. Government Printing Office.
13. Ibid.
14. U.S. Department of Agriculture, Agricultural Research Service. 2012. Nutrient Intakes from Food: Mean Amounts Consumed per Individual, by Gender and Age, *What We Eat in America*, NHANES 2009–2010. Available at www.ars.usda.gov.
15. U.S. Department of Agriculture, U.S. Department of Health and Human Services. 2010.
16. U.S. Department of Agriculture, U.S. Department of Health and Human Services, Marra, M., and A. Boyar. 2009. Position of the American Dietetic Association: Nutrient Supplement. *Journal of the American Dietetic Association* 109: 2073–2085.
17. Todd, J., L. Mancino, and B. Lin. 2010. The Impact of Food Away from Home on Adult Diet Quality, ERR-90, U.S. Department of Agriculture, Economic Research Service.
18. Ibid.
19. Mancino, L., J. Todd, and B. Lin. 2009. Separating What We Eat from Where. Measuring the Effect of Food Away from Home on Diet Quality. *Food Policy* 34: 557–562.
20. United States Department of Agriculture. 2010. *Report of the Dietary Guideline Advisory Committee on the* Dietary Guidelines for Americans, 2010. Available at www.cnpp.usda.gov. Accessed March 2011.
21. Ibid.
22. Centers for Disease Control. 2012. Obesity and Overweight. Available at www.cdc.gov. Accessed February 2012.
23. Ibid.
24. U.S. Department of Health and Preventative Services. 2010. *Healthy People 2020.* Available at www. healthypeople.gov. Accessed February 2013.
25. Fox, S., and M. Duggan. 2013. Health Online 2013. Pew Research Center's Internet & American Life Project. Available at www.pewinternet.org. Accessed February 2013.
26. National Center for Complementary and Alternative Medicine. Updated 2006. 10 Things to Know about Evaluating Medical Resources on the Web. Available at www.nccam.nih.gov. Accessed February 2013.

Feature Box References

1. The Academy of Nutrition and Dietetics. 2012. *Hungry and Overweight: How Is It Possible?* Available at www.hendpg.org. Accessed February 2013.
2. Ibid.
3. Ibid.; USDA. April 2012. The Food Environment, Eating Out, and Body Weight: A Review of the Evidence. *Nutrition Insight 49.* Available at www.cnpp.usda.gov. Accessed February 2013.
4. Debusk, R. M., C. P. Fogarty, J. M. Ordovas, and K. S. Kornman. 2005. Nutritional Genomics in Practice: Where Do We Begin? *Journal of the American Dietetic Association* 105: 589–598.

Two Points of View References

1. Better Business Bureau. 2013. Children's Food and Beverage Advertising Initiative. Available at www.bbb.org. Accessed August 2013.
2. Veerman, J. L., et al. 2009. By How Much Would Limiting TV Food Advertising Reduce Childhood Obesity? *European Journal of Public Health* 19: 365–369; Children Now. 2009. The Impact of Industry Self-Regulation on the Nutritional Quality of Foods Advertised on Television to Children. Available at www.childrennow.org. Accessed August 2013; Harris, J. L., et al. 2013. Redefining "Child-Directed Advertising" to Reduce Unhealthy Television Food Advertising. *American Journal of Preventive Medicine* 44: 358–364.
3. Carter, O. B., et al. 2011. Children's Understanding of the Selling Versus Persuasive Intent of Junk Food Advertising: Implications for Regulation. *Social Science Medicine* 72: 962–968.
4. Graff, S., et al. 2012. Government Can Regulate Food Advertising to Children Because Cognitive Research Shows That It Is Inherently Misleading. *Health Affairs (Millwood)* 31: 392–398.
5. Committee on Food Marketing and the Diets of Children and Youth. Institute of Medicine of the National Academies. 2006. Food Marketing to Children and Youth: Threat or Opportunity? Available at www.nap.edu. Accessed August 2013.
6. Redish, M. H. 2011. Childhood Obesity, Advertising, and the First Amendment. Available at www.gmaonline.org. Accessed August 2013.
7. University of Michigan Health System. 2010. Your Child: Development and Behavior Resources: Television and Children. Available at www.med.umich.edu. Accessed August 2013.
8. Cheeseman, G. M. 2011. McDonald's Stands Its Ground: Advertising to Children Is OK. Available at www.triplepundit.com. Accessed August 2013.
9. Ashton, D. 2004. Food Advertising and Childhood Obesity. *Journal of the Royal Society of Medicine* 97: 51–52.

Chapter 2

1. Institute of Medicine. 2003. *Dietary Reference Intakes: Applications in Dietary Planning.* Washington, D.C.: The National Academies Press. Updated 2013. Available at http://fnic.nal.usda.gov. Accessed February 2013.
2. Davis, C., and E. Saltos. 1999. Chapter 2: Dietary Recommendations and How They Have Changed Over Time. In E. Frazo, ed., *America's Eating Habits: Changes and Consequences.* Agriculture Information Bulletin No. AIB750. Available at www.ers.usda.gov. Accessed September 2005.
3. Lee, P. R. 1978. Nutrition Policy: From Neglect and Uncertainty to Debate and Action. *Journal of the American Dietetics Association* 72: 581–588.

4. U.S. Department of Agriculture. 2010. *2010 Report of the Dietary Guidelines Advisory Committee.* Available at www.cnpp.usda.gov. Accessed February 2013.
5. Ibid.
6. Ibid.
7. Center for Food Safety and Applied Nutrition. 2013. A Food Labeling Guide. Available at www.fda.gov. Accessed March 2013.
8. Food and Drug Administration. 2012. Guidance for Industry: A Food Labeling Guide. Available at www.fda.gov. Accessed March 2013.
9. Ibid.
10. Food Safety and Inspection Service. 2007. A Guide to Federal Food Labeling Requirements for Meat and Poultry Products. Available at www.fsis.usda.gov. Accessed March 2013.
11. Ibid.
12. Food and Drug Administration. 2012. Guidance for Industry: A Food Labeling Guide.
13. Farley, D. 1993. Look for "Legit" Health Claims on Foods. *FDA Consumer Magazine;* 27: 21–28.
14. Center for Food Safety and Applied Nutrition. 2013. Claims That Can Be Made for Conventional Foods and Dietary Supplements. Available at www.fda.gov. Accessed March 2013.
15. Ibid.
16. Ibid.

Feature Box References

1. USDA Nutrition Insights. 2000. Servings Sizes in the Food Guide Pyramid and on the Nutrition Facts Label: What's Different and Why? Available at www.cnpp.usda.gov. Accessed March 2013.
2. USDA Nutrition Insights. 2012. The Food Environment, Eating Out, and Body Weight: A Review of the Evidence. Available at www.cnpp.usda.gov. Accessed March 2013.
3. Young, L. R., and M. Nestle. 2003. Expanding Portion Sizes in the U. S. Marketplace: Implications for Nutrition Counseling. *Journal of the American Dietetic Association* 103: 231–234.
4. Rolls, B. 2003. The Supersizing of America: Portion Size and the Obesity Epidemic. *Nutrition Today* 38: 42–53.
5. Rolls, B., L. S. Roe, and J. S. Meengs. 2006. Larger Portion Sizes Lead to a Sustained Increase in Energy Intake Over 2 Days. *Journal of the American Dietetic Association* 106: 543–549.
6. U.S. Department of Agriculture. 2010. *2010 Report of the Dietary Guidelines Advisory Committee.* Available at www.cnpp.usda.gov. Accessed February 2013.
7. J. M. de Castro. 2003. The Time of Day of Food Intake Influences Overall Intake in Humans. *Journal of Nutrition* 134: 104–111.
8. Ibid.
9. S. H. Holt, J. C. Miller, P. Petocz, and E. Farmakalidis. 1995. A Satiety Index of Common Foods. *European Journal of Clinical Nutrition* 49: 675–690.
10. J. M. Kerver, E. Yang, S. Obayashi, L. Bianchi, and W. Song. 2006. Meal and Snack Patterns Are Associated with Dietary Intake of Energy and Nutrients in U.S. Adults. *Journal of the American Dietetic Association* 106: 46–54.
11. N. K. A. Stockman, T. C. Schenkel, J. N. Brown, and A. Duncan. 2005. Comparison of Energy and Nutrient Intakes among Meals and Snacks of Adolescent Males. *Preventive Medicine* 41: 203–210.
12. Ibid.
13. H. R. Wyatt, G. K. Grunwald, C. L. Mosca, M. L. Klem, R. R. Wing, and J. O. Hill. 2002. Long-Term Weight Loss and Breakfast in Subjects in the National Weight Control Registry. *Obesity Research* 10: 78–82.
14. R. H. Striegel-Moore, D. L. Franko, D. Thompson, S. Affenito, and H. C. Kraemer. 2006. Night Eating: Prevalence and Demographic Correlates. *Obesity* 14: 139–147.
15. F. Halberg. 1989. Some Aspects of the Chronobiology of Nutrition: More Work Is Needed on 'When to Eat.' *Journal of Nutrition* 119: 333–343.
16. N. K. A. Stockman, et al. 2005. Comparison of Energy and Nutrient Intakes.
17. N. L. Keim, M. D. Van Loan, W. F. Horn, T. F. Barbieri, and P. L. Mayclin. 1997. Weight Loss Is Greater with Consumption of Large Morning Meals and Fat-Free Mass Is Preserved with Large Evening Meals in Women on a Controlled Weight Reduction Program. *Journal of Nutrition* 127: 75–82.
18. [illegible]aines, M. Y. Hama, D. K. Guilkey, and B. M. Popkin. 2003. [illegible]d Eating in the United States Is Linked with Greater Energy, Fat, [illegible]ohol Intake. *Obesity Research* 11: 945–949.

19. Hasler, C., and A. Brown. 2009. Position of the American Dietetic Association: Functional Foods. *Journal of the American Dietetic Association* 109: 735–746; IFIC. 2011. Functional Foods. Available at www.ific.org. Accessed March 2013.
20. IFIC. 2011. Functional Foods.
21. Dornlaser, L., and D. Jago. 2011. Functional Foods: Dead or Alive? Mintel International. Available at www.mintel.com. Accessed March 2013.
22. IFIC. 2011. 2011 Functional Foods/Foods for Health Consumer Trending Survey. Available at www.foodinsight.org. Accessed March 2013.
23. Hasler. 2009. Position of the American Dietetic Association: Functional Foods; IFIC. 2011. Functional Foods.
24. Riediger, N., R. Othman, M. Suh, and M. Moghadasian. 2009. A Systemic Review of the Roles of ω-3 Fatty Acids in Health and Disease. *Journal of the American Dietetic Association* 109: 668–679.

Two Points of View References

1. Responsible Reform for the Middle Class. 2010. The Patient Protection and Affordable Care Act Detailed Summary. Available at www.dpc.senate.gov. Accessed August 2013.
2. Robert Wood Johnson Foundation. 2013. Impact of Menu Labeling on Consumer Behavior: A 2008–2012 Update. Available at www.rwjf.org. Accessed August 2013.
3. USDA Economic Research Service. 2011. Will Calorie Labeling in Restaurants Make a Difference? Available at www.ers.usda.gov. Accessed August 2013.
4. U.S. Food and Drug Administration. 2013. Questions and Answers on the New Menu and Vending Machines Nutrition Labeling Requirements. Available at www.fda.gov. Accessed August 2013.
5. Ibid.
6. Robert Wood Johnson Foundation. Impact of Menu Labeling on Consumer Behavior.
7. Stanford Graduate School of Business. 2011. New Stanford Study Shows Posting Calories on Restaurant Menu Boards Lowers Customers' Calorie Counts per Visit. Available at www.gsb.stanford.edu. Accessed August 2013.
8. Ibid.
9. Robert Wood Johnson Foundation. Impact of Menu Labeling on Consumer Behavior.
10. Sapatkin, D. 2013. Restaurants' Nutrition Labels: How Big an Impact? *The Philadelphia Inquirer.* Available at http://articles.philly.com. Accessed August 2013.

Chapter 3

1. Mahan, K., and S. Escott-Stump. 2008. *Krause's Food & Nutrition Therapy.* 12th ed. St. Louis: Saunders Elsevier.
2. Marieb, E. N., and K. Hoehn. 2012. *Human Anatomy and Physiology.* 9th ed. San Francisco: Benjamin Cummings.
3. Tortora, G. J., and B. H. Derrickson. 2011. *Principles of Anatomy and Physiology.* 13th ed. New York: Harper & Row Publishers.
4. Hole, J. W. 1984. *Human Anatomy and Physiology.* 3rd ed. Dubuque, IA: WC Brown Publishers.
5. Marieb. *Human Anatomy and Physiology.*
6. Ganong, W. F. 1977. *Review of Medical Physiology.* 8th ed. Los Altos, CA: Lange Medical Publications.
7. Mahan. *Krause's Food & Nutrition Therapy.*
8. Gropper, S. S., and J. L. Smith. 2012. *Advanced Nutrition and Human Metabolism.* 6th ed. Belmont, CA: Wadsworth Cengage Learning.
9. Guyton, A. C. 1981. *Textbook of Medical Physiology.* 6th ed. Philadelphia: Saunders.
10. Ganong. *Review of Medical Physiology.*
11. Gropper. *Advanced Nutrition and Human Metabolism.*
12. Guyton. *Textbook of Medical Physiology.*
13. Marieb. *Human Anatomy and Physiology.*
14. Mahan. *Krause's Food & Nutrition Therapy.*
15. Gropper. *Advanced Nutrition and Human Metabolism.*
16. Ibid.
17. U.S. Department of Health and Human Services. 2010. Oral Health. Available at www.womenshealth.gov. Accessed March 2013.
18. Ibid.
19. Nelson, J. K., K. E. Moxness, M. D. Jensen, and C. F. Gastineau. 1994. *Mayo Clinic Diet Manual.* 7th ed. St. Louis: Mosby.
20. American Cancer Society. 2012. Esophagus Cancer Overview. Available at www.cancer.org. Accessed May 2013.

21. Anderson, D. M. 2002. *Mosby's Medical, Nursing and Allied Health Dictionary*. 6th ed. St. Louis: Mosby.
22. Nelson, et al. *Mayo Clinic Diet Manual*.
23. National Digestive Diseases Information Clearinghouse, National Institute of Diabetes and Digestive and Kidney Diseases (NIDDK). 2012. Irritable Bowel Syndrome. Available at http://digestive.niddk.nih.gov. Accessed March 2013.
24. National Digestive Diseases Information Clearinghouse, National Institute of Diabetes and Digestive and Kidney Diseases (NIDDK). 2011. Crohn's Disease. Available at http://digestive.niddk.nih.gov. Accessed March 2013.

Two Points of View References

1. Sanders, M. E., et al. 2013. An Update on the Use and Investigation of Probiotics in Health and Disease. *Gut*. Available at doi:10.1136/gutjnl-2012-302504 Accessed March 2013.
2. Chmielewska, A., and H. Szajewska. 2010. Systematic Review of Randomised Controlled Trials: Priobiotics for Functional Constipation. *World Journal of Gastroenterology* 16: 69–75; Marteau P., P. Seksik, and R. Jian. 2002. Probiotics and Intestinal Health Effects: A Clinical Perspective. *British Journal of Nutrition* 88 Suppl 1: S51–S57.
3. Douglas, L. C., and M. E. Sanders. 2008. "Probiotics and Probiotics in Dietetics Practice." *Journal of the American Dietetic Association* 108: 510–521.
4. American Gastroenterological Association, Patient Center. 2008. Probiotics: What They Are and What They Can Do For You. Available at www.gastro.org. Accessed May 2010.
5. McGee, E. 2009. Answers to Your Questions About Probiotics. Available at www.webmd.com. Accessed July 2010.
6. FDA. 2006. Guidance for Industry on Complementary and Alternative Medicine Products and Their Regulation by the Food and Drug Administration. Available at www.fda.gov. Accessed July 2010.
7. American Dietetic Association. 2009. Hot Topics Sheet on Probiotics and Digestion. Available at www.eatright.org. Accessed May 2010.
8. National Center for Complementary and Alternative Medicine. 2012. An Introduction to Probiotics. Available at http://nccam.nih.gov. Accessed May 2013.
9. Joint FAO/WHO Working Group Report on Drafting Guidelines for the Evaluation of Probiotics in Food, London, Ontario, Canada, April 30 and May 1, 2002. Available at www.who.int/foodsafety/fs_management/en/probiotic_guidelines.pdf. Accessed May 2013.

Chapter 4

1. Oldways. 2013. The Heritage Pyramids. Available at http://oldwayspt.org. Accessed March 2013.
2. Johnson, M. 2014. *Human Biology: Concepts and Current Issues*. 7th ed. San Francisco: Benjamin Cummings.
3. Institute of Medicine. 2002. *Dietary Reference Intakes for Energy, Carbohydrate, Fiber, Fat, Fatty Acids, Cholesterol, Protein, and Amino Acids*. Washington, D.C.: The National Academies Press; U.S. Department of Agriculture, Agricultural Research Service. 2012. Nutrient Intakes from Food: Mean Amounts Consumed per Individual, by Gender and Age, *What We Eat in America*, NHANES 2009–2010. Available at www.ars.usda.gov. Accessed March 2013.
4. Ibid.
5. Centers for Disease Control and Prevention. 2012. How to Use Fruits and Vegetables to Manage Your Weight. Available at www.cdc.gov. Accessed March 2013.
6. U.S. Department of Agriculture/Economic Research Service. Food Availability (Per Capita) Data System 2011. Available at www.ers.usda.gov. Accessed March 2013.
7. Fitch, C., and K. Keim. 2012. Position of the Academy of Nutrition and Dietetics: Use of Nutritive and Nonnutritive Sweeteners. *Journal of the Academy of Nutrition and Dietetics*; 112: 739–758.
8. Horn, L., et al. 2010. Translation and Implementation of Added Sugars Consumption Recommendations. *Circulation* 122: 2470–2490.
9. Fitch. 2012. Position of the Academy of Nutrition and Dietetics: Use of Nutritive and Nonnutritive Sweeteners.
10. U.S. Department of Agriculture, U.S. Department of Health and Human Services. 2010. *Dietary Guidelines for Americans, 2010*. 7th ed. Washington, D.C.: U.S. Government Printing Office.
11. Ibid.
12. Horn. 2010. Translation and Implementation of Added Sugars; Johnson, R. K., et al. 2009. Dietary Sugars Intake and Cardiovascular Health. A Scientific Statement from the American Heart Association. *Circulation* 120: 1011–1020.

13. Fitch. 2012. Position of the Academy of Nutrition and Dietetics: Use of Nutritive and Nonnutritive Sweeteners.
14. Ibid.
15. Calorie Control Council. n.d. Reduced-Calorie Sweeteners: Hydrogenated Starch Hydrolysates. Available at www.caloriecontrol.org. Accessed March 2003.
16. Public Health Service, National Toxicology Program. 2000. Report on Carcinogens, 9th ed.
17. Ajinomoto USA, Inc. The History of Aspartame. Available at www.aspartame.net. Accessed October 2010.
18. Fitch. 2012. Position of the Academy of Nutrition and Dietetics: Use of Nutritive and Nonnutritive Sweeteners.
19. March of Dimes. 2013. Birth Defects. Available at www.marchofdimes.com. Accessed March 2013.
20. Ibid.
21. U.S. Library of Medicine. 2011. Phenylketonuria. Available at www.ncbi.nlm.nih.gov. Accessed March 2013.
22. The NutraSweet Company. 2008. Neotame: A Scientific Overview. Available at www.neotame.com. Accessed March 2013.
23. National Digestive Diseases Information Clearinghouse. 2012. Constipation. National Institutes of Health Publication No. 07-2754. Available at http://digestive.niddk.nih.gov. Accessed March 2013.
24. Ibid.
25. National Digestive Diseases Information Clearinghouse. 2012. Diverticulosis and Diverticulitis. National Institutes of Health Publication No. 08-1163. Available at http://digestive.niddk.nih.gov. Accessed March 2013.
26. U.S. Department of Agriculture and the U.S. Department of Health and Human Services. 2010. Report of the Dietary Guidelines Advisory Committee on the *Dietary Guidelines for Americans, 2010*. Available at www.cnpp.usda.gov. Accessed March 2013.
27. Ibid.
28. Ibid.
29. Slavin, J. 2008. Position of the American Dietetic Association: Health Implications of Dietary Fiber. *Journal of the American Dietetic Association* 108: 1716–1731.
30. Ibid.
31. Ibid.
32. National Cancer Institute. 2013. Colorectal Cancer Prevention (PDQ®). Available at www.cancer.gov. Accessed March 2013.
33. National Cancer Institute. 2013. Colorectal Cancer Prevention (PDQ®); Ferguson, L., and P. Harris. 2003. The Dietary Fiber Debate: More Food for Thought. *The Lancet* 361: 1487–1488.
34. Bingham, S., N. Day, R. Luben, P. Ferrari, N. Slimani, T. Norat, et al. 2003. Dietary Fiber in Food and Protection Against Colorectal Cancer in the European Prospective Investigation into Cancer and Nutrition (EPIC): An Observation Study. *The Lancet* 361: 1496–1501.
35. Bingham, et al. 2003. Dietary Fiber in Food and Protection Against Colorectal Cancer; Ferguson. 2003. The Dietary Fiber Debate.
36. Slavin. 2008. Position of the American Dietetic Association: Health Implications of Dietary Fiber.

Feature Box References

1. National Institutes of Health. 2010. NIH Consensus Development Conference: Lactose Intolerance and Health. Available at http://consensus.nih.gov. Accessed March 2013.
2. Ibid.
3. Ibid.
4. USDA/Economic Research Service. 2012. Food Availability (Per Capita) Data System. Available at www.ers.usda.gov. Accessed March 2013.
5. U.S. Department of Agriculture and the U.S. Department of Health and Human Services. 2010. Report of the Dietary Guidelines Advisory Committee on the *Dietary Guidelines for Americans, 2010*. Available at www.cnpp.usda.gov. Accessed March 2013.
6. Ibid.
7. Ibid.
8. Slavin, J., D. Jacobs, L. Marquart, and K. Wiemer. 2001. The Role of Whole Grains in Disease Prevention. *Journal of the American Dietetic Association* 101: 780–785.
9. Whole Grain Council. 2012. Whole Grain Statistics. Available at http://wholegrainscouncil.org. Accessed March 2013.
10. Centers for Disease Control and Prevention. 2012. National Diabetes Fact Sheet, 2011. Available at www.cdc.gov. Accessed March 2013.
11. Ibid.
12. American Diabetes Association. 2011. Diagnosis and Classification of Diabetes Mellitus. Position Statement. *Diabetes Care* 35: 564–571.

13. Ibid.
14. Centers for Disease Control and Prevention. 2012. Prediabetes Facts. Available at www.cdc.gov. Accessed March 2013.
15. Centers for Disease Control and Prevention. 2009. Diabetes Successes and Opportunities for Population-Based Prevention and Control: At a Glance 2009. Available at www.cdc.gov. Accessed January 2010.
16. National Digestive Diseases Information Clearinghouse. 2012. Hypoglycemia. National Institutes of Health Publication No. 09-3926. Available at http://diabetes.niddk.nih.gov. Accessed March 2013.
17. American Diabetes Association. 2003. Tests of Glycemia in Diabetes. *Diabetes Care* 26: S106–S108; National Diabetes Information Clearinghouse. 2001. Diabetes Control and Complications Trial (DCCT). National Institutes of Health Publication No. 02-3874. Available at www.niddk.nih.gov. Accessed April 2003.
18. American Diabetes Association. 2011. Standards of Medical Care in Diabetes—2011. *Diabetes Care* 34: S11–S61.
19. Ibid.
20. Sheard, N., N. Clark, J. Brand-Miller, M. Franz, F. Pi-Sunyer, E. Mayer-Davis, et al. 2004. Dietary Carbohydrate (Amount and Type) in the Prevention and Management of Diabetes. *Diabetes Care* 27: 2266–2271.
21. Ludwig, D. 2002. The Glycemic Index: Physiological Mechanisms Relating to Obesity, Diabetes, and Cardiovascular Disease. *Journal of the American Medical Association* 287: 2414–2423.
22. Roberts, S. 2000. High-Glycemic-Index Foods, Hunger, and Obesity: Is There a Connection? *Nutrition Reviews* 58: 163–169; Foster-Powell, K., and J. Brand-Miller. 1995. International Tables of Glycemic Index. *American Journal of Clinical Nutrition* 62: 871S–893S.
23. Centers for Disease Control and Prevention. 2011. Diabetes Data and Trends. Available at www.cdc.gov. Accessed March 2013.
24. Centers for Disease Control and Prevention 2012. *Diabetes Report Card 2012*: National and State Profile of Diabetes and Its Complications. Available at www.cdc.gov. Accessed March 2013.
25. American Diabetes Association. 2013. Economic Costs of Diabetes in the U.S. in 2012. *Diabetes Care*; 4:1033-1046.
26. Centers for Disease Control and Prevention. 2012. FastStats. Available at www.cdc.gov. Accessed March 2013.
27. Centers for Disease Control and Prevention. 2012. Children and Diabetes. Available at www.cdc.gov. Accessed March 2013.
28. Diabetes Prevention Program Research Group. 2002. Reduction in the Incidence of Type 2 Diabetes with Lifestyle Intervention or Metformin. *New England Journal of Medicine* 346: 393–403.
29. Palmer, C., and Gilbert, J. 2012. Position of the Academy of Nutrition and Dietetics: The Impact of Fluoride on Health. *Journal of the Academy of Nutrition and Dietetics* 112: 1443–1453.
30. National Institute of Dental and Craniofacial Resarch. 2011. Dental Caries (Tooth Decay). Available at www.nidcr.nih.gov. Accessed March 2013.
31. Heller, K., B. Burt, and S. Ekund. 2001. Sugared Soda Consumption and Dental Caries in the United States. *Journal of Dental Research* 80: 1949–1953; American Dental Association. 2002. Diet and Tooth Decay. *Journal of the American Dental Association* 133: 527; Joint Report of the American Dental Association Council on Access, Prevention and Interprofessional Relations and the Council on Scientific Affairs to the House of Delegates. 2001. Response to Resolution 73H-200. Available at www.ada.org. Accessed May 2003.
32. Academy of General Dentistry. 2008. Popular Energy Drinks Cause Tooth Erosion, Study Shows. *ScienceDaily*. Available at www.sciencedaily.com. Accessed May 2010.
33. Duffy, R. 2012. *American Dietetic Association's Complete Food and Nutrition Guide*, 4th ed. Hoboken: John Wiley & Sons; American Dental Association. Early Childhood Tooth Decay (Baby Bottle Tooth Decay). Available at www.ada.org. Accessed March 2013.
34. Moynihan, P., S. Ferrier, and G. Jenkins. 1999. Eating Cheese: Does It Reduce Caries? *British Dental Journal* 187: 664–667; Kashket, S., and D. DePaola. 2002. Cheese Consumption and the Development and Progression of Dental Caries. *Nutrition Reviews* 60: 97–103.
35. Mandel, I. 1996. Caries Prevention: Current Strategies, New Directions. *Journal of the American Dental Association* 127: 1477–1488.
36. United States Department of Agriculture, Economic Research Service. 2012. Table 52—High-Fructose Corn Syrup: Estimated Number of Per Capita Calories Consumed Daily, by Calendar Year. *Sugar and Sweeteners Yearbook 2012*. Available at www.ers.usda.gov. Accessed May 2013.
37. Centers for Disease Control and Prevention. 2012. Adult Obesity Facts. Available at www.cdc.gov. Accessed May 2013.
38. Bray, G. A., S. J. Nielsen, and B. M. Popkin. 2004. Consumption of High-Fructose Corn Syrup in Beverages May Play a Role in the Epidemic of Obesity. *American Journal of Clinical Nutrition* 79: 537–543.
39. Ibid.
40. Forshee, R. A., M. L. Storey, D. B. Allison, W. H. Glinsmann, G. L. Hein, D. R. Lineback, et al. 2007. A Critical Examination of the Evidence Relating High-Fructose Corn Syrup and Weight Gain. *Critical Reviews in Food Science and Nutrition* 47: 561–582.
41. Melanson, K. J., L. Zukley, J. Lowndes, V. Nguyen, T. J. Angelopoulos, and J. M. Rippe. 2007. Effects of High-Fructose Corn Syrup and Sucrose Consumption on Circulating Glucose, Insulin, Leptin, and Ghrelin and on Appetite in Normal-Weight Women. *Nutrition* 23: 103–112.
42. Almiron-Roig, E., and A. Drewnowski. 2003. Hunger, Thirst, and Energy Intakes Following Consumption of Caloric Beverages. *Physiology of Behavior* 79: 767–774.
43. Akhavan, T., and G. H. Anderson. 2007. Effects of Glucose-to-Fructose Ratios in Solutions on Subjective Satiety, Food Intake, and Satiety Hormones in Young Men. *American Journal of Clinical Nutrition* 86: 1354–1363.
44. Bray, et al. 2004. Consumption of High-Fructose Corn Syrup in Beverages.
45. Melanson, K. J., et al. 2007. Effects of High-Fructose Corn Syrup and Sucrose Consumption.
46. Schorin, M. 2005. High-Fructose Corn Syrups Part 1: Composition, Consumption, Metabolism. *Nutrition Today* 40: 248–252.
47. Monsivais, P., M. Perrigue, and A. Drewnowski. 2007. Sugars and Satiety: Does the Type of Sweetener Make a Difference? *American Journal of Clinical Nutrition* 86: 116–123.
48. Ibid.
49. Forshee, R. A., et al. 2007. A Critical Examination of the Evidence.

Two Points of View References

1. Diabetologia. 2013. Drinking One 12-Ounce Sugar-Sweetened Soft Drink a Day Can Increase the Risk of Type 2 Diabetes by 22 Percent, Study Suggests. *ScienceDaily*. Available at www.sciencedaily.com. Accessed May 2013.
2. Shi, Z., E. Dal Grande, A. W. Taylor, T. K. Gill, R. Adams, and G. A. Wittert. 2012. Association between Soft Drink Consumption and Asthma and Chronic Obstructive Pulmonary Disease among Adults in Australia. *Respirology* 17: 363.
3. Centers for Disease Control and Prevention. 2013. Childhood Overweight and Obesity: A Growing Problem. Available at www.cdc.gov. Accessed May 2013.
4. Castillo, M. 2013. Study: NYC Soda Ban Would Affect Overweight People More Than Poor. CBS News. Available at www.cbsnews.com. Accessed May 2013; Wang, Y. C., and S. M. Vine. 2013. Caloric Effect of a 16-Ounce (473-mL) Portion-Size Cap on Sugar-Sweetened Beverages Served in Restaurants. *American Journal of Clinical Nutrition* 98: 261–263.
5. Confessore, N. 2013. Minority Groups and Bottlers Team Up in Battles Over Soda. *The New York Times*. Available at www.nytimes.com. Accessed May 2013.
6. Confessore. Minority Groups and Bottlers Team Up; Castillo. Study: NYC Soda Ban.
7. Wilson, B. M., S. Stolarz-Fantino, and E. Fantino. 2013. Regulating the Way to Obesity: Unintended Consequences of Limiting Sugary Drink Sizes. *PLoS ONE*. 8: e61081.

Chapter 5

1. Institute of Medicine. 2002. *Dietary Reference Intakes for Energy, Carbohydrate, Fiber, Fat, Fatty Acids, Cholesterol, Protein, and Amino Acids*. Washington, D.C.: The National Academies Press.
2. Kris-Etherton, P. M., and S. Innis. 2007. Position of the American Dietetic Association and Dietitians of Canada: Dietary Fatty Acids. *Journal of the American Dietetic Association*; 107: 1599–1611.
3. Harris, W., D. Mozaffarian, E. Rimm, P. Kris-Etherton, L. Rudel, L. Appel, et al. 2009. Omega-6 Fatty Acids and Risk for Cardiovascular Disease. *Circulation* 119: 902–907.
4. U.S. Department of Agriculture, Agricultural Research Services. 2012. Nutrient Intakes from Food: Mean Amounts Consumed per Individual, by Gender and Age. In *What We Eat in America*, NHANES 2009–2010. Available at www.ars.usda.gov. Accessed March 2013.
5. Institute of Medicine. *Dietary Reference Intakes for Energy*.
6. U.S. Department of Agriculture, Agricultural Research Services. 2012. Nutrient Intakes from Food.
7. Institute of Medicine. *Dietary Reference Intakes for Energy*.

8. U.S. Department of Agriculture, U.S. Department of Health and Human Services. 2010. *Dietary Guidelines for Americans, 2010.* 7th ed. Washington, D.C.: U.S. Government Printing Office.

9. Food and Drug Administration. 2010. *Trans Fat Now Listed with Saturated Fat and Cholesterol on the Nutrition Facts Label.* Available at www.fda.gov. Accessed March 2011.

10. U.S. Department of Agriculture. *Dietary Guidelines for Americans.*

11. Ibid.

12. International Food Information Council Foundation. 2012. 2012 Food & Health Survey. Available at www.foodinsight.org. Accessed March 2013.

13. Food Marketing Institute. 2012. Shopping for Health 2012. Available at www.fmi.org. Access March 2013.

14. American Heart Association. 2012. Fat Substitutes. Available at www.heart.org. Accessed March 2012; Mattes, R. D. 1998. Fat Replacers. *Journal of the American Dietetic Association* 98: 463–468.

15. Calorie Control Council. 2013. Fat Replacers. Available at www.caloriecontrol.org. Accessed March 2013; Mattes. Fat Replacers; Wylie-Rosett, J. 2002. Fat Substitutes and Health: An Advisory from the Nutrition Committee of the American Heart Association. *Circulation* 105: 2800–2804.

16. Calorie Control Council. 2013. Fat Replacers.

17. Ibid.

18. Mattes. Fat Replacers.

19. Ibid.

20. Food and Drug Administration. 2003. 21 CFR Part 172. Food Additives Permitted for Direct Addition to Food for Human Consumption; Olestra; Final Rules. *Federal Register.* Available at www.fda.gov. Accessed January 2010.

21. Calorie Control Council. 2006. Olestra. Available at www.caloriecontrol.org. Accessed March 2013; Sandler. R. S., N. L. Zorich, T. G. Filloon, H. B. Wisman, D. J. Leitz, M. H. Brock, et al. 1999. Gastrointestinal Symptoms in 3,181 Volunteers Ingesting Snack Foods Containing Olestra or Triglycerides: A 6-Week Randomized, Placebo-Controlled Trial. *Annals of International Medicine* 130: 253–261; Cheskin, L. J., R. Miday, N. Zorich, and T. Filloon. 1998. Gastrointestinal Symptoms Following Consumption of Olestra or Regular Triglyceride Potato Chips: A Controlled Comparison. *Journal of the American Medical Association* 279: 150–152.

22. Swithers, S., S. Ogden, Davidson, T., and L. Terry. 2011. Fat Substitutes Promote Weight Gain in Rats Consuming High-Fat Diets. *Behavioral Neuroscience* 125: 512–518; Patterson, R. E., A. R. Kristal, J. C. Peters, M. L. Neuhouser, C. L. Rock, L. J. Cheskin, D., et al. 2000. Changes in Diet, Weight, and Serum Lipid Levels Associated with Olestra Consumption. *Archives of Internal Medicine* 160: 2600–2604.

23. U.S. Department of Agriculture, Department of Health and Human Services. 2010. Report of the Dietary Guidelines Advisory Committee for the Dietary Guidelines for Americans, 2010. Available at www.cnpp.usda.gov. Accessed March 2013.

24. Institute of Medicine. *Dietary Reference Intakes for Energy.*

25. U.S. Department of Agriculture. *Trans Fats on the Nutrition Facts Label.* Available at www.fns.usda.gov. Accessed March 2013.

26. U.S. Department of Agriculture, U.S. Department of Health and Human Services. 2010. *Dietary Guidelines for Americans, 2010*; American Heart Association Nutrition Committee. 2006. Diet and Lifestyle Recommendations Revision 2006. *Circulation* 114: 82–96.

27. U.S. Department of Agriculture, U.S. Department of Health and Human Services. 2010. *Dietary Guidelines for Americans, 2010.*

28. Ibid.

29. Ibid.

30. Kramhout, D., E. B. Bosschieter, and C. Coulander. 1985. The Inverse Relation between Fish Consumption and 20-Year Mortality from Coronary Heart Disease. *New England Journal of Medicine* 312: 1205–1209.

31. U.S. Department of Agriculture, Department of Health and Human Services. Report of the Dietary Guidelines Advisory Committee.

32. American Heart Association. 2013. Fish 101. Available at www.heart.org. Accessed March 2013.

33. U.S. Department of Agriculture, Department of Health and Human Services. Report of the Dietary Guidelines Advisory Committee.

34. American Heart Association. Fish 101; Kris-Etherton, P., W. Harris, and L. Appel, 2002. Fish Consumption, Fish Oil, Omega-3 Fatty Acids, and Cardiovascular Disease. *Circulation* 106: 2747–2757.

35. Ibid.

36. U.S. Department of Agriculture, Department of Health and Human Services. Report of the Dietary Guidelines Advisory Committee.

37. American Heart Association. Fish 101.

38. Slavin, J. 2008. Position of the American Dietetic Association: Health Implications of Dietary Fiber. *Journal of the American Dietetic Association* 108: 1716–1731; Brown, L., B. Rosner, W. Willett, and F. Sacks. 1999. Cholesterol-Lowering Effects of Dietary Fiber: A Meta-Analysis. *American Journal of Clinical Nutrition* 69: 30–42.

39. U.S. Department of Health and Human Services. 2005. Your Guide to Lowering Your Cholesterol with TLC. Publication No. 06-5235; National Cholesterol Education Program. 2001. Detection, Evaluation, and Treatment of High Blood Cholesterol in Adults (Adult Treatment Panel III). National Institutes of Health Publication No. 01-3290. Accessed March 2013.

40. U.S. Department of Health and Human Services. Your Guide to Lowering Your Cholesterol.

41. Food and Drug Administration. 2000. FDA Authorizes New Coronary Heart Disease Health Claim for Plant Sterol and Plant Stanol Esters. FDA Talk Paper. Available at http://scienceblog.com. Accessed March 2013.

42. U.S. Department of Health and Human Services. Your Guide to Lowering Your Cholesterol.

43. Tribble, D. L. 1999. AHA Science Advisory. Antioxidant Consumption and Risk of Coronary Heart Disease: Emphasis on Vitamin C, Vitamin E, and β-Carotene. *Circulation* 99: 591–595.

44. U.S. Department of Agriculture, Department of Health and Human Services. Report of the Dietary Guidelines Advisory Committee; Hu, F. B., M. J. Stampfer, J. E. Manson, E. B. Rimm, G. A. Colditz, B. A. Rosner, et al. 1998. Frequent Nut Consumption and Risk of Coronary Heart Disease in Women: Prospective Cohort Study. *British Medical Journal* 317: 1341–1345.

45. Feldman, E. B. 2002. LSRO Report: The Scientific Evidence of a Beneficial Health Relationship between Walnuts and Coronary Heart Disease. *Journal of Nutrition* 132: 1062S–1101S; Center for Food Safety and Applied Nutrition. 2003. Qualified Health Claims: Letter of Enforcement Discretion—Nuts and Coronary Heart Disease. Available at www.fda.gov. Accessed March 2013.

46. Hollenberg, N., and N. Fisher. 2007. Is It the Dark in Dark Chocolate? *Circulation* 116: 2360–2362; Ariefdjohan, M., and D. Savaiano. 2005. Chocolate and Cardiovascular Health: Is It Too Good to Be True? *Nutrition Reviews* 63: 427–430.

47. U.S. Department of Agriculture, Department of Health and Human Services. Report of the Dietary Guidelines Advisory Committee.

48. de Koning Gans, J., Y. Uiterwaal, J. van der Schouw, D. Boer, W. Verschuren, and J. Beulen. 2012. Tea and Coffee Consumption and Cardiovascular Morbidity and Mortality. *Arteriosclerosis, Thrombosis, and Vascular Biology* 30: 1665–1671.

49. Kim, A., A. Chiu, M. Barone, D. Avino, F. Wang, and C. Coleman. 2011. Green Tea Catechins Decrease Total and Low-Density Lipoprotein Cholesterol. A Systematic Review and Meta-Analysis. *Journal of the American Dietetic Association* 111: 1720–1729.

50. U.S. Department of Health and Human Services. 2008. 2008 Physical Activity Guidelines for Americans. Available at www.health.gov. Accessed March 2013.

51. Ibid.

52. Ibid.

53. U.S. Department of Agriculture, Department of Health and Human Services. Report of the Dietary Guidelines Advisory Committee; Rimm, E., A. Klatsky, D. Grobbee, and M. J. Stampfer. 1996. Review of Moderate Alcohol Consumption and Reduced Risk of Coronary Heart Disease: Is the Effect Due to Beer, Wine or Spirits? *British Medical Journal* 312: 731–736.

54. U.S. Department of Agriculture, Department of Health and Human Services. Report of the Dietary Guidelines Advisory Committee; American Heart Association. 2011. Alcoholic Beverages and Cardiovascular Disease. Available at www.heart.org. Accessed March 2013; Goldberg, I. J., L. Mosca, M. R. Piano, and E. A. Fisher. 2001. Wine and Your Heart: A Science Advisory for Healthcare Professionals from the Nutrition Committee, Council on Epidemiology and Prevention, and Council on Cardiovascular Nursing of the American Heart Association. *Circulation* 103: 472–475.

55. American Heart Association. Alcoholic Beverages and Cardiovascular Disease; Rimm, E., and R. C. Ellison. 1995. Alcohol in the Mediterranean Diet. *American Journal of Clinical Nutrition* 61: 1378S–1382S.

56. U.S. Department of Agriculture, Department of Health and Human Services. Report of the Dietary Guidelines Advisory Committee; American Heart Association. Alcoholic Beverages and Cardiovascular

Disease; Mukamal, K. J., K. M. Conigrave, M. A. Mittleman, C. A. Camaro, M. J. Stampfer, W. C. Willett, and E. B. Rimm. 2003. Roles of Drinking Pattern and Type of Alcohol Consumed in Coronary Heart Disease in Men. *New England Journal of Medicine* 348: 109–118.

57. U.S. Department of Health and Human Services. Your Guide to Lowering Your Cholesterol; Jenkins, D. J., C. W. Kendal, A. Marchie, D. A. Faulkner, J. M. Wong, R. de Souza, et al. 2003. Effects of a Dietary Portfolio of Cholesterol-Lowering Foods vs. Lovastatin on Serum Lipids and C-Reactive Protein. *Journal of the American Medical Association* 290: 502–510.

58. U.S. Department of Health and Human Services. Your Guide to Lowering Your Cholesterol; Anderson, J. W. 2003. Diet First, Then Medication of Hypercholesterolemia. *Journal of the American Medical Association* 290: 531–533.

Feature Box References

1. American Heart Association. 2013. Heart Disease and Stroke Statistics—2013 Update. Available at http://my.americanheart.org. Accessed March 2013.

2. Ibid.

3. U.S. Department of Health and Human Services. 2005. Your Guide to Lowering Your Cholesterol with TLC. NIH Publication No. 06-5235. Available at www.nhlbi.nih.gov. Accessed March 2013.

4. Sandmaier, M. Revised 2007. The Healthy Heart Handbook for Women. National Institutes of Health, National Heart, Lung, and Blood Institute. NIH Publication No. 07-2720.

5. Ibid.

6. U.S. Department of Health and Human Services. Your Guide to Lowering Your Cholesterol.

7. American Heart Association. Heart Disease and Stroke Statistics—2013 Update.

8. National Heart, Lung, and Blood Institute. 2010. Smoking and Your Heart. Available at www.nhlbi.nih.gov. Accessed May 2010.

9. American Heart Association. Heart Disease and Stroke Statistics—2013 Update.

10. U.S. Department of Agriculture, U.S. Department of Health and Human Services. 2010. *Dietary Guidelines for Americans, 2010.* 7th ed. Washington, D.C.: U.S. Government Printing Office; U.S. Department of Agriculture, Agricultural Research Service. 2008. Nutrient Intakes from Food: Mean Amounts Consumed per Individual, One Day, 2005–2006. Available at www.ars.usda.gov. Accessed March 2011.

11. Sandmaier. The Healthy Heart Handbook for Women.

12. U.S. Department of Health and Human Services. Your Guide to Lowering Your Cholesterol.

13. Helsing, E. 1995. Traditional Diets and Disease Patterns of the Mediterranean, circa 1960. *American Journal of Clinical Nutrition* 61: 1329S–1337S.

14. Sofi, F., R. Abbate, G. Gensini, and A Casini. 2010. Accessing Evidence on Benefits of Adherence to the Mediterranean Diet on Health: An Updated Systematic Review and Meta-Analysis. *Journal of Clinical Nutrition* 92: 1189–1196.

15. Trichopoulou, A. N., T. Costacou, C. Bamia, and D. Trichopoulos. 2003. Mediterranean Diet, Traditional Risk Factors, and the Rate of Cardiovascular Complications After Myocardial Infarction: Final Report of the Lyon Diet Heart Study. *Circulation* 99: 779–785; Kris-Etherton, P., R. H. Eckel, B. V. Howard, S. St. Jeor, and T. L. Bazzarre. 2001. Lyon Diet Heart Study. Benefits of a Mediterranean-Style, National Cholesterol Education Program/American Heart Association Step I Dietary Pattern on Cardiovascular Disease. *Circulation* 103: 1823–1825.

16. Willett, W. C., F. Sacks, A. N. Trichopoulou, G. Drescher, A. Ferro-Luzzi, E. Helsing, and D. Trichopoulos. 1995. Mediterranean Diet Pyramid: A Cultural Model for Healthy Eating. *American Journal of Clinical Nutrition* 61: 1402S–1406S.

17. Ibid.

18. Willett, et al. Mediterranean Diet Pyramid; Nestle, M. 1995. Mediterranean Diets: Historical and Research Overview. *American Journal of Clinical Nutrition* 61: 1313S–1320S.

19. Nestle. Mediterranean Diets: Historical and Research Overview.

20. Willett, et al. Mediterranean Diet Pyramid; Nestle. Mediterranean Diets: Historical and Research Overview.

21. Keys, A. 1995. Mediterranean Diet and Public Health: Personal Reflections. *American Journal of Clinical Nutrition* 61: 1321S–1323S.

22. Food and Drug Administration. 2013. What You Need to Know About Mercury in Fish and Shellfish: EPA and FDA Advice For Women Who Might Become Pregnant, Women Who Are Pregnant, and Nursing Mothers. Available at www.fda.gov. Accessed March 2013.

23. Ibid.

24. U.S. Department of Agriculture. Food Safety for Pregnant and Breast-Feeding Women. Available at www.choosemyplate.gov. Accessed March 2013.

25. Food and Drug Administration. 2004. What You Need to Know About Mercury in Fish and Shellfish: EPA and FDA Advice for Women Who Might Become Pregnant, Women Who Are Pregnant Women, Nursing Mothers, and Young Children. Available at www.fda.gov. Accessed April 2013.

26. Environmental Protection Agency. 2012. Fish Consumption Advisories. Available at http://water.epa.gov. Accessed March 2013.

27. Ibid.

Two Points of View References

1. Indiana University. 2004. Farmed Salmon More Toxic Than Wild Salmon, Study Finds. *ScienceDaily*. Available at www.sciencedaily.com. Accessed May 2013.

2. Crinnion, W. J. 2011. The Role of Persistent Organic Pollutants in the Worldwide Epidemic of Type 2 Diabetes Mellitus and the Possible Connection to Farmed Atlantic Salmon (*Salmo salar*). *Alternative Medicine Review* 16: 301–313.

3. Monterey Bay Aquarium. 2010. Seafood Watch: Salmon Fact Sheet. Available at www.montereybayaquarium.org. Accessed May 2013.

4. The Cornucopia Institute. 2009. How Farm-Raised Salmon Are Turning Our Oceans into Dangerous and Polluted Feedlots. Available at www.cornucopia.org. Accessed May 2013.

5. Pew Environment Group. 2009. Pew Environment Group Calls for a Crackdown on Unapproved Drug Use by Salmon Farms. Available at www.pewtrusts.org. Accessed May 2013.

6. Monterey Bay Aquarium Seafood Watch. 2013. Seafood Watch: Atlantic Salmon: Farmed Atlantic Salmon. www.montereybayaquarium.org. Accessed May 2013.

7. Ziccarelli, V. 2009. Nutritional Health Benefits of Salmon. Available at www.salmonfarmers.org. Accessed May 2013.

8. Hites, R., and B. Hamilton. 2004. Global Assessment of Organic Contaminants in Farmed Salmon. *Science* 303: 226–229.

9. Ziccarelli. Nutritional Health Benefits of Salmon.

10. Harvard School of Public Health. 2006. Benefits of Eating Fish Greatly Outweigh the Risks, New Study Says. *ScienceDaily*. Available at www.sciencedaily.com. Accessed May 2013.

11. University of California Cooperative Extension. 2010. Commercially Farmed and Wild-Caught Salmon—Bon Appetit! Available at http://seafood.ucdavis.edu. Accessed May 2013.

12. Ibid.

Chapter 6

1. Johnson, M. D. 2014. *Human Biology: Concepts and Current Issues.* 7th ed. San Francisco: Benjamin Cummings.

2. Institute of Medicine. 2002. *Dietary Reference Intakes for Energy, Carbohydrate, Fiber, Fat, Fatty Acids, Cholesterol, Protein, and Amino Acids.* Washington, D.C.: The National Academies Press.

3. Bennion, M. 1980. *The Science of Food.* New York: Harper & Row.

4. Food Safety and Inspection Service. 2011. Poultry: Basting, Brining, and Marinating. Available at www.fsis.usda.gov. Accessed April 2013.

5. Institute of Medicine. *Dietary Reference Intakes for Energy.*

6. National Human Genome Research Institute. 2010. Learning about Sickle-Cell Disease. Available at www.genome.gov; National Institutes of Health. 1998. Genes and Disease: Sickle-Cell Anemia. Available at www.ncbi.nlm.nih.gov.

7. Marieb, E. N. 2004. *Human Anatomy and Physiology.* 6th ed. San Francisco: Benjamin Cummings.

8. Murray, R. K., D. K. Granner, P. A. Mayes, and V. W. Rodwell. 2006. *Harper's Illustrated Biochemistry.* 27th ed. New York: Lange Medical Books/McGraw-Hill.

9. Joneja, J. 2013. *The Health Professional's Guide to Food Allergies and Intolerances.* Chicago: Academy of Nutrition and Dietetics.

10. Astrup, A. 2006. Carbohydrates as Macronutrients in Relation to Protein and Fat for Body Weight Control. *International Journal of Obesity* 30: S4–S9.

11. Vedlhorst, M., A. Smeets, S. Soenen, A. Hochstenback-Waelen, R. Hursel, K. Diepvens, et al. 2008. Protein-Induced Satiety: Effects and Mechanisms of Different Proteins. *Physiology & Behavior* 94: 300–307.

12. Stipanuk, M. 2006. *Biochemical and Physiological Aspects of Human Nutrition.* 2nd ed. Philadelphia: Saunders Elsevier.

13. U.S. Department of Agriculture, Agricultural Research Service. 2012. Nutrient Intakes from Food: Mean Amounts Consumed per Individual,

by Gender and Age. In What We Eat in America, NHANES 2009–2010. Available at www.ars.usda.gov. Accessed April 2013.

14. Ibid.

15. American Dietetic Association, Dietitians of Canada, and the American College of Sports Medicine. 2009. Nutrition and Athletic Performance. *Journal of the American Dietetic Association* 109: 509–527.

16. Economic Research Service (ERS). 2010. Food Availability Per Capita Data System. Available at www.ers.usda.gov. Accessed May 2010.

17. Ibid.

18. U.S. Department of Health and Human Services, National Kidney and Urologic Diseases Information Clearing House. 2013. Kidney Stones in Adults. Available at http://kidney.niddk.nih.gov. Accessed April 2013.

19. Institute of Medicine. *Dietary Reference Intakes for Energy*.

20. Heaney, R. P. 1998. Excess Dietary Protein May Not Adversely Affect Bone. *Journal of Nutrition* 128: 1054–1057.

21. World Cancer Research Fund/American Institute for Cancer Research. 2007. Food, Nutrition, Physical Activity, and the Prevention of Cancer: A Global Prospective. Available at www.dietandcancerreport.org; Key, T. J., N. E. Allen, E. A. Spencer, and R. C. Travis. 2002. The Effect of Diet on Risk of Cancer. *The Lancet* 360: 861–868.

22. Bertstein, M., and N. Munoz. 2012. Food and Nutrition for Older Adults: Promoting Health and Wellness. *Journal of the Academy of Nutrition and Dietetics* 112: 1255–1277.

23. Food and Agriculture Organization of the United Nations. 2012. The State of Food Insecurity in the World 2012. Available at www.fao.org. Accessed April 2013.

24. Nordin, S., M. Boyle, and T. Kemmer. 2013. Position of the Academy of Nutrition and Dietetics: Nutrition Security in Developing Nations: Sustainable Food, Water, and Health. *Journal of the Academy of Nutrition and Dietetics* 113: 581–595.

25. Ibid.

26. Shils. M., A. Olson, M. Shike, and A. Ross. 1999. *Modern Nutrition in Health and Disease*. 9th ed. Baltimore: Williams and Wilkins.

27. Ibid.

28. Ibid.

29. Food and Agriculture Organization of the United Nations. The State of Food Insecurity.

30. American Dietetic Association and Dietitians of Canada. 2009. Position of the American Dietetic Association and Dietitians of Canada: Vegetarian Diets. *Journal of the American Dietetic Association* 109: 1266–1282.

31. Gallup Wellbeing. 2012. Gallup's July 9–12 Consumption Habits Survey. Available at www.gallup.com. Accessed April 2013.

32. Ginsberg, C. 2011. The Market for Vegetarian Foods. Available at www.vrg.org. Accessed April 2013.

33. American Dietetic Association and Dietitians of Canada. Position of the American Dietetic Association and Dietitians of Canada: Vegetarian Diets.

34. Ibid.

35. Ibid.

36. World Cancer Research Fund. American Institute for Cancer Research. 2007. Food, Nutrition, Physical Activity, and the Prevention of Cancer: A Global Perspective. Washington D.C.: AICR.

Feature Box References

1. 2012. Moo-ve Over Milk: Plant Alternatives Primed to Benefit from Protein Supplement Demand. *Euromonitor International*. Available at www.blog.euromonitor.com. Accessed March 2012.

2. 2012. Tests of Protein Powders and Shakes Contain Some Lead Contamination but No Melamine. Available from www.consumerlab.com. Accessed March 2012.

3. 2010. Alert! You Don't Need the Extra Protein or the Heavy Metals Our Tests Found. *Consumer Reports* 75: 24.

4. Maughan, R. J., and S. M. Shirreffs. 2012. Nutrition for Sports Performance: Issues and Opportunities. *Proceedings of the Nutrition Society* 71: 112–119.

5. Graf, S., S. Egert, and M. Heer. 2011. Effects of Whey Protein Supplements on Metabolism: Evidence from Human Intervention Studies. *Current Opinion in Clinical Nutrition and Metabolic Care* 14: 569–580.

6. Spillane, M., N. Schwarz, S. Leddy, T. Correa, M. Minter, V. Longoria, and D. S. Willoughby. 2011. Effects of 28 Days of Resistance Exercise while Consuming Commercially Available Pre- and Post-Workout Supplements, NO-Shotgun® and NO-Synthesize® on Body Composition, Muscle Strength and Mass, Markers of Protein Synthesis, and Clinical Safety Markers in Males. *Nutrition & Metabolism* 8: 78.

7. Culliney, K. 2012. Nutrition Runs Up Front in the US Snack Bar Race: Rabobank. Available at www.bakeryandsnacks.com/. Accessed April 2013.

8. Soyfoods Association of North America. 2012. Sales and Trends. Available at www.soyfoods.org/soy-information/sales-and-trends. Accessed April 2013.

9. United Soybean Board. 2012. Consumer Attitudes About Nutrition, Insights into Nutrition, Health, and Soyfoods. Available at www.soyconnection.com. Accessed April 2013.

10. Ibid.

11. Munro, I. C., M. Harwood, J. J. Hlywka, A. M. Stephen, J. Doull, W. G. Flammn, and H. Adlercrutz. 2003. Soy Isoflavones: A Safety Review. *Nutrition Reviews* 61: 1–33.

12. Sacks, F., A. Lichtenstein, L. Van Horn, W. Harris, P. Kris-Etherton, M. Winston, and the American Heart Association Nutrition Committee. 2006. Soy Protein, Isoflavones, and Cardiovascular Health: An American Heart Association Science Advisory for Professions from the Nutrition Committee. *Circulation* 113: 1034–1044.

13. He, J., M. Wofford, K. Reynolds, J. Chen, C. Chen, Myers, L., et al. 2011. Effect of Dietary Protein Supplementation on Blood Pressure: A Random Controlled Trail. *Circulation* 124: 589–595.

14. American Institute of Cancer Research. 2012. Foods that Fight Cancer. Available at www.aicr.org. Accessed May 2013; Messina, M. J., V. Persky, K. D. R. Setchell, and S. Barnes. 1994. Soy Intake and Cancer Risk: A Review of the In Vitro and In Vivo Data. *Nutrition and Cancer* 21: 113–131; Messina, M. J., and C. L. Loprinzi. 2001. Soy for Breast Cancer Survivors: A Critical Review of the Literature. *Journal of Nutrition* 131: 3095S–3108S.

15. Kushi, L., C. Doyle, M. McCulough, C. Rock, W. Dernark-Wahnedried, E. Bandera, et al. 2012. American Cancer Society Guidelines on Nutrition and Physical Activity for Cancer Prevention: Reducing the Risk of Cancer with Healthy Food Choices and Physical Activity. *A Cancer Journal for Clinicians* 62: 30–67.

16. American Cancer Society. 2013. Soybean. Available at www.cancer.org. Accessed April 2013; Shu, X. O., F. Jin, Q. Dai, W. Wen, J. D. Potter, L. H. Kushi, et al. 2001. Soyfood Intake during Adolescence and Subsequent Risk of Breast Cancer among Chinese Women. *Cancer Epidemiology, Biomarkers & Prevention* 10: 483–488; Maskarinec, G. 2005. Soy Foods for Breast Cancer Survivors. Journal of the American Dietetic Association; 105:1524-8.

17. American Institute of Cancer Research. Foods that Fight Cancer; Maskarinec. Soy Foods for Breast Cancer Survivors; McMichael-Phillips, D. F., C. Harding, M. Morton, S. A. Roberts, A. Howell, C. S. Potten, and N. J. Bundred. 1998. Effects of Soy-Protein Supplementation on Epithelial Proliferation in the Histologically Normal Human Breast. *American Journal of Clinical Nutrition* 68: 1431S–1436S.

18. American Cancer Society. Soybean; American Institute of Cancer Research. Foods that Fight Cancer.

19. American Cancer Society. Soybean.

20. American Institute of Cancer Research. Foods that Fight Cancer.

Two Points of View References

1. The Paleo Diet. 2012. What to Eat on the Paleo Diet. Available at http://thepaleodiet.com. Accessed June 2013.

2. The Vegetarian Resource Group. 2000. Vegetarianism in a Nutshell: Humans Are Omnivores. Available at www.vrg.org. Accessed June 2013.

3. The Paleo Diet. What to Eat on the Paleo Diet; Liu, S., et al. 2000. A Prospective Study of Whole-Grain Intake and Risk of Type 2 Diabetes Mellitus in U.S. Women. *American Journal of Public Health* 90: 1409–1415; Jenkins, D. J., H. Ghafari, and T. M. Wolever, et al. 1982. Relationship between Rate of Digestion of Foods and Post-Prandial Glycaemia. *Diabetologia* 22: 450–455.

4. The Paleo Diet. What to Eat on the Paleo Diet.

5. Ibid.; Centers for Disease Control and Prevention. 2011. Americans Consume Too Much Sodium (Salt). Available at www.cdc.gov. Accessed June 2013; Activist Post. 2012. What Is the Average American Diet? Infographic. Available at www.activistpost.com. Accessed June 2013.

6. U.S. News and World Report. 2013. Health. Health and Wellness. Paleo Diet. Available at http://health.usnews.com. Accessed June 2013.

7. U.S. News and World Report. 2013. Health. Health and Wellness. Paleo Diet. Expert Reviews. Available at http://health.usnews.com. Accessed June 2013; Baik, I., et al. 2013. A Healthy Dietary Pattern Consisting of a Variety of Food Choices Is Inversely Associated with the Development of Metabolic Syndrome. *Nutrition Research and Practice* 7: 233–241.

8. Cunningham, E. 2012. Are Diets from Paleolithic Times Relevant Today? *Journal of the Academy of Nutrition and Dietetics* 112: 8.

9. GoodReads. 2013. Interview with Michael Pollan. Available at www .goodreads.com. Accessed June 2013; Perry, G. H., et al. 2007. Diet and the Evolution of Human Amylase Gene Copy Number Variation. *Nature Genetics* 39: 1256–1260.

Chapter 7

1. Rosenfeld, L. 1997. Vitamine-Vitamin. The Early Years of Discovery. *Clinical Chemistry* 43: 680–685.
2. Young, I. S., and J. V. Woodside. 2001. Antioxidants in Health and Disease. *Journal of Clinical Pathology* 54: 176–186.
3. Dröge, W. 2002. Free Radicals in the Physiological Control of Cell Function. *Physiology Review* 82: 47–95; Traber, M. G., and H. Sies. 1996. Vitamin E in Humans: Demand and Delivery. *Annual Review of Nutrition* 16: 321–347; Young. Antioxidants in Health.
4. National Eye Institute, National Institutes of Health. 2009. Age-Related Macular Degeneration: What You Should Know. Available at www.nei .nih.gov. Accessed May 2009.
5. National Institutes of Health, National Eye Institute. 2011. Age-Related Eye Disease Study—Results. Available at www.nei.nih.gov. Accessed May 2013.
6. National Institutes of Health, Senior Health. 2013. Cataract. Available at http://nihseniorhealth.gov. Accessed May 2013.
7. National Institutes of Health, Senior Health. 2013. Cataract; National Eye Institute. Age-Related Macular Degeneration.
8. American Cancer Society. 2013. Phytochemicals. Available at www.cancer.org. Accessed May 2013.
9. Freeland-Graves, J., and Nitzke, S. 2012. Position of the Academy of Nutrition and Dietetics: Total Diet Approach to Healthy Eating. *Journal of the Academy of Nutrition and Dietetics* 113: 307–317; U.S. Department of Agriculture, U.S. Department of Health and Human Services. 2010. *Dietary Guidelines for Americans, 2010.* 7th ed. Washington, D.C.: U.S. Government Printing Office.
10. U.S. Department of Agriculture. 2005. 2005 Report of the Dietary Guidelines Advisory Committee on the Dietary Guidelines for Americans. Available at www.health.gov. Accessed May 2013.
11. Lee, S. K., and A. A. Kader. 2000. Preharvest and Postharvest Factors Influencing Vitamin C Content of Horticultural Crops. *Postharvest Biology and Technology* 20: 207–220.
12. Pandrangi, S., and L. E. LaBorde. 2004. Retention of Folate, Carotenoid, and Other Quality Characteristics in Commercially Packaged Fresh Spinach. *Journal of Food Science* 69: C702–C707.
13. National Institutes of Health. 2012. Vitamin A. Available at http:// ods.od.nih.gov. Accessed May 2013; Institute of Medicine, Food and Nutrition Board. 2001. *Dietary Reference Intakes: Vitamin A, Vitamin K, Arsenic, Boron, Chromium, Copper, Iodine, Iron, Manganese, Molybdenum, Nickel, Silicon, Vanadium, and Zinc.* Washington, D.C.: The National Academies Press.
14. Institute of Medicine. *Dietary Reference Intakes: Vitamin A.*
15. National Institutes of Health. Vitamin A; Ross, A. C. 1993. Vitamin A as Hormone: Recent Advances in Understanding the Actions of Retinol, Retinoic Acid, and Beta-Carotene. *Journal of the American Dietetic Association* 93: 1285–1290.
16. Bershad, S. V. 2001. The Modern Age of Acne Therapy: A Review of Current Treatment Options. *Mount Sinai Journal of Medicine* 68: 279–286.
17. Institute of Medicine. *Dietary Reference Intakes: Vitamin A;* Ross. Vitamin A as Hormone.
18. Institute of Medicine. *Dietary Reference Intakes: Vitamin A.*
19. Institute of Medicine, Food and Nutrition Board. 2000. *Dietary Reference Intakes: Vitamin C, Vitamin E, Selenium, and Carotenoids.* Washington, D.C.: The National Academies Press.
20. Brown, M., M. Ferruzzi, M. Nguyen, D. Cooper, A. Eldridge, S. Schwartz, and W. White. 2004. Carotenoid Bioavailability Is Higher from Salads Ingested with Full-Fat Than with Fat-Reduced Salad Dressings as Measured with Electrochemical Detection. *American Journal of Clinical Nutrition* 80: 396–403.
21. Institute of Medicine. *Dietary Reference Intakes: Vitamin A.*
22. Ibid. *Vitamin A;* National Institutes of Health. Vitamin A.
23. Ibid.
24. Brinkley, N., and D. Krueger. 2000. Hypervitaminosis A and Bone. *Nutrition Reviews* 58: 138–144; Genaro, P., and L. A. Martini. 2004. Vitamin A Supplementation and Risk of Skeletal Fracture. *Nutrition Reviews;* 62:65–67; Melhus, H., Michaelsson, K. Mark, A. Kindmark, R. Berstrom, L. Holmber, H. Mallmin, A. Wolk, and S. Ljunghall. 1998. Excessive Dietary Intake of Vitamin A Is Associated with Reduced Bone Mineral Density and Increased Risk for Hip Fractures. *Annals of Internal Medicine* 129: 770–778.
25. National Institutes of Health. Vitamin A; Feskanich, D., V. Singh, W. Willett, and G. Colditz. 2002. Vitamin A Intake and Hip Fractures among Postmenopausal Women. *Journal of the American Medical Association* 287: 47–54; Lips, P. 2003. Hypervitaminosis A and Fractures. *New England Journal of Medicine* 348: 347–349; Michaelsson, K., H. Lithell, B. Bvessby, and H. Melhus. 2003. Serum Retinol Levels and the Risk of Fractures. *New England Journal of Medicine* 348: 287–294.
26. National Institutes of Health. Vitamin A; Institute of Medicine. *Dietary Reference Intakes: Vitamin C.*
27. National Institutes of Health. Vitamin A; The Alpha-Tocopherol, Beta-Carotene Cancer Prevention Study Group. 1994. The Effects of Vitamin E and Beta-Carotene on the Incidence of Lung Cancer and Other Cancers in Male Smokers. *New England Journal of Medicine* 330: 1029–1035.
28. National Institutes of Health. Vitamin A; World Health Organization. 2009. Global Prevalence of Vitamin A Deficiency in Populations at Risk 1995–2005. WHO Global Database on Vitamin A Deficiency, Geneva. Available at www.who.int. Accessed in May 2013.
29. National Institutes of Health. 2011. Vitamin E. Available at http://ods .od.nih.gov. Accessed May 2013.
30. Ibid.
31. Ibid.
32. Ibid.
33. U.S. Department of Agriculture. 2012. Nutrient Intakes from Food: Mean Amounts Consumed per Individual, by Gender and Age, What We Eat in America, NHANES 2009–2010. Available at www.ars.usda .gov. Accessed May 2013.
34. National Institutes of Health. Vitamin E.; Miller, E. R., R. Pastor-Barriso, D. Dalal, R. A. Riemersma, L. J. Appel, and E. Guallar. 2005. Meta-Analysis: High-Dosage Vitamin E Supplementation May Increase All-Cause Mortality. *Annals of Internal Medicine* 142: 37–46.
35. Shea, M., and S. Booth. 2008. Update on the Role of Vitamin K in Skeletal Health. *Nutrition Reviews* 66: 549–557; Feskanich, D., P. Weber, W. C. Willet, H. Rockett, S. L. Booth, and G. A. Colditz. 1999. Vitamin K Intake and Hip Fractures in Women: A Prospective Study. *American Journal of Clinical Nutrition* 69: 74–79.
36. Institute of Medicine. *Dietary Reference Intakes: Vitamin A.*
37. National Institutes of Health. 2012. Important Information to Know When You Are Taking Warfarin (Coumadin) and Vitamin K. Available at www.cc.nih.gov. Accessed May 2013.
38. Institute of Medicine. *Dietary Reference Intakes: Vitamin A.*
39. Institute of Medicine. 2011. *Dietary Reference Intakes for Calcium and Vitamin D.* Washington, D.C.: The National Academies Press.
40. National Institutes of Health. 2011. Vitamin D. Available at http://ods .od.nih.gov. Accessed May 2013; Toner, C., C. Davis, and J. Milner. 2010. The Vitamin D and Cancer Conundrum: Aiming at a Moving Target. *Journal of the American Dietetic Association* 110: 1492–1500.
41. Toner. The Vitamin D and Cancer Conundrum.
42. National Institutes of Health. Vitamin D.
43. Ross, A., C. Taylor, A. Yaktine, and H. Del Valle. 2010. *Dietary Reference Intakes for Calcium and Vitamin D.* Committee to Review Dietary Reference Intakes for Vitamin D and Calcium. Available at www.ncbi .nlm.nih.gov. Accessed May 2013.
44. Institute of Medicine. *Dietary Reference Intakes for Calcium and Vitamin D.*
45. Ibid.
46. U.S. Department of Agriculture, Agricultural Research Service. 2012. Nutrient Intake from Food: Mean Amounts Consumed per Individual, by Gender and Age.
47. Institute of Medicine. *Dietary Reference Intakes for Calcium and Vitamin D.*
48. Ibid.
49. Centers for Disease Control and Prevention. 2001. Severe Malnutrition among Young Children—Georgia, January 1997–June 1999. *Morbidity and Mortality Weekly Report.* Available at www.cdc.gov. Accessed April 2012.
50. Gordon, C. M., K. C. DePeter, H. A. Feldman, E. Grace, and S. J. Emans. 2004. Prevalence of Vitamin D Deficiency among Healthy Adolescents. *Archives of Pediatric and Adolescent Medicine* 158: 531–537; Weisberg, P., K. S. Scanlon, R. Li, and M. E. Cogswell. 2004. Nutritional Rickets among Children in the United States: Review of Cases Reported between 1986 and 2003. *American Journal of Clinical Nutrition* 80: 1697S–1705S.
51. Lin, B., and K. Ralston. 2003. Competitive Foods: Soft Drinks vs. Milk. Washington, D.C.: U.S. Department of Agriculture, Economic Research Service. Available at www.ers.usda.gov. Accessed May 2013.
52. Wanger, C., F. Greer, and the Section on Breast-Feeding and Committee on Nutrition. 2008. Prevention of Rickets and Vitamin D Deficiency in

Infants, Children, and Adolescents. *Pediatrics* 122: 1142–1152; Scanlon, K. S. 2001. Vitamin D Expert Panel Meeting. Available at www.cdc.gov.

53. Wharton, B., and N. Bishop. 2003. Rickets. Lancet; 362:1389–1400.

54. Agarwal, K. S., M. Z. Mughal, P. Upadhyay, J. L. Berry, E. B. Mawer, and J. M. Puliyel. 2002. The Impact of Atmospheric Pollution on Vitamin D Status of Infants and Toddlers in Delhi, India. *Archives of Disease in Childhood* 87: 111–113.

55. Institute of Medicine. *Dietary Reference Intakes for Calcium and Vitamin D.*

56. Rosenfeld. Vitamine-Vitamin.

57. U.S. Department of Agriculture, Agricultural Research Service. 2012. Nutrient Intake from Food: Mean Amounts Consumed per Individual, by Gender and Age.

58. U.S. National Library of Medicine, National Institutes of Health. 2012. Beriberi. Medline Plus. Available at www.nlm.nih.gov. Accessed May 2013.

59. U.S. National Library of Medicine, National National Institutes of Health. 2012. Wernicke-Korsakoff Syndrome. Available at www.nlm.nih.gov. Accessed May 2013.

60. Herreid, E. O., B. Ruskin, G. L. Clark, and T. B. Parks. 1952. Ascorbic Acid and Riboflavin Destruction and Flavor Development in Milk Exposed to the Sun in Amber, Clear, Paper, and Ruby Bottles. *Journal of Dairy Science* 35: 772–778.

61. U.S. Department of Agriculture, Agricultural Research Service. 2012. Nutrient Intake from Food: Mean Amounts Consumed per Individual, by Gender and Age.

62. Ibid.

63. Cervantes-Laurean, D., G. McElvaney, and J. Moss. 1999. Niacin. In M. E. Shils, J. Olson, M. Shike, and A. C. Ross, eds., *Modern Nutrition in Health and Disease.* 9th ed. Baltimore: Williams and Wilkins.

64. Institute of Medicine, Food and Nutrition Board. 1998. *Dietary Reference Intakes: Thiamin, Riboflavin, Niacin, Vitamin B$_6$, Folate, Vitamin B$_{12}$ Pantothenic Acid, Biotin, and Choline.* Washington, D.C.: The National Academies Press.

65. Ibid.

66. Ibid.

67. National Institutes of Health. 2011. Vitamin B$_6$. Available at http://ods.od.nih.gov. Accessed May 2013.

68. Ibid.

69. National Institutes of Health. 2012. Folate. Available at http://ods.od.nih.gov. Accessed May 2013; Institute of Medicine. *Dietary Reference Intakes: Thiamin.*

70. Centers for Disease Control and Prevention. 2012. Folic Acid. Available at www.cdc.gov. Accessed May 2013.

71. National Institutes of Health. Folate.

72. Ibid.

73. Institute of Medicine. *Dietary Reference Intakes: Thiamin.*

74. National Institutes of Health. Folate.

75. Ibid.

76. National Institutes of Health. Folate; Ebbing, M., K. Bonaa, O. Nygard, E. Arnesen, P. Ueland, J. Nordrehaug, et al. 2009. Cancer Incidence and Mortality After Treatment with Folic Acid and Vitamin B$_{12}$. *Journal of the American Medical Association* 302: 2119–2126; Cole, B., et al. 2007. Folic Acid for the Prevention of Colorectal Adenomas. A Randomized Clinical Trial. *Journal of the American Medical Association* 297: 2351–2359.

77. Institute of Medicine. *Dietary Reference Intakes: Thiamin.*

78. Ibid. National Institutes of Health. 2011. Vitamin B$_{12}$. Available at http://ods.od.nih.gov. Accessed May 2013.

79. National Institutes of Health. Vitamin B$_{12}$.

80. Institute of Medicine. *Dietary Reference Intakes: Thiamin;* National Institutes of Health. Vitamin B$_{12}$.

81. Institute of Medicine. *Dietary Reference Intakes: Vitamin C.*

82. National Institutes of Health. 2011. Vitamin C. Available at http://ods.od.nih.gov. Accessed May 2013; Iqbal, K., A. Khan, and M. Khattak. 2004. Biological Significance of Ascorbic Acid (Vitamin C) in Human Health. *Pakistan Journal of Nutrition* 3: 5–13.

83. Ibid.

84. National Institutes of Health. Vitamin C; Institute of Medicine. *Dietary Reference Intakes: Vitamin C.*

85. National Institutes of Health. Vitamin C; Rosenfeld. Vitamine-Vitamin.

86. Zempleni, J., S. Wijeratne, and Y. Hassan. 2009. Biotin. *Biofactors* 35: 36–46; Institute of Medicine. *Dietary Reference Intakes: Thiamin.*

87. Glusman, M. 1947. The Syndrome of "Burning Feet" (Nutritional Melagia) as a Manifestation of Nutritional Deficiency. *American Journal of Medicine* 3: 211–223.

88. Sweetmna, L. 2000. Pantothenic Acid and Biotin. In M. H. Stipanuk, ed., *Biochemical and Physiological Aspects of Human Nutrition.* Philadelphia: Saunders.

89. Mock, D. M. 1999. Biotin. In M. E. Shils, J. Olson, M. Shike, and A. C. Ross, eds., *Modern Nutrition in Health and Disease.* 9th ed. Baltimore: Williams and Wilkins.

90. Zeisel, S., and K. da Costa. 2009. Choline: An Essential Nutrient for Public Health. *Nutrition Reviews* 67: 615–623; Institute of Medicine. *Dietary Reference Intakes: Thiamin.*

91. National Institutes of Health. 2004. Carnitine. Available at http://ods.od.nih.gov. Accessed May 2013.

92. American Cancer Society. 2008. Lipoic Acid. Available at www.cancer.org. Accessed May 2013.

93. U.S. Department of Agriculture. 2010. 2010 Report of the Dietary Guidelines Advisory Committee on the Dietary Guidelines for Americans. Available at www.cnpp.usda.gov. Accessed May 2013.

94. Office of Dietary Supplements. National Institutes of Health. 2013. Dietary Supplement Fact Sheet: Multivitamin/mineral Supplements. Available at http://ods.od.nih.gov. Accessed October 2013.

95. Mintel International Group Limited. 2011. Vitamin and Supplement US –December 2011. Available at http://store.mintel.com. Accessed May 2013.

96. Marra, M., and A. Boyar. 2009. Position of the American Dietetic Association: Nutrient Supplementation. *Journal of the American Dietetic Association* 109: 2073–2085.

97. National Institutes of Health. 2011. Dietary Supplements. Available at http://ods.od.nih.gov. Accessed May 2013.

98. United States Pharmacopoeia. USP's Dietary Supplement Verification Program. Available at. Accessed May 2013.

Feature Box References

1. U.S. National Library of Medicine, National Institutes of Health. 2012. Common Cold. Available at www.nlm.nih.gov. Accessed May 2013.

2. National Institute of Allergy and Infectious Diseases. 2011. Common Cold. Available at www.niaid.nih.gov. Accessed May 2013.

3. Hemila, H., and E. Chalker. 2013. Vitamin C for Preventing and Treating the Common Cold. The Cochrane Library. Available at www.thecochranelibrary.com. Accessed May 2013.

4. Ibid.

5. Barrett, B., R. Brown D. Rakel, M. Mundt, K. Bone, S. Barlow, and T. Ewers. 2010. Echinacea for Treating the Common Cold: A Randomized Trial. *Annals of Internal Medicine* 153: 769–777.

6. The Cochrane Library. 2011. Zinc for the Common Cold. Available at www.thecochranelibrary.com. Accessed May 2013.

Two Points of View References

1. Office of Dietary Supplements, National Institutes of Health. 2011. *Dietary Supplement Fact Sheet: Vitamin D.* Available at http://ods.od.nih.gov. Accessed June 2013.

2. L. S. Nield, P. Mahajan, A. Joshi, et al. 2006. Rickets: Not a Disease of the Past. *American Family Physician* 74: 619–626.

3. Ibid; Zeratsky, K. 2012. Vitamin D Toxicity: What If You Get Too Much? Available at www.mayoclinic.com. Accessed July 2013.

4. Trump, D. L., K. Deeb, and C. S. Johnson. 2010. Vitamin D: Considerations in the Continued Development as an Agent for Cancer Prevention and Therapy. *Cancer Journal* 16: 1–9; Garland, C. F., F. C. Garland, and M. F. Holick. 2006. The Role of Vitamin D in Cancer Prevention. *American Journal of Public Health* 96: 252–261.

5. Harvard School of Public Health. 2011. The Nutrition Source: Vitamin D and Health. Available at www.hsph.harvard.edu. Accessed October 2013.

6. Moan, J., A. C. Porojnicu, A. Dahlback, and R. B. Setlow. 2008. Addressing the Health Benefits and Risks, Involving Vitamin D or Skin Cancer, of Increased Sun Exposure. *Proceedings of the National Academy of Sciences of the United States of America* 105: 668–673.

7. American Cancer Society. 2013. Skin Cancer Prevention and Early Detection. Available at www.cancer.org. Accessed June 2013.

8. American Academy of Dermatology. 2013. Vitamin D. Available at www.aad.org. Accessed June 2013.

9. Wolpowitz, D., and B. A. Gilchrest. 2006. The Vitamin D Questions: How Much Do You Need and How Should You Get It? *Journal of the American Academy of Dermatology* 54: 301–317.

10. American Cancer Society. 2007. UV Radiation and Cancer. Available at www.cancer.org. Accessed June 2013.

11. Centers for Disease Control and Prevention. 2013. Skin Cancer: Prevention. Available at www.cdc.gov. Accessed June 2013.

Chapter 8

1. Marieb, E., and Hoehn, K. 2013. *Human Anatomy and Physiology.* 9th ed. San Francisco: Pearson Education, Inc.
2. Sheng, H. 2000. Body fluids and water balance. In Stipanuk, *Biochemical and Physiological Aspects of Human Nutrition.* Philadelphia: W. B. Saunders.
3. Institute of Medicine. 2004. *Dietary Reference Intakes: Water, Potassium, Sodium, Chloride, and Sulfate.* Washington, D.C.: The National Academies Press. Available at www.nap.edu.
4. Ibid; Marieb. *Human Anatomy and Physiology.*
5. Marieb. *Human Anatomy and Physiology.*
6. Ibid.
7. Institute of Medicine. *Dietary Reference Intakes: Water, Potassium, Sodium, Chloride, and Sulfate.*
8. Ibid.
9. Casa, D. J., L. E. Armstrong, S. K. Hillman, S. J. Montain, R. C. Reiff, B. S. E. Rich, W. O. Roberts, and J. A. Stone. 2000. National Athletic Trainers Association Position Statement: Fluid Replacement for Athletes. *Journal of Athletic Training* 35: 212–224.
10. Institute of Medicine. *Dietary Reference Intakes: Water, Potassium, Sodium, Chloride, and Sulfate.*
11. Arnold, D. 2002. To the End, Marathon Was at Center of Student's Life. *The Boston Globe.* April 18, 2002; Aucoin, D. 2002. Tribute to a Fallen Champion of the Needs of the Afflicted. *The Boston Globe.* October 26, 2002; Noakes, T. D. 2003. Overconsumption of Fluids by Athletes. *British Medical Journal* 327: 113–114; Zeller, T. 2007. Too High a Price for a Wii. *The New York Times.* Available at www.nytimes.com. Accessed June 2010; Smith, S. 2002. Marathon Runner's Death Linked to Excessive Fluid Intake. *The Boston Globe.* August 13, 2002.
12. Marieb. *Human Anatomy and Physiology.*
13. Institute of Medicine. *Dietary Reference Intakes: Water, Potassium, Sodium, Chloride, and Sulfate.*
14. Ibid.
15. Ibid.
16. Ibid.
17. Gallagher, M. 2008. The Nutrients and Their Metabolism. In *Krause's Food, Nutrition and Diet Therapy.* 12th ed. St. Louis: Saunders Elsevier.
18. Institute of Medicine. *Dietary Reference Intakes: Vitamin A, Molybdenum, Nickel, Silicon, Vanadium, and Zinc.* Washington, D.C.: The National Academies Press. Available at www.nap.edu.
19. Institute of Medicine. *Dietary Reference Intakes: Water, Potassium, Sodium, Chloride, and Sulfate.*
20. Ibid.
21. Dietary Guidelines Advisory Committee. 2010. Report of the Dietary Guidelines Advisory Committee on the *Dietary Guidelines for Americans, 2010.* Available at www.cnpp.usda.gov. Accessed May 2013.
22. Ibid.
23. Coxson, P., Cook, N., Joffres, M., Hong, Y., Orenstein, D., Schmidt, S., and Bibbins-Domingo, K. 2013. Mortality Benefits from US Population-wide Reduction in Sodium Consumption. *Hypertension* 61: 564–570.
24. Report of the Dietary Guidelines Advisory Committee on the Dietary Guidelines for Americans, 2010. Available on: www.cnpp.usda.gov. Accessed May 2013.
25. Institute of Medicine. *Dietary Reference Intakes: Water, Potassium, Sodium, Chloride, and Sulfate.*
26. U.S. Department of Agriculture. Agricultural Research Service. 2012. Nutrient Intakes from Food: Mean Amounts Consumed per Individual, by Gender and Age, What We Eat in America, NHANES 2009–2010. Available at: www.ars.usda.gov. Accessed May 2012.
27. Lehnhardt, A., and Kemper, M. 2011. Pathogenesis, Diagnosis and Management of Hyperkalemia. *Pediatric Nephrology* 26: 377–384; Sheng. Body fluids and water balance.
28. U.S. National Library of Medicine and National Institutes of Health. 2011. Hypokalemia. Available at www.nlm.nih.gov. Accessed May 2013; Sheng. Body fluids and water balance.
29. Report of the Dietary Guidelines Advisory Committee on the Dietary Guidelines for Americans, 2010. Available on: www.cnpp.usda.gov. Accessed May 2013.
30. Institute of Medicine. 2011. *Dietary Reference Intakes for Calcium and Vitamin D.* Washington, D.C.: The National Academies Press. Available at www.nap.edu.
31. Institute of Medicine. *Dietary Reference Intakes for Calcium and Vitamin D;* Office of Dietary Supplements. 2013. Dietary Supplement Fact Sheet: Calcium. Available at http://ods.od.nih.gov. Accessed May 2013; Institute of Medicine. 1997. *Dietary Reference Intakes for Calcium, Phosphorus, Magnesium, Vitamin D, and Fluoride.* Washington, D.C.: The National Academies Press. Available at www.nap.edu.
32. Office of Dietary Supplements. Dietary Supplement Fact Sheet: Calcium
33. Ibid. Institute of Medicine. *Dietary Reference Intakes for Calcium and Vitamin D;* Miller, G. D., G. D. DiRienzo, M. E. Reusser, and D. A. McCarron. 2000. Benefits of Dairy Product Consumption on Blood Pressure in Humans: A Summary of the Biomedical Literature. *Journal of the American College of Nutrition* 19: 147S–164S.
34. Office of Dietary Supplements. Dietary Supplement Fact Sheet: Calcium; Baron, J. A., M. Beach, J. S. Mandel, R. U. van Stolk, R. W. Haile, R. S. Sandler, et al. 1999. Calcium Supplements for the Prevention of Colorectal Adenomas. *New England Journal of Medicine* 340: 101–107; Wu, K., W. C. Willet, C. S. Fuchs, G. A. Colditz, and E. L. Giovannucci. 2002. Calcium Intake and Risk of Colon Cancer in Women and Men. *Journal of the National Cancer Institute* 94: 437–446.
35. National Kidney and Urologic Diseases Information Clearinghouse. 2013. Kidney Stones in Adults. Available at http://kidney.niddk.nih.gov. Accessed May 2013.
36. Office of Dietary Supplements. Dietary Supplement Fact Sheet: Calcium; Borghi, L., R. Schianchi, T. Meschi, A. Guerra, U. Maggiore, and A. Novarini. 2002. Comparison of Two Diets for the Prevention of Recurrent Stones in Idiopathic Hypercalciuria. *New England Journal of Medicine* 346: 77–84; Bushinsky, D. A. 2002. Recurrent Hypercalciuric Nephrolithiasis: Does Diet Help? *New England Journal of Medicine* 346: 124–125; Curhan, G. C., W. C. Willett, E. B. Rimm, and M. J. Stampfer. 1993. A Prospective Study of Dietary Calcium and Other Nutrients and the Risk of Symptomatic Kidney Stones. *New England Journal of Medicine* 328: 833–838.
37. Office of Dietary Supplements. Dietary Supplement Fact Sheet: Calcium
38. Institute of Medicine. *Dietary Reference Intakes for Calcium and Vitamin D;* Office of Dietary Supplements. Dietary Supplement Fact Sheet: Calcium.
39. Ibid.
40. Ibid.
41. USDA. Agricultural Research Service. 2012. Nutrient Intakes from Food.
42. Dietary Guidelines Advisory Committee. Report of the Dietary Guidelines Advisory Committee on the *Dietary Guidelines for Americans, 2010.*
43. National Institutes of Health. 2000. Osteoporosis Prevention, Diagnosis, and Therapy. NIH Consensus Statement Online. Available at http://consensus.nih.gov. Accessed May 2013.
44. Osteoporosis and Related Bone Diseases—National Resource Center. 2011. Calcium Supplements: What to Look For. Available at www.niams.nih.gov. Accessed May 2013.
45. USDA. Agricultural Research Service. 2012. Nutrient Intakes from Food.
46. Institute of Medicine. *Dietary Reference Intakes for Calcium, Phosphorus, Magnesium, Vitamin D, and Fluoride.*
47. Office of Dietary Supplements. 2009. Magnesium. Available at http://ods.od.nih.gov. Accessed May 2013.
48. Ibid; Appel, L. J., T. J. Moore, E. Obarzanek, W. M. Vollmer, L. P. Svetkey, F. M. Sacks, et al. 1997. A Clinical Trial of the Effects of Dietary Patterns on Blood Pressure. *New England Journal of Medicine* 336: 1117–1124.
49. Office of Dietary Supplements. Magnesium; Harsha, D. W., P. Lin, E. Obarzanek, N. M. Karanja, T. J. Moore, and B. Caballero. 1999. Dietary Approaches to Stop Hypertension: A Summary of Study Results. *Journal of the American Dietetics Association* 99: S35–S39.
50. American Diabetes Association. 2008. Nutrition Recommendations and Intervention for Diabetes. *Diabetes Care* 31: S61–S78; Lopez-Ridaura, R., W. C. Willet, E. B. Rimm, S. Liu, M. J. Stampfer, J. E. Manson, and F. B. Hu. 2004. Magnesium Intake and Risk of Type 2 Diabetes in Men and Women. *Diabetes Care* 27: 134–140.
51. USDA. Agricultural Research Service. 2012. Nutrient Intakes from Food.
52. Institute of Medicine. *Dietary Reference Intakes for Calcium, Phosphorus, Magnesium, Vitamin D, and Fluoride.*
53. Institute of Medicine. *Dietary Reference Intakes: Water.*
54. Gallagher, M. The Nutrients and Their Metabolism.
55. Institute of Medicine. 2001. *Dietary Reference Intakes for Vitamin A, Vitamin K, Arsenic, Boron, Chromium, Copper, Iodine, Iron, Manganese, Molybdenum, Nickel, Silicon, Vanadium, and Zinc.* Washington, D.C.: The National Academies Press. Available at www.nap.edu.
56. Ibid.

57. Office of Dietary Supplements. 2007. Iron. Available at http://ods.od.nih.gov. Accessed May 2013; Beard, J. 2003. Iron Deficiency Alters Brain Development and Functioning. *Journal of Nutrition* 133: 1468S–1472S; Black, M. M. 2003. Micronutrient Deficiencies and Cognitive Function. *Journal of Nutrition* 133: 3972S–3931S.
58. USDA, Agricultural Research Service. 2012. Nutrient Intakes from Food.
59. Ibid.
60. Institute of Medicine. *Dietary Reference Intakes for Calcium, Phosphorus, Magnesium, Vitamin D, and Fluoride.*
61. Britton, H. C., and C. E. Nossamn. 1986. Iron Content of Food Cooked in Iron Utensils. *Journal of the American Dietetic Association* 86: 897–901.
62. Federal Register. 2003. Final Rule - 68 FR 59714, 2003: Iron-Containing Supplements and Drugs, Label Warning Statements and Unit-Dose Packaging Requirements, Removal of Regulations for Unit-Dose Packaging Requirements for Dietary Supplements and Drugs. Updated 2013. Available at www.fda.gov. Accessed May 2013.
63. Institute of Medicine. 2001. *Dietary Reference Intakes for Vitamin A, Vitamin K, Arsenic, Boron, Chromium, Copper, Iodine, Iron, Manganese, Molybdenum, Nickel, Silicon, Vanadium, and Zinc.*
64. Office of Dietary Supplements. Iron.
65. Institute of Medicine. 2001. *Dietary Reference Intakes for Vitamin A, Vitamin K, Arsenic, Boron, Chromium, Copper, Iodine, Iron, Manganese, Molybdenum, Nickel, Silicon, Vanadium, and Zinc*; Turnlund, J. R. 2006. Copper. In Shils, M. E., M. Shike, A. C. Ross, B. Caballero, and R. J. Cousins, eds. *Modern Nutrition in Health and Disease.* 10th ed. Philadelphia: Lippincott Williams & Wilkins; Uaruy, R., M. Olivares, and M. Gonzalez. 1998. Essentiality of Copper in Humans. *American Journal of Clinical Nutrition* 67: 952S–959S.
66. Institute of Medicine. *Dietary Reference Intakes for Vitamin A, Vitamin K, Arsenic, Boron, Chromium, Copper, Iodine, Iron, Manganese, Molybdenum, Nickel, Silicon, Vanadium, and Zinc*; Office of Dietary Supplements. Updated 2011. Zinc. Available at http://ods.od.nih.gov. Accessed May 2013.
67. Office of Dietary Supplements. Zinc; Ibs, K., and L. Rink. 2003. Zinc-Altered Immune Function. *Journal of Nutrition* 133: 1452S–1456S; Schwartz, J. R., R. G. Marsh, and Z. D. Draelos. 2005. Zinc and Skin Health: Overview of Physiology and Pharmacology. *Dermatological Surgery* 31: 837–847; Walravens, P. A. 1979. Zinc Metabolism and Its Implications in Clinical Medicine. *Western Journal of Medicine* 130: 133–142.
68. Russell, R. M., M. E. Cox, and N. Solomons. 1983. Zinc and the Special Senses. *Annals of Internal Medicine* 99: 227–239.
69. The Cochrane Library. 2011. Zinc for the Common Cold. Available at www.thecochranelibrary.com. Accessed May 2013; Caruso, T., C. Prober, and J. Gwaltney. 2007. Treatment of Naturally Acquired Common Colds with Zinc: A Structured Review. *Clinical Infectious Diseases* 45: 569–574.
70. Office of Dietary Supplements. 2011. Dietary Supplement Fact Sheet: Zinc. Available at http://ods.od.nih.gov. Accessed May 2013.
71. Ibid.
72. Prasad, A. 2003. Zinc Deficiency. *British Medical Journal* 326: 409–410.
73. Office of Dietary Supplements. 2012. Selenium. Available at http://ods.od.nih.gov. Accessed May 2013; Combs, G. F. 2005. Current Evidence and Research Needs to Support a Health Claim for Selenium and Cancer Prevention. *Journal of Nutrition* 135: 343–347; Institute of Medicine. 2000. *Dietary Reference Intakes for Vitamin C, Vitamin E, Selenium, and Carotenoids.* Washington, D.C.: The National Academies Press. Available at www.nap.edu.
74. Office of Dietary Supplements. Selenium; Beck, M. A., O. A. Levander, and O. Handy. 2003. Selenium Deficiency and Viral Infection. *Journal of Nutrition* 133: 1463S–1467S; Li, H., M. J. Stampfer, E. L. Giovannucci, J. S. Morris, W. C. Willett, M. Gaziano, and J. Ma. 2004. A Prospective Study of Plasma Selenium Levels and Prostate Cancer Risk. *Journal of the National Cancer Institute* 96: 696–703; Center for Food Safety and Applied Nutrition. 2013. Qualified Health Claims Subject to Enforcement Discretion. Available at www.fda.gov. Accessed May 2013; Wei, W., C. C. Abnet, Y. Qiao, S. M. Dawsey, Z. Dong, X. Sun, et al. 2004. Prospective Study of Serum Selenium Concentrations and Esophageal and Gastric Cardia Cancer, Heart Disease, Stroke, and Total Death. *American Journal of Nutrition* 79: 80–85.
75. Office of Dietary Supplements. Selenium; American Dental Association. 2005. Fluoridation Facts. Available at www.ada.org. Accessed June 2010.
76. Palmer, C., and Gilbert, J. 2012. Position of the Academy of Nutrition and Dietetics: The Impact of Fluoride on Health. *Journal of the Academy of Nutrition and Dietetics* 112:1443–1453.
77. Centers for Disease Control and Prevention. 1999. Achievements in Public Health, 1900–1999: Fluoridation of Drinking Water to Prevent Dental Caries. *Morbidity and Mortality Weekly Report* 48: 933–940. Available at www.cdc.gov. Accessed May 2013.
78. Palmer. Position of the Academy of Nutrition and Dietetics: The Impact of Fluoride on Health.
79. Institute of Medicine. *Dietary Reference Intakes for Calcium, Phosphorus, Magnesium, Vitamin D, and Fluoride.*
80. Office of Dietary Supplements. 2005. Chromium. Available at http://ods.od.nih.gov. Accessed May 2013; American Diabetes Association. 2008. Nutrition Recommendations and Intervention for Diabetes; Hopkins, L. L., O. Ransome-Kuti, and A. S. Majaj. 1968. Improvement of Impaired Carbohydrate Metabolism by Chromium (III) in Malnourished Infants. *American Journal of Clinical Nutrition* 21: 203–211; Jeejeebhoy, K. N., R. C. Clu, E. B. Marliss, G. R. Greenberg, and A. Bruce-Robertson. 1977. Chromium Deficiency, Glucose Intolerance, and Neuropathy Reversed by Chromium Supplementation in a Patient Receiving Long-Term Total Parenteral Nutrition. *American Journal of Clinical Nutrition* 30: 531–538; Mertz, W. 1998. Interaction of Chromium with Insulin: A Progress Report. *Nutrition Reviews* 56: 174–177.
81. Office of Dietary Supplements. Chromium; Cefalu, W. T., and F. B. Hu. 2004. Role of Chromium in Human Health and in Diabetes. *Diabetes Care* 27: 2741–2751.
82. Food and Drug Administration. 2013. Summary of Qualified Health Claims Subject to the Enforcement Discretion. Available at www.fda.gov. Accessed May 2013.
83. Office of Dietary Supplements. Chromium.
84. Ibid.
85. Ibid.
86. Institute of Medicine. *Dietary Reference Intakes for Vitamin A, Vitamin K, Arsenic, Boron, Chromium, Copper, Iodine, Iron, Manganese, Molybdenum, Nickel, Silicon, Vanadium, and Zinc.*
87. Ibid.
88. Ibid.
89. Institute of Medicine. *Dietary Reference Intakes for Vitamin A, Vitamin K, Arsenic, Boron, Chromium, Copper, Iodine, Iron, Manganese, Molybdenum, Nickel, Silicon, Vanadium, and Zinc*; Barceloux, D. G. 1999. Manganese. *Clinical Toxicology* 37: 293–307.
90. Institute of Medicine. *Dietary Reference Intakes for Vitamin A, Vitamin K, Arsenic, Boron, Chromium, Copper, Iodine, Iron, Manganese, Molybdenum, Nickel, Silicon, Vanadium, and Zinc.*
91. Ibid.

Feature Box References

1. U.S. Environmental Protection Agency. 2009. Water on Tap. Available at http://water.epa.gov. Accessed May 2013.
2. Ibid.; U.S. Environmental Protection Agency. 2012. Basic Information about Regulated Drinking Water Contaminants and Indicators. Available at http://water.epa.gov. Accessed May 2013.
3. Centers for Disease Control and Prevention. 2012. Community Water Fluoridation: Statistics 2010. Available at www.cdc.gov. Accessed May 2013.
4. Centers for Disease Control and Prevention. 2012. Bottled Water and Fluoride. Available at www.cdc.gov. Accessed May 2013; Natural Resources Defense Council. 1999. Bottled Water: Pure Drink or Pure Hype? Available at www.nrdc.org. Accessed May 2013.
5. Centers For Disease Control, Fluoride Recommendations Work Group. 2001. Recommendations for Using Fluoride to Prevent and Control Dental Caries in the United States. *Morbidity and Mortality Weekly Report* 50 (RR14): 1–42. Available at www.cdc.gov. Accessed August 2010.
6. American Heart Association. 2013. Heart Disease and Stroke Statistics—2013 Update. *Circulation* 127: e6–e245.
7. American Heart Association. 2011. ACCF/AHA 2011 Expert Consensus Document on Hypertension in the Elderly. *Circulation* 123: 2434–2506; Franklin, S. S., et al. 1997. Hemodynamic Patterns of Age-Related Changes in Blood Pressure. *Circulation* 96: 308–315.
8. National Heart, Lung, and Blood Institute. 2012. High Blood Pressure. Available at www.nhlbi.nih.gov. Accessed May 2013; U.S. Department of Health and Human Services. National Institutes of Health. National Heart, Lung, and Blood Institute. National High Blood Pressure Education Program Coordinating Committee. 2004. The Seventh Report of the Joint National Committee on Prevention, Detection, Evaluation, and Treatment of High Blood Pressure. Available at www.nhlbi.nih.gov. Accessed May 2013.

9. American Heart Association. 2012. About High Blood Pressure. Available at www.heart.org. Accessed May 2013; National Heart, Lung, and Blood Institute. High Blood Pressure.

10. American Heart Association. About High Blood Pressure; U.S. Department of Health and Human Services. 2007. Overweight and Obesity: Health Consequences. Available at www.surgeongeneral .gov. Accessed May 2013; USDA. NIH. NHLBI. National High Blood Pressure Education Program Coordinating Committee. The Seventh Report of the Joint National Committee; Wharton, S. P., A. Chin, X. Xin, and J. He. 2002. Effect of Aerobic Exercise on Blood Pressure: A Meta-Analysis of Randomized Controlled Trials. *Annals of Internal Medicine* 136: 493–503.

11. Xin, X., J. He, M. G. Frontini, L. G. Ogden, O. I. Motsamai, and P. K. Whelton. 2001. Effects of Alcohol Reduction on Blood Pressure: A Meta-Analysis of Randomized Controlled Trials. *Hypertension* 38: 1112–1117.

12. National Heart, Lung, and Blood Institute. 2012. What Is The DASH Eating Plan? Available at www.nhlbi.nih.gov. Accessed May 2013; Harsha, D. W., P. Lin, E. Obarzanek, N. M. Karanja, T. J. Moore, and B. Caballero. 1999. Dietary Approaches to Stop Hypertension: A Summary of Study Results. *Journal of the American Dietetics Association* 99: S35–S39.

13. National Heart, Lung, and Blood Institute. 2006. Your Guide to Lowering Your Blood Pressure with DASH. Available at www.nhlbi.nih .gov. Accessed May 2013.

14. U.S. Department of Agriculture, U.S. Department of Health and Human Services. 2010. *Dietary Guidelines for Americans, 2010.* 7th ed. Washington, D.C.: U.S. Government Printing Office.

15. Patlak, M. 2001. Bone Builders: The Discoveries behind Preventing and Treating Osteoporosis. *The FASEB Journal* 15: 1677.

16. U.S. Department of Health and Human Services, Office of the Surgeon General. 2012. The Surgeon General's Report on Bone Health and Osteoporosis: What It Means To You. Available at www.niams.nih.gov. Accessed May 2013; U.S. Department of Health and Human Services. 2004. *Bone Health and Osteoporosis: A Report of the Surgeon General.* Washington, D.C.: U.S. Department of Health and Human Services, Office of the Surgeon General.

17. Ibid.

18. Ibid.

19. Office of Dietary Supplements. 2013. Dietary Supplement Fact Sheet: Calcium. Available at http://ods.od.nih.gov. Accessed May 2013; U.S. Department of Health and Human Services. *Bone Health and Osteoporosis.*

20. Lewiecki, E. 2011. In the Clinic. Osteoporosis. *Annals of Internal Medicine* 155: ITC1–ITC16; U.S. Department of Health and Human Services. 2004. *Bone Health and Osteoporosis: Osteoporosis in Postmenopausal Women: Diagnosis and Monitoring Evidence.* Report/Technology Assessment No. 28. Agency for Healthcare Research and Quality, 2001. Publication No. 01-E032.

21. Miller, K. K. 2003. Mechanisms by Which Nutritional Disorders Cause Reduced Bone Mass in Adults. *Journal of Women's Health* 12: 145–150.

22. U.S. Department of Health and Human Services. The Surgeon General's Report on Bone Health and Osteoporosis: What It Means To You.

23. Ibid; U.S. Department of Health and Human Services. *Bone Health and Osteoporosis.*

24. Ibid.

Two Points of View References

1. Department of Health and Human Services, Centers for Disease Control and Prevention. 2013. Community Water Fluoridation. Overview. Available at www.cdc.gov. Accessed June 2013.

2. Centers for Disease Control and Prevention. 2008. MMWR Report: Populations Receiving Optimally Fluoridated Public Drinking Water—United States, 1992–2006. Available at www.cdc.gov. Accessed July 2010.

3. Centers for Disease Control and Prevention. 2011. Chronic Disease Prevention and Health Promotion. Oral Health. Preventing Cavities, Gum Disease, Tooth Loss, and Oral Cancers At A Glance 2011. www.cdc.gov. Accessed June 2013.

4. American Dental Association. 2005. *Fluoridation Facts.* Chicago: American Dental Association. Available at www.ada.org. Accessed June 2013.

5. American Dental Hygienists Association. 2010. Fluoride Facts. Available at www.adha.org. Accessed May 2013.

6. American Dental Association. *Fluoridation Facts.*

7. U.S. EPA. 2011. News Releases—Water. EPA and HHS Announce New Scientific Assessments and Actions on Fluoride/Agencies Working Together to Maintain Benefits of Preventing Tooth Decay while Preventing Excessive Exposure. Available at http://yosemite.epa.gov.

8. World Health Organization. 2001. Water-Related Diseases: Fluorosis. Available at www.who.int. Accessed May 2013.

9. Environmental Protection Agency. 2013. Basic Information about Fluoride in Drinking Water. Available at http://water.epa.gov. Accessed May 2013.

10. U.S. Environmental Protection Agency. 2011. New Fluoride Risk Assessment and Relative Source Contribution Documents. Available at http://water.epa.gov. Accessed June 2013.

11. Sierra Club. 2008. Sierra Club Conservation Policies: Policy on Fluoride in Drinking Water. Available at www.sierraclub.org. Accessed May 2013.

12. National Academy of Sciences, National Academies Press. 2006. Fluoride in Drinking Water: A Scientific Review of EPA's Standards. Available at http://www.nap.edu. Accessed May 2013.

Chapter 9

1. Distilled Spirits Councils in the United States. 2007. Distilled Spirits Industry Primer. Available at www.discus.org. Accessed June 2013.

2. Centers for Disease Control and Prevention. 2012. Alcohol and Public Health: General Alcohol Information. Available at www.cdc.gov. Accessed June 2013.

3. National Institute on Alcohol Abuse and Alcoholism. Alcohol and Health. Available at www.niaaa.nih.gov. Accessed June 2013.

4. Mandelbaum, D. G. 1965. Alcohol and Culture. *Current Anthropology* 6: 281–288; National Institute on Alcohol Abuse and Alcoholism. 1992. Moderate Drinking. Available at http://pubs.niaaa.nih.gov. Accessed June 2013.

5. U.S. Department of Agriculture. 2010. Report of the Dietary Guidelines Advisory Committee, 2010. Available at www.cnpp.usda.gov. Accessed June 2013; Goldberg, I. J., L. Mosca, M. R. Piano, and E. A. Fisher. 2001. Wine and Your Heart. A Science Advisory for Healthcare Professionals from the Nutrition Committee, Council on Epidemiology and Prevention, and Council on Cardiovascular Nursing of the American Heart Association. *Circulation* 103: 472–475.

6. Dodd, T. H., and S. Morse. 1994. The Impact of Media Stories Concerning Health Issues on Food Product Sales. *Journal of Consumer Marketing* 11: 17–24.

7. U.S. Department of Agriculture. Report of the Dietary Guidelines Advisory Committee; Goldberg. Wine and Your Heart.

8. U.S. Department of Agriculture. Report of the Dietary Guidelines Advisory Committee.

9. National Institute on Alcohol Abuse and Alcoholism. 2007. Alcohol Alert: Alcohol Metabolism. Available at http://pubs.niaaa.nih.gov. Accessed June 2013.

10. Jones, A. W., and K. A. Jonsson. 1994. Food-Induced Lowering of Blood-Ethanol Profiles and Increased Rate of Elimination Immediately After a Meal. *Journal of Forensic Sciences* 39: 1084–1093.

11. National Institute on Alcohol Abuse and Alcoholism. Alcohol Alert: Alcohol Metabolism.

12. Ibid.

13. National Institute on Alcohol Abuse and Alcoholism. 2004. Alcohol Alert: Alcohol and the Brain. Available at www.pubs.niaaa.nih .gov. Accessed June 2013; National Institute on Alcohol Abuse and Alcoholism. 2000. Alcohol Alert: Imaging and Alcoholism: A Window on the Brain. Available at http://pubs.niaaa.nih.gov. Accessed June 2013.

14. O'Brien, M., T. McCoy, S. Rhodes, A. Wagoner, and M. Wolfson. 2008. Caffeinated Cocktails: Energy Drink Consumption, High-Risk Drinking, and Alcohol-Related Consequences Among College Students. *Academy of Emergency Medicine* 15: 453–460.

15. Ferreira, S., T. deMello, S. Pompeia, and M. deSouza-Formigoni. 2006. Effects of Energy Drink Ingestion on Alcohol Intoxication. *Alcoholism: Clinical and Experimental Research* 30: 598–605.

16. Frezza, M., C. diPadova, G. Pozzato, M. Terpin, E. Baraona, and C. S. Leiber. 1990. High Blood Alcohol Levels in Women: The Role of Decreased Gastric Alcohol Dehydrogenase Activity and First-Pass Metabolism. *New England Journal of Medicine* 332: 95–99.

17. Brooks, P. J., M. A. Enoch, D. Goldman, T. K. Li, and A. Yokoyama. 2009. The Alcohol Flushing Response: An Unrecognized Risk Factor for Esophageal Cancer from Alcohol Consumption. *PLoS Medicine* 6: e1000050. doi:10.1371/journal.pmed.1000050; Makimoto, K. 1998. Drinking Patterns and Drinking Problems Among Asian-Americans and Pacific Islanders. *Alcohol Health & Research World* 22: 270–275.

18. Subgketibm, R., and A. Wolfson. 2009. Alcohol Consumption, Sleep, and Academic Performance Among College Students. *Journal of Studies on Alcohol and Drugs* 70: 355–363; National Institute on Alcohol Abuse

and Alcoholism. 1998. Alcohol Alert: Alcohol and Sleep. Available at www.niaaa.nih.gov. Accessed June 2013.

19. National Institute on Alcohol Abuse and Alcoholism. Alcohol Alert: Alcohol and Sleep; Roehrs, T., D. Beare, F. Zorick, and T. Roth. 1994. Sleepiness and Ethanol Effects on Simulated Driving. *Alcoholism: Clinical and Experimental Research* 18: 154–158.

20. Verster, J., D. van Duin, E. Volkerts, A. Schreuder, and M. Verbaten. 2003. Alcohol Hangover Effects on Memory Functioning and Vigilance Performance after an Evening of Binge Drinking. *Neuropsychopharmacology* 28: 740–746; Swift, R. S., and D. Davidson. 1998. Alcohol Hangover, Mechanisms and Mediators. *Alcohol Health & Research World* 22: 54–60. Available at http://pubs.niaaa.nih.gov. Accessed June 2013.

21. Swift. Alcohol Hangover.

22. Food and Drug Administration. 2013. Acetaminophen and Liver Injury: Q & A for Consumers. Available at www.fda.gov. Accessed June 2013; National Institute on Alcohol Abuse and Alcoholism. Alcohol Alert: Alcohol Metabolism; Swift. Alcohol Hangover.

23. Chen, W., B. Rosner, S. Hankinson, G. Colditz, and W. Willet. 2011. Moderate Alcohol Consumption during Adult Life, Drinking Patterns, and Breast Cancer Risk. *Journal of the American Medical Association* 306: 1884–1890.

24. Muthusami, K., and P. Chinnaswamy. 2005. Effect of Chronic Alcoholism on Male Fertility Hormones and Semen Quality. *Fertility and Sterility* 84: 919–924; USDA. Report of the Dietary Guidelines Advisory Committee; National Institute on Alcohol Abuse and Alcoholism. 2004. Alcohol Alert: Alcohol—An Important Women's Health Issue. Available at http://pubs.niaaa.nih.gov. Accessed June 2013.

25. Lieber, C. S. 2000. Alcohol: Its Metabolism and Interaction with Nutrients. *Annual Review of Nutrition* 20: 394–430.

26. Jarl, J., and U. Gerdtham. 2011. Time Pattern of Reduction in Risk of Oesophageal Cancer Following Alcohol Cessation—a Meta Analysis. *Addiction* 107: 1234–1243; Pelucchi, C., S. Gallus, W. Garavello, C. Bosetti, and C. LaVecchia. 2006. Cancer Risk Associated with Alcohol and Tobacco Use: Focus on Upper Aero-Digestive Tract and Liver. *Alcohol Research & Health* 29: 193–198.

27. Bagnardi, V., M. Blangiardo, C. LaVecchia, and G. Corrao. 2001. Alcohol Consumption and the Risk of Cancer. *Alcohol Research and Health* 25: 263–270.

28. Templeton, A., K. Carter, N. Sheron, P. Gallagher, and C. Verrill. 2009. Sudden Unexpected Death in Alcohol Misuse—An Unrecognized Public Health Issue? *International Journal of Environmental Research and Public Health* 6: 3070–3081.

29. Zakhari, S. 2006. Overview: How Is Alcohol Metabolized by the Body? *Alcohol Research & Health* 29: 245–255; Lieber. Alcohol: Its Metabolism and Interaction with Nutrients.

30. Nolan, J. 2010. The Role of Intestinal Endotoxin in Liver Injury: A Long and Evolving History. *Hepatology* 52: 1829–1835; National Institute on Alcohol Abuse and Alcoholism. 2000. Alcohol and the Liver: Research Update. Available at http://pubs.niaaa.nih.gov. Accessed June 2013.

31. National Institute on Alcohol Abuse and Alcoholism. 2005. Alcohol Alert: Alcohol and the Liver. Available at http://pubs.niaaa.nih.gov. Accessed June 2013.

32. Centers for Disease Control and Prevention. 2012. Alcohol and Public Health. 2012 Fact Sheets—Alcohol Use and Health. Available at www.cdc.gov. Accessed June 2013.

33. Jones, K., and D. Smith. 1973. Recognition of the Fetal Alcohol Syndrome in Early Infancy. *The Lancet* 2: 999–1001; Bertrand, J., R. L. Floyd, and M. K. Weber. 2005. Guidelines for Identifying and Referring Persons with Fetal Alcohol Syndrome. *Morbidity and Mortality Weekly Report* 54 (RR11): 1–10. Available at www.cdc.gov. Accessed June 2013.

34. Centers for Disease Control and Prevention. 2012. Fetal Alcohol Spectrum Disorders. Available at www.cdc.gov. Accessed June 2013; Bertrand. Guidelines for Identifying and Referring Persons.

35. Centers for Disease Control and Prevention. 2012. Alcoholism: Frequently Asked Questions. Available at www.cdc.gov. Accessed June 2013.

36. Centers for Disease Control and Prevention. 2012. Vital Signs. Binge Drinking. Available at www.cdc.gov. Accessed June 2013.

37. National Institute on Alcohol Abuse and Alcoholism. 2012. College Drinking. Available at http://pubs.niaaa.nih.gov. Accessed June 2013.

38. Ibid.

39. Centers for Disease Control and Prevention. 2012. Binge Drinking. Available at www.cdc.gov. Accessed June 2013.

40. White, A. M., D. W. Jamieson-Drake, and H. S. Swartzwelder. 2002. Prevalence and Correlates of Alcohol-Induced Blackouts Among College Students: Results of an E-Mail Survey. *Journal of American College Health* 51: 117–131.

41. National Institute on Alcohol Abuse and Alcoholism. College Drinking.

42. B.R.A.D. 21 website. 2013. Available at www.brad21.org. Accessed June 2013.

43. National Institute on Alcohol Abuse and Alcoholism. 2000. Alcohol Tolerance. Available at http://pubs.niaaa.nih.gov. Accessed June 2013.

44. National Highway Traffic Safety Administration. 2012. Traffic Safety Facts 2011: Alcohol-Impaired Driving. Available at www-nrd.nhtsa.dot.gov. Accessed September 2013.

45. Centers for Disease Control and Prevention. 2011. Drinking and Driving. Available at www.cdc.gov. Accessed June 2013; Centers for Disease Control and Prevention. 2013. Impaired Driving: Get the Facts. Available at www.cdc.gov. Accessed June 2013.

46. National Institute on Alcohol Abuse and Alcoholism. 2012. Underage Drinking. Available at http://pubs.niaaa.nih.gov. Accessed June 2013.

47. Ibid.

48. Centers for Disease Control and Prevention. Binge Drinking.

49. National Highway Traffic Safety Administration. 2013. Traffic Safety Facts 2011: Young Drivers. Available at www-nrd.nhtsa.dot.gov. Accessed September 2013.

50. Centers for Disease Control and Prevention. 2012. Teen Drinking and Driving. Available at www.cdc.gov. Accessed June 2013.

51. American Medical Association. 2003. The Minimum Legal Drinking Age: Facts and Fallacies. Available at www.alcoholpolicymd.com. Accessed June 2013.

52. Wagenaar, A. C., A. L. Tobler, and K. A. Komro. 2010. Effects of Alcohol Tax and Price Policies on Morbidity and Mortality: A Systematic Review. *American Journal of Public Health* 100: 2,270–2,278.

53. Centers for Disease Control and Prevention. 2012. Underage Drinking. Available at www.cdc.gov. Accessed June 2013.

54. Centers for Disease Control and Prevention. Alcoholism: Frequently Asked Questions; National Institute on Alcohol Abuse and Alcoholism. 2007. A Family History of Alcoholism. Available at http://pubs.niaaa.nih.gov. Accessed June 2013.

55. National Institute on Alcohol Abuse and Alcoholism. A Family History of Alcoholism.

56. Alcoholics Anonymous. 2004. Membership Survey. Available at www.aa.org. Accessed June 2013.

57. U.S. Department of Agriculture. Report of the Dietary Guidelines Advisory Committee.

Feature Box References

1. Austin, E., and S. Hust. 2005. The Content and Frequency of Alcoholic and Nonalcoholic Beverage Ads in Magazine and Video Formats November 1999–April 2000. *Journal of Health Communications* 10: 769–785.

2. Johns Hopkins Bloomberg School of Public Health, Center on Alcohol Marketing and Youth. 2012. Youth Exposure to Alcohol Advertising on Television, 2001–2009. Available at www.camy.org. Accessed June 2012.

3. Austin, E., M. Chen, and J. Grube. 2006. How Does Alcohol Advertising Influence Underage Drinking? The Role of Desirability, Identification, and Skepticism. *Journal of Adolescent Health* 38: 376–384.

Two Points of View References

1. Elkind, M. S., R. Sciacca, et al. 2006. Moderate Alcohol Consumption Reduces Risk of Ischemic Stroke. *Stroke* 37: 13; Goldberg, I. J, et. al. 2001. AHA Science Advisory: Wine and Your Heart: A Science Advisory for Healthcare Professionals from the Nutrition Committee, Council on Epidemiology and Prevention, and Council on Cardiovascular Nursing of the American Heart Association. *Circulation*. 103: 472–475.

2. Hanson, D. J. 2013. Alcohol: Problems and Solutions. Available at www2.potsdam.edu. Accessed July 2013.

3. Ibid.

4. Koppes L. L., et al. 2005. Moderate Alcohol Consumption Lowers the Risk of Type 2 Diabetes: A Meta-analysis of Prospective Observational Studies. *Diabetes Care*. 28: 719–725.

5. Walker, C. 2008. Vitamins in Beer. Available at www.aim-digest.com. Accessed July 2013.

6. Centers for Disease Control and Prevention. 2013. Alcohol and Public Health: Frequently Asked Questions. Available at www.cdc.gov. Accessed July 2013.

7. Hingson, R. W., et. al. 2009. Magnitude of and Trends in Alcohol-related Mortality and Morbidity among U.S. College Students Ages 18–24, 1998–2005. *Journal of Studies on Alcohol and Drugs.* Suppl: 12–20.

8. Masten, A., V. Faden, and R. Zucker. 2009. *A Developmental Perspective on Underage Alcohol Use*. Available at http://pubs.niaaa.nih.gov. Accessed July 2013.

9. Ibid.

Chapter 10

1. Centers for Disease Control. 2012. Obesity and Overweight. Available at www.cdc.gov. Accessed June 2013.

2. IFIC Foundation. 2005. Food for Thought VI, Reporting of Diet, Nutrition, and Food Safety News. Available at www.foodinsight.org. Accessed June 2013.

3. Mintel Oxygen. 2012. Diet Trends—US—November 2012. Available at http://oxygen.mintel.com. Accessed June 2013.

4. Centers for Disease Control and Prevention. 2012. Economic Consequences of Overweight and Obesity. Available at www.cdc.gov. Accessed June 2013.

5. Centers for Disease Control and Prevention. 2011. Healthy Weight. Available at www.cdc.gov. Accessed June 2013.

6. Centers for Disease Control and Prevention. Overweight and Obesity; American Medical Association. 2013. AMA Adopts New Policies on Second Day of Voting at Annual Meeting. Available at www.ama-assn.org. Accessed June 2013.

7. National Institutes of Health. 1998. Clinical Guidelines on the Identification, Evaluation, and Treatment of Overweight and Obesity in Adults. Available at www.nhlbi.nih.gov. Accessed June 2013.

8. Ibid.

9. Centers for Disease Control and Prevention. Healthy Weight.

10. Gee, M., L. Mahan, and S. Escott-Stump. 2008. Weight management. In L. Mahan and S. Escott-Stump, eds., *Krause's Food, Nutrition, and Diet Therapy*. 12th ed. Philadelphia: Saunders.

11. Hammond, K. 2008. Assessment: Dietary and clinical data. In L. Mahan and S. Escott-Stump, eds., *Krause's Food, Nutrition, and Diet Therapy*. 12th ed. Philadelphia: Saunders.

12. U.S. Department of Health and Human Services. 2002. A Century of Women's Health, 1900–2000. Available at www.womenshealth.gov. Accessed June 2013.

13. National Institutes of Health. Clinical Guidelines on the Identification, Evaluation, and Treatment of Overweight and Obesity in Adults.

14. Ibid.

15. Ibid.

16. McFarlane, S. I., M. Banerji, and J. R. Sowers. 2001. Insulin Resistance and Cardiovascular Disease *The Journal of Clinical Endocrinology & Metabolism* 86: 713–718.

17. Institute of Medicine. 2002. *Dietary Reference Intakes for Energy, Carbohydrate, Fiber, Fat, Fatty Acids, Cholesterol, Protein, and Amino Acids*. Available at www.iom.edu. Accessed March 2010.

18. Hoffer, L. J. 2006. Metabolic consequences of starvation. In M. Shils, et al., eds., *Modern Nutrition in Health and Disease*. 10th ed. Philadelphia: Lippincott Williams & Wilkins.

19. Mattes, R., J. Hollis, D. Hayes, and A. Stunkard. 2005. Appetite: Measurement and Manipulations Misgivings. *Journal of the American Dietetic Association* 105 (supplement): S87–S97.

20. Smith, G. 2006. Controls of food intake. In M. Shils, et al., eds., *Modern Nutrition*.

21. Mattes. Appetite: Measurement and Manipulations Misgivings.

22. Smith. Controls of Food Intake.

23. Geliebter, A., S. Schachter, C. Lohmann-Walter, et al. 1996. Reduced Stomach Capacity in Obese Subjects After Dieting. *American Journal of Clinical Nutrition* 63: 170–173.

24. Center for Genomics and Public Health. 2004. Obesity and Current Topics in Genetics. Available at http://depts.washington.edu. Accessed June 2013.

25. Hill, J., V. Catenacci, and H. Wyatt. 2006. Obesity: Etiology. In M. Shils, et al., eds., *Modern Nutrition*.

26. Hill. Obesity: Etiology.

27. Bray, G., and C. Champagne. 2005. Beyond Energy Balance: There Is More to Obesity than Kilocalories. *Journal of the American Dietetic Association* 105 (supplement): S17–S23.

28. Brodsky, I. 2006. Hormones and growth factors. In M. Shils et al., eds., *Modern Nutrition*.

29. Hill. Obesity: Etiology.

30. Ibid.

31. Bray. Beyond Energy Balance; Loos, R., and T. Rankinen. 2005. Gene-Diet Interactions on Body Weight Changes. *Journal of the American Dietetic Association* 105 (supplement): S29–S34.

32. Gale, S., T. Van Itallie, and I. Faust. 1981. Effects of Palatable Diets on Body Weight and Adipose Tissue Cellularity in the Adult Obese Female Zucker Rat (fa/fa). *Metabolism* 30: 105–110.

33. Ravussin, E., M. Valencia, J. Esparza, P. Bennett, and L. Schulz. 1994. Effects of a Traditional Lifestyle on Obesity in Pima Indians. *Diabetes Care* 17: 1067–1074; Wang, S., and K. Brownell. 2005. Public Policy and Obesity: The Need to Marry Science with Advocacy. *Psychiatric Clinics of North America* 28: 235–252.

34. The Keystone Group. 2006. The Keystone Forums on Away-From-Home Food, Opportunities for Preventing Weight Gain and Obesity. Available at www.fda.gov. Accessed June 2013.

35. Smith, L., S. Ng, and B. Popkin. 2013. Trends in U.S. Home Food Preparation and Consumption: Analysis of National Nutrition Surveys and Time Use Studies from 1965–1966 to 2007–2008. *Nutrition Journal* 12: 45.

36. U.S. Department of Agriculture, Economic Research Service. 2012. Food and Nutrient Intake Data. Taking a Look at the Nutritional Quality of Foods Eaten at Home and Away from Home. Available at www.fda.gov. Accessed June 2013.

37. Ibid.

38. U.S. Department of Agriculture and U.S. Department of Health and Human Services. 2010. *Dietary Guidelines for Americans, 2010*. 7th ed. Washington, DC: U.S. Government Printing Office.; The Keystone Group. The Keystone Forums on Away-From-Home Food.

39. Ibid.

40. The Keystone Group. The Keystone Forums on Away-From-Home Food; Rolls, B. 1986. Sensory-Specific Satiety. *Nutrition Reviews* 44: 93–101.

41. U.S. Department of Agriculture and U.S. Department of Health and Human Services. *Dietary Guidelines for Americans, 2010*; Rolls, B. 2003. The Supersizing of America. *Nutrition Today* 38: 42–53.

42. Wansink, B. 2006. Ice Cream Illusions: Bowls, Spoons, and Self-Served Portion Sizes. *American Journal of Preventative Medicine* 31: 240–243; Wansink, B. 1996. Can Package Size Accelerate Usage Volume? *Journal of Marketing* 60: 1–14.

43. Rolls, B., L. Roe, and J. Meengs. 2006. Larger Portion Sizes Lead to a Sustained Increase in Energy Intake over 2 Days. *Journal of the American Dietetic Association* 106: 543–549.

44. U.S. Department of Agriculture and U.S. Department of Health and Human Services. *Dietary Guidelines for Americans, 2010*; French, S., M. Story, and R. Jeffery. 2001. Environmental Influences on Eating and Physical Activity. *Annual Reviews of Public Health* 22: 309–335.

45. French. Environmental Influences on Eating.

46. Mummery, W., G. Schofield, R. Steele, E. Eakin, and W. Brown. 2005. Occupational Sitting Time and Overweight and Obesity in Australian Workers. *American Journal of Preventative Medicine* 29: 91–97.

47. French. Environmental Influences on Eating.

48. Wang. Public Policy and Obesity.

49. Lanningham-Foster, L., L. Nysse, and J. Levine. 2003. Labor Saved, Calories Lost: The Energetic Impact of Domestic Labor-Saving Devices. *Obesity Research* 11: 1178–1181.

50. Ibid.

51. Centers for Disease Control and Prevention. 2012. Facts About Physical Activity. Available at www.cdc.gov. Accessed June 2013.

52. Centers for Disease Control and Prevention. 2010. Prevalence and Trends Data. Available at www.cdc.gov. Accessed June 2013; Centers for Disease Control and Prevention. 2005. Trends in Leisure-Time Physical Inactivity by Age, Sex, and Race/Ethnicity—United States, 1994–2004. *Morbidity and Mortality Weekly Report* 54: 991–994. Available at www.cdc.gov. Accessed June 2013.

53. Nielsen Media Research. 2013. Free to Move Between Screens. Available at www.nielsen.com. Accessed June 2013.

54. The Kaiser Family Foundation. 2010. Daily Media Use Among Children and Teens Up Dramatically from Five Years Ago. Available at www.kff.org. Accessed June 2013.

55. National Institutes of Health. Clinical Guidelines.

56. Centers for Disease Control and Prevention. 2013. Eat More, Weigh Less? Available at www.cdc.gov. Accessed June 2013; Mattes. Appetite: Measurement and Manipulations Misgivings; Lissner, L., D. Levitsky, B. Strupp, H. Kalkwarf, and D. Roe. 1987. Dietary Fat and the Regulation of Energy Intake in Human Subjects. *American Journal of Clinical Nutrition* 46: 886–892.

57. Centers for Disease Control and Prevention. Eat More, Weigh Less?; Tohill, B., J. Seymour, M. Serdula, L. Kettel-Khan, and B. Rolls. 2004. What Epidemiologic Studies Tell Us about the Relationship between Fruit and Vegetable Consumption and Body Weight. *Nutrition Reviews* 62: 365–374.

58. Centers for Disease Control and Prevention. Eat More, Weigh Less?; Rolls, B., E. Bell, and E. Thorwart. 1999. Water Incorporated into a Food but Not Served with a Food Decreases Energy Intake in Lean Women. *American Journal of Clinical Nutrition* 70: 448–455.

59. Slavin, J. 2008. Position of the American Dietetic Association: Health Implications of Dietary Fiber. *Journal of the American Dietetic Association* 108: 1716–1731; Burton-Freeman, B. 2000. Dietary Fiber and Energy Regulation. *Journal of Nutrition* 130: 272S–275S.

60. Davis, J., V. Hodges, and B. Gillham. 2006. Normal-Weight Adults Consume More Fiber and Fruit than Their Age- and Height-Matched Overweight/Obese Counterparts. *Journal of the American Dietetic Association* 106: 833–840.

61. Snoek, H., L. Huntjens, L. van Gemert, C. Graaf, and H. Weenen. 2004. Sensory-Specific Satiety in Obese and Normal-Weight Women. *American Journal of Clinical Nutrition* 80: 823–831; Mattes. Appetite: Measurement and Manipulations Misgivings.

62. U.S. Department of Agriculture, U.S. Department of Health and Human Services. *Dietary Guidelines for Americans, 2010*; Saries, W., S. Blair, M. van Baak, et al. 2003. How Much Physical Activity Is Enough to Prevent Unhealthy Weight Gain? Outcome of the IASO Stock Conference and Consensus Statement. *Obesity Reviews* 4: 101–114.

63. Keim, N., C. Blanton, and M. Kretsch. 2004. America's Obesity Epidemic: Measuring Physical Activity to Promote an Active Lifestyle. *Journal of the American Dietetic Association* 104: 1398–1409.

64. Jakicic, J., and A. Otto. 2005. Physical Activity Consideration for the Treatment and Prevention of Obesity. *American Journal of Clinical Nutrition* 82: 226S–229S.

65. Shape Up America! Not dated. 10,000 Steps. Available at www.shapeup.org. Accessed May 2010.

66. Edwards, J., and H. Meiselman. 2003. Changes in Dietary Habits during the First Year at University. *British Nutrition Foundation Nutrition Bulletin* 28: 21–34.

67. Zagorsky, J., and P. Smith. 2011. The Freshman 15: A Critical Time for Obesity Intervention or Media Myth? *Social Science Quarterly* 92: 1389–1407; Graham, M., and A. Jones. 2002. Freshman 15: Valid Theory or Harmful Myth? *Journal of American College Health* 50: 171–173.

68. Kong, A., S. Beresford, C. Alfano, K. Foster-Schubert, M. Neuhouser, D. Johnson, et al. 2012. Self-Monitoring and Eating-Related Behaviors Are Associated with 12-Month Weight Loss in Postmenopausal Overweight-to-Obese Women. *Journal of the Academy of Nutrition and Dietetics* 112: 1428–1435.

69. Schlundt, D., J. Hill, T. Sbrocco, J. Pope-Cordle, and T. Sharp. 1992. The Role of Breakfast in the Treatment of Obesity: A Randomized Clinical Trial. *American Journal of Clinical Nutrition* 55: 645–651.

70. National Institute of Diabetes and Digestive and Kidney Diseases. 2008. Weight Cycling. Available at http://win.niddk.nih.gov. Accessed June 2013; Rosenbaum, M., R. Leibel, and J. Hirsch. 1997. Obesity. *New England Journal of Medicine* 337: 396–407.

71. Ibid.

72. Wing, R., and S. Phelan. 2005. Long-Term Weight Loss Maintenance. *American Journal of Clinical Nutrition* 82: 222S–225S; Rosenbaum. Obesity. Klem, M. L., R. R. Wing, M. T. McGuire, H. M. Seagle, and J. O. Hill. 1997. A Descriptive Study of Individuals Successful at Long-Term Maintenance of Substantial Weight Loss. *American Journal of Clinical Nutrition* 66: 239–246.

73. Ibid.

74. Hill, J., H. Wyatt, G. Reed, and J. Peters. 2003. Obesity and the Environment: Where Do We Go from Here? *Science* 299: 853–897.

75. Hill, J., H. Thompson, and H. Wyatt. 2005. Weight Maintenance: What's Missing? *Journal of the American Dietetic Association* 105: S63–S66.

76. U.S. Department of Health and Human Services. 2008. Physical Activity Guidelines for Americans. Available at www.health.gov. Accessed June 2013.

77. Ibid.

78. Wade, T. D., A. Keski-Rahkonen, and J. Hudson. 2011. Epidemiology of eating disorders. In M. Tsuang and M. Tohen, eds. *Textbook in Psychiatric Epidemiology*. 3rd ed. New York: Wiley, 343–360.

79. Chamorro, R., and Y. Flores-Ortiz. 2000. Acculturation and Disordered Eating Patterns among Mexican American Women. *International Journal of Eating Disorders* 28: 125–129; Crago, M., C. M. Shisslak, and L. S. Estes. 1996. Eating Disturbances among American Minority Groups: A Review. *International Journal of Eating Disorders* 19: 239–248; Kjelsas, E., C. Bjornstrom, and K. G. Gotestam. 2004. Prevalence of Eating Disorders in Female and Male Adolescents (14–15 Years). *Eating Behaviors* 5: 13–25; O'Dea, J., and S. Abraham. 2002. Eating and

Exercise Disorders in Young College Men. *Journal of American College Health* 50: 273 278.

80. Spettigue, W. and K. A. Henderson. 2004. Eating Disorders and the Role of Media. *The Canadian Child and Adolescent Psychiatry Review* 13: 16–19.

81. Rubenstein, S., and B. Cabellero. 2000. Is Miss America an Undernourished Role Model? *Journal of the American Medical Association* 382: 1569.

82. Strober, M., and C. M. Bulik. 2002. Genetic epidemiology of eating disorders. In D. G. Fairburn and K. D. Brownell, eds. *Eating Disorders and Obesity: A Comprehensive Handbook*. 2nd ed. New York: Guilford Press, 238–242.

83. Mangweth, B., J. I. Hudson, H. G. Pope, Jr., A. Hausmagn, C. DeCol, N. M. Laird, and M. T. Tsuang. 2003. Family Study of the Aggregation of Eating Disorders and Mood Disorders. *Psychological Medicine* 33:1319–1323; McElroy, S. L. O., R. Kotwal, and P. E. Keck, Jr. 2006. Comorbidity of Eating Disorders with Bipolar Disorder and Treatment Implications. *Bipolar Disorders* 8:686–695.

84. Altman, S. E., and S. A. Shankman. 2009. What Is the Association between Obsessive-Compulsive Disorder and Eating Disorders? *Clinical Psychology Review* 29:638–646.

85. Woodside, D. B., P. E. Garfinkel, E. Lin, P. Goering, A. S. Kaplan, D. S. Goldbloom, and S. H. Kennedy. 2001. Comparisons of Men with Full or Partial Eating Disorders, Men without Eating Disorders, and Women with Eating Disorders in the Community. *American Journal of Psychiatry* 158: 570–574.

86. Harrop, E. N., and G. A. Marlatt. 2010. The Comorbidity of Substance Use Disorders and Eating Disorders in Women: Prevalence, Etiology, and Treatment. *Addictive Behaviors* 35: 392–398.

87. Reiff, D., and K. Reiff. 1997. *Eating Disorders: Nutrition Therapy in the Recovery Process*. Aspen, CO. Aspen Publishers.

88. Arcelus, J., A. J. Mitchell, J. Wales, and S. Nielsen. 2011. Mortality Rates in Patients with Anorexia Nervosa and Other Eating Disorders. *Archives of General Psychiatry* 68: 724–731.

89. Reiff. *Eating Disorders*.

90. Ibid.

91. Birketvedt, G. S., J. Florholmen, J. Sundsfjord, B. Osterud, D. Dinges, W. Bilker, and A. Stunkard. 1999. Behavioral and Neuroendocrine Characteristics of the Night Eating Syndrome. *Journal of the American Medical Association* 282: 657–663.

92. Birketvedt. Behavioral and Neuroendocrine Characteristics of the Night Eating Syndrome.

93. National Eating Disorders Association. 2013. Treatment. Available at www.nationaleatingdisorders.org. Accessed July 2013.

Feature Box References

1. PRWeb. 2013. Weight Loss Market in U.S. Up 1.7% to $61 Billion. Available at www.prweb.com. Accessed July 2013; Mintel Oxygen. 2012. Diet Trends—US—November 2012. Available at http://oxygen.mintel.com. Accessed June 2013.

2. Freedman, M., J. King, and E. Kennedy. 2001. Popular Diets: A Scientific Review. *Obesity Research* 9: 1S–40S.

3. Dansinger, M., J. Gleason, J. Griffith, H. Selker, and E. Schaefer. 2005. Comparison of the Atkins, Ornish, Weight Watchers, and Zone Diets for Weight Loss and Heart Disease Risk Reduction. *Journal of the American Medical Association* 293: 43–53.

4. Ibid.

5. Seagle, H., G. Strain, A. Makris, and R. Reeves. 2009. Position of the American Dietetic Association: Weight Management. *Journal of the American Dietetic Association* 109: 330–346.

6. Ornish, D. 2004. Was Dr. Atkins Right? *Journal of the American Dietetic Association* 104: 537–542.

7. Denke, M. 2001. Metabolic Effects of High-Protein, Low-Carbohydrate Diets. *The American Journal of Cardiology* 88: 59–61.

8. Ibid.

9. Federal Trade Commission. 2010. Marketers of Unproven Weight Loss Products Ordered to Pay Nearly $2 Million. Available at www.ftc.gov. Accessed June 2013.

10. National Center for Complementary and Alternative Medicine. 2012. Green Tea. Available at http://nccam.nih.gov. Accessed June 2013.

11. National Center for Complementary and Alternative Medicine. 2013. Weight Management. Available at http://nccam.nih.gov. Accessed June 2013; Pittler, M., and E. Ernst. 2004. Dietary Supplements for Body-Weight Reduction: A Systematic Review. *American Journal of Clinical Nutrition* 79: 529–536.

12. National Center for Complementary and Alternative Medicine. 2013. Weight Loss and Complementary Health Practices. Available at http://nccam.nih.gov. Accessed June 2013.

13. Seagle. Position of the American Dietetic Association: Weight Management; National Heart, Lung, and Blood Institute. 1998. Clinical Guidelines on the Identification, Evaluation, and Treatment of Overweight and Obesity in Adults. Available at www.nhlbi.nih.gov. Accessed June 2013.

14. Mariant, M. 2005. Oprah Regrets Her 1988 Liquid Diet. *USA Today* (November). Available at www.usatoday.com. Accessed June 2013.

15. DeWald, T., L. Khaodhiar, M. Donahue, and G. Blackburn. 2006. Pharmacological and Surgical Treatments for Obesity. *American Heart Journal* 151: 604–624.

16. U.S. Food and Drug Administration. 2013. Medications Target Long-Term Weight Control. Available at www.fda.gov. Accessed June 2013.

17. FDA. 2004. *FDA Issues Regulation Prohibiting Sale of Dietary Supplements Containing Ephedrine Alkaloids and Reiterates Its Advice That Consumers Stop Using these Products.* Available at www.cfsan.fda.gov. Accessed June 2012.

18. American Society for Metabolic and Bariatric Surgery. 2013. Metabolic and Bariatric Surgery. Available at http://asmbs.org. Accessed June 2013.

19. Pournaras, D., and C. le Roux. 2010. Ghrelin and Metabolic Surgery. *International Journal of Peptides.* Available at www.hindawi.com. Accessed June 2013.

20. American Society for Metabolic and Bariatric Surgery. Metabolic and Bariatric Surgery.

21. National Eating Disorders Association. 2012. What Is Body Image? Available at www.nationaleatingdisorders.org. Accessed July 2013.

22. Ibid.

23. Ibid.

24. Koran, L. M., E. Abujaoude, M. D. Large, and R. T. Serpe. 2008. The Prevalence of Body Dysmorphic Disorder in the United States Adult Population. *CNS Spectrums* 13: 316–322.

25. Cafri, G., R. Olivardia, and J. K. Thompson. 2008. Symptom Characteristics and Psychiatric Comorbidity among Males with Muscle Dysmorphia. *Comprehensive Psychiatry* 48: 374–379.

26. National Eating Disorders Association. 2012. Enhancing Male Body Image. Available at www.nationaleatingdisorders.org. Accessed July 2013; National Eating Disorders Association. 2012. Every Body Is Different. Available at www.nationaleatingdisorders.org. Accessed July 2013.

Two Points of View References

1. WebMD. Weight-Loss Surgery Health Center. 2012. Facts about Weight-Loss Surgery. Available at www.webmd.com. Accessed June 2013.

2. Mayo Clinic Staff. 2011. Definition of Gastric Bypass Surgery. Available at www.mayoclinic.com. Accessed June 2013.

3. Wolters Kluwer Health, Lippincott Williams & Wilkins. 2012. Obesity Epidemic Means Bariatric Surgery Rates Continue to Rise, Reports *Plastic and Reconstructive Surgery.* Available at www.sciencedaily.com. Accessed June 2013.

4. Centers for Disease Control and Prevention. 2013. Adolescent and School Health: Childhood Obesity Facts. Available at www.cdc.gov. Accessed October 2013.

5. Reeves, G. M., et al. 2008. Childhood Obesity and Depression: Connection between These Growing Problems in Growing Children. *International Journal of Child Health and Human Development* 1: 103–114.

6. Han, J., D. Lawlor, and S. Kimm. 2010. Childhood Obesity. *The Lancet* 375: 1737–1748.

7. Inge, T., J. Bean, et al. 2009. Reversal of Type 2 Diabetes Mellitus and Improvements in Cardiovascular Risk Factors After Surgical Weight Loss in Adolescents. *Pediatrics* 123: 214–222.

8. O'Brien, P., S. Sawyer, et al. 2010. Laparoscopic Adjustable Gastric Banding in Severely Obese Adolescents. *JAMA* 303: 519–526.

9. Cleveland Clinic. 2013. Adolescent Bariatric Surgery. Available at http://weightloss.clevelandclinic.org. Accessed July 2013.

10. Beil, L. 2010. Surgery for Obese Children? *The New York Times.* Available at www.nytimes.com. Accessed July 2013; Ippisch, H., T. Jenkins, T. Inge, and T. Kimball. 2009. Do Acute Improvements in LV Mass and Diastolic Function Following Adolescent Bariatric Surgery Persist at Two Years Post-Op? *Circulation* 120: S474.

11. Beil. Surgery for Obese Children?

12. Ibid.

13. Kaulfers, A. M., et al. 2011. Bone Loss in Adolescents after Bariatric Surgery. *Pediatrics* 127: e956–961.

Chapter 11

1. U.S. Department of Health and Human Services. 2011. Healthy People 2020. Available at www.healthypeople.gov. Accessed April 2013.

2. Whelton, S. P., A. Chin, X. Xin, and J. He. 2002. Effect of Aerobic Exercise on Blood Pressure: A Meta-Analysis of Randomized, Controlled Trials. *Annals of Internal Medicine* 136: 493–503.

3. Alhassan S., K. A. Reese, J. Mahurin, E. P. Plaisance, B. D. Hilson, J. C. Garner, et al. 2006. Blood Lipid Responses to Plant Stanol Ester Supplementation and Aerobic Exercise Training. *Metabolism* 55: 541–549.

4. Janssen, I., P. T. Katzmarzyk, R. Ross, A. S. Leon, J. S. Skinner, D. C. Rao, et al. 2004. Fitness Alters the Associations of BMI and Waist Circumference with Total and Abdominal Fat. *Obesity* 12: 525–537.

5. O'Donovan, G., E. M. Kearney, A. M. Nevill, K. Woolf-May, and S. R. Bird. 2005. The Effects of 24 Weeks of Moderate- or High-Intensity Exercise on Insulin Resistance. *European Journal of Applied Physiology* 95: 522–528.

6. Brooks, G. 2002. Lactate Shuttles in Nature. *Biochemical Society Transactions* 30: 258–264.

7. Kato, T., T. Terashima, T. Yamashita, Y. Hatanaka, A. Honda, and Y. Umemura. 2006. Effect of Low-Repetition Jump Training on Bone Mineral Density in Young Women. *Journal of Applied Physiology* 100: 839–843; Daly, R. M., D. W. Dunstan, N. Owen, D. Jolley, J. E. Shaw, and P. Z. Zimmet. 2005. Does High-Intensity Resistance Training Maintain Bone Mass during Moderate Weight Loss in Older Overweight Adults with Type 2 Diabetes? *Osteoporosis International* 16: 1703–1712; Yung, P. S., Y. M. Lai, P. Y. Tung, H. T. Tsui, C. K. Wong, V. W. Hung, and L. Qin. 2005. Effects of Weight Bearing and Nonweight Bearing Exercises on Bone Properties Using Calcaneal Quantitative Ultrasound. *British Journal of Sports Medicine* 39: 547–551.

8. Karacabey, K., O. Saygin, R. Ozmerdivenli, E. Zorba, A. Godekmerdan, and V. Bulut. 2005. The Effects of Exercise on the Immune System and Stress Hormones in Sportswomen. *Neuroendocrinology Letters* 26: 361–366.

9. Hargreaves, M. 2004. Muscle Glycogen and Metabolic Regulation. *Proceedings of the Nutrition Society* 63: 217–220.

10. Youngstedt, S. D. 2005. Effects of Exercise on Sleep. *Clinics in Sports Medicine* 24: 355–365.

11. U.S. Department of Health and Human Services. 2008. Physical Activity Guidelines for Americans. Available at www.Health.gov. Accessed April 2013.

12. Herbert, R. D., and M. de Noronha. 2007. Stretching to Prevent or Reduce Muscle Soreness after Exercise. *Cochrane Database of Systematic Reviews* 4.

13. Thacker, Stephen B., et al. 2004. The Impact of Stretching on Sports Injury Risk: A Systematic Review of the Literature. *Medicine & Science in Sports & Exercise* 3: 371–378.

14. American College of Sports Medicine. 2011. Quantity and Quality of Exercise for Developing and Maintaining Cardiorespiratory, Musculoskeletal, and Neuromotor Fitness in Apparently Healthy Adults: Guidance for Prescribing Exercise. Position Stand. *Medicine & Science in Sports & Exercise* 43: 1334–1359.

15. Romijn, J. A., E. F. Coyle, L. S. Sidossis, A. Gastaldelli, J. F. Horowitz, E. Endert, and R. R. Wolfe. 1993. Regulation of Endogenous Fat and Carbohydrate Metabolism in Relation to Exercise Intensity and Duration. *American Journal of Physiology - Endocrinology and Metabolism* 265: E380–E391.

16. Costill, D., R. Thomas, R. Robergs, D. Pascoe, C. Lambert, S. Barr, and W. Fink. 1991. Adaptations to Swimming Training: Influence of Training Volume. *Medicine & Science in Sports & Exercise* 23: 371–377; Sherman, W., M. Peden, and D. Wright. 1991 Carbohydrate Feedings 1 Hour Before Exercise Improves Cycling Performance. *American Journal of Clinical Nutrition* 54: 866–870.

17. Coyle, E. F., A. R. Coggan, M. K. Hemmert, and J. L. Ivy. 1986. Muscle Glycogen Utilization during Prolonged Strenuous Exercise When Fed Carbohydrate. *Journal of Applied Physiology* 61: 165–172; Hargreaves, M. Muscle Glycogen and Metabolic Regulation.

18. Burke, L., B. Kiens, and J. Ivy. 2004. Carbohydrate and Fat for Training and Recovery. *Journal of Sports Science* 22: 15–30.

19. American College of Sports Medicine, American Dietetic Association, and Dietitians of Canada. 2009. Nutrition and Athletic Performance Joint Position Statement. *Medicine & Science in Sports & Exercise* 41: 709–731.

20. Ibid.

21. Brownell, K. D., S. N. Steen, and J. H. Wilmore. 1987. Weight Regulation Practices in Athletes: Analysis of Metabolic and Health Effects. *Medicine & Science in Sports & Exercise* 19: 546–556; Horvath, P. J., C. K. Eagen, S. D. Ryer-Calvin, and D. R. Pendergast. 2000. The Effects of Varying Dietary Fat on the Nutrient Intake in Male and Female Runners. *Journal of the American College of Nutrition* 19: 42–51.

22. American College of Sports Medicine, American Dietetic Association, and Dietitians of Canada. Nutrition and Athletic Performance Joint Position Statement.

23. Yaspelkis, B. B., J. G. Patterson, P. A. Anderla, Z. Ding, and J. L. Ivy. 1993. Carbohydrate Supplementation Spares Muscle Glycogen During Variable-Intensity Exercise. *Journal of Applied Physiology* 75: 1477–1485; Coyle, E. F., J. M. Hagberg, B. F. Hurley, W. H. Martin, A. A. Ehsani, and J. O. Holloszy. 1983. Carbohydrate Feeding During Prolonged Strenuous Exercise Can Delay Fatigue. *Journal of Applied Physiology* 55: 230–235.

24. Miller, S. L., K. D. Tipton, D. L. Chinkes, S. E. Wolf, and R. R. Wolfe. 2003. Independent and Combined Effects of Amino Acids and Glucose After Resistance Exercise. *Medicine & Science in Sports & Exercise* 35: 449–455.

25. Koopman, R., D. L. Pannemans, A. E. Jeukendrup, A. P. Gijsen, J. M. Senden, D. Halliday, et al. 2004. Combined Ingestion of Protein and Carbohydrate Improves Protein Balance During Ultra-Endurance Exercise. *American Journal of Physiology - Endocrinology and Metabolism* 287: E712–E720.

26. Ivy, J. L., A. L. Katz, C. L. Cutler, W. M. Sherman, and E. F. Coyle. 1988. Muscle Glycogen Synthesis After Exercise: Effect of Time of Carbohydrate Ingestion. *Journal of Applied Physiology* 64: 1480–1485.

27. Roy, B. D., M. A. Tarnopolsky, J. D. MacDougall, J. Fowles, and K. E. Yarasheski. 1997. Effect of Glucose Supplement Timing on Protein Metabolism After Resistance Training. *Journal of Applied Physiology* 82: 1882–1888.

28. Rasmussen, B. B., K. D. Tipton, S. L. Miller, S. E. Wolf, and R. R. Wolfe. 2000. An Oral Essential Amino Acid-Carbohydrate Supplement Enhances Muscle Protein Anabolism after Resistance Exercise. *Journal of Applied Physiology* 88: 386–392; Zawadzki, K. M., B. B. Yaspelkis, and J. L. Ivy. 1992. Carbohydrate-Protein Complex Increases the Rate of Muscle Glycogen Storage after Exercise. *Journal of Applied Physiology* 72: 1854–1859.

29. Zawadzki. Carbohydrate-Protein Complex; Ivy, J. L., H. W. Goforth, B. M. Damon, T. R. McCauley, E. C. Parsons, and T. B. Price. 2002. Early Postexercise Muscle Glycogen Recovery Is Enhanced with a Carbohydrate-Protein Supplement. *Journal of Applied Physiology* 93: 1337–1344.

30. Karp, J. R., J. D. Johnston, S. Tecklenburg, T. D. Mickleborough, A. D. Fly, and J. M. Stager. 2006. Chocolate Milk as a Post-Exercise Recovery Aid. *International Journal of Sport Nutrition and Exercise Metabolism* 16: 78–91.

31. McAnulty, S. R., L. S. McAnulty, D. C. Nieman, J. D. Morrow, L. A. Shooter, S. Holmes, et al. 2005. Effect of Alpha-Tocopherol Supplementation on Plasma Homocysteine and Oxidative Stress in Highly Trained Athletes Before and After Exhaustive Exercise. *Journal of Nutritional Biochemistry* 16: 530–537; Nieman, D. C., D. A. Henson, S. R. McAnulty, L. S. McAnulty, N. S. Swick, A. C. Utter, et al. 2002. Influence of Vitamin C Supplementation on Oxidative and Immune Changes After an Ultramarathon. *Journal of Applied Physiology* 92: 1970–1977.

32. Dubnov, G., and N. W. Constantini. 2004. Prevalence of Iron Depletion and Anemia in Top-Level Basketball Players. *International Journal of Sport Nutrition and Exercise Metabolism* 14: 30–37.

33. Gropper, S. S., D. Glessing, K. Dunham, and J. M. Barksdale. 2006. Iron Status of Female Collegiate Athletes Involved in Different Sports. *Biological Trace Element Research* 109: 1–14; Dubnov. Prevalence of Iron Depletion.

34. Klesges, R. C., K. D. Ward, M. L. Shelton, W. B. Applegate, E. D. Cantler, G. M. Palmieri, et al. 1996. Changes in Bone Mineral Content in Male Athletes: Mechanisms of Action and Intervention Effects. *Journal of the American Medical Association* 276: 226–230.

35. Krumbach, C. J., D. R. Ellis, and J. A. Driskell. 1999. A Report of Vitamin and Mineral Supplement Use Among University Athletes in a Division I Institution. *International Journal of Sport Nutrition and Exercise Metabolism* 9: 416–425; Herbold, N. H., B. K. Visconti, S. Frates, and L. Bandini. 2004. Traditional and Nontraditional Supplement Use by Collegiate Female Varsity Athletes. *International Journal of Sport Nutrition and Exercise Metabolism* 14: 586–593.

36. Singh, A., F. M. Moses, and P. A. Deuster. 1992. Chronic Multivitamin-Mineral Supplementation Does Not Enhance Physical Performance. *Medicine & Science in Sports & Exercise* 24: 726–732.

37. Gatorade.com. "Gatorade History." Available at www.gatorade.com. Accessed May 2013.

38. C. Rosenbloom, ed. 2000. *Sports Nutrition: A Guide for the Professional Working with Active People.* 3rd ed. Chicago: The American Dietetic Association.

39. Wilk, B., and O. Bar-Or. 1996. Effect of Drink Flavor and NaCl on Voluntary Drinking and Hydration in Boys Exercising in the Heat. *Journal of Applied Physiology* 80: 1112–1117.

40. American College of Sports Medicine. 1996. Position Stand on Exercise and Fluid Replacement. *Medicine & Science in Sports & Exercise* 28: i–vii.

41. McGee, W. 2005. Caffeine in the Diet. National Institutes of Health Medline Plus Medical Encyclopedia. Available at www.nlm.nih.gov.

42. Douglas J. Casa. 2003. Proper Hydration for Distance Running— Identifying Individual Fluid Needs, A USA Track and Field Advisory. Available at www.usatf.org.

43. USA Track & Field. Press Release April 19, 2003. USATF Announces Major Change in Hydration Guidelines. Available at www.usatf.org.

44. Greenhaff, P. L., A. Casey, A. H. Short, R. Harris, K. Söderlund, and E. Hultman. 1993. Influence of Oral Creatine Supplementation on Muscle Torque During Repeated Bouts of Maximal Voluntary Exercise in Man. *Clinical Science* 84: 565–571.

45. Vandenberghe, K., M. Goris, P. Van Hecke, M. Van Leemputte, L. Vangerven, and P. Hespel. 1997. Long-Term Creatine Intake Is Beneficial to Muscle Performance During Resistance Training. *Journal of Applied Physiology* 83: 2055–2063; Kreider, R. B., M. Ferreira, M. Wilson, P. Grindstaff, S. Plisk, J. Reinardy, et al. 1998. Effects of Creatine Supplementation on Body Composition, Strength, and Sprint Performance. *Medicine & Science in Sports & Exercise* 30: 73–82.

46. Mayhew, D. L., J. L. Mayhew, and J. S. Ware. 2002. Effects of Long-Term Creatine Supplementation on Liver and Kidney Functions in American College Football Players. *International Journal of Sport Nutrition and Exercise Metabolism* 12: 453–460; Kreider, R. B., C. Melton, C. J. Rasmussen, M. Greenwood, S. Lancaster, E. C. Cantler, et al. 2003. Long-Term Creatine Supplementation Does Not Significantly Affect Clinical Markers of Health in Athletes. *Molecular and Cellular Biochemistry* 244: 95–104.

47. Wiles, J. D., S. R. Bird, J. Hopkins, and M. Riley. 1992. Effect of Caffeinated Coffee on Running Speed, Respiratory Factors, Blood Lactate and Perceived Exertion During 1500 M Treadmill Running. *British Journal of Sports Medicine* 26: 116–120; Spriet, L. L., D. A. MacLean, D. J. Dyck, E. Hultman, G. Cederblad, and T. E. Graham. 1992. Caffeine Ingestion and Muscle Metabolism During Prolonged Exercise in Humans. *American Journal of Physiology - Endocrinology and Metabolism* 262: E891–E898.

48. Paton, C. D., W. G. Hopkins, and L. Vollebregt. 2001. Little Effect of Caffeine Ingestion on Repeated Sprints in Team-Sport Athletes. *Medicine & Science in Sports & Exercise* 33: 822–825.

49. Crist, D. M., G. T. Peake, P. A. Egan, and D. L. Waters. 1988. Body Composition Responses to Exogenous GH During Training in Highly Conditioned Adults. *Journal of Applied Physiology* 65: 579–584; Foss, M., and S. Keteyian. 1998. *Physiological Basis for Exercise and Sport.* 6th ed. McGraw-Hill: 498.

50. Deyssig, R., H. Frisch, W. Blum, and T. Waldorf. 1993. Effect of Growth Hormone Treatment on Hormonal Parameters, Body Composition, and Strength in Athletes. *Acta Endocrinologica* 128: 313–318; Lange, K., J. Andersen, N. Beyer, F. Isaksson, B. Larsson, M. Rasmussen, et al. 2002. GH Administration Changes Myosin Heavy Chain Isoforms in Skeletal Muscle but Does Not Augment Muscle Strength or Hypertrophy, Either Alone or Combined with Resistance Exercise Training in Healthy Elderly Men. *Journal of Clinical Endocrinology & Metabolism* 87: 513–523.

51. Woodhouse, L. J., S. L. Asa, S. G. Thomas, and S. Ezzat. 1999. Measures of Submaximal Aerobic Performance Evaluate and Predict Functional Response to Growth Hormone (GH) Treatment in GH-Deficient Adults. *Journal of Clinical Endocrinology & Metabolism* 84: 4570–4577.

52. Ekblom, B., and B. Berglund. 1991. Effect of Erythropoietin Administration on Maximal Aerobic Power. *Scandinavian Journal of Medicine and Science in Sports* 1: 88–93.

Feature Box References

1. Tarnopolsky, M. A., S. A. Atkinson, S. M. Phillips, and J. D. MacDougall. 1995. Carbohydrate Loading and Metabolism During Exercise in Men and Women. *Journal of Applied Physiology* 78: 1360–1368.

2. Goforth, W. H., D. Laurent, W. K. Prusaczyk, K. E. Schneider, K. F. Peterson, and G. I. Shulman. 2003. Effects of Depletion Exercise and Light Training on Muscle Glycogen Supercompensation in Men.

American Journal of Physiology - Endocrinology and Metabolism 285: E1304–1311.

3. Houmard, J. A., D. L. Costill, J. B. Mitchell, S. H. Park, R. C. Hickner, and J. N. Roemmich. 1990. Reduced Training Maintains Performance in Distance Runners. *International Journal of Sports Medicine* 11: 46–52.

Two Points of View References

1. World Anti-Doping Agency. 2011. Questions and Answers on 2012 Prohibited List. Available at www.wada-ama.org. Accessed September 2013.
2. NCAA. 2013. 2012–13 NCAA Banned Drugs. Available at www.ncaa.org. Accessed September 2013.
3. Ganio, M. S., et. al. 2009. Effect of Caffeine on Sport-Specific Endurance Performance: A Systematic Review. *Journal of Strength and Conditioning Research* 23: 315–324.
4. McMichael, S. 2010. WADA President to Urge Re-Banning of Caffeine. Available at http://road.cc. Accessed September 2013.
5. Dikos, J. 2010. How to Boost Long-Distance Performance with Caffeine. Available at www.runnersworld.com. Accessed September 2013.
6. Mayo Clinic. 2011. Nutrition and Healthy Eating. Caffeine: How Much Is Too Much? Available at www.mayoclinic.com. Accessed September 2013.
7. Brody, J. 2011. Scientists See Dangers in Energy Drinks. *New York Times*. Available at www.nytimes.com. Accessed September 2013.
8. ACSM Current Comment. 2013. Caffeine and Exercise Performance. Available at www.acsm.org. Accessed September 2013; Mayo Clinic Staff. 2013. Nutrition and Healthy Eating: Carbohydrate-Loading Diet. Available at www.mayoclinic.com. Accessed September 2013.
9. FDA. 2007. Medicines in My Home: Caffeine and Your Body. Available at www.fda.gov. Accessed September 2013.
10. Dikos. How to Boost Long-Distance Performance with Caffeine.
11. FDA. 2013. For Consumers: FDA to Investigate Added Caffeine. Available at www.fda.gov. Accessed September 2013.
12. Silverglade, B., and I. R. Heller. Center for Science in the Public Interest. 2010. Food-Labeling Chaos: The Case for Reform. Available at www.cspinet.org. Accessed September 2013.

Chapter 12

1. USDA. 2012. Global Food Markets, Global Food Industry. Available at www.ers.usda.gov. Accessed May 2013.
2. Gallo, A. 1999. Food advertising in the United States. In Franzao, E., ed., *America's Eating Habits: Changes and Consequences*. Washington, D.C.: United States Department of Agriculture. Available at www.ers.usda.gov. Accessed May 2013.
3. SOS eMarketing. 2009. Red Bull: The Stuff of Beverage Marketing Legends. Available at www.sosemarketing.com. Accessed March 2010.
4. Garner, J. 2009. Using Social Media to Market Your Products: The Case of Red Bull. ComputerWeekly.com. Available at www.computerweekly.com. Accessed March 2010.
5. Blisard, N. 1999. Advertising and what we eat: The case of dairy products. In *America's Eating Habits*.
6. Harmon, A. H., and B. L. Gerald. 2007. Position of the American Dietetic Association: Food and Nutrition Professionals Can Implement Practices to Conserve Natural Resources and Support Ecological Sustainability. *Journal of the American Dietetic Association* 107: 1033–1043; Sobal, J., L. Kahn, and C. Bisogni. 1998. A Conceptual Model of the Food and Nutrition System. *Social Science & Medicine* 47: 853–863.
7. U.S. Environmental Protection Agency. Ag 101: Demographics. Available at www.epa.gov. Updated April 2013. Accessed June 2013.
8. Ibid.
9. U.S. Environmental Protection Agency. 2009. Ag 101: Economic Overview. Updated April 2013. Available at www.epa.gov. Accessed June 2013.
10. U.S. Environmental Protection Agency. Ag 101: Demographics.
11. International Food Information Council. 2009. Food Insight. Background on Agricultural Practices and Food Technologies. Available at www.foodinsight.org. Accessed January 2010.
12. Rickman, D., J. Luvall, J. Shaw, P. Mask, D. Kissel, and D. Sullivan. 2003. Precision Agriculture: Changing the Face of Farming. *GeoTimes*. Available at www.geotimes.org. Accessed January 2010.
13. USDA. 2007. Food Spending in American Households, 2003–2004. Available at www.ers.usda.gov. Accessed June 2013.
14. U.S. Environmental Protection Agency. Ag 101: Economic Overview.
15. Ibid.
16. Ibid.
17. U.S. Environmental Protection Agency. 2009. Agribusiness: Sectors Strategies Program, June 29, 2009. Available at www.epa.gov. Accessed January 2010.

18. Economic Research Service. U.S. Department of Agriculture. 2013. FAQs. Available at www.ers.usda.gov. Accessed November 2013.
19. U.S. Environmental Protection Agency. Agribusiness.
20. U.S. Environmental Protection Agency. 2009. Ag 101: Crop Production. Available at www.epa.gov. Accessed January 2010.
21. Ibid.
22. U.S. Environmental Protection Agency. 2009. Ag 101: Beef Production. Available at www.epa.gov. Accessed January 2010.
23. U.S. Environmental Protection Agency. 2009. Ag 101: Pork Production. Available at www.epa.gov. Accessed January 2010.
24. U.S. Environmental Protection Agency. 2009. Ag 101: Poultry Production. Available at www.epa.gov. Accessed January 2010.
25. Ibid.
26. International Food Information Council. Food Insight. Background on Agricultural Practices and Food Technologies.
27. Hendrickson, M., and H. James. 2008. Does the World Need U.S. Farmers Even If Americans Don't? *Journal of Agricultural and Environmental Ethics* 21: 311–328.
28. United States Department of Agriculture, Economic Research Service. 2013. Outlook for U.S. Agricultural Trade. Available at www.ers.usda.gov. Accessed August 2013.
29. United States Department of Agriculture, Economic Research Service. 2009. Global Food Markets: International Consumer and Retail Trends. Available at www.ers.usda.gov. Accessed January 2010; Regmi, A., H. Takeshima, and L. Unnevehr. 2008. Convergence in Global Food Demand and Delivery. *Economic Research Report No. ERR-56*. Available at www.ers.usda.gov. Accessed January 2010.
30. Popkin, B. 2007. The World Is Fat. *Scientific American*. Available at www.sciam.com. Accessed February 2010; Centers for Disease Control and Prevention. 2013. FastStats: Obesity and Overweight. Available at www.cdc.gov. Accessed August 2013.
31. World Health Organization. 2010. Controlling the Global Obesity Epidemic. Available at www.who.int. Accessed January 2010.
32. United States Department of Agriculture, Economic Research Service. 2013. Value of U.S. Food Imports: Fruits and Fruit Preparations. Available at www.ers.usda.gov. Accessed August 2013.
33. Hendrickson. Does the World Need U.S. Farmers?
34. USDA. 2013. Report on U.S. Agricultural Trade Import Share of Consumption. Available at www.ers.usda.gov. Accessed June 2013.
35. Hendrickson. Does the World Need U.S. Farmers?; Blank, S. 1998. *The End of Agriculture in the American Portfolio*. Westport, CT: Quorum Books.
36. Mundell, E. 2008. U.S. Food Safety: The Import Alarm Keeps Sounding. *U.S. News & World Report*. Available at http://health.usnews.com. Accessed January 2010.
37. Food and Drug Administration. 2010. Ensuring the Safety of Imported Products: Q&A with David Elder. Available at www.fda.gov. Accessed August 2013.
38. Martin, A. 2007. FDA Curbs Sale of 5 Seafoods Farmed in China. *The New York Times*. Available at www.nytimes.com. Accessed January 2010.
39. Regmi. Convergence in Global Food Demand and Delivery.
40. U.S. Environmental Protection Agency. Ag 101: Beef Production.
41. National Oceanic and Atmospheric Administration, National Climatic Data Center. 2008. Global Warming Frequently Asked Questions. Available at www.ncdc.noaa.gov. Accessed January 2010; Pirog, R., et al. 2002. Food, Fuel, and Freeways: An Iowa Perspective on How Far Food Travels, Fuel Usage, and Greenhouse Gas Emissions. Leopold Center for Sustainable Agriculture. Available at www.leopold.iastate.edu; Tompkins Country Relocalization Project. 2005. Implications of Fossil Fuel Dependence for the Food System. *Energy Bulletin*. Available at www.energybulletin.net. Accessed January 2010.
42. Pirog. Food, Fuel, and Freeways.
43. Ibid.
44. Tompkins Country Relocalization Project. Implications of Fossil Fuel Dependence for the Food System; Hendrickson, J. 1996. Energy Use in the U.S. Food System: A Summary of Existing Research and Analysis. Center for Integrated Agricultural Systems, UW-Madison. Available at www.cias.wisc.edu. Accessed January 2010.
45. Harmon. Position of the American Dietetic Association: Food and Nutrition Professionals Can Implement Practices.
46. United States Department of Agriculutre. 2009. USDA Awards More than $5 Million in Grants to Support Local Food Initiatives. Available at www.csrees.usda.gov. Accessed January 2010.
47. Harmon. Position of the American Dietetic Association: Food and Nutrition Professionals Can Implement Practices; Herremans, I., and R. Reid. 2002. Developing Awareness of the Sustainability Concept. *Journal of Environmental Education* 34: 16–20; Brundtland, G. 1987. *Our Common Future*. New York: Oxford University Press; Herrin, M., and

J. D. Gussow. 1989. Designing a Sustainable Regional Diet. *Journal of Nutrition Education* 21: 270–275.

48. FDA, Center for Veterinary Medicine. 2009. Report on the Food and Drug Administration's Review of the Safety of Recombinant Bovine Somatotropin. Available at www.fda.gov. Accessed February 2010.

49. American Cancer Society. 2011. Recombinant Bovine Growth Hormone. Available at www.cancer.org. Accessed October 2013.

50. FDA, Center for Veterinary Medicine. Updated 2009. Steroid Hormones. Available at www.fda.gov. Accessed October 2010.

51. U.S. Environmental Protection Agency. Ag 101: Beef Production.

52. Ibid.

53. FDA, Center for Veterinary Medicine. 2013. National Antimicrobial Resistance Monitoring System. Available at www.fda.gov. Accessed August 2013.

54. FDA, Center for Veterinary Medicine. 2012. Judicious Use of Antimicrobials. Available at www.fda.gov. Accessed August 2013.

55. USDA, Agricultural Marketing Service. 2013. National Organic Program. Available at www.ams.usda.gov. Accessed June 2013.

56. Smith-Spangler, C., et al. 2012. Are Organic Foods Safer or Healthier than Conventional Alternatives? *Annals of Internal Medicine* 157: 348–366.

57. EPA. 2013. What Are Biopesticides? Available at www.epa.gov. Accessed August 2013.

58. Ibid.

59. Beseler, C., L. Stallones, J. Hoppin, M. Alavanja, A. Blair, T. Keefe, and F. Kamel. 2008. Depression and Pesticide Exposures among Private Pesticide Applicators Enrolled in the Agricultural Health Study. *Environmental Health Perspectives* 116: 1713–1719.

60. U.S. Fish and Wildlife Service. 2013. Bald Eagle Fact Sheet. Available at www.doi.gov. Accessed October 2013.

61. U.S. Environmental Protection Agency. 2012. Pesticides and Food: Health Problems Pesticides May Pose. Available at www.epa.gov. Accessed August 2013.

62. U.S. Environmental Protection Agency. 2012. Pesticides and Food: Why Children May Be Especially Sensitive to Pesticides. Available at www.epa.gov. Accessed October 2013.

63. Smith-Spangler. Are Organic Foods Safer or Healthier than Conventional Alternatives?

64. U.S. Environmental Protection Agency. 2012. Pesticides: Environmental Effects. *Ecological Risk Assessments*. Available at www.epa.gov. Accessed August 2013.

65. International Food Information Council. Food Insight. Background on Agricultural Practices and Food Technologies.

66. U.S. Environmental Protection Agency. Updated 2012. Pesticides: Environmental Effects.

67. U.S. Environmental Protection Agency. 2012. Pesticides: Topical and Chemical Fact Sheets. Integrated Pest Management (IPM) Principles. Available at www.epa.gov. Accessed August 2013.

68. Pew Initiative on Food and Biotechnology. 2004. Genetically Modified Crops in the United States. Available at www.pewtrusts.org. Accessed August 2013.

69. International Food Information Council. 2013. Food Insight. Questions and Answers about Food Biotechnology. Available at www.foodinsight.org. Accessed August 2013.

70. International Food Information Council. 2009. Food and Agricultural Biotechnology. Health Impacts in Developing Nations CPE Program. Available at www.foodinsight.org. Accessed January 2010.

71. Fernandez-Cornejo, J., and W. McBride. 2002. Adoption of Bioengineered Crops. *Agricultural Economic Report No. AER-810*. Available at www.ers.usda.gov. Accessed January 2010.

72. USDA, Economic Research Service. 2013. Adoption of Genetically Engineered Crops in the U.S. Available at www.ers.usda.gov. Accessed August 2013.

73. Bruh, C. 2006. Position of the American Dietetic Association: Agricultural and Food Biotechnology. *Journal of the American Dietetic Association* 106: 285–293.

74. The American Oil Chemists' Society. 2012. High-oleic Canola Oils and Their Food Applications. Available at www.aocs.org. Accessed October 2013.

75. Phillips, T. 2008. Genetically Modified Organisms (GMOs): Transgenic Crops and Recombinant DNA Technology. *Nature Education* 1. Available at www.nature.com. Accessed August 2013.

76. Ibid.

77. Ibid.

78. International Food Information Council. 2008 Food Biotechnology: A Study of U.S. Consumer Trends. Available at www.foodinsight.org. Accessed January 2010.

79. Golan, E., L. Mancino, and L. Unnevehr. 2009. Food Policy: Check the List of Ingredients. *Amber Waves*. Available at www.ers.usda.gov. Accessed March 2010.

80. Ibid.

81. O'Neil, C. E., et al. 2010. Whole-Grain Consumption Is Associated with Diet Quality and Nutrient Intake in Adults: The National Health and Nutrition Examination Survey, 1999–2004. *Journal of the American Dietetic Association* 110: 1461–1468.

82. Whole Grains Council. 2009. Report from the Make Half Your Grains Whole Conference, April 2009. Available at http://wholegrainscouncil.org. Accessed June 2013.

83. Golan. Food Policy: Check the List of Ingredients.

84. Ibid.

85. Ibid.

86. Parker, L. 2008. *Commodity Foods and the Nutritional Quality of the National School Lunch Program: Historical Role, Current Operations, and Future Potential*. Washington, D.C.: Food Research and Action Center. Available at www.frac.org. Accessed March 2010.

87. Ibid.

88. Nestle, M. 2002. *Food Policy*. Berkeley: University of California Press.

89. Brownell, K., T. Farley, W. Willett, B. Popkin, F. Chaloupka, J. Thompson, and D. Ludwig. 2009. The Public Health and Economic Benefits to Taxing Sugar-Sweetened Beverages. *New England Journal of Medicine* 361: 1599–1605.

90. Eaton, J. 2009. The Food Lobby's War on a Soda Tax. The Center for Public Integrity. Available at www.publicintegrity.org. Accessed March 2010.

91. USDA. 2013. Meat and Poultry Labeling Terms. Available at www.fsis.usda.gov. Accessed August 2013.

92. USDA, Economic Research Service. 2013. Consumer Demand Drives Growth in the Organic Food Sector. Available at www.ers.usda.gov. Accessed August 2013.

93. Hartman Group. 2012. Organic and Natural Report. Available at www.hartman-group.com. Accessed June 2013.

94. USDA, Agricultural Marketing Service, National Organic Program. 2012. USDA Oversight of Organic Products. Available at www.ams.usda.gov. Accessed August 2013.

95. USDA, Agricultural Marketing Service, National Organic Program. 2013. National List of Allowed and Prohibited Substances. Available at www.ams.usda.gov. Accessed August 2013.

96. USDA, Agricultural Marketing Service, National Organic Program. 2012. USDA Oversight of Organic Products.

97. Smith-Spangler. Are Organic Foods Safer or Healthier than Conventional Alternatives?

98. Ibid.

99. Greene, C., C. Dimitri, B. Lin, W. McBride, L. Oberholtzer, and T. Smith. 2009. Emerging Issues in the U.S. Organic Industry. United States Department of Agriculture, Economic Research Service, Bulletin No. 55. Available at www.ers.usda.gov. Accessed February 2010.

100. USDA, Agricultural Marketing Service, National Organic Program. 2013. International Agreements. Available at www.ams.usda.gov. Accessed June 2013.

101. Greene. Emerging Issues in the U.S. Organic Industry.

Feature Box References

1. Cotner, S., and J. Masabni. 2009. Vegetable Gardening in Containers. AgriLife Extension, Texas A&M System. Available at http://repository.tamu.edu. Accessed August 2013; Iowa State University Extension. 2005. Container Vegetable Gardening. Available at www.extension.iastate.edu. Accessed August 2013.

2. International Food Information Council Foundation. 2013. Food and Health Survey. Available at www.foodinsight.org. Accessed June 2013.

3. USDA, Alternative Farming Systems Information Center. Updated 2007. Special Reference Brief no. SRB 99-02. Available at www.nal.usda.gov. Accessed June 2013.

4. Horrigan, L., R. Lawrence, and P. Walker. 2002. How Sustainable Agriculture Can Address the Environmental and Human Health Harms of Industrial Agriculture. *Environmental Health Perspectives* 110: 445–456.

5. Harmon, A. H., and B. L. Gerald. 2007. Position of the American Dietetic Association: Food and Nutrition Professionals Can Implement Practices to Conserve Natural Resources and Support Ecological Sustainability. *Journal of the American Dietetic Association* 107: 1033–1043; Academy of Nutrition and Dietetics. 2013. Promoting Ecological Sustainability within the Food System. *Journal of the Academy of Nutrition and Dietetics* 113: 464.

6. Brown, L. 2008. *Plan B 3.0. Mobilizing to Save Civilization*. New York: WW Norton & Company.

7. Howard, A. 1940. *The Agricultural Testament*. London: Oxford University Press.
8. Environmental Protection Agency. 2009. What on Earth Is Soil? Available at www.epa.gov. Accessed August 2013.
9. Tagtow, A., and A. Harmon. 2009. *Healthy Land, Healthy Food and Healthy Eaters*. Available at www.uwyo.edu. Accessed February 2010.
10. Hendrickson, M., and H. James. 2008. Does the World Need U.S. Farmers Even If Americans Don't? *Journal of Agricultural and Environmental Ethics* 21: 311–328.
11. Heller, Martin C., and Gregory A. Keolelan. 2000. *Life Cycle-Based Sustainability Indicators for Assessment of the U.S. Food System*. Ann Arbor, MI: Center for Sustainable Systems, University of Michigan, 42; The Sustainable Table, GRACE Communications Foundation. 2009. Local and Regional Food Systems. Available at www.sustainabletable.org. Accessed August 2013.
12. Harmon. Position of the American Dietetic Association: Food and Nutrition Professionals Can Implement Practices.
13. Pimentel, D., P. Hepperly, J. Hanson, D. Douds, and R. Seidel. 2005. Environmental, Energetic, and Economic Comparisons of Organic and Conventional Farming Systems. *BioScience* 55: 573–582.
14. EPA. 2010. Watersense. Available at www.epa.gov. Accessed February 2010.
15. Ibid.
16. Ibid.
17. Pimentel, D., and M. Pimentel. 2003. Sustainability of Meat-Based and Plant-Based Diets and the Environment. *Journal of the American Dietetic Association* 78: 660S–663S.
18. Ibid.

Two Points of View References

1. United States Department of Agriculture, Agricultural Marketing Service. 2013. National Organic Program. Available at www.ams.usda.gov. Accessed August 2013.
2. Dimitri, C., and L. Oberholtzer. 2008. The U.S. Organic Handling Sector in 2004: Baseline Findings of the Nationwide Survey of Organic Manufacturers, Processors, and Distributors. EIB-36, U.S. Department of Agriculture, Economic Research Service.
3. Organic Consumers Association. 2006. *New York Times* Exposes Wal-Mart's Ability to Sell Cheap Organic Milk—It's Coming from Factory Farms. Available at www.organicconsumers.org. Accessed July 2010.
4. S. Ritter. 2009. Pinpointing Trends in Pesticide Use. *Chemical & Engineering News* 87: web exclusive. Available at http://cen.acs.org. Accessed October 2013.
5. M. Roosevelt. 2006. The Lure of the 100-Mile Diet. *Time Magazine* (Sunday June 11, 2006).
6. The Cornucopia Institute. 2010. Wal-Mart in Trouble Again Over Organic Marketing Practices. Available at www.cornucopia.org. Accessed July 2010.
7. M. Pollan. 2006. Letters to Whole Foods CEO John Mackey: My Second Letter to Whole Foods. Available at www.michaelpollan.com. Accessed July 2010.
8. Organic Consumers Association. 2006. What Makes Food Organic? The Twinkie Problem. Available at www.organicconsumers.org. Accessed July 2010.
9. Organic Consumers Association. 2006. Grocery Chains Buying Organic Products from Overseas Undermine Standards and Hurt USA Organic Farmers. Available at www.organicconsumers.org. Accessed July 2010.

Chapter 13

1. U.S. Department of Agriculture, U.S. Department of Health and Human Services. 2010. *Dietary Guidelines for Americans, 2010*. 7th ed. Washington, D.C.: U.S. Government Printing Office.
2. Centers for Disease Control and Prevention. 1999. Safer and Healthier Foods: 1900–1999. *Journal of the American Medical Association* 48: 905–913; Food and Drug Administration. 2009. About the FDA: The Long Struggle for the Law. Available at www.fda.gov. Accessed July 2013.
3. Young. The Long Struggle for the 1906 Law.
4. Johnson, R. 2012. The Federal Food Safety System: A Primer. Available at www.fas.org. Accessed July 2013.
5. Centers for Disease Control and Prevention. Safer and Healthier Foods.
6. Food and Drug Administration. 2013. Food Protection Plan. Available at www.fda.gov. Accessed July 2013.
7. Johnson, M. 2014. *Human Biology: Concepts and Current Issues*. Boston: Pearson Education, Inc.
8. Centers for Disease Control and Prevention. 2013. Norovirus. Available at www.cdc.gov. Accessed July 2013.

9. Ibid.
10. Centers for Disease Control and Prevention. 2003. Public Health Dispatch: Multistate Outbreak of Hepatitis A among Young Adult Concert Attendees, United States, 2003. *Morbidity and Mortality Weekly Report* 52: 844–845.
11. Grice, E. A, H. H. Kong, G. Renaud, et al. 2008. A Diversity Profile of the Human Skin Microbiota. *Genome Research* 18: 1043–1050. Available at http://genome.cshlp.org. Accessed July 2013.
12. Centers for Disease Control and Prevention. 2012. Food Safety. Available at www.cdc.gov. Accessed July 2013.
13. National Center for Zoonotic, Vector-Borne, and Enteric Diseases. 2013. General Information: *Campylobacter*. Available at www.cdc.gov. Accessed July 2013.
14. Ibid.
15. Ibid.
16. National Center for Zoonotic, Vector-Borne, and Enteric Diseases. Updated July 2012. *E. coli*. Available at www.cdc.gov. Accessed July 2013.
17. Ibid.
18. Centers for Disease Control and Prevention. 2006. Traveler's Diarrhea. Available at www.cdc.gov. Accessed July 2013.
19. National Center for Zoonotic, Vector-Borne, and Enteric Diseases. 2009. Salmonellosis. Available at www.cdc.gov. Accessed July 2013.
20. Food Safety and Inspection Service. 2013. Parasites and Foodborne Illness. Available at www.fsis.usda.gov. Accessed July 2013; Food and Drug Administration. 2012. Bad Bug Book. Available at www.fda.gov. Accessed 2013.
21. Ibid.
22. U.S. Department of Agriculture, Animal and Plant Health Inspection Service. 2012. Bovine Spongiform Encephalopathy (BSE). Available at www.aphis.usda.gov. Accessed July 2013.
23. Ibid.
24. Ibid.
25. Food and Drug Administration. 2013. Bovine Spongiform Encephalopathy. Available at www.fda.gov. Accessed July 2013.
26. USDA, Animal and Plant Health Inspection Service. 2006. Bovine Spongiform Encephalopathy Ongoing Surveillance Plan. Available at www.aphis.usda.gov. Accessed July 2013.
27. Ibid.
28. Food and Drug Administration. Bovine Spongiform Encephalopathy.
29. Centers for Disease Control and Prevention. 2013. vCJD. Available at www.cdc.gov. Accessed July 2013.
30. Food and Drug Administration. 2013. Food Safety for Older Adults. Available at www.fda.gov. Accessed July 2013; Buzby, J. C. 2003. Older Adults at Risk of Complications from Microbial Foodborne Illness. *Food Review* 25: 30–35.
31. The Pew Health Group and the American Academy of Pediatrics. 2009. Children and Foodborne Illness. Available at www.pewtrusts.org. Accessed July 2013; Buzby, J. C. 2002. Children and Microbial Foodborne Illness. *Food Review* 24: 32–37.
32. Food and Drug Administration. 2013. Food Safety: It's Especially Important for at-Risk Groups. Available at www.fda.gov. Accessed July 2013.
33. Food and Drug Administration. Bad Bug Book.
34. Ibid.
35. Curtis, V., and S. Cairncross. 2003. Effect of Washing Hands with Soap on Diarrhoea Risk in the Community: A Systematic Review. *The Lancet Infectious Diseases* 3: 275–281.
36. Borchgrevink, C., J. Cha, and S. Kim. 2013. Hand Washing Practices in a College Town. *Environment* 5: 18–24.
37. U.S. Department of Agriculture. 2010. Report of the Dietary Guidelines Advisory Committee on the *Dietary Guidelines for Americans, 2010*. Available at www.cnpp.usda.gov. Accessed July 2013.
38. Godwin, S., F. Chen, and R. Coppings. 2006. Correlation of Visual Perceptions of Cleanliness and Reported Cleaning Practices with Measures of Microbial Contamination in Home Refrigerators. *Food Protection Trends* 26: 474–480.
39. Food Safety and Inspection Service. 2010. Refrigeration and Food Safety. Available at www.fsis.usda.gov. Accessed July 2013.
40. Food Safety and Inspection Service. 1998. Premature Browning of Cooked Ground Beef. Available at www.fsis.usda.gov. Accessed July 2013.
41. Food Safety and Inspection Service. 2011. The Color of Meat and Poultry. Available at www.fsis.usda.gov. Accessed July 2013.
42. The Partnership for Food Safety Education. 2010. Chill: Refrigerate Promptly!. Available at www.fightbac.org. Accessed July 2013.
43. Food and Drug Administration. Bad Bug Book.

44. Food and Drug Administration and U.S. Department of Agriculture. 2000. A Description of the U.S. Food Safety System. Available at www.fsis.usda.gov. Accessed July 2013.
45. Centers for Disease Control and Prevention. Foodborne Disease Active Surveillance Network (FoodNet): FoodNet Surveillance. 2012. Report for 2011. Atlanta, Georgia: U.S. Department of Health and Human Services, CDC.
46. Food and Drug Administration and U.S. Department of Agriculture. A Description of the U.S. Food Safety System.
47. Centers for Disease Control. 2013. PulseNet & Foodborne Diseases Outbreak Detection. Available at www.cdc.gov. Accessed July 2013.
48. Bracket, R. 2006. Statement before the Committee on Health, Education, Labor and Pensions, United States Senate. Ensuring Food Safety: FDA's Role in Tracking and Resolving the Recent *E. coli* Spinach Outbreak. Available at www.hhs.gov. Accessed July 2013; Food and Drug Administration. 2006. FDA Statement on Foodborne *E. coli* O157:H7 Outbreak in Spinach. Available at www.fda.gov. Accessed July 2013.
49. Food and Drug Administration. 2013. Hazard Analysis and Critical Control Points (HACCP). Available at www.fda.gov. July 2013.
50. Food and Drug Administration.2013. FDA Food Code. Available at www.fda.gov. Accessed July 2013.
51. Food and Drug Administration.2013. Talking About Juice Safety: What You Need to Know. Available at www.fda.gov. Accessed July 2013.
52. Centers for Disease Control and Prevention. 2006. Botulism: Control Measures Overview for Clinicians. Available at www.bt.cdc.gov. Accessed July 2013.
53. Food and Drug Administration. 2013. Analysis and Evaluation of Preventive Control Measures for the Control and Reduction/Elimination of Microbial Hazards on Fresh and Fresh-Cut Produce. Available at www.fda.gov. Accessed July 2013.
54. Food and Drug Administration. 2011. Kinetics of Microbial Inactivation for Alternative Food Processing Technologies. High-Pressure Processing. Available at www.fda.gov. Accessed July 2013.
55. U.S. Environmental Protection Agency. 2012. Food Irradiation. Available at www.epa.gov. Accessed July 2013.
56. Ibid.
57. Food and Drug Administration. 2013. Irradiated Food and Packaging: Consumer Information. Available at www.fda.gov. Accessed July 2013.
58. Centers for Disease Control and Prevention. 2009. Food Irradiation. Available at www.cdc.gov. Accessed July 2013; Tauxe, R. 2001. Food Safety and Irradiation: Protecting the Public from Foodborne Infections. *Infectious Diseases* 7: 516–521.
59. Tauxe. Food Safety and Irradiation; Centers for Disease Control and Prevention. Food Irradiation.
60. Food and Drug Administration. Irradiated Food and Packaging:
61. Tauxe. Food Safety and Irradiation.
62. Food and Drug Administration. Irradiated Food and Packaging.
63. Ibid.
64. Food Safety and Inspection Service. 2013. Food Product Dating. Available at www.fsis.usda.gov. Accessed July 2013.
65. Ibid.
66. Grotheer, P., M. Marshall, and A. Simonne. 2005. Sulfites: Separating Fact from Fiction. Institute of Food and Agricultural Sciences, University of Florida. Available at http://edis.ifas.ufl.edu. Accessed July 2013.
67. Ibid.
68. Ibid.
69. Meadows, M. 2003. MSG: A Common Flavor Enhancer. *FDA Consumer* 37: 35.
70. Ibid.
71. Rados, C. 2004. GRAS: Time Tested and Trusted Food Ingredients. *FDA Consumer* 38: 20.
72. FDA. Updated 2010. Food Additives. Available at www.fda.gov. Accessed July 2013.
73. Ibid.
74. Rados. GRAS.
75. Centers for Disease Control and Prevention. 2012. Dioxins, Durans and Dioxin-Like Polychlorinate Biphenyls. Available at www.cdc.gov. Accessed July 2013; Food and Drug Administration. 2013. Questions and Answers about Dioxins and Food Safety. Available at www.fda.gov. Accessed July 2013.
76. Centers for Disease Control and Prevention. 2005. Marine Toxins. Available at www.cdc.gov. Accessed July 2013.
77. Ibid.
78. Ibid.
79. Ibid.
80. Taylor, S. 2006. Food additives, contaminants, and natural toxicants and their risk assessment. In Shils, M., M. Shike, A. Ross, B. Caballero, and R. Cousins. *Modern Nutrition in Health and Disease*. 10th ed. Philadelphia: Lippincott Williams & Wilkins.
81. U.S. Environmental Protection Agency. Updated 2013. Polychlorinated Biphenyls (PCBs). Available at www.epa.gov. Accessed July 2013.
82. Ibid.
83. Ibid.
84. Food and Drug Administration. 2013. Food Defense. What's Your Plan? Available at http://blogs.fda.gov. Accessed July 2013.
85. Centers for Disease Control and Prevention. 2007. Bioterrorism Overview. Available at http://emergency.cdc.gov. Accessed July 2013.
86. Risen, J. 2003. Threats and Responses: Terror Network Plot to Poison Food of British Troops Is Suspected. *New York Times*. Available at www.nytimes.com. Accessed July 2013.
87. Bruemmer, B. 2003. Food Biosecurity. *Journal of the American Dietetics Association* 103: 687–691.

Feature Box References

1. Centers for Disease Control and Prevention. 2013. Vital Signs: *Listeria* Illnesses, Death, and Outbreaks—United States, 2009–2011. *Morbidity and Mortality Weekly Report (MMWR)* 62: 448–452.
2. Centers for Disease Control and Prevention. 2013. Vital Signs: Recipe for Food Safety. Available at www.cdc.gov. Accessed August 2013.
3. Ibid.
4. Centers for Disease Control and Prevention. 2013. *Listeria* (Listeriosis): Prevention. Available at www.cdc.gov. Accessed August 2013.
5. FDA. 2011. *Fish and Fisheries Products Hazards and Controls Guidance*. 4th ed. Available at www.fda.gov. Accessed July 2013.
6. FDA. 2013. Fresh and Frozen Seafood: Selecting and Serving It Safely. Available at www.fda.gov. Accessed July 2013.
7. Ibid.

Two Points of View References

1. Zeratsky, K. Mayo Clinic. 2013. Nutrition and Healthy Eating: What is BPA and What Are the Concerns about BPA? Available at www.mayoclinic.com. Accessed June 2013.
2. U.S. Food and Drug Administration. 2013. Bisphenol A. Available at www.fda.gov. Accessed June 2013.
3. Ibid.
4. DeVries, J. 2006. Chasing "Zero" in Chemical Contaminant Analysis. *Food Safety Magazine*. Available at www.foodsafetymagazine.com. Accessed June 2013.
5. U.S. Food and Drug Administration. Bisphenol A.
6. National Institutes of Health. National Institute of Environmental Health Sciences. 2012. Bisphenol A (BPA). Available at www.niehs .nih.gov. Accessed June 2013; The American Cancer Society. 2008. News and Features: Federal Report Looks at Risks from Plastics and Chemicals. Available at www.cancer.org. Accessed June 2013.
7. Engel, S. M., A. Miodovnik, R. L. Canfield, C. Zhu, M. J. Silva, A. M. Calafat, et al. 2010. Prenatal Phthalate Exposure Is Associated with Childhood Behavior and Executive Functioning. *Environmental Health Perspectives* 118: 565–571.

Chapter 14

1. Hammoud, A., N. Wilde, M. Gibson, D. T. Carrell, and A. W. Meikle. 2008. Male Obesity and Alteration in Sperm Parameters. *Fertility and Sterility* 90: 2222–2225.
2. Eskenazi, B., S. Kidd, A. Marks, E. Sloter, G. Block, and A. Wyrobek. 2005. Antioxidant Intake Is Associated with Semen Quality in Healthy Men. *Human Reproduction* 20: 1006–1012.
3. Centers for Disease Control and Prevention. 2012. Preconception Care and Health Care, Information for Men. Available at www.cdc.gov. Accessed March 2013.
4. Kaiser, L., and L. Allen. 2008. Position of the American Dietetic Association: Nutrition and Lifestyle for a Healthy Pregnancy Outcome. *Journal of the American Dietetic Association* 108: 553–561.
5. Kitsantas, P., and L. R. Pawloski. 2010. Maternal Obesity, Health Status during Pregnancy, and Breast-Feeding Initiation and Duration. *Journal of Maternal and Fetal Neonatal Medicine* 23: 135–141.
6. March of Dimes Foundation. n.d. Eating and Nutrition. Available at www.marchofdimes.com. Accessed March 2013.
7. U.S. Department of Health and Human Services. 2004. *The Health Consequences of Smoking: A Report of the Surgeon General*. Atlanta:

National Center for Chronic Disease Prevention and Health Promotion, Office on Smoking and Health.

8. U.S. Department of Health and Human Services. 2005. U.S. Surgeon General Advisory on Alcohol Use in Pregnancy. Available at www.cdc.gov. Accessed July 2010.

9. National Library of Medicine. National Institutes of Health. 2012. Morning Sickness. Available at www.nlm.nih.gov. Accessed March 2013.

10. Kaiser. Position of the American Dietetic Association: Nutrition and Lifestyle for a Healthy Pregnancy Outcome.

11. National Center for Biotechnology Information, U.S. National Library of Medicine. 2012. Pica. Available at www.ncbi.nlm.nih.gov. Accessed March 2013.

12. Institute of Medicine. 2009. Weight Gain during Pregnancy: Reexamining the Guidelines. Available at www.iom.edu. Accessed March 2013.

13. U.S. Department of Agriculture, U.S. Department of Health and Human Services. 2010. *Dietary Guidelines for Americans, 2010.* 7th ed. Washington, D.C.: U.S. Government Printing Office.

14. Koletzko B., E. Lien, C. Agosoni, et al. 2008. The Roles of Long-Chain Polyunsaturated Fatty Acids in Pregnancy, Lactation, and Infancy: Review of Current Knowledge and Consensus Recommendations. *Journal of Perinatal Medicine* 36: 5–14.

15. Zeisel, S. H., and M. D. Niculescu. 2006. Perinatal Choline Influences Brain Structure and Function. *Nutrition Reviews* 64: 197–203.

16. Shaw, G. M., S. L. Carmichael, W. Yang S. Selvin, and D. M. Schaffer. 2004. Periconceptional Dietary Intake of Choline and Betaine and Neural Tube Defects in Offspring. *American Journal of Epidemiology* 160: 102–109.

17. Institute of Medicine. 2001. *Dietary Reference Intakes for Vitamin A, Vitamin K, Arsenic, Boron, Chromium, Copper, Iodine, Iron, Manganese, Nickel, Silicon, Vanadium, and Zinc.* Washington, D.C.: National Academies Press.

18. USDA. 2013. Health and Nutrition Information for Pregnant and Breast-Feeding Women. Available at www.choosemyplate.gov. Accessed March 2013.

19. Kaiser. Position of the American Dietetic Association: Nutrition and Lifestyle for a Healthy Pregnancy Outcome.

20. March of Dimes Foundation. 2008. Alcohol and Drugs. Available at www.marchofdimes.com. Accessed March 2013.

21. Weng, X., R. Odouli, and D. K. Li. 2008. Maternal Caffeine Consumption during Pregnancy and the Risk of Miscarriage: A Prospective Cohort Study. *American Journal of Obstetrics and Gynecology* 198: 279.e1–e8.

22. Painter, R. C., S. R. de Rooij, P. M. Bossuyt, T. A. Simmers, C. Osmond, D. J. Barker, et al. 2006. Early Onset of Coronary Artery Disease after Prenatal Exposure to the Dutch Famine. *American Journal of Clinical Nutrition* 84: 322–327.

23. Ames, B. N. 2006. Low Micronutrient Intake May Accelerate the Degenerative Diseases of Aging through Allocation of Scarce Micronutrients by Triage. *Proceedings of the National Academy of Sciences* 103: 17589–17594.

24. Wu, G., F. W. Bazer, T. A. Cudd, C. J. Meininger, and T. E. Spencer. 2004. Recent Advances in Nutritional Sciences: Maternal Nutrition and Fetal Development. *Journal of Nutrition* 134: 2169–2172.

25. Stover, P. J., and M. A. Caudill. 2008. Genetic and Epigenetic Contributions to Human Nutrition and Health: Managing Genome-Diet Interactions. *Journal of the American Dietetic Association* 108: 1480–1487.

26. Institute of MedicineWeight Gain during Pregnancy: Reexamining the Guidelines.

27. March of Dimes Foundation. 2012. Physical Activity. Available at www.marchofdimes.com. Accessed March 2013.

28. Centers for Disease Control and Prevention. 2011. Physical Activity, Healthy Pregnant or Postpartum Women. Available at www.cdc.gov. Accessed March 2013.

29. American Diabetes Association. 2013. What Is Gestational Diabetes? Available at www.diabetes.org. Accessed March 2013.

30. Ibid.

31. U.S. Department of Health and Human Services. 2012. Am I at Risk for Gestational Diabetes? Available at www.nichd.nih.gov. Accessed March 2013.

32. National Heart, Lung, and Blood Institute. n.d. High Blood Pressure in Pregnancy. Available at www.nhlbi.nih.gov. Accessed March 2013.

33. Kaiser. Position of the American Dietetic Association: Nutrition and Lifestyle for a Healthy Pregnancy Outcome.

34. Institute of Medicine. 2002. *Dietary Reference Intakes for Energy, Carbohydrate, Fiber, Fat, Fatty Acids, Cholesterol, Protein, and Amino Acids.* Washington, D.C.: National Academies Press.

35. Story, M., and J. Stang, eds. *Nutrition and the Pregnant Adolescent: A Practical Reference Guide.* 2000. Minneapolis, MN: HRSA.

36. Shabert, J. 2000. Nutrition during pregnancy and lactation. In Krause, *Food, Nutrition, & Diet Therapy.* 11th ed. Philadelphia: Saunders.

37. American Academy of Pediatrics. Section on Breast-Feeding. 2012. Breast-Feeding and the Use of Human Milk. *PEDIATRICS* 115: 496–506 doi: 10.1542/peds.2004-2491. Available at http://pediatrics.aappublications.org. Accessed March 2013.

38. Ibid.

39. U.S. Breast-Feeding Committee. 2002. Benefits of Breast-Feeding. Available at www.ehd.org. Accessed March 2013.

40. Economic Research Service. 2001. Economic Benefits of Breast-Feeding: A Review and Analysis. Available at www.ers.usda.gov. Accessed March 2013.

41. Bartick, M., and A. Reinhold. 2010. The Burden of Suboptimal Breast-Feeding in the United States. *PEDIATRICS* 125: e1048–e1056.

42. James, D. C. S., and R. Lessen. 2009. Position of the American Dietetic Association: Promoting and Supporting Breast-Feeding. *Journal of the American Dietetic Association* 109: 1926–1942.

43. American Academy of Pediatrics. Section on Breast-Feeding. Breast-Feeding and the Use of Human Milk.

44. Picciano, M., and S. S. McDonald. 2006. Lactation. In Shils, M. *Modern Nutrition in Health and Disease.* 10th ed. Philadelphia: Lippincott Williams and Wilkins.

45. James. Position of the American Dietetic Association: Promoting and Supporting Breast-Feeding.

46. Ibid.

47. Institute of Medicine. *Dietary Reference Intakes for Energy, Carbohydrate, Fiber, Fat, Fatty Acids, Cholesterol, Protein, and Amino Acids.*

48. Institute of Medicine. Weight Gain during Pregnancy: Reexamining the Guidelines.

49. Institute of Medicine. *Dietary Reference Intakes for Energy, Carbohydrate, Fiber, Fat, Fatty Acids, Cholesterol, Protein, and Amino Acids.*

50. American Academy of Pediatrics. 2012. Things to Avoid When Breast-Feeding. Available at www.healthychildren.org. Accessed March 2013.

51. American Academy of Pediatrics. Section on Breast-Feeding. Breast-Feeding and the Use of Human Milk.

52. Ibid.

53. Heird, W. C., and A. Cooper. 2006. Infancy and Childhood. In Shils, *Modern Nutrition in Health and Disease.* 10th ed. Philadelphia: Lippincott Williams and Wilkins.

54. O'Connor, N. R. 2009. Infant Formula. *American Family Physician* 79: 565–570correct.

55. American Academy of Pediatric Dentistry. 2011. Policy on Early Childhood Caries (ECC): Classification, Consequences and Preventive Strategies. Available at www.aapd.org. Accessed March 2013.

56. Centers for Disease Control and Prevention. 2010. Growth Charts. Available at www.cdc.gov. Accessed March 2013.

57. Institute of Medicine. *Dietary Reference Intakes for Energy, Carbohydrate, Fiber, Fat, Fatty Acids, Cholesterol, Protein, and Amino Acids.*

58. U.S. Department of Agriculture, Department of Health and Human Services. 2010. *Dietary Guidelines for Americans, 2010.* Available at www.health.gov. Accessed March 2013.

59. Institute of Medicine. *Dietary Reference Intakes for Vitamin A, Vitamin K, Arsenic, Boron, Chromium, Copper, Iodine, Iron, Manganese, Nickel, Silicon, Vanadium, and Zinc.*

60. American Academy of Pediatrics. 2008. Prevention of Rickets and Vitamin D Deficiency in Infants, Children, and Adolescents. Available at http://pediatrics.aappublications.org. Accessed March 2010.

61. Centers for Disease Control and Prevention. 2012. Overview: Infant Formula and Fluorosis. Available at www.cdc.gov. Accessed March 2013.

62. American Academy of Pediatrics. Section on Breast-Feeding. Breast-Feeding and the Use of Human Milk.

63. Ibid.

64. American Academy of Pediatrics. 2012. Switching to Solid Foods. Available at www.healthychildren.org. Accessed March 2013.

65. Fleischer, D. M., J. M. Spergel, A. H. Assa'ad, and J. A. Pongracic. 2013. Primary Prevention of Allergic Disease through Nutritional Interventions. *Journal of Allergy and Clinical Immunology: In Practice* 1: 29–36.

66. Ibid.

67. Centers for Disease Control and Prevention. 2010. Botulism. Available at www.cdc.gov. Accessed March 2013.

Feature Box References

1. Slusser, W., L. Lange, V. Dickson, C. Hawkes, and R. Cohen. 2004. Breast Milk Expression in the Workplace: A Look at Frequency and Time. *Journal of Human Lactation* 20: 164–169.
2. Johnson, M. 2006. Letter to the Editor: Twentieth Anniversary Issue. *Journal of Human Lactation* 22: 14.
3. National Council of State Legislatures. 2011. Breast-Feeding Laws. Available at www.ncsl.org. Accessed June 2013.
4. U.S. Department of Health and Human Services, Maternal and Child Health Bureau. 2008. Easy Steps to Supporting Breast-Feeding Employees. Available at www.womenshealth.gov. Accessed June 2013.
5. American Academy of Pediatrics. 2012. Policy Statement: Breast-Feeding and the Use of Human Milk. *PEDIATRICS* 129: e827–e841.
6. National Institute of Allergy and Infectious Diseases. Updated 2012. Food Allergy: Common Food Allergens in Infants, Children, and Adults. Available at www.niaid.nih.gov. Accessed June 2013.
7. Long, A. 2002. The Nuts and Bolts of Peanut Allergy. *New England Journal of Medicine* 346: 1320–1322.
8. Branum, A., and S. Lukacs. 2008. Food Allergy among U.S. Children: Trends in Prevalence and Hospitalizations. *National Center for Health Statistics Data Brief.* Available at www.cdc.gov. Accessed June 2013.
9. Food and Drug Administration. 2006. Food Allergen Labeling and Consumer Protection Act of 2004 (Title II of Public Law 108–282). Report to the Committee on Health, Education, Labor, and Pensions, United States Senate, and the Committee on Energy and Commerce, United States House of Representatives. Available at www.cfsan.fda.gov. Accessed June 2013.

Two Points of View References

1. Health and Human Services Division, Municipality of Anchorage, Alaska. 2008. Why Homemade? Available at hhs.muni.org. Accessed June 2013; Stallone, D., and M. Jacobson, 1995. Cheating Babies: Nutritional Quality and Cost of Baby Food. *CSPI Reports.* Available at www.cspinet.org. Accessed June 2013.
2. Freshbaby.com. Benefits of Homemade Baby Food. Available at http://freshbaby.com. Accessed July 2013.
3. Municipality of Anchorage. Why Homemade?; Stallone. Cheating Babies.
4. Fountain, B., University of Mississippi Extension Service. 2010. Homemade Baby Food Benefits Entire Family. Available at http://msucares.com. Accessed June 2013.
5. USDA, Agricultural Research Service. 2006. The New Food Quality Protection Act, 2006. Available at www.ars.usda.gov. Accessed August 2010.
6. Shaw, G. 2010. Homemade Baby Food: Is it Right for You? *Web MD.* Available at www.webmd.com. Accessed June 2013.
7. Schaefer, E., and N. Fradgley, National Network for Child Care. 1995. Feeding Your Baby. Available at www.nncc.org. Accessed June 2013.
8. Greer, F., and M. Shannon. 2005. Infant Methemoglobinemia: The Role of Dietary Nitrate in Food and Water. *PEDIATRICS* 116: 784–786.

Chapter 15

1. Ministry of Health British Columbia. 2013. Healthy Growth & Weight for Toddlers. Available at www.bestchance.gov.bc.ca. Accessed September 2013.
2. American Academy of Pediatrics. 2004. *Pediatric Nutrition Handbook.* 5th ed. American Academy of Pediatrics.
3. Baker, R. D., F. R. Greer, and the Committee on Nutrition. 2010. Clinical Report—Diagnosis and Prevention of Iron Deficiency and Iron-Deficiency Anemia in Infants and Young Children (0–3 Years of Age). Available at http://pediatrics.aappublications.org. Accessed May 2013.
4. Ibid.
5. Institute of Medicine, Food and Nutrition Board. 1997. *Dietary Reference Intakes for Calcium, Phosphorus, Magnesium, Vitamin D, and Fluoride.* Washington, D.C.: The National Academies Press.
6. Ibid.
7. Institute of Medicine. 2001. *Dietary Reference Intakes for Vitamin A, Vitamin K, Arsenic, Boron, Chromium, Copper, Iodine, Iron, Manganese, Nickel, Silicon, Vanadium, and Zinc.* Washington, D.C.: The National Academies Press.
8. Ibid.
9. Centers for Disease Control and Prevention. 2013. FastStats. Available at www.cdc.gov. Accessed May 2013.
10. Office of Dietary Supplements. 2011. Dietary Supplement Fact Sheet: Vitamin D. Available at http://ods.od.nih.gov. Accessed May 2013.
11. Wagner, C. L., F. R. Greer, and the Section on Breast-Feeding and Committee on Nutrition. 2008. Prevention of Rickets and Vitamin D Deficiency in Infants, Children, and Adolescents. *PEDIATRICS* 122: 1142–1152.
12. Institute of Medicine, Food and Nutrition Board. 2002. *Dietary Reference Intakes for Energy, Carbohydrate, Fiber, Fat, Fatty Acids, Cholesterol, Protein, and Amino Acids.* Washington, D.C.: The National Academies Press.
13. Institute of Medicine, Food and Nutrition Board. 2002. *Dietary Reference Intakes for Water, Potassium, Sodium, Chloride, and Sulfate.* Washington, D.C.: The National Academies Press.
14. American Academy of Pediatrics. 2012. Fruit Juice and Your Child's Diet. Available at www.healthychildren.org. Accessed May 2013.
15. Satter, E. 2003. *Child of Mine: Feeding with Love and Good Sense.* Boulder, CO: Bull Publishing.
16. Larson, N., J. Fulkerson, M. Story, and D. Neumark-Sztainer. 2012. Shared Meals among Young Adults Are Associated with Better Diet Quality and Predicted by Family Meal Patterns during Adolescence. *Public Health Nutrition* 3: 1–11.
17. Abramovitz, B., and L. Birch. 2000. Five-Year-Old Girls' Ideas about Dieting Are Predicted by Their Mothers' Dieting. *Journal of the American Dietetic Association* 100: 1157–1163.
18. Centers for Disease Control and Prevention. 2013. Childhood Obesity Facts. Available at www.cdc.gov. Accessed May 2013.
19. Ibid.
20. Ibid.
21. U.S. Department of Health and Human Services. 2010. *Dietary Guidelines for Americans, 2010.* 7th ed. Washington, D.C.: U.S. Government Printing Office.
22. Henry J. Jaiser Family Foundation. 2010. Generation M2: Media in the Lives of 8- to 18-Year-Olds: Report. Available at www.kff.org. Accessed May 2013.
23. American Academy of Pediatrics. 2013. Media and Children. Available at www.aap.org. Accessed May 2013.
24. U.S. Department of Health and Human Services. 2010. *Physical Activity Guidelines for Americans* Midcourse Report. Strategies to Increase Physical Activity among Youth. Available at www.health.gov. Accessed May 2013.
25. National Association for Sport and Physical Education and the American Heart Association. 2012. 2012 Shape of the Nation Report: Status of Physical Education in the USA. Available at www.aahperd.org. Accessed May 2013.
26. Centers for Disease Control and Prevention. 2012. Diabetes Public Health Resource. Available at www.cdc.gov. Accessed May 2013.
27. Li, S. 2009. Prevalence of Pre-Diabetes and Its Association with Clustering of Cardiometabolic Risk Factors and Hyperinsulinemia Among U.S. Adolescents. *Diabetes Care* 32: 342–347.
28. Rampersaud, G. C., M. A. Pereira, B. L. Girard, J. Adams, and J. D. Metzl. 2005. Breakfast Habits, Nutritional Status, Body Weight, and Academic Performance in Children and Adolescents. *Journal of the American Dietetic Association* 105: 743–760.
29. U.S. Department of Agriculture, Food and Nutrition Service. 2012. National School Lunch Program. www.fns.usda.gov.
30. Office of Dietary Supplements. Dietary Supplement Fact Sheet: Vitamin D.
31. Treuth, M. S., and I. J. Griffin. 2006. Adolescence. In M. Shils, ed., *Modern Nutrition in Health and Disease.* 10th ed. Philadelphia: Lippincott Williams & Wilkins.
32. Centers for Disease Control and Prevention. Childhood Obesity Facts.
33. Treuth. Adolescence.
34. Office of Dietary Supplements. Dietary Supplement Fact Sheet: Vitamin D.
35. Centers for Disease Control and Prevention. FastStats.
36. U.S. Census Bureau. 2012. International Database. Table 094. Midyear Population, by Age and Sex. Available at www.census.gov. Accessed May 2013.
37. U.S. Department of Health and Human Services. *Dietary Guidelines for Americans, 2010.*
38. Office of Dietary Supplements. Dietary Supplement Fact Sheet: Vitamin D.
39. Institute of Medicine. 1998. Vitamin B_{12}. In *Dietary Reference Intakes: Thiamin, Riboflavin, Niacin, Vitamin B_6, Vitamin B_{12}, Pantothenic Acid, Biotin, and Choline.* Washington, D.C.: The National Academies Press.
40. Office of Dietary Supplements. 2007. Dietary Supplement Fact Sheet: Iron. Available at http://ods.od.nih.gov. Accessed May 2013.
41. Office of Dietary Supplements. 2011. Dietary Supplement Fact Sheet: Zinc. Available at http://ods.od.nih.gov. Accessed May 2013.
42. Institute of Medicine, Food and Nutrition Board. *Dietary Reference Intakes for Calcium, Phosphorus, Magnesium, Vitamin D, and Fluoride.*

43. U.S. Department of Health and Human Services. *Dietary Guidelines for Americans, 2010.*

44. Hiza, H. A. B., P. M. Guenther, K. Connell, and C. A. Davis. 2010. Diet Quality of Americans 65 Years and Older. Available at www.fasebj.org. Accessed May 2013.

45. American Heart Association. 2013. Heart Attack and Stroke Statistics. Available at www.heart.org. Accessed May 2013.

46. American Diabetes Association. 2013. Facts about Type 2. Available at www.diabetes.org. Accessed May 2013.

47. National Heart, Lung, and Blood Institute. 2012. What Is High Blood Pressure? Available at www.nhlbi.nih.gov. Accessed May 2013.

48. National Institute of Arthritis and Musculoskeletal and Skin Diseases (NIAMS). 2010. Handout on Health: Osteoarthritis. Available at www.niams.nih.gov. Accessed May 2013.

49. National Center for Complementary and Alternative Medicine. 2008. Questions and Answers: NIH Glucosamine/Chondroitin Arthritis Intervention Trial Primary Study. Available at http://nccam.nih.gov. Accessed October 2013.

50. National Institute of Arthritis and Musculoskeletal and Skin Diseases. 2009. Rheumatoid Arthritis. Available at www.niams.nih.gov. Accessed July 2010.

51. Choi, H. 2005. Dietary Risk Factors for Rheumatic Diseases. *Current Opinion in Rheumatology* 17: 141–146.

52. National Institute on Aging. 2013. Alzheimer's Disease Fact Sheet. Available at www.nia.nih.gov. Accessed May 2013.

53. Ibid.

54. U.S. Department of Agriculture, Economic Research Center. 2012. Food Security in the U.S. Available at www.ers.usda.gov. Accessed May 2013.

55. Administration on Aging. 2009. Older Americans Act. Available at www.aoa.gov. Accessed July 2010.

56. National Institute of Mental Health. 2007. Older Adults: Depression and Suicide Facts (Fact Sheet). Available at www.nimh.nih.gov. Accessed May 2013.

57. National Institute on Aging. 2012. Alcohol Use in Older People. Available at www.nia.nih.gov. Accessed May 2013.

58. U.S. Department of Health and Human Services. *2008 Physical Activity Guidelines for Americans.* Available at www.health.gov. Accessed May 2013.

Feature Box References

1. Centers for Disease Control and Prevention. 2013. Attention-Deficit/ Hyperactivity Disorder (ADHD). Available at www.cdc.gov. Accessed May 2013.

2. U.S. Department of Health & Human Services. National Institutes of Health. 1982. Defined Diets and Childhood Hyperactivity. Available at http://consensus.nih.gov. Accessed May 2013.

3. Kim, Y., and H. Chang. 2011. Correlation between Attention Deficit Hyperactivity Disorder and Sugar Consumption, Quality of Diet, and Dietary Behavior in School Children. *Nutrition Research and Practice* 5: 236–245.

4. American Academy of Pediatrics. 2011. Your Child's Diet: A Cause and a Cure of ADHD? Available at www.healthychildren.org. Accessed May 2013.

5. Centers for Disease Control and Prevention. National Health Statistics Reports. 2013. Changes in Prevalence of Parent-Reported Autism Spectrum Disorder in School-Aged U.S. Children: 2007 to 2011–2012. No. 65. Available at www.cdc.gov. Accessed May 2013.

6. National Institute of Mental Health. 2011. A Parent's Guide to Autism Spectrum Disorder. Available at www.nimh.nih.gov. Accessed May 2013.

7. Mayo Clinic. 2010. Autism. Available at www.mayoclinic.com. Accessed May 2013.

8. American Cancer Society. 2013. Cancer Facts & Figures 2013. Available at www.cancer.org. Accessed May 2013.

9. Ibid.

10. National Cancer Institute. 2011. Secondhand Smoke and Cancer. Available at www.cancer.gov. Accessed May 2013.

11. National Institutes of Health. National Cancer Society. 2010. Chemicals in Meat Cooked at High Temperatures and Cancer Risk. Available at www.cancer.gov. Accessed May 2013.

12. World Cancer Research Fund. American Institute for Cancer Research. 2013. Food, Nutrition, Physical Activity, and the Prevention of Cancer. Available at www.dietandcancerreport.org. Accessed May 2013.

13. American Cancer Society. 2013. Body Weight and Cancer Risk. Available at www.cancer.org. Accessed May 2013.

14. U.S. Department of Health & Human Services. U.S. Food and Drug Adminstration. 2012. Drug Interactions: What You Should Know. Available at www.fda.gov. Accessed May 2013.

15. U.S. Food and Drug Administration. 2009. Dietary Supplements: Tips for Older Dietary Supplement Users. Available at www.fda.gov. Accessed July 2010.

Two Points of View References

1. Winterman, D. 2008. The Towns Where People Live the Longest. *BBC News Magazine.* Available at http://news.bbc.co.uk. Accessed August 2013.

2. Science Daily. 2013. Science Reference. Calorie-Restricted Diet. Available at www.sciencedaily.com. Accessed August 2013.

3. Holloszy, J. O., and L. Fontana. 2007. Caloric Restriction in Humans. *Experimental Gerontology* 42: 709–712.

4. Omodei, D., and L. Fontana. 2011. Calorie Restriction and Prevention of Age-Associated Chronic Disease. *Federation of European Biochemical Societies Letters* 585: 1537–1542.

5. NIH Research Matters. 2012. Calorie Restriction May Not Extend Life. Available at www.nih.gov. Accessed August 2013.

6. Science Daily. Science Reference. Calorie-Restricted Diet.

7. Willcox, D. C., B. J. Willcox, H. Todoriki, J. D. Curb, and M. Suzuki. 2006. Caloric Restriction and Human Longevity: What Can We Learn from the Okinawans? *Biogerontology* 7: 173–177.

8. Maxmen, A. 2012. Calorie Restriction Falters in the Long Run. *Nature: International Weekly Journal of Science* 488: 569.

9. Lawson, W. 2004. The Skinny on Calorie Restriction. *Psychology Today* Available at www.psychologytoday.com. Accessed August 2013; Science Daily. 2010. Science News. Calorie Restriction Leads Scientists to Molecular Pathways That Slow Aging, Improve Health. Available at www.sciencedaily.com. Accessed August 2013.

Chapter 16

1. Nord, M., M. Andrews, and S. Carlson. 2008. Household Food Security in the United States, 2007. United States Department of Agriculture (USDA), Economic Research Report No. (ERR-66), November 2008. Available at www.ers.usda.gov. Accessed January 2009.

2. USDA Economic Research Service. 2012. Household Food Security in the United States in 2011. Available at www.ers.usda.gov. Accessed April 2013.

3. USDA Economic Research Service. 2012. Food Security in the United States: Key Statistics and Graphics. Available at www.ers.usda.gov. Accessed April 2013.

4. USDA Economic Research Service. 2012. Food Security in the U.S.: Measurement. Available at www.ers.usda.gov. Accessed June 2013.

5. Food and Agriculture Organization of the United Nations. 2012. Hunger. Available at www.fao.org. Accessed April 2013.

6. Food and Agriculture Organization of the United Nations. 2012. Undernourished Population. Available at www.fao.org. Accessed April 2013.

7. World Bank. 2013. Poverty Reduction and Equity. Available at web.worldbank.org. Accessed April 2013.

8. United States Census Bureau. 2013. Poverty Data: Poverty Thresholds. Available at www.census.gov. Accessed April 2013.

9. Food and Research Action Center. 2010. Data and Publications. Hunger and Poverty. Available at http://frac.org. Accessed April 2013.

10. United States Census Bureau. 2012. Poverty Data: Income, Poverty and Health Insurance in the United States: 2011—Highlights. Available at www.census.gov. Accessed April 2013.

11. USDA Economic Research Service. 2012. Food Security in the United States: Key Statistics and Graphics.

12. Ibid.

13. Whitaker, R. C., S. M. Phillips, and S. M. Orzol. 2006. Food Insecurity and the Risks of Depression and Anxiety in Mothers and Behavior Problems in their Preschool-Aged Children. *PEDIATRICS* 118: e859–e868.

14. Smith, L. C., and L. Haddad. 2000. *Explaining Child Malnutrition in Developing Countries: A Cross-Country Analysis of International Food Policy.* Washington, D.C.: International Food Policy Research Institute.

15. United Nations Association of the United States of America and the Business Council for the United Nations. 2006. Millennium Development Goals. Available at www.un.org. Accessed June 2012.

16. Ornelas, A., and M. A. Rubin. 2013. Measuring the Real Impact of Sanctions. Available at www.swissinfo.ch. Accessed April 2013.

17. Struble, M. B., and L. Aomari. 2003. ADA Reports: Position of the American Dietetic Association. Addressing World Hunger. *Journal of the American Dietetic Association* 103:1046–1057.

18. Food and Agriculture Organization of the United Nations. 2008. The State of Food Insecurity in the World, 2008. Available at www.fao.org. Accessed April 2010.
19. World Food Programme. 2013. Hunger; What Causes Hunger? Available at www.wfp.org. Accessed April 2013.
20. Food and Agriculture Organization. The State of Food Insecurity in the World, 2008.
21. U.S. Department of Commerce. 2013. U.S. Census Bureau. World POPClock Projection. Notes on the World POPClock and World Vital Events. Available at www.census.gov. Accessed April 2013.
22. Kramer, M. S., and R. Kakuma. 2004. The Optimal Duration of Exclusive Breast-Feeding: A Systematic Review. *Advanced Experimental Medical Biology* 554: 63–77.
23. King, F. S., and A. Burgess. 1993. *Nutrition for Developing Countries*, 2nd ed. Oxford, England: Oxford Medical Publications, Oxford University Press.
24. UNAIDS. 2010. Global Report. Chapter 2. Epidemic Update. Available at www.unaids.org. Accessed June 2013.
25. Maher, D., and C. Eliadi. 2012. Malnutrition in the Elderly: An Unrecognized Health Issue. Available at http://rnjournal.com. Accessed April 2013.
26. Beers, M., R. Porter, T. Jones, J. Kaplan, and M. Berkwits, eds. 2006. Starvation. In *The Merck Manual of Diagnosis and Therapy, Section 1— Nutritional Disorders, Chapter 2: Malnutrition Topics*. Available at www.merck.com. Accessed April 2010.
27. Doctors without Borders. 2012. Malnutrition. What Is Malnutrition? Available at www.doctorswithoutborders.org. Accessed April 2013.
28. Kleinman, R. E., et al. 1998. Hunger in Children in the United States: Potential Behavioral and Emotional Correlates. *PEDIATRICS* 101: 3–10.
29. The World Bank. 2011. Early Child Development. Nutrition. Available at web.worldbank.org. Accessed April 2013.
30. Winicki, J., and K. Jemison. 2003. Food Insecurity and Hunger in the Kindergarten Classroom: Its Effect on Learning and Growth. *Contemporary Economic Policy* 2: 145–157.
31. UNICEF. 2009. Tracking Progress on Child and Maternal Nutrition. Available at www.unicef.org. Accessed April 2013.
32. Halterman, Jill, et al. 2001. Iron Deficiency and Cognitive Achievement Among School-Aged Children and Adolescents in the United States. *PEDIATRICS* 107: 1381–1386. Available at http://pediatrics .aappublications.org.
33. UNICEF. 2013. Improving Child Nutrition. Available at www.unicef.org. Accessed April 2013.
34. Ibid.
35. World Health Organization Media Centre. 2012. Children: Reducing Mortality. Available at www.who.int. Accessed May 2013.
36. Ibid.
37. World Health Organization. 2013. Water Sanitation Health. Water-Related Diseases. Diarrhoea. Available at www.who.int. Accessed May 2013.
38. World Health Organization Media Centre. 2013. Pneumonia. Available at www.who.int. Accessed April 2013.
39. Micronutrient Initiative. 2013. Vitamin A. Available at www.micronutrient.org. Accessed April 2013.
40. Ibid.
41. Food and Agriculture Organization of the United Nations. 2013. Policy Briefs. Female Land Ownership. Available at www.fao.org. Accessed April 2013.
42. World Health Organization Media Centre. 2013. Diarrhoeal Disease. Available at www.who.int. Accessed April 2013.
43. Ibid.
44. CDC. 2008. Household Water Treatment Options in Developing Countries: Solar Disinfection (SODIS). Available at www.cdc.gov.
45. Food and Agriculture Organization of the United Nations. 1995. Annex 4—Micronutrient Fortification of Food: Technology and Quality Control. Available at www.fao.org. Accessed June 2013.
46. King, et al. *Nutrition for Developing Countries.*
47. Struble, et al. Addressing World Hunger.

Feature Box References

1. NCHS Data Brief No. 50, December 2010. Available at www.cdc.gov.
2. Centers for Disease Control and Prevention, Overweight and Obesity. Available at www.cdc.gov. Accessed April 2013.
3. NCHS Data Brief No. 50.
4. Centers for Disease Control and Prevention, Overweight and Obesity.
5. World Health Organization. 2009. World Health Day 2009. Available at www.who.int. Accessed October 2010.
6. BBC News. 2010. Haiti Will Not Die, President Rene Preval Insists. Available at news.bbc.co.uk. Accessed October 2010.
7. Friends of the World Food Program. 2010. Latest Assessment Reveals Widespread Food Insecurity in Haiti. Available at http://friendsofwfp .typepad.com. Accessed October 2010.
8. Food and Agriculture Organization of the United Nations (FAO). 2010. Haiti: Earthquake Flash Appeal, 2010. Available at www.fao.org. Accessed October 2010.
9. Ibid.

Two Points of View References

1. United States Department of Agriculture, Economic Research Service. 2004. Amber Waves: 50 Years of US Food Aid and Its Role in Reducing World Hunger. Available at http://ageconsearch.umn.edu. Accessed April 2013.
2. Center for Global Development. 2009. Cash (or Food?) for Thought: The Debate on Cash versus Food Isn't Over (Yet). Available at www .cgdev.org. Accessed April 2013.
3. Bretton Woods Project. 2010. Farming Furor: World Bank Launches New Agriculture Fund. Available at www.brettonwoodsproject.org. Accessed April 2013.
4. Ibid.
5. Center for Global Development. Cash (or Food?) for Thought.
6. Ibid.
7. A. Gelan. 2006. Cash or Food Aid? A General Equilibrium Analysis for Ethiopia. *Development Policy Review* 24: 601–624.
8. USAid Disaster Assistance. 2010. How Can I Help? Handling Appropriate Commodity Contributions. Available at www1.usaid.gov. Accessed April 2013.
9. Gelan. Cash or Food Aid?; International Policy Network. 2013. New IPN Study Shows Foreign Aid Does More Harm than Good. Available at www.policynetwork.net. Accessed April 2013.
10. USAid Disaster Assistance. How Can I Help?
11. Food First, Institute for Food and Development Policy. 2006. Famine in Africa Means the Poor Can't Buy Food. Available at www.foodfirst.org. Accessed April 2013.

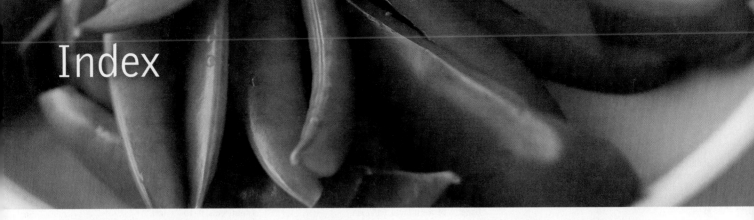

Index

Page references followed by *fig* indicate illustrated figures or photographs; followed by *t* indicates a table.

A

absorption, in GI tract, 72*fig*, 79–81, 80*fig*
Academy of Nutrition and Dietetics (AND), 20, 467
Acceptable Macronutrient Distribution Range (AMDR), 34, 35*t*, 153–154
acesulfame-K (Sunette), 127*t*, 129–130
acetaldehyde, 342
acid, and denaturation, 187
acid erosion, of teeth, 290
acid-base balance, 194
acidosis, 194
acromegaly, 442
active transport, 80, 80*fig*
activity. *See* physical activity
activity level. *See also* disordered eating; physical activity; physical fitness
    basal metabolic rate, 374, 374*fig*, 375*t*
    blood glucose level, 118–119
    body dysmorphic disorder (BDD), 400
    caloric needs, 389*t*
    childhood obesity, 567, 567*fig*, 569–570
    and cholesterol, 163–176, 163*t*
    defined, 414–415
    and Dietary Guidelines for Americans, 36
    and the environment, 379–382, 382*fig*
    Estimated Energy Requirement (EER) for, 34, 375–376
    fat, energy from, 425, 426, 427–428
    and fluid intake, 435–439
    and Mediterranean diet, 168*fig*, 168–170
    and MyPlate, 31*fig*, 38*fig*, 39*fig*, 41*fig*, 42*fig*, 43*fig*, 60*fig*
    and older adults, 577*fig*, 588–589
    and physical activity pyramid, 420*fig*
    during pregnancy, 536–538
    protein, energy from, 195, 429, 444*t*
    timing for, 419, 420*fig*, 421*t*
    and vegetarian diets, 212–213
    and weight management 388, 389*t*
Ad Council, 355
added sugars. *See also* naturally occurring sugars; sugar; sugar substitutes
    defined, 113
    and diabetes, 115–120
    effects of, 115
    finding, 122*fig*, 122–125, 125*fig*, 125*t*
    guidelines for, 126
    HFCS as, 122–124
    lowering, 115
additives, food, 511–514
adenosine triphosphate (ATP), 422, 423*fig*
Adequate Intake (AI), 33*fig*, 34, 35*t*
adolescents, teens. *See also* children; school-age children
    calorie needs for, 563*t*
    and disordered eating, 575

    nutrient needs of, 573
    peer pressure, and eating behavior, 573–574
    pregnancy in, 537
    vitamins, minerals for, 574*fig*, 574–575, 574*t*
adrenaline (norepinephrine), 107
advertising, 24, 346, 355
aerobic, anaerobic exercise, 422
age-related macular degeneration (AMD), 226, 227*fig*, 313
agribusiness, 458–459
agricultural practice, wasteful, 602, 603
air displacement weighing, 371*fig*
airborne emissions, 463*t*
alcohol dehydrogenase, 341
alcohol use and abuse
    about, 338
    and breast-feeding, 543
    CAGE screening tool for, 354
    and cancer, 582
    digestion, absorption of, 340–345, 341*fig*, 343*t*, 344*fig*
    disease of, 352–357, 356–357
    drinking and driving, 354–355
    effects on organs, 349–351, 350*fig*, 351*fig*
    effects on pregnancy, 351–352, 352*fig*, 532
    guidelines for, 37
    health benefits of, 339–340
    and heart health, 174
    and hormones, 347
    and hypertension, 296–297
    and magnesium, 307
    mixed with caffeine, 343
    mocktails, 358
    in older adults, 588
    and overnutrition, malnutrition, 347–349, 348*t*, 349*fig*
    poisoning, 353
    and pregnancy, 526
    progressive effects of, 344*t*
    pros and cons, 359
    reasons for choosing, 338–340, 339*fig*
    serving sizes of, 339*fig*, 340, 340*fig*
    sleep disturbance, hangover, 345, 347
    tolerance for, 354
    underage, 356
    and vitamin deficiency, 245, 250
alcoholic hepatitis, 350
alcoholic liver disease, 350
Alcoholics Anonymous (AA), 357
alcoholism, 352, 356–357
allergens, 195, 550–552, 568
Alli (orlistat), 70, 393
alliums/allicin, 228*t*
alpha-lactalbumin, 540
alpha-linolenic acid, 143*fig*, 144, 152, 158*fig*, 171
alpha-tocopherol, 236
Alzheimer's Disease (AD), 584
amenorhhea, 431, 441
American Academy of Child and Adolescent Psychiatry, 568

American Academy of Pediatrics, 563
American College of Sports Medicine, 437, 437*t*
American diet, quality of, 12–13
American Heart Association (AHA), 22–23
amino acids
    anatomy of, 184–185
    aspartame, neotame as, 129
    essential, nonessential, conditional, 186, 186*t*
    pools, 188, 190, 190*fig*
    profile, 198–199
    structure of, 185*fig*
    supplements for, 202
    synthesis, with DNA, 191*fig*, 192
amniotic fluid, 282
amylase, 78, 102, 103*fig*
amylopectin, 100
amylose, 100
anabolic steroids, 441, 443*t*
anaphylactic reactions, 552
androgenic effect, 441
anemia, 250, 311
anemia
    and exercise, 434
    in infants, 546, 548
    iron-deficiency, 309, 311, 326*t*, 434
    macrocytic, 253, 255
    pernicious, 254, 255
    in pregnancy, 532
    and vitamin deficiencies, 250, 252, 253, 254, 255, 261*t*
anencephaly, 252
Animal and Plant Health Inspection Service (APHIS), 477*t*, 507*t*
animals, raised for food, 460
anorexia nervosa, 397*t*, 399, 431, 575
anthocyanins, 228*t*
antibiotic-resistant bacteria, 470–471
antibiotics, in animal feed, 470–471
antibodies, 194
anti-caking agents, 512
anticoagulant, 236
antidiruretic hormone (ADH), 284
antimicrobials, 471
antioxidants
    in alcohol, 174, 340
    fighting cancer, 581
    and physical fitness, 433
    as preservatives, 511–512
    reservatrol as, 340
    selecting foods with, 172–173
    selenium as, 315
    vitamin C as, 259
    vitamin E as, 236
    vitamins as, 226–227, 227*fig*
anus, 76*fig*, 76–77
apolipoprotein B (ApoB), 166
appendix, 76, 76*fig*
appetite, 83, 195–196, 377–378
arachidonic acid (AA), 152, 541
Armstrong, Lance, 442–443

arsenic, 324*t*
arthritis, 580, 583–584
artificial sweeteners, 126–130, 127*t*
ascending colon, 76, 76*fig*
ascorbic acid. *See also* vitamin C, 256
Asians, alcohol effects on, 344
aspartame (Nutrasweet, Equal), 127*t*, 129
aspartic acid (Asp), 185*fig*
atherosclerosis, 165*fig*, 296
ATP (adenosine triphosphate), 422, 423*fig*
attention deficit/hyperactivity disorder (ADHD), 568
autism spectrum disorder (ASD), 568
Avicel cellulose gel, 161*t*

B

B complex vitamins, 243–255
baby boomers, 576*fig*
Bacillus thuringinensis (Bt), 471, 475
bacteria, and foodborne illness, 491, 495–496, 499*fig*
bacteria, in colon, 76
ballistic stretching, 418
bariatric surgery, 394–395
basal metabolism, metabolic rate, 374, 374*fig*, 375*t*
Beano, 86
Bechler, Steve, 393
behavior modification, 390–391
Belviq, 393
beriberi, 244–245, 245*fig*
beta-carotene, 228*t*, 230, 260*t*
beta-glucan, 59
beta-gluton, 228*t*
Beta-Trim, 161*t*
bicarbonate, 77, 78, 78*t*
bile, 77, 78*t*, 149
binge drinking, 353–354
binge-eating disorder, 397*t*, 401, 575
bioaccumulation, of toxins, 515, 515*fig*, 516
bioavailability
    of minerals, 291
    of vitamins, 228
biodiversity, 467
bioelectrical impedance, 371*fig*
biopesticides, 471
biotechnology, in agriculture
    about, 473–474
    genetic engineering (GE), 474*fig*, 474–475
    and GMOs, 475–476, 476*t*
bioterrorism, 517
biotin, 76, 258, 261*t*
birth defects
    and alcohol, 351–352, 532
    and folate, 251–252
    and gestational diabetes, 535
    and illicit drugs, 532
    and vitamin A, 234, 530
bisphenol A (BPA), 518
blackouts, 353
bleaching, 231, 232*fig*
blood
    blood alcohol concentration (BAC), 342, 343*t*, 354–355
    doping, 442–443
    glucose levels in, 118–119
    iron in, 309
blood pressure. *See* hypertension
BMI. *See* body mass index (BMI)
BMR (basal metabolic rate), 374, 374*fig*, 375*t*
BodPod, 371*fig*
body composition, 415, 416*t*
body dysmorphic disorder (BDD), 400
body image, 400
body mass index (BMI), 368–370, 369*fig*, 378, 529*t*
bolus, 71–73, 72*fig*
bones
    bone mineral density (BMD), 302, 417, 574
    and calcium, 300
    and osteoporosis, 302*fig*, 302–303

borborygmus, 85
boron, 324*t*
bottled water, 287–289, 289*t*
botulism, 550
bovine spongiform encephalopathy (BSE), 497
brain
    effects of alcohol on, 342–343, 344*fig*, 344*t*
    effects of iron on function, 309
    effects of malnutrition on, 605–606
bran, 110–111
breakfast, and calorie intake, 49–50
breast-feeding. *See also* pregnancy
    about, 538
    benefits of, for infants, 540–541
    benefits of, for mothers, 538–540, 539*fig*
    contraindications for, 543
    diet, lifestyle for mother, 541–543
    and early childhood caries, 545
    similarities to formula, 544*t*
    and undernutrition, 604
    at work, 542
broccoli, 58
buffers, protein as, 194
bulimia nervosa, 397*t*, 399, 401, 575
butter, 167, 167*fig*, 170
butylated hydroxyanisole (BHA), 512
butylated hydroxytoluene (BHT), 512

C

caffeine
    affecting fertility, 526*t*
    and breast-feeding, 542
    and exercise, 438, 443*t*, 447
    and hydration, 441
    during pregnancy, 532
CAGE screening tool, 354
calcium
    about, 300–301, 301*fig*
    absorption of, 292
    for adolescents, teens, 574
    importance to exercise, 434–435
    as major mineral, 292
    for older adults, 579
    and osteoporosis, 302*fig*, 302–303
    in pregnancy, 530
    summary of, 325*t*
    for toddlers, preschoolers, 564
calorie-restricted diets, and life span, 590
calories
    balancing, 36, 386
    and diets, 384
    disclosure by restaurants, 61
    and energy balance, 372–374, 373*fig*
    expended during activities, 389*t*
    overconsumption of, 49–50
    and weight loss, gain, 376
Campylobacter jejuni, 470–471, 492*t*, 496, 510
cancer
    and alcohol, 344, 349–350
    and calcium, 300
    defined, 581
    and fiber, 133–134
    and folate deficiency, 252
    and a healthy lifestyle, 581–583
    and high-protein diet, 206
    and obesity, 367
    and physical fitness, 416*t*
    preventing, 582*t*–583*t*
    and selenium, 315
    and sun exposure, 242
    and vegetarian diet, 210
cancer-causing agents, 581
canning, 509
carbohydrate loading, 425, 426
carbohydrate-based fat substitutes, 161, 161*t*

carbohydrates. *See also* fiber, glucose
    about, 98–99
    added sugar guidelines, 125*fig*
    added sugars, finding, 122*fig*, 122–125, 125*fig*, 125*t*
    best food sources for, 108–113
    complex, 100–101
    digesting, 102, 103*fig*
    as energy, 105, 105*fig*
    as energy source for exercise, 422*fig*, 422–425, 423*fig*, 425*t*, 426, 427, 430, 431–433
    and fasting, ketosis, 107–108
    glycogen, 101–102
    minimum daily amount, 109*fig*, 109*t*
    natural vs. added sugars, 113–126, 114*fig*
    as nutrients, 9–10
    and oral health, 121
    simple, 98–99
    substitutions for, 327*t*
    sugar substitutes, 126–130
carboxypeptidase, 78
carcinogenic, 511
carcinogens, 581
cardiorespiratory endurance, 414, 415, 420*fig*, 422
cardiovascular disease (CVD). *See also* heart disease, 164, 166, 580
caries. *See* dental caries; early childhood caries
carnitine, 259
carotenodermia, 235
carotenoids, 12*fig*, 233–235
Carter, Jimmy, 475
cassava, 516
catalysts, 193
cataracts, 226, 227, 227*fig*
cavities. *See* dental caries; early childhood caries
cecum, 76, 76*fig*
celiac disease, 87, 88–89, 90*t*
cell differentiation, 231
cells, 69*fig*
cellulite, 395
cellulose, 112
Centers for Disease Control and Prevention (CDC), 367, 471, 477*t*, 507–508, 568
central obesity, 370
certified label, 480
chemical agents, and foodborne illness, 497
chemical agents, in food, 515–516
chemical digestion, 68–69, 72*fig*
chickens, 460
chickpeas, 198–199
Child and Adult Care Food Program, 609*t*
children. *See also* adolescents, teens; infants; school-age children; toddlers, preschoolers
    food advertising to, 24
    malnourished, 605*fig*, 605–606, 606*t*, 607*t*
    obesity in, 567*fig*, 567, 569
    undernutrition in, 604
Children's Food and Beverage Advertising Initiative, 24
chloride, 292, 308, 308*fig*, 325*t*
chlorophyll, 98, 99
chocolate, 173
cholecystokinin, 78, 378
cholesterol
    and added sugars, 115
    and antioxidants, 172–173
    decreasing LDL, 174*t*
    and fat digestion, 149–150, 150*fig*
    and fiber, 172, 173
    and heart disease, 164
    maintaining healthy levels, 163–176, 163*t*
    minimizing, in diet, 156–157, 156*t*
    on nutrition facts panel, 167*fig*
    and plant sterols, 172
    roles of, 153
    and saturated, *trans* fats, 167, 167*fig*, 170
    transportation of, 151*fig*
choline, 259, 530

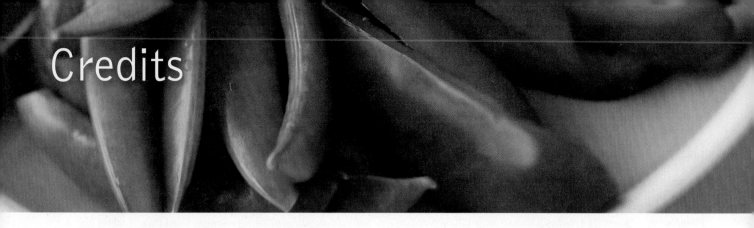

Credits

Pearson; **p. 173:** Comstock/Jupiter Images; **p. 175, top row left:** Neil Rutledge/Alamy; **p. 175, top row right:** Africa Studio/Fotolia; **p. 175, 2nd row left:** Shutterstock; **p. 175, 2nd row right:** Studiotouch/Shutterstock; **p. 175, 3rd row left:** Liz Van Steenburgh/iStockphoto; **p. 175, 3rd row right:** Shutterstock; **p. 175, bottom row left:** iStockphoto; **p. 175, bottom row right:** iStockphoto; **p. 176:** Krasowit/Shutterstock; **p. 178, left:** Comstock/Jupiter Images; **p. 178, right:** Shutterstock; **p. 178, bottom:** ERIC SCHRADER/Pearson; **p. 179, top:** Biophoto Associates/Science Source; **p. 179, bottom:** Erika Craddock/Garden Picture Library/getty images; **p. 181:** Steven Morris/Photolibrary/Getty Images

Chapter 6 **pp. 182–183:** Foodfolio/Alamy; **p. 184:** Foodfolio/Alamy; **p. 187:** Pearson; **p. 189:** John Lund/Tiffany Schoepp/Blend Images/Corbis; **p. 192, top:** Oliver Meckes/Nicole Ottawa/Science Source; **p. 192, bottom:** PhotoAlto/Alamy; **p. 194:** Dr. P. Marazzi/Science Source; **p. 197, right:** Andrew Whittuck/Dorling Kindersley; **p. 197, top:** Ruth Jenkinson/Dorling Kindersley; **p. 197, middle:** Monkey Business Images/Shutterstock; **p. 197, bottom:** Brian Yarvin PhotographyScience Source; **p. 199:** Elena Elisseeva/Shutterstock; **p. 200:** Pearson; **p. 202, top:** Kristin Piljay/Pearson; **p. 202, bottom:** Kristin Piljay/Pearson; **p. 203, top:** Mike Flippo/Shutterstock; **p. 203, bottom:** Kristin Piljay/Pearson; **p. 206:** Mbongo/Fotolia; **p. 207, top:** DAI KUROKAWA/EPA/Newscom; **p. 207, bottom:** Farah Abdi Warsameh/AP Images; **p. 208:** AGE Fotostock; **p. 209:** Elenathewise/Fotolia; **p. 210:** My Vegan Plate by Reed Mangels, PhD, RD; Lindsey Siferd; The Vegetarian Resource Group; www.vrg.org; **p. 211, top:** fotohunter/Shutterstock; **p. 211, bottom:** Valentyn Volkov/Shutterstock; **p. 213:** Pearson; **p. 214, top left:** Lilyana Vynogradova/Fotolia; **p. 214, top right:** Philip Dowell/Dorling Kindersley; **p. 214, bottom left:** Uckyo/Fotolia; **p. 214, bottom right:** Kristin Piljay/Pearson Science; **p. 215, top left:** Akalong Suitsuit/Fotolia; **p. 215, top right:** stockstudios/Shutterstock; **p. 215, bottom left:** Clive Streeter and Patrick McLea/Dorling Kindersley; **p. 215, bottom right:** Kristin Piljay/Pearson; **p. 216, top row left:** ElliotKo/Shutterstock; **p. 216, top row right:** a9photo/Shutterstock; **p. 216, 2nd row left:** Christopher Elwell/Shutterstock; **p. 216, 2nd row right:** dlerick/iStockphoto; **p. 216, 3rd row left:** Lauri Patterson/iStockphoto; **p. 216, 3rd row right:** RoJo Images/Fotolia; **p. 216, bottom row left:** Janet Faye Hastings/Shutterstock; **p. 216, bottom row right:** Serghei Starus/iStockphoto; **p. 217:** Subbotina Anna/Shutterstock; **p. 218, left:** PhotoAlto/Alamy; **p. 218, right:** Monkey Business Images/Shutterstock; **p. 219, top:** Andrew Whittuck/Dorling Kindersley; **p. 219, middle:** DAI KUROKAWA/EPA/Newscom; **p. 219, bottom left:** My Vegan Plate by Reed Mangels, PhD, RD; Lindsey Siferd; The Vegetarian Resource Group; www.vrg.org; **p. 219, bottom right:** Farah Abdi Warsameh/AP Images; **p. 221:** Foodfolio/Alamy

Chapter 7 **pp. 222–223:** Adam Jeffery/Flickr/Getty Images; **p. 224:** Adam Jeffery/Flickr/Getty Images; **p. 225, top left:** Mtsyri/Shutterstock; **p. 225, top right:** Stockbyte/Getty Images; **p. 225, bottom:** Best View Stock/Alamy; **p. 227, top:** National Eye Institute; **p. 227, middle:** National Eye Institute; **p. 227, bottom:** National Eye Institute; **p. 229:** Manceau/SoFood/Alamy; **p. 231:** Timmary/Shutterstock; **p. 232:** Siri Stafford/Getty Images; **p. 233:** Dr. P. Marazzi/Science Source; **p. 234, top:** Envision/Corbis; **p. 234, bottom:** Sarsmis/Shutterstock; **p. 235:** James Stevenson/Science Source; **p. 236, top:** Ian O'Leary/Dorling Kindersley; **p. 236, bottom:** VIPDesign/Fotolia; **p. 237, left:** Rachel Epstein/Photoedit; **p. 237, right:** Jupiter Images - FoodPix - Creatas; **p. 238, top left:** Eye of Science/Science Source; **p. 238, top right:** Ted Kinsman/Science Source; **p. 238, bottom left:** Cristina Pedrazzini/Science Source; **p. 238, bottom right:** Barry Gregg/Keepsake/Corbis; **p. 239:** Suzifoo/iStockphoto; **240, top:** Design Pics Inc./Alamy; **p. 240, bottom:** Zephyr/Science Source; **p. 241:** Shutterstock; **p. 242, left:** Biophoto Associates/Science Source; **p. 242, right:** Michael Littlejohn/Prentice Hall, Inc; **p. 244, top:** Steve Cukrov/Fotolia; **p. 244, left:** Isabelle Rozenbaum/AGE Fotostock; **p. 244, right:** Viktor/Fotolia; **p. 245:** Custom Medical Stock Photo(CMSP) - DNU; **p. 246, top left:** Ralph Morse//Time Life Pictures/Getty Images; **p. 246, top right:** Johner/Getty Images; **p. 246, bottom:** Sea Wave/Fotolia; **p. 247, left:** SPL/Science Source; **p. 247, right:** JJAVA/Fotolia; **p. 248:** Elena Elisseeva/Shutterstock; **p. 249, left:** D. Hurst/Alamy; **p. 249, right:** Dr. M.A. Ansary/Science Source; **p. 250, top:** Photodisc/Getty Images; **p. 250, bottom:** FoodPix/Creatas/Jupiter Images; **p. 251:** Barry Gregg/Spirit/Corbis; **p. 252, left:** Tim Ridley/Dorling Kindersley; **p. 252, right:** Custom Medical Stock Photo; **p. 254, top:** FoodPix/Creatas/Jupiter Images; **p. 254, bottom left:** FoodPix/Creatas/Jupiter Images; **p. 254, bottom right:** Kristin Piljay/Pearson Science; **p. 255, top:** FoodPix/Creatas/Jupiter Images; **p. 255, bottom:** 28/Ocean/Corbis; **p. 256, left:** Dimitri Otis/Taxi/Getty Images;

p. 256, middle: SPL/Science Source; **p. 256, top right:** Barry Gregg/Corbis; **p. 256, bottom right:** Barry Gregg/Keepsake/Corbis; **p. 257, left:** Biophoto Associates/Science Source; **p. 257, right:** Edyta Pawlowska/Shutterstock; **p. 258, top left:** AGE Fotostock; **p. 258, top right:** C Squared Studios/Photodisc/Getty Images; **p. 258, bottom left:** Justin Lightley/Photographer's Choice/Getty Images; **p. 258, bottom right:** Smileus/Shutterstock; **p. 260:** AGE Fotostock; **p. 261, top:** anitasstudio/Fotolia; **p. 261, bottom:** AGE Fotostock; **p. 262, top left:** Jason Stitt/Shutterstock; **p. 262, top right:** Gina Sanders/Fotolia; **p. 262, bottom:** Pearson Education/Pearson Science; **p. 263:** Pearson; **p. 264:** Pearson; **p. 265, top:** Kristin Piljay/Pearson Science; **p. 265, bottom:** GVictoria/Shutterstock; **p. 266:** Pearson; **p. 267, top:** Shutterstock; **p. 267, middle:** Pearson Education/Pearson Science; **p. 267, bottom:** Smal Marina/Shutterstock; **p. 267, right:** U. S. Pharmacopeia; **p. 268:** Pearson Education; **p. 269, top row left:** foodfolio/Alamy; **p. 269, top row right:** Smneedham/FoodPix/Getty images; **p. 269, 2nd row left:** Mariontxa/Fotolia; **p. 269, 2nd row right:** James Nesterwitz/Alamy; **p. 269, 3rd row left:** Ciaran Griffin/Stockbyte/Getty Images; **p. 269, 3rd row right:** iStockphoto; **p. 269, bottom row left:** Olga Popova/Shutterstock; **p. 269, bottom row right:** Mbongo/Fotolia; **p. 270:** Cheryl Casey/Shutterstock; **p. 271, left:** Mtsyri/Shutterstock; **p. 271, middle:** Stockbyte/Getty Images; **p. 271, right:** Sarsmis/Shutterstock; **p. 272, left:** Cristina Pedrazzini/Science Source; **p. 272, right:** Biophoto Associates/Science Source; **p. 273, top:** Isabelle Rozenbaum/AGE Fotostock; **p. 273, middle:** Sea Wave/Fotolia; **p. 273, bottom:** Dr. M.A. Ansary/Science Source; **p. 274, top left:** Photodisc/Getty Images; **p. 274, top right:** Custom Medical Stock Photo; **p. 274, bottom left:** FoodPix/Creatas/Jupiter Images; **p. 274, bottom right:** Edyta Pawlowska/Shutterstock; **p. 275, top left:** Smileus/Shutterstock; **p. 275, top right:** FoodPix/Creatas/Jupiter Images; **p. 275, bottom:** GVictoria/Shutterstock; **p. 277:** Adam Jeffery/Flickr/Getty Images

Chapter 8 **pp. 278–279:** PictureNet/keepsake RF/Corbis; **p. 280:** PictureNet/keepsake RF/Corbis; **p. 281:** Radius Images/Alamy; **p. 282:** Claude Edelmann/Science Source; **p. 284:** Steve HIx/Somos/Thinkstock; **p. 286, top row left:** Sergey Peterman/Shutterstock; **p. 286, 2nd row middle:** George Dolgikh/Shutterstock; **p. 286, 3rd row middle:** Peter Bernik/Shutterstock; **p. 286, bottom row middle:** Jeremy Pembrey/Alamy; **p. 287:** Pearson; **p. 288:** Olinchuk/Shutterstock; **p. 289:** Dynamic Graphics Group/Jupiter Images; **p. 294, top:** Kristin Piljay/Pearson; **p. 294, middle:** Richard Megna/Fundamental Photographs; **p. 294, bottom:** Kristin Piljay/Pearson; **p. 295:** Pearson; **p. 298, top:** keko64/Shutterstock; **p. 298, middle:** Steve Sant/Alamy; **p. 298, bottom:** John Lund/Tiffany Schoepp/Blend Images/Getty Images; **p. 299:** Joe Gough/Shutterstock; **p. 300, top:** M.studio/Fotolia; **p. 300, bottom:** D. Hurst/Alamy; **p. 301, top:** Michael Klein/Peter Arnold/Getty Images; **p. 301, bottom left:** Smit/Shutterstock; **p. 301, bottom middle:** Elena Schweitzer/Shutterstock; **p. 301, bottom right:** motorlka/Fotolia; **p. 302, top:** Office of the Surgeon General; **p. 302, bottom:** Office of the Surgeon General; **p. 304, top:** Vaivirga/Fotolia; **p. 304, bottom:** Nitr/Shutterstock; **p. 305:** Brent Hofacker/Shutterstock; **p. 306, top:** Nick Emm/Alamy; **p. 306, bottom left:** Brent Hofacker/Shutterstock; **p. 306, bottom right:** Ingram Publishing/Alamy; **p. 307, top:** Collage/Image Werks/Corbis; **p. 307, bottom:** Stockbyte/Getty Images; **p. 308, middle:** Brand X Pictures/Jupiter Images; **p. 308, bottom:** Sally Scott/Shutterstock; **p. 309, top:** Comstock/Jupiter Images; **p. 309, bottom:** grafnata/Shutterstock; **p. 310:** C Squared Studios/Photodisc/Getty Images; **p. 311, top:** Eric Grave/Science Source; **p. 311, bottom:** Joaquin Carrillo Farga/Science Source; **p. 312, left:** Smileus/Shutterstock; **p. 312, middle:** bajita111122/Fotolia; **p. 313, top:** Kristin Piljay/Pearson Education; **p. 313, bottom:** lidante/Fotolia; **p. 314:** Medical-on-Line/Alamy; **p. 315, top:** Image Source/Jupiter Images; **p. 315, middle:** Foodcollection/Getty Images; **p. 315, bottom:** papkin/Shutterstock; **p. 318, top left:** Don Farrall/Photodisc/Getty Images; **p. 318, top right:** John A Rizzo/AGE Fotostock; **p. 318, bottom:** NIH/CMSP/Custom Medical Stock Photo — All rights reserved.; **p. 319:** AGE Fotostock; **p. 320, top:** FoodCollection/AGE Fotostock; **p. 320, bottom middle:** Stockbyte/Getty Images; **p. 320, bottom right:** Richard Megna/Fundamental Photographs; **p. 321, left:** CDC/Dr. Hudson; **p. 321, right:** Mike Goldwater/Alamy; **p. 322, left:** Foodcollection/Getty Images; **p. 322, right:** Viktor/Fotolia; **p. 323, left:** Anna Hoychuk/Shutterstock; **p. 323, right:** marco mayer/Shutterstock; **p. 327:** AGE Fotostock; **p. 328, top row left:** Imageman/Shutterstock; **p. 328, top row right:** Nick Emm/Alamy; **p. 328, 2nd row left:** marekuliasz/Shutterstock; **p. 328, 2nd row right:** Valentyn Volkov/Shutterstock; **p. 328, 3rd row left:** Melinda Fawver/Shutterstock;

p. 328, 3rd row right: MaxPhotographer/Shutterstock; p. 328, bottom row left: D. Hurst/Alamy; p. 328, bottom row right: Blue Lemon Photo/Shutterstock; p. 329: Elena Elisseeva/Shutterstock; p. 330: Steve HIx/Somos/Thinkstock; p. 331, left: John Lund/Tiffany Schoepp/Blend Images/Getty Images; p. 331, right: D. Hurst/Alamy; p. 332, top: Stockbyte/Getty Images; p. 332, bottom left: Brand X Pictures/Jupiter Images; p. 332, bottom right: bajita111122/Fotolia; p. 333, top left: Comstock/Jupiter Images; p. 333, top middle: Foodcollection/Getty Images; p. 333, top right: NIH/CMSP/Custom Medical Stock Photo — All rights reserved.; p. 333, bottom left: Foodcollection.com/Alamy; p. 333, bottom middle: Mike Goldwater/Alamy; p. 333, bottom right: Foodcollection/Getty Images; p. 334: Anna Hoychuk/Shutterstock; p. 335: PictureNet/keepsake RF/Corbis

Chapter 9   pp. 336–337: Jamie Grill/Iconica/Getty Images; p. 338: Jamie Grill/Iconica/Getty Images; p. 339, top: Adam Woolfitt/Corbis; p. 339, bottom: Steve Gorton/Dorling Kindersley; p. 340, top: Pearson; p. 340, middle left: johnfoto18/Shutterstock; p. 340, middle right: Foodcollection/Getty Images; p. 340, bottom left: Pearson Education/Pearson Science; p. 340, bottom right: Pearson Education/Pearson Science; p. 341, top: Digital Vision/Getty Images; p. 341, bottom: Alamy; p. 342: Jim Varney/Science Source; p. 343: Joe Raedle/Getty Images; p. 344: Corbis; p. 345: Pearson; p. 346: Fetal Alcohol & Drug Unit (FAS); p. 347: 28/ocean/corbis; p. 348, top row left: Valentyn Volkov/Shutterstock; p. 348, top row right: Joy Brown/Shutterstock; p. 348, 2nd row left: Viktorija/Fotolia; p. 348, 2nd row right: unpict/Fotolia; p. 348, 3rd row left: JJAVA/Fotolia; p. 348, 3rd row right: Danny Hooks/Fotolia; p. 348, bottom row left: iofoto/Shutterstock; p. 348, bottom row right:ampFotoStudio.com/Fotolia; p. 349, left: Richard Megna/Fundamental Photographs; p. 349, right: Richard Megna/Fundamental Photographs; p. 350: Arthur Glauberman/Arthur Glauberman/Science Source; p. 351: Image Source/Corbis; p. 352: Fetal Alcohol & Drug Unit (FAS); p. 354: Pearson Education; p. 355: U.S. Department of Transportation; p. 356: Larry Kolvoord/The Image Works; p. 357: Les/Shutterstock; p. 358, top row left: vsl/Shutterstock; p. 358, top row right: vsl/Shutterstock; p. 358, 2nd row right: Gabe Palmer/Alamy; p. 358, 3rd row left: Denis Komarov/Shutterstock; p. 358, 3rd row left: dibrova/Shutterstock; p. 358, 3rd row right: Denis Komarov/Shutterstock; p. 358, bottom row left: Clive Streeter/Dorling Kindersley; p. 358, bottom row right: ilian food & drink/Alamy; p. 359: ol_vic/Shutterstock; p. 360, top left: Adam Woolfitt/Documentary/Corbis; p. 360, top right: Steve Gorton/Dorling Kindersley; p. 360, bottom: Digital Vision/Getty Images; p. 361, top: Image Source/Corbis; p. 361, bottom: Larry Kolvoord/The Image Works; p. 363: Jamie Grill/Iconica/Getty Images

Chapter 10   pp. 364–365: Donna Day/Big Cheese Photo/Corbis; p. 366: Donna Day/Big Cheese Photo/Corbis; p. 367, top: Bill Aron/PhotoEdit; p. 367, bottom: Dan Kosmayer/Fotolia; p. 368, top left: Bettmann/Corbis; p. 368, top right: Superstock/Glow Images; p. 368, middle: Remy de la Mauviniere/AP Images; p. 368, bottom left: Fairchild Photo Service/Conde Nast/Corbis Entertainment/Corbis; p. 368, bottom right: Harrison G. Pope, Jr. MD; p. 371, top left: Pearson; p. 371, top right: David Madison/Getty Images; p. 371, middle: Mauro Fermariello/Science Source; p. 371, bottom left: Mauro Fermariello/Science Source; p. 371, bottom right: Joe Traver//Time Life Pictures/Getty Images; p. 372: Sam Edwards/OJO Images/Getty Images; p. 373, left: Helder Almeida/Shutterstock; p. 373, top row left: Kenneth Man/Shutterstock; p. 373, top row right: Kenneth Man/Shutterstock; p. 373, middle row left: maga/Shuterstock; p. 373, middle row right: lightpoet/Shutterstock; p. 373, bottom row left: Zurijeta/Shutterstock; p. 373, bottom row right: Brian A Jackson/Shutterstock; p. 377: Laurence Mouton/PhotoAlto/Alamy; p. 378: Ilene MacDonald/Alamy; p. 379: Pearson; p. 380: Inmagine Asia/AGE Fotostock; p. 381: Kristin Piljay/Pearson Education; p. 382: GlowImages/Alamy; p. 383, left: Hurst Photo/Shutterstock; p. 383, right: IS962/Image Source/Alamy; p. 383, bottom: Comstock Images/JupiterImages; p. 383, bottom right: Pearson; p. 384: Evan Vucci/AP Images; p. 387, top all: U.S. Department of Health and Human Services; p. 387, bottom left: Photolibrary/Alamy; p. 387, bottom right upper: Serg64/Shutterstock; p. 387, bottom right lower: Foodcollection RF/Getty Images; p. 388: Ruth Jenkinson/Dorling Kindersley; p. 389, all: Richard Megna/Fundamental Photographs; p. 390: Kimberly Reinick/Fotolia; p. 393: Newscom; p. 394: Corbis; p. 395: LIU JIN/Stringer/Getty Images; p. 398: Redux Pictures; p. 399: David J. Green/Alamy; p. 400: Lucas Allen White/Shutterstock; p. 401: Fuse/Jupiter

Images; p. 402: D. Hurst/Alamy; p. 405, top row left: Darkkong/Shutterstock; p. 405, top row right: Palo ok/Shutterstock; p. 405, 2nd row left: Sharon Day/Shutterstock; p. 405, 2nd row right: Karen Beard/Blend Images/Getty Images; p. 405, 3rd row left: Photolibrary/Getty Images; p. 405, 3rd row right: Denis Vrublevski/Shutterstock; p. 405, bottom row left: Michael Neelon(misc)/Alamy; p. 405, bottom row right: Richard Megna/Fundamental Photographs; p. 406: Kletr/Fotolia; p. 407: Corbis; p. 408, top: Ilene MacDonald/Alamy; p. 408, middle left: Hurst Photo/Shutterstock; p. 408, middle right: IS962/Image Source/Alamy; p. 408, bottom: Comstock Images/JupiterImages; p. 409, top: Serg64/Shutterstock; p. 409, bottom left: Photolibrary/Alamy; p. 409, bottom right: Fuse/Jupiter Images; p. 411: Donna Day/Big Cheese Photo/Corbis

Chapter 11   pp. 412–413: Oliver Eltinger/Corbis; p. 414: Oliver Eltinger/Corbis; p. 415: Dan Dalton/Digital Vision/Getty Images; p. 416, top left: Charles Thatcher/Getty images; p. 416, top right: Arpad/Fotolia; p. 416, bottom left: Tamara Lackey/Getty Images; p. 416, bottom right: Dex Image/Alamy; p. 417, top left: Tetra Images/Getty Images; p. 417, top right: Stockbyte/Getty Images; p. 417, middle left: Ryan McVay/Photodisc/Getty Images; p. 417, middle right: Stockbyte/Getty Images; p. 417, bottom: Stuart Jenner/Shutterstock; p. 418: Creatas/Jupiter Images; p. 423, left: Ariwasabi/Shutterstock; p. 423, top row: Peter Bernik/Shutterstock; p. 423, 2nd row: Koji Aoki/Getty Images; p. 423, 3rd row: Nigel Roddis/EPA/Newscom; p. 423, 4th row: maho/Fotolia; p. 423, 5th row: Colin Underhill/Alamy; p. 423, bottom row: Maridav/Shutterstock; p. 424: Elena Gaak/Shutterstock; p. 428: prudkov/Fotolia; p. 430: Shutterstock; p. 431: Viorel Sima/Fotolia; p. 432: Pearson Education/Pearson Science; p. 434: Tim Hill/Alamy; p. 435, top: Pearson Education/Pearson Science; p. 435, bottom: Image Source/Jupiter Images; p. 437: Pearson Education/Pearson Science; p. 438: Shutterstock; p. 440: Pearson Education/Pearson Science; p. 441: SPL/Science Source; p. 442: Marcelo Sayao/EPA/Newscom; p. 445: Pearson; p. 446, top row left: endeavor/Shutterstock; p. 446, top row right: Whitebox Media/Fotolia; p. 446, 2nd row left: Coleman Yuen. Pearson Education; p. 446, 2nd row right: pink candy/Fotolia; p. 446, 3rd row left: kzww/Shutterstock; p. 446, 3rd row right: oah1611/Fotolia; p. 446, bottom row left: MariusdeGraf/Shutterstock; p. 446, bottom row right: Aleksandar Jocic/Fotolia; p. 447: Kristin Piljay/Pearson; p. 448: Dan Dalton/Digital Vision/Getty Images; p. 449, top: Elena Gaak/Shutterstock; p. 449, bottom: Pearson Education/Pearson Science; p. 450: Pearson Education/Pearson Science; p. 451: Oliver Eltinger/Corbis

Chapter 12   pp. 452–453: FoodPhotography Eising/the food passionates/Corbis; p. 454, left: FoodPhotography Eising/the food passionates/Corbis; p. 454, right: Pearson; p. 456: Maksymowicz/Fotolia; p. 457: Zsolt Nyulaszi/Panther Media/AGE Fotostock; p. 458: Mihalec/Shutterstock; p. 460, top: Bill Barksdale/AgStock Images, Inc./Alamy; p. 460, middle: Mariusz S. Jurgielewicz/Shutterstock; p. 460, bottom: Benjamin J. Myers/Corbis News/Corbis; p. 461: Richard Splash/Alamy; p. 465: Marvin Dembinsky Photo Associates/Alamy; p. 466: Marina Nabatova/Shutterstock; p. 470: Dave Reede/AgStock Images, Inc./Alamy; p. 472: Dennis MacDonald/PhotoEdit; p. 474: Smileus/Shutterstock; p. 475: Scott Camazine/Science Source; p. 476: AGE Fotostock; p. 478: Kristin Piljay/Pearson Education; p. 480: Kristin Piljay/Pearson Education; p. 481, both: Pearson Education; p. 482, top left: Kristin Piljay/Pearson; p. 482, top right: Pearson; p. 482, bottom left: Pearson; p. 482, bottom right: Pearson Education; p. 483: monticelllo/Fotolia; p. 484, top left: Pearson; p. 484, top right: Bill Barksdale/AgStock Images, Inc./Alamy; p. 484, bottom: Marvin Dembinsky Photo Associates/Alamy; p. 485, top: Dennis MacDonald/PhotoEdit; p. 485, bottom left: Kristin Piljay/Pearson Education; p. 485, bottom right: Pearson Education; p. 487: FoodPhotography Eising/the food passionates/Corbis

Chapter 13   pp. 488–489: Hero Images/Corbis; pp. 490: Hero Images/Corbis; p. 491: PHANIE/Science Source; p. 492:Foodcollection.com/Alamy; p. 493, top: E. G. Pors/Shutterstock; p. 493, bottom: Muellek Josef/Shutterstock; p. 495: Jacek Chabraszewski/Shutterstock; p. 496, top: Dr. Gary Gaugler/Science Source; p. 496, middle: Angel Simon/Shutterstock; p. 496, bottom: Eye of Science/Science Source; p. 498: Andrey Starostin/Shutterstock; p. 500: Ivan1981Roo/Shutterstock; p. 501: jathys/Shutterstock; p. 502, top: United States Department of Agriculture; p. 502, bottom: United States Department of Agriculture; p. 504: gmeviphoto/Fotolia; p. 506: Pearson;

p. 507: Anke van Wyk/Shutterstock; p. 510: U.S. Department of Agriculture; p. 511, top: Pearson Education; p. 511, bottom: Pearson Education; p. 512: Africa Studio/Fotolia; p. 515: Ambient Images Inc./Alamy; p. 517: James Cavallini/Science Source; p. 518: as3/Shutterstock; p. 519, top: Dr. Gary Gaugler/Science Source; p. 519, middle: U.S. Department of Agriculture; p. 519, bottom: Pearson Education; p. 520: James Cavallini/Science Source; p. 521: Hero Images/Corbis

Chapter 14   pp. 522–523: Ocean/Corbis; p. 524: Ocean/Corbis; p. 529, left: Andy Crawford/Dorling Kindersley; p. 529, middle: Andy Crawford/Dorling Kindersley; p. 529, right: Andy Crawford/Dorling Kindersley; p. 530: Kristin Piljay/Pearson Education, Inc.; p. 531: Dan Peretz/Shutterstock; p. 532: Kristin Piljay/Pearson Education; p. 534: Kristin Piljay/Pearson; p. 536: Blend Images/SuperStock; p. 538: ZUMA Press/Newscom; p. 539: Stewart Cohen/Blend Images/Getty Images; p. 541: Sally and Richard Greenhill/Alamy; p. 542, top: Chris Rout/Alamy; p. 542, bottom: Pearson; p. 544: © Kayte Deioma/PhotoEdit; p. 545: Martin S. Spiller; p. 549: Dragon Images/Shutterstock; p. 550: Mariusz S. Jurgielewicz/Shutterstock; p. 551, left: Serhiy Kobyakov/Shutterstock; p. 551, right: Serhiy Kobyakov/Shutterstock; p. 552: AGE Fotostock; p. 553, 1st column: Medioimages/Photodisc/Getty Images; p. 553, 2nd column: Andy Crawford/Dorling Kindersley; p. 553, 3rd column: Andy Crawford/Dorling Kindersley; p. 553, 4th column: Andy Crawford/Dorling Kindersley; p. 553, 5th column: American Images Inc/Photodisc/Getty Images; p. 554: Arti_Zav/Fotolia; p. 555, top: Kristin Piljay/Pearson Education; p. 555, bottom left: Blend Images/SuperStock; p. 555, bottom right: Kristin Piljay/Pearson; p. 556, top left: Stewart Cohen/Blend Images/Getty Images; p. 556, top right: ZUMA Press/Newscom; p. 556, bottom left: Sally and Richard Greenhill/Alamy; p. 556, bottom right: Andy Crawford/Dorling Kindersley; p. 557, left: Kayte Deioma/PhotoEdit; p. 557, right: Mariusz S. Jurgielewicz/Shutterstock; p. 559: Ocean/Corbis

Chapter 15   pp. 560–561: Yellowdog/Cultura/Getty Images; p. 562: Yellowdog/Cultura/Getty Images; p. 564: Simon Brown/Dorling Kindersley; p. 565: Huntstock/Creatas/Jupiter Images; p. 566, top: Skip Nall/Alamy; p. 566, bottom: Pearson; p. 570, left: Kadmy/Fotolia; p. 570, right: Monkey Business Images/Shutterstock; p. 572: Mike Booth/Alamy; p. 573: Chris Rout/Bubbles Photolibrary/Alamy; p. 575: Ariel Skelley/Thinkstock; p. 584: Sally and Richard Greenhill/Alamy; p. 585: Tina Manley/Alamy; p. 586: Michael P. Gadomski/Science Source; p. 589, top: USDA/USDA Ag. Research Center; p. 589, bottom: USDA/USDA Ag. Research Center; p. 590: Chris Willson/Alamy; p. 591, top left: Skip Nall/Alamy; p. 591, top right: Monkey Business Images/Shutterstock; p. 591, bottom right: Ariel Skelley/Thinkstock; p. 592: Tina Manley/Alamy; p. 593: Yellowdog/Cultura/Getty Images

Chapter 16   pp. 594–595: Dan Lamont/Encyclopedia/Corbis; p. 596: Dan Lamont/Encyclopedia/Corbis; p. 598: Jane Alexander/Photofusion Picture Library/Alamy; p. 600: Richard Levine/Alamy; p. 601: Abid Katib/Staff/Getty Images; p. 602: Lulu/Fotolia; p. 603: Benjamin J. Myers/Corbis; p. 604: Ladi Kirn/Alamy; p. 605: Jean-Marc Giboux/Getty Images; p. 608, top: ZUMA Press/Newscom; p. 608, bottom: Alain Evrard/Robert Harding; p. 610: Boris Roessler/dpa/picture-alliance/Newscom; p. 611, top: ZUMA Press/Newscom; p. 611, bottom: Pearson; p. 612: Shutterstock; p. 613, bottom left: Ladi Kirn/Alamy; p. 613, bottom right: Jean-Marc Giboux/Getty Images; p. 615: Dan Lamont/Encyclopedia/Corbis

Tolerable Upper Intake Levels (ULs)

Vitamins

Life Stage Group	Vitamin A (μg/d)[a]	Vitamin C (mg/d)	Vitamin D (μg/d)	Vitamin E (mg/d)[b, c]	Niacin (mg/d)[c]	Vitamin B₆ (mg/d)	Folate (μg/d)[c]	Choline (g/d)
Infants								
0–6 mo	600	ND[d]	25	ND	ND	ND	ND	ND
6–12 mo	600	ND	38	ND	ND	ND	ND	ND
Children								
1–3 y	600	400	63	200	10	30	300	1.0
4–8 y	900	650	75	300	15	40	400	1.0
Males								
9–13 y	1,700	1,200	100	600	20	60	600	2.0
14–18 y	2,800	1,800	100	800	30	80	800	3.0
19–30 y	3,000	2,000	100	1,000	35	100	1,000	3.5
31–50 y	3,000	2,000	100	1,000	35	100	1,000	3.5
51–70 y	3,000	2,000	100	1,000	35	100	1,000	3.5
>70 y	3,000	2,000	100	1,000	35	100	1,000	3.5
Females								
9–13 y	1,700	1,200	100	600	20	60	600	2.0
14–18 y	2,800	1,800	100	800	30	80	800	3.0
19–30 y	3,000	2,000	100	1,000	35	100	1,000	3.5
31–50 y	3,000	2,000	100	1,000	35	100	1,000	3.5
51–70 y	3,000	2,000	100	1,000	35	100	1,000	3.5
>70 y	3,000	2,000	100	1,000	35	100	1,000	3.5
Pregnancy								
14–18 y	2,800	1,800	100	800	30	80	800	3.0
19–50 y	3,000	2,000	100	1,000	35	100	1,000	3.5
Lactation								
14–18 y	2,800	1,800	100	800	30	80	800	3.0
19–50 y	3,000	2,000	100	1,000	35	100	1,000	3.5

Note: A Tolerable Upper Intake Level (UL) is the highest level of daily nutrient intake that is likely to pose no risk of adverse health effects to almost all individuals in the general population. Unless otherwise specified, the UL represents total intake from food, water, and supplements. Due to a lack of suitable data, ULs could not be established for vitamin K, thiamin, riboflavin, vitamin B₁₂, pantothenic acid, biotin, and carotenoids. In the absence of a UL, extra caution may be warranted in consuming levels above recommended intakes. Members of the general population should be advised not to routinely exceed the UL. The UL is not meant to apply to individuals who are treated with the nutrient under medical supervision or to individuals with predisposing conditions that modify their sensitivity to the nutrient.

[a] As preformed vitamin A only.

[b] As α-tocopherol; applies to any form of supplemental α-tocopherol.

[c] The ULs for vitamin E, niacin, and folate apply to synthetic forms obtained from supplements, fortified foods, or a combination of the two.

[d] ND = Not determinable due to lack of data of adverse effects in this age group and concern with regard to lack of ability to handle excess amounts. Source of intake should be from food only to prevent high levels of intake.

Data from: DIETARY REFERENCE INTAKES series, National Academies Press. Copyright ©1997, 1998, 2000, 2001, and 2011, by the National Academy of Sciences. These reports may be accessed via www.nap.edu. Courtesy of the National Academies Press, Washington, DC. Reprinted with permission.

Tolerable Upper Intake Levels (ULs)

Elements

Life Stage Group	Boron (mg/d)	Calcium (mg/d)	Copper (µg/d)	Fluoride (mg/d)	Iodine (µg/d)	Iron (mg/d)	Magnesium (mg/d)ᵉ	Manganese (mg/d)	Molybdenum (µg/d)	Nickel (mg/d)	Phosphorus (g/d)	Selenium (µg/d)	Vanadium (mg/d)ᶠ	Zinc (mg/d)	Sodium (g/d)	Chloride (g/d)
Infants																
0–6 mo	NDᵈ	1,000	ND	0.7	ND	40	ND	ND	ND	ND	ND	45	ND	4	ND	ND
6–12 mo	ND	1,500	ND	0.9	ND	40	ND	ND	ND	ND	ND	60	ND	5	ND	ND
Children																
1–3 y	3	2,500	1,000	1.3	200	40	65	2	300	0.2	3	90	ND	7	1.5	2.3
4–8 y	6	2,500	3,000	2.2	300	40	110	3	600	0.3	3	150	ND	12	1.9	2.9
Males																
9–13 y	11	3,000	5,000	10	600	40	350	6	1,100	0.6	4	280	ND	23	2.2	3.4
14–18 y	17	3,000	8,000	10	900	45	350	9	1,700	1.0	4	400	ND	34	2.3	3.6
19–30 y	20	2,500	10,000	10	1,100	45	350	11	2,000	1.0	4	400	1.8	40	2.3	3.6
31–50 y	20	2,500	10,000	10	1,100	45	350	11	2,000	1.0	4	400	1.8	40	2.3	3.6
51–70 y	20	2,000	10,000	10	1,100	45	350	11	2,000	1.0	4	400	1.8	40	2.3	3.6
>70 y	20	2,000	10,000	10	1,100	45	350	11	2,000	1.0	3	400	1.8	40	2.3	3.6
Females																
9–13 y	11	3,000	5,000	10	600	40	350	6	1,100	0.6	4	280	ND	23	2.2	3.4
14–18 y	17	3,000	8,000	10	900	45	350	9	1,700	1.0	4	400	ND	34	2.3	3.6
19–30 y	20	2,500	10,000	10	1,100	45	350	11	2,000	1.0	4	400	1.8	40	2.3	3.6
31–50 y	20	2,500	10,000	10	1,100	45	350	11	2,000	1.0	4	400	1.8	40	2.3	3.6
51–70 y	20	2,000	10,000	10	1,100	45	350	11	2,000	1.0	4	400	1.8	40	2.3	3.6
>70 y	20	2,000	10,000	10	1,100	45	350	11	2,000	1.0	3	400	1.8	40	2.3	3.6
Pregnancy																
14–18 y	17	3,000	8,000	10	900	45	350	9	1,700	1.0	3.5	400	ND	34	2.3	3.6
19–50 y	20	2,500	10,000	10	1,100	45	350	11	2,000	1.0	3.5	400	ND	40	2.3	3.6
Lactation																
14–18 y	17	3,000	8,000	10	900	45	350	9	1,700	1.0	4	400	ND	34	2.3	3.6
19–50 y	20	2,500	10,000	10	1,100	45	350	11	2,000	1.0	4	400	ND	40	2.3	3.6

Note: A Tolerable Upper Intake Level (UL) is the highest level of daily nutrient intake that is likely to pose no risk of adverse health effects to almost all individuals in the general population. Unless otherwise specified, the UL represents total intake from food, water, and supplements. Due to a lack of suitable data, ULs could not be established for vitamin K, thiamin, riboflavin, vitamin B₁₂, pantothenic acid, biotin, and carotenoids. In the absence of a UL, extra caution may be warranted in consuming levels above recommended intakes. Members of the general population should be advised not to routinely exceed the UL. The UL is not meant to apply to individuals who are treated with the nutrient under medical supervision or to individuals with predisposing conditions that modify their sensitivity to the nutrient.

ᵈ ND = Not determinable due to lack of data of adverse effects in this age group and concern with regard to lack of ability to handle excess amounts. Source of intake should be from food only to prevent high levels of intake.

ᵉ The ULs for magnesium represent intake from a pharmacological agent only and do not include intake from food and water.

ᶠ Although vanadium in food has not been shown to cause adverse effects in humans, there is no justification for adding vanadium to food, and vanadium supplements should be used with caution. The UL is based on adverse effects in laboratory animals, and this data could be used to set a UL for adults but not children and adolescents.

Data from: Reprinted with permission from the Dietary Reference Intakes series. Copyright 1997, 1998, 2000, 2001, 2005, 2011 by the National Academies of Sciences, courtesy of the National Academies Press, Washington, D.C. These reports may be accessed via www.nap.edu.